WHERE *to* SKI

and

snowboard

Edited by
Chris Gill
and
Dave Watts

Thomas Cook

Published in Great Britain
by Thomas Cook Publishing
The Thomas Cook Group Ltd
PO Box 227
Thorpe Wood
Peterborough PE3 6PU
United Kingdom

This edition published 1997

10 9 8 7 6 5 4 3 2 1

ISBN 1 900341 17 4

A CIP catalogue entry for this book is
available from the British Library.

Editors Chris Gill and Dave Watts
Assistant editors Mandy Crook,
Ian Porter, Ian Stratford,
Simon Townley, Catherine Weakley
Editorial assistants Alex Barwell,
Ian Crook
Production assistant Oliver Wilshen
Contributors Chris Allan, Alan Coulson,
Nicky Holford, James Hooke,
Tim Perry, Adam Ruck,
Helena Wiesner
Nightlife consultant Bert Walsh
Advertising manager Aubrey Stuart

Photo credits: see page 4
Design by Fox Design Consultants
Production by Guide Editors
Colour reproduction by
Prisma Imaging Limited
Imagesetting by Pindar plc
Printed and bound in Great Britain by
Pindar plc

Contents

Photo credits

About this book

what puts it ahead?

When *Where to Ski* was first published in 1994, it gave the established ski-resort guidebooks a shake-up. It was the first guide to present impartial, no-punches-pulled assessments of resorts in an attractive, reader-friendly format, with full-colour panoramic mountain maps and colour photographs of resorts. Despite the early deadlines of colour printing, it was the first to be based on information – about new lifts, lift pass prices, package holiday programmes – relating to the season ahead rather than the season just gone.

This edition, we reckon, will shake things up again. Of course, the book has been thoroughly updated: in the two years since our last edition, the editors themselves have revisited over 85 resorts to reappraise them – look for the stamp shown in the margin – and every chapter has been revised with the help of reports from readers. We have invested huge amounts of time in finding out about new resort developments for this coming season, summarised in each chapter in a What's New panel like the one shown here.

What's new

boarding

WHAT IT COSTS

But we've also developed the book to make sure we keep one jump ahead of our rivals. Among the key improvements are these:
• we have taken up snowboarding, personally and professionally; even if most of our readers aren't boarders and don't intend to become boarders, we reckon many of their kids will want to – so there's boarding info throughout the book, and each major chapter has a special boarding summary near the start
• we have compiled price ratings for all the major resorts in the book, so you can see at a glance how pricey a holiday in each will be.

There are lots of other improvements, too. Among them:
• reorganised coverage of American resorts – now grouped by region, with introductions to each one and maps of most
• new chapters on resorts in France, Italy, Andorra, Sweden, the US and Canada
• bigger mountain maps and resort photos.

So: the book is comprehensive, detailed, colourful and user-friendly; skim through it yourself and see. But in the end what you want is reliable guidance. If you're an experienced skier or boarder, you'll be able to test us by picking a resort you know well and seeing how accurately we describe and assess it. The quotes on the back cover offer some reassurance. And this is what one reader thought:

'We have skied Europe extensively, and mainly Courchevel in France. Over the last few years we have become increasingly dissatisfied with the lack of service and the attitude of the French. This year, we had added complications – we wanted to take our two-year-old, as well as two older boys who we wanted to put in ski school. With these problems to surmount, we bought your book and read it every night for two months. We finally decided on Whistler. The holiday was fantastic.'

We don't guarantee you'll find your dream holiday through these pages, even if you study them nightly for two months. But our aim is that you should find something close to it. If you're still wavering, remember that you can get your money back (see over the page).

The **Thomas Cook** connection

A word about our new publishers

We are delighted that this third edition of *Where to Ski and Snowboard* (as it is titled from this year) is being published by Thomas Cook Publishing, the publishing arm of the famous travel agency group. Naturally, they specialise in publishing travel guides, and this book fits into their stable perfectly.

We are also working closely with another arm of Thomas Cook, its relatively new Ski Direct telephone booking operation. Much of the content of this new edition is available on the Ski Direct website, and we've negotiated a deal whereby you can get the full cost of this book refunded by the agency. All you have to do is book a 1997/98 or 1998/99 winter-sports holiday through Ski Direct – for details, see facing page.

Thomas Cook Ski Direct was launched in 1995 and is now the biggest specialist ski travel agency in the country. You can use Ski Direct to book skiing and snowboarding holidays provided by practically any UK tour operator – the main exceptions are the very small operators who don't operate through travel agents or who prefer you to book direct.

The Thomas Cook Group can trace its origins back to 5 July 1841, when Thomas Cook, a 32-year-old printer from Market Harborough in Leicestershire, led a party of some 500 temperance enthusiasts on a railway outing from Leicester to Loughborough. This proved to be the birth of the modern tourist industry and, in the course of expanding his business, Thomas Cook and his son John invented many of the features of organised travel that we now take for granted. Over the next 150 years the name Thomas Cook became synonymous with world travel.

The group began arranging winter-sports holidays in the 1890s, with tours to Swiss resorts such as Davos, Grindelwald and St Moritz at a cost of ten guineas each. Skating and tobogganing were the main attractions on these early holidays, but skiing soon became popular. Thomas Cook launched its first winter-sports brochure, featuring six Swiss resorts, in 1908. By the 1920s, tours to France, Italy, Austria, Norway and Sweden were also on offer, and special trains were chartered solely for the use of Cook's clients.

Today the Thomas Cook Group employs over 13,000 people across the globe, providing services to customers at more than 3,000 locations in over 100 countries. Its activities include travel retailing, tour operating and financial services – Thomas Cook is a world leader in traveller's cheques and foreign currency exchange services.

Thomas Cook always believed in the value of the printed word as an accompaniment to travel. His publication The Excursionist was the equivalent of both a holiday brochure and a travel magazine. Today, Thomas Cook Publishing continues to issue one of the world's oldest travel books, the Thomas Cook European Timetable, which has existed since 1873. Updated every month, it remains the only definitive compendium of European railway schedules. The company now publishes a long list of travel guides, to which *Where to Ski and Snowboard* is the latest addition.

Get your
money back

free!

Where to Ski and Snowboard can be yours

We're delighted that our new alliance with Thomas Cook means we can continue to offer readers their money back. Why not take advantage of this offer? **There's no catch!**

You can reclaim the full price of Where to Ski and Snowboard when you book a wintersports holiday for any time in the 1997/98 or 1998/99 seasons. All you have to do is book the holiday through the specialist ski travel agency Thomas Cook Ski Direct. The price of the book will be given as a discount off the cost of your holiday.

Thomas Cook Ski Direct is Britain's biggest ski travel agency. You can buy whatever kind of holiday you want through them, so you're not losing out on choice.

Thomas Cook Ski Direct sells the complete range of package holidays offered by all the bonded tour operators in Britain. With more operators, more resorts and more holidays than anyone else, no one is better placed to find you what you want than Ski Direct.

You could be on the slopes with just one call. Phone Ski Direct on

01733 335513

Claiming your refund

Claiming your refund is easy. Right at the back of the book is a page which comprises two vouchers. When you make your definite booking, tell Ski Direct that you want to claim a refund. Cut out the vouchers and send one to Ski Direct and one to Where to Ski and Snowboard (the addresses are on the vouchers). That's all there is to it. When your final invoice arrives, it will show a refund of the price of the book.

Introduction

the editors ramble

AT LAST: EXCHANGE THAT'S NO ROBBERY

19 January 1996: voucher for 370 at FF7.43: £49.80
27 February 1997: voucher for 362 at FF9.4: £40.13
These two credit card bills for French mountain lunches a year apart
go some way to explaining why the UK's ski holiday industry is
barely able to contain its current glee. After a fair season despite
difficult circumstances, the industry is looking forward to something
of a bonanza next season, as holidaymakers come to appreciate the
magnitude of the change that has overcome the formerly limp
British pound. As we commit these words to silicon in July 1997, the
pound is stronger than it has been for years – it now buys 9.9 French
francs. And a good part of this renewed strength developed in the
early part of the year, in time to affect package holiday pricing.

If the cost of your holidays is something you have to watch, you'll
be interested in the price ratings we give for all the major resorts we
cover in this edition. And in the chapter on the costs of wintersports
holidays (page 36) there's further analysis of what we found.

FAKING IT

There's no such thing as a 'normal' season these days, so identifying
the 1996/97 season as abnormal would be daft. But it certainly was a
curious season. In many Alpine resorts, the only serious falls of snow
were before the season really got under way, and after it finished.
Happily, the quantity that fell at the beginning was enough to see
many resorts through the high season with no serious difficulty.

These days, all resorts really should plan on the assumption that
natural snowfall is unreliable. Happily, that message seems to be
getting through, even to Alpine resorts that have previously lacked
the conviction, the resources or the necessary permission to install
snowmaking. This season, the low resorts of the Ski-Welt (Söll etc)
are among those where you'll find a major step forward in this
respect. And even Kitzbühel seems to have realised that holiday-
makers can't be expected to roll up just because a resort has a famous
downhill course – they want good, reliable snow as well.

TAKING TO THE BOARDS

We admit that we've been putting it off, but last winter your editors
took the plunge and learned to snowboard. Having learned to ski
with the help of the famous book *We Learned to Ski*, by Evans et al,
we're tempted to write a book about it. But we've got our hands full
rewriting this one to make it as useful to snowboarders as to skiers.

People say that boarding is easier to learn – or at least quicker. We
believe the right message is a slightly different one. At first, progress
is faster on skis. But once you crack the basic business of sliding and
turning on a board – once off the nursery slopes – boarders tend to
accelerate quickly to the point where they start to get real excitement
from carving turns on smooth slopes, or in deep snow – a point that
one-week-a-year skiers may take years and years to reach.

A HOUSE DIVIDED?

We're aware that not all everyone will welcome our adoption of snowboarding. 'Pity your book isn't called *Where to Ski without Snowboarders*,' says one correspondent, blissfully unaware of our plans. 'They are an absolute menace, with no regard for anybody else, not even for young children on nursery slopes.'

Sorry, dear reader. But we actually don't go along with that view. Yobs are a menace, and over the years we've been driven to fury by the behaviour of yobs on skis as often as yobs on boards. The fact is that, right now, most of the yobs coming on to the slopes are using boards rather than skis. Like all yobs, they need to be policed and if possible educated. They sure ain't going to go away.

But they sure are going to get older, more mature and more considerate. Some of them are going to have children. Our guess is that, as a result, the gap between the two cultures will narrow, and disappear. Mind you, the philosophers among us say this will be achieved only if we develop a generic term to describe sliding on snow. Then, skiers and boarders will be able to take a 'sliding' holiday in a 'slide' resort, booking it through a 'slide' tour operator and taking lessons from the Ecole de Slide Française. Naturally, their choice will be guided by the latest *Where to Slide*. Suggestions, please.

AND THE WINNER IS ...

We have again analysed where our reporters take holidays. Here are last winter's top 18 resorts, with their previous positions in brackets:

1	Banff, Canada (–)	10	Chamonix, France (12)
2	La Plagne, France (4)		Flaine, France (6)
	Val-d'Isère, France (2)		Serre-Chevalier, France (4)
4	Courchevel, France (1)		Val-Thorens, France (6)
	Méribel, France (8)	14	Aspen, USA (–)
	Alpe-d'Huez, France (7)	15	Gressoney, Italy (–)
7	Selva, Italy (–)		La Thuile, Italy (–)
	Tignes, France (5)	17	St Anton, Austria (–)
	Whistler, Canada (–)		Vail, USA (–)

The rise of Banff to top slot serves to underline the astonishing success of the Canadian Rockies in the British market. Taking Banff and Lake Louise together, we got nearly twice as many reports on them as on any other resort. Some people say Canada is set to displace France as the most popular destination for the British.

For the moment, France continues to dominate our lists. But America and Italy have forced their way in for the first time.

And which resorts are served by the largest numbers of British tour operators? Answers below, with last year's ranking in brackets.

1	Val-d'Isère, France (1)	11	Les Arcs, France (19)
2	Méribel, France (2)	12	Les Deux-Alpes, France (12)
3	Courchevel, France (4)	13	Banff, Canada (10)
4	Chamonix, France (3)	14	Lake Louise, Canada (13)
5	Whistler, Canada (5)	15	Breckenridge, USA (17)
6	Tignes, France (6)	16	St Anton, Austria (18)
7	La Plagne, France (8)	17	Avoriaz, France (16)
8	Verbier, Switzerland (7)	18	Flaine, France (18)
9	Alpe-d'Huez, France (9)	19	Zermatt, Switzerland (3)
10	Val-Thorens, France (11)	20	Serre-Chevalier, France (14)

Club Med

neilson

Crystal HOLIDAYS

Inghams

SWISS TRAVEL SERVICE

SKI DIRECT the ULTIMATE
travel service for SKIERS

Radical

BRINGING POWDER TO

The number of operators going to Val-d'Isère has now reached a mind-boggling 54; even the three bottom-ranking resorts in this list have 21 operators each.

CHOICE AND MORE CHOICE
Meanwhile, at the opposite end of the spectrum, UK tour operators are adding more novel destinations to their programmes. Places that have appeared (or reappeared) on the menus of major operators since our last edition include resorts in the Spanish and French Pyrenees, Sweden, Lapland, Georgia (that's Georgia, ex-USSR, not Georgia, USA) and Serbia. We've got new sections on some of these destinations in this edition – and on areas that have become much more popular, such as New England – but it'll take us a while to catch up on all of them.

If you take a holiday in one of these relatively unknown areas this winter, we'd be especially grateful for a report on what you find. If you do a thorough job of reporting, there's a good chance you'll win a free copy of the next edition – we give a hundred away each year.

AN OLD MESSAGE RENEWED
Everybody knows that north-facing slopes are a good thing, except perhaps in January when the sun is weak and low in the sky. But it's easy to forget just how much more reliable they are than sunny south-facing slopes – in February as well as March and April.

We spent a sunny week in the southern French Alps late last February. We had great conditions in Risoul, Puy-St-Vincent, Serre-Chevalier and Les Deux-Alpes. And then came Alpe-d'Huez.

The difference was, to say the least, striking. There was plenty of snow, as elsewhere, but much of it was thoroughly unpleasant to ski on – thank heaven we weren't trying to snowboard – until approaching lunchtime, when the sun had softened it.

Happily, the big Alpe-d'Huez area includes some shadier slopes, towards Vaujany and on the Signal de l'Homme, so there was good snow to be found, even in the mornings. But we came away viewing Alpe-d'Huez as a better winter choice than a spring one.

GRAVE MISGIVINGS
On that same trip, we spent a day or two in the infamous village of La Grave. This cult resort has a high, steep, glacial mountainside served by one main lift of quite limited capacity. It has no prepared, marked or patrolled pistes, just two recognised routes down, marked out by signs so far apart as to be useless except in perfect weather. The mountain attracts a few hundred skiers and boarders each day.

The lift company, not surprisingly, has difficulty making ends meet. It can't hope to sell more lift tickets to people staying in the village, because there are only a few hundred beds there, so it has to pull in day visitors from other resorts. Ideally, those visitors (who are most unlikely to be experienced in negotiating slopes like those of La Grave) would be led by a mountain guide. But there is only a handful of guides in the resort.

Which explains how the lift company's marketing manager, a charming and energetic chap, has come up with the idea of encouraging British tour operators' 'guides' – or hosts, or escorts, or whatever euphemism is in favour – to take groups from resorts like Les Deux-Alpes and lead them down the slopes of La Grave.

In our view, this is lunacy. On a good day, with fine weather and soft but stable snow, La Grave seems innocent enough. But it's an illusion. What happens if a group gets split up? If a group and its leader get a bit cocky, and stray from the two poorly marked routes? If the weather turns sour? Maybe nothing much; maybe disaster.

Holiday-makers visiting the resort need to observe two golden rules. The first time you go there, go with a mountain guide; and if on later visits you're tempted to do without one, make sure you get good local advice on the state of the snow and the weather.

CHARTERS REVIVAL

One of the key factors in the development of transatlantic winter-sports holidays is, of course, the availability of flights. The boom in holidays to Colorado in the early 1990s was fuelled partly by charter flights to Denver, but scheduled flights then dominated the transatlantic scene until last season, when tour operators realised that by tapping the unused accommodation in and around Banff and laying on charters to Calgary, they could offer real bargains.

One theoretical advantage of charters is that they are cheaper than scheduled flights. Whether that is translated into practice depends on how desperate scheduled airlines are to fill their planes – if holidays to California are a bargain, it's not because of charters but because of excess capacity on scheduled flights. And some of the best bargains to Banff now use scheduled flights – competition in action. There is another attraction to some charters, though: directness.

All the big operators have a wide range of charters across the pond this season – weekend and midweek flights to Calgary (for Banff), Vancouver (for Whistler) and Denver (for Colorado), with some flights from Manchester as well as Gatwick. It's when flying to Denver that the charters really score: there are direct scheduled flights to Vancouver and Calgary, but not (these days) to Denver.

On the other hand, Denver is still a couple of hours' drive from resorts such as Breckenridge and Vail, and the trick with US destinations these days is to fly into the local airport. Vail's Eagle airport is still over half an hour from downtown, but Aspen's airport is within sight of the slopes, and you can now get to it on Northwest Airlines with a single change at Minneapolis. Even so, you don't get into Aspen until 9.40 pm, whereas you can easily get to Denver by around 6pm. Then again ... oh, that's enough of this – get the brochures and see for yourselves.

One thing we know from personal experience is that when charters go wrong, they can go wrong bigtime. A delay that starts out as tolerable can multiply if the aircrew runs out of hours. Scheduled flights do have their attractions.

PICTURE THIS

We've made bigger and better use of photographs in this edition – a trend we hope to extend in future. But it's an uphill struggle.

We take our own pictures when we visit resorts (if the weather is kind), but otherwise we rely heavily on resort tourist offices, with very variable results. Some of the pictures we've included are far from ideal, and in some resorts we haven't been able to get hold of a decent photo at all. For example, it's disappointing that Cortina, to our eyes the most spectacularly scenic resort in Europe, can't provide any worthwhile photographs of its amazing surroundings.

So here's a new departure: an invitation to competent amateur photographers to help us out. As well as reports from readers, we'd like photos from readers. Photos we can use in the next edition, like good reports, will be rewarded with free copies of the next edition – and we don't rule out the possibility of poorly paid 'commissions' to take more pictures. Photos taken in recent seasons will do, as well as up-to-the-minute ones. Drop us a line before sending any pics.

WATCH THIS LACK OF SPACE
Part of the reason that some skiers find boarders a danger, we believe, is simply that the slopes of the Alps are getting busier. Crowding on pistes makes the risk of collision higher, and the development of boarding has coincided with lift improvements throughout the Alps which have cut the time we all waste standing in queues.

One of the pictures below shows a piste last winter in Alpe-d'Huez. We're not actually sure it does full justice to the misery of trying to pick a way down between all those struggling people. It was peak season (French school holidays), and the resort is of course quieter at other times. But the fact is that when a big Alpine resort with efficient lifts is full, there isn't space on the pistes for everyone. We don't have a solution to offer the resorts; for holiday-makers, the solution is to go in low season, or go to north America.

CIVILISATION ADVANCES?
In our last edition we reproduced a picture taken in La Rosière, showing what we took to be a freak occurrence: French (well, mainly French) skiers lining up properly in a long, single-file lift queue of the form commonly seen in Scotland but nowhere else.

But we have seen isolated instances in other resorts since then, and last season – in the height of the high season, mark you – we came upon two similar examples in one week. Both were in the southern French Alps – one in Risoul, the other in Serre-Chevalier. The second of these, shown here, was so spectacularly long that it effectively blocked the mountainside for those wanting to carry on downhill rather than go back up. Thus we find ourselves in the rather unlikely position of hoping that the French go back to their old ways. At least a funnel-shaped queue can be circumnavigated.

High-season queues for the lifts in Serre-Chevalier ↓

High-season crowds on the sunny pistes in Alpe-d'Huez →

What's new?

lifts and snow for '98

Over the next four pages we summarise the main news from the resorts of Europe and north America. For travellers from Britain to the French Alps, there is also some interesting rail news for the 1997/98 season.

LONDON TO THE FRENCH ALPS BY RAIL

A new daytime train service on Saturdays will be going from London Waterloo direct to stations near Courchevel, Méribel, Valmorel, La Plagne, Les Arcs, La Rosière and Val-d'Isère/Tignes. The alternative is less convenient, but gets you two extra days on the slopes (like the established Snowtrain and Motorail services from Calais): you cross to Paris on Friday afternoon and have dinner before boarding a sleeper (couchettes only) which arrives early on Saturday. Return is late on Saturday. All services can be booked via tour operators, and all except the Snowtrain can be booked independently.

AUSTRIA

A new lift pass is being introduced. The Kitzbüheler Alpenskipass will cover the Ski-Welt, Kitzbühel, Alpbach, Schneewinkel and Wildschönau areas, and will be valid for any six days in the season.

HINTERTUX GETS A NEW GONDOLA

The long chair to the mid-mountain Tuxer Ferner Haus was replaced for 1996/97 by the 24-person 'Gletscherbus' gondola, which is not only fast but also insensitive to wind. The short lift on the way down to the valley, at Sommerbergalm, is now a fast 6-person chair.

ISCHGL'S DOUBLE-DECKER CABLE-CAR

In 1996/97 the world's first double-decker cable-car was opened from Samnaun, cutting afternoon queues.

KITZBUHEL SCRAPS THE HAHNENKAMM

For the 1996/97 season the outdated Hahnenkamm cable-car was replaced by a 6-person gondola, ending one of the worst lift queues in the Alps. Two drags were replaced by chairs.

SAALBACH-HINTERGLEMM CUTS THE QUEUES

For 1997/98 the Reiterkogel chair-lift out of Hinterglemm will be replaced by a new cable-car/gondola hybrid. During the previous season the Hochalm drag-lift was replaced by a 6-seater chair-lift.

SERFAUS SPEEDS UP

For 1997/98 two new fast chair lifts replace existing T-bars – a 6-seater to Plansegg and a quad to Alpkopf.

SOLL DOUBLES ITS SNOWMAKLNG

For 1997/98 snowmaking in the Ski-Welt area will be doubled to cover 99 km of slopes – Austria's biggest installation. In 1996/97 two quad chairs replaced drags, one speeding access to Hohe Salve.

FRANCE

CHAMONIX LINKS LE BREVENT TO LA FLEGERE

On the Grands Montets the Bochard chair has been replaced by a gondola with three times the capacity. There is now a cable-car link between Le Brévent and La Flégère slopes.

Les Deux-Alpes opens up Les Gours

Last season the long-awaited Fée chair-lift was opened, serving the new blue and black pistes in the Les Gours sector, and some good off-piste slopes into the Combe de Thuit.

Meribel gets new 8-seater gondola

For the 1997/8 season the Pas du Lac gondola is at last to be replaced by a more powerful 8-seater gondola, hopefully ending the afternoon queues to get back to Courchevel from Mottaret.

Morzine speeds up the circuit

The old chair-lift from Super-Morzine towards Avoriaz was replaced by a fast quad for the 1996/97 season, speeding up access to the main Portes de Soleil circuit from the Morzine gondola.

La Plagne upgrades

For 1996/97 the Borseliers and Rossa drags above Champagny were replaced by fast 6-seater chair-lifts. For 1997/98 the short Quillis drag over to the slopes of Belle Plagne is being replaced by a chair.

La Rosiere improves its links with Italy

The link with Italy will be improved for the 1997/98 season with the Col de la Traversette drag-lift on the French side replaced by a quad chair, and two other crucial lifts having their capacity doubled.

St-Martin-de-Belleville's new quad

A fast new quad chair has replaced the upper lift into the Three Valleys system, speeding up access to the higher slopes.

Tignes solves queue problems

For 1997/98 a new fast 6-seater chair-lift will go from Val Claret to Col de Fresse, speeding access to Val-d'Isère. Across the valley, the queue-prone Grand Huit chair, linking the slopes above Val Claret with those above Le Lac, will be replaced by a fast quad.

Val-Thorens boosts its key cable-car

For 1997/98 the Cîme de Caron cable-car, cause of some of the worst queues in the Three Valleys, is to get bigger cabins. The Moutière chair-lift, below the resort,is being replaced by a fast 6-seater.

Valmorel puts in fast quad

The main Beaudin chair-lift out of the resort will be replaced by a new covered fast quad in time for the 1997/98 season. There will also be a couple of new drag-lifts.

Italy

Cervinia scraps the old gondola

The slow old gondola from the bottom of the long run to Valtournenche is being replaced for the 1997/98 season by a new one with a much higher capacity.

Cortina d'Ampezzo to transform the Cinque Torri

In 1998/99 the quiet, outlying Cinque Torri area is due to be transformed by the replacement of ancient single chairs by a fast quad. Another fast quad is scheduled to link the area with Passo Falzarego, cutting out the need for a shuttle-bus transfer.

Selva/Sella Ronda tackles the queues

For the 1997/98 season the single Costabella chair out of Selva to the Dantercëpies gondola will be replaced by a fast quad, eliminating one of the worst queues on the Sella Ronda circuit. And a new 3-person chair-lift will be built from Plan to the lifts in Selva. A couple of quads are being installed in the Alta Badia. In 1996/97 an 8-seater gondola replaced two slow chairs in the Canazei-Campitello area from Lupo Bianco to Sellajoch.

SWITZERLAND
DAVOS REPLACES THE T-BARS
For the 1997/98 season the Usser Icht T-bar by the race-course on the Jakobshorn will be replaced by a fast quad chair. Another fast quad is also planned to replace the Totalp T-bar on the Parsenn, going from Parsennhütte towards Weissfluhjoch.

FLIMS GETS NEW GONDOLA
For 1997/98 the decrepit gondola out of Flims is being replaced by a new 8-person one which will go to Nagens via mid-stations at Plaun and Scansinas. This will make morning access to the slopes much better, and access to the Laax skiing quicker for Flims residents.

GSTAAD IS LINKED TO THE HORNBERG
Two new chair-lifts, serving two new pistes between Saanenmöser and Zweisimmen, will mean the latter's slopes will be linked into the main Hornberg ski area from the 1997/98 season.

ST MORITZ KEEPS MOVING
Several new fast quads have been installed on Corviglia. For 1997/98 the first stage of the cable-car up to the Corvatsch slopes is being replaced by a much bigger capacity one.

VERBIER HAS SLASHED THE QUEUES
The Tournelle chair-lift on Savoleyres will be replaced by another two-seater, almost doubling its capacity for the 1997/98 season. In recent seasons a new jumbo gondola from Ruinettes to Attelas has eliminated queues at Ruinettes. But don't worry, the queues at Tortin will be as bad as ever.

VILLARS IMPROVES ACCESS
Access to Les Diablerets was made simpler for 1996/97 by the installation of the two-way Perche-Conche chair-lift. For 1997/98 the main access gondola to Roc d'Orsay is to be replaced.

ZERMATT GETS A HUGE NEW CABLE-CAR
A new 150-person cable-car has replaced the earlier 80-person one from Blauherd to Unterrothorn, dramatically reducing queues.

USA
CALIFORNIA
HEAVENLY HAS BIG PLANS
A 6-person fast chair is planned from mid-mountain on the California side to near the top of the Nevada side.

MAMMOTH RACES AHEAD
Three new fast quads are replacing two chairs and a T-bar which serve the race-course area.

COLORADO
Transport and interchangeable lift ticket arrangements between Breckenridge, Vail, Beaver Creek and Keystone are being introduced.

ASPEN OPENS UP HIGHEST TERRAIN IN US
For 1997/98 the existing Ruthie's lift on Aspen mountain will be replaced by the first fast two-person chair-lift in the US. On Snowmass, a new button-lift will go from Big Burn to the top of the Cirque, an area previously accessible only by snowcat or hiking. This will be the highest lift in the US (3812m) and gives Snowmass the biggest vertical drop in the US (1342m).

BRECKENRIDGE SCRAPS SLOW CHAIRS
For 1997/98 two new fast quad chair-lifts are replacing two slow double chairs, one serving the top half of Peak 9, the other the top half of Peak 8 below the bowls.

Keystone opens new districts

There are plans to develop six distinct resort districts. For 1997/98, improvements will centre around River Run, where there will be a new fast quad to supplement the gondola.

Steamboat stays on course

Steamboat is in the middle of a large expansion programme which will add almost 40 per cent to its terrain when complete. A fast quad is replacing the Thunderhead and Arrowhead lifts.

Telluride gets its gondola

The long-awaited gondola linking the old town with the Mountain Village via the top of the mountain opened for 1996/97.

Vail-Beaver Creek leaps ahead

Beaver Creek's terrain was expanded by 30% for 1997 with the construction of the Bachelor Gulch chair-lift and other runs and lifts linking it to Arrowhead. For 1998, the Stump Park lift serving the top half of the main mountain is to be replaced by a fast 6-seat chair. The Arrowbahn fast chair will shift 50% more people. Two fast new lifts out of Vail were built for 1996/97 – the Eagle Bahn gondola at Lionshead and the Riva Bahn chair at Golden Peak.

Winter Park opens up new terrain

For 1997/98 435 acres of new expert terrain will be opened in Vasquez Cirque, west of Parsenn Bowl – open bowls and chutes at the top, glades lower down, served by the Timberline chair.

Utah

Park City replaces gondola

For 1997/98 two fast 6-seater chairs will replace the slow two-stage gondola. Four new runs are being cut near Blueslip Bowl, all equipped with snowmaking.

Snowbird takes flight

For 1997/98 a fast quad is to replace the Gad 1 double chair, the slow alternative to the queue-prone cable-car.

The Rest of the West

Jackson Hole makes things easy

For the 1997/98 season the Bridger gondola will go from the base area to the Headwall, opening up new expert and intermediate terrain previously accessible only by hiking. It will also take pressure off the cable-car, reducing the queues.

Canada

Whistler plays it safe

The Whistler Creek gondola was new for 1996/97. The two others on Whistler Mountain (Green and Redline) are being replaced by more reliable ones for 1997/98. And new black runs have been cut through the trees from West Bowl to Whistler Creekside.

Andorra

Pas de la Casa speeds up

There is a new six-seater high speed chair back from Grau Roig, and a new drag lift up to Collada d'Enradort.

Slicker access at Soldeu

There is now a gondola from the resort base up the main mountain.

Scotland

Major expansion at Nevis Range

Three new lifts have been built, doubling the size of the slopes.

Just to get rid of our cheap image.

No one has ever claimed that our fares are too low. But no one could ever accuse us of stinginess in the area of service and comfort, either. Not to mention reliability and safety. To all those travellers in Europe who may have criticised us for not having blue leather seats in all classes: You'll be happy now. While this increases the value of your Swissair flight, we'd consider it cheap to ask for higher fares. http://www.swissair.com

swissair ✚ world's most refreshing airline.

by **Chris Allan**

Drive to the Alps

and ski where you please

The days when driving from Britain to the Alps was the preserve of the most intrepid of motorists, spurred on by a pioneering spirit, have long gone. The advent of the Channel Tunnel and the tremendous improvements made to the motorway networks in northern France and the Alps have made life much, much easier for the growing number of Brits who decide to drive down. You can now get to most resorts easily in a day. The advantages? It's less hassle, it gives you tremendous freedom once you're in the Alps – the kind of freedom you're probably used to on summer holidays – and it can save money.

If you've never tried driving to the Alps, you don't know what you're missing. For a start, it simplifies the whole business of getting all your kit from here to there: you just load up at one end and unload at the other, without tangling with airport trolleys. If you're taking your family or going self-catering, just think of all the extra things you can cram in that you'd otherwise have to leave behind.

But for us, the freedom factor is the key. If the snow's bad in your resort, or if the lift queues are horrendous, car drivers can try somewhere else. And a car gives a means of escape if it turns out that you don't like the resort you've booked into, or you find the terrain rather limited.

One of the most important plus-points as far as we're concerned is that we can extend the standard six-day holiday by two days while taking only one extra day off work. We do it by crossing the Channel early on a Friday morning and returning nine days later on the Sunday evening. That means we get both Saturdays on the slopes.

Of course, you need accommodation for the Friday night on the way out, and the Saturday night on the way back. On the trip out, we often take advantage of this to spend a day in a different resort before moving on to our final destination late on the Saturday. You could stop off in Chamonix before driving on to Courmayeur, Cervinia or La Thuile in Italy. You could stop off in Valmorel before going on to the Three Valleys or Val-d'Isère. If you're going to Zermatt or Saas-Fee, you could stop off in Wengen or Mürren before putting the car on the train for the half-hour journey through the Lötschberg tunnel, which takes you to the Valais. The possibilities are endless.

After a full day on the slopes on the final Saturday, if you drive towards the Channel for a few hours you won't find Sunday's journey too demanding. In France, you'll be spoiled for choice as far as comfortable and reasonably priced hotels are concerned – particularly in cities such as Mâcon or Strasbourg. You'll be able to enjoy a good, non-resort meal at good non-resort prices. And what better way is there to round off the holiday than a superb French Sunday lunch?

Taking a car means you can tailor your holiday to your needs. You can simply use it for the journey and then forget about it. You can enjoy day trips to other resorts or spend the week touring. It also enables you to escape far from the madding crowd.

Because the quattro four wheel drive system monitors each wheel to de

er and grip when it's needed, the road ahead is always straight.

Audi

Vorsprung durch Technik

AS YOU LIKE IT

If you fancy visiting several resorts, you can use one as a base and make day trips.to nearby places when it suits you. This way, you can still take advantage of the tour operator prices – and get a discount for driving. The discount varies from operator to operator and also depends on whether you go in high or low season – but you can expect to get from around £70 to £120.

The key to turning this kind of holiday into a success is to go for a base which offers easy road access to other resorts. A good choice is the Tirol. The resorts to the east of Innsbruck offer many options for day-trippers. Söll is a convenient base for exploring the other resorts nearby, as well as such resorts as Alpbach and Kitzbühel.

Further east, in Salzburg province, you can use Zell am See as a base for excursions to Bad Gastein and Saalbach, while Flachau is a convenient base for visiting the resorts covered by the Top Tauern lift pass, such as Schladming and Obertauern. Although western Austria is not ideal for this sort of holiday, you could use St Anton as a base and make day-trips to Lech, Zürs, Ischgl and Serfaus.

In the southern French Alps, Serre-Chevalier and Montgenèvre are ideal bases for day-tripping. If the extensive slopes of Serre-Chevalier aren't enough for you, Montgenèvre is within easy reach by car. It's at one end of the Milky Way lift network, which includes Sauze d'Oulx and Sestriere in Italy – you can drive on to them or reach them by lift and piste. On the French side of the border, a few miles south, Puy-St-Vincent is well worth a visit. The major resorts of Alpe-d'Huez and Les Deux-Alpes are also within range. An added bonus is that these resorts share lift-pass arrangements.

The Chamonix valley is an ideal destination for day-trippers. It offers a terrific number of lifts and runs covered by the Mont-Blanc pass – in Chamonix, Megève, Les Contamines, Courmayeur plus a few more. Flaine and its satellites are also fairly accessible – so is Verbier in Switzerland if the intervening passes are open.

You could consider resorts on the Swiss side of the Portes du Soleil, such as Morgins and Champéry, as a base for trips to such resorts as Verbier, Crans-Montana and Chamonix, as well as visiting the Portes du Soleil resorts.

Because the resorts are so remote, Italy provides more of a headache for day-trippers. Courmayeur is a notable exception – with quick access to La Thuile and, through the Mont-Blanc tunnel, to the Chamonix valley. The trip to Cervinia is a rather slow one. And in some parts of the Dolomites it's useful to have a car – to get from Cortina to the Sella Ronda circuit, for example.

Although eastern Switzerland provides more of a challenge to day-trippers, you might find that it's well worth the effort. Lenzerheide is about the best choice of base-camp. Flims, Arosa, Davos and St Moritz are all within striking distance. From St Moritz you could even go over to Livigno in Italy.

AROUND THE ALPS IN SEVEN DAYS

If you want to ski as much of the Alps as possible, consider making a Grand Tour by car, moving every day or two to a different resort and enjoying the complete freedom of going where you want, when you want. Except in high season, there's no need to book any accommodation before you go. So you can decide at the last minute which part of the Alps to visit – where the snow is best, perhaps.

You may have the impression that if you take a touring holiday you'll be spending more time on the road than on the piste. This isn't the case – provided you plan your route carefully. And there's no need to eat into the precious daylight hours. An hour's drive after the lifts have shut is all it takes to travel quite a distance.

Many of the areas that are great for day-trippers are also worth considering if you're going on tour. These include western Austria, the Tirol and the Chamonix valley. Take western Austria, for example; you could start with Lech, Zürs and St Anton, move on to Serfaus and Ischgl, then go down to Obergurgl, perhaps stopping at Sölden on the way.

For the Tarentaise region of France, you could draw up the kind of schedule, albeit fairly hectic, that the keen skier or boarder would drool over. Imagine a week in which you could cover the Three Valleys, La Plagne, Les Arcs, and Val-d'Isère/Tignes.

Italy is far more suitable for tourers than day-trippers provided you're prepared to put up with some slow drives on winding passes. You could start in Livigno, drive to Bormio and then to the Dolomites, visiting Madonna di Campiglio and Selva, and finish your Italian expedition in Cortina.

Eastern Switzerland also offers a very attractive touring holiday. You could start in Davos/Klosters, take in Lenzerheide and Arosa and end up in Flims. You could even include St Moritz if you're prepared to put up with a little extra driving. Again in Switzerland, you could easily combine several resorts in the Bernese Oberland – for example, Gstaad, Adelboden, Grindelwald, Wengen and Mürren. But do remember that the last two are car-free so you'll have to leave your car in Lauterbrunnen.

There's no need to confine yourself to one country. You could imitate the famous Haute-Route by starting in Argentière in France and ending up in Switzerland's Saas-Fee. On the way you could take in Verbier and Zermatt, and even Crans-Montana if time permits.

The major thing that you have to watch out for with a touring holiday is the cost of accommodation. Checking into a resort hotel as an independent traveller for a night or two doesn't come cheap. You can save money by staying down the valley – and you don't even have to drive to the slopes in the morning. For example, you can take the funicular from Bourg-St-Maurice to Les Arcs; a gondola links Brides-Les-Bains to Méribel. You can let the train take the strain in Lauterbrunnen for Wengen and Mürren; and Täsch for Zermatt.

FAR FROM THE MADDING CROWD

If you prefer to escape conversations about England's chances of regaining the Ashes, or the state of the NHS, driving to the Alps has clear advantages. By travelling independently, you can boldly go where not too many Brits have gone before, off the beaten tour operator track. There are hundreds of resorts in the Alps to discover – and in many you'd be unlucky if you heard another British voice.

TRAVEL TIME

The French Alps are the number one destination for most British motorists. The journey time is surprisingly quick. From Calais, for example, you can cover the 900km (560 miles) to Chamonix in just nine hours plus stops – all but the final few miles is on motorways. Although some areas of the Alps are less straightforward to get to, the majority are within a day's driving range provided you cross the Channel early.

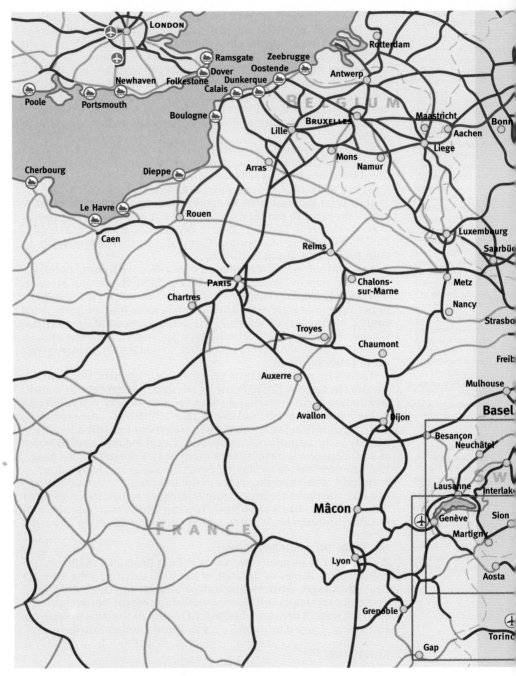

This map should help you plan your route to the Alps. As we've
explained in the text, all the main routes from the Channel and all the
routes up into the mountains funnel through three 'gateways', picked
out on the map in larger type – Mâcon, Basel and Ulm. Decide which
gateway suits your destination, and pick a route to it. Occasionally,
different Channel ports will lead you to use different gateways.

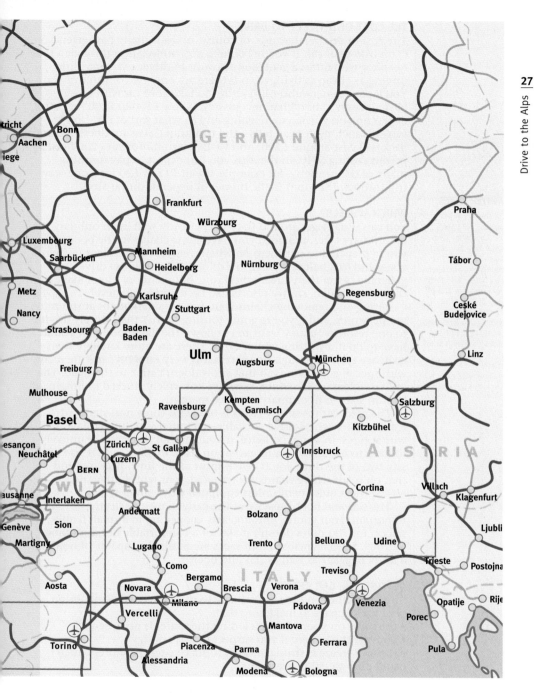

The boxes on the map correspond to the areas covered by the more detailed maps at the start of the main country sections of the book:
Austria page 81
France page 161
Italy page 297
Switzerland page 345.

THE COST OF A TICKET TO DRIVE

The cost of driving depends, of course, on how many passengers you cram into your car. If you're booking accommodation through a tour operator who offers a generous discount to drivers, you may find driving as cheap as flying even if there are only two or three of you. You'll pay from around £130 return to take your car with one passenger on a short channel crossing. Allow £100 to £200 for petrol, depending on where you're going and in what sort of car. Don't forget French motorway tolls – the trip from Calais to Albertville and back will cost around £100. And to use Swiss motorways you need a permit costing SF40. In the Alps you can expect to pay for using many of the tunnels – for example, about £15 or £20 for a one-way trip through the Mont-Blanc tunnel (it depends on car size).

WHICH WHEELS?

You can usually get around the Alps perfectly well in an ordinary car on ordinary tyres, provided you have snow-chains in the boot and you're prepared to put them on whenever it seems prudent (ie before you grind to a halt or slide into a ditch). A front-wheel drive car is generally better than a rear-wheel one, but plenty of Mercs make their way to high, snowy resorts like Lech and Courchevel.

Fitting and removing chains is no fun on a dark night at sub-zero temperatures, and if you're going touring (rather than simply driving to one resort) you may want to cut down the likelihood that you'll have to do it, by fitting winter tyres. These are more knobbly than ordinary tyres (although not necessarily very knobbly) and are made with special compounds so that snow doesn't stick to the tread. The only problem is that winter tyres are not widely stocked in Britain, at least in sizes to fit ordinary cars (see margin).

The ideal car for snowy roads is one with three non-standard features: four-wheel-drive; lockable or limited-slip differentials; and winter tyres. In our experience, if you have all three you're unlikely to have to use snow-chains except on steep inclines, and if you have any two of the three you'll be OK most of the time. Bear in mind that on roads where chains are required, four-wheel drives don't escape the requirement unless equipped with winter tyres.

The size and boot capacity of the car you use are clearly important. Four adults, plus luggage, cooped up in a small family saloon for 700 miles doesn't make for a comfortable or harmonious journey. Special enclosed roof racks are available, capable of holding a lot of baggage as well as skis and boards.

GETTING THE CAR READY

Alpine weather and roads are likely to make unusual demands on your car – it pays to make sure that:
• the tread on your tyres (including the spare) is up to scratch
• you test the battery if you suspect that it's dodgy
• the anti-freeze is strong enough to survive temperatures which could drop to -30°C overnight
• you have a similarly strong solution of winter screenwash
• you check the handbook to see if you need to do anything to adapt the car for cold weather; you may for example, have to adjust the engine air intake, or use a thinner oil
• you fit headlight beam deflectors; if they normally throw a lot of light upwards, fit special fog lights which will be a big help if you have to drive at night in falling snow.

CAR COVER

Even if you have fully comprehensive insurance, it will often be down-graded to third party as soon as you leave the UK, unless you've made arrangements to extend it – allow a week or two for this. Most companies don't charge for such extensions. Although it's no longer compulsory to carry a Green Card in other EU countries, it's a good idea to ask your insurance company for one.

If your car breaks down or is damaged in an accident, you could face a big bill, lengthy delays and utter disruption to your holiday plans. You can buy peace of mind by taking out a breakdown insurance policy, which will cover the cost of things like a replacement hire car. Some UK breakdown insurance policies also cover the Continent, or offer cover as a low-cost option.

SAFE DRIVING

Except in severe weather, you're not likely to come across serious snow conditions except on approach roads to fairly high resorts. Unless you've got a four-wheel-drive car with winter tyres, you'll need chains on the car's driving wheels – not simply to keep you safe and mobile but also to stay on the right side of local laws. You can keep the chains on while you're driving on ordinary roads; but you'll have to drive very slowly and for a limited period only. The instructions should have information about this.

If you've never used chains before, it's well worth having a practice run at putting them on. The first time we had to fit them, we spent a very unhappy hour lying in the road-side slush as the snow came down and our fellow motorists cursed us in a variety of languages as they squeezed past us on a narrow mountain road.

Even if the road surface seems dry and free of ice, still take great care – there could be icy patches on shaded areas. You can't afford to relax in relatively warm weather – there's nothing more treacherous than ice that's melting. Be especially cautious when going downhill. If the road surface is slippery, keep your speed down and brake by using your engine – change down in good time. Brake on the straight, not on bends – otherwise the front wheels may lock and you'll slide straight on. If the back wheels slide and the car starts to spin, steer into the slide.

MOUNTAIN MOTOR MAINTENANCE

Your car will be in for quite a culture shock having, perhaps, left a nice warm garage for overnight temperatures way, way below freezing. So:
• overnight, park on flat ground and in a place where your car will be sheltered from the wind
• leave the car in gear with the hand-brake off; you could have problems if the hand-brake freezes in the 'on' position
• lift the wipers away from the windscreen
• if you're not planning to use the car for a week, it's worth taking it out as departure day approaches, to make sure all is well and top up the battery.

RECOMMENDED ROUTES

From the Channel there are essentially only three 'gateways' into the Alps. For the French and some of the Swiss Alps, you go via the French motorways and **Mâcon**. For most of the Swiss and some of the Austrian Alps you aim for **Basel**. For all of the Austrian Alps you can go via **Ulm** – and for some Austrian resorts it's the only sensible route. Normally, once you've picked your destination you'll be able to see which gateway you need; our maps of Austria (page 81), France (page 161), Italy (page 297) and Switzerland (page 345) will help. Then you can concentrate on deciding how to get to that gateway from a particular port.

Where you have a choice of route, you may wish to bear in mind that German motorways are free, whereas French ones charge tolls that are not negligible (Calais to Albertville and back £100). German ones mostly have no speed limit, making them potentially quicker but rather scary in wet weather. And their petrol stations rarely accept credit cards. To use Swiss motorways, you have to buy a sticker for your windscreen (SF40 for a calendar year). These are sold at the border, and you're expected to buy one unless you have a pretty convincing route-plan involving no motorways.

DESTINATION: FRENCH ALPS

Wherever you're starting from, the gateway is **Mâcon** and the initial target is Beaune. If you're taking the short crossing to Calais, Boulogne or Dunkirk, the route is via Reims, Troyes and Dijon. From Le Havre or Caen your route sounds even simpler: the A13 to Paris then the A6 south. But you have to get through or around Paris. The most direct way around the city is the notorious périphérique – a hectic, multi-lane urban motorway close to the centre, with exits every few hundred yards. But this is not the quickest if is jammed with traffic. The more reliable alternative is to take a series of motorways and dual carriageways through the south-west fringes of Greater Paris. The route (or one of the routes – there are a couple of variants) is signed, but not easy to follow without a detailed map and a good navigator.

At Mâcon, the routes start to diverge; you go east on the A40 for **Geneva** to get to the northern resorts – Chamonix, the Portes du Soleil and so on; take the A43 off the Lyon bypass for **Chambéry** to get to the central Tarentaise mega-resorts; and take the A48 south off that road for **Grenoble** to get to the southern resorts.

DESTINATION: SWITZERLAND

There are two gateways for Switzerland. For the Valais resorts of Champéry, Verbier, Saas-Fee, Zermatt and so on, and those in Vaud such as Villars and Les Diablerets, aim for **Mâcon** and then Geneva. (You may want to consider an alternative route via Besançon, Pontarlier and Lausanne, two-thirds of the way along lake Geneva. Whether this is quicker than the Mâcon-Geneva motorway route depends on the speed of traffic on the route nationale, and how fast you generally drive on French motorways.)

If you're going further east, the gateway is **Basel**. This presents more alternative routes than any other gateway. From Calais the obvious route is via Reims, Metz and Strasbourg, then across the border to the autobahn up the Rhine valley. But from ports further east, other routes are viable – via the Belgian motorways to Luxembourg and into France to pick up the Calais route; or Belgian motorways towards Cologne, then all the way up the Rhine valley. From the Normandy ports, you have a choice of going via Paris to join the Calais route at Reims or heading south, as if for Geneva, and turning left at Beaune. This is the better bet – slightly quicker, more scenic, and better equipped with good places for lunch.

From Basel, the routes diverge: you go on to **Bern** for the Bernese Oberland, and resorts as Wengen and Grindelwald; to **Lucerne** for resorts in central Switzerland; and to **Zürich** for resorts in the Grisons – Davos, Flims and so on.

DESTINATION: AUSTRIA

For the Vorarlberg resorts in western Austria (notably Lech and Zürs) and for St Anton just inside the Tirol, the best gateway may be **Basel** – particularly if starting from the Normandy ports. You drive through Switzerland, and cross into Austria at **Feldkirch**.

But for most purposes the gateway is **Ulm**, between Stuttgart and Munich. From the short-crossing ports there are several ways to get to it, but the basic choice is the same as those for Basel: via France and Strasbourg; via Belgium, Luxembourg and Strasbourg; or via Belgium and the Rhine valley. Our basic advice to those thinking of starting from the Normandy ports is: don't.

From Ulm, routes diverge. For the Vorarlberg and Arlberg resorts, head south to cross into Austria at Bregenz and join the Basel route at **Feldkirch**. For Innsbruck and neighbouring resorts, branch south-east off that route, crossing into Austria between Füssen and **Reutte** and then negotiating the low Fern pass to get to the Inn valley. For resorts further east, carry on through Munich and cross into Austria at **Kufstein** (for resorts in the eastern Tirol – Kitzbühel and neighbours) or **Salzburg** (for resorts in Salzburg province, Styria or Carinthia – Zell am See, Bad Gastein, Schladming, Badkleinkirchheim.)

DESTINATION: ITALY

Italian resorts are spread out over the whole length of the Alpine range. They are reached by passes or tunnels from France, Switzerland or Italy. The possibilities are set out in detail in our introduction to Italian resorts on page 297.

Get next year's edition free

and help make it even better

There are too many resorts for us to visit them all every year, and even in those we do visit there are too many hotels, chalets, bars, nightspots and mountain restaurants for us to hope to see them all. So we are very keen to encourage more people to join our already healthy band of correspondents, who send in reports on their holiday experiences. To encourage readers, we'll be giving away 100 copies of next year's edition to the writers of the best reports.

If you reported on your holiday last year, we'll be sending you a new report form during the season. If you didn't but would like a form, just drop us a line to the address below; no stamp is necessary. But we're always happy to receive reports, whether they are on the form or not. Many reporters would rather use their word processor than struggle to write legibly, and we certainly want to encourage that. But all reports should be clearly set out in a structured way that we can easily handle. (Imagine sifting through a dozen rambling letters to see what people think of a particular ski school, and you'll understand why a clear structure is important.)

The structure we favour is closely related to the structure of the resort chapters of the book – and indeed you'll find it helpful when compiling a report to have the relevant chapter to hand, to see what we've said in this edition. Here are the headings we'd like you to use:

HOW IT RATES
Give the resort marks out of five for:
The slopes
Snow
Extent
Experts
Intermediates
Beginners
Convenience
Queues
Mountain restaurants
The rest
Scenery
Resort charm
Off-slope facilities

OVERVIEW
Summarise the main pros and cons of the resort:
The resort
What did you like?
What did you dislike?
What surprised you?
Who does it suit?
The mountains
What did you like?
What did you dislike?
What surprised you?
Who does it suit?

DETAILED ASSESSMENT
Under each heading, summarise your view of the resort in as much detail as you can. Where appropriate (in the starred sections, probably) give your particular recommendations:
Snow reliability
For experts
For intermediates
For beginners
For cross-country
Queues
Mountain restaurants*
Ski schools*
Facilities for children*
Choice of location*
Chalets*
Hotels*
Self-catering apartments*
Where to eat*
Après-ski*
Off-slope facilities*
Write to:
Where to Ski and Snowboard
FREEPOST
The Old Forge
Norton St Philip
Bath
BA3 6UB

by **Chris Allan**

66 years of sun and snow
from Erna Low

'Young Viennese graduate invites other young people to join her Christmas ski-ing.' That brief ad appeared in the personal columns of the London *Times* in 1932. It was to launch the career of one of the great pioneers of the skiing holiday – Erna Low. Some seven decades on, both she and her company, Erna Low Consultants, are still going strong. In fact, they're the largest UK self-drive tour operator to the French Alps – organising holidays for over 10,000 people last season.

Erna's first group of clients were to boldly go where few British skiers had gone before – Austria. The cost for a fortnight in Sölden was £15 (that's not a misprint). It included full board in the one and only inn, rail travel to and from the resort, ski hire and tuition, and, of course, a lesson in German. Those early skiing trailblazers were a hardy breed – they had to be. They wore stout, leather, lace-up boots which would have turned a skinhead green with envy. Simple straps and ties held boots and wooden skis together – and together they stayed: safety releases were a thing for the wimps of the future, as were lifts. If you wanted to ski, then you carried your skis and walked up and up and up. Hardly surprising that the Stubai and Hintertux glaciers were fairly skier-free.

Homesickness, rather than a desire for entrepreneurial glory, prompted Erna's first sortie into the travel business. In the twenties, she'd left Vienna to study in London, but found that she couldn't afford to visit her family and the Austrian slopes as often as she would have liked. Necessity was to prove the mother of invention, hence that brief ad in 1932. It attracted five enthusiastic clients – enough to help fund Erna's trip home. But that first holiday was far more than a financial success – Erna and her party had a marvellous time. So much so that she decided to offer more skiing holidays. Erna placed great value on the 'personal touch'. She inspected the hotels and knew the guides. In fact, she personally accompanied each group until the mid-1950s.

1932. LONDON. TIMES PERSONAL. "YOUNG VIENNESE GRADUATE INVITES OTHER YOUNG PEOPLE TO JOIN HER CHRISTMAS SKI-ING"

ERNA LOW TOOK HER FIRST PARTY TO AN UNKNOWN SKI-ING COUNTRY–AUSTRIA.

An early Erna Low Ski Party in Fieberbrunn, Austria ➔

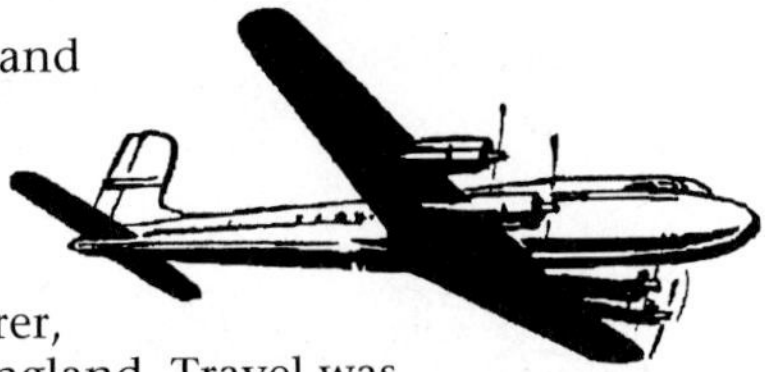

The business flourished in the thirties and Erna Low holidays were well and truly on the map. But the map was to be torn up by one Herr Hitler. During the Second World War, Erna joined the Army's Education Corps as a lecturer, travelling the length and breadth of England. Travel was hardly a burden to Erna; indeed, it provided her with the catalyst for another innovation in the holiday market – the house party. She rented large English houses and boarding-schools and invited paying guests to stay. The atmosphere was informal. The aim was to allow people to meet each other. Sounds familiar? It should do. These English house parties were the forerunner of the chalet holiday. In the early fifties, Erna became the first tour operator to offer them as a holiday option for skiers.

Erna Low invented chalet parties in the 1950s ↓

HOUSE PARTIES

House parties are meant for skiers and beginners of all ages who are travelling alone and want to enjoy an all-round ski holiday with equal emphasis on skiing and apres-ski life.

The Erna Low Travel Service had been launched in 1947 against a backdrop of post-war austerity. Her early brochure featured the slogan, 'To Sun and Snow with Erna Low' – how enticing that must have seemed in that bitterly cold British winter.

Erna's early holidays to Saas-Fee entailed a three-hour ascent by foot or on a mule →

April 14th – April 30th: Saas Fee, Valais, Switzerland.

You could not fail to enjoy an Easter skiing at Saas Fee, one of the highest and most attractive Swiss Alpine villages. The three-hour ascent has to be made by foot or on a mule! Your hotel room will look straight out on to the glaciers. You will enjoy iced drinks and the light wine of the Valais sitting on the sun terrace of the hotel – one of the best I know. Glacier ski touring with guides well known to my parties.

Foreign currency controls were still in place but Erna made life easier for her clients with her 'V' Form scheme – enabling them to pay part of the cost in sterling. In those days, most people travelled by rail. They boarded the train at Victoria Station and arrived in Austria a day later. A long journey, but one made less tedious by another of Erna's ideas – the music car (the prototype for today's disco car on the snowtrain). Thousands made the trip. As package tour holidays began to boom in the sixties, Erna introduced many more flight packages. Innovation has been the hallmark of Erna's career. In the sixties, enterprising skiers were offered the chance to ski in Cyprus, the Lebanon, Morocco and Turkey. Erna Low Ski Counsellors toured the UK, offering advice on resorts, equipment and so on.

ERNA LOW

9 Reece Mews, London SW7 3HE
Information and reservations: 0171 584 2841
Brochure line (24 hours): 0171 584 7820
Fax: 0171 589 9531
e-mail: ernalow@easynet.co.uk
Erna Low Consultants Ltd are members of AITO and licensed by ATOL.

Erna sold her business in 1972, only to buy back her name and the goodwill some three years later. In 1979, she sold the business for a second time. However, Erna had no thoughts of retirement. In 1980, at the age of 72, she launched Erna Low Consultants Ltd. Her first client was La Plagne – Erna became the resort's official UK representative. It was at this time that she was joined by a young graduate, Joanna Yellowlees – now a partner and the company's MD. Flaine was quick to follow La Plagne's example. A few years later, they were joined by Les Arcs.

Erna has never been one to let the grass grow under her feet. Last year, to complement its three dedicated brochures on La Plagne, Les Arcs and Flaine, the company launched its first general French Alps' brochure for 16 years. It offered hotel/apartment holidays in the major French resorts, tailor-made for the independent traveller – go when you want to go, travel how you want to travel. Although Erna Low is already the market leader for self-drive French ski holidays, the company is set to expand even further in the 1997/98 season. It has become the UK ski agent for Pierre & Vacances, the largest apartment agency in France.

During the past seven decades, Erna's contribution to the development of the ski industry has been enormous. Since she placed that first tentative ad in *The Times*, her ideas and expertise have helped to change skiing holidays almost out of all recognition. Back in the thirties, skiers were few and far between. So, the next time you feel sorry for yourself because you're stuck in a lift queue, spare a thought for Erna and those early pisteblazers. Imagine them striding past you and climbing up the mountain. And, when you curse because there's a traffic jam up to your resort, grit your teeth and think of Erna and her clients making the ascent to Saas-Fee by foot or mule. Those were the days.

A brochure from the 1960s ↓

Erna Low has been offering motoring holidays for years and is now the largest UK self-drive tour operator to the French Alps ↓

Erna also invented the forerunner of the today's disco car on the snowtrain →

Cash points

the cost of skiing

Britannia may no longer rule the waves, but we're doing very nicely on the foreign exchange markets. Sterling has risen strongly against the currencies of the major Alpine nations in the last twelve months. When we went to press, the pound was up around 20 per cent against the French and Swiss francs, the schilling and the lira compared to a year ago. For example, last year, £1 stood at 7.7 French francs and 1.9 Swiss francs – by the time we went to press, it had gone up to 9.3 and 2.3 respectively and was still rising. Although sterling has also risen against the American and Canadian dollars, the increase has been less spectacular. So, any skiing Euro-sceptics out there should give some serious thought to the idea of returning to the Alps.

Hurry! Hurry! Hurry! Prices slashed! 'Loadsabargains'! None more so, it would seem, than a package to Europe's most expensive ski hotel – Badrutt's Palace in glitzy St Moritz. When we first reported on the Palace, back in 1994, a week's half-board in high season would have set you back £2,264 per person. It must be said that this figure did include free use of the indoor pool. Last year, the price had fallen to a mere £1,950. And for this coming season, the price has slumped to just £1,680. The pool's still free, but you'll have to pay for use of the Jacuzzi, sauna and solarium. Even with a 35 per cent reduction in price over the past three years, Badrutt's Palace may still be out of your reach. Don't despair, there's always Poiana Brasov – prices have fallen there too. Three seasons ago, a week's half-board in a 2-star hotel cost £219 in low season. This year, you can enjoy staying in Romania's top resort for just £204 in early January.

Between the glitz of St Moritz and the somewhat less glamorous Poiana Brasov you can choose from the hundreds of packages and resorts on offer. Costs will vary enormously depending on the destination and type of accommodation you choose and whether you go in high or low season. The differences become even greater when you add on the cost of lift pass, equipment hire, ski school, eating, drinking and dancing. Skiing is still an expensive business. But you should find your money will go further this coming season.

We've checked the cost of packages to all of the most popular destinations for Brits in Europe and North America. We've also compared the costs of that other necessary item of expenditure for skiers – the lift pass. And we've looked at the cost of eating and drinking on the mountain. For each resort in this book we've given a price rating based on the total cost – see page 41. Here we look in more detail at package and lift pass prices for a range of resorts from the most expensive to the cheapest.

EUROPEAN COSTS

We looked at the brochures of some of the major tour operators and worked out the typical costs of chalets, 3-star and 4-star hotels (including half-board, flights and transfers) for two people sharing a room for the half-term week in February. On page 38, we list them in price order, based on the cost of 4-star hotel packages.

Most of the hotel and chalet prices in Austria and Switzerland that we looked at have actually fallen since last season. Reductions of around £50 per person per week are not unusual. Considerable efforts seem to have been made to woo back those thousands of British skiers who bade a sad *aufwiedersehn* to Austria and Switzerland when the schilling and franc went into orbit against the pound. Not so Italy. Although the lira has remained weak against the pound, hotel package prices in some of the top resorts have risen since last year. It could be that the Italians are cashing in on their reputation as the bargain-basement of Europe's Big Four. Nevertheless, the vast majority of Italian resorts are still relatively cheap. The picture in France is more patchy – some increases, some decreases.

Gone are the days when Switzerland was most the expensive country for skiers. Indeed, only one Swiss resort, St Moritz, made it into the most expensive group, charging around £1,000 for a week's 4-star hotel package. These days, the top French resorts have the strongest presence at the top of the expense table. Courchevel has easily retained its title as Europe's most expensive resort. A week in a 4-star hotel at Courchevel 1850 can set you back around £1,340 – around one-third more costly than its nearest rival Lech. Moving a little down-market to 3-star accommodation can still damage your pocket to the tune of around £980 in Courchevel. Chic Cortina d'Ampezzo's presence in the premier flight, together with that of Courmayeur and Cervinia in the next division, illustrates how the top Italian resorts are moving up the expenses league.

Popular destinations for Brits, such as Verbier, Zermatt, Obergurgl and St Anton, feature in our second division – quite some distance behind the most money-sapping resorts. For example, a week in a 4-star hotel will cost you around one-third less in Verbier than in Courchevel, while a week in a St Anton 3-star hotel will cost around 25 per cent less than one in Val-d'Isère. Eastern Europe is still miles behind in the cost stakes – a week in a 3-star hotel in Poiana Brasov or Borovets is less than half the price of the most expensive resorts.

The price gap between 4-star and 3-star hotels tends to narrow as you move down the expenses league table. However, catered chalet prices are much more evenly spread, making the expensive resorts much more affordable. In the top resorts, standard chalets (not the luxury kind we feature in the chapter starting on page 58) work out very much cheaper than 3-star hotels – and that's before you start adding your wine and bar bill and other extras on to the

hotel cost. Take Val-d'Isère, for example: the difference between a 3-star hotel and a chalet works out at around £230. In Cortina, the difference amounts to around £190. At the other end of the price spectrum, say Soldeu, you'll only save around £50 if you stay in a chalet rather than a hotel. And, in Borovets, you could actually pay more for chalet accommodation.

EUROPEAN PACKAGES	4* Hotel £	3* Hotel £	Chalet £
Courchevel	1340	980	600
Lech	1010	-	570
Cortina d'Ampezzo	1000	740	550
Val-d'Isère	990	850	620
Alpe d'Huez	980	670	540
St Moritz	970	-	-
Verbier	870	680	530
Courmayeur	830	580	450
Zermatt	820	670	590
Cervinia	800	600	-
Obergurgl	790	630	520
St Anton	770	640	600
Wengen	740	600	570
Valmorel	-	680	500
Serre-Chevalier	-	650	510
Kitzbühel	700	540	500
Geilo	640	540	-
Sauze d'Oulx	630	510	470
Soll	630	510	450
Grindelwald	610	540	-
Livigno	580	550	-
Soldeu	530	440	390
Sierra Nevada	490	470	-
Poiana Brasov	-	360	-
Borovets	-	350	360

Notes: All prices are for one week in high season. They're based on half-board, two people sharing a room and include flights and transfers.

Next, the cost of a six-day lift pass. And here, there's very good news for British skiers – the strength of the pound has really made a difference to prices. On page 40, we list, in price order, the cost of 6-day passes for the coming year using the exchange rates that applied when we went to press (see margin copy on page 40); figures in brackets are those for the 95/96 season. In all but five of the resorts in our table, the cost has fallen over the last two seasons. The five exceptions to the falling cost trend are the Italian resorts. Elsewhere, there have been some amazing reductions. Take Verbier and Zermatt for example: two years ago, at £165 and £162, they stood head and shoulders above the rest of the European resorts – this season, the cost has fallen to £122 and £128 respectively. Reductions of £25 to

The original all-inclusive holiday

Club Med

Now in its 49th year, Club Med's continued success lies in the simplicity and power of the Club Med concept which offers the original all-inclusive holiday and a complete antidote to civilisation, whatever your age or inclination and whether you are holidaying as a family group or travelling solo to over 100 destinations worldwide.

Price comparison of the cost of a 7-day holiday in Val d'Isère, France, with an all-inclusive Club Med holiday.	Normal Val d'Isere prices	Typical Club Med holiday
Return airfare London/Geneva	£150	included
Airport and holiday taxes	£23	included
Return coach (or taxi) transfer to resort	£70 (£300)	included
Hotel (3-star equivalent) and breakfast	£350	included
Seven three-course lunches (@ £15)	£105	included
Wine with lunch/dinner (7 bottles @ £4)	£28	included
Seven three-course dinners (@ £20)	£140	included
Lift pass (six days)	£125	included
Lessons (6 days, 2 x 2.5 hours)	£135	included
Night club entrance (5 x £5)	£35	included
Tips to staff etc (7 x £5)	£35	included
Childcare facilities (6 x 4 hours @ £6)*	£144	included
Evening entertainment programme	£?	included
Fully comprehensive insurance	£34	included
Total	**£1,364**	**from £698****

*for illustration only – in fact Val d'Isère is an adult only village unlike the other Club Med villages, and has no childcare facilities available

** or from £644 incl. free flight offer – see below – and depending on the choice of Club Med village which could also feature: equipment hire centre, Club Med bank, boutique, medical centre, bars, speciality restaurant, children's clubs, bridge room, fitness centre, sauna, stretch and relaxation classes, library.

Special offers for this winter

● **ONE IN TWO FLY FREE FROM LONDON** on 4th, 11th, 18th and 25th January, 1st and 22nd February and 1st, 8th, 15th and 22nd March to Les Arcs, Avoriaz, Chamonix, Les Menuires, Méribel, La Plagne, Tignes, Val d'Isère, Villars.

● **NON SKIER REDUCTIONS** throughout the season for adult members of the family at Villars, Pontresina and Chamonix.

● **UNDER FIVES STAY FOR 50%** from 4th January to 8th February and from 1st to 29th March in Avoriaz, Chamonix, Les Menuires, Pontresina and Villars (1 child per paying adult).

PLEASE NOTE that all offers are subject to change and availability and, when expired, the normal prices will be payable. Club Med promotions sometimes cannot be taken in conjunction with each other. See Club Med's winter brochure for details.

For a copy of the brochure call **01455 852202**

For information & reservations call **0171 581 1161**

Club Med Web **http:\\www.clubmed.com**

EXCHANGE RATES
When we went to press:

Austrian Sch 19.37
French Fr 9.31
Italian Lira 2,714
Swiss Fr 2.314
US $ 1.602
Canadian $ 2.225
Spanish Pta 232.11

£30 can be found in resorts such as St Anton, Obergurgl, Grindelwald, St Moritz and Wengen. Lift pass prices have also fallen for French resorts. For example, in Courchevel, Val-d'Isère and Valmorel, you'll pay around £15 less than you did two seasons ago. Prices have also fallen in Romania and, to a lesser extent, Bulgaria. Once again, they're the cheapest by far.

LIFT PASS PRICES

Zermatt	£128 (£162)	**Cortina**	£96 (£84)
Verbier	£122 (£165)	**Serre-Chevalier***	£96 (£102)
Courchevel	£116 (£132)	**Sauze d'Oulx**	£96 (£85)
St Moritz	£111 (£141)	**Cervinia**	£96 (£89)
Lech	£110 (£131)	**Courmayeur***	£92 (£87)
St Anton	£110 (£140)	**Soll**	£90 (£102)
Obergurgl	£108 (£137)	**Livigno***	£88 (£81)
Val-d'Isère	£108 (£123)	**Sierra Nevada**	£73
Alpe d'Huez	£107 (£122)	**Soldeu**	£73 (£83)
Grindelwald	£100 (£127)	**Geilo**	£72
Wengen	£100 (£129)	**Borovets**	£59 (£61)
Valmorel*	£ 99 (£113)	**Poiana Brasov**	£38 (£55)
Kitzbühel	£ 98 (£122)		

Notes: Not all prices for the coming season had been fixed when we went to press. We have adjusted the 1996/97 season price of resorts marked * to estimate the 1997/98 prices.

NORTH AMERICAN COSTS
At first glance, the prices we've listed below will look more expensive than those in the brochures. That's because we've worked out what it would cost for two people sharing a room – brochure prices are often based on four. When you compare prices with Europe, keep in mind that hotel costs exclude dinner, although you can eat out cheaply (or expensively if you like).

Bearing this in mind, hotel packages (excluding food) to north America work out about the same as the top- to mid-range European resorts – despite the trans-Atlantic flight costs. A week in a 4-star hotel in Vail, for example, is roughly the same as in Cortina, Val-d'Isère and St Moritz, and cheaper than Courchevel. A 3-star hotel in Whistler costs about the same as a week in Wengen and Cervinia, and is cheaper than Obergurgl and St Anton. Banff is on a par with Kitzbühel, Grindelwald and Livigno and cheaper than Courmayeur.

NORTH AMERICAN PACKAGES	4* Hotel	3* Hotel	Chalet
	£	£	£
Vail	980	848	700
Park City	860	–	–
Breckenridge	820	750	730
Whistler	730	610	710
Heavenly	700	570	650
Killington	630	580	550
Banff	550	550	600

Unlike north American hotel packages, chalet packages include food. A week in a Breckenridge, Whistler or Vail chalet will cost around £700 – more expensive than the typical European prices we found. Killington and Banff are relatively cheap. But remember that north American chalets are generally more luxurious than European.

When it comes to the cost of a lift pass, the US is in a money-sapping world of its own – we're talking megabucks. Unlike Europe, service always comes with a smile at north American lift stations. Just as well, given that a week in Vail will set you back almost £200. Banff, Breckenridge and Whistler cost around £60 less but are still more expensive than anything Europe can offer.

LIFT PASS PRICES

Vail*	£197	Breckenridge*	£138
Killington*	£168	Banff	£136
Park City	£160	Whistler*	£130
Heavenly*	£158		

Notes: Not all the prices for the coming season had been fixed when we went to press. We have adjusted the 1996/97 season price of resorts marked * to estimate the 1997/98 prices.

Given the air fare costs and the problems of jet lag, it makes sense to go to north America for two weeks rather than one. You can expect to pay around 30 per cent extra for your hotel or chalet – so, proportionately, your holiday becomes cheaper.

MOUNTAIN EATING

Eating and drinking costs on the mountain can vary hugely. Even in plush resorts, such as Courchevel and St Moritz, it is possible to find reasonable prices, though it's also easy to spend a fortune. One reporter in Courchevel was charged £17 for four coffees and a coke. In Norway beware of the booze – a reporter in Geilo found 'cheap' bottles of wine at £30, glasses at £5 and beers costing £4.50.

But detailed price studies by ourselves and reporters show that in most resorts you can eat and drink reasonably without breaking the bank – a budget of £8 to £15 a day should buy you a pasta dish, drink and pudding for lunch wherever you go. We've built major price differences into our resort price ratings outlined below.

Our unique resort price ratings

We've rated each major resort in this book for cost on a scale of one to six. This takes into account the typical cost through the season of a half-board package bought in the UK to a 3- or 4-star hotel (calculated from the big tour operators' brochures), plus the cost of a lift pass and an allowance for lunch in mountain restaurants. For US and Canadian packages, which normally exclude meals, we've added on an amount to cover breakfast and dinner. We assume two people sharing a room.

You'll see that Borovets in Bulgaria gets a ① rating (a total cost of around £350), resorts such as Courchevel, Méribel and Lech get a ((((⑥ (a total cost of around £850 or more). In between, the resorts are divided fairly evenly. Resorts which get a ((⑥ cost slightly less than average, those with a (((④ slightly more.

by **Chris Gill**

Weekends in the mountains

a great return on your time

The British standard winter holiday is a week's trip, giving six days on the slopes. Those six days whizz by; most of us, given the chance, would like to stretch our holiday to seven or eight days (and some of us do, by using scheduled flights, trains or cars rather than charter flights). So at first sight, the idea of going to the Alps for a weekend – even a long weekend, with three or four days on the slopes – doesn't seem mightily attractive.

But look at it another way. It's January. In Britain, it's raining and dreary; in the Alps it's snowing, and the conditions in your favourite resort are ideal. You've a week's holiday booked for March, but that seems an age away. You're too busy at work to have an extra week off now – but you could arrange to take Friday off, and get away promptly on Thursday evening. Bingo! Using the last scheduled flights of the day in each direction and going to a carefully chosen resort, you can get almost three full days' skiing or boarding.

If it was your one trip of the winter, a three-day weekend would doubtless leave you hungry for more. But as an extra trip, a weekend break is a tremendous tonic; you tend to put a lot into it, and get a lot out of it. Once you've done it, you'll want to do it again.

Of course, weekend trips are not cheap. The cost of your flights tends to dominate matters, making the cost per day on the slopes seem high. There's no way round that – but you can console yourself with the thought that you're spending less than if you went for a week.

Whether weekend trips are viable for you depends, first of all, on where you live. If you're not near an airport with late flights to and from Geneva (or another Alpine gateway such as Zurich or Salzburg), you won't be able to employ the classic plan. This is to leave work on Thursday afternoon having done a defensible day's work, in time to catch the last available flight – Swissair's 8pm flight from Heathrow to Geneva, say. With luck and a slick transfer to a close resort – a hire car or a taxi laid on by your tour operator – you'll get to your hotel just before it locks up for the night. On Sunday afternoon, how late you can stay on the slopes will depend on practicalities like changing into street clothes, as well as the transfer and flight timing. If Swissair are still running their 8pm return flight to Heathrow, in some resorts you'll be able to carry on until the close of play. (If the timing dictates an earlier departure, you might want to skip lunch and snack your way through the transfer and the airport.)

Out of your long weekend you'll have got something approaching three days on the slopes, plus two nights on the town, if you have the energy. Gaining an hour on the way back, you'll have no trouble getting to bed early, so that you appear at work on the Monday morning looking refreshed and self-satisfied, rather than whacked and self-satisfied.

The choice of where to aim for is problematic. Ideally, you want somewhere within a short drive of your arrival airport. But by definition, resorts close to major airports are close to large numbers of people poised to hit the slopes on fine weekends, which means queues for the lifts and crowds on the slopes, and competition for hotel beds. (If the forecast is for heavy snow, you can stop worrying about crowds, and start worrying about such things as disrupted flights, roads closed by snow and lifts closed by avalanche danger.)

There is no single solution to this problem. It's tempting to argue

that driving two or three hours from the arrival airport, to a resort that gets less local weekend business, is no big deal and simply means you'll get to bed rather late on the first night. The snag comes on day three, when you have to step out of your bindings three hours before check-in time rather than one hour.

Seen in that light, it seems obvious that resorts close to airports are the ones to focus on. But there aren't many of them. The classic weekend resort for experts, with its steep mountains, deep powder and dozens of cheap hotels, is Chamonix, only an hour from Geneva. Flaine takes about as long from Geneva, but hotel beds aren't so easy to get, except in the depths of low season. It's worth considering Courmayeur in Italy, reached via the Mont Blanc tunnel from Chamonix, if you're thinking of flexing your plastic and hiring a helicopter for a drop or two, but the weekend crowds on the lifts here can be rather extreme. Verbier in Switzerland is two hours from Geneva rather than one, but is another popular destination for weekend trips.

Zurich doesn't have such big, well-known resorts close by. But it does have some excellent smaller ones within a couple of hours' drive, notably Engelberg and Andermatt – another excellent place for experts, with an exceptional snow record. There are lots of resorts within two hours of Salzburg, but not many notable ones within an hour – Schladming and the three-valley system around Wagrain are the main examples. Innsbruck has slopes within minutes rather than hours of the airport, but nothing that seems very compelling to someone looking for an intensely exciting weekend.

For many people, this limited range of resorts, coupled with the risk of queues and crowds, will make the alternative approach more compelling. This is to go for a resort that suits you absolutely, regardless of distance from the airport, and resign yourself to quitting the slopes on Sunday more-or-less at lunch-time. (You'll also need to know that your hotel will keep its doors open for you on the night you arrive.) Resorts such as Courchevel can be reached in well under three hours since the roads from Geneva were improved.

You can obviously fix a weekend trip yourself, with or without the help of a travel agent. But there are several tour operators who specialise in organising short holidays like this. The benefits are that some of them offer catered chalet accommodation as an alternative to hotel rooms; that you may get cheaper flights; and that dealing with a tour operator will certainly simplify the business of arranging your transfer from the airport if you're not planning to hire a car.

Programmes to look at for a wide choice of resort are White Roc, Ski Weekend and Ski Les Alpes. For 1997/98, FlexiSki has added St Anton and Val-d'Isère to Courchevel and Verbier. Collineige and Bigfoot are Chamonix specialists that do a lot of weekend trips. Thomson are running weekend holidays this season. Lots of smaller operators have the flexibility to fix short breaks, and this year Courchevel 1650 specialist Le Ski is formalising that side of its activities under the name Le Ski Specials.

Some of these operators do a lot of 'corporate' business: fixing weekend breaks for companies that want a conference away from the office, or want to reward successful employees or – how shall I put it? – want to show their appreciation to loyal customers. This is all something of a mystery to self-employed writers like us, but if you can persuade your employer or one of your suppliers to treat you to a weekend in Chamonix, we're sure you won't regret it.

Boarding takes off

we're all shredders now

Like it or not, snowboarding is here to stay. It is no longer the exclusive domain of teenagers dressed in grunge, listening to 'heavy metal' and hanging around half-pipes. They might not like their 'lifestyle' sport being muscled in on by wrinklies but that's what's happening. Even the 'forty-something' editors of this esteemed guide have taken up boarding in recent seasons – that's why we decided to change the content and title of the book for this edition to include boarding.

Throughout the book, our boarding summaries of each resort look, in the main, at how suitable or otherwise a resort is for boarders of all standards, but particularly for those of our readers who want to give boarding a go while still going on what is primarily a skiing holiday. But the expert boarder on our staff, Ian (call me Red) Stratford, has also assessed the resorts for experienced boarders and those who want boarder-friendly nightlife as well as fun-parks and half-pipes. We hope we have hit the right tone and level of information for all readers, whether you fancy trying boarding, have snowboarding children or are going in a mixed group of skiers and boarders and want somewhere suitable for everyone. We'd especially welcome feedback for the next edition on how well (or otherwise) we've done this – and how we could improve coverage next time.

HOW WE LEARNED
Dave had done a few hours on a board in the 1995/96 season, mainly in late-April afternoon slush in St Anton and Val-d'Isère. But it was 1997 that we decided had to be the year of the board. So we took ourselves off to Vail in Colorado and enrolled in a two-day boarding camp run by the Delaney brothers (former World and US Amateur snowboarding champions, both of whom came from a skiing background) and aimed firmly at adults rather than kids – the usual age range of people on the course is 30 to 50. By the end of Day 2, Dave was negotiating fairly long blue runs linking several turns; Chris started by using a Quickstick (see overleaf) for support and finished up casting it aside and triumphantly conquering a blue as his last run of the course. The tuition is by a hand-picked selection of excellent, laid-back, young snowboard instructors who allow you to progress at your own pace within groups which average four in size.

After that, Dave persisted with the odd morning or afternoon boarding and took another couple of lessons (again in the US, California this time). We have to say we have been much more impressed with the standard and effectiveness of US tuition compared with the lessons we've had in France and Austria – in a lesson for complete beginners in St Anton, we were taken almost straight to a T-bar, where the whole group fell around and took about ten goes to get up it while the instructor stood smoking cigarettes and chatting to the lift attendant.

Dave finished the season in April by riding down long blues with some steep pitches linking 100 continuous turns without falling. Cool, dude!

So we are now keen boarders as well as skiers. There is no danger of us throwing away our skis and taking to boards full-time. We do, however, enjoy the different feeling that boarding gives compared with skiing – both are great and we intend to continue with both.

WHAT BEGINNERS NEED

If you are going to try to learn to snowboard, you need to choose your resort and slope carefully. There are a number of things which, in our view, make learning to board much easier. Here's what we look for:

• User-friendly lifts. Riding a board up a drag-lift is tricky for an experienced boarder; for a beginner it is a nightmare (with button lifts being even worse than T-bars – with a T-bar you can at least put

one arm of the bar behind one leg and you almost automatically turn sideways as you need to in order to ride the board up). We preferred gondolas and high-speed chairs which virtually stop to allow you to get off – with normal chairs we quite often collapsed in a heap at the top in a rather undignified fashion.

• Gentle, uncrowded slopes. Experienced skiers on a board are beginners again and, just like in those early days of learning to ski, what you want are gentle, wide slopes without crowds and without better skiers and riders racing through.

• Good soft snow or slush. Riding a board on hard or icy snow is even more difficult than skiing on it – two edges are better than one. On the other hand, deep snow, whether powder or thick slush, is easier on a board – its width means it floats more easily on the snow and you only have one edge to worry about. And powder and slush give you a much softer landing when you fall – as you will.

• Decent waterproof clothes and gloves. Proper snowboarding gear is reinforced at key points, such as the bottom and knees, and snowboarding gloves are much tougher than most ski gloves – that's because you spend more time with all these parts of your anatomy in the snow when you're boarding. We found ourselves having to wring out

The Delaney brothers give first-time snowboarders Quicksticks to give them support, help initiate turns and make it easier to get up after a fall. Here's one of the Vail locals trying boarding for the first time.

The Delaneys run camps for all standards from beginner to expert in Vail, Beaver Creek and Aspen. For details:

Delaney Camps,
PO Box 4488,
Boulder,
Colorado 80306

Tel: 001 303 4436868
Fax: 4171077

unpleasantly sodden ski gloves too often – go for Gore-tex or snowboarding gloves from the outset.
• Using extra padding or protection for the bottom and knees softens the pain and bruising of some of the early falls. And we highly recommend wrist-protectors – broken wrists are the most common serious injury in snowboarding because you instinctively put out your hand trying to break your fall.
• Good tuition for a few lessons in the early stages. Contrary to popular opinion we found snowboarding just as difficult to pick up as we did skiing in the early days. But good tuition can help enormously – as we've said, we've been much more impressed with the US instruction we've had than the European. And, in general, most boarders advise going to a specialist snowboard school if possible rather than a ski school which also teaches boarding.
• Specialist snowboard shops are likely to have a wider selection of boards and boots, and better knowledge of the equipment that will suit you best, than ski shops which stock some boards. For advice about equipment, see the snowboarding section of our Equipment chapter which starts on page 51.

We'd recommend beginners who want to give snowboarding a real chance to set aside at least three days (preferably a whole week) of a holiday and devote it to boarding. Trying it for just the odd half-day doesn't work well, but after three days you should have made enough progress to tell whether you'll enjoy it or not.

WHAT EXPERTS NEED
In some ways, experienced boarders need the same as beginners. Most say they prefer chair-lifts to drags, most complain about steep run-offs from fixed-grip chairs and all hate flat sections of slopes where you have to take one foot out of the board and use it to 'scoot' along with – you can't skate and pole along flat bits as you can on skis.

But good boarders also want steeper terrain and most find lumps and bumps fun for jumping off and doing tricks. It's mainly the younger boarders who go for the fun-parks and half-pipes where they can show off their tricks – and the social aspect of it seems as important as the riding itself.

Even after only one week on a board, most people find riding powder easy and great fun and say it is the highlight of their boarding holidays. Although you can't guarantee powder, you do seem to be able to guarantee to enjoy it more on a board than on skis unless you are an advanced skier with previous powder experience.

WHICH RESORT?

Throughout this book we rate each resort for how suitable it is for snowboarders, whether beginners or experts. In general, most resorts (with many Italian resorts unwelcome exceptions) are now making great efforts to attract snowboarders because it is clear that snowboarding is here to stay and that snowboarders will remain important to the economics of running resorts. In the US most of the resorts which used to ban snowboarders have reversed their policies in the last few seasons – most notably Park City, Keystone and Alpine Meadows. The only resorts which persist in banning riders are Taos, Alta and Deer Valley – though boarders are also banned from Aspen Mountain (but not the other three mountains owned by the Aspen Skiing Company).

More and more resorts are gaining reputations as firm boarder favourites including, for example: in Austria, Ischgl, Hintertux, Sölden; in France, Avoriaz, Chamonix (for extreme boarding), Les Arcs, Les Deux-Alpes, Serre-Chevalier; in Switzerland: Leysin, Saas-Fee; in Canada: Whistler; in USA: pretty much everywhere. But read the individual chapters in this book to see how all resorts compare.

THE BASIC JARGON

Snowboarding has its own language and it helps to speak some of it.
Regular: you ride a board with your left leg leading. This will feel more or less comfortable than riding 'goofy' – see below. To find out if you are regular or goofy try getting someone to push you unexpectedly from behind and see which leg you instinctively put forward first to keep your balance. You are also most likely to put this leg in your pants first in the mornings. It's also the foot you put first when you slid on ice as a child.
Goofy: you ride a board with your right leg leading.
Surfer/Shredder: alternative terms for snowboarder.
Fun-park: special area of slopes built and maintained mainly or solely for snowboarders, with jumps, bumps and maybe rails, benches and even VW Beetles to 'jib' off (see below).
Jib: ride over, or on, obstacles such as the rails, benches and cars mentioned above.
Bonk: deliberately hitting and bouncing off obstacles, like oil drums and tree stumps.
Grab: you grab your board with your hand while in mid-air during a jump.
Hit: a jump.
Gap jump: a jump with an empty space between the take-off and the landing. Not clearing the gap usually has detrimental consequences.
Half-pipe: trench carved in the snow with steep sides to ride up and down and do tricks in.
Boarder-cross: race between several boarders down a specially designed course including jumps, where all racers set off at the same time – apart from that, rules are few.
Fakie: riding backwards (with right leg first if you are a 'regular' rider).
360: to do a complete turn on your board so that you turn through a complete 360 degrees.
Ollie: a jump where you use the springiness of your board to gain height, instead of jumping off a ramp or lump of snow.

by **Dave Watts**

Avalanche dangers

go equipped

More and more of us are choosing to ski off-piste. It's easy to explain why: the joy of making first tracks in fresh powder snow, the magical quality of spring snow, the freedom and peace of getting away from the hordes on the pistes, the beauty of being alone in spectacular, high mountain terrain with only your small group, the challenge of tackling steep, unknown terrain.

But the mountains are dangerous, wild, untamed places. And if you go off-piste, you accept the dangers and do so at your own risk – the resort bears no responsibility for your safety (in Europe at least). The dangers are many – unmarked obstacles such as rocks and tree roots, cliffs, crevasses, long falls, trees and ... avalanches.

Every year a large number of people die in avalanches. There are no reliable numbers because resorts are not keen to release details which show them in a bad light. One New Year, when I was in Val-d'Isère, I heard of at least three incidents in which people had been killed on one day alone.

Never, never venture off-piste – even just off the piste – if you are alone. If you have an accident, no one may know until you are reported missing at the end of the day. And the responsible advice is never to go off-piste unless you are with a reliable and qualified local ski instructor or mountain guide.

If you are unlucky enough to be taken by an avalanche, it is imperative that you are found and dug out as rapidly as possible. Statistics from a 1993 study of 322 avalanche accidents by researchers at the University of Innsbruck showed that after 15 minutes 92 per cent of skiers completely buried by snow were still alive. After 45 minutes the survival rate had dropped off drastically to 25 per cent: 75 per cent had already died. The last 25 per cent survived for one more hour on average, and were more likely to freeze to death than die of suffocation. So finding and digging out avalanche victims quickly is the key to saving lives.

One very simple precaution that everyone can take at low (or no) cost is to have Recco reflectors fitted to your gear. Indeed, the Swiss Alpine Club, Swiss Air Rescue and the Federal Institute for the Study of Snow and Avalanches in Davos have jointly recommended that all skiers and snowboarders wear Recco reflectors.

The Royal Marines use them during their winter training in Norway. And in the 1996/97 season, Kitzbühel in Austria invested in 8,000 pairs of reflectors to distribute free to its season pass holders. Recco reflectors now come as standard with every pair of boots sold by Snow+Rock. They are also built into some clothing (eg Nevica, Killy and Tenson). You can buy a pair of reflectors (one for each boot) for only £12.95, a price not even worth bothering about for something which may save your life.

These reflectors do not require any batteries, maintenance or knowledge on the part of the skier or boarder who wears them. They work with portable Recco Rescue System detectors that now weigh

The portable Recco Rescue System detector (bottom) is used by trained rescue staff to find people buried by avalanches who have Recco reflectors fitted to their ski boots (below) or built into their clothing ↓

only 1.7kg and that the rescue services of most major resorts now have. The detectors emit a directional signal on a frequency of 917 MHz. When the signal hits a Recco reflector, even under 10m of snow, the frequency is doubled and sent back to the receiver in the detector; the person carrying out the search is fully trained and expert in using the equipment, and immediately hears a signal on their earphones which enables them to pinpoint the buried victim. The detector can easily be transported in and used from a helicopter searching for victims.

Recco tell us that resorts using their detector system now include such well-known names as Chamonix, Val-d'Isère, Tignes, Verbier, Zermatt, Kitzbühel, Lech, St Anton, Courmayeur, Cortina, the Three Valleys (which has 17 detectors placed at the top of different lifts), the Sella Ronda and Superski Dolomiti regions, Aspen, Vail and Whistler. Some helicopter rescue services which cover many resorts – eg the entire Swiss Alps, the Aosta valley – also carry Recco detectors. Under each resort covered in this book, in the Mountain facts section, we tell you if Recco claim their detectors are in use.

And as well as kitting yourself out with Recco, every off-piste skier and snowboarder should be equipped with and have been trained how to use an avalanche transceiver (or 'beeps'). This is a combined transmitter and receiver. While skiing or riding, everyone in a group has their beeps set on 'transmit'; if there is an avalanche, those not buried by it turn their beeps to 'receive' – they can then receive the signals sent out by their buried colleagues and track them down under the snow. But you need to be very well-trained in transceiver use to do this quickly and effectively.

And as well as all this, there are other essentials that any off-piste group should carry. Preferably everyone in the group – but at least two people as a bare minimum – should have a back pack containing:
• collapsible snow shovel – to dig out avalanche victims, build shelters and do a host of other things
• collapsible avalanche probe – to search for victims
• first-aid kit
• space blanket – to keep warm in an emergency
• whistle – to attract attention
• extra clothing (gloves, hat, sun glasses etc)
• water and high-energy food.
Snow+Rock and other good specialist ski shops sell most of the above individually or as part of an off-piste pack.

Your off-piste guide should always have a radio and keep his or her colleagues elsewhere on the mountain or in the resort aware of the location of their group. Preferably, other group members should also have radios – and these days, digital mobile phones can be useful too if you have to summon help.

by **Dave Watts**

Choosing equipment

the gear you need

For skiing and snowboarding, even more than most sports, having the right equipment is vital. Not only will good gear improve your performance but in the mountains it can save your life too. So make sure you and your family have suitable skis or boards, boots and bindings for your standard and that you have the warm waterproof clothing and other protection from the elements that you might need.

THE CARVING REVOLUTION

Over the past couple of seasons there has been a revolution in ski design. Most of the skis in the shops these days are the new 'shaped', 'carving', 'hourglass', 'super-sidecut' or 'parabolic' skis. Whatever name they go by, the essential thing is that they are wider at the shovel (front) and tail (back) than conventional skis. The idea is that – because of their shape, in particular, the greater sidecut between front and waist – they carve turns more easily and make skiing more fun and easier, whatever your standard.

We have tried many different pairs of 'carving' skis (as we will call them) over the last two seasons and, when we've found the ones right for us, we've loved them. That's where you need to be careful – you need to choose a pair that is right for your standard and style of skiing. There are carvers for intermediates who are still skidding and want to break through that intermediate plateau, there are carvers for all types of advanced skier and there are even race carvers that are used on the World Cup circuit. And find a ski instructor who knows about carving skis to teach you the right technique (they are more common in America than in Europe, in our experience); it would also help to look at a specialist 'carving' video.

All the well-known manufacturers, such as Salomon, Kästle, Rossignol, Head, K2, Atomic, Volkl and Fischer, now have carving skis in their range. When choosing the right pair for you, we suggest you read the results of some highly regarded tests, such as those in *Daily Mail Ski Magazine*, and then get advice from the experts at a shop, such as Snow+Rock. And look for a shop which will give you a ski suitability guarantee and allow you to swap them if they don't suit you (there may be a charge involved).

↑ Carving skis (left) are much wider at the tip and tail than conventional skis (right)

One recent trend has been to fit riser plates on bindings to lift the boot on the ski and increase carving power – only for good skiers ➔

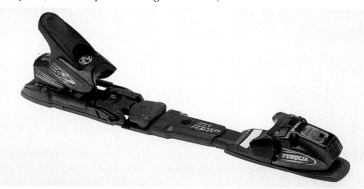

THE BINDING REVOLUTION

Bindings have developed enormously in recent years. One of the main recent trends has been towards improved binding release mechanics which are intended to reduce the epidemic of ligament injuries that has replaced broken legs as the skier's major injury worry in recent years. Salomon, Marker, Rossignol and Tyrolia have all produced new bindings with this in mind. Another trend has been the introduction of riser plates to raise the binding on the ski and increase a good skier's ability to get the ski over on its edge and carve – but take advice about whether your skiing ability is good enough to take advantage of this, and, indeed, whether you'll be able to handle it.

BOOTING UP

Having an uncomfortable or unsuitable pair of ski boots can ruin a ski holiday. We know – we've had a few awful pairs in our time. But over the years the combination of comfort and performance has improved vastly.

A few years ago, rear-entry boots were all the rage. There's little doubt they were good for comfort and the convenience of putting them on, taking them off and adjusting them, but, for the most part, good skiers found they didn't give them enough support and sufficiently precise control between foot and boot. Rear-entries have virtually disappeared from the shelves now (even from the ranges of makes like Salomon and Nordica, which were almost entirely rear-entry at one stage).

Most boots now have four adjustable clips to give you precise fit and control. For intermediates, there are 'mid-entry' boots, which in the main are four-clip boots but with a latching device at the back which allows the upper boot to hinge backwards to make your boots easier to put on and take off. These mid-entry boots are generally more padded for greater comfort, at some cost to precise performance.

More than with any other piece of equipment, you need good advice when buying boots – being fitted by a good boot fitter is invaluable. For years, I struggled with good boots that still, for one reason or another, hurt at times – no matter what I had done to them. Last winter, I went to a boot fitter who examined my feet carefully and selected what he considered the right boot for my shape of foot – the volume of your ankle, your instep, whether your arch is high or low, and a lot of other things determine whether a particular make and model of boot is right for you. After an initial problem on my first outing in them, they were delightfully comfortable for the rest of the season.

As well as good advice, there are some golden rules to follow when being fitted for boots:
• Allow plenty of time – at least a couple of hours and probably more – to try on several models and get properly fitted.
• Shop on a quiet day during the week, when the fitters aren't busy serving several people at the same time.
• Wear ski socks – and only one pair.
• Try different sizes and models – and wear different ones on each foot to get comparisons.
• But before buying, always try on both boots together of the pair you decide on. Adjust them for fit (buckles should be on the first or

second notch) and flex forward repeatedly – you should feel your toes moving away from the front and you should be able to wiggle them, but your heel should be locked in place and not come off the sole. Wear the boots and walk around in them for at least 15 minutes to see if any problems develop.

• Invest in custom-moulded footbeds. These will be moulded to the shape of your foot and give you maximum support when you need it – we've found them a huge help in maximising comfort and performance. You can also now get custom-moulded inner boots – but we have no direct experience of these.

• If possible, get a comfort guarantee that if, despite all your efforts, your boots remain uncomfortable, you get a free refitting service or, at worst, are refitted with an alternative pair.

WHEN TO BUY

We'd recommend beginners to rent for the first week or two of their career – for both skiing and boarding. You progress so quickly that what makes sense on day one almost certainly won't by day six. And rent in the resort rather than the UK, as you can then take back and swap uncomfortable or unsuitable equipment during your week on the slopes. The first thing to consider buying is boots that are custom-fitted to your feet, ensuring greater comfort and control than with knackered rental boots. After that, buy a pair of skis or a snowboard that will allow you to progress for the next few seasons – be ambitious about your planned progress so that you buy equipment that you can grow into.

ANY OLD CLOTHES?

Decent waterproof, breathable clothing to keep you warm and dry on the slopes is essential. If you are a beginner or fair-weather skier or boarder, you'll be able to make do with some of the basic clothing available, but you need gear that has been specially designed for use on snowy mountains. Old jeans or tracksuit trousers just will not do – they'll soon become wet and then freeze. In extreme conditions you could be endangering your life in them. A decent pair of trousers and a decent jacket, both designed specifically for skiing or boarding, are the essentials for beginners. But you'll also need:

• warm clothes under your jacket – layers such as T-shirt, polo-neck shirt and sweater or fleece are best so that you can remove some if you become too hot

• thermal underwear – worth considering if you feel the cold a lot

• long socks which wick away moisture (just wear one pair)

• good-quality ski or snowboard gloves

• a hat – essential because most of your heat loss goes through your head. Headbands and neck warmers are also worth considering – Turtle Fur is incredibly soft and warm, light and quick drying

• good-quality sunglasses and goggles – the sun is incredibly intense at altitude and especially when it is reflected by the snow – never go out without good eye protection

• high-protection-factor suncream – also essential for the same reasons – I never go lower than SPF20 and recommend SPF15 even if you tan easily.

Experienced skiers and boarders who go out in all conditions really need top-quality technical outer clothing made out of quality materials, such as Gore-tex, to keep them protected from extreme

SNOW
+
ROCK

Snowboarding boots can be hard (left) or soft (right). Hard boots are best for carving but soft are more popular with British boarders

Most ski boots now have four clips; rear-entry boots, which were all the rage a few years ago, have virtually disappeared from the market

conditions. There are all sorts of options now available, such as shell jackets with removable fleeces, and jackets and trousers which zip together to give one-piece protection.

And there are huge numbers of accessories and gadgets you can buy to make your time on the slopes more fun. One of my personal favourites is an Avocet watch which, as well as telling the time, has such information available as your current altitude, how many runs you've done since it was last reset and how many vertical metres you've travelled. Swatch Access watches are also very useful if you are going to one of the many resorts that now has the necessary equipment to allow you to use them as a lift pass: a micro-chip in the watch is 'loaded' with the details of your lift pass and at each lift you just point the watch at a scanner and you are let through the gate. You don't even have to lift up your sleeve, let alone dig your old-fashioned pass out of your jacket.

The most essential piece of après-ski wear you'll need is a good pair of stout, waterproof, walking boots with a good sole to give grip on snow and ice.

TAKING CHILDREN
Basically, everything we've said about adult clothing and accessories above applies to children too, only more so. There is nothing more guaranteed to make a young child have a miserable holiday than being cold or wet. And there is now a wide range of fun, colourful children's clothing and accessories available.

A one-piece suit is warm and comfortable (but can be a bit inconvenient for kids when using the loo!). Separate jackets and trousers are more practical for use at home as well as on the slopes. For toddlers, link their gloves with string and thread it through the suit or jacket, otherwise they may get through several expensive pairs in the course of a week.

We would be interested to hear from readers who have bought either in Britain or abroad and have views on which is best – please write to *Where to Ski and Snowboard*, The Old Forge, Norton St Philip, Bath BA3 6LW.

WHY BUY BRITISH?
Snow+Rock have a six-point charter for why it makes sense to buy your ski and snowboard gear in Britain rather than in your resort:
• British ski shops are reputed to be among the most technical and highly trained in the world.
• Britain has a greater international choice of product, not governed by a regional or national bias.
• Do not expect to get the same choice of product or the same range of sizes in a resort shop.
• After sales service is important to British ski shops. You can return to the shop for further boot fitting and adjustment and for ski services. Warranty problems can be dealt with without hassle or cost to the customer.
• You can buy from knowledgeable staff who speak English. Most technicians will have tried and tested the product and are not trying to sell you unknowingly an end of line product or an item which is totally inappropriate for your skiing ability.
• Most British skiers have only two weeks on snow a year at the most. Make the most of your skiing day without wasting time looking for equipment in the resort.

An additional vital accessory for children on the slopes is a good-quality helmet. Children's heads are softer and more vulnerable than adults' and it is essential they wear them until they are at least seven or eight years old. In the US last season we noticed it was becoming more common for older children and even adults to wear helmets too.

SNOWBOARDING GEAR

If you are trying snowboarding for the first time, doing it in your ski clothing is fine (but see the snowboarding chapter starting on page 45 for more tips about accessories). And renting boots and a board is the most sensible move for first-timers. But if you get hooked (as we have), buying specialist gear makes sense.

In general, snowboarding clothing is bigger and baggier than ski clothing, giving the body more room to bend and stretch. And it has more padding and reinforcement in key places, such as the bottom and the knees, which you use a lot more in boarding than in skiing. Having said that, there is now a lot of 'cross-over' clothing around, designed to be used for either boarding or skiing. Snowboarding gloves are, however, generally bigger, longer at the wrist and designed to be much tougher than most ski gloves – to reflect the substantially increased contact with the snow that boarders have.

With boots there is a basic choice between hard and soft boots. Hard boots look pretty similar to ski boots at first sight. They are more popular on the continent than with British or US snowboarders and give you the most precision and greatest control at speed. Most Alpine snowboard racers use hard boots.

Although hard boots might seem most familiar to skiers, we'd recommend trying soft boots. You'll find them remarkably soft and comfortable compared with ski boots and they give you a great feeling of freedom (especially when walking!).

With hard boots, you step in and push your heel back as far as possible, then secure the boot by pulling the toe clip closed against the front of the boot. With soft boots, you use straps over the foot and ankle which are part of the bindings. But in the last few years, a new type of binding has appeared where you click in and out of them rather like you do with ski bindings – as a relative beginner boarder I prefer this type, though some experienced boarders tell me they don't give them enough precise control over the board.

As for boards, there are four main types. Freestyle boards are designed for doing tricks and riding half-pipes – and are not recommended for beginners. Freeride boards are designed for all-mountain, all-terrain use with soft boots and are my recommended type for beginners. Alpine Freecarve boards are designed for cruising and carving on the piste using hard boots and are recommended for beginners who prefer hard boots. Race boards are just what they sound and are definitely not beginner material.

SERVICING YOUR EQUIPMENT

To get the best out of skis and snowboards, you need to have them serviced regularly – to make sure the base is smooth and waxed for a smooth glide and the edges are sharp so that they can grip even on hard snow and ice. We recommend having your equipment serviced before you go on holiday so that you waste no time after you arrive. Then have them serviced again halfway through your week, perhaps.

COURCHEVEL 1850   ST ANTON   VAL D'ISERE   VERBIER

FlexiSki holidays are a
perfect combination of
luxury, value and – as you
might expect – flexibility.
In fact, they tend to put
other ski holidays

in the shade

TELEPHONE
0171-352 0044

Luxury chalets

comfort with charm

In its early days, the catered chalet holiday – a uniquely British idea, where tour operators put their own cooks and housekeepers into private chalets they have taken over for the season – used to be all about charming old buildings and convivial company, and not at all about comfort. You slept in cramped bedrooms separated by paper-thin walls. At tea-time there would be a race to get in the queue for the bathroom you were sharing with six others, to make sure you got some of the limited hot water. For a truly comfortable holiday, you went to a hotel.

But all that has changed. Not only has the standard of catered chalets risen generally, but a new breed of genuinely luxurious chalets has gradually found its way on to the package holiday market. For our money, these luxury chalets now represent the ideal base for a winter holiday with a group of friends, combining privacy with comfort in a way that gives a real sensation of privileged living.

For many British skiers (and increasing numbers of snowboarders), winter holidays mean staying in a catered chalet. What makes the chalet holiday special is the living space – the sitting room and dining room, often a single shared space, in which you and your family or friends can really feel at home. Even a simple chalet can have a warmly welcoming sitting room with a log fire, of course, but in the best chalets, the sitting room is what makes the place irresistible. Ideally, it has oceans of space, picture windows looking out on to fabulous sweeping views, deep sofas in front of that open log fire and a rustic antique cabinet filled with duty-free delights. If, like me, you're the kind of chalet-goer who is disinclined to stir from the fireside after dinner, it's a real treat to pour a cognac and put your feet up in a chalet that has a real sense of style.

Such treats do not, of course, come cheaply. We are talking here about chalets in which a high-season week costs something like

£1,000 a head – in some cases, appreciably more. But then that's what you pay these days for a week in a three-star hotel in Méribel or Courchevel, where many of the chalets are to be found.

It may be the notion of cognac in front of an open fire that is the key attraction of smart chalets, but it's arguable that the biggest single advance that these upmarket chalets represent is in the more functional matter of bathrooms. For years, people who would never dream of booking a hotel room without ensuite bathroom have gone without that simple convenience in the Alps, simply because most chalets didn't have them. Now, lots of chalets do have them, and those who hate the idea of competing for the first bath or the last of the hot water no longer need to confine themselves to hotel holidays. What's more, the bathrooms themselves are often impressively glossy – a world away from the lino-covered floors of yesteryear. (Even so, it's necessary to point out that not all the bedrooms in all the chalets offered by the smarter operators are completely equipped with ensuite bathrooms.)

Many of these upmarket chalets have been designed for occupation by the family that owns them or at least built them – some, indeed, are the summer homes of local families, who move out in November to hibernate in a flat over their ski shop, say. The result is that the bedrooms vary much more than in purpose-built hotel or apartment accommodation. If you're the lucky ones who win the family prize draw or get into the chalet before the rest of your party, you may find yourself in a simply stunning 'master' bedroom with acres of space, an immaculate white carpet and a wall of windows looking out on a deserted valley – and an equally impressive bathroom with spa bath. But it has to be said that some otherwise excellent chalets are slightly let down – in comparison with the four-star and even five-star hotels they compete with on price – by the standard of some of the other bedrooms. Space may be at a premium, even if the furnishings are impressively luxurious. And in some of these chalets, there are sleeping spaces that barely deserve to be called rooms. Make sure you know what you're getting, and who is going to sleep where. (The tour operators who run these places say that their chalet-going customers care much less about this than about having a spacious, comfortable and impressive living room – and who are we to question that?)

The ideal chalet is located right on the piste, so that there is no walking or bus-riding at either end of the day; it is conveniently close to the village centre, so that the shops and bars are handy; but it is tucked away from the main streets, so that there are no problems with noise in the early hours. Some luxury chalets come close, but you can't assume that high quality and a prime position go together automatically. Many of the best chalets are recently built ones which by definition are most likely to be located on the fringes of the resort; that may or may not leave you well placed for the slopes, but it's unlikely to put you close to the evening action. In hilly, tortuous Méribel, for example, some of the new building is going on where the village meets the piste; more is going on at the opposite side, a bus-ride away. Happily, the operators of these chalets mostly operate comprehensive minibus services which more-or-less solve the transport problem, at least in the morning and at tea-time.

Any experienced chalet-goer is aware that nothing makes a bigger contribution to a successful chalet holiday than good food, charmingly served. Chalet operators are well aware that expectations in this department are higher when they are charging £1,000 for a week than when they are charging £500, so you can be reasonably confident of getting good food from any of them. Given the general standard of chalet plonk, you can also be confident of getting better-than-average wine. Some companies have now adopted a policy of staffing their chalets not with teenagers or unemployed graduates, but with slightly older people – couples, often – who are making a career of cooking or hotelkeeping.

In many of the best chalets you will find extras that aren't a traditional part of the chalet concept. Peruse the brochures and you'll find long lists of goodies – morning tea, canapés before dinner, satellite TV, fluffy bathrobes and so on. But to my mind, the big step forward is a boot warmer. If you haven't had the luxury of having your ski boots automatically dried and warmed overnight by one of these gadgets, you haven't lived.

Thanks to the big programmes offered by the major tour operators such as Crystal and Thomson, chalet holidays are available in a much wider range of resorts than they used to be. You can find isolated luxury chalets in all sorts of places, from Austria to Aspen, but the breed in general is still not widespread: most are concentrated in the French resorts of Méribel, Courchevel (close neighbours in the Three Valleys) and Val-d'Isère. Over the last couple of years I have personally visited many of these upmarket chalets (largely, I hasten to add, out of season – I wouldn't want readers to think I spend all winter wallowing in luxury).

Courchevel is well established as the smartest resort in France, so it's not surprising that it has some of the smartest chalets. But tour operators now find it virtually impossible to get their hands on really smart chalets here, so the packaged choice is not super-wide.

Over recent years I've developed a soft spot for Courchevel, and if I'm honest, this is partly because I've been privileged to stay in FlexiSki's Lodge on several occasions. Although the Lodge is chalet-shaped, has only ten rooms and is run along chalet lines (with some British staff), it was built as a little B&B hotel – and is still registered as such, and open for casual trade when space is available. The bedrooms are, as a result, about the best you will find in a chalet; they have room to swing more than one cat, and very stylish bathrooms. The Lodge also has a bar, which forms part of the welcoming sitting/dining room – a fine place to congregate for aperitifs before dinner. I look forward to the day when the dining area can be expanded to give more space in that department.

Ski Scott Dunn has a number of places in Courchevel, of which easily the most impressive is really a very grand apartment, the Cristal de Roche penthouse. This is one luxury chalet that could scarcely be better positioned, being a matter of yards from the very heart of Courchevel 1850. One chalet that appeals to rather specialised tastes is Simply Ski's chalet L'Ancolie, with beautifully fitted bedrooms and an antique-furnished sitting/dining room.

I first got to know the wonderful Three Valleys area by staying in Méribel, and confess to a lingering affection for the place (despite its domination by British visitors). It now offers a greater range of impressively luxurious catered chalets than any other resort, partly as a result of the deliberate move upmarket a few years ago by long-time local specialist Meriski.

COLLINEIGE *The Chamonix specialists*   T **01276 24262**   F **01276 27282**

Collineige have the best quality chalets available in the Chamonix valley. They have had 16 years experience providing holidays to suit individuals, friends, families or corporate clients.

With a permanent Chamonix office, the best connections with professional mountain guides and heliskiing operations, a minibus drop-off service, Collineige provide the complete ski service.

They also offer tailor-made itineraries and have an established weekend programme.

← CHALET LES MAZOTS

SIMPLY SKI *Chalet specialist*   T **0181 742 2541**   F **0181 995 5346**

Simply Ski's 'Chalets of Distinction' offer the ultimate in comfort, fine cuisine and superior service for the discerning skier in some of Europe's most sought-after resorts: Chalet L'Ancolie in Courchevel 1850 is the jewel in our crown, but Chalet Rousillon in Méribel, Chalet Norjeanne in Verbier and Chalet Dauphin in Val d'Isère will all appeal to those who value their creature comforts but prefer the intimacy and informality of a chalet to the stuffy pretension of a grand hotel. Flexible travel options include scheduled BA flights, regional charters, Snowtrain, Eurostar and self-drive.

CHALET NORJEANNE →

YSE LIMITED   T **0181 871 5177**   F **0181 871 5229**

Whatever your definition of luxury, you can find it in a YSE chalet in Val d'Isère. En-suite bathrooms throughout, of course; every facility from satellite TV and saunas to boot warmers; gourmet food and vintage wine; kir; canapés and cognac; freshly squeezed oranges for the morning after (or a full 'heart attack' breakfast if you're up to it), even hampers with champers, smoked salmon, local cheeses – whatever you choose – high in the mountain sunshine.

← MOUNTAIN LODGES

Meriski's big news for 1997/98 is that they are opening a new eight-bedroom flagship property that sounds very Lodge-like – 'not a chalet and not a hotel, but a combination of the best of both worlds'. And it's called, er, the Lodge at Burgin. Burgin is a newly developed upmarket suburb of the resort, next to Belvédère, and Meriski will also be offering a newly built, five-bedroom chalet of a more conventional kind here (Guanaco).

One of my favourites in Méribel is Meriski's four-bedroom Iberis. Two features stand out in this recently built family home: the splendidly spacious, light and tastefully furnished pine-panelled sitting room, with huge floor-to-ceiling windows; and the extravagantly luxurious master bedroom, complete with immaculate white carpet and walk-in wardrobe, vast ensuite bathroom and jacuzzi bath. If you can wangle this room without paying a premium, you're on a winner. The other bedrooms are unremarkable, but well equipped, with good bathrooms and decent storage.

Meriski's Mira Bellum is another captivating place, with an interesting

split-level living space. The bedrooms aren't so widely varying here, though it's still worth making sure that you get one of the two best.

There is no doubt, though, about which is the most spectacularly impressive catered chalet in Méribel: Simply Ski's chalet Brames. It has a two-storey living room with an uninterrupted view up the valley towards Mont Vallon. As we went to press, the owner was trying to sell, but Simply Ski were hoping to have it available.

Val-d'Isère has a good range of impressive chalets – more than a match for Méribel, in some ways. The Ski Company has an impressive enclave of modern luxury places right out at the southern extremity of the resort, with large living rooms and splendid views. And views are just one of the attractions of their spacious and sunny new place down the valley at Ste-Foy, Yellowstone Lodge, which is being sold in a package with Top Ski off-piste guiding.

If you are more interested in good living rooms than views, consider YSE's Mountain Lodges – Vieux Cret and Maison du Rocher. These two adjacent and ancient houses offer no picture windows, but a warm, enveloping atmosphere. The two have a below-stairs connection, but are best viewed as separate and slightly different units. The chief attraction in each case is a splendidly atmospheric and comfortable living room, with ample leather sofas, stone walls and full hi-fi/TV apparatus. The Vieux Cret has its living room at the top of the house, with a cute mezzanine (with sofa-beds) between the rough beams in the very apex of the roof, and straightforward, adequate bedrooms beneath. The Maison du Rocher reverses the formula, with some of the beds squeezed into the rafters.

Ski Scott Dunn has several properties here, but the only ones I'm familiar with are their Squaw Valley apartments (also featured by Finlays). These deeply comfortable places are distinguished from a real chalet only by the fact that you pad along carpeted corridors and stairways to get to the outside world. For many people, the key attraction is likely to be the location: although only a few yards from snow and lifts, Squaw Valley is right in the heart of the village.

Of the chalets in other parts of the Alps, several are in the Ski Company's portfolio. Sadly, one of the best, the wonderful old Chalet Gueret just outside Morzine, was destroyed by fire last season. Probably the most distinctive – though not necessarily what most people expect of an Alpine retreat – is Villa Terrier, an Edwardian house in Chamonix. This is a town replete with characterful old houses, and Collineige has more than its share in its programme. I have to confess that I haven't visited any of them, but Prarion, near the Flégère lift, looks a gloriously spacious and charming house – certainly the only 'chalet' I know of with a piano in the living room.

The catered chalet holiday isn't such an obviously appealing formula in north America, given the amazing range of tempting restaurants you can sample at modest cost; but on the other hand, there are some impressive and highly suitable properties available. Ski Independence has one of the biggest chalet programmes, with properties in Breckenridge, Crested Butte and Vail, and now two in Whistler. They embrace a range of styles, from places lost in the woods to the company's premier chalet, the clapboard-style Victoria, close to the centre of Breckenridge. The latest addition in Whistler, chalet Pakalolo, has the right ingredients – central wood-burning fire, private hot tub. It may or may not have the antique drinks cabinet, but Ski Independence does lay on a tot of Drambuie as a digestif.

Get wired now

for access to the latest info

We hope you're enjoying your perusal of Where to Ski and Snowboard, and that you'll find it really helpful in the perenially tricky process of deciding where to go next winter. A book like this remains the best way to immerse yourself in a wide and deep pool of information, which is what you need when weighing up ski resorts; there's no more convenient way of having so much information instantly accessible. But there's no denying that other media have their attractions – and we're developing ways of using them to complement the book.

As editors and publishers who plan to survive into the next millennium, we're well aware that there are now electronic alternatives to the printed page – and we've looked at them carefully. We've considered creating a multimedia CD-ROM resort guide, and been put off by the high initial costs (and the limited success of existing guides in that format). Publishing on the Internet, on the other hand, we're very excited about.

Slightly to our surprise, we were among the first UK travel guide producers to jump on to the Internet bandwagon. Back in the autumn of 1995 – shortly after our last paper edition was published – we were persuaded by IdeaNet, Paris-based Website developers, that the Internet was going somewhere, and that we ought to be aboard. So, over the last two winters, our resort information has appeared on IdeaNet's award-winning SkiIN site.

It turns out that IdeaNet were right – although they may have been a bit optimistic about the bandwagon's departure time. Now that reasonably fast modems are affordable, the World Wide Web is a great way to obtain information, and a viable medium for publishing it. And as the British and European markets catch up with the American one, we believe the Web will become a major channel for carrying out all sorts of transactions – such as booking holidays.

If you're still not 'wired', the information on the next page will help you understand what all this is about, and to appreciate why you should be getting plugged in to the Internet. If you already have net access, you'll probably be interested to hear what we're up to.

Some of the content of the book will probably still be published by IdeaNet on its multilingual SkiIn site. But from now on our information will also form a part of some other sites, too – including one run by our publishers, Thomas Cook. What's more, we now have our own site, which gives access to the SkiIn and Thomas Cook Ski Direct sites – and contains a lot of unique stuff too.

We've conceived our site in the form of a magazine called *Snow Zone*. We plan to produce new editions monthly from September to December, and weekly through the season to Easter. *Snow Zone* is designed to complement this book; it harnesses the strengths of the World Wide Web to do things we can't do here.

The Web offers instant publishing – so we'll have current snow reports, resort updates, travel news, late-booking bargains. Whereas space is always in short supply in a book like this, Web 'space' is virtually free – so we'll have room for features on all aspects of skiing, with great photos, and we'll be able to accumulate them in a growing archive. We'll have information on skiing and boarding equipment and clothing, World Cup racing and so on.

The Web is interactive – the user can take actions which determine what gets displayed on-screen – so we're planning systems to help you narrow your holiday choices. Specify what you're looking for in a resort, chalet or hotel, and you'll get a ready-made short-list. And to turn the tables, there's an opportunity for you to file reports on resorts you have visited recently.

Initially we're publishing *Snow Zone* specifically to meet the needs of people based in Britain, with features on travel from Britain to the Alps and Rockies, and special deals from UK tour operators. The address is **http://www.snow-zone.co.uk**. In due course, we plan to develop a parallel edition that will be more international in outlook, with information that's equally valuable whether you're visiting the site from California, Canberra or Cambridge. The address will be **http://www.snow-zone.com**.

The magazine also reproduces some of what's in this book, as a taster for the benefit of those who don't have a copy. It contains some of the reference stuff that you'll find at the back of the book – such as parts of the resort Directory (including information on major resorts, for which we give only a page reference in the printed Directory). And, like any self-respecting website, *Snow Zone* has pages of links to other worthwhile sites.

We aim to make *Snow Zone* an indispensable part of the run-up to winter for the keen skier or boarder. Take a look at **http://www.snow-zone.co.uk** or **http://www.snow-zone.com**, and let us know what you think – you'll find e-mail links on the pages.

THE INTERNET AND THE WORLD WIDE WEB EXPLAINED

The Internet is a global network of linked computers on which information of many kinds is stored and accessible. Unless your place of work has computers that are themselves part of this network, you get access to the Internet by arranging an account with a firm set up for the purpose (an Internet Service Provider or Access Provider), and using a gadget called a modem to connect your computer to that firm's computers over an ordinary phone line (what is quaintly called dial-up access). The account will cost you around £150 a year, the modem around £100. The several magazines devoted to the Internet are the best place to start looking for both.

The Internet is very useful for exchanging messages (e-mail) with other users, but the really exciting aspect of it is the World Wide Web. The key concept of the Web is a simple but very powerful one – the hyperlink. Click your mouse button while the on-screen pointer is over a word or an image that is designated as a hyperlink, and you call up another page of information which may originate from a quite different source. On that page, there will probably be further links that you can activate the same way. And so on, and on.

There is all sorts of information available on the World Wide Web, from recipes to guidance from government departments – practically all of it free. Three of our favourite 'sites' are Railtrack's interactive train timetable, the Electronic Yellow Pages, and a comprehensive measurements converter put up by a Russian student. There are links to these sites (and others we like that are nothing at all to do with skiing or snowboarding) within *Snow Zone*.

Choosing your resort

get it right first time

Unless you're lucky enough to live within weekend driving distance of major mountains, you probably get to go skiing or boarding only once or twice a year – and then only for a week at a time. So choosing the right resort is crucially important. This book is designed to help you do just that. Here is some advice on how to use it to best effect.

Lots of factors need to be taken into account. The weight you attach to each of them depends on your own personal preferences, and on the make-up of the group you are going on holiday with. In the next chapter, you'll find over 20 shortlists of resorts which are outstanding in various key respects. For many people, cost will be an important factor; that's why (in addition to giving you a shortlist of budget resorts) we've devoted a whole chapter to it, earlier in the book, and why we've started each resort chapter with a clear price rating, giving a unique at-a-glance picture of which resorts are in your price range, and which are better left alone.

St-Martin-de-Belleville is a charming hideaway which is part of the biggest linked lift network in the world – the Three Valleys ↓

Each resort chapter is organised in the same way, to help you choose the right resort. This short introduction explains how they work. At the end of it, for easy reference, is a page summarising what each major resort chapter contains.

WHICH RESORT?

We start each chapter with a one-line verdict, in which we aim to sum up the resort in a few words. If you like the sound of it, you might want to go next to our new What it Costs rating, in the margin. These ratings, ranging from ① to ⓒⓒⓒⓒⓒ, reflect the total cost of a week's holiday from Britain, including a typical package of flights plus half-board accommodation, lift pass and meals and drinks on the spot. As you might expect with a six-point scale, 3 means on the low side of average, 4 means on the high side. Below that, in the How it Rates section, we rate each resort from 11 points of view – the more stars the better. (All these star ratings are brought together in one chart, on pages 75 to 79, following the resort shortlists.) Still looking at the information in the margin, in most chapters we have a What's New section; this is likely to be of most use and interest in resorts you already know – perhaps resorts you've resolved to stay away from until they fix some fundamental problem with the lift network.

For major resorts, the next thing to look at is our lists of the main good and bad points about the resort and its slopes, picked out with ➕ and ➖. These lists are followed by a summary in **bold type**, in which we've aimed to encapsulate the essence of the place and to weigh up the pros and cons, coming off the fence and giving our view of who might like it. These sections should give you a good idea of whether the resort is likely to suit *you,* and whether you should read our detailed analysis of it. Then, we have a special new summary of the resort from the particular point of view of snowboarders – whether the slopes present special attractions or problems, how much you can expect to have to use drag-lifts, whether you'll find specialist schools and shops in the resort.

You'll know by now whether this is, for example, a high, hideous, purpose-built resort with superb, snowsure skiing for all standards of skier but absolutely no nightlife, or whether it's a pretty, traditional village with gentle wooded skiing ideal for beginners if only there was some snow. We then look at each aspect in more detail.

THE RESORT

Resorts vary enormously in character and charm. At the extremes of the range are the handful of really hideous modern apartment-block resorts thrown up in France in the 1960s – step forward, Les Menuires – and the captivating old traffic-free mountain villages of which Switzerland has an unfair number. But it isn't simply a question of old versus new. Some purpose-built places (such as Valmorel) can have a much friendlier feel than some traditional resorts with big blocky buildings (eg Davos). And some places can be remarkably strung out (eg Vail) whereas others are surprisingly compact (eg Wengen).

The landscape can have an important impact – whether the resort is at the bottom of a narrow valley (eg Ischgl) or on a shelf with panoramic views (eg Crans-Montana). Some places are working towns as well as ski resorts (eg Bormio). Some are full of bars, discos and shops (eg St Anton). Others are peaceful backwaters (eg Arabba). Traffic may choke the streets (eg Châtel). Or the village may be traffic-free (eg Mürren).

In this first section of each chapter, we try to sort out the character of the place for you. Later, in the Staying There section, we tell you more about the hotels, restaurants, bars and so on.

THE MOUNTAINS

The slopes Some mountains and lift networks are vast and complex, while others are much smaller and lacking variation. The description here tells you how the area divides up into different sectors and how the links between them work.

Snow reliability A crucial factor for many people, and one which varies enormously. In some resorts you don't have to worry at all about there being a lack of snow, while others (including some very big names) are notorious for treating their paying guests to ice, mud and slush. Whether a resort is likely to have decent snow on its slopes normally depends on the height, the direction most of the slopes face (north good, south bad), its snow record and how much artificial snow it has (we list this figure in Mountain Facts).

For experts, intermediates, beginners Most (though not all) resorts have something to offer beginners. But remarkably few will keep an expert happy for a week's holiday. As for intermediates, whether a resort will suit you really depends on your standard and temperament. Places such as Cervinia and Obergurgl are ideal for those who want easy cruising runs, but have little to offer intermediates looking for more challenge. Others, such as Sölden and Val-d'Isère, may intimidate the less confident intermediate who doesn't know the area well.

For cross-country We don't pretend that this is a guide for avid cross-country skiers. But if you or one of your group wants to try it, our summary here will help you gauge whether the resort is worth considering or a wash-out. It looks not just at the amount of cross-country available but also at its scenic beauty and whether or not the tracks are likely to have decent snow (many are at low altitude).

Queues Another key factor. Most resorts have improved their lift systems enormously in the last ten years, and monster queues are largely a thing of the past. But there are notable exceptions – such as Verbier.

Mountain restaurants Here's a subject that divides people clearly into two opposing camps. To some, having a decent lunch in civilised surroundings – either in the sun, contemplating amazing scenery, or in a cosy hut, sheltered from the elements – makes or breaks their holiday. Others regard a prolonged mid-day stop as a waste of valuable time, as well as valuable spending money. We are firmly in the former camp. We get very disheartened by places with miserable restaurants and miserable food (eg many resorts in America); and there are some resorts that we go to regularly partly because of the cosy huts and excellent cuisine (eg Zermatt).

Schools and guides This is an area where we rely heavily on readers' reports of their own or their friends' experiences. The only way to judge a ski school is by trying it. Reports on schools are always extremely valuable and frequently record disappointment.

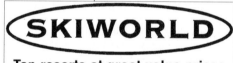

Facilities for children If you need crèche facilities don't go to Italy. In other countries, facilities for looking after and teaching children can vary enormously between resorts. We say what is available in each resort, including what's on offer from UK tour operators – often the most attractive option for Brits. But, again, to be of real help we need reports from people who've used the facilities.

STAYING THERE

In some resorts, such as St Anton and Zermatt, choosing where in the resort to stay is very important – otherwise you might end up with long treks to and from the lifts or being woken at 2am by noisy revellers. We tell you what to take into account.

How to go The basic choice is between catered chalets, hotels and self-catering accommodation. The catered chalet holiday remains a peculiarly British phenomenon. A tour operator takes over a chalet (or a hotel in some cases), staffs it with young Brits (or antipodeans), fills it with British guests, provides half-board and free wine, and lets you drink your duty-free booze without hassle. You can take over a complete chalet, or share it with other groups. It is a very economical way of visiting the expensive top resorts – see our chapter on costs.

Hotels, of course, can vary a lot but, especially in France and Switzerland, can work out very expensive. In north America, rooms are often capable of sleeping four, and UK tour operators are inclined to base their standard brochure prices on the assumption that you fill all available bed spaces. Watch out for supplements.

Apartments can be very economical but French ones, in particular, tend to be very small – it's not unusual for brochure prices to be based on four people sleeping in a one-room studio, for example. To be comfortable, pay extra for under-occupancy.

We also look at what's available for independent travellers who want to fix their own hotels or self-catering accommodation. With hotels we've given each a price rating from ① to ⑤ – the more coins, the pricier the hotel.

Staying up the mountain / down the valley If there are interesting options for staying on the slopes or in valley towns, we've picked them out. The former is often good for avoiding early-morning scrums for the lifts, the latter for cutting costs considerably.

Eating out The range of restaurants varies widel. Even some big resorts, such as Les Arcs, may have little choice because most of the clientele stay in their apartments or chalets. Others, such as Val-d'Isère, have a huge range available, including national and regional cuisine, pizzas, fondues and international fare. American resorts generally have an excellent range of restaurants – everyone eats out.

Après-ski Tastes and styles vary enormously. Most resorts have pleasant places in which to have an immediate post-skiing beer or hot chocolate. Some then go dead. Others have noisy bars and discos until the early hours. And, especially in Austrian resorts, there may be a lot of events such as tobogganing and bowling that are organised by British tour operator reps. We are largely dependent for this section on hearing from reporters who are keen après-skiers.

Off the slopes In some resorts, there is really nothing to do during the day but hit the slopes or stay in bed. In others, such as Seefeld, there are more people walking, skating, curling and swimming than there are skiing or boarding. Excursion possibilities vary widely. And there are great variations in the practicality of meeting skiers and boarders for lunch up the mountain.

Resort shortlists

to simplify the decision

We are always being asked 'Which is your favourite resort?' There's no simple answer to that question because it depends crucially on what we are looking for on a particular trip. If it's miles and miles of varied piste skiing, it has to be the Three Valleys; if it's great lift-served off-piste, it has to be Val-d'Isère/Tignes or Chamonix; if it's stunning scenery and a pretty, peaceful village, it has to be Wengen or Mürren; if it's a combination of village, scenery and skiing, it's Zermatt; if it's US charm with decent, varied slopes, it's Aspen; and so on... In reality, most of these only just make it to the top of the list, with a bunch of rivals close behind.

So, to choose the ideal resort for your own holiday, you first need to identify the key things which are most important to you. Then the ratings, general summary and lists of pros and cons at the start of each resort chapter will help you spot resorts to suit you. But for a real shortcut, here are lists of the best ten or so resorts for 21 different categories. Most lists embrace European and North American resorts, but some we've confined to the Alps, because America has too many qualifying resorts (eg for beginners) or because America does things differently, making comparisons invalid (eg for off-piste).

Here's a clue to the identity of the resort shown below: it figures in at least one shortlist ↓

SOMETHING FOR EVERYONE
Resorts with everything from reassuring nursery slopes to real challenges for experts
Alpe d'Huez, France p167
Les Arcs, France p175
Aspen, Colorado p432
Courchevel, France p202
Flaine, France p215
Lech/Zürs, Austria p109
Mammoth, California p427
Vail, Colorado p460
Val-d'Isère/Tignes, France p277/271
Val-Thorens, France p291

INTERNATIONAL OVERSIGHTS
Resorts that deserve as much attention as the ones we go back to every year, but don't seem to get it
Alta, Utah p 472
Andermatt, Switzerland p349
Bad Gastein, Austria p85
Les Contamines, France p201
Cortina d'Ampezzo, Italy p309
Ischgl, Austria p 98
Ste-Foy-Tarentaise, France p264
Sun Valley, Idaho p487
Telluride, Colorado p459
Western Safari, p514

RELIABLE SNOW IN THE ALPS
Alpine resorts with good snow records or lots of snowmaking, and high or north-facing slopes
Argentière, France p185
Cervinia, Italy p304
Courchevel, France p202
Hintertux, Austria p97
Lech/Zürs, Austria p109
Obergurgl, Austria p121
Saas-Fee, Switzerland p382
Val-d'Isère/Tignes, France p277/271
Val-Thorens, France p291
Zermatt, Switzerland p407

OFF-PISTE WONDERS
Alpine resorts where, with the right guidance and equipment, you can have the time of your life
Alpe d'Huez, France p167
Andermatt, Switzerland p349
Argentière/Chamonix, France p185
Davos/Klosters, Switzerland p361
La Grave, France p221
Lech/Zürs, Austria p109
St Anton, Austria p133
Val d'Isère/Tignes, France p277/271
Verbier, Switzerland p393
Zermatt, Switzerland p407

BLACK RUNS
Resorts with steep, mogully, lift-served slopes within the safety of the piste network
Alta/Snowbird, Utah p472/479
Andermatt, Switzerland, p349
Les Arcs, France p175
Argentière/Chamonix, France p185
Aspen, Colorado p432
Jackson Hole, Wyoming p483
Taos, New Mexico p488
Telluride, Colorado, p459
Val d'Isère/Tignes, France p277/271
Zermatt, Switzerland p407

CHOPAHOLICS
Resorts where you can quit the conventional lift network and have a day riding helicopters or cats
Alagna, Italy p319
Aspen, Colorado p432
Banff, Canada p500
Crested Butte, Colorado p445
Grand Targhee, Wyoming p486
Lech/Zürs, Austria p109
La Thuile, Italy p342
Verbier, Switzerland p393
Whistler, Canada p 508
Zermatt, Switzerland p407

HIGH-MILEAGE PISTE-BASHING
Extensive intermediate slopes with big lift networks
Alpe d'Huez, France p167
Davos/Klosters, Switzerland p361
Flims/Laax, Switzerland p368
Milky Way: Sauze d'Oulx (Italy), Montgenèvre (France) p328/241
La Plagne, France p251
Portes du Soleil, France/Switz. p259
Sella Ronda/Selva, Italy p333
Three Valleys, France p270
Val-d'Isère/Tignes, France p277/271
Whistler, Canada p508

MOTORWAY CRUISING
Long, gentle, super-smooth pistes to bolster the frail confidence of those not long off the nursery slope
Les Arcs, France p175
Aspen, Colorado p432
Breckenridge, Colorado p439
Cervinia, Italy p304
Cortina, Italy p309
Courchevel, France p202
Megève, France p225
La Plagne, France p251
La Thuile, Italy p342
Vail, Colorado p460

RESORTS FOR BEGINNERS
Alpine resorts with gentle, snowsure nursery slopes and easy runs to progress to
Alpe d'Huez, France p167
Les Arcs, France p175
Cervinia, Italy p304
Courchevel, France p202
Isola 2000, France p222
Montgenèvre, France p241
Pamporovo, Bulgaria p523
La Plagne, France p251
Saas-Fee, Switzerland p382
Soldeu, Andorra p521

MODERN CONVENIENCE
Resorts where there's plenty of slope-side accommodation to make life easy in those heavy boots
Les Arcs, France p175
Avoriaz, France p181
Courchevel, France p202
Flaine, France p215
Isola 2000, France p222
Les Menuires, France p230
Obertauern, Austria p126
La Plagne, France p251
Valmorel, France p286
Val-Thorens, France p291

WEATHERPROOF SLOPES
Alpine resorts with snowsure slopes if the sun shines, and trees in case it doesn't
Courchevel, France p202
Courmayeur, Italy p314
Flims, Switzerland p368
Montchavin/Les Coches, France p251
Schladming, Austria p144
Selva, Italy p333
Serre-Chevalier, France p265
Sestriere, Italy p341
La Thuile, Italy p342
Zermatt, Switzerland p407

BACK-DOOR RESORTS
Cute little villages linked to big, bold ski areas, giving you the best of two different worlds
Les Brevières (Tignes), France p271
Champagny (La Plagne), France p251
Falera (Flims), Switzerland p368
Leogang (Saalbach), Austria p127
Montchavin (La Plagne), France p251
Le Pré (Les Arcs), France p175
St-Martin, France p263
Samoëns (Flaine), France p215
Stuben (St Anton), Austria p133
Vaujany (Alpe d'Huez), France p167

SNOWSURE BUT SIMPATICO
Alpine resorts with high-rise slopes, but low-rise, traditional-style buildings
Andermatt, Switzerland p349
Arabba, Italy p333
Argentière, France p185
Ischgl, Austria p98
Lech/Zürs, Austria p109
Méribel, France p233
Obergurgl, Austria p121
Obertauern, Austria p126
Saas-Fee, Switzerland p382
Zermatt, Switzerland, p407

SPECIALLY FOR FAMILIES
Resorts where you can easily find accommodation surrounded by snow, not by traffic and fumes
Les Arcs, France p175
Avoriaz, France p181
Flaine, France p215
Isola 2000, France p222
Montchavin (La Plagne), France p251
Mürren, Switzerland p378
Saas-Fee, Switzerland p382
Serfaus, Austria p149
Valmorel, France p286
Wengen, Switzerland p402

BUDGET BALANCING
Resorts where cheap packages, cheap lifts, cheap drinks and meals will mean a cheap holiday
Bardonecchia, Italy p300
Arinsal, Andorra p517
Borovets, Bulgaria p524
Gressoney, Italy p319
Kranjska Gora, Slovenia (Directory)
Livigno, Italy p320
Poiana Brasov, Romania p528
Sauze d'Oulx, Italy p328
Sierra Nevada, Spain p522
Soldeu, Andorra p521

SPECIAL MOUNTAIN RESTAURANTS
Alpine resorts where the mountain restaurants can really add an extra dimension to your holiday
Alpe d'Huez, France p167
La Clusaz, France p197
Courmayeur, Italy p314
Kitzbühel, Austria p103
Megève, France p225
Saalbach-Hinterglemm, Austria p127
St Johann in Tirol, Austria p140
St Moritz, Switzerland p387
Selva, Italy p333
Zermatt, Switzerland p407

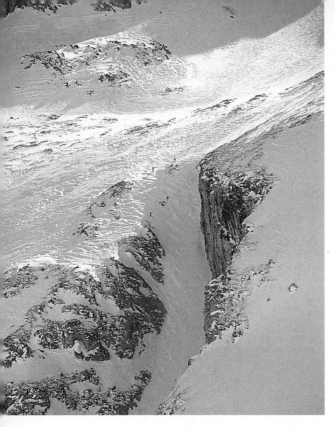

↑
High above La Grave

VILLAGE CHARM
Resorts with traditional character that enriches your holiday – from mountain villages to mining towns
Alpbach, Austria p84
Champéry, Switzerland p351
Courmayeur, Italy p314
Crested Butte, Colorado p445
Lech, Austria p109
Mürren, Switzerland p378
Saas-Fee, Switzerland p382
Telluride, Colorado p459
Wengen, Switzerland p402
Zermatt, Switzerland p407

LIVELY NIGHTLIFE
Alpine resorts where you'll have no difficulty finding somewhere to boogy, and someone to do it with
Chamonix, France p185
Ischgl, Austria p98
Kirchberg, Austria p103
Kitzbühel, Austria p103
Saalbach, Austria p127
St Anton, Austria p133
Sölden, Austria p150
Soldeu, Andorra p521
Val d'Isère, France p277
Verbier, Switzerland p393

OTHER AMUSEMENTS
Resorts where those not interested in skiing or boarding can still find plenty to do
Bad Gastein, Austria p85
Chamonix, France p185
Cortina, Italy p309
Davos, Switzerland p361
Kitzbühel, Austria p103
Megève, France p 225
St Moritz, Switzerland p387
Seefeld, Austria p148
Wengen, Switzerland p402
Zell am See, Austria p157

DECENT MOUNTAIN RESTAURANTS
US resorts which have at least one mountain restaurant that would survive in the Alps
Aspen, Colorado p432
Beaver Creek (Vail), Colorado p460
Deer Valley, Utah p478
Keystone, Colorado p449
Steamboat, Colorado p454
Sun Valley, Idaho p 487
Winter Park, Colorado p467

DRAMATIC SCENERY
Resorts where the mountains are not just high and snowy, but precipitous too
Banff, Canada, p500
Chamonix, France p185
Cortina, Italy p309
Courmayeur, Italy p314
Jungfrau resorts (Grindelwald, Mürren, Wengen), Switzerland p373/378/402
Heavenly, California p420
Saas-Fee, Switzerland p382
St Moritz, Switzerland p387
Selva, Italy p333
Zermatt, Switzerland p407

Resort ratings at a glance

The following five pages bring together the ratings we give each resort for eleven key characteristics. You'll find these ratings at the start of each resort chapter too. Use the tables here to compare resorts directly for the aspects which are most important to you. You'll be able to see at a glance which resorts come out top and bottom of the pile.

AUSTRIA

	Alpbach	Bad Gastein	Ellmau	Fieberbrunn	Hintertux	Ischgl	Kitzbühel	Lech
Page	84	85	91	96	97	98	103	109
Snow	**	***	*	**	*****	****	**	****
Extent	*	****	****	*	**	***	****	****
Experts	*	***	*	*	***	***	***	****
Intermediates	**	****	****	**	***	****	****	****
Beginners	****	**	****	****	*	**	**	****
Convenience	**	**	***	**	**	***	**	***
Queues	***	***	****	****	***	***	**	***
Restaurants	***	****	**	**	**	**	****	**
Scenery	***	***	***	***	***	***	***	***
Resort charm	*****	***	***	****	***	****	****	****
Off-slope	***	****	***	***	*	***	*****	***

	Mayrhofen	Neustift	Niederau	Obergurgl	Obertauern	Saalbach-Hinterglemm	St Anton	St Johann in Tirol
Page	115	119	120	121	126	127	133	140
Snow	***	*****	*	*****	****	***	****	**
Extent	**	**	*	**	**	****	****	**
Experts	*	**	*	**	***	**	*****	*
Intermediates	***	***	**	***	****	****	***	***
Beginners	**	**	****	****	*****	***	*	***
Convenience	*	*	***	****	****	****	***	***
Queues	*	***	****	*****	****	***	**	***
Restaurants	***	**	**	**	***	****	***	****
Scenery	***	***	***	***	***	***	***	***
Resort charm	***	****	***	****	**	****	****	***
Off-slope	****	***	**	**	**	**	***	***

	Schladming	Seefeld	Serfaus	Sölden	Söll	Westendorf	Zell am See
Page	144	148	149	150	151	156	157
Snow	***	**	***	****	*	**	**
Extent	***	*	***	***	****	*	**
Experts	**	*	**	**	*	*	**
Intermediates	****	**	***	****	****	**	***
Beginners	****	*****	****	**	***	****	***
Convenience	**	*	***	***	**	***	**
Queues	****	***	***	**	***	****	**
Restaurants	****	***	***	***	**	***	***
Scenery	***	***	***	***	***	***	***
Resort charm	****	****	****	**	***	****	***
Off-slope	****	*****	***	**	**	**	****

FRANCE

	Alpe-d'Huez	Les Arcs	Avoriaz	Chamonix	Châtel	La Clusaz	Les Contamines	Courchevel
Page	167	175	181	185	192	197	201	202
Snow	****	****	***	****	**	**	****	****
Extent	****	***	*****	***	*****	***	**	*****
Experts	****	****	***	*****	***	**	**	****
Intermediates	****	****	****	**	****	****	***	*****
Beginners	*****	****	****	*	**	***	***	*****
Convenience	****	****	****	*	**	***	**	****
Queues	***	***	**	**	***	***	**	****
Restaurants	****	*	****	***	***	****	****	****
Scenery	****	***	***	*****	***	***	***	***
Resort charm	*	*	**	****	***	****	****	**
Off-slope	**	*	*	*****	**	***	**	***

	Les Deux-Alpes	Flaine	La Grave	Isola 2000	Megève	Les Menuires	Méribel	Montgenèvre
Page	210	215	221	222	225	230	233	241
Snow	****	****	***	***	**	****	****	***
Extent	***	****	**	**	*****	*****	*****	****
Experts	***	****	*****	**	*	****	****	**
Intermediates	**	*****	*	***	****	*****	*****	****
Beginners	***	*****	*	*****	***	***	***	*****
Convenience	***	*****	***	*****	**	*****	***	****
Queues	**	****	****	***	***	****	****	****
Restaurants	*	**	**	**	*****	***	****	**
Scenery	****	****	****	***	***	***	***	***
Resort charm	**	*	***	*	****	*	***	***
Off-slope	**	*	*	*	****	*	***	*

	Morzine	La Plagne	Puy-St-Vincent	Risoul	La Rosière	St-Martin-de-Belleville	Ste-Foy	Serre-Chevalier
Page	245	251	260	261	262	263	264	265
Snow	**	****	***	***	***	***	***	****
Extent	*****	****	**	***	***	*****	*	****
Experts	***	***	***	**	**	****	****	***
Intermediates	****	*****	***	****	***	*****	***	****
Beginners	***	*****	***	****	*****	***	**	****
Convenience	**	*****	*****	****	***	***	***	***
Queues	***	***	****	****	***	****	*****	***
Restaurants	***	**	***	**	*	****	*	***
Scenery	***	***	***	***	***	***	***	****
Resort charm	***	*	**	**	***	****	***	***
Off-slope	***	*	*	*	*	*	*	**

FRANCE (continued) – ITALY

	Tignes	Val-d'Isère	Valmorel	Val-Thorens	Vars
Page	271	277	286	291	295
Snow	*****	*****	***	*****	***
Extent	*****	*****	***	*****	***
Experts	*****	*****	**	****	**
Intermediates	*****	*****	****	*****	****
Beginners	**	***	*****	****	***
Convenience	****	***	*****	*****	****
Queues	****	****	****	***	****
Restaurants	**	**	**	****	**
Scenery	***	***	***	***	***
Resort charm	*	***	****	*	**
Off-slope	*	**	**	**	**

ITALY

	Bardonecchia	Bormio	Cervinia	Cortina d'Ampezzo	Courmayeur	Gressoney-la-Trinité	Livigno	Madesimo
Page	300	301	304	309	314	319	320	324
Snow	**	***	*****	***	****	***	****	***
Extent	***	**	***	***	**	***	**	*
Experts	*	*	*	**	***	**	**	***
Intermediates	***	***	****	***	****	****	***	**
Beginners	**	**	*****	*****	**	**	****	***
Convenience	**	***	***	*	*	****	**	***
Queues	***	***	***	***	****	****	****	***
Restaurants	***	****	***	****	****	**	***	**
Scenery	***	***	****	*****	****	****	***	***
Resort charm	*	****	**	****	****	***	***	**
Off-slope	**	****	*	*****	***	*	**	*

	Madonna di Campiglio	Pila	Sauze d'Oulx	Selva	Sestriere	La Thuile
Page	325	326	328	333	341	342
Snow	***	***	**	****	****	****
Extent	***	**	*****	*****	****	***
Experts	**	**	**	***	***	**
Intermediates	****	****	****	*****	****	****
Beginners	****	***	**	****	***	****
Convenience	**	***	**	***	****	***
Queues	***	****	***	***	***	****
Restaurants	****	***	***	****	**	*
Scenery	****	***	***	*****	***	***
Resort charm	***	***	**	***	*	***
Off-slope	***	**	*	***	*	**

SWITZERLAND – ANDORRA – BULGARIA – NEW ZEALAND

	Adelboden	Andermatt	Arosa	Champéry	Crans-Montana	Davos	Engelberg	Flims
Page	348	349	350	351	356	361	367	368
Snow	**	****	***	**	**	****	***	***
Extent	***	*	**	*****	***	*****	**	****
Experts	**	****	*	***	**	****	***	***
Intermediates	***	**	***	****	****	*****	***	*****
Beginners	****	*	****	**	***	***	**	****
Convenience	***	***	***	*	**	**	*	***
Queues	***	**	****	****	***	***	***	***
Restaurants	**	*	****	***	**	***	***	***
Scenery	***	***	***	****	****	***	***	***
Resort charm	****	****	**	****	**	**	***	***
Off-slope	****	**	****	***	****	*****	***	***

	Grindelwald	Gstaad	Mürren	Saas-Fee	St Moritz	Verbier	Villars	Wengen
Page	373	377	378	382	387	393	401	402
Snow	**	*	***	*****	****	***	**	**
Extent	***	****	*	**	*****	*****	**	***
Experts	***	**	***	***	****	*****	**	***
Intermediates	*****	***	***	****	****	***	***	****
Beginners	***	***	**	*****	**	**	****	***
Convenience	**	*	***	***	**	**	***	***
Queues	**	***	***	***	**	**	***	***
Restaurants	***	***	**	***	****	***	***	****
Scenery	*****	***	*****	****	****	****	***	*****
Resort charm	****	****	*****	*****	*	***	****	*****
Off-slope	****	****	***	****	*****	***	****	****

		ANDORRA		Pas de la Casa	BULGARIA	NEW ZEALAND
	Zermatt	Arinsal	Soldeu		Borovets	Queenstown
Page	407	517	521	520	524	536
Snow	****	***	***	***	**	**
Extent	****	*	**	**	*	*
Experts	*****	*	*	*	*	***
Intermediates	****	**	***	***	**	***
Beginners	*	****	****	****	****	***
Convenience	*	***	***	****	****	*
Queues	***	***	***	***	**	***
Restaurants	*****	*	*	***	*	*
Scenery	*****	***	***	**	***	****
Resort charm	*****	*	*	*	**	**
Off-slope	****	*	*	*	*	*****

Ratings at a glance

UNITED STATES – CANADA

	Alta	Aspen	Breckenridge	Copper Mountain	Crested Butte	Heavenly	Jackson Hole	Keystone
Page	472	432	439	444	445	420	483	449
Snow	*****	*****	*****	*****	****	***	***	*****
Extent	*	****	**	**	**	***	**	**
Experts	****	****	***	***	****	***	*****	***
Intermediates	***	*****	****	****	***	****	***	****
Beginners	***	*****	****	****	****	****	***	****
Convenience	****	**	***	****	***	*	***	**
Queues	***	****	****	****	****	***	**	****
Restaurants	**	***	**	*	*	*	*	***
Scenery	****	***	***	***	***	****	***	***
Resort charm	***	****	***	*	****	*	****	**
Off-slope	*	****	***	*	**	**	**	**

	Killington	Mammoth Mountain	Park City	Smugglers' Notch	Snowbird	Steamboat	Stowe	Sun Valley
Page	491	427	473	495	479	454	496	487
Snow	****	****	****	****	*****	****	****	***
Extent	**	***	***	*	*	**	*	***
Experts	***	****	****	***	*****	***	***	***
Intermediates	***	****	****	***	***	****	****	****
Beginners	****	****	****	****	**	*****	****	***
Convenience	*	**	***	*****	*****	***	*	**
Queues	****	****	****	****	**	****	****	****
Restaurants	*	*	**	*	*	***	**	****
Scenery	***	***	***	***	***	***	***	***
Resort charm	**	**	***	**	*	**	****	***
Off-slope	*	*	***	*	*	**	*	***

					CANADA		
	Taos	Telluride	Vail	Winter Park	Banff	Jasper	Whistler
Page	488	459	460	467	500	507	508
Snow	****	****	*****	*****	*****	****	****
Extent	**	**	****	***	****	*	****
Experts	*****	****	****	****	***	***	*****
Intermediates	***	***	*****	****	****	***	*****
Beginners	**	*****	*****	*****	***	****	****
Convenience	***	****	***	*	*	*	****
Queues	****	*****	***	****	*****	****	*****
Restaurants	*	**	**	***	*	*	*
Scenery	***	***	***	***	****	***	***
Resort charm	***	****	****	**	***	***	***
Off-slope	**	**	***	*	***	***	**

A guide to our major resort chapters

What you'll find in the margins of major resort chapters

· REVISITED · BY THE EDITORS (R)

Since the last edition, we have personally revisited the vast majority of the resorts covered – and these are identified by this symbol. With the other resorts, we have updated all resort details and incorporated many reporters' observations.

WHAT IT COSTS ((((3))))

The cost of visiting each resort is rated on a scale of one to six, reflecting the typical price of a one-week trip based on a half-board package bought in the UK, plus a lift pass and an allowance for lunch in mountain restaurants. We assume two people sharing a room – even in the US, where package prices are often based on four people sharing.

HOW IT RATES

Star-ratings summarising our view of the resort in 11 different respects, including how well it suits different standards of skier/boarder.

What's new

Recent and imminent developments in the resort, particularly new lifts.

MOUNTAIN FACTS

Key information such as altitudes, the quantity and difficulty of pistes (slope area in north America) and extent of snowmaking.

LIFT PASSES

Essential information about lift passes including prices (normally for the 1997/98 season) in the local currency.

SCHOOLS/GUIDES

Details of classes and private lessons including prices (normally for the 1997/98 season) in the local currency.

CHILDCARE

Kindergarten and nursery facilities, with contact telephone numbers.

GETTING THERE

What's involved in getting there by air or by rail.

UK PACKAGES

The UK package holiday firms offering holidays in the resort (contact details at the back of the book).

ACTIVITIES

Cinemas, swimming pools, galleries, sports and other resort facilities.

TOURIST OFFICE

International phone and fax numbers of the tourist office (the lift company in north America). Normally, substitute a zero for the +code if calling from within the country concerned.

What you'll find in the main body text

One-line summary

At the top of the chapter, an instant snapshot of the resort.

➕ Plus points, and

➖ Minus points

We pick out the main pros and cons to consider before making a decision.

Extended summary in bold type.

We give a clear view of who we think will like the resort, and who won't.

boarding

We summarise the special attractions and drawbacks of the place – facilities such as fun-parks and half-pipes, types of lift, character of the slopes.

The resort

We outline the main characteristics and style of the resort village or town.

The mountains

We start by summarising the character of the slopes – who they suit. Our maps show the resort's own gradings of runs (so those in the US are different from those in Europe). We mark fast or high capacity lifts:

Ⓕ fast chair-lift

Ⓖ gondola

Ⓒ cable-car

Ⓕ funicular

Under THE SLOPES we explain the lift network. We assess SNOW RELIABILITY, then evaluate the slopes for EXPERTS, INTERMEDIATES and BEGINNERS. We review CROSS-COUNTRY possibilities. Under QUEUES, we pinpoint inadequate lifts. Then we weigh up the MOUNTAIN RESTAURANTS, SCHOOLS AND GUIDES, and FACILITIES FOR CHILDREN.

Staying there

Under HOW TO GO we summarise the accommodation available, and make recommendations. Sections follow summarising EATING OUT and APRES-SKI possibilities. Under OFF THE SLOPES we look at the resort for people who don't want to ski or board.

Austria

Austria used to be the favourite destination of British skiers. But that has changed over the last few years – France has raced ahead of it and Italy claimed similar numbers last season. Austria suffered because the soaring value of the schilling made it an expensive place to holiday for the cost-conscious, especially compared with Italy; the resorts were slow to put in artificial snowmaking, even though most of them suffered poor cover on their low-altitude slopes; and as British skiing standards improved, people started looking for more challenging places to visit. Now France claims 25 per cent of the market compared with Austria and Italy's 20 per cent each. But Austria is beginning to make a resurgence. The pound was back to 20 schillings when we went to press, making Austria competitive again and the authorities have finally started to install more snow-guns. And Austria remains unbeatable for its unique and jolly après-ski.

Austria has a huge number of resorts, large and small. And one thing all of them have in common is reliably comfortable accommodation – whether it's in four-star hotels with pools, saunas and spas, or in great-value family-run guest houses, of which Austria has thousands. Chalet and self-catering packages are less widely available.

Most Austrian resorts are real, friendly villages on valley floors, with skiing and boarding on the wooded slopes above them. They have expanded enormously since the war, but practically all the development has been in traditional chalet style, and the villages generally look good even without the snow that is the saving grace of many French and even some Swiss resorts.

The skiing is often quite limited. There are many Austrian resorts that a keen skier could explore fully in half a day. Those who start their skiing careers in such resorts may not be worried by this; those who have developed a taste for bigger areas find the list of acceptable Austrian resorts quite a short one.

Unfortunately, several of the resorts on that shortlist bring you up against another problem – low altitude, and therefore poor snow conditions. Kitzbühel is at 760m, Söll at 700m, Zell am See at 775m. The top heights of Austrian resorts are relatively low, too – typically 1800m to 2000m, and snowmaking is still not all that widespread.

The resorts of the Arlberg area, at the western end of the Tirol – St Anton, Lech and Zürs, stand apart from these concerns, with excellent snow records and extensive skiing. And there are other resorts where you can be reasonably confident of good snow, such as Obergurgl and Ischgl, not to mention the year-round slopes on glaciers such as those at Hintertux, Neustift and Kaprun. But for most other resorts our advice is to book late, when you know what the snow conditions are like.

Snowboarders don't need big areas; and snowboarding in slushy snow is not as unpleasant as skiing in it. So it's not surprising that boarding in Austria is booming.

Nightlife is an important feature of Austrian holidays for many regular visitors. It ranges from lively bars, through Tirolean evenings and activities organised by UK tour operator reps, to much more sophisticated discos, nightclubs and even some casinos in resorts such as Lech, Ischgl and Kitzbühel.

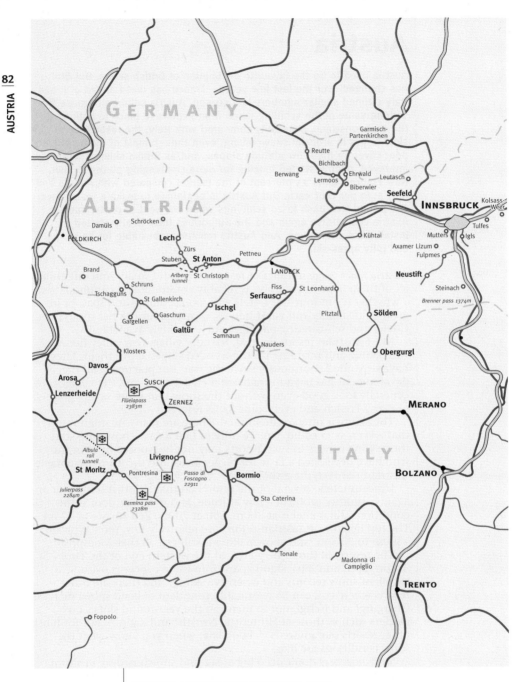

GETTING AROUND THE AUSTRIAN ALPS

The dominant feature of Austria for the ski driver is the thoroughfare of the Inn valley, which runs through the Tirol from Landeck via Innsbruck to Kufstein. The motorway along it extends, with one or two breaks, westwards to the Arlberg pass and on to Switzerland.

The Arlberg – which divides Tirol from Vorarlberg, but which is

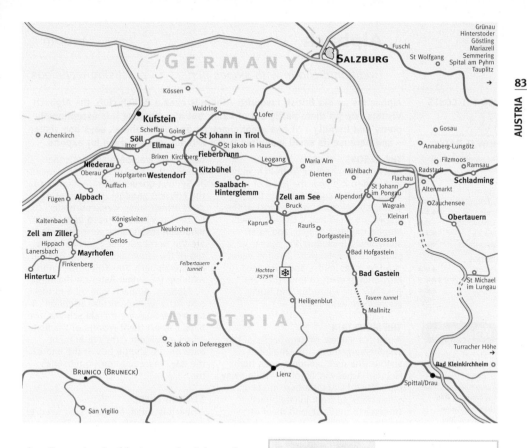

also the watershed between Austria and Switzerland – is one of the few areas where driving plans are likely to be seriously affected by snow. The east–west Arlberg pass itself has a long tunnel underneath it; this isn't cheap, and you may want to take the high road when it's clear, through Stuben, St Christoph and St Anton. The Flexen pass road to Zürs and Lech (which may be closed by avalanche risk even when the Arlberg is open) branches off just to the west of the Arlberg summit.

At the eastern end of the Tirol, the Gerlos pass road from Zell am Ziller over into Salzburg province (1628m) can be closed. Resorts in Carinthia such as Bad Kleinkirchheim are easily reached by motorway thanks to the Tauern and Katschberg tunnels. Or you could drive over the Radstädter Tauern pass through Obertauern (1740m), or use the car-carrying rail service from Böckstein to Mallnitz.

Alpbach

1000m

Traditional charm with slopes perfect for practising technique

HOW IT RATES

The slopes

Snow	**
Extent	*
Experts	*
Intermediates	**
Beginners	****
Convenience	**
Queues	***
Restaurants	***

The rest

Scenery	***
Resort charm	*****
Off-slope	***

What's new

A new half-pipe and fun-park for boarders opened for the 1996/97 season. The new Alpbach Aktiv school welcomes both skiers and boarders.

MOUNTAIN FACTS

Altitude	830m-2025m
Lifts	20
Pistes	45km
Blue	15%
Red	70%
Black	15%
Artificial snow	20km

UK PACKAGES

First Choice Ski, Inghams, Made to Measure, Sloping Off

TOURIST OFFICE

Postcode A-6236
Tel +43 (5336) 5211
Fax 5012

Alpbach is an old British favourite – there is even a British club, the Alpbach Visitors. We go there partly out of habit, but also because it is exceptionally pretty and friendly – 'it has great character and atmosphere', says one visitor – and because its small mountain is not without interest, even for experts.

THE RESORT

Alpbach is captivating both in summer and winter. It's near the head of a valley, looking south towards the Wiedersbergerhorn, where most of the slopes are. Traditional chalets crowd around the little church, and open snow fields (including the nursery slopes) are yards away. The Inn valley is a few miles north, and trips east to Kitzbühel or west to Innsbruck are possible. The Hintertux and Stubai glaciers are within reach.

THE MOUNTAIN

Alpbach's **slopes**, on two flanks of the Wiedersbergerhorn, are small and simple. The main gondola goes from isolated Achenwirt (830m), a mile away but served by shuttle bus and taxis. Slower lifts go from Inneralpbach (1050m) to the east, and meet at Hornboden (1890m), then two drags take you to 2025m. The small area at Reith is on the lift pass. **Snowboarders** will like the natural lumps and bumps as well as the new fun facilities.

Alpbach cannot claim great **snow reliability**; but at least most slopes face north. The village nursery slope and, increasingly, other runs have artificial snow. 'Alpbach works very hard to keep its pistes well groomed and safe', comments one regular visitor, who is enthusiastic despite never having encountered good snow.

Alpbach isn't ideal for **experts**, but the reds and the two blacks are not without challenge, and runs of 1000m vertical are not to be sniffed at. There are a couple of off-piste routes to the valley, short tours are offered, and the schools take the top classes off-piste.

There is great **intermediate** terrain; the problem is that it's limited. This resort is for practising technique on familiar slopes, not high mileage.

Beginners love the sunny, handy nursery slopes. Higher slopes can be used, but not for confidence-building: most longer runs are red.

Pretty **cross-country** trails rise up beyond Inneralpbach (1050m); the most testing is 9km and climbs 300m.

Serious **queues** are rare, thanks to the efficient gondola. But the resort does attract some weekend trade.

The area has squeezed in many **mountain restaurants**. Recommended are the Hornboden self-service at the top of the mountain, the cosy Bögalm at Inneralpbach, the Kolberhof, and the Asthütte (or Kafner Aste) for the sun.

Alpbach, Alpbach Innertal and the new Activ (with particular attention to snowboarding) are the **ski schools**. We have had excellent reports of the first. All take **children** – they're brought back on the shuttle bus at the end of the day. There are non-ski nurseries too.

STAYING THERE

Alpbach is small, so there's no need to worry about where you stay. The very centre is most convenient, both for the bus and for après-ski. The backwater of Inneralpbach is convenient for the slopes, and suits families.

Hotels and pensions dominate in UK packages. Of the smart 4-star places, the Alpbacherhof and historical Böglerhof get most votes. But simpler Haus Thomas, Haus Theresia, Haus Angelika and Haus Leirerhäusl are recommended by visitors. Some self-catering is offered – and the Alpbach Visitors Club provides an inside track.

For **eating out** the Reblaus, Jakober and Hotel Post are recommended, as is the Wiedersbergerhorn in Inneralpbach – worth a taxi-ride. For self-caterers there are two good supermarkets.

The **après-ski** is typically Tirolean, with lots of noisy tea-time beer-swilling in the bars of central hotels such as the Jakober. In the evening the Waschkuch'l is good for a quiet drink. The Birdy Bar, Böglerkeller and Weinstahdl have late night dancing.

There is much to amuse **off the slopes**, including swimming, curling (400m from the centre), pretty walks, and trips to Innsbruck and beyond.

Bad Gastein 1000m

Cruise the pistes and soak in the spas

WHAT IT COSTS

((€3))

HOW IT RATES

The slopes

Snow	★★★
Extent	★★★★
Experts	★★★
Intermediates	★★★★
Beginners	★★
Convenience	★★
Queues	★★★
Restaurants	★★★★

The rest

Scenery	★★★
Resort charm	★★★
Off-slope	★★★★

What's new

For 1997/98 the valley lift pass will also cover snowsure Mallnitz-Ankogel, 30 minutes away by train or bus in Carinthia.

The new hotel Metro Ferienclub Bellevue opened for the 1996/97 season.

⊕ Four separate, varied areas with, between them, a huge number of slopes on one pass

⊕ Great for confident intermediates, with lots of long, challenging reds

⊕ More snowsure than most low-altitude Austrian resorts, with artificial snow and the high Sportgastein area as back-up

⊕ Lots of good, atmospheric, traditional mountain restaurants

⊕ Plenty of off-slope facilities, especially related to its origin as a spa resort

⊕ Unusual setting, architecture and ambience for a winter resort

⊖ Slopes don't really suit beginners or timid intermediates

⊖ Biggest and smallest areas accessed direct from Bad Gastein but other two a bus-ride away. Buses can be infrequent and crowded and having a car would be handy

⊖ Sedate spa-town atmosphere not to everyone's taste and can suffer from local traffic on the narrow streets

⊖ Bus-rides or steep walks to the slopes or après-ski from some accommodation

The Gastein valley has some of Austria's best and most extensive slopes for intermediates. We have always been impressed with it, and yet it is very little known on the British market. Perhaps that is because of its unusual character. Bad Gastein grew up as a spa town with large, austere stone buildings. It is built in a deep gorge, with a steep road winding down from top to bottom. The atmosphere is elegant, but slightly faded. The après-ski matches the village – no Tirolean lederhosen-clad knees-ups here. Elegant tea rooms, sophisticated bars and a casino are more the style. The spa facilities are those you'd expect of a town born because of its hot springs and health cures. It's a far cry from a standard chalet-style Austrian farming village.

But then so are the slopes. There are lovely long runs, above and below the tree line – mostly steepish reds. It's much more of a place for confident skiers and boarders than timid intermediates. And there's a lot of it. The biggest local area, reached by gondola from the top of town, is linked to that of nearby Bad Hofgastein to form an impressively large circuit. There's also a smaller, local area on the opposite side of the valley – usually quiet and ideal for bad-weather days because of its tree-lined runs. And then there's snowsure Sportgastein further up the valley, and the big Dorfgastein–Grossarl circuit down the valley. Add together all these areas and there's more than enough to keep even the keenest piste-basher happy for a week.

So it's really a question of whether you fancy the spa-type town rather than winter-resort atmosphere. The main alternative places to stay are Bad Hofgastein (another spa town) and quiet, rustic Dorfgastein (see end of chapter).

boarding *Among Bad Gastein's well-heeled visitors boarding might seem out of place, but the resort is starting to embrace the sport, at least on the slopes. There's no special school (tuition is through ski school), but there are two half-pipes – one on the Stubnerkogel above the town, the other at Sportgastein, and the Gastein valley tends to host lots of events. Only the main lifts are chairs and gondolas – most of the rest are drags, particularly above Bad Hofgastein. And there are few easy slopes, so it's not ideal for beginners. There's a fair amount to do in the evenings, but it's not as much fun as other Austrian resorts.*

MOUNTAIN FACTS

Altitude 840m-2685m
Lifts   53
Pistes   250km
Blue   24%
Red   66%
Black   10%
Artificial snow   40km
Recco detectors used

LIFT PASSES

97/98 prices in
schillings
**Gastein Super Ski
Pass**
Covers all lifts in
Gastein valley and
Grossarl, and buses,
trains and road tolls
between the resorts.
Beginners Day- and
points-tickets for
baby lifts.
Main pass
1-day pass 400
6-day pass 1,990
(low season 1,490 –
25% off)
Senior citizens
Over 65 male, 60
female: 6-day pass
1,790 (10% off)
Children
Under 15: 6-day pass
1,190 (40% off)
Under 6: free pass
Short-term passes
Single ascent on
selected lifts, time
card (2, 3 and 4
hours) and half-day
passes available.
Alternative periods
5 skiing days in 7,
and 12 skiing days in
14 passes available.
Notes Discounts for
families, students
(under 26) and
groups of over 20.
Alternative passes
Gastein Super Ski
Pass only available
for 1½ days or more.
Passes for shorter
periods cover only
Bad Gastein/Bad
Hofgastein. Single
ascent passes
available for lifts in
Dorfgastein and
Sportgastein.

The resort

Bad Gastein sits at the head of eastern
Austria's Gastein valley. It is an old
spa that had its heyday many years
ago; it has spread widely, but still has
a compact core. Its central buildings
are a bizarre combination (smart,
modern, hotel–shopping–casino
complex, baroque town hall and
concrete multi-storey car park) and it
has a cramped horseshoe layout set in
what is virtually a gorge, complete with
waterfall crashing beneath the main
street. The thick surrounding woods
lend charm, and the main road and
railway bypass the centre.

From the upper part of Bad Gastein
resort. Winter visitors will feel most at
home in the area around the railway
station and main lift.

Bad Gastein is a formal place.
People tend to dress smartly for hotel
evening meals, and the general
ambience is sophisticated, quiet
and relaxed.

The mountains

On the whole, this is an area that suits
confident intermediates best; most of
the slopes are graded red, and rightly
so. Where there is a blue option, it is
not always a very attractive one – and
not always as easy as a timid
intermediate might hope.

Buses and trains covered by the lift
pass run between the spread-out
slopes. But they can be overcrowded
and a bit of a scrum. Rail excursions
are easy to Zell am See and St Johann
im Pongau. Drivers can visit snowsure
Obertauern and Kaprun.

THE SLOPES
Extensive but fragmented
The extensive main slopes are made
up of two distinct sectors, above Bad
Gastein, and the large but less well
known area of Bad Hofgastein. Mid-
way between them is a link via the
side valley of Angertal.

From the upper part of Bad Gastein
a gondola goes up to **Stubnerkogel**,
from where you can head back to the
resort or down to Angertal. This valley
has lifts going up to **Schlossalm** above
Bad Hofgastein, from where a variety
of pistes lead off in different
directions. The runs back to Angertal
are south-facing and low, but well
covered by artificial snowmakers.

The much smaller **Graukogel** area
lies at the other side of Bad Gastein. It
is a steep, straightforward mountain
with just three lifts. With pistes set in
broad swathes through the forest, the
area is a great asset in bad weather
and quiet at other times.

Reached by bus or train, high, wild
Sportgastein, 9km away, has the best
snow in the area, and is served by an
eight-person gondola; but there are
few pistes: red and blue variants of a
long run down the narrow mountain.
Dorfgastein (8km north) and, in the
next valley, Grossarl share another
extensive area of red and blue runs.

SNOW RELIABILITY
Good for a low-altitude resort
Although the area is essentially of
typically Austrian low altitude, there is
a battery of snowmakers in crucial
sections, and the higher sector of
Sportgastein is an important fallback.
This part of the Alps has a good snow
record in relation to its height, and
there are a lot of slopes above mid-
station height.

FOR EXPERTS
More fast cruises than challenge
The terrain is really better suited to
advanced intermediates than to true
experts. There are few black runs but
there are long, interesting reds with
steepish terrain for great fast cruising.

The Graukogel has the World Cup
slopes, and provides some challenge
on its upper slopes. The route between
Stubnerkogel and Bad Gastein is fairly
steep, and often icy, with plenty of
room for off-piste excursions on the
open, top section.

Sportgastein is worth the trip –
there are off-piste possibilities on the
front of the mountain, and a long off-
piste trail off the back drops almost
1500m from Kreuzkogel to Heilstollen
in the valley (on the bus route).
Dorfgastein has the least demanding
slopes in the area, but there is a fine
black run down to the village.

FOR INTERMEDIATES
Not for leisurely cruiser
Good intermediates will love all the
areas on the lift pass – more than
enough to keep you happy for a week.
A particular delight is the beautiful
8km run, well away from the lifts, from
Höhe Scharte down to Bad Hofgastein.
The open north-facing slopes of
Stubnerkogel down into Angertal are

good, for both interest and snow cover. The same is true of the Graukogel runs. None of the slopes is boringly easy.

But the area as a whole is uncomfortably challenging for early intermediates. The Grossarl and Schlossalm sectors have less demanding pistes than other sectors, and the open bowl around the main cluster of restaurants at Schlossalm is reassuringly blue in gradient. Most intermediates will enjoy the network of red runs above Dorfgastein and Grossarl, as well as the whole Schlossalm sector.

↑ Cancer-inducing sunshine above, cancer-curing radioactive water below; can't be Bad

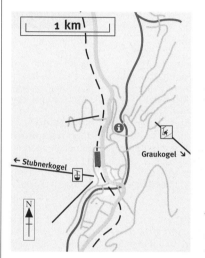

EASE THOSE ACHES AND PAINS

Bad Gastein boasts 17 thermal springs – the ideal place to relax if you have overdone it on the slopes. The spas are supposed to have a regenerative effect thanks to the high radon content. They are also marketed as a beauty treatment, but we cannot comment on their usefulness in this capacity.

There is also an underground 'healing gallery' where the humidity, high temperature and concentration of radon 'make you feel years younger'.

CHILDCARE

Both ski schools run ski kindergartens.

There is a kindergarten at the Grüner Baum hotel, taking children aged 3 to 8, from 9.30 to 4pm. Skiing is available, with a special lift. A free shuttle bus is offered.

SCHOOLS/GUIDES

96/97 prices in schillings

Badgastein
Manager Werner Pflaum
Classes 6 days
6hr: 10am-4pm, 1hr lunch; 3hrs: 1pm-4pm
6 full days: 1,690
Children's classes
Ages: up to 14
6 full days including lunch: 2,600
Private lessons
55 mins
450 for 55 mins; each additional person 120

Luigi
Manager Luigi Kravanja
Classes 6 days
5hr 15min: 10am-3.15 with 1hr lunch
6 full days: 1,450
Children's classes
Ages: 4 to 14
6 full days including lunch: 1,950
Private lessons
1hr or full-day
450 for 1hr; each additional person 105

GETTING THERE

Air Salzburg, transfer 2hr. Linz or Munich, transfer 3½hr.

Rail Mainline station in resort.

FOR BEGINNERS
Unsuitable slopes

Inadequate nursery slopes are dotted around. Only the good school makes this resort in any way suitable.

FOR CROSS-COUNTRY
Extensive, if low and fragmented

There is an impressive 90km of trails, but all are along the valley floor, making only the small loop at Sportgastein reasonably reliable for snow. Another drawback is the scattered nature of the loops. Bad Hofgastein is by far the best base for cross-country skiing, with long trails stretching almost to Bad Gastein.

QUEUES
Buses are the problem

There are few problems outside the peak season in late February. The powerful gondola at Sportgastein put paid to the queues there when conditions were poor elsewhere.

Morning queues to get out of the valley and for the Bad Hofgastein mid-station cable-car are the worst. Bus queues can be a problem too. Buses between villages are infrequent, and Bad Gastein's in-village transport (essential for some accommodation) is unreliable and erratic.

MOUNTAIN RESTAURANTS
One of the pleasures of this area

Numerous atmospheric, traditional huts are dotted around. Good value and good food are the norm. Bad Gastein's places are more expensive than those in the rest of the valley, but still cheap compared to most of the Alps.

Bad Hofgastein's smart Schlossalm has a large terrace, plus yodelling! All jolly are the Aeroplanstadl on the 8km Höhe Scharte run, Hamburger Skiheim, at Schlossalm (with 'barbecue in the snow'), and the Panoramastube in Dorfgastein. The Wengeralm, also above Dorf, is a cosy, upmarket refuge with a good terrace. Two new restaurants were built at Sportgastein, as part of the gondola's construction.

SCHOOLS AND GUIDES
English widely spoken

English speakers make up a small proportion of guests here, and your class size may well depend on how many of the limited number of your fellow Brits having tuition happen to be at your ability level. The two schools do have good reputations, but

we lack recent reports. In the past the main Schi & Rennschule has been praised for its enthusiastic instructors with good English, plus optimal use of time and good division of abilities.

The tuition at Schischule Luigi concentrates on guiding, touring, snowboarding and children.

FACILITIES FOR CHILDREN
Reasonable

Bad Gastein hardly seems an ideal resort for small children, but there are facilities for all-day care, of which the ski kindergarten at the Grüner Baum sounds the most inviting.

Staying there

Getting around Bad Gastein is not easy, so it is worth picking your location with care. For getting to the slopes, the best place to stay is in the upper part of town, close to the Stubnerkogel gondola station.

HOW TO GO
Packages mainly to hotels

Although apartments make up nearly 15 per cent of the total beds available, British tour operators sell mainly hotel-based packages. The nearest thing to a chalet is Ski Miquel's Tannenburg, a traditional old hotel run as a chalet-hotel. It is a short walk from the gondola and offers good value for money – although wine is extra.

Hotels This is an upmarket spa resort, and it has lots of smart hotels with excellent spa facilities – almost as many 4-stars as 3-stars.

©©©⑤ **Elizabeth Park** Luxury hotel popular with Brits looking for excellent facilities, style, comfort and formality. Unfortunately, poorly placed for the slopes, but does run a courtesy bus.

©©©④ **Salzburger Hof** 4-star with excellent spa facilities, a longish walk from the village gondola.

©©©④ **Schillerhof** Reliable 4-star in good position, opposite Graukogel lift.

©©©④ **Wildbad** 4-star within reasonable walking distance of the main lift.

©©©④ **Grüner Baum** Splendidly secluded Relais & Châteaux place, tucked away in the Kötschachtal.

©©③ **Mozart** Well placed for buses. Good food.

©©③ **Alpenblick** Good value, informal 3-star; well placed for the slopes.

Self-catering Plenty of apartments are available for rent but you have to book them directly.

UK PACKAGES

Crystal, First Choice
Ski, Inghams, Made
to Measure, Ski
Miquel

Bad Hofgastein
Crystal, Inghams,
Made to Measure

ACTIVITIES

Indoor Fitness centre
(swimming, sauna,
gym), thermal baths,
squash, bridge,
tennis, bowling,
indoor golf, darts,
casino, museum,
theatre, concerts
Outdoor Natural ice
rinks (skating and
curling), sleigh rides,
horse-riding, ice
climbing, toboggan
runs, ski-bob, 35km
cleared paths

EATING OUT
Something for most tastes

There is a fair range of restaurants,
including surprisingly fine Chinese and
seafood places. The Bellevue Alm is
one of the liveliest places to eat at,
while the à la carte menus at the 3-star
hotels Nussdorferhof and Mozart are
good value.

APRES-SKI
Varied, but no oom-pah-pah

Soaking in one of the spas is a
popular activity – see the feature on
spas.

There are elegant tea rooms,
sophisticated dances, numerous bars,
discos and casinos, but the general
ambience is rather subdued.

This part of Austria has not
imported the informal Tirolean-style
'oom-pah-pah'; neither are there any
lively bands. The tea-dance at the
Bellevue Alm is the only real
concession to Kitzbühel-style fun. The
best tea-rooms are the Causerie, in the
Elizabeth Park and the Wiener
Café/Pilsstube in the Salzburger Hof.
The Weismayr, Eden's Bar and
Manfreda's Bar are pleasant for a quiet
drink. The Hexen Haüsl is a more
informal little wooden schnaps bar.

Haggenblooms has live music and
gets full of young Swedes out to have
a good time. The Bunny Bar is more
sophisticated than its name suggests.
The various functions in the Grüner
Baum are the most informal hotel
entertainment, but the elegant Ritz and
Felsen bars in the Satzburger Hof and
the Elizabeth Park respectively are
more typical of the scene later on.

The Gatz and the Blockhaüsl are the
main clubs. The casino gives you a
generous amount of free chips, so
those with will-power and/or luck can
have a surprisingly inexpensive couple
of hours there. Bowling and a casino
trip are likely to be organised by tour
operator reps.

OFF THE SLOPES
Great variety of things to do

Provided you don't mind the style of
the place, Bad Gastein has a lot to
offer off the slopes, whether you're
active or not. The spa facilities are
superb – see the feature panel.

The Gastein Healing Gallery is a
highlight – a train takes you down into
an old gold-digging tunnel where you
have the opportunity to lie on benches
inhaling radon in steam-room-like heat

and humidity for a couple of hours!
The Rock Pool is a large indoor pool
hewn out of the rock, heated naturally
by hot springs.

Meeting up the mountain is no
problem for pedestrians, though
getting to the best mountain
restaurants isn't easy.

There are organised coach trips to
Kitzbühel, Salzburg and Goldegg
Castle, and trains run to the resorts of
Zell am See and St Johann im Pongau.

Bad Hofgastein 860m

Bad Hofgastein is a sizeable quiet, old
spa village set out spaciously in a
broad section of the valley. It has an
impressive old Gothic church,
traditional-style buildings, elegant
quiet hotels, narrow alleys and a
babbling brook. Everything is kept in
pristine order.

Although rather sprawling, the
village has a pleasant pedestrianised
area which acts as a central focus.
Because of the spa 'cures' there's a
relatively high number of people just
pottering about during the day,
notably at the curling rinks in Kurpark.
The place looks very pretty in the
evenings, under the soft glow of night
lamps. The large public spa building,
the Kurzentrum, is the only relative
blot on the landscape, though it's not
exactly an eyesore.

The best location to stay is in the
pedestrian zone, which is relatively
handy for most things including the
slopes. However, convenience for the
slopes is not generally a strong point
and a high proportion of hotels are a
long walk from the single village lift
station. Many people catch the inner-
village shuttle-bus.

Buses to the other Gastein valley
resorts are infrequent (half-hourly to
Bad Gastein, hourly to Dorfgastein,
twice daily to Sportgastein), and in the
past reporters have found the
timetable in Dorfgastein particularly
difficult to decipher.

Bad Hofgastein's lift is a short
funicular that takes you up to a mid-
station (1302m), above which most of
the slopes are found. Here, you have a
choice between a cable-car and two-
stage chair. Both the funicular and the
much lower capacity cable-car can
generate big queues (30 minutes in
rush hour during peak season is not
unusual). At such times, the chair is an
obvious alternative to the cable-car
and there's closed-circuit TV at the

TOURIST OFFICE

Postcode A-5640
Tel +43 (6434) 25310
Fax 253137

funicular base station which shows you the situation up at the cable-car.

Beginners staying in Bad Hofgastein have to catch a bus to the limited nursery area over at Angertal.

Bad Hofgastein makes a fine base for cross-country skiers when its lengthy valley-floor trails have snow.

We have received complimentary reports of the two schools in the past, but haven't heard from recent visitors. One is based at Angertal, and runs the village ski kindergarten there, which can be very inconvenient for parents. Lack of many English-speaking children to play with may be another drawback.

Bad Hofgastein is essentially a hotel resort. They tend to be large, good quality and many have their own fine spa facilities. Some are within easy walking distance of the funicular, a few provide courtesy transport, and most of the rest are close to bus stops.

The Palace Gastein is a big 4-star with superb leisure facilities, including pool and thermal baths. The elegant Germania is similarly comfortable.

The high-quality Norica is atypically modern in design, but is well positioned in the pedestrian zone. The Alpina is another well located 4-star, five minutes from the slopes. The Astoria is well appointed but quite poorly positioned and doesn't supply courtesy transport.

The Kürpark has been popular for its good food, service and location in the pedestrian zone – but our reports are not recent. Gasthof Reiter is poorly positioned but provides a useful inexpensive, informal B&B.

There is a good range of restaurants, and many hotels offer good formal dining. The Moserkeller is an intimate restaurant, and Pension Maier one of the better informal places. The Pyrkerhöhe, on the slopes just above town, is worth an evening excursion. The Tele Pizza Bar cooks outside on an open fire at lunchtimes in fine weather. It's also good inside in the evenings, as are the Tschickeria and Da Dimo pizza and pasta places.

Après-ski is very quiet by Austrian standards. Some reporters have been disappointed; others have loved the peacefulness.

There are, however, a few animated places around. The Picolo ice bar in the centre of town is lively immediately after the lifts close. Frankie's bar is quite lively and popular with locals. Evergreen has a friendly atmosphere.

Visions is a spacious modern disco, while Match Box and C'est la Vie had loud music and were full of teenagers when we looked in.

Most of Bad Hofgastein's clientele prefer something more sedate. Café Weitmoser is an historic little castle popular for its cakes at tea-time. The outdoor bar of the Ostereicher Hof is a pleasant spot to catch the last of the sun. Another atmospheric tea-time rendezvous is the Tennishalle. Later, the West End bar is a cosy place for a quiet drink. The Glocknerkeller in Pension Zum Toni and the Rondo bar in Hotel Käruten have live music in a low-key ambience.

The Bad Gastein casino provides free taxis to and from town. A bowling evening is organised by tour reps.

The Kurzentrum is the centrepiece of the things to do off the slopes, being arguably an even more impressive spa facility than that of Bad Gastein. It has an impressive thermal pool, and offers a range of therapies Other off-slope amenities include artificial and natural ice skating, indoor tennis, squash, sleigh rides. Lovely walks and riding.

Dorfgastein 830m

Those who wish to try the Gastein valley slopes but prefer not to stay in large, commercialised villages should consider Dorfgastein. Prices are lower, and the atmosphere more friendly and informal – a contrast to its rather cold setting sheltered from the sun.

The extensive slopes are more suitable for early intermediates than the steeps above Bad Gastein. Runs are long and varied, amid lovely scenery. Unfortunately the low-altitude nursery slopes can be cold and icy. Bad Hofgastein's funicular is 15 minutes away by bus (infrequent and sometimes crowded).

Those not interested in venturing that far can buy a local pass costing 75 per cent of the Gastein Valley lift pass price.

There are a few shops and après-ski places, a five- or ten-minute walk or short bus-ride from the slopes. Café St Ruperb is a nice village pizzeria.

The Kirchenwirt and Romerhof are comfortable hotels. Pension Schihause is cheaper, does good food, and is next to the slopes.

There is an outdoor heated pool with sauna-solarium, a bowling alley and a ski kindergarten.

Ellmau 800m

A quiet base from which to access the extensive Ski-Welt area

WHAT IT COSTS

(((③)))

HOW IT RATES

The slopes

Snow	*
Extent	****
Experts	*
Intermediates	****
Beginners	****
Convenience	***
Queues	****
Restaurants	**

The rest

Scenery	***
Resort charm	***
Off-slope	***

What's new

For 1997/98 artificial snowmaking in the Ski-Welt area is being doubled to cover 99km – making it the most extensive snowmaking system in Austria. And a new lift pass is being introduced. The Kitzbüheler Alpenskipass will cover Ski-Welt, Kitzbühel, Alpbach, Schneewinkel and Wildschönau, and will be valid for any six days over the season.

- ➕ Extensive, pretty, easy slopes
- ➕ Cheap by Austrian standards
- ➕ Quiet, charming family resort – more appealing than neighbouring Söll
- ➕ Excellent nursery slopes (but see minus points)
- ➕ Heavy investment in new snowmaking equipment taking place

- ➖ Very poor snow record; increased snowmaking so far doesn't completely compensate
- ➖ When snow is in short supply, queues can be a problem – and transport to nearby resorts is poor
- ➖ Lack of nightlife other than rep-organised events
- ➖ Little for experts

Like nearby Söll, Ellmau gives access to the large, unthreatening Ski-Welt circuit (some still call it the Grossraum). The resort is a pleasant, quiet alternative to Söll, and offers more holiday amenities than other neighbours such as Scheffau. Its nursery slopes and main lifts are more convenient than most in this area.

In the past holiday-makers' reports on Ellmau have always mentioned lack of snow as a problem. However, recent investment in snowmakers seems to be making a difference. A 1997 visitor comments, 'massive investment in artificial snow and new lifts have improved the situation considerably. It's now normally possible to get down to Brixen on artificial snow rather than using the gondola for most of the season, though cruising through green fields of grazing sheep seems a bit odd!' And the snowmaking in the Ski-Welt area is being doubled for the 1997/98 season.

boarding *The extensive Ski-Welt area could be a good boarder destination but it doesn't seem to go out of its way to attract them – Westendorf has the only half-pipe in the area, is not linked to the rest of the area, and is way over the other side of the mountain from Ellmau. But Ellmau is a good place to give boarding a try – the local slopes are easy, you can stick to the funicular and chair-lifts when you get off the nursery slopes and if the slopes go slushy the boarding gets easier. Nightlife is in rather short supply – again good for a family with some members learning to board but a disaster area for hardcore boarders looking for a rave.*

MOUNTAIN FACTS

Altitude	620m-1830m
Lifts	90
Pistes	250km
Blue	37%
Red	53%
Black	10%
Artificial snow	99km

LIFT PASSES

97/98 prices in schillings

Ski-Welt Wilder Kaiser-Brixental
Covers all lifts in the Wilder Kaiser-Brixental area, from Going to Westendorf.

Beginners Points cards for lifts available (25 points 70). Small drags are 5 points.

Main pass
1-day pass 360
6-day pass 1,745

Children
Under 15: 6-day pass 960 (45% off)
Under 5: free pass

Short-term passes
Single ascent, half-day passes up to noon and from 11am, noon and 2pm to the end of the day.

Alternative periods
Passes available for 5 skiing days in 7, 7 days in 10 and 10 days in 14.

Notes Discounts for physically disabled skiers and children with a Kinderkarten (child's card) of 70%.

Alternative passes
Ellmau ski pass covers 16 local lifts (adult 6-day 1,415). Kitzbüheler Alpenskipass covers lots of resorts in the East Tirol (adult 6-day 1,990)

The resort

Ellmau sits at the north-eastern corner of the Ski-Welt, between St Johann and Wörgl. Although a sizeable resort, and becoming more commercialised each year, it remains quiet and pretty, with traditional chalet-style buildings, welcoming bars and shops, and a picturesque old church. Its Alpine charm is spoilt a little by the main road along its edge, and by a frequent lack of snow on rooftops and streets.

By Austrian standards the nightlife is rather tame, and although off-slope diversions have improved, the village doesn't really amount to more than a pleasant dormitory for slope users.

The mountains

The Ski-Welt is reputedly the largest mountain circuit in Austria. It links to Going, Scheffau (covered in this chapter), Söll, Itter, Hopfgarten and Brixen. But it hardly compares in size, and certainly not in quality, to St Anton, Ischgl, Saalbach or the Gastein valley. Most runs are short, and not difficult. Westendorf is covered by the Ski-Welt pass, though separate. Kitzbühel, Waidring, Fieberbrunn and St Johann are within easy range for day-trips and are covered by the Kitzbüheler Alpenskipass.

THE SLOPES
Slow links to the rest of Ski-Welt
At least Ellmau is close to the best slopes in the area, above Scheffau. The funicular railway on the edge of the village (served by the free shuttle bus) takes you up to Hartkaiser, from where a fine long run leads down to Blaiken (Scheffau's lift station). A choice of gondola or two-stage chair goes back to Brandstadl, the start of three varied, long alternatives back to Blaiken.

Immediately beyond Brandstadl, the slopes become rather bitty; an array of short runs and lifts link Brandstadl to Zinsberg. From there, excellent, long, south-facing pistes lead down to Brixen. Then a short bus-ride takes you to Westendorf's pleasant separate area. Part way down to Brixen you can head towards Söll – either by the steep Hohe Salve or by avoiding the latter using a series of easy runs. Hohe Salve also provides access to a long, west-facing run to Hopfgarten. If you

want to include the fine long run down to Itter in your tour, it's best to do so before getting to Hochsöll.

Returning to Ellmau is a time-consuming business. Getting back to Blaiken via the Süd drag is quicker, but the buses to Ellmau are irregular.

Ellmau and Going share a pleasant little area of slopes on Astberg, slightly apart from the rest of the area and well suited to the unadventurous and to families. One piste leads to the funicular for access to the rest of Ski-Welt. The main Astberg chair is rather inconveniently positioned, midway between Ellmau and Going.

SNOW RELIABILITY
Now with more artificial help
Ellmau has a poor snow record, though the resort – and the Ski-Welt as a whole – is trying to counter this by installing more snow-guns. Of the extra 49km of new snowmaking for 1997/98 in the Ski-Welt, 12km will be in Ellmau and Going. The north-facing Eiberg area above Scheffau holds its snow well. Or you can travel to Waidring's high Steinplatte area – covered by the new regional lift pass.

FOR EXPERTS
Not suitable
There's a steep plunge off the Hohe Salve summit, and a little mogul field between Brandstadl and Neualm, but the area isn't really suitable except for those prepared to seek out worthwhile off-piste opportunities. The Morderer ski route from Branstadl down to Scheffau is a highlight.

FOR INTERMEDIATES
Great for cruisers and families
In good snow, good intermediates will enjoy the runs to Brixen, and on Hohe Salve. Groups of mixed ability can enjoy a variety of runs above Blaiken, while moderate cruisers have fine runs down to the valley villages, including long ones alongside the Ellmau funicular. Ellmau is particularly well placed for timid intermediates with the quiet, easy slopes of Astberg on hand.

FOR BEGINNERS
One of the best Ski-Welt villages
Ellmau has an array of good nursery slopes – snow permitting. East of the village is a vast area of gentle slopes that spreads across to Going. The area next to the funicular station, west of the village, is smaller but still very

CHILDCARE

The Ist School has a playroom open from 9am. The Hartkaiser school opened a ski nursery last season. The Top-Ski school welcomes children and provides lunchtime care on request. There is also a village non-skiing kindergarten

SCHOOLS/GUIDES

96/97 prices in schillings

1st Ellmau
Manager Friedl Fuchs
Classes 6 days
4hr: 10am-noon and 2pm-4pm
6 full days: 1,280
Children's classes
Ages: 3 to 14
6 full days: 1,230
Private lessons
Hourly or full day (4hr)
450 for 1hr; each additional person 180

Ellmau-Hartkaiser
Manager Dietmar Maier
Classes 6 days
4hr: 10am-noon and 2pm-4pm
6 full days: 1,300
Children's classes
Ages: 3 to 14
6 full days: 1,250
Private lessons
Hourly or full day
450 for 1hr; each additional person 200

Top
Manager Hans Peter Haider
Classes 6 days
4hr: 10am-noon and 2pm-4pm
6 full days: 1,300
Children's classes
Ages: 3 to 15
6 full days: 1,250

satisfactory, with the Astberg chair opening up a more snowsure plateau at altitude. The Brandstadl-Hartkaiser area has another section of short, easy runs. Near-beginners looking for a rest from drag-lifts have a nice long piste running the length of the funicular.

FOR CROSS-COUNTRY
Plenty of valley trails

When there is snow, there are long, quite challenging trails along the valley to St Johann and Kirchdorf, and an easier one to Scheffau and via Söll to Itter. But trails at altitude are lacking.

QUEUES
Few local problems

Again, snow-cover dominates the analysis. With good snow, the worst queues are quite distant from Ellmau. Hochsöll can be a bottleneck – particularly the Hohe Salve chair. The Blaiken gondola gets oversubscribed at weekends and when snow is poor elsewhere. At such times, everyone wants to head for Eiberg's reliable snow, and the higher lifts on and around Eiberg may suffer bad queues.

The poor valley bus service and the roundabout links between Hartkaiser and the rest of the Ski-Welt are more of a problem, causing greater delays in practice than any lift queues.

MOUNTAIN RESTAURANTS
Stick to the little huts

'Little huts good, big huts bad' is a simple but fairly accurate description. The smaller places are fairly consistent in providing wholesome, good-value food in pleasant surroundings, although perhaps only the one at Neualm deserves special mention. The larger self-service restaurants are rather functional (the Jochstube at Eiberg is an exception, and now has an Igloo bar attached) and suffer queues. Going is a good spot for a quiet lunch.

SCHOOLS AND GUIDES
Good on the whole

The school has a good reputation except that classes tend to be very large. As well as the main school there is a mountaineering school organising daily tours in the Wilder Kaiser group as well as the Kitzbühel mountains.

FACILITIES FOR CHILDREN
Fine in theory

Ellmau is an attractive resort for families, and kindergarten facilities seem satisfactory. We have no recent reports on how they work in practice.

Staying there

Ellmau has a compact centre, but its accommodation is scattered. Hotel position is quite important: those keen to hit the slopes as early as possible will want to be close to the funicular. Après-skiers will want to be more central, close to the village facilities and up to 20 minutes' walk or a bus-ride from the funicular. Near-beginners might want to be near the Astberg chair, half-way between Ellmau and Going. The main nursery slopes are also at the Going end of the village, beside the school, but there are some by the road to the funicular.

HOW TO GO
Lots of chalet-style hotels

Ellmau is essentially a hotel and pension resort, though there are apartments that can be booked locally. **Hotels** Ellmau is typical of Austrian resorts that have expanded since World War II, with many comfortable, modern, chalet-style hotels, largely indistinguishable at first sight.
((((⑤ **Bär** Elegant but relaxed Relais & Châteaux chalet that seems almost out of place in Ellmau – twice the price of any other hotel.
(((③ **Hochfilzer** Central, well equipped and once described by a reporter as 'the best encountered in 22 years'.
((③ **Christoph** Large, comfortable, multi-facility place in secluded position on the outskirts – quite handy for the funicular.
((③ **Sporthotel** Similar in style to the Christoph, but opposite the school and main nursery slopes.
((③ **Alte Post** Pleasant and central, though not self-evidently 'alte'.
((② **Pension Claudia** Good bedrooms, next to the school.
① **Gasthof Au** Cheapest place in town, five minutes from the funicular and ten from the centre.
Self-catering There is a wide variety. Basically you get what you pay for. The Bauer Annemarie is under the same management as the hotel Christoph and equally well placed for lifts. Conveniently close to the nursery slopes is Feyersinger Martin.

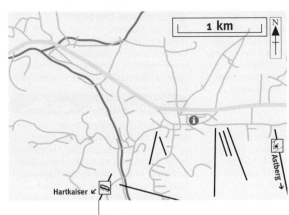

1 km

N

Hartkaiser ↙

Astberg →

WHERE TO EAT
Hotel-dominated

Most people are on half-board so there are not many restaurants. The hotel Hochfilzer has a reputation for good food and is open to non-residents. The Lobewein and Buchingerstüberl are worth a visit. Café Bettina, midway between the funicular and town, is good for afternoon coffee and cakes.

APRES-SKI
Limited but varied programme

The rep-organised events include bowling, sleigh rides, Tirolean folklore and inner-tubing, but there is little else. The Memory bar is lively, but not for those who hate passive smoking.

The mountains you're on may be gentle, but the ones you have in view (the Wilder Kaiser range) are not ↓

OFF THE SLOPES
Excellent sports centre

The Kaiserbad leisure centre is good. There are many excursions available, including Innsbruck, Salzburg, Rattenburg, Vitipeno or even Venice (six hours each way). St Johann in Tirol is a nice little town only a few miles away by bus. Other facilities are very limited. Valley walks are spoilt by the busy main road.

Scheffau 745m

Scheffau is one of the most attractive of the Ski-Welt villages: a rustic little place complete with pretty white church, it is spacious yet not sprawling, and has a definite centre. It is tucked away a kilometre off the busy main Wörgl road, which increases the charm factor at the cost of slope convenience (the Ski-Welt lifts are at Blaiken, on the opposite side of the main road). The nursery slopes are in the village, however, and this makes Scheffau a poor choice for mixed-ability parties – though one regular visitor finds even real beginners can make it up to Brandstadl by the end of the week. When the snow conditions are very good it is possible to get down to the main road from the village. If convenience is all important to you, you have the option of staying in Blaiken, where there are several more hotels.

UK PACKAGES

Airtours, Crystal, First Choice Ski, Inghams, Neilson, Thomson

Scheffau am Wilden Kaiser Crystal, First Choice Ski, STS, Thomson

GETTING THERE

Air Salzburg, transfer 2hr.

Rail Wörgl (18km), St Johann in Tirol (10km), Kufstein (20km), bus to resort.

PACKAGES

Airtours, Crystal, Inghams, Neilson, Rank STS, SkiBound, Thomson

Scheffau Crystal, First Choice Ski, Thomson

ACTIVITIES

Indoor Swimming pool, sauna, solarium, tennis, squash, bowling, billiards, ski museum, theatre
Outdoor Winter hiking, natural ice rink, curling, toboggan run, sleigh rides, cleared walking paths, paragliding, hang-gliding, mountaineering school

TOURIST OFFICE

Postcode A-6352
Tel +43 (5358) 2301
Fax 3443

A gondola and parallel two-stage chair give rapid and generally queue-free access directly to the Ski-Welt's best (and most central and snowsure) section of pistes. This makes Scheffau (or more accurately Blaiken) arguably the best place to stay if you want to hit every run on Austria's largest mountain circuit.

The pistes above Blaiken are some of the longest and steepest in the Ski-Welt. Nearby Eiberg is the place to go when snow is poor, and the slopes are more extensive since drags were replaced by four-seater chairs.

Links from Ellmau and Söll are awkward (or impossible) when snow is poor, which is another attraction of being based in Scheffau or Blaiken. It remains to be seen whether this is improved by new snow-guns.

The village nursery slope is adequate when snow-cover is good enough. Higher slopes suitable for novices are an inconvenient and expensive distance away up the main mountain, though there are plenty of options for improving beginners.

Given full snow-cover there are few queuing problems, but delays can be long when poor conditions elsewhere force Söll, Hopfgarten and Brixen guests into the Scheffau section. At such times the two-stage valley chair can be a useful alternative to the oversubscribed gondola – though the VIP pass you get when you stay in Sheffau means you can slide past day trippers in the queue.

The school is well regarded but groups can be large and bilingual. A visitor reports that 'a mixed group of Dutch and English with a Dutch instructor can be a lot of fun'.

Hotels dominate the accommodation scene. The 4-star Alpin Tirol is one of the best and has the only pool in town. The new Kaiser is also recommended. Gasthof Weberbauer is a lovely, olde-worlde place at the centre of the village – but not so near the gondola. The Wilder Kaiser is the best hotel at Blaiken. Nearby are the good value gasthofs Waldhof (right next to the gondola), Aloisia and Blaiken.

There is a distinct lack of village restaurants, and those staying in B&B places are advised to book tables well in advance. There are two pizzerias. Regulars find Scheffau friendly and restful. Après-ski is unlikely to draw Blaiken residents up the hill. Pub Royal is the only bar with much animation, though the Kaiseralm disco livens up at weekends. The usual rep-organised events such as bowling and tobogganing are available.

Walking apart, there is little to do off the slopes. Tour ops organise trips to Innsbruck (the Swarovski Crystal factory is just outside) and Salzburg.

Scheffau is a good family choice: both the ski kindergarten and non-ski nursery have good reputations.

Going 775m

Going is a tiny, attractively rustic village, well placed for the limited but quiet slopes of the Astberg and for the vast area of nursery slopes between here and Ellmau. Prices are low by Austrian standards, but it's not an ideal place for covering the whole of the Ski-Welt on the cheap.

Going is ideal for families looking for a quiet time, particularly if they have a car for transport to Scheffau or St Johann when the Astberg's low runs lack snow.

Fieberbrunn 800m

Pretty village and slopes, ideal for beginners

WHAT IT COSTS

HOW IT RATES

The slopes

Snow	**
Extent	*
Experts	*
Intermediates	**
Beginners	****
Convenience	**
Queues	****
Restaurants	**

The rest

Scenery	***
Resort charm	****
Off-slope	***

What's new

In 1996/97 the slopes gained a few metres vertical by the construction of a new quad chair at the top, replacing the old Sonnenmulde drag.

MOUNTAIN FACTS

Altitude	800m-2020m
Lifts	14
Pistes	40km
Blue	34%
Red	50%
Black	16%
Artificial snow	7km

TOURIST OFFICE

Postcode A-6391
Tel +43 (5354) 6304
Fax 2606

Beginners could do worse than try Fieberbrunn, with its good nursery slopes, pretty tree-lined pistes and jolly Tirolean atmosphere. But any decent intermediates will soon tire of its limited and unexciting slopes.

THE RESORT

Fieberbrunn is a non-commercialised, atmospheric and attractive resort, even though it sprawls along the valley road for 2km. It has classic Tirolean charm: wooden chalets, pretty church, cosy bars and coffee shops, sleighs, tea dances and friendly locals.

Much of the village is also pleasantly set back from the road and railway, so that peace is interrupted only by church bells. Light sleepers can stay in hotels out near the main lift-station, served by regular but sometimes crowded buses from the village. But beginners should stay in the centre near the nursery slopes. The resort is popular with the Dutch but has few British visitors these days.

THE MOUNTAINS

The **slopes**, with their 40km of piste (not including neighbouring St Jakob), are best for beginners and leisurely intermediates who like very pretty resorts. The tree-lined runs are attractive but don't offer much variety. Most pistes are on north-facing slopes which now reach 2020m. For **snowboarders** there are a 100m half-pipe and a fun-park on Streuböden. Fieberbrunn also hosts the ISF European championships every year.

Fieberbrunn has better **snow-cover** than is usual at this altitude, claiming 'Schneewinkl' status, and it now has snowmakers on two runs from mid-mountain. Nearby Waidring's Steinplatte (on the same lift pass) has particularly snow-reliable slopes.

Fieberbrunn holds little to attract **experts** or good **intermediates**. Its prettiest runs are the Doischberg reds, which would be blue in many resorts. The Streuböden runs to the village are pleasant cruising territory, and the Reckmoos chair accesses steeper, open slopes. Some of the most popular runs can get very crowded at weekends. Guided off-piste excursions, including some towards Kitzbühel, are popular.

Beginners have broad nursery slopes conveniently close to the village

centre. Graduation to the long, gentle Streuböden runs is comfortable.

There are 40km of good trails for **cross-country** skiers.

Weekday **queues** are rare outside the morning rush for the Streuböden lifts. The new chair-lift on the top slope has cut out any delays there. But when less fortunate resorts in the Tirol are short of snow, Fieberbrunn can be invaded by visitors. Sunny weekends are also busy, but overcrowded pistes are a greater problem than queues.

The good **mountain restaurants** are found at the Streuböden mid-station and at Reiteralm.

The two **ski schools** have a high reputation, but classes can be large.

Children's facilities include a ski kindergarten which takes children from age of 4. There is no longer a non-ski kindergarten, but there is baby-sitting.

STAYING THERE

Fieberbrunn is essentially a hotel resort. The 3-star Lindauhof is near the main slopes. Probably the top hotel, on the other side of town, near the railway station, is Schloss Rosenegg, with a swimming pool. More central, cheaper places include the 3-star Metzgerwirt and Grosslehen and pension Pirker.

Restaurants are mainly hotel-based. The candlelit Weinstubli in the Rosenegg is good for a splurge. Hotel Alte Post has a particularly pleasant restaurant. La Pampa is an excellent specialist Mexican establishment.

Après-ski is liveliest at 4pm. The Enzianhütte, Lindauhof and Siglu snow bar at the foot of the slopes are atmospheric; the first two have good tea dances. Later, the expensive Londoner Pub is popular but overloud. Riverhouse is classier, with quieter music and live shows.

Off the slopes, there's quite a bit to do, with an adventure pool, skating, sleigh rides and cleared walks – and an illuminated toboggan run. Train excursions are possible to Salzburg, Innsbruck and Kitzbühel.

WHAT IT COSTS

(((3)))

HOW IT RATES

The slopes

Snow	*****
Extent	**
Experts	***
Intermediates	***
Beginners	*
Convenience	**
Queues	***
Restaurants	**

The rest

Scenery	***
Resort charm	***
Off-slope	*

What's new

The long chair to the mid-mountain Tuxer Ferner Haus was replaced for 1996/97 by the 24-person 'Gletscherbus' gondola, which is not only fast but also insensitive to wind. The short lift you have to take on the way down to the valley, at Sommerbergalm, is now a fast six-person chair.

MOUNTAIN FACTS

Altitude	1500m-3250m
Lifts	20
Pistes	86km
Blue	35%
Red	55%
Black	10%
Artificial snow	none

TOURIST OFFICE

Postcode A-6293
Tel +43 (5287) 8506
Fax 8508

Hintertux has one of the best glaciers in the world. It's popular with national ski teams for summer training. In winter, it provides guaranteed good snow even when the resorts of the nearby Zillertal are suffering badly.

THE RESORT

Tiny Hintertux is bleakly set at the dead-end of the Tux valley. Ringed by steep mountains except to the north, the village is often in shade. It is little more than a small collection of hotels and guest-houses; there is another, smaller group of hotels near the lifts, which lie a 15-minute walk away from the village, across a car park which fills with day-visitors' cars and coaches, especially when snow is poor in lower resorts. The nearest bank, doctor and chemist are in Lanersbach, 5km down the valley (see Mayrhofen chapter).

THE MOUNTAINS

Hintertux's **slopes** are fairly extensive and, for a glacier, surprisingly challenging. The main lifts rise in four stages up the east side of the north-facing glacier. A gondola and chair go to Sommerbergalm, where a fast quad chair serves the slopes below Tuxer Joch; from the top of this sector, an excellent secluded off-piste run goes down to the village. Two gondolas go on up to Tuxer Ferner Haus, beside the glacier, one the fast new one. Then it's fiercely cold chairs only to 3050m and finally to Gefrorene Wand ('frozen wall') at 3250m. There are links across to another 1000m-vertical chain of lifts below Grosser Kaserer on the west, and behind Gefrorene Wand is the area's one sunny piste. Descent to the valley involves a short ascent to Sommerbergalm on the way, now achieved by a fast six-seater chair-lift.

There are two year-round **snowboard** half-pipes on the glacier, and a fun-park at Hinteranger.

The glacier is of course snowsure, and the other slopes are high and face north, making for reliable **snow-cover**.

There is more to amuse **experts** here than on any other glacier, with justifiably black runs on the west, and steep slopes beneath glacier level.

The area particularly suits good or aggressive **intermediates**. The long runs down from Gefrorene Wand and Kaserer are tests. Moderate intermdiates love the glacier, and there is a pleasant tree-lined run to the valley from Sommerbergalm.

This is not a resort for **beginners**. But there are nursery slopes down the valley at Madseit and Juns.

Cross-country trails are located between Madseit and Lanersbach.

There are few **queues** until Hintertux is invaded by visitors from lower, less snowsure resorts, when there can be long queues at the bottom station. Queues on the mountain have been partly relieved by the two new lifts.

Queues for the inadequate glacier-area **mountain restaurants** can be even worse. The one at Tuxer Joch is less crowded, but hardly for gourmets. Gletscherhütte, at the top, has great views but is very expensive.

The **ski school** has a good reputation and English is widely spoken. There's a **children's** section and Lanersbach has a nursery.

STAYING THERE

Most **hotels** are large and expensive and have spa facilities, but there are also more modest pensions. Close to lifts are the 4-star Neuhintertux and 3-star Vierjahreszeiten, neither cheap. Pensions Jörglerhof, Kössler and Willeiter are in the heart of the village.

There are plenty of **apartments**. The 3-star Nennerhof is the highest quality and best-placed, in the centre.

Restaurants are hotel-based, so pricey. The Berghof and Alpenhof have good reputations. The Vierjahreszeiten is pleasant and informal.

There is very little **nightlife**. The Rindererhof has a lively tea dance.

The spa facilities are excellent, but some walks are relatively uninspiring. In general, for **off-slope** activities you're much better off in Mayrhofen.

Being based in **Lanersbach** has its pluses, especially for drivers, who can get to the glacier in 10 minutes, or head down the Ziller valley. Lanersbach has more amenities – see Mayrhofen chapter.

Ischgl

1400m

Wide French-style slopes above a genuine Tirolean village

WHAT IT COSTS

(((((5))

HOW IT RATES

The slopes

Snow	****
Extent	***
Experts	***
Intermediates	****
Beginners	**
Convenience	***
Queues	***
Restaurants	**

The rest

Scenery	***
Resort charm	****
Off-slope	***

The slopes rise steeply from the narrow Paznaun valley that Ischgl is set in ↓

● Old Tirolean village which has grown quite large but retained much of its atmosphere and charm

● High slopes by Austrian standards, with reliable snow record

● Lots of good intermediate runs, extending over the Swiss border to duty-free Samnaun

● Lively après-ski

● Despite the abundance of high-speed chairs, still quite a number of long T-bars

● Not ideal for beginners, for various reasons

● Rather expensive, particularly initial package price (and few tour operators to choose between)

Ischgl deserves to be better known and more popular with the British. It has most of the ingredients that make Austrian resorts popular – a traditional village, lively nightlife, and a choice of smartly rustic hotels or modest B&Bs. And to this familiar recipe Ischgl adds important extras: by Austrian standards its slopes are extensive (linked to Samnaun in Switzerland), well served by a fair number of high-speed chair-lifts and high, with good, reliable snow.

So what's the problem? It appears to be limited availability of package holiday rooms, rather than any drawback to the resort itself. It's also one of the most expensive Austrian resorts. But for a group of mixed-ability intermediates, it's worth putting on your short-list.

boarding *Ischgl was one of the first Austrian resorts to embrace boarding, starting with hosting the 1991 European Championships. Between Idalp, the main station above the town, and Idjoch, a chair-ride further up, is the well-established half-pipe and board park. The lifts are generally boarder-friendly; where there is a drag, there's often a chair option. The area is well-suited to beginners and intermediates; experts will love Ischgl after fresh snow, but nearby St Anton is even better. The town is lively at night, mainly thanks to the large numbers of hard-drinking Scandinavians and Germans.*

The resort

The village is tucked away in the long, narrow Paznaun valley south-west of Landeck. The lower, steep, wooded, north-facing slopes and the village get almost no sun in early season.

The main street is virtually traffic-free, making it a pleasant place for an early evening stroll. The architecture is a mixture of old original buildings, traditional Tirolean-style hotels and shops, and modern recent additions. Like the valley, the village is long and narrow, but you can walk from one end to the other in 10 minutes or so. It's far from flat, though – and the ups and downs can be quite treacherous when there's snow or ice on the ground.

There's a good selection of bars, an excellent sports centre and a fair number of shops to stroll round.

Many high-speed chairs have been installed in recent years and the slopes are now well served. In 1996/97 the world's first double-decker cable-car was opened from Samnaun, cutting queues there. And a new floodlit toboggan run opened from Idalp to Ischgl.

The resort has its first 5-star hotel, the Trofana Royal, near the Silvrettabahn.

MOUNTAIN FACTS

Altitude 1400m-2870m
Lifts   42
Pistes   200km
Blue   25%
Red   60%
Black   15%
Artificial snow 48km
Recco detectors used

The mountains

Ischgl is a fair-sized, relatively high, snowsure area ideal for intermediates. Most pistes are red, with very few black or easy blue runs. Being able to pop over to duty-free Samnaun in Switzerland adds spice to the area. The Silvretta lift pass covers this area plus Galtür, and smaller Kappl and See – all linked by an infrequent bus service. Visiting St Anton is easy with a car.

THE SLOPES
Cross-border cruising
The main slopes start at the top of three gondolas. From both ends of the village you can get up to the sunny **Idalp** plateau at 2310m, where the schools and guides meet. At the east end of town the third gondola goes about 300m higher to Pardatschgrat, from where it's an easy run down to Idalp – with the alternative of testing red and black runs towards Ischgl. Lifts radiate from Idalp, leading to a wide variety of mainly north-west- and west-facing intermediate runs.

A short piste brings you to the lifts serving the **Höllenkar** bowl, leading up to the area's south-western extremity at Palinkopf. There are further lifts beyond Höllenkar, on the slopes of the Fimbatal.

The mountain ridge above Idalp forms the border with Switzerland. On the Swiss side the hub of activity is

Alp Trida at 2265m, surrounded by south- and east-facing runs. From here an enjoyable, scenic red run goes down to the hamlet of Compatsch, from where there is an infrequent bus to Ravaisch, for the cable-car back, and Samnaun.

From the Palinkopf area there is a very beautiful run to Samnaun itself, down an unspoilt valley. It is not difficult, but doesn't always have ideal snow conditions and is prone to closure by avalanche risk.

SNOW RELIABILITY
Very good
All the slopes, except the runs back to the resort, are above 2000m and much of those on the Ischgl side are north-west- or north-facing. So snow conditions are often good here even when they're poor elsewhere (which can lead to crowds when bus-loads of visitors arrive from lower resorts). The run from Idalp back down to Ischgl has

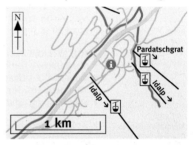

LIFT PASSES

VIP Skipass
Covers all lifts in Ischgl, Samnaun and Mathon and local buses.

Main pass
1-day pass 385
6-day pass 1,930
(low season 1,755 – 9% off)

Senior citizens
Over 60: 6-day pass 1,450 (25% off)

Children
Under 15: 6-day pass 1,190 (38% off)
Under 6: free pass

Short-term passes
Single and multi-ascent passes for main cable-cars; half-day pass from 11.30 (350), trial ticket from 2pm (210).

Alternative periods
5 skiing days in 7, 10 days in 14 and 10 days in the season.

Notes VIP skipass is only available to those staying in Ischgl, Samnaun or Mathon on presentation of guest card. Discounts for physically disabled and groups.

Alternative passes
Silvretta skipass covers Ischgl, Samnaun, Galtür, Kappl and See (adult 6-day 2,470), 68 lifts and use of ski bus; See is 15km away.

artificial snowmaking facilities all the way, with most of the variants from the mid-station of the gondolas benefiting from artificial snow.

FOR EXPERTS
Some attraction

Ischgl can't compare with nearby St Anton for exciting slopes, and many of the runs marked black on the piste map barely deserve their rating. But there is plenty of challenging and beautiful off-piste to be found with the help of a guide – and because there are fewer experts around, it doesn't get tracked out as much as it would in a more 'macho' resort. The wooded lower slopes of the Fimbatal, near the Paznauner Taya restaurant, are delightful in a snowstorm – and since the glades are used as pasture in the summer, you needn't worry about damaging infant trees.

The best steep piste is the Fimba Nord run from Pardatschgrat towards Ischgl. If snow conditions are poor near the bottom, you can do the top half of this repeatedly by catching the gondola at the mid-station.

FOR INTERMEDIATES
Something for everyone

Most of the slopes are ideal for intermediates. No matter what your standard, you should be able to find runs to suit you.

At the tough end of the spectrum our favourite runs are those from Palinkopf down to Gampenalp and on along the valley to the secluded restaurant at Bodenalp. You can now do the top of these runs repeatedly, using the chair-lift up from Gampenalp to Palinkopf. Sadly this fairly recent innovation also means the runs are no longer away from civilisation.

There are also interesting and challenging runs (some marked black) down the Hollspitz chair, and from both the top and bottom of the drag-lift from Idjoch up to Greitspitz.

For easier motorway cruising, there is lots of choice, including the Swiss side, where the runs from the border down to Alp Trida should prove ideal. So should the runs that take you back to Idalp on the return journey. But there are frequent moans from intermediates about the red runs down to Ischgl itself; neither is easy, and conditions can be tricky despite the artificial snow.

FOR BEGINNERS
Not ideal

Beginners go up the mountain to Idalp, where there are good sunny nursery slopes and a short beginners' drag-lift – and good snow as some compensation for the inconvenience. The blue runs on the east side of the bowl offer pleasant progression. But away from this area there are few runs ideal for the near-beginner. You'd do better to learn elsewhere and come to Ischgl after getting two or three years' experience. If you want to stay in the Paznaun valley area, Galtür would be a better choice.

FOR CROSS-COUNTRY
Plenty in the valley

There is 28km of cross-country track in the Paznaun valley between Ischgl, Galtür and Wirl. This tends to be pretty sunless, especially in early season, and is away from the main slopes, which makes meeting downhillers for lunch rather inconvenient. We've also seen people doing cross-country high up in the Fimbatal, towards Gampenalp, though this isn't an official trail. Galtür is a better cross-country skier's choice, with 60km of loops.

QUEUES
Still some bottlenecks

There can be lengthy waits at key lifts at peak times. The main Silvrettabahn gondola can be a problem during the morning peak, especially when people are being bussed in from other resorts. We've managed to avoid this on our visits by taking one of the two gondolas at the other end of the village, but we're told this isn't always a foolproof method.

The notorious wait out of Samnaun has been addressed by the astonishing double-decker cable-car (by some way a world record). But the planned new lift from its arrival point to Greitspitz has not yet materialised, meaning the lifts up from Alp Trida are still crowded early afternoon.

MOUNTAIN RESTAURANTS
Mostly large and crowded

In general, Ischgl isn't the place to go for either culinary delights or charming, small mountain restaurants. The clear exception, at least on the latter score, is the Paznauner Taya, above Bodenalp – an exceptionally rustic chalet imported from eastern Austria, and understandably very popular. There is

SCHOOLS/GUIDES

96/97 prices in schillings

Ischgl-Silvretta
Manager Edi Zangerl
Classes 6 days
4hr: 10.30-12.30 and
1.30-3.30
6 full days: 1,500
Children's classes
Ages: from 5
6 full days including
lunch: 1,980
Private lessons
Half- (2hr) or full-day
(4hr)
1,100 for half-day;
each additional
person 150

CHILDCARE

The childcare facilities are all up the mountain at Idalp. There's a ski kindergarten for children aged 3 to 5; from age 5 they go into a slightly more demanding regime in an 'adventure garden'; lunch is included in both arrangements, which are open 6 days a week. Toilet-trained children can be left at a non-ski nursery; lunch is available.

GETTING THERE

Air Innsbruck, transfer 2hr. Zurich, transfer 5hr.

Rail Landeck (30km); frequent buses from station.

table service upstairs and often a band playing on the large terrace. Down in Fimbatal (most easily reached via the long runs from Palinkopf) is the quieter rustic restaurant (with table service) at Bodenalp. It's also an enjoyable walk from the gondola mid-station.

The main restaurant at Idalp has a big self-service cafeteria, and a good table-service alternative (with an outdoor terrace with splendid views). There's also a smaller, crowded self-service nearby. The restaurant at Pardatschgrat tends to be quieter.

The restaurants on the Swiss side at Alp Trida are pleasant, and La Marmotte has pricey table service as well as self service. There is a huge sunny terrace with an outdoor bar and barbecue. They take schillings, but don't forget the prices are marked in Swiss francs – and aren't cheap.

SCHOOLS AND GUIDES
Language problems
The school meets up at Idalp and starts very late (10.30 to 12.30 and 1.30 to 3.30). In the past we've heard from both supporters and critics of the school, but have no recent reports. There are few British here, and the standard of English of the instructors is likely to be variable.

As well as normal lessons the school organises off-piste tours – this area is one of the best in the Alps for touring.

FACILITIES FOR CHILDREN
High-altitude options
Taking small children up the mountain with you rather than leaving them behind at village level is an unusual arrangement, but we have no first-hand reports of the service they actually provide. The ski kindergarten opened a few seasons ago.

Staying there

On or near the main street is the best place to stay. Both the main lift stations are an easy walk from there and the nightlife is on your doorstep. Beware of accommodation set up the steep hillside (some roads are so steep that tour operators' coaches may not make it to the door) or across the bypass road at the far side of the valley floor from the main village – though this does have the advantage of getting more sun.

HOW TO GO
Expensive packages
As is the norm in Austria, you pay for altitude. Much of the accommodation is expensive, particularly the mostly upmarket places sold through tour operators. There is, however, a big choice of cheaper little pensions.

Travelling most of the way by train is easy – the nearby town of Landeck has a main-line station.
Hotels Ischgl has a splendid selection of hotel and B&B accommodation, ranging from the luxurious and expensive to the plain but comfortable and good-value.
((((⑤ **Madlein** Convenient and quiet. Near the two quieter gondolas. Modern family-run chalet in traditional style. Reportedly comfortable rooms. Facilities include swimming pool, sauna, steam room and solarium. Nightclub and disco.
(((((⑤ **Solaria** Near the Madlein and just as luxurious, but with a 'friendly family atmosphere'. Splendid carved wooden ceiling to restaurant, and wood-panelled wine bar. Swimming pool, sauna, steam room, solarium, fitness room and squash courts.
((((④ **Goldener Adler** Traditional 250-year-old hotel right in the middle of the village. Wood-panelled and painted restaurant. Sauna, steam room, jacuzzi and solarium.
((((④ **Sonne** One of Ischgl's oldest hotels. Well modernised, but with some very small rooms. In the centre of the village. Lively stube, with traditional squeeze-box music. Sauna, steam room, jacuzzi, solarium.
(((③ **Astoria** Comfortable B&B hotel that faces the main Silvrettabahn gondola.
(((③ **Christine** Probably the best B&B in town. Right opposite the end of the main run down from Idalp. One of the liveliest cafés at the end of the day.
(((③ **Erna** Small, central B&B. Firmly recommended by a reporter who has holidayed in Ischgl 20 times.
((② **Alpenrose** Popular, good-value pension close to Pardatschgratbahn.
Self-catering Some attractive apartments are available – but you'll have to book them independently.

EATING OUT
Plenty of choice
Our favourite places for dinner are the traditional Austrian restaurants and stubes, of which there's a wide choice. The Goldener Adler probably serves the best food around and has a splendid traditional dining room. The Wippas

stube in the Sonne is lively and serves good food. For pizza there's the very popular and 'excellent' Nona and the Trofana-Alm, which is as much a bar as a restaurant, and for fondue the Kitzloch with its galleried tables overlooking the dance floor. La Bamba is a restaurant-bar serving Mexican specialities. The Grillalm, Salner and Tirol are also popular eateries.

APRES-SKI
Very lively
Ischgl is one of the liveliest resorts in the Alps, both immediately after leaving the slopes and after dinner.

At tea-time the Café Christine gets packed and does great coffee and cakes, as well as alcohol. If you get up to dance to the disco music, make sure someone is saving your seat for you, unless you're happy to join the stand-up crush for the rest of the time.

The Kitzloch at the bottom of the run down from Pardatschgrat is just as lively and a bit more rowdy – dancing on tables and communal congas are common. Niki's Stadl across the road is worth a visit too, with comedy spots as well as music. In good weather the ice bar of the Elisabeth hotel by the Pardatschgratbahn is popular. The Post hotel also has a busy outdoor bar beneath a giant umbrella. The Wippas stube at the hotel Sonne also gets crowded and has live music but no dancing. Other places for tea dancing include the Wunderbar of the hotel Madlein and the Trofana-Alm.

Most places are dominated by Scandinavians and Germans who are mainly interested in the drink and music. There are, however, few stylish discos in which to strut your stuff. The main exception is the Wunderbar, which becomes a sophisticated club in the evenings with international floor shows and disco nights.

OFF THE SLOPES
Fair by high-village standards
Although the resort is best suited to those keen to hit the slopes, there's no shortage of off-slope activities. There are plenty of walks (24km of marked paths) and a splendid sports centre with an interesting pool and sauna, steam room and solarium. There's another sports centre in Galtür with swimming, tennis and squash.

It's easy to get around the valley and to Landeck by bus. But meeting friends on the slopes for lunch

presents problems: the restaurants at the top stations of the gondolas are crowded and characterless.

STAYING DOWN THE VALLEY
Too far without a car
Ischgl is fairly isolated. We don't recommend staying down in the main valley unless you have a car and want a touring holiday. Landeck is the nearest big town. It has good shopping and is well positioned for trips to the surrounding resorts, including Serfaus, Nauders, Sölden and St Anton.

Galtür 1585m
You could consider staying up the valley instead, in Galtür. It is a charming, peaceful, traditional village clustered around a pretty little church, amid impressive mountain scenery. Quieter, sunnier and considerably cheaper than Ischgl, it is a good base for a quiet family holiday. There are good 3-star and 4-star hotels – the Ballunspitz has been recommended by visitors. The nightlife is not too animated, but there are a few jolly bars and good food in the hotels.

Galtür's own slopes are not particularly challenging, but its black runs are ideal for intermediates, and there are fine nursery slopes, plus plenty of 'graduation' pistes for improvers. The school also has a high reputation. If you intend to be in Ischgl most of the time, bear in mind that the bus service isn't frequent. The last bus home is disappointingly early in the evening and tends to be a real crush.

Off-slopes facilities are limited, but there is a superb sports centre with pool, tennis and squash and a natural ice rink.

Samnaun 1840m
The main attraction of staying in Samnaun is to use the slopes of Ischgl-Samnaun without the worst of the queues. The village itself is nothing special and consists of not much more than a handful of shops and hotels. It is very quiet. Its duty-free status makes it a useful stopover for those who want to restock on booze and tobacco. If you're touring around in a car, it's also a cheap place to fill up.

Kitzbühel 760m

Wonderful town and extensive slopes, but unreliable snow

WHAT IT COSTS

《《③

HOW IT RATES

The slopes
Snow	**
Extent	****
Experts	***
Intermediates	****
Beginners	**
Convenience	**
Queues	**
Restaurants	****

The rest
Scenery	***
Resort charm	****
Off-slope	*****

What's new

For the 1996/97 season the outdated Hahnenkamm cable-car was replaced by a six-person gondola, ending one of the worst lift queues in the Alps. Two drags were replaced by chairs.

For the 1997/98 season the new gondola will open on Friday and Saturday nights until 11pm to allow dining at the table-service restaurant at the top. An extra 20km of piste will be covered by snow cannon. And a new Kitzbhüheler Alpenskipass will be available covering 720km of pistes and 262 lifts in resorts such as the Ski-Welt (Söll, Ellmau etc), Alpbach, Niederau, St Johann and Fieberbrunn.

The end of the Hahnenkamm is nigh
→

- Vibrant nightlife
- Plenty of off-slope amenities, both for the sporty and the not-so-sporty
- Large, attractive, varied slopes offering a sensation of travel both on and off-piste
- Beautiful medieval town centre (but see minus points)
- A surprisingly large amount of cheap and cheerful accommodation
- Jolly mountain restaurants

- Unreliable snow (though increasing amount of snowmaking)
- Surprisingly little expert terrain
- Disjointed slopes, with quite a lot of bussing to get around them
- Town's charm spoilt by heavy traffic
- Disappointing nursery area
- Crowded pistes

Kitzbühel is an impressive name to drop in the pub. Every *Ski Sunday* viewer knows that the Hahnenkamm race is the most challenging on the World Cup circuit, helping the resort to cultivate a reputation as a rather special resort. But the race course is irrelevant to holiday-makers, and completely untypical of Kitzbühel's slopes. And there is nothing very special about coping with ice and slush or bare slopes. We have visited Kitz countless times, and rarely found decent snow on the lower slopes. It does get good snow at times, and has recently made serious investments in lifts (not least the new, faster Hahnenkamm gondola) and snowmaking. But Kitzbühel's low altitude and the spread-out nature of the slopes means that its problems won't go away.

The resort is very far from exclusive. It has its expensive, elegant hotels, but it also has a huge amount of hotel and pension accommodation that is quite inexpensive – and not surprisingly attracts quite a few low-budget visitors, many of whom are young and intent on a good time.

We have received fewer reports on Kitzbühel lately, but enthusiasts enjoy its unique combination of historic town and extensive slopes.

boarding *Kitzbühel has been slow off the mark with boarding, keeping to its image of World Cup Downhill venue/skier party town. Things are slowly changing, and now there is a fun-park, including half-pipe, on the Kitzbüheler Horn, an area with few drag-lifts. Half of all lifts in the area are drags, but all main lifts are gondolas and chair-lifts – the area suits beginners and intermediates well. The town is lively at night, with plenty of bars and clubs; the Londoner Pub is the main place with boarder appeal.*

MOUNTAIN FACTS

Altitude 800m-2000m
Lifts   60
Pistes   158km
Blue   50%
Red   42%
Black   8%
Artificial snow 30km
Recco detectors used

LIFT PASSES

97/98 prices in
schillings
Kitzbühel
Covers all lifts in
Kitzbühel, Kirchberg,
Jochberg, Pass Thurn,
Bichlalm and Aschau,
linking buses, and
swimming pool.
Beginners Points
cards valid on 15
mainly drag-lifts
(adult 12 point card
100).
Main pass
1-day pass 410
6-day pass 1,890
(low season 1,700 –
10% off)
Senior citizens
Over 60: 6-day pass
1,510 (20% off)
Children
Under 15: 6-day pass
945 (50% off)
Under 4: free pass
Short-term passes
Single ascent tickets
for the major lifts;
hourly refunds on day
tickets; day tickets
can be bought in half-
hourly steps from
11am.
Notes 5% reduction
for groups of over 15
people. The season
pass is valid in
Gstaad and
Davos/Klosters.
Alternative passes
Kitzbüheler Alpen-
Skipass covers 5
large ski areas –
Schneewinkl (St
Johann), Ski Region
Kitzbühel, Skiwelt
Wilder Kaiser,
Bergbahnen
Wildschönau and
Alpbachtal (adult 6-
day, 1,990).

The resort

Set at a junction of broad, pretty
valleys, Kitzbühel is a large, animated
town, with local slopes on each side.
The beautiful walled medieval centre –
complete with quaint church, cobbled
streets and attractively painted
buildings – is traffic-free during the
day. But the much-publicised old town
is only a small part of Kitz; the resort
spreads widely, and busy roads girdle
the old town reducing the charm factor
markedly. Visitors used to peaceful
little Austrian villages are likely to be
disappointed by its urban nature. For
those who like it, the sophisticated
towny ambience is what 'makes' Kitz.

The mountains

Snow and lift queues permitting, the
mountain suits intermediates well.
Although experts can find things to do,
there are many better places for them.
Kitz's total area is large, and includes
access to sizeable Kirchberg. Lots of
resorts in the Tirol can be reached by
car or train – and if you buy the wide-
ranging Kitzbüheler Alpenskipass you
are covered to visit many of them.

THE SLOPES
Big but bitty
Kitzbühel has four piste areas, two of
them just connected. The **Hahnenkamm**
is by far the largest, and accessible
from the town. It is reached via a
gondola or two chair-lifts, from the top
of which a choice of steep and gentle
runs lead down into Ehrenbachgraben;
from there several chair-lifts fan out.
One takes you to the gentle peak of
Steinbergkogel, the high point of the
sector at 1975m. Beyond is the slightly
lower peak of Pengelstein. On the far
side of Pengelstein several long runs
lead down to the west of the resort;
shuttle buses link their end-points at
Aschau and Skirast with Obwiesen,
Kirchberg and Kitz. From Obwiesen, a
slow series of lifts take you to
Ehrenbachhöhe, the focal point of the
Hahnenkamm sector. You can also get
to the Hahnenkamm via a gondola at
Klausen, on the road to Kirchberg.
    Pengelstein is the start of the 'ski
safari' route to Kitzbühel's most
remote but snowsure area, **Jochberg-
Pass Thurn**. The piste from Pengelstein
finishes at Trampelpfad, a short walk
from the Jochberg lifts. A parallel piste

from Steinbergkogel ends at
Hechenmoos – more than a walk from
Jochberg. Jochberg-Pass Thurn is a fine
area, despite short runs. By local
standards the slopes are high, and
have the best snow in the area – well
worth the excursion even when snow is
acceptably good lower down. Runs
lead to Pass Thurn, the terminus of the
shuttle bus, where it is well worth
ending the day to ensure a bus seat.
    The very small **Bichlalm** area is of
little interest except for getting away
from the crowds and working on your
suntan. When conditions are good, the
top station (Stuckkogel) accesses an
off-piste route to Fieberbrunn. A train
returns you to Kitz.
    The **Kitzbüheler Horn** is equally
sunny, with repercussions for snow-
cover, but many slopes are above the
1270m-high mid-station, accessed by a
modern gondola starting close to the
railway station, but some way from the
centre. The second stage leads to a
sunny bowl at around 1660m, but the
alternative cable-car takes you up to
the summit of the Horn, from where a
fine, solitary east-facing piste leads
down into the Raintal on the far side,
with a chair-lift returning to the ridge.
There are widely spread blue, red and
black runs back towards town.
    The piste map could be greatly
improved, especially by the addition of
altitudes and mountain restaurants.

SNOW RELIABILITY
Limited guarantees
Kitzbühel's slopes have one of the
lowest average heights in the Alps, and
when snow disappears from its wealth
of valley-bound pistes, the area is
drastically reduced in size. Long lift
queues result, and many mountain
restaurants become inaccessible. Such
problems are sadly common. The
introduction of snowmakers in recent
years has improved matters, notably
on the main Hahnenkamm piste early
in the season, but most of the area
remains unprotected. The best plan is
to book late when snow-cover is
known to be good. Otherwise, take a
car for snow-searching excursions
(which may take you far afield).

FOR EXPERTS
Plan to go off-piste
Steep pistes are concentrated in the
ring of runs down into the bowl of
Ehrenbachgraben, the most direct of
which are challenging mogul fields.

SCHOOLS/GUIDES

97/98 prices in schillings

Hahnenkamm
Manager Helmut Egger
Classes 6 days
4hr: 2hr am and pm
6 full days: 1,550
Children's classes
Ages: up to 14
6 full days including lunch: 2,280
Private lessons
On request.

Kitzbüheler Horn
Manager Wasti Zwicknagl
Classes 6 days
4hr: 2hr am and pm
5 full days: 1,500
Children's classes
Ages:
5 full days including lunch: 2,590
Private lessons
On request.

Red Devils
Manager Rudi Sailer
Classes 6 days
4hr: 2hr am and pm
6 full days: 1,550
Children's classes
Ages: 4 to 11
6 full days including lunch: 2,820
Private lessons
On request.

Total
Manager Ernst Hinterseer
Classes 6 days
4hr: 9.30-11.30 and 1pm-3pm
6 full days: 1,550
Children's classes
Ages: 4 to 11
6 full days: 2,230
Private lessons
On request.

Nearby is the Streif red, the basis for the famous Hahnenkamm Downhill race – see the feature panel below. When conditions allow there is plenty of off-piste potential, some of it safely close to pistes, some requiring guidance.

FOR INTERMEDIATES
Lots of alternatives
The Hahnenkamm area is prime intermediate terrain. Good intermediates will want to do the World Cup downhill run, of course, but the long 1000m-vertical red to Klausen from Ehrenbachhöhe is equally satisfying. The long runs down to the Kirchberg–Aschau road make a fine end to the day; earlier, they are rather spoilt by the lack of return lifts.

The east-facing Raintal runs on the Horn provide perhaps the best 'yo-yo' slopes in the whole area for good intermediates, though the long runs back to town from the ridge are disappointingly easy.

The runs above Jochberg are particularly good for mixed abilities, with plenty of varying routes from the top of the mountain down to Wirtsalm. Less adventurous types have some fine runs either side of Pengelstein, including the safari route, and the Hieslegg piste above Aschau. The short high runs at the top of the Pass Thurn area are ideal if you're more timid. There are also easy routes down to both Pass Thurn and Jochberg. Much of the Horn and Bichlalm is also cruising territory, including very long glides to town when snow conditions allow.

FOR BEGINNERS
Not ideal
The Hahnenkamm nursery slopes are no more than adequate, and prone to poor snow conditions. The Horn has a high, sunny nursery-like section, and precocious learners will soon be cruising home from there on the long Hagstein piste. There are also plenty of easy runs to progress to.

FOR CROSS-COUNTRY
Plentiful but low
There are nearly 40km of trails dotted about, but all are at valley level and prone to lack of snow. When the snow is good, try the quiet Reith area.

QUEUES
Still a drawback
The replacement of the impossibly slow Hahnenkamm cable-car means Kitzbühel's lift system is no longer such a dinosaur. The speedy six-person gondola has vastly reduced the morning queues. However, elsewhere on the mountain bad snow conditions can lead to queues. And once up, both the Horn and the Hahnenkamm overcrowded pistes are even more of a problem than queues. Reporters have also complained about the poor piste map and warning signs for closed or icy pistes being in German only.

MOUNTAIN RESTAURANTS
A highlight
'One of the reasons we keep going back,' says one of our Kitz regulars. There are many restaurants, none of them marked explicitly on the resort piste map. Avoid the large self-service places and stick to the smaller huts.

THE HAHNENKAMM DOWNHILL

Kitzbühel's Hahnenkamm downhill race, held in mid-January each year, is the toughest as well as one of the most famous on the World Cup circuit. On the race weekend the town is packed and there is a real carnival atmosphere, with bands, people in traditional costumes and huge (and loud) cowbells everywhere.

The victory celebrations in the Londoner Pub are legendary – and the winner traditionally serves behind the bar.

The race itself starts with a steep icy section before you hit the famous Mausfalle and Steilhang, where even Franz Klammer used to get worried. The course (now thankfully served by snow-guns) starts near the top of the new gondola and drops 860m to finish amid the noise and celebrations right on the edge of town. Ordinary mortals can try all but the steepest parts of the course after the race weekend, whenever the snow is good enough.

CHILDCARE

All four schools cater for small children, offering lunchtime supervision as well as tuition on baby slopes – generally from age 3. There is no non-ski nursery, but babysitters and nannies can be hired.

GETTING THERE

Air Salzburg, transfer 1½hr. Munich, transfer 2hr. Innsbruck, transfer 1½hr.

Rail Mainline station in resort. Postbus every 15 mins from station.

On the Horn the Hornköpfl has good food, reasonable prices, sunny terraces and few queues. Alpenhaus is good for a lively lunch, the Gipfelhaus quieter with 'good views and food'. The Bichlalm in the next-door sector is also good if you want some peace. In the Pass Thurn–Jochberg sector the Jägerwurzhütte and Trattenbachalm are recommended, Panoramaalm has great views. The Ochsalm, Seidalm and Brandseit in the Hahnenkamm sector are good – and there are many others. The new Hochkitzbühel table-service restaurant at the top of the gondola is more expensive than most but has good food and friendly service.

SCHOOLS AND GUIDES
Off-piste guiding a bargain

There are now several competing schools. The original school, Rudi Sailer's famous Red Devils, runs regular off-piste guiding groups – an excellent way to explore outside the pistes without the usual expense of hiring a guide. In contrast to the 200-strong Red Devils, the other schools emphasise their small scale and personal nature. Ernst Hinterseer's Total school is the best established of the newcomers – started in 1989/90 – and includes video analysis.

FACILITIES FOR CHILDREN
Not an ideal choice

Provided your children are able and willing to take classes, you can deposit them at any of the four schools. The Total school has the advantage of supervision until 5pm.

Staying there

The size of Kitz makes choice of location important. Staying in the old town has advantages other than aesthetic. It's reasonably equidistant from the two main lift stations either side of town, both being within walking distance. However, the Hahnenkamm is very much the larger (and more snowsure) of the two areas, and many visitors prefer to be as close as possible to its gondola. Beginners should be aware that the Hahnenkamm nursery slopes are often lacking in snow, and then novices are taken up the Horn.

The bus service around town is good, but the sheer weight of numbers and the congested one-way system often make journeys slow and uncomfortably crowded. Having a car is very useful for quick access to the Pass Thurn–Jochberg and Bichlalm areas and the Klausen gondola, which is relatively queue-free.

HOW TO GO
Mainly hotels and pensions

Kitz is essentially a hotel resort, and UK package offerings reflect this.
Chalets A few tour operators run chalet-hotels here.
Hotels There is an enormous choice, with 4-star and 3-star hotels forming the core of the resort.
(((((5) **Tennerhof** Much-extended, luxuriously converted farmhouse in big garden with renowned restaurant. Beautiful panelled rooms.

UK PACKAGES

Airtours, Austrian Holidays, Bladon Lines, Crystal, Fairhand Holidays, First Choice Ski, Independent Ski Links, Inghams, Lagrange, Made to Measure, Neilson, PGL Ski Europe, STS, Ski Choice, Ski Club of GB, Thomson

Kirchberg Crystal, Fairhand Holidays, Lagrange, Ski Choice, Top Deck

ACTIVITIES

Indoor Aquarena Centre (2 pools, sauna, solarium, mud baths, aerated baths, underwater massage – free entry with lift pass), indoor tennis hall, 2 squash courts, fitness centre, beauty centre, bridge, indoor riding school, local theatre, library, museum, chess club, casino
Outdoor Ice-rink (curling and skating), horse-riding, sleigh rides, toboggan run, ballooning, ski-bobs, flying school, wildlife park, hang-gliding, paragliding, 40km of cleared walking paths (free guided tours), copper mine tours

TOURIST OFFICE

Postcode A-6370
Tel +43 (5356) 2155
Fax 2307

(((((5) **Schloss Lebenberg** Modernised 'castle' with smart pool, and free shuttle bus to make up for secluded but inconvenient location. Free nursery for kids aged 3-plus.
((((**Goldener Grief** Historic inn, elegantly renovated; vaulted lobby-sitting area, panelled bar, casino.
((((**Weisses Rössl** Smartly traditional, with a welcoming bar–sitting room area (open fire); food can be good.
(((**Schweizerhof** Comfortable chalet in unbeatable position right by Hahnenkamm gondola.
(((**Maria Theresia** Big, comfortable modern chalet.
(((**Hahnenhof** Small converted farmhouse retaining rustic charm.
(((**Strasshofer** An old favourite – 'central, family-run, friendly, good food, quiet rooms at back'.
① **Mühlbergerhof** Small, friendly pension in good position.
Self-catering Although there are plenty of apartments in Kitz, very few are available through tour operators. Many of the best (and best-positioned) places are attached to hotels. The 4-star Garni Ludwig and 3-star Garni Christophorus, Haselsberger and Pension Hillebrand all have good apartments close to the gondola.

EATING OUT
Something for everyone
There is a wide range of restaurants to suit all pockets, down to good-value pizzerias and fast food outlets (even McDonald's). Some of the 4-star hotels have excellent restaurants; the Weisses Rössl and Maria Theresia are recommended. But the Unterberger Stuben vies with the Schwedenkapelle for the 'best in town' award. Good, cheaper, less formal places include the Huberbräustube, Sportstüberl and Zinnkrug. Goldene Gams does a good fondue and has live entertainment.

APRES-SKI
A main attraction
Nightlife is a great selling point of Kitz. There's something for all tastes from throbbing bars full of the young, free and single, to quiet little places popular with local workers, nice cafés full of calories and self-consciously smart spots for fur-coat flaunting.

Much of the action starts quite late; immediately after the slopes close the town is jolly without being much livelier than many other Tirolean resorts – try the Mockingstube, near the gondola, which often has live music. Cafés Praxmair, Kortschak and Langer are among the most atmospheric tea-time places, where many a diet has been ruined by their cakes and pastries. Later the lively English-style Big Ben bar is a focal spot, and Das Lichtl is also popular. Royal, Olympia, K&K and Take 5 are the main discos. The Londoner Pub is the loudest, most crowded place in town, with sing-along and dance-along guitar music. It's run largely by Australians and is something of an acquired taste; it's been described as 'crowded, smoky, expensive but probably my favourite après-ski bar'.

Tour reps organise plenty of the usual events, and there's also a casino for more formal entertainment.

OFF THE SLOPES
Plenty to do
The Aquarena leisure centre is very impressive, with two pools, sauna, solarium and various health activities. One of the many other diversions is a surprisingly worthwhile museum. The railway also affords plenty of scope for excursions (to Salzburg and Innsbruck, for example) and there are a number of rep-organised coach trips available.

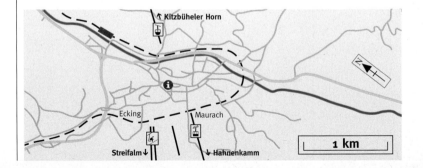

Kirchberg 850m

Anyone going to Kirchberg expecting a quiet, rustic little haven from which to access Kitzbühel's slopes will be sadly disappointed. Kirchberg is a large, spread out, crowded, lively, commercialised village very popular with young Brits, Scandinavians and Germans. It suffers similar traffic congestion and inconvenient layout to its famous neighbour, without the compensating medieval town centre. Nor are prices much lower here.

There is a choice of schools: here as in Kitz there is a Total school. Meeting points are spread about. Beginners, for example, start over on the Gaisberg mountain, on the opposite side of town from the main area. There are non-ski and ski kindergartens at Obwiesen, 2.5km out of town, near the Elisabeth–Zeinlach hotel complex. Total's Snow Adventure ski kindergarten will keep children until 5pm. The village Krabbelstube crèche accepts babies.

Like Kitz, Kirchberg is essentially a hotel-pension resort, with a wide choice of modern chalet-style places available. Choice of location is important. Beginners have slopes within walking distance of the village, but the more experienced wishing to avoid crowded bus journeys should look for a hotel a couple of kilometres out of town near the Maierl chair.

The 3-star Elisabeth and Zeinlach twin-hotel complex, even further out at Obwiesen, provides the best slope-side accommodation. These hotels are particularly good for families, with shared games and playroom amenities, and kindergartens on hand (see above). Those preferring a central village location will appreciate the 4-star multi-amenity Tiroler Adler, which has a fine leisure complex and a bus stop right outside. The 3-star Landhaus Brauns is also comfortable and has a good position by the nursery slopes.

Nightlife is very lively, to the point of rowdiness at times. The best bars in town for good, lively fun and atmosphere are Le Moustache, Vis a Vis and Charlie's Club. Habitat is a cheaper, more basic place full of Brits. The Londoner is a raucous spot catering for rich teenagers. All the usual Tirolean-style entertainment is available, plus rep-organised sleigh rides etc.

Kirchberg does not have as much entertainment off the slopes as Kitzbühel does, but still provides plenty to do – including the same range of excursion possibilities.

Lech   1450m

Charming luxury for the rich and famous

WHAT IT COSTS

$(((((6)))$

HOW IT RATES

The slopes
Snow	****
Extent	****
Experts	****
Intermediates	****
Beginners	****
Convenience	***
Queues	***
Restaurants	**

The rest
Scenery	***
Resort charm	****
Off-slope	***

➕ Picturesque Alpine village

➕ Fair sized, largely intermediate piste network

➕ Excellent off-piste terrain

➕ Easy access to the tougher slopes of St Anton and other Arlberg resorts

➕ Sunny slopes with excellent snow record and extensive snowmaking

➕ Lively après-ski scene

➕ Very chic resort, good for posing and people-watching

➕ Some captivating hotels and restaurants

➖ Very expensive, and credit cards not always accepted by hotels, shops, restaurants or lift pass office

➖ Surprising dearth of atmospheric mountain restaurants other than in Oberlech

➖ Very few tough pistes

➖ Somewhat antiquated lift system

➖ Blue runs back to the village are rather steep for nervous novices

Lech is one of the most glamorous and expensive resorts in Austria. It shares a mountain with neighbouring and equally upmarket Zürs. The slopes could fairly easily be linked with those of neighbouring St Anton. The fact that they haven't been emphasises the difference between Zürs' and Lech's rich and royal visitors and the hoi polloi of its equally famous neighbour.

Lech is for those who don't mind fur coats, do like well groomed, snowsure, easy pistes and are content to enjoy a winter holiday in pampered comfort and style in a traditional Alpine village. There are challenging slopes available (mainly off-piste) and the tougher slopes of St Anton are only a short bus- or car-ride away. But it is the part-timer, who enjoys the après and the strolling as much as the winter sports, who will get the most out of the resort. It helps to have a deep pocket.

 Lech's upper-crust image has not stood in the way of its snowboarding development, and it continues to improve its facilities. Chairs and cable-cars, with hardly any drags, and perfectly manicured pistes make the area ideal for beginner and intermediate boarders – lessons are with the local ski school. There's also a good fun-park above the town at the Schlegelkopf, with jumps, a half-pipe and a quarter-pipe, and more confident boarders should hire a guide and track some powder. The town slips back to being an up-market ski destination in the evenings – bars tend to be in 4-star hotels populated by 'the beautiful people', rather than packed bierkellers pumping out lager and loud music in equal quantities.

What's new

New snowmaking has been installed over the last few seasons, including on the lower runs to the village and up to the Kriegerhorn.

For 1997/98 the Rüfikopf cable-car will open every Thursday evening for access to a mountain casino at the top station. Drinks are served on the journeys and profits from the roulette and blackjack go to support skiing for the disabled.

Any winnings have to be spent in the restaurants, cafés and bars of Lech (you are given vouchers).

There will also be a new ski bus, free to lift pass holders.

The resort

Lech is Austria's answer to glitz-and-glamour resorts such as Courchevel and Zermatt – people come here to be seen. It lies at the end (in winter) of a small, high valley leading off the main Switzerland–Innsbruck motorway near St Anton. The village offers cosy old-world Austrian charm with modern convenience. Buildings are larger than the typical small chalets, but there is an onion-domed church and covered wooden bridge over the river.

The main street is bordered on one side by the Lech, a gurgling river, and by enticing and pricey shops on the other. In good weather it is a picture of open-air cafés, dancing in the street and a fashion show of fur coats and horse-drawn carriages, with good views of the mountains on all sides.

While some of the best hotels are right in the centre, they are not obtrusive. There are no towering monstrosities in Lech and the village remains picturesque despite its growth and popularity. Princess Diana is

MOUNTAIN FACTS

Altitude	1445m-2450m
Lifts	86
Pistes	260km
Blue	30%
Red	40%
Black	30%
Artificial snow	18km
Recco detectors used	

Lech's best-known celebrity but there are many others. Princess Caroline of Monaco goes to neighbouring Zürs.

The clientele is largely German and Austrian, with very few Brits. The fur coat count is one of the highest in the Alps. And it helps to be able to afford a helicopter transfer out if the high Flexen Pass on the road in and out is shut – which it can be for days on end after an exceptional snowfall. The top hotels are owned by a few families and have large numbers of regular guests who come back year after year.

The first settlers in Lech came from the Valais region of Switzerland in the 11th century. The village is named after the river Lech – originally the 'Licca', which means stonewater. Skiing started in the early 1900s. The Lech school was founded in 1925 and the first T-bar was built in 1939. Lech's most famous son is Patrick Ortlieb, Albertville Olympic Downhill champion in 1992. He was born and learned his skiing in Oberlech.

Oberlech is a small, traffic-free collection of 4-star hotels and chalets set on the piste above Lech and served by a cable-car which works until late at night, allowing access to Lech's much livelier nightlife and shopping. If you stay there, luggage is delivered efficiently from Lech to your hotel via the underground tunnels, leaving you free for the short, snowy walk from the cable-car.

Zug is a hamlet, 3km from Lech, which connects with the Lech–Oberlech area. The small amount of accommodation is mostly bed and breakfast with one 4-star hotel, the Rote Wand, which serves the best Kaiserschmarren (a delicious pancake and fruit dessert) in the Arlberg. From Lech, Zug makes a good night out: you can take a horse-drawn sleigh for a fondue at the Rote Wand, Klosterle or Auerhahn, followed by a visit to the Rote Wand disco.

The mountains

For such an upmarket resort the lift systems in Lech and connected Zürs are surprisingly antiquated. Perhaps that's because its clientele are there mainly for a relaxing and social winter break, not to clock up as many miles as possible between dawn and dusk. The runs also flatter leisurely cruisers, with a lot of gentle, wide blues and reds. As well as Lech and Zürs, the Arlberg lift pass covers St Anton, St Christoph and Stuben, all reachable by car or local bus.

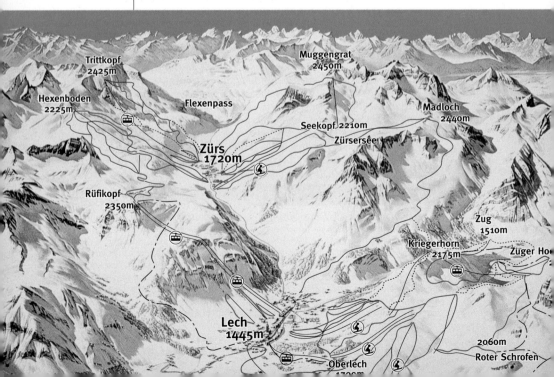

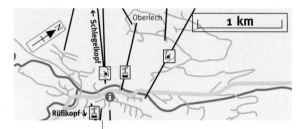

THE SLOPES
One-way traffic
The main slopes centre on **Oberlech**, 300m above Lech, and reached from the village by chair-lifts as well as the cable-car. The wide, open slopes are perfect for intermediates and the area, served by 16 lifts, also accesses off-piste for experts. **Zuger Hochlicht** is the highest point of this sector, at 2380m, and views from here, and Kriegerhorn below, are stunning. As at St Anton, the toughest runs here are now classed as 'ski routes' or 'high-touring routes' rather than pistes, with all the resulting confusion (see the St Anton chapter). The only official pistes back to the main slopes from Zuger Hochlicht are now gentle blues, and the only way down to Zug is one of the ski routes.

To get to Zürs and the linked Lech–Zürs–Lech circuit, you take the **Rüfikopf** cable-car from the centre of town, opposite Lech's main piste area. From the top there are long cruisey pistes, via a couple of lifts, down to Zürs. The circuit can be done only in a clockwise direction so in school holidays and other busy periods the linking lifts and runs can get crowded.

All the slopes at Zürs are above the tree line, with two areas on either side of the village. The more difficult runs are off the top of **Trittkopf** (the same side as the runs down from Lech).

On the other side of the valley, chairs go up to **Seekopf** and Zürsersee with intermediate runs down. There's a chair up to Muggengrat (at 2450m the highest point of the Zürs area) from below Zürsersee. This has a blue back under it and a lovely long red away from all the lifts back down to Zürs. But most people head for the Madloch–Joch chair. This accesses the long red run all the way back to Lech. You can peel off part way down and head for Zug and the chair-lift up to the Kriegerhorn above Oberlech.

SNOW RELIABILITY
One of Austria's best
Lech and Zürs both get a lot of snow, but Austrian weather station records show a big difference between them despite their proximity. Lech gets an average of almost 8m of snow between December and March, almost twice as much as St Anton and three times as much as Kitzbühel, but Zürs gets half as much again as Lech. The altitude is high by Austrian resort standards and there is excellent snowmaking on Lech's sunny lower slopes.

This combination, together with excellent grooming, means that the Lech–Zürs area normally has good coverage from December until April. And the snow is frequently better here than on St Anton's predominantly south-facing slopes.

One of the few resorts to offer Austrian Alpine charm at an impressive altitude →

LIFT PASSES

97/98 prices in schillings

Arlberg Ski pass
Covers all St Anton, St Christoph, Lech, Zürs and Stuben lifts, and linking bus between Rauz and Zurs.

Beginners Limited day passes covering a few lifts; adventurous second-week skiers need an area pass.

Main pass
1-day pass 465
6-day pass 2,130
(low season 1,920 – 10% off)

Senior citizens
Over 65 male, 60 female: 6-day pass 1,850 (13% off)

Children
Under 15: 6-day pass 1,290 (39% off)
Under 6: free pass

Short-term passes
Single ascent tickets on some lifts throughout Arlberg. Half-day tickets (adults 345) from noon, afternoon 'taster' tickets (190) from 3pm. Day tickets have by-the-hour reimbursement.

Notes 6-day pass prices are for Arlberg 'Special' pass, available to adults and children staying in the Arlberg area (normal adult 6-day pass, 2,310). Main pass also covers Klösterle (10 lifts), 7km west of Stuben. Discounts during wedel, firn and snow crystal weeks. 'Snowman' season pass for under 6s and over 80s is only 100.

FOR EXPERTS
Off-piste is main attraction

There are no black pistes on the piste map, only the two types of off-piste route referred to above. The official recommendation is to visit these with a guide, though many ignore the advice. The truth is that experts will get a lot more out of the area if they do have a guide. There is plenty of excellent off-piste that isn't marked on the map, much of it accessed by long traverses. Especially in fresh snow, it can be wonderful.

Many of the best runs start from Zuger Hochlicht or the Steinmähder chair, which finishes just below it. Some routes involve a short climb to access bowls of untracked powder. From the Kriegerhorn there are shorter off-piste runs down towards Lech and a very scenic long run down to Zug. There are also good runs from Salober Kopf at the northern end of the area. One of the problems with all these, however, is that most are south- or west-facing and can suffer from getting a lot of sun.

At the end of the season, when the snow is deep and settled, the off-piste off the shoulder of the Wöstertäli from the top of the Rüfikopf cable-car down to Lech can be superb. There are also good runs from the top of the Trittkopf cable-car in the Zürs sector, including a tricky one above the Flexen Pass down to Stuben.

Experts will also enjoy cruising some of the steeper red runs and will want to visit St Anton during the week, where there are more challenging pistes as well as more off-piste.

Heli-lifts are available to a couple of remote spots.

FOR INTERMEDIATES
Flattering variety for all

The pistes in the Oberlech area are nearly all immaculately groomed blue runs, the upper ones above the trees, the lower ones in wide swathes cut through them. It is ideal territory for leisurely cruisers not wanting surprises. And even early intermediates will be able to take on the circuit to Zürs and back, the only red run involved being the beautiful long (and not at all difficult) piste back to Lech from the top of the Madloch chair in Zürs.

More adventurous intermediates should take the Steinmähder chair to just below Zuger Hochlicht, or the cable-car all the way up, and from

there take the scenic red run all the way to Zug (the latter part on a 'ski route' rather than a piste). And if you feel ready to try some off-piste, enthusiastic reporters recommend Lech as the place to try it!

Zürs has many more interesting red runs, on both sides of the valley. We particularly like the west-facing reds down from the Trittkopf cable-car and the usually quiet run back to Zürs from the Muggengrat chair, which starts in a steep bowl.

FOR BEGINNERS
Easy slopes in all areas

The main nursery slopes are in Oberlech, but there is also a nice isolated area in the village dedicated purely to beginners. There are good, easy runs to progress to, both above and below Oberlech.

FOR CROSS-COUNTRY
Picturesque valley trail

There are two cross-country trails in Lech. The longer one is 15km; it begins in the centre of town and leads through the beautiful Zug valley, following the Lech river and ending up outside Zug. The other begins behind the church and goes to Stubenbach (another hamlet in the Lech area). In Zürs there is a 3km track starting at Zürs and going to the Flexen Pass. This starts at 1600m and climbs to 1800m.

QUEUES
Some bottlenecks at peak times

The region proudly boasts that it limits numbers on the slopes to 14,000 a day for a more enjoyable experience. Our most recent reporters seem to bear this out as they had little problem with queues, experiencing only brief congestion. One reporter did find the lifts prone to closure by wind, and expressed concern that queues could be bad at peak times.

Our experience has been that even early starters may well find queues at the Rüfikopf cable-car as the morning rush heads off to Zürs. Similarly the crucial Madloch chair at the top of the Zürs area generates queues of people going to Lech. The problem is that the circuit goes only one way, so everyone is headed in the same direction. Other bottlenecks can include the Zuger Hochlicht lift, Trittkopf cable-car and getting up from Zürs to Seekopf.

The Oberlech region rarely causes any problems.

CHILDCARE

There are ski kindergartens in Lech (21610) and Oberlech (3236) taking children from age 3, from 9am to 4pm.

SCHOOLS/GUIDES

96/97 prices in schillings

Lech and Oberlech
Classes 6 days
4hr: 10am-noon and 1pm-3pm
6 full days: 1,570
Children's classes
Ages: 3½ to 12
6 full days: 1,440
Private lessons
Full day only
2,150 for 1 day; each additional person 160

GETTING THERE

Air Zürich, transfer 3hr. Innsbruck, transfer 2hr.

Rail Langen (15km); 12 buses daily from station, buses connect with international trains.

MOUNTAIN RESTAURANTS
Not enough

A lack of cosy Alpine restaurants sends many frustrated lunchers back to Lech and Zürs to be sure of an enjoyable meal. One of the best mountain restaurants is Seekopf (reached by the Seekopf chair-lift) which has a lovely sun terrace. Also popular is the self-service Palmenalpe above Zug, but it does get very crowded. There are a few good places set prettily around the piste at Oberlech but all get crowded; our favourite is the Goldener Berg. You may be lucky enough to find a live band playing, as we did in 96/97. For a gourmet blow-out in Zürs, Chesa Verde in the hotel Edelweiss and the hotel Hirlanda's restaurant both feature in Gault-Millau but are not cheap. The hotel Rote Wand in Zug serves more casual fare. Café Schneider in Lech serves good local dishes.

SCHOOLS AND GUIDES
Excellent in parts

The ski schools of Lech, Oberlech and Zürs all have good reputations – the instructors speak good English, as they are used to foreigners. Group lessons are divided into no less than 12 ability levels, which augurs well for optimum use of time. One 96/97 visitor enjoyed 'the best tuition I have ever had'. In peak periods it might be as well to book in advance as many of the instructors are hired regularly every year by an exclusive clientele. A recent reporter found that even when booking ahead, getting what you want can be unreliable when instructors are so in demand, so make sure you get confirmation of your requirements when booking.

FACILITIES FOR CHILDREN
Oberlech's fine, but expensive

Oberlech does make an excellent choice for families who can afford it, particularly as it's so convenient for the slopes. The Sonnenburg and the Goldener Berg at least have in-house kindergartens. Reporters tell us the Oberlech school is great for children old enough for lessons, with small classes, good English spoken and lunch offered. However, one reporter found the ski kindergarten for younger children was 'old fashioned, without exciting toys and games'.

Lech is big enough for some of the cheaper accommodation to be quite a walk from the lifts. Unless you're heavily into nightlife, staying up in Oberlech is very attractive. Reporters have recommended both the Goldener Berg and the Berg for food, service, comfort, facilities (pool and sauna) and views from your own balcony.

HOW TO GO
Luxury dominates

Hotels There are several 5-star hotels, and dozens of 4-star and 3-star ones, but also countless more modest places charging a tenth of the 5-star rates.
((((⑤ **Arlberg** A favourite with certain royal(ish) persons. Elegantly rustic chalet, centrally placed. Pool.
(((④ **Krone** One of the oldest buildings in the village, in a prime spot by the river.
(((④ **Tannbergerhof** Splendidly atmospheric inn on main street, with outdoor bar and hugely popular disco (tea-time as well as later). Pool.
(((④ **Sonnenburg** (Oberlech) Luxury on-piste chalet (popular for lunch). Good children's facilities. Pool.
(② **Haus Angerhof** Beautiful ancient pension, with wood panels and quaint little windows.
(② **Haus Fernsicht** Pension with spa facilities.
(② **Haus Rudboden** Right by the nursery slopes.
Self-catering There are no apartments available through tour operators.
Chalets There are a couple of catered chalets run by British tour operators, including one in Zug (Inghams).

EATING OUT
Not necessarily expensive

There are over 50 restaurants in Lech with nearly all of them being in hotels. For reasonably priced meals try the Montana, which has an excellent wine cellar, the Krone, Ambrosius (above a shopping arcade), or the Post, which serves Austrian nouvelle-type food. The Madlochblick has a typically Austrian restaurant, very cosy with good solid food. For pasta and other Italian fare there is Pizza Charly. In Oberlech there is a good fondue at the Alte Goldener Berg, a tavern built in 1432. In Zug the Rote Wand is excellent for fondues and a good night out. Also try the Alphorn, the Klosterle and the Café Olympia.

UK PACKAGES

Bladon Lines, Chalets 'Unlimited', Inghams, Made to Measure, Ski Arrangements, Ski Choice, Ski Les Alpes, Ski Total, White Roc

Zug Bladon Lines, Inghams

Zürs Made to Measure, Ski Arrangements

ACTIVITIES

Indoor Tennis, squash, hotel swimming pools and saunas, cinema, museum, art gallery, bowling, hotel spas (massage and balneotherapy) **Outdoor** 25km of cleared walking paths, toboggan run (from Oberlech), natural ice rink (skating, curling), sleigh rides, billiards, helicopter rides

TOURIST OFFICE

Postcode A-6764
Tel +43 (5583) 21610
Fax 3155

APRES-SKI
OK but pricey

The umbrella bar of the Berg hotel at Oberlech is popular immediately after slopes close. Then the 'beautiful people' head for Krones ice bar, which has a lovely setting by the river, or to the outdoor bar of the Tannbergerhof.

Inside the Tannbergerhof, there's a tea dance disco. Dancing in the streets is quite common. The other main discos are the Arlberg Hotel's Scotch Club (owned and run by former Olympic champion, Egon Zimmermann), and those in the hotels Almhof-Schneider and Krone. The latter's Side Step specialises in 60s and 70s music. The Pfefferkörnd'l is a good place for a drink, and is particularly popular for its après-ski cocktails and gourmet snacks. You can get a steak or pizza there until late. For a change of scene after the slopes close, there's the champagne bar in Oberlech's Hotel Montana, or later the Rote Wand in Zug has a disco.

Taxi James is a shared mini-bus taxi which charges a flat fare for any journey in Lech/Zürs – you phone and it picks you up within half an hour.

OFF THE SLOPES
Poseurs' paradise

Many visitors to Lech don't indulge in sports. If you're armed with limitless funds the shopping possibilities are enticing, and the main street is often filled with fur-clad browsers. Strolz's plush emporium in the centre of town is a good place to up the rate at which you're spending schillings.

It's easy for pedestrians to get to Oberlech or Zug to meet friends for lunch on the slopes – or for them to glide back to the village. The village outdoor bars make ideal posing positions – but make sure you are immaculately groomed or you'll feel out of place. An excursion to St Anton, to see how the other half live, is possible, though Lech clientele may feel more at home getting off the bus at chic St Christoph. For the more active there are 25km of walking paths and a variety of sporting activities – the walk along the river to Zug is especially beautiful.

Zürs 1720m

Ten minutes' drive towards St Anton from Lech, Zürs is almost on the Flexen Pass, with good snow virtually guaranteed. Zürs was a tiny hamlet used for farming during the summer only until (in the late 1890s) the Flexen Pass road was built and Zürs began to develop, entering the winter sports scene in the early 20th century.

The village is even more exclusive than Lech, with no hotels of less than 3-star standing, and a dozen 4-star and 5-star hotels around which life revolves. But the opulence is less overt here. There are few shops. Nightlife is quiet, though there are discos in the Edelweiss, Mara and Zürserhof hotels. There's also a piano bar in the Alpenhof and a good après-ski watering hole is Gerhard's Bar. Later on, Matthie's Stub'l and Kaminestub'l are worth trying. Serious dining means the Zürserhof and the Lorünser – make sure your wallet will stand a visit before you go. For something cheaper try spaghetti in the basement of the hotel Edelweiss. Princess Caroline (who stays at the Lorünser) once managed to get spaghetti here at 5am.

Zürs has its own school, but many of the instructors are booked for the entire season by regular clients, and more than 80 per cent of them are hired privately. The resort also has its own kindergarten.

Mayrhofen 630m

For keen skiers, the last resort – but a British favourite

WHAT IT COSTS

$$(((3)$$

HOW IT RATES

The slopes

Snow	★★★
Extent	★★
Experts	★
Intermediates	★★★
Beginners	★★
Convenience	★
Queues	★
Restaurants	★★★

The rest

Scenery	★★★
Resort charm	★★★
Off-slope	★★★★

➕ Excellent children's amenities

➕ Lively après-ski – but it's easily avoided if you prefer peace

➕ Wide range of off-slope facilities

➕ Snowsure by Tirol standard, with the added safety net of the Hintertux glacier nearby

➕ Various nearby areas on the same lift pass, and reached by free bus

➕ The new high-capacity Penken gondola is a significant improvement over the old queue-ridden cable-car

➖ Slopes in two completely separate sectors

➖ No slopes at village level, even for beginners

➖ Inconveniently situated lifts, some out of town, can mean long walks and bus-rides at the ends of the day

➖ The Ahorn sector is still served by a slow cable-car

➖ Sprawling, commercialised village

➖ Little to challenge experts

➖ Small, crowded local slopes

Mayrhofen is a British favourite which wears two distinctly different hats. Many young or youngish visitors like it for its lively nightlife. But it's also an excellent family resort: its amenities include highly regarded kindergartens and a fun pool with special children's area. Fortunately, the liveliest of the nightlife is confined to a few very popular places, easily avoided by families in such a large resort.

But there are other considerations. Even though the long-promised new gondola up to the Penken finally materialised for the 1995/96 season, and speeds access to this sector from town, the Ahorn cable-car has not been modernised, and both lifts are still out of the centre. On the other hand, the Zillertal pass covers all the resorts in the valley, including the excellent glacier at Hintertux. If you plan to spend a lot of time at the glacier, it may be worth trying a nearer base – such as Lanersbach, described at the end of this chapter.

What's new

A new gondola up to the Penken opened in 1995, making access to the main sector of the slopes much less painful.

For 1997/98 a new quad chair is planned in the Horberg-Gerent area of Penken.

boarding *Mayrhofen is not ideal for learning to snowboard, just as it isn't for learning to ski, because of the drawbacks of the nursery slopes. For intermediates, the slopes are good and the gondolas and chair-lifts mean that few drags have to be negotiated. For the experienced boarder there is a half-pipe and a fun-park on the Gerent slopes at the top of the Penken area. The Hintertux glacier, further up the valley, provides a snow guarantee that's hard to beat and is a boarder friendly place (except for the drag-lifts), with two permanent half-pipes – it is especially good on powder days, after the sun has come out. And Mayrhofen's budget prices and lively nightlife make it popular.*

MOUNTAIN FACTS

Altitude	630m-2250m
Lifts	31
Pistes	99km
Blue	26%
Red	53%
Black	21%
Artificial snow	4½km

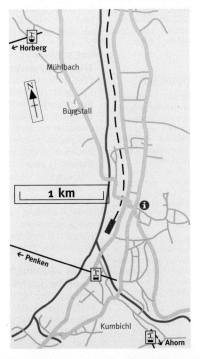

LIFT PASSES

Mayrhofen/Zillertal
Coverage depends on period – see notes.
Main pass
1-day pass 350
6-day pass 1,965
Children
Under 14: 6-day pass 1,180 (40% off)
Under 6: free pass
Short-term passes
Passes available from 11am, noon and 2pm.
Alternative periods
Zillertaler skipass available for 4 days skiing in 6, 5 days in 7, 6 days in 7 and 10 days in 14.
Notes Up to 3-day passes covers Penken, Horberg-Gerent and Ahorn areas only; 4-day and over includes all 154 Ziller valley lifts (including Hintertux glacier), 455km of piste, skibus and railway. Reduced pass price for 14- to 18-year-olds (6-day 1,580)
Alternative passes
Zillertaler skipass also available without Hintertux glacier (6 days 1,650 for adults, 990 for children).

CHILDCARE

All four ski schools run children's classes, and ski kindergartens where lunch is provided – Spiess at Ahorn, Gager, Total and Everest at Penken. All take children aged 4 to 12 or 14, and appear to operate only until the end of ski teaching at 3.30.

Wuppy's Kinderland non-skiing nursery at the fun pool complex takes children aged 3 months to 7 years, 8am to 6pm.

The resort

Mayrhofen is a large resort sitting in the flat-bottomed Zillertal – big enough to be called a town, but not towny in character. It's essentially a traditional little village of a few bars, restaurants, hotels and sports shops – multiplied twenty-fold. As the village has grown, architecture has been kept traditional, but the place is so sprawling and commercialised it isn't really charming.

The main street is surrounded by almost every kind of tourist amenity – except lifts. The new Penken lift station, like the old one, is on the edge of the village centre, while the Ahorn cable-car is out in the suburbs, about 1km from the centre.

Despite its 'lively' image, Mayrhofen is not dominated by lager louts. They exist, but tend to gather in a few easily avoided bars. The central hotels are mainly slightly upmarket, and overall the resort feels pleasantly civilised.

The mountains

Of Mayrhofen's two mountains Penken is mainly suitable for intermediates, and Ahorn only for beginners. Neither has much for experts. A frequent free bus serves other resorts covered by the pass, notably Hintertux, Lanersbach and Gerlos – but we hear you need be up early to beat the queues.

THE SLOPES
Highly inconvenient
Lifts to the two main sectors are a bus-ride apart, and you often have to take them down as well as up. The only trail from mountains to village is an unpisted run from **Ahorn**, and changing mountains or lunching in the village means a serious waste of slope time. **Penken** is also accessible via the Hippach and Finkenberg gondolas, a couple of kilometres either side of the resort. You can get back to them on snow if cover is good. The Finkenberg run is only a path. The unpisted Hippach trail is the best in the area for experts, but is rarely in good condition.

SNOW RELIABILITY
Good by Austrian standards
Although the highest lift goes no higher than 2280m, the area is reasonably good for snow-cover because (apart from the unreliable valley runs) all of Mayrhofen's slopes

are above 1580m. There is also one of the best glaciers in the Alps within day-trip range, at Hintertux.

FOR EXPERTS
Not ideal
Mayrhofen itself doesn't have much for experts. But there are worthwhile challenges to be found, including off-piste areas, you can go touring, and reporters staying here and visiting the other resorts on the pass have been more than happy. The long unpisted run to Hippach is the only testing local slope, and is rarely in good order.

FOR INTERMEDIATES
Problematic
Mayrhofen's slopes are small enough to disappoint avid piste-bashers, yet just difficult enough to be unappetising for nervous intermediates. If you fall between the two, its short, mainly open runs spread across the Penken and next-door Gerent may suit you.

If you're willing to travel each of the main mountains covered by the Ziller valley pass is large and varied enough for an interesting day out.

FOR BEGINNERS
Overrated: big drawbacks
Despite its reputation for teaching, Mayrhofen is not ideal for beginners. The Ahorn nursery slopes are excellent – high, extensive and sunny – but it's a tiresome journey to reach them. The overcrowded slopes and restaurant add to the hassle. The Penken nursery area is less satisfactory.

FOR CROSS-COUNTRY
Go to Lanersbach
In theory there is a fine 20km trail along the valley to Zell am Ziller, plus small loops conveniently in, or close to, the village. But snow at 600m is not reliable. Vorderlanersbach has a much higher, more snowsure trail running to Madseit.

QUEUES
Getting there
The new Penken gondola has tripled the lift's capacity – it now carries 2,000 people per hour, and can cope with high winds. It also ends higher than the old lift, cutting out an irritating walk up to the chair-lifts. The new lift has ended one of the worst morning and evening queues in the Alps. But nothing has been done to address the lengthy queues for the Ahorn cable-car.

SCHOOLS/GUIDES

97/98 prices in schillings

Uli Spiess
Manager Uli Spiess
Classes 6 days
4hr: 10am-noon and 1pm-3pm
6 full days: 1,490
Children's classes
Ages: 4 to 14
6 full days including lunch: 2,230
Private lessons
Hourly and daily
500 for 1hr; each additional person 200

Manfred Gager
Manager Manfred Gager
Classes 6 days
4hr: 10am-noon and 1.30-3.30
6 full days: 1,450
Children's classes
Ages: 4 to 14
6 full days including lunch: 2,170
Private lessons
Hourly and daily
500 for 1hr; each additional person 200

SMT Mayrhofen Total
Manager Max Rahm
Classes 6 days
4hr: 10am-noon and 1pm-3pm
6 full days: 1,490
Children's classes
Ages: 4 to 14
6 full days including lunch: 2,210
Private lessons
Hourly and daily
500 for 1hr; each additional person 200

Mount Everest
Manager Peter Habeler
Classes 6 days
4hr: 10am-noon and 1pm-3pm
6 full days: 1,490
Children's classes
Ages: 5 to 14
6 full days including lunch: 2,270
Private lessons
Hourly
500 for 1hr; each additional person 200

Once away from the busy area near the Penken lift, slopes are surprisingly queue-free. Buses to and from the more out-of-town gondolas are often crowded, especially the Finkenberg one, which also serves Hintertux.

MOUNTAIN RESTAURANTS
Penken good, Ahorn bad
Most of Penken's many mountain restaurants are attractive, sunny and serve good-value food – Vroni's has been recommended. The Ahorn has only one restaurant – inadequate for the hordes of beginners using it.

SCHOOLS AND GUIDES
You name it, they do it – well
Mayrhofen's popularity is founded on its four ski schools, which between them provide a wide range of services, now of course including snowboard lessons. We have received many positive reports on many of them in the past (though recent reporters haven't used the schools). There's also guiding around the Zillertal, and tours with the Mount Everest school to the Hoher Riffler and Rastkogel summits.

FACILITIES FOR CHILDREN
Excellent but inconvenient
Mayrhofen has put childcare at the centre of its pitch, and all the facilities are excellent. However, we prefer to take our offspring to resorts where they don't have to be bussed around and ferried up and down the mountain.

Staying there 🔑

In such a large sprawling village, with two widely separated lifts, location is important. The original centre of the village, around the market, church and bus/railway stations, is now on the edge of things. The most convenient area is on the main street, as close as possible to the Penken gondola.

HOW TO GO
Plenty of mainstream packages
There is a wide choice of hotel holidays available from UK tour operators, but few catered chalets.
Hotels There are dozens of cheap pensions, but most Brits stay in the larger, better hotels. Most of the hotels packaged by UK tour operators are centrally located close to village amenities but a fair walk from the Penken gondola, and a bus-ride from the Ahorn lift.

(((((5) **Elisabeth** The resort's only 5-star hotel, an opulent chalet in a fair position near the post office.
(((4) **Manni's** Well-placed, smartly done out; pool.
(((4) **Kramerwirt** Lovely Tirolean hotel simply oozing character.
(((3) **Sporthotel Strass** Best placed of the 4-stars, very close to the Penken gondola. Lively bar, disco, fitness centre, solarium, pool and children's playroom, but rooms lack style.
(((3) **Waldheim** Smallish, cosy 3-star gasthof, close to the Penken lift.
(((3) **St Georg** Poorly positioned for amenities, but ideal for those wanting a multi-facility quality hotel in peaceful surroundings.
(((3) **Jägerhof** Another peaceful hotel with good facilities, mid-way between the two lifts.
(1) **Claudia**, **Monika** Cheap little twin guesthouses in a good position.
(1) **Kumbichl**, **Kumbichlhof** Adjoining pensions, next to the Ahorn cable-car.

EATING OUT
Wide choice
Most visitors are on half-board, but there is a large choice of restaurants catering for most tastes and budgets. The Hotel Rose has a particularly good, informal restaurant.

APRES-SKI
Lively but not rowdy
Nightlife is a great selling point. Mayrhofen has all the standard Tirolean-style entertainments such as folk dancing, bier kellers and tea-dances, along with bowling, sleigh rides, tobogganing and several lively bars and discos. Mo's American theme bar, Sportsbar and the Sporthotel's Arena video disco are particularly rocking places to go later on in the evening. The latter has live bands, and you may be charged to get in. Although après-ski is lively, it usually avoids becoming too rowdy; try Rundum or Papageno (in the hotel Elizabeth) if you're after more Manhattan than Mayerhofen.

OFF THE SLOPES
Good for all
The village travel agency arranges trips to Italy, and Innsbruck is easily reached by train. There are also good walks and sports amenities. Pedestrians have no trouble getting up the mountain to meet friends.

GETTING THERE

Air Salzburg, transfer
3hr. Munich, transfer
2½hr. Innsbruck,
transfer 1hr.

Rail Local line
through to resort;
regular buses from
station.

UK PACKAGES

Airtours, Crystal,
Equity Total Ski, First
Choice Ski, Inghams,
Made to Measure,
Neilson, Ski
Arrangements,
Snowcoach, Thomson,
Timescape Holidays

Finkenberg Crystal

ACTIVITIES

Indoor Bowling,
adventure pool, 2
hotel pools open to
the public, massage,
sauna, squash, fitness
centre, indoor tennis
centre at Hotel
Berghof (3 courts,
coaching available),
indoor riding-school,
pool and billiards,
stamp-swapping,
cinema

Outdoor Natural
skating-rink, curling,
horse-riding, horse
sleigh rides and
racing, 45km cleared
paths, hang-gliding,
paragliding,
tobogganing (2 runs
of 2.5km),
snowrafting, ski-bobs

TOURIST OFFICE

Postcode A-6290
Tel +43 (5285) 6760
Fax 6411633

Finkenberg 840m

Finkenberg is a welcome alternative to Mayrhofen, being a much smaller, quieter village with good access to and from the Penken. It is no more than a collection of traditional-style hotels, bars, cafés and private homes awkwardly dispersed along a steep section of the busy main road between Mayrhofen and Lanersbach. There are two distinct halves – the original village around the church, and a cluster of buildings conveniently close to the gondola station, just over five minutes' walk away.

The gondola gives queue-free access to the Penken (those based in Mayrhofen tend to use the Hippach gondola rather than this one as an alternative to the Penken) and a speedy ride home for beginners (and everyone else when the Katzenmoos path is not open).

Finkenberg has a nursery slope in the village which, given good snow, means that beginners do not need to buy the full lift pass. But it's a sunless spot, and good conditions are far from certain at this altitude.

Cross-country skiers have to get a bus up to Lanersbach.

There are two schools. Klauss-Kroll has a particularly good reputation.

Like Mayrhofen, Finkenberg prides itself on giving children a good time. But it is not for young tots: there is no non-ski crèche and the ski nursery doesn't take children under age four.

All hotels are within walking distance of the gondola, and many of the more distant ones run minibuses to the lift station. Restaurants are mostly hotel-based.

Finkenberg is quiet in the evenings. The main après-ski spots are Pub Laternall and Cafe Zum Fink'n, and there are rep-organised events such as tobogganing and bowling. Mayrhofen is a short taxi-ride away and offers a far wider choice of evening action.

Swimming, curling and ice-skating are available, and the local walks have been recommended, but those not using the slopes find themselves spending a lot of time in Mayrhofen.

Lanersbach 1300m

Lanersbach is an attractive, spacious, traditional village spoilt only a little by the busy road up to Hintertux, which passes the main lift. Happily, the area around the pretty church is hidden away off the road, yet within walking distance of the lift. The village is small and uncommercialised, but has all you need in a resort. And prices are low.

The slopes of Eggalm, accessed by a cable-car, have a high point of 2300m at Beil, and a small network of pleasantly varied, mostly wooded pistes leading back to the village and across to the Rastkogel sector, above nearby Vorderlanersbach. This sector (also accessed by its own modern gondola) goes higher (top station 2500m) but is not so pretty or interesting. The two sectors total 33km of piste. Snow conditions are usually good, at least in early season; by Austrian standards, these are high slopes, but the Vorderlanersbach sector, in particular, gets a lot of sun.

There are no pistes to challenge experts, but there is a fine off-piste route starting a short walk from the Lanersbach top station and finishing at the village. Intermediates will enjoy the wonderfully uncrowded, well groomed runs. Lanersbach's nursery slope is rather small, and finding an English-speaking instructor can be a problem.

This is the best base in the area for cross-country, with 23km of trails running up the valley to Madseit.

Lanersbach is essentially a hotel resort. The Lanersbachhof is a multi-amenity olde worlde 4-star close to the lifts but is also on the main road. The cheaper 3-star Pinzger and Alpengruss are similarly situated. The 3-star Bergkristall is central, but reasonably close to the cable-car. Restaurants are mainly hotel-based. and nightlife is quiet by Austrian standards.

Off-slope facilities are fairly good considering the size of the resort. Some hotels have pools, jacuzzis and fitness rooms open to non-residents. Outside the village is a tennis centre with squash and ten-pin bowling. Mayrhofen is a worthwhile excursion and Salzburg is just within range.

The non-ski nursery takes children from age two, the school from four. Lanersbach is generally child-friendly, though a lack of English-speaking supervision, tuition and other children to play with could be a problem.

WHAT IT COSTS

(((3)))

HOW IT RATES

The slopes

Snow	*****
Extent	**
Experts	**
Intermediates	***
Beginners	**
Convenience	*
Queues	***
Restaurants	**

The rest

Scenery	***
Resort charm	****
Off-slope	***

MOUNTAIN FACTS

Altitude	1000m-3210m
Lifts	30
Pistes	55km
Blue	60%
Red	31%
Black	9%
Artificial snow	7km

What's new

A couple of years ago the Eisgratbahn gondola up to the middle of the glacier was upgraded, and a new restaurant was built at Gamsgarten. For 1997/98, a table-service section is being added there.

The Daunferner slope on the glacier will be specially prepared for carving. A new Fun Street area for boarders will be prepared near the Eisgrat top station.

UK PACKAGES

Alpine Tours, Crystal, Inghams, Made to Measure, Ski Valkyrie

TOURIST OFFICE

Postcode A-6167
Tel +43 (5226) 2228
Fax 2529

Neustift has its own little area of slopes where unadventurous intermediates can potter happily, but it's the Stubaigletscher – 20km away and one of the best glaciers in Austria – or the world – that earns Neustift its place in this book.

THE RESORT

Neustift is a very attractive, traditional Tirolean village half-way along the Stubai valley. It is the closest large community to the Stubai glacier, but there are other resorts down the valley. Fulpmes (with its satellite village of Telfes) has more extensive local slopes. Milders has some slopes too. The Stubai lift pass covers all these resorts, the glacier and the linking shuttle bus. The service to the glacier is inadequate – half-hour intervals and insufficient capacity.

THE MOUNTAINS

Neustift's local **slopes** are a narrow chain of runs and lifts – mainly drags – from Elferhütte at 2080m down to the village. Except for one short blue run at altitude, the pistes are all red. This area is on the south-east side of the valley; there is a nursery area at village level, on the other side.

The Stubai glacier is a much more extensive area of blue and red runs (and one short black) between 3200m and 2300m. The glacier is broken up by rocky peaks, giving more sense of variety than is normal on a glacier, but the landscape is harsh. There is also a lovely route (Wilde Grub'n) down from the glacier via a deserted bowl to the valley station at 1750m. Start at the top of the glacier and you have a descent of about 1450m and 14km.

On the glacier, **snow reliability** is not a problem. Our regular reporter goes each year in May to round off the season, and most of the area is open in summer. The lower local slopes face roughly north, but are of typically modest Austrian altitude. The sunny village nursery slopes are unreliable.

The village slopes do not have much for **experts**, and the glacier does not have the challenge of Hintertux's. But there are some good long runs, including a 4km itinerary route down the east side of the glacier.

For **intermediates**, the local slopes are neither easy nor extensive – so the main appeal is to the confident intermediate who wants to practise technique rather than get around. The glacier is splendid territory.

This is not a resort for **beginners**; the village nursery slopes are attractive, but too sunny – though they do have snowmakers.

The glacier attracts **snowboarders** in increasing numbers, and it now has a fun-park. There is a half-pipe on the lower village slopes.

There are 100km of **cross-country** trails in the Stubaital, including some reached by the lifts serving Fulpmes and Milders, and some on the glacier.

In the past, there have been serious **queues** for the access lifts to the glacier – worst, of course, when snow is short elsewhere – but the upgraded gondola must have helped a lot.

The **mountain restaurants** are a mixture of primitive mountaineering huts and impersonal cafeterias. There are great views from the cute little cabin at Jochdohle (at 3150m, Austria's highest restaurant), and the Dresdner Hütte at 2300m is recommended as charming and uncrowded.

There are **ski schools** both in Neustift itself and at the glacier. Guides are available. **Children** can be looked after all day.

STAYING THERE

If you fly into Innsbruck, you can be in the resort an hour later. There are lots of 4-star and 3-star **hotels**. The 3-star Tirolerhof is excellent – comfortable and relaxed, good food. It has its own ski school and hire shop. The central 4-star Sonnhof is also recommended. For families, a visitor suggests the 4-star Gasteigerhof in Gasteig, with pool.

Most **restaurants** are hotel-based. Visitors recommend Bellefonte's pizzas, and the atmospheric Hoferwirt. **Après-ski** is focused on the Romanstuben and the Hully Gully.

Neustift has quite a lot to offer **off the slopes**: tennis, squash and bowling. All the villages have impressive toboggan runs. Innsbruck is only minutes away by bus.

Niederau

830m

A family resort with friendly slopes

WHAT IT COSTS

(2)

HOW IT RATES

The slopes

Snow	*
Extent	*
Experts	*
Intermediates	**
Beginners	****
Convenience	***
Queues	****
Restaurants	**

The rest

Scenery	***
Resort charm	***
Off-slope	**

What's new

Niederau's big step forward was the construction of a fast (but low capacity) gondola to the top of the mountain in 1995. For 1997/98 there will be snowmaking on the Tennladen slope.

MOUNTAIN FACTS

Altitude	830m-1900m
Lifts	30
Pistes	42km
Blue	35%
Red	56%
Black	9%
Artificial snow	1km

UK PACKAGES

Alpine Tours, First Choice Ski, Inghams, Neilson, PGL Ski Europe, Thomson

Auffach Alpine Tours, PGL Ski Europe

Mühltal Alpine Tours

Oberau First Choice Ski, Inghams, PGL Ski Europe, Thomson

TOURIST OFFICE

Postcode A-6311
Tel +43 (5339) 8255
Fax 2433

An attractive village, small but spread out, with a small but quite varied area of runs, that has a strong British following. Good for families and beginners, so long as there is decent snow. Sadly, this is far from guaranteed.

THE RESORT

Niederau is a popular example of what Austria does so well: the unspoilt, hassle-free, family winter resort. It's more convenient than Waidring and Fieberbrunn, cheaper and prettier than Obergurgl, and less commercialised than Westendorf. It has a lovely valley setting and chalet-style buildings, but a cluster of restaurants and shops opposite the Markbachjoch gondola is the nearest thing to a focal point. Few hotels are more than five minutes' walk from a main lift, though. Roads are quiet, except on Saturdays.

The resort suits families looking for a friendly, unsophisticated but civilised atmosphere. A faithful following of Brits return each year.

The Wildschönau lift pass includes the higher area of Auffach and the nursery slopes in and around Oberau on the col between the two.

THE MOUNTAINS

The small local **slopes** are spread over a broad, wooded mountainside which does not rise above 1600m. Access is via chair or 8-person gondola – these are just a few minutes' walk apart, in central Niederau. The Markbachjoch gondola goes up to a novices' plateau at 1500m and the area's steepest runs, back to the village. Easier runs to Niederau open up from the plateau. The chair doesn't go so high, but is followed by a steep drag to the high-point of Lanerköpfl (1600m). A choice of red runs descend back to the village. For **snowboarders**, there are half-pipes at Schatzberg and Hahnkopf.

A reliable half-hourly bus (free) goes to Auffach. Its sunny slope area goes up to 1900m, with a vertical of 1000m. The main lift is a two-stage gondola. There are few **queues** in either area.

The low altitude means that **snow reliability** is poor – and if you can't use the runs to Niederau, the piste area becomes tiny. Snowmaking is at last being introduced, but not on a big scale. Auffach has much more upper-mountain terrain.

The few black runs don't have much appeal for **experts**, though Stock and Hochberg deserve respect.

Good **intermediates** may find the ungroomed gully black runs awkward and the area too small to keep them interested for more than a day or two – though the red runs do merit their status. The long main Auffach piste is attractive.

Niederau seems suitable for **beginners**, with excellent nursery slopes at the foot and top of the mountain, but the low ones lose the sun each afternoon, and there aren't many really easy long runs to go on to.

The 35km of **cross-country** trails along the valley are good when snow is abundant, and there is a new 6km trail on top of Markbachjoch.

Mountain restaurants are scarce but good, causing lunchtime queues. Many people lunch in the village.

The **ski schools** have a good reputation but classes can be large.

The ski kindergarten and non-ski nursery take **children** from age three.

STAYING THERE

The 4-star Sonnschein, part of the 'Silent Hotel' chain, is reported to be the best hotel, with a pool open to the public. The Vicky and Schneeberger are well-placed 3-stars; the former has the lovely Drift In bar. The Staffler is a lively, central 2-star. Bergwett and Lindner are good-value B&Bs. Haus Jochum is spacious, comfortable **self-catering** close to the Tennladen drag.

Hotels Alpenland and Wastl-Hof are reputed to be good for **eating out**.

Niederau has a nice balance of **après-ski**, neither too noisy for families nor too quiet for the young and lively. Bobo's ice bar is popular at tea-time. Later, the Almbar is lively, and open till 1am, or there's the Dorfstubn disco, featuring karaoke once a week.

Off the slopes there are excellent sleigh rides, horse-riding, organised walks and the Slow Train Wildschönau – on wheels rather than rails. Try the trip to the unspoilt Kundl Gorge.

Obergurgl 1930m

High, snowsure slopes with loyal clientele

WHAT IT COSTS

((((4)

HOW IT RATES

The slopes

Snow	*****
Extent	**
Experts	**
Intermediates	***
Beginners	****
Convenience	****
Queues	*****
Restaurants	**

The rest

Scenery	***
Resort charm	****
Off-slope	**

➕ Glaciers apart, one of the Alps' most reliable resorts for snow – especially good for a late-season holiday

➕ Excellent area for beginners, timid intermediates and families

➕ Normally queue- and crowd-free

➕ Retains village charm despite modern development

➕ Jolly tea-time après-ski

➖ Small area with no tough pistes

➖ Very bleak setting, with no sheltered slopes for bad weather

➖ Few off-slope amenities except in hotels

➖ Quiet nightlife by Austrian standards

➖ For a small Austrian resort, rather expensive

A dedicated group of visitors go back to Obergurgl every year. They love its high, snowsure, easy intermediate slopes, its end-of-the-valley seclusion and civilised atmosphere, its jolly tea-time après-ski and its comfortable, expensive hotels. You need to book early to avoid disappointment.

But the Obergurgl-Hochgurgl area is certainly not to everyone's taste – ours included, we have to admit. And while Where to Ski reporters who are regulars of the resort love it, those on their first visit are more cautious with their praise.

So what's the downside? The slope area is small and almost entirely easy, and the setting is high, treeless and can be cold and bleak in early season and poor weather. It also lacks variety, making the area feel even more limited. Keen piste-bashers will have explored it all in a day or two – going off-piste with a guide or the school will be the main attraction after that. The village itself is made up primarily of hotels, with little in the way of shops or a vibrant nightlife. Those expecting something even remotely akin to other high Austrian resorts such as Ischgl or Lech will be sadly disappointed.

boarding *Obergurgl is a traditional ski destination, attracting an affluent and (dare we say it?) 'older' clientele, but the resort has made a good attempt at accommodating snowboarding. There is a fun-park in the Obergurgl area, but the 150m half-pipe is up at Hochgurgl, which seems a bit perverse. The resort has a low proportion of drag-lifts, which makes it good for beginners too, and some off-piste potential. Evenings tend to be a bit tame for boarders – fever-pitch is usually a 'Conga' around the bar.*

What's new

A new quad lift is being installed to replace the Roskar chair to Gaisberg going all the way up to Roskar mid-station.

A new cable-car linking Obergurgl and Hochgurgl is planned, but is unlikely to make an appearance for years yet.

The resort

Obergurgl is based on a traditional old village, set in a remote, bleak spot, the dead end of a long road up past Sölden. It is the highest parish in Austria and is usually under a blanket of snow from November until May. The surrounding mountains are bleak, with an array of avalanche barriers giving them a forbidding appearance. Obergurgl has no through-traffic and few day visitors, and the village centre is usually traffic-free.

Despite its small size, this is a village of hotels. At the entrance to the resort is a cluster of hotels near the main gondola, which takes you to all the local slopes. The road then passes another group of hotels around the ice rink, up the hillside to the left, before coming to the village proper. This starts with an attractive little square with church, fountain, and the original village hotel (the Edelweiss und Gurgl). Just above there's a chair lift to the local slopes.

Village atmosphere is jolly during the day and immediately after the slopes close, but can be subdued later at night; there are some nightspots, but most people stay in their hotels. The resort is popular with British families and well-heeled groups looking for a relaxing winter break.

Hochgurgl, a bus-ride away, is little more than a handful of hotels at the foot of its own slopes.

MOUNTAIN FACTS

Altitude 1800m-3080m
Lifts	23
Pistes	110km
Blue	32%
Red	50%
Black	18%
Artificial snow	9km

LIFT PASSES

97/98 prices in
schillings
Obergurgl ski pass
Covers all lifts in
Obergurgl, Untergurgl
and Hochgurgl, and
local ski-bus.
Beginners Lift pass or
points card.
Main pass
1-day pass 420
6-day pass 2,090
(low season 1,840 –
12% off)
Senior citizens
Over 60: 6-day pass
1,280 (39% off)
Children
Under 16: 6-day pass
1,280 (39% off)
Under 8: free pass
Short-term passes
Half-day (from 11am,
noon, 1pm or 2pm).
Alternative periods
5 days skiing in 7 and
11 days skiing in 14
passes available.

The mountains

For a well-known and popular resort, Obergurgl's slopes are surprisingly small and lacking interest or challenge for adventurous intermediates or better. You also don't get a sense of travel, as you do in bigger Alpine resorts: you just go up and down north-west facing slopes, not from area to area or down into a valley and up the other side. There are, however, some good off-piste runs to explore with a guide.

The lift pass is very expensive for the extent of slopes and number of lifts. Recent reports about piste-marking are varied, though reporters still comment that runs are not always well marked, and life can be made trickier than it should be by unmarked rocks, steep drops, and easy paths crossing steeper runs.

For a day out to other slopes, it's a short bus or car trip to Sölden, and a long car trip to Kuhtai (a worthwhile high area near Innsbruck). Much closer is the tiny touring launch-pad of Vent.

THE SLOPES
Fragmented cruising
The lift pass covers the two separate areas of Obergurgl and Hochgurgl. **Obergurgl** is the smaller. It is in two sections, well linked by piste in one direction, more loosely in the other.

The Festkogl gondola from near the village entrance goes to the highest area. This is served by two drags and two chairs, one of which reaches 3035m. From these runs you can head back to the gondola base or over to

Gaisberg, which has a high point of 2670m reached by a long, slow chair. There are four other short lifts here, and also one that comes up from Obergurgl's village square. Follow this access lift back to town and you can pole or walk to the Festkogl gondola and start the circuit again. We've observed before that improving the Gaisberg-Festkogl connection would be a good thing, so we're pleased to hear that a new chair-lift to achieve that is planned for 1997/98.

The regular and reliable free shuttle bus goes to Untergurgl. From there a chair-lift goes to **Hochgurgl** (also reachable by car, or by bus that leaves a few times a day). Another chair-lift takes you from Hochgurgl to the heart of its mountain, served by four drags. Two chair-lifts up from here take you to the spectacular views of the Italian Dolomites and the 3080m Wurmkogel summit.

A single tree-lined run leads down from Hochgurgl to the bottom of the Untergurgl chair and the bus home.

Recent visitors tell us the piste map is difficult to follow and say they've found significantly different versions.

SNOW RELIABILITY
Excellent
Obergurgl has high slopes and is arguably the most snowsure of Europe's non-glacier resorts. It has a justifiably popular mid-December white week, and regular late-season visitors who book well in advance. But there are virtually no tree-lined runs, wind and white-outs can shut the lifts and, especially in early season, severe cold can curtail enthusiasm.

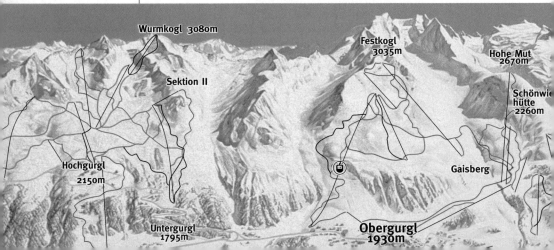

Wurmkogl 3080m

Sektion II

Festkogl
3035m

Hohe Mut
2670m

Schönwie
hütte
2226m

Hochgurgl
2150m

Gaisberg

Untergurgl
1795m

Obergurgl
1930m

SCHOOLS/GUIDES

97/98 prices in
schillings

Obergurgl
Classes 6 days
4hr: 10am-noon and
2pm-4pm
6 full days: 1,630
Children's classes
Ages: from 5
6 full days including
lunch: 2,610
Private lessons
Half- and full day
1,450 for half-day, for
1 to 2 people

Hochgurgl
Classes 5 days
4hr: 10am-noon and
2pm-4pm
5 full days: 1,490
Children's classes
Ages: from 5
5 full days: 1,490
Private lessons
Half- and full day
1,450 for half-day, for
1 to 2 people

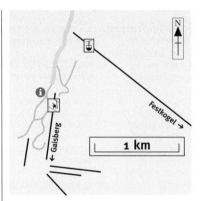

Gaisberg ←   Festkogel →

1 km

N

FOR EXPERTS
Not generally recommendable

There is a fair amount of enjoyable off-
piste to be found with a guide –
especially from Obergurgl – and the
top school groups often go off-piste at
times when there is little avalanche
danger. This is a well-known area for
ski touring.

The most challenging official piste is
the Hohe Mut mogul field beneath the
slow, old chair-lift at Gaisberg. But this
is often irritatingly awkward rather than
pleasurable, being icy, worn and
difficult to follow in places. Other
blacks are rather overgraded – they
could easily be red – and there are few
challenges. Experts will soon tire of
cruising the mainly short runs, no
matter how powdery the snow. We do
have reports of very challenging
touring to be had on the glaciers at
the head of the valley, and trips to
Sölden by local bus are possible.

FOR INTERMEDIATES
Good but limited

There is some perfect intermediate
terrain here, made even better by the
normally flattering snow conditions.
The problem is there's not much of it.
Keen piste-bashers will quickly tire of
travelling the same runs and be itching
to catch the bus to Sölden, down the
valley – unfortunately there is no pass-
sharing arrangement.

Hochgurgl has the bigger area of
easy runs, and these make good
cruising. For more challenging
intermediate runs head to the Vorderer
Wurmkogellift, on the right as you look
at the mountain.

The run down from Hochgurgl to the
bus stop at Untergurgl is about the
only tree-lined piste in the area, and
about the only long run served by
artificial snow. Less confident
intermediates can find this tricky but
necessary unless they want to wait for
an infrequent Hochgurgl bus or take an
expensive taxi home.

The Obergurgl area has more red
than blue runs but most offer no great
challenge to a confident intermediate.
The area served by chair-lifts at the top
of the Festkogl gondola is easy
cruising. And there is a long enjoyable
run down the length of the gondola,
with a scenic off-piste route in the
adjoining valley.

In the Gaisberg area, there are very
easy runs in front of the Nederhütte
and back towards town. The bottom
drag-lifts here serve very short but
sometimes surprisingly tricky and
bumpy runs.

Obergurgl is tiny, but
it's not *that* tiny: as
you might deduce
from the church spire
peeping over the hill,
most of the village is
hidden from view in
this shot →

CHILDCARE

The ski schools at Obergurgl and Hochgurgl take children over the age of 5, but do not offer any special care arrangements.

The village kindergarten takes children from the age of 2.

The Alpina and Austria hotels (among others) have in-house kindergartens.

GETTING THERE

Air Innsbruck, transfer 2hr. Salzburg, transfer 3hr. Munich, transfer 4hr.

Rail Train to Ötz; regular buses from station, transfer 1½hr.

FOR BEGINNERS
Fine for first-timers or improvers

There is an adequate nursery slope above the village, and the Gaisberg run under the chair out of town can be completed as soon as a modicum of control is achieved.

Near beginners can travel from the top of the four-person Wurmkogel chair to Hochgurgl village (600m vertical) without any problems. The quality of the snow at Obergurgl makes the area a good (but relatively expensive) choice for beginners compared with most lower Austrian resorts.

CROSS-COUNTRY
Limited but snowsure

Four small loops: two at Obergurgl, one at Untergurgl and another at Hochgurgl give just 13km of trail. They are, however, relatively snowsure and all pleasantly situated, the lower ones run along the river. Tuition is available.

QUEUES
No problems

Lift queues are rare – even at Christmas and New Year. The resort is too remote to attract day trippers, and its authorities do not encourage 'bussing-in' when lower villages are struggling for snow.

MOUNTAIN RESTAURANTS
Little choice

Compared with most Austrian resorts, mountain huts are not very numerous and not very special. At Gaisberg the Nederhütte is jolly, and often with live music; David's is friendly, cheerful, good value and recently refurbished – and the Schönwieshütte, a 10-minute walk from the piste is in a beautiful setting. So is the tiny hut at the top of the Hohe Mut chair. At Hochgurgl, the tiny hut at Wurmkogel has stunning views into Italy and basic food. Many people return to Obergurgl and Hochgurgl for lunch. Hotels Edelweiss and Jenewein in Obergurgl are convenient, if expensive. Café Josl is cheaper. In Hochgurgl, hotel Riml has excellent reasonably priced food.

SCHOOLS AND GUIDES
Mainly good news

We've had nothing but good reports of the Obergurgl school in the last couple of years, with good English spoken and excellent tuition and organisation: 'highly efficient, very thorough testing of pupils before being put into a class',

'big effort to make school fun'. But we've also been hearing that class sizes have climbed to as many as 15.

FACILITIES FOR CHILDREN
Check out your hotel

For a village with obvious appeal to families, Obergurgl doesn't seem to put itself out to cater for children. There is no ski kindergarten for tots who want to start early, and no special arrangements for lunchtime care of young children attending classes. But many hotels offer childcare of one sort or another, and the Alpina is particularly recommended.

Staying there

The Festkogl gondola area at the village entrance is the best place for getting to the slopes and for ease of access by car. However, it's a long walk or a shuttle bus from the village centre and the nursery slopes.

Accommodation around the ice rink is perched above the village, with very steep, sometimes treacherous walks to and from other amenities. It's a very short slide to the chair-lift and a pole, walk or slide to the Festkogl gondola.

Many of Obergurgl's middle-aged clientele much prefer the convenience of staying in the village centre, being close to the Gaisberg lift and well placed for the shuttle bus. Drivers have underground parking bang in the centre of town.

HOW TO GO
Plenty of good hotels

Virtually all package accommodation is in hotels and pensions, but there are one or two catered chalets and a number of comfortable apartments. Demand for rooms in Obergurgl exceeds supply, and for once it is true that you should book early to avoid disappointment.

Hotels Obergurgl's accommodation is of high quality: most of its 30 hotels are of 4-star rating, and none is less than 3-star.

Within each rating, hotels are uniformly comfortable. In our fat file of reports we have hardly any complaints. The main ones come from couples staying in the Deutschmann who had to share tables.

(((4 Edelweiss und Gurgl
The focal hotel – biggest, oldest, among the most appealing; on the central square. Pool.

UK PACKAGES

Airtours, Bladon Lines, Crystal, First Choice Ski, Independent Ski Links, Inghams, Made to Measure, Thomson

Hochgurgl Inghams

ACTIVITIES

Indoor Swimming pool (at Hotel Muhle, open to the public), saunas, whirlpools, steam baths, massage, bowling, pool and billiards, squash, table tennis, shooting range
Outdoor Natural skating rink (open in the evenings), curling, sleigh rides

TOURIST OFFICE

Postcode A-6456
Tel +43 (5256) 466
Fax 353

(((④) **Alpina** Big, smart chalet with excellent children's facilities – kindergarten and playroom. Pool.
(((④) **Jenewein** Recently refurbished, friendly staff, excellent food; good central position next to main lift.
(((④) **Gamper** Best rooms very comfortable, good food; at far end of village, past the square.
(((④) **Crystal** If you don't mind the ocean-liner appearance, one of the best hotels in the Festkogl lift area.
(((③ **Fender** Good all-rounder with friendly staff; central
(((③ **Wiesental** Comfortable, well positioned, good value.
(((③ **Granat-Schlössl** Amusing pseudo-castle, surprisingly affordable.
(((② **Alpenblume** Good B&B hotel well-placed for Festkogl lift.
(((② **Haus Gurgl** B&B near Festkogl lift; friendly, pizzeria, same owners as Edelweiss und Gurgl.
Hochgurgl has equally good hotels.
(((⑤ **Hochgurgl** The most luxurious in the area – the only 5-star. Pool.
(((③ **Laurin** Well equipped, traditional rooms, excellent food.
Self-catering The Lohmann is a high-standard large modern apartment block, well placed for the slopes, less so for the village centre below. The 3-star Pirchhütte Garni has apartments close to the Festkogl gondola, and the Wiesental hotel has more central ones.

EATING OUT
Wide choice, limited range
Hotel dining rooms and à la carte restaurants dominate. The commendable Pic Nic is the only independent restaurant, and hotel Madeleine has a good separate pizzeria. Hotel Alpina has a particularly good reputation for its food, while the restaurant at the Gasthof Gamper is pleasantly cosy.

APRES-SKI
Lively early, quiet later
Obergurgl is reasonably animated immediately after the slopes close, but things are pretty quiet later on. The Nederhütte mountain restaurant has a lively tea dance three times a week, and the Umbrella Bar outside the Edelweiss hotel is popular when the weather is good.

Later on, the crowded Krumpn's Stadl barn is the liveliest place in town with live music on alternate nights – it's also recommended for its fondues. The Josl, Jenewein, Gurgl and Edelweiss hotels have atmospheric bars. Discos are uninspiring, but hotel Alpenland's bowling alley is popular.

Hochgurgl is very quiet at night except for Toni's Almhütte bar in the Olymp Sporthotel – one of three places with live music. Hotel Hochfirst has a disco but it's difficult to believe much atmosphere is generated.

OFF THE SLOPES
Very limited
There isn't much to do during the day. Innsbruck is over two hours by post-bus. Sölden (20 minutes away) has a leisure centre and shopping facilities. Pedestrians can walk to restaurants in the Gaisberg area to meet friends for lunch. The Hochfirst hotel has a good health centre.

STAYING IN HOCHGURGL
Very quiet
The usual advantages of staying part way up a mountain are convenience for the slopes, good snow and no queues. Obergurgl itself scores well in these, but Hochgurgl does have some good hotels, including the most luxurious one in the area (the hotel Hochgurgl). It is even quieter than Obergurgl – great if that's what you're looking for.

Obertauern 1740m

Small but varied area, with great snow record

WHAT IT COSTS

((((5)

HOW IT RATES

The slopes
Snow	****
Extent	**
Experts	***
Intermediates	****
Beginners	*****
Convenience	****
Queues	****
Restaurants	***

The rest
Scenery	***
Resort charm	**
Off-slope	**

MOUNTAIN FACTS

Altitude	1640m-2335m
Lifts	25
Pistes	120km
Blue	50%
Red	35%
Black	15%
Artificial snow	50km

UK PACKAGES

Crystal, Inghams, Made to Measure, Neilson, Ski Club Europe, Thomson

TOURIST OFFICE

Postcode A-5562
Tel +43 (6456) 7252
Fax 7515

Obertauern's excellent snow record takes precedence for some over its lack of charm and limited mountain. It has a small intermediate circuit, good beginners' slopes and some challenges. It's crowded when snow in lower resorts is poor.

THE RESORT

In the land of postcard resorts grown out of rustic villages, Obertauern is something of an oddity – a mainly modern development at the top of the Tauern pass road. Built in (high-rise) chalet-style, it's not unattractive – but here is no real central focus of shops and bars, and a lack of local transport.

THE MOUNTAINS

The Tauern pass road divides the **slopes** into two unequal parts, well-linked to make a user-friendly circuit that can be travelled clockwise or anti-clockwise. However, reporters complain about the piste map and poor and out-of-date piste information. Most pistes are on the sunny slopes to the north: a wide, many-faceted basin of mostly gentle runs, with a few steepish moguled pitches punctuated by long schusses. Vertical range is limited and runs are short. Visitors used to big areas will soon see it all. There is a **snowboard** fun-park at Plattenkarlift.

Zehnerkar and Gamsleiten to the south-west have Obertauern's highest and most difficult runs. Even here, though, the top station is less than 600m above the resort. You can travel the circuit in a couple of hours.

The resort exploits the exceptional **snow reliability** record of its high bowl. In the unlikely event of a shortage, there is plenty of snowmaking too.

Experts naturally incline towards the south-west slopes. There are some genuinely steep pisted and off-piste runs from the Gamsleiten chair, but it is prone to closure by wind and avalanche danger. For more challenge and longer descents join guided tours to peaks above the top lifts.

For **intermediates** the biggest draw is Obertauern's circuit. Stay low for easier pistes, or try the tougher runs higher up. The central point of the north side is Hochalm, from where the Seekareck and Panorama chairs take you to challenging, often mogully runs. The chair to Hundskogel leads to a red and a black. And over at the Plattenkar

quad there are two splendid reds.

Obertauern has very good nursery slopes for **beginners,** close to the village. After the first couple of lessons you can go up the mountain, because the Schaidberg chair leads to a drag-lift serving a high-altitude beginners' slope and it is an easy run back home. There is a 15km **cross-country** loop in the heart of the resort.

When neighbouring resorts don't share Obertauern's good snow, non-residents arrive by the bus-load. The lift system is erratic – on the circuit, slow two-person chairs may follow high-speed quads, so some big **queues** can build up.

The **mountain restaurants** are plentiful and good, but crowded. The Kringsalm is recommended.

Of the several **schools and guides**, most tour operators use the Krallinger – and its kindergarten. We have good reports of both, despite large classes. But one regular rates the Grillitsch school 'much the best', though another reports mixed-ability classes.

STAYING THERE

Practically all **accommodation** is in hotels (mostly 3-star and 4-star) and guest-houses. Location is not a major consideration. The 4-star Enzian is welcoming, with good food and an outstanding wine cellar. The Edelweiss, Petersbuhel, Gamsleiten and Alpina are also recommended.

Eating out is mostly in hotels (the Enzian is recommended) and the busy après-ski bars at the foot of the north-side lifts. The Hochalm restaurant at the top of the quad chair sometimes serves early-evening meals. **Après-ski** is lively and varied. The Latschnstub'n has a terrace, music and dancing and is good at tea-time. Later the Lutzeralm has farmyard-style decor and a disco. The Taverne has various bars, a pizzeria and disco.

Off the slopes there's a sports centre (no pool, but with tennis). Salzburg is an easy trip. For lunch, the Kringsalm can be reached on foot.

Saalbach-Hinterglemm 1000m

Attractive villages, lively nightlife and good intermediate runs

WHAT IT COSTS

((((4))))

HOW IT RATES

The slopes

Snow	***
Extent	****
Experts	**
Intermediates	****
Beginners	***
Convenience	****
Queues	***
Restaurants	****

The rest

Scenery	***
Resort charm	****
Off-slope	**

➕ Large, well-linked, intermediate circuit with a good mix of open and tree-lined runs

➕ Little walking to the lifts from central accommodation

➕ Saalbach is a big but pleasant, affluent village, lively at night

➕ Both village centres traffic-free

➕ Atmospheric mountain restaurants all over the mountain

➕ Sunny slopes

➕ Large snowmaking installation and excellent piste maintenance

➖ Large number of low, south-facing slopes that suffer from the sun

➖ Not much for experts

➖ Nursery slopes in Saalbach are not ideal – sunny, and busy in parts

➖ Saalbach has now spread along the valley and some accommodation is far from central

➖ Can get rowdy at night in Saalbach

Like many Austrian resorts Saalbach-Hinterglemm has a pretty, traditional-style village and very lively nightlife but unlike many it combines this with a very extensive circuit of slopes on both sides of a valley, and runs are linked by an efficient modern lift system. Its slopes resemble a French resort more than a traditional Austrian one – with the added advantage of excellent traditional mountain restaurants dotted around.

The only real downside is the snow. Although it has impressive snowmaking and claims to be in a 'snow-pocket', one side of the valley faces south and these slopes, especially the lower ones, deteriorate quickly in good weather.

Saalbach's après-ski is lively – even rowdy – and dominated by Scandinavian and German visitors. These days, as a reporter found, the bars are swarming with young Brits travelling on cheap package holidays.

boarding *Saalbach is great for boarding – the mix is just right. Slopes are extensive, lifts are mainly chairs and gondolas (though there are some connecting drags), and there are pistes to appeal to beginners, intermediates and experts alike. For experienced boarders there's good off-piste terrain, a large half-pipe on the Bernkogel above Saalbach, and another in the small but good fun-park at Hochalm above Hinterglemm. And to cap it all, pretty good nightlife.*

What's new

For 1997/98 the Reiterkogel chair-lift out of Hinterglemm will be replaced by a new cable-way with several gondola cabins going up as a group. This will make getting out of the centre of Hinterglemm in the morning a much quicker affair.

During the previous season the old Hochalm drag-lift was replaced by a six-seater covered chair-lift.

The resort

Saalbach and Hinterglemm, their centres 4km apart, expanded along a narrow dead-end valley floor until, a few years ago, they adopted a single identity. Their slopes are spread across north- and south-facing mountainsides, with lifts and runs connecting the villages via both sides.

Saalbach is one of the most attractive winter villages in Austria. Wedged into the narrow valley, with pisted slopes

The village looks as good in the daytime as it does at night ➔

MOUNTAIN FACTS

Altitude 930m-2095m
Lifts 60
Pistes 200km
Blue 50%
Red 33%
Black 17%
Artificial snow 17km
Recco detectors used

LIFT PASSES

97/98 prices in
schillings
**Saalbach-
Hinterglemm-Leogang**
Covers all the lifts in
Saalbach,
Hinterglemm and
Leogang, and the ski
bus.
Main pass
1-day pass 400
6-day pass 1,940
(low season 1,700 –
12% off)
Senior citizens
Over 65 male, 60
female: 6-day pass
1,175 (39% off)
Children
Under 15: 6-day pass
1,175 (39% off)
Under 7: free pass
Short-term passes
Day pass refundable
by the hour; day pass
price reduced hourly
from 11am; single and
return tickets on main
lifts.
Notes 6-day pass for
15- to 19-year-olds
1,765. Special rates
for children
accompanied by
parents – first child
ski pass is full price,
the second at a 50%
discount and all
subsequent passes
are free.

coming right down to the village centre, its traditional-style buildings are huddled together around a classic onion-domed church. Most buildings are modern reproductions – the main exceptions are the Post Inn and the church – and the result is pretty close to Austrian charm with French convenience.

Saalbach is quite upmarket, with some large, expensive hotels, and a few cheap and cheerful pensions. The attractive main street is lined with hotels, restaurants and shops, festooned with fairy lights and comes complete with gigantic snowman. The village centre is mainly traffic-free.

Hinterglemm is a more scattered, less appealing collection of hotels and holiday homes, with a small, traffic-free zone in the centre. It offers a cheaper, though not inexpensive, alternative to Saalbach, with far better access to the north-facing slopes.

The resort has a youthful atmosphere and attracts a cosmopolitan clientele, from Germany, Scandinavia and the UK.

Leogang is a quiet village in the next valley to the north, its long, north-facing slopes forming a spur from the main area.

The mountains

The slopes form a 'circus' almost exclusively suitable for intermediates, much of it on lightly wooded slopes. Few runs are likely either to bore the aggressive intermediate or worry the timid one. There are sufficient open sections and changes of pitch and direction to give pistes variety, but not many genuinely black pistes.

Several resorts in Salzburg province are reachable by road – Bad Hofgastein, Kaprun and Zell am See, the last a short bus-ride away.

THE SLOPES
User-friendly circuit
The complete circuit of the valley can only be travelled anti-clockwise – going clockwise, at Vorderglemm there is no way up the slope on the opposite side of the valley. You can do a truncated clockwise circuit, crossing to the south side of the valley at Saalbach itself. The valley floor is very narrow, so there is very little walking necessary when changing hillsides. Where you end up at the end of the day is not important because of the excellent bus service which runs every 20 minutes,

though you might have to wait slightly longer at Vorderglemm.

A good deal of the south-facing slopes are above 1400m, albeit with rather short runs. Five sectors can be identified – from west to east, **Hochalm**, **Reiterkogel**, **Bernkogel**, **Kohlmaiskopf** and **Wildenkarkogel**. The last connects via Schönleitenhütte to Leogang – a small, high, open area, leading to a long, narrow north-facing slope down to Leogang village, broadening towards the bottom. An eight-person gondola brings you most of the way back.

The connections across Saalbach-Hinterglemm's south-facing slopes work well: when traversing the whole hillside you need to descend to the valley floor only once, whichever direction you go. This occurs at Saalbach itself, where a very short walk across the main street gets you from the Bernkogel piste to the Kohlmaiskopf lift and vice versa. Both these runs are well endowed with snowmakers to ensure the link normally remains open, and there is a choice of lifts going up, including a multi-cabin cable-way to Kohlmaiskopf.

The north-facing slopes are different in character – two more distinct mountains, with long runs from both to the valley. Access from Saalbach is by a solitary, queue-prone cable-car to **Schattberg**. The high, open, sunny slopes behind the peak are served by a fast quad chair.

From Schattberg, long runs go down to Saalbach village, Vorderglemm and Hinterglemm. From the latter, lifts go not only to Schattberg but also to the other north-facing mountain, **Zwölferkogel**, served by a two-stage eight-person gondola. Drags serve open slopes on the sunny side of the peak, and a little-used gondola provides a link from the south-facing Hochalm area.

SNOW RELIABILITY
Better than most of the Tirol
Saalbach's array of snowmakers cover several main runs on the lower half of the mountain, on both sides of the valley. The resort also claims to be in a 'snow pocket'. Good piste maintenance helps to keep the slopes in the best possible condition, but an altitude range of 900m to 2100m is only a slight advance on Kitzbühel. As 60 per cent of runs face south, Saalbach suffers when the sun comes out.

SCHOOLS/GUIDES

96/97 prices in schillings

Hannes Füstauer
Classes 6 days
4hr: 10am-noon and
1pm-3pm
6 full days: 1,550
Children's classes
Ages: from 5
6 full days: 1,550
Private lessons
Hourly and daily
550 for 1hr, for 1 to 2
people; each
additional person 100

Wolfgang Zink
Classes 6 days
4hr: 10am-noon and
1pm-3pm
6 full days: 1,550
Children's classes
Ages: from 6
6 full days: 1,550
Private lessons
Hourly and daily
550 for 1hr, for 1 to 2
people; each
additional person 100

Willi Fritzenwallner
Classes 6 days
4hr per day
6 full days: 1,550
Children's classes
Ages: from 6
6 full days: 1,550
Private lessons
Hourly
550 for 1 to 2 people;
each additional
person 100

FOR EXPERTS
Little steep stuff

There are few testing slopes. Off-piste guides are available, but snow conditions and forest tend to limit the potential. The long (4km) run beneath the length of the Schattberg cable-car is the only truly black run, but even this is far from really challenging.

Worthwhile runs are the 5km Schattberg West-Hinterglemm red (and its scenic 'ski route' variation), and the Zwölferkogel-Hochalm link. Now that it is served by two gondolas, Zwölferkogel is where the more proficient will spend most time.

FOR INTERMEDIATES
Paradise

This area is ideal for both the great British piste-basher, eager to clock up the miles, and the more leisurely cruiser. The south-facing pistes have mainly been cut through the pine forest at an angle, allowing movement across the area on easy runs.

For those looking for more of a challenge, the most direct routes down from Hochalm, Reiterkogel, Kohlmaiskopf and Hochwartalm are good fun. All the south-facing slopes are uniformly pleasant and, as a result, everyone tends to be fairly evenly distributed over them. Only the delightful blue from Bernkogel to Saalbach gets really crowded at times. The alternative long ski route is very pleasant, taking you through forest and meadows.

The north-facing area has some more challenging runs, and a section of relatively high, open slopes around Zwölferkogel, which often have good snow. None of the black runs is beyond a competent intermediate, while the long pretty cruise from Limbergalm to Vorderglemm gets you away from lifts for most of the time and is particularly quiet and pleasant first thing in the morning.

FOR BEGINNERS
Best for improvers

Saalbach's two nursery slopes are very well positioned for convenience, right next to the village centre. But they are both south-facing, and the upper one gets a lot of intermediate traffic taking a short-cut between the Kohlmaiskopf and Bernkogel areas. The lower one is very small, but the lift is free.

Alternatives are trips to the short, easy runs at Bernkogel and Schattberg.

There is also a little slope at the foot of the Schattberg but the school seems loath to use it – so it's great for pottering about on your own at lunchtime. It's rather sunless and a little steeper than the other nursery areas, but perfectly usable.

Hinterglemm's spacious nursery area is separate from the main slopes. Being north-facing, it is much more reliable for snow later on in the season, but it consequently misses out on the sun in midwinter.

There are lots of easy blue runs to move on to, in all sectors of the area.

FOR CROSS-COUNTRY
Go to Zell am See

Trails run beside the road along the valley floor from Saalbach to Vorderglemm and between Hinterglemm and the valley end at Lindlingalm. In midwinter these trails get very little sun, and are not very exciting. The countryside beyond nearby Zell am See offers more scope.

QUEUES
Busy, but only one long delay

The Schattberg cable-car is an obvious problem, with waiting routine in the morning peak period. Otherwise, much depends on snow conditions. When all runs are in good shape there are few problems, other than small morning peak queues to leave Saalbach. When snow conditions are poor, the Bernkogel chair and the following drag get very busy, as do any lifts servicing the better snow.

Saalbach-Hinterglemm does not get as overrun at weekends as other Tirolean resorts – it's less accessible for the Munich hordes than the Ski Welt area and its neighbours.

MOUNTAIN RESTAURANTS
Excellent quality and quantity

The south-facing slopes are liberally scattered with attractive little huts that serve good food. And they do not simply rely on good weather; many have pleasant rustic interiors and an animated atmosphere.

The Panorama on the Kohlmaiskopf slope, Waleggeralm on Hochalm and Turneralm close to Bründelkopf serve particularly good food. The little Bernkogelalm hut, overlooking Saalbach, has a great atmosphere. The large hut above the main Saalbach nursery slope gets packed at 4pm, when customers disco dance before

CHILDCARE

Some of the ski schools take children from age 4 or 5 and can provide lunchtime care – there are special areas in both villages.

Several hotels have nurseries, and some in HInterglemm are open to non-residents, including the Egger, Glemmtalerhof, Lengauerhof and Theresia. The Glemmtalerhof is part of a group of 'Partner-hotels' which operate a shared nursery.

going home to change. There is a new umbrella bar at the top of the Zwölferkogel gondola which reporters say is good for sun lounging.

On the north-facing slopes there are relatively few places. The Gipfelhütte at Schattberg West is adequate. We had great Tiroler Rösti, served in the pan, at the place between the chair-lifts on the way down. Ellmaualm, at the bottom of the Zwölferkogel's upper slopes, is a quiet, sunny retreat with good food but suspect loos.

SCHOOLS AND GUIDES
An excess of choice
We're all in favour of competition between schools but visitors to Saalbach-Hinterglemm may feel that they are faced with rather too much of this good thing. Two or three schools offers a choice; eight or nine begins to look like a recipe for confusion. It

certainly makes life difficult for the editors of resort guides: the few reports we have are all on different schools, half of them not clearly identified. But some students of Wolfgang Zink (aka Ski Pro) tell us they made excellent progress.

FACILITIES FOR CHILDREN
Hinterglemm tries harder
Saalbach doesn't go out of its way to sell itself to families, although it does have a ski kindergarten. Hinterglemm, perhaps seeing itself as more of a family resort, has some good hotel-based nursery facilities – the one at the Theresia is reportedly excellent. Hotels in both resorts are identified in the resort literature as 'child-friendly' if they conform to a long list of requirements, ranging from electric socket covers in bedrooms to provision of ice-skates.

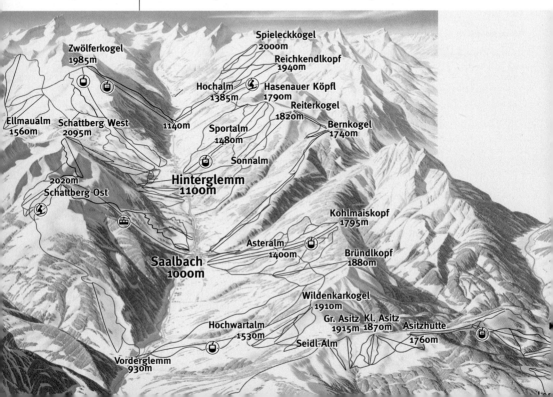

GETTING THERE

Air Salzburg, transfer 2hr. Munich, transfer 3½hr.

Rail Zell am See; hourly buses from station, transfer ½hr.

UK PACKAGES

Airtours, Crystal, First Choice Ski, Inghams, Made to Measure, Neilson, PGL Ski Europe, PGL Teenski, STS, Ski Club Europe, Ski Leogang, Sloping Off, Thomson

Leogang Ski Leogang

ACTIVITIES

Indoor Swimming pools, sauna, massage, solarium, bowling, billiards, tennis, squash (Hinterglemm) **Outdoor** Floodlit tobogganing, sleigh rides, skating, ice hockey, curling, 35km of cleared paths, paragliding

Staying there 🔑

The walk to lifts from Saalbach's central hotels is minimal. Unfortunately Saalbach has seen a fair amount of expansion in recent years, and many of the cheaper hotels used by British tour operators tend to be situated in the least convenient part of the village. In Hinterglemm itself, position isn't so important. Most of the accommodation is near a lift.

HOW TO GO
Cheerful doesn't mean cheap

Chalets Crystal has the only catered chalets that we are aware of in the main resorts – in central Hinterglemm. It offers a relatively cheap alternative to the mostly expensive hotels.

Hotels There are a large number of hotels in Saalbach, mainly 3-star and above. Most of the more expensive ones have excellent positions in the village centre, whereas the cheapest places tend to be along the road to Hinterglemm – or in Hinterglemm itself, which is rather less ritzy than Saalbach. Be aware that some central hotels are affected by disco noise.

Saalbach

⟨⟨⟨⟨4 **Alpenhotel** Luxurious, with a wealth of facilities, including an open-fire lounge, disco, pub and small pool.

⟨⟨⟨⟨4 **Berger's Sporthotel** Liveliest of the top hotels, with a popular daily tea dance, good bar and disco. Good pool.

⟨⟨⟨⟨4 **Kendler** Position second to none, right next to the Bernkogel chair. Classy, expensive, good food.

⟨⟨⟨⟨4 **Saalbacher Hof** Retains a friendly feel despite its large size.

⟨⟨⟨3 **Haider** Best-positioned of the 3-stars, right next to the main lifts.

⟨⟨⟨3 **König** Slightly cheaper 3-star, particularly well placed for school and nursery slopes.

Hinterglemm

⟨⟨⟨⟨4 **Theresia** Hinterglemm's top hotel, and one of the best-equipped for families. Out towards Saalbach, but nursery slopes nearby. Pool.

⟨⟨⟨3 **Wolf** Small but well-equipped 4-star in the the nursery-sharing scheme. 'Especially good' food, excellent position. Pool.

⟨⟨2 **Pension Austria** Half-way between the villages, and so good value by local standards for those who don't mind catching a bus every morning.

⟨⟨2 **Pension Spatz** Good value, friendly welcome, good position near the centre of the village.

Self-catering There's an enormous choice of apartments for independent travellers.

EATING OUT
Wide choice of hotel restaurants

Saalbach-Hinterglemm is essentially a half-board resort, with relatively few non-hotel restaurants. Peter's restaurant, at the top of Saalbach's main street, is atmospheric and serves excellent meat dishes cooked on hot stones. The Wallner Pizzeria on the main street is good value. The Auwirt hotel on the outskirts of Saalbach has an à la carte restaurant that is better than the hotel's 3-star status would suggest. The simple Hochleiten hotel in Hinterglemm also has a surprisingly good restaurant. Otherwise general hotel standards and style are reflected in their restaurants.

APRES-SKI
Excellent but expensive

Après-ski is very lively, pretty much from immediately after the slopes close until the early hours, perhaps quietening down a bit at dinner time while most people are tucking-in back at their hotels.

In Saalbach the tiny Zum Turn (next door to the church and cemetery) is an atmospheric former medieval jail – everyone arrives at 4pm and many are still there at 11pm. The Pub on the main road out of town is packed with young Brits enjoying the karaoke. The Neuhaus Taverne and Crazy Bear have live music. Bobby's Bar is cheap, and has bowling. Kings Disco livens up after midnight. The Panther Bar has jungle decor, discreet music and well-heeled clientele. Zum Herrn'Karl, Hellis and Bergers are also popular.

In Hinterglemm there are a number of ice bars, including the Schirm in the centre of town, which are busy straight after the lifts close. Later on, the Londoner is the biggest attraction – live and disco music, smart, friendly, with a plastic card you collect on the way in and buy your drinks on. Bla Bla is small, modern and smart, with reasonable prices. The Alm Bar has good music and some dancing.

Tour operator reps organise tobogganing, sleigh-rides and bowling.

TOURIST OFFICE

Postcode A-5753
Tel +43 (6541)
680068
Fax 680069

OFF THE SLOPES
Surprisingly little to do

Saalbach is not very entertaining if you're not into winter sports. There are few shops other than supermarkets and equipment places. Walks tend to be restricted to the paths alongside the cold cross-country trails or along the Saalbach toboggan run to Spielberghs. But there are excursions by bus and train (or car) to Kitzbühel and Salzburg.

Leogang 800m

Leogang is an attractive, although rather scattered, farming community-cum-mountain resort. The lack of any central focus has repercussions: many of the hotels are a long way from the main lifts, and the bus service is disappointingly infrequent.

Leogang is, however, a much less expensive alternative to Saalbach-Hinterglemm. It is also far quieter, smaller and less commercialised than its neighbours. Situated on the St Johann-Bischofshofen road, and having a mainline railway station, Leogang is also better placed for independent travel access and for taking day excursions. One visitor reported that the snow was better in Leogang than the rest of the area.

The link with Saalbach is fairly reliable: the gondola towards Asitz is followed by a couple of short pistes and lifts, with all the slopes above a lofty 1590m. These pistes are red, but not difficult. Less experienced intermediates can amuse themselves on the blue slopes served by the first stage of the gondola, or on the separate little area situated closer to the village centre.

Beginners have good nursery slopes, conveniently placed just above the village. If the snow is poor, the higher slopes are not too steep, though icy conditions can be a problem for novices.

Leogang is the best of the local villages for cross-country. There are 25km of trails, with a connection to Saalfelden, plus a panoramic high-altitude trail which links through to other resorts. Given good snow, trails are kept in fine condition.

The Leogang Altenberger school has a high reputation – 'highly recommended, with excellent service and tuition'. There is a non-ski crèche, and children can start school at four years old.

Ski Leogang runs a catered chalet in a converted farmhouse in Hütten, a tiny hamlet west of Leogang, which is better positioned for the slopes and the gondola than the main village. Visitors report comfort and character with great catering and entertainment.

There are convenient hotels in each price category. The luxury Krallerhof has its own nursery lift which can be used to get across to the main lift station. The 4-star Salzburgerhof, and much simpler Gasthof Asiztstuberl, are the best-placed hotels, within a two-minute walk of the gondola. Gasthof Stockinggut is a fine 3-star, within reasonable walking distance of the main lift, and also has a good free minibus service to the slopes. The informal Rupertus is better placed, right next to the gondola, and closer to the village.

Restaurants are hotel-based. The Krallerhof has the excellent food you would expect. The much cheaper Gasthof Hüttwirt has a high reputation for wholesome Austrian home cooking.

The rustic old farming chalet Kralleralm is very much the focal tea-time and evening rendezvous. Its atmosphere seems to please everyone, which is just as well, there being very little else available. The Stockinggut does, however, have an entertainment programme including a cow-milking competition! Excursions to the pleasant nearby town of Saalfelden and the lovely city of Salzburg are the main attractions off the slopes. Other facilities include swimming and tennis.

St Anton

An Austrian resort to rival the best in France

WHAT IT COSTS

((((5)

HOW IT RATES

The slopes

Snow	****
Extent	****
Experts	*****
Intermediates	***
Beginners	*
Convenience	***
Queues	**
Restaurants	***

The rest

Scenery	***
Resort charm	****
Off-slope	***

What's new

In the 1996/97 season an 'information team' of five with multi-lingual skills was put on the slopes to help people and to control unruly skiers and boarders. Our reporters generally found them very useful.

For 1997/98 the ski bus between Rauz and Zürs will be free (though you'll still have to pay if you get on in St Anton). The local St Anton buses are already free. No new lifts are planned for 1997/98 but those who haven't visited St Anton for a few years will be pleased to find new high-speed quad chairs replacing some slow, old T-bars and the tiny St Christoph cable-car.

- ➕ Extensive slopes for adventurous intermediates and experts
- ➕ Heavy snowfalls, backed up by snowmakers, generally give good cover despite sunny slopes
- ➕ Much-improved lift system has greatly reduced queuing problems
- ➕ Easy rail access, direct from Britain
- ➕ The liveliest, most varied après-ski around (but see minus points)
- ➕ Despite resort expansion, village retains distinct Tirolean charm

- ➖ Slopes don't suit beginners or timid intermediates
- ➖ Pistes can get very crowded
- ➖ Long walks or bus-rides to lifts from much accommodation
- ➖ All the tough stuff is off-piste
- ➖ Surprisingly little to amuse off the slopes
- ➖ Nightlife can get rowdy, with noisy drunks in the early hours

St Anton has, along with Wengen and Mürren, a strong British tradition. From the 1920s, successive generations learned to ski here, adopting the distinctive 'feet together' Arlberg style. Sir Arnold Lunn helped start the Kandahar race here in 1928. The resort has remained popular with good British skiers.

It has also become one of the world's Meccas for ski bums. That's a reflection of the wonderful, tough off-piste runs available in the bowls below the Valluga – the best that Austria has to offer. In good snow conditions they are superb. Sadly, conditions are often less than perfect except just after a fall, because of their south-facing aspect. But if you are lucky with the snow you'll have the time of your life. There's a lot to offer adventurous intermediates too, both locally and at Lech and Zürs, a short bus-ride away.

There are lots of late-night discos and bars. The resort is an ideal choice for the hard-drinking, disco-loving, keen-for-action holiday-maker who can stand the pace of getting to bed late and being up for the first lift. But it's not for those who like a quiet life and gentle, uncrowded pistes.

boarding *Though steeped in skiing tradition, St Anton is moving with the times and improving facilities for boarders. Although we don't recommend it to beginners, it is one of the best freeride areas in the world, with lots of steep terrain and hits. The Rendl area is where the snowboard facilities are: a new fun-park and a 100m half-pipe. The top of this area has a lot of T-bars but a gondola is the main lift up and elsewhere chairs and cable-cars are the main lifts. Tuition is provided by the ski schools, as well as the specialist Snowboard Academy. A book could be written about the nightlife.*

The resort

St Anton is at the foot of the road up to the Arlberg pass, at the eastern end of a lift network that spreads across to St Christoph and above the pass to Rauz and Stuben. The resort is a long, sprawling mixture of traditional and modern buildings crammed into a narrow valley, between a busy road and mainline railway – a town in size but in character a very overgrown village full of tourism-related facilities.

It is an attractively bustling place, full of life, colour and noise, and positively teeming with a lively young international clientele. Although it is crowded and commercialised, St Anton is full of character, and its traffic-free main street retains Alpine charm and traditional-style buildings.

The resort's main slopes start with a central cable-car, just beyond the rail tracks. This leads to the Valluga area. On the other side of the main road a gondola goes to the Rendl area.

MOUNTAIN FACTS

Altitude	1305m-2650m
Lifts	85
Pistes	260km
Blue	30%
Red	40%
Black	30%
Artificial snow	20km
Recco detectors used	

The mountains

St Anton vies with Val-d'Isère for the title of 'resort with most undergraded slopes'. There are plenty of red pistes which would be black in many other resorts, and plenty of blues which would be red. Strangely, there are no black pistes. There are very popular black runs marked on the piste map but they are all given off-piste status. Some are classified as 'high-touring routes' – this means they are not marked, not groomed, not patrolled and not protected from avalanche danger. There are also some 'ski routes'. These have some markers, are groomed occasionally in part, but are not patrolled and are protected from avalanches only in 'the immediate vicinity of the markers'.

The piste map says that high-touring routes require 'extensive mountain experience and expert guidance' and ski routes are recommended only for people with 'good Alpine experience or with an instructor'. And yet between them these grades of run cover most of the best runs for experts. And they are commonly used by holiday-makers without the services of an instructor or guide – many people who visit St Anton couldn't afford one. One visitor commented, 'The lack of marked black runs is discouraging. When we were there the routes of the old black runs were clear and well used. It is entirely unreasonable to expect everyone to

take guides on these routes, and it seems irresponsible to ignore the fact that people will go on them. They run the risk of alienating those who want to move off red runs but are not quite ready to take on anything and everything. On some of the ski routes there were snow cannons. This doesn't fit with the theory that you are on your own.' Another reporter tells a worrying tale of being badly lost on an avalanched ski route that was not marked as closed at the start.

In the last edition we said the resort was reviewing its piste grading system, converting some existing reds to blacks and blues to reds. Unfortunately we're still waiting – and hoping the resort will do something more to help people decide whether off-piste routes are safe. Marking more of the restaurants on the piste map would also be useful.

If you want to go further afield, regular buses go (at reasonable cost) to Zürs and Lech, which share yet more extensive slopes covered by the Arlberg lift pass. Serfaus, Nauders, Ischgl and Sölden are feasible outings.

THE SLOPES
Large linked area
St Anton's slopes are made up of several sectors, all except one of which are linked, on a predominantly south-facing mountain.

Starting on the east, you have the choice of a four-person chair or a funicular up to **Gampen**. From there pistes lead back to St Anton and

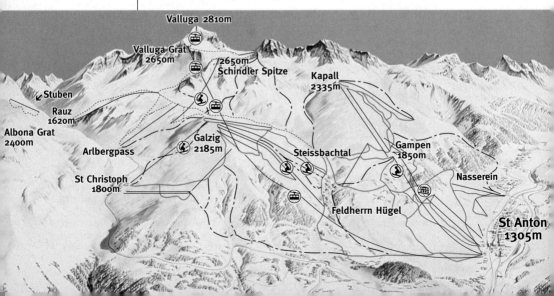

Nasserein, or in the opposite direction across to the links with the Valluga–Galzig area. Or you can go up higher to **Kapall** and head down unmarked routes – ending up at the same places.

A four-person chair is the quickest link to **Galzig**. This brings you out just above the mid-station of the cable-car up from St Anton. From here you can travel in most directions, including back to town, down to **St Christoph** (from where there's a high-speed quad back up) or back to Feldherrn Hügel. At peak periods the blue pistes down from here are some of the most crowded we've come across.

From Galzig you can get up to St Anton's most famous slopes, the bowls below the **Valluga**, by taking the second stage of the cable-car or going up the Schindlergrat three-person chair, which delivers you to the same height (2650m) but on a different peak. There's a tiny third stage of the Valluga cable-car which takes you up to 2810m, but this is mainly for sightseeing. The only run down from there is off the back, off-piste to Zürs. You are not allowed to take skis or a board up the lift without a guide.

From both the second stage of the cable-car and the Schindlergrat chair, you can take the long, beautiful but busy ski route to Rauz, at the western end of St Anton's own slopes.

From Rauz you cross the road and along to Stuben, where a slow two-stage chair-lift takes you to the quiet, mainly north-facing **Albona** area.

The final area, **Rendl**, is separate and reached by gondola from just outside town (there are buses from the village, but it's an easy walk). Six lifts (many T-bars) serve the west-facing runs at the top here, with a single north-facing piste returning to the gondola bottom station. One reporter was told by her instructor that the going is often rocky here, as the mountain has more loose rock than the other side.

SNOW RELIABILITY
Generally very good cover

If the weather is coming (as it often is) from the west or north-west, the Arlberg gets it first, and as a result St Anton and its neighbours get heavy

If you don't like high cable-cars, you won't like the Vallugabahn ↓

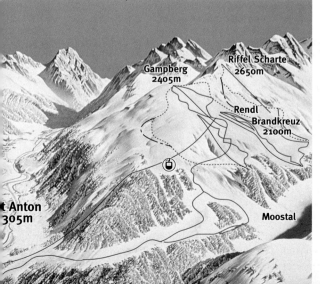

Gampberg
2405m

Riffel Scharte
2650m

Rendl
Brandkreuz
2100m

Anton
305m

Moostal

LIFT PASSES

97/98 prices in schillings

Arlberg Ski Pass
Covers all St Anton, St Christoph, Lech, Zürs and Stuben lifts, and linking bus between Rauz and Zürs.

Beginners Limited pass covering beginners' lifts.

Main pass
1-day pass 465
6-day pass 2,130
(low season 1,920 – 10% off)

Senior citizens
Over 65 male, 60 female: 6-day pass 1,850 (13% off)

Children
Under 15: 6-day pass 1,290 (39% off)

Short-term passes
Single ascent tickets on some lifts throughout Arlberg. Half-day tickets (adults 345) from noon, afternoon 'taster' tickets (190) from 3pm. Day tickets have by-the-hour reimbursement.

Notes 6-day pass prices are for Arlberg 'Special' pass, available to adults and children staying in the Arlberg area (normal adult 6-day pass, 2,310). Main pass also covers Klösterle (10 lifts), 7km west of Stuben. Discounts during wedel, firn and snow crystal weeks. 'Snowman' season pass for under 6s and over 80s is only 100.

falls of snow. They often have much better conditions than other resorts of a similar height, and we've had great snow here as late as April in the last couple of seasons. But many of the slopes face south- or south-east, causing icy or heavy conditions at times. It's vital to time your runs off the Valluga to get decent conditions.

The lower runs are now well equipped with artificial snowmaking, which ensures the home runs remain open (but not necessarily enjoyable).

FOR EXPERTS
One of the world's great areas

St Anton vies with Chamonix, Val-d'Isère and a handful of others for the affections of experts. It has some of the most consistently challenging and extensive slopes in the world. The jewel in the crown is the variety of off-piste in the bowls beneath the Valluga – see feature panel below.

Lower down, very difficult trails lead off in almost every direction from the Galzig summit. Osthang is an extremely tough, long mogul field that leads down to Feldherrn Hügel. Not much less challenging are trails down to Steissbachtal, St Christoph and past Maiensee towards the road. These lower runs can be doubly tricky if the snow has been hit by the sun.

The Kandahar Men's Downhill course is a long run between Gampen and town. There are countless opportunities for going off-piste in the Kapall–Gampen area, including the beautiful Schöngraben unmarked route to Nasserein.

The Rendl area across the road has plenty of open space beneath the top

lifts and, with an accompanying guide, there is some delightful fun to be had off the back of this ridge.

The Albona mountain above Stuben has north-facing slopes that hold good powder and some wonderful, deserted off-piste descents including beautifully long runs to Langen (where you can catch the train) and back to St Anton.

On top of all this, bear in mind that many of the red runs on the piste map are long and challenging too.

The ultimate challenge, though, is perhaps to go with a guide off the back of the third stage of the Valluga. The initial pitch is very, very steep. But once you have negotiated that, the run down to Zürs is very beautiful and usually deserted.

FOR INTERMEDIATES
Some real challenges

St Anton is well suited to good, adventurous intermediates. They will be able to try the Mattun run from Vallugagrat (see below). The red run from Schindler Spitze to Rauz is very long, tiring, varied (over 1000m vertical) and ideal for good (and fit) intermediates. Alternatively, turn off from this part-way down and take the – usually crowded – Steissbachtal to the lifts back to Galzig.

The Kapall–Gampen section is also interesting, with sporty bumps among trees on the lower half. From Kapall to town (over 1000m vertical), keeping to the left of the Kandahar funicular and ending up on a run called Fang is fun.

Less adventurous intermediates will find St Anton less to their taste. There are few easy cruising pistes. The most obvious are the blues from Galzig.

THE VALLUGA RUNS

The off-piste runs in the huge bowl beneath the summit of the Valluga, and reached by either the Schindlergrat chair or the second stage of the Valluga cable-car, are justifiably world famous. In good snow, this whole area is an off-piste delight for experts.

Except immediately after a fresh snowfall, you can see tracks going all over the mountain – and some of the descents look terrifying. There are two main high-touring routes down marked on the piste map – both long, steep, often mogulled descents. The Schindlerkar gully is the first you come to, and the steeper. For the wider, somewhat easier Mattun run, you traverse over further at the top. Both these feed down into the Steissbachtal gully where there are lifts back up to Galzig. The Scweinströge starts off in the same direction as the red ski route, but you traverse the shoulder of the Schindler Spitze and down a narrow gully.

Our only reservation about this area is its sunny aspect. The snow can deteriorate very rapidly after a snowfall and so ice and slush are too often encountered.

SCHOOLS/GUIDES

97/98 prices in schillings

Arlberg
Manager Richard Walter
Classes 6 days
4hr: 2hr am and pm, from 9.30
6 full days with guest card: 1,580
Children's classes
Ages: 4 to 14
6 full days with guest card and including lunch: 2,400
Private lessons
Half or full day
2,220 for full day; each additional person 170

St Anton
Manager Franz Klimmer
Classes 6 days
4½hr: 9.30am-noon and 1pm-3pm
6 full days with guest card: 1,520
Children's classes
Ages: 6 to 14
6 full days: 1,500
Private lessons
Half or full day
3,050 for full day; each additional person 160

CHILDCARE

The kindergarten at the Jugendcenter (2526) takes toilet-trained children aged 30 months to 14 years, from 9am to 4.30. Ski tuition with the Arlberg ski school in a special snow-garden is available for children aged 4.

These are reasonably gentle but get very crowded, particularly at peak times. The blue to St Christoph, served by drag-lifts, is probably the best bet. The narrowish blues between Kapall and Gampen can have some challenging bumps. Intermediates looking for easy cruising will find the best by taking the bus to Lech.

In the Rendl area a variety of trails suitable for good and moderate intermediates criss-cross, including a lovely long tree-lined run (over 1000m vertical from the top) back to the valley gondola station. This is the best run in the whole area when visibility is poor, though it has some quite awkward sections.

FOR BEGINNERS
A lousy choice
St Anton has neither decent nursery slopes nor easy runs for beginners to progress to. Experts and intermediates who are desperate to visit the Arlberg but are taking novices on holiday would be better off staying in Lech or Zürs and taking the bus to Rauz when they want to try St Anton.

FOR CROSS-COUNTRY
A suitable valley
There are a couple of uninspiring trails near town in the valley, another at St Jakob 3km away, and a pretty trail through trees along the Verwalltal to the foot of the Albona area. There is also an insignificant little loop at St Christoph. Snow conditions are usually good, but St Anton is not really a cross-country resort. Total trails 40km.

QUEUES
Improved, but still a problem
Queues are not the problem they once were after the replacement of several bottleneck lifts by high-speed quads. But they can still be tiresome in peak season and at weekends – when up to 20 minutes is not unusual for some lifts. Several of our reporters have suggested abandoning the main lifts for other chairs and T-bars.

Perhaps worse than the queues in busy periods are the crowded trails that you'll encounter – we were there one March weekend where we had to continuously look all round before making a turn to make sure we didn't hit anyone; we could have done with wing mirrors.

MOUNTAIN RESTAURANTS
Plenty of choice
Look out for the little table-service huts, which have much more going for them than the characterless cafeterias. Two of the best are just above town, the Sennhütte and Rodelhütte. The Rendl Beach is also worth a visit. The Mooserwirt serves typical Austrian food, and the Krazy Kanguruh burgers, pizzas and snacks. The goulash soup at the Taps Bar next to Krazy Kanguruh has been recommended, and the Kaminstube gets beautiful sunset views.

Having lunch in St Christoph or Stuben is also a useful idea. The St Christoph choices include the excellent but expensive Hospiz Alm, where you can sit in a slide which delivers you to the lavatories, the good value Almbar just above it and Traxl's ice bar at the Maiensee Hotel. In Stuben reporters say that the views from the Albonagrathütte are worth the short walk to get to it, and that the Albona is quiet and friendly.

SCHOOLS AND GUIDES
Great for experts
The relatively new St Anton school has brought much-needed competition to the Arlberg school, which had slipped from its previously high standards during the 1980s. Nowadays both schools get good reports for tuition and standard of English spoken, though we had a lousy snowboard lesson here where an instructor took a class of beginners straight to a T-bar and then stood smoking and chatting to the lift attendant as we all tumbled around. Few schools are as well geared-up for teaching experts though.

Past reporters who have hired a guide to the off-piste at the top of the Valluga have had a great day.

FACILITIES FOR CHILDREN
Getting better
St Anton might not seem an obvious resort for family holidays, but there are no good reasons to avoid it if the area suits you. The resort works increasingly hard to accommodate families' needs: the youth centre attached to the Arlberg school is excellent, and the special slopes both for tots (at the bottom) and bigger infants (up at Gampen) are well done. Reports on these facilities would be very welcome.

Mark Warner has a chalet-hotel which has a crèche.

← Galzig ↑ Gampen

Nasserein

1 km

Oberdorf

St Jakob

ⓘ

↓ Rendl

GETTING THERE

Air Innsbruck, transfer 1¼hr. Zurich, transfer 3hr.

Rail Mainline station in resort.

Staying there 🔑

The village itself is fairly compact, but it's worth being careful about location. Staying near the main lifts has clear advantages, unless street noise disturbs you. Much accommodation 'in' St Anton is really in the quieter suburb of Nasserein, a short free bus-ride or 15-minute walk from the centre and the nightlife. It isn't too inconvenient for the slopes when there's resort-level snow. A drag-lift and short slide takes you to the main lifts, and you can get back to your door from Gampen.

St Anton spreads up the hill to the west of the centre, towards the Arlberg pass. Places up here in and beyond Oberdorf can be 20 minutes' walk from the centre – but quite convenient for the slopes, if snow-cover is good.

HOW TO GO
Austria's main chalet resort
There's a wide range of places to stay, from quality hotels to cheap and cheerful pensions and apartments. What sets St Anton apart from other

Not the Assistant Editor (Snowboarding), high above St Anton ↓

Austrian resorts for Brits is the number of chalets, which are fairly expensive, though few are particularly luxurious and many are well away from the centre up the hill or at Nasserein. There are chalets in the centre but they are virtually all apartment-based.

Hotels There is one 5-star hotel, lots of 4-stars and 3-stars and a great many cheaper B&Bs around the valley.

(((((5) **St Antoner Hof** Best in town, but its position on the bypass is less than ideal except for curling (the rink is opposite) and motoring. Pool.

((((4) **Schwarzer Adler** Centuries-old inn on main street. Widely varying bedrooms.

(((4) **Neue Post** Comfortable if uninspiring 4-star at the centre of affairs, close to both lifts and nightlife.

((((4) **Kertess** Charmingly furnished, slightly further up the hill (hotel shuttle to lifts). Pool.

((((4) **Sport** Good central position, with varied bedrooms, good food. Pool.

(((3) **Grischuna** Welcoming family-run place in peaceful position up the hill west of the town; close to the slopes, five minutes to the cable-car.

(((3) **Valluga** About the cheapest of the 3-stars, but rather on the edge of things on the bypass.

(((3) **Goldenes Kreuz** A comfortable B&B hotel half-way to Nasserein, well positioned for cruising home.

Self-catering There are plenty of apartments available but package deals are few and far between.

STAYING DOWN THE VALLEY
Nice and quiet
Beyond Nasserein is the more complete village of St Jakob. It's reached by pistes, but is dependent on the free shuttle-bus in the morning. The Brunnenhof is an attractive little hotel with a good rustic restaurant. The Gletscherblick and Pfeffermühle are well-run, friendly family hotels.

Pettneu is a quiet village further down the valley, with slopes that most suit beginners. It's best for drivers.

UK PACKAGES

Airtours, Austrian Holidays, Bladon Lines, Chalet World, Chalets 'Unlimited', Crystal, First Choice Ski, FlexiSki, Independent Ski Links, Inghams, Made to Measure, Mark Warner, Powder Byrne, Simply Ski, Ski Arrangements, Ski Club of GB, Ski Equipe, Ski Les Alpes, Ski Total, Ski Valkyrie, Ski-Val, St Anton Ski Company, Thomson, White Roc

Pettneu Crystal

ACTIVITIES

Indoor Swimming pool (also hotel pools open to the public, with sauna and massage), tennis, squash, bowling, museum, cinema in Vallugasaal
Outdoor 20km of cleared walks, natural skating rink (skating, curling), sleigh rides, tobogganing, paragliding

TOURIST OFFICE

Postcode A-6580
Tel +43 (5446) 22690
Fax 2532

EATING OUT
Mostly informal

You live fast and eat hard to make up for it in St Anton. Plain, filling fare is the norm, with numerous places such the Fuhrmannstube, Amalienstüberl, Trödlerstube and the Reselehof and Alt St Anton in Nasserein serving healthy portions of traditional Austrian home-cooking. The Bahnhof restaurant is said to be excellent value, especially for fondue. Dixies is the place for a lively American Western-style meal in modern surroundings and Bobo's serves good Mexican. A most atmospheric place for dinner is the wood-panelled museum, where as well as enjoying up-market food and wine, you can learn the history of the resort. And one reporter recommends an evening trip to the Rodel Alm above Nasserein. It may involve walking up to 30 minutes, but the traditional Austrian fare, beer, schnapps and toboggan run down make up for it. We're also told booking is essential.

APRES-SKI
Throbbing till late

Every form of informal fun is available from karaoke to late discos; from 'English' pub-style bars to local live bands. Sophisticates are less well provided for. The infamous Krazy Kanguruh remains popular at the end of the afternoon. But the Mooserwirt is even more so – live band, usually packed out, dancing on the beams in ski boots. Several reporters have enjoyed the live bands at the S'Gräbli, followed by a trip down the piste in the dark. The Underground bar has a great atmosphere and live music, but gets terribly full. The Hazienda is equally lively and popular, and the Piccadilly pub is good for those who want a home from home. Reporters enjoyed Scotty's atmosphere, and Kartouche for dancing. The Drop In throbs into the early hours. The Stanton in the centre of town is also popular. If you want to concentrate on drinking rather than dancing, Pub 37 is a bit quieter.

OFF THE SLOPES
Not very relaxing

St Anton is a sprawling resort, not especially attractive outside the centre, and with surprisingly little to offer off the slopes. Many of the most attractive mountain restaurants are not readily accessible by lift for pedestrians. The centre is lively with a fair selection of shops. Getting by bus to the other Arlberg resorts is easy but buses tend to run only early morning and late afternoon, making excursions a long day. Lech would arguably be a better, if pricier, base, with more to do off the slopes. St Anton's railway station does at least allow easy access to Innsbruck.

St Christoph 1780m

A small, exclusive collection of hotels, restaurants and bars right by the Arlberg Pass with drag-lifts and a chair-lift to the slopes. Good for a nice lunch. Expensive and deadly quiet to stay in. The most expensive hotel of all – the most expensive in the whole area – is the huge Arlberg-Hospiz.

Stuben 1410m

Stuben is an interesting alternative to St Anton, quite the opposite of the large, noisy resort. Dating back to the 13th century, it's a small unspoilt village where personal service and quiet friendliness are the order of the day. Modern developments are kept to a minimum. The only concessions to the new era are a few unobtrusive hotels, a school, two bars, a couple of banks and a few little shops. The old church and traditional buildings, usually snow-covered, make Stuben a really charming Alpine village.

The north-facing local slopes retain snow well, though the queue-free but slow village chair can be a cold ride. A quicker and warmer way to get to St Anton in the morning, if you have a car, is to drive down the road to Rauz. Lech and Zürs are nearby, accessed by infrequent but timetabled buses.

Stuben has sunny nursery slopes separate from the main slopes, but lack of progression runs make it unsuitable for beginners. Evenings are quiet, but several places have a pleasant atmosphere. Willie's Stubli is the most animated. Hotels Mondschein and Albona have bars with dance areas. The S'Murmele and Gasthof Berghaus bars are quieter. Most people stay here on half-board, but the Sport Café is a good-value pizza place for those in B&B. The charming old Post is a very comfortable 4-star renowned for its fine restaurant. Haus Erzberg is a good pension. Kolerhaus is a simple, inexpensive B&B.

Stuben doesn't offer much off the slopes except eating and drinking.

St Johann in Tirol 650m

Relax on easy runs with plenty of pit stops

WHAT IT COSTS

(((3)))

HOW IT RATES

The slopes
Snow	**
Extent	**
Experts	*
Intermediates	***
Beginners	***
Convenience	***
Queues	***
Restaurants	****

The rest
Scenery	***
Resort charm	***
Off-slope	***

What's new

A new lift pass is being introduced. The Kitzbüheler Alpenskipass will cover Ski Welt (Söll, Ellmau, Brixen etc) Kitzbühel, Alpbach, Schneewinkel (St Johann, Fieberbrunn, Steinplatte, Waidring etc) and Wildschönau (Niederau) – 760km of pistes and 262 lifts in total.

➕ Most accommodation reasonably close to lifts

➕ Slopes liberally endowed with restaurants

➕ Plenty of off-slope activities and things to do in the evening

➕ Easy to visit neighbouring resorts

➕ Highly regarded for both ski and snowboard schools

➕ Few Brits by Tirol standards

➕ Good snow record for height

➖ Very small area, with little to interest experts

➖ Busy town makes it unsuitable for families with small children

➖ Weekend crowds from Germany

➖ Can be especially busy when nearby resorts with less reliable snow are suffering

In some ways St Johann falls between two stools. Its slopes are small and predominantly easy. Yet it is a far from ideal choice for families and others who traditionally turn to the Tirol for 'small and friendly' resorts – the town is too busy to suit them. But with no fewer than 18 mountain restaurants, fairly convenient lifts and plenty of off-slope facilities, St Johann is a fine choice for leisurely part-timers who like to spend as much time pottering about having coffee and lunch as they do actually cruising the slopes.

St Johann also suits the most energetic of holiday-makers who want to tour around visiting surrounding resorts and have plenty of evening entertainment awaiting their return.

boarding *St Johann is home to some of the top boarders – see Schools and Guides section – and it has a half-pipe. But keen freeriders may find the small area limiting and want to visit other nearby resorts. For beginners and intermediates the slopes are suitably gentle and the top to bottom gondola and number of chair-lifts means drag-lifts are largely optional. Although boarders are in a minority, the nightlife is lively.*

The resort

St Johann is a sizeable town with a life other than as a resort. The compact centre is wedged between a railway track, main roads and converging rivers. It is fairly attractive and has some traditional character, with a main street full of old wooden chalet buildings. The 5-minute walk between central hotels and the lift involves picking your way through town traffic and clambering over railway tracks. But when you get there the main gondola does access the whole mountain.

St Johann has sprawling industrial and residential suburbs. Lifts at the hamlet of Eichenhof to the east are convenient for the slopes, but it's a trek along a busy road to the centre of town. Lifts also start from the separate village of Oberndorf, to the west.

MOUNTAIN FACTS
Altitude	670m-1700m
Lifts	18
Pistes	60km
Blue	41%
Red	47%
Black	12%
Artificial snow	7km

The mountain

St Johann's small local slopes are on the north-facing side of the Kitzbüheler Horn – the 'back' side of Kitzbühel's 'second' and smallest mountain. It would be easy to link the two resorts' slopes, but up-market Kitzbühel appears to have no desire to be joined to its poorer neighbour. That said, it's only a 10-minute car or train ride to Kitz. A new lift pass covers Kitzbühel and many other local resorts. And Leogang, Zell am See and Kaprun's glacier are all within reach.

THE SLOPES
Small and easy
The main access lift is a gondola which transports you to the top of the slopes at **Harschbichl** (1700m). From there, a choice of north-facing pistes lead back

LIFT PASSES

97/98 prices in schillings

St Johann lift pass
Covers all lifts and ski bus.

Beginners Points card, and half-day passes for nursery drags.

Main pass
1-day pass 345
6-day pass 1,740
(low season 1,570 – 10% off)

Children
Under 15: 6-day pass 970 (44% off)
Under 6: free pass

Short-term passes
Half-day, (morning pass valid till 12.30, afternoon pass valid from 12.30), 'late sleeper' pass from 11am, 'try out' pass from 2pm.

Alternative periods
5 in 6 days and 11 in 13 days.

Notes 6-day pass also covers Fieberbrunn, Steinplatte, Waidring and other small resorts.

Alternative passes
Kitzbüheler Alpen-Skipass covers 5 large ski areas – Schneewinkl (St Johann), Ski Region Kitzbühel, Skiwelt Wilder Kaiser, Bergbahnen Wildschönau and Alpbachtal (adult 6-day, 1,990).

ACTIVITIES

Indoor Swimming, sauna, steam baths, solarium, 2 indoor tennis halls, fitness centre, massage, bowling
Outdoor Artificial skating rink, curling, sleigh rides, floodlit toboggan run, 40km cleared paths, ballooning, sightseeing flights

---

through the trees towards town. Two chair-lifts and the mid-station of the gondola allow you to 'yo-yo' the upper part of the mountain. There are more chairs and drags lower down. The top-station and one of the chairs also access a sunnier sector of west-facing pistes that lead down to a car park just above the hamlet of Oberndorf, served by another chair.

None of the runs is particularly challenging and average intermediates could cover the whole area in a day.

SNOW RELIABILITY
Altitude problems
Lack of altitude is an obvious problem. But St Johann is on by far the snowier side of the Kitzbüheler Horn – its snow pocket location 'steals' some of Kitzbühel's snow. This, together with its largely north-facing slopes, means that St Johann often has better conditions than its famous neighbour (and the nearby Ski Welt). Snowmakers cover one piste from 1400m to town, with both red off-shoots to the valley chair also endowed.

Several nearby resorts, such as Waidring's Steinplatte, are fairly snowsure if St Johann is suffering. The glacier at Kaprun has guaranteed snow but gets very crowded when snow is scarce elsewhere. The Hintertux glacier and Obertauern are worth an hour's drive at such times.

FOR EXPERTS
Totally unsuitable
There is nothing here to challenge an expert. The long black run on the piste map is really a moderate red – and is often closed because of the effects of the strong afternoon sun. Your best hope would be a solid week of snow, so you can practice powder technique.

FOR INTERMEDIATES
A small amount for all
The slopes are pleasantly varied, with something for everyone. Decent intermediates have a fairly direct-running piste between Harschbichl and town (runs 1b and 2b), and the black mentioned above. There are some easier red runs, but the best of them (3a and 4b) are served by long drags. The Penzing piste (6a) is served by a more comfortable chair. The less adventurous have many options, with the long meandering run between the mid-station of the gondola and town completely covered by snowmakers.

FOR BEGINNERS
Good when snow is abundant
The main nursery slopes are excellent but have no snowmakers. The slopes served by the second stage of the chair out of town have much more reliable snow and suit beginners with some dry slope experience. Near-beginners and fast learners have a fine easy run (2a) from the mid-station of the gondola back to the bottom.

CROSS-COUNTRY
Excellent valley trails
Given good snow St Johann is one of the best cross-country resorts in Austria. A wide variety of trails totalling 74km fan out from the cross-country centre beyond the main road.

QUEUES
Good except when 'invaded'
Queues are relatively rare except at weekends, during 'Fasching' week (mid-February) and any time Kitzbühel is struggling for snow, when the gondola can get long morning queues. The second stage of the Eichenhof drag will also get queues. But pistes becoming crowded is a bigger worry.

MOUNTAIN RESTAURANTS
Amazing array
With 18 restaurants spread over just 60km of piste, St Johann must have the densest array of huts of any sizeable resort in Europe. Needless to say, most are pleasantly uncrowded and competitively priced. None is worthy of special mention, but many are very welcoming.

SCHOOLS AND GUIDES
Good attitude
The St Johann and Eichenhof schools have a good reputation for English, tuition and friendliness, though large classes can be disappointing.

The snowboard section, 'White Wave', has its own half-pipe. (Three world-class performers are based here.) There's a large cross-country set-up and off-piste guides are available.

FACILITIES FOR CHILDREN
Good resort and hotel amenities
St Johann is keen to attract families and has first-class facilities for children. The village nursery, geared to the needs of workers rather than visitors, offers exceptionally long hours. We have no recent reports of how this all works in practice.

GETTING THERE

Air Salzburg, transfer 1½hr. Munich, transfer 2hr. Innsbruck, transfer 2hr.

Rail Mainline station in resort.

UK PACKAGES

Crystal, PGL Ski Europe, Ski Choice, Ski Club Europe, Thomson

Kirchdorf Crystal, Snowcoach

Oberndorf Lagrange

Waidring Thomson

Staying there

Most accommodation is central, but hotels beyond the railway track close to the lifts are best for the slopes. There is plenty of parking here and traffic noise is negligible. The railway is not far away, but not a problem. Cross-country skiers are better placed for their trails at the other side of town.

HOW TO GO
Plenty of hotel packages
British tour operators concentrate on hotels plus a few pensions but there are numerous apartments available.
Hotels All hotels are 3- or 4-star. The 4-stars are best-placed for the slopes. There are dozens of B&B pensions.
Brückenwirt Smartest in town, but wrong side for the slopes.
Fischer Central family-run 3-star.

1 km

Harschbichl

Goldener Löwe Vast, central 200-bed 3-star. It has widely differing rooms, the simplest offering excellent value.
Post House 13th century inn on the main street.
Park Comfortable 4-star right next to gondola and school. 'Excellent.'
Sporthotel Austria Ditto, with more amenities, including a pool.
Moser Much smaller, cosier main-street hotel in the same price range as the Löwe's cheaper rooms.
Kaiserblick A modest B&B in a quiet spot, yet close to amenities.
Self-catering The Alpenblick (expensive), Gratterer (mid-range) and Helfereich (very cheap) are some of the best-situated apartments.

EATING OUT
Large range of options
The restaurants stick mostly to good old-fashioned Austrian cooking. The Huber-Bräu is a working brewery where you taste local beers before moving on to good food. The Bären, hotels Post and Park, plus the Rettenbachstuberl specialise in tasty Tirolean dishes. The Lemberg, Lowengrill and the Crystal and Fischer hotels serve international cuisine as well as Austrian fare. For a special meal, locals have assured us the Ambiente is a fine establishment. Non-Austrian places recommended by locals are the Rialto for pizza, and the Hasianco for Mexican and pizza.

APRES-SKI
Plenty for all tastes
Ice bars and tea dancing greet you as you come off the slopes, and St

Kitzbuheler Horn
2000m

Harschbichl
1700m

Jodlalm
1500m

Bergstation Penzing
1465m

Eichenhof

St Johann in Tirol
650m

Ob

SCHOOLS/GUIDES

97/98 prices in schillings

St Johann
Manager Ulli Arpe
Classes 6 days
4hr: 10am-noon and
1.30-3.30
6 full days: 1,390
Children's classes
Ages: from 4
6 full days including
lunch: 1,950
Private lessons
Hourly, half- or full
day
450 for 1hr, for 1 to 2
people; each
additional person 110

Eichenhof
Manager Hermann
Leitner
Classes 6 days
4hr: 10am-noon and
1.30-3.30
6 full days: 1,350
Children's classes
Ages: from 4
6 full days including
lunch: 1,910
Private lessons
Hourly or full day
460 for 1hr, for 1 to 2
people; each
additional person 110

CHILDCARE

Both ski schools have
special areas for
children aged 4 or
more to take lessons,
and can provide
lunchtime care. The
St Johann school's
kindergarten takes
younger children from
9.30 to 4pm. It has a
fairytale playground
and a special
Dwarfs' Express
snowmobile lift.

The Eichenhof ski
school cares for
children under 4
years.

There's a free
children's party at
Café Rainer in the
resort centre every
Friday afternoon.

TOURIST OFFICE

Postcode A-6380
Tel +43 (5352) 62218
Fax 65200

Johann is lively without the rowdiness of some neighbouring Tirolean resorts.

Café Max ice bar, at the bottom of the main piste, has friendly service, music and a large umbrella. Popular Bunny's offers live music, as does Café Rainer. De Klomp is popular with locals, rustic, friendly and good for a quiet drink. Platzl is a comfortable late night bar with excellent service. La Scala and Die Firma are disco bars, and Pub Max a teenage video bar.

Tour reps organise sleigh-rides, tobogganing and Tirolean and nine-pin skittles evenings. The resort also puts on a show most evenings, ranging from snowboarding demonstrations and glühwein to festival hall concerts.

OFF THE SLOPES
A very good choice
There is plenty on offer, including an excellent public pool, indoor tennis, an artificial ice-rink and 40km of cleared walks. There is also more worthwhile shopping in St Johann than is usual in a winter resort. Train excursions to Salzburg, Innsbruck, and to a lesser extent Kitzbühel, are interesting.

Waidring 780m
The nursery slopes are right in the centre of this quiet, unspoilt, friendly Tirolean village, making it ideal for beginners. Also, the school has a reputation for good spoken English and enjoyable lessons. Beginners spend most of the week in the nursery area before graduating to the main slopes, the Steinplatte (10 minutes away by bus). Waidring has a good snow record for its height, and the slopes suit near novices and timid intermediates. Buses go to St Johann and Fieberbrunn (both on the area lift pass) and to Ellmau and Kirchberg. Cross-country skiers have 30km of trails. The ski kindergarten is open all day and baby-sitting can be arranged for young ones.

The area is wonderfully uncrowded on weekdays, and two fast quad chairs ensure minimal queueing even at weekends. Mountain restaurants are pleasant. Try the Stellenalm on the piste back to the car park. Cafés Schneidermann and Weinstube are good for lunch in the village.

The Waidringerhof is a central 4-star hotel with a pool. The Tiroler Adler is good value; Gasthof Brücke is popular for good food, value and friendliness. Nightlife centres around such events as

sleigh rides, tobogganing and an instructors' ball. The Keller Bar of hotel Post is good for a quiet drink, and Café Schneidermann has a civilised atmosphere.

Kirchdorf 640m
Kirchdorf is very similar to Waidring – quiet and traditional, with handy nursery slopes. It's five minutes by bus from St Johann, 20 from the Steinplatte, and a weekly pass includes a day in Kitzbühel. Kirchdorf also has a day-care centre that accepts children as young as three months. Both this and the ski kindergarten are open all day. There's a specialist cross-country ski school and 80km of trails.

Après-ski is livelier than in Waidring, with several bars and a good disco at the Wintersteller. For eating try the Gasthof Zur Mauth, Zehenthof and Giovanni's. The 3-star Wintersteller is one of the best hotels. The Tasma has leisure facilities and a bar with open fire. Gasthof Oberhabachhof is simple but handy for the slopes. Gasthof Marienstetten is poorly positioned but has a children's playground.

This must be the only slope in St Johann with no restaurant in view ↓

Schladming
745m

Pretty old town with good, if fragmented, intermediate slopes

HOW IT RATES

The slopes

Snow	***
Extent	***
Experts	**
Intermediates	****
Beginners	****
Convenience	**
Queues	****
Restaurants	****

The rest

Scenery	***
Resort charm	****
Off-slope	****

⊕ The different mountains add up to extensive slopes by Austrian standards

⊕ Charming town with a life independent of tourism

⊕ Excellent nursery slopes

⊕ Very short airport transfer

⊕ Excellent snowmaking operation and superb piste maintenance

⊕ Very sheltered slopes, among trees

⊕ Close to snowsure Obertauern and Dachstein glacier

⊖ Unconnected slopes are individually small, and buses between them infrequent

⊖ Nursery slopes (at Rohrmoos) are inconvenient unless you stay beside them – and beginners are expected to pay for a full lift pass

⊖ Little for experts

⊖ The slopes lack variety – one mountain is much like the others

To link or not to link, that is the question. Schladming gets rave reviews from most of its customers, in most respects – not least for its uncommercialised, pretty town centre. One constant whinge is the as yet unconnected mountains. But it may be this very inconvenience that keeps Schladming pleasantly unspoilt and uncrowded. If and when the projected linking lifts are put in place, Schladming will have a total area to rival those of Kitzbühel and Söll in the Tirol; but it may also come to suffer the same overcrowding and vulgarity.

Meanwhile, Schladming has another major plus-point. Its huge early investment in snowmakers stands in stark contrast to the belated efforts of its Tirolean competitors to give holiday-makers something other than grass, slush and ice.

What's new

The first-rate snowboard fun-park and boarder-cross slope was new in 1996/97.

There seems to be little progress on the long-mooted idea of linking the separate mountains by lifts.

boarding *Schladming makes a good destination for most boarders, as it has good facilities and a diverse nightlife. Most lifts on the spread-out mountains are gondolas or chairs, with some short drags around. The central mountain of Planai has an excellent fun-park and half-pipe, and the specialist school Blue Tomato is run by former European and six-times Austrian champion snowboarder, Gerfried Schuller. The area is ideal for beginners and intermediates, though there is little to draw the expert boarder bar the between-the-trees powder.*

The resort

The old town of Schladming has developed both slopes and industry without spoiling its charming centre. The woodyard, brewery and railway station are separated from town by a river, and the main road bypasses the town. The modern sports centre, tennis halls and Sporthotel, plus lift stations are on the outskirts. The main gondola to Planai starts close to the centre, but the suburb of Rohrmoos, where chair-lifts access the slopes of Hochwurzen is a drive out of town, as are Haus and Pichl, access for two more areas.

Most shops, restaurants and bars (and some appealing hotels) are gathered around the traffic-free main square, which is prettily lit at night.

The mountains

All four of the local hills have been developed for skiing and boarding. Most pistes are on the wooded north-facing slopes that line the main valley, with some going into the side valleys at higher altitudes. The runs are consistently easy reds, ideal for the intermediate majority.

Your lift pass includes a fifth area at Galsterbergalm, above Pruggern, and other small areas at Stoderzinken, Ramsau and the Dachstein glacier. The glacier is a 45-minute bus-ride, and has only a handful of runs, but the views are superb. The Top Tauern pass also covers other resorts such as St Johann im Pongau, Flachau and snowsure Obertauern

MOUNTAIN FACTS

Altitude	745m-2015m
Lifts	86
Pistes	152km
Blue	29%
Red	61%
Black	10%
Artificial snow	48km

LIFT PASSES

97/98 prices in schillings

Skiparadies Dachstein-Tauern
Covers all lifts in the Dachstein/Tauern region and ski bus.

Main pass
1-day pass 385
6-day pass 1,890
(low season 1,760 – 7% off)

Children
Under 15: 6-day pass 1,040 (45% off)
Under 5: free pass

Short-term passes
Half-day from 11am, noon and 1.30, 'trial' ticket valid for 2½hr.

Alternative periods
1½- and 2½-day passes.

Notes Discounts for groups, families and senior citizens on request.

Alternative passes
Day passes for Ramsau/Dachstein (excluding the glacier), Galsterbergalm and Stoderzinken ski areas only; Top-Tauern Skicard covers Dachstein/Tauern, Obertauern, Lungau and Sportwelt Amadé.

THE SLOPES
Series of poorly connected sectors

Planai, Reiteralm and Hauser Kaibling are the main sectors; Hochwurzen has fewer runs, but Rohrmoos, at its foot, has valley-level nursery slopes.

The gondola to **Planai** is on the east edge of town. There is a little open section at the top, but most runs are through forest. One run branches towards Rohrmoos at the foot of **Hochwurzen**, but you have to get a lift down (and up) to complete the link. A two-stage chair rises above Rohrmoos to a cable-car for the upper slopes.

Hauser Kaibling, a bus-ride away, is accessed by a gondola and a small cable-car from either side of Haus village. A small open section at the top has the only real off-piste in the area.

Rieteralm lies beyond Hochwurzen; it is accessed by a chair from Pichl, or the Gleiming gondola.

A recent reporter comments that timetables for the buses linking the mountains can be confusing, and not all buses are free with your lift pass.

SNOW RELIABILITY
Excellent in cold weather

Schladming's impressive snowmaking operation makes it a particularly good choice for early holidays; for late holidays it doesn't have the required altitude, but the northerly orientation of the slopes and superb maintenance help keep the slopes in good shape longer here than in some neighbouring resorts. The run to Pichl is the only valley run in the area without full artificial snow cover – very impressive.

FOR EXPERTS
Strictly intermediate stuff

Schladming's status as a World Cup downhill venue doesn't make it macho. The slopes are almost all gentle, the steep finish to the Men's Downhill course being an exception, and the moderate mogul slopes at the top of Planai another. Hauser Kaibling's off-piste can be good, but it's rather limited. Excellent piste grooming and quiet slopes at off-peak times allow you to get up some speed – the Women's World Cup run is great fun.

FOR INTERMEDIATES
Generally flattering runs

The two World Cup pistes, and the red that runs parallel to the Haus Downhill course, are ideal for fast intermediates. The open sections at the top of Planai

and Hauser Kaibling also have some challenging slopes. Moderate cruisers have the whole area at their disposal. Many concentrate on Planai, but Reiteralm has some of the best runs. Hauser Kaibling is the best mountain for the more timid, with a lovely meandering blue running from top to bottom and a quiet, easy little section with good snow at the summit. Runs are well-bashed, so intermediates will find the slopes generally flattering.

FOR BEGINNERS
Good, particularly for improvers

Complete beginners start on the extensive, but inconvenient and low-altitude Rohrmoos nursery area – and they are expected to pay for a full lift pass. Another novice area near the top of Planai is more convenient for most people and has better snow.

FOR CROSS-COUNTRY
Extensive network of trails

Given sufficient snow-cover there are 250km of trails in the area. Schladming has loops along the main valley floor, beyond the the Alpine slopes, to Moosheim and Mandling respectively. The Untertal and Obertal valleys, between Planai and Hochwurzen, have more trails. Further afield there are more snowsure trails at Stoderzinken, and the Dachstein glacier has small loops with spectacular views. The 1999 World Cross-country Championships are being held at Ramsau, a 20-minute bus-ride from Schladming.

QUEUES
One or two bottlenecks

The Planai gondola can suffer delays on peak-season mornings. The main Haus lift also experiences short queues at such times. However, there are few other problems. Surprisingly, given its proximity to less snowsure resorts, Schladming does not suffer too badly from invasions when conditions are generally poor. Those in search of snow tend to go higher.

MOUNTAIN RESTAURANTS
Plenty of nice places

There are attractive restaurants in all sectors, though Planai probably has the edge – Mitterhaus at the extremity of the piste system is particularly pleasant, Onkel Willy's is popular for its live music, open fire, indoor nooks and crannies and large terrace, and the Schladmingerhütte at the top of the

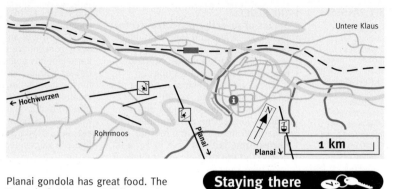

SCHOOLS/GUIDES

96/97 prices in schillings

WM Schladming
Classes 5 days
4hr: 2hr am and pm
5 full days: 1,400
Children's classes
Ages: from 4
5 full days including lunch: 2,000
Private lessons
1hr, 2hr or 4hr
500 for 1hr; each additional person 200

Schladming-Rohrmoos/Tritscher
Classes 5 days
4½hr: 10am-noon and 1.30-4pm
5 full days: 1,400
Children's classes
Ages: 4 to 14
5 full days including lunch: 2,000
Private lessons
1hr (between normal course times), half-day or full day
500 for 1hr; each additional person 200

Snowboard School Dachstein Tauern
Classes 5 days
5 full days: 1,700
Children's classes
Ages: from 5
Private lessons
1hr or 4hr
450 for 1hr; each additional person 150

Planai gondola has great food. The Knapphof at Hauser Kaibling is also good, and has many racing mementos on show as it's owned by Helmut Höflehner's family. The Imbisstube is good for lunch if you're in Reiteralm.

SCHOOLS AND GUIDES
Satisfaction likely
There are two main schools, which have good reputations. Charly Kahr's WM Schladming school proudly claims local boy Arnold Schwarzenegger as a regular client. Beginners at Rohrmoos should join the Tritscher school.

Snowboarders are well catered for by a specialist school. Ramsau is the best place to get cross-country tuition.

FACILITIES FOR CHILDREN
Rohrmoos is the place
The extensive gentle slopes that make up the suburb of Rohrmoos could have been designed to build up youngsters' confidence. Whether in the nursery or proper classes, this is where we would head with children. That's the theory; reports on the practice welcome.

Staying there

Much accommodation is central, but some hotels and most apartments are on the outskirts. Staying on the east fringe of town is handy for the Planai gondola. But the walk from central hotels to the lift is no great burden.

Rohrmoos has doorstep slopes for beginners, peace and quiet, plus good-value hotels. But there is little to do but hit the slopes in the daytime and drink in the evenings – Schladming is further away than tour operators using Rohrmoos would have you believe.

HOW TO GO
Packages means hotels
Packaged accommodation is in hotels and pensions, but there are plenty of apartments for independent travellers.
Hotels Most of the accommodation is in modestly priced pensions but there are also a few more upmarket hotels. Staying at the resort entrance, near the Planai and Rohrmoos chairs, is good value. The hotels here are cheaper than their centrally placed opposition.

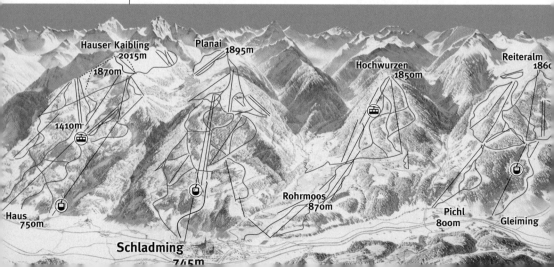

CHILDCARE

Ma Petite Ecole takes children aged 1 to 10, from 7am to 4pm.

At Rohrmoos, the Stocker nursery (61188) takes children from 18 months. There is also a Kinderwelt nursery (61301).

Children in ski school can be looked after from 9am to 5pm.

GETTING THERE

Air Salzburg, transfer 1½hr.

Rail Mainline station in resort.

UK PACKAGES

Crystal, Equity School Ski, Equity Total Ski, Made to Measure, Neilson, PGL Ski Europe, STS, Ski Club Europe

ACTIVITIES

Indoor Swimming, sauna, bowling, indoor tennis court, squash, museum
Outdoor Ice skating, curling, 6km toboggan run, sleigh rides, 50km of cleared paths in the Schladming and surrounding area, paragliding

TOURIST OFFICE

Postcode A-8970
Tel +43 (3687) 22268
Fax 24138

(((④ Sporthotel Royer Big, smart, comfortable multi-amenity place, on the outskirts but within walking distance of the main Planai lift.
((③ Alte Post Characterful old inn with best position in town – on the main square, a few minutes from gondola. Very good food, but some rooms are rather small by 4-star standards.
((③ Stadttor Similarly priced, although less charming and well placed, but with more creature comforts. Special deals for families.
((③ Neue Post Large rooms, good food, in centre of town.
((③ Schladmingerhof Bright, modern chalet in peaceful position, a bus-ride from centre in Untere Klaus.
Self-catering Ferienhaus Girik is the best-positioned apartment house in town, close to the gondola.

EATING OUT
Plenty of choice

There is a wide choice of informal places. The Kirchenwirt hotel restaurant has excellent home-cooking. Giovanni's does the best pizza. Others worth a visit are the Gasthof Brunner ('good value'), Talbackschenke ('good grills and atmosphere'), Vorstadtstub'n, Falbach and Lisi's. The Jaegerstubl in the hotel Neue Post is good, but more expensive, while the Alte Post is the best place for a blow-out meal.

APRES-SKI
Pleasantly animated

Après-ski in Schladming used to be quiet by Austrian standards, but seems to get livelier every year. It has its own brewery and brew pub.

Numerous cafés and bars have a jolly atmosphere immediately after the lifts close. The tea dance at the Touralm on Hochwurzen is great fun. Charley's Treff umbrella bar opposite the Planai is lively immediately after the slopes shut, as is the Siglu (in a big plastic igloo-like bubble).

Beizel is a smart, beautiful bar attracting a varied age group. Hangl Bar mostly attracts the over 30s with its wooden decor and middle of the road music – the back room has special nights such as karaoke and evergreen. The Pub has a nautical theme, loud music and a quiet room at the rear. La Porta is more sophisticated, while Raudis is a scruffy hard rock bar.

Our favourite bar was the Gondel Treff with an international football theme (lots of scarves draped around), big screen video for sports matches, a friendly teetotal host (Johann) and various gimmicks such as motorised lollipops and tequila mit worm – popular with locals and Dutch.

The Sondarbar is a central disco with a great DJ and three bars including a quieter one at the rear.

OFF THE SLOPES
Good for all but walkers

Those not looking for on-slope action should still find adequate diversions. Some mountain restaurants are easily reached on foot (though single gondola rides are very expensive). The town shops and museum are worth a look. Schladming has a railway station, making trips to beautiful Salzburg very easy. Buses run to the old walled town of Radstadt. For the more active, the public swimming pool and ice rink are supplemented by excellent sport facilities at Sporthotel Royer.

Haus 750m

Unlike Rohrmoos, Haus is a real village with a life of its own. It has a fair amount of accommodation plus its own schools and kindergartens.

The Hauser Kaibling lifts are a little out of town, but the user-friendly nursery area is more handily placed between town and gondola station.

Haus is a railway stop, so excursions are easy, but off-slopes activities are better in Schladming. The same could be said if you're looking for nightlife.

Hotel prices are generally lower here. The Gurtl is a small, friendly, excellent-value hotel with good food. The Hauser Kaibling is a good, more upmarket place.

Seefeld 1200m

Limited mountain with great off-slope facilities

WHAT IT COSTS

((③))

HOW IT RATES

The slopes

Snow	**
Extent	*
Experts	*
Intermediates	**
Beginners	*****
Convenience	*
Queues	***
Restaurants	***

The rest

Scenery	***
Resort charm	****
Off-slope	*****

MOUNTAIN FACTS

Altitude	1180m-2065m
Lifts	21
Pistes	25km
Blue	75%
Red	25%
Black	0%
Artificial snow	10km

What's new

A toboggan run from the Gschwandtkopf area, complete with lift and a hut at the top, should be ready for the 1997/98 season.

UK PACKAGES

Austrian Holidays, Crystal, First Choice Ski, Inghams, Made to Measure, Thomson

TOURIST OFFICE

Postcode A-6100
Tel +43 (5212) 2313
Fax 3355

Seefeld rates highly for cross-country, and is also one of the best mountain resorts for off-slope activities – particularly curling, skating and swimming. For downhillers there are literally hundreds of better resorts in this book.

THE RESORT

Seefeld is a classic post-war Tirolean tourist development: chalet-style and with the warm glow of wood skillfully applied to interiors and exteriors alike. It is very well designed and has a large pedestrian-only central sector that is prettily lit at night and very pleasant to stroll around. It attracts well-heeled Germans of (or approaching) pensionable age; these people can afford to go more or less where they like, so it is in a sense fashionable.

Seefeld sits on an elevated plateau, not far from Innsbruck, to which it is linked by rail. Ehrwald and Garmisch (over the border in Germany) are easy to reach, and car trips to the Stubai and Zugspitz glaciers are worthwhile.

THE MOUNTAINS

Seefeld's **slopes** consist of two main sectors, both on the outskirts and reached from most hotels by regular, free shuttle bus. Gschwandtkopf is a rounded hill with 300m of intermediate vertical down two main slopes. Rosshütte is a more extensive but still very limited area – **snowboarders** will find the fun-park and 100m half-pipe here. A funicular goes up to 1800m, and a cable-car then goes up to 2100m. There is one main slope, also served by three drags. Runs go down from Rosshütte into the adjacent Hermannstal, with return by chair or the funicular. From Rosshütte another cable-car goes to the shoulder of Härmelekopf at 2050m, whence there is an excellent red run to the village.

With reasonable altitudes by Austrian standards and a serious snowmaking installation in both main sectors, **snow reliability** is not a serious problem. But most of the slopes are sunny in the morning or afternoon, affecting snow quality – particularly on Rosshütte.

The Rosshütte sector has some genuine challenges for **experts** – seriously steep off-piste routes, with and without climbing. These are great for visitors popping out from Innsbruck

for the day, but no basis for a week-long holiday.

Only the most timid of **intermediates** should think of coming here. Gschwandtkopf is tiny, and Rosshütte is a two-run area.

This is an excellent resort for **beginners** – particularly those who are not dead set on becoming ace downhillers by the end of week one. The central village nursery slopes are broad and gentle; there is also a beginners' slope at Gschwandtkopf, but the slope and its lift get very busy.

The excellence of Seefeld's **cross-country** trails is one of the reasons why Innsbruck has been able to hold the Winter Olympics twice. More recently, the Nordic World Championships have been held here. It is one of Europe's best resorts for cross-country with 200km of trails.

Lift **queues** are rarely a problem.

Mountain restaurants are adequate, but many people lunch in the village.

Reports on the **ski school** say instruction and standard of English are good; **children** are cared for all day, and there's a non-ski kindergarten.

STAYING THERE

The upmarket nature of the resort shows in the range of **hotels**. There are seven 5-star places, and almost 30 4-stars. In 1997 we stayed at the 4-star Hiltpolt – very comfortable with good food (try to get a corner room with big semi-circular windows). Of the many pensions the Felseneck and Haus Kerber have been recommended.

Most **restaurants** are hotel-based. There's a lively **après-ski** scene; many bars have live music (Chris Barber's jazz band was on when we were there). Graham's Bar has been recommended for early evening music and happy hour. Four hotels have tea-dancing. There's a Casino.

Seefeld has great **off-slope facilities**. They are far too numerous to list, but include tennis courts, skating rinks and 40 curling lanes. The superb pool has areas for non-swimmers and children.

Serfaus 1430m

Attractive village with good-sized mountain

Serfaus offers the charm and nightlife of a typical Austrian village but with extensive slopes, fairly reliable snow and the huge benefit of being largely traffic-free. The resort deserves to be better known on the British market.

WHAT IT COSTS

((((4)

HOW IT RATES

The slopes

Snow	★★★
Extent	★★★
Experts	★★
Intermediates	★★★
Beginners	★★★★
Convenience	★★★
Queues	★★★
Restaurants	★★★

The rest

Scenery	★★★
Resort charm	★★★★
Off-slope	★★★

What's new

For 1997/98 two new high-speed chair lifts replace existing T-bars – a 6-seater to Plansegg and a 4-seater to Alpkopf.

MOUNTAIN FACTS

Altitude	1200m-2685m
Lifts	21
Pistes	80km
Blue	38%
Red	49%
Black	13%
Artificial snow	15km

UK PACKAGES

Made to Measure

Ladis Alpine Tours

TOURIST OFFICE

Postcode A-6534
Tel +43 (5476) 6239
Fax 6813

THE RESORT

Serfaus is attractive and friendly with chalet-style buildings. It is largely traffic-free, with a big car park on the outskirts and a unique underground railway from there to the lifts, stopping off in the village en route. Few hotels are too far from a station. This allows traditional charm to be preserved while reducing the effort of getting from one end of the long village to the slopes at the other end. A skating rink, sleighs and an old church add to the charm.

Most visitors are well-heeled Germans and Dutch, who give the numerous bars and cafés a jolly atmosphere. Serfaus has few British visitors, but deserves more. The sunny shelf setting adds to the attraction.

THE MOUNTAINS

Though its **slopes** aren't as impressive as at nearby Ischgl, Serfaus is a decent area, served by lifts less prone to wind and queues. The 80km of sunny pistes spread west from the resort. The area is long and thin and reaches a respectable 2685m. Most of it is above the tree line and served by drags.

The underground drops you at the main lifts, from where a gondola and cable-car take you to the mid-station. A second stage of the gondola rises to Lazid at 2350m. There are long reds from here to the village, and drags to the highest Mindersjoch sector.

There's the slopes of neighbouring Fiss to explore, too, linked in both directions. It's smaller than the Serfaus area, but is somewhat steeper. There is a **snowboard** fun-park at Komperdell.

The high average height, and snowmakers on four important pistes plus the children's nursery area, make Serfaus reasonably **snowsure**.

There are few challenging slopes for **experts**, on-or off-piste, but it is a good area for touring.

Good **intermediates** have a couple of short, steep runs between Lazid and the mid-station, while the most testing of the long runs is the pretty Alpkopf-village piste. Most of the area has ideal runs for average intermediates. The less experienced have wonderful long runs from Plansegg to the village, dropping gently almost 1000m vertical.

Both the village and mid-station nursery slopes are good, and there is ample opportunity for **beginners** to progress. The **schools and guides** have a good reputation but there have been complaints about standards of English.

The 60km of excellent **cross-country** includes very pretty trails at altitude.

The two new chairs for 1997/98 and the earlier replacement of the Lazid chair by a second-stage of gondola mean that mid-station **queues** are no longer large. The Scheid drag can be a bottleneck in the early morning.

The seven **mountain restaurants** are adequate for the size of the area. The Masiner, on Mindersjoch, is atmospheric, and has a good ice bar. Taking a trip down the cross-country trail from Alpkopf is well worth it for a quiet lunch at Rodelhütte.

Facilities for **children** are excellent. The crèche and ski kindergarten are open all day. Our one concern would be the lack of English-speaking children to play with.

STAYING THERE

Most accommodation is in comfortable chalet-style **hotels**. Hotel Löwen is a charming old hotel with a tasteful modern wing and lots of facilities. The Alte Schmeide is closest to the slopes. The Post is an attractive, central 3-star. There are plenty of centrally positioned pensions, too.

Restaurants are mainly hotel-based. Many hotels have a good 'farmer's buffet' once a week. Alte Serfaus is a jolly restaurant and bar. **Après-ski** is lively and traditional. Patschi's is the most popular of the dance bars. Four discos liven up late.

There is not much to do **off the slopes**, though some hotels have pools and sauna, and there are beautiful walks. Pedestrians can easily ride the gondola to meet friends for lunch and interesting car trips are possible.

Sölden
1380m

Fairly extensive, convenient area with throbbing nightlife

WHAT IT COSTS

((((4))))

HOW IT RATES

The slopes

Snow	****
Extent	***
Experts	**
Intermediates	****
Beginners	**
Convenience	***
Queues	**
Restaurants	***

The rest

Scenery	***
Resort charm	**
Off-slope	**

MOUNTAIN FACTS

Altitude	1380m-3060m
Lifts	32
Pistes	101km
Blue	42%
Red	44%
Black	14%
Artificial snow	10km
Recco detectors used	

UK PACKAGES

Crystal, Made to Measure

TOURIST OFFICE

Postcode A-6450
Tel +43 (5254) 22120
Fax 3131

Sölden is best suited to those who enjoy lively après-ski, challenging intermediate runs and reliable snow. The slopes are large and easy to get around, but don't expect Tirolean charm, or many tough or easy runs.

THE RESORT

Despite its traditional TIrolean-style buildings and tree-filled valley, Sölden is a large traffic-filled place which sprawls along both sides of a main road and river. It attracts a young, lively crowd – mostly Germans. If you're looking for quiet evening ambience, stay in Hochsölden.

THE MOUNTAINS

Sölden's **slopes** are made up of two similar-sized sectors separated by a small valley. A high-capacity two-stage gondola, at the southern edge of town, whisks you up to the top of the 3060m Gaislachkogl. From here you can reach Gaislachalm at the southern extremity of the slopes and Gampealm in its centre. From the latter a chair goes up to the slopes above Hochsölden – also reached via lifts at the northern end of the village. Both sectors have runs through trees to the village. There's a **snowboard** fun-park and half-pipe at Giggijoch and a half-pipe that's open in spring on the Rettenbach glacier.

Most of the area is over 2100m – a good height for Austria – so Sölden is fairly **snowsure**. Its two glaciers don't usually open in winter (the road there is prone to avalanches). But if spring is early, they are a useful fall-back.

Sölden has a reputation for being suitable for **experts**, though there is not much to challenge them. But there is a mountain guides' office in Sölden, and at the top of the valley is one of the Alps' premier touring areas.

Nearly all of Sölden's slopes are red runs for adventurous **intermediates**. There are several easy blacks, and the long, quiet piste down to Gaislachalm is ideal for speed freaks. Giggijoch and Rotkogl, above Hochsölden, are good if you prefer a more moderate pace, but Sölden is not really for timid types.

The **beginners** slopes are situated inconveniently – just above the village at Innerwald; and prone to poor snow. Near-beginners can start at the top of the Giggijoch gondola.

There are a couple of uninspiring

cross-country loops by the river, plus a small area at Zwieselstein. The one factor in Sölden's favour is altitude.

Thanks to the upgrading of its lifts, Sölden has few **queues**. But delays can still be lengthy when the resort is full.

The **mountain restaurants** tend to get very crowded and the quality of the food is nothing special. We like the two in the Gaislachalm area best.

In our few reports on the **ski schools**, Sölden is recommended for flexibilty in changing lessons and for private tuition. We've had no reports about Total Vacancia, which offers half-day tuition, or the new Öztal 2000. Phillippe Imhof runs snowboard camps.

There is no proper day-care nursery for **children**, and kindergartens keep rather short hours. Children old enough for lessons can be looked after all day.

STAYING THERE

The two main lifts are out at the edges of town so staying in the geographic centre is inconvenient. Most tour operators use Sölden's better **hotels**. The Central is the best and one of the biggest in town. The Granat is the best B&B hotel, well placed off the road. Self-catering **apartments** at the Posthausl are good quality. Cheaper and quieter are the Gerhard opposite the Innerwald chair. For peace and quiet, stay in Innerwald or Hochsölden.

For **eating out,** the good-value Café Hubertus does everything from snacks to full meals. The Nudeltopf and Café Corso vie for the title of 'best pizzas in town', and the Hotel Birkenhof's restaurant is pleasantly traditional.

If you want happening **après-ski** Sölden has numerous bars, live bands and discos. Every night there is a toboggan evening, with drinking and dancing before an exciting 6km run back to town from the Gaislachalm mountain restaurant.

Given Sölden's size there is little to do **off the slopes**. Trips to Innsbruck and Igls are possible. Mountain bikes are available and there is a sports centre, swimming pool and ice rink.

Söll

700m

Artificial snow saves the day – they hope

WHAT IT COSTS

(((3)))

HOW IT RATES

The slopes

Snow	*
Extent	****
Experts	*
Intermediates	****
Beginners	***
Convenience	**
Queues	***
Restaurants	**

The rest

Scenery	***
Resort charm	***
Off-slope	**

What's new

In 1996/97 two new four-seater chairs replaced drag-lifts, one speeding up the journey from Hochsöll to Hohe Salve, the highest point in the Ski-Welt. A beginners lift was extended.

And on-mountain helpers were introduced to advise guests on routes and control reckless skiing and boarding.

For 1997/98 artificial snowmaking in the Ski-Welt area is being doubled to cover 99km – making it the most extensive snowmaking system in Austria. And a new lift pass is being introduced. The Kitzbühheler Alpenskipass will cover Ski-Welt, Kitzbühel, Alpbach, Schneewinkel and Wildschönau, and will be valid for any six days over the season.

If you hit Söll with this much snow around, congratulations →

⊕ Extensive, pretty, easy-intermediate slopes

⊕ Short airport transfers and easy road access

⊕ Plenty of cheap and cheerful pensions for those on a budget

⊕ Improved lift system has reduced queues

⊕ Local slopes are the highest and steepest in the Ski-Welt area

⊖ Very poor recent snow record (but lots of snowmaking being installed)

⊖ Long walks or inefficient bus to the lifts from most accommodation

⊖ Little for experts

⊖ Local slopes are the most crowded in the Ski-Welt

⊖ Poor links to the most snowsure section of the Ski-Welt

⊖ Mostly short runs in local sector

Söll has had to overcome two horrendous reputations in recent years. In the 1980s it gained notoriety as prime lager-lout territory, rivalling Sauze d'Oulx for booze and fights. It cleaned up its act here, partly with the help of the strong Austrian schilling, which drove the budget boozers to new destinations such as Andorra. These days its pretty scenery and attractive traditional village attracts families more than hordes of singles.

Its other problem was snow – its low altitude, sunny slopes and a succession of poor snow years meant there was often a dearth of the white stuff. The slopes were too often slushy or bare, not just in Söll but also throughout the extensive Ski-Welt circuit it is part of. Söll is now tackling that problem big-time. For the 1997/98 season artificial snowmaking in the Ski-Welt will have doubled to cover an impressive 99km – more than in any other Austrian ski area.

What difference that makes in practice depends on how often it's cold enough to use the snow cannon. With good snow Söll can be a great place for a holiday cruising attractive and undemanding pistes. Let's hope the snowmaking is effective – more news in the next edition.

boarding *Söll is a good place to try out boarding: slopes are gentle and there are plenty of gondolas and chairs. For decent boarders it's more limited – the slopes of the Ski-Welt are tame, there are no half-pipes or fun parks and fresh powder is not the norm – but you can still have fun in the evening.*

MOUNTAIN FACTS

Altitude	620m-1830m
Lifts	90
Pistes	250km
Blue	37%
Red	53%
Black	10%
Artificial snow	50km

LIFT PASSES

97/98 prices in schillings
Ski-Welt Wilder Kaiser-Brixental
Covers all lifts in the Wilder Kaiser-Brixental area from Going to Westendorf, and the ski-bus.
Beginners Points tickets (100 points 280). Most beginner lifts cost from 5 to 10 points.
Main pass
1-day pass 360
6-day pass 1,745
Children
Under 16: 6-day pass 970 (44% off)
Under 6: free pass
Short-term passes
Single ascent on some lifts, half-day passes up to noon and from 11am, noon and 2pm to the end of the day.
Alternative periods
5 in 7 days, 7 in 10 days and 10 in 14 days.
Alternative passes
Hohe Salve pass available (1455 6-day pass for adults, 825 for children) covers Söll, Itter, Hopfgarten and Kelchau (30 lifts, 69km piste). Kitzbüheler Alpen-Skipass covers 5 large ski areas – Schneewinkl (St Johann), Ski Region Kitzbühel, Skiwelt Wilder Kaiser, Bergbahnen Wildschönau and Alpbachtal (adult 6-day, 1,990).

The resort

Söll is a small, friendly village, though development has left it feeling rather cramped. Everything (except the slopes) is to hand, and new buildings have a traditional design. The pretty scenery of the wide valley adds to Söll's charm, and it benefits from being off the main road through the Tirol.

Unfortunately the main gondola is a 15-minute walk from the centre across a busy road, and further from some accommodation. What's more, the shuttle bus service is poor. There is some accommodation near the lifts.

The mountains

The Ski-Welt may be the largest linked area in Austria, but that doesn't make it a Trois Vallées. It covers Hopfgarten, Brixen, Scheffau and Ellmau, but is basically a typically small, low, pastoral Austrian hill multiplied several times. One section is much like another, and most slopes best suit intermediates. Runs are short and scenery attractive rather than stunning – although the panoramic views from the Hohe Salve are impressive on a clear day.

Westendorf is separate, but covered by the area pass, and by the new and far-reaching Kitzbüheler Alpenskipass. The latter also covers many other resorts easily reached by car including Kitzbühel, Schneewinkel (includes St Johann, Fieberbrunn, Steinplatte, Waidring), Niederau and Alpbach – an impressive total of 262 lifts and 760km of pistes.

THE SLOPES
Short run network
A gondola takes all but complete beginners up to the shelf of Hochsöll, where there are a couple of short lifts and connections in several directions.

A two-stage chair rises to Rigi, from where you can head to Hopfgarten or Itter, or get a further chair to the high point of Hohe Salve – also accessed directly by chairs (including a new quad) from Hochsöll. Hohe Salve is the start of runs down to Kälbersalve – steep at first, and south-facing – and then on to Brixen, or up by chair to Zinsberg. You can access Eiberg, the Ski-Welt's most snowsure area, from the latter. This protracted route is tiresome and crowded when snow is in short supply; but a cable-car from

Hochsöll offers an alternative, cutting out the tricky Hohe Salve.

From Zinsberg you also access fun, long runs from Brandstadl to Blaiken.

SNOW RELIABILITY
More artificial help
With a very low average height, and important links that get a lot of sun, the Ski-Welt's poor snow record is a real weakness – one that it is trying to tackle by doubling its artificial snow capacity for the 1997/98 season. At 99km it will be Austria's biggest artificial snow installation. How much difference it makes in practice depends on temperatures being cold enough to use it effectively. At best, it could transform the attractiveness of the area. The best natural snow in the region tends to be in the Eiberg area.

FOR EXPERTS
Not a lot
The plunge straight off Hohe Salve towards Hochsöll and the black run alongside the Brixen gondola are the only challenging pistes. There are further blacks in Scheffau and Ellmau, but most experts will need to seek amusement off-piste – from Scheffau's Brandstadl down to Söll, for example.

FOR INTERMEDIATES
Something for everyone
The most direct of the runs between Brandstadl and Blaiken, the Hohe Salve red and the pistes down to Brixen suit good intermediates. Moderate cruisers have an enormous choice. With good snow, the lower woodland runs down to Söll, Hopfgarten and Itter are interesting slopes. The runs down to Ellmau are enjoyable, but it's a bit of a trek to get over there. Early intermediates have plenty of cruising terrain on the higher slopes between Hochbrixen and Brandstadl. The varied long runs from Zinsberg down to Brixen are good for groups of mixed abilities.

FOR BEGINNERS
OK when snow is good
The nursery slopes are between the main road and the gondola station, and are perfectly adequate when snow is abundant – gentle, spacious and uncrowded. In poor snow the Hochsöll area is used. Near-beginners and fast learners can get home to the bottom station when the meandering blue from Hochsöll is not too icy.

SCHOOLS/GUIDES

97/98 prices in schillings

Söll-Hochsöll
Manager Sepp Embacher
Classes 5 days
2hr or 4hr: 10am-noon and 2pm-4pm
5 full days: 1,290
Children's classes
Ages: 5 to 14
5 full days: 1,250
Private lessons
Hourly or full day (4hr)
460 for 1hr; each additional person 150

Austria
Manager Hans Wohlschlager
Classes 6 days
4hr: 10am-noon and 2pm-4pm
6 full days: 1,280
Children's classes
Ages: 5 to 14
6 full days: 1,220
Private lessons
Hourly or daily
460 for 1hr; each additional person 170

CHILDCARE

The ski schools take children from age 5, starting them off in special snow-gardens. The Söll-Hochsöll school's is next to Gasthof Eisenmann, on the nursery slopes; while based here, children can be looked after from 9.30 to 4.15. Once they progress to Hochsöll, care has to be arranged with the instructor.

Next to the main ski kindergarten, the same school now operates a Mini Club for children aged 3 to 5 – fun and games, with skiing available. It is open 6 days a week, 9.30 to 4.30.

FOR CROSS-COUNTRY
Neighbouring villages are better
Söll has 35km of local trails but they are less interesting than those between Hopfgarten and Kelchsau or the ones around and beyond Ellmau. Lack of snowcover is a big problem.

QUEUES
Much improved
Continued introduction of new lifts has greatly improved this once queue-prone area, most recently the new quad Hochsöll-Hohe Salve chair. The Blaiken gondola is to be avoided on weekend mornings. However, most delays are directly related to conditions: when snow is in short supply, the linking lifts to and from Zinsberg and Eiberg get busy.

MOUNTAIN RESTAURANTS
Good, but crowded
There are quite a few jolly little chalets dotted about, but those at Hochsöll, in particular, can get very busy. The otherwise pleasant Stockalm, Kraftalm and Grundalm are also prone to crowds. The Alpenrose, near the top of Hohe Salve, has a good sun terrace, generous portions and reasonable prices. Further afield the Neualm, half-way down to Blaiken, is one of the best huts in the Ski-Welt. The Jochstube at Eiberg is self-service but has a good atmosphere and excellent Tiroler Gröstl. The Filzalm above Brixen is a good place for a quick drink on the way back from the circuit – but don't miss the last lift connection.

SCHOOLS AND GUIDES
The usual reservations
The 'red' Austria school and the bigger Söll-Hochsöll school have fairly good reputations, though you may find classes over-large and poor spoken English. We have no recent reports, however. Söll-Hochsöll is more widely used by tour operators.

FACILITIES FOR CHILDREN
Fast becoming a family resort
Söll has fairly wide-ranging facilities – the Söll-Hochsöll ski kindergarten, a Mini Club, which looks after children aged 3 to 5 who don't want to spend all day on the slopes, and a special kids-only drag and slope on the opposite side of the village to the main lifts. Reports welcome.

There is some accommodation out near the lifts but most is in or around the village centre. Being on the edge of town nearest the lifts is the best for those who are prepared to walk to the slopes. The other side of town is better for those who prefer the bus, since you can board there before it gets too crowded. Be aware that some guest-houses are literally miles from the centre and lifts, and that the shuttle bus does not serve every nook and cranny of this sprawling community.

HOW TO GO
Mostly cheap, cheerful gasthofs
There is a wide choice of simple gasthofs, pensions and B&Bs, and an adequate amount of better-quality hotel accommodation – mainly 3-star. There are apartments, but Söll is not a big catered chalet resort.
Hotels
(((3) **Greil** The only 4-star – attractive place, but out of the centre on the wrong side for the lifts and pool.
(((3) **Postwirt** Attractive and central old 3-star that is a hub of the nightlife.
(((3) **Bergland** Small 3-star, well placed mid-way between the village and lifts.
(((3) **Theresa** Comfortable, 'superb' food, but a 10-minute walk out of the centre on the wrong side.
(((3) **Panorama** 3-star far from lifts but with own bus stop; wonderful views; pleasant rooms; best cakes around.
(((3) **Ingeborg** Next to the lifts.
((2) **Feldwebel** Central 2-star.
((2) **Schirast** Next to the lifts.
((2) **Garni-Tenne** B&B gasthof between centre and main road.
Self-catering The central Ferienhotel Schindlhaus has nice accommodation, though the best apartments in town are those attached to the Bergland hotel. There are many other options.

EATING OUT
A fair choice
Some of the best restaurants are in hotels. The Greil and Postwirt are good but the Schindlhaus is said to be the best. Hotel Alpenschloss, up the hill above Söll, is supposed to have a very good restaurant too. Café Einstein and the Brunhof cook excellent pizzas, while other places worth a visit include the Dorfstub'n, Venezia and Al Dente.

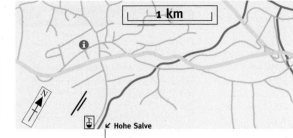

↙ Hohe Salve

APRES-SKI
Seen better (or worse) days
Söll is not as raucous as it used to be
but it's still lively. Pub 15 is a bit of a
sleazy remnant of the old days, but is
lively. Vis A Vis is a more pleasant,
civilised bar. The bar of the Postwirt
has a singalong and the Mirabell is a
quieter alternative for a convivial drink.
The Whisky Mühle is a large disco
which can get a little rowdy. The Klaus
is a smaller nightclub, with a friendlier
atmosphere. One fun evening activity
is the toboggan run from Hochsöll. And
for a romantic evening you can hire the
Gerhard Berger VIP gondola, complete
with leather upholstry, curtains and a
champagne bucket.

OFF THE SLOPES
Not bad for a small village
You could spend a happy day in the
wonderfully equipped Panoramabad:
taking a sauna, swimming, lounging
about. The baroque church would be
the pride of many tourist towns. There
are numerous coach excursions,
including trips to Salzburg, Innsbruck
and even Vipiteno over in Italy. Walks
are quite pretty.

GETTING THERE

Air Salzburg, transfer
2hr. Innsbruck,
transfer 1½hr.

Rail Wörgl (13km) or
Kufstein (15km); bus
to resort.

Hopfgarten 620m
Hopfgarten is an unspoilt, friendly and
traditional resort tucked away several
kilometres from the busy Wörgl road.
Most hotels are within five minutes'
walk of the queue-free chair that
accesses Rigi and Hohe Salve – the
high-point of the Ski-Welt. The resort's
great weakness is that you're unlikely
to be able to get home to 620m on the
south-west-facing slope – but there's
more artificial snow for 1997/98. The
village is a good size: small enough to
be intimate, large enough to have
plenty of off-slope amenities.

When snow allows, the runs down
to Hopfgarten and the nearby villages
of Brixen and Itter are some of the
best in the Ski-Welt. The fine, and
relatively snowsure, runs above
Scheffau are irksomely distant.

For a change of scene, and perhaps
less crowded pistes, take a bus to
Westendorf (see separate chapter) or
Kelchsau, both on the Ski-Welt pass.

There is a convenient beginner
slope in the village, but it is sunny as
well as low, so lack of snow-cover is
likely to mean excursions up the
mountain to the higher blue runs – at
the cost of a lift pass.

Hopfgarten is one of the best cross-
country bases in the area. There are
fine trails to Kelchsau (11km) and
Niederau (15km), and the Itter-Bocking
loop (15km) starts nearby.
Westendorf's trails are also close.

No large British tour operators go to
Hopfgarten, but all the Australians with
Contiki Travel mean English is widely
spoken in the two schools.

UK PACKAGES

Airtours, Crystal, First Choice Ski, Inghams, Neilson, Ski Club of GB, Ski Hillwood, Thomson

Brixen Alpine Tours

Hopfgarten Contiki

Cheap and cheerful gasthofs, pensions and little private B&Bs are the norm here. The exceptions are the comfortable but rather expensive hotel Hopfgarten and Sporthotel Fuchs, both well placed for the main lift. Also centrally placed, and better value, are numerous little gasthofs such as the Krone and Oberbräu. The Lukas is one of the best-positioned B&Bs.

Après-ski is generally quiet, though a lively holiday can usually be ensured if you go with Aussie-dominated Contiki Travel. Lift Stubl has a good tea-time atmosphere, while the Silver Bullet is the main rendezvous later. The Tirolean evening is popular. Though most of the restaurants are hotel-based, there are exceptions, including a Chinese and a pizzeria.

The village has off-slope amenities including swimming, riding, bowling, skating, tobogganing and parapenting. The railway makes trips to Salzburg, Innsbruck and Kitzbühel possible.

Hopfgarten is a family resort, providing a fine nursery in the hotel Hopfgarten which is open to non-residents. Children are taken from 3 years. The ski kindergarten takes them from 4, and staff are friendly.

Itter 700m

Itter is a tiny village half-way around the mountain between Söll and Hopfgarten, with nursery slopes close to hand and a gondola just outside the village into the Ski-Welt, via Hochsöll. A hotel, half a dozen gasthofs and a similar number of B&Bs provide accommodation. There's a school with hire shop, and when conditions are good this is a good beginner's resort.

Brixen 795m

Brixen im Thale is a very scattered roadside village at the south-east edge of the Ski-Welt, close to Westendorf. It may not be pretty, but it has a queue-free, high-capacity gondola and a chain of snowmakers on its main piste. This is some compensation for the inconvenience of the place: its main hotels are clustered around the railway station, a bus-ride from the lifts.

When snow-cover is good, Brixen has some of the best slopes in the Ski-Welt. All three pistes leading down to the lifts are fine runs in different ways: a black provides an interesting short cut from Hohe Salve; an unpisted route runs the length of the village gondola; and a much easier, prettier piste with

ACTIVITIES

Indoor Swimming, sauna, solarium, massage, bowling, squash
Outdoor Natural ice rink (skating, curling), sleigh rides, horse-riding, 3km floodlit toboggan run, para-gliding, hang-gliding

artificial snow leads home from Holzalm. An easy route home for the end of the day is a lovely long, away-from-the-lifts run finishing close to the village centre. There's also a very small area of north-facing runs, including the nursery slopes, on the other side of the village. A free bus runs to Westendorf every 45 minutes.

Brixen is a better base for experts than any other Ski-Welt resort. Two of the three runs to the village are challenging, and tend to be icy. The Hohe Salve black is another test.

Intermediates will find plenty to do, either trying the interesting runs down to Brixen, Itter and Hopfgarten, or going over to Scheffau.

The nursery slopes are across the valley at Kandleralm – an inconvenient bus-ride from the village. They are secluded and shady, but meeting up with friends for lunch is a hassle. At the top of the gondola is some of the best terrain for improving novices.

Brixen is one of the best cross-country villages in the Ski-Welt. There is a long trail to Kirchberg, and more leisurely loops that circumnavigate nearby Westendorf. A 5km loop up the mountain at Hochbrixen provides fine views and fairly reliable snow.

The surprisingly large ski school runs the usual group classes, and mini-group sessions for five to seven people. Lack of English-speaking tuition can be a problem.

Brixen has plenty of hotels. The multi-amenity 4-star Alpenhof and Sporthotel, and the cheaper 3-star Hetzenauer are in the nearest thing to a village centre, some way from the lifts. The 3-star Gasthof Brixnerwirt and the less expensive Mairwirt are better placed for the slopes, though still a lengthy walk from the gondola. Several little pensions are isolated near the lifts and so are very inexpensive.

Restaurants are mainly in hotels – the Sporthotel and Alpenhof have the best. The Loipenstub'n and Brixner Thalhof are less pricey, cosier places. Après-ski is quiet, but livelier Westendorf is a short taxi-ride away.

Off-slope activities include tennis, the sports facilities of the Alpenhof and Sporthotel and excursions to Salzburg, Innsbruck and Kitzbühel.

Brixen is not as suitable for children as other Ski-Welt resorts, but it does have an all-day ski kindergarten with optional lunch time supervision.

TOURIST OFFICE

Postcode A-6306
Tel +43 (5333) 5216
Fax 6180

Westendorf   800m

Lively, friendly resort with access to the Ski Welt

WHAT IT COSTS

HOW IT RATES

The slopes

Snow	**
Extent	*
Experts	*
Intermediates	**
Beginners	****
Convenience	***
Queues	****
Restaurants	***

The rest

Scenery	***
Resort charm	****
Off-slope	**

What's new

The amount of artificial snow in the resort has been almost doubled, to around 23km for the 1997/98 season.

MOUNTAIN FACTS

Altitude	800m-1865m
Lifts	14
Pistes	40km
Blue	38%
Red	62%
Black	0%
Artificial snow	23km

UK PACKAGES

Crystal, First Choice Ski, Inghams, Neilson, Thomson

TOURIST OFFICE

Postcode A-6363
Tel +43 (5334) 6230
Fax 2390

Westendorf is part of the Ski Welt pass-sharing arrangement (along with Söll, Ellmau, Brixen and others) but not on the main circuit. Its own slopes are not uninteresting (except to experts), and its friendliness wins many repeat visitors.

THE RESORT

The village is a compact Tirolean charmer, complete with attractive onion-domed church and sleighs. It attracts more Germans than Brits, and more Dutch than either.

THE MOUNTAINS

The local **slopes** form a small section of leisurely cruising. A two-stage gondola takes you to Talkaser (1760m), from where various north-west-facing runs go back to the resort. Short west- and east-facing pistes run below the two low peaks of Choralpe (1820m) and Fleiding (1890m), either side of Talkaser. A couple of red runs from Fleiding go down past the lifts to hamlets served by buses. There's a **snowboard** half-pipe. The main Ski Welt area is nearby at Brixen; there's a good bus service.

Westendorf's **snow reliability** is a bit better than some other Ski Welt resorts. And it is doubling its snowmaking facilities for the 1997/98 season – over half its pistes will now be covered.

Essentially Westendorf is far from suitable for **experts**, but some are happy pottering about off-piste. Leisurely **intermediates** have a fair number of pretty, uncrowded slopes. Most pistes are of blue difficulty, whatever their official grading.

Early intermediates and confident **beginners** have nice runs both between the mid-station and village, and alongside the Choralpe chair. The extensive nursery slopes are Westendorf's pride and joy.

There are 30 km of local **cross-country** trails. One links up with the Brixen route to Kirchberg. Snow-cover is a big problem.

Given good conditions, **queues** are rare except at Fasching, and far less of a problem than in the main Ski Welt area. If poor weather closes the upper lifts, queues do become long.

Of the **mountain restaurants,** Alpenrosenhütte is woody and warm, with good food; Brechhornhaus is

quiet; Gassnerhof is good but you have to catch a bus back to town.

The three **ski schools** have quite good reputations, though classes can be over-large and may cram English and Dutch together.

Westendorf sells itself as a family resort and amenities are good. Both the crèche and the ski kindergarten are open all day, but apparently close when demand tails off. Ski school takes **children** up to the age of 15.

STAYING THERE

Although the village is small, location is worth considering. Staying in the centre puts you close to the village nursery slopes, and a five-minute walk from the lifts to the main area, on the edge of the village. But staying on the other side of the village, further from the lifts, may be preferable to putting up with the church bells at 6am.

There are central 4-star **hotels** – the Jakobwirt and the 'excellent' Schermer – and a dozen 3-star ones, but most reporters stay in more modest guest-houses. Pension Wetti is popular and away from the church bells. Pension Ingeborg is highly recommended and next to the gondola. The Schermhof **apartments** are of good quality.

Most of the best **restaurants** are in hotels– the Schermer, Post Mesnerwirt and Jakobwirt are good. A taxi to Berggasthaus Stimlach is well worth it, as is the sleigh ride to the Almaheuf.

Nightlife is lively, but it's a small place with limited options. Kibo's Café is pleasant at tea-time. Hausberger has the best coffee and cakes. Gerry's is about the liveliest bar, and the Dutch meeting place. The new Wonderbar is great after dinner, with music and a mixed clientele. Also try In a Moment and the Mesnerkeller for live music. The discos liven up at weekends.

Off the slopes there are excursions by rail or bus to Innsbruck, Salzburg and Kitzbühel. Walks and sleigh rides are very pretty. The adventurous can try paragliding – or learn to speak German on the weekly course.

Zell am See 775m

Charming lakeside town, varied slopes and glacier option

WHAT IT COSTS
③

HOW IT RATES

The slopes
Snow	**
Extent	**
Experts	**
Intermediates	***
Beginners	***
Convenience	**
Queues	**
Restaurants	***

The rest
Scenery	***
Resort charm	***
Off-slope	****

What's new

The gondola from Schüttdorf now goes nearly all the way to the top of the mountain, to Breiteck, in three stages. And snowmakers have been installed all the way down the sunny piste back to Schüttdorf.

The new Schmittentunnel now takes through traffic underneath the town and has enormously reduced traffic problems.

MOUNTAIN FACTS

Altitude	760m-2000m
Lifts	60
Pistes	130km
Blue	38%
Red	50%
Black	12%
Artificial snow	9½km
Recco detectors used	

➕ Pretty, tree-lined slopes with great views down to the lake

➕ Lively, but not rowdy, nightlife

➕ Charming old town centre with beautiful lakeside setting

➕ Lots to do off the slopes

➕ Huge range of cross-country trails

➕ Kaprun glacier nearby

➕ Varied terrain including a couple of steep black runs

➖ Sunny, low slopes often have poor conditions despite snowmakers

➖ Trek to lifts from much accommodation, and sometimes crowded buses

➖ Less suitable for beginners than most small Austrian resorts

➖ The Kaprun glacier gets horrendous queues when it is most needed

Zell am See is an unusual resort – not a rustic village like most of its small Austrian competitors, but a lakeside town with a charming old centre that seems more geared to summer than winter visitors. It's a pleasant place – made more so by the opening of the tunnel taking the through traffic out of the main street.

Zell's slopes have a lot of variety and challenging terrain for a small area, but not enough to keep a keen intermediate or better happy for long. And the slopes are very sunny, making the snow rather unreliable. Though Zell is within easy reach of the Kaprun glacier so are many low-altitude resorts, all of which run buses there if snow is in short supply. The result can be horrendous queues.

Zell makes an attractive base for holiday-makers who enjoy travelling around. Having a car makes it easy to visit numerous other resorts – including Saalbach-Hinterglemm, Badgastein-Bad Hofgastein, Wagrain, Schladming and Obertauern.

boarding *Zell is well suited to boarders: the mountain above the town has a high proportion of chairs, gondolas and cable-cars and there's a good fun-park and half-pipe. There's also plenty of life in the evenings. Plus, the Kaprun glacier has a half-pipe and fun-park, with more powder in its wide, open bowl – but it also has a high proportion of drag-lifts.*

The resort

Zell am See is a long-established, year-round resort town set between a large lake and a mountain. Its charming, traffic-free medieval centre is on a flat promontory, and the resort has grown up around this attractive core. A gondola at the edge of town goes up one arm of the horseshoe-shaped mountain, but Zell's cable-cars are 2km away. Access by another gondola at Schüttdorf is 3km away. Most places to stay are a long walk from the town gondola. There is more accommodation out by the main cable-car station.

You can also stay in Schüttdorf. Some of the accommodation here is close to the gondola (which now goes directly to the highest part of the slopes), but the place is less appealing than Zell itself, especially for nightlife.

The mountains

Despite claims to the contrary, the extent of Zell's horseshoe of slopes is not large and the area is best suited to intermediates. Easier runs are along the ridge, with steeper pistes heading down into the centre. Kaprun's glacier slopes are only a few minutes by bus; Saalbach and Bad Hofgastein are easily reached by bus and train respectively and, at a push, Wagrain and Obertauern are car trips.

THE SLOPES
Varied but limited
The town gondola takes you to Mittelstation. From there it's either an easy or a steep run to the double cable-car station. Or, take a chair up to Hirschkogel, meeting the gondola up from Schüttdorf – which can then take

LIFT PASSES

97/98 prices in schillings

Europa-Sportregion Kaprun-Zell am See
Covers all lifts in Zell and Kaprun, and buses between them.
Beginners Points card or limited pass.

Main pass
1-day pass 400
6-day pass 1,970 (low season 1,820 – 8% off)

Senior citizens
Over 65 male, 60 female: 6-day pass 1,780 (10% off)

Children
Under 15: 6-day pass 1,180 (40% off)
Under 6: free pass

Short-term passes
Half-day pass from 11.30 for Zell only; reduces in price by the hour through the day.

Alternative periods
5 in 7 days and 10 in 14 days.

Notes Day pass vaild on Zell am See, Schmittenhöhe and Thumersbach only (33 lifts).

GETTING THERE

Air Salzburg, transfer 2hr. Munich, transfer 3hr.

Rail Station in resort.

CHILDCARE

All three ski schools take children from age 4 and offer lunchtime care. The Areitbahn school runs a snow kindergarten and play room for children from age 3, from 9am to 4.30. This is up at Areitalm (handy for Schüttdorf residents).

There are two village nurseries. Ursula Zink (56343) takes children from age 3, from 9.30 to 3.30; younger children looked after on an hourly basis. Feriendorf Hagleitner (57187) takes children from age 12 months, from 10am to 4pm.

you to a drag to the Schmittenhöhe top-station. This is also where the main valley floor cable-car brings you. A gentle cruise and a single short drag-lift moves you to Sonnkogel. Here several routes lead down to Sonnalm mid-station – the top of the other cable-car from the valley. A piste runs from here to the valley floor. At the end of the day you can take a gentle piste from the cable-cars back to town.

SNOW RELIABILITY
Increased artificial support
Zell am See's slopes get a lot of sun and the snow can suffer as a result. But except for the Sonnkogel-Sonnalm area, the lower slopes are now well-covered by snowmakers, which have recently been installed all down the sunny home run to Schüttdorf.

The Kaprun glacier is snowsure but suffers from horrendous queues when visitors are bussed in from lower, snowless resorts.

FOR EXPERTS
Two tremendous blacks
Zell has more steep slopes than most resorts this size, but can't entertain an expert for a week. All but one run back to the valley are black. When we were last there both black runs 1 and 2 were immaculately groomed each night. It was fabulous speeding down them – and they were deserted first thing.

Off-piste opportunities are limited.

FOR INTERMEDIATES
Bits and pieces for most grades
Good intermediates have a choice of fine, long runs, but this is not a place for high-mileage. All black pistes are within a brave intermediate's capability. There's a lovely cruising run between Areit and Schüttdorf when conditions are good. Some of Sonnkogel's pistes are also suitable. The timid can cruise the ridge all day or head past Mittelstation and on to Zell's cable-cars on an easy blue.

FOR BEGINNERS
Two low nursery areas
There are small nursery slopes at the cable-car area and at Schüttdorf, both covered by snowmakers. Near-beginners and fast learners have plenty of short, easy runs at Schmittenhöhe, Brieteckalm and Areitalm. Some are used by complete beginners when snow conditions are poor lower down, but it means buying a lift pass.

FOR CROSS-COUNTRY
Excellent if snow allows
The valley floor has extensive trails, including a superb area on the Kaprun golf course. Unfortunately, there is very little at altitude except a 2km loop at the top of the Zell gondola.

QUEUES
Not normally a problem
Zell am See doesn't have many problems except at peak times, when the Schmittenhöhe cable-cars are geneally the worst hit. The gondola from Schüttdorf was extended up to Breiteck for the 1996/97 season (with mid-stations at Mittelstation and Hirschkogel), reducing queues at Hirschkogel.

When snow is poor there are few daytime queues at Zell – many people are away queueing at Kaprun – but getting down by lift at the end of the day can involve delays.

MOUNTAIN RESTAURANTS
Plenty of little refuges
There are plenty of cosy, atmospheric huts. Among the best are Glocknerhaus (below Hirschkogel), Kettingalm, Areitalm, Pinzgauer and Brieteckalm. The Berghotel restaurant at Schmittenhöhe is good, but expensive. Its bar, with loud music, is lively. And the restaurant at the Schüttdorf gondola station is reported as 'very good, clean and with plenty of seating both inside and out'.

SCHOOLS AND GUIDES
A wide choice, with specialists
The number of schools in the area has doubled in the last few years – there are now six. We have no reports as to how this has affected the previously good teaching. One school specialises in snowboarding. There are also specialist cross-country centres at Schüttdorf and at Kaprun.

FACILITIES FOR CHILDREN
Schüttdorf's the place
We have no recent reports on the workings of the childcare provisions, but staying in Schüttdorf has the advantage of direct gondola access to the Areitalm snow-kindergarten, and fairly convenient access to one of the two village nurseries (Ursula Zink is at Zeller-Moos, just outside Schüttdorf).

UK PACKAGES

Airtours, Altours Ski, Bladon Lines, Crystal, Fairhand Holidays, First Choice Ski, Inghams, Lagrange, Neilson, On The Piste Travel Ltd, PGL Ski Europe, PGL Teenski, STS, Ski Choice, Ski Leogang, Thomson

Kaprun Airtours, Crystal, Inghams, Neilson

Schüttdorf Airtours

Staying there

Choice of location is tricky, and will depend on your priorities. Our three favourite strategies would be to stay: in a beautiful lakeside setting (which gets you on the shuttle bus before it's too crowded); at the upper edge of the town centre (walking distance from the Zell gondola); or near the cable-car stations at Sonnenalm.

Schüttdorf has easy access to the top of the mountain, but it is a characterless dormitory with little else

The view of Zell and its lake; and yes, there is skiing on the mountains beyond →

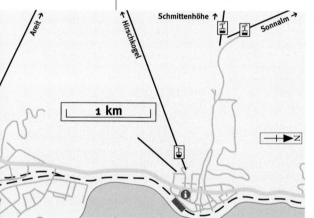

SCHOOLS/GUIDES

97/98 prices in schillings

Schmittenhöhe
Courses start Sunday and Monday
Classes 6 days
Full day: from 9.30
6 full days: 1,600
Children's classes
Ages: from 4
6 full days: 1,600
Private lessons
Hourly or daily
550 for 1hr; each additional person 100

Wallner-Prenner
Courses start Sunday and Monday
Classes 6 days
Full day: from 9.30
6 full days: 1,600
Children's classes
Ages: from 4
6 full days: 1,600
Private lessons
Hourly or daily
550 for 1hr; each additional person 100

Areitbahn
Courses start Sunday and Monday
Classes 6 days
Full day: from 9am to 4.30
6 full days: 1,600
Children's classes
Ages: from 4
6 full days: 1,600
Private lessons
Hourly or daily
550 for 1hr; each additional person 100

ACTIVITIES

Indoor Swimming, sauna, solarium, fitness centre, spa, tennis, squash, bowling, museum, art gallery, cinema, lessons in self-defence and judo, library, massage, ice skating
Outdoor Riding, skating, curling, floodlit toboggan runs, plane flights, sleigh rides, shooting range

TOURIST OFFICE

Postcode A-5700
Tel +43 (6542) 770
Fax 72032

going for it. Though closer to Kaprun this is, perversely, a drawback unless you have a car. Trying to get on a glacier bus is tough, as they tend to be full when they leave Zell. Families wishing to use the Areitalm nursery and cross-country skiers stand to gain most from staying in Schüttdorf.

HOW TO GO
Choose charm or convenience
There is a very wide range of hotels or pensions, and apartments, but tour operators have ignored the latter.
Hotels There's a broad range of hotels and guest-houses. 4-star hotels outnumber 3-stars.
(((④ **Salzburgerhof** Best in town – the only 5-star. Nearer lake than gondola, but has courtesy bus and pool.
(((④ **Tirolerhof** Excellent, friendly 4-star chalet in the old town. Good pool, jacuzzi, steam room – and food.
(((④ **Eichenhof** On the outskirts of town, but popular and with a minibus service, great food and lake views.
(((④ **Alpin** Modern 4-star chalet next to the Zell gondola.
(((④ **Zum Hirschen** Comfortable, 4-star, easy walk to gondola, sauna, steam, splash pool, popular bar.
(((④ **Schwebebahn** Attractive 4-star in secluded setting by cable-cars.
(((③ **Berner** 4-star by the Zell gondola.
((② **Hubertus** B&B near Zell gondola.
((② **Margarete** B&B next to cable-car.
Self-catering The budget Karger Christine apartments are near the Zell gondola. Apartment Hofer is mid-range and close to the Ebenberg lift (linking to the gondola). More comfortable are the 3-star Diana and Seilergasse (both in the old centre) and the Mirabell, which is close to the Zell gondola.

STAYING UP THE MOUNTAIN
Widely spread choices
As well as the big hotel at the top of the Schmittenhöhe cable-car, there are a couple of mountain restaurants with rooms. Breiteckalm is high up on the southern arm of the resort, Sonnalm is at the northern arm mid-station.

EATING OUT
Plenty of choice
Zell has more non-hotel places than is usual in a small Austrian resort. The Ampere is quiet and sophisticated; Guiseppe's is a popular Italian with excellent food; and Kupferkessel and Traubenstüberl both do wholesome regional dishes. There are Chinese

restaurants in Zell and Schüttdorf. Car drivers can try the good value Finkawirt, across the lake at Prielau, or the excellent Erlhof.

APRES-SKI
Plenty for all tastes
Après-ski is lively and varied. Tea-dances and high-calorie cafés are popular; and there are bars and discos a-plenty. When it's sunny Schnapps Hans ice bar outside the Berghotel at Schmittenhöhe really buzzes, with loud music, singing and dancing on the bar. The Diele disco bar rocks; Crazy Daisy on the main road has two crowded bars and Evergreen has a live band and 60s and 70s music. Viva disco allows no under 18s and advertised erotic shows on our visit. Other places include the smart Hirschkeller, the cave-like Lebzelter Keller and the Sportstuberl with old ski photos on the walls.

OFF THE SLOPES
Spoilt for choice
There is plenty to do in this year-round resort. The train trip to Salzburg is a must, Kitzbühel is also well worth a visit and Innsbruck is within reach.

You can often walk across the frozen lake to Thumersbach, plus there are good sports facilities, a motor museum, sleigh rides and flights.

Kaprun 785m
Kaprun is a spacious village with lots of Tirolean charm. There is a small area of slopes on the outskirts of the village, and a separate nursery area – both suited to early intermediates.

The glacier is a bus-ride away, and accessed by either an underground funicular or a gondola which is met by a quad chair. The main slopes are in a big bowl above. Pistes are mainly gentle blues and reds with one tougher run from the very top at 3029m. Snow is nearly always good and the area is one of the better summer glacier areas, as well as a winter fallback. The drawback is the queues, which can be appalling when crowds are bussed-in.

Off-slope activities are good, and include a fine sports centre. Nightlife is quiet, but the Baum, Yeti and Nindl bars are the liveliest. Good restaurants include the Dorfstadl, the Bella Musica and the Schlemmerstuberl. The Orgler, Mitteregger and Tauernhof are three of the best hotels. Good cheaper hotels include Abendruh and Heidi.

France

France has now overtaken Austria as the most popular destination for British skiers and snowboarders. And it is by far the most popular country with readers of this book. It's not difficult to see why: France has the biggest linked ski areas in the world; for keen piste-bashers who like to cover as many miles in a day as possible, these are unrivalled. Most of these big areas are also at high altitude, ensuring high-quality snow and good coverage for a long season – in marked contrast to the vast majority of Austrian resorts, for example. France has a mixture of some of the toughest, wildest slopes in the Alps, and some of the longest, gentlest and most convenient beginner runs. The French mountains take some beating. French resort villages can't be quite so uniformly recommended; but, equally, they don't all conform to the standard image of soulless, purpose-built resorts, thrown up without concern for appearance during the building boom of the 1960s and 70s.

And this season, France has another big plus point going for it – British visitors will all find it astonishingly cheaper because of the rise in the pound against the franc. After several years of a falling pound, France was in serious danger of becoming unaffordable, just as Switzerland had become. Prices were becoming an important issue in reader reports. If exchange rates stay as they were when we went to press, that danger has now been averted. Beers which cost £4 a pint last season will cost only £3 in the winter of 1997/98 – we'll drink to that!

Of course the other Alpine countries have become cheaper for British visitors too. And, indeed, as our analysis of costs in the earlier chapter shows, French resorts head the costs league table; comparable standards of accommodation in France generally cost more than they do in Switzerland. So, while France remains expensive in relative terms, it has, thankfully, become more affordable again for British visitors. That means that we will continue to go there in big numbers. And the main way of making France even more affordable is to take a chalet holiday, as our earlier chapter showed. France is home to more catered chalets run by British tour operators than any other country – and by a very large margin. And the chalets on offer range from budget to luxury. Whichever end of the price scale you opt for, you can be sure you are getting a good deal compared with a hotel of the same standard.

Château d'Oex • Gstaad • Adelboden
Lenk
Leysin • Leukerbad
THONON • Les Diablerets Crans-Montana
La Chapelle- Villars Anzère SIERRE VISP
d'Abondance Morgins SION
GENEVA Châtel SWITZERLAND
Morzine Avoriaz Champéry
Les Gets Verbier Saas Fee
Praz-de-Lys MARTIGNY
Morillon Zermatt
Samoëns
Les Carroz
Flaine Le Tour
Le Chinaillon Argentière Cervinia
Le Grand- Chamonix Valtournenche
ANNECY Bornand Combloux Les Houches Mt Blanc Champoluc Gressoney-
LA CLUSAZ Praz- Le Betex St-Gervais tunnel la-Trinité
-sur- St Nicolas de Veroce
Notre-Dame-de- Arly Megève MONT
Bellecombe Les Contamines BLANC Courmayeur
Les Saisies AOSTA
ALBERTVILLE Arèches La Thuile
CHAMBÉRY La Rosière
Bourg-St-Maurice Villaroger
AIME Les Arcs Ste-Foy
Vallandry
Montchavin Peisey-
MOÛTIERS Les Coches Nancroix
Combelouvière Brides-les- La Plagne Tignes
Valmorel Bains Champagny Val-d'Isère
St-François- La Tânia
Longchamp Courchevel
St-Martin- Méribel Pralognan Bonneval
Les Sept-Laux La Toussuire de-Belleville Les Menuires
GRENOBLE Le Corbier St-Jean-de- Val-Thorens Val-Cenis
Villard-de-Lans Les Karellis MAURIENNE
Chamrousse Vaujany La Norma FRANCE
Oz-Station Valmeinier MODANE
Villard- Alpe-d'Huez Valloire Valfréjus
Reculas Auris Fréjus tunnel
BOURG- La Grave Bardonecchia
D'OISANS Col du Lauteret
Les Deux-Alpes Sauze d'Oulx
Cesana Torinese
Serre-Chevalier Sestriere TURIN
Claviere
Briançon Montgenèvre
Puy-St-Vincent ITALY
Superdévoluy
Orcières-Merlette
Off the map:
Pra-Loup
GAP Risoul Vars ↓ La Foux-d'Allos
Auron
Les Orres Isola 2000

0 ——————— 30
Scale in km

GETTING AROUND THE FRENCH ALPS

Pick the right gateway – Geneva, Chambéry or Grenoble – and you can hardly go
wrong. The approach to Serre-Chevalier and Montgenèvre involves the 2058m Col
du Lauteret; but the road is a major one, and kept clear of snow or reopened
quickly after a fall. Crossing into Switzerland from Chamonix involves two closure-
prone passes – the Montets (1461m) and Forclaz (1527m). When necessary, one-
way traffic runs beside the tracks through the rail tunnel beneath the passes.

ANY STYLE OF RESORT YOU LIKE

The main negative factor, which we hinted at on page 161, is the monstrous architecture of some of the purpose-built resorts. Certainly, France has its fair share of Alpine eyesores, such as Les Menuires, central La Plagne, Flaine, Tignes and Les Arcs. The redeeming features of places like these are the splendid quality of the slopes they serve, the reliability and quality of the snow, and the amazing piste-side convenience of most of the accommodation. But the French have learnt the lesson that new development doesn't have to be tasteless to be convenient – look at Valmorel, Belle Plagne and Les Coches, for example.

If you prefer, there are genuinely old, mountain villages to stay in, linked directly to the big base areas. These are not usually as convenient for the slopes, but they give you a feel of being in France rather than a winter-holiday factory. Examples include Montchavin or Champagny for La Plagne, Vaujany for Alpe-d'Huez, St-Martin-de-Belleville for the Three Valleys and Les Carroz or Samoëns (a short drive from the slopes) for Flaine. There are also old villages with their own slopes which have developed as resorts while retaining their ambience – such as Serre-Chevalier and La Clusaz.

And France has Alpine centres with a long mountaineering and skiing history. Chief among these is Chamonix, which sits in the shadow of Mont Blanc, Europe's highest peak, and is the centre of the most radical off-piste terrain in the world.

France has advantages in the gastronomic stakes. While many of its mountain restaurants serve fast food, it is generally possible to find somewhere to get a half-decent lunch. In the evening, most resorts have restaurants serving good, traditional, French food as well as regional specialities. And the wine is decent and affordable.

The one big drawback of many French resorts (though not all) is the lack of nightlife. But nightlife isn't important to many British holiday-makers. Of the people who fill in questionnaires on French resorts for us, 90 per cent say they can't help us with the nightlife section because they spend a hard day on the slopes and all they want to do after dinner is to fall into bed.

France is unusual among European countries in helping people decide which runs to try by using four grades of piste instead of the usual three – a system of which we approve. The very easiest runs are graded green and, except in Val-d'Isère, they are reliably gentle. Blue, red and black follow. (Note that under Mountain facts in our major resort chapters, we've lumped green and blue runs together because that's what Swiss, Austrian and Italian resorts do – beginners should bear in mind that some blues can be quite challenging.)

One good development over the last few years has been the end of the monopoly of the Ecole de Ski Français. Most resorts now have at least one competing winter-sports school, often aimed at non-French visitors, and this has raised teaching standards (and standards of spoken English and customer care) considerably. One major grouse that still applied when we went to press, however, was the French refusal to allow British-qualified instructors on to their slopes without taking extra tests set by the French. This issue has been rumbling on for years. Essentially, under EU law, someone who has qualified to follow a profession in one EU country should be allowed freedom of movement to practise it in another. But the French are

currently still trying to argue that skiing and snowboarding are
different because they are dangerous activities and are insisting on
extra tests. Many British instructors, however, believe that this is
merely an excuse to exercise the usual French protectionism, with
the aim of keeping foreigners out in order to keep French nationals
in jobs. Lots of young people in France would like to become ski
instructors, and only a small proportion succeed.

One aspect of running a resort that the French are, at last,
becoming increasingly conscious of is the need to give friendly,
helpful customer service. We are not saying that they do it – just that
they are becoming aware of it. When we were in Courchevel last
season, one of the lift company's senior staff had just come back
from the US and was instituting new programmes based on US
customer care – asking employees to talk to guests if they met them
on lifts and so on. He thought it was too much to ask them to smile
as well though! We don't believe France will ever get near US service
standards – but even if they get a fraction of the way there, it will be
a huge leap forward.

↑ High, huge, snowsure slopes with accommodation conveniently close to lifts and runs are the main reasons that French resorts have become increasingly popular with British visitors. Most of the resorts that fit the bill aren't attractive to look at – even from a paraglider.

Alpe-d'Huez 1860m

An impressive all-rounder; just a pity it faces south

WHAT IT COSTS

((((5)

HOW IT RATES

The slopes

Snow	****
Extent	****
Experts	****
Intermediates	****
Beginners	*****
Convenience	****
Queues	***
Restaurants	****

The rest

Scenery	****
Resort charm	*
Off-slope	**

What's new

After a bout of heavy investment a few years ago, Alpe d'Huez seems to be in a period of what you might call consolidation. So no big news this year; but you may wish to note that the number of snow-guns has now reached an impressive 400, covering runs totalling 21km.

Not a pretty sight: looking across the lower end of Alpe d'Huez, towards Les Bergers ↓

➕ Extensive, high, sunny slopes, with many excellent runs for all standards

➕ Vast, gentle, sunny nursery slopes right next to the resort

➕ Efficient, modern lift system

➕ Grand views of the peaks in the Ecrins national park

➕ Some good, surprisingly rustic mountain restaurants

➕ Short walks to and from the slopes

➕ Vaujany offers a pleasant, unspoilt alternative base

➖ In sunny weather the many south-facing runs can be icy early in the day and slushy in the afternoon

➖ Many of the tough runs are very high, and inaccessible or very tricky in bad weather

➖ Some main intermediate runs get badly overcrowded in high season

➖ Messy modern resort with a hotch-potch of architectural styles, no central focus and very little charm

➖ Practically no woodland runs

There are few places to rival Alpe-d'Huez for the extent and variety of terrain – in good conditions, it's one of our favourites. At altitude it has some great tough runs (on and off-piste) amid spectacular, high-mountain scenery. Lower down it has extensive intermediate terrain, and the nursery slopes are simply the best.

But you're very dependent on the weather. The lack of woodland runs is not unusual in a high French resort, but bad-weather problems are accentuated by the concentration of most of the tough runs at the top of the area, served by a closure-prone cable-car. More serious still in late season is the threat of warm weather, which can make your mornings miserably hard work, however alluring the prospect of slushy moguls in the afternoons. Late-season holiday-makers booking in advance are safer in less sunny resorts.

There's a lot to be said for staying in Vaujany – a pleasant old village at the foot of the shadiest part of the mountain, with a huge queue-free cable-car up into the heart of the Alpe-d'Huez domain.

boarding *Alpe-d'Huez caught on to boarding early – it built a half-pipe in 1988 – but now seems rather half-hearted about it. There's now no regular half-pipe, and looking at the resort information for 1997 you wouldn't think any alternative to skiing existed. Maybe they're reluctant to push boarding because they know that the icy morning conditions that can prevail here in sunny weather are even more miserable on a board than on skis; but what about the afternoons? Another drawback for carvers is that many pistes are unpleasantly busy in high season. But it's not all negative. The off-piste is vast and varied; the terrain park seems to have found a permanent home beside the low-speed nursery slope zone; apart from the nursery slopes, there are hardly any drag-lifts to contend with; and when we were last there the resort was hosting a freestyle competition. There is a bit of board culture in the resort, centred on the Planète Surf shop, home of the Ecole de Surf des Neiges. And there are some good pool halls and video arcades.*

MOUNTAIN FACTS

Altitude 1350m-3330m
Lifts   85
Pistes   220km
Green/Blue   46%
Red   30%
Black   24%
Artificial snow   21km
Recco detectors used

LIFT PASSES

97/98 prices in francs
Grandes Rousses
Covers all lifts in
Alpe-d'Huez, Auris,
Oz, Vaujany and
Villard Reculas.
Beginners Daily lift
passes for reducec
areas. Beginner pass
covers 16 lifts (55),
Altitude 2000 covers
39 lifts (100)
Main pass
1-day pass 189
6-day pass 1,000
Senior citizens
Over 60: 6-day pass
700 (30% off)
Children
Under 16: 6-day pass
700 (30% off)
Under 5: free pass
Notes Pass for 6 days
or more includes one
day's skiing at each
of the Grande Galaxie
resorts (Les Deux
Alpes, Serre-Chevalier,
Puy-St-Vincent and
the Milky Way) and
free entrance to the
sports centre.
Alternative passes
Passes for Auris only
(15 lifts), Oz only (10
lifts), Vaujany only (10
lifts), Villard-Reculas
only (8 lifts), Oz-
Vaujany (19 lifts) and
Moyenne Altitude (39
lifts). A pedestrian
pass costs 350.

The resort

Alpe-d'Huez is a large village spread across an open mountainside, high above the Romanche valley, east of Grenoble. It is a large, amorphous resort which lacks a definite centre. It was one of the venues for the 1968 Grenoble Winter Olympics, and then grew quickly in a seemingly unplanned way. Its buildings come in all shapes, sizes and designs – including a futuristic church (which hosts regular organ concerts). The nearest thing to a central focus is the main Avenue des Jeux in the geographic centre, where you'll find the swimming pool, ice skating and some of the shops, bars and restaurants. The rest of the resort spreads out in a triangle, with lift stations at two of the apexes. There's an efficient (but under-publicised) free bus service, and a bucket lift (with a piste beneath it) running from bottom to top.

Slightly away from main body of the resort (and linked by chair-lift) are the 'hamlets' – apartment blocks, mainly – of Les Bergers and L'Eclose. There is also accommodation down the hill in Huez, also linked by lift to the resort.

Many reporters have remarked on the surprising friendliness of the place, and in terms of ambience, this once quiet 'typically French' resort gets more animated and interesting each year. It now has an extremely good Palais des Sports, with lots of activities on offer, and 32 bars, 44 restaurants and three discos to choose from.

The mountains

Alpe-d'Huez ranks alongside giants like Val-d'Isère or La Plagne for extent and variety of its slopes. The piste map understates the challenge of these slopes: there are some red runs that would be black in other resorts, and a few blues that would be red.

THE SLOPES
Several well-linked areas
The slopes can essentially be divided into four sectors, with good connections between them.

The biggest sector is directly above the village, on the slopes of **Pic Blanc**. There is sport here for everyone, from excellent tough pitches at the top to vast, gentle beginner slopes at the bottom. The Grandes Rousses gondola

(with massive stand-up cabins) goes up in two stages from the top of the village to 2700m. From the mid-station, a couple of slow, old chair-lifts serve long and testing red and black runs. Above the top gondola station, a cable-car goes up to 3330m on Pic Blanc itself, where the runs are genuinely black.

There is a glacier on the back of the mountain, served in summer by a short chair-lift. In winter, Pic Blanc is the starting point of the longest piste in the Alps (see feature, facing page).

The Sarenne gorge separates the main resort area from **Signal de l'Homme**. There are lifts from the gorge into the runs, and a down-and-up lift from the Bergers part of the village. From the top you can take excellent north-facing slopes back down towards the gorge, or down south to Auris or west to the old hamlet of Chatelard.

The other end of town from Signal de l'Homme is the small **Signal** sector, reached by drag-lifts next to the main gondola or a by a chair lower down. Runs go down the other side of the hill to the old village of Villard-Reculas. The long drag-lift back is tricky in parts and sheds a fair number of its riders.

The **Vaujany-Oz** sector consists largely of north-west-facing slopes, accessible from Alpe-d'Huez via good red runs from either the mid-station or the top of the big gondola. At the heart of this sector is the mid-station of the two-stage cable-car from Vaujany, at Alpette. From here a disastrously sunny blue goes down to Oz, and a much more reliable blue goes north to the Vaujany home slopes around Montfrais, to meet the gondola up from Vaujany. The links back to the Alpe-d'Huez slopes are made by the top cable-car from Alpette, or a gondola from Oz.

Outings by road are feasible to other resorts covered on the lift pass, including Serre-Chevalier, Les Deux-Alpes (also linked by helicopter) and Montgenèvre.

SNOW RELIABILITY
Affected by the sun
Alpe-d'Huez is unusual – and unique among major purpose-built resorts in the Alps – in having mainly south- or south-west-facing slopes. The strong southern sun means that later in the season conditions may alternate between slush and ice on the greater part of the area (which is below

It's no surprise that most ski runs that are seriously steep are also seriously short, at least when measured along the slope or horizontally, as on a map. (The vertical dimension, of course, is something else.) Look at the exceptionally long runs in the Alps, and they tend to be graded blue, or red at the most. The Parsenn runs to Klosters and neighbouring villages, for example – typically 12km to 15km long – are manageable in your first week. Even the longest lift-served off-piste run in the world, Chamonix's Vallée Blanche, doesn't include steepness in its attractions.

So you could be forgiven for being sceptical about the 'black' run from the top of the Pic Blanc to the Sarenne gorge. Even though the vertical is an impressive 2000m, a run claiming to be up to 16km in length means an average gradient of only 11% – well within the typical steepness of a blue run. Macho-hype on the part of the lift company, presumably?

Not quite. The average gradient may be silly, but the Sarenne is a run of two halves. The top half is a genuine black, and the bottom half is virtually flat (boarders beware). The main challenge is the steep mogul-field starting just below the top lift station; after that, things are much gentler, even before you get to the path proper. But the first half is a demanding and highly satisfying run (with stunning views) that any keen skier will enjoy – at least when the conditions are right. We last skied it in bad weather after a week of sunshine. In white-out conditions, the initial mogul-field was a nightmare; lower down, the run was rock-hard – there's nothing worse than a sunny run with no sun.

Incidentally, the piste map shows two variations on the main Sarenne run, but in several visits (not always in white-outs) we have seen no sign of them.

2300m) – and even the top slopes of Pic Blanc are not immune. Although there are shady slopes in the Vaujany and Signal de l'Homme sectors, the degree of exposure to the sun is a real drawback of the area as a whole.

In more wintery circumstances the runs are relatively snowsure, and the natural stuff is backed up by extensive snowmaking on the main runs down both the Alpe-d'Huez gondolas and in the Vaujany and Oz sectors.

FOR EXPERTS
Plenty of blacks and off-piste
This is an excellent resort for experts, with long and testing black runs (and reds that ought to be black) as well as serious off-piste options.

The slope beneath the Pic Blanc cable-car, usually an impressive mogul-field, is reached by a 200m tunnel from the back side of the mountain. The start of the run is often awkward, with block-like moguls. Beyond that the slope is of ordinary black steepness, but can be very tricky because it gets a lot of sun; early in the day you may find rock-hard moguls, especially in good weather late in the season. The run splits into three part-way down, with two of the variants requiring the use of the short Lac Blanc chair-lift to

get back to the cable-car station.

The long Sarenne run on the back of the Pic Blanc is described above. There are several off-piste variants. Other very long off-piste routes that take you well away from the pisted area (so a guide is essential) lead all the way down from Pic Blanc to Vaujany, over 2000m vertical below, or to the piste area above Vaujany. In other directions there are runs that end in remote spots where you need a taxi back. Or a helicopter: as elsewhere in France, heli-lifts to mountain tops are forbidden, but heli-pickups from the valleys are allowed.

There is good off-piste is several other sectors, too – notably from Signal towards Villard-Reculas and Huez, and from Signal de l'Homme in various directions – the slopes of Les Orgières, above Auris, are a particular favourite of locals. And there's abundant off-piste on the lower half of the mountain that is excellent in good snow conditions, including lovely runs through scattered trees and bushes at the extreme northern edge of the area above Vaujany.

Some of the upper red pistes are tough enough to give experts a challenge. These include the Canyon and Balme runs accessed by the Lievre

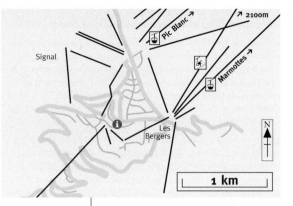

Blanc chair-lift from the gondola mid-station – runs which are unprepared and south-facing (late in the day, perhaps best tackled on a board), and steep enought to be graded black in many resorts. Above this, the Clocher de Macle chair serves another series of steep black runs including the beautiful long, lonely Combe Charbonniere.

FOR INTERMEDIATES
Much improved
Additions to the slopes in recent years have increased the number of suitable runs between the tough and easy extremes.

Good intermediates now have a fine selection of runs all over the area. In good snow conditions the variety of the runs is difficult to beat. Every

section has some challenging red runs to test the adventurous intermediate. The most challenging are the Canyon and Balme runs, mentioned above. There are lovely long runs down to Oz and to Vaujany. The off-piste among the bushes and trees above Vaujany, mentioned above, is a good place to start your off-piste career in good snow. The Villard-Reculas and Signal de l'Homme sectors also have long challenging reds. The Chamois red from the top of the gondola down to the mid-station is beautiful but quite narrow, and miserable when busy and icy. Fearless intermediates should enjoy most of the super-long black runs from Pic Blanc.

For less ambitious intermediates, there are usually blue alternatives. The main Couloir blue from the top of the big gondola is a lovely run, well served by snowmakers, but it does get extremely crowded (and scary because of that) at times.

There are some great cruising runs above Vaujany; but it's not easy for early intermediates to get over to the Vaujany sector from Alpe-d'Huez, except by riding down the Oz gondola. The blue down to the mid-station of the Vaujany gondola is picturesque and well-served by snowmaking.

Early intermediates will also enjoy the gentle slopes leading back to Alpe-d'Huez from the main mountain, and the Signal sector.

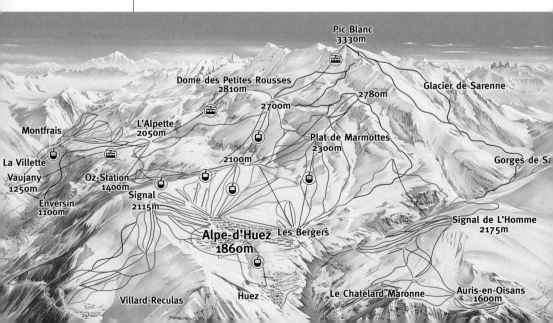

FOR BEGINNERS
Good facilities

The large network of green runs immediately above the village is as good a nursery area as you will find anywhere – its only flaw is that it carries a lot of through-traffic. A large area embracing half-a-dozen runs has been declared a low-speed zone protégée, but the restriction is not policed and so doesn't achieve much. Add to the quality of the slopes the convenience, availability of good tuition, a special lift pass covering 15 lifts and usually reliable snow, and Alpe-d'Huez is difficult to beat. There's another good beginners' area with gentle green runs at the top of the Vaujany gondola, and small slopes in Oz and Auris.

FOR CROSS-COUNTRY
High-level and convenient

There are 50km of trails, with two easy loops and two demanding circuits, all at around 2000m and consequently relatively snowsure. All trails are within the Alpine domain and a cross-country user's pass costs 165 francs.

QUEUES
Generally few problems

Even in French holiday periods, when the main pistes can be unbearably crowded, the modern lift system ensures there are few queues. The main ones are usually for the lifts serving the high tough runs – the Pic Blanc cable-car and Lièvre Blanc chair. Console yourself with the thought that the runs would be a lot less enjoyable

---

Selected chalets and club hotels in Alpe d'Huez   ADVERTISEMENTS

SCHOOLS/GUIDES

97/98 prices in francs

ESF
Classes 6 days
5½hr: 9.40-12.40 and
2.30-5pm
6 full days: 920
Children's classes
Ages: 4 to 12
6 full days: 800
Private lessons
Hourly
175 for 1hr, for 1 to 2
people

International
Classes 6 days
4½hr: 2½hr am, 2hr
pm
6 full days: 1,085
Children's classes
Ages: 5 to 12
6 full days: 910
Private lessons
Hourly
175 for 1hr, for 1 to 2
people

CHILDCARE

The main schools
both run ski
kindergartens.

The ESF Club des
Oursons, at Les
Bergers and near the
main gondola (476
803182), takes
children from age 4,
ski school hours. The
Eterlous kindergarten
(476 804327) has a
private slope area
and takes children
aged 2½ to 14 all
day; it also offers a
child-minding service
(until 6pm) for babies
of 6 months or more.

The SEI (476 804277)
runs the Baby-Club
children aged 3 to 4,
and the Club des
Marmottes for those
aged 5 to 12.

The Club Med nursery
takes children from 4,
with or without
tuition.

if the lifts were improved. The cable-car is often closed by bad weather. Queues can sometimes build up for the gondolas out of the village, but the main gondola shifts its queue impressively quickly. The bottom section of the Vaujany cable-car never suffers from queues; nor do the gondolas out of Oz.

MOUNTAIN RESTAURANTS
Some excellent rustic huts

Mountain restaurants are generally good – even self-service places are welcoming, and there are many more rustic places with table service than you expect to find in French purpose-built resorts. One of our favourites is the Chalet du Lac Besson, a peaceful haven with good food on the cross-country circuit north of the big gondola mid-station, accessible to adventurous downhillers from the Chamois red run.

The pretty Forêt de Maronne hotel at Chatelard, below Signal de l'Homme, is delightful and has a good choice of traditional French cuisine. The Combe Haute, at the foot of the Chalvet chair in the gorge towards the end of the Sarenne run, is welcoming but gets very busy. The terrace of the Perce-Neige, just below the Oz-Poutran gondola mid-station, attracts crowds. The Plage des Neiges at the top of the nursery slopes is one of the best places available to beginners. The Bergerie at Villard-Reculas has good views and is highly recommended by reporters. The Alpette and Super Signal places are also worth a visit. Chantebise 2100, at the mid-station of the big gondola, offers slick and cheerful table service. The Cabane du Poutat, half-way down from Plat de Marmottes, is recommended for good food and service.

The restaurants in the Oz and Vaujany sectors tend to be cheaper. At Montfrais, Les Airelles is a rustic hut, built into the rock, with a roaring log fire, classical music and excellent good-value food.

SCHOOLS AND GUIDES
Contrasting views of the schools

The sound reputation the ESF once enjoyed here has been lost of late. We've had reports of 14 or 15 people in group classes and mixed views on standards of English – beginners seem particularly unhappy. In contrast, the International school limits classes to eight, and standards of English are

reported high. Ski évolutif is an option. International Masterclass is an independent operation run from the SEI offices by a Brit, Stuart Adamson, and is highly recommended by recent reporters; 'small, friendly and helpful,' says one. The Bureau des Guides also has a good reputation – very useful for experts who want to try the excellent off-piste.

FACILITIES FOR CHILDREN
Good reports

We've had rave reviews in the past of the International School's classes for children ('started the week snowploughing nervously down greens, ended up skiing parallel down reds … only three in the class') and reports continue to be full of praise. The ESF, on the other hand, has not impressed reporters. One parent commented: 'It consisted of 20 wailing infants trailing after a grumpy 60-year-old'.

Staying there

Staying close to one of the gondolas is useful, and most accommodation used by British operators is well placed for piste access. Les Bergers, at the eastern entrance to the resort, is convenient for the slopes (it has its own nursery area) but is a trek from most of the other resort facilities. Being near the village bucket-lift is handy if you're not close to the slopes. And there is a free bus service.

HOW TO GO
Something of everything

Chalets There are not many classic chalets in Alpe d'Huez, but quite a few chalet-hotels – hotels that have been taken over by UK chalet operators.
Hotels There are more hotels than is usual in a high French resort, and a clear downmarket bias, with more 1-stars than 2- or 3-stars, and only one 4-star. There is a huge Club Med at Les Bergers.
(((4 **Royal Ours Blanc** Central. Luxurious inside, with lots of warm wood. Good food. Superb fitness centre. It runs a free minibus to the lifts.
(((3 **Au Chamois d'Or** Good facilities, modern rooms (some with balconies), one of the best restaurants in town and well placed for main gondola.
(((3 **Cimes** South-facing rooms with balconies, excellent food; close to cross-resort lift and pistes.

GETTING THERE

Air Lyon, transfer 3hr. Geneva, transfer 4hr. Grenoble, transfer 1½hr.

Rail Grenoble (63km); daily buses from station.

UK PACKAGES

AA Ski-Driveaway, Airtours, Alpine Options Snowtrain and Skidrive Holidays, Altours Ski, Chalets 'Unlimited', Club Med, Crystal, Erna Low, Fairhand Holidays, First Choice Ski, Inghams, Lagrange, Made to Measure, Motours, Neilson, On The Piste Travel Ltd, PGL Ski Europe, Ski Arrangements, Ski Club Europe, Ski Club of GB, Ski Leisure Direction, Ski Miquel, Ski Valkyrie, Ski trek, Skiworld, Stena Line Holidays, Thomson, Travelscene Ski-Drive

Auris-en-Oisans Fairhand Holidays, Lagrange

Vaujany Alpine Options Snowtrain and Skidrive Holidays, Erna Low, Made to Measure, Ski Peak, Ski Valkyrie

ACTIVITIES

Indoor Sports centre (tennis, gym, squash, aerobics, body-building, climbing wall), library, cinema, swimming pool, billiards, bridge
Outdoor Artificial skating rink (skating and curling), 30km of cleared paths, outdoor swimming pool, hang-gliding, paragliding, all-terrain carts, quad-bikes

TOURIST OFFICE

Postcode 38750
Tel +33 476 803541
Fax 476 806954

((3) **Grandes Rousses** Comfortable, excellent food, friendly staff; close to pistes and lifts.
(2) **Beausoleil** The best-situated 2-star, offering good value.
(2) **Gentianes** Close to the Sarenne gondola in Les Bergers; a wide range of rooms, the best of them comfortable.
Self-catering There is an enormous choice of apartments, though most British operators' allocations are in the same few, mostly simple, blocks.

The Rocher Soleil apartments are in a different class from most, offering unusually comfortable, spacious accommodation with good communal facilities including access to a heated outdoor pool. Their position, opposite the Sarenne gondola in Les Bergers, is convenient and quiet.

The Pierre et Vacances places are much more central, but are not up to the usual standards of the chain. They remain, however, better than some apartments in this resort.

EATING OUT
Good value
Alpe-d'Huez has dozens of restaurants, many of which are of high quality – and good value by French resort standards. The Pomme de Pin is one of the best. The Crémaillère is highly recommended by a frequent visitor for its excellent food; it gives aperitifs gratis and even lays on a free taxi there and back. Au P'tit Creux gets a similarly positive review for excellent food, ambience and value. The Genepi is a nice old friendly place with good cuisine. Au Vieux Guide also has admirable food, though the animal skins used for decor are an acquired taste. The Fromagerie and Edelweiss are others worth a try. The Origan, Tremplin and Pizzeria Pinocchio have good, wholesome Italian fare, the last possibly having the best pizza in town.

APRES-SKI
Getting better all the time
Regular visitors tell us that the village is now more reliably animated that it once was, and that you can count on a lively time in some of the bars even in low season. Among these are likely to be the basement bars of chalet-hotels run by British tour operators, notably Crystal's Vallée Blanche (a newcomer, replacing the Utop disco) and Neilson's Chamois (the Underground – an established favourite).

The little Avalanche bar is popular with locals and is often lively, thanks to its resident singer. The P'tit Bar de l'Alpe takes some beating for atmosphere, and also has a fun singer. The Sporting is a large but friendly French rendezvous which has a live band. The Ménandière, Charly's and Le Chalet are other popular places, often with live music. The two or three discos liven up whenever the French are in town en masse. The Igloo is popular with locals, is not too big and has loud music. English films are shown occasionally in the cinema, the ice rink is open till 11pm, and the village swimming pool closes at 7pm.

OFF THE SLOPES
Good by purpose-built standards
There is a wide range of facilities, including a new indoor pool, older open-air heated pools, Olympic-size ice rink and splendid sports centre. Be warned: take proper trunks – Bermuda-style shorts are reportedly banned from the pool. There's also a winter driving school. Shops are numerous, but limited in range. A helicopter ride to Les Deux-Alpes might be an amusing diversion. A car is useful for interesting excursions to Grenoble and Briançon. It's a pity that the better mountain restaurants aren't easily accessible to pedestrians.

Vaujany 1250m
Vaujany is a tiny rural village perched on the hillside opposite its own sector of the domain, above Montfrais. Thanks to hydro-electric riches, it has a giant 160-person cable-car that whisks you, in two stages, to 2800m, from where an easy red takes you into the heart of the Alpe-d'Huez lift system at the bottom of the Pic Blanc cable-car. If you hate morning queues this is the place to be – no-one has ever seen the cable-car full.

The first stage gives you direct access to both the Oz and Vaujany sectors. There's also a gondola from Vaujany direct to the bottom of the Montfrais runs and nursery slopes, with a mid-station at La Villette, an even smaller hamlet than Vaujany (just one tiny bar-restaurant). There's a run back to La Villette, but you normally have to ride from there down to Vaujany.

For years the piste map has shown an itinerary route from the Montfrais area down to Enversin, below the village. This is now a black piste, ending at a short lift across the valley and up to the village; sadly it was closed for lack of snow when we last visited.

Vaujany has four simple hotels. The Rissiou is run by a British tour operator (Ski Peak). It has a popular bar (frequented by the lift operators and ski instructors), pleasant dining room which serves excellent French cuisine (and good inexpensive wines), and fairly basic bedrooms. The staff are friendly and the maitre d'hôtel is efficient and pleasantly eccentric. Ski Peak also has catered chalets in Vaujany and La Villette and some self-catering accommodation. It runs a minibus to ferry guests around.

The Cîmes, over the road, is less rustic but useful for a change of bar scenery. The Etendard, by the lift station, and Grandes Rousses, in the village above the road, are run by a Belgian tour operator and cater for a young, lively crowd – the Etendard bar gets noisy and packed at the end of the day. There are two nightclubs.

There's an open-air ice rink, well-stocked sports shop, small supermarket, a couple of restaurants and a few chickens wandering the streets. And there's a bit of (tasteful) development going on up the mountainside.

Vaujany has its own ski school – we've had a glowing report of it this year (only three in a class of beginners). And there's a big, brand-new day nursery by the lift station.

Oz-Station 1350m

Oz is a purpose-built little place up in the heart of the main resort area, above the attractive original old village of Oz-le-Oisans. Its two large apartment blocks, which are the focus of the place, have been built in a sympathetic style, with much use of wood and stone. The village also benefits from being the only resort in the area with trees on all sides.

It has the basics required of a tiny, family resort – good access to the slopes, ski school, sports shops, nursery slopes, a couple of bar-restaurants and a supermarket. There is a choice of gondolas moving away in different directions, from where you can set off to all points in double-quick time. The main run home is liberally endowed with snow cannon.

Auris 1600m

Auris is a series of wood-clad, chalet-style apartment blocks with a few shops, bars and restaurants. Beneath it is the original old village, complete with attractive, traditional buildings, a church and all but one of the resort's hotels. This is a pleasant base for those with a car. They can nip up to the upper village to set off locally, and also have speedy access to the valley for excursions to neighbouring resorts such as Serre-Chevalier. The upper village is pleasantly set close to the thickest woodland in the area. It's a fine family resort, with everything close to hand, including a nursery that takes children from 18 months and a ski kindergarten for 4- and 5-year-olds. There's also a ski school.

Evenings are unsurprisingly quiet, with just four bar-restaurants to choose from. The Beau Site, which looks like an apartment block, is the only hotel in the upper village. Down the hill, the attractively traditional Auberge de la Forêt, hotel Emaranches and a selection of gîtes give you a feel of 'real' rural France. Over the hill, in a secluded spot, is a fourth hotel – the cosy open-fired Forêt de Maronne.

A 'down and up' chair takes skiers and boarders over to Alpe-d'Huez, but there are plenty of local slopes to explore, for which there is a special lift pass. This covers 45km of piste for just over half the cost of the full area pass. Most of the sport is intermediate, though Auris is also the best of the local hamlets for beginners.

Villard-Reculas 1500m

Villard is a secluded village, complete with an old church, set on a small shelf wedged between an expanse of open snowfields above and tree-filled hillsides below. It's a farming community, with just the bare essentials of a 'resort' – one hotel, a few apartment buildings, supermarket and a couple of bars and restaurants. Its local slopes are linked over the mountain to Alpe-d'Huez, and essentially have the character of the large resort in microcosm – good village nursery slopes and mostly steep, sunny intermediate runs. One surprise is the lack of snowmakers, often leaving the runs home icy and patchy.

Les Arcs

1600m-1200m

Purpose-built for a holiday on the slopes – and little else

WHAT IT COSTS

((((5))

HOW IT RATES

The slopes

Snow	****
Extent	***
Experts	****
Intermediates	****
Beginners	****
Convenience	****
Queues	***
Restaurants	*

The rest

Scenery	***
Resort charm	*
Off-slope	*

What's new

Les Arcs, conceived as a one-company operation, has spent recent years re-inventing itself as a more conventional resort. On the slopes, the main recent improvement has been in the number and quality of mountain restaurants. For the 1996/97 season, the 2300 drag-lift above Plan-Peisey was replaced by a new quad chair.

+ Fairly easy access to the slopes from much of the accommodation, with traffic kept safely away

+ Excellent tough runs, on and off piste, on the Aiguille Rouge

+ Opportunity for skiing beginners to learn by the évolutif method

+ Excellent children's facilities

+ Few queues except above Arc 2000

+ Splendid views of Mont Blanc massif

+ Quite a few pretty tree-lined runs

– Villages are purpose-built and lack traditional charm

– Very quiet in the evenings

– Few off-slope diversions

– Some apartment buildings are quite a walk from lifts, and some are so big that the walk along the corridors to the snow is not negligible

– Nearly all accommodation is in apartments; there's a lack of catered chalets and budget hotels – except down in Bourg-St-Maurice

Les Arcs is a classic purpose-built French resort, with all the usual advantages and drawbacks. If a short walk from front-door to lift base is your priority – and not village atmosphere or animation – put it on the short-list. For train freaks, Les Arcs has the further attraction that it is the only high-altitude French resort reachable by rail: the TGV to Bourg-St-Maurice connects with a funicular that takes you straight to Arc 1600. (For the two other Arcs it's a taxi, though.)

Les Arcs' terrain isn't in quite the same league as the Three Valleys, La Plagne or Val-d'Isère/Tignes for sheer extent, but within its slightly smaller area it contains an impressive variety, including some of the longest descents in the Alps. For a keen mixed-ability group, it is a strong candidate.

boarding *Les Arcs calls itself 'the home of the snowboard'. Local boy Regis Rolland played a big part in popularising the sport (not least with his 'Apocalypse Snow' movies), and the resort is constantly developing its boarding facilities. Some boarders are doubtless attracted by the budget self-catering accommodation, but also by the great mix of terrain served mainly by boarder-friendly lifts (though getting around can involve some long traverses). Arc 2000 and Vallandry have great smooth runs for beginners and carvers. There's a park and half-pipe, and a couple of specialist board schools (linked to shops): In Extremis, in 1800, and Tip-top, down in Bourg-St-Maurice.*

Apartments don't come much closer to the snow than this – Arc 1800 (Villards) →

MOUNTAIN FACTS

Altitude 1200m-3225m
Lifts   77
Pistes   150km
Green/Blue   54%
Red   32%
Black   14%
Artificial snow   12km
Recco detectors used

LIFT PASSES

97/98 prices in francs
**Massif Aiguille Grive-
Aiguille Rouge**
Covers all lifts in Les
Arcs and Peisey-
Nancroix, including
funicular from Bourg-
St-Maurice.
Beginners Five free
lifts; one in 1600 and
two each in 1800 and
2000.
Main pass
1-day pass 212
6-day pass 995
(low season 690 –
31% off)
Senior citizens
Over 60: 6-day pass
845 (15% off)
Over 75: free pass
Children
Under 14: 6-day pass
845 (15% off)
Under 7: free pass
Short-term passes
Half-day afternoon
(adult 150). Half-day
(am or pm) passes for
each area (adult 105).
Single and return
tickets on most lifts
for walkers.
Notes All passes over
1 day cover La Plagne
and allow 1 day in La
Rosière-La Thuile and
Tignes-Val d'Isère. 6-
day pass and over
allows one day each
in the 3V, Pralognan-
la-Vanoise and Les
Saises. 10% reduction
on weekly pass for
families, 5% reduction
on presentation of
previous season's
pass.
Alternative passes
Two half-, 1- and 2-
day passes (140, 175,
330) are available;
one covers Arc 2000
and Villaroger (44
lifts), the other Arc
1600, 1800 and
Peisey Vallandry (28
lifts).

The resort

Les Arcs is made up of three modern
resort units, linked by road, high
above the railway terminus town of
Bourg-St-Maurice in the Isère valley.
The three villages have a lot in
common: they are dreary, purpose-
built, apartment-dominated places,
offering doorstep access to the snow
with no traffic hazards, but lacking
Alpine charm, off-slope activities, and
evening animation.

Much the largest of the three
'villages', with the largest network of
lifts (including the area's only gondola)
is Arc 1800. It has three sections (each
with about as many beds as the two
other Arcs), though the boundaries are
indistinct. Charvet and Villards are
dominated by low-rise apartment
blocks the size of ocean liners. More
pleasant on the eye is Charmettoger, at
the periphery of the resort as a whole,
with smaller, wood-clad buildings
nestling among trees – though most
recent development has taken place at
this southern end of the resort. The
nearest things 1800 has to a central
focus is the Hotel du Golf, set more or
less where Charvet meets Villards. The
main village slopes and a couple of
main lifts are just outside the door,
and the village nursery and mini-club
are nearby. The two arcades that
house most of 1800's shops, bars and
restaurants are either side. And it's the
pivot of après-ski activity.

Arc 2000 is just a few hotels,
apartment blocks and the Club Med,
huddled together in a bleak spot, with
little to commend it but immediate
access to the highest, toughest skiing.

Arc 1600 (these days strictly known
as Arc Pierre Blanche) was the original
Arc (opened in December 1968) and
remains our favourite. It has the
advantage of being at the top of the
Bourg-St-Maurice funicular, giving
quick and easy access to civilisation
for shopping, TGV trains and trips to
other resorts. 1600 is set in the trees
and has a friendly, small-scale
atmosphere; and it enjoys good views
along the valley and towards Mont
Blanc. The central area is particularly
good for families: uncrowded, compact,
and set on even ground. But things are
even quieter here at night than they
are during the day. And beware the
outlying bits, which may be much less
convenient.

The mountains

Les Arcs' piste network is not huge – it
is much smaller that that of
neighbouring La Plagne, for example.
But its terrain is notably varied; it has
plenty of runs suitable for experts as
well as beginners and intermediates,
and a good mixture of high, snowsure
slopes and accessible low-level
woodland runs ideal for bad weather.

THE SLOPES
Well planned, and varied
The slopes are very well laid out, and
moving around is quick and easy.
There are runs down into each of the
villages, and Arc 2000 has runs
descending below village level, to the
lift-base, restaurant and car-park
complex at Pré-St-Esprit, at about
200m lower. Each village has a number
of lifts fanning out, and virtually any
lift will do to gain height, after which
there are countless runs criss-crossing
the mountainsides to other sections.

Arc 1600 and Arc 1800 share a west-
facing mountainside laced with runs
leading down to one or other village.
At the southern end are runs down
through woods to Plan-Peisey and
Vallandry, mountainside outposts
above the more substantial village of
Peisey-Nancroix.

From various points on the ridge
above 1600 and 1800 you can head
down into the Arc 2000 bowl. On the
opposite side of this bowl, lifts take
you to the highest runs of the area,
from the Aiguille Rouge (3225m) and
the Grand Col (2835m) at its shoulder.
As well as a variety of steep runs back
to Arc 2000, the Aiguille Rouge is the
start of a lovely long run (over 2000m
vertical and 7km long) right down to
the hamlet of Le Pré near Villaroger.
This is arguably the longest
continuously interesting piste in the
Alps. You can also reach Le Pré from
below Arc 2000, via a short drag-lift. A
chair brings you back up.

All three resorts have a floodlit
piste, officially open twice a week.

Day trips are possible on the Les
Arcs lift pass to La Rosière across the
valley, Val-d'Isère/Tignes, the Three
Valleys, Pralognan-la-Vanoise and Les
Saises. You can spend any number of
days in La Plagne, and there are long-
term plans to link the two resorts by
building lifts across the Nancroix
valley. Don't hold your breath.

CHILDCARE

The ESF branches in all three stations take children from 3. The International school's Club Poussin in 1800 starts at 4.

At Arc 1600 the Garderie at the hotel de la Cachette (479 077050) runs three clubs for children from 4 months to 11 years, from 8.30 to 6pm, with ski lessons available.

At Arc 1800 various schemes running from 8.45 to 5.45 are offered by the Pommes de Pin (479 415542). The Nurserie takes childrem aged 1 to 3, the Garderie those aged 3 to 6, and children aged 3 to 9 can have lessons through the two clubs based at the Garderie.

At Arc 2000 Les Marmottons (479 076425) takes children aged 2 to 6 from 8.30 to 5pm, with lessons for those aged 3 to 6.

The Club Med (2000) has full childcare facilities – this is one of their 'family villages'.

SNOW RELIABILITY
Good – plenty of high runs

A high percentage of the runs are above 2000m and a fair amount on north-facing slopes – though those above 1600 and 1800 get the afternoon sun. While the highest slopes from the Aiguille Rouge are more suitable for good skiers, there are easy north-facing runs starting from 2600m. There is limited artificial snow on some runs back to 1600, 1800 and Peisey, but none down to Le Pré.

FOR EXPERTS
Challenges on- and off-piste

Although it does not have the macho reputation of Chamonix, Verbier or neighbouring Val-d'Isère, Les Arcs has a lot to offer experts – at least when the high lifts are open (the Aiguille Rouge cable-car, in particular, is often shut in bad weather).

There are a number of truly black pistes above Arc 2000, and a couple in other areas. The Aiguille Rouge-Le Pré black piste is superb, with remarkably varying terrain throughout its vertical drop of over 2000m. There is also a great deal of off-piste potential, in various parts. There are steep pitches on the front face of the Aiguille Rouge, and secluded runs on the back side, towards Villaroger – the Combe de l'Anchette, for example. A short climb to the Grand Col from the chair-lift of the same name gives access to several routes, including a quite serious couloir and a more roundabout route over the Glacier du Grand Col. The wooded slopes above 1600 are another attractive possibility – and there are open slopes all over the mountain.

FOR INTERMEDIATES
Plenty for all standards

One strength of the area is that most main routes have easy and more difficult alternatives, making it good for mixed-ability groups. There are plenty of challenges, yet less confident intermediates are able to move around without getting too many nasty surprises. An exception is the solitary Comborcières black from Deux Tetes down to Pré-St-Esprit. This long mogul field justifies its rating and can be great fun for strong intermediates, but it is often clogged up by near-novices out of their depth, tempted to take this very direct route from Arc 1600 to the slopes of Arc 2000.

The woodland runs at either end of the domain, above Peisey and Le Pré, and the bumpy Cachette red down to 1600, are also good for better intermediates. Those who enjoy speed will like Peisey: its well groomed runs are remarkably uncrowded much of the time. Those blessed with more confidence than technique should avoid the Le Pré black, which has a narrow section demanding technical proficiency rather than guts.

The lower half of the mountainside is good for mixed-ability groups, with a choice of routes through the trees. The red runs down from Arpette and Col des Frettes towards 1800 are quite steep but usually well groomed.

Cautious intermediates have plenty of cruising terrain. Many of the runs around 2000 are rather bland and prone to overcrowding. The blues above 1800 are nice, though busy, motorways, while the easier of the pistes down to Plan-Peisey are pleasantly quiet. The pretty Mont Blanc run is a lovely glide.

FOR BEGINNERS
1800 best for complete novices

There are nursery slopes conveniently situated just above all three villages. The ones at Arc 1600 (open at night) are rather steep for complete beginners, while those at 2000 get crowded with intermediate through-traffic at times. The sunny, spacious runs at 1800 are best. Fast learners can take the gondola up to Col de la Chal for 'top of the world' views and good snow on the easy runs towards 2000.

FOR CROSS-COUNTRY
Very boring locally

Short trails, mostly on roads, close to all three villages, is all you can expect unless you travel down to the Nancroix valley's 40km of pleasant trails.

QUEUES
2000 is the main problem area

There are few queues except at Arc 2000. Even when snow is good in other sections, too many people seem to make a bee-line for the runs above the highest village. Not surprisingly, the Aiguille Rouge cable-car attracts more people than it can handle. The lifts above Plan-Peisey can get busy, too. At holiday times overcrowded pistes can be as big a problem as queues. The Grand Col quad chair installed a couple of years ago has made this area rather congested.

SCHOOLS/GUIDES

96/97 prices in francs

ESF
Classes 6 days
3hr: am or pm
6 half-days: 630
Children's classes
Ages: 3 to 13
6 half-days: 630
Private lessons
Hourly
180 for 1hr, for 1 or 2
people

International (Arc Adventure)
Classes 6 days
5hr: 2½hr am and pm
6 full days: 780
Children's classes
Ages: 4 to 13
6 full days: 780
Private lessons
Hourly
170 for 1hr

Virages
Classes 6 days
3hr per day
6 3hr days: 670
Children's classes
Ages: from 3
6 3hr days: 680
Private lessons
Hourly
185 for 1hr

TEST YOUR NERVE ON THE FLYING KILOMETRE

One of the special features of Les Arcs is the 'flying kilometre' course, as used in the speed skiing event in the 1992 Albertville Olympics. Various world speed records have been set here, including the current women's skiing record and the men's records for descent on snowboards and (seriously) mountain bikes – although the current men's skiing record of 241 km/hr was set on the shorter, steeper course at Vars in the southern French Alps. But what makes the course especially interesting for holiday skiers is that you can have a go on it (as you can on the one in Vars).

About 8,000 people a year do so, and accidents are reassuringly rare (and rarely serious). You go from some way below the competition start at the top, and the stopping area is very wide, flat and (like the course itself) immaculately groomed. You get a mini-medal for averaging 90kph between the timing posts, a bronze medal for 110kph, silver for 130kph, and gold for 150kph; they say you're sure to get a bronze unless you resort to a snowplough. Go late in the season for the highest speeds (or for the best chance of seeing the pros breaking records). One run, including hire of helmet, goggles and special long, straight skis, costs FF60; an all-day pass is FF120. It takes a long time to prepare the course after a snowfall (it's too steep for a piste-basher), so don't be surprised to find it closed.

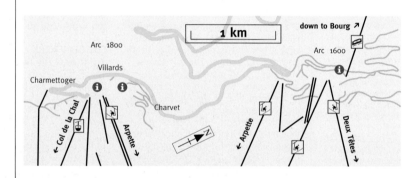

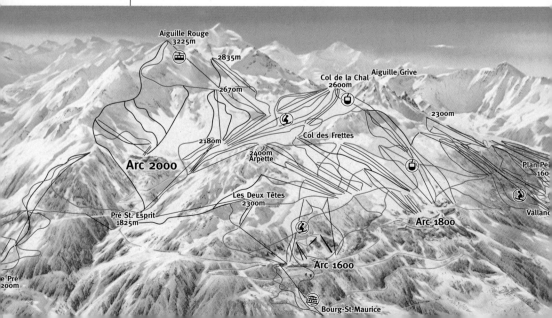

GETTING THERE

Air Geneva, transfer 3½hr. Lyon, transfer 3½hr. Chambery, tranfer 2½hr.

Rail Bourg-St-Maurice; frequent buses and direct funicular to resort.

UK PACKAGES

AA Ski-Driveaway, Airtours, Club Med, Crystal, Erna Low, Fairhand Holidays, Independent Ski Links, Inghams, Lagrange, Made to Measure, Motours, On The Piste Travel Ltd, PGL Ski Europe, Ski Activity, Ski Amis, Ski Club of GB, Ski Leisure Direction, Ski trek, Skiworld, Stena Line Holidays, Thomson, Travelscene Ski-Drive, UCPA, Vanilla Ski, Virgin Snow, avant-ski

Peisey-Nancroix Peisey Holidays, Ski Hiver

ACTIVITIES

Indoor Squash (3 courts 1800), Chinese gymnastics, saunas (1600, 1800), solaria, multi-gym (1800), bridge (1800, 1600), cinemas, amusement arcades, music, concert halls, fencing (2000), bowling (1800)
Outdoor Natural skating rinks (1800 and 2000), floodlit skiing, luge run, speed skiing (2000), ski-jump, climbing wall (1800), organised snow-shoe outings, 10km cleared paths (1800 and 1600), hang-gliding, horse-riding, sleigh rides, helicopter rides to Italy

MOUNTAIN RESTAURANTS
An improving choice

The resort villages are easily accessible for lunch, and restaurants higher up on the slopes are neither numerous nor very attractive. But the newly built one at the Col de la Chal, at the top of the gondola, has fabulous views, at least. The Poudreuse, above the trees near the top of the Vallandry chair-lift, is one of the best, but gets busy.

There are more worthwhile lunch spots below the main villages The large place at Pré-St-Esprit (below 2000) has a good sun terrace and (by local standards) cheap pizza and pasta. The 500-year-old Belliou la Fumée next door – named after the hero of a Jack London novel – has a rustic atmosphere and good food, though the welcome could be warmer. La Ferme, further down at Le Pré, has a nice terrace and good prices. Chez Léa in Le Planay serves simple food in rustic surroundings.

SCHOOL AND GUIDES
Ski évolutif recommended

The ESF ski school is renowned for being the first in Europe to teach ski évolutif, where beginners learn parallel turns right from the start on short skis, cutting out snowploughs and gradually moving on to longer and longer skis. Such tuition is available only to the over 12s. Tuition is also available in powder, mogul and racing techniques.

The International school (also known as Arc Adventure) in Arc 1800 has impressed reporters over the years. It also operates in 2000. This seems a better bet than the ESF – which we've had mixed reports of in all three villages.

We have had glowing reports this year of the Optimum ski courses, using British instructors, based in a catered chalet in Le Pré.

FACILITIES FOR CHILDREN
Good reports

We continue to get good reports on the Pommes de Pin facilities in Arc 1800 – 'great care and attention paid to children, patient approach to teaching' – with no repetition this year of the earlier findings that advance bookings were a waste of time. Comments on the children's ski school classes are favourable, too – 'nearly all instructors spoke English, classes went smoothly'.

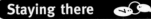

Staying there

Les Arcs is essentially a convenience resort, and in 1600 and 2000 you need not worry much about where you are based. But self-caterers staying in 1800 should beware: some of its apartment blocks have been built down the fall line, stretching away down the hillside for such a distance that some apartments are a long walk from the snow. Charmettoger doesn't suffer from this problem, but it has few facilities and is quite far from the children's facilities and ski school.

HOW TO GO
Geared towards self-catering

Although all the big UK tour operators come here, their accommodation is limited – mostly rough-and-ready apartments. The charter train to Bourg-St-Maurice used by UK tour operator is very convenient, with one of the shortest transfers to any resort. There is a Club Med 'village' at Arc 2000.
Chalets There are hardly any catered chalet holidays in Les Arcs.
Hotels The choice of hotels in Les Arcs is gradually widening, particularly at the upper end of the market. All-in packages of full-board accommodation and lift pass can be attractive.
《《④ **Mercure** (1800) Recently built, and locally judged to be worth four stars rather than its actual three.
《《③ **Golf** (1800) A super-pricey 3-star; the best in Les Arcs, with recently renovated rooms, sauna, gym, kindergarten and covered parking.
《《③ **La Cachette** (1600) Smartly renovated in 1995, with something of the style of an American resort hotel.
《《③ **Trois Arcs** (1600) Central.
《② **Aiguille Rouge** (2000) Daily free ski guiding.
Self-catering Over three-quarters of the resort beds are in apartments, mostly tight on space, so paying extra for under-occupancy is a sound investment. Given the lack of nightlife, atmosphere and off-slope facilities, cable TV may be worth considering, even if you wouldn't normally watch television on holiday. The Ruitor apartments are some of the best, in one of the smaller blocks at the foot of the slopes, close to a lift. They are well equipped and nicely situated, among trees between Villards and Charmettoger. The Nova residences in Villards, which house a kindergarten

and mini-club, and the Pierre et Vacances places, the Arnoise and Grand Arbois, are about the best of the rest on the British package market.

EATING OUT
Cook it yourself
Most people cook for themselves, which is pretty wise. Le Green restaurant in the Hotel du Golf has haute cuisine at sky-high prices. The Gargantus in 1800 is a welcome exception to the general mediocrity in the more informal places. L'Equipe specialises in Savoyard dishes. Casa Mia does good pizza and pasta. Le Grenier des Arcs, in 1800, has been recommended for good food at modest prices. A surprisingly popular outing is to drive half-way down the mountain to the welcoming and woody Bois de Lune, at Montvenix (479 071792).

APRES-SKI
Early to bed?
The Hotel du Golf in 1800 is the centre of what nightlife there is, with quite a few bars and clubs in Villards and Charvet. Rock Hill and Apocalypse are recent recommendations. The cinemas at 1800 and 1600 have English-

language films once or twice a week. The Blue Bar, an American-style cocktail joint, is the focus in 2000. It has occasional live music and stays open till late. In 1600 the bar opposite (and belonging to) the hotel La Cachette has games machines, pool and live bands, and can be quite lively even in low season.

OFF THE SLOPES
Very poor
Les Arcs is not the place for an off-the slopes holiday. There is very little to do and it doesn't even have a swimming pool. A shopping trip to Bourg-St-Maurice, preferably on Saturday for the market, and a few walks are the main options available.

Bourg-St-Maurice 840m
Staying in Bourg-St-Maurice has its advantages. It's a real French town, without much charm, but with cheaper hotels and restaurants and easy access to other resorts for day trips. The funicular goes straight to Arc 1600 in seven minutes. There are modest hotels with much lower prices than you'll find up the mountaim. But those without a car will find the walk from town to the funicular a trek in ski boots.

Le Pré 1200m
A charming, rustic little hamlet with a chair-lift up towards the Arc 2000 domain. It has a few small bars and restaurants but not much more, and is a short drive from Villaroger on the road between Bourg-St-Maurice and Val-d'Isère. The Aiguille Rouge restaurant has been recommended.

Peisey-Nancroix 1350m
This small village dates back to AD1000, though its most striking feature is the fine baroque church. The other, mostly old, buildings house a small selection of shops, restaurants and bars, a short drive above the main Moutiers-Bourg road. The main tree-lined runs of Les Arcs start a five-minute gondola ride above the village, at Plan-Peisey-Vallandry. Getting home off-piste is feasible.
  Reporters who have stayed here recommended it highly for its very French atmosphere and pretty tree-lined easy red runs home. The only criticism seems to be that more and more people are discovering the place.

Avoriaz 1800m

The best base on the Portes du Soleil circuit for snow

WHAT IT COSTS

((((5)

HOW IT RATES

The slopes

Snow	***
Extent	*****
Experts	***
Intermediates	****
Beginners	****
Convenience	****
Queues	**
Restaurants	****

The rest

Scenery	***
Resort charm	**
Off-slope	*

➕ Good position on the main Portes du Soleil circuit, giving access to very extensive, quite varied runs for all grades from novices to experts

➕ Generally has the best snow in the Portes du Soleil

➕ Accommodation right on the slopes

➕ Excellent family apartments

➕ Resort level snow and ski-through, car-free village give Alpine ambience

➕ Good children's facilities

➕ Easy car access, short airport transfer

➖ Whole of Portes du Soleil area is low for a major French resort, with resulting risk of poor snow even at top and bare slopes lower down

➖ Disappointing lift bottlenecks and some crowded pistes, especially in local Avoriaz area

➖ Non-traditional architecture, which some find ugly

➖ Little to do off the slopes

➖ Few alternatives to self-catering

➖ Pricey by local standards

For access to the impressive Portes du Soleil piste network, Avoriaz has clear attractions. In a low-altitude area where snow is not reliable, it has the best there is – on relatively high, north-facing slopes of varying difficulty, including some of the most challenging terrain in the Portes du Soleil.

But there are drawbacks. First, the character of the village: we don't mind sleeping in purpose-built resorts to get instant access to high-altitude snow, but there is no really high-altitude terrain here. The Portes du Soleil has several attractive low-altitude villages, and we'd rather be based in one – Swiss Champéry, for preference. Secondly, cost: Châtel and Morzine are cheap by French standards; Avoriaz is not. Queues can be a nuisance, too, but they affect those exploring the Portes du Soleil from other bases just as much as they affect those based in Avoriaz – more so, in fact.

What's new

A high-speed quad chair-lift replaced a slow old double towards Avoriaz from Super-Morzine for the 1996/97 season. And a slightly improved route-marking system was added to the Portes du Soleil piste maps.

boarding *Avoriaz has the distinction of being Europe's snowboarding capital, the British championships have been held here and the first British chalet aimed specially at snowboarders opened here. From early on in the sport's development it has been a rider haven, and continues to improve its service. Lifts have been upgraded, and now just a few (mainly avoidable) drags are left. There's an excellent fun-park just above the village near the 'Bleue du Lac' piste in the Arare area, and a 100m half-pipe further down. There's a specialist snowboard school, and a snowboard village for children aged 6 to 16. There's also a limited area pass for boarders. The blocks of self-catering accommodation may suit the budget boarder willing to pack people in. Nightlife revolves around the couple of bars that manage an atmosphere.*

The resort

Avoriaz is a purpose-built resort perched impressively above a dramatic, sheer rock face. Cars and coaches have to stop at the edge of town, and horse-drawn sleighs or snow-cats transport holiday-makers and their luggage to the accommodation. This adds up to a surprising amount of traffic at times, some of it fast moving (and we have had complaints about the horse mess and smell). The village

MOUNTAIN FACTS

Altitude	1165m-2275m
Lifts	228
Pistes	650km
Green/Blue	54%
Red	33%
Black	13%
Artificial snow	11km
Recco detectors used	

is set on a considerable slope, but there are chair-lifts and elevators in buildings and moving around on foot is straightforward except when pathways are icy.

Avoriaz usually has snow all over its byways, and being able to glide around town adds to the convenience. Pistes, lifts and off-slope activities are close to virtually all accommodation.

The village is composed of angular, dark, wood-clad high-rise buildings, mostly apartment blocks. Reactions to

LIFT PASSES

97/98 prices in francs
Portes du Soleil
Covers all lifts in all 12 resorts, and shuttle buses.
Beginners Reduced price (and area) pass (1-day 104, 6-day 475).
Main pass
1-day 203
6-day pass 928
Senior citizens
Over 60: 6-day pass 612 (34% off)
Children
Under 16: 6-day pass 612 (34% off)
Under 5: free pass
Short-term passes
Ascent and return on the télépherique (adult 61).
Alternative passes
Pass covering the 42 lifts of Avoriaz only: 160 per day.

SCHOOLS/GUIDES

97/98 prices in francs
ESF
Classes 6 days
5hr: 2½hr am and pm
6 full days: 800
Children's classes
Ages: 4 to 11
6 full days: 650
Private lessons
1hr, 1½hr or 2hr
170 for 1hr, for 1 to 2 people; 3 to 6 people 215 per hour

L'Ecole de Glisse
Classes 6 days
2hr, am or pm
6 half-days: 500
Private lessons
1hr or 2hr
170 for 1hr; 330 for 2hr

the architecture vary but the place has a distinct style, unlike the dreary cuboid blocks thrown up in the 1960s in Flaine and Les Menuires.

When snow-covered, the compact village has an Alpine feel despite the architecture. It is also pleasantly cosmopolitan, with the numerous British joined by Scandinavians, Germans and Spaniards. The evenings are not especially lively, which is just as well as much of the accommodation is close to the bars and nightclubs.

Avoriaz is above the established valley resort of Morzine, to which it is linked by piste and lift. It also has good links to Châtel in one direction and Champéry in the other. Car trips are possible to Flaine and Chamonix.

The mountains

The slopes closest to Avoriaz are bleak and tree-less but relatively (note that word) snowsure. They suit all grades, from novice to expert. There is quick access to the most challenging runs in the Portes du Soleil. The whole circuit can be done by intermediates. It breaks down at Châtel, where a bus or long walk is necessary, depending on the direction of travel (see below). The areas of Morzine and Les Gets are part of the Portes du Soleil network but are not on the core circuit. They are accessed from the far side of Morzine – most easily reached by taking the bus from Les Prodains.

THE SLOPES
Short runs and plenty of them
The village has lifts and pistes fanning out in all directions. Staying close to Avoriaz assures the comfort of riding mostly chair-lifts – some other parts of the Portes du Soleil (particularly around Champoussin and Super-Châtel) have a lot of drags. Facing the village are the slopes of **Arare-Hauts Forts**; these are essentially short 'yo-yo' runs, but when the snow conditions allow there are long, steep runs down to Les Prodains.

The lifts off to the left go to the **Chavanette** sector on the Swiss border – a broad, undulating bowl. Beyond the border at the col is the infamous Swiss Wall – a long and impressive mogul slope with a tricky start, but not the terror it is cracked up to be unless it is icy (it gets a lot of sun). Lots of people doing the circuit (or returning to Champéry) ride the chair down. At

the bottom of the Wall is the open terrain of Planachaux, above Champéry, with links to the even bigger open area around Les Crosets and Champoussin. There are several ways back from this sector, but the most amusing is the chair up the Wall, with a grandstand view of those struggling down beneath you.

Taking a lift up from Avoriaz (or traversing from some of the highest accommodation) takes you to the ridge behind the village, where pistes go down into the **Lindarets-Brocheaux** valley, from where lifts and runs in the excellent Linga sector lead to Châtel. Getting back is basically a matter of retracing your steps, although there are several options from Lindarets.

Morgins is the resort opposite Avoriaz on the circuit, and the state of the snow may encourage you to travel anticlockwise rather than clockwise, so as to avoid the low, south-facing slopes down from Bec de Corbeau.

SNOW RELIABILITY
High resort, low slopes
Although Avoriaz is high, its slopes don't go much higher – and some parts of the Portes du Soleil circuit are much lower. Considering their altitude, the north-facing slopes between Hauts Forts and Avoriaz hold their snow well. Chavanette also has fairly snowsure slopes. Elsewhere don't be surprised to find poor conditions – especially over the border on the south-facing Swiss slopes.

Piste maintenance can be slack, but snow-guns have been introduced in some places, including on the great blue run from the top of the cable-car down to Les Prodains.

FOR EXPERTS
Several testing runs
The tough terrain is rather dotted about. The challenging runs down from Hauts Forts to Prodains (including a World Cup downhill course) are excellent. There is a tough red, and several long, truly black runs, one of which cuts through trees – particularly useful in poor weather. Two chair-lifts serve the lower 'yo-yo' runs, which snow-guns help to keep open. The Swiss Wall at Chavanette will naturally be on your agenda, and Châtel's Linga sector is well worth the trip. It's not a great area for off-piste adventures, but there is plenty of snow just outside the pistes in all of these sectors.

182

CHILDCARE

Les P'tits Loups (450 740038) takes children aged 3 months to 5, from 9am to 6pm; indoor and outdoor games, and so on.

The Village des Enfants (450 740446) takes children aged 3 to 16, from 9am to 5.30, combining tuition with lots of other activities.

The Club Med in Avoriaz is one of their 'family villages', with comprehensive childcare facilities.

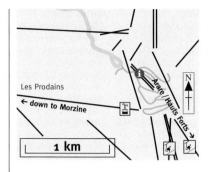

The heart of Avoriaz, in more ways, than one: the children's snow garden ↓

FOR INTERMEDIATES
Virtually the whole area

Although some sections lack variety, the Portes du Soleil is excellent for all grades of intermediates when snow is in good supply. Timid types not worried about pretty surroundings need not leave the Avoriaz sector; Arare and Chavanette are gentle, spacious, above the tree-line bowls. The Linderets area and on down to Ardent is also easy, with pretty runs through the trees. Champoussin has a lot of easy runs, reached without too much difficulty via Les Crosets and Pointe de l'Au. Better intermediates have virtually the whole area at their disposal. The runs down to Pré-la-Joux and L'Essert on the way to Châtel, and those either side of Morgins, are particularly attractive. The long, sunny runs down to Grand-Paradis near Champéry are a must when snow conditions allow; they offer great views. Good intermediates may want to take on the Wall, but the chair to Pointe de Mossette from Les Lindarets is an easier route to Champéry.

FOR BEGINNERS
Convenient and good for snow

The nursery slopes seem small in relation to the size of the resort, but are adequate because so many visitors are intermediates. The slopes are sunny, yet good for snow, and link well to longer, easy runs.

FOR CROSS-COUNTRY
Varied, with some blacks

There are 45km of trails, a third graded black, mainly between Avoriaz and Super-Morzine, with other fine trails down to Lindarets and around Montriond. The only drawback is that several trails are not loops, but 'out and back' routes.

QUEUES
Long at peak times

There are a disappointing number of bottlenecks. In mid- and late-season, long queues form for the lifts to Arare and Chavanette at peak times, and to get to the top of the village in the early evening (although the six-person chair has made things a lot better). Weekends can be particularly busy as people pour in to their holiday apartments. Crowds on the pistes can be even worse than queues for the lifts, with care having to be taken to avoid collisions.

GETTING THERE

Air Geneva, transfer 2hr.

Rail Cluses (42km) or Thonon (45km); bus and cable-car to resort.

UK PACKAGES

AA Ski-Driveaway, Airtours, Chalet Snowboard, Club Med, Crystal, Erna Low, Fairhand Holidays, First Choice Ski, Inghams, Lagrange, Made to Measure, Motours, Neilson, On The Piste Travel Ltd, Ski Arrangements, Ski Choice, Ski France, Ski Leisure Direction, Ski trek, Stena Line Holidays, Thomson, Travelscene Ski-Drive

Ardent Ski trek

ACTIVITIES

Indoor Health centre 'Altiform' (sauna, gym, jacuzzi), squash, turkish baths, cinema, bowling
Outdoor Paragliding, hang-gliding, snow-shoe excursions, dog-sleigh rides, walking paths, sleigh rides, skating, snow-scooter excursions, quad-bikes, helicopter flights

TOURIST OFFICE

Postcode 74110
Tel +33 450 740211
Fax 450 741825

MOUNTAIN RESTAURANTS
Good choice over the hill
Avoriaz has a poor reputation for mountain restaurants because of the mediocre places close to the village, but there are plenty of good places slightly further afield. The chalets in the hamlets of Les Lindarets – surely one of the great concentrations of mountain restaurants in the Alps – and Les Marmottes are generally charming. A particular Lindaret favourite is the Cremaillerie which specialises in chanterelle mushrooms. Others worth a visit are at the top of the Chavanette chair, Pré-la-Joux and Super-Châtel.

SCHOOLS AND GUIDES
Good, but watch the queues
The ESF ski school has a good reputation, but classes can be large and queues may cut down tuition time. The Ecole de Glisse and the Avoriaz section of the British Alpine School, made up of BASI-qualified instructors, provide useful competition. Emery is a specialist snowboard school.

FACILITIES FOR CHILDREN
'Annie Famose delivers'
The central Village des Enfants, run by Annie Famose, is a key part of the appeal of Avoriaz for many families. Its facilities are excellent – a chalet full of activities and special slopes complete with Disney characters. Recent reports have been full of praise. Children aged 3 to 16 can be looked after for a whole week without parental involvement – sounds marvellous. For the 1995/96 season a snowboard village was opened exclusively for children aged 6 to 16. It has 10 hectares of special terrain, with jumps etc. The car-free village of Avoriaz must be one of the safest in the Alps, but there are still sleighs, skiers, snowboarders and snow-cats to watch out for.

Staying there 🗝

The main consideration when choosing where to stay in this steep village is your evening habits. By day you can get around using lifts, but at night you may have to walk home uphill (or nip in and out of apartment blocks using their internal lifts).

The resort is nominally divided into half a dozen 'villages'. The Village-de-la-Falaise is the most recent area of development; it is separate from the rest, close to the entrance car parks.

HOW TO GO
Self-catering dominates
Alternatives to apartments are few.
Chalets There are several available, comfortable and attractive but mainly designed for small family groups. Boarders could check out Chalet Snowboard at Les Prodains, near the cable-car to the main resort.
Hotels There is not much choice of hotels, but there is a Club Med village.
⟨⟨C3⟩ Dromonts The original Avoriaz construction. In the middle of the resort, reasonably well placed for the slopes and après-skiing.
⟨⟨C3⟩ Hauts-Forts Close to bottom of village, easy walk up in evening.
Self-catering Most apartments tend to be cramped if the full allocation is taken up. Many of the better ones are in the new Falaise area, by the resort entrance, fairly convenient for most things. There is a new apartment block here, Le Neva. The Elinka & Malinka is better equipped than most. Other Falaise apartments are simple but slightly more spacious. At the top of the resort – good for views and access to the slopes but little else – the Sirius apartments are reasonable.

EATING OUT
Good; booking essential
There are more than 30 restaurants in the resort itself. The hotel Dromont's Bistro has some of the best French cuisine in town. Booking is essential. L'Igloo is also good, but expensive. L'Ortolan, in the Elinka & Malinka complex, is friendly and good value (by local standards). And brunch in US1 is also good value.

APRES-SKI
Lively, but not much choice
Nightlife lacks variety, but a few bars have a good atmosphere, particularly during the early-evening happy hour that some operate. Le Choucas and The Place are lively and have bands, Le Tavaillon and Le Fantastique are worth a visit. Happy hour in US1 (which also stays open late) is popular, as is the Midnight Express nightclub (free entry, pricey drinks).

OFF THE SLOPES
Not much at the resort
Those not interested in the slopes would be better off staying in Morzine, which has much more going on, including shops, sports facilities, riding and plenty of good walks.

Chamonix 1035m

High drama among Europe's highest peaks

WHAT IT COSTS

((((4))))

HOW IT RATES

The slopes

Snow	****
Extent	***
Experts	*****
Intermediates	**
Beginners	*
Convenience	*
Queues	**
Restaurants	***

The rest

Scenery	*****
Resort charm	****
Off-slope	*****

What's new

On the Grands Montets the Bochard chair has been replaced by a gondola with three times the capacity, and artificial snow has been installed in this area. The black Chamois run from Bochard can now be groomed. The mid-mountain complex at Lognan has been rebuilt with new, expanded cafeteria facilities.

There is now a cable-car link between Le Brévant and La Flégère slopes. A new quad chair has been put in at La Tête de Balme.

Les Houches was not included in the Chamonix area lift pass in 1996/97, and may not be for 1997/98. The Chamonix sports centre was renovated during the summer of 1997.

➕ A lot of very tough terrain, especially off-piste

➕ Unforgettable cable-car ride to the Aiguille du Midi, leading to the most famous off-piste route of all – the Vallée Blanche

➕ Amazing views of the Mont Blanc massif and surrounding glaciers

➕ Town steeped in Alpine traditions, with lots to do off the slopes

➕ Well-organised and extensive cross-country trail system

➕ Easy access by road, rail and air

➖ Several separate mountains – a lot of driving or bussing required, and mixed ability groups are likely to have to split up

➖ Pistes in each individual area are quite limited

➖ Hardly any slope-side accommodation

➖ Runs down to the valley floor are often closed due to lack of snow

➖ Popularity means crowds and queues

➖ Bad weather can shut the best runs

Chamonix could not be more different from France's well-known, purpose-built mountain resorts. There is no huge area of well-connected lifts and groomed pistes. Unless you are content to use just one area and pick your place to stay accordingly, you have to drive or take a bus each day to your chosen mountain, although the new cable-car linking Le Brévant to La Flégère has improved things a little. There is all sorts of terrain, but it offers more to interest the expert than anyone else, and to make the most of the area you need a mountain guide rather than a piste map. Chamonix is neither convenient nor conventional, but it is special and – understandably – a Mecca for experts.

The slopes and the scenery are dramatic: the Chamonix valley cuts deeply through Europe's highest mountains and glaciers. The views are stunning and the runs are everything really tough terrain should be – not only steep, but high and long. If you like perfectly manicured pistes accessed by queue-free bubbles, stick to the Trois Vallées; but if you like your snow and your scenery on the wild side, give Chamonix a try. But be warned: there are those who try it and never go home – lots of them.

boarding *Chamonix is the same for advanced snowboarders as for advanced skiers; a place of pilgrimage. Head for Argentière and the Grands Montets for the hairiest action – there's also a fun-park and a half-pipe here, and a natural half-pipe a kilometre long at Le Tour, the furthest point up the Chamonix valley. There are quite a few drags at La Tour, though the rest of the ski areas are equipped mainly with cable-cars and chairs. If you do do the Vallée Blanche, you may find yourself scooting, as it's flat in places. Chamonix isn't the best place to learn to board. Staying in the town itself will certainly guarantee a satisfactory week (or season) of nightlife.*

The resort

Chamonix is a busy town with hundreds of hotels and restaurants, visitors all year round, a lively Saturday market and generally lots of bustle.

The centre of town is full of atmosphere, with cobbled streets and squares, beautiful old buildings and a

fast-running river. Sadly, unsightly modern buildings have been built on to its periphery (especially in the Chamonix Sud area near the Aiguille du Midi cable-car station) and some of its lovely old buildings have been allowed to fall into disrepair. Sadly, too, traffic clogs the streets surrounding the pedestrianised centre. But the views of the mountains of the

MOUNTAIN FACTS

Altitude 1035m-3840m
Lifts   49
Pistes   140km
Green/Blue   35%
Red   45%
Black   20%
Artificial snow   4km
Recco detectors used

LIFT PASSES

97/98 prices in francs
Cham'Ski pass
Covers all areas in the
Chamonix Valley
except Les Houches,
the bus services
between them.
Beginners Cham'Start
5 days in 6 pass
covers all green and
blue runs (625),
Cham'Baby 6-day
pass covers the same
for 4- to 11-year-olds
(470).
Main pass
1-day pass 230
6-day pass 930
Senior citizens
Over 60: 6-day pass
791 (15% off)
Children
Under 12: 6-day pass
651 (30% off)
Under 4: free pass
Notes 6-day passes
now cover Grands
Montets cable-car, but
only for two ascents.
Additional ascents
cost extra (28 for 1
ascent, 450 for 20).
Cham'Junior pass for
12- to 15-year-olds (6-
days 791).
Alternative passes
Ski-pass Mont Blanc
covers all lifts in the
13 resorts of the Mont
Blanc area (700km of
piste) and
Courmayeur in Italy (6
days 1080 for adults,
756 for children).

Mont Blanc massif on one side and the Aiguilles Rouge on the other more than make up for that.

Vantage points in the town and, even better, on the surrounding slopes, offer an overwhelming spectacle of mountains and glaciers. The town squares and pavement cafés are busy most of the day, and shoppers and sightseers sip their drinks and stare at the glaciers pouring down the mountainsides. It all makes for a very agreeable and distinctively French atmosphere.

The shops in Chamonix cover the range from those dealing in high-priced, high-tech equipment to some surprisingly tacky souvenir shops. But it remains essentially a town for mountain men rather than poseurs.

Strung out for 20km along the Chamonix valley are several areas, some with attached villages – from Les Houches at one end to Argentière and Le Tour at the other. Chamonix is at the centre of it all.

There are regular buses to and from all the lifts but we've had mixed reports of their reliability. Having a car is very useful and means you can get easily to other resorts covered by the Mont Blanc pass, such as Megève, Les Contamines and Courmayeur in Italy. Swiss resorts such as Verbier are also within reach over the Col des Montets.

The mountains

Once you get over the initial impression that the place is hopelessly disconnected, you come to realise that there is actually a reasonable variety of slopes available. There is excellent tough terrain on the pistes at Les Grands Montets and Le Brévent and some classic off-piste routes, many over the glaciers that dominate much of the higher terrain. Some of these routes suit confident and guided intermediates quite well and some are best reserved for those with outrageous hairstyles and a 'bad' attitude. Intermediates are best served at La Flégère, Le Tour and Les Houches. Several of the beginners' areas need snow-cover down to the valley floor to be operational.

A dispute between lift companies led to the Les Houches slopes not being included in the Chamonix area lift pass during 1996/97. When we went to press the situation looked likely to be the same for 1997/98.

THE SLOPES
Very fragmented

For those who really like getting about a bit, the Mont Blanc lift pass covers 14 resorts, 25 areas of slopes, over 200 lifts and 700km of piste. The resorts covered extend far beyond the Chamonix valley – including St-Gervais, Megève, Les Contamines, and even Courmayeur in Italy.

The areas within the Chamonix valley – and there are a dozen of them – are either small, low, beginners' areas or are much higher up on the valley side, with cable-car or gondola access from the valley floor. The modern six-seater gondola for **Le Brévent** departs a short but steep walk from the centre of town, and the cable-car above it takes you to the summit at 2525m. At **La Flégère**, like Le Brévent, the runs are mainly between 2000m and 2500m and the views across to Mont Blanc are themselves worth the price of the lift pass. In 1996/97 a 50-person cable car linking La Flégère and Le Brévant went into operation, greatly improving the convenience of getting around the slopes on that side of the valley.

There have recently been improvements to the system at **Les Grands Montets** above Argentière but the top cable-car to the 3300m summit is still relatively low-capacity. The area above Les Houches is served by a cable-car to **Bellevue** and a gondola to **Prarion**; there are no runs above 2000m but there are links over to St-Gervais. The runs at **Col de Balme**, above Le Tour, are mostly at opposite ends of a wide, sunny bowl reached by gondola and chair-lift.

To get the most out of each area you'll need the local area piste map – the valley map is not sufficiently detailed. We are particularly impressed with the Grands Montets piste map, produced by Iain Cleaver, the Briton in charge of marketing the Grands Montets. It includes brief descriptions of each run, with assessment of suitability for different standards of ability, a history of the area, advice on safety and a feedback form to send to the lift company – and all in French and English versions.

Most of our reporters have been more impressed than they expected with the piste grooming, but not with the signposting of the runs.

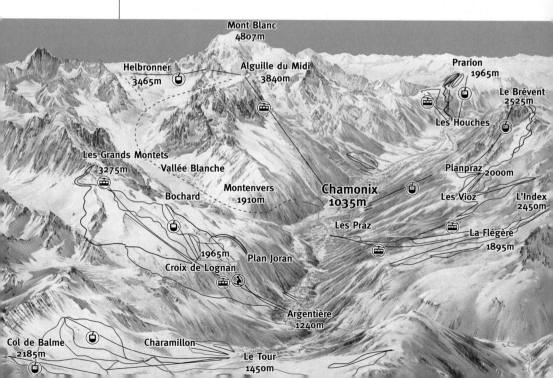

Every competent skier should do it once: the start of the Vallée Blanche →

SNOW RELIABILITY
Good high up; poor low down
The top runs on the north-facing slopes above Argentière are almost guaranteed to have good snow, and the season normally lasts well into May. Finding the top lift shut because of the weather is more of a worry. The Col de Balme area above Le Tour has a snowy location and a good late-season record. The largely south-facing slopes of Brévent and Flégère and the low-altitude slopes of Les Houches can suffer in warm weather and runs to the resort are frequently closed. There is now snowmaking at Bochard on Les Grands Montets as well as some of the smaller areas.

FOR EXPERTS
Head for the Grands Montets
Les Grands Montets above Argentière is justifiably renowned for its extensive steep terrain. A supplement is charged for each ride on the top cable-car – though two free rides are now included

Mont Blanc 4807m

Helbronner 3465m

Alguille du Midi 3840m

Prarion 1965m

Le Brévent 2525m

Les Houches

Les Grands Montets 3275m

Vallée Blanche

Bochard

Montenvers 1910m

Chamonix 1035m

Planpraz 2000m

Les Vioz

L'Index 2450m

Les Praz

La Flégère 1895m

1965m

Plan Joran

Croix de Lognan

Argentière 1240m

Col de Balme 2185m

Charamillon

Le Tour 1450m

SCHOOLS/GUIDES

97/98 prices in francs

ESF
In both Chamonix and
Argentière
Classes 6 days
4½hr: 9.45-noon and
2.15-4.30
6 full days: 800
Children's classes
Ages: 4 to 12
6 days: 9am-5pm,
including supervised
lunch: 1,350
Private lessons
1hr, 2hr, half- or full
day
190 for 1hr, for 1 or to
2 people; 230 for 3 to
4 people

in a six-day pass. If you've got the legs and lungs, climb the 121 steep metal steps to the observation platform at the top and take in the stunning views and stimulating air. Bear in mind that it's a long way down again – 200 more steps once you are down to the cable-car before you hit the snow.

The black pistes – Point de Vue and Pylones – start with a narrow and lumpy section and are then long and exhilarating. The Point de Vue sails right by some dramatic sections of glacier, with marvellous views of the crevasses. The off-piste routes from the top are numerous and often dangerous; the Pas de Chèvre joins with the Vallée Blanche, but only after a fairly epic journey, and there's a scenic route through the Argentière

glacier. From the new Bochard gondola, you can head down the Combe de la Pendant bowl for 1000m vertical of wild, unpisted mountainside. The continuation down the valley side to Le Lavancher is equally testing and suffers frequently from lack of snow on the steep sections. To get the best out of the area you really need to have a local guide. Without one you either stick to the relatively small number of pistes or you put your life at risk.

At Le Brévent there's more to test experts than it might first seem from the map – there are a number of variations on the runs down from the summit; some are steep and icy and the couloir routes are very steep and very narrow. The runs in the sunny Col de La Charlanon are uncrowded and

THE VALLÉE BLANCHE

This is a trip you do for the stunning views and glacial scenery rather than the challenge of the run, which is easy and well within the capability of the average intermediate. It is a classic tour, not to be missed by anyone who is there when conditions are right – though expect crowds of people and be prepared for flat and uphill sections.

Go in a guided group – despite the ease of the runs, dangerous crevasses lurk to swallow those not in the know – and prepare for extreme cold at the top. It does get extraordinarily busy at times – going early on a weekday gives you the best chance of avoiding the worst of the crowds.

The cable-car is a stunning ride that takes you to 3790m. There are snack-bars and the '3842' restaurant, if time allows. Across the bridge from the arrival station on the 'Piton Nord' is the 'Piton Central' and the highest point of the Aiguille du Midi – the view of Mont Blanc from the summit terrace should not be missed.

A tunnel through the rock and ice of the 'Piton Central' delivers skiers to the top of the infamous ridge-walk down to the start of the run. Many parties rope up for this walk and a fixed guide-rope provides further security. You might still feel envious about those strolling nonchalantly down in crampons – you may wish you'd stayed in bed.

After that the run seems a doddle; mostly effortless gliding down gentle slopes with only the occasional steeper, choppy section to deal with. So stop often and enjoy the surroundings fully – no written description or amateur photography can do it justice. The views of the ice, the crevasses and seracs are simply mind-blowing.

There are many variants on the classic route, all of which are more difficult and more hazardous – the 'Vraie Vallée' is for experts only and the 'Envers du Plan' is a direct descent down to the Refuge du Requin – the mountain hut where everyone takes a break and admires the recently negotiated ice fall. Snow conditions may well not allow skiing the full 24km route back down to Chamonix, in which case the station at Montenvers (1910m) is the target. A short gondola links the edge of the glacier to the station where everyone piles on to the train for Chamonix.

Book your guide or sign up for a group trip the day before at the Maison de la Montagne or other ski school offices.

CHILDCARE

The ESF runs ordinary classes for children aged 6 to 12. For children aged 4 to 6 there are lessons in a snow-garden. And children in either category can be looked after all day (and amused when not on the slopes) from 8.45 to 5pm.

The day-care centre at the Maison pour Tous (450 531224) takes children aged 18 months to 6 years from 8.15 to lunchtime.

The Panda Club takes children aged 6 months to 12 years. For those up to 18 months there is a crèche in Chamonix (450 558612). Older babies are taken here or in Argentière (450 540476), where the club has its own slopes, open to children aged 3 or more.

Some of the more expensive hotels will provide child-minding – the Alpina is one. Club Med has comprehensive in-house arrangements – their place here is one of their 'family villages', with a crèche taking babies from 4 months.

GETTING THERE

Air Geneva, transfer 1½hr. Lyon, transfer 3½hr.

Rail Station in resort, on the St Gervais-Le Fayet/Vallorcine line.

include one marked red run and lots of excellent off-piste if the snow is good.

At La Flégère there are several good off-piste routes flanking the main area and a pretty tough run back to the village when snow-cover permits. Le Tour boasts little tough terrain on-piste but there are good off-piste routes from the high points to the village and over into Switzerland.

FOR INTERMEDIATES
It's worth trying it all

For early or less-confident intermediates, the best areas are at the two extreme ends of the Chamonix valley. The slopes of the Prarion-Bellevue system above Les Houches weave gently through the trees and are the least likely to intimidate anyone. The area is good for intermediates wanting to build confidence. Likewise, the Col de Balme area above Le Tour is good for easy cruising and usually free from crowds.

A trip to Courmayeur in Italy one day makes an interesting change. Try it when the weather's bad in Chamonix – the sun is often shining on the other side of the Mont Blanc tunnel.

More adventurous intermediates will also want to try the other three main areas, though they may find the Grands Montets tough going and crowded. The bulk of the terrain at Le Brévent and La Flégère provides a sensible mix of blue and red runs; at Le Brévent the slopes have been redesigned to achieve this. If the weather is good then you shouldn't miss a guided trip down the Vallée Blanche, perfectly within a competent intermediate's capability.

FOR BEGINNERS
Best if there's snow in the valley

If there is snow low down, the nursery lifts at La Vormaine, Les Chosalets, Les Pelerins and Le Savoy are fine for teaching first-timers; learners will not be bothered by speed-merchants. The Planards and Glacier du Mont Blanc lifts both benefit from snowmaking and also provide some progression from the nursery areas.

But beginners would really be better advised to learn elsewhere, and come to Chamonix when they can appreciate the tough high-mountain terrain that is its hallmark.

FOR CROSS-COUNTRY
A good network of trails

Most of the 42km of prepared trails lie along the valley between Chamonix and Argentière. There are green, blue, red and black loop sections and the full tour from Chamonix to Argentière and back is 32km. All these trails are fairly low and fade fast in spring sun.

QUEUES
Fewer problems

The new Bochard gondola on Les Grands Montets has removed one main bottleneck but there are still long queues for the top cable-car here.

At the end of the day, when the runs have been closed, the lifts down can get busy – especially the cable-cars. And in poor weather, Les Houches may be the only area open and the queues for the Bellevue cable-car can be bad. But in good weather Les Houches can be very quiet.

MOUNTAIN RESTAURANTS
Stunning views

The Panoramic restaurant at the top of Brévent enjoys the best views and also does a six-course 'gastronomic' menu. The food's fine but the place is dull. The Altitude 2000 is a straightforward self-service joint with a sunny terrace, as is the bar-restaurant at La Flégère.

On the Grands Montets the Plan Joran serves good food and has a table- as well as a self-service section.

At Le Tour, the Col de Balme refuge needs a bit of uphill work to get there, but it wouldn't be as nice if it didn't. The restaurants in the Prarion-Bellevue area are pleasant and good value.

SCHOOLS AND GUIDES
The place to try something new

The schools here are particularly strong in some specialist fields – off-piste, glacier and couloir skiing, ski touring, snowboarding and cross-country. English-speaking instructors are plentiful. At the Maison de la Montagne in Chamonix, there is the main ESF office and also the HQ of the Compagnie des Guides de Chamonix Mont Blanc, which has taken visitors to the mountains for 150 years.

Competition is provided by a number of smaller, independent guiding and teaching outfits such as Stages Vallençant and Yak and Yeti Services. And there are many internationally qualified British guides who base themselves in Chamonix.

UK PACKAGES

AA Ski-Driveaway, Airtours, Bigfoot, Bladon Lines, Chalet Beaumont, Chalets 'Unlimited', Chinook-It, Club Med, Collineige, Crystal, Erna Low, Fairhand Holidays, First Choice Ski, HuSki, Independent Ski Links, Inghams, Lagrange, Made to Measure, Motours, Neilson, Peak Ski, Poles Apart, Powder Byrne, Ski Arrangements, Ski Club of GB, Ski Esprit, Ski France, Ski Leisure Direction, Ski Les Alpes, Ski Valkyrie, Ski Weekend, Ski trek, Skiworld, Stanford Skiing, Stena Line Holidays, The Ski Company, The Ski Company Ltd, Thomson, Travelscene Ski-Drive, White Roc, avant-ski

Argentière Bigfoot, Chalets 'Unlimited', Collineige, Crystal, Fairhand Holidays, Lagrange, Motours, Poles Apart, Ski Bumpy Trails, Ski Club of GB, Ski Valkyrie, Snowline Skiing, Stanford Skiing, White Roc

Les Houches Barrelli Ski, Chalets 'Unlimited', Fairhand Holidays, Lagrange, Motours

FACILITIES FOR CHILDREN
Better than they were
The Panda Club is used by quite a few British visitors and reports have been enthusiastic – though there have been reservations expressed about the Argentière base being inconvenient for meeting up with your children for the afternoons. The Club Med crèche seems to go down well.

Staying there

The obvious place to stay is in Chamonix itself – it's central, has all the amenities going and some of the slopes are close at hand. For those who intend to spend most of their time in one particular area such as Argentière, Les Houches or Le Tour, staying near there obviously makes sense. Whatever the choice, no location is convenient for everything, so be prepared for some commuting – a car is a huge advantage, especially for visiting other resorts on the Mont Blanc lift pass. The Chamonix bus runs frequently between Chamonix and the different local areas, but only till about 7pm. It's free to lift-pass holders.

HOW TO GO
Pile into the car and drive
Given the value of having a car in the resort and the good road links to Chamonix, it is worth driving there.
Chalets Many are run by small outfits that cater for this specialist market. Quality tends to be quite high and value-for-money good. The Ski Company Ltd has the one very expensive place in town (featured in *Tatler's* World's Top 50 Villas to Rent!). Bigfoot also has an upmarket operation. Collineige has the largest selection – all of them very comfortable. Cheaper places are offered by HuSki and several big tour operators such as Crystal and Inghams. Childcare specialists Ski Esprit also have a place.
Hotels The place is full of hotels, many of them modestly priced, and the vast majority are small, with fewer than 30 rooms. If you have a car, location isn't crucial. There is a Club Med 'village'.
((((4) **Albert 1er** Smart, expensive, traditional chalet-style hotel with much the most ambitious food in town (Michelin star).
((((4) **Auberge du Bois Prin** A small modern chalet with a big reputation; great views; bit of a hike to the centre;

a shorter one to the Brévent lift.
((((4) **Mont Blanc** Central, luxurious.
((((4) **Jeu de Paume** (Lavancher) Alpine satellite of a chic Parisian hotel: a beautifully furnished modern chalet half-way to Argentière.
(((3) **Alpina** Much the biggest in town: modernist–functional place just north of centre; child-minding available.
(((3) **Labrador and Golf** (Les Praz) Scandinavian-style chalet close to the Flégère lift.
(((3) **Sapinière** Traditional hotel with good food; run by long-established Chamonix family; reasonable site on the Brévent side of town.
(((3) **Vallée Blanche** Smart low-priced 3-star B&B hotel, handy for centre and Aiguille du Midi cable-car.
((2) **De L'Arve** By the river, just off main street; smallish recently refurbished rooms.
((2) **Richemond** Lovely old building and nice grounds, near the centre.
((2) **Pointe Isabelle** Not pretty, but central location; friendly staff, good plain food, well-equipped bedrooms.
((2) **Roma** Simple but satisfactory B&B hotel in hassle-free location on south side of centre; friendly patron.
(1) **Faucigny** Cottage-style; in centre of Chamonix; cheap.
Self-catering There are hundreds of properties for renting throughout the valley – chalets, apartments and rooms (some on a B&B basis). Those that find their way into UK package brochures are typically in large purpose-built blocks, usually in Chamonix Sud – convenient but charmless. The Balcons du Savoy look much better, are well situated and have use of a swimming pool, steam room and solarium. The Splendid & Golf apartments in Les Praz have been created from the tasteful restoration of the old hotel of that name – the Flégère cable-car is nearby.

EATING OUT
Plenty of quality places
The good hotels all have good restaurants – the Eden at Les Praz and Bois Prin in Chamonix are first-rate – and there are many other good places to eat. The Sarpe is a lovely 'mountain' restaurant and The Impossible is rustic but smart and features good regional dishes. The Monchu is good for Savoyarde specialities, and along the Rue des Moulins there are several more pleasant places to choose from. There are a number of ethnic

Chamonix

ACTIVITIES

Indoor Sports complex (sports hall, weight training, table tennis), indoor skating and curling rinks, ice hockey, swimming pool with giant water slide, saunas, 2 indoor tennis courts, 2 squash courts, fitness centre, Alpine museum, casino, 3 cinemas, library, 10-pin bowling

Outdoor Ski-jumping, snow-shoe outings, mountain biking, hang-gliding, paragliding, flying excursions, heli-skiing

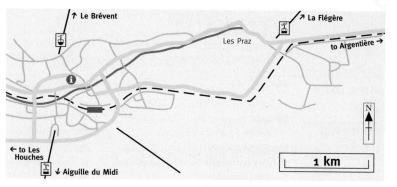

restaurants – Mexican, Spanish, Japanese, Chinese etc – and lots of brasseries and cafés. For something completely different try the restaurant of the catering college – the students get to pract
ise and you get good food at a knockdown price.

APRES-SKI
Lots of bars and music
The sports centre and swimming pools have been in a derelict condition because of severe flooding but were renovated during the summer of 1997 and should be open in time for the new season. There is also a ten-pin bowling alley.

Many of the bars around the pedestrianised centre of Chamonix get busy for a couple of hours at sundown. Later on there are numerous lively venues. The Cantina has live music and is open late. There are plenty of bars and brasseries for a quieter drink too.

There's a lively variety of nightclubs and discos. The casino features both English and French roulette – and if you don't know the difference, you shouldn't be there.

OFF THE SLOPES
An excellent choice
There's more off-slope activity here than in many resorts, and in spring it's a very pleasant place for a stroll by the river or for pedestrians to take a cable-car trip to admire the scenery at closer quarters. Scenic flights offer superb all-round views but are not for the nervous flier. Excursion possibilities are numerous – Annecy, Geneva, Courmayeur and Turin are within striking distance and the St-Gervais–Martigny railway line runs through the valley. The Alpine Museum is an interesting diversion and there are good sports facilities.

Argentière 1240m
The old village is in a lovely setting towards the head of the valley – the Glacier d'Argentière pokes down towards it and the Aiguille du Midi and Mont Blanc still dominate the scene down the valley. There's a fair bit of modern development spread around the main street but it still has a certain cachet that brings people back year after year. Many of the winter residents these days are young, happy and broke, but there's also a smattering of more seasoned Alpine visitors. The small village of Le Tour, just beyond Argentière, is quiet and picturesque, and the place most likely to have snow in the streets.

A number of the hotels are simple, inexpensive and handy for the village centre – less so for the slopes – but the Grands-Montets is a large chalet-style building, right next to the piste and the Panda Club for children.

Restaurants and bars are informal and inexpensive. The Office is the happening place in Argentière, from breakfast till late.

Les Houches 1010m
Les Houches is an unremarkable village, which sprawls along a busy main road. Views of Mont Blanc are impressive, but the shadow of the massif makes it a dark, cold place.

Ski and non-ski kindergartens are available for children.

TOURIST OFFICE
Postcode 74400
Tel +33 450 530024
Fax 450 535890

Châtel

1190m

A distinctively French base for touring the Portes du Soleil

What's new

The last couple of seasons has seen Châtel's snowmaking capacity more than double – there are now 25 mobile snow-guns capable of creating over 40 hectares of artificial snow. An improved piste map of the area has also been introduced.

A quad chair-lift from Torgon to the Tour de Don is relatively new – together with a new restaurant at the top from which to admire the Portes du Soleil's best views (aptly named the Panoramique).

We are told there are plans to replace the slow chair at Pré la Joux with a new quad – but have been given no definite date.

- ⊕ Very extensive, pretty, intermediate terrain – the Portes du Soleil
- ⊕ Wide range of cheap and cheerful, good-value accommodation
- ⊕ Easily reached – close to Geneva, and one of the shortest drives from the Channel
- ⊕ Pleasant, lively, French-dominated old village, still quite rustic in parts
- ⊕ Local slopes relatively queue-free
- ⊕ Good views

- ⊖ Both resort and top of skiing are low for a French resort, with resulting risk of poor snow
- ⊖ Inconvenient nursery slopes
- ⊖ Time-consuming journey to Avoriaz to get to the best snow in the area
- ⊖ Queues can be a problem on the Portes du Soleil circuit
- ⊖ Congested village traffic, especially at weekends

Like neighbouring Morzine, Châtel offers a blend of attractions that is uncommon in France – an old village with plenty of facilities, cheap accommodation by French standards, and a large ski area on the doorstep. Châtel's original rustic charm has been largely eroded by expansion in recent years, but some of it remains, and the resort has one obvious advantage over smoother Morzine: it is part of the main Portes du Soleil circuit.

The circuit actually breaks down at Châtel, but this works in the village's favour. Whereas those doing the circuit from other resorts have the inconvenience of waiting for a bus mid-circuit, Châtel residents have the advantage of being able to time their bus-rides to avoid waits and queues. Those mainly interested in the local slopes should also consider Châtel. For confident intermediates, Châtel's Linga has few equals in the Portes du Soleil, while the nearby Torgon section has arguably the best views. The Chapelle d'Abondance slopes are pleasantly uncrowded at weekends, when many other sections are crowded. Châtel is not, however, ideal for beginners – the nursery slopes are up at Super-Châtel.

 Avoriaz is the hardcore boarder destination in the Portes du Soleil. But Châtel is not a bad place to learn or to go to as a budget option or as part of a mixed group of skiers and boarders. Most local lifts are gondolas or chairs and there's a fun-park and half-pipe at Super Châtel. There are a couple of lively bars to spend the evenings in.

The resort

Châtel lies near the head of the wooded Dranse valley, at the north-eastern limit of the French-Swiss Portes du Soleil ski circuit.

It is a much expanded and now quite large but nonetheless attractive old village. New unpretentious chalet-style hotels and apartments rub shoulders with old farmhouses where cattle still live in winter and milk and cheese are sold.

Although there is a definite centre, the village sprawls along the road in from lake Geneva, and the diverging roads out – up the hillside towards Morgins and along the valley towards the Linga lifts at L'Essert.

Lots of French and Swiss holiday-makers take cars and use them, and the centre gets clogged with traffic during the evening rush-hour, and even more so at weekends. The other main French Portes du Soleil resorts – Avoriaz and Morzine – are quite easily reached on skis, but not by road. A few kilometres down the valley is the rustic village of La Chapelle-d'Abondance (see end of chapter).

MOUNTAIN FACTS

Altitude	1200m-2200m
Lifts	228
Pistes	650km
Green/Blue	51%
Red	40%
Black	9%
Artificial snow	11km

LIFT PASSES

97/98 prices in francs
Portes du Soleil
Covers all lifts in all
12 resorts, and
shuttle buses.
Main pass
1-day pass 203
6-day pass 928
Senior citizens
Over 60: 6-day pass
612 (34% off)
Children
Under 16: 6-day pass
612 (34% off)
Under 5: free pass
Short-term passes
Morning and
afternoon passes for
the Portes du Soleil
(both 138), and for
Châtel only (morning
92, afternoon 109).
Alternative periods
5 non-consecutive
days pass for Châtel
only available (adult
610).
Notes Discounts for
holders of the Carte
Neige (5%), families
(15%) and family
Carte Neige (22%).
Carte Neige gives
insurance cover and
discounts at ESF, ice
rink and some shops.
Alternative passes
Châtel pass covers 50
lifts in Châtel, Linga,
Super-Châtel,
Barbossine, Torgon
and the link to
Morgins (adult 6-day
pass 660).

The mountains

The Portes du Soleil as a whole is classic intermediate terrain, and Châtel's local slopes are very much in character. Confident intermediates, in particular, will find lots to enjoy in the Linga sector.

THE SLOPES
The circuit breaks down here

Châtel sits between two sectors of the Portes du Soleil circuit, linking the two with a frequent, free bus service. **Super-Châtel** is directly above the village – an area of open and lightly wooded easy terrain where beginner classes take place, accessed by a choice of gondola or two-stage chair from the top of the village. From here you can tour over to the quiet little Torgon sector or move clockwise around the Portes du Soleil circuit, crossing the Swiss border to Morgins and then Champoussin and Champéry, before crossing back into France above Avoriaz.

The **Linga** sector starts a bus-ride out of the village, and leads more directly to Avoriaz. For intermediates and above Linga has some of the most interesting runs in the Portes du Soleil, though the best of it leads back in the direction of Châtel and is therefore not used by those in a hurry to reach Avoriaz or do the complete anti-clockwise circuit. If time is of the essence it is quicker to avoid Linga altogether by staying on the bus to Pré-la-Joux. From here it's a short lift and schuss to the hamlet of Plaine Dranse; then a single lift and run to

Les Linderets, where there is a choice of final lifts towards Avoriaz.

Recent reports indicate that the new map of the area makes finding your way around much easier than before.

SNOW RELIABILITY
Poor – the main drawback

The main drawback of the whole Portes du Soleil region is that, for a big French ski area, it is low. So snow quality can suffer if it is warm. And Châtel itself is at only 1200m – 600m lower than Avoriaz – and runs home can be tricky or shut, especially from Super-Châtel. The Châtel area will have 25 mobile snow-guns for the 1997/98 season (a doubling of capacity in the last two seasons), used mainly at Super-Châtel and on the runs down from Linga and to Pré-la-Joux. These last two are mainly north-facing and generally have the best local snow – a regular visitor tells us there has been good snow at Pré-la-Joux until May in the last three seasons. But another reporter tells of the snow being like a 'damp pudding' in March and pistes to Morgins and Les Lindarets being closed.

FOR EXPERTS
Some challenges

The best steep runs – on and off-piste – are in the Linga and Pré-la-Joux area. Beneath the Linga gondola and chair, there's a pleasant mix of open and wooded ground which follows the fall line fairly directly. And there's a genuine black mogul field between Cornebois and Plaine Dranse which a recent reporter describes as 'steeper and narrower than the infamous Swiss

193

Châtel

Wall'. An unpisted trail from Super-Châtel towards the village is also fun. And the challenging Hauts Forts sector beyond Avoriaz is within reach.

Pierre Tardival Extreme Clinics are held in Châtel each year and he doesn't seem to have any problem finding local off-piste terrain he considers steep enough (this is the man who climbed up and skied down Everest!).

FOR INTERMEDIATES
Some of the best runs in the PdS
When conditions are right the Portes du Soleil is an intermediate's paradise. Good intermediates need not venture far from Châtel; Linga has some of the best red runs in the whole area. But

A view of Châtel ↓

the Champéry-Avoriaz sector also beckons. The moderately skilled can do the whole circuit without any problems, and will particularly enjoy the runs around Les Lindarets and Morgins. Even timid types can do the circuit, provided they take one or two short-cuts and ride chairs down trickier bits. The chair from Les Lindarets to Pointe de Mossette provides a red run into the Swiss area which is a lot easier than the 'Swiss Wall' from Chavanette and also speeds up the whole journey.

Leaving aside attempts to complete the whole circuit in both directions, there are rewarding out-and-back expeditions to be made clockwise to the wide open snowfields above Champoussin, beyond Morgins, and anti-clockwise to the Hauts-Forts runs above Avoriaz.

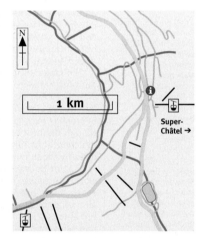

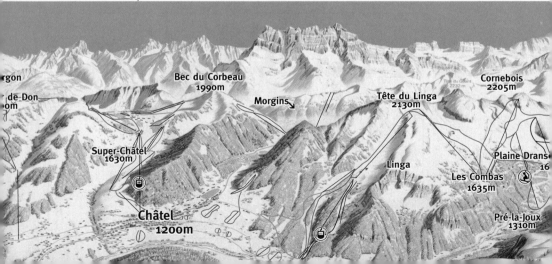

CHILDCARE

The ESF runs a ski kindergarten for children aged 5 or more, with lunch provided.

Le Village des Marmottons (450 733379) takes children from age 14 months to 10, from 8.30 to 5.30, with ski tuition for those aged 3 or more.

ACTIVITIES

Indoor Swimming pool, bowling, cinema, library
Outdoor Skating rink, paragliding, horse-drawn carriage rides, helicopter rides, dog-sledding, snow-shoe excursions, visits to the farm

FOR BEGINNERS
Inconvenient slopes
The nursery slopes are fine, but they are in an inconvenient position up at Super-Châtel. Near-beginners not wanting tuition have some nice runs around Super-Châtel and nearby Tour de Don, and there's some gentle terrain above Pré-la-Joux.

FOR CROSS-COUNTRY
Pretty, if low, trails
There are plenty of pretty trails along the river and through the woods on the lower slopes of Linga (42km), but snow-cover can be a problem.

QUEUES
Lots of bottlenecks can occur
Queues vary enormously according to conditions and time of year. Given good snow in January, there are no problems apart from a couple of notorious bottlenecks in Avoriaz. Poor conditions from February onwards can cause more widespread delays. Beginners can face bad queues to get down from Super-Châtel, and people getting to and from Avoriaz face constant delays en route. Pré-la-Joux is a particular black spot (we hear the slow chair here is due for replacement but have no firm date for this).

MOUNTAIN RESTAURANTS
Variable
There are atmospheric chalets to be found, notably at Plaine Dranse (Chez Crépy, Tame aux Marmottes, Pierre aux Loups and Chez Dennis have all been recommended). The Perdrix Blanche down at Pré-la-Joux scarcely counts as a mountain restaurant, but is nevertheless an attractive spot for lunch. Super-Châtel is less well-endowded but Portes du Soleil at the bottom of the Cocs drags is much better than the big place at the top of the gondola.

SCHOOLS AND GUIDES
Getting better
Recent reports suggest that schools and instruction in Châtel seem to have improved in recent years. The International school includes some British instruction. The Ski McGary courses received glowing reports, but those tempted to join the Pierre Tardival Extreme Clinics offered by the McGary school should be sure they are up to the challenge.

FACILITIES FOR CHILDREN
Increasingly sympathetic
The Marmottons nursery has good facilities, including toboggans, painting, music and videos, and children are reportedly happy here.

Staying there

Snow conditions permitting, it is possible to make your own way back to town from Super-Châtel and Linga. The most convenient place to stay is close to the Super-Châtel lifts. The nursery slopes are served by these lifts, and timid intermediates are likely to prefer the terrain towards Morgins. A central position also has its advantages for those aiming for the more challenging runs of Linga and Avoriaz: getting on the navette here may add a few minutes to your journey, but at least you get a seat before the bus gets crowded.

HOW TO GO
A wide choice, including chalets
Although this is emphatically a French resort, the days are long gone when packages from Britain were difficult to track down.
Chalets A fair number of UK operators have places here, including some Châtel specialists.

SCHOOLS/GUIDES

97/98 prices in francs

ESF
Classes 6 days
2hr am or pm
6 half-days: 470
Children's classes
Ages: 5 to 16
6 half-days: 410
Private lessons
1hr or 1½hr
175 for 1hr, for 1 to 2;
3 to 4 people: 230

International
Classes 6 days
3hr: 9am-noon or
2pm-5pm; 2hr: noon-
2pm
6 mornings: 660
Children's classes
Ages: from 8
6 afternoons: 660
Private lessons
1hr or 2hr
175 for 1hr, each
additional person 15

Stages Henri Gonon
Courses can include 6
days' accommodation,
pass and 5 half-days'
tuition
Classes 5 days
3hr per day
5 days: 600
Children's classes
Ages: 5 to 16
5 days: 500
Private lessons
1hr
150 for 1 to 2 people

GETTING THERE

Air Geneva, transfer
1½hr.

Rail Thonon les Bains
(42km).

UK PACKAGES

Chalets 'Unlimited',
Fairhand Holidays,
First Choice Ski,
Freedom Holidays,
Lagrange, Made to
Measure, Ski
Addiction, Ski Club of
GB, Ski Leisure
Direction, Ski Rosie,
Snowfocus, Snowise,
Travelscene Ski-Drive

TOURIST OFFICE

Postcode 74390
Tel +33 450 732244
Fax 450 732287

Hotels Practically all of the hotels are 2-stars, mostly friendly chalets, wooden or at least partly wood-clad, and none of the trio of moderate 3-stars is particularly well placed. A recent reporter recommends staying at Les Cornettes in La Chapelle (see below) in preference to the village hotels.

③ **Macchi** Modern chalet, most central of the 3-stars.

③ **Fleur de Neige** Well-maintained and welcoming old chalet on edge of centre; Grive Gourmande restaurant does about the best food in town.

③ **Lion d'Or** Right in centre, good reputation.

② **Belalp** Very comfortable, with excellent food.

① **Kandahar** One for peace-lovers: a Logis, down by the river, a walkable distance from the centre.

Self-catering Many of the better places are available through Châtel- and self-drive specialists. The Gelinotte (out of town but close to the Linga lifts and children's village) and Les Erines (central and close to the Super-Châtel gondola) look good. The Flèche d'Or apartments are not so well positioned, either for lifts or shops. The Aveniers is right by the Linga gondola.

EATING OUT
Fair selection

There is an adequate number and range of restaurants. Les Cornettes in La Chapelle-d'Abondance has been highly recommended for its 'excellent cuisine'. The Vieux Four, in an old farm building, has a reputation for the best steaks in Châtel, together with views of the restaurant's donkey behind a plate glass window. The Fleur de Neige hotel has a good restaurant. The Perrier serves Savoyard specialities. La Ripaille, almost opposite the Linga gondola, has been highly recommended by a recent reporter, especially for its fish.

APRES-SKI
All down to bars

Châtel is getting livelier, especially at weekends. The Tunnel bar, which used the be the Slalom, is very popular with the British and has a DJ or live music every night. The Isba bar is popular, too. La Godille – close to the Super-Châtel gondola and popular at tea-time – has a more French feel. Otherwise there's a bowling alley, and one of the cinemas shows English-language films

a few times a week. The Dahu disco, just out of town on the road to Morgins, livens up at weekends.

OFF THE SLOPES
Better to stay in Morzine

Those with a car have some entertaining excursions available: Geneva, Thonon and Evian. Otherwise there is a little to do but take some pleasant walks along the river. Those not keen on hitting the slopes would find more to do in Morzine. The Portes du Soleil as a whole is less than ideal for those not using the slopes who like to meet their more active friends for lunch: skiers and boarders are likely to be above some distant resort at lunchtime.

La Chapelle-d'Abondance
1010m

This unspoilt, rustic farming community, complete with old church and friendly locals, is 5km along a beautiful valley from Châtel. It's had its own quiet little north-facing area of easy wooded runs for some years, but has recently been put on the PdS map by a new gondola and three chair-lifts that now link it to Torgon and from there, Super-Châtel. This new section remains essentially only a spur of the PdS circuit. But, taken together with Chapelle's own little area, it is worth exploring – good at weekends when Châtel gets crowded.

Lack of English-speaking instructors is reported to be a big drawback to using the local ESF school, which also runs a ski kindergarten. There is no non-ski nursery. Nightlife is virtually non-existent: just a few quiet bars, a cinema and torchlit descents. However, there are a number of good, reasonably priced restaurants, notably the Cornettes and the Alpage.

La Chapelle makes the occasional appearance in tour operator brochures, but most accommodation has to be booked independently. The hotel Cornettes has been very highly recommended for its facilities, convenience and cuisine. The Alpage and Chabi are other hotel options. The Airelles apartments have received a favourable report.

La Clusaz   1100m

Great for late-booking Francophiles

WHAT IT COSTS

((((4)

HOW IT RATES

The slopes

Snow	**
Extent	***
Experts	**
Intermediates	****
Beginners	***
Convenience	***
Queues	***
Restaurants	****

The rest

Scenery	***
Resort charm	****
Off-slope	***

What's new

Through traffic has been eliminated from the old-town centre, which is a great improvement. The number of snow-guns has been increased.

➕ Traditional mountain village, with character retained despite development into fairly major resort

➕ Extensive, interesting slopes, best for beginners and intermediates

➕ Very French atmosphere

➕ Very short transfer time from Geneva and easy to reach by car from UK

➕ Attractive mountain restaurants

➖ Snow conditions unreliable because of low altitude (for France)

➖ Not enough challenges to keep experts happy for a week

Few other major French resorts are based around what is still, essentially, a genuine mountain village rather than a purpose-built resort. It exudes Gallic charm and atmosphere, despite its expansion in recent years. It is proud of its winter sports heritage, which includes local boy Edgar Grospiron, who won gold for bumps skiing at the Albertville Olympics.

Combine that with a fairly large, spread-out, mainly intermediate piste area with five separate interlinked sectors and you've got a good basis for an enjoyable, relaxed week, especially if you're a Francophile.

La Clusaz has one big problem – its height, or rather the lack of it. Snowmaking has been installed in recent years, but it's on a modest scale and prebooking a holiday here remains a slightly risky business.

boarding *Not an ideal boarder destination as there are still quite a lot of drag-lifts around, especially higher up, past the main gondolas and chairs. But there is a fun-park on Etale, Sno' Acadamie is a specialist snowboard school and Backside a specialist snowboard shop. The beginners' slopes are good, being covered by short chair-lifts and there is a special snowboard lift pass. During the week the resort is quiet, and livens up only at the weekend. There are a couple of livelier bars and discos, but none with much boarder appeal.*

The resort 🏠⛪🎿

MOUNTAIN FACTS

Altitude	1100m-2490m
Lifts	56
Pistes	132km
Green/Blue	71%
Red	25%
Black	4%
Artificial snow	4½km

La Clusaz was once frequented almost entirely by the French. But it has developed into a major international resort – for both summer and winter seasons.

The village is built at the junction of a number of narrow wooded valleys, which means that it has had to grow in a rather rambling and sprawling way. But it has retained the charm of a genuine French mountain village and the planners have successfully avoided the monstrous architecture that has been inflicted on many other French resorts. The village has been developed around the original old stone and wooden chalet buildings and, for the most part, the new buildings have been built in similar

style and blend in well. The centre comes complete with large old church, fast-flowing mountain stream and a sympathetically designed modern shopping centre. Around this, narrow roads and alleys run in a confusing mixture of directions. The old-town centre has now been closed to traffic which is a great improvement although the main highway still gets busy.

La Clusaz has a friendly feel to it. The villagers welcome visitors every Monday evening in the main square with vin chaud and the local Reblochon cheese. There's a weekly market, and there are several typically French bars, ranging from the type you'd expect in any rural French village to modern ones with loud rock music.

For much of the season La Clusaz is a quiet and peaceful place for a

LIFT PASSES

96/97 prices in francs
La Clusaz pass
Covers all lifts in La Clusaz.
Beginners Points cards cover all lifts (60 points 97).
Main pass
1-day pass 147
6-day pass 730
(low season 630 – 14% off)
Senior citizens
Over 60: 6-day pass 550 (25% off)
Children
Under 16: 6-day pass 550 (25% off)
Under 4: free pass
Short-term passes
2hr pass, half-day passes from 9am to 1pm and from 11am, 12.30 or 2.30 to the end of the day.
Notes 6-day pass and over covers 40 lifts of Le Grand Bornand (6km away). Reductions for families, groups and holders of the Carte-Neige La Clusaz, which provides insurance cover and reductions in some shops.

SCHOOLS/GUIDES

97/98 prices in francs

ESF
Classes 6 days
4hr: 9am-11am, 3pm-5pm
5 full days: 770
Children's classes
Ages: 5 to 12
5 full days: 615
Private lessons
Hourly
180 for 1 to 3 people;
235 for 4 to 5 people

holiday. But in peak season and at weekends the place can get packed out with French and Swiss families and the singles crowd. It is one of the most accessible resorts from Geneva – good for short transfer times but bad for crowds.

Les Etages is a much smaller accommodation centre above the main town, where two of the ski sectors meet.

You can get a lift pass which also covers Le Grand Bornand, a charming village a 10-minute bus-ride away with quite extensive slopes, well worth exploring for a day or two. If you're taking a car you might consider basing yourself there.

The mountains

Like the village, the pistes at La Clusaz are rather spread out – which makes it all the more interesting. There are five main areas, each interconnecting with at least one of the others.

THE SLOPES
Five interlinked areas
Several lifts in the village have lifts giving access to the predominantly west- and north-west facing slopes of the **Aiguille** mountain. From there you can head for the **Balme** area on a choice of off-piste trail or easy green track. La Balme has the resort's highest runs (normally the best snow) and a speed skiing track. From La Balme there are more woodland tracks which, perhaps with a bit of poling, take you back to the village.

Going the other way from L'Aiguille leads you to the **Etale** area via another choice of easy runs and the Transval cable-car, which has been built to shuttle people between the two areas in both directions. From the bottom of L'Etale, you can head back along another path to the village and the cable-car up to the fourth piste area of **Beauregard** which, as the name implies, has splendid views and catches a lot of sunshine.

From the top of Beauregard you can link via yet another easy piste and a two-way chair-lift with the fifth area of **Col de la Croix-Fry/Col de Merdassier/Manigod**. You can get from here to L'Étale.

SNOW RELIABILITY
Variable because of low altitude
Most of the runs are west or north-west facing and tend to keep their snow fairly well. That's fortunate, because most of the area is below 2000m. The best snow is usually at La Balme where the north-west-facing slopes reach over 2400m. The resort itself is only just over 1000m and the runs back can be dependent on artificial snow – which has been installed in recent years and added to each season. The main lifts down from Beauregard and Crêt du Merle will carry people down as well as up.

FOR EXPERTS
Limited
The best terrain for experts is at La Balme, where a number of fairly challenging runs lead from the top lifts back down to the top of the gondola. But the only black in the area is the speed skiing piste which leads right back down to the bottom.

On L'Aiguille, there are a couple of good off-piste itinéraires – the Combe du Fernuy towards La Balme and the Combe de Borderan towards Les Etages. There's a black run down the face of Beauregard that can be tricky in poor snow conditions. And the red run from the top of Etale is fairly steep at the top. Other than that, experts will find La Clusaz pretty tame.

FOR INTERMEDIATES
Good if snow is good
Most intermediates will love La Clusaz if the snow conditions are good. Early intermediates will delight in the gentle slopes at the top of Beauregard and over on La Croix-Fry, where there's a network of gentle tree-lined runs. And they'll be able to travel all over the area on the gentle green linking pistes, where poling or walking is more likely to be a problem than any fears about steepness.

L'Etale and L'Aiguille have more challenging but wide blue runs. The best snow is usually on the top half of the mountains here.

More adventurous intermediates will prefer the steeper red slopes and good snow of La Balme, from the top of which there are wonderful views. This is a fairly substantial area with good lifts (a high-capacity gondola from the bottom linking to a fast quad chair).

FOR BEGINNERS
Splendid beginner slopes
The best nursery slopes are up the mountain at the top of the Beauregard cable-car and at Crêt du Merle. The Beauregard area has lovely gentle green runs to progress to, including one long run round the mountain right back to the village.

FOR CROSS-COUNTRY
Excellent
La Clusaz has much better cross-country facilities than many resorts, with a total of 70km of loops of varying difficulty. The main area is near the lake at Les Confins, reached by bus. There's also a lovely area at the top of the Beauregard cable-car.

QUEUES
Not a problem
Except on peak weekends or if the lower slopes are shut because of snow shortage, lift queues aren't a problem. The worst bottleneck used to be the top half of La Balme. But the slow old chair was replaced by a fast quad a few seasons ago.

MOUNTAIN RESTAURANTS
High standard
Mountain restaurants are one of the resort's strong points. There are lots of them and, for the most part, they are rustic and charming, and serve good, reasonably priced – often Savoyard – food. We have had excellent reports on the Télémark above the chair lift to l'Etale and Les Chenons at the bottom of La Balme. There are several other good restaurants higher up in the Aiguille sector, of which the Bercail is said to be the best. At night you can get to it by sledge. The restaurant at Beauregard by the cross-country trail is sunny and peaceful, with good food. Le Neve at Le Rosey has also been highly recommended.

Chalets and rocky ridges – La Clusaz is a good-looking resort ↓

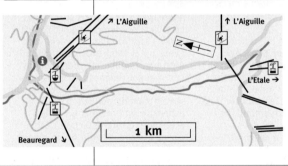

CHILDCARE

The ESF runs a ski kindergarten for children aged 5 to 12, at normal class hours.

The two all-day kindergartens operate 8.30 to 6pm. The Club des Mouflets (450 326950) offers creative activities and indoor games for non-skiing children aged 8 months to 4½ years, (babies looked after in a special section). The Champions' Club (450 326950) takes from age 3½ to 6 for indoor and outdoor games, with the option of supervised skiing (with French instructors) for ages 3½ to 5.

GETTING THERE

Air Geneva, transfer 1½hr. Lyon, transfer 2½hr.

UK PACKAGES

Aravis Alpine Retreat, Erna Low, Fairhand Holidays, First Choice Ski, Lagrange, Made to Measure, Motours, Silver Ski, Ski Amis, Ski Arrangements, Ski Leisure Direction, Ski Valkyrie, Ski Weekend, Stena Line Holidays

ACTIVITIES

Indoor Various hotels have saunas, massage, jacuzzi, weights rooms, aerobics, sun beds and swimming pools
Outdoor Ice skating, paragliding, hang-gliding, micro-light flights, snow-shoe excursions, snowmobile rides, winter walks

TOURIST OFFICE

Postcode 74220
Tel +33 450 326500
Fax 450 326501

SCHOOLS AND GUIDES
Mixed reports
There are tales of large classes and poor instruction in group lessons, but we've heard from some satisfied customers too – especially those who took private lessons. Locals say Croix Fry is better organised than La Clusaz.

FACILITIES FOR CHILDREN
Excellent – in theory
The childcare arrangements seem carefully considered, but we have had mixed reports about the kindergarten. Generally, however, the resort is one where families can feel at home – provided they keep away from the traffic on the main highway.

Staying there 🔑

Much of the accommodation is a fair walk from an access lift to the runs and the bus system is somewhat erratic. It's best to stay close to the start of one of the main access lifts near the centre of town. Or car drivers could consider staying in rustic Le Grand Bornand 6km away (and with its own slopes covered by the La Clusaz 6-day lift pass).

HOW TO GO
Decreasing choice of packages
Some of the big tour operators have dropped La Clusaz in recent seasons but there's still a fair choice. The drive from the Channel and the transfer from Geneva airport are both among the shortest of any resort.
Chalets There is quite a range of chalets including some charmingly rustic ones.
Hotels Small, friendly 2-star family hotels are the mainstay of the resort.
(((3) **Beauregard** Best in town – comfortable, big by local standards; on the fringe of the village. Pool.
(((3) **Alp'Hôtel** Comfortable modern chalet close to the centre, with one of the better restaurants. Pool.
(((3) **Alpen Roc** Big but stylish, central and comfortable, although one reporter called his room 'very cramped'. Pool.
(((3) **Croix-Fry** In a peaceful spot with good views, just beyond the col of the same name, on the fringe of the piste area – a rare French example of a really cosy, rustic chalet.
(((3) **Vieux Chalet** In a splendid piste-side setting overlooking the village, this is a wonderful spot for a meal and has a handful of pleasant rooms. The

food is some of the best in town.
((2) **Christiania** Traditional, simple family hotel in the centre. Quiet, small rooms, and decent food.
Self-catering There's quite a good choice, including (unusually) some self-catering chalets as well as apartments. Some are out of town and best for those with a car.

EATING OUT
Good choice
There's a wide choice of restaurants in town, with a number of others a short drive away, including the Vieux Chalet, which does some of the best food in the resort. The St Joseph at the Alp'Hôtel is highly recommended. L'Ecuelle is the place to go for good seafood, or steak that you cook yourself on a little brazier on the table. La Cordee and L'Outa are unpretentious places that are great value for money. At the other end of the price scale is the more formal Symphonie restaurant in the hotel Beauregard. We're told the best food in the area is at the Ferme du Lormay.

APRES-SKI
Very quiet except at weekends
La Clusaz is a typically quiet French family resort during the week, but livens up at weekends. Le Pressoir is a focal bar, popular for sports videos and draught Guinness. L'Ecluse disco has a glass dance-floor with a floodlit stream running beneath it. (It is expensive and there is no early evening entrance reduction.) Other discos are cheaper but by no means inexpensive. Other entertainments include floodlit skiing and ice-skating, and there's a cinema.

OFF THE SLOPES
Quite good
The village is a pleasant enough place for a stroll. It's easy for pedestrians to get to several mountain restaurants for lunch. There are good walks along the valleys and a day in Annecy is a pleasant excursion.

STAYING UP THE MOUNTAIN
Cheap and panoramic
The Relais de l'Aiguille at Crêt du Loup has five adequate bedrooms that are about the cheapest in the resort.

Les Contamines
1160m

A friendly village at the snowy shoulder of Mt Blanc

WHAT IT COSTS

((((4)

HOW IT RATES

The slopes

Snow	****
Extent	**
Experts	**
Intermediates	***
Beginners	***
Convenience	**
Queues	**
Restaurants	****

The rest

Scenery	***
Resort charm	****
Off-slope	**

What's new

A new kindergarten taking children from 2½ is promised for the 1997/98 season.

MOUNTAIN FACTS

Altitude	1165m-2485m
Lifts	27
Pistes	120km
Green/Blue	37%
Red	40%
Black	23%
Artificial snow	3km
Recco detectors used	

UK PACKAGES

Chalets 'Unlimited', Fairhand Holidays, Lagrange, Ski Activity, Ski Total, Skiworld

TOURIST OFFICE

Postcode 74170
Tel +33 450 470158
Fax 450 470954

- ➕ Traditional unspoilt French village
- ➕ Fair-sized intermediate area
- ➕ Good snow record for its height
- ➕ Lift pass covers several nearby resorts, easily reachable by road

- ➖ Limited for experts and beginners
- ➖ Not for nightlife lovers
- ➖ Piste area a bus-ride from main village
- ➖ Can be some lengthy queues

Les Contamines is an unspoilt village with pretty wooden chalets, weekly market in the village square and prices typical of rural France rather than resorts. Its local slopes offer substantial, surprisingly snowsure, intermediate terrain. It is included in the Mont Blanc area lift pass, which also covers the neighbouring resorts of Chamonix, Megève and Courmayeur.

THE RESORT

The village is compact but the lifts are a bus-ride or long walk from the centre. There is accommodation by the lift at Le Lay, but staying in this uninspiring spot defeats the purpose of choosing this charming resort. A car is useful but the Mont Blanc lift pass gives free access to the local and regional buses.

THE MOUNTAINS

From Le Lay a two-stage gondola climbs up to the **slopes**. Another gondola leads from a little further up the valley. Above these, a sizeable network of open, largely north-facing pistes fans out. You can drop over the ridge at Col du Joly (2000m) to a series of south-facing runs – with these, the area totals a respectable 120km. There is a **snowboard** fun-park and half-pipe.

Many of the runs are above 1800m and north- or north-east-facing, and the mass of Mont Blanc is said to trigger heavy snowfalls, making for reliable **snow conditions**.

The steep western section has black runs which are enjoyable but not terribly challenging for **experts**. The main attraction is the substantial off-piste potential – do take a guide. You also have the other Mont Blanc resorts – notably Chamonix.

The black runs are manageable for good **intermediates**. Other runs are ideal for people of average ability, with the best from the gondola's top station to its mid-station.

In good snow, the village nursery area is adequate for **beginners**. There are other areas at the mid-station and top of the gondola, but no long greens

to progress to.

There are **cross-country** trails of varying difficulty totalling 29km.

Queues in the morning at the gondola can be a problem, especially when people are bussed in from other resorts. Some lifts higher up can have queues, but these have been reduced by the introduction of more fast quads.

The lift company wickedly leaves off the piste map those lovely rustic **mountain restaurants** which it doesn't own. La Ferme du Ruelle is a jolly barn. Chalet du Col du Joly has great views. Best of all are two cosy chalets – Roselette and Buche Croisée.

We have had mixed reports on the **ski school**. Some parents thought their children's classes too strict and overcrowded. There are excursions to other resorts, including a guided group to the famous Vallée Blanche.

There is a new all-day kindergarten for **children** from the age of 2¼, and the ski school takes children from the age of 4.

STAYING THERE

A number of operators run catered **chalets** here, and there are a dozen modest **hotels**.

There are various restaurants and crêperies in town. **Après-ski** is quiet but there are several bars, some with live jazz on later, others which get a reasonable crowd at tea-times. There are also a couple of discos.

There are good walks and a natural ice-rink, but St-Gervais (10 minutes by bus), Megève and Chamonix have more to offer **off the slopes**. You can take a train ride up from St-Gervais on the Mont Blanc tramway.

Courchevel

1300m-1850m

Gourmet skiing and boarding – for those who can afford it

WHAT IT COSTS

(((((6)

HOW IT RATES

The slopes

Snow	★★★★
Extent	★★★★★
Experts	★★★★
Intermediates	★★★★★
Beginners	★★★★★
Convenience	★★★★
Queues	★★★★
Restaurants	★★★★

The rest

Scenery	★★★
Resort charm	★★
Off-slope	★★★

➕ Extensive, varied local terrain to suit everyone from beginners to experts – plus the rest of the Three Valleys

➕ Great, easy runs for near-beginners

➕ Lots of slope-side accommodation

➕ Impressive lift system, particularly above Courchevel 1850

➕ Excellent piste maintenance, and widespread use of snowmakers

➕ Wooded setting is pretty, and useful in bad weather

➕ Appealing old village at 1300

➕ Some great restaurants, and good après-ski by French standards

➖ Some pistes get unpleasantly busy

➖ Generally charmless villages – the upper suburbs of 1850 being a conspicuous exception – with intrusive traffic in places

➖ 1850 is the most expensive resort in the Alps (prices in the other villages are much lower)

➖ Little to do away from the slopes (during the day, at least)

Courchevel 1850 – the highest of the four components of this big resort – is the favourite Alpine hangout of the Paris jet set, who fly directly in to the mini-airport in the middle of the slopes. Its top hotels and restaurants are among the best in the Alps, and the most expensive. But don't be put off: a holiday here doesn't have to cost a fortune (especially in the lower villages), the atmosphere is not particularly exclusive, and the slopes are excellent. Courchevel is the most extensive and varied sector of the whole Three Valleys, with everything from long gentle greens to steep couloirs. Many visitors never leave the Courchevel sector; but there is good access to the rest of the Three Valleys, too.

Courchevel 1300 is a pleasant village, and the posh bits of 1850 are stylishly woody, but overall the resort is no beauty. Well, nothing's perfect. Courchevel's long list of merits is enough to attract more and more Brits; but it remains much more French than Méribel, over the hill – as well as having better snow.

What's new

Courchevel is heavily into offering new sensations, whether on skis or boards, and for 1996/97 built a sort of fun-park for skiers (though boarders can use it too) on the gentle slopes below Verdons – huge 'dunes' and 'canyons' of snow.

boarding *Courchevel already gets a lot of business from boarders, and sees the long-term value of attracting young people – so it's continuing to invest in facilities for boarders. Add that to the great terrain, and you have a compelling board resort. There's a snowboard park and half-pipe (on the Plantrey piste), a terrain park below the Verdons lift station (see What's new) and we're told to expect further developments for 1998. Chairs and gondolas are the norm, and if there is a drag-lift, there's usually a chair alternative. As part of its campaign to acquire boarder-cred, 1850 has developed a funky little youth-shopping centre called 'Prends ta luge et tire toi', complete with cyber café.*

The resort

Courchevel is made up of four villages known by their altitudes. A road winds up the hill, linking 1300 (also known as Le Praz) via 1550 and 1650 to 1850; bus services (covered by the lift pass) link the villages. La Tania, newly built a few km along the mountainside from 1300, makes a fifth base. The villages differ widely in piste access, character and facilities.

1850 is by far the largest, and is very much the focal point of the area, with most of the nightlife and off-piste facilities. It is conspicuously upmarket, with some very smooth hotels on the slopes just above the village centre and among the trees in the Jardin Alpin, and a spreading area of smart private chalets just to the east, across the Bellecôte piste.

The jet set are able to retreat to these woody suburbs. The centre of

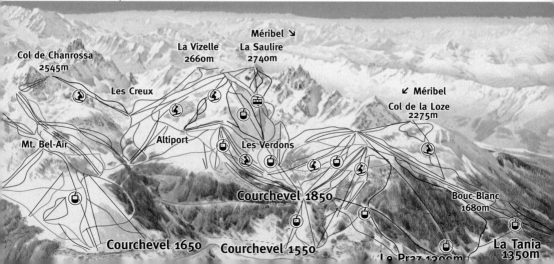

The top of Courchevel's domain, and one of the links with Méribel – La Saulire ➔

the the village itself is a rather messy sprawl that has a surprising amount of traffic and fumes in the centre – and the initial impression as you drive in from 1650 is distinctly tacky.

1650 is dominated by large apartment blocks lining the road through to 1850, and has little in the way of facilities. The slopes above 1650 are linked to those above 1850 at only two points, making this a relatively inconvenient base for access to the rest of the Three Valleys.

1550 is a very quiet dormitory, a gondola-ride beneath 1850. It has the advantage of having essentially the same position in the area as 1850, with much cheaper accommodation and restaurants. But if you want to go out in the evening, it is a long drive to 1850 by road. Although small, it's a

scattered place, with some accommodation a fair distance from the gondola.

1300 (or Le Praz) is the most attractive of the resorts. It's a traditional village set amid woodland, although the charm factor has been undermined by expansion triggered by the 1992 Olympics, including the building of the Olympic ski jump. It's still a quiet place, with good links into the runs above 1850, and has the advantage of tree-lined slopes on its doorstep for bad weather. 1300 has a nursery slope with a free drag-lift but no ski school, which means that beginners need a lift-pass to ride up and down to and from 1850. Near-beginners wanting access to long easy runs also face rides down as well as up: the pistes back to 1300 are red

Col de Chanrossa 2545m

La Vizelle 2660m

La Saulire 2740m

Méribel ↘

↙ Méribel

Col de la Loze 2275m

Les Creux

Mt. Bel-Air

Altiport

Les Verdons

Courchevel 1850

Bouc-Blanc 1680m

Courchevel 1650

Courchevel 1550

Le Praz 1300m

La Tania 1350m

MOUNTAIN FACTS

Altitude 1300m-3200m
Lifts 200
Pistes 600km
Green/Blue 49%
Red 37%
Black 14%
Artificial snow 80km
Recco detectors used

LIFT PASSES

97/98 prices in francs
Three Valleys
Covers all lifts in Courchevel, La Tania, Méribel, Val-Thorens, Les Menuires and St-Martin-de-Belleville.
Beginners 12 free lifts in the Courchevel valley.
Main pass
1-day pass 220
6-day pass 1,080
(low season 972 – 10% off)
Senior citizens
Over 60: 6-day pass 864 (20% off)
Over 75: free pass
Children
Under 16: 6-day pass 810 (25% off)
Under 5: free pass
Short-term passes
Half-day passes (from 12.30) for Courchevel valley (adult 135) and the 3 Valleys (adult 165).
Notes 6-day pass and over valid for one day each in Tignes-Val-d'Isère, La Plagne-Les Arcs, Pralognan-la-Vanoise and Les Saisies. 70- to 75-year-olds get a 50% discount on pass price (6-day pass 540). Reductions for families.
Alternative passes
Vallée de Courchevel pass covers 67 lifts and 150km of piste around Courchevel and La Tania (adult 6-day 880).

204

FRANCE

and black, and at this altitude conditions are often poor.

The new accommodation centre of **La Tania** is nearby – it's purely a quiet, small, purpose-built base with lower prices than Courchevel.

The mountains

There are three sections to the local slopes, though everywhere is so well linked that it is essentially just one big network. The central 1850 section is suitable for all, the wooded 1300 area suits experts best, while 1650 has mainly very easy slopes. Runs lead back to all the villages, but the runs to 1300 can close due to lack of snow. Piste maintenance is superb, snowmakers ae abundant and the major lifts are modern, fast and comfortable – though there are a surprising number of ancient drag-lifts, too. The area is also very well laid out. The main complaint we've had is that many people find the piste map hard to follow because it is too small.

Many reporters recommend buying only a Courchevel pass, and buying daily extensions when you want to go off into the rest of the Three Valleys to visit Méribel, Mottaret, St-Martin-de-Belleville, Les Menuires or Val-Thorens – all linked by lifts and intermediate pistes. Champagny is an easy road outing, giving quite fast access into the whole La Plagne area.

THE SLOPES
Highly varied

The **1850** section is the largest, with a great network of lifts and pistes spreading out from the village, which is very much the focal point. The main axis of the area is the Verdons gondola, leading to a second gondola to La Vizelle and a (nearly) parallel cable-car up to **La Saulire** (2740m), one of the two gateways to Méribel and all points to Val-Thorens. Both of these high points give access to a wide range of intermediate and advanced terrain, including a number of couloirs.

To the right, looking up the mountain, the Chenus gondola from 1850 goes up towards the second departure point for Méribel, the **Col de la Loze**. Easy and intermediate runs go back to 1850, with more difficult runs in the woods above La Tania and **1300** – splendid slopes when snow is in good supply.

To the left of the Verdons gondola is the gentle **Biollay** sector, reached by the Jardin Alpin gondola, which also serves some of the higher hotels. This is great beginner terrain, and gives access to 1650.

The **1650** area offers a good mixture of intermediate and beginner slopes, with the genuinely steep Chanrossa black at the top making one of the two links with 1850's Saulire and Biollay. Neither link is easy: the drag connecting to the blue and green runs

THE STEEPEST PISTES IN EUROPE?

The Alps are the place to go for dramatic mountains and really adventurous (or even dangerous) off-piste runs. For serious challenges within the safety of the protected, patrolled piste network, on the other hand, American resorts generally have the edge. There are very few pistes in the Alps that would stand comparison with the steepest double-black-diamond trails of Telluride, Aspen or Park City. But in Courchevel there are three.

The runs are the three couloirs that drop from the ridge of La Saulire down towards Verdons and the base station of the cable-car that gives access to them. Even the easiest, the Grand Couloir, is steep by Alpine standards, and although it is not especially narrow, it offers a genuine sense of adventure – not least because of the unnervingly narrow ridge you have to negotiate from the cable-car station. The middle one, the Emile Allais, is steeper. The most difficult, from every point of view, is the Téléphérique, which, as you might expect, goes down beneath the cable-car. The combination of steepness, narrowness and worrying rocks is enough to give you plenty to think about, but you also have to add the fact that you're in full view of those riding up in the cable-car.

Notoriously 'steep' black runs like the Swiss Wall at Avoriaz come nowhere near the Téléphérique, which is the steepest and most intimidating piste we have found in the Alps. If you find one steeper, we'd be interested to hear about it.

of the Biollay sector is unpleasantly steep, and apparently not open to children. Getting to and from the Méribel valley from 1650 is more of an effort than from elsewhere.

SNOW RELIABILITY
Very good
The combination of Courchevel's orientation (its slopes are north- or north-east-facing), its height, an abundance of snowmakers and excellent piste maintenance usually guarantees good snow down to at least the 1850 and 1650 villages, and to Bouc Blanc (1680m), above La Tania. On countless visits we have found that the snow is usually much better than in neighbouring Méribel, which gets more sun.

FOR EXPERTS
Some black gems
Tough runs appear to make up only a small proportion of the terrain but there is plenty to interest experts, even without exploring the Three Valleys.

There is a lot of steep terrain, on- and off-piste, on the shady slopes of La Vizelle, both towards Verdons and towards the link with 1650, with the quite difficult Chanrossa run nearby. Some of the reds on Vizelle verge on black steepness. The Saulire cable-car

gives access to Courchevel's three famed couloirs – see the feature on the facing page. For a change of scene and a real test of stamina, a couple of long (700m vertical), genuinely steep blacks cut through the trees down to 1300. (If they ever cut a run down the fall-line on this slope, it will be a run to be reckoned with.)

There is lots of off-piste terrain served by the lift system, with the steepest pitches, not surprisingly, close to the black pistes. With guidance there are some excellent slopes accessible with a bit of climbing – for example, off-piste couloirs on La Saulire, and high, north-facing slopes right at the top of the 1650 sector, reached by climbing from Chanrossa.

FOR INTERMEDIATES
Paradise for all levels
All grades of intermediates love Courchevel. Novices have wonderful long runs above 1650 in the Pyramide/Grand Bosses areas. The Biollay sector also has fine, gentle slopes, leading down to the two easy home runs on either side of the Jardin Alpin.

Those of average ability can negotiate most of the red runs without too much difficulty. Our favourite is the long, sweeping Combe de la Saulire run from top to bottom of the cable-car. This is especially pleasant first thing in the morning, when it is immaculately groomed and free of crowds. (It's a rather different story at the end of the day.) The Creux run behind La Vizelle is another splendid, fast long red, while Marmottes from Vizelle itself is more challenging. The Bouc Blanc runs through the trees towards La Tania are particularly attractive. This section also has fine red runs down to the 1850 area, with easier blues running alongside. Over at 1650, the reds on Mt Bel Air and Signal are excellent, and rarely crowded.

Excursions to Méribel and the rest of the Three Valleys can be undertaken by confident intermediates. The route via Col de la Loze is easier than via La Saulire, but more exposed to sun.

FOR BEGINNERS
Great graduation runs
There are excellent nursery slopes above both 1650 and 1850. At the former, lessons are likely to begin on the short drags close to the village, but quick learners will soon be able to go from close to the top of the 1650

Sadly, Courchevel 1850 doesn't look as good as this from all angles – facing page →

facing page →

SCHOOLS/GUIDES

97/98 prices in francs

ESF in 1850
Classes 6 days
5hr: 9.30am-noon and 2.30-5pm; 2½hr: am or pm
6 full days: 1,125
Children's classes
Ages: from 4
6 full days: 875
Private lessons
2½hr morning, 2hr lunchtime, 2½hr afternoon, 7hr full day
1,350 for full day, for 1 to 4 people

ESF in 1650
Classes 6 days
4½hr: 9.30am-noon and 3pm-5pm; am (2½hr) or pm (2hr)
6 full days: 900
Children's classes
Ages: from 3
6 full day: 720
Private lessons
2½hr morning, 2hr lunchtime, 2hr afternoon, 7hr full day
1,450 for full day, for 1 to 6 people

ESF in 1550
Classes 6 days
3hr: am or pm
6 mornings: 840
Children's classes
Ages: from 3
6 full days: 960
Private lessons
3hr morning, 3hr afternoon, 7hr full day
1,450 for full day, for 1 to 6 people

Ski Academie
Classes 5 days
2½hr: am
5 mornings: 510
Children's classes
Ages: from 4
5 mornings: 510

Ski Masterclass
British-run ski school
Classes 5 days
2hr: am or pm
5 days: 695
Children's classes
Ages:
5 days, 3hr am or pm: 840

area all the way down to the village. The best nursery area at 1850 is at Pralong, above the village, near the airstrip. An easy green links this area with the runs above 1650, so adventurous novices have the opportunity to move far afield. The Bellecôte green run down into 1850 is an excellent long, gentle slope – though it would be better for beginners if it was quieter. It is served by the Jardin Alpin gondola, and by a drag-lift which is one of a dozen free beginner lifts in Courchevel. 1550 and 1300 have small nursery areas, but most people go up to 1850 – the 1300 slope is not reliably open.

FOR CROSS-COUNTRY
Long wooded trails

All the villages have some cross-country, but 1300 is by far the most suitable, with trails through the woods towards 1550, 1850 and Méribel. Given sufficient snow, there are also several loops around the village.

QUEUES
Superb lift system copes well

Even at New Year and Easter, when 1850 in particular positively teems with people, queues are minimal, thanks to the excellence of the lift system. The Verdons gondola had its capacity doubled a few years ago, alleviating this old bottleneck, and the fast-moving queues for the huge Saulire cable-car have been all but eliminated by the upgrading for 1995/96 of the parallel Vizelle gondola.

Most complaints from people based in Courchevel concern lifts in the other valleys. But the famously inadequate gondola back from Méribel-Mottaret is at last due for replacement.

MOUNTAIN RESTAURANTS
Good but expensive

Mountain restaurants are plentiful and pleasant by French standards, but prices are high – and a striking proportion of recent reporters say they rely on picnics or chocolate for lunch. It is possible to economise, if you can be bothered. For example, bar prices in hotel Courcheneige on the Bellecôte piste are half what you pay beside the slopes in central 1850. (If you want to eat at village level, you'll pay less by getting away from the lift station – or by going on down the piste, to 1550.)

The big Chalet de Pierres, on the Verdons piste just above 1850, is one

of the highlights for those inclined to extravagance – a comfortable and smooth place in traditional style (waiters in Alpine uniform, even), doing excellent food (including superb cakes) with about the highest prices of all. Only a little way behind this in the swank stakes comes the Cap Horn, near the airstrip. Much better value are the busy self-service restaurant nearby, with good food and a fine terrace, and the Verdons – well placed for piste-watching. The Chenus is an atmospheric self-service place. Le Casserole, above 1650 at the foot of the Grandes Bosses drags, is a good self-service place. Mont Bel-Air, a bit higher up, is an excellent place, with efficient and cheerful table-service, and a splendid tiered terrace; booking advised. A trip down to the Bistrot du Praz at 1300 is recommended for a blow-out on a bad-weather day. Bouc Blanc above La Tania is recommended for 'lovely' food and good views.

SCHOOLS AND GUIDES
Size is everything

Courchevel's three branches of the ESF, at 1850, 1650 and 1550, add up to the largest ski school in Europe, with a

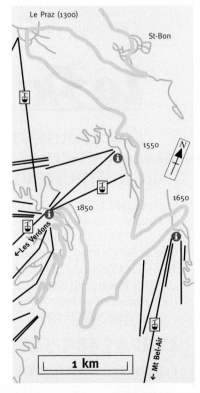

Le Praz (1300)

St-Bon

1550

1850

1650

← Les Verdons

Mt Bel-Air →

1 km

Selected chalets in Courchevel

SIMPLY SKI *Chalet specialist*   T **0181 742 2541**   F **0181 995 5346**

Simply Ski offer a choice of 9 chalets in Courchevel, ranging from the comfortable to the luxurious and sleeping from 8 to 21 guests. At Courchevel 1850, we offer Chalet L'Ancolie, rated by the Sunday Times as one of the Top 20 chalets in the world, as well as a selection of chalet apartments in the popular Forum. Our chalets in picturesque Le Praz/Courchevel 1300 are ideal for families, offering easy access to our own Snowdrop Crèche and Snowflake Club. All our chalets offer friendly chalet staff and Cordon Bleu cuisine with free Appellation Contrôlée wines. Scheduled BA flights, regional charters, Snowtrain and self-drive.

CHALET SENECHAL →

SKI OLYMPIC *Great value chalets*   T **01302 390120**   F **01302 390787**

With 5 chalets and 3 chalet hotels in Courchevel and Méribel, Ski Olympic have a great choice to suit all needs.

Chalet Monique, for example, is a superb chalet with 12 en-suite rooms. Here operates the exclusive 'chalet service plus' with enhanced level of service and cuisine, while the chalet hotels are great for groups and families. A nanny service is available in both resorts. Every property also has a resident guide whose services are available 4/5 days each week.

Other resorts featured by Ski Olympic are: Tignes, La Plagne (Les Coches), La Rosière and Meribel.

← CHALET MONIQUE   CHALET MORS →

CHILDCARE

There are kindergartens in 1850 (479 080847) and 1650 (479 083584) which take children from age 2, until 5pm. The ESF branches in all three main parts of the resort have ski kindergartens; minimum age is 3 in 1550 (479 082107) and 1650 (479 082608) and 4 in 1850 (479 080772).

UK PACKAGES

Airtours, Bladon Lines, Chalet World, Chalets 'Unlimited', Crystal, Erna Low, Fairhand Holidays, Finlays, First Choice Ski, FlexiSki, Independent Ski Links, Inghams, Lagrange, Le Ski, Lotus Supertravel, Made to Measure, Mark Warner, Motours, Neilson, PGL Ski Europe, Powder Byrne, Silver Ski, Simply Ski, Ski Activity, Ski Arrangements, Ski Choice, Ski Esprit, Ski France, Ski Leisure Direction, Ski Les Alpes, Ski Olympic, Ski Scott Dunn, Ski Trois Vallees, Ski Weekend, Ski trek, Ski-Val, Skiworld, Stena Line Holidays, The Ski Company, Thomson, Travelscene Ski-Drive, White Roc, avant-ski

La Tania AA Ski-Driveaway, Alpine Action, Crystal, Erna Low, Fairhand Holidays, Inghams, Lagrange, Motours, Neilson, Ski France, Ski Leisure Direction, Ski trek, Stena Line Holidays, Thomson

Le Praz Ski Trois Vallées

total of almost 500 instructors. Of course, this is a reflection of the number of people taking private lessons in this affluent resort. As elsewhere, the number of pupils in a class depends on demand; in the past we have had reports of a group of 25 in the February peak. That apart, people seem generally content with the standards of instruction and English. The school contains mountain guides who can take you on some exciting excursions (eg the Glacier de Gébroulaz – see pic on page 235).

Ski Academy, an independent group of French instructors, aims to offer 'a more personal, friendly service', and claim their dozen or so instructors speak 'fluent English'. 'Adequately clear English' would be nearer the mark, in our experience, but the school has another attraction: it operates a maximum class size of seven.

FACILITIES FOR CHILDREN
Lots of chalet-based options

There is an excellent-looking ski kindergarten in 1850, which has generated positive reports from British families. There are English-speaking instructors, and the general atmosphere is 'jolly'. A recent report on children's classes in the ESF is also full of praise – 'amazing results'.

An in-house crèche in a catered chalet with British nannies is an alternative that many families have found attractive. Several chalet operators provide services of this kind, mainly in the lower resort villages, and in our experience (as in that of reporting readers) these arrangements always seem to work well.

Staying there 🔑

The choice of which part of Courchevel to go to depends on how much importance you attach to nightlife (1850 best), charm (1300 best) or the quality and price of your accommodation.

In all three of the higher resorts, there is accommodation close to the lifts and runs. The prime place to stay is close to the main lift station at 1850 or on the runs leading down to it. A number of chalets and hotels are pleasantly sited among the trees that surround the village or on the slopes up towards the airport – ideal for access to the slopes, but making evening trips into town a bit of a trek.

HOW TO GO
Value chalets and apartments

Huge numbers of British tour operators go to Courchevel, with a wide choice of accommodation.

Chalets There are plenty of chalets available from dozens of UK tour operators, including some very comfortable ones and a few that are genuinely luxurious. There are places in La Tania, 1300, 1550 and 1650, as well as the main resort of Courchevel 1850. As usual in a French resort with a stock of ageing hotel buildings, there are also some chalet-hotels run by UK tour operators.

Our favourite place to stay in 1850 (when the budget allows) is FlexiSki's Lodge – an exceptionally comfortable and charming cross between a chalet and a small hotel (you can take a room by the night). Simply Ski's L'Ancolies is a conventional but rather special chalet, elegantly furnished, and with numerous mod cons.

Hotels There are nearly 50 hotels in Courchevel, mostly at 1850. Three-quarters of these are graded 3-star and above, though some would have lower ratings in other countries.

((((5) **Bellecôte** (1850) Our favourite among the more swanky places – it offers some Alpine atmosphere as well as sheer luxury.

((((5) **Mélezin** (1850) Superbly stylish and luxurious – and in an ideal position beside the bottom of the Bellecôte home slope.

((((4) **Grandes Alpes** (1850) In pole position, on the piste right next to the main lifts.

((((4) **Rond Point** (1850) Recently revived after a prolonged closure – a relaxed family atmosphere and an excellent central position.

((((4) **Lodge** (1850) Cute little British-run chalet-hotel in a good position above the resort. Bookable through FlexiSki in UK.

(((3) **Courcheneige** (1850) Pleasantly informal, large chalet in quiet position on the piste above the resort, with a popular lunchtime terrace.

(((3) **Ducs de Savoie** (1850) Pleasant, wood-built; well placed in the trees for skiing to the door, but only five minutes' walk from the village.

(((3) **Sivoliere** (1850) No beauty, but charming and comfortable inside and pleasantly set among pines.

(((3) **Golf** (1650) Pleasant, good-value 3-star, in a superb position on the piste next to the gondola station.

GETTING THERE

Air Geneva, transfer 3½hr. Lyon, transfer 3½hr. Chambery, transfer 2½hr. Direct flights to Courchevel altiport from London at weekends only (contact tourist office for details).

Rail Moûtiers (24km); transfer by bus or taxi.

ACTIVITIES

Indoor Artificial skating rink, bridge, chess, squash, swimming and saunas (hotels), gymnasium, health and fitness centres (swimming pools, sauna, steam-room, Jacuzzi, water therapy, weight-training, massage), bowling, exhibitions (galleries in 1850 and 1650), cinema, games rooms, billiards, language courses **Outdoor** Hang-gliding, paragliding, flying lessons, parachuting, floodlit skiing, ski jumping, toboggan runs, snow-shoe excursions, snowmobile rides, dog-sleigh rides, 35km cleared paths, 2km toboggan run, curling, ice-climbing, flight excursions

TOURIST OFFICE

Postcode 73122
Tel +33 479 080029
Fax 479 081563

③ **Ancolies** (1550) 'A real find,' says an American visitor, impressed by the warmth and hospitality of the staff and the excellent food.
② **Chanrossa** (1550) This attractive 2-star is a friendly, well placed hotel.
② **Peupliers** (1300) Well placed and cheap by local standards.

Self-catering There's a large selection of apartments in 1850, 1650 and La Tania, though high-season packages can get sold out early. Some UK tour operators have apartments in the smart and superbly positioned Forum complex in 1850; watch out, though, for cramped windowless bedrooms.

EATING OUT
You pay for quality
Restaurants are, in the main, high in quality and price. Self-caterers on a budget may be forced to cook for themselves whether they want to or not. Despite the resort's international outlook, practically all the cuisine is French – a couple of Italian places is as adventurous as it gets.

Among the best, and priciest, restaurants are the Michelin 2-stars Chabichou and Bateau Ivre in 1850. The 'friendly' Bercail also has a high reputation, notably for seafood. Other recommendations for Savoyard food include the cosy La Saulire (aka Jacques' bar – booking essential) and its sister restaurant La Fromagerie; and the good-value Chardon Bleu and Mazot – 'very traditional'.

Many staying in 1850 venture to the other villages in search of lower prices. The Chanrossa hotel restaurant and the Cortona pizza place in 1550 are good value by local standards. Also recommended are the Lizard and the Plouc (for eat-in or take-away pizza) at 1650. Bistrot du Praz in 1300 is pricey but excellent.

APRES-SKI
1850 has it
If you want nightlife, it's got to be 1850. There are some exclusive night clubs, such as La Grange and Les Caves, with top Paris cabaret acts and sky-high prices. The Bergerie does themed evenings – food, music, entertainment two or three times a week. The recently opened piano/champagne bar of the Cendrée Italian restaurant is proving popular. The more down-to-earth Bar L'Equipe seems to be readers' favourite

nightspot; opinions are divided on the Wednesday karaoke sessions. Jacques, L'Arbe, Tee-Jay's and the (relatively) cheap and cheerful Potinière are also popular bars.

The Croisette cinema has a couple of English-language films each week. Concerts take place from time to time.

The lower villages are quieter, though buses run late enough for cinema and bar excursions to 1850. It's a pity that the gondola between 1550 and 1850 doesn't run in the evening.

The 1650 scene has livened up in recent years, not least because of the number of rowdy Brits it is attracting. The Signal bar is renowned for its views at the back and its incredibly strong Mutzig; this and Rocky's bar are described by one recent visitor as 'like Blackpool on a bad night – strictly for the eight-pints-a-night drinker'. Le Plouc is an intimate, welcoming French bar with good music. Even the uninspiring Green Club livens up occasionally these days. A reporter tells us of a 'buzzing' boarders' bar, but doesn't name it.

In 1550 the Chanrossa bar is British-dominated, the Taverne 'French and friendly'.

In 1300 the pizzeria tucked away in the shopping mall is the social hub, with live music and modest prices.

OFF THE SLOPES
1850 isn't bad
Courchevel isn't an ideal all-round winter resort. The range of activities available has improved in recent years – the new Forum sports centre in 1850 is an asset – but the villages are not particularly pleasant places in which to spend time, shopping is limited, and excursion possibilities even more so. A pedestrian lift pass for the gondolas and buses in the Courchevel and Méribel valleys makes it easy to get around the area and meet companions for lunch on the slopes. And you can take joy-rides from the altiport, and try to spot your friends below.

Les Deux-Alpes   1650m

Twin attractions of snow and fun

WHAT IT COSTS

((((4)

HOW IT RATES

The slopes

Snow	****
Extent	***
Experts	****
Intermediates	**
Beginners	***
Convenience	***
Queues	**
Restaurants	*

The rest

Scenery	****
Resort charm	**
Off-slope	**

- ➕ High, snowsure slopes, including an extensive glacier area
- ➕ Varied high-mountain terrain, from motorway cruising to seriously steep blacks and off-piste slopes
- ➕ Efficient, modern lift system
- ➕ Excellent, sunny nursery slopes
- ➕ Stunning views of the Ecrins peaks
- ➕ Lively, varied nightlife
- ➕ Wide choice of hotels

- ➖ Piste network modest by French mega-resort standards – and badly congested in places
- ➖ Only one easy run back to the resort – a busy zig-zag path; others are red or black, and often ruined by sun
- ➖ Virtually no woodland runs
- ➖ Spread-out, traffic-choked resort
- ➖ Few appealing mountain restaurants

We have a love–hate relationship with Les Deux-Alpes. We love the high-Alps feel of its main mountain, and the good snow to be found on the large proportion of the runs that lie above 2100m and face north. Choked though it is by traffic, we quite like the buzz of the town – arriving here is a bit like driving into Las Vegas from the Nevada desert – and we understand the appeal of the resort's vibrant nightlife. We are less enamoured of the congestion that results from having a very efficient lift system above a very big resort, serving a piste area that, in practice, is quite modest in size – if you discount the sunny, steep and ice-prone slopes directly above the village, and if you bear in mind that most of the glacier is a giant nursery slope.

Crowding apart, keen intermediates spoilt by high-mileage French mega-resorts (and not up to the excellent off-piste) will simply find the area rather small.

 Les Deux-Alpes has been attracting snowboarders for quite a while, and has built up a good reputation. Beginners start on the slopes just in front of the resort, and are usually taught how to use the numerous drags at this level early on. Higher up the mountain in the Toura sector, where most lifts are chairs, a 'surf' park was opened last season, with tables and barbie stuff as well as a half-pipe. At the top, there's the glacier (access is by T-bar or funicular), which has a half-pipe in summer. With cheap and plentiful accommodation, and noisy, lively nightlife in the bars and discos, it's a well-deserved reputation.

What's new

Last season the long-awaited Fee chair-lift was opened, serving the new blue and black pistes in the Les Gours sector – welcome additions to what is still a rather confined piste network. There's a new restaurant at the bottom, following the equally welcome construction of the splendid Chalet de la Toura the previous year. If this carries on, we'll have to consider awarding Les Deux Alpes two stars for mountain restaurants, not one.

The resort

Les Deux-Alpes is a narrow village sitting on a high, remote col. Access is from the Grenoble-Briançon road to the north or by gondola from Venosc. The village is a long, sprawling collection of hotels, apartments, bars and shops, most lining the busy main street and the parallel street that completes the one-way traffic system. Although there is no centre as such, and lifts are spread fairly evenly along the village, a couple of focal points are evident.

The resort has grown up haphazardly over the years, and there is a wide range of building styles, from old chalets through monstrous 1960s blocks to more sympathetic recent developments.

France does have worse-looking resorts, though not many. Fans point out that it looks better as you drive out than as you drive in, because all the apartment buildings have their balconies facing the remote southern end of the resort.

The lively ambience helps to distract you from the look of the place. Bars, restaurants and nightclubs that originally catered for young French weekenders now cater equally well for the growing contingent of young Brits in search of fun. The resort is popular with Italians too, especially at weekends and in summer.

MOUNTAIN FACTS

Altitude 1300m-3570m
Lifts 63
Pistes 200km
Green/Blue 62%
Red 28%
Black 10%
Artificial snow 4km
Recco detectors used

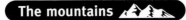

The mountains

For a big resort, Les Deux-Alpes has a disappointingly small piste area, despite recent improvements. Although extremely long and tall (it rises almost 2000m) it is also very narrow, with just a few runs on the upper part of the mountain, served by a few long, efficient lifts. Many of the higher blue runs are easy and crowded and most of the red and black runs rising above the resort are steep, and tricky in the poor snow conditions that often apply. The area has considerable attractions for experts (largely off-piste). For novices, there are very easy green runs on the glacier, as well as good village nursery slopes.

THE SLOPES
Long, narrow and fragmented

The western **Pied-Moutet** side of Les Deux-Alpes is relatively little-used. It is served by lifts from various parts of town but reaches only 2100m. As well as the short runs back to town which get the morning sun, there's an attractive, longer north-facing run off the back which goes down through the trees to the small village of Bons. This is one of only two tree-lined runs in

↑ If you don't spot the sign, you could be in trouble

LIFT PASSES

Super ski pass
Covers all lifts in Les Deux-Alpes, entry to swimming pool and skating rink.
Beginners 3 free lifts; 'Première trace' pass covers 19 lifts.
Main pass
1-day pass 182
6-day pass 908
(low season 817 – 10% off)
Senior citizens
Over 60: 6-day pass 681 (25% off)
Children
Under 13: 6-day pass 681 (25% off)
Under 4: free pass
Short-term passes
Half-day 145
Notes 6-day pass includes one day's skiing in Alpe-d'Huez, Serre-Chevalier, Puy-Saint-Vincent and the Milky Way.
Alternative passes
3 limited area passes: 'Ski première trace' covers 19 lifts (86 per day), 'Ski sympa' covers 27 lifts (107 per day), 'Grand ski' covers 39 lifts (138 per day).

Les Deux-Alpes – the other going down to another low village, Mont-de-Lans, and reachable from either sector.

On the main, **eastern side** of the valley, the broad, steep slope immediately above the village offers a series of relatively short, testing runs, down to the nursery slopes ranged at the bottom of the hill.

Most of the runs back down to the resort deserve a black rating. They are usually mogulled and often icy early and late in the day because they get the afternoon sun. The resort has had some difficulty coming to terms with this. For some years, some of these runs – notably Sapins and Diable – have been marked black on the ground but red on the piste map. In 1995, at last, the piste map was brought into line with the facts.

The ridge above the village has lifts and gentle runs along it, and behind it the deep, steep Combe de Thuit. Lifts span the combe to the main mid-mountain station at 2600m, passing over the smaller lift junction of Lac du Plan in the process. The middle section, above and below 2600m, is made up primarily of blue cruising runs and is very narrow. At one point, there is essentially just a single run down the mountain – a broad ledge which skirts the Combe de Thuit back to the 'home' ridge. There are various chair-lift-served diversions you can take from the main channel, and it is now possible to avoid the Thuit ledge by taking the roundabout Gours run to the bottom of the combe, where a new lift takes you up to the 'home' ridge. This pleasant run passes the base of the new Fée, serving a new black run as well as the blue Gours.

The top **Glacier de Mont-de-Lans** section, served by drag-lifts and the warmer underground funicular, has some fine, very easy runs which afford great views and are ideal for beginners and the less adventurous. You can go from the top here all the way down to Mont-de-Lans – a descent of 2268m vertical which, as far as we know, is the world's biggest on-piste vertical.

The six-day pass covers a day in each of Alpe-d'Huez, Serre-Chevalier, Puy-St-Vincent and the Milky Way resorts from Montgenèvre to Sauze d'Oulx. All are easily reached by car, road conditions permitting. Helicopter trips to Alpe-d'Huez are easily arranged and good value (FF350 return). You can get to La Grave by walking from

the top of the Les Deux-Alpes domain, but at present there is no lift-pass-sharing arrangement.

SNOW RELIABILITY
Excellent on higher slopes

The snow on the higher slopes is normally very good, even in a poor winter – one of the main reasons for Les Deux-Alpes' popularity. Above 2200m most of the runs are north-facing, and the top glacier section guarantees good snow. You should worry more about bad weather shutting the lifts, or extremely low temperatures high up, than about snow shortage.

But the runs just above the village face west, so they get a lot of afternoon sun and can be icy at the beginning and end of the day. Artificial snow on some of the lower slopes helps keep them usable.

FOR EXPERTS
Off-piste is the main attraction

With good snow and weather conditions, the area offers wonderful off-piste sport.

There are several good off-piste runs within the lift network, including a number of variations from underneath the top stage of the Jandri Express down to the Thuit chair-lift. The best-known ones are now marked on the piste map. The easy gunbarrel of Les Gours is now a piste, but the new Fée chair has opened up new off-piste possibilities into the Combe de Thuit. There are also more serious routes that end well outside the lift network, with verticals of over 2000m.

The Tête Moute chair-lift, from the top of the Diable gondola, serves the steepest black run around. The brave can also try off-piste variations here between the rocks.

FOR INTERMEDIATES
Limited cruising

Les Deux-Alpes can disappoint intermediates. A lot of the runs are either fairly tough or boringly bland. The steep runs just above the resort put off many. As one of our reporters (who classes himself as an 'advanced' skier) said, 'I myself fell from top to bottom. I was lucky. A girl in the "Tour of the Pistes" group broke her back. You cannot afford to be complacent getting back to the village.'

The runs higher up generally have good snow, and aggressive

SCHOOLS/GUIDES

97/98 prices in francs

ESF
Classes 6 days
3hr: am; 2½hr: pm
6 mornings: 720
Children's classes
Ages: 6 to 12
6 mornings: 600
Private lessons
1hr over lunchtime or
full day Sunday
180 for 1hr, for 1 to 4
people

International St-Christophe
Classes 6 days
2½hr: am or pm
6 mornings: 660
Children's classes
Ages: 6 to 12
6 mornings: 520
Private lessons
1hr over lunchtime
195 for 1hr, for 1 to 4
people

CHILDCARE

Both ski schools run
kindergartens on
more-or-less identical
terms – taking
children aged 4 to 6
until 5pm. The ESF
(476 792121) is
slightly more
expensive and does
lunch only on
request, but starts at
9.15am whereas the
ESI de St Christophe
(476 790421) starts at
9.30am. The Crèche
du Village offers an
excellent service for
babies from 6 months
to 2 years, from
8.30am to 5.30pm.
Garderie du
Bonhomme de Neige
for children aged 2 to
6 years.
List of babysitters
available from the
tourist office.

intermediates can enjoy great, fast
cruising, especially on the mainly
north-facing pistes served by the chair-
lifts off to the sides. You can often
pick gentle or steeper terrain in these
bowls as you wish, but avid piste-
bashers will explore all there is to offer
in a couple of days. Most of our
reporters made use of their lift passes
to take excursions to Alpe-d'Huez and
Serre-Chevalier.

Less confident intermediates will
love the quality of the snow and the
gentleness of most of the runs on the
upper mountain. Their problem might
lie in finding the pistes too crowded,
especially if snow is poor in other
resorts and people are bussed in. At
the end of the day, you can ride the
Jandri Express down.

FOR BEGINNERS
Good slopes
The nursery slopes beside the village
are spacious and gentle. The run along
the ridge above them is excellent, too.
The glacier also has a fine array of very
easy slopes – but bear in mind that
bad weather can close the lifts to get
up there.

FOR CROSS-COUNTRY
Needs very low-altitude snow
There are three small, widely dispersed
areas. Le Petite Alpe, near the entrance
to the village, has a couple of
snowsure but very short trails. Given
good snow, Venosc (950m), reached
by a gondola down, has the only
worthwhile picturesque ones. Total trail
distance is 20km.

QUEUES
Can be a problem
Les Deux-Alpes has a great deal of
hardware to keep queues minimal. But
the village is large, and peak morning
queues can be long for the Jandri
Express and Diable gondolas. The
Jandri queue moves quickly and, if you
are headed for the top, it is worth
using that lift to avoid further queues
for the second stage.

Problems can also occur when
people are bussed in from
neighbouring resorts when snow is in
short supply. At such times the lower
slopes at Les Deux-Alpes are likely to
be out of action too, causing even
longer queues for the Jandri Express.
The top lifts are prone to closure if it's
windy, putting pressure on the lower
lifts.

MOUNTAIN RESTAURANTS
100% improvement recently
There are mountain restaurants at all
the major lift junctions, but they are
generally pretty poor. La Pastorale, at
the top of the Diable gondola, has for
years been the only recommendable
place (despite huge queues for the
loo). But a couple of years ago the
scene was transormed by the
construction of the splendid Chalet de
la Toura, in the middle of the domain
at about 2600m, with a big terrace, a
welcoming woody interior and efficient
table-service throughout. Another new
restaurant, La Refuge de la Fée, was
opened last year at the bottom of the
new Fée lift.

SCHOOLS AND GUIDES
One of the better ESFs
There are two schools, both of which
have good reputations for standards of
tuition and English, although class
sizes can be large. The School of
Adventure section will take you to
nearby resorts on the lift pass.

FACILITIES FOR CHILDREN
Fine for babies
Babies can safely be entrusted to the
village crèche, and there are chalet-
based alternatives run by UK tour
operators.

 **Staying there**

Alpe de Venosc, at the southern end of
town, has many of the nightspots and
hotels, the most character, the fewest
cars and the best shops. It also has
immediate access via the Diable
gondola to the tough terrain around
Tête Moute, but getting to other parts
of the mountain is a roundabout
business compared with going up the
Jandri Express. This starts from the
geographical centre, where there is a
popular outdoor ice rink and some
good restaurants and bars. The village
straggles north from here, becoming
less convenient the further you go. 'Le
Village' consists of a cluster of
apartments, a sports centre, a chair-lift
and little else, and is an inconvenient
distance from the rest of town.

HOW TO GO
Wide range of packages
Les Deux-Alpes has something for most
tastes, including that rarity in high-
altitude French resorts, reasonably
priced hotels.

UK PACKAGES

Airtours, Alpine Options Snowtrain and Skidrive Holidays, Chalet Freestyle, Chalet Snowboard, Chalets 'Unlimited', Crystal, Equity School Ski, Equity Total Ski, Fairhand Holidays, First Choice Ski, Inghams, Lagrange, Made to Measure, Motours, Ski Amis, Ski Arrangements, Ski Club Europe, Ski Club of GB, Ski Leisure Direction, Ski Valkyrie, Ski trek, Skiworld, Sloping Off, Thomson, UCPA

Mont-de-Lans Alpine Options Snowtrain and Skidrive Holidays

GETTING THERE

Air Lyon, transfer 3½hr. Grenoble, transfer 2hr. Chambery, transfer 3hr. Geneva, transfer 4½hr.
Rail Grenoble (70km); 4 daily buses from station.

ACTIVITIES

Indoor 2 sports centres; Club Forme (squash, swimming pool, sauna, jacuzzi), Tanking Centre (floatation chambers, physiotherapy, pressotherapy, sauna, jacuzzi, turkish baths)
Outdoor Ice skating, swimming pool, snow-shoe excursions

TOURIST OFFICE

Postcode 38860
Tel +33 476 792200
Fax 476 790138

Chalets There are a number of catered chalet packages available from UK tour operators, but some use cramped apartments rather than real chalets.
Hotels There are over 30 hotels, of which the majority are 2-star or below.
(((3) **Bérangère** Smartest in town, although dreary to look at, with Michelin-starred restaurant and pool; on-piste, but at the less convenient north end of resort.
(((3) **Farandole** Better placed for nightlife and shopping, and within comfortable walking distance of the Diable bubble and east-facing slopes.
((2) **Chalet Mounier** Smartly modernised. Good reputation for its food, and well placed for the Diable bubble and nightlife.
((2) **Souleil'Or** Looks like a lift station, but appearances are deceptive. Pleasant and comfortable, and well placed for the Jandri Express gondola.
((2) **Brunerie** Cheap and cheerful, large 2-star Logis with plenty of parking and quite well positioned.
Self-catering Many of the apartments are stuck out at Le Village, at the north end of the resort, so it is well worth shopping around for more centrally situated ones.

STAYING DOWN THE VALLEY
Close to the foot of the final ascent to Les Deux-Alpes are two near-ideal places for anyone thinking of travelling around to Alpe-d'Huez, La Grave and Serre-Chevalier, both Logis de France – the cheerful 13-room Cassini at Le Freney, and the even more appealing 10-room Panoramique, at Mizoën.

EATING OUT
Plenty of choice
The village restaurants are much better than those up the mountain. The Bérangère has a Michelin star and Chalet Mounier has a reputation for some of the best food in town. Le Petit Marmite has good food and atmosphere at reasonable prices. Booking is essential. Patate and Crêpes à Gogo are recommended. Visitors on a budget can get a relatively cheap Italian meal at either Vetrata or the Spaghetteria.

APRES-SKI
Unsophisticated fun
Les Deux-Alpes is one of the liveliest of French resorts, with plenty of bars to choose from. The Rodeo has a mechanical bucking bronco which

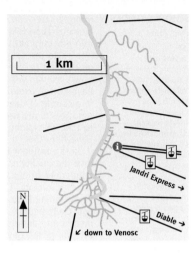

attracts great numbers of rowdy après-skiers, many of them Brits. Mike's (which tour operators use a lot for quiz nights) and the Windsor are other noisy British enclaves. Smokey Joe's is recommended for its FF10 dice throwing – what you throw determines what drink you get! Bar Brazillienne is recommended for 'great music and tremendous atmosphere'. There are plenty of quieter places around too, and discos that get lively late at night.
The resort has contrived a couple of ways of dining at altitude – you can snowmobile to the glacier and back, eating on the way (you're allowed one glass of wine), or at full moon you can ski or board back to town after dinner.

OFF THE SLOPES
Not recommended
Les Deux-Alpes is not a particularly good choice for people not hitting the slopes. It is quiet during the day, the shopping is uninspiring and the village is rather cut off, with little public transport for excursions.
The pretty valley village of Venosc is well worth a visit by gondola, and you might be tempted to take the helicopter flight with skiers or boarders in your party to Alpe-d'Huez (though there's even less to amuse you there).
For the active there are plenty of sports facilities, and these now include the Pumper – a sort of bungy jump in reverse that catapults you into the air.
Only one of the decent mountain restaurants is easily accessible to pedestrians, and you can't count on skiers or boarders coming back to the village for lunch if the lower slopes are icy, as they often are.

Flaine

A high, white wilderness with links to the real world

WHAT IT COSTS

(((3)))

HOW IT RATES

The slopes

Snow	****
Extent	****
Experts	****
Intermediates	*****
Beginners	*****
Convenience	*****
Queues	****
Restaurants	**

The rest

Scenery	****
Resort charm	*
Off-slope	*

➕ Big, varied area, with off-piste challenges for experts as well as extensive intermediate terrain

➕ Reliable snow in the main bowl

➕ Compact, convenient, mainly car-free village, right on the slopes

➕ Excellent facilities for children

➕ Scenic setting, and glorious views

➕ Short transfer from Geneva airport

➖ Dreary architecture

➖ Not much nightlife

➖ Little to do off the slopes

So long as you don't care about the uncompromising architecture or lack of lively evening ambience, Flaine has a lot going for it. Many people, especially those with children, love it.

There is some very pleasant and convenient accommodation. If you want to spend a holiday with your kids, there is everything to help you – and the ski schools have improved in recent years. Flaine has slopes that intermediates will love, and lots of them; with its links to Samoëns, Morillon and Les Carroz, the Grand Massif lives up to its name. Flaine caters well for beginners too, with free access to nursery slope lifts. But there is also challenging terrain for experts – particularly for those prepared to take guidance and go off-piste.

What's new

Perhaps the biggest news from Flaine is that there are some faint stirrings of a nightlife scene.

There is no sign yet of a lift up from Sixt, reachable on-piste since the blue run on the left of the map was expensively created a couple of seasons ago. The ownership of the Flaine lift company is about to change, which could bring welcome investment and development.

MOUNTAIN FACTS

Altitude	700m-2480m
Lifts	80
Pistes	265km
Green/Blue	39%
Red	46%
Black	15%
Artificial snow	5km
Recco detectors used	

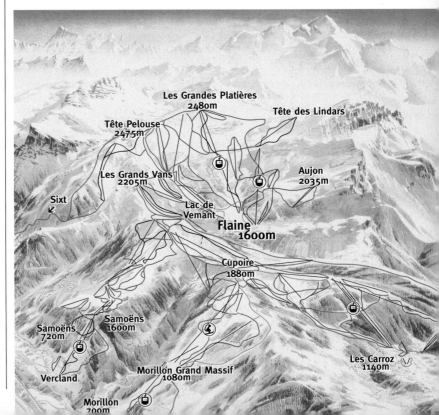

boarding *Flaine's mountain suits boarders quite well – there are smooth cruising/carving runs, bumpy terrain and plenty of off-piste, including woods if you get outside the main bowl, and the chance to get heli-lifts back to base from remote spots. But the everyday lifts aren't ideal – the main lift is a gondola, and there are some chairs, but there are many more drags, some unavoidable if you want to get around the whole area. There's a fun-park with half-pipe – location depends on the snow conditions. And the ESF runs a special fun-park for kids, Fantasurf Land, a great idea for a family-oriented resort like this. BackSide is the local specialist shop, right in the central Forum.*

The resort

In our unofficial vote for Ugliest Resort in the Alps, Flaine was narrowly beaten by Les Menuires. Like 'Les Manures', it has a nickname based on how horrid it looks: 'Phlegm'. The concrete massifs that are its buildings were conceived in the sixties as 'an example of the application of the principle of shadow and light'. They look particularly shocking the first time you see them from the approach road – a mass of blocks nestling at the bottom of a bleak but impressive snowy bowl. The one good thing about these blocks is that from the slopes you can hardly see them, as they blend into the rocky grey hillside.

In common with other French Alpine carbuncles, efforts have been made to improve Flaine's looks. The recent development of Hameau-de-Flaine is built in a much more attractive chalet style – but is inconveniently situated a good 15-minute walk or a short bus-ride from the slopes. Many of the hotels and apartments have been smartened up internally too.

Whatever the aesthetic qualities of Flaine, from the convenience point of view the planners made no mistakes with the layout. There is supermarket and speciality food shopping close to all the Forum and Forêt accommodation; sports hire shops are a short hop away; the lifts are easy to get to, and trips to organise lift passes, school and so on are no problem. It is also easy to get to, being only 70km from Geneva, with a very short airport transfer (around 90 minutes)

There are two main parts to the main resort. The hotels, and some apartments, are set in the lower part, Forum. The focus of this area is a snow-covered square with buildings on three sides, with the fourth side being the piste back from the slopes. Watch out for skiers and boarders when you're strolling from the hotels on one side to the bars and shops on the other. Flaine Forêt has its own bars and shops and most of the apartment accommodation. Neither centre is very lively at night.

There are children all over the place; they are catered for with play areas, and the resort is supposed to be traffic-free. This has become pretty lax, in fact, and there is an uncomfortable amount of traffic around; but the central Forum itself, leading to the pistes, is pretty safe.

The mountains

With its 265km of pistes, the Grand Massif claims to be the third largest resort in France (behind the Three Valleys and Espace Killy – the Franco-Swiss Portes du Soleil doesn't count). Whatever the truth of that, the Grand Massif is a genuinely impressive area with plenty of scope for any standard of skier or boarder, provided you can get to all of it – the greater part of the domain lies outside the main Flaine bowl.

THE SLOPES
A big white playground

The day begins for most people at the **Grandes Platières** high-capacity stand-up gondola, which speeds you in a single long stage up the north face of the Flaine bowl to the 2480m high-point of the Grand Massif, and a magnificent view of Mont Blanc.

Most of the runs are reds (though there are some blues curling away to the right as you look down the mountain, and one direct black). There are essentially four or five main ways down the barren, treeless, rolling terrain back to Flaine, or to chairs in the middle of the wilderness going back to the summit.

On the far right, a broad cat-walk leads to the experts-only **Gers** bowl. A long, winding blue piste has been created from the bottom to the outskirts of Sixt (770m), which has its

LIFT PASSES

97/98 prices in francs
Grand Massif
Covers all the lifts in Flaine, Les Carroz, Morillon, Samoëns and Sixt.
Beginners Four free lifts. Ski pass for beginners covers more 3 lifts (89 per day for adults, 65 for children).
Main pass
1-day pass 177
6-day pass 860
Senior citizens
Over 60: 6-day pass 640 (26% off)
Children
Under 11: 6-day pass 580 (33% off)
Under 5: free pass
Notes Discount on all ski-passes for 12- to 15-year-olds (6-day 640).
Alternative passes
Flaine area only (1-day pass 155 for adults, 110 for children).

SCHOOLS/GUIDES

97/98 prices in francs

ESF
Classes 6 days
4hr: 10am-noon and
2.30-4.30
6 full days: 700
Children's classes
Ages: 3 to 12
6 full days: 590
Private lessons
1hr, 2hr or 6hr
190 for 1hr, for 1 to 2
people

International
Classes 6 days
4hr: 9.30-11.30 and
2.30-4.30
6 full days: 695
Children's classes
Ages: 4 to 12
6 full days: 565
Private lessons
1hr, 2hr or full day
180 for 1hr

Flaine Super Ski
Advanced skiers only

**Independent
instructors**
Hired by the day,
hour or week;
contact Guy Pezet
450 478454

own little west-facing area offering red and black slopes of 700m vertical. The creation of this piste, a massive undertaking in itself, is to be followed, one day, by the construction of a lift back into the Flaine slopes. In the meantime there is a regular shuttle bus service back to Samoëns or Morillon.

Back at Grandes Platières, the alternative is to head left down the long red Méphisto (all the reds in this area have diabolic names – Lucifer, Belzebuth etc) to the **Aujon** area. This opens up another sector of the bowl, again mostly red runs but with some blues further down. The lower slopes here are used as slalom courses. This sector is also reachable by gondola or drag-lifts from below the resort.

The pistes in the Flaine bowl are mostly punchy medium-length runs. For a collection of longer cruises, head out of the bowl via the Grands Vans chair, reached from Forum by means of a slow bucket lift (aka télébenne or 'yogurt pots'). From the top, you go over the edge of the bowl and have a choice of three different resorts to head towards, each with its own lifts and runs. The lie of the land hereabouts is complicated, and the piste map does not represent it clearly.

In good snow there is a choice of

blues and reds winding down to **Les Carroz** (1140m) or **Morillon** (700m), the latter with a half-way point at 1100m – Morillon Grand Massif. There are only mogully blacks and reds down towards **Samoëns 1600** and on down to Vercland, a couple of miles from Samoëns itself.

Getting back to the crucial Grands Vans drag-lift for the return to Flaine can be complicated, so don't leave it too late. Over the years, many reporters have complained about this bent drag-lift, and rightly; in a premier-league area, a key end-of-day connection like this should not depend on a tricky button-lift.

Arrival back in Flaine can cause a problem: some reporters have complained that it's difficult to get between the top of the resort and Forum. The trick is to loop round away from the buildings and approach from under the gondola.

It is possible to visit the slopes of Chamonix and neighbouring resorts by road, or even to make a quick trip to Italy through the Mont Blanc tunnel.

SNOW RELIABILITY
Usually keeps its whiteness
The main part of Flaine's slopes lie on the wide north- and north-west-facing flank of the Grandes Platières. Its direction, along with a decent height, means that it keeps the snow it receives. There is now snowmaking on the greater part of the Aujon sector and on the nursery slopes. The runs towards Samoëns 1600 and Morillon are north-facing too, but the lower parts are frequently unpleasant or impassable. The Les Carroz runs are west-facing and can suffer from strong afternoon sun, but one of the runs has snowmaking. So do the slopes close to Samoëns 1600 and Morillon Grand Massif. Several reporters have complained that the Grand Massif needs better snowmaking facilities, and we have complaints of lax grooming of blue runs.

FOR EXPERTS
Great fun with guidance
Flaine's family-friendly reputation tends to obscure the fact that it has some seriously testing terrain. But much of it is off-piste and, although some of Flaine's off-piste runs look like they can safely be explored without guidance, this impression is mistaken. The Flaine bowl is riddled with rock

crevasses and potholes, and should be treated with the same caution that you would use on a glacier. There have been some tragic cases of off-piste skiers coming across nasty surprises, including a British skier falling to his death only yards from the piste.

All the black pistes on the map deserve their grading. The Diamant Noir, down the line of the main gondola, is a testing 850m descent, tricky because of moguls, narrowness and other people rather than because of great steepness; the first pitch down from the summit plateau is one of the most unnerving, with spectators applauding on the overhead chair-lift.

To the left of the Diamant Noir as you look down are several short but steep off-piste routes through the crags of the Grandes Platières.

The Lindars Nord chair serves a shorter slope that often has the best snow in the area, and some seriously steep gradients if you look for them.

The Gers drag-lift, outside the main bowl beyond Tête Pelouse, serves great expert-only terrain. The piste going down the right of the drag is a proper black, but by departing from it you can find slopes of up to 45°. To the left of the drag is the impressive main Gers bowl – a great horseshoe of about 550m vertical, powder or moguls top to bottom, all off-piste. You can choose your gradient, from steep to very steep. As you look down the bowl, you can see more adventurous ways into the bowl from the Grands Vans and Tête de Veret lifts.

There are further serious pistes on the top lifts above Samoëns 1600.

Touring is a possibility in the Desert de Platé area, behind the Grandes Platières, and there are some scenic off-piste routes from which you can be retrieved by helicopter – notably the Combe des Foges, next to Gers. Make sure the pilot gives you the exciting ride home, not the tame one.

FOR INTERMEDIATES
Something for everyone
Flaine is ideal for confident intermediates, with a great variety of pistes (and usually the bonus of good snow conditions, at least above Flaine itself). The diabolically named reds which dominate the Flaine bowl are not really as hellish as their names imply – they tend to gain their status from short steep sections rather than overall difficulty, and they're great for improving technique. There are gentler cruises from the top of the mountain – Cristal, taking you to the Perdrix chair which goes back up to the top, or Serpentine, all the way home.

The connections with the slopes outside the main bowl are graded blue but at least one blue-run reporter found them tricky. Once outside the bowl all intermediates will enjoy the long tree-lined runs down to Les Carroz, as long as the snow is good. You can choose between red routes or slightly easier blues, one of which constantly underpasses and flies over the road out of Flaine, allowing races with the coach drivers!

A trip to Morillon Grand Massif will yield some pleasure for those who want to clock up the kilometres; the journey to Samoëns 1600 is suited more to the better intermediate who likes the odd dose of moguls.

FOR BEGINNERS
Very good
There are excellent nursery slopes right by the village, served by free lifts which make a pass unnecessary until you are ready to go higher up the mountain. There are no very long green runs to progress to, but some gentle blues (see For intermediates).

CROSS-COUNTRY
Very fragmented
The Grand Massif as a whole claims 64km of cross-country tracks but little of that total is around Flaine itself. The majority is on the valley floor and dependent on low snow. Two 3km loops lie below the resort and a 600m practice loop is off the road to Les Carroz. There are extensive tracks over the mountain between Morillon and Les Carroz, with some tough uphill sections. Samoëns 1600 has its own tracks and would make the best base for cross-country enthusiasts.

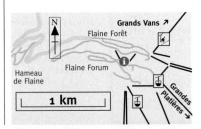

CHILDCARE

Both schools operate ski kindergartens. The ESF's Rabbit Club (450 908100) takes children aged 3 to 12, until 5pm. The SEI's Club de la Souris Verte (450 908441) takes children aged 3 to 12, until 5pm. The hotel Club Aquarius (450 908166) has a nursery for babies aged 3 months to 2 years. The ESF's Rabbit Club will pick up children from Club Aquarius for lessons, and deliver them at the end of the class. There is also an independent nursery, the Petits Loups (450 908782).

GETTING THERE

Air Geneva, transfer 1¼hr.

Rail Cluses (30km); regular bus service.

UK PACKAGES

Airtours, Crystal, Erna Low, Fairhand Holidays, First Choice Ski, Independent Ski Links, Inghams, Lagrange, Made to Measure, Motours, Neilson, On The Piste Travel Ltd, Ski Choice, Ski Club of GB, Ski Leisure Direction, Ski Safe Travel, Ski trek, Solo's, Stena Line Holidays, Thomson, Travelscene Ski-Drive

Les Carroz Fairhand Holidays, Lagrange, Stanford Skiing

Morillon Fairhand Holidays, Lagrange, PGL Ski Europe, STS

Samoëns Fairhand Holidays, Lagrange, Stena Line Holidays

QUEUES
Few real problems

There are three obvious crush points when the resort is full. The main one is the Grandes Platières gondola at the start of the day, but it is an efficient lift and the queue moves quickly, even if it does feel like 'the Northern Line at rush hour'.

Other bottlenecks – again only at holiday times – are the chair towards Samoëns and the twin drags back towards Flaine. Otherwise, reporters say queues are rare, although some of the lifts are ageing and some appear to be 'steam-driven', and the resort does get a weekend influx.

MOUNTAIN RESTAURANTS
Not a lot

In the Flaine bowl, there are few restaurants above the resort's upper outskirts. The Desert Blanc, at the top station, is a run-of-the-mill, two-room self-service snackery, with a terrace overlooking Mont Blanc. The Blanchot, at the bottom of the Serpentine run, is popular and rustic, with basic food.

At Forum level, across the piste from the main gondola, is a pair of chalets containing the welcoming and comfortable Michet, with very good Savoyard food and table service, and the self-service Eloge – friendly but with very limited food. Up the mountain, at Forêt level, Chalet Bissac has a good atmosphere, traditional decor, a huge warming fire, self service and excellent plain food. The nearby Cascade is self-service, modern and stylish, with a good terrace and amazing hi-tech loos, but the food is disappointing. The Chalet L'Epicea has a rustic atmosphere and has received rave reviews from one reporter.

Outside the bowl, the Oasis, above Morillon, and the Chalet des Molliets beside the road up from Les Carroz, are recommended.

SCHOOLS AND GUIDES
On the up?

Both the International and ESF schools have improved dramatically in recent years according to most reports, although class sizes are on the large side and the standard of English patchy. There are several small specialist schools, of which Flaine Super Ski is one, and a group of independent instructors. We can testify to the excellence of at least one of the group – Guy Pezet.

FACILITIES FOR CHILDREN
Parents' paradise? Possibly

Flaine prides itself on being a family resort, and the number of English-speaking children around is a definite bonus according to most reporters. The International Ski School has had the best reviews while opinions on the ESF for children remain mixed.

The hotel Les Lindars, traditionally popular with British families because of its special facilities – nursery, all-day crèche, ski school pick-up and drop-off service, children's dining-room, in-house babysitters, even an automatic nappy-dispenser – has changed its style as well as its name. As Club Aquarius it is now much more of a French club operation (all-in packages with lift pass) but is still available through some UK tour operators. Some other accommodation units have children's clubs.

Flaine is an excellent resort for families, not so good for anyone concerned about traditional village atmosphere ↓

ACTIVITIES

Indoor Top Form centre (swimming pool complex with sauna, solarium, gymnasium, massage), arts and crafts gallery, cinema, auditorium, concerts, indoor climbing wall
Outdoor Natural ice-rink, snow-shoe excursions, hang-gliding, paragliding paraskiing, helicopter rides, snow scooters, high mountain outings, ice-driving car circuit

TOURIST OFFICE

Postcode 74300
Tel +33 450 908001
Fax 450 908626

UK Representative

Erna Low Consultants
9 Reece Mews
London SW7 3HE
Tel 0171 584 2841
Fax 0171 589 9531

Staying there

As a purpose-built resort, Flaine is convenient regardless of where you stay, except in Hameau-de-Flaine.

HOW TO GO
Plenty of apartments
Accommodation is overwhelmingly in self-catering apartments. These are mostly based on the Forêt level and linked by lift to the shops at Forum.
Chalets There are few catered chalet options, but they include a couple of attractively traditional Scandinavian-style huts in Hameau.
Hotels There are just four hotels, all located around Forum.
(((3) **Totem** The smartest hotel, with prices to match. Modern, stylish, great views of Aujon skiing, excellent food; but the rooms are unremarkable at best and some of the staff unhelpful.
((2) **Club Aquarius** Formerly Les Lindars – see Facilities for Children. Reports on the new regime welcome.
((2) **Flaine** Renovated recently
(1) **Aujon** Large and impersonal, but good value, and liked by most visitors. One reporter says it is 'declining'.
Self-catering Most favoured by the many Brits visiting Flaine is the recently renovated Forêt. Apartments are attractively woody inside and there are hotel facilities such as a restaurant, bar and kindergarten. A similar set-up which is almost as popular is the Grand Massif. Both are right next door to the Forêt shopping centre. At Hameau, there are high-standard, roomy apartments, more comfortable than anything in the main village.

EATING OUT
Mostly fast food
Most people eat in their apartments or hotels (The Totem also takes outside bookings), but there are more interesting alternatives, and hotel residents are encouraged to use them – vouchers are available as part payment for your meal out. The bulk of the eateries are downmarket pizzerias and burger bars. For a more refined meal, the Perdrix Noire in Forêt is a good bet – smart, busy and friendly. The Michet (see Mountain restaurants) is open in the evening. In the mid-range, Trattoria is a good Italian, Chez la Jeanne is the best pizza restaurant. Chez Daniel offers Savoyard specialities such as pierrade.

APRES-SKI
Signs of life
Recent reports suggest that the après ski scene is picking up. The resort is no longer limited to family groups, and some bars show signs of life.
The White Grouse pub is boisterous: extreme sports videos compete with rock music and punters trying to get pints in before the end of happy hour.
Later, the more French Cîmes Rock is the only really lively joint, with live bands. Nightclubs include the 'seedy' Diamant Noir.

OFF THE SLOPES
Curse of the purpose-built
As with most purpose-built resorts, there are few walks, and no town to explore. Not recommended.

Les Carroz 1140m
This is a spacious, sunny, traditional, family resort where life revolves around the village square with its pavement cafés and interesting little shops. It has a 'lived-in' feel, with more animation than Flaine.
The gondola and chair-lift go straight into the Grand Massif area – but there's a steep 300m walk from the village centre.
Apartments make up a high percentage of the beds available, but there are plenty of hotels.
The village centre has a pleasant atmosphere, and the ski school's torchlit descent is something of a highlight – it's preceded by fireworks and concludes with vin chaud and live jazz in the square.
Les Carroz is best for self-drivers who want to stay in a genuine village near the snow reliability of Flaine.

Samoëns 720m
This is probably the most beautiful resort in France. It's certainly the only one to be listed as a 'Monument Historique'. Medieval fountains, rustic old buildings, an ancient church – it's all there. In the centre of the village is an impressive 8.5-acre botanical garden with thousands of plants from around the world. The traditional-style bars and restaurants give you a feel for 'real' rural France.
The slopes are a bus-ride away, but most people here have cars. The local terrain is generally testing, except around the mid-station of Samoëns 1600, and only confident skiers should consider basing themselves here.

La Grave
1450m

A superb mountain for good skiers

La Grave enjoys legendary status among experts. It's a quiet, old village with less than 1,000 beds and just one serious lift – a small cable-car/gondola serving a high, wild and entirely off-piste mountainside. The result: an exciting area that's refreshingly crowd-free – they never get more than 1,500 people on the mountain, and sometimes there are only 150. Strictly, you ought to have a guide – but in good weather hundreds of people (families included) go it alone.

WHAT IT COSTS

(((3)))

HOW IT RATES

The slopes

Snow	★★★
Extent	★★
Experts	★★★★★
Intermediates	★
Beginners	★
Convenience	★★★
Queues	★★★★
Restaurants	★★

The rest

Scenery	★★★★
Resort charm	★★★
Off-slope	★

What's new

La Grave does not change much and that is half the charm of the place. But the lift company has a new marketing manager with some wild ideas – so watch this space.

MOUNTAIN FACTS

Altitude 1450m-3550m
Lifts 4
Pistes 5km
Green/Blue 100%
(This figure relates to pistes; practically all the skiing is off-piste)
Artificial snow none
Recco detectors used

UK PACKAGES

Ski Club of GB, Ski Valkyrie, Ski Weekend

TOURIST OFFICE

Postcode 05320
Tel +33 476 799005
Fax 476 799165

THE RESORT
La Grave is an unspoilt mountaineering village set on a steep hillside facing the impressive glaciers of majestic La Meije, the last major European peak to be conquered by mountaineers. Like most French mountain villages it's drab, and the busy road through to Briançon further reduces its charm. But it still has a rustic feel, and prices in the handful of small hotels, food shops and bars are low by resort standards. The lift station is central, but when poor weather closes the slopes – on average, two days a week – a car is useful for access to other resorts.

THE MOUNTAIN
An eccentric two-stage gondola/cable-car hybrid (with an additional station at a pylon half-way up the lower stage) ascends into the **slopes** and finishes at 3200m. Above that, a short walk and a drag-lift give access to a further drag serving twin blue runs on a glacier slope of around 350m vertical. But the reason that people come here is to explore the legendary off-piste slopes back down towards La Grave. There are no defined, patrolled, prepared, avalanche-protected pistes – just a wild, north-facing mountainside with two marked itinéraires from the top to the pylon lift-station at 1800m.

The Chancel route is mostly of red-run gradient; the Vallons de la Meije, more testing but not too steep. People take these routes without a guide or avalanche protection equipment, but we couldn't possibly recommend it.

There are many more demanding runs away from the itinéraires, including couloirs that range from the straightforward to the seriously hazardous, and long descents from the glacier to the valley road below the village, with return by taxi, bus, or strategically parked car. The danger from crevasses, cliffs, avalanches and bad weather is considerable, and guidance is essential.

The chances of finding powder **snow** on La Grave's high, north-facing slopes are good, but there are no pistes to fall back on if conditions are tricky.

Only **experts** should contemplate a stay here – and then only if they are content to sit tight or struggle over the Col du Lautaret to Serre-Chevalier in bad weather. The itinéraires get ploughed into a piste-like state, and adventurous **intermediates** could tackle the Chancel, but that's scarcely the basis of a decent holiday. **Beginners** should go elsewhere.

There are no special **snowboarding** facilities. La Grave has a couple of **cross-country** loops (total 12km); the longer goes to Les Freaux. A further 18km are available near Villar d'Arene.

There are short **queues** only at weekends – at the bottom station first thing, and at the mid-station later.

Surprisingly, there are three decent **mountain restaurants**, the best the Evariste Chancel climbing refuge half-way down the Chancel itinéraire.

There are half a dozen **guides** in the village, offering a good range of services through their bureau.

Children's babysitting can be arranged through the tourist office.

STAYING THERE
There are several simple **hotels**. The Edelweiss is a comfortable, friendly, family-run 2-star with good home cooking. **Self-catering** studios are bookable through the tourist office.

Most people **eat** in their hotels, though there are alternatives. The standard tea-time **après-ski** gathering place is the central Glaciers bar, known to habitués as chez Marcel; it is not riotous. The Candy Ass bar has music, but doesn't get much business. Anyone not using the slopes will find La Grave much too small and quiet.

Isola 2000

2000m

Snow right on your doorstep, just above the Côte d'Azur

A scheduled flight and a short (90km) transfer from Nice, with some decent from-the-door access to the slopes, Isola is high on convenience as well as altitude. Like many purpose-built French resorts, it has been extended in a sympathetic style. But its original buildings are irredeemably block-like.

WHAT IT COSTS

(((4)

HOW IT RATES

The slopes
Snow	***
Extent	**
Experts	**
Intermediates	***
Beginners	*****
Convenience	*****
Queues	***
Restaurants	**

The rest
Scenery	***
Resort charm	*
Off-slope	*

What's new

There is a new sports centre and more snowmaking for 1997/98.

MOUNTAIN FACTS

Altitude	1840m-2610m
Lifts	24
Pistes	120km
Green/Blue	54%
Red	35%
Black	11%
Art. snow	165 guns
Recco detectors used	

UK PACKAGES

Made to Measure

TOURIST OFFICE

Postcode 06420
Tel +33 493 231515
Fax 493 231425

THE RESORT

Isola is one of the many small, high, purpose-built resorts in the French Alps, but it is further south than the rest, with access via Nice. On clear days you can see the sea.

Built by a British property company at the end of the 1960s, Isola aimed itself squarely at the family market. Front de Neige is a complex of apartments, shops, bars, restaurants and a couple of hotels that makes up the core of the resort, with nursery slopes and lifts on the doorstep.

Various owners have since worked hard to glamorise the image of the resort with new hamlets of more luxurious, wood-clad apartment blocks. But the main complex has become tatty, with shops closing down.

THE MOUNTAINS

The piste map shows three areas of **slopes**, St Sauveur, Pélevos and Levant. Really it is one linked area in a horseshoe shape around the resort. Due to the great base height of Isola – the lowest of the slopes is at 1840m – most of the runs are above the tree line. The main access point is the gondola from the centre of the complex to Pélevos at 2320m, and from there all three areas can be accessed more or less directly. There is a **snowboard** fun-park and half-pipe.

Isola can get different weather from other major French resorts. Sometimes it has masses of **snow** when the rest of the French Alps have none; at other times it misses out. It has installed extra snowmaking for 1997/98. Regular visitors say that they never find all the lifts open, but there is always snow – and plenty of sun. The north-facing slopes of St Sauveur and Pélevos keep their snow well.

Experts head for St Sauveur, which has Isola's longest and most challenging runs, as well as its best off-piste runs. There are good blacks here – and from the chair to Mont Mené. The Pélevos area is an interesting cluster of red and blue runs where **intermediates** can take their pick of difficulty. The more adventurous can try the challenging St Sauveur sector, where there is a choice of steep reds and blacks. The south-facing slopes below the Col de la Lombarde, in the Levant sector, are also intermediate.

There are excellent nursery slopes for **beginners** right in the heart of the resort, and an easy progression to greens, then blues, nearby.

There is a 4km loop just above the village, but little else to recommend Isola to **cross-country** enthusiasts.

The only central main lift, the gondola, is prone to **queues** at peak times. Weekend day-trippers from Nice, cause more bottlenecks.

There is only a handful of **mountain restaurants**. The best is the excellent Génisserie at the foot of St Sauveur.

The ESF **ski school** has a good reputation for its English and its teaching – both in the traditional way and ski évolutif – but, as ever, class size is a gripe among reporters.

Isola has an all-day crèche, and a snow garden for **children** starting out. English is widely spoken.

STAYING THERE

Accommodation is largely in **self-catering** apartments but there are several **hotels**.

The number of British operators serving Isola 2000 has declined and, with it, the vitality of the **après-ski** scene outside high season and weekends, when people from the Riviera arrive. That's the time to go to the two discos.

Despite its Aquavallée pool complex, new sports centre and ice driving circuit, Isola is hardly the place for someone not taking to the slopes. But trips to the Riviera and the casinos in Monte Carlo are easy.

Maurienne valley

Everything from cute old villages to 1960s monstrosities

WHAT IT COSTS

3

MOUNTAIN FACTS

Valloire/Valmeinier

Altitude	1430m-2600m
Lifts	33
Pistes	150km
Green/Blue	49%
Red	34%
Black	17%
Artificial snow	10km

Valfréjus

Altitude	1550m-2735m
Lifts	12
Pistes	52km
Green/Blue	70%
Red	10%
Black	20%
Artificial snow	none

Val-Cenis

Altitude	1400m-2800m
Lifts	22
Pistes	80km
Green/Blue	50%
Red	40%
Black	10%
Artificial snow	10km

Go to the southern extremity of the Val-Thorens piste network or set off ski-touring northwards from La Grave, and you come to the same place: the Maurienne valley – a great curving trench cut by a river appropriately called the Arc. This backwater of the French Alps has over 20 winter resorts, but only a handful have any international market – Valloire and Valfréjus the best-known among them. They range from pleasant old valley villages to resorts purpose-built in the 1960s for the convenience of skiers. About all they have in common is piste and lift networks that are rather limited in size, and participation in a lift-pass deal that allows you to have a day each in any five resorts at very low cost. We gave it a try, with mixed results. Three resorts left a favourable impression, and they are covered here. The others are covered in our Directory.

Many of these resorts are close enough to be linked together – and in the boom years of the 1970s, grand plans were formulated to link Valfréjus with Valmeinier and Valloire to the west, and with Bardonecchia in Italy. Michelin maps started to show a lift going right up to the Pointe du Fréjus on the Italian border, and Valfréjus painted 'Bardonecchia' on its gondola cabins. But they never built the lift, and it's no longer on the maps.

It's also worth noting that Orelle – a non-village in the valley bottom – has a big gondola up to the Val-Thorens lift network. So a trip to the Maurienne can include a visit to Europe's highest resort and some of its best snow.

Different though they are, in winter all of these resorts are of little appeal to anyone not intent on skiing or boarding. Outings to Chambéry are possible, but it's quite a drive, especially while a new railway line *and* a new motorway are being forced through the lower Maurienne valley.

VALLOIRE 1430m

Valloire is the best-known of the Maurienne resorts internationally, and it offers the most extensive slopes, shared with the twin stations of Valmeinier 1500 and 1800. The village has a rustic French feel to it and retains a life as a farming community. The resort is quite a drive up from the valley. Despite considerable development, it has retained a feeling of 'real' France, complete with impressive old church, crêperies, fromageries, reasonable prices, villagey atmosphere and friendly locals.

The 150km of piste are spread over three similar-sized, lightly wooded areas: Sétaz – shady slopes, part open and part wooded, directly above the village and served by gondola to Thimel at mid-mountain; Crey du Quart – broad, open, west-facing slopes reachable from the village or from Sétaz by chair-lift; and Valmeinier – mainly west-facing slopes in the next valley (beyond Crey du Quart), with just four main lifts. The slopes are almost entirely intermediate, Les Karellis (a 45-minute drive) being better for more taxing runs (and for superior snow and scenery).

Reliable snow-cover is not a strong point. Important links are too low, sunny and lacking artificial snow to ensure that the whole area is reliably accessible. The main piste to the village is served by snowmaking, while the Valmeinier area holds snow well.

Valloire is very much an intermediate area, with plenty of options for all standards in all three sectors. The Crey du Quart section is particularly good for an easy day. Sétaz has several black runs, but they don't represent much of a challenge for experts. The mogul field down to Valmeinier 1500 is steeper.

The limited village nursery areas are adequate in low season when snow cover is good. Otherwise, there are good nursery slopes up the mountain, at the top of the Sétaz gondola, but a full lift pass is needed to reach them.

There are few queue problems when snow-cover is complete, but some bottlenecks when it is not. The village gondola gets busy for a short period when ski school starts.

Mountain restaurants are in very short supply but are of good quality. The Thimel is perhaps the best.

UK PACKAGES

Valloire Fairhand Holidays, First Choice Ski, Lagrange, Snowcoach

Valmeinier Fairhand Holidays, Lagrange, Motours

Valfréjus Fairhand Holidays, Lagrange, Made to Measure, Motours, Ski trek

Val-Cenis Equity Total Ski, Hannibals, On The Piste Travel Ltd

TOURIST OFFICES

Valloire

Postcode 73450
Tel +33 479 590396
Fax 479 590966

Valmeinier

Postcode 73450
Tel +33 479 568048
Fax 479 592817

Valfréjus

Postcode 73500
Tel +33 479 053271
Fax 479 050146

Val-Cenis

Postcode 73480
Tel +33 479 052366
Fax 479 058217

There's a fair choice of hotel and apartment accommodation. The Grand (3-star) and Christiania (2-star) are the best hotels, and both are well placed.

Most of the restaurants are pizza and fondue joints. The Crêperie and Asile des Fondues are perhaps the best of these. The Gastilleur has the best French cuisine in town.

Après-ski is quiet, though far from dead. There are bars to suit most tastes, and a couple of discos which warm up at weekends.

VALFREJUS 1550m
Valfréjus is a small and unusual modern resort – built in the woods, with most of the slopes higher up above the tree line.

The resort is a compact and quite pleasant affair built on a quite narrow, shady shelf, with woods all around. There are several apartment blocks of less than monster size grouped around the main lift station, and individual chalets dotted around the hillside.

There are runs of all grades back towards the village, but the focus of the slopes is Plateau d'Arrondaz, at 2200m, reached by gondola. Above here are steep, open slopes – genuine bumpy blacks, with excellent snow – on Punta Bagna (2735m) served by the second stage of the gondola, and gentler blue runs from Col d'Arrondaz. From both the top and the col there are also sunny intermediate runs on the back side of the hill, with chair-lifts back to both high-points or the option of the glorious long blue Jeu run (with plenty of off-piste variations along the way) back to the village – a top-to-bottom descent of almost 1200m vertical.

Snow cover in the main open area is pretty reliable, and there's a good chance of complete cover to village level even without artificial assistance. Within its small area, Valfréjus has something for everyone (there are nursery slopes both at mid-mountain and village level). Near beginners might welcome more easy blues, but it would be a good place for a confident intermediate to get in some serious practice on good snow. Experts may be interested to know that heli-lifts are advertised, presumably setting you down a few centimetres over the border in Italy, to make it legal.

There are decent restaurants at both stations of the gondola – a handsomely woody self-service at the top, table-service both inside and out at the mid-station.

The 2-star Auberge du Charmaix is the main hotel, right in the centre of the village, with a pleasant restaurant. Prices are modest, but if you want to pay even less you can stay down in the railhead town of Modane.

Après-ski is confined to a couple of bars, a disco in one of the apartment blocks and an occasional cabaret.

VAL-CENIS 1400m
Val-Cenis is a marketing concept rather than a place. It represents a couple of pleasant villages in the Haute Maurienne, the high and remote part of the valley.

Lanslebourg is a long, linear place, speading along the Route Nationale 6 (a dead-end in winter, when the Col du Mont-Cenis is closed and becomes part of the slopes). It's pleasant enough, but no great beauty. A couple of km up the valley, Lanslevillard is more captivating – off the road, randomly arranged and rustic, and split into three parts.

There are lifts up into the north-facing slopes from no less than five points along the valley, including Lanslebourg and both major parts of Lanslevillard. The main one, a gondola, starts between the two villages, on the fringes of Lanslevillard, and goes up to the main mid-mountain congregation area at 2100m, where there there is a rustic self-service restaurant.

There are intermediate runs heading more or less straight down through the woods to the valley, and easy ones winding down – including a splendid green following the hairpin road up to the Col. Above mid-mountain are a good range of runs to suit every standard, served by chairs and drags. From the top station at 2800m,there is a good, mogulled black down the shady front face, a challenging red on the shoulder of the mountain and a sunny away-from-the-lifts black over to the Col, where a couple of drags serve a slightly separate area of red and blue runs. All in all, a very enjoyable area for a short stay.

There are modest hotels in both villages, of which the best is the 3-star Alpazur. It does good food, and there is a range of simple eating-out alternatives. Après-ski is quiet.

There is skating, paragliding and snowmobiling, but not much else to do off the slopes.

Megève

1100m

One of the traditional old winter holiday towns

WHAT IT COSTS

((((5)

HOW IT RATES

The slopes

Snow	**
Extent	*****
Experts	*
Intermediates	****
Beginners	***
Convenience	**
Queues	***
Restaurants	*****

The rest

Scenery	***
Resort charm	****
Off-slope	****

➕ Extensive, very pretty slopes ideal for intermediates

➕ Charming old village centre

➕ Gourmet mountain lunches in attractive surroundings

➕ Excellent for cross-country

➕ Plenty of things to do off the slopes

➖ Often poor snow, especially low down

➖ Three separate mountains, two linked by lift but not by piste

➖ Not many challenging pistes

Megève used to be France's most fashionable winter sports village, popular with its chic clientele for its gentle, woodland runs, rustic charm, pretty scenery, attractive mountain restaurants, lovely walks, sophisticated nightlife and friendly locals. It has certainly lost that title now to Courchevel but still attracts its fair share of Beautiful People, complete with fur coats and fat wallets, there as much for the posing as the sport.

Megève's pretty tree-lined runs are ideal for gentle intermediate cruising and gourmet lunching. And it's said that there's a swing away from purpose-built resorts back to traditional villages with character. Fine and dandy if you're going to jump in the car and thrash down from Paris when the snow's good. But for those booking a holiday six months ahead, Megève is simply too low, and unreliable for snow.

boarding *Boarding doesn't really fit with Megève's traditional, rather staid, up-market image. But it does have two fun-parks – one on Mont d'Arbois and the other at Rochebrune – and the area is really rather good for freeriding. If the snow is heavy, it doesn't matter as much to a boarder as a skier. And it's a good place to try boarding for the first time, with plenty of fairly wide, gentle runs and a lot of chair-lifts and gondolas; though there are a fair number of drag-lifts, they are generally avoidable. Nightlife can be sophisticated (there's a casino), but there are a few noisy bars as well.*

What's new

Megève was slow to install artificial snowmaking but now it has started, it is expanding its capacity each year – with new snow guns being put in for 1997/98.

A new casino is also planned for the coming season. And a new hotel, The Lodge Park, is opening in the heart of the village in 'western America' style.

MOUNTAIN FACTS

Altitude	1050m-2350m
Lifts	81
Pistes	300km
Green/Blue	30%
Red	45%
Black	25%
Artificial snow	27km
Recco detectors used	

The resort

Megève is very much a tale of two cities. It is in a lovely sunny setting and has a beautifully preserved traditional medieval centre, which is pedestrianised and comes complete with open-air ice rink, horse-drawn sleighs, cobbled streets and a fine church. There are lots of smart clothing, jewellery, food, antique and gift shops.

Megève has expanded enormously and is surrounded by a strangulation of modern roads and traffic. Thankfully, the main Albertville–Chamonix road bypasses the centre, and there are expensive underground car parks. But the cars are a problem – especially at weekends when the crowds arrive and at the end of the day when people are driving back from excursions.

The clientele are mainly well-heeled French couples and families, who come here as much for an all-round winter holiday and for the people-watching potential as for the slopes themselves. The nightlife is, as you'd expect for such a resort, lively and varied.

The mountains

Megève's slopes are predominantly easy intermediate cruising, much of it prettily set in the woods. But there are tough runs to be found.

THE SLOPES
Pretty but low

There are three separate areas, two of them linked by cable-car – but not by pistes. The two linked areas are Rochebrune and Mont d'Arbois. A gondola within walking distance of central Megève serves both areas. From the mid-station, you can catch

LIFT PASSES

97/98 prices in francs

Rocharbois-Mont Joly
Covers all lifts on
Rochebrune, Côte
2000, Mont d'Arbois,
Megève, St-Gervais,
Mont Joux and Mont
Joly.

Beginners Pay by the
ride.

Main pass
1-day pass 170
6-day pass 832
(low season 724 –
13% off)

Senior citizens
Over 60: 6-day pass
665 (20% off)

Children
Under 12: 6-day pass
665 (20% off)
Under 4: free pass

Short-term passes
Half-day pass
available morning or
afternoon.

Alternative passes
Mont-Blanc Evasion
pass covers all lifts in
Megève, St-Gervais,
St-Nicolas and
Combloux, available 2
days or over (2-day
pass 342 for adults,
273 for children).
Mont Blanc pass
covers all lifts in the
13 resorts of the Mont
Blanc area (700km of
piste and 190 lifts)
and the buses
between them, plus
Courmayeur in Italy 4
days out of 6 (6 days
1080 for adults and
756 for children). Jaco
pass valid for Le
Jaillet, Christomet and
Combloux.

the cable-car, followed by a gondola,
up to Mont d'Arbois (1840m), or you
can carry on up the gondola to
Rochebrune (1750m).

Rochebrune can also be reached
directly by an ancient cable-car from
the southern edge of town. From
Rochebrune you can go up to Alpette
(1880m), the starting point for
Megève's historic downhill course. A
network of gentle, wooded, east-facing
slopes, served by drag-lifts and a high-
speed quad, take you across to Côte
2000 – the sector's furthest and
highest point, at 2015m.

Mont d'Arbois is Megève's largest
and most interesting area. It's also
accessed by another gondola starting
at Princesse, way out to the north-east
of town. From the top, you can take
north-facing slopes to Le Bettex and
on down to St-Gervais at around
900m. Yet another two-stage gondola
returns you to Mont d'Arbois, with its
mid-station at Le Bettex. You can work
your way over to Mont Joux and
Megève's highest (2350m), most
snowsure slopes – a small area.

The third, and quietest, area is **Le
Jaillet**, accessed by gondola from just
outside the northern edge of town.
Above the top of the gondola (1600m)
are predominantly easy, east-facing
pistes. The high-point is Christomet to
the west, served by a two-stage chair.
In the other directions, a series of
long, tree-lined runs and lifts serves
the area above Combloux. St-Gervais
and Le Bettex share Megève's main
area. The Mont Blanc lift pass covers
many other resorts, including the
Chamonix valley and Courmayeur in
Italy.

SNOW RELIABILITY
The area's worst feature

The problem with Megève is that the
slopes are low and sunny, with very
few runs above 2000m. So in a poor
snow year, or in a warm spell, snow
cover and quality can suffer badly. And
because the resort itself is so low, it
often rains there when it is snowing in
higher places. The relatively snow-sure
Mont Joly and Le Bettex sections are
very small.

The good news is that the resort
has belatedly started to install artificial
snow and is increasing the area
covered for 1997/98. Some runs are
now entirely covered, including the
long red Olympique run at Rochebrune.
But a recent reporter says that

snowmaking didn't seem to be used
enough, even though it was cold
enough during the four weeks they
were in the resort. Piste grooming, on
the other hand, was good.

FOR EXPERTS
Off-piste is the main attraction

The Mont Joly and Mont Joux sections
offer the steepest slopes. The top chair
here serves a genuinely 33° black run,
and the slightly lower Epaule chair has
some steep runs back down and also
accesses some good off-piste, as well
as pisted, runs down to St-Nicolas-de-
Véroce. There is an off-piste route
down to neighbouring Les Contamines
from here, too.

The steep area beneath the second
stage of the Princesse gondola can be
a play area of powder runs among the
trees. Côte 2000 has a small section of
steep runs, including some off-piste.

Because few 'powder hounds' go to
Megève, you can often find untracked
powder days after the last snowfall.

FOR INTERMEDIATES
Superb if the snow is good

Good intermediates will enjoy the Mont
d'Arbois area best. The black runs
below the Princesse gondola are
perfectly manageable. The runs served
by the Grand Vorassel drag and the
most direct route between Mont
d'Arbois and Le Bettex are also
interesting. Similarly testing are the
steepest of the Jaillet sector pistes
above Combloux. Nearby, the
Christomet bowl is probably the best
area for mixed abilities, with the same
lift giving access to three widely
differing runs.

Those of moderate ability are
particularly well suited to Megève. A
plethora of comfortable reds lead
down to Le Bettex and Princesse from
Mont d'Arbois, while nearby Mont Joux
accesses long, similar-standard runs to
St-Nicolas. Alpette and Côte 2000 are
other suitable sections.

Even the timid can get a great deal
of mileage in. All main valley-level lifts
have easy routes down to them
(although the Milloz piste to the
Princesse mid-station is a little steep).
There are some particularly good, long,
gentle cruises between Mont Joux and
Megève via Mont d'Arbois. But in all
sectors, you'll find easy, well-groomed
blue runs – the main problem you are
likely to come across is poor quality or
thin snow-cover.

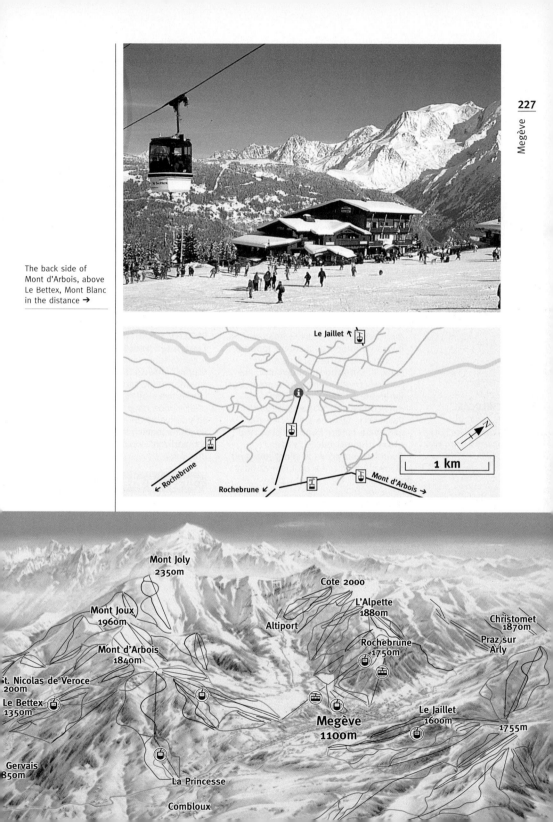

The back side of
Mont d'Arbois, above
Le Bettex, Mont Blanc
in the distance →

Le Jaillet ↖

← Rochebrune

Rochebrune ↙

Mont d'Arbois →

1 km

Mont Joly
2350m

Cote 2000

L'Alpette
1880m

Mont Joux
1960m

Altiport

Christomet
1870m

Praz sur
Arly

Mont d'Arbois
1840m

Rochebrune
1750m

St. Nicolas de Veroce
200m

Le Bettex
1350m

Megève
1100m

Le Jaillet
1600m

1755m

Gervais
850m

La Princesse

Combloux

SCHOOLS/GUIDES

97/98 prices in francs

ESF
Classes 6 days
4hr: 9.30am-11.30am
and 3pm-5pm
5 half days: 450
Children's classes
Ages: 5 to 12
6 full days: 750
Private lessons
Hourly or daily
190 for 1hr, for 1 to 2
people

International
Classes 6 days
2hr: 10am-noon, 1pm-
3pm and 3pm-5pm;
3hrs: 10am-1pm
6 mornings (2hr): 580
Children's classes
Ages: 4 to 12
6 full days: 780
Private lessons
Hourly or daily
185 for 1hr, for 1 to 2
people

CHILDCARE

There are four
kindergartens dotted
around the sprawling
resort, all offering
skiing. Age limits and
hours vary. Alpage
(450 211097), next to
the Mont d'Arbois
gondola: ages 3 to 6,
until 5.30. Caboche
(450 589765) at the
Caboche gondola
station: ages 3 to 10,
until 5.30pm.
Meg'Loisirs (450
587784) is a
comprehensive
nursery: ages 1 to 6,
until 6pm or even
7pm. Princesse (450
930086), out at the
Princesse gondola:
ages 3 to 6, until
5pm.

GETTING THERE

Air Geneva, transfer
1hr. Lyon, transfer
2½hr.

Rail Sallanches
(13km); regular buses
from station.

FOR BEGINNERS
Several nursery areas
The large number of very easy runs
makes Megève a good choice for near-
beginners and there are plenty of nice
little nursery areas. Unfortunately all of
them are prone to poor snow
conditions – in which case you're
better off going to Jaillet or Mont
d'Arbois.

FOR CROSS-COUNTRY
An excellent area
There are 75km of varied trails spread
throughout the area, some of which
are at reasonable altitude
(1300m–1550m). Meeting up with
Alpine skiers or walkers at one of the
many mountain huts is a particular
attraction of this area.

QUEUES
Quiet during the week
Megève is relatively queue-free during
the week, except at peak holiday time.
It was described by a recent reporter
as 'the quietest resort I have ever
known'. But school holiday and sunny
Sunday crowds can mean some delays;
the Petite Fontaine lift in the
Rochebrune sector is a particular
bottleneck. Queues are noticeably
genteel, a far cry from the push and
shove of more macho resorts.
Overcrowded pistes at Mont Joux and
Mont d'Arbois are a problem at busy
periods.

MOUNTAIN RESTAURANTS
The long lunch lives
Megève is one of the great skiing
gourmet venues. The Mont d'Arbois
area is particularly well endowed with
mountain restaurants.
  Several of the little old chalets
around St-Nicolas have both great
charm and fine food, while L'Alpage at
Les Communailles beneath Mont Joux
is worth a visit, and is particularly
recommended for good salads and the
plat du jour. The Club House at Mont
d'Arbois is a nice place, but popular
with the Megève poseurs with dogs
and fur coats – as is Idéal Sports. The
Igloo is expensive, but does excellent
and interesting food (such as ostrich
and buffalo) and has a fine sun terrace
facing Mont Blanc.
  Self-service places are cheaper and
less leisurely, but still reasonably good
quality. Chez Tartine is a very friendly
self-service spot at the Princesse mid-
station. Le Rosay on Mont Joux is also

friendly and generally quite good. The
Igloo has both self-service and table-
service sections; the staff in both are
helpful and there are wonderful views
of Mont Blanc. Further afield, Côte
2000 is a former farm popular for its
atmosphere, friendly service and good
quality and Radaz is similar, while La
Caboche is handily placed for an end-
of-day drink. Forestier and Alpette are
other recommended spots. In the Jaillet
sector the Supérior is good.

SCHOOLS AND GUIDES
Adventurous
The two schools both have broad
horizons, offering expeditions to the
Vallée Blanche and heli-skiing (in Italy)
as well as conventional tuition. The
International school advertises outings
to the Grands Montets at Argentière
and appears to be more popular
generally than its rival, the ESF.

FACILITIES FOR CHILDREN
Language problems
A comfortable, low-altitude resort like
Megève attracts lots of families who
can afford day-care. The facilities seem
impressive – all four kindergartens
offer a wide range of activities as an
alternative to the slopes. Lack of
English-speaking staff (and
companions) could be the main
drawback.

Staying there

Staying in the traffic-free centre of
town gives you the best atmosphere
and puts you within walking distance
of the Chamois gondola.

HOW TO GO
Few packages
Relatively few British tour operators go
to Megève. Although it's a chic resort
with several 4-star hotels, there are
simpler, charming hotels and good-
value chalets around. Apartments can
be expensive but are of a good
standard.
Chalets A few UK tour operators offer
catered chalets.
Hotels Megève may not be France's
smartest resort any longer, but it still
attracts enough affluent visitors to
sustain some exceptionally stylish and
welcoming hotels.
((((4 **Mont Blanc** Megève's traditional
leading hotel – very elegant and
fashionable. Right in the centre, and
close to the main gondola.

UK PACKAGES

Chalets 'Unlimited', Fairhand Holidays, Lagrange, Made to Measure, Motours, Simon Butler Skiing, Ski Barrett-Boyce, Ski Les Alpes, Ski Weekend, Stanford Skiing, White Roc, avant-ski

St-Gervais Fairhand Holidays, Lagrange, MasterSki, PGL Ski Europe, Snowcoach, Snowman Holidays

ACTIVITIES

Indoor 'Palais des Sports' (climbing wall, swimming pool, sauna, solarium, skating, gym), judo, classical and contemporary dance classes, music lessons, bridge, tennis, yoga, archery, language classes, museum, library, cinemas, pottery, casino, concert and play hall, body-building hall, table-tennis, tennis
Outdoor 50km of cleared paths, snow-shoe excursions, skating rink, riding, sleigh rides, plane and helicopter trips, paragliding, curling, horse-riding, rock-climbing, mountaineering

TOURIST OFFICE

Postcode 74120
Tel +33 450 212728
Fax 450 930309

(((4) **Chalet du Mont d'Arbois** Prettily decorated, former Rothschild family home, now a Relais & Chateaux hotel in a secluded position near the Mont d'Arbois gondola.
(((3) **Fer à Cheval** French rustic-chic at its best, with a warmly welcoming wood-and-stone interior. Excellent food, and a fitness centre to redress the balance. Close to the centre, but now only a 3-star.
(((3) **Grange d'Arly** Wrong side of the road, but still quite close to the centre – a beautifully furnished chalet.
(((3) **Ferme Hôtel Duvillard** Smartly restored farmhouse, perfectly positioned for the slopes, at the foot of the Mont d'Arbois gondola.
((2) **Sapins** Comfortable logis on edge of town, close to the main gondola.
Self-catering There are some very comfortable and well positioned apartments available.

EATING OUT
Very French

Megève is a très chic French town whose restaurants are mainly high-quality, if expensive. Michel Gaudin is probably the best in town and does very good-value set menus. The restaurants in the Fermes de Marie, Chalet du Mont d'Arbois, Mont Blanc and Mont Joly are also good but much more expensive. The Tire Bouchon, Sapinière and Pizzeria del Mare are good value. The Phnom-Penh serves food rather different from normal French cuisine.

APRES-SKI
Plenty to try

Nightlife is lively, and less formal than it used to be. The Sapinière bar is an animated tea-time place and the Chamois has been recommended. The Puck is an atmospheric locals' bar, Le Club de Jazz (formerly the Cinque Rues) is a very popular jazz club-cum-cocktail bar, while Harries Bar is an informal rendezvous popular for its wide range of beers, a weekly live band, karaoke and satellite TV. The Conga is another lively spot.

A new casino will open for the 1997/98 season. The weekly broomball match between the British and French on the open-air ice rink is a good chance to let your hair down.

OFF THE SLOPES
Lots to do

There is something for most tastes, with an impressive sports centre, a central outdoor ice rink, plenty of outdoor activities and a weekly market. Excursions to Annecy, Chamonix and even Courmayeur are possible. Walks are excellent outside town, with 50km of marked paths, much at high altitude. Meeting friends on the slopes for lunch is easy.

STAYING IN OTHER RESORTS
A couple of alternatives

Praz-sur-Arly (1035m) and Notre-Dame-de-Bellecombe (1130m) are much cheaper options for independent car travellers.

Praz is a small, quiet place, but has hotels, restaurants, bars, sports club, ski school and ski kindergarten. It has a fair-sized slope of its own, with short, mainly easy, north-facing runs.

Notre-Dame is further along the road past Praz, a pleasant village with mainly apartment accommodation, simple hotels, and several bars and restaurants. It has its own varied, pretty area and a ski school.

St-Gervais 850m

St-Gervais is a handsome, 19th-century spa town set in a narrow river gorge, half-way between Megève and Chamonix, at the turn-off for Les Contamines. It has direct access to the Mont d'Arbois slopes via a 20-person gondola from the centre of town. At the mid-station is Le Bettex (1400m), a small collection of hotels, private chalets and new apartments, more conveniently situated for the runs but with little evening animation.

You can go up in the opposite direction from St-Gervais, towards Mont Blanc, on a rack-and-pinion railway which takes you to Les Houches. The only way back to St-Gervais from here on the snow is off-piste, and there's frequently not enough snow. St-Gervais and Le Bettex both have their own ski schools.

Its position makes St-Gervais a good base for touring the different resorts of the Mont Blanc region.

Les Menuires
1850m

Lift your eyes to the mountains – and keep them there

WHAT IT COSTS

(4)

HOW IT RATES

The slopes
Snow	****
Extent	*****
Experts	****
Intermediates	*****
Beginners	***
Convenience	*****
Queues	****
Restaurants	***

The rest
Scenery	***
Resort charm	*
Off-slope	*

➕ Probably the cheapest place to stay in the famously extensive Three Valleys area – biggest in the world

➕ Some great local slopes

➕ Lots of slope-side accommodation

➕ Extensive artificial snowmaking

➖ The ugliest resort in the Alps

➖ Main intermediate and beginner slopes get a lot of sun; artificial snow turns into artificial slush

➖ Nursery slopes are busy as well as over-exposed to the sun

Les Menuires is hideous, at least to our eyes. One day, we confidently predict, they'll simply knock the whole thing down and start again. But not everyone agrees – and it is certainly the bargain base for the Three Valleys, with the bonus of immediate access to the excellent, challenging slopes on La Masse, rarely visited by visitors from the other valleys.

 Les Menuires gets a fair number of boarding visitors – not surprising since it gives relatively economical access to such a huge area of terrain. There is plenty here for every style of rider. Lots of chairs and gondolas in the massive lift system, but be warned – there are some flattish sections of piste to negotiate in places. And we'd certainly recommend beginners to go somewhere with more secluded nursery slopes and better snow. There's a fun-park just above the main village. Les Bruyeres is the part of the resort to head for – that's where you'll find the specialist Pro Shop.

What's new

They keep adding snow guns – the total is now up to 300. There is a new quad chair at St Martin, and some new places to stay.

SCHOOLS/GUIDES

97/98 prices in francs

ESF
Classes 6 days
5½hr: 3hr am, 2½hr pm; half-day am or pm
6 full days: 930
Children's classes
Ages: up to 12
6 full days: 790
Private lessons
Hourly
180 for 1 or 2 people

International
Classes 6 days
2½hr am or pm
6 half-days: 670
Children's classes
Ages: up to 14
6 half-days: 595
Private lessons
Hourly
179 for 1 or 2 people

The resort

The resort itself is ugly – in our view the worst in the Alps – but some reporters quite like the place. The original centre at La Croisette is particularly horrendous. Newer outposts of Reberty and Les Bruyères are better. But most accommodation does enjoy slope-side convenience.

The new outposts have their own shops and bars. The main centre has a claustrophobic indoor shopping complex. Some pleasant bar and restaurant terraces face the slopes.

The mountains

Les Menuires has two main attractions: La Masse, a challenging mountain that is off the beaten Three Valleys track, and can be peaceful when Les Menuires is packed with people; and the swift links to the rest of the Three Valleys. It suits all standards except complete beginners. But local runs for intermediates and beginners are spoilt by the orientation of the main slopes, which get the full force of the afternoon sun; despite considerable artificial snowmaking, they can be icy early in the day and heavy later.

THE SLOPES
A good base for the Three Valleys
Les Menuires and St-Martin-de-Belleville share a local area with 120km of runs and 50 lifts. The west-facing slopes have the vast bulk of the runs. The main gondolas take you up to the **Mont de la Chambre** (2850m), from where you can head back towards the resort or down to Val-Thorens or the Méribel slopes. Chairs and drags serve the local slopes, and you can work your way north by piste and lift, and make your way down to the charming old village of St-Martin-de-Belleville (see separate chapter).

The north-east-facing slopes of **La Masse** (2805m) usually have excellent snow on the top half and are served by a two-stage high-capacity gondola.

SNOW RELIABILITY
Cover guaranteed but not quality
La Masse's height and orientation ensure good snow for a long season.

The opposite, west-facing slopes are supplied with abundant artificial snow (the resort boasts 300 snow guns). But although cover there is guaranteed – so long as the weather is cold enough to make snow – the quality of the snow is often found wanting, especially

MOUNTAIN FACTS

Altitude 1300m-3200m
Lifts 200
Pistes 600km
Green/Blue 49%
Red 37%
Black 14%
Artificial snow 80km
Recco detectors used

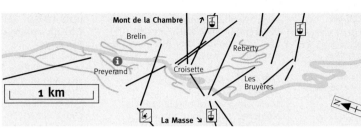

LIFT PASSES

97/98 prices in francs
Three Valleys
Covers all lifts in
Courchevel, La Tania,
Méribel, Val-Thorens,
Les Menuires and St-
Martin-de-Belleville.
Beginners 6 free lifts;
beginners pass covers
11 lifts (1-day 104)
Main pass
1-day pass 220
6-day pass 1,080
(low season 972 –
10% off)
Senior citizens
Over 60: 6-day pass
864 (20% off)
Over 75: free pass
Children
Under 16: 6-day pass
810 (25% off)
Under 5: free pass
Short-term passes
Half-day passes (from
12.30) available for
Les Menuires and St-
Martin-de-Belleville
(adult 133), 3 Valleys
(adult 165).
Notes 6-day pass and
over valid for one day
each in Tignes-Val-
d'Isère, La Plagne-Les
Arcs, Pralognan-la-
Vanoise and Les
Saisies. 70- to 75-
year-olds get a 50%
discount on pass
price (6-day pass
540). Reductions for
families.
Alternative passes
Vallée des Belleville
pass covers 75 lifts
and 240km piste in
Val-Thorens, Les
Menuires and St-
Martin (adult 6-day
1010). Les Menuires
and St-Martin pass
covers 45 lifts and
120km of piste (adult
6-day 885).

on the lower slopes.

Lift passes for six days or more also give you a day in Val-d'Isère/Tignes and La Plagne or Les Arcs. But it's quite a drive to these resorts.

FOR EXPERTS
Hidden treasures

La Masse has some of the steepest and quietest pistes in the Three Valleys – most people doing the 'circuit' skip it. Long reds and blacks come down either side of the top stage of the gondola. Other steep blacks, usually mogulled, are served by the Dame Blanche and Lac Noir chairs.

From the top there are also some marvellously scenic itinéraires. The wide, sweeping, but not too steep, Lac du Lou takes off down towards Val-Thorens. Others lead off in the opposite direction to various villages from which you need transport back, but the Les Yvoses run takes you back into the Les Menuires lift system.

Easy access to the rest of the Three Valleys means good skiers are spoilt for choice. Within an hour of leaving your door you can be on the steepest slopes of Méribel or Val-Thorens. Courchevel won't take much longer.

FOR INTERMEDIATES
600km of pistes to choose from

The Three Valleys is an intermediate's paradise. The local slopes at Les Menuires are virtually all blue and red. Because most slopes face west, the snow is often better elsewhere. But with good snow, you may find little reason for leaving the local area.

There are both pistes and itinéraires down into Méribel, and five different peaks you can approach it from. Even a second- or third-timer should have no problem cruising from valley to valley. In poor snow conditions the attractions of Val-Thorens become evident, and there's blue-run access via the Montaulever drag as well as red runs from the top of the mountain.

FOR BEGINNERS
Try elsewhere

Although there are wide and gentle slopes for beginners, we think you'd be better off for your first winter-sports holiday in a resort which offers more of a real Alpine atmosphere and is easier on the eye. While others can get away from Les Menuires into beautiful Alpine scenery, beginners are stuck with it. And the snow quality is a worry. We've

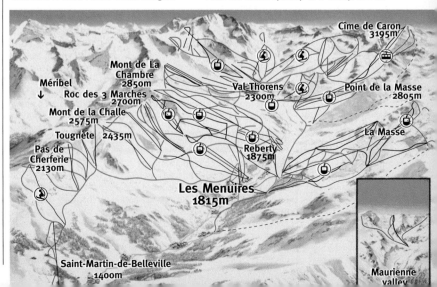

CHILDCARE

The ESF-run Village des Schtroumpfs (479 006379) takes children aged 3 months to 7 years. It has a nursery for babies, a Baby Club for toddlers and a leisure centre for older children, with indoor and outdoor activities and ski lessons for children aged 2½ or more.

At Reberty-les-Bruyères, the Marmottons offers similar facilities, and the SEI runs a ski kindergarten.

GETTING THERE

Air Geneva, transfer 3½hr. Lyon, transfer 3½hr. Chambery, transfer 2½hr.

Rail Moûtiers (27km); regular buses from station.

UK PACKAGES

AA Ski-Driveaway, Club Med, Crystal, Erna Low, Fairhand Holidays, First Choice Ski, Inghams, Lagrange, Made to Measure, On The Piste Travel Ltd, Ski Club Europe, Travelscene Ski-Drive, Virgin Snow

ACTIVITIES

Indoor Library, games room, 2 cinemas, fitness centres
Outdoor 2 outdoor heated swimming pools, microlight flights, hang-gliding, guided walks, snow-scooters, artificial skating rink, snow-shoe excursions, paragliding, guided tours, horse-drawn carriage rides

TOURIST OFFICE

Postcode 73440
Tel +33 479 007300
Fax 479 007506

seen beginners struggling on ice first thing and in thick slush later on. The blue slopes above the resort can get extremely crowded.

FOR CROSS-COUNTRY
Valley hike

There are 28km of prepared trails along the valley floor between St-Martin and half-way between Les Menuires and Val-Thorens.

QUEUES
Can be bypassed

Queues are not much of a probem provided the Mont de la Chambre gondola does not break down. A new detachable quad has been installed at St Martin, speeding the process of getting back from lunch there.

MOUNTAIN RESTAURANTS
Have lunch in St-Martin

The restaurant at the top of the first stage of the La Masse gondola is fairly pleasant. But a lot of people prefer to head for the restaurants of the old village of St-Martin-de-Belleville. The Bouitte, in nearby Saint-Marcel, is typically French and delightful for a blow-out. It's reachable off-piste (follow the signs). The chef, René, will even drive you to Saint-Martin, Les Menuires or Val-Thorens after lunch.

SCHOOLS AND GUIDES
Overcomes language barrier

Reporters are full of praise, despite English not being widely spoken, and we have reports of children enjoying themselves in multinational classes which have a guaranteed maximum size of ten.

FACILITIES FOR CHILDREN
All-embracing

This is very much a family resort, and the childcare arrangements seem well organised. The general view is that it is a good place for children to be introduced to the snow.

Staying there 🔑

Despite the fact that the resort is designed for convenient access to the slopes, you may wish to think quite hard about location. The central area around La Croisette is best for shops and après-ski. But the 'village' has several component parts with fewer facilities, and overall well over 1km in length.

HOW TO GO
Cheap, rough-and-ready packages

Most of the big UK tour operators go to Les Menuires. They have a fair selection of hotels and apartments. There are, perhaps surprisingly, no catered chalets. There is a Club Med above Reberty.

Hotels It comes as a slight surprise to find that there are some quite smart hotels here – although none above 3-star grading, and none with a pool.
⑬ **Ours Blanc** Best in town: a wood-clad, chalet-style 3-star on the slopes above Reberty 1850.
⑬ **Latitudes** 3-star on the lower fringe of Les Bruyères.
② **Menuire** Neat, well equipped place on southern fringe of the resort; but we have had some negative reports.
Self-catering Apartments are cheap but not cheerful. It's a classic French budget resort, so paying extra for under-occupancy is wise. L'Orée des Pistes and Residence Le Villaret are among the least objectionable. The latter has a communal lounge with open fire, and a TV/video room. The Pierre et Vacances places are not up to the usual standard, but are better than some other apartments in the resort.

EATING OUT
Good authentic French cuisine

Though some restaurants lack atmosphere at times, there's no shortage of good food. Savoyard specialities and 'real' French food are the order of the day. Most of our reporters seem happy to stay in their hotel restaurant and bar.

APRES-SKI
Improving but still very limited

The young people who are attracted here by low prices have done their best to bring a spark of life to the nightlife scene, but it's still pretty quiet. Le Challenge bar has live music. La Mousse and Le Passeport are also popular. The Liberty disco in Les Bruyères was modernised last year.

OFF THE SLOPES
Forget it

Les Menuires is a resort for keen piste-bashers who want to explore the world's most extensive slopes on a budget. It's not the place for those who do not take to the slopes themselves, though there are some pretty walks.

Méribel

1400m-1700m

The best-looking base for the wonderful Three Valleys

WHAT IT COSTS

(((((6)

HOW IT RATES

The slopes
Snow	****
Extent	*****
Experts	****
Intermediates	*****
Beginners	***
Convenience	***
Queues	****
Restaurants	****

The rest
Scenery	***
Resort charm	***
Off-slope	***

➕ In the centre of the biggest linked piste network in the world – ideal for intermediates who love covering the miles, but plenty for experts, too

➕ Modern, constantly improved lift system means little queueing and rapid access to all slopes

➕ Good piste grooming and snowmaking

➕ Village purpose-built in pleasing chalet-style architecture

➕ Some slope-side accommodation (in Méribel as well as Mottaret)

➖ Main village spread out, straggling along a long, winding road that is mostly well away from the slopes

➖ Expensive

➖ Mottaret satellite is rather lifeless

➖ Not the place to go for any sensation of being a traveller in France – too many Brits

For keen piste-bashers who dislike tacky purpose-built resorts, Méribel is difficult to beat. It is slap in the middle of the Three Valleys – the biggest inter-linked winter-sports area in the world. With 200 lifts and 600km of pistes, and endless off-piste possibilities, it is difficult to be bored in a fortnight here. Fans of Courchevel and Val-Thorens sniff at Méribel's local slopes but, since Mont Vallon and the top of the valley were opened up some years ago, Méribel can stand comparison on most counts.

You won't like it if you don't like sharing the slopes with hordes of Brits. And it's not cheap – indeed, the 1992 Olympic Games seem to have prompted the resort to move significantly upmarket. Several very comfortable and expensive hotels were built for the Games and others were renovated; the place is now much more of a rival than it once was for traditionally swanky Courchevel. But don't be put off: one of us learned to ski here, the other visited it on his second trip, and we both go back whenever we can.

boarding *Méribel may not be a classic boarder resort – it's a bit too smart for that – but the terrain locally and further afield has lots to offer, you rarely have to take a drag-lift, and the resort is doing its bit by organising a fun park and two half-pipes. There are no less than three specialist shops – Oxygène Surf, Surfer of Fortune and Surf Academy – and it would be surprising if you didn't feel at home in at least one of the lively Brit-dominated bars.*

What's new

The 1996/97 season saw the completion of the splendid Olympic Centre, which now has a 12m climbing wall, 25m pool with children's area, medical centre and a big nursery. More snow guns were installed, notably on the Georges Mauduit black run.

For 1997/98, the Pas du Lac gondola, which for years has had trouble shifting the afternoon crowds out of Mottaret towards Courchevel, is at last to be replaced by a more powerful 8-seater gondola.

The resort

Méribel occupies the central valley of the Three Valleys system and consists of two main resort villages.

The original resort of Méribel-les-Allues (now known as Méribel-Centre) is built on a single steepish west-facing hillside with the home piste running down beside it to the main lift stations at the valley bottom. All the buildings are wood-clad, low-rise, chalet style, making this one of the most tastefully designed of French purpose-built resorts. A road winds up from the village centre at about 1400m

to the Rond Point des Pistes at about 1650m, and goes on through woods to the outpost of the Altiport (an airport with snow-covered runway and little planes with skis) at around 1700m.

The resort was founded by a Brit, Peter Lindsay, in 1939, and has retained a strong British presence ever since. It has grown enormously over recent years, and although some accommodation is right on the piste, much of the newer building is more than a walk away. One clear exception is Belvédère, an upmarket enclave built on the opposite side of the home piste (there's a tunnel for road access).

MOUNTAIN FACTS

Altitude	1300m-3200m
Lifts	200
Pistes	600km
Green/Blue	49%
Red	37%
Black	14%
Artificial snow	80km
Recco detectors used	

There are collections of shops and restaurants at a couple of points on the road through the resort – Altitude 1600 and Plateau de Morel. The hotels and apartments of Altiport enjoy splendid isolation in the woods, and are convenient for some of the slopes.

The satellite village of Méribel-Mottaret was developed in the early 1970s, further up the valley. The original development was beside the piste on the east-facing slope, but in recent years the resort has spread up the opposite hillside and further up the valley. Both sides are served by lifts for pedestrian access – but the gondola up the original village stops at 7.30pm and it's a long, tiring walk up to the top. Mottaret looks modern, despite wood-cladding on its apartment blocks. Even so, it is much more attractive than many other resorts built for slope-side convenience. Mottaret has many fewer shops and bars and much less après-ski than Méribel-Centre.

For the Olympics, a new gondola was built from Brides-les-Bains, an old spa town way down in the valley, which served as the Olympic Village for the games, up to Méribel-Centre. There's a mid-station at the old village of Les Allues, which has put it back on the map as a possible place to stay.

The mountains

The main attraction of Méribel is the runs of the immense Three Valleys region, so read the entries for Courchevel, Les Menuires and Val-Thorens as well as this one.

It's keen piste-bashers who will get the best out of what Méribel has to offer. The grooming of the slopes is about the best in the Alps, and there is endless cruising to be had – as well as more challenging terrain. The lift system is very efficient, and planned to cut out walks and climbs. The piste grading is not always entirely reliable.

THE SLOPES
Highly efficient lift system

The Méribel valley runs north–south. On the eastern side, gondolas leave both Méribel and Mottaret for **La Saulire** at around 2700m. From here you can head back down towards either village or down the other side in a choice of directions to join the Courchevel runs.

From Méribel-Centre a gondola rises

to **Tougnète**, on the western side of the valley, from where you can get down to Les Menuires or St-Martin-de-Belleville. You can also head for Mottaret from here. From there, a chair then a drag take you to another entry point for the Les Menuires runs.

The Mottaret area has seen rapid mechanisation over the last decade. The **Plattières** gondola rises up the valley to the south, ending at yet another entry point to the Les Menuires area. To the east of this, a totally new area was opened up a few years ago by the building of a big stand-up gondola to the top of **Mont Vallon** at nearly 3000m. There are wonderful views from the top – see facing page. A high-speed quad from near this area goes south up to **Mont de la Chambre**, giving direct access to Val-Thorens.

Lift passes for six days or more also give you a day in Val-d'Isère-Tignes (just over an hour away), La Plagne or Les Arcs (30 and 45 mins respectively).

SNOW RELIABILITY
Great piste-maintenance

The Méribel slopes aren't the highest in the Three Valleys, and snow conditions are often better elsewhere. But the grooming of the runs is excellent and the lower runs now have a substantial amount of snowmaking. So lack of snow here is rarely a problem, though ice or slush low down at the end of the day can be. It's the west-facing La Saulire side, which gets the afternoon sun, where conditions deteriorate first – but then you can always go to the Courchevel slopes. The north-west-facing slopes above Altiport generally have decent snow. At the southern end of the valley, towards Les Menuires and Val-Thorens, a lot of the runs are north-facing and keep their snow well.

FOR EXPERTS
Exciting choices

The extent of the Three Valleys area means experts are well catered for. In the Méribel valley one of the places to head for is Mont Vallon. The long, steep, mogulled Combe de Vallon run here is graded red, but often presents plenty of challenge. And there's a beautiful itinéraire (strangely, not marked on the piste map) in the next valley to the main pistes, leading to the bottom of the gondola.

The slopes down from the top of

Tantalising view from Mt Vallon: the slopes in the foreground may be out of bounds, but the ocean of snow beyond – the Glacier de Gébroulaz – can be reached by climbing from Val-Thorens ➔

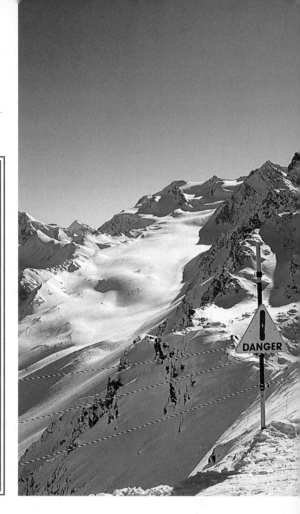

DANGER

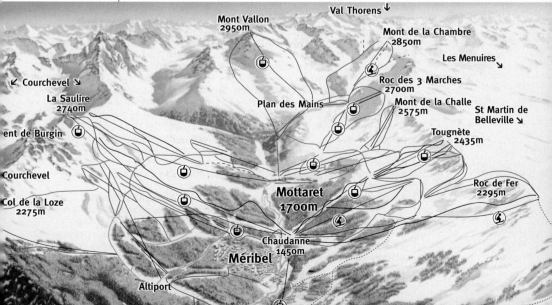

Val Thorens ↓

Mont Vallon 2950m

Mont de la Chambre 2850m

Les Menuires ↘

← Courchevel ↘

Roc des 3 Marches 2700m

La Saulire 2740m

Plan des Mains

Mont de la Challe 2575m

St Martin de Belleville ↘

ent de Burgin

Tougnète 2435m

Courchevel

Roc de Fer 2295m

Col de la Loze 2275m

Mottaret 1700m

Chaudanne 1450m

Méribel

Altiport

LIFT PASSES

97/98 prices in francs
Three Valleys
Covers all lifts in Courchevel, La Tania, Méribel, Val-Thorens, Les Menuires and St-Martin-de-Belleville.
Beginners One free lift in Mottaret and one in Méribel; reduced price lift pass with beginners' lessons.
Main pass
1-day pass 220
6-day pass 1,080 (low season 972 – 10% off)
Senior citizens
Over 60: 6-day pass 864 (20% off)
Over 75: free pass
Children
Under 16: 6-day pass 810 (25% off)
Under 5: free pass
Short-term passes
Half-day passes (from 12.30) available for Vallée de Méribel (adult 135) and 3 Valleys (adult 165).
Notes 6-day pass and over valid for one day each in Tignes-Val-d'Isère, La Plagne-Les Arcs, Pralognan-la-Vanoise and Les Saisies. 70- to 75-year-olds get a 50% discount on pass price (6-day pass 540). Reductions for families.
Alternative passes
Vallée de Méribel pass covers 150km of runs in Méribel and Mottaret (adult 6-day 880, child 6-day 660).

the Val-Thorens sector were all off-piste when we old hands first visited Méribel. Since the new lifts were installed up here, there are two pistes back from Val-Thorens, but still plenty of opportunity for getting off-piste in the wide open bowls.

A good mogul run is down the side of the double Roc de Tougne drag-lift which leads up to Mont de la Challe. And there is a steep black run all the way down the Tougnète gondola back to Méribel-Centre – apart from a shallow section near the mid-station, unrelenting most of the way.

At the north end of the valley the La Face run was built for the women's downhill in the 1992 Olympics. Served by a two-stage fast quad, it makes a splendid cruise when it is freshly groomed, and you can terrify yourself just by imagining what it must be like to go straight down.

On the La Saulire side, there are a couple of black runs marked on the piste map. But neither is as steep or demanding as those on the opposite side of the valley.

Throughout the area there are good off-piste opportunities. The ESF runs excellent-value guided groups.

FOR INTERMEDIATES
Paradise found
Méribel and the rest of the Three Valleys is a paradise for intermediates; there are few other resorts where a keen piste-basher can cover so many kilometres so easily. Virtually every slope in the Three Valleys region has a good intermediate run down it, and to describe them would take a book in itself. If you're an intermediate, don't miss it!

For less adventurous intermediates, the run from the second station of the Plattières gondola back to Mottaret is ideal, and used a lot by the ski school. It is a gentle, north-facing, cruising run which is well groomed and generally has good snow.

Even those with only moderate experience should find the runs over into the other valleys well within their capabilities, opening up further vast amounts of intermediate runs. Go to Courchevel for the better snow.

Virtually all the pistes on both sides of the Méribel valley will suit more advanced intermediates. Most of the reds are on the difficult side.

FOR BEGINNERS
Not ideal
Méribel isn't ideal for beginners. The resort lacks good nursery slopes set apart from the main areas. There is a small one at Rond Point, mainly used by the children's ski school.

But the best area for beginners is at Altiport, now accessible direct from the village at Altitude 1600 by chair-lift. There is a gentle out-of-the-way area here which can be treated as a nursery slope. And, once you can tackle a drag-lift, you can get up to one of the best and most attractively situated green pistes we know, the Blanchot – gentle, wide and tree-lined, with little through-traffic.

FOR CROSS-COUNTRY
Scenic routes
The main area is in the woods near Altiport. There is about 17km of prepared track here, a pleasant introduction to those who want to try cross-country for the first time.

There is also a track round the frozen lake at Mottaret, and for the more experienced there is an 8km itinéraire from Altiport to Courchevel.

QUEUES
Virtually non-existent
The huge investment in lifts that has been made consistently over the years has paid off in making the area virtually queue-free despite the huge numbers of people. If you do come across a queue, there is generally an alternative route available.

The old four-person Pas du Lac gondola from Mottaret towards Courchevel has been generating afternoon queues for as long as we can remember, but is at last to be replaced for the 1997/98 season. In any case, you can avoid the queue at Mottaret by taking the gondola from Méribel-Centre or the chair from Altiport to Col de la Loze.

The Plattières gondola at Mottaret can also get crowded at ski school time, when the school gets priority. Simply avoid the peak period.

MOUNTAIN RESTAURANTS
Places you won't want to leave
There is lots of choice by the standards of most French purpose-built resorts. The Pierres Plates, at the top of the La Saulire gondolas, has magnificent views and you can watch hang-gliders taking off, though the

SCHOOLS/GUIDES

97/98 prices in francs

ESF
in Méribel and
Mottaret
Classes 6 days
5hr: 9.30-noon and
2.15-4.45
5 full days: 987
Children's classes
Ages: 5 to 13
5 full days: 777
Private lessons
1hr or 2hr, lunchtimes
only
285 for 1½hr, for 1 to
2 people

International
In Méribel and
Mottaret
Classes 6 days
4½hr: 9.30-noon and
2.45-4.45
5 full days: 840
Children's classes
Ages: 5 to 12
5 full days: 662
Private lessons
1hr to 2½hr,
lunchtimes only
185 for 1 hr

Ski Cocktail
Classes 6 days
2hr am or 2hr pm
6 mornings: 750
Children's classes
Ages: 6 to 12
6 half days: 895
Private lessons
on request

Magic in Motion
English-speaking
school with course
maximum of 7
people.

CHILDCARE

The ESF runs P'tits
Loups kindergartens
at both Méribel and
Mottaret, with snow
gardens (lifts,
inflatable characters
etc) for children aged
3 to 5. Open 9am to
5pm.

Les Saturnins in the
Olympic Centre
building in Méribel
takes children aged
18mths to 3, offering
indoor games and
handicrafts, sledging
and other outdoor
activities.

food is nothing special. Chardonnet, at
the mid-station of the Mottaret
gondola, has table-service and
excellent food but is expensive.
Rhododendrons, at the top of the
Altiport drag, has a modern but
atmospheric wooden dining room. The
Altiport hotel has a great outdoor
buffet in good weather and the 'best
tarts in town' but, again, is expensive.
Les Crêtes, below the top of the
Tougnète gondola, is family-run, has
good service and is one of smallest
mountain restaurants in the Three
Valleys. La Sittelle, above the first
section of the Plattières gondola, has
decent food and magnificent views
towards Mont Vallon. Les Castors, at
the main Méribel lift station, scarcely
counts as a mountain restaurant, but
earns praise for good, affordable food
including 'exquisite' carbonara.

SCHOOLS AND GUIDES
No shortage of instructors
The three main schools all have plenty
of English-speaking instructors.
    The ESF is by far the biggest, with
over 300 instructors. It has a special
International section, run by Pat
Graham, with instructors speaking
good English. We've had few reports
recently, but they have generally been
favourable; it's best to book in
advance in high season.
    Ski Cocktail is French-run, but along
business rather than the usual
cooperative lines. Reports are generally
encouraging; for example: 'Good
tuition. Well organised, conscientious,
friendly instructors with a good sense
of humour.' They appear to keep
classes down to reasonable numbers.
    But this year the rave reviews are
reserved for Magic in Motion, who
teach only in English. 'Fantastic tuition
and good group size, with courses to
meet all needs,' says one report. 'Use
of time was excellent,' says another of
her 'expensive but value-for-money'
private lesson.
    As well as standard group and
private lessons, there are some
interesting alternatives. For example,
the ESF runs off-piste guided tours.

FACILITIES FOR CHILDREN
Lots of choice
Despite our fat file of reports on
Méribel, none deals first-hand with the
resort's childcare facilities. Several
chalet operators run their own crèches,
with British nannies.

Staying there

You need to pick where you stay with
some care, according to your own
priorities. From the point of view of
easy access to the piste, Mottaret is
hard to beat, but even here there are
better and worse spots.
    For those who prefer chalet
accommodation, a more villagey
ambience and a greater choice of
shops, bars and restaurants, the best
place would be around or just above
the village centre of Méribel. The main
thing to check is how far your
accommodation is from the piste – a
fair amount is a long hike (and the
resort is built on a hill, remember). The
local buses are now free, and many UK
tour operators run their own minibus
services to the lifts.

HOW TO GO
Huge choice but few bargains
Package holidays with all types of
accommodation are easy to find both
with big UK tour operators and smaller
Méribel specialists. There is a Club
Med, occupying the swanky new Aspen
Park hotel at Rond-Point.
Chalets Méribel has more chalets
dedicated to the British market than
any other resort.
    There are lots of merely comfortable
chalets, but what really distinguishes
Méribel is the range of luxurious ones.
Simply Ski have a couple of very
luxurious chalets – including (as far as
they knew when we went to press) the
spectacular chalet Brames. Local
specialists Meriski have a good
selection of places at the top end of
the market, including some splendid
new places for 1997/98 and an old
mountain refuge up the east-facing
slopes, isolated after the lifts shut.
    Mottaret chalets tend to be towards
the lower end of the Méribel market
but most of them are more convenient
than many of their Méribel-Centre
counterparts.
Hotels Méribel has some excellent
hotels with reputations for high-quality
accommodation and food. But they
don't come cheap. A lot of renovation
and repositioning went on at the time
of the Olympics, and there are now
lots of smart hotels with health and
fitness facilities.
(((⑤ **Antares** Best in town; beside the
piste at Belvedere. Ambitious cooking.
Pool, fitness room etc.

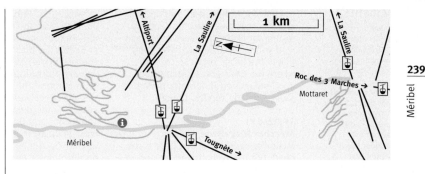

GETTING THERE

Air Geneva, transfer 3½hr. Lyon, transfer 3½hr. Chambery, transfer 2½hr.

Rail Moûtiers (18km); regular buses to Méribel.

UK PACKAGES

AA Ski-Driveaway, Airtours, Alpine Action, Altours Ski, Bladon Lines, Chalet World, Chalets 'Unlimited', Club Med, Crystal, Erna Low, Fairhand Holidays, First Choice Ski, Independent Ski Links, Inghams, Lagrange, Lotus Supertravel, Made to Measure, Mark Warner, Meriski, Motours, Neilson, Poles Apart, Powder Byrne, Silver Ski, Simply Ski, Ski Activity, Ski Arrangements, Ski Beat, Ski Bon, Ski Choice, Ski France, Ski Leisure Direction, Ski Les Alpes, Ski Olympic, Ski Scott Dunn, Ski Trois Vallees, Ski Valkyrie, Ski trek, Skiworld, Snowcoach, Snowline Skiing, Solo's, Stena Line Holidays, The Ski Company Ltd, Thomson, Travelscene Ski-Drive, White Roc, avant-ski

Brides-les-Bains
Crystal, Erna Low, Lagrange, Motours, STS, Ski Leisure Direction, Stena Line Holidays

Mottaret AA Ski-Driveaway, Crystal, Ski Leisure Direction, Ski trek, Skiworld, Stena Line Holidays, Thomson

(((((5) **Chalet** Luxurious, beautifully furnished wooden chalet at Belvedere, with lovely rooms and all mods cons – outdoor pool, fitness room etc.

(((((4) **Grand Coeur** Our favourite almost-affordable hotel in Méribel. Just above the village centre. Welcoming, mature building with plush lounge. Magnificent food. Huge jacuzzi, sauna, etc.

(((((4) **Altiport** Modern and luxurious hotel, isolated at the foot of the Altiport lifts. Convenient for access to Courchevel, not for Val-Thorens.

(((((4) **Mont Vallon** The best hotel at Mottaret, with a reputation for good food, and excellently situated for the Three Valleys pistes. Pool, sauna, jacuzzi, squash, fitness room, etc.

(((((4) **Chaudanne** One of the oldest Méribel hotels, but completely renovated a couple of years ago, with a sports centre – pool, and the rest. Excellent food.

(((((4) **Grangettes** Near the lift station. Good food; friendly staff.

(((((3) **Adray Télébar** Welcoming piste-side chalet with pretty, rustic rooms, good food and popular sun terrace.

(((((3) **Orée du Bois** Just off the piste at Rond Point, convenient for the slopes but not for nightlife. Old hotel offering good value for money. Sauna, steam room and jacuzzi.

(((((2) **Roc** A good value B&B hotel, in the centre, with a bar-restaurant and crêperie below.

Self-catering There is a huge number of apartments and chalets to let in both Méribel-Centre and Mottaret. Take care to make sure that the place you book is conveniently situated and not too 'compact'.

EATING OUT
Fair choice

There is a reasonable selection of restaurants, from ambitious French cuisine to relatively cheap pizza and pasta. For the best food in town, in plush surroundings, there is nothing to beat the top hotels – the Antares, Grand Coeur ('so pleased we ate there several times,' says one reporter), Allodis and Chaudanne. Other recommendations from reporters include Chez Kiki – 'good food and atmosphere'; Jardin d'Hiver – 'great char grills'; Les Castors – 'best French fare'; La Taverne – 'surprisingly good'.

Alternatives worth a try include the Galette, the Glacier and the Refuge, or the Cave, Plantin and Cro Magnon, all

Méribel-Mottaret, with the early afternoon sun striking the west-facing slopes ↓

ACTIVITIES

Indoor Parc des Sports Méribel (skating rink, swimming pool), Forme Mottaret (spa, sauna, gym), library, bowling, billiards, video club, bridge, fitness centres, jacuzzi, 2 cinemas, concert hall
Outdoor Flying lessons and excursions, snow-mobiles, snow-shoe excursions, para-gliding, hang-gliding, 10km of cleared paths, motor-trikes, sleigh rides

popular for raclette and fondue. One reporter recommended the Crocodile restaurant in the Hameau at Mottaret.

If you fancy an outing, you could follow the locals down to Les Allues, where the Croix Jean-Claude serves good-value food in a pretty dining room – patchy service, though.

APRES-SKI
Méribel has come to life

Méribel's après-ski scene used to be dead, but it has improved beyond all recognition in the last few years, not least because of the number of British-run places that have developed. And the big news in 1997 was that the dear old Saints-Pères disco, on the roadside on the way out of the resort, was transformed into a clone of Dick's Tea Bar, the famous British-owned bar/disco in Val-d'Isère. (The 'brand' is now owned by the company behind Meriski, the British chalet operator specialising in Méribel.) 'Clone' isn't quite right, actually: the new place has been thoughtfully designed to suit a range of needs. Even late at night it is possible (just) to hold a conversation if you pick your spot.

Unlike the original in Val-d'Isère, the new Dick's Tea Bar is remote from the slopes and, despite lowish prices from 4pm to 9.30, it's never going to be ideal for immediate après-ski drinking. At close of play, the Rond Point bar (aka Yorkie's, after the previous owner) is usually packed – happy hour starts at 4pm – and it generally has live music a couple of times a week. Jack's, with a sun terrace opposite the ice-rink, is also very popular, especially with resort staff (possibly because they get a 50 per cent discount); prices are said to be modest, even for the super-strong Mutzig beer (happy hour here starts at 5pm).

There's a ring of bars around the main square that do good business at tea-time (it's only a short stagger down the steps from the main piste beside the village). La Taverne gets packed with Brits, and now has a quieter downstairs bar. Just across the square is The Pub, with videos, pool and sometimes a band. The Capricorne (more Mutzig) attracts a more cosmopolitan crowd and Le Refuge (a little way down the road towards the lifts) is that rare thing in Méribel: a place where you'll be understood if you use your French.

Later on, live music brings in the

crowds at the Pub, Artichaud (a sort of bar/club hybrid), French Connection and Rond Point. There is late dancing at Scott's (next to the Pub) and, of course, Dick's Tea Bar (free entry and sub-disco drinks prices until 11.30).

In Mottaret the bars at the foot of the pistes get packed at tea-time – especially the terraces on a sunny day. The Rastro and DownTown are the most popular, though reporters inform us that Zig Zag has lower prices. Later on, Plein Soleil sometimes has live music, and the Rastro disco is the main venue for late revellers.

Both villages have a cinema which shows new films in English up to three times a week.

OFF THE SLOPES
Flight of fancy

Méribel is essentially a resort for people who want to go skiing or boarding, rather than languishing in the village. But as purpose-built French resorts go, it is one of the most attractive architecturally, and not a bad choice for someone with no interest in the slopes. Méribel-Centre has a good public swimming pool near the lift station. You can also take joy-rides in the little plane which operates from the Altiport. The cinema often shows films in English. The pedestrian's lift pass covers all the gondolas and cable-cars in the Méribel and Courchevel valleys, and makes it very easy for pedestrians to get around the mountain and meet friends for lunch. The buses are free.

STAYING DOWN THE VALLEY
The old village and a revived spa

If you want a quiet time, some UK tour operators have places in the old village of Les Allues, down the road from the resort and connected by the gondola up from Brides-les-Bains. There are a couple of bars and a good-value, well renovated hotel which serves good food in the area – the Croix Jean-Claude. Rooms are small, though.

Brides-les-Bains itself is an old spa town which served as the Olympic village at the 1992 Winter Games and is now trying to turn itself into a winter as well as summer resort. It's cheap and has some simple hotels and a casino. But it's dead in the evening. And the long gondola ride to Méribel is tedious, and not covered by the lift pass. If you are driving, it makes a good base for visiting other resorts.

TOURIST OFFICE

Postcode 73551
Tel +33 479 086001
Fax 479 005961

Montgenèvre
1850m

Not a pretty pass, but an admirably snowy one

REVISITED · BY THE EDITORS

WHAT IT COSTS
((3))

HOW IT RATES

The slopes

Snow	***
Extent	****
Experts	**
Intermediates	****
Beginners	*****
Convenience	****
Queues	****
Restaurants	**

The rest

Scenery	***
Resort charm	***
Off-slope	*

What's new

For 1996/97 the popular Brousset drag was replaced by a quad chair and the snowmaking coverage was extended down to that lift from the Prarial chair out of the village.

There is still no bank but there is now a cash machine at the tourist office.

MOUNTAIN FACTS

Altitude	1850m-2580m
Lifts	24
Pistes	65km
Green/Blue	48%
Red	33%
Black	19%
Artificial snow	6km

➊ Good, convenient nursery slopes, with easy progression to longer runs

➊ Few queues on weekdays

➊ Most accommodation close to slopes, and some right on them

➊ Good snow record, and local slopes largely north-facing

➊ Attractive old village centre tucked away off main road

➊ Great potential for car drivers to explore other nearby resorts

➖ Local prices high compared to neighbouring Italy

➖ Poor base for exploring the Italian Milky Way resorts

➖ Slow lifts, short runs and continual pass-checking can be irritating

➖ Main road and tatty bars reduce village charm and family appeal

➖ Little to do off the slopes

➖ Little to challenge experts on-piste

Montgenèvre is set at one end of the extensive Milky Way network, reaching over to Sestriere and Sauze in Italy. It is not the ideal base for exploring the area – it's a time-consuming trek from much of the best terrain, and lift-pass arrangements make regular visits across the border expensive. You can deal with the first of these by taking a car (which also facilitates day-trips to other French resorts such as Serre-Chevalier and La Grave). But Montgenèvre is also worth considering on its own merits. It's a convenient and pleasant village with a fair-sized area of intermediate slopes, particularly attractive to beginners and near-beginners wanting to do some longer runs on (normally) excellent snow.

boarding *There's plenty to attract boarders to Montgenèvre, with good local beginner slopes, and long runs on varied terrain for intermediates. There's a fun-park with half-pipe on the lower slopes, and there are some excellent off-piste areas for more advanced boarders. But many of the lifts in the area are drags, and you will have to use them to get around – getting over to Sestriere and back involves lots (and a flat green run to skate along as well). Snow Box is the local specialist shop.*

The resort

Montgenèvre is a narrow roadside village set on a high pass only 2km from the Italian border. At first glance it appears a rather inhospitable place – a collection of tatty-looking bars and restaurants lining the side of the sometimes windswept and often busy main road over the col.

But appearances are deceptive. Tucked away off the main road is a charming old village, complete with quaint church and friendly natives. Being covered in snow for much of the season accentuates the charm factor, as do the pleasantly wooded mountains either side of the village. The slopes are convenient, despite the road. There is little walking to be done in this compact village, where all accommodation is less than five minutes from a lift. Furthermore, the underrated Chalvet area is on the same side of the road as the village. For their part, the cheap and cheerful cafés and bars add an animated atmosphere sometimes missing from French resorts. There is no bank but there is a limited post office exchange service and now an automatic cash machine at the tourist office.

The mountains

Montgenèvre's local slopes are best suited to leisurely intermediates, with lots of easy cruising on blues and greens, both above and below the tree line. The local upper slopes are bland, but the runs gain in interest further afield. Intermediates who like to cover a bit of ground will want to cross into Italy to tour the whole of the Milky Way (see the chapters on Sestriere and Sauze d'Oulx).

LIFT PASSES

97/98 prices in francs

Montgenèvre
Covers Montgenèvre lifts only.

Beginners One free drag-lift. Points cards available. 'Petit Réseau' day pass covers 7 lifts (adult 90). 'Debutant' pass (6-day 470) available with ski school.

Main pass
1-day pass 130
6-day pass 680
(low season 560 – 18% off)

Senior citizens
Over 60: 6-day pass 510 (25% off)

Children
Under 12: 6-day pass 510 (25% off)
Under 6: free pass

Short-term passes
Single ascent for foot passengers of Le Chalvet. Half-day pass up to and from 1pm (adult 103).

Notes 6 day-pass and over allows free days at Alpe-d'Huez, Les Deux-Alpes, Puy-Saint-Vincent and Serre-Chevalier. Reductions for families. Extensions by the day to main pass for the Voie Lactée (adult 50)

Alternative passes
Montgenèvre-Mont de la Lune (Clavière) (adults 135 per day). Voie Lactée (Milky Way) covers Montgenèvre, Clavière, Cesana, Sansicario, Sauze d'Oulx, Grangesises, Borgata, Sestriere, (adults 199 per day).

CHILDCARE

The Halte Garderie takes children aged 1 to 4, from 9am to 5.30pm. Meals you provide can be administered.

The ESF's kindergarten takes children aged 3 to 5.

THE SLOPES
Slow going

The two sets of slopes are accessed from opposite sides of the village. The south-facing slopes of Le Chalvet lead straight up from the village. The major sector, the north-facing slopes of Les Anges and Le Querelay with the nursery slopes at the bottom, are across the main road from the village.

This sector has a high-altitude link to the slopes above Clavière and so to the rest of the Milky Way. The link involves a long drag-lift with a 200m walk at the top, followed by a mogul-field (red on some maps, black on others) – not ideal for intermediates. The alternative is to head for the chair-lift out of Clavière, either by plodding across valley cross-country loops or by descending from the Chalvet area and walking across the village.

Once you've got to Clavière, getting to and from the slopes of Sauze and Sestriere via Cesana and Sansicario is time-consuming, involving countless slow chairs and drags. You often get the feeling you are doing a lot of travelling and clock-watching without having much fun. Indeed, getting to Sestriere and back in a day is scarcely worthwhile, now that the only access is via Col Basset. (They've done away with the lifts and runs on Monte Fraiteve that in the past allowed you to bypass Sauze d'Oulx in both directions, apparently on the feeble grounds that the slope above Sestriere was too sunny to be reliably open.)

The best way to get to these other resorts and enjoy some time there is to travel by car. Serre-Chevalier and Puy-St-Vincent, with lift-pass sharing arrangements, are also easily reached by car, and well worth an outing each.

SNOW RELIABILITY
Excellent locally

Montgenèvre has an excellent snow record, attracting dumps when westerly storms come up the valley to the pass. The high, north-facing slopes naturally keep their snow better than the south-facing area but both have snowmaking on the main village-bound piste. The sunny link from the top of Le Prarial to the Brousset chair is now covered, too. Sestriere is also snowsure, thanks to its altitude and huge snowmaking installation. The pistes either side of the connecting Cesana valley are often bereft of snow, but chair-lifts make the connection.

FOR EXPERTS
Limited, except for off-piste

There are very few challenging pistes in the Montgenèvre-Clavière-Cesana sectors. Many of the runs are overgraded on the piste map, with none of the blacks being much more than tough reds in reality. There is, however, ample opportunity for off-piste excursions when snow conditions are right.

There's a lonely, north-east-facing bowl on the Chalvet side, served by a drag-lift from below the gondola mid-station, that is superb in good snow and has a black and red run too, with a chair to bring you back up.

On the major sector, both the runs from the top drag-lift on the Franco-Italian border can be fun. Unfortunately, there is no returning lift on the Italian side (you get back to Montgenèvre via lower lifts, just above Clavière). The open section between Montanina and Sagna Longa on the Italian side is another good powder area. Drivers should visit Sestriere for the most challenging runs.

FOR INTERMEDIATES
Plenty of cruising terrain

The overgraded blacks are just right for adventurous intermediates, though none holds the interest for very long. The pleasantly narrow tree-lined runs to Clavière from Plan del Sol, the steepest of the routes down in the Chalvet sector (including the lonely bowl mentioned for experts above) and the Montquitaine-Clavière piste (by the chair linking Clavière with Montgenèvre) are all fine in small doses. The Sagna Longa blacks are particularly uninteresting. Tours to the rest of the Milky Way are rewarding, offering a real sensation of getting around the mountains on the snow.

Average intermediates will enjoy the red runs, though most are short. The longest are down from the top of the Chalvet sector and from the Franco-Italian border.

Getting to Cesana via the lovely sweeping run starting at the top of the Coche drag (red on some maps, black on others) and heading home from La Coche via Plan del Sol is easier than the gradings suggest, and these can be tackled by less adventurous intermediates, who also have a wealth of cruising terrain high up at the top of the north-facing Anges and Querelay slopes above Montgenèvre. These are

SCHOOLS/GUIDES

96/97 prices in francs
ESF
Classes 6 days
5hr: 9.15-11.45 and
14.15-16.45
6 half-days: 515
Children's classes
Ages: Up to 12
6 half-days: 485
Private lessons
Hourly or daily
165 for 1hr; for 2-3
people 198

served by several upper lifts, but you have the option of continuing right down to the village. These long, gentle slopes are just as flattering as the famous motorways of Courchevel and Cervinia.

Further afield, getting down to Clavière from the top of the Coche drags on the Italian border is a beautifully gentle cruise.

FOR BEGINNERS
Good for novices and improvers
There is a fine selection of convenient nursery slopes with reliable snow at the foot of the north-facing area. Progression to longer runs could not be easier, with a very easy green starting at Les Anges (2460m) and finishing at the roadside 600m below.

FOR CROSS-COUNTRY
Having a car widens horizons
Montgenèvre is the best of the Milky Way resorts for cross-country enthusiasts, but it's useful to have a car. There are just two trails locally, totalling 20km, but a further 30km of track starts 8km away in the Clarée valley. One village trail is an easy loop that takes you parallel to the road, through the golf course, to the border post just outside Clavière; the other is a steeper route that climbs through woods in the opposite direction.

Downtown Montgenèvre, seen from the the gentle slopes across the through-road ↓

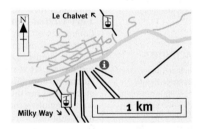

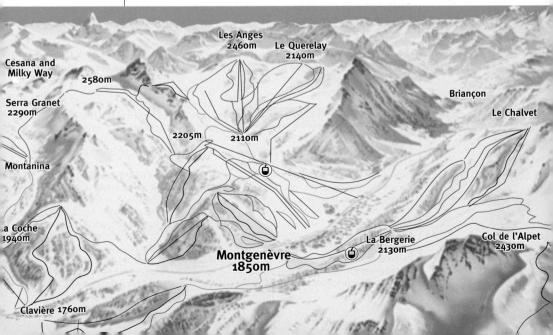

GETTING THERE

Air Turin, transfer 2hr. Grenoble, transfer 3hr. Lyon, transfer 4¹⁄₂hr.

Rail Briançon (10km) or Oulx (17km); 3 or 4 buses per day from station.

UK PACKAGES

Airtours, Crystal, Equity School Ski, Equity Total Ski, Fairhand Holidays, First Choice Ski, Lagrange, Made to Measure, Motours, Ski Etoile, Thomson

Cesana Torinese First Choice Ski, PGL Ski Europe

Clavière Crystal, Equity School Ski, Equity Total Ski, First Choice Ski, Neilson, PGL Ski Europe

ACTIVITIES

Indoor Library, cinema
Outdoor Natural skating rink, curling, hang-gliding, para-gliding, snow-scooters, sledge runs

TOURIST OFFICE

Postcode 05100
Tel +33 492 215252
Fax 492 219245

QUEUES
No problems most of the time

The slopes are wonderfully uncrowded during weekdays, provided surrounding resorts have snow. At weekends and when nearby Bardonecchia is snowless, some lifts become oversubscribed. However, the improved links between Sauze d'Oulx and the impressive artificial snow of Sestriere now make bussing in from the former less likely. There is now a quad chair at Brousset behind Le Prarial – but apart from that, the lifts can be old and slow, with no improvements planned for 1997/98.

MOUNTAIN RESTAURANTS
Head for Italy

Restaurants are in very short supply locally. Most people travel back to the village for lunch. The Ca del Sol café-bar does a good pizza. There are several nice spots in Italy. L'Edelweiss at Les Chalmettes has received good reviews.

SCHOOLS AND GUIDES
Very varied reports

Comments on the school vary greatly, from very good to very poor. They tend to push pupils hard, which suits some but not others. One reporter was complimentary about the instructors' enthusiasm for the mountains but some beginners have been disappointed with the teaching.

FACILITIES FOR CHILDREN
Pity about the traffic

The intrusive main road apart, Montgenèvre would seem a fine family resort. Reports on the school's children's classes continue to be complimentary of both class size and spoken English.

Staying there 🔑

There are hotels, chalets and apartments available, all of which are cheap and cheerful places. Don't expect to find much luxury here. Location is unimportant, as Montgenèvre is small.

HOW TO GO
Limited choice

UK tour operators concentrate on catered chalets, though a few apartments are also available and one or two operators now package hotels as well.

Chalets Several UK tour operators have catered chalets here, mainly cheap and cheerful.
Hotels There are a handful of simple places offering good value.
② **Valérie** Rustic old 3-star in the village centre.
② **Napoléon** 3-star on the roadside.
① **Chalet des Sport** About the cheapest hotel rooms in the Alps.
① **La Grange** Another cheap and cheerful place with tiny rooms and basic food. The older part of the hotel is in line for renovation.
Self-catering Résidences La Ferme d'Augustin are simple, ski-to-the-door apartments on the fringes of the main north-facing slopes, five minutes' walk (across the piste) from town.

EATING OUT
Cheap and cheerful

There are a dozen places to choose from, mostly pizzerias. The Ca del Sol and the Tourmente are recommended. The Estable, Napoli and Transalpin serve good pizza. Chez Pierrot and the Jamy are the only ones with an authentic French feel. The 3-star Napoleon is the only hotel with a restaurant open to non-residents, but it's yet another pizzeria! A trip to Clavière is worthwhile – the cheaper prices will pay for the taxi fare.

APRES-SKI
Mainly bars, but fun

The range is limited. Le Graal is a friendly, unsophisticated place; the Ca del Sol bar is a cosy place with an open fire. The Blue Light is the better of the discos. The Refuge and the Jamy are the focal café-bars at tea-time.

OFF THE SLOPES
Very limited

There is a weekly market and you can walk the cross-country routes, but the main attraction is a bus-trip to the beautiful old town of Briançon.

STAYING IN OTHER RESORTS
Only for the dedicated

Cesana and Clavière are small, unappealing villages with few facilities. Cesana is a 15-minute walk from its lifts. Clavière's nursery slope is small and steep but uncrowded and snow-reliable. There are longer runs suitable for progression. Both resorts are best for dedicated intermediates keen to make the most of the Milky Way slopes without much après-ski.

Morzine

A lively, year-round resort linked by lift to the Portes du Soleil

WHAT IT COSTS
((((4)

HOW IT RATES

The slopes

Snow	**
Extent	*****
Experts	***
Intermediates	****
Beginners	***
Convenience	**
Queues	***
Restaurants	***

The rest

Scenery	***
Resort charm	***
Off-slope	***

➕ Part of the vast Portes du Soleil lift network

➕ Larger local piste area than other Portes du Soleil resorts

➕ Good nightlife by French standards

➕ Quite attractive old village – a stark contrast to Avoriaz

➕ One of the easiest drives from the Channel or Le Shuttle terminal (a car is very useful here)

➕ Few queues locally (but see minus points)

➖ Avoriaz queues slow down access to Portes du Soleil circuit

➖ Bus-ride or long walk to lifts from much of the accommodation

➖ Poor snow record, with few snowmakers

➖ Low altitude or very inconvenient nursery slopes

➖ Very little for experts if Avoriaz Prodains runs are closed

➖ Weekend crowds

Morzine is a long-established French resort, popular for its easy road access, traditional atmosphere and gentle tree-filled slopes, where children do not get lost and bad weather rarely causes problems. For keen piste-bashers wanting to travel the Portes du Soleil circuit, the main drawback to staying in Morzine is the strong possibility of poor local snow conditions, and the frustration involved in getting to, and through, queue-prone Avoriaz.

Such problems can, however, be avoided by taking a car. A little-used gondola awaits at Ardent, a short drive from Morzine; from there, you can tour the circuit clockwise via Châtel, missing out Avoriaz. If snow is poor, Avoriaz is normally the first thought – but it's everyone else's first thought too. If you have a car, you have the alternative of visiting nearby Flaine, a resort far better than Avoriaz at coping with crowds looking for snow. Morzine is one of the easiest resorts to drive to from the Channel – there is a motorway from Calais to nearby Cluses, and Le Shuttle has made it an even more attractive proposition.

boarding *Avoriaz is the hardcore boarder destination in the Portes du Soleil – and that's where the fun-park and half-pipe are. There's not much terrain to interest experienced boarders in the more immediate Morzine-Les Gets area. But with few drag-lifts, and its interesting, tree-lined area, the local Morzine slopes are good for beginners and intermediates. Chalet Snowboard – the first specialist snowboard tour operator – sited its first chalet in Morzine, but out near the Les Prodains cable-car for swift access to Avoriaz.*

What's new

The old chair-lift from Super-Morzine towards Avoriaz was replaced by a high-speed quad for the 1996/97 season, speeding up the process of getting into the main Portes du Soleil circuit from the Morzine gondola.

The resort

Morzine is a large, traditional, mountain town which sprawls amorphously on both sides of a river gorge and on several levels. Under a blanket of snow, its chalet-style buildings look charming, and in spring the village quickly takes on a spruce appearance. But at this altitude in France, the blanket of snow often gives way to slush and mud, which is somewhat less appealing.

Perhaps because the French share our view that the resort suits car drivers, there are lots of them, and the resort suffers traffic problems because of them.

The old centre of Morzine is next to the river, but most resort amenities are clustered up the hill around the Le Pléney lifts.

Accommodation is widely scattered, and a good bus service operates on six routes around the town, giving access to outlying lifts, including the Prodains ones towards Avoriaz.

Morzine is essentially a family resort. Consequently village ambience tends to be fairly subdued.

MOUNTAIN FACTS

Altitude	975m-2020m
Lifts	219
Pistes	650km
Green/Blue	54%
Red	33%
Black	13%
Artificial snow	12km

LIFT PASSES

97/98 prices in francs
Portes du Soleil
Covers all lifts in 12 resorts, and shuttle buses.
Main pass
1-day pass 203
6-day pass 928
Senior citizens
Over 60: 6-day pass 612 (34% off)
Children
Under 16: 6-day pass 612 (34% off)
Under 5: free pass
Short-term passes
Half-day passes available for the Portes de Soleil (adult 138), Super-Morzine-Avoriaz (adult 127) and Morzine-Gets (adult 109).
Notes Discounts for groups of 13 or more and holders of the Carte Neige.
Alternative passes
Morzine-Les Gets pass covers 85 lifts (adult 6-day 726, child 545); 6-day pass including 5 days in Morzine-Les Gets and 1 day in Portes du Soleil (809 adults, 591 children).

The mountains

The local slopes, like those of the main Portes du Soleil area, suit intermediates well, with excellent areas for beginners and near-beginners too.

THE SLOPES
No need to go far afield

Morzine is not an ideal base for the Portes du Soleil circuit (for descriptions of the slopes there, see the Avoriaz, Châtel and Champéry chapters). But it has a good local area too.

A cable-car and parallel gondola rise from the edge of central Morzine to **Le Pléney**, where numerous routes return to the valley, including a run down to Les Fys – a quiet junction of chairs which access **Nyon** and, in the opposite direction, the ridge separating the Morzine from the **Les Gets** slopes. Nyon is also accessed by cable-car, situated a bus-ride out of Morzine, and is connected to the slopes of Les Gets higher up the valley that separates the two, with a lift up from Le Grand Pré to Le Ranfolly.

The Nyon sector has two peaks – Pointe de Nyon and Chamossière – accessible from Nyon and Le Grand Pré respectively. Connections between Pléney and Nyon are not easy for the uninitiated, owing to an inaccurate piste map and poor piste directions. Returning from Les Gets has to be via Le Ranfolly, from where you can get home to Morzine without using a lift, via a path to central Morzine.

Beyond Les Gets is another small sector, chiefly of interest to Les Gets residents, on the front and back of Mont Chéry. The walk across the resort from the bottom of the Chavannes sector is a bearable one.

A third area starts at **Super-Morzine**, accessed from town by gondola. A series of pistes and lifts transports you to Avoriaz. This section is very much an access route, used mainly by Morzine clientele moving to and from Avoriaz. The alternative is a bus-ride or short drive to Les Prodains, from where you can get a cable-car to Avoriaz or a chair-lift into the **Hauts Forts** slopes above it.

By bus or car you can also get to Ardent, where a gondola accesses Les Linderets. From here you can get lifts towards Châtel, Avoriaz or Champéry. Car trips to Flaine, Chamonix and even Courmayeur are also feasible.

SNOW RELIABILITY
Poor

Morzine has a very low average height, and when snow disappears from the valley, both of the main areas become very small and unconnected. Snowmakers have been introduced to the area – most noticeably on the runs linking Nyon and Le Pléney, and on red and blue runs back to town – but many more would be needed to make this a reasonably snowsure area.

FOR EXPERTS
Limited

The run down from Pointe de Nyon is challenging, but it is the cable-car at Les Prodains which is the place to head for, taking you up to Avoriaz. The Hauts Forts black runs, including the World Cup downhill course, are excellent. Unfortunately, these runs are sometimes closed due to lack of snow. The far end of the Chamossière section occasionally has some good off-piste possibilities.

FOR INTERMEDIATES
Something for everyone

Good intermediates will enjoy the challenging reds and blacks down from the Chamossière and Pointe de Nyon high points. Mont Chéry – remote from Morzine on the far side of Les Gets – has some fine steepish runs which are worth heading for.

Those of average ability have a great number of runs to choose from, though most are rather short. Le Ranfolly accesses a series of good cruising runs on the Les Gets side of the ridge, and a nice piste back to Le Grand Pré. Le Pléney has a compact network of pistes that are ideal for groups with mixed abilities: mainly moderate intermediate runs, but with some easier alternatives for the more timid, and a single challenging route for the aggressive. Nyon's slopes are rather bitty for those not up to at least Chamossière runs.

Less experienced intermediates have plenty of options on Le Pléney, including a snow-gun-covered cruise from the summit back to the main lift station. Heading from Le Ranfolly to Le Grand Pré is another nice run. And making your way down to Les Gets from Le Pléney is particularly easy when conditions allow (the run is south-facing).

There are plenty of early intermediate slopes around the area →

SCHOOLS/GUIDES

97/98 prices in francs

ESF
Classes 6 days
5hr: 9.30-noon and
2.30-5pm; 2½hr: am
or pm
6 half-days: 540
Children's classes
Ages: Under 12
6 full days including
lunch: 1,280
Private lessons
Hourly
170 for 1 to 2 people

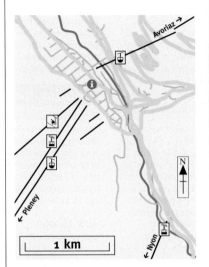

1 km

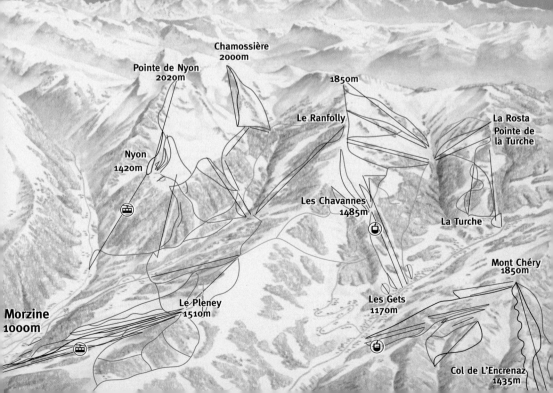

Chamossière
2000m

Pointe de Nyon
2020m

1850m

Le Ranfolly

La Rosta
Pointe de
la Turche

Nyon
1420m

Les Chavannes
1485m

La Turche

Mont Chéry
1850m

Le Pleney
1510m

Les Gets
1170m

Morzine
1000m

Col de L'Encrenaz
1435m

CHILDCARE

The Halte Garderie l'Outa (450 792600) takes children aged 2 months to 4 years, from 8.30am to 6pm. From age 3 they can have one-hour introductory lessons. The Centre de Loisirs takes children aged 4 to 12, ferrying them to and from ESF lessons.

GETTING THERE

Air Geneva, transfer 1½hr. Lyon, transfer 3½hr.

Rail Cluses or Thonon (30km); regular bus connections to resort.

UK PACKAGES

Bladon Lines, Chalets 'Unlimited', Challenge Activ, Crystal, Fairhand Holidays, First Choice Ski, Inghams, Lagrange, Made to Measure, Mountain Highs, Ski Chamois, Ski Choice, Ski Esprit, Ski France, Ski Valkyrie, Ski Weekend, Snowline Skiing, Thomson, White Roc

Les Gets AGD Travel, Chalets 'Unlimited', Fairhand Holidays, Fantiski, Made to Measure, Ski Famille, Ski Hillwood, Ski Les Alpes, Ski Total

FOR BEGINNERS
Good for novices and improvers

The village nursery slopes are wide, flat and convenient, and benefit from snow guns. Fast learners have the inconvenience that the slightly longer, steeper runs are over at Nyon. However, adventurous novices also have the option of easy pistes around Le Pléney. Near-beginners can get over to Les Gets via Le Pléney, and return via Le Ranfolly. The slopes at Les Gets suit near-beginners well.

FOR CROSS-COUNTRY
Good variety

There is a wide variety of cross-country trails, not all at valley level. The best section is in the pretty Vallée de la Manche beside the Nyon mountain up to the Lac de Mines D'Or where there is a good restaurant at the end of a fast descent. The Pléney-Chavannes loop is pleasant and relatively snow-reliable. A network of trails runs between Super-Morzine and Avoriaz, and around Montriond lake.

QUEUES
Few problems when snow is good

Queues are not a problem in the local area. The Nyon cable-car and Belvédère drag (Le Pléney) are weekend bottlenecks. Queues to and from Avoriaz are much improved in recent times, but are still bad when snow is in short supply. Bottlenecks in the Avoriaz sector make exploring the Portes du Soleil circuit a rushed affair for those without a car.

MOUNTAIN RESTAURANTS
Within reach of some good huts

The nice little place at the foot of the d'Atray chair is perhaps the best of the local huts. Les Lindarets, Les Marmottes and Plaine Dranse are not too far and have some of the best restaurants in the whole Portes du Soleil. The Restaurant des Crêtes de Zore above Super-Morzine is good, but most pass it by in their haste to get to or from Avoriaz.

SCHOOLS AND GUIDES
British ski school here

The British Alpine Ski School, featuring BASI-qualified instructors, is based in Morzine and Les Gets and we have good reports of it. It is used by several British tour operators. But we lack feedback on the ESF operation here.

FACILITIES FOR CHILDREN
Stick to Ski Esprit

We have always been quite impressed by the facilities of the Outa crèche, but in the past have received reports of poor spoken English and low staff ratios. Ski Esprit's facilities for children here are comprehensive, with three in-chalet crèches, an afternoon Snow Club for children attending morning ski school and their own tuition scheme, using specially contracted instructors.

Staying there

As the extensive network of bus routes implies, Morzine is a town where getting from A to B can be tricky. It is well worth making sure that your accommodation is near the lifts that you expect to be using, which for most visitors means the gondola and cable-car to Le Pléney.

HOW TO GO
Good-value hotels and chalets

The tour operator market concentrates on cheap and cheerful hotels and chalets. Independent travellers have a wider choice, notably of apartments.
Chalets There's a wide choice, with something to suit all tastes and tour operators ranging from the smallest to the biggest. Position varies enormously: you can be in the centre of town or right on the edge of the slopes; many are on the outskirts, however, without either convenience.

Sadly, the Ski Company Ltd's wonderful old chalet in Essert-Romand was burned down last winter and was in the process of being rebuilt at the time we went to press.
Hotels The range of hotel accommodation is wider than it at first appears – the handful of 3-star hotels includes some quite smooth ones. But the core of the resort is its modest accommodation – dozens of 2-stars and quite a lot of 1-stars. If there is a resort with more hotels in the Logis de France group (13 at the last count), we have yet to find it.
((((4) **Dahu** Best in town: upmarket 3-star, complete with comfortable, elegant public areas and good restaurant and pool complex. Some distance from all lifts and public buses except the Ardent route, but with private shuttle. Pool.
((((4) **Airelles** Central 3-star close to Pléney lifts and both Prodains and Nyon bus routes. Good pool.

ACTIVITIES

Indoor Skating, curling, bowling, cinemas, sauna, massage, gym, table tennis, fitness track, swimming pool
Outdoor Horse-riding, sleigh rides, paragliding, snow-shoe classes, artificial climbing wall, tennis

TOURIST OFFICE

Postcode 74110
Tel +33 450 747272
Fax 450 790348

(((④ **Champs Fleuris** Comfortable 3-star right next to Pléney lifts. Pool.
(((③ **Tremplin** Slightly simpler, but just as close to the lifts.
(((③ **Bergerie** Rustic, old-fashioned chalet with a few rooms and many more studios, in centre.
((② **Côtes** Simple, upwardly mobile 2-star, with more studios than rooms. Recently installed pool compensates for poor position on the edge of town.
((② **Equipe** One of the better 2-stars, superbly placed next to the Pléney lift.
Self-catering The Télémark apartments offer high-quality accommodation, and are close to the Super-Morzine gondola.

EATING OUT
A fine choice
Morzine is a gourmet's resort. The expensive La Chamade has high-quality French cuisine, Café Chaud is an atmospheric place that does good fondue, Les Airelles has a fine restaurant known for its hot buffets and is open to non-residents, and Le Dahu also has good food.

APRES-SKI
One of the livelier French resorts
Nightlife is good by French standards, though far from wild. Le Dixie is of the most animated bars and has

occasional live music, Eurosport/MTV and Murphy's on tap. Boppers could try Laury's or Le Wallington, a ten-pin bowling alley-cum-disco-cum-pool-hall-cum-bar. There are also two cinemas, Le Colibri and Le Rex.

OFF THE SLOPES
Quite good; excursions possible
There is a fine sports centre with a large ice rink. Les Gets has a swimming pool and some of the hotels have their own. Buses runs to Thonon, which is a useful shopping excursion, and car owners can drive to Geneva, Annecy or Montreux. There are lots of very pretty walks, and other activities include horse-drawn sleigh rides, horse-riding, saunas and parapenting.

Les Gets 1170m

Les Gets is not a sensible base for exploring the Portes du Soleil circuit, but its local slopes have a far larger, denser array of pistes than any of the resorts on the circuit, and is perfectly adequate for many intermediates. The good children's facilities, pleasant trees, French ambience, convenience, nice village restaurants, fine nursery slopes and reasonable prices make Les Gets an excellent choice for families and others looking for a civilised, atmospheric holiday venue. Weekend crowds are a drawback, but lack of snow is a more serious one. Snowmakers would greatly improve the appeal of Les Gets.

Les Gets is a little old village of mainly traditional chalet buildings, 6km from its larger neighbour, Morzine. Although the village has a scattered appearance, most of the facilities are conveniently close to the main lift station. It is on a through road (Cluses–Morzine to Avoriaz), but traffic does not intrude too much, bypassing most of the village. There is a fair amount of nightlife but most places are quiet except at weekends when the atmosphere becomes more chic.

As well as the area shared with Morzine, Les Gets has slopes on Mont Chéry, on the other side of the village, accessed by gondola and parallel chair from the edge of the resort, with a further chair leading to the summit. Much of this section gets too much sun, but at least most of it is reasonably high.

Beyond Mont Chéry summit is Les Gets' steepest skiing, down the back of the mountain. These are 'yo-yo' runs served by a solitary returning chair.

The quite good village nursery slopes are convenient for most accommodation, but Chavannes has better and more snow-reliable ones. Progression to pistes is simple, with a very easy run between Chavannes and the resort, and a couple of nicely meandering routes from La Rosta. Easy pistes between Le Ranfolly and Les Chavannes, and down to La Turche, mean confident beginners can get a lot of mileage in without getting any lifts in a downward direction.

Cross-country skiers would be better off in Morzine, which has an excellent array of trails. But Les Gets has a good variety of loops on Mont Chéry and Les Chavannes – a total of 46km.

Reports on the ski schools have been generally favourable but group sizes can be large. Beginners should shop around if conditions are less than perfect, looking for lessons at Chavannes. One family found the ESF 'wonderful' for their children aged 5 and 8 but a 'horrible experience' for their son aged 3. There's a branch of the British Alpine Ski School here.

The Ski Alpin pass covers all Les Gets, Nyon and Pleney lifts. The local ticket saves a fair amount on the cost of a Portes du Soleil pass, and is worth considering for the less-experienced if snow conditions are good.

Many visitors stay in private chalets, quite a few of which are on the British market in catered form. Most are pleasant, comfortable, no-frills places. There are surprisingly few hotel beds and apartments available.

All the hotels are 3-star and below, mostly cheap and cheerful old 2-stars.

The Crychar, 100m from central Les Gets at the foot of the slopes, is one of the best. The Ours Blanc is comfortable and central, and known for its good food. The Labrador, of similar standard, is closer to the edge of town, though still an easy walk from the Chavannes chair. The Praz Du Soleil is a simple, but pleasant good-value apartment five minutes from the main lifts. The hotel Bellevue at the bottom of the slopes is the natural rendezvous point.

Les Gets has a surprisingly wide variety of places to eat. Most of the hotels have worthwhile restaurants. The Tyrol and the Schuss are good pizza places. The rustic Vieux Chêne is popular for its Savoyard specialities. The Flambeau and Tourbillon are also recommended.

Nightlife is quiet, particularly on weekdays. The Pub Irlandaise can get lively. Dream's Bar (formerly the Magnetic Theatre) has live music. The Igloo is a small disco, popular with locals, and the Jeckyll and Hyde is a less crowded alternative.

Morzine is a better choice for people not using the slopes, although Les Gets has a good fitness centre with swimming, saunas, massage, weights and so on, and an artificial ice rink. Outings to Geneva, Lausanne and Montreux are possible.

There is a non-ski nursery for children aged 3 months to 2 years, and two ski-kindergartens. Ski Espace's 'Ile des Enfants' is reputedly the better of the two, and is open from 8am to 6pm, taking children from 3 years old. ESF's Club Fantaski has been criticised for inattentive supervision and having a roadside slope used by adults.

La Plagne

1800m-2100m

A variety of villages spread across a vast playground

WHAT IT COSTS

$(((($5$)

HOW IT RATES

The slopes

Snow	****
Extent	****
Experts	***
Intermediates	*****
Beginners	*****
Convenience	*****
Queues	***
Restaurants	**

The rest

Scenery	***
Resort charm	*
Off-slope	*

- ➕ Extensive slopes, best suited to intermediates
- ➕ Excellent nursery slopes
- ➕ High, and pretty snowsure
- ➕ Purpose-built resort units are convenient for the slopes, and some are not unpleasant
- ➕ Attractive, traditional-style villages lower down share the slopes
- ➕ Wooded runs of lower resorts are useful in poor weather
- ➕ Good cross-country trails

- ➖ Few sustained challenging pistes
- ➖ Persistent lift bottlenecks in the high resorts
- ➖ Lower villages often suffer from poor snow conditions – sunny Champagny especially
- ➖ Unattractive architecture in some of the higher resort units
- ➖ Not many green runs for nervous beginners to go on to
- ➖ Nightlife very limited

In terms of size, La Plagne's terrain and lift network ranks alongside those of Val d'Isère/Tignes and the Three Valleys, yet the resort doesn't enjoy the same status. What it lacks, more than anything, is the macho factor: it has very few black runs, and scores of blues. For most intermediates that is, of course, just the ticket – a largely unthreatening area, offering a real sensation of travel between the widely spread resort villages. And there is some great off-piste terrain which is underexploited. So even experts can be kept happy here, provided they get the necessary guidance. But there are also a number of irritating and long-standing weaknesses in the lift network, which in the end lead us to agree with one recent, highly experienced reporter who reached the conclusion that La Plagne has a slightly jaded, second-division feel.

What's new

The main changes have been in the Champagny sector. For 1996/97 the Borseliers and Rossa drags were replaced by fast 6-seater chair-lifts. For 1997/98 the short Quillis double drag giving access to the slopes above Belle Plagne is being replaced by another chair. A new fun-park is being built on the Col de la Forcle slope above Bellecôte.

boarding *La Plagne's area is pretty good territory, whatever you're looking for. There's a good mix of long, easy runs and high, open slopes with many off-piste variations – the guides can take you on some really mind-blowing trips. (Watch out for some flat areas, though, particularly from Roche de Mio back to Champagny.) The resort is building a fun-park for this winter. For beginners and carvers there are splendid smooth runs in several sectors. Most lifts are gondolas or chairs, though there are still some difficult-to-avoid drag-lifts.*

The camera cannot lie: pretty La Plagne (ie a carefully framed shot of Belle Plagne, the best-looking part of a multi-part resort) ➔

MOUNTAIN FACTS

Altitude	1250m-3250m
Lifts	111
Pistes	210km
Green/Blue	66%
Red	28%
Black	6%
Artificial snow	10km
Recco detectors used	

LIFT PASSES

97/98 prices in francs
La Plagne
Covers all lifts in La
Plagne and
Champagny-en-
Vanoise.
Beginners Free baby-
lift in each centre.
Main pass
1-day pass 216
6-day pass 1,005
(low season 755 –
25% off)
Senior citizens
Over 60: 6-day pass
755 (25% off)
Children
Under 16: 6-day pass
755 (25% off)
Under 7: free pass
Short-term passes
Half-day pass (158).
Single ascent on
inter-area links.
Notes 6-day pass and
over covers Les Arcs
for duration of pass,
and one day each in
Tignes-Val d'Isère, the
Three Valleys,
Pralognan-la-Vanoise
and Les Saisies.
Reductions for
groups.
Alternative passes
Limited passes
available in the main
areas (La Plagne,
Champagny,
Montchavin).
'Discovery' passes in
each area.

The resort

La Plagne consists of no fewer than 11 separate 'villages'; seven are purpose-built at altitude in the main bowl, on or above the tree line and linked by road, lifts and pistes; the other four are widely spaced in the valleys outside the bowl.

Even the resorts built up the mountain vary considerably in style and character. The first to be built, in the 1960s, was Plagne Centre, at around 2000m – still the focal point for shops and après-ski. Typical of its time, it consists of big ugly blocks and dark, depressing passageways which house the shops, bars and restaurants.

Above it, and linked by cable-car, is the even more obtrusive Aime la Plagne – with its single great apartment block in the shape of a giant chalet. Below these two, and somewhat out of the way, is Plagne 1800, a more tasteful but rather dull (and full of Brits) chalet-style development.

A short walk above Plagne Centre is the newest incarnation of La Plagne, Plagne Soleil, still as yet small but with its own shops and very convenient for the slopes.

Plagne Villages is an attractive collection of small-scale apartment and chalet developments built in traditional Savoyard style and around 50m higher than Plagne Centre. Again, it is very convenient for the slopes.

The large apartment buildings of Plagne Bellecôte, on the other hand, are built an inexplicably awkward walk below the local lifts. Above it is Belle Plagne – as its name suggests, built in a pleasing style, with something of the Disneyesque neo-Savoyard look of Valmorel, and entirely underground parking.

Accommodation in all these developments on the mountain is largely self-catering, and popular with French families, who pack the resort during peak season weeks. In low-season it can be eerily empty. There are some hotels in Plagne Centre.

Then there are the lower resorts in the valleys – the old villages of Montchavin and Champagny, on opposite sides of the slopes area, and the newly developed villages of Les Coches (near Montchavin) and Montalbert. For a description of each, see the end of this chapter.

The mountains

La Plagne is an ideal resort for all intermediates. There are wide motorways for early intermediates and long excursions for the more adventurous. Beginners are well catered for by good schools that operate on easy, accessible nursery slopes. Day trips to Les Arcs are easy, to Val-d'Isère, Tignes or the Three Valleys more time-consuming.

THE SLOPES
Multi-centred; can be confusing

La Plagne boasts 210km of pistes over a wide terrain that can be broken down into seven distinct but inter-linked sectors. From Plagne Centre you can take a lift up to **Biolley**, from where you can head back to Centre, to Aime la Plagne or down gentle runs to **Montalbert**, from which you ride several successive lifts back up. But the main lift out of Plagne Centre leads up to **Grande Rochette**. From here there are good sweeping runs back and an easier one over to Plagne Bellecôte, or you can drop over the back into the predominantly south-facing **Champagny** (from which a lift arrives back up at Grande Rochette and another brings you out much further east). From the Champagny sector there are great views over to Courchevel, across the valley.

From Plagne Bellecôte and Belle Plagne, the main gondola heads up to **Roche de Mio**, where runs spread out in all directions. You can head back down towards La Plagne proper, or down towards Champagny in one direction and **Montchavin** in the other. Montchavin can also be reached by taking a chair from Plagne Bellecôte. If you change gondolas at Roche de Mio, you go down to the mid-station at Col de la Chiaupe (there are no runs down to it in that direction) then up again to the **Bellecôte glacier**, start of some of the steepest slopes in the area. You have to catch the gondola at the mid-station to get back to Roche de Mio.

SNOW RELIABILITY
Good except in low-lying villages

Most of La Plagne's runs are snowsure, being at altitudes between 2000m and 2700m on the largely north-facing open slopes above the purpose-built centres. The Bellecôte glacier drags are normally shut in winter.

SCHOOLS/GUIDES

97/98 prices in francs

ESF
Schools in all centres.
Prices do vary; those
given here are for
Plagne Centre
Classes 6 days
2½hr, 3hr, 5hr, 6hr,
depending on centre
and time of day and
season
6 full days: 850
Children's classes
Ages: Up to 16
6 full days: 745
Private lessons
1hr, 1½hr, 2hr
185 for 1hr

Eric Laboureix
Ski and mountain
sports school in Belle
Plagne
Classes 6 days
am or pm
6 half days: 830
Children's classes
Ages: Up to 14
6 full days: 1,190
Private lessons
Hourly
195 for 1hr

Oxygène
Private school in
Plagne Centre
Classes 6 days
am or pm
6 full days: 885
Children's classes
Ages: Up to 14
5 full days: 725
Private lessons
Hourly
210 for 1hr

Runs down to the valley resorts can cause more problems, and you may have to take the lifts home at times. This is particularly true of the Champagny sector, where the two home runs are both south-facing and quickly lose their snow in warm weather. The runs down to Les Coches and Montchavin are north-facing and have artificial snow – just about the only snowmaking in the whole area. Grooming is patchy, with some runs kept in good shape, others neglected.

FOR EXPERTS
A few good blacks and off-piste

There are two exceptional black runs leading down from the Bellecôte glacier, both of which take you away from the lift system and are beautiful long runs with a vertical drop of over 1000m. A chair-lift takes you back to the mid-station of the glacier gondola. The other long black run is the Emile Allais down from above Aime la Plagne through the forest, finishing at 1400m, with a couple of drag-lifts taking you back up. This is surprisingly little-used, north-facing and very enjoyable in good snow. But it's not as seriously steep as the shorter Coqs and Morbleu runs in the same sector.

The long, sweeping Mont de la Guerre red run, with a 1250m vertical drop down from Grande Rochette-Les Verdons to Champagny, is also a beautiful run in good snow – a rare event because of its orientation.

There are other good long reds to cruise around on. But experts will get the best out of La Plagne if they hire a guide and explore the vast off-piste potential. There are very popular off-piste variants from the Bellecôte glacier black run down to the restaurant at Les Bauches (a drop of over 1400m), from where you can ride chairs back to the main slopes above Les Pierres Blanches, or cruise down to Montchavin. You can also head down off-piste to Peisey-Nancroix and take the lifts up to the Les Arcs slopes.

Another beautiful and out-of-the-way off-piste run from the Bellecôte glacier is over the Col du Nant glacier and down into the valley of Champagny-le-Haut.

Unfortunately, the glacier gondola can be closed by high winds or poor weather – and after a snowfall the black runs from the top may remain closed for days because of avalanche danger. These problems greatly reduce the area's interest for experts.

In fresh snow, those who enjoy picking their way through woods in search of fresh light powder will not be disappointed by the forests above Montchavin and Montalbert.

FOR INTERMEDIATES
Great variety

Virtually the whole of La Plagne's area is a paradise for intermediates, with blue and red runs wherever you look. Your main choice will be whether to

TRY THE OLYMPIC BOBSLEIGH RUN

If the thrills and spills of a day on the slopes aren't enough, you can round it off by having a go on the 1992 Winter Olympics bob-sleigh run. The floodlit 1.5km run drops 125m, has 19 bends and you can go in a proper four-man 'taxi-bob' (FF460 in 1997) or in a special driverless bob raft (FF175). You can also get combination tickets covering the bob-run and other activities – eg a session on a snowmobile, or a couple of goes on the speed skiing course at Les Arcs.

Most people, not surprisingly, take the cheaper option, and find the ride quite thrilling enough. The bob raft is padded and mounted on wide skids that keep the speed down to a mere 75–80kph; the ride takes around one and a half minutes.

With the taxi-bob, you are one of two passengers wedged between the driver and brakeman. You reach a maximum speed of 100–105kph and the ride lasts about 50 seconds. The pressure in some turns can be as high as 3g – not recommended if you're suffering from heart, vascular or back problems (thus neatly ruling out your editors), or if you're pregnant.

Prices include the loan of a helmet and a diploma. Additional insurance is available (yours may not be valid). The course is generally open to tourists from Tuesday to Sunday from 5pm to 8pm (from 2pm on Tuesday and Friday) from Christmas to mid-March – though the season may be shorter if it's not cold enough. The taxi-bob doesn't operate every day.

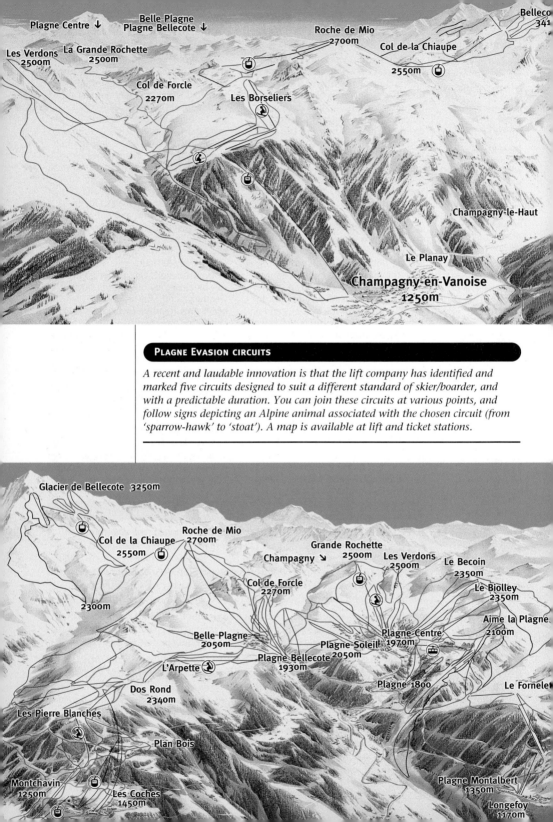

Plagne Centre ↓

Belle Plagne
Plagne Bellecote ↓

Roche de Mio
2700m

Col de la Chiaupe

Belleco
341

Les Verdons
2500m

La Grande Rochette
2500m

2555m

Col de Forcle
2270m

Les Borseliers

Champagny-le-Haut

Le Planay

Champagny-en-Vanoise
1250m

PLAGNE EVASION CIRCUITS

A recent and laudable innovation is that the lift company has identified and marked five circuits designed to suit a different standard of skier/boarder, and with a predictable duration. You can join these circuits at various points, and follow signs depicting an Alpine animal associated with the chosen circuit (from 'sparrow-hawk' to 'stoat'). A map is available at lift and ticket stations.

Glacier de Bellecote 3250m

Col de la Chiaupe
2555m

Roche de Mio
2700m

Grande Rochette
2500m

Champagny ↘

Les Verdons
2500m

Le Becoin
2350m

2300m

Col de Forcle
2270m

Le Biolley
2350m

Aime la Plagne
2100m

Belle Plagne
2050m

Plagne Soleil
2050m

Plagne-Centre
1970m

L'Arpette

Plagne Bellecote
1930m

Dos Rond
2340m

Plagne 1800

Le Fornele

Les Pierre Blanches

Plan Bois

Plagne Montalbert
1350m

Montchavin
1250m

Les Coches
1450m

Longefoy
1170m

UK PACKAGES

AA Ski-Driveaway, Altours Ski, Chalet World, Chalets 'Unlimited', Club Med, Crystal, Erna Low, Fairhand Holidays, First Choice Ski, Independent Ski Links, Inghams, Lagrange, Made to Measure, Mark Warner, Motours, Neilson, Silver Ski, Simply Ski, Ski Activity, Ski Beat, Ski Club of GB, Ski France, Ski Leisure Direction, Ski Les Alpes, Ski trek, Skiworld, Solo's, Stena Line Holidays, Thomson, Travelscene Ski-Drive, UCPA, Virgin Snow

Belle Plagne Bladon Lines, Motours, On The Piste Travel Ltd, Travelscene Ski-Drive

Champagny Barrelli Ski, Fairhand Holidays, Lagrange, Made to Measure, Motours, Ski Leisure Direction, Stena Line Holidays

Les Coches AA Ski-Driveaway, Chalets 'Unlimited', Crystal, Fairhand Holidays, Lagrange, Made to Measure, Motours, On The Piste Travel Ltd, Ski Esprit, Ski Leisure Direction, Ski Olympic

Montalbert Ski Amis

Montchavin Chalets 'Unlimited', Fairhand Holidays, Lagrange, Made to Measure, Simply Ski, Ski Esprit

settle for one area for the day and explore it thoroughly, or just cruise around the pistes that form the main arteries of the network.

For early intermediates there are plenty of gentle blue motorway pistes in the main La Plagne bowl, and a long, interesting run from Roche de Mio back to Belle Plagne which includes a long, dark (and often very cold) tunnel. In poor weather the best place to be is in the trees on the gentle runs leading down to Montchavin-Les Coches or to Montalbert. The easiest way over to Champagny is from the Roche de Mio area rather than Grande Rochette.

Better intermediates have lots of delightful long red runs to try. Roche de Mio to Les Bauches is a drop of 900m. There are challenging red mogul pitches down from the glacier to the mid-station of the gondola at Col de la Chiaupe. And the main La Plagne bowl has enjoyable reds in all sectors. The Champagny sector has a couple of tough reds – Kamikaze and Hari Kiri – leading from Grande Rochette. The long Mont de la Guerre red is a satisfying run for adventurous intermediates.

FOR BEGINNERS
Excellent facilities for the novice
La Plagne is a good place to learn, with generally good snow and above-average facilities for beginners, especially children. Each of the main centres has nursery slopes on its doorstep. There are not many long green runs to progress to, but no shortage of easy blues.

CROSS-COUNTRY
Open and wooded trails
There are close to 100km of prepared and marked cross-country pistes in La Plagne and its surrounding satellites. The most beautiful of these are the 35km set out in the Champagny-le-Haut valley. Here the pistes loop and wind through wild countryside, often in good sunny conditions. The north-facing areas have more wooded trails that link the various centres. There is a 12km route around Les Coches-Montchavin and a longer, 25km route that begins low down at Longefoy (1350m) and winds up through Montalbert to Plan Bois at 1700m. Plagne Bellecôte, Belle Plagne and Plagne Villages are similarly linked by a less arduous, 24km route.

QUEUES
Bottlenecks in high season
When the resort is full there can be big queues to get out of the high-altitude centres at the start of the day. The old gondola from Plagne Bellecôte via Belle Plagne to Roche de Mio is still a bad bottleneck, despite the alternative roundabout ways available. The higher gondola can also get oversubscribed when snow is poor lower down (and the return pistes can get crowded). The gondola from Plagne Centre to Grande Rochette can also generate queues (after lunch as well as first thing). The old Colorado chair-lift next door to it has been replaced by a fast six-seater, but frustratingly it does not reach the ridge above Champagny. Two other six-seaters have been installed on the top slopes of the Champagny sector, replacing the Borseliers and Rossa drags (and liberating extra slope-space in the process). There are several lifts which can generate queues that you can't avoid, once you've descended to them – at Plagne 1800 and Les Bauches for example.

MOUNTAIN RESTAURANTS
An improving choice
Mountain restaurants are numerous, varied and seldom crowded, as many people prefer to descend to one of the resorts – particularly Champagny or Montchavin / Les Coches – at the end of the morning. Some pleasant new restaurants have been built both in the main bowl and on the Montchavin slopes. Two great rustic restaurants in which to hole up in poor weather for a long lunch of Savoyarde dishes are Le Sauget, above Montchavin, and Aux Bons Vieux Temps, just below Aime la Plagne. Reservations may be required at either. The restaurant at the top of the Champagny gondola is also recommended – friendly staff, both table and self-service, beautiful views from the terrace over to Courchevel, good basic cooking. The Little Breton café at the bottom of the Quillis lift at the start of the Lavasset piste has also been highly recommended.

SCHOOLS AND GUIDES
Adequate for all levels
Each centre has its own ESF school which is generally well run and offers classes for all standards. Groups can be large in peak season. Instructors speak English of varying standard. Reports on the tuition are generally

CHILDCARE

There are ESF ski kindergartens in all the high resort units, generally taking children from age 3. The ESF also runs all-day nurseries in most of the villages, mostly taking children aged 2 to 6 (18 months to 3 years in Belle Plagne). In Centre, independent nursery Marie Christine does much the same.

The deal in the outlying satellite villages is similar, except that in Montchavin and Les Coches very young skiers are handled by the Nursery Club, the ESF taking over at age 4.

positive. The Oxygene school in Centre has impressed some observers – including UK tour operators based in Plagne 1800, who find them more responsive than the ESF. Ski évolutif is popular as are snowboarding and monoski lessons, which are said to be of a high standard. Alternative and specialist schools are good value.

FACILITIES FOR CHILDREN
Good choice

Children are well catered for. The nursery at Belle Plagne is 'excellent, with good English spoken'. The Club Med at Aime la Plagne is one of their 'family' villages. La Plagne and its satellites are fast becoming the chalet-crèche capital of the Alps – several UK tour operators run them.

Staying there

Slope-side accommodation is the norm in the high-altitude resorts. This means unless you miss a crucial linking lift, you can nearly always get home on the snow. There is, however, an efficient bus system linking the resorts, which runs until after midnight and might tempt you to explore the après-ski in different areas. Most people, however, are happy to use the après-ski facilities most immediately accessible.

HOW TO GO
Plenty of packages

For a resort which is very apartment-dominated, there is a surprising number of attractive chalets available through British tour operators. There are few hotels, but some attractive, simple 2-stars in the lower villages. There is a Club Med 'village' at Aime la Plagne. Accommodation in the outlying satellite resorts is described at the end of the chapter.

Chalets There's a large number available, though many are of a similar standard, type and position – fairly simple, small and in 1800.

Hotels There are very few, all of 2-star or 3-star grading. Probably the most comfortable place, if you're looking for a package, is Club Med, up at Aime la Plagne.

② **Graciosa** Well-run 14-room hotel in Plagne Centre.

② **Eldorador** Adequate hotel in Belle Plagne – spacious rooms, generous buffet breakfast.

Self-catering La Plagne is the ultimate apartment resort, but many of the blocks are similar in standard. In-house communal facilities such as lounges, restaurants and the like are not as commonplace here as in most French purpose-built resorts. Fortunately, many tour operators have allocations in the above-average Pierre et Vacances apartments in Belle Plagne.

EATING OUT
Emphasis on convenience

Throughout the resort there is a good range of restaurants, with something to suit most pockets and tastes, but the emphasis is on less expensive pizzeria-style dining which suits the self-catering family. Some satellite villages cater more for the diner interested in the regional dishes: raclette and Savoyard fondue restaurants are popular (La Ferme in Plagne Bellecôte is recommended).

Le Matafan in Plagne Centre is popular for its traditional French cuisine in a more formal setting. Hotel Les Glières, in Champagny, serves good Savoyard food in friendly rustic surroundings.

Aux Bons Vieux Temps (also mentioned under Mountain Restaurants) at Aime 2000 is open in the evening. One reporter, however, was not too impressed by the food at dinner.

GETTING THERE

Air Geneva, transfer 3½hr. Lyon, transfer 3½hr. Chambery, transfer 2½hr.

Rail Aime (18km) and Bourg-St-Maurice (35km) (Eurostar service to Bourg available); frequent buses from station.

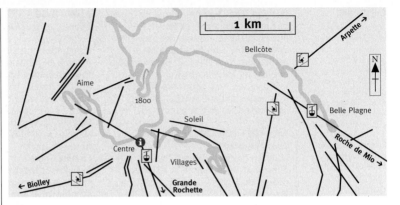

ACTIVITIES

Indoor Sauna and solarium in most centres, skating (Bellecôte), squash (1800), fitness centres (Belle Plagne, 1800, Centre, Bellecôte), cinemas, bowling **Outdoor** Heated swimming pool (Bellecôte, Aime), bob-sleigh (La Roche), 30km marked walks, paragliding, skidoos, climbing, skating, hang-gliding, snow-shoe excursions

TOURIST OFFICE

Postcode 73211
Tel +33 479 097979
Fax 479 097010

APRES-SKI
Nothing exclusive or original

La Plagne has a wide range of après-ski amenities catering particularly for the younger crowd. Each centre produces a weekly events bulletin listing special forthcoming events, particularly those run by the hotel 'animateurs'. There is an ice rink and outdoor heated pool at Plagne Bellecôte, ten-pin bowling and electronic golf at Belle Plagne, and most large hotels or apartment blocks have games rooms. In Belle Plagne, Matt's is the one genuine bar, with no restaurant attached. The King Café is the liveliest bar in Plagne centre and sometimes has live music.

OFF THE SLOPES
OK for the active

Off-slope activities have evolved throughout La Plagne to offer the visitor a strong alternative to bashing the pistes. As well as the sports and fitness facilities, winter walks along marked trails during the March and April sunshine are particularly pleasant. It's also easy to get up the mountain on the gondolas, which both have restaurants at the top.

The Olympic bob-sleigh run is a popular evening activity. Excursion possibilities are limited.

STAYING IN OTHER RESORTS
A good plan

Montchavin is a relatively unspoilt old farming community where rustic timber haybarns and cowsheds are much in evidence. Restaurant terraces set in orchards at the foot of the slopes add to the scene. There are adequate shops, a kindergarten and a school. Reaching the La Plagne slopes involves four lifts but the local slopes are well-endowed with snowmakers, a cheap local lift pass covers 30km of mostly easy, pretty, sheltered runs, with nursery slopes at village level and up at Plan Bois. Those who do venture further afield can return from Roche de Mio (2700m) in one lovely long swoop. Après-ski is quiet, but the village doesn't lack atmosphere and has a couple of nice little bars. The Bellecôte is a modest hotel with a decent restaurant, the Boule de Neige.

Les Coches is a sympathetically designed modern resort that several reporters have liked for its 'small, quiet and friendly' feel. It has its own school and kindergarten, and arrangements are much the same as at Montchavin.

Montalbert is a traditional village with quicker access into the main area – though it's a long way from here across to the Bellecôte glacier. The local slopes are easy and wooded – a useful insurance against bad visibility. The Aigle Rouge is a simple hotel.

Champagny-en-Vanoise is a charming old village in a pretty wooded setting. The south-facing local slopes mean you often have to get a gondola home at the end of the day, but Champagny is better placed than any of the other outlying villages for access into the main area and well placed for an outing to Courchevel. There are routes from the gondola station to summits above Centre and Bellecôte, the former being a particularly speedy affair using just one further lift. Given good snow, there are lovely runs home from above Centre (2500m). There are several hotels, of which the two best are both Logis. The Glières is a rustic old hotel with varied rooms, a friendly welcome and good food. L'Ancolie is smarter, with modern facilities.

Portes du Soleil

The Portes du Soleil vies with the Three Valleys for the title of World's Largest Ski Area, but its slopes are very different from those of Méribel, Courchevel and neighbours. It is spread out over a much larger area, most of which forms part of a central circuit straddling the French–Swiss border; smaller areas branch off from that circuit. The runs are great for keen intermediates who like to travel long distances in a leisurely fashion. There are few of the tightly packed networks of runs that encourage you to stay put in one area – though there are exceptions in one or two places. The slopes are also low by French standards, with top heights in the range 2000m to 2300m – and some important links in the circuit are low, sunny and short of snowmakers.

259

The main resorts and the slopes are described in four chapters: in France, Avoriaz, page 181, Châtel, page 192, Morzine and Les Gets, page 245; and in Switzerland, Champéry (and other small resorts nearby), page 351.

Purpose-built **Avoriaz** has the most snowsure slopes – north-facing and the highest in the area, but still uncomfortably low by French standards. (Avoriaz has quite an impressive vertical range, but most of it is below the resort, not above it.) It also has the most densely packed section of runs, and good lift links to Champéry, Châtel and Morzine; and it's especially good for families, with a big snow-garden right in the heart of the car-free village. But prices are rather high by local standards.

The other villages are attractive in many ways, but less snowsure. The other French resort on the main circuit of lifts and runs is **Châtel**. Given good snow, it has some of the best runs in the area, and it's not too far by lift and piste from the higher, steeper slopes of Avoriaz. Although an old and quite characterful village, it's a busy, traffic-jammed place. Although low, it has a good beginner area at mid-mountain, with a gondola you can ride up and down.

Morzine is close to Avoriaz, and linked by lift but not quite by piste. It's a summer as well as a winter resort – a pleasant, bustling little town with good shops and restaurants, busy traffic, lots of walking to the lifts, plenty to do. The local slopes are extensive, and shared with the slightly higher, quieter, village of **Les Gets**. You can use Morzine as a base to ski the main Portes du Soleil circuit, but it's not ideal.

Champéry is peaceful and attractive – a classic Swiss charmer, just off the main circuit with a cable-car link and a run to the valley (though not directly to the village). The lack of village nursery slopes may be a drawback for families and beginners. **Champoussin** and **Les Crosets** are purpose-built mini-resorts set on the very extensive open slopes between Champéry and Morgins, with fairly direct links over to Avoriaz as well – so in terms of access to skiing, at least, they have a lot to recommend them. **Morgins**, in contrast to Champéry, has excellent village slopes – but they are low and very sunny, and although its more serious local runs are enjoyable and prettily wooded, they are also limited in extent.

Puy-St-Vincent 1400–1600m

Under-rated little modern resort with some serious slopes

WHAT IT COSTS

(((3)))

HOW IT RATES

The slopes
Snow ***
Extent **
Experts ***
Intermediates ***
Beginners ***
Convenience *****
Queues ****
Restaurants ***

The rest
Scenery ***
Resort charm **
Off-slope *

MOUNTAIN FACTS

Altitude 1400m-2700m
Lifts 15
Pistes 50km
Green/Blue 50%
Red 42%
Black 8%
Artificial snow 7km

UK PACKAGES

Fairhand Holidays,
Lagrange, Ski Club
Europe, Snowbizz

TOURIST OFFICE

Postcode 05290
Tel +33 492 233580
Fax 492 234523

Puy-St-Vincent's ski area is not big by Alpine standards, but we like it a lot – more, to be honest, than we expected. It offers a big vertical and a lot of variety, including steep stuff. There are excellent high-altitude cross-country trails, and the two purpose-built resort villages are not eyesores. People are friendly and prices are low by French standards.

THE RESORT

Puy-St-Vincent proper is an old mountain village on the fringes of the Ecrins massif, not far south-west of Briançon. The modern resort of PSV is a two-part affair – the minor part, Station 1400, is just along the mountainside at 1400m; the major part, Station 1600, is a few hairpins (or a chair-lift-ride) further up (guess the altitude). There are buildings in various styles dotted around the mountainside, but the main monolith at the foot of the lifts is unusual – boldly styled to resemble a mountain range, and largely finished in white. We and our one recent reporter found PSV friendly ('even the lift operators') and well run.

THE MOUNTAINS

Within its small area, PSV packs in a lot of variety, with runs of all colours from green to black that justify their gradings. There are gentle **slopes** between the two villages, but most of the runs are above 1600. A gondola goes up to the tree line at around 2000m. Entertaining red runs go back down, and a green takes a less direct route. The main higher lift is a long chair to 2700m, serving excellent open slopes of red and genuine black steepness. The shorter Rocher Noir drag serves another steep slope, but also accesses splendid cruising runs that curl around the eastern edge of the area through the woods back to 1600. These runs are also accessed by a fast quad chair from just below 1600.

A short run above 1600 is floodlit in the early evening 3 or 4 times a week. **Snowboarders** have a fun-park with half-pipe at 1600, but are not allowed on the Rocher Noir drag-lift.

The 6-day Grande Galaxie lift pass covers a series of major resorts beyond Briançon. More to the point for most visitors is that it also covers the lifts above the valley hamlet of Pelvoux, 10 minutes' drive away. It has blue, red and black runs, often used for race-training, and a vertical of over 1000m served by a chair and a drag.

The slopes face north-east and are reasonably **reliable for snow**, with snowmaking on one run down to 1400 and on a couple of slopes above 1600.

The black runs are short but genuinely challenging for **experts**, and there are off-piste routes to be tackled with guidance. There are itinéraires outside the piste network, including one to the valley bottom – doubtless amusing in good snow.

Provided the limited extent doesn't worry you, it's an excellent area for **intermediates** who welcome a challenge – but there aren't many very easy runs. **Beginners** should be happy on either of the nursery slopes, and on the long green run from 2000m.

There are splendid **cross-country** routes between 1400m and 1700m, ranging from green to black difficulty.

There is a modern but pleasantly woody and reasonably priced **restaurant** at mid-mountain, but in good weather the sunny terraces at 1600 are the natural place to head for.

You have a choice of French and International **ski schools**. There are **nurseries** in both villages, and both schools run ski kindergartens. Under fives go free on the lifts.

STAYING THERE

Purpose-built and compact it may be, but 1600 (where most of the **accommodation** is located) is not perfectly laid out; beware walks to the lift. 1600 consists entirely of apartments; a reader recommends the Podium. There are some apartments down in 1400, and three cheap hotels.

The half-dozen bar-restaurants in each village meet both **eating out** and **après-ski** needs. The place is not quite devoid of things to do **off the slopes**, but not far off: snow-shoe expeditions and paragliding are about all there is.

Risoul

1850m

Villagey modern resort in an attractive southern setting

261

Reasonable prices, convenience, good snow, few queues (outside French school holidays) and extensive slopes shared with Vars: Risoul has a lot going for it, particularly for intermediates, beginners and families. And it's one of the more attractive purpose-built resorts, with something like a village feel.

WHAT IT COSTS

(((3)))

HOW IT RATES

The slopes

Snow	★★★
Extent	★★★
Experts	★★
Intermediates	★★★★
Beginners	★★★★
Convenience	★★★★
Queues	★★★★
Restaurants	★★

The rest

Scenery	★★★
Resort charm	★★
Off-slope	★

What's new

The Risoul/Vars snowmaking setup was extended for 1997; both resorts now have coverage on several runs to the villages.

A new 2-star hotel, the Chardons Bleus, is to open for the 1997/98 season.

MOUNTAIN FACTS

Altitude	1660m-2750m
Lifts	56
Pistes	170km
Green/Blue	56%
Red	34%
Black	10%
Artificial snow	4km

UK PACKAGES

Crystal, Fairhand Holidays, First Choice Ski, Lagrange, Motours, Neilson, Ski Arrangements, Thomson, Travelscene Ski-Drive

TOURIST OFFICE

Postcode 05600
Tel +33 492 460260
Fax 492 460123

THE RESORT

Risoul, purpose-built in the late 1970s, is a quiet, apartment-based resort, popular with families. Set among the trees, with excellent views over the Ecrins national park, it is made up of wood-clad buildings – mostly bulky, but with some concessions to traditional style. It has a busy little main street – surprisingly not traffic-free – and an array of restaurant terraces facing the slopes. The village lacks many resort amenities – a pool, notably – and the slopes are short of modern lifts and mountain restaurants. Reporters comment on the friendliness of the natives. Watch out for long airport transfers.

THE MOUNTAINS

The **slopes**, mainly north-facing, spread over several minor peaks and bowls, and connect with the sunnier slopes of neighbouring Vars via the Pointe de Razis (2570m) and the lower Col des Saluces. Together, they amount to one of the biggest domains in the southern French Alps. The upper slopes are open, but those leading back into Risoul are attractively wooded, and good for bad-weather days.

The top of the slopes above Vars reach 2750m. The link can be made in both directions by using drag-lifts, which have the advantage that wind is unlikely to close the link.

Risoul's slopes are entirely above 1850m and mostly north-facing, so despite its southerly position **snow reliability** is reasonably good. There is a fair amount of snowmaking.

Risoul does not offer much to interest **experts**. The main top stations access a couple of steepish descents, and there are six black runs in all. There are some good off-piste opportunities if you have a guide, especially in the trees.

The whole area is best suited to **intermediates**, with some good long reds and blues in both the Risoul and Vars sectors. Virtually all Risoul's runs head towards the village, making it difficult to get lost in even the worst of weather. So intermediate children can be let off the leash with the minimum of worry.

Beginners have good, convenient, nursery slopes with a free lift, easy pistes to move on to.

There are a couple of short **cross-country** loops, including a trail along the top ridge of the Alpine area.

There is a **snowboarders'** fun-park with half-pipe beside one of the chair-lifts out of the village.

Outside French school holidays, Risoul has impressively quiet slopes, with few **queues**.

There are few **mountain restaurants** and none worth noting; most people return to the village terraces for lunch.

There is a choice of **ski school** – ESF or Internationale – and our few recent reports are positive about both.

Risoul is very much a family resort. It provides an all-day nursery for **children** over six months. Both ski schools operate ski kindergartens, using an impressive special area slightly above the village, reached by a special child-friendly lift.

STAYING THERE

Nearly all Risoul's visitors stay in apartments – though a second **hotel** is due to open for 1997/98. **Chalets** are becoming more widely available from UK operators.

There's plenty of choice for **eating out**, from pizzerias to good French food, and it's mostly good value. More expensive are the Traderidera and Assiette Gourmande.

Après-ski is limited to a cinema and a few quiet bars. The best are the Licorne, Cimbro, Chérine, l'Eterlou, Thé 'n Thé and L'Ecureuil.

Risoul is not recommended for those who plan to spend their time **off the slopes** – though excursions to Briançon are possible.

La Rosière

1850m

Pop over to Italy from the sunniest slopes in the Tarentaise

La Rosière is not well known internationally. For beginners, intermediates and families, it's worth considering. It's attractive and cheaper than many resorts.

WHAT IT COSTS

((((4)

HOW IT RATES

The slopes

Snow	***
Extent	***
Experts	**
Intermediates	***
Beginners	*****
Convenience	***
Queues	***
Restaurants	*

The rest

Scenery	***
Resort charm	***
Off-slope	*

What's new

The link with Italy will be vastly improved for the 1997/98 season with the Col de la Traversette drag-lift being replaced by a quad chair with a moving carpet and three other crucial lifts all having their capacity increased.

There is a new snowboard park, near the top of the Roches-Noires lift.

MOUNTAIN FACTS

Altitude	1150m-2640m
Lifts	37
Pistes	135km
Green/Blue	45%
Red	37%
Black	18%
Artificial snow	10km

UK PACKAGES

Erna Low, Ski Olympic, Vanilla Ski

TOURIST OFFICE

Postcode 73700
Tel +33 479 068051
Fax 479 068320

THE RESORT

La Rosière has been built in traditional chalet style beside the road which zig-zags its way up to the Petit St Bernard pass to Italy from Bourg-St-Maurice and Seez in the valley. The village makes a pleasant contrast with the stark architecture of resorts such as Les Arcs and La Plagne across the valley. All the buildings are attractive and many are dotted around discreetly in the woods. But there isn't much except accommodation and a few shops. Expect peace, quiet and friendly locals, but not a lively nightlife.

THE MOUNTAINS

The link with Italy means it has plenty of **slopes** for such a little-known resort, with the home slopes being largely on the south-facing flank of the mountain above the town.

The chair and drag out of the village take you into the heart of the slopes, from where a series of drags and chairs spread across the mountain takes you up to **Col de la Traversette** (2400m). From there, you can get over the ridge and to the lifts which link with **Italy** at Belvedere (2640m). These top lifts are prone to being closed by wind or heavy snow. There is a new **snowboard** fun-park and half-pipe at the top of the Roches-Noires lift.

Snow reliability is surprisingly good despite its south-facing direction, relatively low height (most of the slopes are between 1850m and 2400m) and most of the area's artificial snow being on the Italian side.

There is little excitement for **experts**. The steepest terrain is on the lowest slopes, down the Marcassin run to Le Vaz (1500m) and Ecudets or Eterlou to Les Ecudets (1150m). Other than that, there are some good off-piste itinéraires to be explored with a guide.

For **intermediates**, La Rosière would be nothing special on its own, but there's lots to explore if you take into account its links to La Thuile.

Apart from the lowest runs down to below the main village, the bottom half of La Rosière's slopes are mainly gentle, open, blue and green runs, ideal for early intermediates to brush up their technique. The top half of the mountain, however, below Le Roc Noir and Col de la Traversette, boasts steeper and more interesting red runs.

The red over the ridge from Col de la Traversette has good snow and views, but is narrow for its top section. Weaker intermediates can avoid it by taking the Chardonnet chair down.

For **beginners**, La Rosière has good nursery slopes and short lifts at the main slopes above the village and at the altiport.

La Rosière has four **cross-country** trails totalling 12km, set around the tree line in the altiport area.

Queues are not usually too much of a problem but it is much busier than on the Italian side.

The only real **mountain restaurant** is the Plan du Repos, at mid-mountain. There is a couple of bars near the top which are fine for picnics. Many people descend to the village for lunch.

Views are divided on local **ski schools**. The ESF has been praised.

Children's facilities tend to be good, especially the snow garden of the Village des Enfants.

STAYING THERE

The most convenient accommodation is in the main village, near the lifts, or just below, in Le Gollet or Vieux Village. There is also some by the other main lift up, in Les Eucherts, and more in rural hamlets further down the mountain. There are half a dozen 2-star hotels and prices are low. There are some ancient hamlets where you can rent gîtes, or you can stay in the valley village of Seez or the bigger town of Bourg-St-Maurice. There's a wide choice of **restaurants**, many of which have been praised in reports.

Après-ski is limited to a couple of bars in town. There is little **off-slope** entertainment, apart from scenic flights and a cinema. Walks are good, but only 3km of them are marked.

Saint-Martin-de-Belleville   1400m

The sharpest imaginable contrast to nearby Les Menuires

WHAT IT COSTS

(((4)))

HOW IT RATES

The slopes

Snow	***
Extent	*****
Experts	****
Intermediates	*****
Beginners	***
Convenience	***
Queues	****
Restaurants	****

The rest

Scenery	***
Resort charm	****
Off-slope	*

What's new

For 1997/98 the upper lift into the Three Valleys system is being replaced by a fast quad chair.

UK PACKAGES

ABT Ski, Chalets 'Unlimited', Chalets de St Martin, Poles Apart, Solo's, Virgin Snow

TOURIST OFFICE

Postcode 73440
Tel +33 479 089309
Fax 479 089171

St-Martin is a traditional Savoyard village, with old church, small square and old wood and stone buildings, a few miles down the valley from Les Menuires. As a quiet, inexpensive base for exploration of the Three Valleys, it's very attractive.

THE RESORT

In 1950 St-Martin didn't even have running water or electricity. Later, while new resorts were developed nearby, St-Martin remained a bit of a backwater. But in the late 1980s chair-lifts were built, linking it to the slopes of Les Menuires. The resort has been developed, of course, but without losing its rustic character.

THE MOUNTAINS

Two chair-lift rides – the upper one now a fast quad – take you to the ridge separating Les Menuires from Méribel, from which point the whole of the Three Valleys is accessible.

Snow reliability locally is not good, although there is now snowmaking on the lower slopes. The local slopes are pleasant blues and reds, mainly of interest to **intermediates** – though there are large areas of gentle off-piste for **experts** to explore. It's not a bad place for **beginners**. **Queues** are not much of a problem. There are **cross-country** trails along the valley floor. There are no special facilities for **snowboarders**.

One of the best **mountain restaurants** in the area is La Bouitte in St-Marcel. It is very French, and a great

place for a slap-up meal. A lot of people based in other resorts visit St-Martin for lunch.

The **ski school** is said to have some instructors with poor English. We've had good reports of the **kindergarten**, which is being expanded in time for the 1997/98 season.

STAYING THERE

A new Grangeraies district has been built to extend the accommodation at the foot of the slopes. It blends in well, in contrast to new developments elsewhere in the valley. There are a few hotels – the Alp'Hôtel and the Edelweiss are traditional-style 3-stars – and a good variety of apartments. Brewski's, a chalet-hotel, run by ABT Ski, is convenient for the slopes, with a sauna, jacuzzi, bar and restaurant.

St Martin is known for its **restaurants** – there were 12 at the last count, some in hotels – including traditional places and a pizzeria.

Après ski is livening up as young Germans and Scandinavians discover the resort. The Pourquoi Pas piano bar is popular, as is Brewski's bar, which has live music twice a week. Unfortunately, there is not much else to do **off the slopes**.

Sainte-Foy-Tarentaise — 1550m

Secret off-piste haven for those in the know

WHAT IT COSTS

HOW IT RATES

The slopes

Snow	***
Extent	*
Experts	****
Intermediates	***
Beginners	**
Convenience	***
Queues	*****
Restaurants	*

The rest

Scenery	***
Resort charm	***
Off-slope	*

What's new

The whole 'resort' is new and deserted. It's a wonder how it keeps going, considering how few lift tickets they sell.

MOUNTAIN FACTS

Altitude	1550m-2620m
Lifts	5
Pistes	25km
Green/Blue	23%
Red	54%
Black	23%
Artificial snow	none

UK PACKAGES

Altours Ski, Le Relais, Ski Arrangements, Ski Weekend, The Ski Company Ltd

TOURIST OFFICE

Postcode 73640
Tel +33 479 069519
Fax 479 069509

This small area in the Tarentaise has been developed only since 1990. The millions who flock to the nearby mega-resorts never give it a thought. But those in the know are well rewarded. It is an undiscovered, uncrowded gem with some wonderful off-piste slopes for experts and intermediates.

THE RESORT

There isn't one; that's the charm of this place; it's a good place to visit when staying at one of the big resorts nearby, such as Val d'Isère or Les Arcs, to get away from the crowds for a day or two. Ste-Foy is a tiny mountain hamlet of a few buildings – the largest houses the ticket office, shop and café. It's set 8km off the main road between Val-d'Isère and Bourg-St-Maurice: turn off at the village of the same name.

THE MOUNTAIN

Off-piste guides from Val d'Isère regularly make pilgrimages to Ste-Foy's deserted **slopes**, which spread over the mountainside directly above the village and on both sides of the three chair-lifts which rise, one above the other, from 1550m to the Col de l'Aiguille (2610m). The top lift – the Aiguille – gives access to almost 600m vertical of runs above the tree line and to superb, long off-piste routes on the back of the mountain. The lower two chairs serve a number of pleasant green, blue and red runs through the trees and back to the base station. The area is as good for **snowboarding** as it is for skiing.

The slopes are north- or west-facing. **Snow reliability** is good on the former but can suffer on the latter. Because of the lack of crowds, a fresh fall of powder is cut up less quickly than in the larger resorts: you can make fresh tracks days after the latest storm.

Experts can pass many a happy hour on Ste-Foy's slopes. It's not the pistes that you come for but the off-piste, for which you must have a guide. There are wonderful runs off the back down through deserted villages to the road between Ste-Foy and Val d'Isère and a splendid route which starts with a hike and takes you through trees and over a stream down to the tiny village of Le Crot. And there's plenty of off-piste scope on the front face too, as well as a couple of black, and several red, pistes.

Intermediates should have a field-day at Ste-Foy. There's 1000m vertical of uncrowded red runs – ideal for confidence building, sharpening technique or clocking up the miles. The higher slopes are the more difficult ones – the Aiguille run is a superb test for confident intermediates.

For **beginners** there is a small drag-lift near the base station; after which it's a case of getting on the Grand Plan chair and looping down on the Plan Bois trail – a pleasant, gentle track through trees and the only real beginners' run. But this isn't really a resort for beginners.

There are no prepared **cross-country** trails, but you can lay some original tracks through the woods.

The three chair-lifts are all quads, and there are never any **queues** – it's not unusual for the highest chair to be so quiet that it's only started up when someone needs a ride.

There are two rustic **mountain restaurants** at the top of the first chair, both converted from barns and serving good food. The café next to the ticket office serves pizzas, meals and snacks, and has a large terrace overlooking the valley. There is one other good, rustic bar-restaurant, housed near the bottom of the first chair.

There is a **ski school** and there's a good chance classes will not be too large. There are few, if any, facilities for **children**, however.

STAYING THERE

Hotel Monal, in the village of Ste-Foy at the turn-off in the valley, is a basic, well-run auberge with good food, and there's a lot of accommodation in Bourg-St-Maurice. The Ski Company Ltd has a new luxury chalet at the slopes and there's a chalet for snowboarders called Chalet Number One. But most people stay in one of the major resorts and take a day trip to Ste-Foy. On a busy day, there may be a short-lived **après-ski** scene in one of the bars.

Serre-Chevalier   1350m-1500m

Surprise! Big, French, but full of character

WHAT IT COSTS

((((3))))

HOW IT RATES

The slopes

Snow	****
Extent	****
Experts	***
Intermediates	****
Beginners	****
Convenience	***
Queues	***
Restaurants	***

The rest

Scenery	****
Resort charm	***
Off-slope	**

➕ Fairly big area, ideally suited to intermediate cruising

➕ Interesting mixture of wooded runs (ideal for blizzards) and open bowls

➕ One of the few big French areas based on old villages with character

➕ Good-value and atmospheric old hotels, restaurants and chalets

➕ Buses link all the villages, so you can end the day wherever you like

➕ Lift pass covers several other major resorts easily reached by car

➖ A lot of indiscriminate new building, which looks awful from the slopes

➖ Lots of slow, old lifts higher up

➖ Not many tough pistes

➖ Serious queues in French holidays

➖ Possibly the most misleading piste map in the Alps

➖ Limited nightlife

➖ Busy road runs through the resort villages, with jams at times

➖ Few off-slope diversions

Serre-Chevalier is less well known internationally than most major French resorts. It deserves better. If you love old French villages with a genuinely French atmosphere and traditional restaurants, hotels and crêperies, try it. It is one of the few resorts with the sort of ambience that you might choose for a summer holiday – a sort of Provence in the snow.

And the slopes are equally likeable. Although there are runs on only one side of the long valley, it is split into different segments, so you really feel you are travelling around as you tour them on pistes and lifts. In good snow conditions there are excellent off-piste opportunities to keep experts happy, as well as intermediates. What really sets the area apart from the French norm is the woodland runs, making Serre-Chevalier one of the best places to be when snow is falling – though there are plenty of open runs, too.

boarding *Serre-Chevalier is a snowboarding hot-spot, but has few snowboard-specific facilities. There is a board park but it is over-shadowed by the fabulous off-piste and snow reliability of the area. The pisted areas suit intermediates, but the area is popular mainly with advanced boarders because of the powder. The pistes have plenty of diversity, with open and tree-lined runs, though there are some flat sections between lifts, which are annoying. The main lifts are chairs and gondolas but there are a lot of difficult-to-avoid drag-lifts around as well, some making the links between the main areas. Evenings are quiet but there's usually at least one bar in each centre which is fairly lively.*

What's new

Serre-Chevalier went through a phase of installing powerful new lifts from the valley several years ago. But little has changed since and there are a lot of slow, old lifts on the top half of the mountains that badly need updating.

The resort

As one reporter puts it, Serre-Chevalier is 'much nicer than most French resorts'. It is made up of a string of 13 villages set on a valley floor running roughly east–west below the north-facing ski slopes. The three main villages are Monêtier (Serre-Chevalier 1500) to the west, Villeneuve (1400) in the middle and Chantemerle (1350) to the east, spread over a distance of 5km and linked by regular buses. All the villages have charming old hamlets as well as modern development.

Monêtier is the smallest, quietest and most unspoilt of the main villages, with a Provençal feel to its narrow streets, stone buildings with shutters and small square with a fountain. New building, in sympathetic style, has taken place on the other side of the main road, near the lifts.

Villeneuve has three major gondolas out of the village. The central area of new development near the lifts is fairly charmless. But the hamlet of Le Bez is peaceful and traditional, with old small stone chalets and barns. Across the main road and river the old

MOUNTAIN FACTS

Altitude 1350m-2780m
Lifts 72
Pistes 250km
Green/Blue 42%
Red 46%
Black 12%
Artificial snow 13km
Recco detectors used
— helicopter-based

LIFT PASSES

96/97 prices in francs
Grand Serre-Chevalier
Covers all lifts in
Briançon, Serre-
Chevalier and Le
Monêtier.
Main pass
1-day pass 175
6-day pass 875
Senior citizens
Over 60: 6-day pass
585 (33% off)
Over 70: free pass
Children
Under 13: 6-day pass
585 (33% off)
Under 6: free pass
Notes Passes of 6
days or more give
one day in each of
Les Deux-Alpes, Alpe-
d'Huez, Puy-St-
Vincent and Voie
Lactée (Milky Way).
Reductions for
families.
Alternative passes
Passes covering
individual areas of
Serre-Chevalier (adult
6-day 750), Briançon
(adult 6-day 575) and
Le Monêtier (adult 6-
day 625).

FRANCE 266

village of La Salle is a traditional village of stone houses, bars, hotels, restaurants and crêperies.

Chantemerle has some tasteless modern buildings in the centre and along the main road. The old sector is a couple of minutes' walk from the lifts with a lovely church and most of the restaurants, bars and small hotels.

Briançon is not strictly Serre-Chevalier but is linked to the same ski area and offers a fair amount of accommodation. It feels like a town (in fact it is the highest in France) rather than a mountain resort. The modern section, in the valley surrounding the lift station, has a wide selection of shops, bars, hotels and restaurants. Higher up is the fortified old town with narrow cobbled streets, well worth an excursion even if you are staying elsewhere. Many of the best restaurants are in the old town. The profusion of barracks reflects the town's historic role as guardian of the link between France and Italy.

The mountains

Serre-Chevalier's slopes are ideally suited to intermediates, with miles of easy cruising blues and reds, both above and below the tree line. Trees cover almost two-thirds of the mountainside; the runs here are very pretty and offer some of France's best wooded routes if the weather is poor. Mixed ability groups are likely to find something to suit everyone, with the added advantage that it is easy to meet up for lunch. But we find the piste map infuriatingly unclear and imprecise.

The six-day area lift pass also covers a day's skiing in each of Les Deux-Alpes, Alpe-d'Huez, the Milky Way ski area and Puy-St-Vincent.

THE SLOPES
Interestingly varied and pretty

Serre-Chevalier's 250km of pistes are spread in four main sectors above the Grenoble-Briançon highway.

From **Monêtier** in the west, two chair-lifts take you to mid-mountain and further lifts to the highest point in the Serre-Chevalier area (2780m), from which you can link with the other sectors. Heading from Monêtier towards Villeneuve, the main link is a red piste which is much more interesting than the narrow, flattish tracks you take when travelling in the other direction.

Both **Villeneuve** and **Chantemerle** have a choice of major lifts into the slopes, and a network of chairs and drags makes getting between these sectors easy. This area forms the heart of the Serre-Chevalier domain.

From the area above Chantemerle a pair of drag-lifts takes you to the link with **Briançon** slopes. From there you can get down to the edge of town – a long run with great views of the valley and the town of Briançon itself. A gondola brings you back.

SNOW RELIABILITY
Good – especially upper slopes

Most of the slopes face north or north-east and therefore hold their snow well, especially high up (and much of the skiing is above 2000m). Long runs down into Briançon and Chantemerle have artificial snow-making, as do a shorter run down to Monêtier and a couple of sections above Villeneuve.

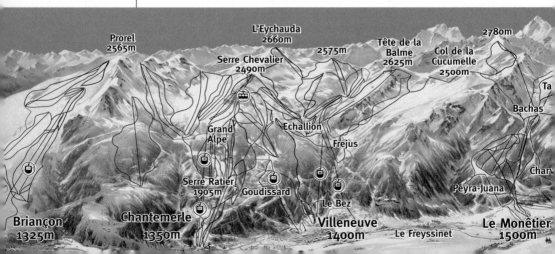

FOR INTERMEDIATES
Ski wherever you like

Serre-Chevalier's slopes are ideally suited to intermediates, who can buzz around from piste to piste and area to area without worrying about coming across anything too surprising or challenging. Looking at the piste map it might appear that red runs far outnumber blues. But most of the reds are at the easy end of the grading scale, and even nervous intermediates should have no problems with most – especially in the light of the intensive grooming that goes on.

There's plenty to challenge the more adventurous intermediate, though. Many of the runs are wide enough to be able to choose a faster pace. The Cucumelle run in the Fréjus sector is a beautiful long red run with a challenging initial section. In the bowls, you can normally pick your own route – to offer as much challenge as you are looking for. And many of the runs down to the valley, including the Olympique down to Chantemerle and the Grande Gargouille towards Briançon, have steep pitches. The runs either side of the little-used Aiguillette chair in the Chantemerle sector are quiet, enjoyable fast cruises.

FOR BEGINNERS
Good at Villeneuve

All three main villages have nursery areas at the bottom of the slopes (though at Chantemerle it's small, and you generally go up to Serre Ratier or Grande Alpe). Villeneuve has good slopes, and excellent green runs to progress to above the tree line at the top of the Fréjus gondola. The Chantemerle sector is less suitable, but also has some easy high runs. Both these sectors have green paths that wind down from mid-mountain; whether they are worth taking is another question. All of Monêtier's easy runs are at resort level, next to the excellent nursery slopes.

SCHOOLS/GUIDES

96/97 prices in francs

ESF
In all centres
Classes 6 days
5hr: 3hr am and 2hr pm; half-day am or pm
6 full days: 820
Children's classes
Ages: Up to 12
6 full days: 730
Private lessons
Hourly
170 for 1 to 2 people

International
Group lessons and special courses
Classes 6 days
am or pm
6 mornings: 540
Children's classes
Ages: up to 12
6 mornings: 480
Private lessons
Hourly
170

Montagne Adventure
Off-piste and ski touring lessons

Compagnie des Guides de l'Oisans
Off-piste, ski touring, climbing and ice climbing tuition

Montagne à la carte
Off-piste, ski touring, heliskiing, climbing

Serre Che Concept
Off-piste specialist tuition

↑ The French school holidays at their peak – post-lunch crowds at the mid-mountain station of Serre-Ratier

FOR EXPERTS
Head off-piste

There are long black pistes down to Villeneuve, Chantemerle and Monêtier, but none is fearsomely steep. About the best is the beautiful Tabuc run which takes you away from the lifts, around the side of the mountain, through woods to Monêtier. This is generally narrow and in places genuinely steep, but levels out towards the bottom. In poor snow and with big moguls it could be very tricky.

The top bowls above Villeneuve and Chantemerle have a few black runs. The two from the top of the Eychauda drag and the wide Balme run are good.

But the main interest for experts is the off-piste, both above and through the trees. In good snow this can be superb. Highlights include: Tête de Grand Pré to Villeneuve (involving a climb from Cucumelle); Croix de la Noire to Chantemerle (short climb); off the back of l'Eychauda to Puy-St-André (isolated and beautiful, taxi-ride home); l'Yret to Monêtier via Vallon de la Montagnolle (steep at the start, very beautiful). And the off-piste Mecca of La Grave is only a few miles away.

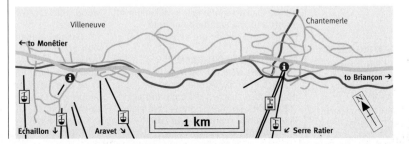

CHILDCARE

Each of the three main villages has its own non-ski nursery that takes children all day (9am to 5pm) or for a half-day. At Villeneuve, Les Schtroumpfs (492 247095) caters for kids from age 6 months; meals not provided. At Chantemerle, Les Poussins (492 240343) takes them from age 8 months; meals provided. At Monêtier, Garderie de Pré-Chabert (492 244575) takes them from age 18 months (6 months out of school holiday times); meals not provided.

GETTING THERE

Air Turin, transfer 2½hr. Grenoble, transfer 2½hr. Lyon, transfer 4hr.

Rail Briançon (6km); regular buses from station.

FOR CROSS-COUNTRY
Excellent if the snow is good

There are 45km of tracks along the valley floor, mainly following the gurgling river between Monêtier and Villeneuve and going on up towards the Col du Lautaret.

QUEUES
Avoid French school holidays

More than most resorts, Serre-Chevalier seems to be severely affected by the presence of French families during the February holidays, when there are serious queues to get up and around all sectors of the slopes. The isolated Aiguillette chair, at the extreme eastern side of the Chantemerle sector, is the place to escape the crowds.

At other times there are few problems. There is an impressive range of big lifts giving access from the valley to the slopes – though the Pontillas gondola from Villeneuve has a much less impressive capacity than its 20-person cabins would imply.

MOUNTAIN RESTAURANTS
Few, but quite good

For such a traditional French resort and large area, mountain restaurants are relatively thin on the ground, especially in the Briançon sector. The big Grande Alpe restaurant offers good value. The rustic Bachas, above Monêtier, has a good sun terrace with table service of drinks and good views. There's a choice at both Serre Ratier, above Chantemerle, (Jaques A is an excellent self-service) and at Echaillon, above Villeneuve. The welcoming Pi Mai in Fréjus, just off the Cucumelle run, does pricey table service.

SCHOOLS AND GUIDES
Highly recommended

We have received a number of reports on the Ecole de Ski Buissonnière – all of them full of praise. One reporter describes it as the best school he has ever known, another says it is worth going to Serre-Chevalier for this school alone. Classes are small, a maximum of eight) and the standards of both English and tuition are very good.

FACILITIES FOR CHILDREN
Facilities at each village

The Ecole de Ski Buissonière (see above) also teaches children and again the reports are full of praise. We also have positive reports about Les Schtroumpfs in Villeneuve.

Staying there

The central resorts of Chantemerle and Villeneuve are more convenient for getting on to the main slopes than the two extremities, Monêtier and Briançon. And the link between the Monêtier and Villeneuve slopes relies on high chair-lifts that can be closed by wind. But frequent buses run along the valley, so location isn't crucial.

More important to the feel of your holiday will be whether you stay in an 'old' or 'new' part of the resort. What makes Serre-Chevalier different from competing French resorts is the old-world charm and French ambience of the traditional hamlets and villages. If you are a Francophile, go for accommodation in one of the rustic areas, not a modern suburb.

HOW TO GO
A good choice of packages

There's a surprisingly wide choice of UK tour operators for a resort which is still not widely known internationally.
Chalets Several major UK tour operators offer chalets in the diffeent parts of the resort. Crystal's chalet Jerome has been highly recommended by a reporter, with an open-fire lounge and a sunny terrace with good views, but it is a rather tiring uphill walk from the lifts.
Hotels One of the features of this string of little villages is that it has a range of attractive, modest hotels.
In Monêtier:
(((3) **Auberge du Choucas** Smart wood-clad rooms, and a stone-vaulted restaurant with good food.
In Villeneuve:
((2) **Lièvre Blanc** Former coaching inn, with a large stone-vaulted bar. Being steadily improved by British owners; popular with UK operators; has its own guide and hire shop.
((2) **Christiania** Traditional hotel on main road, crammed with ornaments.
((2) **Vieille Ferme** Stylish conversion – wood, tiles and white walls – on edge of village.
((2) **Cimotel** Modern and charmless, with good-sized but simple rooms and 'excellent' food. Next to the piste and close to a main lift.
(1) **Le Chatelas** Prettily decorated simple chalet right on the river (once a sawmill); small, cheap rooms.
In Chantemerle:
((2) **Plein Sud** Modern; pool and sauna.

UK PACKAGES

Altours Ski, Crystal, Equity Total Ski, Fairhand Holidays, First Choice Ski, Hannibals, Inghams, Lagrange, Made to Measure, Motours, Neilson, On The Piste Travel Ltd, PGL Ski Europe, Ski Club Europe, Ski Club of GB, Ski Miquel, Sloping Off, Thomson, Travelscene Ski-Drive

Briançon Lagrange, Motours

ACTIVITIES

Indoor Swimming pool, sauna, fitness centres, cinemas, bridge
Outdoor At Chantemerle: skating rink, ice driving circuit, paragliding, cleared paths, snow-shoe walks. At Villeneuve: horse-riding, cleared paths, paragliding, snow-shoe walks. At Monêtier: skating rink, cleared paths. Also hang-gliding, husky dog-sleigh rides

② **Boule de Neige** Comfortable 2-star in the old centre.
① **Ricelle** Charming, but tucked away in Villard-Laté on the other side of the valley from the slopes. Good food at modest prices.
Self-catering There are plenty of modern apartment blocks in the new parts of Villeneuve, Chantemerle and Briançon. Few have much charm.

STAYING UP THE MOUNTAIN
Worth considering
The chalet-hotel Serre Ratier, at the mid-station of the cable-car out of Chantemerle, does full board at reasonable rates.

EATING OUT
Unpretentious and traditional
In Monêtier, the Auberge du Choucas has the best sophisticated eating. The Alliey is more of a family restaurant, and it has an excellent wine cellar.

In the old part of Villeneuve, La Pastorale has an open-fire grill and good-value menu. The Marotte is a tiny stone building with classic French cuisine ('anyone staying in Villeneuve and not eating here needs their head examining', said one reporter). The Noctambule specialises in fondue and raclette. And there are a couple of good crêperies – the Bretonne and the Petit Duc. Over in Le Bez, Le Bidule is 'really excellent'.

In Chantemerle, Amphore has good pizzas and grills. The Couch Ou is good value for fondue and raclette and has a pizzeria upstairs. The Crystal is candlelit, and is the smartest (and most expensive) place in town. The Clos has a wide choice of food and Kandahar is a charming little pizzeria. The charmingly rustic Ricelle offers amazing value for money.

APRES-SKI
Quiet streets and few bars
Serre-Chevalier isn't the place to go for wild nightlife. The village streets are usually deathly quiet, and having a car is handy if you want to try the scattered bar scene. In Villeneuve the Lièvre Blanc is popular with Brits, and L'Iceberg is a pub-style bar frequented by teenagers. The Frog is a cramped, uninspiring place. In Chantemerle, the Yeti is focal for everyone. The bar in the Clos hotel is better for a quiet drink. The discos rarely come to life except at weekends.

OFF THE SLOPES
Nothing special
Serre-Chevalier doesn't hold many attractions off the slopes, and it's certainly not the place for avid shoppers. But the old town of Briançon is well worth a visit. And there are plenty of activities on offer. The swimming pool in the hotel Sporting in Villeneuve is open to non-residents from 3pm to 9pm.

Briançon 1325m
Briançon is linked by gondola to the Serre-Chevalier slopes. It has a lovely 17th-century upper quarter, complete with impressive fortifications, narrow cobbled streets and typically French provincial restaurants, auberges and patisseries. However, the area surrounding the lift station, at the opposite and lower end of town, is an ugly urban sprawl, full of busy roads, large car parks and petrol stations.

The gondola, followed by a choice of short lifts, brings you to the link to the rest of the Serre-Chevalier slopes. The east-facing local slopes (all intermediate) are the sunniest in the area, but snowmakers ensure that the main pistes down to the gondola mid-station (1625m) stay open throughout the season, and the run to town remains complete for much of it.

The school has a high reputation, though the lack of English speakers is a drawback. The nursery and kinder-garten will care for children all day.

Packages are mostly geared towards car-driving self-caters, but independent travellers have plenty of modestly priced hotels available. The Vauban is a very comfortable 3-star; Mont Brison is a good B&B.

There are numerous restaurants; some of the best are in the old part. One reporter gave the Auberge de la Paix a rave review. Le Passe Simple, Le Péché Gourmand and L'Entrecôte are worth a try. The old town itself is the main off-slope attraction – there are wonderful views if you climb up through the ramparts. There is ice-skating and swimming, and Grenoble is a worthwhile excursion.

TOURIST OFFICE

Postcode 05240
Tel +33 492 249898
Fax 492 249884

The Three Valleys

Despite competing claims, notably from the Portes du Soleil, the sheer quantity of lift-served terrain in the Trois Vallées puts it in a league of its own. There is nowhere like it for a keen skier or boarder who wants to cover as much mileage as possible while rarely taking the same run repeatedly. And it has a lot to offer everyone from beginner to expert.

The runs of the three valleys and their resorts are dealt with in five chapters. The four major resorts are Courchevel, page 202, Méribel, page 233, Les Menuires, page 230, and Val-Thorens, page 291. Saint-Martin-de-Belleville, a small village along the mountainside from Les Menuires, now gets its own chapter on page 263.

None of the resorts is cheap. **Les Menuires** is the cheapest but it is also the ugliest, and lacks decent accommodation. The slopes around the village get too much sun for comfort, but close by across the valley are some of the best (and quietest) challenging pistes in the Three Valleys on its north-facing La Masse. Its near neighbour, **St-Martin-de-Belleville**, is a small traditional village with good-value accommodation – and now with improved lift links into the rest of the area.

At 2300m **Val-Thorens** is the highest resort in the Alps, and at 3200m the top of its slopes is the high-point of the Three Valleys. The snow in this area is almost always good, and it includes two glaciers where that's guaranteed. But the setting is bleak and the lifts are vulnerable to closure in bad weather. The purpose-built resort is very convenient. Visually it is not comparable to Les Menuires, thanks to the smaller-scale design and more thorough use of wood cladding, but it still isn't to everyone's taste.

Méribel's purpose-built satellite, **Mottaret**, is the best-placed of all the resorts for getting to any part of the system in the shortest possible time. It's now quite a spread-out place, with some of the accommodation a long way up the hillsides – great for access to the slopes, less so for access to nightlife. **Méribel** itself is 200m lower, and has long been a favourite for the British, especially those going on chalet holidays. It is the most attractive of the main Trois Vallées resorts, built in chalet style beside a long winding road up the hillside. Parts of the resort are very convenient for the slopes and the village centre; parts are very far from either.

Courchevel 1850 is the most fashionable resort in France, and the most expensive resort in the Alps. Despite these considerations, it is well worth thinking about – though holiday-makers without deep pockets are probably better off based in one of the less expensive resort villages (1300, 1550 and 1650). They don't have the same choice of nightlife and restaurants, and only 1550 enjoys the same central location in the lift system. The slopes around Courchevel are thought by many to be the best in the Three Valleys, with runs to suit all standards and some of the most immaculately groomed pistes you'll find anywhere. The snow tends to be better than in neighbouring Méribel, because many of the slopes are north-facing.

La Tania is a small place built for the 1992 Olympics, along the mountainside from Courchevel 1300 on the road to Méribel. Consisting mainly of apartment blocks, it has few facilities and little nightlife, but it is a good-value option.

Tignes

Great skiing, but a village that could be on the moon

WHAT IT COSTS

((((((6)

HOW IT RATES

The slopes

Snow	*****
Extent	*****
Experts	*****
Intermediates	*****
Beginners	**
Convenience	****
Queues	****
Restaurants	**

The rest

Scenery	***
Resort charm	*
Off-slope	*

What's new

For 1997/98 a new high-speed six-seater chair-lift is due to be running from Tignes Val Claret to Col de Fresse. This will make getting to Val d'Isère from Val Claret much quicker than on the slow, old Tufs chair.

And the slow, old Grand Huit chair which links the slopes above Val Claret with those above Le Lac on the Aiguille Percée side will be replaced by a high-speed quad, solving the queue problem here.

➕ One of the best areas in the world for lift-served off-piste runs

➕ Huge area, with great terrain for intermediates and experts

➕ Good snow guaranteed for a long season

➕ Highly convenient, with very little walking to the slopes

➕ Good lift system, with swift access to slopes of Val-d'Isère

➖ Ugly and now rather tatty buildings – traffic can be a problem, too

➖ Bleak, treeless setting

➖ Little skiing below the tree line – and it's inaccessible from Tignes if the high lifts are closed

➖ No green runs for beginners to progress to

➖ Limited après-ski

➖ Poor mountain restaurants

The appeal of Tignes is simple: good snow, spread over a wide area. If that's what you want from a winter holiday, and you don't want much nightlife or off-slope diversions, if you don't care about long lunches in charming restaurants or about the aesthetic appeal of the place where you are staying, Tignes is one of the best choices you can make.

Tignes and Val-d'Isère together form the enormous Espace Killy – a Mecca for experts, and ideal for adventurous intermediates. Whereas Val-d'Isère has a huge British presence, Tignes is much more French. It is also even more reliable for snow: set at 2100m, it is one of Europe's highest resorts, with good snow right back to the resort for most of the season.

Access to the highest runs was greatly improved a few years ago by the opening of a fast underground funicular and fast quad chairs almost to the top. And access to Val d'Isère from the runs to the bottom of these lifts will be improved for 1997/98.

boarding *This is a big area, with a big boarder reputation. Snowsure (if a bit flat) boarding on the glacier gives way to steep tree-hopping above the lowest part, Tignes-les-Brévières. In between, the lift system is modern, with lots of chair and gondola links, and long, wide pistes to blast down, with powder between them to play in. The glacier is a good place for near-beginners to practise. There's a fun-park and a half-pipe and Kebra Surfing (in Le Lac) and Surf Feeling (in Val-Claret) are specialist snowboard schools/shops. Hiring a guide and exploring the off-piste is recommended for good boarders. There is now a special boarders' guide to the resort available. Val Claret is the only part that has any life, let alone nightlife. There are a couple of bars worth going to – just follow the noise.*

Not a single tree in sight, and scarcely a single pitched roof, either ↓

MOUNTAIN FACTS

Altitude 1550m-3500m	
Lifts	100
Pistes	300km
Green/Blue	62%
Red	29%
Black	9%
Artificial snow	24km
Recco detectors used	

LIFT PASSES

97/98 prices in francs
L'Espace Killy
Covers all lifts and
resort buses in Tignes
and Val d'Isère.
Beginners Free lifts
on all main nursery
slopes; special
beginners' half-day
pass.
Main pass
1-day pass 217
6-day pass 1,005
Senior citizens
Over 60: 6-day pass
850 (15% off)
Over 75: free pass
Children
Under 13: 6-day pass
705 (30% off)
Under 5: free pass
Short-term passes
Half-day pass from
12.30 (adult 151,
Super Tignes pass
135).
Alternative periods
14 non-consecutive
days pass available.
Notes 1-day pass and
over valid for one day
in La Plagne-Les Arcs.
6-day pass and over
valid for one day each
in the Three Valleys,
Pralognan-la-Vanoise,
Les Saisies and
Valmorel. On 3- to 15-
day passes, pass
reimbursed if all lifts
are shut due to bad
weather. Discount on
new passes on
presentation of
previous season's
pass. Extra discount
for senior citizens
aged 70 to 74 (6-day
505, 50% off).
Alternative passes
Super Tignes ski pass
covers the lifts on the
Tignes side of the
Espace Killy only
(adult 6-day 855).

The resort

Tignes was created before the French
discovered how to make purpose-built
resorts look acceptable. It has two
main centres – Le-Lac and Val-Claret –
and both are just plug-ugly. They're
now looking very tatty in places, too.
But at least the traffic is now being
restricted in the centre.

Large concrete blocks, some wood-
clad, some not, set beside a wide
road, don't make for an aesthetically
pleasing holiday base. But they are
very convenient for the slopes. And a
free ski-bus links Le Lac, Val-Claret and
accommodation not accessible directly
from the slopes. Both centres have
their own shops, restaurants and bars
and are linked on skis.

Some tour operators have places in
Le Lavachet, 10 minutes' walk from Le
Lac. It's more villagey, with a compact
horseshoe of small restaurants. It also
has the best bar in Tignes, and mainly
slope-side accommodation.

Below the resort are two smaller
settlements, different in style. Tignes-
les-Boisses is quietly set in the trees
near a military camp. Tignes-les-
Brévières is a renovated old village at
the lowest point of the Tignes slopes.
A regular free bus service connects all
the villages until midnight.

The mountains

The runs of the Espace Killy have few
rivals for the attention of experts.
There is almost limitless off-piste as
well as on-piste challenge.
Intermediates too will have a great
time here, with mile after mile of
cruising runs linked by efficient lifts.

Also see the chapter on Val d'Isère
for a summary of the slopes there.

Tignes has all-year-round runs on its
3500m Grande Motte glacier. And the
resort height of 2100m generally
means good snow-cover right back to
base for most of the long season.

The main drawback of the area is
that it can become unusable in bad
weather. There are no woodland routes
except towards Tignes-les-Boisses and
Tignes-les-Brévières – a tiny fraction of
the total area, and reachable only by
road if the high lifts are closed.

There's a tendency for runs to be
undergraded – so it was good to see
some recent piste map changes (some
blues becoming red; some reds, black).

THE SLOPES
High, snowsure and varied

Tignes' biggest asset is the **Grande
Motte** glacier. Access is easy thanks to
the underground funicular from Val-
Claret, which whizzes you up to over
3000m in six minutes. The snow up
here, with a cable-car taking you up a
further 500m, is always good, even on
the warmest spring day. There are
chairs and drags to play on, as well as
beautiful long runs back to the resort
and a link over to Val-d'Isère.

A high-capacity gondola from Le Lac
and a new (for 1997/98) high-speed
chair from Val Claret take you up to
slopes which go down to Val d'Isère.
The gondola goes to **Tovière**, the chair
to **Col de Fresse** – and from both you
can also head back to Tignes.

Going up the opposite side of the
valley takes you to an area of drags
and chair-lifts serving predominantly
east-facing runs – splendid for early-
morning sun – and leading to some
delightful off-piste runs down the other
side to the La Plagne and Les Arcs
areas. The east-facing slopes split into
two main sectors, linked in both
directions – **Col du Palet** and **Aiguille
Percée**. From the latter, you can
descend on blue, red or black runs to
the old village of Tignes-les-Brévières,
from which there's an efficient
gondola back.

A six-day pass covers a day in
several other resorts, including Les
Arcs or La Plagne and the Three
Valleys.

SNOW RELIABILITY
Difficult to beat

Few resorts can rival Tignes for reliably
good snow-cover. The whole region,
not just the glacier area, usually has
good cover from November to May.
The sunniest lower slopes now have
substantial snowmaking facilities.

FOR EXPERTS
An excellent choice

There's no lack of challenge here for
experts. On piste, our favourite run is
the Vallon de la Sache black from
Aiguille Percée down to Tignes-les-
Brévières. This long run takes you
down a secluded valley, right away
from the lifts, with beautiful views. It
isn't particularly steep or narrow
except for a couple of short pitches,
and is manageable by adventurous
intermediates. There are also off-piste
variants, for which you need a guide.

SCHOOLS/GUIDES

97/98 prices in francs

ESF

Classes 5 days
6hr: 9am-noon and
1.45-4.45; 3hr: am or
pm
5 full days: 920
Children's classes
Ages: 4 to 12
5 full days: 870
Private lessons
Hourly or daily
180 for 1hr, between
noon and 2.30,
otherwise 230

Evolution 2
Classes 5 days
am or pm
4 half-days: 400
Children's classes
Ages: 5 to 14
5 half-days: 590
Private lessons
Hourly or daily
180 for 1hr

OTHER SCHOOLS

International
Snow Fun
Ski Action
Kebra Surfing
Surf Feeling

The other long black run, from Tovière to Tignes-le-Lac, is steep and heavily mogulled at the top and bottom but has a long easy section in the middle. Parts of this get a lot of afternoon sun.

But it is the off-piste possibilities that make Tignes an excellent area for experts. Go with one of the off-piste groups that the schools organise and you'll have a wonderful time.

One of the big adventures is to head for Champagny (linked to the La Plagne area) or Peisey-Nancroix (linked to the Les Arcs area) – very beautiful runs, and not too difficult. Your guide will organise return transport.

Another favourite descent of ours is the Tour de Pramecou, from the Grande Motte glacier. After some walking and beautiful away-from-it-all runs, you end up on a steep, smooth north-facing slope which takes you back to Val-Claret. There are other descents across the glacier to the bottom of the two Leisse chairs, which take you back up to the arrival point of the funicular.

The off-piste served by the Col des Ves chair is often excellent. To the left (looking up) there are wonderfully secluded, scenic and challenging descents. On the right, lower down, is a less heavily used and gentler area, ideal for off-piste initiation.

Then there's the whole of the Val-d'Isère slopes to sample, too – see that chapter.

FOR INTERMEDIATES
One of the best

Only the Three Valleys has intermediate runs in greater quantity than L'Espace Killy. But there's more than enough here to keep even the keenest intermediate happy for a fortnight. And, in the unimaginable event that you did get bored, remember that a six-day or longer pass covers a day in the Three Valleys and a day in La Plagne or Les Arcs too.

Tignes' local slopes are ideal intermediate terrain. The red and blue runs on the Grande Motte glacier nearly always have superb snow. The glacier run from the top of the cable-car is a very gentle blue. The Leisse red run down to the double chairs can get very mogulled but has good snow. The long red run all the way back to town is a delightful long cruise – so long as it isn't too crowded – and has a lot of snowmaking guns on the lower

section to ensure good cover.

From Tovière, the Campanules red and the blue 'H' run to Val-Claret are both enjoyable cruises and generally well groomed. But again, they can get very crowded. The direct way down from the top to Tignes-le-Lac is a steep black mogul field, but there are red and blue alternatives.

On the other side of the valley, we particularly like the Ves red run from the Col des Ves chair – the highest point of Tignes' non-glacier runs at 2845m. After an initial mogul field the run becomes an interesting undulating and curvy cruise, usually with good snow and a few moguls. It's never crowded because of the low capacity of the double chair which serves it.

The runs down from Aiguille Percée to Tignes-les-Boisses and Tignes-les-Brévières are also scenic and enjoyable. There are red and blue options as well as the beautiful black Vallon de la Sache which adventurous intermediates shouldn't miss (see For Experts, above). Brévières is a good place for a mid-morning break, especially if you need to recover from the Sache run.

The runs down from Aiguille Percée to Le Lac are gentle, wide blues. The Bluets red from the top of the Aiguille Rouge chair is a more interesting and challenging alternative.

Then there's the whole of the Val-d'Isère slopes to sample, too – see that chapter.

FOR BEGINNERS
Little attraction

The nursery slope in Le Lac is convenient, snowsure and gentle, and is kept nicely separate from the main area by a man-made bank of snow. There are, however, no green runs at all to progress to, and the blues near both main villages get fairly crowded with people hurtling through to the lift stations. In poor weather, because of the height and lack of trees, beginners could find it cold and intimidating. We really think beginners would be better off going elsewhere.

FOR CROSS-COUNTRY
Interesting

The Espace Killy has 44km of cross-country trails. There are tracks on the frozen Lac de Tignes, along the valley between Val-Claret and Tignes-le-Lac, at Les Boisses and Brévières and up the mountain on the Grande Motte.

CHILDCARE

The Petits Lutins kindergartens in Le Lac and Val-Claret (479 065127) take children aged 3 months to 6 years.

The recently opened hotel Diva in Val-Claret (479 067000) has a nursery taking children from age 18 months.

The Marmottons kindergarten in Le Lac (479 065167) takes children from 2 to 10, with skiing with Evolution 2 instructors for those aged 3½ or more.

QUEUES
Very few

The new Grande Motte funicular and parallel high-speed chairs have removed the worst bottleneck. But there can still be hordes of people waiting for the funicular. If there are, it's often quicker to take the chair. The worst queues now are usually for the cable-car above the funicular. Half-hour waits here are still common, especially when lower snow is poor. Inevitably, the improvements to the lifts have increased pressure on the pistes, to the point where the run down from the Grande Motte can be seriously unpleasant. In late afternoon, queues can build up for the slow Tovière chairs to return from Val-d'Isère – the high-speed quad to Col de Fresse is a much quicker route. And a new high-speed six-seater chair will link Val Claret with the Col de Fresse for the 1997/98 season, eliminating queues for the slow, old Tufs chair to Tovière. Progression across the mountainside

from the Col du Palet sector towards the Aiguille Percée has depended on the inadequate Grand Huit chair in the past, but a new, faster four-seat chair should be fully operational for the 1997/98 season.

MOUNTAIN RESTAURANTS
Neither cheap nor cheerful

Mountain restaurants are not a highlight. The big one at the top of the funicular has great panoramic views and a huge terrace, which is invaded every few minutes by the next funicular-full of people clumping across to the piste.

The Chalet du Bollin restaurant, at the top of the short Bollin chair from Val-Claret, is probably the best in the main area, with table service and a good plat du jour. The restaurant just above the mid-mountain lift junction going up to Col du Palet is pleasant, with a big terrace. And the place next to the Grand Motte chair-lift is good.

In Les Brévières it's much cheaper

GETTING THERE

Air Geneva, transfer 4½hr. Lyon, transfer 4½hr. Chambery, transfer 3½hr.

Rail Bourg-St-Maurice (25km); regular buses or taxi from station.

to walk round the corner into the village than eat at one of the two places by the piste. La Sachette is recommended. Les Boisses has the best restaurant in the area in La Cordée.

Reporters continue to protest at the practice of charging even big-spending customers FF2 for using the toilet.

SCHOOLS AND GUIDES
Enormous choice

At the last count there were ten schools, plus various independent instructors. The ESF and Evolution 2 are the main ones, with sections in both resort centres. Evolution 2 has received the best reports recently, with class sizes put at a maximum of eight and standards of English good. It may

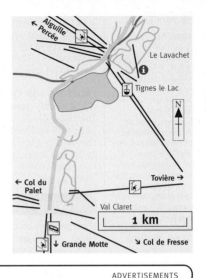

Selected chalets and club hotels in Tignes

CRYSTAL   T **0181 399 5144**   F **0181 390 6378**

SKI OLYMPIC *Great value chalets*   T **01302 390120**   F **01302 390787**

UK PACKAGES

Altours Ski, Bladon Lines, Chalets 'Unlimited', Club Med, Crystal, Erna Low, Fairhand Holidays, First Choice Ski, Independent Ski Links, Inghams, Lagrange, Made to Measure, MasterSki, Motours, Neilson, On The Piste Travel Ltd, Ski Activity, Ski Amis, Ski Arrangements, Ski Beat, Ski Choice, Ski Club of GB, Ski France, Ski Leisure Direction, Ski Olympic, Ski Valkyrie, Ski trek, Skiworld, The Ski Company, Thomson, Travelscene Ski-Drive, UCPA, Virgin Snow, avant-ski

ACTIVITIES

Indoor 'Vitatignes' in Le Lac (balneotherapy centre with spa baths, sauna etc), 'Espace Forme' in Le Lac, Fitness Club in Val-Claret (body-building, aerobics, squash, golf practice and simulation, sauna, hammam, Californian baths, jacuzzi, swimming pool, massage), cinema, covered tennis court, bowling, climbing wall, 'La Banquise M and M's' for children (ice skating, snow sliding, solarium, snow activities, climbing activities) **Outdoor** Natural skating-rink, hang-gliding, paragliding, helicopter rides, snow-mobiles, husky dog-sleigh rides, diving beneath ice on lake, heli-skiing

TOURIST OFFICE

Postcode 73320
Tel +33 479 400440
Fax 479 400315

also be worth trying one of the smaller schools. Based in Le Lac, Stages 2000 specialises in off-piste tuition; Association 9 Valleys does mostly inter-resort circuits and extreme skiing.

FACILITIES FOR CHILDREN
Apparently good
The Hotel Diva's children's clubs have been well received. The English standard is good and children appear to be well looked after. We have also had good reports on the Marmottons kindergarten.

Staying there

Location isn't crucial, especially as Val Claret, as well as Le Lac, will now have swift access to the Val d'Isère slopes.

HOW TO GO
Disappointing range of options
Although all three main styles of accommodation are available through tour operators, there isn't a lot of choice in any category, especially for those who like their creature comforts.
Chalets The choice of catered chalets is very limited in comparison to many other major French resorts. Many chalets are also surprisingly inconvenient for the slopes and tend to be reasonably comfortable but far from luxurious. Ski Olympic's Chalet Rosset has been recommended by a reporter as an exception 'superb, with a lovely lounge with views but a bit of an uphill plod at the end of the day'.
Hotels The few hotels are small and simple, or (in a couple of cases) small and quite luxurious.
((((4) **Ski d'Or** Smooth little Relais & Châteaux hotel; a modern chalet in Val-Claret, with the best food in town.
(((3) **Curling** Tastefully renovated for the Olympics; in Val-Claret.
(((3) **Campanules** Big modern chalet in Le Lac, with well equipped rooms.
(((3) **Diva** Opened a few years ago and enthusiastically recommended for 'spacious rooms, helpful staff and superb food'. Close to the funicular.
((2) **Terril Blanch** Well run place next to the lake.
((2) **Neige et Soleil** Excellent family-run place in Le Lac – central, clean, cosy, comfortable, with good food.
Self-catering In upper Val-Claret, close to the Tovière chair, the Residence Le Boursat apartments are about the best on offer – not too cramped, reasonably well equipped and have a communal

lounge. The Chalet Club in Val-Claret is a collection of simple studios, but has the benefit of free indoor pool, sauna and in-house restaurant and bar.

EATING OUT
Good places dotted about
Le Lavachet has a cluster of quite nice places; we have had good reports of the Osteria and the (expensive) Orée du Maquis. Finding anywhere with some atmosphere is difficult in Le Lac, though some of the food is good. The Tocade has also been praised. The Ski d'Or, Bouf'Mich and Winstub (Alsatian cooking) are three of the better places in Val-Claret. Those on a budget here should try the Italian at the Pignatta. But the Cordée in Les Boisses is a must if you have a car – unpretentious surroundings, great traditional French food and cheap.

APRES-SKI
Early to bed
Tignes is desperately quiet at night, though Val-Claret has some early-evening atmosphere and 'happy hours' are reported to be popular. The Wobbly Rabbit is popular with Brits – but was up for sale when we went to press. The Corniche is more cosmopolitan, with live music.
Le Lac is virtually dead, even immediately after coming off the slopes – though there is a cinema with bowling and video games for the kids.
Late revellers head for Harri's in Lavachet, the most animated bar in town, though it's quite large and takes some filling before it warms up. The satellite TV here is popular.

OFF THE SLOPES
Forget it
Despite the range of alternative activities, Tignes is a resort for those who want to use the slopes, where anyone who doesn't is liable to feel like a fish out of water.

STAYING DOWN THE VALLEY
Only for visiting other resorts
See the Val-d'Isère chapter; the same considerations apply broadly here. But bear in mind that there are rooms to be had in simple hotels on the edge of the Tignes slopes. Most comfortable is the 2-star Melezes at Les Boisses, but there are even simpler alternatives in the same hamlet (the Cordée and Marais) and in Les Brévières (the Perdrix Rouge and the Génépy).

Val-d'Isère

On and off-piste playground with reliable snow

WHAT IT COSTS

ⓒⓒⓒⓒⓒ **6**

HOW IT RATES

The slopes

Snow	*****
Extent	*****
Experts	*****
Intermediates	*****
Beginners	***
Convenience	***
Queues	****
Restaurants	**

The rest

Scenery	***
Resort charm	***
Off-slope	**

➕ Huge area linked with Tignes, with runs for all standards

➕ Some of the best lift-served off-piste runs in the world

➕ High altitude means snow is more or less guaranteed

➕ Wide choice of schools for on and off-piste lessons and guiding

➕ Wide range of package holidays, of every kind

➕ For a high resort, the town is attractive, and very lively at night

➖ Piste grading understates the difficulty of many runs

➖ You're quite likely to need the bus at the start or end of the day

➖ British visitors and residents can be dominant, especially in low season

➖ Not much chance of getting on the slopes when the weather is bad

➖ Crowds come from lower resorts when snow is poor – and some key lifts at altitude need improvement

➖ Disappointing mountain restaurants

Val is one of the world's best resorts for experts – attracted by the extent of lift-served off-piste – and for confident intermediates keen to clock up the miles. But you don't have to be particularly adventurous to enjoy the resort – both the editors of this guide have had successful holidays here with mixed family groups, including beginners. The relaxed attitude to piste grading and grooming does mean that early intermediates must be steered to the right runs.

The drawbacks listed above are mainly petty complaints. For some visitors, dependence on the bus may matter, even though the free service is one of the best in the Alps. Ironically it has become more important recently because of lift improvements: lots of people based in central Val now start their day with a bus-ride to the super-quick funicular at La Daille.

The village was improved enormously in appearance and ambience for the 1992 Olympics. One of our main reservations is its domination (especially in low season) by the British; but for others this is a plus-point – it results in a vibrant après-ski scene in which English-speakers can feel perfectly at home.

boarding *Val d'Isère is good for boarders, though Tignes is a more popular boarder destination. Most of the main lifts are cable-cars, chair-lifts and gondolas, with very few drag-lifts. But there are a few flat areas where you'll need to scoot or walk. Experts will revel in the off-piste and there's a fun-park at La Daille and a half-pipe at the bottom of the Bellevarde piste. There are several specialist snowboard shops and schools. The village nursery area is ideal for trying boarding for the first time and Le Fornet is good to progress to (avoiding the drag-lift on Solaise). Val d'Isère's nightlife is difficult to beat.*

What's new

For 1997/98 a new high-speed six-seater chair-lift is due to be running from Tignes Val Claret to Col de Fresse. This will make getting back to Val d'Isère much quicker than on the slow, old Tufs chair.

A new babysitting service is due to open and a new ESF kindergarten is promised.

Tours of a farm near the town centre are being organised in early evening to see local cheeses such as St Avalin (unique to Val d'Isère) and Tomme de Savoie being made.

The resort

Val-d'Isère spreads along a remote valley which is a dead-end in winter. It is a classic ribbon development. As you drive in from La Daille – a convenient but hideous slope-side apartment complex – the apartments and chalets lining the road increase in density, and then give way to shops, bars, restaurants and hotels. As you approach the centre, the legacy of the 1992 Olympics becomes more evident:

new wood- and stone-cladding, culminating in the tasteful pedestrian-only Val Village complex and the few remnants of the original old village.

There is a lot of traffic around, making the centre feel towny rather than villagey. Still, many first-time visitors find the resort much 'prettier' than they expected.

Beyond Val-d'Isère the valley road continues 3km to the old hamlet of Le Fornet – with its own cable-car, another possible base for a holiday.

MOUNTAIN FACTS

Altitude 1550m-3500m
Lifts   100
Pistes   300km
Green/Blue   62%
Red   29%
Black   9%
Artificial snow   24km
Recco detectors used

The mountains

For experts, there are few areas to rival L'Espace Killy (as the linked areas of Val d'Isère and Tignes are known). Its attractions are as much its splendid off-piste runs as its groomed runs. But there are significant on-piste challenges too. Intermediates of all standards will find enough to keep them interested for several visits – though there are complaints about overcrowded pistes at peak periods. Contrary to popular opinion, there are some good areas for novices too. Piste grooming has improved enormously.

There's been a bit of building since this was taken, but the bumps on Solaise don't change
↓

THE SLOPES
Vast and varied

Val-d'Isère's slopes divide into three main sectors. **Bellevarde** (2770m) is the mountain which is home to Val-d'Isère's famous Men's Downhill course – the OK piste, which opens each season's World Cup programme in early December. You can reach Bellevarde by the funicular from La Daille or by cable-car or high-speed chairs from Val.

From the top you can get back down to the main lifts, play on a variety of drags and chairs on the top half of the mountain or take a choice of lifts to get to the Tignes slopes.

Solaise is the other mountain accessible directly from the centre of Val-d'Isère. The Solaise cable-car was Val's first major lift – begun illicitly during the Occupation in 1940 and finished in 1942. The parallel high-speed quad Solaise Express chair-lift takes you a few metres higher. Once up, a short drag takes you over a plateau and down to a variety of chairs which serve this very sunny area of predominantly gentle pistes.

From near the top of this area you can catch a drag or chair over to the third main area, above and below the Col de l'Iseran (with runs up to 3300m on the Pissaillas glacier), which can also be reached by cable-car from Le Fornet in the valley. The chair-lift is spectacular: it climbs over a narrow ridge and then drops suddenly down the other side. You can also ride the chair-lift back if you don't want to catch the bus from Le Fornet. The drag-lift isn't the easy option, though. It's short and steep. At the top you head through a narrow tunnel leading to an awkward black run which is often closed. The runs here are predominantly easy, with spectacular views and access to the region's most beautiful off-piste sections.

The ski area links with that of Tignes. A six-day lift pass gives a day's skiing in Les Arcs or La Plagne, plus the Trois Vallées – easily reached by car. Other resorts nearby are Ste-Foy and La Rosière.

SNOW RELIABILITY
Unbeatable

In years when lower resorts have suffered, Val-d'Isère has rarely been short of snow. Its height of 1850m means you can almost always get back to the village, especially because of

LIFT PASSES

97/98 prices in francs

L'Espace Killy
Covers all lifts and
resort buses in Tignes
and Val d'Isère.
Beginners 11 free
beginners' lifts on
main nursery slopes.
Main pass
1-day pass 217
6-day pass 1,005
Senior citizens
Over 60: 6-day pass
850 (15% off)
Over 75: free pass
Children
Under 13: 6-day pass
705 (30% off)
Under 5: free pass
Short-term passes
Half-day pass from
12.30 (adult 151).
Alternative periods
14 non-consecutive
days pass available.
Notes 6-day pass and
over valid for one day
each in the Three
Valleys, Pralognan-la-
Vanoise, Les Saisies
and Valmorel. On 3-
to 15-day passes,
pass reimbursed if all
lifts are shut due to
bad weather.
Discount on new
passes on
presentation of
previous season's
pass. Extra discount
for senior citizens
aged 70 to 74 (6-day
505, 50% off).

the snowmaking facilities on the lower slopes of all the main routes home.

Many of the slopes are north-facing (or northish) and plenty are between 2300m and 3000m, even ignoring the higher glacier skiing.

FOR EXPERTS
One of the world's best

Val-d'Isère is one of the top resorts in the world for experts. The main attraction is the huge range of beautiful off-piste possibilities – see feature panel below.

There are excellent pistes for experts, too. Many of the red and blue runs – even one or two greens – are steep enough to get mogulled, so the small number of blacks is not the limitation it might seem.

On Bellevarde the famous Face run is the main attraction – mogulled from top to bottom, but not worryingly steep. Epaule is the sector's other black run – where the moguls are hit by long exposure to sun and can be slushy or rock-hard too often for our liking. On Solaise the main attractions for bump enthusiasts are the runs back down under the lifts to the village. There are several ways down: all steep, though none fearsomely so.

Apart from all this, there's Tignes' slopes to explore – as much again.

FOR INTERMEDIATES
Quantity and quality

Val-d'Isère has as much to offer intermediates as it does experts. But the less experienced should be aware that many runs are under-graded. This continues to be a complaint of many of our reporters.

In the Solaise sector is a network of gentle blue runs ideal for building confidence. And there are a couple of beautiful runs from here through the woods to Le Laisinant, from where you catch the bus – these are ideal for bad weather, though prone to closure in times of avalanche danger.

The runs in the Col de l'Iseran

OFF-PISTE PARADISE

L'Espace Killy has some of the most extensive lift-served off-piste skiing in the world. The piste map shows the start of over 20 of the classic off-piste runs and there are dozens more and endless variations.

They are best explored with a professional guide because of the avalanche and other hidden dangers, such as cliffs to fall off and rivers to fall in. But many of the more popular runs are skied into an almost piste-like state soon after a fresh snowfall – here, again, a guide will be able to show you the less well-known and less often skied routes.

Our favourite off-piste routes include:

– Col Pers from the top of the glacier above Le Fornet. You traverse over to a big, wide, fairly gentle bowl with glorious views. There are endless variants on the way down. Most bring you out just below the source of the Isère river, where you drop into the very beautiful, narrow Gorges du Malpasset and ski on top of the frozen Isère back to the Le Fornet cable-car. This is a good area for spotting chamois grazing in the sun on the rocky outcrops above you.

– Tour de Charvet from the top of the Grand Pre chair-lift in the Bellevarde sector. The easiest route starts with a long traverse in a huge bowl, before dropping into a narrow gorge which you ski along before the long run-out to the Manchet chair up to the Solaise sector.

– Tour de Pramecou from the Grand Motte area in Tignes. After a long, flat section at the top and a couple of short climbs between downhill sections you end up at the top of a long, steep, wide, north-facing slope where the snow is usually excellent and swoop down that to the Carline piste back down to the bottom of the Motte.

You can literally spend a whole week here off-piste skiing different runs every day. We recommend the Alpine Experience and Top Ski guided groups: you can join a group of your standard for off-piste skiing every morning (8.45 until 1pm). Afternoons tend to be more conventional lessons to improve technique.

SCHOOLS/GUIDES

97/98 prices in francs

ESF
Classes 6 days
5½hr: 3hr am, 2½hr pm
6 full days: 1,070
Children's classes
Ages: from 4
6 full days: 795
Private lessons
1hr, mornings, afternoons, or whole day

Snow Fun
Classes 6 days
3hr am and 2½hr pm
5 mornings: 490
Children's classes
Ages: up to 13
6 full days: 760
Private lessons
Hourly or daily
170 for 1hr

Top Ski
Specialise in slalom, mogul and off-piste courses for small groups (max 6)
Classes 4 days
4hr: 9am-1pm; 2hr: 2pm-4pm
4 full days: 1,300
Private lessons
am (8.45-1pm), pm (2pm-4.30) or full-day (8.45-4.30)

Alpine Experience
Specialise in off-piste guiding and teaching for small groups (max 6)

sector are flatter and easier – ideal for early and hesitant intermediates. Those marked blue at the top of the glacier could really be graded green.

Bellevarde has a huge variety of runs ideally suited to intermediates of all standards. From Bellevarde itself there is a choice of green, blue and red runs of varying pitch. And the wide runs from Tovière normally give you the choice of groomed piste or moguls.

A snag for early intermediates is that runs back to the valley can be testing. The easiest way is to head down to La Daille, where there is a green run – but it should be graded blue (in some resorts it would be red), and gets very crowded and mogulled at the end of the day. None of the runs from Bellevarde and Solaise back to Val itself is really easy.

The blue Santons run from Bellevarde takes you through a long, narrow gun-barrel which often has people standing around plucking up courage, making things even trickier.

On Solaise there isn't much to choose between the blue and red ways down – they're both mogulled and narrow in places. At the top, there's no option other than the red mogul run in full view of the lifts. It's just a question of choosing how big you want your moguls – the largest are on your right. Many early intermediates sensibly choose to ride the lifts down – take the chair for a spectacular view.

FOR BEGINNERS
OK if you know where to go

Val-d'Isère has a superb nursery slope right by the centre of town. What's more, the lifts serving it are free – no coupons, never mind a lift pass.

Once you get off the nursery slopes, there are some easy runs, but you have to know where to find them; many of the greens would be blue, or even red, in other resorts. One experienced Val-d'Isère instructor admitted: 'We have to have plenty of green runs on the piste map, even if we haven't got many green slopes – otherwise beginners wouldn't come to Val d'Isère.'

A good place for your first real runs off the nursery slopes is the Madeleine green run on Solaise. The Col de l'Iseran runs are also gentle and wide; they're less easily accessible but the snow is normally the best around.

There are no easy runs back to the valley – you'll have to ride down.

FOR CROSS-COUNTRY
Limited

There are a couple of loops towards La Daille and another out past Le Laisinant. More picturesque is the one going from Le Châtelard (on the road past the main cable-car station) to the Manchet chair. But keen cross-country enthusiasts should go elsewhere.

QUEUES
Few problems

Queues to get out of the resort have been pretty much eliminated by the building of the funicular and high-speed chair-lifts up the mountains as alternatives to the two main cable-cars. The Boisses lift out of Tigne Les Boisses, however, closes between 12 and 2pm, which creates queues for the Sache gondola.

At the end of the day, there's usually a wait for the chair back from Col de l'Iseran to Solaise. To get to Tignes, it's quicker to take the high-speed quad to Col de Fresse than the slow Tovière chairs.

Returning from Val-Claret at the end of the day will be much quicker in future thanks to a new high-speed six-person chair-lift direct to Col de Fresse. The Col de Fresse drag-lift is closed to boarders.

If you plan to go back next year, keep your lift pass as you may get a reduction.

MOUNTAIN RESTAURANTS
Getting better

The mountain restaurants mainly consist of big self-service places with vast terraces at the top of major lifts.

La Fruitière at the top of La Daille gondola is relatively new and probably the best. It is done out like a dairy and serves generous portions of classic French food at reasonable prices. Service is friendly and the cheese trolley highly recommended. La Folie Douce is the more functional self-service section above – again, popular with reporters.

The Crech'Ouna just across the slope from the funicular station at La Daille, is a charming, civilised place and now has an outside terrace too. But the food is not all it used to be.

Other recommendations: Le Tufs, just below Crech'Ouna – a newer table-service restaurant, terrace, good pizzas and Savoyard fare; Trifollet, about halfway up the La Daille gondola – table service, great pizzas, terrace

CHILDCARE

Garderie Isabelle (479 411282) at La Daille takes children from age 2½, from 8.30 to 5.30. The Petit Poucet (479 061397) in the Residence les Hameaux at Val takes children aged 3 to 8, from 9am to 5.30. Both provide indoor and outdoor activities and delivery to and collection from ski school.

Snowfun's Club Nounours takes children aged 3 to 6 for lessons of 1hr 30 mins, 2hr or 3hr. Older children can be left in classes all day.

The ESF runs a ski nursery for aged 4 up, with rope tows and a heated chalet.

GETTING THERE

Air Geneva, transfer 4½hr. Chambery, transfer 3½hr. Lyon, transfer 4½hr.

Rail Bourg-St-Maurice (33km); regular buses from station.

overlooking the men's downhill piste; Clocheton, near the cross-country course at Le Châtelard – peaceful, with good views; Marmottes, in the middle of the Bellevarde bowl – big sunny terrace, self-service.

An alternative is to head into town, to a reataurant overlooking the nursery slopes. Our favourite is the big terrace of the Brussels. Bananas does good burgers, steaks, salads and has a small terrace. When at Col de l'Iseran, the most pleasant plan for lunch is to descend to the rustic Arolay at Le Fornet – especially on a wintry day.

SCHOOLS AND GUIDES
A very wide choice

There is a huge choice of schools (15 in the resort brochure) plus private instructors to choose from. We continue to get poor reports on ESF, although some people are happy with them. We've had lots of satisfied Snow Fun pupils: their guides seem to 'know their snow'. We have also had good reports on Alpine Experience, Evolution 2 and Top Ski, who all specialise in taking people off-piste in small groups which they put together – excellent for the more experienced who want to make the most of Val-d'Isère's vast off-piste possibilities. We've had great days off-piste with both Alpine Experience and Top Ski.

Mountain Masters has a reputation for 'inner skiing' teaching methods, has small classes and video analysis.

The Hors-Limites school is said by one reporter to offer 'the best snowboard tuition in the Alps'.

All the schools have teachers who speak good English – in many cases it's their native language. In peak periods it's best to book in advance, especially with some of the off-piste schools who have only a handful of teachers each. Heli-trips can be arranged – you are taken to Italy because they are banned in France.

↑ La Daille: monstrous apartment blocks (background) and traditional chalet-restaurants (foreground)

FACILITIES FOR CHILDREN
Good tour op possibilities

The resort crèches are small, get booked up early and don't cater for the under-2s and many people prefer to use the tour operator facilities.

We have personal experience of the incompetence and indifference of the ESF nursery; stay away.

A new Bibou babysitting service is due to start in 1997/98.

Staying there 🔑

The location of your accommodation isn't crucial. Free shuttle buses run along the main street linking the main lift stations. It is one of the most efficient bus services we've come across; even in peak periods, you never have to wait more than a few minutes. But in the evenings frequency plummets and it may be quicker to walk. Dedicated après-skiers will want to be within walking distance of the town centre. The development up the side valley beyond the main lift station is mainly attractive; some accommodation is a pleasant stroll from the centre, but the farthest flung are a long slog – you need a car or a tour operator that provides transport.

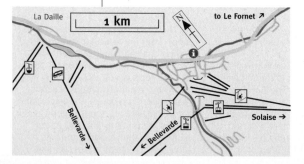

La Daille   1 km   to Le Fornet ↗

Bellevarde →

← Bellevarde

Solaise →

SIMPLY SKI *Chalet specialist*   T **0181 742 2541**   F **0181 995 5346**

Simply Ski offer a choice of five chalets in Val d'Isère sleeping from 8 to 32 guests. Chalet Dauphin is Simply Ski's 'Chalet of Distinction' in Val d'Isère, offering superior levels of comfort, cuisine and service in a prime location. Our largest chalet, Chalet Lores, offers a friendly and sociable atmosphere with its spacious lounge and bar. All our chalets offer fine cuisine accompanied by free Appellation Contrôlée wines, served by friendly chalet staff. Ski leader service free of charge. Flexible travel options include scheduled BA flights, regional charters, Snowtrain, Eurostar and self-drive.

← CHALET DAUPHIN

FINLAYS   T **01835 830562**   F **01835 830550**

Finlays offers a choice of seven chalets in Val d'Isère, all of them in the centre of town and all but one at the edge of the main piste. Sizes vary from 6 to 20, and the majority of bedrooms have private facilities.

We also have chalets in Courchevel 1850 and 1550.

Call us for details and a brochure.

CHALET RATON LAVEUR →

YSE LIMITED   T **0181 871 5117**   F **0181 871 5229**

YSE are the Val d'Isère specialists. They offer more chalets there than anyone else, but only go to Val d'Isère, so it is easy for them to remain efficient and personal, especially with John Yates-Smith in Val d'Isère and Fiona Easdale in London.

YSE's chalets are divided into five price bands, from very civilised catered apartments in a three-star résidence hôtelière to the ultra-smart Mountain Lodges, and including Val d'Isère's most comfortable chalet hotel.

← MOUNTAIN LODGES

ACTIVITIES

Indoor Swimming pool, sports hall (basketball, volleyball, table tennis, badminton, trampoline and gymnastics), library, bridge, health centres in the hotels Christiania, Brussel's and Le Val d'Isère (sauna, hammam, jacuzzi, body building, massages, solarium etc), cinema

Outdoor Walks in Le Manchet valley and Le Fornet, natural skating rink, curling, hang-gliding, quad bikes, all-terrain karts, ice driving, snow-mobiles, paragliding, shoe-snow outings, heli-skiing, microlight trips, bungee jumping

HOW TO GO
Lots of choice

More British tour operators go to Val-d'Isère than to any other resort except Méribel. The choice of chalets and chalet-hotels, in particular, is vast. There is a Club Med 'village'.

Chalets There is everything from budget chalets to the most luxurious you could demand. The resort has a fair number of chalet operators who don't go anywhere else, the most prominent of which are YSE and Val d'Isère Properties.

Both these include some luxury places in their portfolios, as do Simply Ski, Ski Scott Dunn, Finlays and The Ski Company Limited (which has a group of luxury chalets with fabulous views over the Manchet valley – a long way out of town).

YSE also have what is probably the most comfortable chalet-hotel, the Crêtes Blanches. This could be rivalled in 1997/98 by Mark Warner's decision to run the former 4-star Sofitel hotel as a chalet-hotel.

The best-value chalets tend to be away from the centre, at Le Fornet, Le Châtelard and Le Laisinant. Le Ski have a good choice here.

Hotels There are 40 to choose from, mostly 2- and 3-star, but for such a big international resort surprisingly few are notably attractive.

((((4) **Christiania** Recently renovated big chalet, probably best in town. Chic, with friendly staff. Sauna.

((((4) **Latitudes** Modern, stylish. Piano bar, nightclub. Leisure centre: sauna, steam room, whirl-pool, massage.

((((4) **Blizzard** Renovated for Olympics. Indoor-outdoor pool behind. Convenient.

(((3) **Grand Paradis** Excellent position. Good food.

(((3) **Brussels** Excellent position. Large terrace, which is popular for lunch. Leisure centre.

(((3) **Savoyarde** Rustic decor. Leisure centre. Good food. Rooms a bit small.

(((3) **Kandahar** Smart, newish building above Taverne d'Alsace on main street.

(((3) **Sorbiers** Modern but cosy B&B.

(((3) **Samovar** In La Daille. Traditional hotel with good food.

((2) **Kern Basic** but good value.

Self-catering There are thousands of properties to choose from. UK operators offer lots of them, but they tend to get snapped up by early bookers. Local agency Val-d'Isère Agence has a particularly good brochure. As in all French resorts, most apartments are small, but you can find bigger places if you scour the brochures. UK operator Val-d'Isère Properties has a good selection and Finlays is geared up to offer self-catering places.

The Rocher Soleil apartments are worth considering, with their satellite TVs, heated outdoor pool, leisure centre, lounge, bar and restaurant.

EATING OUT
Plenty of good, affordable places

Restaurants here have to satisfy the still predominantly French market, so standards are high and prices lower than in London. Although there are, among the 70-odd restaurants, some which specialise in Italian, Alsatian, Tex-Mex, even Japanese food, most offer good French dishes.

You can get a good meal for less than £15 in numerous very pleasant places, such as the very popular Perdrix Blanche (everything from Savoyard to sushi), and Taverne d'Alsace.

The Crech'Ouna is worth a visit (see Mountain restaurants) if only for the lovely dining room. But our favourite is the newcomer, the Chalet du Cret, off the main road on the way to La Daille.

UK PACKAGES

TOURIST OFFICE

Postcode 73155
Tel +33 479 060660
Fax 479 060456

Set in a beautifully renovated 300-year-old stone farmhouse with splendid wooden beams, it serves a fixed price menu (not cheap) starting with a magnificent hors-d'oeuvres trolley, choice of main dish and dessert – with an excellent wine list.

The best restaurants in the centre of town are the Solaise, Grande Ourse or the hotels Savoyard and Tsanteleina.

Those on tight budgets should try the pizzas in Chez Nano, next to Dick's T-bar, or the Pacific, next to the Moris pub, which serves generous portions of pasta and seafood. G-Jay's serves a good, all-day breakfast.

APRES-SKI
Very lively

Nightlife is surprisingly energetic, given that most people have spent a hard day on the slopes. There are lots of bars but you can save money by following the happy hour crawl from bar to bar, as prices change at different times.

Bananas, G-Jays and the Moris pub fill up as the slopes close and Bar Jacques and the Perdrix Blanche bar are popular with locals. The Pacific has big-screen Sky TV – good for watching big sporting events. Several British-run chalet hotels have bars that get very lively at times. In La Daille the Brighton Rock (run by SkiBound) has cheap happy-hour beer. For a French rather than British atmosphere, try Brasserie des Sports or Boubou's. Taverne d'Alsace is good for comfortable relaxing.

There are lots of late bars, many with music and dancing into the early hours. The famous Dick's T-Bar seems now to be more popular with young, drunken Swedes than with Brits. Couleur Café and Café Face have become more trendy, the latter with good music and a kitchen theme to the decor. Aventure, next to Killy Sports, has household decor, including a fridge, a bath and a bed – it serves good food in a separate eating area. Victors is a Swedish-run restaurant which turns into a bar later on – black and white decor and stainless steel loos. Club 21 is popular with French and stays open latest, though it can be rather seedy with topless dancers and the like.

For those who like a quieter time, there are hotel bars, piano bars and cocktail lounges.

OFF THE SLOPES
Not much, except for sporty types

Val is primarily a resort for those keen to get on to the slopes There are not many other diversions, and it can be difficult getting those who are out on the snow to commit themselves to a pedestrian-accessible lunchtime rendezvous.

The best walks are up the Manchet valley. The range of non-skiing activities is quite wide. But the mainstream facilities are surprisingly poor, although there is a swimming pool which has now been renovated. They could do with a smart new sports centre.

The range of shops is better than in most French resorts.

STAYING DOWN THE VALLEY
Not a great idea

Val-d'Isère is a long way up its dead-end valley. If you're driving out to the Alps you could consider staying half an hour away in rustic Ste-Foy (which has its own delightful and deserted slopes), or even further away in Bourg-St-Maurice. But if you do that you'll really want to consider exploring different resorts each day rather than just Val-d'Isère.

Valmorel

1400m

Disneyland in the Alps

HOW IT RATES

The slopes

Snow	★★★
Extent	★★★
Experts	★★
Intermediates	★★★★
Beginners	★★★★★
Convenience	★★★★★
Queues	★★★★
Restaurants	★★

The rest

Scenery	★★★
Resort charm	★★★★
Off-slope	★★

What's new

The main Beaudin chair-lift out of town will be replaced by a new covered high-speed quad in time for the 1997/98 season. This will cut the journey time by around two-thirds and should solve the queue problem in the village. There will also be a couple of new drag-lifts.

There are six new snow guns: four beneath the gondola, two in the children's snow gardens.

Electronic lift pass processing was introduced last season.

⊕ Fairly extensive slopes provide something for everyone

⊕ The most sympathetically designed French purpose-built resort

⊕ Largely slope-side accommodation

⊕ Beginners and children particularly well catered for

⊕ One of the most accessible of the Tarentaise resorts

⊕ Relatively cheap package holidays

⊖ Few challenging runs

⊖ Fairly low in altitude, so good snow not guaranteed

⊖ Little variety in accommodation and in restaurants and bars

⊖ A couple of bottlenecks mar a good lift system

This is the purpose-built resort where they got it right. Built from scratch in the mid-1970s, Valmorel was intended to look and feel like a mountain village: a traffic-free main street with low-rise hamlets grouped around it and along the lower slopes, and traditional Savoie stone and wood materials throughout. The end-result is an attractive, friendly sort of place, even if it does have a 'Disneyland' feel to it.

The slopes are extensive by most standards – though Valmorel can't rival its huge neighbours, the Three Valleys or Val-d'Isère-Tignes. But with good snow conditions and the whole system open, there's enough here to keep everyone except experts happy. As the snow conditions deteriorate, the variety of available runs reduces rapidly and the flaws in the lift system can start to show through.

Unashamedly aimed at the middle ground (intermediates, families and mixed-ability groups), Valmorel does have considerable appeal because it has been so well put together.

boarding *Valmorel is a good place to try boarding for the first time – there's a separate beginners' slope and gentle runs to progress to served by chairs and gondolas. There's a fun-park and half-pipe when snow permits but few slopes (except off-piste) to challenge advanced boarders, who should look towards one of the bigger neighbours. Nightlife is far from throbbing in this family-oriented resort.*

The resort

Valmorel, a short drive from Moûtiers, is the main resort in 'Le Grand Domaine' – a ski area that links the Tarentaise with the Maurienne, by way of the Col de la Madeleine. Happily for Valmorel and its visitors, the place was built with more than just convenience in mind – it also manages to look pretty good. Bourg-Morel is the heart of the resort – a traffic-free street where you'll find most of the shops, the restaurants, visitor information – just about everything – in a 200m stretch. It's pleasant and usually lively, with a distinctly family feel. And the slopes are right at hand, with the main pistes back and chair-lift out meeting at the end of the street. Nearby is an information board showing lift and piste status, and what's on locally.

Dotted around the hillside, but not very far from the Bourg-Morel centre, are the six 'hameaux' which contain most of the accommodation. Most of it is self-catering and of a reasonably high standard.

We've had a report of a jolly New Year's Eve in town, with lots of fireworks, a parade and torch jugglers.

MOUNTAIN FACTS

Altitude 1200m-2550m
Lifts	50
Pistes	163km
Green/Blue	69%
Red	19%
Black	12%
Artificial snow	7km

A rarity: a modern French resort built to be in harmony with its surroundings →

The mountains

Beginners and intermediates will take to it. Those looking for more of a challenge will find it more limited. Variety is provided by a number of sectors of quite distinctive character, and the system is big enough to provide interesting, if hardly epic, exploratory trips to its farthest boundaries. Some visitors find the piste map inadequate, especially for the Longchamps sector, and there are a couple of long, awkward drag-lifts.

THE SLOPES
A big system in miniature

The 50 lifts and 163km of piste spread out in an interesting arrangement over a number of minor valleys and ridges either side of the Col de la Madeleine, with Valmorel at the eastern extremity of the system and runs coming down into the village on three sides.

The most heavily used route out of the village is via the **Beaudin** chair which takes you over the main pistes back. This lift is to be replaced in time for the 1997/98 season. From the top of the chair a network of lifts and

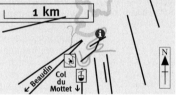

FRANCE

LIFT PASSES

/97 prices in francs
Le Grand Domaine
Covers all lifts in
Valmorel and St-
François Longchamp.
Beginners Limited
area lift pass covers
beginner lifts and
runs.
Main pass
1-day pass 167
6-day pass 898
(low season 711 –
21% off)
Senior citizens
Over 60: 6-day pass
768 (14% off)
Children
Under 13: 6-day pass
768 (14% off)
Under 4: free pass
Short-term passes
Half-day from 11.30
(146) and 12.30 (124).
Saturday morning
until 1pm (124).
Alternative passes
Valmorel Domaine
covers 33 lifts in
Valmorel only (6 days
857 for adults, 722
for children).

pistes takes you over to the **Col de la Madeleine** and beyond that to Lauzière (the highest point of the ski area at 2550m) or the slopes of **Saint-François** and **Longchamp** at the far western end of the area.

The Pierrafort gondola for the **Mottet** sector and the Crève-Cœur chair for the **Gollet** area take off from Hameau-du-Mottet at the top end of the village. Both have their own runs back towards the village, or the more experienced can work their way over to the Beaudin and Madeleine sectors (tough runs down only). There's an easy link in the other direction.

Adjacent to the village there are nursery areas with good easy runs.

All the mega-ski areas of the Tarentaise are within reasonable driving distance – the Trois Vallées, La Plagne, Les Arcs and even Val-d'Isère-Tignes. An off-piste tour through a number of these resorts starts from the Col du Mottet above Valmorel.

SNOW RELIABILITY
Sort of average

With a top station of 2550m and many of the runs below 2000m, good snow conditions are not guaranteed. Lower runs are frequently closed, and even Lauzière, which has the system's high point but faces south, can suffer quite quickly during sunny spells. Mottet is north-facing and usually has the best snow.

Artificial snowmaking covers the almost 600m vertical from Beaudin down to village level. And more is being installed for 1997/98.

FOR EXPERTS
Better than you might think

Although not renowned for its tough slopes, there are challenging runs. Gollet is usually a good place for moguls – plenty of them, but not too big and not too hard. In 1997 we did a great off-piste run from here with a guide, which started with a long traverse from the top of the drag-lift and ended right down in the village of Les Avanchers, way below Valmorel, passing through forests and over streams on the way.

There are steep black runs below the top section of the Mottet chair and some interesting off-piste variants. From the drag-lift up towards the Madeleine sector, there are a couple of fine runs (one off-piste) which generally have good snow.

The Lauzière chair can seem a bit of a trek, but once there you'll probably find it under-used and a lot of fun, provided it hasn't suffered too much sun. There are three marked runs and plenty of acreage in which to pick your own route – there are some steep pitches and often some big bumps. You can also explore a lovely deserted north-facing off-piste run here if you hire a guide – in 1997 we found long stretches of great powder over a week after the last snowfall.

Touring is a popular activity in the region, and trips such as the Nine-Valley safari can be organised.

FOR INTERMEDIATES
Plenty to keep you busy

Lots of scope, though a lot of people seem to mill around Beaudin and the Arenouillaz drag and Biollène chair – the adjacent runs are quite friendly. The runs down into the Celliers valley are more testing, particularly the two reds served by the Madeleine chair, which are too difficult for early intermediates to cope with comfortably.

The main thoroughfare back to the village – from Beaudin along the line of the snow cannons – is graded blue then red, and the red stretch can be quite daunting at the end of the day. The artificial snow tends to pile up in surprisingly large heaps, as do tired beginners.

For a day out, the slopes around Saint-François-Longchamp are within easy striking distance, and form a big area of mainly broad, flattering runs.

The red route from the top of Mottet is outstandingly boring on the upper half – more push-and-walk than anything else – but the views are some compensation, and the lower half is much better.

The runs back to the village, served by the Pierrafort gondola, are graded blue but are long, interesting and in parts tricky.

The adjacent Gollet slopes also provide plenty of scope for good intermediates to amuse themselves.

FOR BEGINNERS
An excellent choice

Valmorel suits beginners – there are dedicated learning areas right by the village for both adults (at Bois de la Croix) and children (in the snow garden of the children's club), and lots of expertise among the instructors.

SCHOOLS/GUIDES

96/97 prices in francs

ESF

Classes 6 days
2½hr am or pm
6 half-days: 585
Children's classes
Ages: 4 to 12
6 half-days: 545
Private lessons
Hourly
174 for 1 or 2 people

GETTING THERE

Air Geneva, transfer
3½hr. Lyon, transfer
3½hr. Chambery,
transfer 2½hr.

Rail Moûtiers (18km);
regular buses from
station.

CHILDCARE

Saperlipopette (479
098445) provides
care for children aged
from 6 months to 7
years, from 8.30 to
5pm. Those aged 18
months to 3 are given
'a gentle and amusing
first experience with
the snow'. Those
aged 3 to 7 have
indoor activities as
well as ski classes
(divided into three
levels), and there is a
snow play area for
those who do not
wish to ski.

The terrain does not allow extensive nursery areas in the valley, so progress from novice to beginner usually sees the children heading for the top of the Pierrafort gondola and the adults for the Beaudin sector.

The lifts accessing these areas can be used to return to the village.

If the snow-cover is complete, there is a very pleasant green run through the trees down to Combelouvière.

FOR CROSS-COUNTRY
Inconvenient and not extensive

Valmorel is not the place for aficionados; more for those giving it a try. Trails adding up to 23km, at a number of different locations in the valley (and therefore likely to have a limited season only), can be reached by special bus from Valmorel itself.

QUEUES
Occasional (avoidable) problems

The main Beaudin chair out of the village has been a problem in the past. But the new high-speed replacement for 1997/98 should cut the queues – and hopefully ease the pressure on the gondola, too.

Once into the slopes, there are only two bottlenecks to worry about – the Madeleine chair, which provides the only access to the Saint-François and Lauzière side, and the Frêne drag, almost as critical to the return journey. Simply avoid them at peak times.

MOUNTAIN RESTAURANTS
Fair to middling

There are half a dozen or so mountain restaurants, none of them either appalling or wonderful. The Altipano at the top of the gondola has been recommended by recent reporters for good food and value for money, though it lacks much atmosphere. Prariond, lower down, is livelier but more expensive, with good food and loud music. L'Arbet at the top of Lanchettes sells reasonably priced food.

SCHOOLS AND GUIDES
Good, especially for first-timers

We've had several good reports this year on the school. Instructors generally speak good English and are enthusiastic and imaginative. The main criticism is the familiar one that classes can be too large – plus the fact that English-speaking classes are sometimes held in the afternoons only.

Teaching for first-timers and for children is a speciality of the resort, and likely to produce good results.

FACILITIES FOR CHILDREN
First-rate but book early

Saperlipopette is a comprehensive childcare facility. Reports vary wildly, however. One parent told us: 'Our four-year-old couldn't wait to get to Saperlipopette each day but our six-year-old refused to go back after one day on the grounds of boredom.'

Another parent was very unhappy with the whole organisation. She told us: 'It was run like a battery chicken farm. Children were given numbers and ordered around. The staff seemed very cold and impersonal.' This reporter's four-year-old daughter became 'more and more distraught with each visit'.

Prices vary with the seasons. Advance booking is essential except for very quiet times.

Staying there

Valmorel is a traffic-free resort, with drop-off points for the accommodation. At the bottom end of Bourg-Morel is the base station of the Télébourg, a cross-village lift providing access to the 'Hameau-du-Mottet'.

Between the other hameaux and Bourg-Morel, walking doesn't take long – but some of the pathways should be graded red. Hameau-du-Mottet probably wins the convenience contest – it is at the top of the Télébourg, and access to main lifts and from return runs is good.

A car is of no use in the resort but very handy for trips to other resorts of the Tarentaise.

HOW TO GO
Take a package for value

Self-catering packages are the norm in Valmorel, though there are quite a few catered chalets available too. There are few hotels in Valmorel, but tour operators have an allocation in most of them. If you're travelling independently and prefer quieter more traditional rustic surroundings, Les Avanchers is a possibility.

Chalets Though there are more on the market each year, the range isn't wide – most are actually catered apartments.

Hotels There are only three hotels, and only the central hotel du Bourg expects casual callers – the others, up the hill

UK PACKAGES

AA Ski-Driveaway,
Altours Ski, Bladon
Lines, Crystal, Equity
School Ski, Equity
Total Ski, Fairhand
Holidays,
Independent Ski
Links, Inghams,
Lagrange, Made to
Measure, Motours,
Neilson, Ski Leisure
Direction, Stena Line
Holidays, Thomson,
Travelscene Ski-Drive

ACTIVITIES

Indoor Cinema
Outdoor Snow-shoe
outings, 12km of
prepared walks,
floodlit skiing,
paragliding

TOURIST OFFICE

Postcode 73260
Tel +33 479 098555
Fax 479 098529

a little way, basically cater for people staying the week on half-board.
《《③ **Planchamp** Best in town, family run, with a good French restaurant.
《② **Hotel du Bourg** Simple place in the middle of Bourg-Morel – not recommended by this year's reporter.
《② **La Fontaine** Across the piste from the Planchamp.
Self-catering Most people do – 8,500 apartment beds are distributed throughout the six hamlets and they are generally well-equipped. While it's great having a view over the piste, the downside of certain locations in Mottet and Planchamp is the proximity of some very noisy snow guns: the sound-proofing is not quite good enough for light sleepers.

EATING OUT
Good enough but rarely thrilling
You can check out the menus of most of Valmorel's restaurants in 15 minutes wandering up and down the main street. The pattern soon emerges – pizzas, pasta, fondues and a smattering of Savoie fare. There's also couscous and galettes available; not a huge variety but enough, and you're likely to get decent food and fair value. Many of the places need to be booked for any chance of a seat at a reasonable time.

The restaurant of hotel Planchamp is a relatively upmarket place with prices to match. The Vadrouille does local dishes and has a lively atmosphere. The Petit Savoyarde is a mid-range place recommended by reporters. The Grenier in Mottet offers a bit of everything, in a slightly different location. Locals also recommend the Grange (formerly La Galette), the Perce Neige and tex-mex at Jimbololo. A pizza or shared fondue in the popular Chez Albert or the Petit Prince is the best bet if you're on a tight budget.

APRES-SKI
Unexciting
Immediate après-ski is centred on the outdoor cafés at the end of Bourg-Morel and Le Grenier. Both are lively spots. The after-dark activities are, like everything else, concentrated around that main street. Café de la Gare has live music, Ski Roc and Petit Prince are popular with locals, while the Perce-Neige frequently gets packed and boisterous. Cocktails can be enjoyed in more polished surroundings at the Shaker in hotel La Fontaine. There's one disco, Jeans, which is often neglected but occasionally buzzes.

You may catch the occasional musical event at the village hall, or a street parade (there's a Mardi Gras with medieval costumes and fireworks). A two-screen cinema and a wine-tasting evening are other possibilities.

OFF THE SLOPES
Pleasant but boring
It's not a great place to hang around if you're not using the slopes– there are some marginal activities which, together with the usual café-based pastimes, can help to pass a few days. There are some cleared walks around the village and at the top of all the main lifts; and there's a pretty baroque church and some good lunch venues in Les Avanchers. Several mid-mountain restaurants are accessible to pedestrians, and it's also quite a practical proposition for those using the slopes to return to the village for a lunchtime meet.

Snow-shoe treks and dog-sleigh trips can be organised – you can even learn to 'mush' the dogs.

STAYING DOWN THE VALLEY
Appealing
There are several small hotels in Les Avanchers handy enough if you prefer the ambience of the old village, and you have a car.

Val-Thorens 2300m

Europe's highest resort, with guaranteed good snow

WHAT IT COSTS

((((5)

HOW IT RATES

The slopes

Snow	*****
Extent	*****
Experts	****
Intermediates	*****
Beginners	****
Convenience	*****
Queues	***
Restaurants	****

The rest

Scenery	***
Resort charm	*
Off-slope	**

What's new

For 1997/98 the Cîme de Caron cable-car is to get bigger cabins – a bold development, since they're already among the world's biggest. The Moutière chair-lift – accessing many of the best slopes from below the resort – is being replaced by a fast six-seater.

- Extensive local slopes to suit all standards, and good access to the rest of the famous Three Valleys
- The highest resort in the Alps, with north-facing slopes guaranteeing good snow for a long season
- Compact village with direct slope access from most accommodation

- Purpose-built style doesn't suit all tastes, although efforts to make the village more attractive have helped
- Can be bleak in bad weather – not a tree in sight
- Not much to do off the slopes
- Some very busy piste intersections
- Not queue-free, although new lifts will help in future

For the enthusiast looking for the best snow, it's difficult to think of anywhere better than Val-Thorens. It has the highest slopes in the Three Valleys (up to 3200m) and a couple of glaciers, guaranteeing good snow conditions for a long season – October to May (the glaciers are open in summer as well).

The resort was purpose-built in the early 1970s. It has always been one of the more attractive French high-altitude efforts, with less low-rent accommodation than usual; and efforts to smarten the place up further have paid off – it's now mainly car-free, trees have been planted and the compact design, with friendly squares, makes it feel more pleasant than most rivals.

boarding *The best resort-level snow in Europe appeals to boarders as well as skiers – and pulls in considerable numbers. There are pistes to suit all abilities, and the good snow is great for beginners and carvers. For free-riders, there's plenty of off-piste choice, though if you want trees you'll have to travel. The lifts are now mainly chairs and gondolas, though one or two drags remain. There's a fun-park towards the bottom of the Caron sector, served by a fast chair, but you have to leave the valley to find a half-pipe. Nightlife centres around bars and a couple of discos which, because of all the young people in the resort (especially Scandinavians), are usually noisy and entertaining.*

MOUNTAIN FACTS

Altitude 1300m-3200m
Lifts 200
Pistes 600km
Green/Blue 49%
Red 37%
Black 14%
Artificial snow 80km
Recco detectors used

LIFT PASSES

97/98 prices in francs
Three Valleys
Covers all lifts in
Courchevel, La Tania,
Méribel, Val-Thorens,
Les Menuires and St-
Martin-de-Belleville.
Beginners 4 free lifts
in Val-Thorens.
Main pass
1-day pass 220
6-day pass 1,080
(low season 972 –
10% off)
Senior citizens
Over 60: 6-day pass
864 (20% off)
Over 75: free pass
Children
Under 16: 6-day pass
810 (25% off)
Under 5: free pass
Short-term passes
Half-day passes (from
12.30) available for
Val-Thorens lifts
(adult 128) and the 3
Valleys (adult 165).
Notes 6-day pass and
over valid for one day
each in Tignes-Val-
d'Isère, La Plagne-Les
Arcs, Pralognan-la-
Vanoise and Les
Saisies. 70- to 75-
year-olds get a 50%
discount on pass
price (6-day pass
540). Reductions for
families.
Alternative passes
Vallée des Belleville
pass covers 75 lifts
and 240km piste in
Val-Thorens, Les
Menuires and St-
Martin (adult 6-day
1010). Val-Thorens-
only pass covers 31
lifts and 120km of
piste (adult 6-day
810).

The resort

Val-Thorens is built high above the tree line on a west-facing mountainside at the head of the Belleville valley. It is a classic purpose-built resort, with lots of slope-side accommodation. But it is not as hideous as some – notably Les Menuires, just down the road. The buildings are mainly medium-rise and wood-clad, and some are distinctly stylish. The village has streets that are now largely traffic-free (although fume-filled on Saturdays). There are shopping arcades, a fair choice of bars and restaurants, and a good sports centre. Despite the northerly orientation of the slopes, the village is quite sunny. A reliable, free bus service makes getting around quite easy.

The mountains

Take account of its abundance of high slopes, the extent of its local slopes and the easy access to the other resorts of the Three Valleys, and the attraction of Val-Thorens to enthusiasts becomes clear. The main disadvantage is the lack of trees. Val-Thorens can be bleak in cold weather – and heavy snowfalls or wind can shut practically all the lifts and slopes.

THE SLOPES
High and snowsure
The resort has a wide piste going right down the front of it leading down to a number of different lifts out. The biggest is the enormous Funitel de **Péclet** gondola, with 25-person cabins. This takes you to one of the two glaciers, each with its own lifts.

The larger **Montée du Fond** area can be reached from Péclet or directly from the resort. From the top of a network of ideal intermediate runs you can descend into the relatively new 'Fourth Valley', the **Maurienne**. The slopes extend half-way down to the valley, and a 12-person gondola now comes up from Orelle in the valley bottom. If the lira ever gets stronger, expect Italians to pour through the Fréjus tunnel and up this lift.

The **Cîme de Caron** cable-car to the highest lift-served point in the Three Valleys, at 3200m, can be reached from the Montée du Fond area or by taking a gondola or fast chair from below the village.

Going the opposite way up from the resort leads you to the Méribel slopes via two chair-lifts. Les Menuires can be reached using these lifts too, or by taking the easy Boulevard Cumin along the valley floor.

SNOW RELIABILITY
Difficult to beat
Few resorts can rival Val-Thorens for reliably good snow cover – accounted for by its altitude and the north-facing direction of most of its slopes. The only place where you are likely to find poor snow is on the west-facing runs on the way back from an excursion to the Méribel valley and on the south-facing runs down into the Maurienne valley. But the addition of snow guns has helped alleviate what few problems there were.

FOR EXPERTS
Few big challenges on-piste
Val-Thorens' local slopes are primarily intermediate terrain. But you'll enjoy racing down the good snow on predominantly red runs. The runs down from the Cîme de Caron cable-car are the most challenging – with the red around the side narrower than the black down the face, and almost as steep. The Cascades run back into town from the Péclet direction is also worth trying, and served by a fast 6-seater chair. The Marielle Goitschel run down from the connection with Méribel is one of the easiest blacks we've come across – but its snow suffers from being south-facing and from the traffic travelling to Val-Thorens.

There are three good itinéraires. Two lead to the bottom of the chair in the Maurienne valley. And the long Lac du Lou itinéraire leaves from the summit of the Cîme de Caron and joins the run from the La Masse area of Les Menuires. There is also a great deal of unmarked off-piste area, for which you will need a guide.

FOR INTERMEDIATES
Unbeatable quality and quantity
Although Val-Thorens is not in the centre of the Three Valleys, it will take a decent intermediate only 90 minutes or so to get to Courchevel at the far end, if not distracted by the endless runs on the way. The scope for intermediates throughout the Three Valleys is enormous.

The local slopes in Val-Thorens are some of the best intermediate terrain in the region. Most of the pistes are

SCHOOLS/GUIDES

97/98 prices in francs

ESF
Classes 6 days
3hr: am; 2½hr: pm
6 mornings: 690
Children's classes
Ages: 4 to 12
6 mornings: 595
Private lessons
Hourly
170 for 1 to 2 people

International
Known as Ski Cool
Classes 6 days
3hr, am or pm
6 mornings: 700
Children's classes
Ages: up to 12
5 mornings: 540
Private lessons
Hourly or daily
190 for 1hr, for 1 to 2
people

OTHER SCHOOLS

Ski Surf Nature
Prosneige
Espace Goitschel

CHILDCARE

Marielle Goitschel's
Children's Village
(479 000047) takes
children aged from 3
to 16, from 9am to
5.30, 7 days a week.
The ESF can provide
all-day care and offers
classes for children
from age 2. It also
runs Mini club crèches
in two locations, at
the top and bottom
of the resort, taking
children from age 3
months.

GETTING THERE

Air Geneva, transfer
3½hr. Lyon, transfer
3½hr. Chambery,
transfer 2½hr.

Rail Moûtiers (37km);
regular buses from
station.

easy cruising reds and blues, made
even more enjoyable by the usually
excellent powdery snow.

The snow on the red Col run is
always some of the best around. The
blue Moraine below it is gentle and
popular with the schools. The runs on
the top half of the mountain are
steeper than those back into the
resort. The Montée du Fond 1 and 2
lifts serve a good variety of red runs.
Adventurous intermediates shouldn't
miss the Combe du Caron black run
underneath the cable-car: it is very
wide and usually has good snow.

FOR BEGINNERS
Good late-season choice
The slopes at the foot of the resort are
very gentle and provide convenient,
snowsure nursery slopes. There aren't
any ideal long green runs to progress
to, but the blues back into town are
very easy. Because of the resort's
height and bleakness, beginners can
find it cold early in the season and
intimidating in bad weather.

FOR CROSS-COUNTRY
Try elsewhere
Val-Thorens is a poor base for cross-
country, with only 4km of local trails.

QUEUES
A few bad lift bottlenecks
The lift system is far from perfect.
There are some state-of-the-art lifts,
but also lots of antiquated ones – and
even some of the more modern ones
generate queues. The biggest queues
are at the slow, old, two-person Col
chair (now fed by a high-speed quad,
so it's not surprising queues build up)
and for the Cîme de Caron cable-car.
Hour-long queues have been reported
– more than one reporter has spent a
week in the resort without riding the
cable-car once, because the queues
were so off-putting. Happily, its
capacity is to be increased for the
1997/98 season.

There can also be long queues for
the 3 Vallées 1 and Plein Sud chair-lifts
back towards Méribel in mid-afternoon,
and for the short village lift at the end
of the day. The Côtes Brune and Plain
Main chairs are also possible bottlenecks. Reporters who've been here in
high season when snow has been in
short supply elsewhere tell us that
queues can become a significant
problem, particularly if people are
bussed in from lower resorts.

MOUNTAIN RESTAURANTS
Lots of choice
Moutière, just below the top of the
chair of the same name, is one of the
more reasonably priced of Val-Thorens'
mountain huts (which are generally
expensive). We like the Chalet de
Génépi, on the run down from the
Moraine chair, and so do several of our
reporters. It has great views, an open
fire, good soup and, if you're lucky, a
medley of sixties hits.

The Plan Bouchet refuge in the
Maurienne valley is very popular and
welcoming, but bar service can be
slow. You can stay the night there too.

On the other side of the valley, the
Chalet Plain Sud, below the chair of
the same name, has excellent views.
The Chalet de Thorens at the bottom
of the Fond 1 and Moraine lifts has
been praised for the quality of its food
and reasonable prices.

SCHOOLS AND GUIDES
Plenty of courses
There are two main schools, the ESF
and the International (known as Ski
Cool), which between them offer a
wide range of options. We've had good
reports of private lessons with both
schools. As well as the usual group
lessons, the ESF have shorter duration,
smaller-class sessions (two hours for
five days, with a maximum of eight).
They also have a Trois Vallées group
for those who want to cover a lot of
ground while receiving tuition. This is
available by the day or the week, and
can include off-piste. Ski Cool also
offer numerous courses, with the
bonus of class sizes guaranteed not to
exceed ten. They specialise in teaching
beginners, who get an extra day's
tuition (six instead of five), and offer
an 'Evoluski' package that includes
equipment hire and lift pass. Tuition is
ski évolutif: you start on short skis and
work your way up. Ski Cool also have
off-piste courses. There are several
specialist guiding outfits.

FACILITIES FOR CHILDREN
Not impressed
In the past we have recommended the
ESF crèche at the top of the village.
Some reporters are happy with it, one
describing the style of tuition as 'brutal
but effective'. Others have described it
as 'complete chaos', and report having
to rescue children abandoned on the
slopes. Thomson's Peter Polar Bear
Club is 'absolutely excellent'.

UK PACKAGES

AA Ski-Driveaway, Airtours, Altours Ski, Bladon Lines, Crystal, Erna Low, Fairhand Holidays, First Choice Ski, Independent Ski Links, Inghams, Lagrange, Made to Measure, Motours, Neilson, On The Piste Travel Ltd, Ski Choice, Ski France, Ski Leisure Direction, Ski Les Alpes, Ski Valkyrie, Ski trek, Skiworld, Stena Line Holidays, Thomson, Travelscene Ski-Drive, UCPA, Virgin Snow, White Roc

ACTIVITIES

Indoor Sports centre (tennis, squash, climbing wall, roller, golf simulator, swimming pool, saunas, jacuzzi, volley ball, weight training, table tennis, fitness, badminton, football), games rooms, music recitals, cinema, beauty centre
Outdoor Walks, snow-mobiles, snow-shoe excursions, para-gliding

TOURIST OFFICE

Postcode 73440
Tel +33 479 000808
Fax 479 000004

Even if your resort is effectively on the slopes, it's still nice to have lunch somewhere that's *really* on the slopes
→

Staying there 🗝

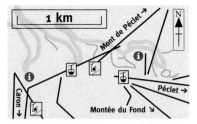

Everywhere is convenient for the slopes, but there are two distinct parts of the village, separated by a nursery slope. There is more animation in Péclet than in the lower Caron.

HOW TO GO
Surprisingly high level of comfort
Accommodation is of a higher standard than many French purpose-built villages, with plenty of choice too.
Chalets These are catered apartments, and many are quite comfortable.
Hotels There are plenty of hotels, mainly 3-stars. Most are grouped around the nursery slope.
(((((5)) **Fitz Roy** Swanky but charming Relais & Châteaux place with lovely rooms and about the best food in town. Pool. Well placed.
(((((4)) **Val Thorens** Welcoming and comfortable; next door to the Fitz Roy.
(((((3)) **Sherpa** Highly recommended for pleasant atmosphere and excellent, substantial food. Less-than-ideal position at the top of the resort.
(((((3)) **Bel Horizon** Friendly, family-run 3-star, popular with reporters – 'cuisine wonderful'; south-facing rooms. On piste near bottom of resort.
Self-catering There is a wide range of options, including apartments of a higher standard than usual in France.

EATING OUT
Surprisingly wide range
Val-Thorens has something for most tastes – there's even a glossy guide to the local restaurants. At the top of the

range, gourmets will enjoy the Fitz Roy hotel and Chalet des Glaciers. Sherpa is another hotel with fine cuisine. Reporters have recommended the Montana in Caron. Tavern le Scapin du Lou is a nice brasserie. Matafan, El Gringo's Café and the Temples du Soleil pizzeria are informal places. The Galoubet in the Place du Caron has been praised for its steaks.

APRES-SKI
Getting there
Val-Thorens is livelier at night than many of our reporters expected. Most people recommend the Ski Rock Café (with karaoke), El Gringo's (with a pub and karaoke as well as its good Mexican restaurant) and the Frog and Roast Beef (with cheap food and live music). The Lincoln, Viking and Malaysia cellar bar (live music) were also mentioned. There are three discos.

OFF THE SLOPES
Forget it
Val-Thorens is basically about skiing and boarding. There's a good sports centre and you can get up to some of the mountain restaurants, but not the best, by lift. The swimming pool is small, overcrowded and expensive.

Vars

1850m

A less attractive alternative to Risoul – except for speed-skiers

WHAT IT COSTS

(((3))

HOW IT RATES

The slopes

Snow	***
Extent	***
Experts	**
Intermediates	****
Beginners	***
Convenience	****
Queues	****
Restaurants	**

The rest

Scenery	***
Resort charm	**
Off-slope	**

What's new

The Risoul/Vars snowmaking setup was extended for 1997; both resorts now have coverage on several runs to the villages.

MOUNTAIN FACTS

Altitude	1660m-2750m
Lifts	53
Pistes	170km
Green/Blue	55%
Red	34%
Black	11%
Artificial snow	4km

UK PACKAGES

Fairhand Holidays, Lagrange, Motours

TOURIST OFFICE

Postcode 05560
Tel +33 492 465131
Fax 492 465654

Vars is a purpose-built resort in the southern French Alps, its sunny slopes linked to the shadier ones of Risoul to form a fair-sized area – largely of intermediate steepness, but topped by the world's fastest speed-skiing course.

THE RESORT

Vars includes several small, old villages (of which one, Vars-Ste-Marie, has lifts into the slopes) on or near the road running southwards towards the 2111m Col de Vars. But for winter visitors it mainly consists of purpose-built Vars-les-Claux, higher up the road. The resort has convenience and reasonable prices in common with Risoul, but is bigger and has far more in the way of shops, restaurants, hotels, nightlife and other amenities such as squash and saunas. There are a lot of block-like apartments, but Les Claux is not a complete eyesore, thanks mainly to surrounding woodland. There are two centres: the original and geographic one where the main gondola starts, with most of the accommodation and shopping, and Point-show – a collection of bars, restaurants and shops, at another main lift station, 10 minutes' walk away. The resort is very French, and locals are friendly to those making some attempt at the native tongue.

THE MOUNTAINS

There are **slopes** on both sides of the village, linked by pistes and by chair-lift at the lower end of Les Claux. The wooded, west-facing Peynier area is much the smaller of the two sectors, and reaches only 2275m – though there is a reasonable descent down to Ste-Marie at 1660m. The main slopes are in an east-facing bowl beneath the Crête de Chabrières (2750m) with direct links to the slopes of Risoul at the top and lower down at the Col des Saluces. The speed skiing course is at the top (you can have a go at it, via the ski school), with one or two black slopes nearby. Beneath it are easy runs, open at the top but descending into trees towards the village, with areas of red runs on either side.

The main slopes get the morning sun, and are centred around the 2000m mark, so **snow reliability** is not particularly good, although there is quite a large area of snowmaking.

There is little of challenge for **experts**, though the Crête de Chabrières top section accesses some off-piste, an unpisted route and a tricky couloir at Col de Crevoux.

Most of the area is fine for **intermediates**, with a good mixture of comfortable reds (including long ones down to Ste-Marie) and easy blues, particularly in the main bowl.

Beginners have a nursery area of free lifts conveniently close to central Vars, with plenty of 'graduation' runs throughout the area. Quick learners will be able to get over to Risoul by the end of the week.

There is a terrain park for **snowboarders**, but no half-pipe.

There are **cross-country** trails that start at the edge of town, but those above Ste-Marie are more extensive. **Queues** are rare outside the French holidays, and even then Vars is not overrun as some family resorts are.

There are few **mountain restaurants**, and none worth noting. Most people eat in Vars or Risoul.

At the **ski school**, the lack of English-speaking tuition is an obvious problem. The well-equipped crèche takes **children** aged 18 months to four years. The school also has a nursery and a ski kindergarten.

STAYING THERE

Les Claux is dominated by **apartment** accommodation. Of the **hotels**, Le Caribou is the smartest place in town (with a swimming pool). L'Ecureuil is an attractive modern chalet (with no restaurant). There are more hotels in the lower villages, including Ste-Marie.

The range of **restaurants** is impressive, with numerous good-value pizzerias, crêperies and fondue places, and places like Chez Plumot doing proper French cuisine.

Après-ski is quite animated at tea-time, but less so after dinner, except during holidays and weekends when the two discos warm up.

Off-slope amenities are rather disappointing, given the size of Vars.

The French Pyrenees

It took us a long time to get round to visiting the resorts of the French Pyrenees – mainly because we had the idea that they were second-rate compared with the Alps. Well, it is certainly true that they can't compete in terms of size of ski area with the mega-resorts of the Trois Vallées and La Plagne. But don't dismiss them: they have considerable attractions, including price – hotels cost half as much as in the Alps and beers up the mountain at FF12 can't be bad.

We went with several pre-conceived ideas, not least that the Pyrenees are hills compared with the mountains of the Alps. Not true: the Pyrenees are serious mountains, and have dramatic picturesque scenery too. They are also attractively French. Unlike the big plastic mega resorts, many Pyrenean bases have a rustic, rural Gallic charm.

The biggest ski area is shared by **Barèges** and **La Mongie**. Between them they have 120km of runs (only 30km less than Les Arcs, for example) and 50 lifts. The runs are best suited to intermediates, with good tree-lined runs above Barèges and open bowl skiing above La Mongie. The best bet for an expert is to try off-piste with a guide – one beautiful run away from all the lifts starts with a scramble through a hole in the rocks. There are atmospheric mountain huts dotted around the slopes. Barèges is a spa village set in a narrow, steep-sided valley, which gets little sun in mid-winter. It's also the second oldest ski resort in France and the pioneer of skiing in the Pyrenees. Accommodation is mainly in basic 1-star and 2-star hotels. Its rather drab buildings and one main street grow on you, though there's little to do in the evenings other than visit the thermal spa and a restaurant (of which there are a good number serving solid local fare). La Mongie, on the other hand, is a purpose-built resort reminiscent of the Alps.

Cauterets is another spa town but a complete contrast with Barèges. It is much bigger (18,000 beds compared with 3,500) and set in a wide, sunny valley. It is a popular summer destination and even in March we were able to sit at a pavement café with a drink after dinner. It feels rather like a town in Provence rather than a ski resort. Indeed it wasn't until 1964 that skiing started here when the cable-car to the slopes 850m above the town was built – you have to ride down as well as up. There are only 30km of slopes, set in an open, semi-circular bowl that can be cold and windy. A decent intermediate could cover all the runs in a day and there's little to challenge an expert. But Cauterets' jewel is its cross-country, set a long drive or bus-ride from town at Pont d'Espagne and served by a gondola. It is the start of the Pyrenees National Park and the old smugglers' route over the mountains between France and Spain. The 36km of snowsure cross-country tracks run up this beautiful deserted valley, beside a rushing stream and a stunning waterfall.

The other major Pyrenean resort is **St-Lary-Soulan**, a traditional village with houses built of stone, with a cable-car at the edge going up to the slopes, of which there are 80km, suiting mainly intermediates. There's a satellite called **St-Lary-Espiaube** which is purpose-built and right at the heart of the slopes, up the road from the old village.

All the areas welcome snowboarders but Cauterets provides the most facilities and is the Pyrenees' leading boarding resort.

Italy

For a few years now Italy has been a booming winter destination. Most people were attracted initially by price; while the French franc, Austrian schilling and Swiss franc soared, the lira plummeted even more than the pound – so Italy became cheaper while other Alpine countries were finding themselves priced out of the market. But now Italy is losing some of its price advantage as the other currencies fall and Italian lift companies, hoteliers and restaurateurs cash in on the boom. So Italy will have to compete with other countries on quality, not just price.

Italy has some enduring attractions. Food and wine always were first-rate, the atmosphere always was jolly, the scenery always was splendid – in the Dolomites, simply stunning. But 10 or 20 years ago Italian lift companies had the reputation of being a bit of a joke.

Not any more. Now, lift systems are modern; snowmaking – which the Italians were early to catch on to – is very widespread; piste grooming is of a consistently high standard. The value side of the value for money equation is one you need not worry about.

Although there aren't huge numbers of them (on the international market, at least), Italian resorts vary as widely in characteristics as they do in location – and they are spread along the length of the Italian border, from Sauze and neighbours (just across the French border from Montgenèvre), all along the Swiss border to the Dolomites, an area that used to be part of Austria. There are high, snowsure ski-stations and charming valley villages, and mountains that range from one-run wonders to some of the most extensive domains in the world.

Since the last edition of this book we've made three major tours of Italian resorts, and we have been impressed by all the aspects mentioned in the introduction above – and especially with the scenery (an aspect which tour operator brochures tend to neglect).

A lot of Italian runs, particularly in the north-west, seem flatteringly easy. This is partly because the piste grooming is immaculate, and also because piste grading seems to overstate difficulty. Nowhere is this clearer than in La Thuile (located in Italy, despite its French name). Its mountain connects (just) with that of La Rosière (across the valley from Les Arcs) and, when we last visited, venturing from the Italian side to the French side was like moving from the shelter of harbour to the open sea. Red runs on the La Thuile side were virtually motorways; at La Rosière, they offer challenging moguls.

We have also been struck by the way Italian resorts continue to be weekend-oriented. Except in the Dolomites, which depend largely on German custom, resorts can be quiet as the grave during the week, especially in low season, and come to life on Friday night or Saturday morning when the weekenders from Italy's affluent northern plain arrive. If, like us, you quite like having the hotel bar to yourself (not to mention the pistes), this is a real advantage.

In general, Italians don't take their skiing or boarding too seriously. Some lifts may still close for lunch, and mountain restaurants are generally welcoming places serving satisfying food and wine, encouraging leisurely lunching. Pasta – even in the most modest establishment – is delicious. And eating and drinking on the mountain is still much cheaper than in other Alpine resorts.

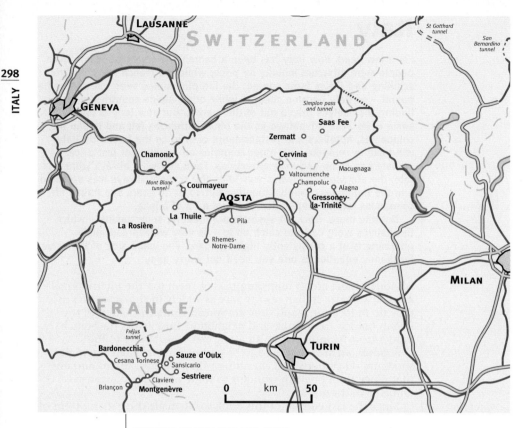

DRIVING IN THE ITALIAN ALPS

There are four main, widely separated geographical groupings of Italian resorts. Getting to some of these resorts is a very long haul, and if you want to go from one area to another it can involve very long drives.

The handful of resorts to the west of Turin – Bardonecchia, Sauze d'Oulx, Sestriere and neighbours in the Milky Way region – are easily reached from France via two major routes: the Fréjus tunnel from Modane, or via the good road over the pass that the resort of Montgenèvre sits on.

Further north, and about equidistant from Milan and Turin, are the resorts of the Aosta valley – Courmayeur, Cervinia and La Thuile the best-known among them. Courmayeur is the easiest of all Italian resorts to reach from Britain, thanks to the Mont Blanc tunnel from Chamonix in France. The road down the Aosta valley is a major thoroughfare carrying heavy goods traffic, but the roads up to some of the other resorts are quite long, winding and (at least in the case of Cervinia) high. The Aosta valley can also be reached from Switzerland via the Grand St Bernard tunnel. The approach is high, and may require chains.

To the east is a string of scattered resorts, most close to the Swiss border, many in isolated and remote valleys involving long drives up from the nearest Italian cities, or high-altitude drives from Switzerland. The links between Switzerland and Italy are more clearly shown on our Switzerland map at the beginning of that section. The

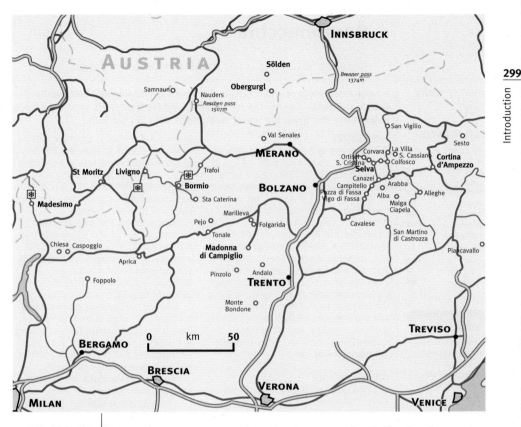

major routes are the St Gotthard tunnel between Göschenen, near Andermatt, and Airolo – the main route between Basel and Milan – and the San Bernardino tunnel reached via Chur.

Finally, further east still, are the resorts of the Dolomites. Getting there from Austria is easy, over the Brenner motorway pass from Innsbruck. But getting there from Britain is a very long drive indeed – allow at least a day and a half. We drove to Cortina for a week's holiday in 1997 and are not sure we'd want to do it again. Even though we believe driving is the best way of getting to the mountains, we wouldn't lightly drive there and back except as part of a longer tour. It's also worth bearing in mind that once you arrive in the Dolomites, getting around the intricate network of valleys linked by narrow, winding roads can be a slow business – not helped by impatient Italian driving.

Bardonecchia 1310m

Plenty of leisurely cruises and a market-town flavour

WHAT IT COSTS

HOW IT RATES

The slopes
Snow	**
Extent	***
Experts	*
Intermediates	***
Beginners	**
Convenience	**
Queues	***
Restaurants	***

The rest
Scenery	***
Resort charm	*
Off-slope	**

What's new

There are two new four-seat chair lifts from Campo Smith and Pian del Sole. This should reduce morning and weekend waits here.

MOUNTAIN FACTS

Altitude	1290m-2750m
Lifts	23
Pistes	140km
Blue	55%
Red	41%
Black	4%
Artificial snow	13km

UK PACKAGES

Airtours, Crystal, Equity School Ski, Equity Total Ski, First Choice Ski, Motours, Neilson, PGL Ski Europe, STS, Sloping Off, Stena Line Holidays

TOURIST OFFICE

Postcode 10052
Tel +39 (122) 99032
Fax 980612

A fairly extensive area worth considering as a base for touring other nearby French and Italian resorts. The local slopes, and the town itself, tend to be fairly quiet during the week, but lots of weekenders pour in from Turin.

THE RESORT

Bardonecchia is a sizeable old railway town, set in a beautiful wide valley, at the entrance to the Fréjus road tunnel that links France and Italy. It has two separate areas of slopes either side of town, both a bus-ride away. This description could almost be of Chamonix, but Bardonecchia is far from similar. It's a middling sort of place, with reasonable prices, moderate nightlife and useful slopes. The resort lacks classic mountain charm, but has traditional market-town character. But the frequent lack of resort-level snow and the intrusive railway rather detract. Valfréjus, Valloire, the Milky Way resorts (Sauze etc) and Serre-Chevalier are reachable by car.

THE MOUNTAINS

The two areas of **slopes** differ in some ways. The larger one is a wide section of low (little above 2000m), tree-lined, north-facing runs above three valley lift stations – Campo Smith on the edge of town, Les Arnauds and Melezet. Jafferau is a tall, thin mountain of long, partly open, west-facing runs. Chairs are generally antiquated and there are no bottom-to-top lifts. Jafferau is less popular, yet it has sunnier slopes and is certainly emptier at weekends when the Torinese hit town. All runs lead back to the town chair-lift, the top-to-bottom piste descending an impressive 1460m from the high-point of 2750m.

The area doesn't have a particularly good **snow record** but there are plenty of relatively snowsure runs above the middle stations, and the main pistes above Campo Smith and Melezet have snowmaking top-to-bottom. Jafferau quickly loses snow below mid-station.

In Campo Smith-Melezet, the highest run, which can have moguls, and a medium-length black from Pra Magnan are the best for **experts**. There is some off-piste in the trees when conditions allow. Jafferau is worth a visit for the long top-to-bottom reds.

Virtually the whole 140km is suitable for **intermediates**. Good

intermediates should head for Jafferau, where a network of fine runs finishes at the mid-station. There is a wealth of reds in the other area – flying down the tree-lined red from the top station to Campo Smith is great fun. There are plenty of leisurely cruises.

Campo Smith and Melezet have nursery areas, but the inconvenience of Bardonecchia and lack of special lift pass are disadvantages for **beginners**. For **boarders** there is a fun-park and half-pipe but there are a lot of awkward drag-lifts to cope with.

A varied, valley-level **cross-country** trail goes for miles in both directions from just above Campo Smith; Melezet is a starting point for other long trips. Although the lifts are antiquated there are few **queues** during the week.

Mountain restaurants are generally pleasant and uncrowded.

The large **ski school** has a good reputation, except for over-large classes. Recent reports indicate that more instructors speak English.

For **children**, there is a non-ski nursery and an all-day ski kindergarten at Campo Smith.

STAYING THERE

Accommodation is almost exclusively in **hotels**. Recent visitors recommend the 3-star Asplenia (10 minutes from Campo Smith towards town) for good food, comfort, efficiency and friendliness. The Park Hotel Rosa (4-star) is 10 minutes' walk from both the town centre and Campo Smith. The Ronco **apartments** are inexpensive and only minutes' walk from Campo Smith.

There are numerous **restaurants** and pizzerias but some of the best places are in hotels. Loc Cá Fiore, at Campo Smith, is handy for Ronco-dwellers.

Being a working town, Bardonecchia lacks the usual **après-ski**. Some bars are good for a quiet drink. New ones include La Botte, Nuovo Trau (with billiards) and Il Pik Bo for wine tasting.

Off the slopes there's a weekly market, tennis and swimming. Trips to more exciting Turin are easy.

Bormio

1225m

A tall, narrow mountain with a rather narrow appeal

WHAT IT COSTS

(2)

HOW IT RATES

The slopes
Snow	***
Extent	**
Experts	*
Intermediates	***
Beginners	**
Convenience	***
Queues	***
Restaurants	****

The rest
Scenery	***
Resort charm	****
Off-slope	****

➕ Good mix of high, snowsure pistes and woodland runs with artificial snow, giving some excellent long runs when conditions are right

➕ Several good neighbouring resorts on same lift pass

➕ Attractive medieval town centre – quite unlike any other winter resort

➕ Good mountain restaurants

➖ Slopes all of medium steepness

➖ Rather confined main mountain, with second area some way out

➖ Many slow lifts up the mountain, despite modern access lifts

➖ Long airport transfers

➖ Crowds and queues on Sundays

➖ Central hotels inconvenient

Bormio is a highly unusual resort. If you like cobbled medieval Italian towns and don't mind a lack of Alpine resort atmosphere, you'll find the centre very appealing – though you're unlikely to be staying right in the middle. The slopes, too, suit a rather specific and perhaps rather uncommon breed of visitor: you need to enjoy red runs and very little else, but you need to be happy with a limited range of them – unless, that is, you're prepared to take the bus out to Val di Dentro, or make longer outings, to Santa Caterina.

boarding *Bormio attracts some boarders, but it has no special appeal. The slopes are too steep to make first-time boarding enjoyable, and there's little to attract experienced boarders either: no park or pipe (though there is a half-pipe at Santa Caterina, 12km away); little enthusiasm from the ski schools to teach boarding; and a mainly skier orientation on the slopes. At least the main area's lifts are mostly chairs, gondolas or cable-cars – though there are some drags. Nightlife is sedate and really gets going only at the weekend.*

The resort

Bormio began life as a Roman spa, and still has thermal baths. It's in a remote part of Lombardy, at the foot of the Stelvio pass, close to the Swiss and Austrian borders – and a hefty four hours from the airport. The 17th-century town centre is wonderfully preserved, with cobbled streets, markets and old façades for today's shops, restaurants and cafés. Bormio is not as dreary and formal as many European spas. It's colourful, and promenading is an important evening pastime, but it's not as lively as some Italian resorts, such as Courmayeur.

Between the town centre and the local chair-lift and gondola (over the river on the southern edge of town) is a characterless urban sprawl – mainly made up of hotels built to be near the slopes. Staying here saves most of a 15-minute walk or a bus-ride. The free shuttle bus is reliable, but many people walk. There are more slopes well west of town, served by lifts at Oga, Le Motte or Val di Dentro.

The mountains

Bormio has good (but limited) slopes for confident intermediates who like long runs, with a nice mix of high, snowsure pistes and lower wooded slopes. Beginners, intermediates who prefer blue runs and experts are less well provided for.

Both the piste map and the piste marking need substantial improvement.

THE SLOPES
One-dimensional

The main slopes are tall (vertical drop 1800m) and narrow. Most pistes face north-west and head to town. The two-stage **Cima Bianca** cable-car goes from bottom to top (3010m) of the slopes via the mid-station at **Bormio 2000**. An alternative gondola goes to **Ciuk** (1620m). Above the mid-stations all runs are served by drag- and chair-lifts.

Lifts above **Oga** and **Val di Dentro** make this once insignificant area, a short bus-ride out of Bormio, a useful addition to Cima Bianca. It is now large enough to merit one or more day-trips.

MOUNTAIN FACTS

Altitude	1225m-3010m
Lifts	28
Pistes	62km
Blue	36%
Red	46%
Black	18%
Artificial snow	8½km

ACTIVITIES

Indoor 2 museums, library, thermal baths, squash, swimming pool, sauna, massage, sports hall, skating rink

Outdoor Ski-bob, toboggan run, walks in the Stelvio National Park

LIFT PASSES

97/98 prices in lire
Alta Valtellina
Covers all lifts in Bormio, Valdisotto, Valdidentro (all in local area), Santa Caterina (12km away) and Livigno (40km away), plus one free day in St Moritz.
Main pass
1-day pass 47,000
6-day pass 245,000 (low season 220,000 – 10% off)
Senior citizens
Over 65: 6-day pass 170,000 (31% off)
Children
Under 14: 6-day pass 170,000 (31% off)
Notes Day pass price covers Bormio lifts only.
Alternative passes
Up to 3-day pass for Bormio only (adult 3-day pass 130,000).

CHILDCARE

Children's ski classes are offered by some of the ski schools, but there are no special arrangements for all-day care, and no non-ski kindergartens.

Half the runs face east and are not high, but some face north. The mainly tree-lined pistes are very pleasant.

Day-trips further afield add interest to Bormio. Santa Caterina (20mins by bus), Livigno (1½hr) and buses to them are covered by the Valtellina lift pass. A six-day pass includes a day in St Moritz (3 hours away). The Passo Tonale glacier is easily reached by car.

SNOW RELIABILITY
Good above mid-station
Runs above Bormio 2000 are usually snowsure, and the snowmaking facility on the lower slopes is impressive. The high, shaded, north-facing slopes of Santa Caterina (1735m to 2725m) usually have good snow, and are not far away. However, the summer slopes of Passo Stelvio aren't open in winter.

FOR EXPERTS
Rather limited
There is little to challenge on Bormio's small mountain. Long, steep off-piste routes between Cima Bianca and the

Ornella drag to the west are feasible in good conditions. Otherwise there are a couple of short black runs. Bormio is said to be one of Franz Klammer's favourite resorts; but it's the length of the runs, not their difficulty or extent, that have impressed him.

FOR INTERMEDIATES
A few options for all grades
The 1985 World Championship Men's Downhill course starts with a steep plunge, but otherwise is just a tough red, ideal for strong intermediates. Stella Alpina, down to 2000, is another fairly steep piste.

Many runs are less tough – ideal for most intermediates. The longest is a superb top-to-bottom cruise, excellent for less aggressive types. The Oga area is also suitable for early intermediates. Santa Caterina has good intermediate slopes too.

FOR BEGINNERS
Many better Italian resorts
There are small nursery areas at both Ciuk and 2000, but novices would be better off at nearby Santa Caterina or Livigno. Near-beginners have a nice, quiet little area beneath 2000, using the Ornella drag, but no very flattering pistes to move on to.

FOR CROSS-COUNTRY
Go to Santa Caterina
There are some trails either side of Bormio, towards Piatta and beneath Le Motte and Val di Dentro, but cross-country skiers would be better off at snowsure Santa Caterina.

QUEUES
Much improved
Bormio has had a reputation for queues – though improvements to the lifts and the opening of Oga-Le Motte area have greatly improved matters. But both sections of the cable-car suffer delays in the morning peak period and on Sundays. And when the lower slopes are incomplete, queues form to ride the gondola down at the end of the day. Otherwise there are few problems except during carnival week (end of February).

MOUNTAIN RESTAURANTS
Good fare everywhere
The mountain restaurants are uniformly good for value and food. Even the efficient self-service at 2000 has a good choice of dishes. At La Rocca,

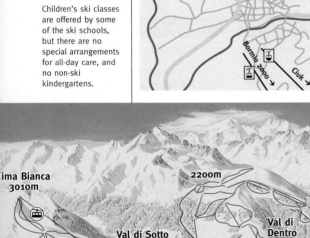

SCHOOLS/GUIDES

96/97 prices in lire

Bormio 2000
Classes 6 days
2hr: 9am-11am, 11am-1pm or 2pm-4pm
6 2hr days: 150,000

Nazionale
Classes 6 days
2½hr: 10am-12.30
6 2½hr days: 150,000
Private lessons
Hourly or daily
50,000 per hour; each additional person 10,000

Sertorelli
Italian-speaking instructors only.
Classes 6 days
2½hr
6 2½hr days: 170,000

OTHER SCHOOLS

Anzi
Capitani
Alta Valtellina
Fondo Alta Valtellina

GETTING THERE

Air Bergamo, transfer 4hr.

Rail Tirano (40km); regular buses from station.

UK PACKAGES

Airtours, Altours Ski, Crystal, First Choice Ski, Inghams, Neilson, PGL Ski Europe, Thomson, Winterski

CRYSTAL HOLIDAYS

helped us to compile the Eating out and Après-ski sections. Our thanks to them.

TOURIST OFFICE

Postcode 23032
Tel +39 (342) 903300
Fax 904696

above Ciuk, there is a welcoming chalet and a smart, modern place with table or self-service. Cedrone, at 2000, has a good terrace and a play area for children. The Baita da Mario, at Ciuk, is a very welcoming table-service restaurant. The Oga area has two huts, one of them set among trees on the run to Val di Dentro.

SCHOOLS AND GUIDES
Short lessons
There are six schools, some with outposts at 2000 and one based at Ciuk. Most Brits get sent to Scuola Alta Valtellina by their tour operators. We have a recent good report of their helpful and fun tuition. All the schools seem to limit their classes to half-day sessions, which some reporters think too short.

FACILITIES FOR CHILDREN
Typically Italian – limited
There is no crèche or ski kindergarten. But the Sertorelli and Bormio 2000 schools, at least, seem to make some effort to cater for children. The latter has a roped-off snow garden at its mid-mountain chalet.

Staying there

Bormio is big enough for location to be of some importance. You choose between convenient locations on the lift side of the river and the vitality of the town. Several major hotels are on Via Milano, leading out of town, which is neither convenient nor atmospheric.

HOW TO GO
Probably on a hotel package
Bormio is not a chalet resort, but there are plenty of apartments. However, hotels dominate the package market.
Hotels Most of Bormio's 40-plus hotels are 2-star and 3-star places, though there are a handful of 4-stars.
④ **Palace** Only luxurious place in town, on the Via Milano.
③ **Baita dei Pini** Best placed of top hotels: on the river, equidistant from lifts and centre. Excellent food, good facilities, fitness room and a piano bar.
③ **Posta** In the pedestrian heart of the town, rated a 4-star but with some 'pretty basic' rooms.
② **San Lorenzo** Friendly 3-star on edge of old town.
② **Ambassador Chalet** Welcoming place close to the gondola.
② **Derby** Large, attractive 3-star.

① **Piccolo Mondo** Small, basic but friendly B&B place with good breakfasts, close to Ciuk lift.
① **Dante** Good-value, central 2-star.
Self-catering The plain, modern Residence Jolly is close to the centre. The modern, well-equipped Cristallo apartments have been recommended, but are away from the lifts.

EATING OUT
Plenty of choice
There's a wide selection of restaurants. The atmospheric Taulà does excellent modern food with great service – at a price, but worth it. The Kuerc is also pricey but popular. Primo Piatto, in the Piccolo Mondo hotel, and the Vecchia Combo are also worth a try. There are excellent pizzerias, including the Jap – in a vault near the main square.

APRES-SKI
Tea-time promenading
Nightlife is fairly subdued. Many people just like to do early evening promenading and visit the elegant Mozart tea-room, with classical music. More hectic is a stop at the Rocca mountain café for a 'Bombardino' (hot advocat, brandy, whiskey and cream), and then on to town in the gathering darkness. Bar Cristallo is a popular rendezvous at the bottom of the piste. Just around the corner is the relaxing terrace of the Jolly Bar. Or try Bar Nevada, next to the cable-car station. Clem's Pub and the Piano Bar are two of the livelier after-dinner spots. Shangri-La is a friendly bar. La Terra is the karaoke joint. The Kings Club, the only disco, gets busy at weekends.

Every Wednesday there's a floodlit ski race open to all. Tour reps organise a trip to the Roman baths, snowmobile rides and a quiz evening.

OFF THE SLOPES
Take in the thermals
Bormio offers plenty of distractions, including thermal baths, riding and walks in the Stelvio National Park. Ritzy St Moritz and duty-free Livigno are popular excursions.

STAYING UP THE MOUNTAIN
Contrasting possibilities
The modern Girasole, at Bormio 2000, is simple but well run, with a warm welcome and lots of events to counter the isolation. The Baita da Mario at Ciuk is quieter and more traditional in style. Both can be reached by road.

Cervinia 2050m

Mile after mile of high-altitude snowsure cruising

WHAT IT COSTS

((((4)

HOW IT RATES

The slopes

Snow	*****
Extent	***
Experts	*
Intermediates	****
Beginners	*****
Convenience	***
Queues	***
Restaurants	***

The rest

Scenery	****
Resort charm	**
Off-slope	*

What's new

The slow old gondola from the bottom of the long run to Valtournenche is being replaced for the 1997/98 season by a new one with a much higher capacity.

➕ Extensive mountain with miles of long, gentle runs, usually with excellent snow

➕ Ideal for early intermediates and anyone who isn't looking for steep challenges or nasty surprises

➕ High, sunny and snowsure slopes amid impressive scenery

➕ Link with Zermatt in Switzerland provides more of the same type of slopes and some spectacular views

➖ Very little to interest good or aggressive intermediates and above

➖ Almost exclusively above-the-tree-line slopes, with little possible in bad weather

➖ Lifts prone to closure by wind, particularly early in the season

➖ Village not unpleasant in the centre, but an eyesore in general

➖ Tiresome walk to main lifts from much of the accommodation

➖ Few off-slope amenities

What brings people to Breuil Cervinia (as the resort now styles itself) in winter in the 20th century is what brought climbers to the original village of Breuil in the 19th century: altitude. For climbers it was a launch-pad for assaults on the nearby Matterhorn (Monte Cervino). For winter sports, it offers an unusual combination: slopes that are both gentle and extensive; sunny and snowsure.

For cruisers who like to cover the miles without worrying about the slopes being too steep, there is nowhere like it. But experts should steer clear. They'll find the slopes tame and the link with Zermatt disappointing because it doesn't access Zermatt's best slopes.

boarding *Cervinia has great slopes for learning to snowboard – gentle, wide and usually with good snow. And the main lifts around the area are chairs, gondolas and cable-cars, but there are many drags as well – if you go all the way down to Valtournenche, you'll have to catch at least four to get back. But there's not much to interest better boarders and there are no special facilities such as half-pipe or fun-park – so it is not surprising that boarders in Cervinia are in a definite minority. Nightlife is fairly limited.*

The resort

Cervinia is at the head of a long valley up from the Aosta valley on the Italian side of the Matterhorn. The old climbing village developed into a winter resort in a rather haphazard way, and it has no consistent style of architecture. It's an uncomfortable hotch-potch, neither pleasing to the eye, nor as offensive as the worst of the French purpose-built resorts. The centre is pleasant, compact and traffic-free. But surrounding apartment blocks and hotels make the village feel less friendly and welcoming.

A lot of people stay near the centre, at the foot of the nursery slopes. A series of drags takes you from here to the slopes. But the main gondola and cable-car are an awkward uphill walk away. There is more accommodation further out at the Cielalto complex and on the road up to it.

As well as the usual shops there are some very smart Italian clothes shops and jewellers, with upmarket Italian prices to match. The resort fills up with day-trippers and weekenders from Milan and Turin at peak periods. As well as their money they bring cars, making the village surprisingly traffic- and fume-ridden at times.

The resort is expensive by Italian standards, but no longer for the rich and trendy. There is a lively clientele, and a high proportion of Brits.

There are surprisingly few off-slope amenities, such as kindergartens, marked walks and swimming and spa facilities. And for those staying out of the centre there are some awkward walks and no bus – though some hotels have courtesy buses.

MOUNTAIN FACTS

Altitude	1525m-3480m
Lifts	34
Pistes	120km
Blue	40%
Red	48%
Black	12%
Artificial snow	7km

The mountains

Cervinia's main slopes are on a high, large, open, sunny, west-facing bowl. It has Italy's highest pistes and some of its longest (13km from Plateau Rosa down to Valtournenche – with only a short drag-lift part-way). Nearly all the runs are accessible to intermediates. The weather is more of a problem than steepness. If it's bad, the top lifts often close because of high winds. And even the lower slopes may be unusable because of poor visibility. There are few woodland pistes.

The slopes link to Valtournenche further down the valley (covered by the lift pass) and Zermatt over in Switzerland (daily supplement payable). Day trips by car are possible to Courmayeur, La Thuile and the Monte Rosa resorts of Champoluc (good off-piste) or Gressoney.

THE SLOPES
Very easy

Cervinia has the biggest, highest, most snowsure area of easy pistes we've come across. A gondola and ancient cable-car leave from above the village centre, though it's a steep climb up to them. These take you to the main mid-mountain base of **Plan Maison** (2555m). From there a further gondola and cable-cars go up to **Plateau Rosa** (3480m) and the link with Zermatt.

From Plateau Rosa you can go left on a blue run to a large network of drag- and chair-lifts serving Cervinia's easiest slopes and linking back to Plan Maison again. Don't miss the sign to Italy and the left turn near the top, otherwise you'll end up on the **Zermatt** lift system – paying the supplement. This area can also be accessed by drags from the village centre and you can head back there or to the gondola and cable-car station.

If you go right at Plateau Rosa you take the splendid wide Ventina run, which you can take all the way down to Cervinia (8km). Or you can branch off left down towards **Valtournenche**. The slopes here are served by a number of lifts above the initial gondola from Valtournenche to Salette at 2245m. The top of the Ventina run can be done several times by taking the giant 140-person cable-car. And there's a chair to play on – but no other lifts serve this sector and you can't get back to Plan Maison (though

you can take the gondola down to there if you like).

There is also the small, little-used **Cieloalto** area, served by three lifts to the south of the cable-car at the bottom of the Ventina run. This can be very useful in bad weather as it has the only trees in the area.

From Plan Maison a cable-car used to go to **Furggen** (3490m) and access Cervinia's steepest slopes. But this old lift has closed, and no-one is saying if and when a replacement will be built.

The slopes just above the village are floodlit some evenings.

SNOW RELIABILITY
Superb

The mountain is one of the highest in Europe and, despite getting a lot of afternoon sun, can usually be relied upon to have good snow conditions. Lifts being closed due to wind is a bigger worry.

The village nursery slopes and bottom half of the Ventina run have snowmaking facilities.

FOR EXPERTS
Forget it

This is not the resort for experts. There are several black runs dotted about but most of them would be graded red elsewhere. The beautiful, long, lonely piste from Furggen was the only worthwhile run, and with the cable-car out of action it's no longer accessible.

Experts paying the Zermatt supplement in search of tough runs will be disappointed – especially if the links are closed, as they often are with the high winds. The Trockener Steg-Schwarzsee area close to Cervinia has a great many easy runs and only a few challenging pistes. Getting to and from the other, more challenging areas on a day-trip isn't practical.

FOR INTERMEDIATES
Miles of long, flattering runs

Virtually the whole area can be covered comfortably by average intermediates. And if you like wide, easy, motorway pistes, you'll love Cervinia. It has more long, flattering runs than any other resort. The high proportion of red on the piste map is misleading: most of them would be graded blue elsewhere.

The easiest slopes are on the left as you look at the mountain. From top to bottom here, there are gentle blue runs and almost equally gentle reds in the

SCHOOLS/GUIDES

96/97 prices in lire

Cervino
Classes 6 days
2hr 50min: 10am-
12.50
6 days: 190,000
Children's classes
Ages: any
6 days: 190,000
Private lessons
Hourly
50,000 for 1 or 2
people; each
additional person
5,000

CHILDCARE

The ski school runs a
snow garden with
mini-lift at the foot of
the Cretaz slopes and
1 mini lift in Plan
Maison. Care
arrangements 10am to
1pm. There is not a
non-ski kindergarten.

GETTING THERE

Air Turin, transfer
2½hr. Geneva,
transfer 2½hr.

Rail Châtillon (27km);
regular buses from
station.

beautiful scenery at the foot of the
south face of the Matterhorn.

The area on the right as you look at
the mountain is best for adventurous
intermediates. The Ventina run is a
particularly good fast cruise. The long
run down to Valtournenche is easy for
most of its length. Good intermediates
will be capable of the black runs.

The trip over to Zermatt will bring
you first of all to even gentler
motorways than on the Cervinia side,
but then to some more challenging
pistes around Schwarzsee.

There's also the bonus of even
more spectacular scenery. The view of
the Matterhorn from the Swiss side is
the classic one you see in all the
pictures (you wouldn't recognise it
from the Cervinia side), and the view
of the glacier when you ride the Klein
Matterhorn cable-car to Europe's
highest pistes is breathtaking.

If you want to have a look at the
village of Zermatt, allow plenty of time.
The run down can be tricky, the lifts
back time-consuming.

FOR BEGINNERS
Pretty much ideal
Complete beginners will start on the
good village nursery slope, and should
graduate quickly to the fine flat area
around Plan Maison and its gentle
green runs. Fast learners will be able
to cover a great deal of ground by the
end of the week, and end up on the
blue run that goes all the way from top
to bottom of the mountain. The very
easy runs down to Salette, on the way
to Valtournenche, are a must.

FOR CROSS-COUNTRY
Hardly any
There are a couple of short trails, but
this is not a cross-country resort.

QUEUES
Can still be problems
Although much improved recently,
there are still some antiquated lifts,
and the system still has drawbacks.
Access to the Plan Maison mid-station
is crucial for most people, so the two
main access lifts get oversubscribed in
peak season and at busy weekends –
even though they jointly carry 2,850
people an hour. The alternative is a
roundabout series of drags and chairs.

There can be queues for many lower
lifts when the upper lifts are shut due
to high wind, restricting people to the
bottom half of the mountain.

MOUNTAIN RESTAURANTS
Good choice
The food in mountain restaurants is
generally good, wholesome stuff, and
helpings are liberal. But the toilet
facilities can be primitive. The
restaurants are cheaper and less
crowded on the Valtournenche side –
and, in our experience, serve good
food. A recent reporter enjoyed Lo
Barancon Dou Tene for efficient service
and good loos. The Motta, at the top
of the drag-lift of the same name, has
an excellent local speciality (Suppa di
Valdostani – bread, cheese and
vegetable soup). On the Cervinia side,
the Etoile on the Rocce Nere piste has
good pasta and a terrace. Baita Cretaz,
near the bottom of the Cretaz pistes, is
good value and has excellent service
and presentation. The British-run Igloo,
at the top of the Bardoney chair just
off the Ventina piste, is busy and has a
UK-style loo. Les Clochards, on the
edge of town, does tasty pasta and the
Bontadini da Lombard, on the blue run
back from Plateau Rosa, has good
main courses and glüwein.

SCHOOLS AND GUIDES
Getting better
Cervinia has one main school, the
Cervino. Recent reporters had no
complaints about tuition or standard of
English spoken – both criticised in
earlier years. Classes do tend to be
large, and some reporters found they
were doing too much waiting around.
There is a separate school up at the
satellite of Cieloalto.

FACILITIES FOR CHILDREN
Do-it-yourself
Children's classes in the school is
about it. The slopes, with their long
gentle runs, should suit families.

Staying there

Most visitors to Cervinia accept that
it's not a very convenient resort and
put up with some walking (there's no
public bus service). Central hotels are
quite convenient for the Cretaz drags,
but not for the main gondola station.
There are more convenient hotels,
some of them mentioned below.

HOW TO GO
Plenty of hotel packages
Most of the big tour operators come
here, providing between them a wide
selection of hotels, though other types

of accommodation are rather thin on the ground.

Hotels There are almost 50 hotels, mostly 2- or 3-star, with half a dozen 4-stars.

(((((5) **Cristallo** Luxury 4-star with pool, sauna, massage. A reporter found it a little faded, but service and food are great. Free bus to lifts.

(((((4) **Hermitage** Small, luxurious Relais et Château just out of the village on the road up to Cielalto. Great view, pool, free bus to lifts.

Cervinia is no beauty, but does have a bit of village atmosphere →

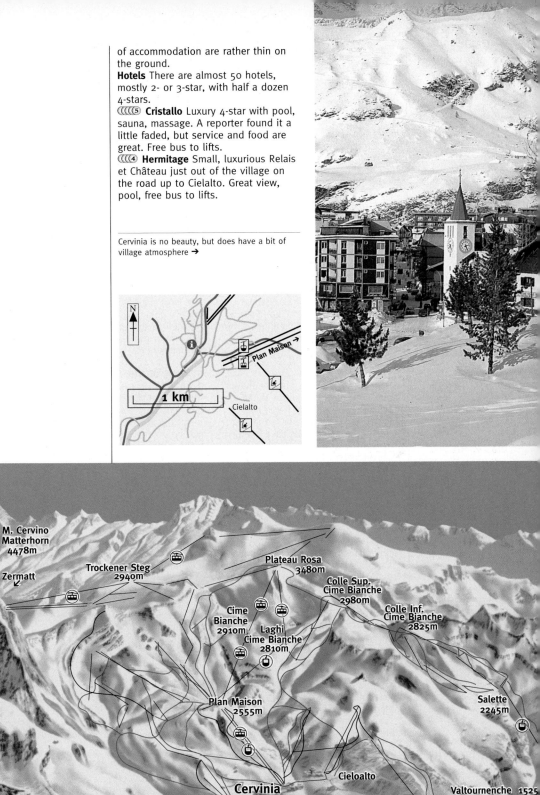

UK PACKAGES

Airtours, Crystal, First Choice Ski, Inghams, Lagrange, Ski trek, Thomson

(((④ **Punta Maquignaz** Captivating chalet-style 4-star, in centre near Cretaz lifts.

(((③ **Sporthotel Sertorelli** Excellent food, large buffet breakfast, sauna and jacuzzi. Ten minutes from lifts.

(((③ **Excelsior Planet** Pleasant, central 3-star with a pool.

(((③ **Furggen** Modern hotel above the resort on the Cretaz slopes, with good food and the slopes at your door.

((② **Breithorn** Good food. One of a number of good-value (by local standards) 2-stars.

((② **Marmore** Clean, warm, with good food; easy walk to the lift stations.

Self-catering There are many apartments in the resort but few are available through British tour operators. The Cristallino apartments are fairly simple but guests have use of the fine facilities of the Cristallo next door. The Residence La Pineta is of a similar standard, five minutes from the gondola and cable-car.

EATING OUT
Expensive for Italy

Cervinia's 50 or so restaurants allow plenty of choice, though the range of food isn't vast. It helps if you like pasta, pizza or polenta-based meals. Some of the best hotels have good, but expensive, restaurants open to non-residents.

The Chamoix and Matterhorn are excellent, but are particularly pricey. The Grotta belies its unfortunate name with good food. Casse Croute serves probably the biggest, and best, pizzas in town. Copa Pana serves pizza in a lively atmosphere. La Bricole and La Nicchia have been recommended for grills and steaks. An evening out at the Baita Cretaz mountain hut makes a nice change.

APRES-SKI
Disappoints many Brits

Plenty of lively Brits come here looking for action but there isn't much to do but tour the mostly fairly ordinary bars. The Café Whymper, White Rose and Copa Pan apparently have a pleasant atmosphere, good prices and serve generous measures.

The Dragon Bar is a major congregating spot for Brits. Satellite TV, videos, lager and karaoke are provided. The Pellissier Bar and Yeti Pub are other places popular with Brits. More cosmopolitan bars that can have atmosphere are Lino's and Café

ACTIVITIES

Indoor Hotel with swimming pools and saunas, fitness centre **Outdoor** Natural skating rink (until March), bob-sleigh run, paragliding, hang-gliding, mountaineering, walks, heli-skiing

TOURIST OFFICE

Postcode 11021
Tel +39 (166) 949136
Fax 949731

des Guides (with mementos of the owner's mountaineering trips to the Himalayas and a happy hour). The Scotch Club has occasional live music, but it doesn't really get going till after midnight. The discos liven up at weekends and according to one recent visitor the Garage and La Chimera seem to be the most popular late night places. There are several tour-rep-organised events such as snowmobiling, quiz nights and various evening meals – with fondue, pizza and local specialities.

OFF THE SLOPES
Little attraction

There is little to do. The pleasant town of Aosta is reached easily enough, but it's a four-hour round trip. Village amenities include pools, fitness centre and large natural ice rink. The walks are disappointing. The mountain restaurants that are reachable by gondola or cable-car hold little interest for pedestrians.

STAYING UP THE MOUNTAIN
To beat the queues

Up at Plan Maison, the major lift junction 500m vertical above the resort, Lo Stambecco is a 50-room 3-star hotel ideally placed for early nights and early starts.

Less radically, the Cime Bianche is a rustic 3-star chalet on the upper fringes of the resort (in the area known as La Vieille).

STAYING DOWN THE VALLEY
Great home run

Valtournenche, 9km down the road, is cheaper than Cervinia, has a genuine Italian atmosphere and a fair selection of simple hotels, of which the 3-star Bijou is the best. For 1997/98 its ancient gondola into the slopes is being replaced by one of much higher capacity, which should handle the queues even on busy weekends. But the drag-lifts above it mean it takes quite a time to reach Cervinia. The exceptionally long run back down, however, is a nice way to end the day. (It involves a short drag, so you can't leave it too late.) The main street through the village is very busy with cars going to and from Cervinia.

Cortina d'Ampezzo 1220m

Simply the world's most beautiful winter playground

WHAT IT COSTS

ⓒⓒⓒⓒⓒ 5

HOW IT RATES

The slopes
Snow	★★★
Extent	★★★
Experts	★★
Intermediates	★★★
Beginners	★★★★★
Convenience	★
Queues	★★★
Restaurants	★★★★

The rest
Scenery	★★★★★
Resort charm	★★★★
Off-slope	★★★★★

➕ Magnificent Dolomite scenery – perhaps the most dramatic of any winter resort

➕ Marvellous nursery slopes and good long cruising runs, ideal for nervous intermediates

➕ Access to the vast area covered by the Dolomiti Superski pass

➕ Attractive, although rather towny, resort, with lots of upmarket shops

➕ Good off-slope facilities, as you might expect of an Olympic venue

➕ Remarkably uncrowded slopes

➖ Several separate areas of slopes, which are inconveniently spread around all sides of the resort and linked by buses

➖ Expensive by Italian standards

➖ Gets very crowded during Italian holidays

➖ Very little for experts

Nowhere is more picturesque than chic Cortina, the most upmarket of Italian resorts. Dramatic pink-tinged peaks rise sheerly from the top of the slopes, giving picture-postcard views from wherever you are.

Cortina's slopes are fine for its regular upmarket visitors from Rome and Milan, many of whom have second homes here and enjoy the strolling, shopping, people-watching and lunching as much as the odd leisurely excursion on to the slopes. For complete beginners and leisurely intermediates, the splendid nursery slopes and long easy runs are ideal. For keen piste bashers, Cortina's fragmented areas can be frustrating; but the (time consuming) access to the Sella Ronda and other Dolomiti Superski resorts is some compensation. For experts the slopes are limited, with few tough runs and the best of those liable to poor snow conditions because they face south.

 Despite its up-market chic, Cortina is a good resort for learning to board. The Socrepes nursery slopes are wide, gentle and served by a high-speed quad chair-lift. And progress on to the resort's other easy slopes is simple because you can get around in all areas using just chairs and cable-cars – though there are drags, they can be avoided. There is no half-pipe or fun-park and little off-piste to interest experienced boarders. And hardcore boarders might find the chic shops, beautiful people and expensive nightlife a bit hard to stomach.

What's new

For years Cortina did little to update its ancient lift system. But that has all changed in recent years. 1996/97 saw the opening of a high-speed quad chair to replace the existing slow one from Rio Gere to Son Forca on Cristallo. Falloria also has an efficient high-speed quad and Socrapes has three.

In 1998/99 the quiet, outlying Cinque Torri area is due to be transformed by the replacement of ancient single-person chairs by a high-speed quad. Another high-speed quad is scheduled to link the area with the Passo Falzarego slopes, cutting out the need for a shuttle-bus transfer.

The resort

In winter, more people come to Cortina for the clear mountain air, the stunning views, the shopping, the cafés and to pose and be seen than come for the winter sports – 70 per cent of all Italian visitors don't bother taking to the slopes. Cortina attracts the rich and wealthy from the big Italian cities, many of whom have second homes here. Fur coats and glitzy jewellery are the norm – even among the young.

The resort itself is a widely spread town rather than a village, with exclusive chalets scattered around the woods and the roads leading off into the countryside. The centre is the traffic-free Corso Italia, full of chic designer clothes and jewellery shops, art galleries and furriers – finding a ski shop can seem tricky. In early evening, the street is a hive of activity, with everyone parading up and down in their finery, window-shopping, people-watching and making calls on mobile phones. Seeing anyone dressed for the slopes at 5pm is very much a rarity but the cobbles and picturesque church add to the typically Italian atmosphere. Luckily, all this glamour doesn't mean Cortina has to be expensive.

Surrounding the centre is a horrendous one-way system, often

traffic-clogged and stinking of fumes –
a nasty contrast to the stunning
scenery everywhere else you look.

Unlike the rest of the Dolomites,
Cortina is pure Italy. It has none of the
Germanic traditions of Selva and the
Sud Tirol, and doesn't attract many
German visitors.

The mountains

Cortina first leapt to fame as host of
the 1956 Winter Olympics. At the time,
it was very modern, now it feels dated.
Its widely spread areas are nothing like
the classic modern French purpose-
built resorts. The lifts to the two main
areas of slopes are a fair way from the
centre, and at opposite sides of town.
Other lifts are a lengthy bus-ride away.

If you fancy a trip further afield, **San
Cassiano** is not far to the west, with
links from there to **Corvara** and the
other Sella Ronda resorts.

THE SLOPES
Inconveniently fragmented
All Cortina's smallish separate areas
are a fair trek from the town centre.
The largest is **Socrepes**, accessed by
chair- and drag-lifts a bus-ride away. It
links with **Tofana**, Cortina's highest
area, also reached by two stage cable-

car from just outside the town centre.

On the opposite side of the valley is
the tiny **Mietres** area. Another cable-car
from the east side of town leads to the
Faloria area, from where you can head
down to the chairs that lead up into
the limited but dramatic runs beneath
the **Cristallo** peak.

Other tiny areas are reachable by
road. The cable-car from Passo
Falzarego (2150m) up to Lagazuoi
(2750m) accesses a beautiful red run
to Armentarola. On the way to Passo
Falzarego is the tiny but spectacular
Cinque Torri area. Its excellent, north-
facing slopes are served by ancient
single-seater chairs, but the 98/99
season should see them replaced by a
fast quad. Another quad should link
the area with Passo Falzarego.

An advantage of fragmented areas
is that pistes tend to be uncrowded
with few queues. But we've had
complaints about the different versions
of the piste map, all of which seem out
of date and missing important runs.

A car is very helpful to make the
most of other areas on the Dolomiti
Superski pass. But the bus service is
good, and tour operators offer a good
selection of day trips to other areas.

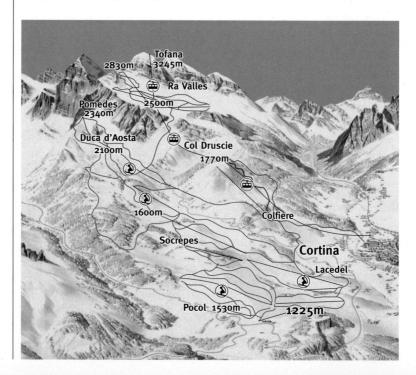

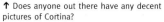

↑ Does anyone out there have any decent pictures of Cortina?

LIFT PASSES

97/98 prices in lire
Cortina d'Ampezzo
Covers all lifts in
Cortina, San Vito di
Cadore, Auronzo and
Misurina, and ski-
buses.
Main pass
1-day pass 52,000
6-day pass 260,000
(low season 226,000
– 13% off)
Senior citizens
Over 60: 6-day pass
182,000 (30% off)
Children
Under 15: 6-day pass
182,000 (30% off)
Under 8: free pass
Notes Discount prices
for senior citizens and
children for 2-day
passes and over only.
Alternative passes
Dolomiti Superski
pass covers 464 lifts
and 118km of piste
in the Dolomites
(adult 6-day 286,000).

SNOW RELIABILITY
Lots of artificial help
Cortina has invested heavily in artificial snow, so expect good cover on the Socrepes slopes and the south-facing runs of the Cristallo area. But in 1997 the link between Tofana and Socrepes was closed because of lack of snow on a key south-facing slope – which made the areas even more fragmented. The natural snowfall record is erratic – the snow here can be good when it's poor on the north side of the Alps.

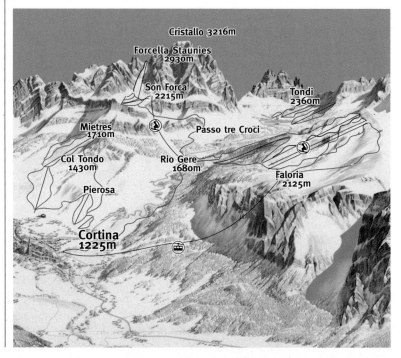

SCHOOLS/GUIDES
96/97 prices in lire

Cortina
Classes 6 days
2½hr: 9.30am-noon;
2hr: noon-2pm
6 2½hr days: 270,000
Children's classes
Ages: under 15
6 full days (9.30-3.30)
including lunch:
900,000
Private lessons
Hourly
60,000 for 1hr; each
additional person
14,000

Azzurra Cortina
Classes 6 days
3½hr: 9.15am-1pm;
3hr: 1pm-4pm; 6½hr:
9.15-4pm
6 3½hr days: 390,000
Private lessons
Hourly
62,000 for 1hr; each
additional person
20,000

CHILDCARE
Both schools offer all-day classes for children – the Cortina school from 9.30 to 3.30, the Azzurra school from 9am to 4pm.

FOR EXPERTS
Limited
The run down from the second stage of the Tofana cable-car at Ra Valles goes through a gap in the rocks, and a steep, narrow, south-facing section gives wonderful views of Cortina, deep down in the valley. It's often tricky because of poor snow conditions.

Cortina's other steep run goes from the top of the Cristallo area at Forcella Staunies. A chair-lift takes you to a steep, south-facing couloir, often shut due to avalanche danger or poor snow.

Other than these two runs (both shut on our 1997 visit) there's little to keep experts happy for a week.

FOR INTERMEDIATES
Fragmented and not extensive
If you like cruising in beautiful scenery and don't mind repeating the same runs you'll get the most out of Cortina. But don't expect a huge linked area.

The red runs at the top of Tofana are short, but normally have the best snow. The highest are at over 2800m and mainly face north. But be warned: the only way down is by the tricky black run described above or cable-car. The reds from the linked Pomedes area are longer and offer good cruising.

Faloria has a string of fairly short north-facing reds – we loved Vitelli around the back away from all signs of lifts. And the Cristallo area that you can get to from here has just one long red, served by a new high-speed quad.

It is well worth making the trip to Cinque Torri for wonderful, deserted fast cruising on usually excellent north-facing snow. The Hidden Valley run from Lagazuoi at the top of the Passo Falzerego cable-car to Armenterola is a must – a very easy red and one of the most beautiful runs we've come across. It offers isolation amid sheerly rising pink-tinged Dolomite peaks and frozen waterfalls. Make time to stop at the atmospheric Scotolino refugio near the end, then it's a long pole, skate or walk to the welcome sight of a horse-drawn sled with ropes attached which tows the weary to Armenterola. Shared taxis take you to Passo Falzerego (if you've time, try the slopes of Alta Badia, accessed from Armenterola).

FOR BEGINNERS
Wonderful nursery slopes
The Socrepes area has some of the biggest nursery slopes and best progression runs we have seen.

However, a reporter gave a mixed report on the standard of tuition in beginners' lessons. Also, some of the forest paths marked blue can be icy and intimidating. But you'll find ideal gentle terrain on the main pistes.

FOR CROSS-COUNTRY
One of the best
Cortina has 74km of trails, mainly in the woods towards Dobbiaco. There are also trails below the Cristallo area.

QUEUES
No problem for early birds
Most Cortina holiday makers rise late, lunch lengthily and leave the slopes early – if they get on them at all. That means few lift queues and generally uncrowded pistes. And out of peak season, the resort can be extremely quiet. 'Lack of queues was one of the highlights of our holiday,' said one recent reporter. Another visited the Sella Ronda but soon hurried back to Cortina and the solitude.

MOUNTAIN RESTAURANTS
Good, but get in early
Lunch is a major event for many Cortina visitors. At weekends you often need to book or turn up very early to be sure of a table. Many restaurants can be reached by road or lift, and pedestrians arrive as early as 10am to sunbathe and admire the views. Although prices tend to be high in the swishest establishments, we've found plenty of reasonably priced, simple fare. The up-market El Camineto, where white-jacketed waiters ministered to your needs, was mysteriously burned down a couple of years ago and the cause was still being investigated in 1997. The Pic de Tofana, nearby, is recommended, as is the Rifugio Pomedes, up the mountain.

The Socrepes sector has several hotels along the road going up its edge – including the best restaurant in the resort, the Michelin-starred Tivoli.

At Cristallo the Rio Gere at the base of the quad chair and Son Forca, with fabulous views at the top of it, are both worth a visit.

The restaurants at Cinque Torri, the Scoiattoli and the Rifugio Averau, offer fantastic views as well as good food, and, unusually, are non-smoking. The restaurant at Lagazuoi, a hike up from the top of the Pazzo Falzerego cable-car has a similar attraction of views and no smoking.

SCHOOLS AND GUIDES
Tuition not always in English
With such an upmarket Italian clientele, we'd expect tuition to be good – and we have a few enthusiastic reports. It seems some instructors speak English well, but one reporter stopped taking lessons as none of them was teaching her level. There is a guiding school, the Gruppo Guide Alpine, which offers off-piste, touring and special high altitude weeks.

FACILITIES FOR CHILDREN
Better than average
By Italian standards childcare facilities are outstanding, with a choice of all-day care arrangements for children of practically any age. Given the very small number of British visitors, you can't count on good spoken English. Also, the fragmented area can make travelling around with children difficult.

Staying there 🔑

There's a wide range of hotels in the centre and scattered in the outskirts. None is likely to be convenient. To get the most out of the town, staying in the centre and resigning yourself to a bus-ride to the lifts is the best bet. If you have a car, your choice is wider.

HOW TO GO
Now with more packages
Hotels dominate the market but the last couple of season have seen Crystal and Ski Equipe open catered chalets.
Hotels There's a big choice, especially at the luxury end where there are two 5-star and 15 4-star hotels. But the resort is not really exclusive: there are cheaper places – down to 1-star and 2-star pensions.
((((⑤ **Miramonti** Spectacularly grand hotel in extensive grounds, 2km south of town. Pool.
(((④ **Poste** Reliable 4-star, at the heart of the town.
(((④ **Ancora** Elegant public rooms, right on the traffic-free Corso Italia.
(((④ **Parc Victoria** Rustic 4-star with small rooms but good food (especially the pasta course), at the Faloria end of the town centre.
((③ **Olimpia** Comfortable B&B hotel in centre, close to Faloria lift.
((③ **Menardi** Welcoming roadside inn, a long walk from centre and lifts.
Self-catering There are some chalets and apartments – usually out of town – available for independent travellers.

EATING OUT
Huge choice
There's an enormous selection, both in town and a little way out, doing mainly Italian food. The very smart and pricey El Toulà is in a beautiful old barn, just on the edge of town. Many of the best restaurants are further out – such as the Michelin-starred Tivoli, Meloncino (a charming chalet), Leone e Anna, Rio Gere and Baita Fraina. Reasonably priced central restaurants include the Cinque Torri and Da Franco for pizza and pasta, and Mezcal, which does drinks, snacks and tex-mex food.

APRES-SKI
Lively in high season
Cortina is a lively social whirl in high season, with lots of well-heeled Italians staying up very late (which is why the slopes are so quiet). Don't go on the early evening walkabout if the sight of fur coats upsets you.

Bar Lovat is one of several popular, high-calorie tea-time spots. Bar Cristallino is an elegant spot where young and old rub shoulders. The Enoteca is a welcoming wine bar, popular with locals at the end of the day. Fe is another wine bar, with good decor, which is also busy later. The most happening bar is the Clipper, with a bob-sleigh in the door, and lots of designer beer. The discos can have atmosphere – as long as you get there after 11pm. Some of the best are the Metro, Hyppo and Limbo.

OFF THE SLOPES
A classic resort
Along with St Moritz, Cortina rates as one of the leading resorts if you're happier off the slopes. The setting is stunning, the town attractive, the shopping extensive, the mountain restaurants easily accessible by road (a car is handy). And there's plenty more: ice skating, dog-sledding, major ice hockey matches and even an ice disco on the Olympic ice rink. If you're there at the right time, you can watch sleds careering down the Olympic bobsleigh run. There's horse jumping and polo on the snow occasionally.

Cortina also has several museums and art galleries, including the Mario Rimoldi, which houses the largest private collection in Italy of painting and sculptures by leading modernists.

Trips to Venice are easily and inexpensively organised, where you'll find rather cheaper shopping.

GETTING THERE
Air Venice, transfer 3hr.

Rail Calalzo (35km) or Dobbiaco (32km); frequent buses from station.

UK PACKAGES
Chalets 'Unlimited', Crystal, Inghams, Powder Byrne, Ski Club of GB, Ski Equipe

ACTIVITIES
Indoor Swimming pool, saunas, museums, art gallery, cinema, indoor tennis court, public library
Outdoor Olympic ice-stadium (2 rinks), curling, ice hockey, sleigh rides, horse-riding school, ski-bob run, olympic ski jump, 6km walking paths, toboggan run, heli-skiing

TOURIST OFFICE
Postcode 32043
Tel +39 (436) 3231
Fax 3235

Courmayeur 1225m

A seductive village on the sunny side of Mont Blanc

WHAT IT COSTS
((((4)

HOW IT RATES

The slopes

Snow	****
Extent	**
Experts	***
Intermediates	****
Beginners	**
Convenience	*
Queues	****
Restaurants	****

The rest

Scenery	****
Resort charm	****
Off-slope	***

What's new

The only lift news from Courmayeur is negative: the gondola from the suburb of Dolonne is no longer operating, which is a pity. Quite apart from the convenience for residents on that side of the resort, anyone doing the off-piste runs to Dolonne from Cresta d'Arp or Plan Checrouit now faces a walk or a taxi-ride into the main village.

➕ Charming, traditional village, with car-free centre and stylish shops

➕ Stunning views of Mont Blanc massif

➕ Pleasant range of intermediate runs

➕ Comprehensive snowmaking

➕ Good mountain restaurants

➕ Lively, but not rowdy, evening atmosphere and nightlife

➕ One of the shortest, easiest drives from UK, and short airport transfers

➖ Lack of nursery slopes and easy runs for beginners to progress to

➖ No tough pistes

➖ Relatively small area, with mainly short runs

➖ Slopes very crowded on Sundays

➖ Tiresome walk and cable-car journey between village and slopes

Courmayeur is very popular, especially at weekends, with the smart Italian set from Milan and Turin. It's easy to see why: not only is it very easy to get to, thanks to the road up to the Mont Blanc tunnel, but it is certainly the most captivating of the Val d'Aosta resorts.

The scenery, the charm and the nightlife must influence the many Brits who go there, too. Certainly, the slopes themselves are unlikely to be the main draw, given their limited range of difficulty, inconvenient location across the valley from the village and, particularly, their limited size. A keen piste-basher will cover Courmayeur in a day, then wonder what to do for the rest of the week.

Courmayeur makes a good day-trip from Chamonix (the weather on the southern side of Mont Blanc can be quite different from that on the northern side), or a jolly week for those who want to party as much as hit the slopes. It also appeals to those with quite different ambitions, who want to explore the spectacular Mont Blanc massif with the aid of a guide, and other local peaks with the aid of a helicopter.

boarding *Courmayeur's pistes suit intermediate boarders, and most areas are easily accessible by novices as the main lifts are cable-cars, chairs or gondolas – but it's all a bit steep for beginners. The biggest draws for the more experienced are the off-piste routes. Guides take groups from the top of the main slopes, or on to the flanks of Mont Blanc, or all the way to Chamonix via the Vallée Blanche. Like a lot of Italian resorts, Courmayeur has no park or pipe; unlike other Italian resorts, it still manages to attract quite a few boarders, and you shouldn't find yourself in too much of a minority. Nightlife is lively in a stylish kind of way, and there's plenty of diversity in the bars.*

The resort

Courmayeur is a traditional old Italian mountaineering village which, despite the nearby Mont Blanc tunnel road and proliferation of modern hotels, has retained much of its old-world feel.

The village has a charming traffic-free centre of attractive shops, cobbled streets, and well-preserved buildings, the church being the most impressive. An Alpine museum and a statue of a famous, long-dead mountain rescue hero add to the historical feel.

The centre has a great atmosphere, focused around the Via Roma. As soon as the lifts close, people pile into the numerous bars, which include some very civilised places. Others wander in and out of the many small shops, which include a salami specialist and a good bookshop. At weekends people-watching is part of the evening scene, as ski jackets are outnumbered by the fur coats of the Milanese and Torinese.

The village extends away from the centre in several directions, and its huge cable-car is right on the edge.

MOUNTAIN FACTS

Altitude 1295m-2755m
Lifts   28
Pistes   100km
Blue   50%
Red   40%
Black   10%
Artificial snow   15km
Recco detectors used

LIFT PASSES

96/97 prices in lire
Courmayeur Mont Blanc
Covers all lifts in Val Veny and Checrouit, and the lifts on Mont Blanc up to Punta Helbronner.
Beginners Free nursery lifts at Plan Checrouit and top of Val Veny cable-car (which can be paid for by the ride).
Main pass
1-day pass 48,000
6-day pass 245,000
(low season 212,000 – 13% off)
Short-term passes
Single ascent on some lifts and half-day pass available.
Notes Passes of 6 or more days are valid for one day in the Chamonix valley.
Alternative passes
Valle d'Aosta area pass covers all lifts in Courmayeur, Gressoney, Alagna, Champoluc, La Thuile, Pila, Cervinia and Valtournenche (adult 6-day 255,000). Mont-Blanc ski region pass covers all lifts in 13 resorts around Mont Blanc.

The mountains

The main slopes suit intermediates, with few difficult or easy runs, but it is a surprisingly small area for such a well known, large resort. The pistes are varied in character if not in gradient, and pretty. Piste marking and maintenance could be improved.

THE SLOPES
Small but interestingly varied

The slopes are separate from the village: you have to ride a cable-car at the start and end of the day. This, the only lift from Courmayeur itself, transports you to the bottom of the slopes at Plan Checrouit (where you can store your equipment).

There are two distinct sections, both almost entirely for intermediates. The north-east-facing **Checrouit** area catches the morning sun, and has open, above-the-tree-line pistes. The 25-person, infrequently running Youla cable-car goes to 2625m, the top of Courmayeur's pistes. There is a further cable-car to Cresta d'Arp (2755m). This serves only long off-piste runs – and you can go up there only with a guide.

↑ One of Courmayeur's principal pleasures: refreshments

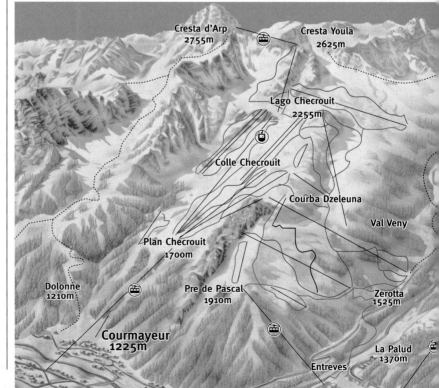

SCHOOLS/GUIDES

97/98 prices in lire
Monte Bianco
Classes 6 days
3hr: 10am-1pm
6 half-days: 210,000
Children's classes
Ages: from 4
6 half-days: 190,000
Private lessons
Hourly
50,000 for 1 to 2
people; each
additional person
5,000

Most people follow the sun over to the north-west-facing slopes towards **Val Veny** in the afternoon. These are interesting, varied and tree-lined, with great views of Mont Blanc and the Brenva glacier. Connections between the two areas are good, with many alternative routes. The Val Veny slopes are also directly accessible by cable-car from Entrèves, a few miles outside Courmayeur.

A little way beyond Entrèves, up Val Ferret, is La Palud, where a cable-car goes up in three stages to Punta Helbronner, at the shoulder of **Mont Blanc**. You can do the famous Vallée Blanche run to Chamonix from here – spectacularly scenic, and not difficult – without the horrific initial ridge walk you encounter on the Chamonix side. Or you can tackle other off-piste runs on the Italian side of the massif. None of these glacier runs should be undertaken without a guide.

La Thuile is an easy drive to the south, and Cervinia is reachable.

SNOW RELIABILITY
Good for most of the season

Courmayeur's slopes are not high – mostly between 1700m and 2250m. Those above Val Veny face north or north-west, so keep their snow well, but the Plan Checrouit side is rather too sunny for comfort in late season. There is snowmaking on most of the main runs, so good coverage in midwinter is virtually assured.

FOR EXPERTS
Off-piste is the only challenge

Courmayeur has few challenging pistes. The only black – the Competizione, on the Val Veny side – is not difficult, and few moguls form elsewhere. But if you're lucky enough to find fresh powder you can have fantastic fun among the trees.

Classic off-piste runs go from Cresta d'Arp, at the top of the lift network, in three directions – a clockwise loop via Arp Vieille to Val Veny, with close-up views of the Miage glacier; east down a deserted valley to Dolonne or Pré St Didier; or south through the Youla gorge to La Thuile.

On Mont Blanc, the Vallée Blanche is not a challenge (though there are more difficult variations and the views are stunning), but the Toula glacier route on the Italian side from Punta Helbronner to Pavillon most certainly is, often to the point of being

dangerous. There are also heli-drops available on the peaks above Val Ferret, north-east of the resort, or on various nearby glaciers.

FOR INTERMEDIATES
Ideal gradient but limited extent

The whole area is suitable for most intermediates, but it is small. The avid piste-basher will find it very limited.

The open Checrouit section is pretty much go-anywhere territory, where you can choose your own route and make it as easy or difficult as you like. The blue runs here are about Courmayeur's gentlest. On the Val Veny side, the red pistes running the length of the Bertolini chair are more challenging and very enjoyable. These pistes link in with the pretty, wooded slopes heading down to Zerotta.

The Zerotta chair dominates the area, with numerous alternatives starting at its top. It's a good area for mixed abilities, with runs of varying difficulty meeting up at several places on the way down to Zerotta.

The Vallée Blanche, although off-piste, is easy enough for adventurous, fit intermediates to try.

FOR BEGINNERS
Consistently too steep

Courmayeur is not well suited to beginners. There are several nursery slopes but none is ideal. The area at Plan Checrouit gets crowded and there are few easy runs for the near-beginner to progress to. The small area served by the short Tzaly drag, just above the Entrèves cable-car top station, is the most suitable beginner terrain, and it tends to have good snow.

FOR CROSS-COUNTRY
Beautiful trails

There are good trails dotted around Courmayeur. The best are the four covering 20km at Val Ferret, to which there is a bus service. Dolonne also has two short trails, and a skiable path runs from Entrèves to Zerotta, which is useful for meeting up with Alpine types for lunch. Total trails 35km.

QUEUES
Weekend cable-car black spots

The lift system is generally excellent. The Checrouit and Val Veny cable-cars suffer queues only at weekends, and even these can be beaten with an early start. Most patience is needed when waiting for the infrequently running

CHILDCARE

The Kinderheim at Plan Checrouit (845073) takes children from age 6 months, from 9.30 to 4pm. Children taking lessons can be deposited at the ski school in Courmayeur at 9am, and looked after for the whole day (lesson am, play pm).

GETTING THERE

Air Geneva, transfer 2hr. Turin, transfer 2hr.

Rail Pré-St-Didier (5km); regular buses from station.

Youla cable-car. Otherwise, no problems. Overcrowded slopes at the weekends, particularly down to Zerotta, are a greater problem.

MOUNTAIN RESTAURANTS
Lots – some of them good

The area is lavishly endowed with 27 establishments ranging from rustic on-piste huts to larger self-service places at main lift stations. Most restaurants do table service of delicious pizza and pasta, but there are also snack bars selling little more than hard sandwiches and cardboard pizza, and relying on views and sunshine to fill their terraces.

One of the better snack bars is Courba Dzeleuna, at the top of Dzeleuna chair. Several restaurants are excellent. Château Branlant, next to the Chiecco drag at Plan Checrouit, is recommended for good food, atmosphere, friendly service and good views of struggling beginners. Maison Vieille, at the top of the chair of the same name and run by the charming Giacomo, is a welcoming rustic place with good food. The pick of the restaurants at Plan Checrouit is the hotel Christiania – book a table downstairs, where you can savour the superb food in peace.

On the other side of the mountain in Val Veny is another clutch of places worth noting – La Zerotta, at the foot of the eponymous chair; the Petit Mont Blanc, nearby; the atmospheric Monte Bianco climbing refuge, along the mountainside; and the jolly Grolla, further along still.

SCHOOLS AND GUIDES
Classes not a strong point

Reports on the school vary widely, with some criticism of chaotic organisation. We have no recent comments on the standard of English spoken, but 'the instructor didn't give enough personal attention', says one report. There is a thriving guides' association ready to help you explore the area's off-piste; it has now produced a helpful booklet showing the main possibilities.

FACILITIES FOR CHILDREN
Good care by Italian standards

The resort's childcare arrangements are well ahead of the Italian norm, but Courmayeur is far from an ideal resort for a young family.

Staying there

The cable-car station is on the southern edge of town, a fair distance from much of the accommodation. There is no shuttle bus alternative to walking. Once up the mountain, there is another short walk to the other lifts before you can get on the slopes.

Having accommodation close to the cable-car is obviously advantageous. But don't stay too close to the Mont Blanc road, which can be very noisy. However, having this major route on the doorstep does afford particularly easy access if you're a driver. Most hotels have some parking spaces. Parking at the village cable-car is very limited, but drivers can go to Entrèves, a few kilometres away, where there is a large car park at the Val Veny cable-car. Buses, infrequent but timetabled, link Courmayeur with La Palud, just beyond Entrèves, for the Punta Helbronner–Vallée Blanche cable-car.

HOW TO GO
Plenty of hotels

Courmayeur's long-standing popularity ensures a wide range of packages, mainly in hotels. Interski stay out of town and bus people in. Courmayeur isn't a major chalet resort, but one or two UK operators have places.

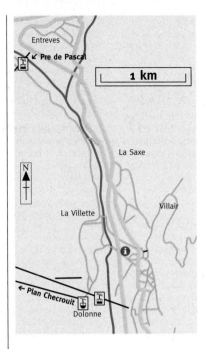

Entreves

Pre de Pascal

1 km

La Saxe

N

La Villette

Villair

Plan Checrouit

Dolonne

UK PACKAGES

Airtours, Bladon Lines, Crystal, First Choice Ski, Independent Ski Links, Inghams, Interski, Mark Warner, Motours, Neilson, Ski Activity, Ski Weekend, Skiworld, Stena Line Holidays, Thomson, White Roc, Winterski

ACTIVITIES

Indoor Swimming pool and sauna in Hotel Royal and at Pré-St-Didier (5km), skating rink, Alpine museum, cinema, bridge, library
Outdoor Walking paths in Val Ferret and Dolonne, paragliding

TOURIST OFFICE

Postcode 11013
Tel +39 (165) 842060
Fax 842072

Hotels There are nearly 50 hotels in Courmayeur, evenly distributed between the star ratings.
(((4) **Gallia Gran Baita** Newly opened place with antique furnishings and panoramic views. Pool.
(((4) **Pavillon** Comfortable 4-star near cable-car, with a pool. Friendly staff.
(((4) **Palace Bron** Small but tall, elegantly furnished chalet above the town at Plan Gorret.
(((3) **Berthod** Friendly, family run hotel near centre.
(((3) **Grange** Rustic, stone-and-wood farmhouse at Entrèves.
((2) **Edelweiss** Friendly, cosy, good-value place close to the centre.
((2) **Lo Scoiattolo** Good rooms, good food, shame about the position – at opposite end of town from cable-car.
Self-catering There is quite a lot of self-catering accommodation available to those who book independently.

EATING OUT
Jolly Italian evenings
There is a great choice of restaurants, both in downtown Courmayeur and within taxi-range in neighbouring villages and valleys; there's a handy promotional booklet describing many of them (in English as well as Italian). The touristy but very jolly Maison de Filippo in Entrèves is famous for its fixed-price, 36-dish feast. Further out,

at Val Ferret, Chalet Proment (Floriano's) is attractively rustic, with a warm welcome and wonderful local cooking. For a serious meal out in town, reporters recommend the Cadran Solaire; we've been impressed by Pierre Alexis. The Tunnel pizzeria serves huge pizzas and is very popular, so book well in advance.

APRES-SKI
Stylish bar-hopping
Courmayeur has a lively evening scene, centred on a series of bars in and around the main street. Our favourites are the Roma, the back room of the Caffe della Posta, and the upper room of Steve's Bar Privé, all with comfy armchairs to collapse in. Ziggy's is also popular, and the Cadran Solaire is where the big money from Milan and Torino accumulates. The Red Lion is worth a visit if you're missing English pubs. There is a disco or two.

OFF THE SLOPES
Much improved for sporty types
If you're not interested in hitting the snow you'll find the village pleasant and may find the shops diverting. There are some interesting excursions – by cable-car up to Punta Helbronner and by bus to Aosta (great for shopping) or Chamonix. It's easy to go up the main cable-car to Plan Checrouit to meet friends for lunch. There is now a large sports complex with everything you could wish for – except a pool. Reporters found ice hockey matches very exciting to watch.

STAYING UP THE MOUNTAIN
Why would you want to?
Visiting Courmayeur and not staying in the charming village seems perverse – if you're that keen to get on the slopes in the morning, this is probably the wrong resort. But the Christiania at Plan Checrouit (see Mountain restaurants) has simple rooms; you need to book way in advance.

Gressoney
1640m

Extensive, attractive slopes, especially off-piste

HOW IT RATES

The slopes

Snow	***
Extent	***
Experts	**
Intermediates	****
Beginners	**
Convenience	****
Queues	****
Restaurants	**

The rest

Scenery	****
Resort charm	***
Off-slope	*

MOUNTAIN FACTS

Altitude	1640m-2970m
Lifts	30
Pistes	70km
Blue	31%
Red	63%
Black	6%
Artificial snow	18km

UK PACKAGES

Crystal, Inghams, Ski trek

Alagna Ski Club of GB, Ski Weekend

Champoluc Crystal

TOURIST OFFICE

Postcode 11020
Tel +39 (125) 366143
Fax 366323

Gressoney is at the heart of the Monterosa area – Italy's little-known answer to the Three Valleys. The pistes are less extensive and mostly easy (and link only two of the three valleys, in fact), but they offer the same sensation of travelling around, amid impressive scenery – and there's excellent off-piste.

THE RESORT
Gressoney la Trinité is a quiet, neat little village a bus-ride from the outpost of Stafal at the head of the central valley. Gressoney St Jean, a more substantial village (with shops) 5km down the valley, has its own, limited, slopes, separate from the main system.

The main resort in the east valley is Champoluc; to the west it's Alagna. Road trips to Cervinia, La Thuile and Courmayeur are possible. Buses covered by the lift pass run half-hourly from La Trinité to Stafal and St Jean.

THE MOUNTAINS
The **slopes** of Monterosa are relatively extensive, and very scenic. The pistes are almost all easy (and very well groomed). The terrain is undulating and fragmented; runs are attractively varied, but many lifts serve only one or two pistes. The lifts are impressively modern, with several high-speed chair-lifts. There are lifts out of La Trinité, but the main linking lifts are at the head of the valley, at Stafal.

La Trinité's local slopes are centred on the sunny shelf of Gabiet (2300m). Chairs and drags serve the area below it, and above it a long 12-person gondola goes up to Passo dei Salati (3000m). From here, a serious off-piste run makes the link with the pistes of the Alagna valley – you may need a guide to get there. You can descend to Orsia or Stafal (both in the Gressoney valley), where chair-lifts go up towards the Colle Bettaforca (2705m), the link with the Champoluc valley. There are no special facilities for **snowboarders**.

The **snow reliability** is good, thanks to altitude and extensive snowmaking, especially on west-facing runs.

There is not much to interest **experts**, apart from one black of 700m vertical (most blacks on the badly printed piste map turn out to be blue). At Alagna there is a long black run (roughly 7km for only 850m vertical)

from the top of the cable-car at Punta Indren (3260m). But there is great off-piste from the high-points of the lift system in all three valleys, and some excellent heli-drops.

For **intermediates** who like to travel, the area is great, with long runs from the ridges down into the valleys.

Beginners are adequately catered for on the lower slopes at La Trinité, but Champoluc's sunny area at Crest (1950m) is better.

There are long **cross-country** trails around St Jean, and shorter ones up the valley; Brusson, in the Champoluc valley, has the best trails in the area.

Only at weekends, when the Italians arrive, are there **queues**. The **mountain restaurants** are adequate. Reporters recommend making the off-piste trip to the Vieux Crest, above Champoluc.

The **ski schools** don't get much chance to practise English, but classes are small. Facilities for **children**, are lacking, but the area suits them.

STAYING THERE
If you want to be on the slopes first thing, and don't mind isolation, **accommodation** at Stafal is best. The 4-star Monboso is a big modern chalet-style hotel. At La Trinité, half a mile outside the village, reporters recommend the Jolanda Sport and the Dufour, at the foot of the slopes.

Eating out possibilities are limited. **Après-ski** is very quiet; some discos may open up at weekends. Go elsewhere for **off-slope activities**.

STAYING IN THE OTHER VALLEYS
Champoluc is another attractive, quiet chalet-style village with a handful of hotels and only a couple of shops. The hotel Villa Anna Maria is a charming creaky wooden chalet, tucked away amid trees a short walk from the lifts.

Only those with plans to go off-piste should make **Alagna** their base. The pistes are very limited, and don't include the connection to Gressoney.

Livigno

1815m

Lowish prices and highish altitude – a tempting combination

WHAT IT COSTS

(((3)))

HOW IT RATES

The slopes
Snow	****
Extent	**
Experts	**
Intermediates	***
Beginners	****
Convenience	**
Queues	****
Restaurants	***

The rest
Scenery	***
Resort charm	***
Off-slope	**

- ➕ High altitude plus snowmaking ensures a long season and a good chance of snow to resort level
- ➕ Large choice of beginners' slopes
- ➕ Modern and improving lift system, with few queues
- ➕ Cheap by the standards of high resorts, with the bonus of duty-free shopping – a great place to treat yourself to new equipment
- ➕ Cosmopolitan, friendly village with some Alpine atmosphere
- ➕ Long, snowsure cross-country trails

- ➖ No difficult pistes
- ➖ Long airport transfers
- ➖ Links across the valley depend on buses, overcrowded at peak times
- ➖ Village is very long and straggling, and a bit prone to tattiness
- ➖ Very few off-slope amenities
- ➖ Bleak, windy setting – not a good place to be in bad weather
- ➖ Lack of really comfortable hotels bookable through UK tour operators
- ➖ Nightlife can disappoint – it's not as lively as many people expect

Livigno is not an outstanding resort in any respect, and it is not an easy place to get to or to get around. But it offers the unusual combination of a fair-sized intermediate area of slopes, high altitude and fairly low prices. Despite its vaunted duty-free status, hotels, bars and restaurants are not much cheaper than in other major Italian resorts, but shopping is. It cannot compete with eastern Europe on cost, but as a relatively snowsure alternative to the Pyrenees or to the smallest, cheapest resorts in Austria, Livigno seems very attractive.

The scale of the duty-free shopping in the resort may come as a surprise – there are countless camera and clothes shops. It's a pleasant enough place in which to spend time, although it looks a bit of a mess, taken as a whole.

boarding *Livigno attracts a fair number of boarders and young people generally, though it doesn't go far out of its way to attract them – there's a 90m long half-pipe in the Mottolino area, but otherwise little for advanced freestylers. The area has excellent beginner slopes, but the lifts serving most of them are drags. Intermediates and carvers will like the longer, higher runs, accessed mainly by cable-cars and chairs, and the terrain provides plenty of lumps and jumps. Galli's pub tends to be the centre of après-boarding activity.*

The resort

Livigno is an amalgam of three villages in a wide, remote valley near the Swiss border. It is really just a continuous string of hotels, bars and supermarkets lining a single street. The buildings are small in scale and mainly traditional in style, giving the village a pleasant atmosphere. The original hamlet of San Antonio is the nearest thing Livigno has to a centre. Here, the main street and those at right angles linking it to the busy bypass road are nominally traffic-free; but this is Italy, so the traffic ban is not entirely effective. (There is a petrol station right in the middle, spoiling the surroundings of

the central and historic Alpina hotel.) The road that skirts the 'traffic-free' area is constantly busy, and becomes intrusive in the northernmost hamlet of Santa Maria, 1km away. Germans arriving in Livigno to hit the duty-free shops as well as the slopes add to traffic nuisance. The third hamlet, San Rocco, is about 3km further south.

Lifts go to both sides of the valley slopes from the northern end of the resort, and you can get to the western slopes from San Rocco too. The local bus services, running on three colour-coded routes, are free and frequent, but are sometimes confusing, get overcrowded at peak times morning and afternoon and stop early evening.

What's new

Not much to report since the quad chair linking Costaccia to Carosello was opened a couple of seasons ago – a boon if you're based at the north end of the resort.

MOUNTAIN FACTS

Altitude	1815m-3000m
Lifts	30
Pistes	110km
Blue	42%
Red	46%
Black	12%
Artificial snow	none

LIFT PASSES

96/97 prices in lire
Alta Valtellina
Covers all lifts in
Livigno, Bormio
(40km away, but 1hr
30 mins by a very
poor road),
Valdidentro (30km
away) and Santa
Caterina (50km away).
Main pass
1-day pass 48,000
6-day pass 235,000
(low season 210,000
– 11% off)
Senior citizens
Over 65: 6-day pass
160,000 (32% off)
Children
Under 13: 6-day pass
160,000 (32% off)
Short-term passes
Afternoon pass for
Livigno only (35,000).
Notes Day pass price
is for Livigno lifts
only. 6-day pass and
over is valid for one
day in St Moritz and
Engadine.
Alternative passes
Livigno only pass for
up to 2 days (adult 2-
day 90,000).

SCHOOLS/GUIDES

96/97 prices in lire
Livigno Inverno/Estate
Classes 6 days
2hr: 9am-11am or
11am-1pm
6 2hr days: 115,000
Children's classes
Ages: from 4
6 2hr days: 115,000
Private lessons
Hourly
42,000 for 1hr; each
additional person
6,000

OTHER SCHOOLS

Livigno Italy
Azzurra Livigno
Livigno Soc. Coop.

The mountain

The slopes appeal mainly to beginners and intermediates. They are extensive in comparison with many other cheap and cheerful destinations. Scanners that read your lift pass through your clothes make life easier. The pass covers Bormio and Santa Caterina, an easy drive if the high pass is open, and a 6-day pass covers a day in St Moritz – getting there via a road tunnel to the north is more reliable, if busy.

THE SLOPES
Improved links

There are three areas, all of them suitable for moderate and leisurely intermediates, and two of them are reasonably well linked.

The ridge of **Mottolino** is reached by an efficient gondola from Teola, a tiresome walk or a short bus ride from San Antonio. As well as north-west-facing runs back towards Livigno from Monte della Neva, the high point at 2660m (reached by an antique chair that can be fiercely cold), there are north-east-facing pistes and lifts on the other side of the ridge, above Trepalle, on the road to Bormio.

On the other side of the valley, closer to town, chairs in the middle of a row of nursery slopes take you up to **Costaccia** (2370m), where a long high-speed quad chair-lift goes along the ridge towards the **Carosello** sector. The linking runs between these sectors – particularly the one back from Carosello to the top of Costaccia – are not runs you would take for pleasure; depending on the snow conditions and the wind, energetic poling may be needed. Carosello is usually accessed by the optimistically named Carosello 3000 gondola at San Rocco, which goes up to 2750m. Most runs return towards the valley, but there are a couple on the back of the mountain, on the west-facing slopes of Val Federia.

Signposting is patchy and information about which lifts are running is hard to come by.

SNOW RELIABILITY
Very good, despite no glacier

Livigno's slopes are high (you can spend most of your time around 2500m), and with snow guns on the lower slopes of Mottolino and Costaccia, the season is long.

FOR EXPERTS
Not recommended

The piste map shows a few black runs but these are not steep – and recent reporters who visited early in the season found them all in bad condition and closed. There is off-piste to be done, but not many people do it.

FOR INTERMEDIATES
Flattering slopes

Few pistes follow the fall line directly, so good intermediates looking for a challenge could be disappointed. Trying the off-piste may be the best option. The runs on the back of Carosello down to Federia are more challenging, and bumpy. Moderate intermediates have virtually the whole area at their disposal. The long run beneath the Mottolino gondola is one of the best. Leisurely types have several long cruises. Passo d'Eira-Teola, Monte della Neve-Sponda and Costaccia's easy runs are all enjoyable. The run beneath the new Vetta chair, at the top of the Costaccia sector, is a splendid slope for confidence-building – 1.5km long, dropping only 260m.

FOR BEGINNERS
Excellent but scattered slopes

A vast array of nursery slopes along the sunny lower flanks of Costaccia, and other slopes around the valley, make Livigno excellent for novices – although some of the slopes at the northern end are on the steep side. There are lots of longer runs suitable for fast learners and near-beginners.

CROSS-COUNTRY
Good snow, bleak setting

Long snowsure trails (50km in total) follow the valley floor, making Livigno a good choice, though the scenery is bleak. Staying in Santa Maria is best, being close to a nicer trail along the Val Federia. There is a specialist cross-country school, and the resort organises major cross-country races.

QUEUES
Few problems these days

Lift queues are not a problem apart from short delays for the Carosello gondola in peak season. There has been a lot of investment in fast new chairs at Carosello and Mottolino, so queues up the mountain are not a worry. Overcrowded pistes at Mottolino at weekends, are a greater problem, as are queues for buses and restaurants.

MOUNTAIN RESTAURANTS
More than adequate

While there are few great culinary delights by the standards of some Italian resorts, many reporters have commented on the consistent pleasures of the huts. The self-service places at the top of Mottolino and Carosello are acceptable and there are some more charming places lower down. One of the best is not marked on the piste map – Mama's at Passo d'Eira, at the low point of the Mottolino ridge. The welcoming Tea del Vidal is at the base of the same sector, making Mottolino the best bet for serious lunchers, though Costaccia's Tea del Plan is also pleasantly rustic and sunny, with good food. And Tea Bork, in the trees near the bottom of Carosello, offers good value, and great food in a Tirolean-style atmosphere. If you're in the Carosello area, lunch in the valley at the hotel Sporting (close to the gondola station) is popular – excellent cheap pizza. The Bellavista is another resort-level recommendation.

It's all about snow↓

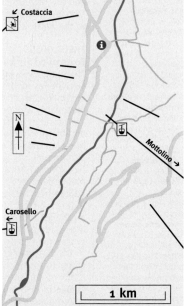

CRYSTAL HOLIDAYS

helped us to compile the Eating out and Après-ski sections. Our thanks to them.

GETTING THERE

Air Bergamo, transfer 5hr.

Rail Tirano (48km), Zernez (Switzerland, 28km); regular buses from station.

UK PACKAGES

Airtours, Crystal, First Choice Ski, Inghams, Neilson, Panorama, Ski Club of GB, Thomson

CHILDCARE

There are no all-day care facilities.

ACTIVITIES

Indoor Sauna, gym, body-building, games room, cinema
Outdoor Cleared paths, skating rink, snow-mobiles, horse-drawn sleigh rides, paragliding, mountaineering

TOURIST OFFICE

Postcode 23030
Tel +39 (342) 996379
Fax 996881

SCHOOLS AND GUIDES
Short lessons a drawback

There are several schools. English is widely spoken, and recent reports are generally favourable. But one reporter notes a reluctance to get beginners off the nursery slopes and up the mountain.

FACILITIES FOR CHILDREN
Bring your own

The schools run children's classes, but (as so often in Italy) there are no special arrangements for all-day care, with or without tuition. One reporter's five-year old was put in a class with adults – and thoroughly enjoyed it.

Staying there

In such a long village, with fragmented slopes, the location of accommodation can be important. Tour operators tend to be a little vague, stating that a particular hotel is 'close to the lifts'; find out which lifts. Beginners should avoid San Rocco (the Carosello end of town), because your school is a bus-ride away in San Antonio. The latter is the best all-round location now there is lift access via Costaccia to Carosello – though it will still be quicker to take a bus out to the Carosello gondola.

HOW TO GO
Lots of hotels, some apartments

Livigno has an enormous range of hotels and a number of apartments. There are some attractively priced catered chalets from UK operators.
Hotels Most of the hotels are small 2- and 3-star places, with a couple of 4-stars out of the centre.
(((3) **Intermonti** Huge, modern 4-star with all mod cons (including a pool); some way from the village, on the slopes of Mottolino – reachable on snow by going off-piste.
(2) **Europa** One of the better 3-stars, within walking distance of the Mottolino gondola and village centre.
(2) **Bivio** Bang in the centre of things, close to schools and lifts; the only hotel in central Livigno with a pool.
(2) **Steinbock** Nice little place, far from major lifts but only five minutes' walk from some nursery slopes.
(2) **Teola** Quiet place, a little way up Mottolino slopes; recommended (despite small bedrooms) for good food and friendly staff.
(2) **Larice** Stylish little 3-star well placed for Costaccia lifts and slopes.

(2) **Montanina** Good central 2-star.
(2) **Gimea** Quiet B&B 300m from Carosello gondola.
(2) **Camana Veglia** Charming old wooden chalet with popular restaurant, well placed in Santa Maria.
(1) **Silvestri** Well liked, reasonably handy for lifts, schools and nightlife.
Self-catering All the big tour operators that come here have apartment options. Most are cheap and cheerful.

EATING OUT
Value for money

Livigno has an appetising range of attractively traditional, unpretentious restaurants, many hotel-based. Hotel Concordia has some of the best cooking in town, and the Camana Veglia restaurant is superior to the hotel's 2-star rating. Mario's has one of the largest menus in town, serving seafood, fondue and steaks in addition to the ubiquitous pizza and pasta. The Bellavista is a charming little restaurant. Bait dal Ghet has excellent pizzas, the Rusticana wholesome, cheap food.

APRES-SKI
Lively, but disappoints some

It's not that there isn't action in Livigno, but simply that the scene is quieter than some people expect in a duty-free resort. Also, the best places are dotted about, leaving the village lacking evening atmosphere. The San Rocco end of town is quiet. At tea-time the Tea del Vidal, at the bottom of Mottolino, gets lively. Most people return to their hotels for a quiet drink. Galli's pub, in San Antonio (not to be confused with the Galli in San Rocco), is popular with Brits. Most after-dinner nightlife doesn't get going until after 10pm. Galli's is again popular. Foxi's cellar video bar is more Italian and stylish. Mario's is another good video bar, with an organist (livelier than it sounds!). The Underground pub is a cheap and cheerful, noisy place.

OFF THE SLOPES
Disappointing but improving

Livigno does not have many off-slope amenities. Walks are uninspiring and there is no sports centre or public swimming pool. The few hotel pools are kept for the exclusive use of guests. Excursions to Bormio and St Moritz are popular things to do.

323

Livigno

Madesimo 1545m

Respectable altitude, some traditional charm and low prices

HOW IT RATES

The slopes

Snow	***
Extent	*
Experts	***
Intermediates	**
Beginners	***
Convenience	***
Queues	***
Restaurants	**

The rest

Scenery	***
Resort charm	**
Off-slope	*

MOUNTAIN FACTS

Altitude 1545m-2890m	
Lifts	23
Pistes	43km
Blue	35%
Red	45%
Black	20%
Artificial snow	9½km

UK PACKAGES

Crystal, Inghams, Neilson, Thomson

TOURIST OFFICE

Postcode 23024
Tel +39 (343) 53015
Fax 53782

Madesimo's mountain has something for everyone, from a decent nursery slope to the Canalone – a classic Alpine black run. Great for Italian weekenders. If you're planning a week, though, it's far from ideal: beginners will not find the progression to real runs easy, and others are likely to find the terrain limited.

THE RESORT

Madesimo sits in a remote, pretty side valley, a three-hour drive north from Bergamo, which ends in a very dramatic hairpin-bend ascent. The village claims 17th-century origins and has restaurants in old farm buildings to prove it. But the rest of the village is a piecemeal modern development. Pitched roofs and timber are evident, but so is concrete. The delightful central church, narrow streets and little shops appear to be overlooked by an airport control tower (the hotel Torre).

THE MOUNTAIN

A two-stage cable-car is the primary lift to the **slopes**, with chair and drag alternatives to the first section. Most runs return to the village, but the top station accesses pistes on the far side of the mountain. You can cut across the wide mountainside to an isolated group of lifts and runs at Motta, also reachable by cable-car from the valley town of Campodolcino.

The altitude of Madesimo's slopes is respectable, but the runs – facing almost east and west – get too much sun for **snow** to be very reliable.

Experts need the upper cable-car to be open for access to the famous Canalone run, a long, sweeping black run which is relatively shady, keeps its snow well, and is nowhere near as terrifying as the locals make out. In theory there is also an itinerary to Campodolcino, a run of 1900m vertical.

The best **intermediate** runs also start from the top station, dropping into the beautiful Valle di Lei, on the morning-sun side of the mountain. The reds from the cable-car mid-station are very pleasant, passing through pretty woodland. The nursery slopes are fine, but improving **beginners** have few really easy pistes to graduate to: some of the blue runs have steeper sections that can prove awkward.

There are no special facilities for **snowboarders**.

There's plenty of **cross-country**

skiing dotted around the area, but you need a car to reach most of it.

There are weekend **queues** for the cable-car, but otherwise few lift delays.

The **mountain restaurants** are not particularly appealing.

Having been popular with British school groups, the **ski school** has plenty of English-speaking instructors.

There are no public **children's facilities**, but the Cascata e Cristallo hotel has a Mini club for infants.

STAYING THERE

The village spreads for some way along both sides of a river, with the old centre and lifts on the eastern side, and many of the hotels and apartments on the other. The main lifts are at the southern end, the nursery slopes about 500m away at the northern end.

A fair choice of **hotels** is available. The Emet is the more traditional of the two 4-stars; the Cascata e Cristallo is a large, modern, multi-amenity place. The small modern 3-star Ferrè is highly recommended by readers; it has a popular après-ski bar. The Andossi is attractive and friendly. You can also get **self-catering** apartments.

Eating out is one of Madesimo's delights. Taverna Verosa is good value, atmospheric and popular for pizzas cooked over an open fire. Osteria Vecchia is a charming, traditional place with some of the best food in town. Dogana Vegia serves tasty specialities in a 17th-century building. The Cantinone, next to the hotel Andossi, is a smart white-walled bar-restaurant, with an exceptional wine list.

Après-ski is fairly quiet. There are several pleasant cafés for a tea-time cappuccino and cakes. The piano cellar bar in the Meridiana and the Ferrè are other focal spots. The Facsimile Videoteque and Queen's are discos that liven up at weekends. Tour reps organise several events.

There's not much to do **off the slopes** – walks and excursions.

Madonna di Campiglio　　1520m

Extensive intermediate slopes amid stunning scenery

WHAT IT COSTS

((((4)

HOW IT RATES

The slopes

Snow	***
Extent	***
Experts	**
Intermediates	****
Beginners	****
Convenience	**
Queues	***
Restaurants	****

The rest

Scenery	****
Resort charm	***
Off-slope	***

MOUNTAIN FACTS

Altitude	1550m-2505m
Lifts	51
Pistes	150km
Blue	43%
Red	41%
Black	16%
Artificial snow	71km

UK PACKAGES

Altours Ski, Crystal, Inghams, Sloping Off, Solo's, Thomson, Winterski

Folgarida Altours Ski, Equity School Ski, Equity Total Ski, Winterski

Marilleva Equity School Ski, Equity Total Ski, Ski Club Europe, Winterski

TOURIST OFFICE

Postcode 38084
Tel +39 (465) 442000
Fax 440404

Madonna is rather like Cortina – a pleasant Dolomite village with an affluent, almost exclusively Italian, clientele. In contrast Folgarida and Marilleva, with which Madonna shares its slopes, have a lot of British school and group visitors.

THE RESORT
Madonna is a modern, but pleasant, traditional-style village that has spread widely across its prettily wooded valley beneath the impressive Brenta Dolomites. It is on a through-road, but most traffic is local and bypasses the focal piazza. There is more development about 1km south, and a frozen lake between the two.

Madonna attracts an affluent, but young, Italian clientele. It has almost as many 4-star hotels as 3-stars, and the kind of smart clothes shops you find in Courmayeur and Cortina. Many visitors potter about the village during the day, and promenading is an important early evening ritual.

THE MOUNTAINS
The terrain is mainly intermediate, both above and below the tree line. There are three areas of **slopes** around Madonna itself, each with a handful of lifts and runs. A cable-car from the edge of the village serves Cinque Laghi to the west, a gondola Pradalago to the north, and a less convenient gondola Monte Spinale to the east. Just outside the village and 130m vertical above it, another gondola serves Passo Groste – the highest area, reaching 2505m, and also accessible via Spinale. Pradalago is linked by lift and piste to Monte Vigo (2180m), where the slopes of Folgarida and Marilleva also meet.

Although many of the runs are sunny, they are at a fair altitude, and all three resorts have invested heavily in snowmakers. As a result, **snow reliability** is reasonable.

Madonna's status as a World Cup racing resort should not lead **experts** to expect a lot. The 3-Tre race-course is the only steep run – but it is steep, as our nightlife consultant found when he tumbled over 200 metres on it. Pista Nera is a good mogul field in the Folgarida section, and the Spinale and Groste areas can have good off-piste.

Cinque Laghi, Madonna's racing mountain, is ideal for good

intermediates. Moderate intermediates will love the area, and have no difficulty exploring most of the network. The tree-lined runs above Folgarida are particularly lovely. Groste and Pradalago have long easy runs, though the former can get crowded.

It's a good resort for **beginners**, provided they don't mind taking a bus out to the excellent main nursery slopes at Campo Carlo Magno (run by a separate lift company). There are fine long runs to progress to.

Snowboarding is popular here and there is a fun-park and half-pipe.

Madonna is big on **cross-country** quality if not quantity. The 30km of trails are very pretty, running through the woods over the pass towards Folgarida. There is a specialist school.

Except at Christmas and New Year, there are few **queues**.

The **mountain restaurants** are a highlight, serving good food in civilised settings, with lovely views.

With several **ski schools** in operation, classes tend to be multi-standard and multi-lingual.

STAYING THERE
There is a shuttle bus, but it's not free and doesn't run at night – so in this spread-out resort it's worth thinking about location. There is a wide choice of **hotels**. The 3-star Christiania B&B hotel takes some beating for convenience. Hotel Bellavista is a friendly, excellent 2-star right by the Pradalago lift. The Lorenzetti is a luxury 4-star on the edge of town but with free daytime transport. Some self-catering is sold by tour ops.

There are 20 **restaurants** to choose from, limited mainly to Italian dishes. Belvedere da Lele, Le Roi and Stube Diana are recommended.

Après-ski can be lively. Bars include the lovely Franz-Joseph Stube, The Pub and the StorkDes Alpes is the smartest venue in town and has live music.

Off the slopes, window-shopping and walking are most popular, but you can also skate and swim.

Pila

1800m

Secret snowsure slopes above cute, ancient town

Pila is virtually unknown outside Italy. It offers a worthwhile surprise to those who pay it a visit. A fair-sized area of well-groomed, snowsure slopes rises around a purpose-built resort, linked by gondola to an old Roman town below.

WHAT IT COSTS

HOW IT RATES

The slopes

Snow	***
Extent	**
Experts	**
Intermediates	****
Beginners	***
Convenience	***
Queues	****
Restaurants	***

The rest

Scenery	***
Resort charm	***
Off-slope	**

MOUNTAIN FACTS

Altitude	1550m-2710m
Lifts	13
Pistes	70km
Blue	43%
Red	41%
Black	16%
Artificial snow	5km

UK PACKAGES

Crystal, Interski, Ski trek

TOURIST OFFICE

Postcode 11100
Tel +39 (165) 521148
Fax 521437

THE RESORT

Pila is a modern, car-free, purpose-built resort right on the slopes and high for an Italian resort at 1800m. Its architecture is a mix of chalet-style buildings and large apartment blocks typical of a French resort. There are genuinely old buildings dotted around the area as well as new constructions.

Below the resort at 1370m, and connected by an 18-minute gondola ride or an 18km drive on a winding road, is the regional capital of Aosta, which was founded by the Romans in 25BC, and the city's 'Historical Guide' lists 25 'important' historical buildings. The centre is traffic-free, with cobbled streets and alleys lined with shops and cafés catering largely for local rather than tourist trade and a huge church and central square.

The whole area is virtually unknown on the international market and the vast majority of visitors are Italian. Other resorts in the Aosta valley, such as Courmayeur, La Thuile and Cervinia, are within easy day-trip distance for those with a car and are covered by the Aosta valley lift pass.

THE MOUNTAINS

The terrain is an interesting mix of **slopes** above and below the tree line, with stunning views from the top (2750m) from Mont Blanc in the west to the Matterhorn and Monte Rosa in the east. Chair-lifts and a cable-car fan out from the village and there are runs for all standards. It's a good resort for snowboarding, with mainly chair-lifts, wide pistes for freeriding, good off-piste and a half-pipe.

Most of the slopes are north- or north-east facing and above 2000m, so **snow reliability** is good. And there's some artificial snow.

Experts will find Pila's slopes limited. There are steep pistes and mogul fields at the top and some good off-piste. But not huge amounts.

But the slopes are ideal for all standards of **intermediate** with great cruising on red and blue runs. A keen piste-basher could cover all the runs in a day or two but there is more variety here than in nearby Courmayeur.

It's a good resort for **beginners**, with a nursery area right on your doorstep and wide, easy, well-groomed runs to progress to.

There are only 8km of prepared **cross-country** trails but these are at altitude and so snowsure.

Except at weekends, when Italians in the know pour on to the slopes, there are few **queues**.

There are several good **mountain restaurants**. Our favourite was the rustic Lo Bautson (which means cowshed) – where the Penne all'Arrabiata was one of our best ever.

The only **ski school** reports we've had are of the Interski operation, which features mainly British instructors – satisfied customers only.

STAYING THERE

The choice is between staying at the resort and in Aosta. The former is more convenient for the skiing, the latter for old-town atmosphere, visiting other resorts and price. Most of the resort **hotels** and apartments are right on the slopes and there are several pizza and pasta **restaurants** as alternatives to those in the hotels and apartment complexes. **Après-ski** is quiet during the week but at weekends the Karaoke at the Bar Brimod and the disco at the KU liven up.

In Aosta most **hotels** are 3-star, near the centre and an easy 10-minute walk from the gondola. We stayed in the reasonable 4-star Europe. There's also a Holiday Inn. There's a good choice of **restaurants** which cater mainly for locals. **Après-ski** largely means local bars, but there are a couple of discos. And there's a casino in nearby St Vincent.

Off the slopes, Aosta is a far more interesting base than Pila for people not intending to hit the slopes. It has lots of shops, sights, bars and streets to wander around. And there are ice hockey matches to watch.

Sauze d'Oulx 1510m

'Suzy does it' still, but with more dignity than in the past

WHAT IT COSTS

(((3)))

HOW IT RATES

The slopes

Snow	**
Extent	*****
Experts	**
Intermediates	****
Beginners	**
Convenience	**
Queues	***
Restaurants	***

The rest

Scenery	***
Resort charm	**
Off-slope	*

➕ Extensive and uncrowded slopes, great intermediate cruising

➕ Linked into Milky Way

➕ Mix of open and tree-lined runs is good for all weather conditions

➕ Entertaining nightlife

➕ Some scope for off-piste adventures

➕ One of the cheapest major resorts there is – and more attractive than its reputation suggests

➖ Brashness and Britishness of resort will not suit everyone

➖ Lots of old lifts, making progress around the slopes slow

➖ Crowds at weekends

➖ Very few challenging pistes for experts

➖ Poor snow reliability in late season

➖ Steep walks around the village, and an inadequate shuttle bus service

We've revisited Sauze d'Oulx twice since the last edition and have been very impressed with its extensive, ideal intermediate terrain. Slopes are attractively varied, prettily wooded and, on our visits, were well-groomed and maintained. Although there is little to challenge experts, some of the slopes were deserted enough to allow enjoyable high-speed cruising. Short school hours and the need to ride lifts to the main nursery slopes make it less attractive to beginners.

Sauze d'Oulx is still remembered for the reputation that it had in the early 1980s of being prime lager-lout territory. Its nickname – 'Suzy does it' – only increased expectations. And a lot of people avoided it because of that reputation (and some severe snow shortages). Sauze has now justifiably regained its popularity as a budget destination for, mainly young, Brits. While it still has bars and shops conspicuously aimed at the British it now offers an affordable combination of extensive slopes and animated nightlife for those who want a lively, but not wild, time.

And those for whom nightlife matters little – families, for example – needn't stay away. Like us, most reporters seem to like the resort more than they expected.

What's new

No new lifts this season but those who haven't visited for a few years will be delighted to find three high-speed quad chairs dotted around the slopes, including the main lift up to Sportinia. But lots of other lifts badly need updating.

boarding *Sauze has good snowboarding slopes – it's got local tree-lined slopes (with space in the trees too), high, undulating, open terrain, and links to other resorts in the Milky Way. But although it has a fair number of chair-lifts, there are also lots of drags – a serious drawback for inexperienced riders. There's no park or pipe, but the amount and variety of terrain makes up for this. Sauze's mainly young visitors ensure lively, entertaining nightlife.*

The resort

Sauze d'Oulx sits on a gentle mountain shelf facing north-west across the Valle di Susa. It's not immediately obvious, but Sauze has an attractive old core, with narrow, twisting streets and the occasional carved stone drinking fountain; houses have huge stone slabs serving as roof slates.

Most of the resort, however, is modern and undistinguished, made up of block-like hotels, relieved by the occasional chalet, spreading down the steep hillside, from the foot of the slopes to the village centre and beyond. Despite the shift in clientele,

the centre is still quite lively at night, with late-closing bars that are usually quite full, as well as a handful of discos that do most of their business at the weekend.

Out of the bustle of the centre, where most of the bars and nightclubs are located, there are quiet, wooded residential areas full of secluded apartment blocks, and a number of good restaurants are also tucked out of the way of the front line. Chair-lifts go from the top of the village and from two points on its fringes. There's also a chair from nearby Jouvenceaux.

Traffic roams freely through the village, which can be congested

MOUNTAIN FACTS

Figures relate to the
whole Milky Way area

Altitude	1390m-2825m
Lifts	97
Pistes	400km
Blue	12%
Red	67%
Black	21%
Artificial snow	65km

LIFT PASSES

97/98 prices in lire
La Via Lattea
Covers all lifts in
Sauze d'Oulx,
Sestriere, Sansicario,
Cesana and Clavière.
Beginners Points
book (85 points
100,000), with lifts
costing from 1 to 12
points.
Main pass
1-day pass 50,000
6-day pass 260,000
(low season 210,000
– 19% off)
Senior citizens
Over 60: 6-day pass
234,000 (10% off)
Children
Under 13: 6-day pass
234,000 (10% off)
Under 8: free pass
Short-term passes
Some single ascent
passes and afternoon
pass.
Notes Includes one
free day in each of:
Alpe-d'Huez, Les Deux
Alpes, Serre-Chevalier
and Puy-St-Vincent.
One day extension for
Montgenèvre (18,000).
One day extension for
Pragelato (10,000).
Alternative passes
La Via Lattea VIP card
also covers
Montgenèvre and
Pragelato.

morning and evening as cars vie for
convenient parking spaces or the
quickest way out of town. The roads
become slushy and dirty during the
day and icy and treacherous at night –
hazardous as there are few pavements.
Free buses run around the resort, but a
few reporters complain of them being
infrequent and crowded, and the ones
to Jouvenceaux stop as soon as the
lifts close.

Sauze is surrounded by trees, and
on a good day the views across the
Valle di Susa, to the towering
mountains forming the border with
France, can be spectacular.

The mountains

Sauze's mountains provide excellent
intermediate terrain. The piste grading
fluctuates from year to year, if you
believe the resort's map – and we're
not sure we've caught up with the
latest changes from blue to red and
red to blue. But most reporters agree
that many runs graded red or even
black should really be graded blue;
challenges are few, and far between.
(The same might be said of the whole
extensive Milky Way area, of which
Sauze is one extreme.)

THE SLOPES
Big and varied enough for most
Sauze's local slopes are spread across
a broad wooded bowl above the
resort, ranging from west- to north-
facing. The main lifts are chairs, from
the top of the village up to **Clotes** and
from the western fringes to **Sportinia** –
a sunny mid-mountain clearing in the
woods, with a ring of restaurants and
hotels (see Staying up the mountain)
and a small nursery area.

The high-point of the system is
Monte Fraiteve. From here you can
travel west on splendid broad, long
runs to **Sansicario** – and on to chair-
lifts near **Cesana Torinese** which link
with **Claviere** and then **Montgenèvre**, in
France, the far end of the Milky Way
(though both are reached more quickly
by car). You can travel back to Sauze
on some of the steepest terrain in the
area. But there is no longer a piste
south to **Sestriere** – you get there from
the lower point of Col Basset. If you
have a car you can go beyond
Montgenèvre to Briançon, Serre
Chevalier and Bardonecchia.

As in so many Italian resorts, piste
marking, direction signing and piste

map design are not taken seriously.
But maintenance seems good most of
the time.

The linked slopes of Sestriere and
Montgenèvre are dealt with separately.

SNOW RELIABILITY
Can be poor, affecting the links
Sauze's biggest problem is that many
of the slopes get a lot of afternoon
sun. At these modest altitudes, late-
season conditions are far from reliable.
Recent reporters found the icy, bare
slopes at vital link points problematical
earlier in the season, too – particularly
from M Fraiteve. There's snowmaking
on a couple of slopes, notably the key
home run from P Rocca via Clotes to
the village.

FOR EXPERTS
Head off-piste
Very few of the pistes are challenging.
The best slopes are at virtually
opposite ends of Sauze's local area – a
high, north-facing run from the
shoulder of M Fraiteve, and the sunny
slopes below M Montcrons. The main
interest is in going off-piste. There are
plenty of minor opportunities within
the piste network, but the highlights
are long, top-to-bottom descents of up
to 1300m vertical from M Fraiteve,
ending (snow permitting) at villages
dotted along the valleys. The best-
known of these runs (which used to be
marked on the piste map) is the Rio
Nero, down to the road near Oulx.
When snow low down is poor, some of
these runs can be cut short at
Jouvenceaux or Sansicario.

FOR INTERMEDIATES
Splendid cruising terrain
The whole area is ideal for confident
intermediates who want to clock up
the kilometres. For the less confident,
the piste map doesn't help because it
picks out only the very easiest runs in
blue – there are many others they
could manage. The Belvedere and
Montcrons sectors at the east of the
area are served only by drags but offer
some wonderful, uncrowded high
cruising, some of it above the tree line.

The long runs down to Sansicario
and down to Jouvenceaux are splendid
confidence boosting intermediate
terrain. The run down to Sestriere gets
a lot of sun but is worth it for the
somewhat more challenging
intermediate terrain on the opposite
side of the valley.

SCHOOLS/GUIDES

96/97 prices in lire

Sauze Sportinia
Classes 6 days
3hr: 10am-1pm
6 3hr days: 190,000
Children's classes
Ages: from 6
6 3hr days: 190,000
Private lessons
Hourly
50,000 for 1hr

Sauze d'Oulx
Classes 6 days
3hr: 10am-1pm
6 3hr days: 190,000
Children's classes
Ages: from 6
6 3hr days: 190,000
Private lessons
Hourly
50,000 for 1hr

Sauze Project
Italian-speaking
school only.

CHILDCARE

The village
kindergarten (858396)
has English and
Italian staff and takes
children aged from 6
months to 6 years,
from 9am to 5pm.
You have to provide
lunch, but it can be
heated up.

At the higher levels, where the slopes are above the tree line, the terrain often allows a choice of route. Lower down are pretty runs through the woods, where the main complication can be route-finding. The mountainside is broken up by gullies, and pistes that appear to be quite close together may in fact have no easy connections between them.

FOR BEGINNERS
There are better choices
Sauze is not ideal for beginners: its village-level slopes are a bit on the steep side and the main nursery area is up the mountain, at Sportinia. Equally importantly, the mornings-only classes don't suit everyone.

FOR CROSS-COUNTRY
Severely limited, even with snow
There is very little cross-country skiing, and it isn't reliable for snow.

QUEUES
Slow lifts the biggest problem
There can be 10-minute waits at Sportinia when school classes are setting off, or immediately after lunch, but otherwise the system has few bottlenecks. More of a problem are the ancient, slow lifts even though high-speed quads – such as the ones up to Sportinia, Triplex and Col Basset – are more in evidence these days. It can seem to take an age to get to the top of the mountain in the morning via Clotes. This route is not yet blessed with fast lifts. Breakdowns on drag-lifts may also be a nuisance.

MOUNTAIN RESTAURANTS
Some pleasant possibilities
Restaurants are numerous, and generally pleasant. The hotel Capricorno, at Clotes, is one of the most civilised and appealing lunch-spots in the Alps. It is not cheap, though. There are more modest mid-mountain restaurants across the mountainside, with the main concentration at Sportinia, where service is friendly. The Capanina and the Genevris at the bottom of the Chardonnet lifts at Belvedere were most popular with recent reporters.

SCHOOLS AND GUIDES
Tuition variable, large classes
We always used to get good reports about the schools here, but some recent reporters found a lack of good

---

English spoken and large classes. Some found the tuition satisfactory, others were disappointed. Classes are only half-day, but are three hours' tuition. Reporters on the school in Sansicario found the instruction enthusiastic and useful, and said the instructors spoke good English.

FACILITIES FOR CHILDREN
Consider Neilson
As well as the resort kindergarten, there is the possibility of plugging into the arrangements Neilson offer at the hotel des Amis, down in Jouvenceaux: a crèche for children aged 6 months to 2 years and a children's club for those aged 3 to 8.

Staying there

Most of the hotels are reasonably central, but the Clotes lift is at the top of the village, up a short but steep hill, and the Sportinia chair is an irritatingly long walk beyond that. There is a shuttle bus, but it is infrequent and unreliable, and gets very crowded in the morning peak.

HOW TO GO
Packaged hotels dominate
All the major mainstream operators offer hotel packages here, but there are also one or two chalets. Most of the big tour operators have at least one chalet here.

Hotels Simple 2-star and 3-star hotels form the core of the holiday accommodation, with a couple of 4-stars and some more basic places.
(((3) **Capricorno** Small, charming; at Clotes (see Staying up the mountain).
(((3) **La Torre** Cylindrical landmark 200m below centre. Excellent rooms and buffet-style food; free wine; mini-buses to lifts.
((2) **Hermitage** Neat chalet-style hotel in about the best spot for the slopes – beside the home piste from Clotes.
((2) **Stella Alpina** Right at the foot of the slopes, just below the Clotes chair-lift. Well run – friendly and lively (and home to the popular New Scotch Bar).
((2) **Gran Baita** Comfortable place in quiet, central back-street, with excellent food and good rooms, some with spectacular sunset views from their balconies.
((2) **Biancaneve** Pleasant, with smallish rooms. Close to the centre.
((2) **Des Amis** Down in Jouvenceaux, but close to bus stop; small, simple

Long views across the resort →

GETTING THERE

Air Turin, transfer 2hr.

Rail Oulx (5km); frequent buses.

hotel run by Anglo-Italian couple, with childcare facilities offered through Neilson.

Self-catering There are apartments and chalets available, some through UK tour operators.

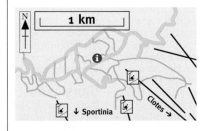

EATING OUT
Caters for all tastes and pockets
Typical Italian banquets of five or six courses can be had in the upmarket Don Vincenzo and Il Cantun restaurants. The Italian chef at the Del Falco cooks a particularly good three-course 'skiers' menu'. In the old town, Del Borgo serves perhaps the best pizza in town, and has a very friendly atmosphere. Nearby is La Griglia, which is full of character and does a good steak. Il Lampione is the place to go for 'pub grub' – good-value Chinese, Mexican and Indian food. We have a report that Sago's provides delicious, filling and economic fare.

UK PACKAGES

Airtours, Bladon Lines, Crystal, Equity Total Ski, First Choice Ski, Inghams, Neilson, Panorama, Ski Club of GB, Thomson, Winterski

ACTIVITIES

Indoor Bowling, cinema, sauna, massage
Outdoor Artificial skating rink, floodlit tobogganing, torchlit descents, heli-skiing from Sestriere

TOURIST OFFICE

Postcode 10050
Tel +39 (122) 858009
Fax 850497

APRES-SKI
Suzy does it with more dignity

Once favoured almost solely by large groups of youngsters, some of whom were very rowdy, the number and atmosphere of Sauze's bars now impresses reporters young and old.

The Assietta terrace is popular for catching the last rays of the sun at the end of the day. The more discerning then move on to the excellent New Scotch Bar, while nearby the once-famous Andy Capp's Pub still attracts punters looking for a 'home from home'. Il Lampione, in the old town is highly recommended for crêpes.

After dinner, more places warm up. One of the best is the smart, atmospheric cocktail bar Moncrons, which holds regular quiz nights. We also like the late-night Osteria, under Andy Capp's, which is popular with Italians and workers. The Cotton Club provides good service, directors chairs, video screen and draught cider. The Rock Café has as many Italian clients as Brits. Upstairs is popular with an older crowd, and downstairs has karaoke. Gossips is a bit of a hike but has live music every night. It has a rowdy, mainly British clientele and Italian staff. Gran Trun also has live music and reminded us of a Majorcan barbecue venue, with bottles on the wall and white stucco decor. Of the discos, Banditos is a walk away, and popular with Italians. Schuss runs theme nights and drink promotions – and Brits get in free.

Tour reps organise activities including torchlit descents, bowling and 'broomball' on the ice rink.

OFF THE SLOPES
Go elsewhere

Sauze is not a particularly pleasant place in which to while away the days if you don't want to hit the slopes. Shopping is limited, there are no gondolas or cable-cars for pedestrians and there are few off-slope activities.

STAYING UP THE MOUNTAIN
You pays your money . . .

In most resorts, staying up the mountain is an amusing thing to do and is often economical – but usually you pay the price of accepting simple accommodation. Here, the reverse applies. The 4-star Capricorno, up at Clotes, is one of the most comfortable hotels in Sauze, certainly the most attractive and by a wide margin the most expensive. It's a charming little chalet beside the piste, with a smart restaurant and terrace (a very popular spot for a good lunch on the mountain) and only eight bedrooms.

Not quite in the same league are the places up at Sportinia. Crystal are running a couple of them now as jumbo chalets. They also have a smaller chalet here.

Reporters who stayed here enjoyed the isolation and easy access to the slopes – but you can't get down to town after 4pm.

Sansicario 1700m

If any resort is ideally placed for exploration of the whole Milky Way, it is Sansicario. It is a modern, rather soulless, purpose-built, self-contained resort mainly consisting of apartments linked by monorail to the little shopping precinct. The 40-room Rio Envers is a comfortable, quite expensive hotel. Visitors recommend the Chalmettes for its views and food at lunchtime, and the Pinoteca in the evening for fondue and grappa. There's not really much nightlife.

Selva/Sella Ronda   1565m

Spectacular Dolomite resort ideal for intermediates

WHAT IT COSTS

ⓒⓒⓒ④

HOW IT RATES

The slopes
Snow	****
Extent	*****
Experts	***
Intermediates	*****
Beginners	****
Convenience	***
Queues	***
Restaurants	****

The rest
Scenery	*****
Resort charm	***
Off-slope	***

➕ Vast network of connected slopes – suits intermediates particularly well

➕ Stunning, unique Dolomite scenery

➕ Superb snowmaking and grooming

➕ Jolly mountain huts with good food

➕ Many new lifts with just a few bad Sella Ronda circuit bottlenecks

➕ Good nursery slopes

➕ Excellent value

➖ Small proportion of tough runs

➖ Lifts and slopes can be crowded especially on Sella Ronda circuit

➖ High proportion of short runs, not so many long ones

➖ Not the most attractive of villages

➖ Erratic snow record; slopes vulnerable to warm weather

➖ Main language is German, which detracts from jolly Italian feel

The slopes of the Sella Ronda have been revolutionised over recent years by heavy investment in both the lift system and artificial snowmaking. Both are now among the best and most extensive in Europe. Combine that with extraordinarily picturesque Dolomite scenery, a lift pass which covers over 460 lifts and 1100km of runs, cheap Italian prices and jolly mountain refuges, and you have a compelling case for going on holiday there.

Only experts who find a lack of challenging runs frustrating will be disappointed with the slopes. If what you want is a feeling of travelling around great scenery, there's little to beat the Sella Ronda – a trip around the Gruppo Sella massif easily covered in a day by an average intermediate. On the way round you will hit many separate local slopes worth exploring – but also crowds and queues.

If you don't want to stay in Selva there are plenty of smaller, quiet, attractive places on the circuit to base yourself in.

boarding *Selva is one of the few Italian resorts to build a half-pipe and fun-park; but they are away from the main pistes, by the chair-lift leading to the summit of the Seceda. The main lifts out of Selva are all gondolas or chairs and you can do the Sella Ronda clockwise using only one drag – though the anti-clockwise route has more. As with the skiing, the area will mainly suit beginners and intermediates, with little to challenge experts. And for boarders there are some frustratingly flat sections where you'll have to scoot or walk. There are enough lively bars to have a good time in the evenings.*

What's new

For the 1997/98 season the single Costabella chair out of Selva to the Dantercëpies gondola will be replaced by a high-speed quad, eliminating one of the worst queues on the Sella Ronda circuit. And a new 3-person chair-lift will be built from Plan to the lifts in Selva, allowing people to avoid poling along a flat section of the circuit. A couple of quads are being built in the Alta Badia.

This continues the recent radical improvement in the area's lift system. In 1996/97 the most notable new lift was an eight-seat gondola replacing two slow chairs in the Canazei-Campitello area from Lupo Bianco to Sellajoch, eliminating another bottleneck.

A proposed underground rail link between the Campinoi and the Col Raiser gondolas has been delayed.

The resort

Selva is a long roadside village, almost merged with the next village of Santa Cristina. It suffers from traffic but has traditional-style architecture and an attractive central church. And it enjoys a lovely setting among trees beneath the impressive pink-tinged walls of the Gruppo Sella massif and Sassolungo. The area is famous for its wood carvings and you'll see them all over.

Despite its World Cup fame (as Val Gardena, the name of the valley) and animated atmosphere, Selva is neither upmarket nor brash. It's a good-value, lively but civilised family resort.

Gondolas rise in two directions. One east from the top of the nursery slopes towards Colfosco and Corvara and the clockwise Sella Ronda route; the other south from the village to Ciampinoi and the anti-clockwise route.

The free buses that run around the resort are usually packed – some reporters preferred shared taxis.

The local Ladino dialect has resisted being absorbed into either German or Italian. The main language, however, is German – as are most of the visitors. Place names are normally given in both German and Italian. Selva is also known as Wolkenstein and the Gardena valley as Gröden. For many years the area was under Austrian rule and the influence is still strong.

MOUNTAIN FACTS

Altitude	1230m-2520m
Lifts	81
Pistes	175km
Blue	30%
Red	60%
Black	10%
Artificial snow	90km

LIFT PASSES

97/98 prices in lire
Dolomiti Superski
Covers 464 lifts and
118km of piste in the
Dolomites, including
all Sella Ronda
resorts.
Main pass
1-day pass 58,000
6-day pass 286,000
(low season 249,000
– 13% off)
Senior citizens
Over 60: 6-day pass
228,800 (20% off)
Children
Under 18: 6-day pass
200,000 (30% off)
Under 6: free pass
Alternative passes
Val Gardena pass
covers all lifts in
Selva Gardena, S
Cristina, Ortisei and
Alpe di Siusi, and ski-
bus between Selva
Gardena and Ortisei.

The mountain

The slopes here cover a vast area, all
amid stunning scenery and practically
all ideally suited to intermediates who
don't mind shortish runs. You can set
off for the day, pick an area that takes
your fancy and explore the local area.
Or you can set off round the Sella
Ronda circuit – see below.

It's an easy road trip to Cortina,
covered by the Dolomiti Superski pass.

THE SLOPES
High mileage piste excursions

A gondola and parallel-running chair
go up from Selva to **Ciampinoi**, from
where several pistes spread out across
the mountain and lead back down to
Selva, **Santa Cristina** and **Plan de
Gralba**. These include the famous
World Cup Downhill run which takes
place in mid-December each year. From
Plan de Gralba, you can head off
towards **Passo Sella**, **Canazei** and the
rest of the Sella Ronda.

Across the valley from the Ciampinoi
gondola is a chair that links with the
Dantercëpies gondola. This accesses
the Sella Ronda in the opposite
direction or you can return to Selva on
the Ladies Downhill. From the top you
head down to **Colfosco**, then lifts link
with **Corvara** and from there to **Arabba**
and the rest of the Sella Ronda.

There are several linked areas that
are not directly on the Sella Ronda
circuit that are worth exploring. The
biggest is the **Alta Badia** area to the
west of Corvara, from which you can
get down to **San Cassiano** and **La Villa**.

Local to Selva is the **Seceda** area,
accessed by a gondola a bus-ride from
town. You can head back down to the
bottom of here or to **Ortisei**. And from
Ortisei a cable-car goes up the other
side of the valley to **Alpe di Siusi** and
its virtually flat plateau of easy runs,
cross-country and walks.

SNOW RELIABILITY
Excellent when it's cold

The slopes are not high. There's very
little above 2200m. Most are between
1500m and 2000m. And the Dolomites
miss out on many of the snowstorms
which affect the Alps to the north. But

THE SELLA RONDA

*The Sella Ronda is one of the world's classic circuits for intermediates and above.
The journey around the Sella massif, among spectacular Dolomite scenery, is
easily managed in a day by even an early intermediate. We did it last season in
just three and a half hours plus some diversions and hut stops.*

*The slopes you travel along are almost all easy and take in Colfosco, Corvara,
Arabba and Canazei. You can do the circuit clockwise by following very clearly
marked orange arrows and direction boards or anti-clockwise by following the
green boards. We preferred the clockwise route which is slightly quicker and
avoids a tedious series of four drag lifts from Colfosco towards Selva. Reporters
agree this way is also better for interesting slopes. There's now a good free map of
the Sella Ronda, complete with contour lines so you can get a good idea of how
the land lies.*

*The whole journey involves around 23km of skiing or boarding and around 14km
of lift riding. The lifts take a total of about two hours (plus any queuing). But be
warned: it can be crowded (both on the pistes and on the lifts) on busy days, with
hordes of people having the same idea as you. 'Just like the M25,' said one
reporter. Set out early and, if possible, choose low season or a Saturday.*

*To make the journey more enjoyable we suggest experts take time out for some
diversions on the way. The long runs down from Ciampinoi to Santa Cristina
and Selva, from Dantercepies to Selva, from the top of the Boe gondola back
down to Corvara and the runs from the top of the Arabba gondola are
particularly entertaining. Take in all those in a day round the circuit and you'll
have had a good day! Intermediates could take time out to explore the off-the-
circuit Alta Badia area. Groups of different standards can do the circuit and
arrange to meet along the way. There are plenty of welcoming refugios at which
to take a break.*

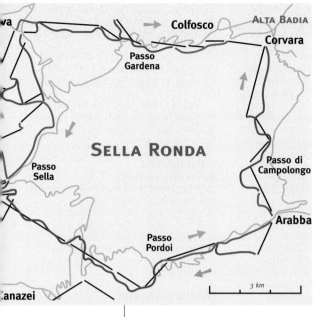

Colfosco

ALTA BADIA

Corvara

Passo
Gardena

SELLA RONDA

Passo
Sella

Passo di
Campolongo

Arabba

Passo
Pordoi

Canazei

3 km

the area has invested heavily in snowmaking and now has one of the largest capacities in Europe, covering 90km of runs. Only the high Arabba, Passo Sella and Pordoi sections lack cannons. All other areas have snowmakers on at least the main runs to resorts, and almost all Selva's local pistes are liberally endowed. Good piste grooming adds to the effectiveness of the snowmaking.

The only problem therefore arises in poor snow years when temperatures are too high to make snow. We have experienced excellent pistes here in times of severe natural snow shortage. And the Marmolada glacier near Arabba is now open most of the winter for great snow and views, but it is not included in the lift pass.

FOR EXPERTS
Staying in Arabba is better
Arabba has the best steep slopes, though it's rather distant from Selva with a lot of bland runs en route. The

335

Selva/Sella Ronda

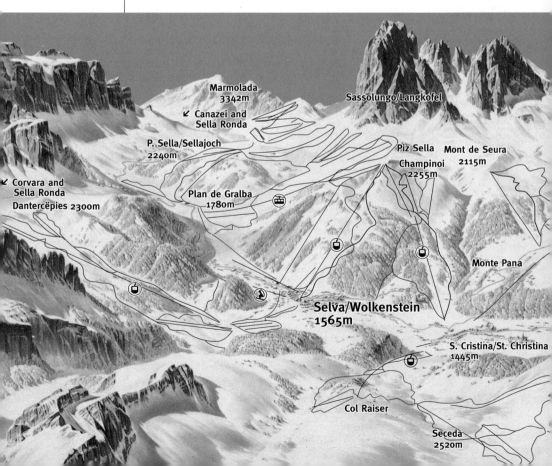

Marmolada
3342m

Sassolungo/Langkofel

↙ Canazei and
Sella Ronda

P. Sella/Sellajoch
2240m

Piz Sella   Mont de Seura
Champinoi   2115m
2255m

↙ Corvara and
Sella Ronda
Dantercëpies 2300m

Plan de Gralba
1780m

Monte Pana

Selva/Wolkenstein
1565m

S. Cristina/St. Christina
1445m

Col Raiser

Seceda
2520m

SCHOOLS/GUIDES
97/98 prices in lire

Selva Gardena
Classes 6 days
4hr: 9am-1pm or 1pm-
5pm; 2hr: 11am-1pm
6 4hr days: 230,000
Children's classes
Ages: 4 to 12
6 6hr days: 395,000
Private lessons
Hourly
54,000 for 1hr for 1
person; each
additional person
10,000

Ortisei
Classes 6 days
3hr: am or pm
6 3hr days: 200,000
Children's classes
Ages: from 3
6 4hr days: 230,000
Private lessons
Hourly
53,000 for 1hr for 1
person; each
additional person
10,000

S Cristina
Classes 6 days
2hr: am and pm
6 3½hr days: 225,000
Children's classes
Ages: from 2½
6 4hr days: 230,000
Private lessons
Hourly
53,000 for 1hr for 1
person; each
additional person
10,000

north-facing blacks and reds from Porta Vescovo back to Arabba are served by an efficient high-capacity gondola and are great fun. The Val Gardena World Cup piste, the 'Saslonch', is one of several steepish runs between Ciampinoi and both Selva and Santa Cristina. Unlike many World Cup pistes it is kept in racing condition, for Italian team practices, but is open to the public much of the time. It's especially good in January, when it's not too crowded. The unpisted trail from the top of the Saltaria chair on Alpe Di Siusi down to Santa Cristina is not difficult, but pleasantly lonely.

For the daring there is also exciting off-piste to be explored with a guide. The run from Sass Pordoi (the highest point around at 2950m) to Colfosco finishes in the spectacular narrow descent through the Val Mezdi. For the not so daring, a trip in the terrifying cable-car is worth it for the view.

Overall, off-piste is limited because of the sheer-drop nature of the tops of the mountains in the Dolomites.

In general, experts might find the region as a whole too tame, especially if they are looking for a lot of steep challenges or moguls.

FOR INTERMEDIATES
A huge network of ideal runs
The Sella Ronda region is renowned for its easy slopes. The runs down from Dantercëpies to Colfosco and Corvara, and across the valley from there in the Alta Badia are superb for early or unadventurous intermediates – it is a big area of confidence-boosting runs. These are easily reached from Selva, though returning home from Dantercëpies may be a little daunting. Riding the gondola down is an option. Nearer to Selva itself, the runs in the the Plan de Gralba area are nice and gentle. The Alpe di Siusi runs above Ortisei are rather flat, but pleasant for timid intermediates.

Average intermediates have a very large network of suitable pistes, though there are few long runs. The beautiful swoop down the far side of the Seceda massif from Cuca to Ortisei is a good long run. The Plan de Gralba area, the runs either side of the Saltaria chair, and the main pistes down to La Villa and San Cassiano are other particularly nice cruises.

Recent reporters rave about the spectacular 'hidden valley', reached via

a cable-car at Lagazuoi to which you get a bus or shared taxis from Armentarola. See the Cortina chapter for more details.

The runs back down to the valley direct from Ciampinoi are a bit more challenging, as are the descents from Dantercëpies to Selva.

And of course most intermediates will want to do the Sella Ronda circuit at least once during a week – see feature panel earlier.

FOR BEGINNERS
Great slopes, but ...
Near-beginners have numerous runs, and the village nursery slopes are excellent – spacious, convenient, and kept in good condition. In fact a recently visiting beginner thoroughly recommends the area. However, we have varying reports about the school – see opposite.

FOR CROSS-COUNTRY
Beautiful trails
There are over 70km of trails all enjoying wonderful scenery. The 12km trail up the Vallunga-Langental valley is particularly attractive, with neck-craning views all around. The largest section of trails (40km) has the advantage of being at altitude, running between Monte Pana and Seiseralm, and across Alpe di Siusi.

QUEUES
Much improved: a few problems
New lifts have vastly improved this once badly queue-prone area. Bottlenecks are no longer as common and, except for peak periods, most areas are now fairly queue-free. One of the worst queues – for the single chair from Selva to the Dantercëpies gondola – will be eliminated for the 1997/98 season by its replacement by a high-speed quad. Another – for the chairs from Lupo Bianco near Canazei to Passo Sella – was solved by a new eight-seater gondola in 1996/97.

But in busy periods the chair-lifts from Arabba in both directions can still be a problem, as can the long, cold drag-lifts from Colfosco to Selva.

And you may find the crowds on the pistes worse than the queues.

MOUNTAIN RESTAURANTS
One of the area's highlights
Our reporters are unanimous in their praise for the mountain huts – there are lots of them all over the area and

CHILDCARE

The ski school runs a kindergarten for children aged 1 to 4, with skiing available for the older children. Those attending proper ski school classes can be looked after all day.

GETTING THERE

Air Verona, transfer 3hr. Innsbruck, transfer 3hr.

Rail Chiusa (27km), Bressanone (35km), Bolzano (40km); frequent buses from station.

UK PACKAGES

Bladon Lines, Crystal, First Choice Ski, Inghams

Arabba Inghams, Neilson, Ski Beach Villas

Campitello Crystal, First Choice Ski, Inghams

Canazei Crystal, First Choice Ski, Inghams, Neilson

Kastelruth Inntravel

La Villa Neilson, Ski Beach Villas

San Cassiano First Choice Ski

Val Gardena Waymark Holidays

virtually all offer good food, atmosphere and value for money.

In Val Gardena: The Panorama is a small, cosy, rustic sun-trap at the foot of the Dantercëpies drag. On the way down to Plan de Gralba from Ciampinoi, the Vallongia Rolandhütte is tucked away on a corner of the piste. In the Plan de Gralba area the top station of the cable-car does excellent pizza slices; the Comici is atmospheric with a big sun terrace; Piz Seteur is beautifully situated but can get very full. Further west the restaurant above the Col Raiser gondola has a large sun terrace with marvellous views.

Colfosco area: The triumvirate of little huts – Forcelles, Edelweiss and Pradat – are all very pleasant.

Alta Badia: The Piz Sorega above San Cassiano gets very busy. Nearby Las Vegas is smaller and more atmospheric – lots of stuffed creatures, if you like that sort of thing. Pride of place must go to Trappers' Home – a Wild West mountain hut with totem pole, tepee, country music and a Harley Davidson in the basement. Cherz above Passo di Campolongo has great views of Marmolada (and a beautiful big St Bernard).

Around Arabba: Bec de Roces and Col de Burz are both sun-traps. Capanna Bill, on the long run down to Malga Ciapella, has stunning views of the Marmolada glacier.

Above Canazei: there are at least six huts dotted around the Belvedere bowl. Lower down, Lupo Bianco is a notable rendezvous point and sun-trap. As well as restaurants, there are lots of little snow bars for a quick grappa.

SCHOOLS AND GUIDES
Don't count on English

Lack of English-speaking instruction may be a problem. Recent reporters give us varying accounts. If you are lucky enough to be in a suitable group and to get a good English-speaker or understand German or Italian, the lesson is likely to be useful. Selva has a good reputation for standards of tuition and private lessons are reported to be very good.

FACILITIES FOR CHILDREN
Good by Italian standards

There are comprehensive childcare arrangements, but English is not routinely spoken. That said, we have reports of very enjoyable lessons, and children longing to return

Selva is the biggest and liveliest of the places to stay right on the Sella Ronda circuit. Ortisei is the administrative centre of the Val Gardena – pretty, and more of a complete community – but it is not so convenient for the slopes. For a brief description of the other villages on or near the circuit, see the end of this chapter.

In Selva itself, the most convenient position to stay is near one of, or between, the two main gondolas. There is a free, regular bus service throughout the valley until early evening, but reporters say this can get very oversubscribed.

HOW TO GO
Increasing number of packages

Selva and the Sella Ronda area has made a comeback in British tour operators' programmes after being dropped for several years. There is now quite a wide choice of catered chalets, and some of the properties are good quality, with en-suite bathrooms. **Hotels** There are 10 4-stars, over 30 3-stars and numerous lesser hotels. Few of the best hotels are well positioned.
(((3) **Gran Baita** Large, luxurious sporthotel, with lots of mod cons including indoor pool. A few minutes' walk from centre and lifts.
(((3) **Aaritz** Best-placed of the 4-stars, opposite the gondola.
((2) **Astor** Family-run chalet in centre, below nursery slopes. Good value.
((2) **Olympia** Well positioned, central 3-star.
((2) **Solaia** 3-star chalet, superbly positioned for lifts and slopes.
Self-catering There are plenty of apartments to choose from – some more convenient than others. We have excellent reports of the Villa Gardena and Isabelle apartments (the latter attached to the Gran Baita hotel).

EATING OUT
Plenty of good-value choices

Selva offers the best of both Austrian and Italian food at prices to suit all pockets. The higher-quality restaurants are mainly hotel-based. The Antares and Laurin have particularly good menus while the Olympia is renowned for its fondues. The Bellavista is recommended for good pasta. Da Rino has some of the best pizzas in town (it's worth booking).

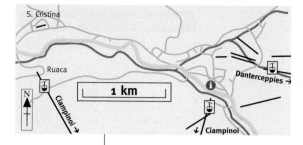

ACTIVITIES

Indoor Swimming, sauna, solaria (in hotels), bowling alley, squash, artificial skating rink, ice hockey, museum, indoor golf, concerts, cinema, billiards, tennis
Outdoor Sleigh rides, torch-light descents, horse-riding, extensive cleared paths around Selva Gardena and above S Cristina and Ortisei

TOURIST OFFICE

Postcode 39048
Tel +39 (471) 795122
Fax 794245

The slopes around Selva are impressive, but it's the views that are such a knockout
↓

APRES-SKI
Above average for a family resort
Nightlife is lively and informal, though the village is so scattered there is little on-street atmosphere. La Stua is a popular après bar on the Sella Ronda route, with accordion music later on. For a civilised early drink try the good value ski-school bar at the base of the Dantercëpies piste. Café Mozart on the main street is highly recommended for ice-cream and cakes. The Luisl and Laurin kellers are thigh slapping, lively bars. Hotel Stella's bar has atmosphere but the disco is costly for a bop. The Dali and Savoy Keller are other discos. La Bula is a quieter piano bar.

OFF THE SLOPES
Good variety
There's a sports centre and some lovely walks. There are sleigh rides on Alpe di Suisi. The charming town of Ortisei is well worth a visit for its large hot-spring swimming pool, shops, restaurants and lovely old buildings. Numerous good restaurants, nicely scattered around the different sections of the mountains, can be reached by

pedestrians by gondola or cable-car. Car-drivers have Bolzano and Innsbruck within reach and tour-operators do trips to Cortina.

Ortisei 1235m
Ortisei is a charming market town with a life of its own, but its local slopes aren't on the main Sella Ronda circuit. It's full of lovely old buildings, pretty churches and pleasant shops. The lift to the south-facing slopes is very central, but if you wish to start on the north-facing Alpe di Siusi slopes you have to negotiate the busy main road that skirts town. The nursery area, school and kindergarten are at the foot of these slopes, but there's a fair range of family accommodation on the piste-side of the road. The fine public indoor pool and ice rink are also here. The quickest way to get to Selva and the Sella Ronda circuit is by bus or car.

There is hotel and self-catering accommodation to suit all tastes and pockets and there are many good restaurants, mainly specialising in local dishes. The immediate après-ski is quite jolly, and many bars keep going till late.

Corvara 1570m
Corvara is the most animated Sella Ronda village east of Selva, with plenty of hotels, restaurants, bars and sports facilities. It's well positioned for the slopes with village lifts heading off in different directions to reasonably equidistant Selva, Arabba and San Cassiano. The main shops and some hotels are clustered around a small

central piazza, but the rest of the place sprawls along the valley floor.

Ardent après-skiers should visit the Posta Zirm, which has great tea dances – tour operators often organise transport back from here to other resorts to allow a weekly bop here.

Colfosco 1645m

Colfosco is a smaller, quieter version of Corvara, 2km away. It has a fairly compact centre with a sprawl of large hotels along the road towards Selva. It's connected to Corvara by a horizontal-running chair-lift. In the opposite direction, a series of drag-lifts head off to the Passo Gardena and on to Selva.

There are several large hotels that between them provide plenty of services.

San Cassiano 1530m

San Cassiano is a pretty little village, set in an attractive, tree-filled valley. It's a quiet, slightly upmarket resort, full of well-heeled Italian families and comfortable hotels, but little else. The local slopes, the Alta Badia, though sizeable and fully linked, are something of a spur of the main Sella Ronda circuit. Moving further afield is a tiresome business for adventurers who want to do the circuit.

Among the best hotels in each category are the Rosa Alpina (4-star), Tyrol (3-star), Alexander (2-star), Plang (1-star) and Jasmin (B&B). The Ciasa La Ro and Ciasa Ulli are good apartments.

The tea dance in Corvara's Posta Zirm is a must for those wanting something lively. Stop there at the end of the day, taxi home afterwards. Later nightlife is very limited. The Rosa Alpina hotel has dancing and there's a bowling alley in the Diamant hotel. Walking in the pretty scenery is the main off-slope activity. Swimming is the other. There is no nursery or ski kindergarten.

La Villa 1435m

La Villa is similar to neighbouring San Cassiano in most respects – small, quiet, pretty, unspoilt – but is slightly closer to Corvara, making it rather better placed for the main Sella Ronda circuit. And there is a home piste which features on the World Cup circuit. Village amenities include pool, bowling, ski kindergarten (no nursery), and ice skating on a frozen lake.

Canazei 1440m

Canazei is a sizeable, bustling, pretty, roadside village of narrow streets, rustic old buildings, traditional style hotels and nice little shops, set in the Sella Ronda's most heavily wooded section of mountains. It has reasonably animated nightlife and plenty going on generally – and is highly recommended by the many reporters who've visited recently. It is not, perhaps, an ideal choice for some British families because of the busy road and lack of English spoken in the school (one instructor took all the English visitors says one reporter, and was excellent) and nursery facilities.

A 12-person gondola is the only mountain access point, but it shifts the queues (which can be long) quickly. A single piste back to the village is linked to runs returning from both Selva and Arabba, but it is often closed. The village nursery slope is inconveniently located, but it's unlikely to be used after day one. The local Belvedere slopes are uniformly easy and dotted with mountain restaurants.

There are no luxury hotels, but the 3-star Croce Bianca offers elegant comfort and old-world charm. It's also central and close to the lift. The much cheaper Diana is a charming place, five minutes from the village centre. The friendly, comfortable Azola is a long walk from the gondola. The Astoria is a good choice and there are some catered chalets available on the British market.

There are numerous restaurants. The Stala, Principe (El Pael), Rosticceria Melester and Te Cevana are all worth a try. For early après-ski the beautiful La Stua dei Ladins is a peaceful oasis, with candlelit tables and excellent cakes. Rosengarten, by the church, has good service and sandwiches, an agricultural theme and rock music. The Husky pub, Speckkeller and Black Cat disco are all worth a visit, as is Peter's Konditore when the sun is out and on the terrace.

There's a fair amount to do off the slopes. Walks are beautiful, clothes shopping worthwhile. There's a good pool, sauna, Turkish baths, and skating in neighbouring Alba. There's an all-day nursery and ski kindergarten.

Campitello 1445m

This is smaller and quieter than next door Canazei and still very unspoilt, with little English spoken.

By the high standards of the Sella Ronda, the village is nothing special to look at, particularly when there's little snow – which is much of the time – but still pleasant. It's remarkably quiet during the day, having no slopes to the village.

A cable-car takes you up into the Sella Ronda circuit. If you don't wish to return by lift at the end of the day, you can take the piste to Canazei and catch a bus.

The Rubino is an elegant 4-star hotel well placed close to the cable-car. The good 3-star Sella Ronda is also very convenient for everything. The 3-star Enrosadira is less well positioned, a tiring uphill walk from the cable-car. Pension Festil is similarly placed but offers a useful cheap and cheerful B&B option. Campitello is lively – we had trouble getting near the bar of the throbbing Da Giulio in the early evening. The Tontin pub is an alternative. Neighbouring Pozza has ice skating and floodlit slopes. There are no children's facilities.

Arabba 1600m

Arabba is a small traditional village, uncommercialised to the point where basic resort infrastructure is in short supply. But the lifts into the Sella Ronda in both directions make it very convenient. It is much more of a serious skier's and boarder's destination than its sunny, family-oriented neighbours. The high north-facing slopes have the best natural snow and steepest pistes in the Dolomites. The nearby Marmolada glacier is open most of the winter (for a supplement to your lift pass) and guarantees good snow. The Rifugio Passo Fedaia at its foot has been recommended by reporters for pasta and wild mushrooms.

Apartment-conversion chalets and self-catering accommodation are available.

The 4-star Sport is the best hotel. The Porta Vescovo is a large, comfortable, multi-amenity 3-star with the only pool in town. The Evaldo is a simpler 3-star. Albergo Pordoi is a 2-star with character, and Garni Erika is a pleasant 1-star.

Venues for eating out are limited. Al Forte, 3km out of town, is best. Al Tablé, 7 Sass and Ru De Mont are cheap and cheerful pizzerias.

The après-ski is also very limited – but cheap. The Al Fegole bar is the smartest place in town. Bar Peter, and the bars of Pension Erika and Albergo Pordoi, are others worth a try. The Delmonego family's bar-caravan, at the bottom of the piste, is the tea-time rendezvous.

Sestriere　　　　　2000m

Modern resort with access to the Milky Way

Sestriere was built for snow – high, with north-west-facing slopes – and it now has very extensive snowmaking facilities. Sestriere's international profile has been raised since it hosted the 1997 World Championships.

WHAT IT COSTS

(((3)))

HOW IT RATES

The slopes

Snow	****
Extent	****
Experts	***
Intermediates	****
Beginners	***
Convenience	****
Queues	***
Restaurants	**

The rest

Scenery	***
Resort charm	*
Off-slope	*

MOUNTAIN FACTS

Figures relate to the whole Milky Way area

Altitude	1390m-2825m
Lifts	97
Pistes	400km
Blue	12%
Red	67%
Black	21%
Artificial snow	65km

UK PACKAGES

Airtours, Club Med, Crystal, Equity Total Ski, Lagrange, Motours, Neilson, Stena Line Holidays

Grangesises Stena Line Holidays

Sansicario Equity School Ski, Equity Total Ski

TOURIST OFFICE

Postcode 10058
Tel +39 (122) 755444
Fax 755171

THE RESORT

Sestriere was the Alps' first purpose-built resort. It sits on a broad, sunny and windy col at 2000m. Neither the site nor the village looks very hospitable, though the buildings have benefited from recent investment.

THE MOUNTAINS

Sestriere is at one extreme of the big Franco-Italian Milky Way area. The local **slopes** have two main sectors: Sises, directly in front of the village (which has a brightly floodlit piste), and more varied Motta, above Borgata – 2km to the north-east and 150m lower.

Drag- and chair-lifts predominate on the local north-west-facing slopes. Access to Sansicario and the rest of the Milky Way is via the gondola from Borgata to Col Basset, at the top of the Sauze d'Oulx area, and a drag-lift back up to Monte Fraiteve.

With most of the local slopes facing north-west and ranging from 1840m to 2820m, it is fair to expect them to have **snow-cover** for most of the season, even without the snowmaking that covers practically all of the Sises sector and about half of Motta.

There is a fair amount to amuse **experts** – steep pistes served by the drags at the top of both sectors, and off-piste opportunities in several directions from here and from the lifts on Monte Fraiteve.

Both sectors also offer plenty for **intermediates,** who can also expect to explore practically all of the Milky Way areas, time permitting. The terrain is excellent for **beginners**, with several nursery areas and the gentlest of easy runs down to Borgata.

There are two **cross-country** loops covering a total of 15km.

There are no special **snowboarding** facilities.

The lifts are mainly modern, with several quad chairs, but **queues** for the main lifts occur at the weekends and holidays – it's better if you stay off the main routes. The lifts from Borgata to Sestriere become crowded at the end of the day, as everyone using Motta or returning from Sauze uses this link.

The local **mountain restaurants** are fair – the one at Sises is best – but there are better ones further afield.

Lack of spoken English can be a problem with the **ski schools**. An all-day crèche takes **children** aged 3 to 6.

STAYING THERE

Sestriere is not the most convenient of purpose-built resorts, but location is not crucial. If you want to make use of Sestriere's nightlife or shops, don't be tempted to stay in Borgata. Most **accommodation** is in apartments, but there are a dozen hotels, mostly of 3-star or 4-star status. The central 4-star Grand Hotel Sestriere is an ugly low building, but is comfortable and well placed. Just out of the village (but not far from a lift, and with courtesy transport) is the luxurious Principi di Piemonte. The Savoy Edelweiss is a central, attractive 3-star. The distinctive round towers of the Torre and Duchi d'Aosta are occupied by Club Med.

The Bellavista apartments, at the entrance to the resort, are 10 minutes' walk from both main lifts, and run 46 ends nearby.

The numerous 3- and 4-star hotels offer plenty of options for **eating out**. The Gargote and the Last Tango grill have good Italian and French food across the price range. Last year a visitor discovered Lu Peyrôl for home-made ravioli and atmosphere.

Après-ski is lively at weekends, quiet at other times. The Prestige and Palace are just two of the many little bars that liven up. The Rendezvous is a cosy piano bar. The Black Sun piano-bar-cum-disco and the Tabata club are great fun at weekends. The Pinky is perhaps the best of the relaxed bars that double as pizzerias or snack joints, with lots of low sofas in the classic Italian style. There is a fair amount to do **off the slopes**, but it is not a very attractive place, despite some smart shopping. There is no indoor swimming pool.

La Thuile 1450m

Little-known resort with extensive slopes and link with France

WHAT IT COSTS

(((3)))

HOW IT RATES

The slopes

Snow	****
Extent	***
Experts	**
Intermediates	****
Beginners	****
Convenience	***
Queues	****
Restaurants	*

The rest

Scenery	***
Resort charm	***
Off-slope	**

➕ Fair-sized area with good lift system linked to La Rosière in France

➕ Excellent beginner and easy intermediate slopes

➕ Unusual mix of purpose-built accommodation at foot of slopes and more villagey atmosphere of the old town, a 10-minute walk away

➖ All the seriously tough pistes are low down, and most of the low tree-lined runs are tough

➖ Mountain restaurants very disappointing

➖ Not the place for lively après-ski

La Thuile is surprisingly little known on the British market. It deserves better. The slopes best suit beginners and intermediates not seeking challenge, but are not devoid of interest for experts, particularly if the snow conditions are good, when there is the choice of venturing off-piste above the Petit St Bernard pass between France and Italy (closed in winter) or trying the short but serious blacks through the trees above the village.

boarding *These are great slopes for learning to board. You can confine yourself to riding chair-lifts and the gondola and most of the slopes are very easy with good snow. The only question mark is the standard of English for instruction. For more experienced boarders La Thuile has less going for it except the link with France and the off-piste possibilities, though there is a fun-park and half-pipe near the Gran Testa lift. Rich boarders could go heli-boarding on the Ruitor glacier!*

What's new

The link with France will be vastly improved for the 1997/98 season with the Col de la Traversette drag-lift on the French side being replaced by a quad chair with a moving carpet and two other crucial lifts having their capacity doubled.

The 1996/97 season saw 48 new snow guns covering 3km of one of the main red pistes back to the village.

MOUNTAIN FACTS

Altitude	1150m-2640m
Lifts	33
Pistes	135km
Green/Blue	44%
Red	36%
Black	20%
Artificial snow	13km

The resort

La Thuile looks and feels like a typical French purpose-built resort such as La Plagne or Tignes, but with a distinctly Italian atmosphere. At the foot of the lifts is a modern complex, with places to stay, leisure centre, bars, shops and restaurants. A fast chair or gondola take you up the mountain, and there are more high-speed chairs to the top.

Cross the river and things are very different. La Thuile started life as a mining town but then large parts of it fell into disrepair until the slopes were developed. Much of the old village has been restored and new buildings tastefully added. But parts are still in ruins, with a 'ghost town' feel to them. There are reasonable restaurants and bars but not many entertaining shops.

The mountains

For a little-known resort, La Thuile has surprisingly extensive slopes. And it is normally very uncrowded, with quiet pistes and no lift queues. Many runs are marked red, but deserve no more than a blue rating. The lift system is

excellent in general, and the lift pass is electronic. The slopes can be very cold, especially early in the season – many runs face north.

The slopes link with La Rosière, over the border in France. Courmayeur is easily reached by car, Chamonix is just through the Mont Blanc tunnel and Cervinia is about an hour away.

THE SLOPES
Big and gentle

The lifts out of the village take you to **Les Suches** (2200m), with black runs going back down directly to the village through the trees, and reds taking a more roundabout route. From here chairs and drags take you to the top of the mountain and a number of different gentle bowls accessed from **Chaz Dura** (2580m). You can also drop down over the back from here to the Petit St Bernard road.

The link to to **La Rosière** in France is via Belvedere (2640m) and the Col de Traversette (2400m). In contrast with La Thuile the French slopes are largely south-facing. Although the runs in France tend to be steeper, the snow in Italy tends to be better.

LIFT PASSES

96/97 prices in lire

**Dominio
Internazionale**
Covers all lifts in La
Rosière and La
Thuile.
Beginners One baby-
lift in village. Points
tickets (50 points
65,000).
Main pass
1-day pass 49,000
6-day pass 237,000
(low season 211,000
– 11% off)
Children
Under 11: 6-day pass
192,000 (19% off)
Under 4: free pass
Short-term passes
Half-day pass (adult
34,000), passes for
2hrs (28,000) or 3hrs
(36,000).
Alternative periods
6-day (non-
consecutive) pass
available (adult
273,000).
Alternative passes
Valle d'Aosta pass
covers La Thuile,
Courmayeur,
Gressoney,
Champoluc, Alagna,
Cervinia,
Valtournenche and
Pila (adult 6-day
255,000).

SNOW RELIABILITY
Good
Most of La Thuile's slopes are north- or
east-facing and above 2000m, so the
snow generally keeps well. There's also
a decent amount of snowmaking both
above the tree-line and on the runs
home. You can check the conditions at
Les Suches via a camera and screens
around the resort.

FOR EXPERTS
Rather limited
The only steep pistes are those down
through the trees from Les Suches
back to the resort. The steepest of
these, the Diretta, is serious stuff.
    The best of the rest, for experts, is
the area above the Petit St Bernard
road, where there is some genuinely
black terrain and plenty of off-piste.
You'll find many red runs overgraded.
    An added attraction of La Thuile, for
those who can afford it, is its heli-trips.
One of the best is a drop on to the
Ruitor glacier, with a 20km run into
France, ending at La Rosière.

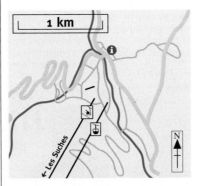

FOR INTERMEDIATES
Something different
La Thuile has some good intermediate
runs, and its link with La Rosière in
France adds adventure. Together, the
two resorts are a large and varied area,
with over 130km of runs. However,
timid intermediates are best off staying
on home ground: the start of the route
back from La Rosière is a short but
tricky red, and most of La Rosière –
particularly the top half of the
mountain – is fairly challenging.
    On the Italian side, the bowls above
Les Suches have many gentle, blue
and red runs, ideal for cruising and
practising. There are also long reds
through the trees back to the resort.
    The red runs on the other side of
the top ridge, down towards the Petit
St Bernard road, offer a greater
challenge for more adventurous
intermediates. But La Thuile's slopes
suit less ambitious intermediates best.

FOR BEGINNERS
Good, but slopes can be crowded
There are nursery slopes at village
level and at Les Suches. There's a
good gentle green run above Les
Suches to progress to, and some
shallow blues. But nothing is
segregated from the main slopes.
Recent reporters enjoyed the less
crowded slopes above the Belvedere
lift more. Remember too that the runs
down to the resort are red and black.

FOR CROSS-COUNTRY
Varied choice
La Thuile has 16km of tracks of varying
difficulty on the valley floor.

QUEUES
Very rare
The resort has a very effective lift
system for the number of visitors,
starting with a gondola and parallel
high-speed chair up to Les Suches. You
can usually walk straight on to any of
the lifts, except during peak weekends.

MOUNTAIN RESTAURANTS
Disappointing
We couldn't find a decent lunch up the
mountain when we visited La Thuile,
and recommend heading back to town.
We tried Rascard, just off the nursery
slope (take the drag-lift up) – see
Eating Out. Although there are several
ristorantes marked on the piste map,
most serve little more than sandwiches
and snacks. If you are coming to Italy

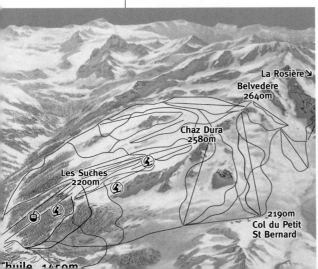

SCHOOLS/GUIDES

96/97 prices in lire

La Thuile
Classes 6 days
2½hr: 10am-12.30;
2hr: 1pm-3pm
6 2½hr days: 163,000
Children's classes
Ages: from 6
6 2½hr days: 163,000
Private lessons
1hr
50,000 for 1 person

CHILDCARE

There are no all-day
childcare
arrangements.

GETTING THERE

Air Geneva, transfer
2½hr. Turin, transfer
2½hr.

Rail Pré-St-Didier
(10km); regular buses
to resort.

UK PACKAGES

Bladon Lines, Crystal,
First Choice Ski,
Independent Ski
Links, Inghams,
Interski, Lagrange,
Motours, Neilson, Ski
Valkyrie, Thomson

ACTIVITIES

Indoor Skating rink, 2
swimming pools,
gymnasium,
amusement arcade,
solarium, sauna,
jacuzzi, massage,
amusement arcade,
billiards, squash,
football pitch
Outdoor Winter walks,
heli-skiing

TOURIST OFFICE

Postcode 11016
Tel +39 (165) 884179
Fax 885196

for the pasta, you'd be better off going elsewhere. The self-service cafeteria at Les Suches lacks atmosphere but serves good home-made Italian food. Just below there's a pleasant hut.

SCHOOLS AND GUIDES
Good but foreign
Reporters we've heard from praise the school for reasonably sized classes and fair instruction. Their reservation is that some of the instructors don't speak good English.

FACILITIES FOR CHILDREN
OK when they're older
La Thuile doesn't seem to cater much for children. A recent reporter told us the kindergarten appears to require parental supervision, but school starts at six years – and we've heard of youngsters who've had a good time.

Staying there 🔑

The modern Planibel complex at the foot of the lifts is most convenient for the slopes. But many people find this rather soulless and prefer to stay in the old town over the river (served by a free bus) or in one of the more traditional buildings nearer the slopes.

HOW TO GO
Some choice of packages
The number of tour operators going to La Thuile is increasing.
Hotels Choice is between the swanky but characterless 4-star Planibel, three 3-stars and 10 simpler places.
(((4) **Planibel** American-style 'resort hotel' with all mod cons, including underground parking. Right at the base of the lifts. Pool.
(((3) **Eden** Comfortable modern hotel in traditional wood and stone style, very close to lifts and the Planibel centre.
((2) **Chalet Alpina** Simple place with the atmosphere of a catered chalet, on the outskirts of the resort.
Self-catering The Planibel apartments receive much praise from reporters. They're spacious, well-equipped, handy for the slopes and great value. Not surprisingly, they book out early.

EATING OUT
Limited, but consistently good
La Thuile doesn't have a lot of restaurants but we've received

positive reports on most of them. At Rascard, we had superb home-made pasta with wild-boar bolognaise. La Fordze has also been recommended for excellent food. The Bricole and La Raclette do good cheese dishes such as fondue. The always-busy Lo Creton, Spaghetteria and Grotta vie for the title of Best Cheap and Cheerful Pizza and Pasta place. The Maison de Laurent and Tufeja are also popular. Booking at all of these is advisable.

APRES-SKI
Early to bed
The main bar to fill up after the lifts close is the Buvette. The Bouchon in the Planibel is a piano bar, which is open until late. The Rendezvous bar has karaoke but the Bricolette and Bricole are more atmospheric. The Bricole and Fantasia discos warm up at the weekend.

OFF THE SLOPES
Limited options
The Planibel complex has excellent leisure facilities including a huge pool, but there's few attractive walks or shops. Excursions to Courmayeur and Chamonix can be organised. It's easy for pedestrians to ride up the gondola for lunch, but not very enticing.

Switzerland

Switzerland is home to some of our favourite resorts. For sheer charm and spectacular scenery, the 'traffic-free' villages of Wengen, Mürren, Saas Fee and Zermatt take some beating. Many resorts have impressive slopes too – including some of the biggest, highest and toughest runs in the Alps. So we're delighted that Switzerland is becoming affordable again thanks to the substantial recent fall in the Swiss franc; and what you get for your money is first class.

Downhill skiing in its modern form was invented in Wengen and Mürren, which were persuaded to open their summer railways in winter to take their British guests up the mountain. They remain firm favourites with their regular British visitors, who return every year to savour the special atmosphere of these tiny villages and their awesome views of the Eiger, Mönch and Jungfrau.

While France is the home of the purpose-built resort, Switzerland is the home of the traditional mountain village which has transformed itself from farming community into year-round holiday centre. Many of Switzerland's most famous mountain resorts are as popular in the summer as in the winter, or more so. This creates places with a much more lived-in feel to them and a much more stable local community. Many are still run and dominated by a handful of families who were lucky or shrewd enough to get involved in the early development of the area.

This has its downside as well as advantages. The ruling families are able to stifle competition and prevent newcomers from taking a slice of their action. New ski schools, competing with the traditional school, are much less common than in other countries, for example. And in many resorts, British tour operators are severely restricted in the amount of guiding they can offer their guests – a popular service which the schools see as taking business away from them.

Swiss resorts have a reputation for efficiently relieving you of your money. And the reputation is well earned. Nothing is cheap; but the quality of the service you get for your money is generally high. Swiss hotels are some of the best in the world. The trains run like clockwork to the advertised timetable. The food is almost universally of good quality, and much less stodgy than in neighbouring Austria. And Switzerland is no longer more expensive than many fashionable French and Austrian resorts. In Switzerland you get what you pay for: even the cheapest wine, for example, is not cheap; but it is reliable – duff bottles are very rare.

Perhaps surprisingly for such a long-established, traditional, rather staid skiing country, Switzerland has gone out of its way to develop facilities for and attract snowboarders. It is one of the most boarder-friendly of all Alpine nations.

GETTING AROUND THE SWISS ALPS

Access to practically all Swiss resorts is fairly straightforward when approaching from the north. Many of the high passes that are perfectly sensible ways to get around the country in summer are closed in winter, which can be inconvenient if you are moving around from one area to another. There are car-carrying rail tunnels beneath the passes either side of Andermatt (Furka leading westwards to Brig, and Oberalp leading eastwards to Sedrun, Flims and Chur).

St Moritz is more awkward to get to. The main road route is over the Julier pass. This is normally kept open, but at 2284m it is naturally prone to heavy snowfalls that can shut it for a time. The fall-back is the car-carrying rail tunnel under the Albula pass.

These car-carrying rail services are painless unless you travel at peak times, when there may be long queues – particularly for the Furka tunnel from Andermatt, which offers residents of Zürich the

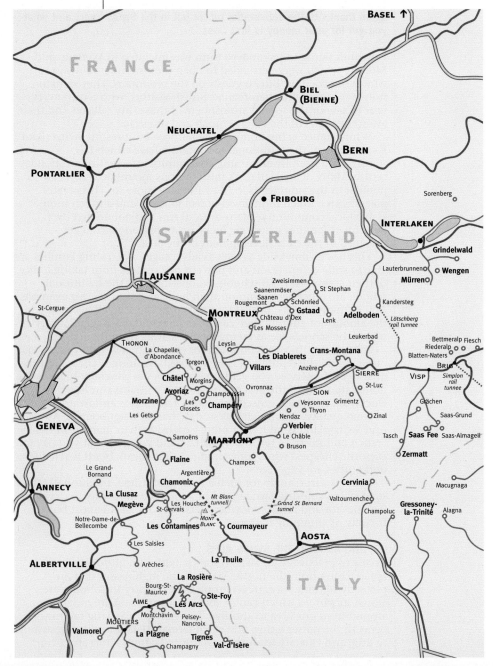

shortest route to the Valais resorts (Zermatt etc). Another rail tunnel service that's very handy is the Lötschberg tunnel, linking Kandersteg in the Bernese Oberland with Brig in the Valais. There's no quicker way from Wengen to Zermatt.

There is a car-carrying rail tunnel linking Switzerland with Italy – the Simplon. But most of the routes to Italy are kept open by means of road tunnels. See the Italy introduction for more information.

Scale in km

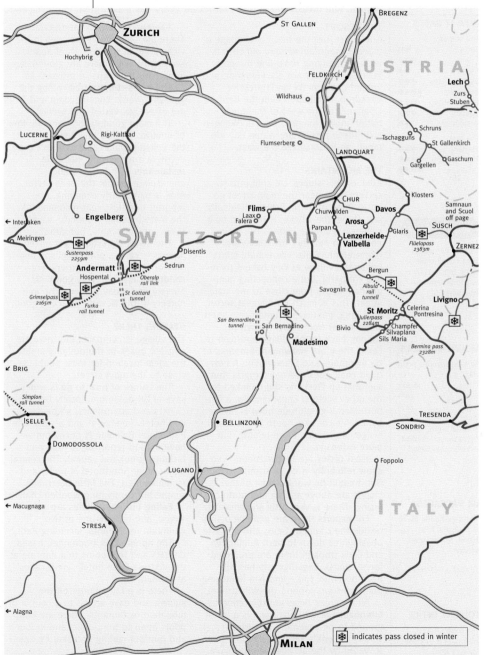

Adelboden   1355m

Chocolate-box village with fragmented slopes

WHAT IT COSTS

(((3)))

HOW IT RATES

The slopes

Snow	**
Extent	***
Experts	**
Intermediates	***
Beginners	****
Convenience	***
Queues	***
Restaurants	**

The rest

Scenery	***
Resort charm	****
Off-slope	****

What's new

The old two-seater Geils Luegli chair is being replaced by a fast four-seater to Pommerngrat.

MOUNTAIN FACTS

Altitude	1070m-2355m
Lifts	50
Pistes	160km
Blue	48%
Red	44%
Black	8%
Artificial snow	1km

Recco detectors used
— helicopter-based

UK PACKAGES

Inghams, Kuoni, Made to Measure, Plus Travel, Swiss Travel Service

TOURIST OFFICE

Postcode CH-3715
Tel +41 (33) 673 8080
Fax 673 8002

Adelboden is unjustly neglected: for intermediates who find relaxing, pretty surroundings more important than convenience for the slopes, it has a lot of appeal. And investment in lifts over recent years has meant great improvements.

THE RESORT

Adelboden has the traditional image of a Swiss mountain village: old chalets with overhanging roofs line the quiet main street (cars are discouraged), and 3000m peaks make an impressive backdrop. Adelboden is in the Bernese Oberland, to the west of the much better-known Jungfrau resorts (Wengen etc). These resorts are within day-trip range, as is Gstaad to the west.

THE MOUNTAINS

Adelboden's **slopes** are split into six sectors. Lifts near the main street go up to three of them. Schwandfeldspitz, just above the village, is reached by a cable-car–gondola hybrid. The main gondola to nearby Hochsthorn and more remote Geils-Sillerenbühl starts below the village at Oey (where there is a car park), but a connecting mini-gondola starts from close to the main street. This is much the biggest sector, with long, gentle runs (and some short, sharp ones) from 2200m down to 1450m, back to the village and over to Lenk. There are **snowboard** funparks at Hahnenmoos and Sillerenbühl. A new quad chair goes to Pommerngrat, but the drag up Fleckli is still unlinked to the other sectors. Engstligenalp, a flat-bottomed high-altitude bowl is reached by a cable-car 4km south of the resort; Elsigenalp is even more remote, but more extensive.

Most pistes are below 2000m – so **snow reliability** is not a strong point. But it could be worse: most of the slopes are above 1500m and north-facing. There is very little snowmaking.

For **experts** there are genuine blacks beside the chairs at Geils, and off-piste possibilities down to both Adelboden and Lenk (though there are protected forest areas). Engstligenalp has off-piste potential too – and is a launching point for tours around the Wildstrubel.

All six areas deserve exploration by **intermediates**. At Geils there is a lot of ground to be covered – and trips across to Lenk's gentle Betelberg area (covered by the lift pass) are possible.

Beginners are well catered for. There are good nursery slopes in the village and at the bottom of nearby sectors. At Geils there are gloriously long, easy blue runs to progress to.

The **cross-country** trails along the valleys towards Engstligenalp and Geils are extensive, varied and scenic.

The main gondola isn't entirely free of **queues**. If snow low down is poor, the Engstligenalp cable-car can't cope.

There are pleasant **mountain restaurants** with terraces and immaculate loos in the Geils sector. Aebi is particularly charming. A reporter from last year recommends the Metschstand, 'wonderful views, sunny, small, simple, but good'.

The Swiss **ski schools** get mixed reports – 'caring, good English', but 'mix of abilities within group'. For **children** there is a 'very good' ski nursery and a day nursery. The free nursery at the Nevada Palace is good.

STAYING THERE

The village is compact, and there are efficient buses to the outlying areas; the ideal location for most people is close to the main street.

The choice of **how to go** is wide: several UK operators, locally bookable chalets and apartments, 30 pensions and hotels (mainly 3- and 4-star). The Park Hotel Bellevue is pricey but we have a good report of its food and facilities (pool and sauna). The central 3-star Adler Sporthotel is pretty and recommended. The little Bären is a simple but captivating wooden chalet.

Eating out possibilities are quite varied, and include one or two mountain restaurants, including Aebi.

The **après-ski** is traditional, based on bars and tea-rooms (tea dancing at the Viktoria Eden hotel, 'great cakes' at Schmidt's).

There is a fair amount **off the slopes**, and easy access to a couple of mountain restaurants. There are hotel pools open to the public, and indoor and outdoor curling and skating rinks.

Andermatt   1445m

An old-fashioned resort with some great off-piste

349

WHAT IT COSTS

((((3))))

HOW IT RATES

The slopes

Snow	****
Extent	*
Experts	****
Intermediates	**
Beginners	*
Convenience	***
Queues	**
Restaurants	*

The rest

Scenery	***
Resort charm	****
Off-slope	**

MOUNTAIN FACTS

Altitude	1445m-2965m
Lifts	13
Pistes	56km
Blue	29%
Red	42%
Black	29%
Artificial snow	none
Recco detectors used	
— helicopter-based	

UK PACKAGES

Made to Measure

TOURIST OFFICE

Postcode CH-6490
Tel +41 (41) 887 1454
Fax 887 0185

Andermatt used to be a firm favourite with the British, but as other areas developed it got left behind. The village is now rather a backwater, and its lift system limited – but giving access to some great, steep off-piste slopes.

THE RESORT
A familiar name among pre- and immediately post-war British skiers, Andermatt is now terra incognita to all but a few of the old brigade and a sporty minority of committed off-piste adventurers. Its primary livelihood now is the army, and the village seems slightly run-down. But it is attractive, with wooden houses lining the dog-leg main street, which runs from railway to cable-car stations.

THE MOUNTAINS
The main two-stage cable-car serves magnificent, varied **slopes** on the open, usually empty, slopes of Gemsstock, and there are three more areas along the valley: Nätschen, Winterhorn (above Hospental) and Realp. The valley railway is the only link between Andermatt and the latter two sectors, and in winter the only link with resorts to the east (Davos, St Moritz) and west (Zermatt and other Valais resorts). You can put your car on some trains.

Andermatt has a reputation for **reliable snow**, fully justified in our experience.

It is most definitely a resort for **experts**. The top Gemsstock cable-car serves two main slopes: the north-facing bowl beneath it is a glorious, long black slope (about 800m vertical), usually with excellent snow, in which there is usually one marked run down, and countless off-piste routes; the Sonnenpiste, curling around the back of the mountain to the mid-station, scarcely deserves its black grading (and indeed used to be red), but is a fine open run nevertheless. From mid-mountain to the village there is a genuine black, not fearsomely steep but heavily mogulled. There are plenty of guides for off-piste adventure and safaris, and heli-trips. Unfortunately the Gemsstock cable-car can take a while to get going after a heavy snowfall, but Nätschen and Winterhorn both provide black runs and off-piste opportunities while you wait.

Intermediates needn't be put off the Gemsstock: the Sonnenpiste can be tackled, and there is a pleasant red run at mid-mountain, served by a drag. Winterhorn's deceptively modest lift system offers all standards of piste down the 900m vertical, while Nätschen's south- and west-facing mountain is mostly open – perfect for confidence-building.

There is an isolated nursery slope at Realp, and the lower half of Nätschen has a good, long easy run back to the village. But essentially this is not a resort for **beginners**.

There is a **snowboard** funpark and half-pipe on the Gemsstock. And there is a 20km **cross-country** loop between Andermatt and Realp.

Although the Gemsstock cable-car was upgraded some years ago, it can still generate morning **queues** in the village, and at mid-mountain when conditions are attractive. And if it's quiet, the cable-car waits ages for a decent load before ascending.

The few **mountain restaurants** are dull. Lunch is for wimps, of course, but it's best taken in the village.

The excellent work of the Swiss **ski school** is rather overshadowed by the high reputation of Alpine Adventures Mountain Reality, a specialist off-piste guiding outfit run by the famous Alex Clapasson, who also happens to run the lift company.

There are no special facilities for **children**; but there are slopes they can handle at Nätschen.

STAYING THERE
Andermatt's **accommodation** is in small, cosy 2-star and 3-star hotels. The central Gasthaus Zum Sternen is an attractive old chalet with a popular and lively restaurant and bar. The 3-star Sonne, between the centre and the lift, is welcoming and comfortable. The 2-star Bergidyll, next door, is a British favourite.

Après-ski revolves around cosy local bars, and finishes early. There's little to do **off the slopes**.

Arosa

1800m

Classic all-round winter holiday resort

WHAT IT COSTS

((((4))))

HOW IT RATES

The slopes

Snow	***
Extent	**
Experts	*
Intermediates	***
Beginners	****
Convenience	***
Queues	****
Restaurants	****

The rest

Scenery	***
Resort charm	**
Off-slope	****

MOUNTAIN FACTS

Altitude	1800m-2655m
Lifts	16
Pistes	70km
Blue	38%
Red	57%
Black	5%
Artificial snow	8km

Recco detectors used
– helicopter-based

What's new

Double indoor tennis courts were new in 1996/97. There is now a kids' snow playground, as well as a board park.

UK PACKAGES

Freedom Holidays, Inghams, Kuoni, Made to Measure, Plus Travel, Ski Choice, SkiGower, Swiss Travel Service

TOURIST OFFICE

Postcode CH-7050
Tel +41 (81) 377 5151
Fax 377 3135

The classic image of a winter sports resort is perhaps an isolated, snow-covered Swiss village, surrounded by big, beautiful mountains, with skating on a frozen lake, horse-drawn sleighs jingling through the streets, and people in fur coats strolling on mountain paths. Arosa is just that.

THE RESORT

High and remote, Arosa is in a sheltered basin at the head of a beautiful wooded valley, in contrast to the open slopes. A long, winding road or rail journey brings you from Chur. Obersee, at the centre, is drab though its lakeside setting adds charm. The rest of Arosa is scattered, with a hill separating Obersee from the older, prettier Innerarosa – which also has a chair, drag and (away from the village) a gondola. Arosa is quiet; its relaxed ambience attracts an unpretentiously wealthy clientele of families and older people. Some accommodation is a long walk from the lifts, but there's a free, frequent shuttle bus.

THE MOUNTAINS

For such a well-known resort, Arosa's **slopes** are tiny and unchallenging. The slopes are spread widely over two main sectors. The **Weisshorn** faces mainly south and south-east. Tschuggen, half-way to the Weisshorn peak, is the major lift junction, reachable from both Obersee and Innerarosa. An inconveniently sited gondola below Innerarosa is the main access to the east- and north-east-facing slopes of the **Hörnli** sector. Drags and chair-lifts allow you to travel either way between the two sectors.

There is a **snowboard** park and a half-pipe at Carmennahütte. You can get to Davos-Klosters, Flims and Lenzerheide by road. The latter also reachable off-piste.

Although there are no very high slopes, and they get a lot of sun, Arosa has relatively good **snow reliability**. All the best south-facing pistes are above 2000m and the shadier Hörnli slopes usually hold their snow well.

Arosa isn't the resort for a keen **expert**. The most interesting opportunity is to ski off-piste to and from Lenzerheide via Hörnli.

This is a good area for **intermediates** who want to take it easy

and aren't looking for high mileage or much challenge.

For beginners the Tschuggen nursery slopes are excellent and usually have good snow, but get a lot of through traffic. Innerarosa has a quieter but more limited area usually reserved for children.

Although it lacks the sheer length of trails of many resorts, Arosa (with 29km) has some of the best, varied **cross-country** loops in the Alps.

With so many part-timers, plus a well laid out lift system, Arosa does not suffer many **queues**. There can still be waits for the improved Weisshorn cable-car.

Some of the **mountain restaurants** are very good, but there are too few of them. Consequently they get crowded. Carmennahütte is the best, while Tschuggenhütte is a rustic little refuge with a nice sun terrace

There's a big **ski-school** and a lot of demand for private lessons by the affluent Arosa guests. Arosa seems a good choice for a family holiday, and several hotels have kindergartens for the **children.**

STAYING THERE

It's a spread-out place, but where you stay is not that important as there is an excellent shuttle bus. Innerarosa has the advantage of lifts to both sectors. Arosa is a hotel resort, with a high proportion of them 3- and 4-stars. Most restaurants are hotel-based. For a true gourmet experience, the tiny wood-panelled Zum Wohl dining room in the unprepossessing Hotel Anita is an expensive treat that has to be booked. **Après-ski** is lively. The Carmenna hotel by the ice rink has well priced drinks and live jazz. Later the popular bar of the Eden hotel has live music. There are plenty of **off-slope** alternatives. You can get a pedestrian's lift pass, and many mountain restaurants are reachable via 35km of cleared, marked walks. Sleigh rides in the mountains are beautiful.

Champéry
1050m

A Swiss charmer, with fair access to the Portes du Soleil

WHAT IT COSTS
©©(3)

HOW IT RATES

The slopes

Snow	**
Extent	*****
Experts	***
Intermediates	****
Beginners	**
Convenience	*
Queues	****
Restaurants	***

The rest

Scenery	****
Resort charm	****
Off-slope	***

➕ Charming rustic village with impressive mountain views

➕ Very extensive slopes, linking with Avoriaz and Châtel in France

➕ Quiet, relaxed place – yet plenty to do off the slopes

➕ Easy access for independent travellers – by car, train, or plane and train

➖ Local slopes suffer from the sun – facing south-east – though the resort now has some snowmakers

➖ No runs back to the village – and sometimes none back to the valley

➖ Beginners face hassle and expense getting up to Planachaux, which is not as gentle as it could be

➖ Not many tough slopes nearby

Champéry is one the prettiest of villages, with narrow streets, pleasantly rustic wooden buildings, informal cafés, nice little shops, and a friendly atmosphere – certainly a most appealing base for the main Franco-Swiss Portes du Soleil circuit. Unfortunately, it is also one of the least reliable Swiss resorts for snow, with sunny slopes mainly lying between 1600m and 2200m. However the resort has invested in snowmakers recently, mainly on the lower slopes at Planachaux. But, of course, temperatures must be low for them to be used successfully.

With good transport links and sports facilities, Champéry is great for part-timers and off-slope activities, or for families looking for a quiet time in a lovely place, especially if they have a car. But it also deserves consideration if you simply put character before convenience. The north-facing slopes of Avoriaz, just across the French border, are only four lift-rides away – and we have found fresh powder there when Champéry's lower slopes were bare and its upper ones slushy.

boarding *Champéry is not the best choice in the Portes du Soleil for a keen boarder. Although there is a fun-park in Les Crosets, there's a much bigger and better one (and a half-pipe) in Avoriaz. A lot of the lifts in the local Champéry area are drags – you may not need to take one to get to Avoriaz, but you will to return. For beginners the local slopes are a cable-car ride away and they aren't great when you get to them either. And nightlife is quiet.*

The resort

Set beneath the dramatic Dents du Midi, Champéry is the stuff of picture-postcards. The main street is lined with old wooden chalets housing most of the hotels, bars and restaurants, liberally adorned with Swiss flags.

An attempt has been made to provide the facilities demanded by today's holiday-makers without spoiling the old-world charm. Down a steepish hill, away from the main street, are the cable-car, excellent

MOUNTAIN FACTS

Altitude	1050m-2280m
Lifts	219
Pistes	650km
Blue	51%
Red	41%
Black	8%
Artificial snow	11km

Recco detectors used
— helicopter-based

Main street during the morning rush-hour ↓

LIFT PASSES

97/98 prices in Swiss francs

Portes du Soleil
Covers all the lifts in 12 resorts.

Beginners Points card (adult 50-point card 30).

Main pass
1-day pass 48
6-day pass 219

Senior citizens
Over 60: 6-day pass 145 (34% off)

Children
Under 16: 6-day pass 145 (34% off)
Under 7: free pass

Short-term passes
Half-day pass from noon (adult 33).

Notes Reductions for families.

Alternative passes
Half-day (to and from noon), 1- and 2-day passes available for 35 lifts and 100km of piste in Champéry, Les Crosets, Champoussin and La Foilleuse (Morgins) (adult 1-day 36).

sports centre and a convenient new terminus for the narrow-gauge railway.

The village has a friendly, relaxed atmosphere; it would be ideal for families if it wasn't separated from its slopes by a steep, fragmented mountainside. You can get back to Grand Paradis, 2km up the valley, on snow (assuming there's enough cover).

The mountains

Champéry's local slopes are as friendly and relaxing as the village, at least for intermediates. It is far from ideal for absolute beginners. Experts can cover vast amounts of ground on the Portes du Soleil piste circuit, which takes in the French resorts of Avoriaz and Châtel as well as the Swiss ones of Champoussin, Les Crosets, and Morgins – just be careful to leave enough time to get back. The last four are also easily reached by car, as are the off-piste possibilities of Verbier, Chamonix and Les Diablerets.

THE SLOPES
Extensive and sunny
The village of Champéry is not quite part of the main Portes du Soleil circuit (see overall summary on page 259) but its slopes are – the sunny bowl of **Planachaux**, way above the village, with a couple of runs leading down to the valley at **Grand Paradis**, a short bus-ride from Champéry.

There are no pistes to Champéry itself, though on rare occasions local conditions allow off-piste trips. Planachaux is rather featureless, and most people quickly move on – at least as far as next-door Les Crosets. You can explore the Portes du Soleil by travelling west towards Avoriaz or north-east to Champoussin, Morgins and Châtel.

There are three ways to get to Avoriaz – via a chair-lift from the eastern side of the Planachaux bowl to Chavanette (check out the infamous 'Swiss Wall' mogul field as you ride up) or via one of two lifts from Les Crosets (one being the revamped Pointe de Mossette gondola). Allow plenty of time to return from Avoriaz.

Queues form at some lifts, and the run home is usually either closed or made awkward by poor snow. Getting to the top of the Champéry cable-car to ride down is a roundabout business.

The easy Champoussin runs are best reached by chair-lift (a walk across the

Les Crosets car park) to Pointe de l'Au. Then a network of short runs and lifts goes to Champoussin and Morgins.

A day at Villars/Les Diablerets and at Crans-Montana is covered on the lift pass, if you want to make the trips.

For more on Avoriaz see page 181; for Châtel see page 192.

SNOW RELIABILITY
Better in France
The snow on the north-facing French side of the area is usually better than on the sunnier Swiss side to the south. And getting to Avoriaz's north-facing slopes when conditions are poor can be unpleasant for early intermediates.

Champéry has just 13 mobile snow-guns to cover the area it shares with Les Crosets. This isn't enough to handle the size of the area needing attention.

FOR EXPERTS
Few local challenges
Champéry is not well placed for reaching the tough runs of the Portes du Soleil. The Swiss Wall, on the Champéry side of Chavanette, is an intimidatingly long, steep slope, but not nearly as terrifying as its various names suggest; the main difficulty is at the very top, which can be icy when snow is in short supply or may have moguls the size of small cars when it is in abundance.

There's a limit to how many times you will want to battle the Wall, and it's quite a trek to the Hauts Forts above Avoriaz – the main black-run sector in the Portes du Soleil.

There's lots of scope for off-piste at Chavanette and on the broad slopes of Les Crosets and Champoussin.

FOR INTERMEDIATES
Wonderful if snow is good
Confident intermediates have the whole of the Portes du Soleil at their disposal. There are a huge number of possibilities to enjoy without straying across the border.

The runs home to Grand Paradis are as good as any when the snow conditions allow, and enjoyable by all intermediates. It's not worth dwelling too long around the bland Planachaux area, but Les Crosets is a junction of several fine runs.

The pistes down from Pointe de Mossette and Grand Conche are good direct runs ideal for competent, or simply confident, intermediates. The

SCHOOLS/GUIDES

97/98 prices in Swiss francs

Swiss
Classes 5 days
3hr: 9.30-12.30
5 half-days: 120
Children's classes
Ages: from 3 to 7
5 days including lunch: 260
Private lessons
Hourly, half-daily or daily
50 for 1hr, for 1 or 2 people

CHILDCARE

The ski school runs a ski kindergarten for children aged 4 to 7, from 9.15 to 4.30.

The non-ski kindergarten takes children aged 6 months to 5 years, from 9am to 5pm – Maison des Schtroumpfs (741066).

GETTING THERE

Air Geneva, transfer 2hr.

UK PACKAGES

Chalets 'Unlimited', Made to Measure, Piste Artiste, Plus Travel, Ski Les Alpes, White Roc

Champoussin
Snowline Skiing

Morgins Chalets 'Unlimited', Ski Morgins

runs back from Pointe de l'Au also hold the interest. Champoussin has a network of short, easy pistes ideal for leisurely cruising.

Those 'doing the circuit' tend to find these uninteresting and time consuming, so don't bother with them, leaving them nicely uncrowded for nervous performers. Beyond, the runs down to Morgins are delightful tree-lined meanders, and are certainly the place to go in poor visibility. If need be, you can get from Planachaux to Morgins using just two lifts.

FOR BEGINNERS
Go elsewhere if you have a choice
Despite its good school, Champéry is far from ideal for beginners. An expensive cable-car ride takes novices to the steepish Planachaux runs, on the shortest of which they receive tuition. Beginners with a car can reach the far more suitable Champoussin slopes reasonably quickly.

FOR CROSS-COUNTRY
Very poor
A 7km loop is advertised, but it's very unreliable for snow and also not well maintained.

QUEUES
Few local problems
The cable-car comfortably copes with the village's quite low demand. When snow is good, weekend crowds can be a problem – hence the car park opposite the cable-car station – but Avoriaz's queues are a greater concern, and we've had reports that the pistes are becoming more crowded, especially around Les Crosets.

MOUNTAIN RESTAURANTS
Wide choice, some highlights
The local area is very good in terms of numbers of mountain restaurants, though few are particularly memorable. Chez Coquoz at Planachaux is recommended for its traditional atmosphere and good cheesy specialities.

Chez Marius (or Clavets) is a pleasant halt on the way down to Grand Paradis. Chez Gaby, above Champoussin, has been reported as 'a table-service delight' in the past. Further afield, the refuges at Marmottes-Les Lindarets are worth heading for (see Avoriaz chapter).

SCHOOLS AND GUIDES
No worries
The few (now rather ancient) reports that we've had on the school are free of criticism and tell of a surprising number of instructors who speak good English.

FACILITIES FOR CHILDREN
Some, but few reports
We've had few reports on either the ski kindergarten or the non-ski one.

Staying there

Although only a small village, most accommodation is not particularly well located for the slopes. The cable-car station is on the outer fringes of town, some way from many hotels. The result, surprisingly for a small resort, is that the shuttle bus is quite important – fortunately it is fairly efficient – and that having your own transport can be an advantage.

HOW TO GO
Limited packages available
Champéry is one of the easiest resorts to get to – by car, train or plane.

There's a limited range of hotels and catered chalets available through tour operators. The number of UK chalet operators going to Champéry has decreased in recent years – however, there are still a few catered chalets available.

Hotels There's a good spread of accommodation from 4-star to B&B and prices are low by comparison with many smarter Swiss resorts.
(((③ **Champéry** Biggest and best in town, but hardly in the luxury bracket despite 4-star rating – a pleasantly comfortable chalet on the main street.
(((③ **Suisse** Rival adjacent 4-star.
(((③ **Beau Séjour** Comfortable, traditional 3-star at the southern end of the main street.
((② **National** Classic Swiss villa-style hotel on the main street, with neatly renovated bedrooms.
((② **Paix** Creaky old chalet near the Beau Séjour.
((② **Alpes** Ditto, but in a slightly inconvenient position. Recent reporters found it quiet and friendly with good food though rather sparse rooms.
(① **Souvenir** Central 1-star which does the cheapest half board you'll find.
Self-catering Some apartments are available to independent travellers.

ACTIVITIES

Indoor Swimming pool, ice skating and curling rink, Sunfit fitness centre (sauna, solarium, body building, physiotherapy)
Outdoor Para-gliding, cleared walking paths, bungy jumping

EATING OUT
A fair choice

Two of the best places are just outside the village. Cantines des Rives, on the other side of the valley, is a taxi-ride away. It's a beautiful traditional chalet specialising in fondue and raclette. Similarly distant is the Grand Paradis. It serves excellent, if pricey, local specialities. The stuffed animals decorating the place may be off-putting for some.

There are impressive, pricy gourmet restaurants in the Hotel Suisse. Good, less expensive places are the Vieux Chalet and the restaurants of the Hotel des Alpes and Hotel National. For a less formal ambience it's best to try the local specialities of the Farinet, Café du Centre or Hotel du Nord, and the pizza at Cime de l'Est.

Once a week the restaurant at the top of the cable-car is open in the evening with special departures from and to the base-station.

APRES-SKI
Something for everyone

Champéry has a convivial atmosphere at tea-time, but things are fairly sedate later in the evening.

The Pub is the liveliest place in town, with noisy jukebox music earlier before a disco starts in the basic little downstairs bar around midnight. It's frequented mostly by resort workers and a few locals.

Far cosier places are the pleasantly informal bars in the hotel Suisse. The Bar des Guides is a pre-dinner watering hole with interesting relics and photographs of pre-war skiing. The

Mines d'Or is a cellar bar, mainly frequented by instructors, that's good for a mellow late drink.

The Farinet is a spacious cellar night-club with upstairs restaurant which is good fun when there are enough people to give it atmosphere – mostly at weekends. Most Brits prefer it to the simpler Levant disco, which is more of a locals' place.

OFF THE SLOPES
Excellent for the energetic

The Portes du Soleil has a general drawback for pedestrians, in that anyone on the the slopes other than beginners is very unlikely to want to hang around (or return to) the local area for lunch. But, that aside, Champéry is very attractive for the those who don't insist on a lot of animation in the village.

Walks, particularly along to Val d'Illiez, are very pleasant, and the

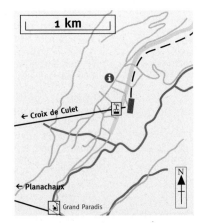

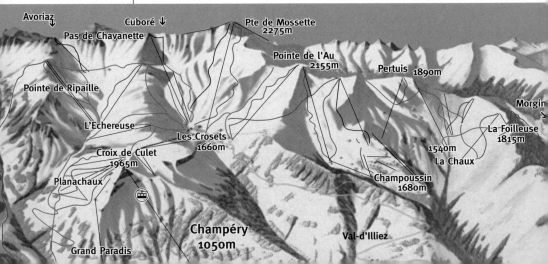

narrow-gauge railway allows excursions to Montreux, Lausanne and Sion.

There is a good range of activities in this small village, thanks to the excellent sports centre.

Les Crosets 1660m

Les Crosets has a prime position within the Portes du Soleil, but to stay there you would have to be very keen. It's little more than a multi-lift station and car-park, with a couple of hotels and restaurants supposedly making it a mini-resort.

It could be good only for car-driving hermits who might find it a useful base with the option to visit Champéry if they get bored. Hotel Télécabine is a homely place, which reputedly provides good evening meals.

Champoussin 1580m

Champoussin is, theoretically at least, a good choice for a family looking for a quiet, user-friendly base – no through traffic, convenient for the slopes enough altitude to have snow in the village often, no noisy late-night revellers, rustic-style buildings and the comfortable Ambassador hotel with all mod cons (and a disco). It also has recommended restaurants in Le Poussin and Gabi.

A few years ago, however, we had a report from a very bitter visitor who certainly felt her choice of resort had been a mistake. Her family's holiday was spoilt by problems with a poorly-run, impersonal school and a children's Miniclub where apparently kids spent much of their time standing around, no English was spoken and the unpleasant supervisor was seen shaking a small child.

They fared little better at their swish hotel; it had variable food and a shortage of staff, making for almost non-existent service, and the accommodation they'd booked was not available. And all this was supervised by an unrepentant Basil Fawlty figure. Perhaps it was just a bad week, we speculated; but we wondered whether it was worth the risk of finding out.

Well, some readers have felt it was. One returned a report praising the friendliness of the natives, the lively atmosphere created by the many Dutch visitors, 'stupendous views of the Dents du Midi', the proximity to the slopes, the child-friendly attitude of the comfortable Alpage hotel (two restaurants, pool, gym, disco) and the

progress his daughter made in the multi-lingual Miniclub.

Our most recent report was enthusiastic about the resort and particularly the private snowboard lessons. Little is revealed, however, about the children's facilities. The Miniclub seemed understaffed, and Snowline Holidays provide fun children's activities (such as a chocolate hunt) in the evenings.

Morgins 1350m

Morgins can disappoint many visitors. Attracted there by visions of a quiet little Swiss village with great mountains on its doorstep, visitors are surprised to find a scattered resort where some accommodation is a fair walk from one or both of the Portes du Soleil lifts.

Although reasonably attractive, the village is not in the same league as Champéry for charm, and even those looking for peace and quiet may find too much of a good thing here. The bland local slopes lead visitors to look further afield; but with poor snow conditions affecting links, an irritating series of short lifts, and lack of public transport to Châtel, this is often easier said than done.

Those expecting typical Swiss efficiency are also surprised to find poor local piste grooming and marking.

Morgins is best suited to those with a car. They can drive to Les Crosets for the highest and best of the Swiss Portes du Soleil slopes, or to the Linga gondola at Châtel.

If you're not interested in 'doing the circuit' you can buy the cheaper Evasion lift pass which still covers Morgins, Champoussin, Super-Châtel, Torgon and La Chapelle-d'Abondance. Cross-country enthusiasts have 20km of pleasant trails.

The large 3-star Bellevue is a modern hotel, but built in traditional style, and has been praised by reporters in the past for its friendliness and comfort. There are a couple of worthwhile restaurants but not much else in the way of nightlife. Off-slope amenities include indoor tennis, horse riding and a natural ice-rink.

Crans-Montana

1500m

Take your binoculars and hope for fresh snow

WHAT IT COSTS

((3))

HOW IT RATES

The slopes

Snow	**
Extent	***
Experts	**
Intermediates	****
Beginners	***
Convenience	**
Queues	***
Restaurants	**

The rest

Scenery	****
Resort charm	**
Off-slope	****

➕ Large piste area suitable for all, except if you prefer black runs

➕ Splendid wooded setting with magnificent panoramic views

➕ Fair number of woodland slopes – good for bad weather

➕ Modern, well designed lift system, with few queues

➕ Golf course provides excellent, gentle nursery slopes

➕ Very sunny slopes (see right)

➕ Excellent cross-country trails

➖ Snow badly affected by sun except in early season

➖ Towny resort centres composed partly of big chalet-style blocks but mainly of dreary cubic blocks – and therefore entirely without Alpine atmosphere

➖ Bus-rides or long, uphill walks to lifts from much of the accommodation

➖ Not many challenging pistes

When conditions are right – clear skies above fresh, deep snow – Crans-Montana takes some beating. The mountains you bounce down with the midday sun full on your face are charmingly scenic, the slopes broken up by rock outcrops and forest. The mountains you gaze at – Zermatt's Matterhorn just discernible among them – are mind-blowing. When conditions are right, mountain-lovers may forgive Crans-Montana anything – in particular, its inconvenient, linear layout and the ugly, towny style of its twin resort centres.

Sadly, conditions are more often wrong than right. Except in the depths of winter, the strong midday sun quickly bakes the pistes. For someone booking six months ahead, this is enough to keep Crans-Montana off the short-list. For those who can time a visit according to the weather – and are content to avert their eyes from the architecture – the resort is worth serious consideration.

boarding *Despite Crans-Montana's staid, middle-aged image, boarding still manages to make an in-road. There are plenty of broad, smooth pistes, lots of underexploited off-piste, and good specialist facilities. Aminona is the main area for experienced boarders, with a half-pipe and fun-park – we hear it's even got a fashionable buried VW Beetle – but there's another pipe in the more central Cry-d'Err area. There are no specialist schools, but the Swiss ski school has plenty of boarding instructors – and there are two specialist shops, Avalanche in Montana and Pacific Surf in Crans. The main lifts are chairs and gondolas, and the drag-lifts are usually avoidable with good planning. Together with the generally flattering slopes, that makes it a good place for beginner and intermediate boarders – and, of course, slush is good for learning to board in! But avoid the ice first thing in the morning. Nightlife tends to be a fairly civilised affair, too staid for hard-core teenage boarders.*

What's new

Crans-Montana dealt with our main reservation about its lift network – queues to get up to the best snow – in 1995, with the opening of its impressive double-cable 30-person gondola to Plaine Morte. No doubt that left the coffers depleted.

The resort

Crans-Montana celebrated 100 years as a resort in 1993, but is far from being a picturesque Swiss chocolate-box village. Set on a broad shelf facing south across the Rhône valley, it is really two villages, their centres a mile apart and their fringes now merging. Strung along a busy road, the resort's many hotels, villas, apartments and smart shops are mainly ugly blocks with little traditional Alpine character.

Fortunately, the resort's many trees help to hide some of the architectural excesses, and make some areas positively attractive. And its wonderful setting means you get a lot of sun as well as superb views to the great mountains beyond the Rhône. There are several lakes and two golf courses, one home to the Swiss Open.

The resort is reached by good roads, and by a funicular railway up from Sierre to Montana. It depends heavily on summer conference business, which sets the tone even in winter. Hotels tend to be comfortable but formal, village facilities varied but daytime-oriented; and visitors middle-aged and dignified. In the evenings there's little Alpine-village atmosphere.

Gondolas go up to the main slopes from both villages. Crans is the more up-market, with expensive jewellery shops, a casino, and a high fur-coat count. It is well situated for the pretty golf course area, which has baby lifts for complete beginners, a cross-country trail and lovely walks. Montana has cheaper restaurants and bars, and a more efficient lift accessing the slopes. There are other lift base stations and places to stay further east, at Les Barzettes and Aminona.

MOUNTAIN FACTS

Altitude 1500m-3000m
Lifts	41
Pistes	160km
Blue	38%
Red	50%
Black	12%
Artificial snow	15km

Recco detectors used

LIFT PASSES

97/98 prices in Swiss francs
Crans-Montana-Aminona
Covers all lifts in Crans-Montana and Aminona and the ski-bus.
Beginners Points card
Main pass
1-day pass 54
6-day pass 255
Senior citizens
Over 65: 6-day pass 154 (40% off)
Children
Under 16: 6-day pass 154 (40% off)
Under 6: free pass
Short-term passes
Half-day from 11.15 (adult 42) or 12.30 (adult 36); 2hr afternoon pass from 2pm (adult 31).
Alternative periods
8 non-consecutive days (adult 369).

The mountains

Although it has achieved some prominence in ski-racing – it's again hosting the climax of the World Cup series in March 1998 – Crans-Montana is not a bravo's resort. Its pistes suit intermediates well, with few challenges and no nasty surprises. Beginners are well catered for.

THE SLOPES
Interestingly fragmented
Crans-Montana's 160km of piste are spread over three well-linked areas, all equally suitable for intermediates of varying abilities and persuasions.

Cry d'Err is the largest sector – an open bowl descending into patchy forest, directly above Montana. Cry d'Err itself is the meeting point of many lifts and the starting point of the cable-car up to the sector high-point of Bella Lui (2545m). Cry d'Err is served directly by two gondolas – one carrying 2200 people per hour from just above central Montana, the other carrying less than half that number from just above Crans. Both have mid-stations; the one above Montana delivers beginners to the high-altitude nursery slopes served by the twin Verdets drags. A third gondola goes from the west side of Crans to Chetzeron, with a drag above going on to Cry d'Err.

The next sector, reached directly from Les Barzettes by another 2200p/h gondola, is focused on Les Violettes, starting point of the newish gondola

up to the Plaine Morte glacier. There are three linking routes from Cry d'Err to the **Violettes-Plaine Morte** sector. One, starting at Bella Lui (or, strictly, at Col du Pochet, a short run and drag beyond) is officially 'for experts only' as it is off-piste; but it is largely a traverse, made awkward only by wave-like bumps and narrowness in places. Bella Lui is also the start of the Men's Downhill race course (Piste Nationale), which passes Cry d'Err, finishing at Les Barzettes. The third option is an easy path across from the Verdets drags, near the bottom of the Cry d'Err sector. It's high enough to reach the low mid-station of the Violettes gondola.

The third sector is above **Aminona** at the eastern-end of the slopes. This is linked to Les Violettes and there's a gondola up from the valley.

Anzère is nearby to the west, though the slopes aren't linked. You can make expeditions to Zermatt and Verbier, or smaller Grimentz and Ovronnaz, by road or rail.

SNOW RELIABILITY
The resort's main drawback
Crans-Montana's slopes go up to glacier level at 3000m, but this is misleading; the runs on the Plaine Morte glacier are very limited and, excellent though it is, the solitary run down from there does not make this a snowsure area as a whole. Few of the other slopes are above 2250m, and practically all get a lot of direct sun. Late in the season, at least, this makes for slush in the afternoons, rock-hard ice in the mornings, and a tendency for snow to disappear. There is now snowmaking on four runs on the lower half of the mountain – one to Violettes, two to Montana and one to Crans. We applaud these efforts; but it is a losing battle.

FOR EXPERTS
Lacks challenging pistes
There are few steep pistes. The only moguls worthy of the name are on the short but often quiet run served by the Toula lifts. There's plenty of off-piste in all sectors, but particularly beneath Chetzeron and La Tza; guides are usually easy to book.

The Piste Nationale course is far from daunting taken at 'normal' speed, but has some enormous jumps just above Les Marolies. The direct run from La Tza to Plumachit is fairly testing in places, especially when icy.

FOR INTERMEDIATES
Lots of attractive, flattering runs
Crans-Montana is very well suited to intermediates. Pistes are mostly wide and, although red dominates the map, many of the red runs don't justify the grading. They also tend to be uniform in difficulty from top to bottom, with few nasty surprises for the nervous. Avid piste bashers enjoy the length of many runs, plus the fast lifts and good links that allow a lot of varied mileage.

The 11km run from Plaine Morte to Les Barzettes starts with superb top-of-the-world views and powder snow, and finishes among pretty woods. There are several truly contrasting variants of the bottom half from Les Violettes. But many people love the top half so much ('my favourite run in Europe') they do it repeatedly – a practical proposition now that the big gondola has cut waiting times (though, of course, this also means more people on the piste).

The short runs from Bella Lui to just below Cry d'Err have some of the best snow and quietest slopes in the area, and provide fine views of awesome Montagne de Raul. The Piste Nationale is a good test of technique, with plenty of bumps but also lots of room. The quietest area, and good for groups of varying intermediate standards, is the Petit Bonvin sector above Aminona. Three long runs of varying difficulty go from La Tza to Aminona, and there are also drags up at Petit Bonvin serving short, easy runs with good snow.

FOR BEGINNERS
Plenty to offer the first-timer
There are three excellent nursery areas, with slopes of varying difficulty. Complete beginners have very gentle slopes on the golf course next to Crans. Cry d'Err has an area of relatively long, easy runs, with up-the-mountain views and atmosphere as well as better snow. But the runs aren't just for beginners, and you do need a full lift pass. The Verdets-Grand Signal run is steeper, and the drag-lift can get terribly icy. Near-beginners can try the little run up at Plaine Morte – great snow, great views.

FOR CROSS-COUNTRY
Excellent high-level trails
There are 17km of pretty, easy trails (skating-style as well as classic) on and

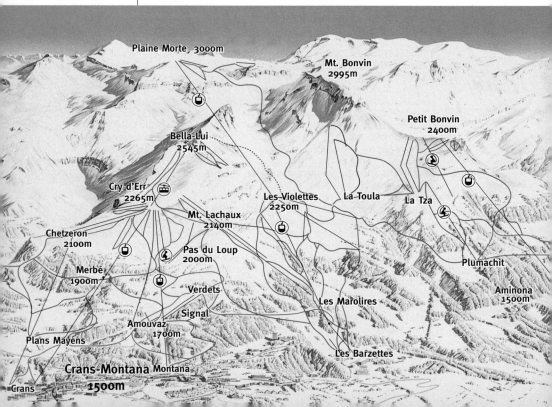

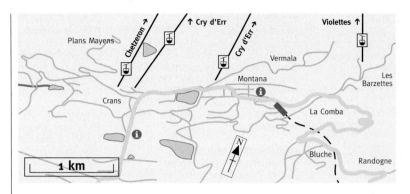

around the golf course. But what makes Crans-Montana particularly good for cross-country is its high-level route, in and out of woods, across the whole mountainside from Plans Mayens to beyond Aminona – a 15km round-trip. Plaine Morte has a further 12km available in the summer.

You have to buy a vignette (valid in all other Swiss resorts too), which gets you a 50 per cent discount on the lifts up to Plaine Morte.

QUEUES
Recent transformation
Access to the glacier – and, more importantly, the excellent red run of over 1000m vertical back down – did involve long waits. But in December 1995 the impressive Funitel stand-up gondola opened, with five times the capacity of the old cable-car. Recent reporters say you never wait longer than five minutes. Minor remaining irritations include short queues for the Barmaz chair-lifts up to Les Violettes from La Toula, and sometimes at Cabane des Bois. Delays are longer when snow lower down is in poor condition. On the other hand, the low-capacity gondola to Merbé becomes over-subscribed when wind closes the other major lifts. Crans-Montana does not get overrun at weekends.

MOUNTAIN RESTAURANTS
Disappointing for a smart resort
Mountain restaurants are generally undistinguished, but at least they tend to be table service. They're expensive, with main meals better value than snacks. Only the Cry d'Err sector offers much choice. The Merbé, at the Crans-Cry d'Err gondola mid-station, is the most attractive, with table service of good food in a pleasant setting just above the tree-line. Bella Lui's terrace

(with service) offers good views. The Chetzeron eatery allows picnics provided you buy a drink.

Petit Bonvin has perhaps the best of the self-service places, with superb views. The Plumachit restaurant, towards the bottom of the sector, has a large sun terrace in a pretty setting. Reporters recommend the Ratrac in Aminona for atmosphere. There is not much choice in the Violettes sector, but the small hut 50m from the main cafeteria at Violettes itself gets a rave review (be there early for a seat on the terrace), and there's a welcoming little hotel opposite the bottom station.

The craggy mountainside is one of the attractions of the area ↓

SCHOOLS/GUIDES
97/98 prices in Swiss francs

Swiss
Classes 5 days
3hr: 9.30-12.30
5 days: 155
Children's classes
Ages: from 3
5 days: 155
Private lessons
Hourly
50 for 1hr

CHILDCARE

The Montana ski school runs a kindergarten with skiing available up at Signal (411480) for children aged 3 to 6, from 9am to 4.45.

There are several other kindergartens. In Crans, Bibiland (418142) takes children from age 2. In Montana, Fleurs des Champs (412367) takes children aged 2 months to 12 years; and Les Coccinelles (412423) takes children aged 3 to 16.

GETTING THERE

Air Geneva, transfer 3hr.

Rail Sierre (15km), Sion (22km); regular buses to resort.

UK PACKAGES

Fairhand Holidays, Inghams, Kuoni, Lagrange, Made to Measure, PGL Ski Europe, Plus Travel, Ski Club of GB, Ski Weekend, Swiss Travel Service

Aminona Lagrange

ACTIVITIES

Indoor Hotel swimming pools, tennis, bowling, bridge, squash, concerts, cinema, casino, skating, curling
Outdoor Toboggan run, ski-bob, horse-riding

TOURIST OFFICE

Postcode CH-3962
Tel +41 (27) 485 0404
Fax 485 0460

SCHOOLS AND GUIDES
Good reports
Both local branches of the Swiss school attract favourable comments: 'Small class sizes, imaginative tuition with individual instruction'. Cry d'Err is a common rendezvous spot. Note the unusual hours (see margin). Private lessons are easily booked, both for on- and off-piste.

FACILITIES FOR CHILDREN
Adequate, but few reports
The resort facilities for children seem to be adequate, especially in Montana. Sadly, childcare specialists Ski Esprit no longer operate their chalet here.

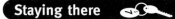

Staying there

Crans-Montana is quite sprawling. The free shuttle bus links the villages and satellite lift stations during the day, but there's no evening service. Though frequent at peak times buses can get very crowded, and they don't cut out walks. The gondola-stations are above the main road, a tiring enough walk from many hotels to warrant paying to store equipment at the lift station. The best choice of location for most people would be near the Montana gondola.

HOW TO GO
Much more choice on your own
The independent traveller has a wide choice of hotels and apartments, and some are available through UK tour operators. We are not aware of any catered chalet holidays.
Hotels This conference resort has 52 mainly large, comfortable, expensive hotels. 42 have three or more stars.
(((((5) **Crans-Ambassador** Huge luxury place with distinctive 'chalet' roof-line, near the Montana gondola. Pool.
((((4) **Hauts de Crans** Smart modern hotel in excellent position up above Montana. Pool.
((((4) **Aïda Castel** Beautifully furnished in chic rustic style, with hand-painted furniture and pine panelling. Between the two resort centres. Outdoor pool.
(((4) **Le Green** Well placed near the Crans lifts; small, modern and chic.
(((3) **La Foret** Highly recommended. Almost at Les Barzettes, with minibus to lifts. Pool and splendid views.
(((3) **National** Perfectly placed for the Crans-Cry d'Err gondola; 'quiet, comfortable, good food'.
(((3) **Au Robinson** B&B only; well placed near the National, in Crans.

(1) **Petit Paradis** Five minutes from Montana in Bluche, a family-run auberge with a welcoming restaurant.
Self-catering There are many apartments available, particularly to independent travellers. Supermarkets in Montana are surprisingly cheap.

EATING OUT
Plenty of alternatives
There is a good variety of restaurants from French to Chinese and Lebanese, although prices tend to push British self-caterers into pizzerias or supermarkets. Almost all the cheaper restaurants are in Montana. Most do good filling *rösti*. The Carnozet has been recommended in the past for excellent fondue. The Au Robinson hotel restaurant is good, reasonably priced, and open to non-residents. The Gréni is a welcoming restaurant on the western fringe of Montana. The Cervin up at Vermala is unusually rustic.

APRES-SKI
Can be ritzy, but otherwise quiet
The resort boasts plenty of après-ski places, but people seem loath to use them. The Pub Georges & Dragon is by far the liveliest, most crowded bar; surprisingly, as it's in Crans, it has the cheapest beer in town. A recent report says the outdoor ice rink in Montana is the liveliest place to be on a Friday and Saturday evening: 'The best disco and most impressive light show in town; you can just sit and watch if you want.' We also hear that Amadeus is a good, lively bar in Montana. For peace and quiet, there are quite a few piano bars. The two cinemas change films every couple of days, and some play in English. Bridge is played from 3pm in the Aïda-Castel.

OFF THE SLOPES
Excellent, but little charm
There are plenty of off-slope activities to keep you busy; lovely walks through and around the golf course, among novice downhillers and cross-country skiers. Swimming is available in about a dozen hotels. Sierre is only a funicular-ride away for serious shopping, while the larger town of Sion is only a few minutes further by rail. Montreux is also within reach. Mountain restaurants are mainly at gondola and cable-car stations, so everyone can easily meet others for lunch at altitude.

A big town surrounded by a great Alpine playground

WHAT IT COSTS

((((5))))

HOW IT RATES

The slopes

Snow	****
Extent	*****
Experts	****
Intermediates	*****
Beginners	***
Convenience	**
Queues	***
Restaurants	***

The rest

Scenery	***
Resort charm	**
Off-slope	*****

Pros

- ➕ Very extensive slopes
- ➕ Some superb long and mostly easy runs away from the lifts
- ➕ Lots of off-piste, with lots of marked itineraries and some short tours
- ➕ Good cross-country trails
- ➕ Excellent sports facilities, pretty walks, good range of shopping
- ➕ Some captivating mountain restaurants above Klosters
- ➕ Klosters is attractively villagey

Cons

- ➖ Dreary block-style buildings of Davos spoil the views
- ➖ Davos is a huge, city-like resort, rather plagued by traffic and lacking Alpine atmosphere
- ➖ The slopes are spread over five or six essentially separate areas
- ➖ Some access lifts are inefficient, leading to queues, and T-bars are common

Once popular with Brits, Davos is a rather specialised taste these days (and British visitors are hugely outnumbered by Germans). Few resorts in the world have more extensive slopes, or offer more for all standards. But the area has its drawbacks: it is split into five or six unlinked sectors, and relatively ancient lifts serve many of them. Those prepared to accept such drawbacks normally do so as the price of staying in a captivating Alpine village. But Davos is far from that.

Whether you forgive the flaws and fall for the resort depends on how highly you value three plus-points: the distinctive, long intermediate runs of the Parsenn area; being able to visit a different sector every day; and the considerable off-piste potential. We like all three, and we always look forward to visiting.

But you don't have to stay in Davos to enjoy its slopes: Klosters offers a much more captivating alternative. Despite royal connections, it is not exclusive – on the contrary, it has exceptionally welcoming places to stay. It is less well placed than Davos for exploring all the mountains, but just as handy for the Parsenn.

boarding *Although the nursery slopes are not ideal, the long easy runs of the Parsenn are good for near-beginner boarders and you can avoid drags if you plan your runs properly and use the cable-cars and funiculars. But intermediate and advanced boarders will get the most out of Davos's vast terrain and off-piste potential. The established boarder mountain is the Jakobshorn, with its half-pipe, fun-park and funky Jatz Bar nearby – but there are a lot of long drag-lifts and the Parsenn now also has a fun-park and half-pipe. There are several cheap and cheerful hotels specially for snowboarders, including the Snowboardhotel Bolgenschanze which organises a lot of après-board action too.*

What's new

For the 1997/98 season the Usser Icht T-bar by the race course on the Jakobshorn will be replaced by a high-speed quad chair. Another high-speed quad is also planned to replace the Totalp T-bar on the Parsenn from Parsennhütte towards Weissfluhjoch.

Plans for the long-overdue replacement of the ancient Parsennbahn funicular by a jumbo gondola had no firm date attached when we went to press.

The resort

Davos is set in a broad, gently sloping valley, with its slopes either side. Arguably it was the very first place in the Alps to develop its slopes. The railway up the Parsenn was one of the first built for skiers (in 1931), and the first drag-lift was built on the Bolgen nursery slopes in 1934. But Davos was already a health resort; many of its luxury hotels used to be sanatoriums. Sadly that's just what they look like. There are still several specialist clinics here, and they and the big business in conferences make Davos feel like the town it is (it's often called the highest town in Europe). It is not Switzerland's biggest winter resort however: in terms of beds at least, Crans-Montana is much bigger, and Verbier slightly so.

Davos shares its slopes with Klosters, down the hill. It has two main centres, Dorf and Platz, about 2km apart. Easiest access to the slopes is from Dorf to the main Parsenn area, via the funicular railway, or from Platz to the Strela and Jakobshorn areas.

MOUNTAIN FACTS

Altitude	810m-2845m
Lifts	55
Pistes	344km
Blue	30%
Red	40%
Black	30%
Artificial snow	21km
Recco detectors used	
— helicopter-based	

The mountains

The slopes here have something for everyone, though experts and nervous intermediates need to choose their territory with care. Trips are possible by car or rail to St Moritz and Arosa, or by car to Flims and Lenzerheide.

THE SLOPES
Vast and varied

If you wanted you could hit a different mountain in Davos every day for a week. In practice, you don't: the minor areas tend to be neglected by most visitors – but they are worth checking out, and are all the better for neglect.

The ancient Parsennbahn funicular from Davos Dorf (due to be replaced by a jumbo-gondola) takes you to the major lift junction of Weissfluhjoch (2660m), at one end of the **Parsenn**. At the other is Gotschnagrat, reached by cable-car from Klosters. Between the two is the wide, open Parsenn bowl. From Davos Platz, a funicular takes you up to Schatzalp, at the base of the **Strela** area. A cable-car from the top of it offers a back-door to Weissfluhjoch.

Across the valley, **Jakobshorn** is reached by cable-car from Davos Platz; this is the main snowboarders' hill. **Rinerhorn** and **Pischa** are reached by bus or (in the case of Rinerhorn) train.

Beyond the main part of Klosters, a gondola goes up from Klosters Dorf to the sunny, scenic **Madrisa** area.

Lift passes are monitored electronically, without the need to take them out of your pocket.

SNOW RELIABILITY
Good, but not the best

Davos is high by Swiss standards. Its mountains go respectably high too – though not to glacial heights. Not many of the slopes face directly south, but not many face directly north either – mainly the long runs on the back of the Parsenn. So snow reliability is no more than fair. The south-east-facing pistes down to Dorf from Weissfluhjoch are the ones most at risk. There is some artificial snowmaking capacity but not a lot.

FOR EXPERTS
Plenty to do, on- and off-piste

A glance at the piste map may give the misleading impression that this is an intermediate's resort. In fact blacks are largely in the wooded lower slopes of several sectors, which means excellent visibility when snow is falling – the Meierhofer Tälli run to Wolfgang is excellent – but rough going when snow is thin. There are two exceptions: the trio of runs at the southern extremity of the Strela area, and the runs from Gotschnagrat directly towards Klosters – around the infamous Gotschnawang slope. The Wang run is a seriously steep ski route (marked on the map but not prepared or controlled – and rarely open, in our experience). Drostobel is less scary, though the overall gradient is little different.

The main appeal, however, is the excellent off-piste and short tours – as a recent expert reporter confirms. Practically all the sectors now have at least one marked itinerary to the valley – an excellent arrangement which allows experts to escape the crowds without paying for guidance. Rinerhorn is the exception – but that has an excellent black piste of 1000m vertical that amounts to much the same thing.

Arosa can be reached much more quickly on snow than by road or rail, but requires a return by rail via Chur. From Madrisa you can make tours to Gargellen in Austria's Montafontal. This means an exhausting one-hour walk on skins or snowshoes on the way back.

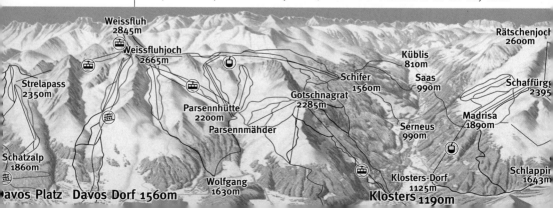

LIFT PASSES

97/98 prices in Swiss francs

Rega area
Covers all Davos and Klosters, the railway in the whole region and buses between the resorts.
Beginners Single and return tickets on main lifts in each area.
Main pass
1-day pass 52
6-day pass 259
(low season 207 – 20% off)
Senior citizens
Over 65 male, 62 female: 6-day pass 207 (20% off)
Children
Under 16: 6-day pass 155 (40% off)
Under 6: free pass
Short-term passes
Half-day passes, up to and from 12.30, for each area (Jakobshorn, adult 35).
Alternative periods
Passes for 8 days (Rinerhorn, adult 230) and 15 days (Rinerhorn, adult 377) in the season, but only for limited areas.
Notes Day pass price is for Parsenn, Pischa, Schatzalp and Gotschna only.
Alternative passes
A confusing array of passes covering limited areas (Jakobshorn, Rinerhorn, Pischa and Schatzalp, and other combinations).

FOR INTERMEDIATES
A splendid variety of runs
For intermediates of any temperament or tendency, this is a great area. But its greatest appeal is to those who like to get around, with long runs to the valleys and the stimulating prospect of covering several different areas.

The epic runs to Klosters and other places (described in the feature box) pose few difficulties for a confident intermediate or even an ambitious near-beginner (one of the editors did the run to Klosters on his third day on skis). And there are one or two other notable away-from-the-lifts runs to the valley that are more than just woodland paths. In particular, you can travel from the top of Madrisa back to Klosters Dorf via the beautiful Schlappin valley.

FOR BEGINNERS
Platz is the more convenient
The Bolgen nursery slope is adequately spacious and gentle, and a bearable walk from the centre of Platz. But Dorf-based beginners face more of a trek out to Bünda – unless staying out at the hotel of the same name.

There is no shortage of easy runs to progress to, spread around all the sectors. The Parsenn sector probably

has the edge, with long, easy runs in the main Parsenn bowl, as well as in the valleys down from Weissfluhjoch.

FOR CROSS-COUNTRY
Long, scenic valley trails
Davos has a total of 75km of trails running in both directions along the main valley and reaching well up into Sertigtal and Dischmatal. There is a cross-country ski centre and special ski school on the outskirts of the town.

QUEUES
Still a problem in places
The ancient Parsennbahn railway generated queues when we first visited Davos 20 years ago, and it's still doing the same today. Thankfully it's due to be replaced by a jumbo gondola in a couple of seasons. The Schatzalpbahn – the roundabout, alternative way to Davos' main slopes – suffers queues too, as do the lifts at the base of the Jakobshorn. In Klosters, queues for the Gotschna cable-car have been much reduced by a doubling of its capacity, but can still be a problem at weekends. Reporters recommend avoiding the crowds by simply not going to Parsenn and Jakobshorn at the weekends, and heading for Madrisa, Rinerhorn or Pischa instead.

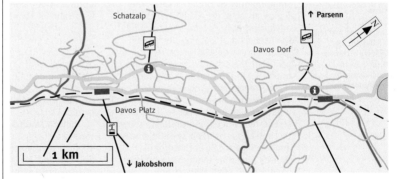

CHILDCARE

The ski school runs the Pinocchio nursery at Bünda, on the outskirts of Davos Dorf, taking children from age 3, from 8.30 to 4.30. Children can stay in the nursery, play about on skis or take proper ski school classes.

The Berghotel Schatzalp has its own ski nursery – see Staying up the mountain. The hotel Derby in Dorf has an indoor kindergarten.

SCHOOLS/GUIDES

96/97 prices in Swiss francs

Swiss
Classes 5 days
4hr: 2hr am and pm
5 full days: 185
Children's classes
Ages: 4 to 16
5 full days: 185
Private lessons
Half-day or full-day
145 for half-day

MOUNTAIN RESTAURANTS
Stay low down
The main high-altitude restaurants are dreary self-service affairs, but the Strelapass hut is recommended as particularly enjoyable on a warm sunny day, with good views and 'excellent' food. There are other compelling places at or approaching valley level – notably the rustic Conterser Schwendi and Serneuser Schwendi in the woods on the way down to the Klosters valley from the Parsenn. These are great places to end up as darkness falls – Klosters Schwendi, at least, sells wax torches to illuminate your final descent to the village. The Skilife, down from Totalp, is suggested as a great stop for either food or a rest (you can eat your own food) 'if you like pop music'. The Jatz Bar near the boarders' fun-park on Jakobshorn is wild – decked out like a desert island, complete with mock palm trees, parrot and pirate.

There are peaceful restaurants at or near the bottom of the Pischa, Jakobshorn and Rinerhorn sectors. And the station restaurants at Saas and Kublis are pleasant places to wait.

SCHOOLS AND GUIDES
Don't count on English
We lack recent reports, but, given the small number of British visitors that Davos attracts, it's likely that the more advanced, at least, are likely to find themselves in a German-dominated group. In the past a Davos regular has said that the school is well organised, but that the instructors vary widely.

The 'deep snow' classes guarantee no more than six participants, with half a day a week given over to avalanche rescue techniques and understanding the behaviour of deep snow. Seniors and teenagers can both enrol in classes aimed at them. Snowboarders have a keen specialist school.

FACILITIES FOR CHILDREN
Not ideal
Davos is a rather spread-out place in which to handle a family – and indeed the school's nursery is in a slightly isolated spot, at Dorf's Bünda nursery slope, inconvenient for dropping off and picking up. A recent reporter tells us the school is 'well organised, but even good instructors forget at times that your child doesn't speak German'. Our instinct, if the budget will stand it, would be to stay at the Berghotel Schatzalp (see Staying up mountain).

Staying there

Davos is a big, spread-out resort and although transport is good, with buses around the town as well as the railway linking Dorf and Platz to Klosters and other villages, location is important. Dorf has direct but currently queue-prone access to the Parsenn; Platz has lifts to Jakobshorn and Strela, the big sports facilities, the smarter shopping and more evening action.

HOW TO GO
Hotels dominate the packages
Although most bed space in Davos is in apartments, hotels dominate the UK package holiday market.

Hotels A dozen 4-star and about 30 3-star places form the core of the Davos hotel trade, though there are a couple of 5-stars and quite a few cheaper places, including B&Bs.

(((((5) **Fluela** The more atmospheric of the two 5-star hotels, in central Dorf, and quite well placed to beat the Parsenn queues. Pool.

((((4) **Golfhotel Waldhuus** As convenient for winter langlaufers as for summer golfers. Quiet, modern, tasteful. Pool.

(((3) **Parsenn** Davos needs more hotels that look like this attractive chalet, right opposite the Parsenn railway in Dorf.

(((3) **Bahnhof Terminus** We stayed here in '97. Friendly, three restaurants including a great Chinese, good sauna, right by bus stop in Platz.

(((3) **Davoserhof** One of our favourites: small, old, beautifully furnished, with excellent food; well placed in Platz.

((2) **Alte Post** Traditional and cosy; in central Platz.

((2) **Hubli's Landhaus** 5km out at Laret, towards Klosters. Quiet country inn with sophisticated, expensive food.

Self-catering The Allod Park apartments are in a dreary block, but are reasonably comfortable, and in a happy medium position, mid-way between the Parsenn and Strela lifts.

STAYING UP THE MOUNTAIN
Especially appealing for families
The Berghotel Schatzalp, on the tree-line about 300m above Davos Platz and reached by funicular (free to guests), is a 4-star hotel to rival any in the resort, complete with pool and sauna. The Strela slopes just above have something for everyone, but the Berghotel is especially interesting for the nursery slope right next to it – and

GETTING THERE

Air Zürich, transfer 3hr.

Rail Station in Davos Platz.

UK PACKAGES

Freedom Holidays, Inghams, Kuoni, Made to Measure, Plus Travel, Ski Choice, Ski Les Alpes, Ski Weekend, SkiGower, Swiss Travel Service, White Roc

Klosters Kuoni, Made to Measure, Plus Travel, Powder Byrne, Ski Club of GB, Ski Les Alpes, Ski with Julia, SkiGower, The Ski Company Ltd, White Roc

the hotel runs its own crèche (evenings as well as daytime) with tuition available. Schatzalp is also the start of the local toboggan run, a mini-Cresta.

EATING OUT
Wide choice, mostly in hotels

Most of the better restaurants are in hotels. The Davoserhof's restaurant is one of the best in town, both for food and ambience. Chinese food is trendy here – the lavish Zauberberg restaurant in the Central and the Golden Dragon in the Bahnhof Terminus are two of the best in this category.

Good-value places include the Pizzeria Padrino, Mona Lisa, Da Elio and the Gentiana (with an upstairs *stübli*). The Alte Post has a restaurant doing pasta, fondue and raclette.

An evening excursion for dinner out of town is popular. Teufi, Schatzalp (reached by a funicular) and Islen are all good places. Our favourite would have to be the wholesome local fare in the basic old Landhaus in Frauenkirch.

APRES-SKI
Lots on offer, but quiet clientele

There are plenty of bars, discos and nightclubs, but we're not sure how some of them make a living. Davos guests tend to want the quiet life. The off-slope activities and numerous cafés and bars give Davos a pleasant tea-time atmosphere, but things are subdued after dinner. High calories are consumed with enthusiasm at cafés Weber and Schneider. A civilised drink can be had at several hotels – the Derby's attractive Paluda bar; the Corner bar of the Post Morosani; the piano bars in the Central and Europe. A reporter mentions that people have started to use the recently introduced temporary 'tent-like' bars for a couple of beers on coming off the slopes. Carlos has a popular outside terrace.

The liveliest place in town is the rustic little Chämi bar. Its taped pop music and strange decor is popular with the young crowd. It's one of the few spots to retain a spark of life late in the evening. The Scheuten is another interesting place where Ranch meets Jungle decor, with live music and popular with locals. The X Bar is a smart mixture of Parisienne Brasserie with a touch of Pancho Villa and attracts a mixed age group. A recent reporter tells of a bar known as the 8.15 which sells large beers for the same price as a small beer elsewhere, but 'has sticky carpets and several drunks'.

Nightclubs tend to be sophisticated, expensive and lacking atmosphere during the week. The most popular are the Cabanna, the Pöstli (which was very lively and had a good live band when we visited) and the Europe.

Bolgenschanze is the biggest snowboarder hang-out and runs various theme evenings.

THE PARSENN'S SUPER-RUNS

The runs from Weissfluhjoch that head north, on the back of the mountain, make this area special for many visitors. The pistes that continue northward to Schifer and then to Kublis, Saas and Serneus, and the one that curls around the mountain to Klosters, are graded red but are not difficult. What marks them out is their sheer length (10–12km) and the sensation of travel they offer.

Until ten years ago, only the very top 2.5km and 400m vertical of this enormous snow field could be done over and over; once below Kreuzweg, you had to go down to the valley and catch the train home. Usually, you did it towards the end of the day, dawdling in the rustic restaurants in the woods on the lower reaches. The long Schiferbahn gondola changed all that – you can now 'yo-yo' 1100m vertical as often as you like. Some long-standing visitors regret the change, but there is the added advantage that the lower runs, below the Schifer gondola station, are quieter.

The longest runs are the marked but unpatrolled routes to Fideris and Jenaz, the latter being 18km from Weissfluhjoch, according to official figures. Start at the Weissfluh summit and you can add another kilometre, as well as another 200m vertical. But these are not continuous runs: they require skins or snowshoes for a couple of short ascents, and payment for the use of the lifts at Fideriser Heuberge on the way.

ACTIVITIES

Indoor Artificial
skating rink, fitness
centre, tennis,
squash, swimming,
sauna, cinema,
museums, galleries,
libraries
Outdoor Over 80km of
cleared paths (mostly
at valley level),
natural skating rink,
curling, toboggan run,
horse-riding, hang-
gliding, sleigh rides,
para-gliding

TOURIST OFFICE

Postcode CH-7270
Tel +41 (81) 415 2121
Fax 415 2100

The Klosters valley –
only a few km from
Davos, but a world
away in style ↓

OFF THE SLOPES
Great apart from the buildings

Provided you're not fussy about
building style, Davos can be
unreservedly recommended for off-
slope fun. The towny resort has shops
and other diversions, and transport
along the valley (covered by the tourist
tax) and up onto the slopes is good –
though the best of the mountain
restaurants are well out of range for
pedestrians. The sports facilities are
excellent; the natural ice rink is said to
be Europe's biggest, and is
supplemented by artificial rinks both
indoor and outdoor.

Spectator sports include speed
skating as well as hockey. And there
are lots of marked walks up on the
slopes as well as around the lake and
along the valleys.

Klosters 1190m

In a word association game, Klosters
might trigger 'Prince of Wales'. The
world's TV screens have shown him
skiing there countless times. In 1988
he was almost killed there in an off-
piste avalanche that did kill one of his
companions, and now the enlarged
cable-car to Gotschna – which takes
you to the Parsenn area shared with
Davos – is named after him.

Don't be put off. We don't know
why HRH likes to ski in Klosters
particularly, but it is certainly not
because the place is the exclusive
territory of royalty and aristocracy.

It's a comfortable, quiet village with
a much more appealing Alpine flavour
than Davos, despite its lower altitude.
Klosters Platz is the main focus – a
collection of upmarket, traditional-style
hotels around the railway station, at
the foot of the steep, wooded slopes
of Gotschna. The road to Davos passes
through, and traffic can be a nuisance.

The village spreads along the valley
road for quite a way before fading into
the countryside; there's then a second
concentration of building in the even
quieter village of Klosters Dorf, from
where a gondola goes up to Madrisa.

Although there are some nursery
lifts at valley level, the sunny slopes of
Madrisa are more appealing. There is a
ski kindergarten up there. The hotel
Vereina has a non-ski kindergarten,
taking very young children on request.

Klosters' upmarket image is
reinforced by the upmarket UK tour
operators who go there – The Ski
Company Ltd and Powder Byrne.

There are some particularly
attractive hotels. The central Chesa
Grischuna is irresistible, combining
traditional atmosphere (carved wood
everywhere) with modern comfort
– and a lively après-ski bar.

The less central Wynegg is a
favourite with British visitors, with a
warmly welcoming panelled dining
room and good-value bedrooms. The
Vereina is a 'slightly faded' grand
hotel, with 'friendly, helpful staff and
very good food'. In Dorf, the Albeina
has been recommended.

The evenings are quiet, but not
entirely lifeless. The huts in the woods
above the village attract lots of people
on their last run of the day, particularly
the Serneuser Schwendi. In the village,
the Chesa Grischuna is a focus of
activity from tea-time onwards, with its
piano bar, bowling and expensive but
popular restaurant.

The Wynegg is also popular
immediately after the lifts close, and
for more affordable dinners. An
alternative for eating out is the
Walserhof (a rival to the Chesa
Grischuna) and there are other more
modest places.

In the late evening the bars of the
hotels Kaiser and Vereina are popular.
The Casa Antica is a small but popular
disco. The Kir Royale, under the hotel
Silvretta Park, is bigger and more
brash. The Funny Place, under the Piz
Buin, is more grown-up and expensive.

Klosters is an attractive base for
walking and cross-country skiing, but
has little else to offer off the slopes.
The hotels Pardenn and Sport have
pools, and there is curling.

Engelberg 1050m

One of the biggest verticals in the Alps

Engelberg makes a great weekend retreat for the residents of Lucerne, less than an hour away. Despite impressive and distinctive mountains towering 2000m above the village, it attracts few foreign visitors – partly, we guess, because its slopes are rather inconveniently fragmented.

WHAT IT COSTS

(((3)))

HOW IT RATES

The slopes

Snow	***
Extent	**
Experts	***
Intermediates	***
Beginners	**
Convenience	*
Queues	***
Restaurants	***

The rest

Scenery	***
Resort charm	***
Off-slope	***

MOUNTAIN FACTS

Altitude	1050m-3020m
Lifts	25
Pistes	82km
Blue	30%
Red	60%
Black	10%
Artificial snow	2km

Recco detectors used
— helicopter-based

UK PACKAGES

Freedom Holidays, Kuoni, Made to Measure, SkiGower, Swiss Travel Service

TOURIST OFFICE

Postcode CH-6390
Tel +41 (41) 637 3737
Fax 637 4156

THE RESORT

Engelberg is a long-established year-round resort – bustling, towny and home to an impressive 12th-century monastery, surrounded by spectacular mountains. Much of the old-world charm of the original village has been diluted by modern development, but away from the town the valley is very scenic. Engelberg is rather isolated from other resorts, but you can get to Andermatt and to the Jungfrau region.

THE MOUNTAINS

The **slopes** are in contrasting sectors on either side of the village. For the main sector, a regular, free shuttle bus takes you across the valley to a two-stage gondola to the shelf of Trübsee (1800m). Above this a two-stage cable-car rises to Titlis at over 3000m, the second stage having the novelty of revolving cabins for optimal scenery-gazing. Below the summit are some short drags serving red and black slopes; descent to Stand (2430m) is via a single steep piste, with an easier red from there down to Trübsee. Across the frozen lake, a separate set of lifts serve good red runs above and below Jochpass (2205m). There is a roundabout run back to the valley.

The Brunni area, accessed by a cable-car from the edge of town, has a small network of sunny pistes between Schonegg (2040m) and Ristis (1600m), and occasionally a run back to town.

High, north-facing Titlis is **snowsure** (high drags stay open into June). The Brunni sector is much less reliable.

For **experts**, the big attraction is off-piste – the famous Laub. This steep wall drops 1000m from the shoulder of Titlis – superb when conditions are right, dangerous when they aren't. The slopes suit confident **intermediates**, though they are not very extensive; there are not many very easy slopes. There are nursery slopes in various places, but they involve lift-rides – the resort is not ideal for **beginners**.

The resort attracts quite a few **snowboarders**; the place to head for is Jochpass, where there's a fun-park and half-pipe when snow allows. Engelberg is good for **cross-country**, with 30km of trails amid lovely scenery at Trübsee and along the valley.

Queues and overcrowded pistes are likely at weekends and holiday times – New Year crowds from Lucerne can create queues measured in hours.

Mountain restaurants are plentiful. Most are friendly and inexpensive by Swiss standards. The Titlis restaurant is good (though not its snack bar), and the cosy Sporthotel Trübsee has a vast sun terrace overlooking the frozen lake. Reporters have enjoyed the traditional, friendly Untertrübsee.

Unusually, the Swiss **ski school** has competition – the Neue Schischule, plus several specialist boarding schools. There is a **kindergarten** up at Ristis. Hotels Regina Titlis and Edelweiss have supervised crèches.

STAYING THERE

Most package **accommodation** is in hotels, with chalets and apartments to rent locally. The 4-star Sporthotel (with fewer amenities than its claimed 'mini-resort' status suggests) is up at Trübsee. The elegant 4-star Hess has nice rooms and good food. Among the 3-stars, Edelweiss is poorly placed but has good children's facilities, and the Crystal and Engelberg are central.

Eating out is mostly in hotels, though there are alternatives. Engel's Stübli is recommended for tasty inexpensive food.

Après-ski is good, particularly at weekends, with lots of live music. The Alpenclub and Banklialp have extensive folklore programmes. The Casino appears to be a lively nightclub.

Engelberg has plenty to do **off the slopes**, with good sports facilities, a monastery tour, glassworks and trips to Lucerne and Zurich. For vicarious thrills, watch ski jumpers in training.

Flims

1100m

A splendid spacious area that deserves to be better known

WHAT IT COSTS

(((4)

HOW IT RATES

The slopes
Snow	***
Extent	****
Experts	***
Intermediates	*****
Beginners	****
Convenience	***
Queues	***
Restaurants	***

The rest
Scenery	***
Resort charm	***
Off-slope	***

What's new

Flims and neighbouring Laax have continually improved their lifts over the years and now have an impressive system.

For 1997-98 the decrepit gondola out of Flims is being replaced by a new 8-person one which will go to Nagens via mid-stations at Plaun and Scansinas.

This will make morning access to the slopes much better and access to the Laax skiing very much quicker for Flims residents.

There will also be much-needed snowmaking on the Flims slopes. And there are plans in future years to replace drag-lifts below La Siala with a six-seater chair.

1997-98 also sees the opening of a new disco called the Arena near the base of the new gondola.

- ➕ Extensive, varied slopes suitable for all but experts
- ➕ Impressive lift sytem
- ➕ Virtually queue-free on weekdays
- ➕ Fair number of slopes above 2000m, partly offsetting effects of their sunny south-east orientation
- ➕ Lots of wooded runs for bad-weather days

- ➖ Sunny orientation can cause icy or slushy pistes and shut runs to the resort
- ➖ Buses or long walks to lifts necessary from much of the accommodation
- ➖ Very subdued in the evenings
- ➖ Village very spread out, which detracts from its charm
- ➖ Weekend crowds

We've visited Flims/Laax twice since the last edition and have been hugely impressed by the extensive intermediate slopes (with an impressive 220km of pistes – much more than, for example, the Jungfrau region or Kitzbühel). The resort is very popular with weekenders and has invested in some smart new lifts, including high-speed quads and even a high-speed six-seater chair as well as a jumbo gondola from the main Laax base station. But it can be very quiet during the week and it is virtually unknown outside the Swiss and German markets. It deserves better.

There are very long runs from the tops of three different interconnected mountains, amid stunning scenery – all ideal for adventurous intermediates. And there's plenty to play around on in all areas. The two main drawbacks are its sunny orientation, which can soon spoil the snow on the lower part of the mountain, and the lack of any sense of real alpine charm in any of the alternative places to stay. They aren't ugly – just lacking in the chocolate-box charm you might look for in Switzerland.

boarding *Flims/Laax is a truly snowboard-friendly area, and for several years has actively cultivated the snowboarder market, building special facilities and running major events. Most lifts are chairs, gondolas or cable-cars, though there are some drags. There are fun-parks and half-pipes in both the Crap Sogn Gion and Vorab glacier areas and the Snowboard Garage is both specialist school and shop. The slopes are well suited to beginners and intermediates, and a few steeper sections and between-the-pistes powder gives them all-round appeal. The evenings are quiet, but as the slopes close, the Crap Bar at the Laax base station is popular with boarders (and with cyber-surfers on its internet terminals).*

The resort

Flims is made up of two villages over a kilometre apart on a sunny, wooded mountain terrace. Dorf is by far the larger and more animated, sprawling along a busy main road lined with shops, hotels, restaurants and bars. Waldhaus is a sedate, sophisticated huddle of hotels – some quite grand – attractively set among trees. Both resorts look traditional, with almost all hotels of the wooden chalet variety.

Dorf is best placed for the slopes, with the smart new gondola and a chair on its western outskirts. The slopes spread across the mainly south-east facing mountain to a second lift base-station at Murschetg (1.5km from Waldhaus), an outpost of Laax. From Laax itself there's an efficient jumbo gondola and less efficient cable-car. There's also a high-speed quad at Falera, 5km from Waldhaus. Given the resort is so spread out, it's surprising there's no shuttle bus. But a combination of hotel courtesy buses, post buses and regional buses serve well. Some hotels in Dorf are near the lifts, but most are a long walk away.

MOUNTAIN FACTS

Altitude 1100m-3020m
Lifts   32
Pistes   220km
Blue   29%
Red   45%
Black   26%
Artificial snow   6km
Recco detectors used
— helicopter-based

LIFT PASSES

96/97 prices in Swiss
francs
White Arena
Covers all lifts and
buses between Flims,
Laax and Falera.
Main pass
1-day pass 54
6-day pass 270
Senior citizens
Over 65 male, 62
female: 6-day pass
215 (20% off)
Children
Under 16: 6-day pass
135 (50% off)
Under 6: free pass
Short-term passes
Half-day from 12.15
(adult 44).
Alternative periods
Passes for 8 non-
consecutive days
(adult 400).
Notes Discount for 16-
to 20-year-olds (6-day
pass 215).

The mountains

Flims has extensive, underrated, varied slopes: some long runs and some high peaks, including a small glacier area. Because of its sunny aspect, the lower runs deteriorate quickly and it's often impossible to get back to Flims on snow (though the black run down to Murschetg is served by snow guns). In poor visibility there are plenty of tree-lined runs.

Trips are possible via Chur, by public transport or car, to Lenzerheide, Davos–Klosters and Arosa.

THE SLOPES
Impressive and well planned

There are essentially four sectors, each suitable for all grades but expert. The slopes are very well planned, and moving around them is straightforward, even more so after the replacement of the gondola from Flims.

The new gondola has two mid-stations, the first at Plaun, where you can get out and catch a high-speed six-person chair to **Crap Sogn Gion** at the heart of the Laax slopes. From here you can go down towards Murschetg, Laax or Falera or catch a cable-car up to **Crap Mesegn**. This area is the biggest section of slopes and is served by eleven lifts.

If you carry on in the gondola there's another mid-station at Scansinas before you hit the top at Nagens (2127m) – alighting at either of these will allow you to get over to **La Siala** (via drag-lifts if you choose the Scansinas option). From La Siala (2810m) there's a blue run to the high **Vorab glacier** area (where the top lift reaches 3020m).

There is also a link via a two-way, two-stage gondola between the Vorab glacier and Crap Mesegn. And there's a slope linking Crap Mesegn with Plaun.

The **Cassons** sector above Flims Dorf is the smallest, particularly when runs to the village are incomplete. It's reached by the chair from the village, then a further chair or drag up to the cable-car to the peak (2675m). It is linked via piste and lift with Nagens and Grauberg.

The piste map shows each type of lift clearly (eg 4-seater chair) and the time it takes to ride – an excellent idea which makes planning your routes and meeting others on time very easy.

SNOW RELIABILITY
Poor lower down, good higher up

Due to its sunny aspect, Flims is far from snowsure top to bottom. There is snowmaking on runs from Crap Sogn Gion – the black race course down to Murschetg, a red to Curnius, a red to Plaun, and on a run to Startgels. And more snowmaking is being installed in the Flims sector for 1997/98. But even if you have to ride the lifts down lower sections, there are lots of slopes above 2000m which usually enjoy decent snow except in late season.

FOR EXPERTS
Bits and pieces

There is a fair amount to challenge, but it's rather dotted about, with the added frustration that some of it is on short sections of otherwise easy pistes. The toughest run is the steep, unpisted Cassons black, reached by a steep climb from the top of the cable-car near the village. An off-piste trip from the Cassons summit looks tempting but don't even think about it without a guide. You could go over a cliff.

One of the great pleasures of the whole area is the men's World Cup downhill course from Crap Sogn Gion to Murschetg. It's so long (1000m vertical) and pretty that doing it repeatedly using the Murschetg cable-car doesn't get boring – and it's not so vulnerable to the sun now that it has snowmakers. The Nagens–Startgels run is short but steep.

The off-piste is generally between pistes, but in such an extensive area there is plenty of such terrain. Ruschein, at the western extremity of the area, is the best sector. And the long Sattel piste from Vorab – see below – is a good, beautiful starting point. Note that many of the black runs are really no more than 'dark red'.

FOR INTERMEDIATES
Paradise for all

In general this is a superb area for all standards of intermediate. When conditions allow, the area just above Flims is splendid for easy cruising. But the real highlight for early intermediates is heading over to the Vorab glacier and back on blue and red runs. On the way back you can take the cable-car from Grauberg to Startgels to avoid the awkward runs in this area.

More adventurous intermediates have most of the area to choose from.

SCHOOLS/GUIDES

96/97 prices in Swiss francs

Swiss
Classes 5 days
4hr: 2hr am and pm
5 full days: 175
Children's classes
Ages: up to 12
5 full days: 175
Private lessons
Half- or full-day
130 for half-day

There's a wonderful descent of over 1700m vertical on reds and blues if you start at La Siala and go all the way down to Flims. The easier of two runs from Cassons is a lovely trip along the shoulder of the mountain into a valley and on to Startgels, a 1000m vertical trip. The run from Crap Sogn Gion to Larnags via Curnius is also great fun.

Good intermediates will enjoy the superb and beautiful Sattel black run from the glacier to Ruschein at the extreme west of the area. It starts with a challenging mogul field but develops into a fast cruise and is one of the longest, most beautiful runs around.

The Crap Sogn Gion to Plaun routes are interesting, being quite steep and sheltered – and are some of the few runs not to almost directly face the sun.

Less confident intermediates have to watch out for some easy runs that have short steep sections (normally marked black on the map). Two links between Siala and Flims (Platt 'Alva and Stretg) and the run from the bottom of the Grisch drag down to Plaun (Sogn Martin) are examples.

FOR BEGINNERS
Plenty of options
There's a good nursery area in Dorf, and an alternative at Startgels when snow is poor. Quick learners can soon move further afield – getting the bus to the lovely easy runs above Falera is a good option. There's plenty of tuition in English.

FOR CROSS-COUNTRY
One of the best
An excellent choice. There are 60km of beautiful, well marked, mainly forest trails. Loops range from 3km to 20km. The cross-country ski school, centred at Waldhaus, has a good reputation, and organises group classes. 3km of trail are floodlit. The only drawback is the possibility of poor snow.

QUEUES
Some delays
There is generally little queuing during the week, but we have a report of 20-minute and longer waits for the Cassons, Crap Sogn Gion and Crap Masegn cable-cars. The resort is busier at weekends, with coach loads of day visitors arriving at Murschetg. But delays out of Flims in the morning are rare and should be eliminated by the new gondola. The chair towards La Siala can generates queues, as can the slow 2-person Alp Ruschein chair and some of the T-bars. Lifts closing

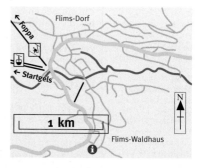

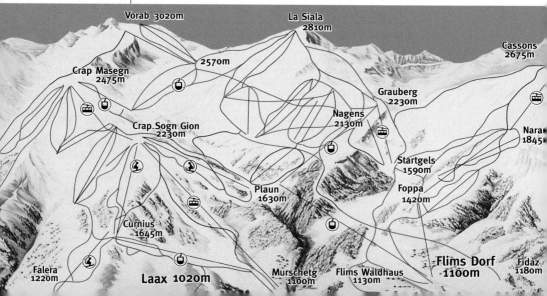

CHILDCARE

The ski school runs ski kindergartens taking children from age 4 – in Flims from 9am to 4.30, in Laax from 8.30 to 4.30. Childcare in Falera is 'on request'.

Several hotels claim special facilities for children. The Park Hotel Waldhaus has its own crèche, and an independent crèche may be operating in the Adula.

Flims

GETTING THERE

Air Zürich, transfer 3hr.

Rail Chur (22km); regular buses to resort.

UK PACKAGES

Freedom Holidays, Kuoni, Made to Measure, Plus Travel, Powder Byrne, Ski Choice, Ski Weekend, Swiss Travel Service, White Roc

Laax Made to Measure

because of wind was a common complaint among reporters – the chair on the glacier almost never opens (there are T-bars too).

MOUNTAIN RESTAURANTS
Good, wide selection

Mountain restaurants are numerous and generally good, if expensive. The large cafeterias at Curnius, Sogn Gion and Vorab are clean, efficient and serve good wholesome food. Nagens has another good high-altitude place, with live music, but the nicest refuges are lower down. The Spaligna below Foppa, the Tegia at Larnags, and the Runcahöhe where the Stretg piste flattens out and crosses the path down from Startgels are among the best.

SCHOOLS AND GUIDES
Plenty of English tuition

The school has a good reputation and standards of English are reported to be good too.

FACILITIES FOR CHILDREN
Expensive option

Not surprisingly, given the low number of British visitors, we lack reports on the resort childcare arrangements. If you want pre-skiing children to be looked after, you have to stay at the very expensive Park Hotel Waldhaus.

Staying there

Although it might seem best to stay near the lifts in Dorf, in practice most of the better hotels in Waldhaus (and the remote bits of Dorf) run efficient courtesy buses to and from the slopes. These satisfy most guests, especially as many don't often venture out on the town after dinner. And do consider staying in Laax, Murschetg or rustic Falera – all have speedy access to the heart of the Laax slopes.

HOW TO GO
Few tour operators

Only a handful of tour operators feature Flims.
Hotels Flims has over 30 hotels. The majority are either 3-star or simple B&B places, the latter tending to book up long in advance. Of six top hotels, five are in Waldhaus. Grading of hotels is accurate – you get what you pay for.
((((5) **Park** Enormous and very comfortable, but rather institutional, 5-star in wooded grounds at Waldhaus; a courtesy bus is vital in the morning,

but there are runs to the door. Pool.
((((4) **Crap Ner** The only 4-star in Dorf, but well away from the lifts and just as inconvenient as Waldhaus. But it's a friendly hotel with spacious rooms and superb food. The hotel's courtesy bus is very efficient. Good pool and sauna.
((((4) **Adula** Big, highly recommended 4-star in Waldhaus. Good pool.
(((3) **Grischuna** Pretty little 3-star just outside Dorf, and close to the lifts.
(((3) **Curtgin** Attractive, quiet place on edge of town, quite near the lifts.
(((3) **Albana Sporthotel** Modern 3-star beside lifts, with focal après-ski bar.
(((3) **Waldeck** Neat 3-star place in Waldhaus, with pleasant restaurant.
Self-catering Minerva in Waldhaus has by far the nicest of the limited apartments available.

EATING OUT
Varied options

Flims has a wide variety of restaurants, mostly in hotels. Italian, Chinese, local specialities and nouvelle cuisine are some of the main choices on offer. The good value (by local standards) Chesa does a nice fondue, and has a lovely open fire. The National, by the bus station, has good fish dishes. The Meiler hotel restaurant also has a good reputation. Something a bit different is going up to the Spaligna mountain restaurant, with a toboggan run home. Little China is a good Chinese, and the Alpina Garni (Waldhaus) is very good value – and does good pizzas.

APRES-SKI
Not a strong point

Flims is very quiet après-ski. The Spaligna trip mentioned under Eating out is the highlight of the week. The Iglou bar at the base of the gondola is packed when the slopes close, as is the Stenna-Bar, opposite, which has has a tea dance. Just across the road the Albana Pub is popular with a young crowd. Later, the focal spot is also in Dorf, at the hotel Bellevue's Caverna, an atmospheric old wine vault. A new Arena disco is opening for 1997/8, near the gondola station. The Park hotel is the centre of limited action in Waldhaus, having an old cellar with entertainer, and the Chadafo bar with dancing to live music. The Segnes and Bellavista bars are quiet. The sophisticated Viva Club comes to life at weekends.

ACTIVITIES

Indoor 4 hotel swimming pools open to public, saunas, 2 indoor tennis courts, covered hall with ice-skating and 4 curling rinks, fitness centres (including Prau La Selva), table tennis, whirlpool, solarium **Outdoor** 60km of cleared paths, riding, natural skating rinks, curling, sleigh rides, toboggan runs, ski-bob, para-gliding, hot-air ballooning, hang-gliding

TOURIST OFFICE

Postcode CH-7018
Tel +41 (81) 920 9200
Fax 920 9201

OFF THE SLOPES
Lots to do

There are plenty of things to do. The enormous sports centre has a huge range of activities, including shooting – and 'guest cards' from hotels and the tourist office provide a discount. Flims also has some of the best and most extensive (60km) marked walks of any winter resort. Historic Chur is a short bus-ride away. Other good trips are to the impressive church at Zillis, and to the Rhine canyon, which is nature at its best. The Glacier Express train from Chur to Andermatt takes you through some wonderful scenery.

STAYING UP THE MOUNTAIN
Space station St John

Even though there are entire resorts that are higher, the prospect of staying 1100m above Murschetg, in the ultra-modern 3-star Crap Sogn Gion, is an exciting one. It has all mod cons, including a pool. You can also stay above Flims in the more traditional Berghaus Nagens – it has dormitories as well as comfortable double rooms.

Laax 1020m

Laax is a quiet, spacious old farming community which has retained a lot of its original character; much of its modern development has taken place a short bus-ride away at Murschetg. This modern complex has been built at the base of the lifts and has its own hotels, shops and restaurants for those who want convenience for the slopes above all else. Though the oldest house in Laax dates from 1615, and the setting is pleasant enough, the village is no more than routinely charming.

The Murschetg cable-car (which generates peak-time queues) gives speedy access to Crap Sogn Gion, the main mid-station of the whole area. An efficient jumbo gondola, followed by a fast quad chair, is an alternative route up the mountain. Runs lead back to Murschetg from Sogn Gion and Curnius; the routes converge at Larnags, where the village gondola has a joining station – useful for rides down when snow is becoming patchy.

Cross-country skiers visiting the area should stay in Laax. A fine trail network of 60km starts nearby.

Laax has its own school and ski kindergarten, run by the well known downhill racer Conradin Cathomen.

Most of the hotels are in the 3-star and 4-star categories. Although a few

of those are large and modern, some semblance of traditional style has usually been attempted, and the thick pine forest which surrounds Murschetg also helps to hide the worst architectural excesses.

The Vallarosa and Signina are Murschetg 4-stars – very user-friendly and comfortable. The 4-star Arena Alva is a more attractive building in the old village, with its own transport to the lifts. The Bellaval is a pretty, traditional 3-star in the village centre. We've enjoyed staying at the charming, central old Posta Veglia, with its lively stubli and piano bar, and at the traditional Larisch, set well back off the busy bypass. A good central B&B is the Cathomen.

Restaurants are mostly hotel-based. The Laaxer Bündnerstuben in the Posta Veglia is best for a meal in traditional surroundings. The limited nightlife scene centres around the Bistro Bar in the Capricorn hotel, live music in the Vallarosa bar or Laaxerhof, and, again, the Posta Veglia. At Murschetg the Crap bar gets packed when the lifts close – popular with snowboarders.

As at Flims, there's a fair amount to do off the slopes. The 60km of cleared walks are one highlight. Other facilities include a riding academy, curling and skating on a nearby lake or artificial rink, sleigh rides, indoor pool, squash and a little museum.

Falera 1220m

Along the road from Flims, beyond Laax, lies the attractively rustic village of Falera. It's a traditional, quiet little place, complete with two lovely old churches, and benefits from being traffic-free (parking is free at the entrance to the village). Sitting on a sunny plateau, it has good views over three valleys. Everything is close to hand, including the school, ski kindergarten (by arrangement) and fast quad chair to the slopes. The onward connections from Curnius is by fast quad too, so Falera is quite an attractive base if you want a quiet time, even if you're the keenest to get on the slopes in the morning.

Accommodation is mostly in apartments, but the two hotels have plenty of beds between them. La Siala is a large 4-star with pool and sauna and its Spielkeller is the only real nightspot. It also has apartments. The Encarna is a much simpler, atmospheric place.

Grindelwald   1035m

Traditional mountain town in spectacular scenery

REVISITED · BY THE EDITORS

WHAT IT COSTS
(((3)

HOW IT RATES

The slopes

Snow	**
Extent	***
Experts	***
Intermediates	*****
Beginners	***
Convenience	**
Queues	**
Restaurants	***

The rest

Scenery	*****
Resort charm	****
Off-slope	****

What's new

A winter hiking path now links Kleine Scheidegg with Männlichen. There are new indoor swimming pool, sauna, steambath, whirlpool, massages, and solarium facilities at Parkhotel Schoenegg. There is a new pub at Bellevue hotel, and a new budget dormitory at Restaurant First.

+ Dramatically set in magnificent scenery beneath the towering north face of the Eiger

+ Extensive slopes, ideal for intermediates

+ Traditional mountain village with long mountaineering history

– Village gets very little sun in winter

– Few challenging pistes for experts

– Inconvenient for visiting Mürren

– Not ideal for beginners – village nursery slopes often short of snow

– Snow cover unreliable, with little artificial help

– Slow train and gondola, with some long queues, especially at weekends

Grindelwald is a much expanded, traditional mountain village, set at the bottom of some of Europe's best climbing terrain, with the north face of the Eiger towering dramatically above. The main mountain is shared with Wengen and has stunning views – unmatched except perhaps by those from Mürren.

In good conditions, the slopes match the scenery – at least for intermediates. Experts will find the pistes unexciting, and beginners may find the snow on the lower slopes poor or non-existent. Poor snow reliability is a main drawback: the slopes are low and there's hardly any artificial snow on the Grindelwald side.

But it has a loyal following of people for whom getting on the slopes is only one part of a winter holiday. Our most recent enthusiastic reporters were over 70, and say 'Grindelwald suits people who enjoy the mountains and real Alpine villages, and don't need difficult runs all the time. OAPs, in fact!' Families, too.

Then there's the question of whether to stay here or in Wengen. On balance, we'd go for Wengen. Its 'traffic-free' village is prettier and more relaxing. And it has much quicker access to Mürren and its more exciting slopes.

boarding *Grindelwald's local area, First, has a lot of drag-lifts, but there's a half-pipe just below Oberjoch (the highest point), accessible by gondola and chair. The Kleine Scheidegg-Männlichen area is well equipped, with a half-pipe on the Männlichen and the excellent Snow Valley terrain park – a wide natural gully by the Wixi chair above Wengernalp. Intermediates will enjoy the area most – the beginners' slopes can be bare, while experts will hanker for the steep, off-piste slopes of Mürren, some distance from Grindelwald. There are two specialist snowboard schools/shops – Backside and Madhouse. Nightlife caters mainly for the more affluent, middle-aged visitors.*

The resort

Grindelwald is set either side of the road along the foot of a narrow valley. Buildings are primarily traditional Swiss chalet style. Towering mountains rise sheerly from the valley floor, and the resort gets very little sun in early season. It can feel claustrophobic.

The resort shares the main Kleine Scheidegg-Männlichen slopes with Wengen. From Grund, near the western end of town, you can get to Kleine Scheidegg by cog railway, or to Männlichen by gondola. The slopes of First, on the opposite side of the valley, are reached by a gondola just to the east of the village centre.

At weekends the train and gondola to the main area can get very crowded with coachloads of day visitors.

Grindelwald can feel very jolly at times, such as during the ice-carving festival in January, when large and beautiful tableaux are on display. The village is more lively at night than the other Jungfrau resorts of Wengen and Mürren. There's live music in several bars and hotels, but it isn't a place for bopping every night until dawn.

SWITZERLAND

MOUNTAIN FACTS

Altitude 945m-2970m
Lifts   45
Pistes   188km
Blue   30%
Red   50%
Black   20%
Artificial snow   15km
Recco detectors used
— helicopter-based

SCHOOLS/GUIDES

97/98 prices in Swiss
francs

Swiss
Classes 5 days
4hr: 10am-noon and
2pm-4pm
5 full days: 192
Children's classes
Ages: 3 to 14
5 full days: 192
Private lessons
2½hr or 5hr
170 for 2½hr

The mountains

See Wengen (page 402) for a general
description of the main mountain.
Grindelwald's separate, mainly south-
facing First area is served by a three-
stage gondola. The slopes are best for
intermediates and can be marvellous in
fresh snow (which, sadly, melts fast).

Trips to other resorts are not very
easy, but you can get to Gstaad by rail
and road, and Adelboden by road.

SNOW RELIABILITY
Poor

Grindelwald's low altitude – the slopes
go down to below 1000m and few are
above 2000m – and few snowmakers
mean this is not a resort to book up
months in advance. And it's not the
place for a late season holiday.

FOR EXPERTS
Very limited

See the chapter on Wengen. The main
interest is off-piste. On-piste, the black
run from Männlichen to Grindelwald
must qualify as one of the most overgraded runs in the world. The black
run on First beneath the gondola back
to town is tougher, especially when the
snow has suffered from too much sun.
Getting to the tougher, higher slopes
of Mürren is a lengthy business unless
you've got a car – Wengen is a much
better base in that respect.

FOR INTERMEDIATES
Ideal intermediate terrain

See the chapter on Wengen for the
ideal intermediate slopes the resorts
share. In good snow they're perfect.

First has very gentle slopes right at
the top. In good snow, they make a

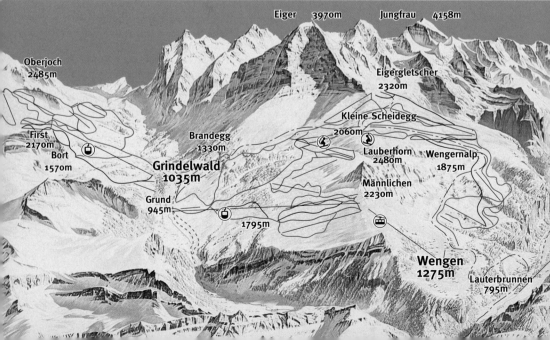

LIFT PASSES

97/98 prices in Swiss francs

Jungfrau Top Ski Region
Covers all lifts in Wengen, Mürren and Grindelwald, trains between them and Grindelwald ski-bus.
Beginners Points card (adult 100 points 46, lifts cost 4 to 10 points).
Main pass
1-day pass 50
6-day pass 232
Senior citizens
Over 62: 6-day pass 209 (10% off)
Children
Under 16: 6-day pass 116 (50% off)
Under 6: free pass
Short-term passes
Single ascent tickets for most lifts. Half-day pass for First (adult 38), Kleine Scheidegg-Männlichen (adult 40) and Mürren-Schilthorn (adult 38).
Alternative periods
3 days in 7 pass available (133).
Notes Day pass price for Kleine Scheidegg-Männlichen area only (100km of piste, 20 lifts), as Jungfrau Top Ski Region pass is only available for 2 days or over. Discounts for teenagers 16 to 20 (6-day 186) and groups.
Alternative passes
1- and 2-day passes available for First (adult 2-day 90), Mürren-Schilthorn (adult 2-day 90) and Kleine Scheidegg-Männlichen (adult 2-day 95).

GETTING THERE

Air Zürich, transfer 3hr. Bern, transfer 1½hr.

Rail Station in resort.

---

splendid intermediate playground, and are worth a day or two of your time – although many visitors head straight for the main mountain. The high point is 2485m – just higher than the Lauberhorn lift takes you, and there's a lovely long red run all the way back to Grindelwald on the far eastern side.

FOR BEGINNERS
In good snow, wonderful
Grindelwald's gentle slopes make ideal beginner territory, with a splendid blue run through the trees to progress to once off the nursery slopes. It goes right from the top of the train at Kleine Scheidegg down to Grund. But you can just do parts of it by using train stops such as Brandegg and Alpiglen.

If the snow is poor, it's not good to be a beginner in Grindelwald. The main nursery slopes are at low altitude at the foot of the sunny First area.

FOR CROSS-COUNTRY
The best in the Jungfrau region
There are between 25km and 32km of prepared tracks, depending on snow conditions. Almost all of this is in the valley floor at around 1000m, so in good snow it's delightful. In poor snow there may be hardly any trails usable.

QUEUES
Can be dreadful at weekends
The queues for the gondola and train at Grund can be very bad, especially when weekend visitors pour in.

If all of the slopes are open, lift queues higher up are not a problem. But if snow is short on the lower slopes, queues build up higher up.

MOUNTAIN RESTAURANTS
More choice on the Wengen side
See the Wengen chapter for restaurants on the main mountain. At First the restaurant at Bort does very good rösti.

SCHOOLS AND GUIDES
One of the better Swiss schools
We lack recent reports, but in the past they have consistently suggested standards are high, with small classes and good English spoken.

FACILITIES FOR CHILDREN
Good reputation
A past reporter who put four children through the Grindelwald mill praised caring and effective instructors.

Staying there 🔑

The most convenient place to stay for the slopes is at Grund. But this is out of the centre and rather charmless.

There's a wide range of hotels in the heart of the village, handy enough for everything else, including the First area, at the foot of which are nursery slopes, ski school and kindergarten.

HOW TO GO
Limited range of packages
The hotels UK tour operators offer are mainly at the upper end of the market, but traditional little B&B pensions and self-catering apartments are widely available to independent bookers.
Hotels One 5-star, a dozen 4-stars, and a good range of more modest places.
((((5) Regina The one 5-star. Big and imposing; right next to the railway station. Nightly music in the bar. Pool.
(((4) Schweizerhof Beautifully decorated 4-star chalet at west end of centre, close to station. Pool.
(((4) Bodmi Little chalet right on the village nursery slopes.
((3) Hirschen Excellent family-run 3-star in central position at foot of nursery slopes.

The cute rustic foreground isn't entirely typical of Grindelwald; the dramatic mountain backdrop certainly is ↓

CHILDCARE

The ski school takes children aged 3 to 14, and they can be looked after at lunchtime in the Children's Club kindergarten at the Bodmi nursery slopes. This takes children from age 3, from 9.30 to 4pm. It apparently ceases to function if snow shortage closes the nursery slopes.

In February there is an organised programme of activities for children of secondary school age.

UK PACKAGES

Inghams, Kuoni, Made to Measure, Plus Travel, Powder Byrne, Swiss Travel Service, Thomson

ACTIVITIES

Indoor Sports centre (swimming pool, sauna, solarium, massage), indoor skating rink, curling, bowling, cinema
Outdoor 80km of cleared paths, train rides to Jungfraujoch, tobogganing, snow-shoe excursions, sleigh rides, paragliding, snowrafting, glacier tours, devalkarts

TOURIST OFFICE

Postcode CH-3818
Tel +41 (33) 854 1212
Fax 854 1210

(((③ **Fiescherblick** Hospitable chalet on eastern fringe of village, five minutes from the First gondola.
(((③ **Derby** Popular, modern 3-star right on the station.
((② **Tschuggen** Modest chalet in central position below nursery slopes.
① **Lehmann's Herbage** Simple, friendly, comfortable B&B recommended by our reporter in his 70s.
① **Wetterhorn** Cosy, simple chalet way beyond the village, with great views of the glacier.
Self-catering One independent reporter recommended the apartments of the hotel Hirschen for comfort and space.

EATING OUT
Hotel based

There's a wide choice of good hotel restaurants, but cheaper pizzeria-style places are in short supply. The Latino, specialises in home-made Italian cooking.

Among the more attractively traditional places are: the Gepsi in the Eiger; Schmitte in the Schweizerhof; Challi-Stubli in the Kreuz; and the Alte Post. The Fleischerblick has been recommended for a special occasion.

The Kirchbuhl is good for vegetarians, the Bahnhof in the Derby for fondue and raclette. Hotel Spinne has good restaurants for almost all tastes – the Mercato for Italian, Mescalero for Mexican, a Chinese and the candlelit Rôtisserie for a special romantic meal. Hotel Belvedere has a gourmet French restaurant.

APRES-SKI
Relaxed

It's fairly subdued, though there's no shortage of live music. The Regina has a sophisticated dance band, and the Derby has live entertainment, including country and western. The Spinne has reputedly the best of the two discos. There's also a cinema, plus ice hockey and curling matches to watch.

OFF THE SLOPES
Plenty to do, easy to get around

There are many cleared paths with magnificent views, including a new winter hiking path between Männlichen and Kleine Scheidegg. It's also easy for pedestrians to get around the mountain – there's a special (though expensive) pedestrian lift pass. A trip to Jungfraujoch is spectacular (see below), and excursions by train to Interlaken are easy, and Bern possible. Day trips to Mürren are long-winded as you have to change three times, with a lengthy wait at the first change. Helicopter flights are available.

STAYING UP THE MOUNTAIN
Several possibilities

Grindelwald, like Wengen, gives easy rail access to Kleine Scheidegg, where there are quite pricey rooms at the Kleine Scheidegg hotel and cheap dormitory space above the station buffets. There are also dormitories at the nearby Grindelwaldblick. The Bort, at the gondola station in the middle of the First area (1570m), is perhaps the most attractive of all.

THE JOURNEY TO THE TOP OF EUROPE

From Kleine Scheidegg you can take a train journey through the heart of the Eiger to the highest railway station in Europe – Jungfraujoch at 3454m.

We found the journey itself a bit of a let down – you're in a tunnel for most of the trip. You stop part way up to get out of the train and look out of a viewing gallery carved into the sheer north face of the Eiger, with magnificent views down the Grindelwald valley and over to Männlichen. The climbers were roped in here in the film The Eiger Sanction.

You arrive in a big restaurant complex. There's a fascinating 'ice palace' carved in the glacier with beautiful ice sculptures and slippery walkways, an outdoor 'plateau' to wander around and a panoramic viewing tower called the Sphinx. But watch out for the altitude. At almost 3500m the air is thin and we met people having breathing and balance problems.

The return trip costs around £20 if you have a Jungfrau region lift pass for three days or more, but around three times that from Wengen or Grindelwald if you don't. Journey time from these two resorts is around one hour 30 minutes; from Kleine Scheidegg it's 51 minutes.

Gstaad 1050m

Surprisingly unpretentious, with extensive, pretty slopes

WHAT IT COSTS

ⓒⓒⓒⓒⓒ 5

HOW IT RATES

The slopes

Snow	*
Extent	****
Experts	**
Intermediates	***
Beginners	***
Convenience	*
Queues	***
Restaurants	***

The rest

Scenery	***
Resort charm	****
Off-slope	****

What's new

Two new chair lifts serving two new pistes between Saanenmöser and Zweisimmen, will mean the latter's slopes will be linked into the main Hornberg ski area from the 1997/98 season.

MOUNTAIN FACTS

Altitude	950m-3000m
Lifts	69
Pistes	250km
Blue	60%
Red	30%
Black	10%
Artificial snow	2km

Recco detectors used
— helicopter-based

UK PACKAGES

Made to Measure, SkiGower

Château d'Oex Ski Valkyrie

TOURIST OFFICE

Postcode CH-3780
Tel +41 (33) 748 8181
Fax 748 8183

Gstaad is renowned as a jet-set resort, but for 'ordinary' holiday-makers too it is civilised, crowd-free and rustic, with beautiful scenery, quality hotels and great off-slope facilities. However, it's not convenient, snowsure or cheap.

THE RESORT

Gstaad is a traditional, year-round resort in a spacious, sunny setting. The bustling main street is lined with hotels, smart shops and cafés – only local traffic detracts from an otherwise pleasant and relaxing village. The Montreux-Oberland-Bernois (MOB) railway accesses numerous surrounding villages, and is close to much of the accommodation.

THE MOUNTAINS

Three of the unconnected areas of **slopes** have local lifts reached by shuttle bus. Wasserngrat and Wispile are both small 'yo-yo' areas. Eggli is more complex. From Eggli you can get to Videmanette, and on to Rougemont, in French-speaking Switzerland.

The larger Hornberg sector is a short train trip from Gstaad. The departure points at Schönried and Saanenmöser are not much less convenient than Gstaad's local lift stations; you just need to study the MOB and shuttle-bus timetables, and time your day accordingly.

There are **snowboard** funparks and half-pipes at Saanenmöser, Saanersloch and the Diablerets glacier.

A lack of altitude and snowmakers is bad for **snow-cover**, but all areas have north-facing slopes. The Diablerets glacier (15km away and covered by the lift pass) is snowsure, but limited.

Few runs challenge **experts**. Black runs rarely exceed red difficulty, and some should be blue. There are some off-piste possibilities, and the blacks above the Col du Pillon are genuine. The run described below, from the glacier, is worth an hour of anyone's time, and heli-trips are available.

Intermediates will find the Wispile and Wasserngrat reds and blacks entertaining, and more challenging runs in the Hornberg sector. Leisurely types have plenty of choice above Saanenmöser. The adventurous should take a trip to the Diablerets glacier for the splendid red run down. After a slightly tricky start, this becomes a glorious swooping run, down a deserted valley which keeps its snow very well.

For **beginners**, nursery slopes at the bottom of Wispile are only adequate. Saanenmöser has plenty of runs for precocious learners.

The 60km of **cross-country** trails are very pretty, but virtually all are at valley level and prone to loss of snow.

Time lost on buses or trains is more of a problem than **queues**, except at peak times.

Mountain restaurants are plentiful and most are attractive, if pricey. The Berghaus Wasserngrat – a small chalet with a big terrace – is the most captivating of all.

English is more widely spoken by the **ski school** than in many Brit-free zones. It has a good reputation too. The **kindergarten** offers limited hours, and the only nursery appears to be in the Palace hotel.

STAYING THERE

It's best to forget convenience for the slopes and stay in the heart of Gstaad. Most of the **hotels** are at least 3-star. The 5-star Palace is extravagantly swish, with secluded grounds. The Olden is a charming, family-run chalet, right in the centre; and the Rutti is the cheapest hotel in Gstaad, 10 minutes from the centre. There is a wide choice of **self-catering** options.

Restaurants are mainly in hotels, and pricey. During 'the season', **nightlife** is lively both at tea-time and for having a bop later on. Saanen's slopes are floodlit three nights a week.

Gstaad's **off-slope** activities rival those on. There is a tennis centre and swimming pool, and there are 50km of pretty, cleared walks. The buses and MOB train make getting around easy for those not hitting the slopes.

It's worth considering **staying outside** Gstaad. Schönried and Saanenmöser are better placed for the slopes; Rougemont is most attractive; and Chateau d'Oex gets more British visitors, and is unspoilt.

Mürren 1650m

Stupendous views, an epic run, and a chocolate-box village

HOW IT RATES

The slopes

Snow	***
Extent	*
Experts	***
Intermediates	***
Beginners	**
Convenience	***
Queues	***
Restaurants	**

The rest

Scenery	*****
Resort charm	*****
Off-slope	***

➕ Tiny, charming, traditional 'traffic-free' village, with narrow paths and chocolate-box chalets

➕ Stupendous scenery, best enjoyed on the challenging run from the panoramic Schilthorn

➕ Good sports centre

➕ Good snow high up, even when the rest of the region is suffering

➖ Extent of local pistes very limited no matter what your level of expertise

➖ Lower slopes can be in poor condition and served by some awkward T-bars

➖ Quiet, limited nightlife

➖ Like all other Swiss 'traffic-free' villages, Mürren is gradually admitting more service vehicles

Mürren is one of our favourite resorts – for a short visit, at least. There may be other Swiss mountain villages that are equally pretty, but none of them enjoys views like the ones that Mürren gives across the deep valley to the Eiger, Mönch and Jungfrau massifs: simply breathtaking.

But it isn't just the views that keep us going back to Mürren. The Schilthorn run draws us back like a magnet whenever we're driving through the Oberland. Our visits are normally one-day affairs; holiday makers, we concede, are likely to want to explore the extensive intermediate slopes of Wengen and Grindelwald, across the valley. Getting there takes time; but who cares, given the scenery?

It was in Mürren that the British more-or-less invented modern skiing. Sir Arnold Lunn organised the first ever slalom race here in 1922. Twelve years earlier his father, Sir Henry, had persuaded the locals to open the railway in winter so he could bring the first winter package tour here. British families have been going back to Mürren ever since.

boarding *Like other Swiss resorts, Mürren has a traditional image, but it is trying to move with the times, and offer a more snowboard-friendly attitude. This may be at odds with the resort's usual clientele, but the facilities speak for themselves; the major lifts are cable-cars and chair-lifts (though there are some key drag-lifts too), and there's a fun-park and half-pipe below Engetal. The terrain above Mürren is suitable mainly for good free-riders – it's steep, with a lot of off-piste routes. Intermediates will find the area tough and limited, but nearby Wengen is ideal, and is much better for beginners. At night, Mürren is quiet, with not much scope for raving.*

What's new

Only if you haven't visited for several years will you find much new.

Two new chair-lifts were built below Engetal in the early-1990s to allow repeated use of the reliable snow on the higher runs without tackling the infamous Kanonenrohr. A plan for a third lift back up to Birg, avoiding an awkward T-bar, has been shelved.

The resort 🏘

Mürren is set on a shelf 800m above the Lauterbrunnen valley, opposite Wengen, and can only be reached by cable-car from Stechelberg, or funicular and then railway from Lauterbrunnen. Once you get there you can't fail to be struck by Mürren's tranquillity and beauty. The tiny village is made up of paths and narrow lanes weaving between tiny wooden chalets and a handful of bigger hotel buildings. The roofs and paths are normally snow-covered for a long season, giving the village a really traditional Alpine feel.

Two further stages of the cable-car take you up to the high slopes of Birg and the Schilthorn, nearby drag-lifts go to the main lower slopes, and an ancient funicular halfway along the village accesses the rest of the slopes.

Even in peak season, Mürren feels peaceful and quiet. And although in our summary above we protest against the gradual 'traffic' increase, Mürren still isn't plagued by electric carts and taxis as most other traditional 'traffic-free' resorts now are.

It's not the place to go for lively nightlife, shopping or showing off your latest gear to admiring hordes. It is the place to go if you want tranquillity and stunning views.

MOUNTAIN FACTS

Altitude	945m-2970m
Lifts	41
Pistes	188km
Blue	30%
Red	50%
Black	20%
Artificial snow	15km

Recco detectors used – helicopter-based

SCHOOLS/GUIDES

97/98 prices in Swiss francs

Swiss
Classes 6 days
2hr: 10am-noon
6 days (12hr): 130
Children's classes
Ages: from 4
6 days (12hr): 130
Private lessons
Half-day (2hr) or full-day (5hr)
100 for 2hr afternoon

The mountain

For such a well-known resort, Mürren's slopes aren't extensive – and many are tricky unless you're an expert. But it has one of our favourite runs in the world. And intermediates happy to travel to Wengen-Grindelwald will find plenty of options. These resorts are covered on the Jungfrau area pass, and easily (if not quickly) reached.

THE SLOPES
Small but interesting

There are three connected areas at the bottom of the mountain. The biggest is **Schiltgrat**, served by three drag-lifts behind the cable-car station. You can also get there from the top of the ancient funicular which goes to the nursery slope at **Allmendhubel** – and

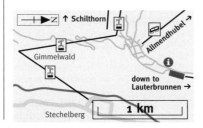

↑ An idyllic hideaway, and one of our favourite places for a short stay

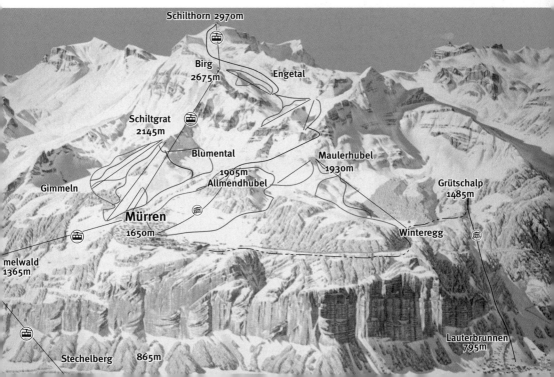

LIFT PASSES

97/98 prices in Swiss francs

Jungfrau Top Ski Region
Covers all lifts in Wengen, Mürren and Grindelwald, trains between them and Grindelwald ski-bus.
Beginners Points card (adult 100 points 46, lifts cost 4 to 10 points).
Main pass
1-day pass 50
6-day pass 232
Senior citizens
Over 62: 6-day pass 209 (10% off)
Children
Under 16: 6-day pass 116 (50% off)
Under 6: free pass
Short-term passes
Single ascent tickets for most lifts. Half-day pass for First (adult 38), Kleine Scheidegg-Männlichen (adult 40) and Mürren-Schilthorn (adult 38).
Alternative periods
3 days in 7 pass available (133).
Notes Day pass price for Mürren-Schilthorn area only (35km of piste, 12 lifts), as Jungfrau Top Ski Region pass is only available for 2 days or over. Discounts for teenagers 16 to 20 (6-day 186) and groups.
Alternative passes
1- and 2-day passes available for First (adult 2-day 90), Mürren-Schilthorn (adult 2-day 90) and Kleine Scheidegg-Männlichen (adult 2-day 95).

GETTING THERE

Air Zürich, transfer 3½hr. Bern, transfer 1½hr.

Rail Lauterbrunnen; transfer by mountain railway and tram.

also leads to **Maulerhubel**. There's a chair-lift to there from the Winteregg stop on the railway, too. These lower slopes take you up to around 2000m.

Much more interesting are the higher slopes reached by cable-car. The first stage takes you to Birg at 2675m, and the **Engetal** area. The final stage takes you up to the 2970m summit of the **Schilthorn** and the Piz Gloria revolving restaurant, made famous by the James Bond film *On Her Majesty's Secret Service*. In good snow you can go all the way from here (via Engetal and one drag-lift) to Lauterbrunnen at 795m – a distance of almost 16km and vertical drop of 2175m. The Inferno race (see box below) takes place in January over this course. But below Winteregg it's all pretty boring paths.

Thanks to two relatively new chair-lifts below the Engetal experts can now enjoy a long, testing run from the Schilthorn without descending all the way to the village, while intermediates have many more snowsure slopes available than they used to. But plans for a third new lift, up to Birg, have been shelved leaving an annoying walk up from the end of the other two chairs to the old T-bar.

SNOW RELIABILITY
Good on the upper slopes
The Jungfrau region does not have a good snow record. But when Wengen-Grindelwald (and Mürren's lower slopes) have problems, the Schilthorn and Engetal often have packed powder snow because of their height and the north-facing direction of the Engetal. Piste grooming seems haphazard, except at Winteregg.

FOR EXPERTS
One wonderful piste
The run from the top of the Schilthorn starts with a steep, but not terrifying, mogul-field. But it flattens into some gentle slopes followed by a schuss to Engetal, below Birg. Then there's a wonderful wide run with stunning views over the valley to the Eiger, Mönch and Jungfrau. Since the new chair-lifts were built you can try these upper runs several times without risking going down to poorer snow.

If you ignore the lifts you hit the Kanonenrohr (or gunbarrel). This is a very narrow shelf with solid rock on one side, and a steep drop on the other (protected by nets, thankfully). After an open slope and scrappy zig-zag path, you can head through trees into the village, or to the lower slopes.

A short serious mogul run takes you from Schiltgrat to the village (the Kandahar), but experts are more likely to be interested in the off-piste runs into the Blumental, both in this sector (the north-facing Blumenlucke run) and from Birg (the south-east-facing Tschingelchrachen), or the more adventurous runs from the Schilthorn.

FOR INTERMEDIATES
Limited, but Wengen nearby
Keen piste-bashers will need to make a few trips to the ideal intermediate terrain of Wengen-Grindelwald. The best easy cruising run in Mürren is the blue down to Winteregg. The reds on the other low slopes can get mogulled, and snow conditions can be poor. The area below Birg is high and fairly shady, and snow is normally good.

THE INFERNO RACE

Every January hundreds of racers enter the spectacular Inferno race from the top of the Schilthorn at 2970m right down to Lauterbrunnen at 795m – a vertical drop of 2175m and a distance of almost 16km. The racers start in pairs at 30-second intervals and the fastest finish the course in around 15 minutes, but anything under half an hour is very respectable. And this includes an uphill section where the racers have to run up beside a drag-lift they are not allowed to ride. Apart from seven gates, you can choose your own route down the mountain.

The race was started by Sir Arnold Lunn in 1928 when he and his friends climbed to the top of the Schilthorn, spent the night in a mountain hut and then raced each other down in the morning. For many years the race was organised by the British-run Kandahar Club and there is still a strong British presence among the competitors.

CHILDCARE

The ski school takes children from age 4.

The nursery in the sports centre no longer cares for babies. It now takes children aged 3 or more all day, but those aged 2 to 3 for mornings only. There are few places, so it's advisable to book in advance through the tourist office.

UK PACKAGES

Chalets 'Unlimited', Inghams, Kuoni, Made to Measure, Plus Travel, Ski Club of GB, Swiss Travel Service

Lauterbrunnen Ski Miquel, Top Deck

ACTIVITIES

Indoor 'Alpine Sports Centre Mürren' swimming pool, whirlpool and children's pool, library, children's playroom, gymnasium, squash, sauna, solarium, steambath, massage, fitness room
Outdoor Artificial skating rink (curling, skating), toboggan run to Gimmelwald, 15km cleared paths

TOURIST OFFICE

Postcode CH-3825
Tel +41 (33) 856 8686
Fax 856 8696

FOR BEGINNERS
Go elsewhere
The nursery slopes, at Allmendhubel at the top of the funicular, are fine. But once you get off those, there are no good, easy runs to graduate to. The Winteregg run and the area around Birg are about the easiest. Beginners would be better off at Wengen, across the valley.

FOR CROSS-COUNTRY
Forget it
There is one small cross-country loop above the village in the Blumental, and extensive loops along the valley floor from Lauterbrunnen or Stechelberg. But snow is unreliable at valley height. There are many better resorts for cross-country enthusiasts.

QUEUES
Generally not a problem
Mürren doesn't get as crowded as Wengen and Grindelwald. There are rarely queues except, occasionally, for the cable-cars. These usually arise when snow shortages bring visitors from less fortunate resorts.

MOUNTAIN RESTAURANTS
Disappointing at altitude
Piz Gloria's revolving restaurant has a fabulous 360° panorama of peaks and lakes. But the service, food and atmosphere are disappointing.

Lower down, we like the Suppenalp in the Blumental – rustic and away from the lifts, with good views and a large sun terrace. And it's easy to get back to Mürren for lunch, where our favourite is the small sun terrace at the back of the Bellevue hotel, near the foot of the funicular – get there early to be sure of a table. Views are stunning and the alcoholic cakes well worth trying.

SCHOOLS AND GUIDES
Now reliable?
The school has had a patchy reputation but, according to recent reports, is currently delivering the goods: 'very good instructor, excellent English, six people of similar standard in the group, very good tuition'.

FACILITIES FOR CHILDREN
Half-hearted
Mürren doesn't have ideal terrain for infants to find their feet, and the facilities seem to echo this, offering only limited care.

Mürren is so small that location is not a concern. Nothing is more than a few minutes' walk.

HOW TO GO
Mainly hotels, packaged or not
A handful of operators offer packages.
Hotels There are fewer than a dozen hotels, but they range widely in style.
(((④ **Mürren Palace** Victorian pile near railway station – the 'best' in town.
(((④ **Eiger** Plain-looking 'chalet' blocks next to railway station; good blend of efficiency and charm; pool.
((③ **Alpenruh** Attractively renovated chalet next to the cable-car station.
(② **Alpenblick** Simple, small, modern chalet near railway station.
Self-catering There are plenty of chalets and apartments in the village for independent travellers to rent.

STAYING DOWN THE VALLEY
A cheaper option
See the Wengen chapter for options in Lauterbrunnen and Interlaken. If you want to use both Wengen and Mürren, Lauterbrunnen in particular is a good budget place to stay. It has a resort (rather than town) atmosphere and access to and from both main resorts until late (covered by your lift pass).

EATING OUT
Mainly in hotels
The rustic Stägerstübli is the main alternative to hotels – a popular bar as well as restaurant. The hotels Bellevue, Eiger and Palace are said to be good.

APRES-SKI
Quiet
Most activity is hotel based. The Tachi in the Eiger is lively, and the Balloon bar in the Palace and the Belmont are good for a civilised après-ski drink. The Stägerstübli is the place to meet locals. Teenagers fill up the little Blienilichäller disco until it closes.

OFF THE SLOPES
Tranquillity but not much else
Other than admiring the peace and beauty, there isn't a lot to amuse. There is a very good sports centre, with a splendidly set outdoor ice rink.

It's no problem for friends to get down to the village for lunch. The only problem with meeting at the top of the cable-car is the expense.

Saas-Fee

1800m

An attractive car-free village with slopes on top of the world

WHAT IT COSTS

((((4)

HOW IT RATES

The slopes

Snow	*****
Extent	**
Experts	***
Intermediates	****
Beginners	*****
Convenience	***
Queues	***
Restaurants	***

The rest

Scenery	****
Resort charm	*****
Off-slope	****

- ➕ Good percentage of high-altitude, snowsure slopes
- ➕ Two high-speed lifts improved access to highest slopes
- ➕ Spectacular setting amid high peaks and glaciers
- ➕ Traditional, 'traffic-free' village
- ➕ Good facilities – even a slope where skis and snowboards are banned

- ➖ Disappointingly small area
- ➖ Glacier stifles off-piste potential
- ➖ Much of the area is in shadow in mid-winter – cold and dark
- ➖ Bad weather can shut the slopes
- ➖ Parts of the village are inconvenient for the slopes
- ➖ Rocky home runs need good snow-cover

People fall for Saas-Fee in a big way. It's got lots of Swiss charm and the setting is stunning – impressive glaciers and 4000m peaks surround the place.

Unfortunately the dramatic surroundings make Saas-Fee's slopes rather less spectacular than its scenery – the steep terrain and glaciers severely restrict the area's development. The tight ring of high peaks can also make the village seem dark and cold in mid-winter, which is good for the snow, not so good for those wanting to sit on restaurant terraces. So Saas-Fee is not without its faults – but it's too good to be ignored. In particular, its snow is too good to be ignored, especially if you're taking a late holiday. With much of the area above 2500m, snow conditions are often excellent when many other resorts are struggling to keep runs open. The question is: can you put up with a limited choice of runs and the occasional lunchtime shiver in exchange for perfect packed powder?

 Saas-Fee has encouraged snowboarding in a big way and in the summer, in particular, its year-round glacier slopes are dominated by boarders. There are three half-pipes and an excellent fun-park with just about every conceivable obstacle. While its gentle glacier slopes are ideal for learning to board, unfortunately only the main access lifts are boarder-friendly (gondolas, cable-cars and a funicular); nearly all the others are drag-lifts. As well as the specialist Paradise snowboard school, the local Swiss ski school takes its boarding activities seriously. Expert freeriders may be frustrated by the limits imposed on off-piste riding by the glacier and its gaping crevasses. But the nightlife doesn't disappoint – for a start, the Popcorn board shop has its own built-in bar.

What's new

Like many Alpine resorts, Saas-Fee made the big investments it needed to make a few years back, and can perhaps afford to relax for a while. Not much has happened since 1996-97, when the glacial fun-park was created (see boarding section, right) and the new hotel Gletscherblick was opened.

MOUNTAIN FACTS

Altitude	1800m-3620m
Lifts	27
Pistes	100km
Blue	25%
Red	50%
Black	25%
Artificial snow	2km
Recco detectors used	
— helicopter-based	

The resort

Like nearby Zermatt, Saas-Fee is car-free (there are car parks at the entrance to the resort) but somewhat plagued by electric vehicles. On most other counts, Saas-Fee and its more exalted neighbour are a long way apart in style. Saas-Fee still feels like a village, with attractive old chalets, cow sheds and narrow streets.

Of course there are some very smart hotels (plus many more modest ones) and plenty of good eating and drinking places. But there's little of the glamour and greed that, for some, spoil Zermatt – and even the electric taxis here are driven at a more considerate pace.

The village may be chilly in January, but when the spring sun is beating down, Saas-Fee is a quite beautiful place in which to just stroll around and relax, admiring the impressive view.

Depending on where you're staying and which way you want to go up the mountain, you may do more marching than strolling. It's a long walk (or costly taxi) from one end of the spread-out village to the other. Three major lifts start from the southern end of the village, at the foot of the slopes, and there are lots of hotels and apartments up to 1km away, or more. But the modern Alpin Express starts below the centre, quite near the entrance to the resort.

The village centre has the school and guides' office, the church and a few more shops than elsewhere, but doesn't add up to much of a focus. On a sunny day, though, the restaurant terraces fronting the nursery slopes at the far end of the village are a magnet, with breathtaking views up to the horseshoe of 4000m peaks – you can see why the village is called 'The Pearl of The Alps'.

Tall mountains cast long shadows across Saas-Fee, especially in mid-winter →

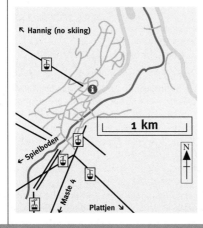

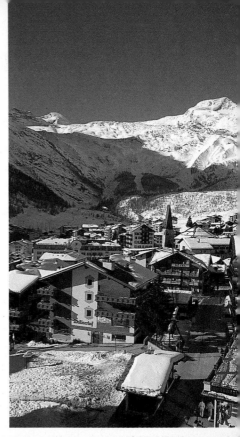

LIFT PASSES

97/98 prices in Swiss francs

Saas Fee area
Covers all lifts in Saas Fee only.
Beginners Village area pass covers 5 beginners' lifts.
Main pass
1-day pass 56
6-day pass 260
Senior citizens
Over 62: 6-day pass 240 (8% off)
Children
Under 16: 6-day pass 150 (42% off)
Under 6: free pass
Short-term passes
Single and return tickets on most main lifts. Half-day pass from noon (adult 46).
Notes Discount for groups of 20 or more.
Alternative passes
Separate passes for each of the other ski areas in the Saastal (Saas Grund, Saas Almagell, Saas Balen). Pass for all four villages in the Saastal also available, and includes free ski-bus between them.

SCHOOLS/GUIDES

97/98 prices in Swiss francs

Swiss
Classes 5 days
3hr: 10am-1pm
5 full days: 163
Children's classes
Ages: from 5
5 full days: 163
Private lessons
Hourly or daily
55 for 1hr for 1 to 2 people

The mountain

The main Felskinn-Längfluh area has been improved by some modernisation of the lift system, though there are still bottlenecks, and many visitors complain about the number of drag-lifts. The slopes are set in classic Alpine surroundings, with something for everyone but, for some, simply not enough kilometres of piste. However, the other resorts of Saas-Almagell, Saas-Balen and Saas-Grund are a short bus-ride away, and covered by the lift pass.

Day trips to Zermatt, Grächen and Crans-Montana are realistic options.

Saas-Fee is one of the leading resorts for mountaineering and touring. Several nearby peaks can be climbed and the extended Haute Route from Chamonix ends at Saas-Fee.

THE SLOPES
A glacier runs through it

Saas-Fee's smallest area, **Plattjen**, is reached by a 'rather quaint' (as one reporter put it) gondola from the southern end of the village. This small intermediates' hill has only one chair-lift apart from the gondola.

The main **Felskinn-Längfluh** area can be reached in three ways. The Felskinn cable-car, starting a short drag-lift away from the foot of the pistes, takes you directly to Felskinn at 3000m and the entrance to the Metro Alpin (an underground funicular which hurtles to what can be a literally breathtaking 3500m). From the top two drags access the high point of 3620m.

The efficient 30-person Alpin Express gondola also takes you to Felskinn, starting from the edge of the village between the slopes and parking area. It has a mid-station at Maste 4 (where you have to change cabins).

From the same station as the Plattjen lift, another gondola leaves for Spielboden. This is met by a cable-car which takes you up to Längfluh.

Felskinn and Längfluh are squeezed out to opposite fringes of an off-limits glacier area. The old snowcat service connecting the two has been improved by a drag-lift from Längfluh to a point where you can get down to Felskinn. It is very long at a reported 11 minutes ('why didn't they put in a chair'). The Längfluh and Felskinn sectors are served mainly by drag-lifts, and you can get down to the village from both.

The nursery slopes are at the edge of the village and are quite extensive.

SNOW RELIABILITY
Good at the highest altitudes

Most of Saas-Fee's slopes face north and many are above 2500m, making this one of the most snow reliable resorts in the Alps. The glacier is open all year round. Even so, recent visitors complain of rocks and stones on the lower slopes, no matter what the time of year. Snow cannons on the nursery slopes normally ensure they stay in working order, but our reports suggest it's a good idea to stay high, especially as it seems grooming is haphazard.

FOR EXPERTS
A few good challenges on-piste

There is not much steep stuff, but sufficient technical challenge to keep experts busy for a while. The highest drag-lift, on the left above Felskinn, serves two short, steep blacks and one easy one. The lift itself is a bit of a challenge – we've been lifted off the ground here. The short Spielboden drag delivers you to the top of an equally short, steep and lumpy slope – and in full view of an expectant terrace audience. The slopes around the top of Längfluh often provide good powder. The long runs to the village from both Längfluh and Felskinn have some genuinely black sections which can be especially tricky in icy conditions. Saas-Fee's glacier puts limits on the off-piste – crevasse danger is extreme, and experts must be content with the pistes or take a guide for limited off-piste or extensive touring. Late-season tours are a big feature in this region. The black runs and trees on Plattjen are worth exploring.

FOR INTERMEDIATES
Enough to do; plenty to see

Plattjen has a variety of runs, all of them fine for ambitious intermediates. Those looking for long cruising runs should head for Mittelallalin. The top half of the mountain, down as far as Maste 4 (the end of the first stage of the Alpin Express), is ideal too, with usually excellent snow.

Gradients range from gentle blue confidence-building slopes to steeper reds which can build up smallish bumps. We particularly like the runs at the top of the Metro first thing on a late-season morning – but they can be mind-numbingly cold in early season.

The 1800m vertical descent from the top down to the village is great if you want to prove your stamina. Either way, via Felskinn or via Längfluh, it's superb. The runs on the bottom half of the mountain all have tricky sections and can have thin snowcover. It may be a good idea to take a lift down.

FOR BEGINNERS
A nice place to start
There's a good, large out-of-the-way nursery area right at the edge of the village. Those ready to progress can head for the gentle blues on Felskinn just above Maste 4 – the return trip is best completed by Alpin Express. There are further gentle blues at the very top of the mountain, from where you can head down the glacier to Längfluh – again, use the lifts to return to base.

There's a useful pass for beginners who aren't ready to go up the mountain, allowing access to all the short lifts at the edge of the village.

FOR CROSS-COUNTRY
Good local trail and lots nearby
There is one short (8km) pleasant trail at the edge of the village. It snakes up through the woods, providing about 150m of climb and nice views. There are more options in the valley.

QUEUES
Some long queues on new lifts
We had hoped that the construction of the Alpin Express all the way up to Felskinn would stop complaints about appalling queues at the main lifts. However our reporters found 15-minute

to half-hour waits possible both in the village and at the Maste 4 mid-station.

MOUNTAIN RESTAURANTS
A couple of gems
The revolving restaurant at Mittelallalin is justifiably famous (see box below). The good café beneath it doesn't rotate but is cheaper. The best of the huts are slightly off the beaten track: the Berghaus Plattjen (not to be confused with the place at the top of the Plattjen lifts) and the Gletscher-Grotte, half-way down from Spielboden. Both have excellent food and a lovely old, smoky hut kind of ambience – especially good when the weather's foul. The Britanniahütte is a real mountain refuge, awkward to get to but, if you're up to the trek, best for mountain atmosphere and views. At Spielboden there's a large terrace with good views of some tricky slopes. At Längfluh the terrace has splendid views of huge crevasses in the glacier.

SCHOOLS AND GUIDES
Attitude problems
It's the Swiss school or nothing. We have no recent reports – but previous ones indicated over-large classes, with a wide range of abilities in a class, and some instructors with limited English.

FACILITIES FOR CHILDREN
Half-hearted
Neither the school nor the non-ski kindergarten take children under 5. One solution is to use one of the hotels with an in-house kindergarten.

CHILDCARE
The ski school takes children from age 5, and can provide lunchtime care. The kindergarten at the Hotel Berghof (572484) takes children from age 2½ to 6, from 9am to 5pm.

A couple of 3-star hotels – the Alphubel and the Europa Minotel – have their own kindergartens.

EUROPE'S HIGHEST LUNCH?

There is something beautifully Swiss about the idea of a revolving restaurant – and, sure enough, all three pivoting pubs in the Alps are to be found in Switzerland. "Customers complaining that they're not getting a share of the views? We can't have that – and we can't expect them to switch tables. Only one thing for it: we'll have to spin the whole restaurant about once an hour." Actually, of course, they don't spin the whole restaurant: the bit of floor with the tables on it revolves while the stairs stay put (along with the windows and the windowsill – and any gloves you thoughtlessly put down on it).

Two years after Saas-Fee built the Alps' highest funicular railway in 1984, it crowned that achievement with what is certainly the world's highest revolving restaurant – a good 500m higher than the one on Mürren's Schilthorn, the Piz Gloria of the James Bond movie On Her Majesty's Secret Service – and possibly Europe's highest eatery of any kind.

We don't rate the views from Mittelallalin particularly highly. But it's an amusing novelty that most visitors enjoy trying once. If you're going, do it properly and reserve a table next to the windows – phone 957 1771.

GETTING THERE
Air Geneva, transfer 3½hr.

Rail Brig (38km); regular buses from station.

UK PACKAGES
Crystal, Independent
Ski Links, Inghams,
Kuoni, Made to
Measure, PGL Ski
Europe, Plus Travel,
Ski Choice, SkiGower,
Swiss Travel Service

Staying there 🔑

Staying near one of the main lifts
makes most sense. If you do end up at
the wrong (north) end of the village –
and most budget accommodation is
there – you can ease the pain by
storing equipment near the lifts.

HOW TO GO
Check the location
Quite a few UK tour operators sell
holidays to Saas-Fee, offering an
excellent range of hotel
accommodation. But there are
surprisingly few chalet holidays.
Hotels 50-plus hotels mean lots of
choice. The great majority are 3-star,
with half a dozen 4-stars and a similar
number of 2-stars. There are also many
lesser-graded but comfortable places.
⟨⟨⟨⟨5⟩ **Fletschhorn** Elegant chalet, far
from the village in the wrong direction,
but in a lovely tranquil setting – and
with fabulous food (Michelin star).
⟨⟨⟨4⟩ **Walliserhof** Lively, ritzy 4-star,
smart but reported as friendly. Pool.
⟨⟨⟨4⟩ **Schweizerhof** Stylish place in
quiet, but not convenient, position just
above centre (can leave kit at
Saaserhof). 'Excellent' food. Pool.
⟨⟨3⟩ **Beau-Site** 'First-rate' but quiet
4-star in central, but not convenient,
position. Good food. Pool.
⟨⟨3⟩ **Saaserhof** Modern chalet in good
position, just over the river from the
nursery slopes. Sauna and whirlpool.
⟨⟨3⟩ **Ambassador** Modern chalet, well
placed close to the nursery slopes.
⟨⟨3⟩ **Alphubel** At the wrong end of
town, but one of the best bets for
families, with its own kindergarten.
⟨⟨3⟩ **Hohnegg** A more rustic alternative
to the Fletschhorn, in a similarly
remote spot; only eight rooms.
⟨2⟩ **Belmont** The most appealing of the
hotels looking directly on to the
nursery slopes.
⟨2⟩ **Zur Mühle** Rustic restaurant with
three bedrooms, well placed by the
river bridge.
Self-catering A number of the least
attractive looking buildings at the
north end of the village, remote from
the slopes, house apartments which
are featured by UK tour operators.
Fortunately, the apartments themselves
tend to be spacious, clean and well-
equipped. They aren't convenient for
the slopes, but independent travellers
can choose better situated apartments.

ACTIVITIES
Indoor Bielen Leisure
centre (swimming,
jacuzzi, steam bath,
solarium, sauna,
massage, tennis, gym,
whirlpool), cinema,
museum, concerts,
badminton
Outdoor 20km cleared
paths, natural skating
rink (skating, curling,
ice-hockey), toboggan
run

TOURIST OFFICE
Postcode CH-3906
Tel +41 (27) 958 1858
Fax 958 1860

EATING OUT
No shortage – some high class
Gastronomes will probably want to
head for the Michelin-starred
Fletschhorn (see Hotels) or the
Hohnegg – their high reputations and
high prices are widely judged to be
justified. Most hotel restaurants
welcome non-residents and usually
offer set meals at a good price. The
food tends to be traditional – the
Belmont and the Tenne are typical; the
latter also has charcoal grill
specialities. Boccalino is cheap and
does pizzas – book or get there early.
Alp-Hitta specialises in rustic food and
surroundings. The Skihütte is a good
bet for both lunch and dinner. The
hotel Dom's splendid restaurant
specialises in endless varieties of *rösti*.
Locals assure us that the following are
all good: Arvu-Stuba, Zur Mühle, the
Gorge, the Feeloch and the Ferme.

APRES-SKI
Excellent and varied
For that tea-time drink the best places
are near the lifts, where it's usually
pretty lively for at least a couple of
hours. Nesti's ski-bar, Zur Mühle and
the little snowbars are all popular.
Later on, Nesti's and the Underground
keep going till 1am. The Arts Club is
smarter and more sophisticated, with
live music. The Metro Bar is like being
in a 19th century mineshaft and is
popular with locals; the Happy Bar has
huge wood carvings and heavy music;
Popcorn is popular early and after 9pm
with the younger boarding crowd. The
Metropole has a disco and three other
bars. For a quieter drink, try the
Roadhouse, the tiny Sissy Bar or the
traditional Christiana Stubl.

OFF THE SLOPES
A mountain for pedestrians
It's easy for pedestrians to travel
around the mountain on the gondolas
and cable-car. There is a whole
mountainside, the Hannig, where
eating, drinking, sunning, walking,
tobogganing and parapenting take
priority. Skiers and boarders are
banned. In the village, the splendid
Bielen leisure centre boasts a 25m
pool, indoor tennis courts and a
lounging area with sunlamps which
turn on and off at intervals. A close
look at the glacier is a must – the
views from the terrace at Längfluh are
tremendous; whereas the ice-caves at
Mittelallalin left us cold.

St Moritz

1800m

Luxury living – on and off the flatteringly easy slopes

WHAT IT COSTS

HOW IT RATES

The slopes

Snow	****
Extent	*****
Experts	****
Intermediates	****
Beginners	**
Convenience	**
Queues	**
Restaurants	****

The rest

Scenery	****
Resort charm	*
Off-slope	*****

What's new

Several new high-speed quads have been installed on Corviglia in the last few years.

For the 1997/98 season the first stage of the cable-car up to the Corvatsch slopes is being replaced by a much bigger capacity one which should ease the queues here.

There will be a new fun-park for snowboarders at Pontresina's local hill Languard.

⊕ Beautiful panoramic scenery

⊕ Off-slope amenities second to none – including the Cresta Run

⊕ Extensive, varied slopes

⊕ Fairly snowsure, thanks to altitude and extensive snowmaking

⊕ Good après-ski, for all tastes

⊕ Good mountain restaurants

⊕ Celerina is an attractive villagey alternative to staying in St Moritz

⊕ Painless rail access via Zürich

⊖ Views sometimes blighted by hideous block buildings

⊖ Dorf has little Alpine character

⊖ No proper nursery slopes at resort level – except at Celerina

⊖ You have to get a bus, train or car to most areas

⊖ Runs on two main mountains all fairly easy and much the same

⊖ Difficult road access and long overland airport transfers

⊖ Expensive

St Moritz is Switzerland's most famous 'exclusive' winter resort: glitzy, pricey, fashionable and, above all, the place to be seen – it's the place for an all-round winter holiday, not just downhill skiing. The slopes on the two main mountains are almost uniformly easy intermediate – and flattering to the pampered clientele. We don't rate it highly for complete beginners, nor for experts (unless they want to venture off-piste) but there is some compensation in the off-slope diversions, which are unrivalled. And for langlaufers, it is superb.

The town of St Moritz itself is surprisingly unattractive. It is far removed from the chocolate-box image of the Swiss mountain resort, all wooden huts and cows with bells round their necks. Here, many of the buildings resemble council flats (extremely neat and clean ones – this is Switzerland, after all).

St Moritz itself may be unattractive to look at, but its setting is spectacular – beside the lowest in a long chain of lakes at the foot of the 4000m Piz Bernina. This is one of those areas where our progress on the mountain is regularly interrupted by the need to stand and gaze. It may not have quite the drama of the Jungfrau massif, or the Matterhorn, or the Dolomites, but its wide and glorious mountain landscapes are equally special. And the langlauf, walking and other activities on the frozen lake give it a real 'winter wonderland' feel.

Stunning mountains, lakes and tower blocks: that's St Moritz →

MOUNTAIN FACTS

Altitude 1720m-3300m
Lifts 55
Pistes 350km
Blue 16%
Red 71%
Black 13%
Artificial snow 15km
Recco detectors used
— helicopter-based

LIFT PASSES

97/98 prices in Swiss francs
Upper Engadine
Covers all lifts in St Moritz, Celerina, Surlej, Sils Maria, Maloja, Lagalb, Diavolezza, Pontresina, Punt Muragl, Samedan, Müsella and Zuoz, and the swimming pools in St Moritz and Pontresina.
Main pass
1-day pass 54
6-day pass 258
Children
Under 16: 6-day pass 129 (50% off)
Under 6: free pass
Short-term passes
Half-day pass from 11.45 (adult 45).
Alternative periods
5 (adult 248) or 10 (adult 418) days' skiing in the season.
Notes Discount for groups of 15 or more. Ski pass also valid in Gstaad Superski region, and gives one day's skiing in Livigno.
Alternative passes
Half-day and day passes for individual areas within the Upper Engadine.

boarding *Though doing its best to put boarders off with high prices, a distinct lack of grunge in its glitzy image, and a paucity of special facilities the terrain in St Moritz turns out to be quite favourable. The main boarding domain is above the town on Corviglia. Only the Corvatsch area has links that rely on drags – otherwise, most lifts are chairs, gondolas, cable-cars and trains. The extent of well-groomed cruising runs should appeal to any hard-booter, and there are three specialist snowboard shops. Beginners are less well cared for, though there's a special school (The Wave). At night, there are a few places you don't have to wear a dinner jacket to get in.*

The resort

St Moritz has two distinct parts. Dorf is the fashionable main part, on a steep hillside above the lake. It's a busy, compact town with two main streets lined with boutiques selling Rolex watches, Cartier jewellery and Hermes scarves, a few side lanes and a small main square. A funicular takes you from Dorf to the main slopes of Corviglia, also reached from down the road at Celerina, and from Dorf's other half, the spa resort of St Moritz Bad, spread around one end of the lake.

Everything here is less prestigious. Many of the modern buildings, are uncompromisingly rectangular and very damaging to the otherwise superb views. In winter the lake is used for eccentric activities including polo, 'ice golf' and even cricket.

Other slopes, at Corvatsch, are reached via lifts at Surlej, on the fringe of Silvaplana, and Sils Maria. Cross-country skiing is the main activity around the outlying villages of Samedan and Pontresina.

The town clientele is typified by the result of the annual Cresta Run race, which finishes at Celerina (which also has a gondola into the Corviglia slopes). In the top 29 on our '97 visit were three Lords, one Count, one Archduke and a Baronet – but the race was won by a Swiss, without a title.

The mountains

Like the resort, most of the slopes are made for posing. There are lots of long and generally wide flatteringly well-groomed runs, with varied terrain. There's an occasional black run, but few are seriously steep. But there is tough off-piste, and it doesn't get tracked out as it does in more macho resorts. Beginners' slopes are few and far between. Trips to other resorts such as Lenzerheide and Davos are possible, but not easy.

THE SLOPES
Big but broken up

There are several distinct areas which add up to a substantial 350km of pistes. The main slopes, shown on our piste maps, are nearby Corviglia-Marguns and Corvatsch-Furtschellas, a bus-ride away (although you can get back to Bad on snow). Diavolezza, Piz Lagalb, Alp Languard and a few more distant bits and pieces make up the rest. Some of these areas are well worth an outing. It helps to have a car, although the free bus service is reported to be efficient.

From St Moritz Dorf a two-stage monorail train goes up to **Corviglia**, a fair-sized area with slopes facing east and south. The peak of Piz Nair, reached from here by cable-car, splits the area – the sunny runs towards the main valley, and less sunny ones in the bowls to the north. From Corviglia you can head down (snow permitting) to Dorf and Bad, and via the lower lift junction of Marguns to Celerina.

From Surlej, a few miles from St Moritz, a two-stage cable-car (with a new higher-capacity first-stage for 1997/98) takes you to up to the north-facing slopes of **Corvatsch**. From there you have a choice of red runs to Murtel and Alp Margun. From the latter you can work your way over to **Furtschellas**, also reached by cable-car from Sils Maria. Runs go down to Sils Maria and Surlej, and to Bad.

Diavolezza (2978m) and Lagalb (2959m), the main additional areas, are on opposite sides of the road to the Bernina pass to Italy, less than half an hour away by bus. **Diavolezza** has excellent north-facing pistes of 900m vertical, down under its big (125-person) main cable-car, and a very popular off-piste route, off the back of the mountain, across a glacier and down a valley beneath Piz Bernina to Morteratsch. **Lagalb** is a smaller area with quite challenging slopes, with an 80-person cable-car serving the west-facing front slope of 850m vertical.

SCHOOLS/GUIDES

97/98 prices in Swiss francs

St Moritz
Classes 6 days
4hr: 10am-noon and
1.30-3.30
6 full days: 230
Children's classes
Ages: from 5
6 full days: 230
Private lessons
Half-day (2hr) or full-day (5hr)
140 for half-day

Suvretta
Small groups of 4 to 6 people
Classes 6 days
2hr, 3hr, 4hr or full-day (5hr)
1 full day: 66
Children's classes
Ages: up to 15
3 days (4hr): 170
Private lessons
Hourly or daily
80 for 1hr between noon and 1pm

SNOW RELIABILITY
Reasonable

This corner of the Alps has a rather dry climate, but the altitude means that any precipitation is likely to be snowy. There is snowmaking in every sector: several easy slopes around Corviglia are covered, as is an excellent 800m vertical red run on Corvatsch (Murtel to Surlej), much of the 900m vertical face of Diavolezza and part of Lagalb.

FOR EXPERTS
Dispersed challenges

If you're looking for challenges you're liable to find St Moritz disappointing on-piste. Red runs (many of which are no more than blues) far outnumber the black, and mogul fields are few and far between. The few serious black runs are dotted about different sectors.

The blacks at Lagalb and Diavolezza are the most testing pistes. The direct Minor run down the Lagalb cable-car has 850m vertical of non-stop moguls.

There are plenty of opportunities to venture a little way off-piste in search of challenges – there is an excellent north-facing slope immediately above the Marguns lift junction, for example. Experts often head for the tough off-piste runs on Piz Nair, such as Guinness (down into the Val Suvretta) and Niarchos (named after the Greek who is a major shareholder in the lift company), or on the Corvatsch summit. More serious expeditions can be undertaken – such as down the splendid Roseg valley from Corvatsch. The off-piste potential, particularly from Corviglia and Corvatsch, is all the better for being relatively little exploited. Instructors are allowed to guide only on certain slopes; for the Roseg valley run, for example, you have to take a proper mountain guide.

FOR INTERMEDIATES
Good but flattering

St Moritz is great for intermediates. Most of the pistes are easyish reds that could well have been graded blue.

One of the finest runs is the Hahnensee, from the northern limit of the Corvatsch lift system down to St Moritz Bad – a black-graded run that is of red difficulty for most of its 6km length and 900m vertical drop. It's a five-minute walk from the end of the run to the cable-car up to Corviglia.

Diavolezza is mostly intermediate. There is an easy open slope at the top, served by a fast quad chair, and a splendid long intermediate run back down under the lift, with mogulled variants. The popular off-piste run to Morteratsch requires a bit of energy and nerve. After a gentle climb, you have to cross the glacier on a narrow ledge, with crevasses waiting to gobble you up on the right should you slip. When we did it in '97, there were ice-picks and shovels at intervals along the path, put there by the enterprising proprietors of the beautifully laid out, welcoming ice bar which greets you at the end of the 30-minute slog. After that, it's downhill through the glacier all the way – with splendid views.

Lagalb has more challenging pistes.

FOR BEGINNERS
Not much to offer

St Moritz is not ideal for beginners. It sits in a deep, steep-sided valley, with very little space for nursery slopes at the lower levels. Beginners start up at Salastrains or Corviglia, or slightly out of town, at Suvretta. Celerina has good, broad nursery slopes at village level. Progression from the nursery slopes to intermediate runs is rather awkward, as these invariably include the odd difficult section.

THE CRESTA RUN

No trip to St Moritz is really complete without a visit to the Cresta Run. It's the last bastion of Britishness (until recently, payment had to be made in sterling) and male chauvinism (women have been banned since 1929 – for their own good, of course).

Any adult male can pay around £200 for five rides on the famous run (helmet and lunch at the Kulm hotel included). Watch out for the Shuttlecock corner – that's where most people come off, and the ambulances ply for trade. You lie on a toboggan (aptly called a 'skeleton') and hurtle head-first down a sheet ice gully from St Moritz to Celerina. David Gower, Sandy Gall and many others are addicts. Fancy giving it a go?

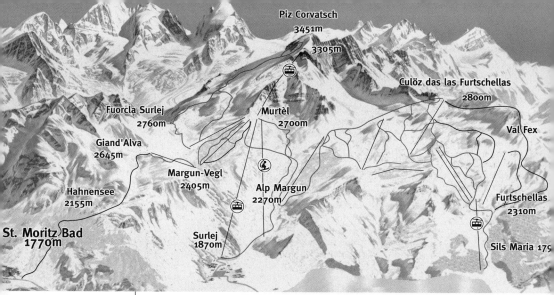

Piz Corvatsch
3451m
3305m
Culöz das las Furtschellas
2800m
Fuorcla Surlej
2760m
Murtèl
2700m
Val Fex
Giand'Alva
2645m
Margun-Vegl
2405m
Alp Margun
2270m
Furtschellas
2310m
Hahnensee
2155m
St. Moritz Bad
1770m
Surlej
1870m
Sils Maria 179

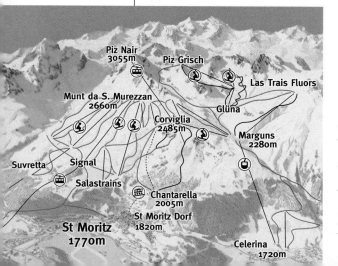

Piz Nair
3055m
Piz Grisch
Las Trais Fluors
Munt da S. Murezzan
266om
Corviglia
2485m
Glüna
Marguns
2280m
Suvretta
Signal
Salastrains
Chantarella
2005m
St Moritz Dorf
1820m
St Moritz
1770m
Celerina
1720m

UK PACKAGES

Club Med, Inghams, Kuoni, Made to Measure, Plus Travel, Powder Byrne, Ski Club of GB, Ski with Julia, SkiGower, Swiss Travel Service

Celerina Made to Measure

Champfér Made to Measure

Sils Maria Made to Measure

Silvaplana Made to Measure

FOR CROSS-COUNTRY
Excellent; go to Pontresina

The Engadine is one of the premier regions in the Alps for cross-country, with 150km of trails of all levels of difficulty, amid splendid scenery and with pretty reliable snow. Pontresina is a great location, and has good skating and curling rinks and swimming pools. There are floodlit loops too.

QUEUES
Crowds can be a problem

St Moritz has invested heavily in new lifts designed to meet international expectations. High-speed quad chairs with bubble covers are now common – six-seat chairs are beginning to appear. But it's also true that the area as a whole is over-dependent on cable-cars

– most not of huge capacity – both for getting up the mountain from resort level and for access to the peaks from mid-mountain. Queues can be the result, though our reporters have had good experiences lately. The enlarged cable-car from Surlej to Murtel should ease one bottleneck. Some cable-cars have a system to pre-allocate space.

MOUNTAIN RESTAURANTS
Some special places

Mountain restaurants are plentiful, and include some of the most glamorous in Europe. Prices can be high, and reservations are advisable, especially if you want to sit in particular spots. But there are plenty of cheaper places too.

On Corviglia, the highlight is the Marmite; but it is outrageously expensive. And don't expect much Alpine charm for your money: the Marmite is housed in the Corviglia lift station, known locally as the highest post office in Switzerland because of its bright yellow paint. At the far west of the lift network, behind Piz Nair, is an attractive chalet, Lej de la Pesch.

On the Corvatsch side, Fuorcla Surlej is a delightfully secluded spot, as is Hahnensee, on the lift-free run of the same name down to St Moritz Bad – a splendid place to pause in the afternoon sun on the way home. On stormy days, the most captivating place is the extremely rustic Alpetta, at Alp Margun (table service inside).

The hotel-restaurant up at Muottas Muragl, between Celerina and Pontresina, is well worth a visit. It has truly spectacular views overlooking the

CHILDCARE

The St Moritz ski school operates a pick-up service for children. Both schools provide all-day care.

Children aged 3 or more can be looked after in hotels – there are nurseries in the Carlton, the Parkhotel Kurhaus and the Schweizerhof, open from 9am to 4.30 or 5pm.

valley, as well as good food. But the best time to go is at sunset; the funicular runs half-hourly.

The restaurant at Morteratsch (end of the off-piste run from Diavolezza) is splendid – sunny, by the cross-country area and tiny railway station and with excellent, good-value grub.

SCHOOLS AND GUIDES
Internal competition
The St Moritz and Suvretta schools are apparently both branches of the national Swiss school. They also run The St Moritz Experience, a school specialising in powder. We lack recent reports on them. Some of the posh hotels have their own instructors, for private lessons only.

FACILITIES FOR CHILDREN
Hotel-based nurseries
Children wanting lessons have a choice of the two schools, but others must be deposited at one of three hotels with nurseries: the Parkhotel Kurhaus close to the cable-car in Bad, and two others up in Dorf. Club Med has its usual good facilities. A recent reporter found 'good sub-nursery slopes at Marguns and Diavolezza for the two- and five-year-old beginners in our party'.

Staying there

For high society you will want to stay in Dorf. If economy matters, you will probably have to stay in Bad – or stay at home. You can find convenient accommodation in either part of the resort, but not easily. Bad has the advantage that you can get back to it from Corvatsch and Corviglia. But Celerina is our preferred base.

HOW TO GO
More packages than you expect
More than a handful of tour operators package the resort, but independent

travellers have much more choice. There is a branch of Club Med – and its all-inclusive deal is one way to cut the impact of high prices.

Hotels Over half the hotels are of 4-star and 5-star quality – the highest concentration of high-quality hotels in Switzerland.

We don't actually like any of the famous 5-star places, but if forced to choose would prefer the glossy, secluded Carlton or the even more secluded Suvretta House to the rather staid Kulm or the Gothic Badrutt's Palace.

(((④ **Crystal** Big 4-star in Dorf, as close to the Corviglia lift as any.

(((④ **Schweizerhof** 'Relaxed' 4-star in central Dorf, five minutes from the Corviglia lift, with 'excellent food and very helpful staff'.

(((④ **Albana** 4-star in Dorf, with walls adorned by hundreds of big game trophies bagged by proprietor's family.

(((③ **Monopol** Good value (in St Moritz terms) 4-star in centre of Dorf. Pool and sauna.

(((③ **Nolda** One of the few chalet-style buildings, close to the cable-car in St Moritz Bad.

EATING OUT
Mostly chic and expensive
It's easy to spend £50 a head eating out in St Moritz – without wine. Even the Swiss complain about the prices.

But the Soldanella hotel has a set menu which is good value for money; the Steffani is also inexpensive for St Moritz; as is the cosy restaurant of the Belvedere, with great views of the lake. We liked the excellent Italian food at the down-to-earth, atmospheric Cascade in Dorf – only SF85 for two including wine for two courses each in '97. But the best food is supposed to be out at Champfèr, at Jöhri's Talvo.

On a clear day late in the season, an evening up the funicular at Muottas

GETTING THERE

Air Zürich, transfer 4hr.

Rail Mainline station in resort.

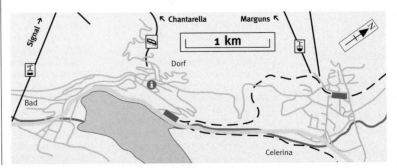

ACTIVITIES

Indoor Curling, swimming, sauna, solarium, tennis, squash, museum, health spa, cinema (with English films), aerobics, beauty farm, health centre, Rotary International club
Outdoor Ice skating, sleigh rides, ski jumping, toboggan run, hang-gliding, golf on frozen lake, Cresta run, 150km cleared paths, greyhound racing, horse-riding and racing, polo tournaments, cricket tournaments, ski-bob run, paragliding

Muragl is recommended for a splendid sunset followed by a good dinner in the hotel's unpretentious restaurant.

APRES-SKI
Caters for all ages
There was an enormous variety of après-skiing age groups in St Moritz. The fur coat count is high – people come to St Moritz to be seen, though the Cresta men have no truck with fashion and all that sissy stuff.

At tea-time, if you can tear yourself away from the bars up the mountain, the obvious venue is the famous Hanselmann's, for cakes.

Pit Stop is the favourite hang-out for boarders, with minimalist decor and a concrete floor. The three bars in the Scweizerhof are all popular after dinner: the Mule Bar has a country and western theme and live music, the Stubli has louder music and a younger crowd, the Piano Bar is for the chic with jacket and tie. The Cresta Bar, at the Steffani, is popular with the British, while the Cave below it is louder, livelier and younger.

The two most popular discos are the Vivai (expensive) and the famous Kings at the Palace (even more expensive and jackets and ties required).

OFF THE SLOPES
Excellent variety of pastimes
Even if you lack the bravado or masculinity for the Cresta Run, there is lots to do. In midwinter the snow-covered lake provides a playground for bizarre events like ice cricket, golf – with red balls on 'white greens', ice polo and greyhound racing. After February the lake starts to thaw.

Some hotels run special activities. The hotel Corvatsch offers a 'curling week'; the Carlton a 'health spa week'; and the Europa even holds rock and roll dance courses.

Other options are hang-gliding instruction, indoor tennis and even trips to Italy (Milan is four hours away by car). The public pool in Bad is worth a visit.

St Moritz has a reputation for being sunny – some 322 sunny days a year, according to the tourist board statistics – so there are many outside eating facilities, even at resort level.

Try the Sunny Bar of the Kulm hotel, which is south-facing and overlooks the lake. Many Cresta riders have lunch there.

STAYING UP THE MOUNTAIN
Excellent possibilities
Next door to each other at Salastrains, just across the mountainside from Chantarella, are two chalet-style hotels, the 3-star hotel Salastrains, with 60 comfortable beds, and the slightly simpler and much smaller Zuberhütte. Great views, and no queues.

Celerina 1730m
At the bottom end of the Cresta Run, Celerina is an unpretentious, villagey if rather quiet resort, with good access to Corviglia. It is a sizeable village with a lot of second homes, many owned by Italians (the upper part is known as Piccolo Milano). There are also some appealing small hotels – as well as a couple of bigger 4-stars.

Pontresina 1780m
Pontresina is a small sedate base – another marked contrast to nearby St Moritz – an excellent base for the extensive cross-country skiing on its doorstep.

It's a sheltered, sunny village with essentially a single narrow street of traditional old buildings, spoilt somewhat by the sanitorium-style of architecture that blights this whole area. Position of accommodation is relatively unimportant – all the skiing involves a bus- or car-ride.

Five minutes away towards Celerina is the Muottas Muragl area, where a funicular railway serves a tiny mountain-top area with marvellous views and a single long run to the bottom station. Pontresina's own hill, Languard, has a single long piste and, somewhat surprisingly, a new fun-park for snowboarders.

Much is made of Pontresina being a cheaper place to stay than St Moritz, but cheaper doesn't mean cheap – hotels are still very expensive, with little in the way of self-catering options. There is another Club Med here, in addition to the one in St Moritz.

Dining is mostly hotel-based and nightlife is very quiet.

For those not taking to the slopes, there are the numerous facilities of St Moritz close by, while Pontresina has a free skating rink, swimming pool (covered by the lift pass), sauna and massage facilities, sleigh rides, horse-drawn buses and a cinema. Walking is the main pursuit, with 140km of cleared paths throughout the Engadine.

TOURIST OFFICE
Postcode CH-7500
Tel +41 (81) 837 3333
Fax 837 3377

Verbier

Paradise for nightlife-loving powder hounds v

WHAT IT COSTS

((((4))))

HOW IT RATES

The slopes

Snow	***
Extent	*****
Experts	*****
Intermediates	***
Beginners	**
Convenience	**
Queues	**
Restaurants	***

The rest

Scenery	****
Resort charm	***
Off-slope	***

➕ Extensive, challenging slopes with a lot of off-piste potential

➕ Lively nightlife

➕ Wide range of chalet holidays available

➕ Hardly any drag-lifts

➕ Fewer queues than there used to be

➕ Sunny, panoramic setting, and great views from the highest slopes

➕ Good off-piste and other advanced-level tuition

➕ Much improved piste grooming in recent seasons

➖ Still bad queues at u... bottleneck

➖ Overcrowded pistes in certain areas

➖ Sunny lower slopes, and still very little artificial snowmaking

➖ Piste signing still inadequate

➖ Busy traffic in centre

➖ Some long walks/rides to lifts

➖ Poorly positioned for exploration of the whole Four Valleys network

We have been very critical of Verbier in the first two editions of *Where to Ski* – as have our reporters. Since the last edition we have been on inspection visits three times and both we and reporters have seen significant improvements. The piste grooming, lift queues and school have all got better – and in 1996/97 the resort even cut the price of its lift pass (previously Europe's most expensive). Verbier is trying hard to retain its international visitors. But significant grouses remain, including a couple of appalling lift queue bottlenecks, a poor piste map (which we are told will be improved for 1997/98) and piste marking and some very crowded intermediate slopes.

Intermediates who know where to go (mainly the less crowded Savoleyres area) can have a good time – but there are lots of resorts which have much more to offer the keen piste-basher: the Trois Vallées, Val d'Isère and Whistler to name just three. It is really the experts who want to hire a guide and explore the off-piste who will get the most out of Verbier's slopes. And, of course, those who want to enjoy Verbier's famous nightlife and restaurants.

boarding

As with its skiing, Verbier is one of Europe's best off-piste and extreme boarding resorts for those able and willing to pay for a guide or join a group. The main area is served by gondolas, cable-cars and chairs, with no drag-lifts at all; and there are two fun-parks (one near Ruinettes and the other near Gentianes) and a half-pipe at Gentianes. Verbier itself is the best place for boarders to stay – the outlying villages tend to be connected by drags. Less experienced boarders should try Savoleyres, though there are some drag-lifts here. There is a specialist snowboard school and two specialist snowboard shops. Verbier is also attractive for its nightlife, which gets pretty wild at times.

What's new

The Tournelle chair-lift on Savoleyres will be replaced by another two-seater, almost doubling its capacity for the 1997/98 season.

In recent seasons a new jumbo gondola from Ruinettes to Attelas has eliminated queues at Ruinettes and piste grooming has been substantially improved.

There are plans to replace the notorious old Tortin gondola with a new eight-person one but no date had been fixed when we went to press.

The resort

Verbier is an amorphous, still-expanding sprawl of chalet-style buildings, which retains some charm by not having too much concrete in evidence, and being impressively set on a wide, sunny, tree-filled balcony beneath spectacular peaks. It's a fashionable, yet informal, very lively place which teems with a young (20s rather than teens) cosmopolitan clientele. But it's no longer exclusive. Sloanes rub shoulders with Essex girls, and the Scandinavians party alongside the Brits.

The centre of town, where most of the typical touristy shops and hotels (but not chalets) are, is set around the Place Centrale. Much of the nightlife is here too, though bars are rather scattered – there's not much evening street life. The main lift station is 500m (40m vertical) away, and the secondary Savoleyres area is reached by a lift a bus-ride from the centre.

More chalets and apartments are built each year, with much of the recent development inconveniently situated along the bus route to the Savoleyres lifts. There's a good sports centre and an efficient free bus service.

The mountains

Verbier is at one end of long, strung out, interconnected slopes. The main area of local slopes suits experts best because of the steepness and the quality of the off-piste. The Four Valleys extend to Nendaz, Thyon, La Tzoumaz, Siviez and Veysonnaz. Other small areas reached by bus are covered by the lift pass, including Bruson – also reached by riding a gondola down to Le Châble and taking a bus from there. Chamonix and Champéry (part of the Portes du Soleil circuit) are a car trip away.

THE SLOPES
Very spread out

Our recent reporters consistently moan about the poor piste map, 'one of the worst I've ever seen', and piste marking, 'almost impossible not to get lost on bad weather days'. The tourist office assure us that both these are being improved. Verbier has two local areas. **Savoleyres** is the smaller one, mainly suited to beginners and intermediates and reached by a gondola from the northern end of town. This area is underrated and under-used (our recent reporters have spent some of their best hours on its crowd-free slopes, and we had a great time in 1997 cruising its well-groomed

pistes). It has a pleasant mix of open and tree-lined runs and some of the better mountain restaurants. From the top (2355m) you can head down to La Tzoumaz. When conditions are good you can also get back to Verbier on south-facing slopes, but these deteriorate quickly.

Verbier's main slopes are reached by lifts from the opposite end of town, where two gondolas rise to **Ruinettes** and one carries on to **Attelas**. The ancient, small cable-car from Ruinettes to Attelas was replaced a few seasons ago by a 30-person jumbo gondola.

From Attelas you can head back down to town or Ruinettes, over to La Chaux or down to Lac des Vaux. La Chaux is served by a number of chair-lifts and is the departure point of a huge cable-car up to Col de Gentianes and the glacier area of **Mont-Fort**.

A second, much smaller cable-car then goes up to the high point of the Four Valleys at 3330m. All the lifts to and around Col des Gentianes are accessible only if you buy the 'Général' pass. If the weather is doubtful, it may be best to get the basic Four Valleys pass and pay the daily Mont-Fort supplement whenever you need it.

From Mont-Fort you can travel all the way down to **Tortin**, a run of almost 1300m vertical, the lower half of which is now defined as off-piste. From here a cable-car returns to Col des Gentianes. An ancient gondola also leaves from Tortin for Chassoure, from where you can get down to Lac des Vaux. A chair-lift from Lac des Vaux returns to Chassoure and the off-piste mogul run down to Tortin. Other chairs return you to Attelas. From Attelas a cable-car takes you to Mont-Gelé, for steep off-piste runs only.

Tortin is the gateway to the rest of the Four Valleys. From there you head down to **Siviez**. Take the chair up to

MOUNTAIN FACTS

Altitude 1300m-3330m
Lifts 100
Pistes 400km
Blue 32%
Red 42%
Black 26%
Artificial snow 35km
Recco detectors used

Serious queue for the Tortin gondola – an everyday event ↓

the left there and you are entering the long, thin **Nendaz** sector. Take the chair to the right and you are heading for the **Thyon** and **Veysonnaz** sectors, reached by a couple of lifts and a long, easy run along the mountain. Both these sectors suit intermediates best. The way back from both sectors involves retracing your footsteps to Siviez and then Tortin.

Allow plenty of time for the queues – you don't want to be stranded in the wrong valley because, although it's not far from Verbier to Siviez on snow, it is by road. There is no bus back – and it's a very expensive taxi-ride.

SNOW RELIABILITY
Limited glacier
The slopes of the Mont-Fort glacier always have good snow. The runs to Tortin are normally snowsure too. But nearly all this is steep, and much of it is now off-piste. Most of Verbier's main local slopes are west-facing, get the hot afternoon sun and are below 2500m – so they can be in poor condition at times.

The north-facing slopes of Savoleyres and Lac des Vaux are normally much better than the rest – as they were when we visited in February '97.

FOR EXPERTS
The main attraction
Verbier has some superb tough slopes, many of them off-piste and needing a

↑ Chalets, chalets and more chalets: Greater Verbier is at your feet

guide. The very extreme, almost impossible, couloirs between Mont-Gelé and Attelas and below the Attelas gondola are some of the toughest of all. There are safer, more satisfying off-piste routes from Mont-Gelé to Tortin and La Chaux.

The front face of Mont-Fort is a

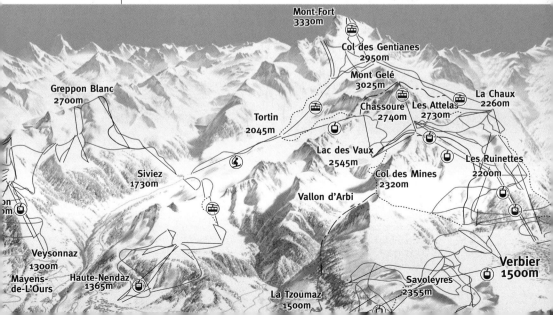

Mont-Fort 3330m
Col des Gentianes 2950m
Mont Gelé 3025m
La Chaux 2226m
Greppon Blanc 2700m
Chassoure 2740m
Les Attelas 2730m
Tortin 2045m
Lac des Vaux 2545m
Les Ruinettes 2200m
Siviez 1730m
Col des Mines 2320m
Vallon d'Arbi
Veysonnaz 1300m
Verbier 1500m
Mayens-de-L'Ours
Haute-Nendaz 1365m
Savoleyres 2355m
La Tzoumaz 1500m

LIFT PASSES

97/98 prices in Swiss francs

General Four Valleys
Covers all lifts and ski buses in Verbier, Mont-Fort, Bruson, Champex-Lac, La Tzoumaz, Nendaz, Veysonnaz and Thyon.
Beginners Station pass covers 6 beginner lifts.
Main pass
1-day pass 56
6-day pass 282
Senior citizens
Over 65: 6-day pass 169 (40% off)
Children
Under 16: 6-day pass 85 (70% off)
Short-term passes
Half-day pass from 11am (adult 51) or 12.30 (adult 44).
Alternative periods
10 non-consecutive day pass (excluding Mont-Fort, adult 468).
Notes Reductions for students, families and groups. Children up to 6 years free; 16-20 years 20% off.
Alternative passes
Limited passes for Savoleyres-la Tzoumaz-Bruson-Champex-Thyon-Veysonnaz-Nendaz and Four Valleys without Mont-Fort.

SCHOOLS/GUIDES

97/98 prices in Swiss francs

Swiss
Classes 6 days
4hr 45min: 9.15-11.45 and 2.10-4.30
6 half-days: 119
Children's classes
Ages: 3 to 12
6 half-days: 119
Private lessons
Hourly, half- or full-day
58 for 1hr for 1 to 2 people

wonderful, tough mogul field. It is all of black steepness, although some (but not all!) piste maps misleadingly show a red variant. But there is some choice of gradient – from seriously steep to intimidatingly steep. Occasionally you can get from Mont-Fort all the way to Le Châble off-piste. You can also head off-piste down to Siviez via one of two spectacular couloirs off the back of Mont-Fort. The North Face of Mont-Fort is one of the hottest of expert runs.

Some of what used to be black runs are now itinerary routes – visitors complain at the re-grading, especially as they seem to be treated like pistes and are not difficult enough to merit taking a guide. Both itinerary routes to Tortin (one from the bottom of the drags below Col des Gentianes and the other under the Tortin gondola) are long, rewarding and heavily mogulled.

There is often off-piste powder around the north-facing slope from Gentianes to Tortin – and those willing to shoulder their skis and walk up a steep slope near the start (Staircase to Heaven) are rewarded by usually good powder in a quiet valley parallel to the main run. Attelas is the start of shorter off-piste runs towards the village.

A couple of long, but easy, off-piste routes go from Lac des Vaux via Col des Mines. One is a popular short cut back to town, but the other is very beautiful, passing through Vallon d'Arbi and the woods before finishing at La Tzoumaz. In our recent experience, however, these have rarely been open – a piste-basher needs to form a ledge to traverse along to reach the runs, otherwise the traverse is very frightening, with a sheer drop on one side and ice and rocks under foot.

The World Cup run at Veysonnaz is a steepish, often icy, red, ideal for really speeding down. There is also an entertaining off-piste run from Greppon Blanc at the top of the Siviez–Thyon sector down to Leteygeon. An hourly bus (covered by the lift pass) brings you back to Thyon. Allow a full day for this excursion. There are also organised tours and heli-trips.

FOR INTERMEDIATES
Go to Savoleyres
Many keen piste-bashing intermediates find Verbier disappointing. The intermediate slopes in the main area are concentrated between Attelas and the village, above and below Ruinettes, plus the little bowl at Lac des Vaux

and the slopes served by the chairs at La Chaux. This is all excellent and varied intermediate territory. But there isn't much of it – this whole area is no bigger than Alpbach, for example – and it is used by half of those staying in one of Switzerland's largest resorts. As a result, it is often very crowded, especially the otherwise wonderful sweeping red from Attelas to Ruinettes served by the jumbo gondola.

We recommend intermediates to make much more use of the much less crowded Savoleyres area. This has good intermediate pistes, usually better snow and many fewer people (especially on Sundays). It is also a good hill for mixed abilities, with variations of many runs to suit most standards of intermediate except the very inexperienced.

The best snow for intermediates is normally on the summer area served by two drag-lifts on the Mont-Fort sector. Early intermediates will probably want to take lifts down as well as to it, though the red run down to La Chaux is not too steep.

A trip across to the Bruson area is also worthy of a day's excursion.

FOR BEGINNERS
A poor choice
Verbier's nursery slopes are inconveniently positioned (between Savoleyres and town) and get a lot of sun (but also have a lot of snowmakers). Near-beginners and fast improvers have few options, especially if they do not want to buy a full lift pass. A couple of runs to La Chaux are easy enough, but get too crowded.

FOR CROSS-COUNTRY
Surprisingly little on offer
Verbier is limited for cross-country. There's a 4km circuit in Verbier, 4km at Ruinettes-La Chaux and 30km down at Le Châble/Val de Bagnes.

QUEUES
Not the problem they were
So say reporters from the 1996/97 season, no matter when they visited. The jumbo gondola from Ruinettes to Attelas has virtually eliminated queues at Ruinettes but it has increased the overcrowding on the pistes back down. Queues at Tortin for both the ancient bubble and the cable-car, and for the Mont-Fort cable-car are still as bad as ever – not going there is the only way to avoid them. On a low-season Friday

GETTING THERE

Air Geneva, transfer 2½hr.

Rail Le Châble (7km); regular buses to resort or gondola.

CHILDCARE

The ski school's Kids Club kindergarten, on the slope Les Moulins, has its own drag-lift and takes children from aged 3 from 8.30 to 5pm.

The Schtroumpfs non-ski kindergarten (771 6585), close to the middle of the resort, takes children of any age up to 4 years (older ones by arrangement), from 8.30 to 5.30.

in March '97 we waited 20 minutes for the lift to the top of Mont-Fort and 40 minutes for the cable-car from Tortin (the gondola queue looked longer).

At the main bottom lift station at Medran, the queue problem seems to have improved with more people taking the six-person gondola to Ruinettes to meet the new lift to Attelas rather than wait for the slower four-person gondola which starts down in Le Châble and carries on all the way up to Attelas.

Peak-season weekends can bring more general queue problems.

MOUNTAIN RESTAURANTS
Very disappointing in main area

There are not enough huts, which creates queues, overcrowding and high prices. Savoleyres is the best area. The hotel by the Tzoumaz chair takes some beating for value and lack of crowds. Also worth trying are Chez Simon ('simple and cheap') and La Marmotte ('wicked, excellent rösti' says one reporter – we tried it too and agree wholeheartedly).

In the main area, the rustic Chez Dany at Clambin, on the off-piste run down from the La Chaux area, is about the best, but is a bit tricky to get to at times. It is open at night too. Carrefour

is popular and well situated at the top of the nursery slopes.

The Tortin has good pasta, and a visit puts off standing in the lift queue for a while. The Cabane de Mont-Fort, between La Chaux and Les Gentianes, is cheerful, with good food and views, but gets very busy. Violon d'Ingres, at Ruinettes, is a large table-service place, popular with several reporters.

SCHOOLS AND GUIDES
Good reports

Verbier is an excellent place for experts, in particular, to get tuition. Several reporters are complimentary about the off-piste lessons. These can be part of a Ski Adventure course (five full days) or a La6!! course (four half-days 9am-1pm) with a mountain guide. More than 20 guides are available for heli-trips, which include trips to Zermatt and the Aosta valley. The Vallée Blanche at Chamonix, Monte Rosa tours and a trip to Zinal are cheaper excursions. If you prefer speeding down the piste, there are plenty of race competitions organised. Verbier is also quite big on snowboard and telemark tuition.

And recent visitors say the school's standards are good for both intermediates' classes and children's classes – even though not much English was spoken in the latter.

FACILITIES FOR CHILDREN
Wide range of options

The school's facilities in the resort are good, and the resort attracts quite a lot of families. The playground up at La Chaux has also received favourable reports. Although it is not used exclusively by the school, space on the bus back is limited, and priority is given to school groups. Visitors say it can be difficult to organise children in time for the 9.15 start and it's a good idea to stay near the Medran lift where classes start.

The possibility of leaving very young babies at the Schtroumpfs nursery is valuable. British families have the option of travelling with family-oriented chalet operators – Ski Esprit and Mark Warner both have crèches and Simply Ski has a nanny service you can arrange in advance.

There are considerable reductions on the lift pass price for families with production of your passports.

SIMPLY SKI

helped us to compile the Eating out and Après-ski sections. Our thanks to them.

UK PACKAGES

Airtours, Bladon Lines, Chalet World, Chalets 'Unlimited', Crystal, Fairhand Holidays, FlexiSki, Freedom Holidays, Independent Ski Links, Inghams, Lagrange, Made to Measure, Mark Warner, Neilson, Peak Ski, Plus Travel, Simply Ski, Ski Activity, Ski Choice, Ski Club of GB, Ski Esprit, Ski Les Alpes, Ski Mates, Ski Verbier, Ski Weekend, Ski with Julia, Skiworld, Swiss Travel Service, Thomson, White Roc, avant-ski

Staying there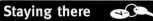

Staying at the top of the resort, close to the Medran lift station, is convenient for the slopes and sufficiently distant from nightlife to avoid late evening noise. However, the supermarkets are a tiresome walk from the lift area.

The free shuttle bus service is mostly good and reduces the inconvenience factor, and there are several routes running around the network of busy (congested at weekends) streets. Some accommodation has quite an infrequent service. There is now a night bus too, running until 11.30pm for four francs a trip.

HOW TO GO
Plenty of options
Verbier is the chalet-party capital of the Alps. It has a higher proportion of chalets than any other resort. Given the size of the place there are surprisingly few apartments and pensions available, though those on a budget have inexpensive B&B options in Le Châble. Hotels are expensive in relation to their grading.
Chalets There are chalets available for most types of holiday maker. Small ones, ideal for a family or small group of friends to have exclusive use of, are particularly common. There are also large chalets good for groups, places handy for the slopes, and others slap bang in the centre of Verbier's lively nightlife. Prices are generally surprisingly low.

There are not, however, many options for luxury lovers. Simply Ski's Norjeanne is a notable exception – set near the sports centre it is owned by a Count and Countess and beautifully furnished. Flexiski's Bouvreuil is also owned by a Count (they must be big in Verbier), furnished with antiques and plush sofas and well positioned, mid-way between Place Centrale and the lifts.
Hotels There are half a dozen 4-star places, a dozen 3-star and a handful of simpler places.
(((④ **Rosalp** The place to stay if you can afford it, not least for the food in Roland Pierroz's Michelin-starred restaurant, which is the best you'll find in a Swiss resort. Good position mid-way between centre and lifts.
(((④ **Montpelier** Very comfortable

4-star, but out of town (a courtesy bus is provided).
(((④ **Vanessa** Central 4-star with spacious apartments as well as rooms.
(((④ **Rois Mages** Smart little B&B hotel in secluded setting, up near the Savoleyres lift.
(((③ **Rotonde** Much cheaper, well positioned 3-star between centre and lifts; some budget rooms.
(((③ **Chamois** 3-star close to lifts.
(((③ **Poste** Well placed 3-star mid-way between centre and lifts; the only hotel pool. Some rooms rather small.
(((③ **de Verbier** Central 3-star, popular with tour operators and their clientele; renowned for good food; atmospheric, but 'olde worlde' decor is a little in need of refurbishment.
((② **Auberge** Well placed 2-star, mid-way between centre and lifts.
((② **Farinet** Central 3-star B&B hotel.
Self-catering Apartments through tour operators are very thin on the ground. Self-caterers usually book direct. The comfortable Richemont and Troika apartments are close to the nursery slopes, a trek from the main lifts. The similar standard Blizzard is mid-way between Place Centrale and lifts.

The Vieux Verbier apartments have a position second to none for the slopes, next to the main lift station. Close to the town centre are the simple Carina places. The La Bagnardise apartments on the quiet, convenient Chemin de Vernes get a good report.

EATING OUT
Very big choice
There is a very wide range of restaurants. Hotel Rosalp is clearly the best (and most expensive) in town, and among the best in Switzerland, with an awesome wine cellar to match its excellent Michelin-starred food – splash out on the seven course Menu Gastronomique if you can afford it.

Two-star hotel Chalet Phénix has a surprisingly good Chinese restaurant. Au Fer à Cheval is a very popular pizza/salad/breakfast place that's full of life. Arguably the best-value Italian food in town, however, is at Al Capone's out near the Savoleyres gondola. The Spaghetti House is another inexpensive place.

The Farinet restaurant is atmospheric and has good food at affordable prices. For Swiss specialities, try the Relais de Neige, Robinsons, Le Caveau, Vieux Verbier by the Medran lifts or Les Esserts by the

ACTIVITIES

Indoor Sports centre (swimming, skating, curling, squash, sauna, solarium, steam bath, jacuzzi), fitness centre, cinema, ice hockey, artificial skating rink, indoor golf
Outdoor Ski-bob, 20km cleared walking paths, para-gliding, hang-gliding, mountaineering, jogging tracks

nursery slopes.

The Grotte à Max does a vast variety of rösti plus unusual meats such as ostrich and kangaroo. Harold's is Verbier's 'fast-food' outlet – it's less clinical and more fun than McDonald's.

APRES-SKI
Throbbing but expensive

It starts with a 4pm visit to Offshore, for people-watching and hot chocolate (no alcohol sold). Then it's on to the Mont Fort pub, if you're young, loud and British. Last season the Nelson was popular with locals. The Farinet is particularly good in spring, its live band playing to the audience on a huge, sunny terrace – there's now a conservatory-type cover over it when it's cold. Au Fer à Cheval is a fun place full of locals and regular Verbier-ites.

After dinner the Mont Fort pub is a very lively pick-up joints, popular with Brits and locals alike. Crock No Name often has live music (when it jacks its

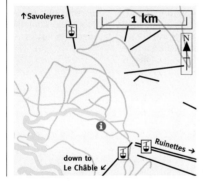

↑Savoleyres

1 km

N

Ruinettes →

down to
Le Châble ↙

drink prices up), and is entertaining for its cosmopolitan crowd. The Garage is a small cellar bar, decked out with car seats and number plates and King's is a quiet, candle-lit cellar bar with 60s decor. Bar New Club is a sophisticated Piano Bar, with comfortable seating and a more discerning clientele. Jacky's Bar is a classy haunt frequented by big spenders on their way to the Farm Club.

The Farm is an outrageously expensive nightclub which nonetheless is very popular, especially with balding geriatrics with much younger girls in tow – tables are difficult to book. Punters buy bottles of spirits (200SF for vodka) and mixers come free. It's packed with rich Swiss on Fridays and Saturdays and has more Brits on Tuesdays (chalet girls day off on Wednesdays!).

More within the pocket of most Brits is the noisy, glitzy Marshalls Club, which sometimes has live music. Tara Club is less smart but the noise level is more conducive to conversation, and it has a friendly atmosphere and arranges theme nights, such as 70s and Medics nights. Scotch is the cheapest disco in town and popular with teenagers and snowboarders. Big Ben is another cheaper place, popular with youngsters. Harry's Bar is good for a midnight burger.

Something a bit different is to snowmobile up to Chez Dany or La Marmotte for a good evening meal in the mountains, followed by a torchlit descent. It's great fun.

Selected chalets in Verbier

OFF THE SLOPES
No great attraction
Verbier has an excellent sports centre and some nice walks, but otherwise very little if you don't want to hit the slopes. Montreux is an enjoyable train excursion from Le Châble, and Martigny is worth a visit for the Roman arena and museums. It's easy to walk to some of the lower mountain restaurants to meet up with friends for lunch, and you can reach restaurants at most of the gondola top stations.

STAYING IN OTHER RESORTS
A lot going for them
There are advantages to staying in the other resorts of the Four Valleys. For a start, you can avoid the worst of the Tortin queues if you set off early, spend the day in the Verbier area and wave to the crowds on your way home.

Secondly, they are substantially cheaper for both accommodation and incidentals. What you lose is the Verbier ambience and its range of restaurants, bars and nightlife. If you don't really care about those elements, staying elsewhere is well worth considering. Unfortunately British tour operators no longer offer packages to any of them.

Veysonnaz and Thyon are both small resorts, with mainly apartment accommodation. Veysonnaz is by far the more attractive – an old village complete with church. It has adequate bars, cafés and restaurants, a disco, sports centre with swimming pool, and school and guides. Thyon is little more than a functional, ugly, purpose-built place.

Nendaz is a far larger resort, with an enormous number of beds available, mainly in apartments. There are plenty of amenities, including a skating rink, sports centre with swimming, fitness centre and squash, cafés, restaurants, discos, crèche and school and guides.

Le Châble is a village just a gondola-ride from Verbier. As changing gondola cars is not necessary for moving on to Ruinettes and Attelas, access to the slopes can be just as quick (or even quicker) from the queue-free valley. Le Châble is particularly convenient for those travelling by train or drivers who want to visit other resorts too. The Giétroz, Poste and Ruinette are all simple, adequate hotels.

Villars 1300m

Let the train take the strain

With its mountain railway, gentle low-altitude slopes and year-round tourist trade, Villars is the kind of resort that has been rather overshadowed by modern mega-resorts. But for a relaxing family holiday – perhaps involving a range of activities off the slopes – this formula has clear attractions.

WHAT IT COSTS

((((4)

HOW IT RATES

The slopes

Snow	**
Extent	**
Experts	**
Intermediates	***
Beginners	****
Convenience	***
Queues	***
Restaurants	***

The rest

Scenery	***
Resort charm	****
Off-slope	****

What's new

Access to Les Diablerets was made simpler for 1997 by the installation of the two-way Perche-Conche chair-lift.

For 1998 the main access gondola to Roc d'Orsay is to be replaced. And a half-pipe is promised for boarders.

MOUNTAIN FACTS

Altitude	1130m-2970m
Lifts	45
Pistes	120km
Blue	35%
Red	55%
Black	10%
Artificial snow	none

Recco detectors used
— helicopter-based

UK PACKAGES

Club Med, Kuoni, Made to Measure, Ski trek, Swiss Travel Service

TOURIST OFFICE

Postcode CH-1884
Tel +41 (24) 495 3232
Fax 495 2794

THE RESORT

Villars sits on a sunny shelf at 1300m, looking south-west across the Rhône valley towards the mountains of the Portes du Soleil. A busy high street lined with all sorts of shops gives Villars the air of a pleasant, reassuring small town; all around are chalet-style buildings, with just two or three block-like large hotels.

There is now an improved link with Les Diablerets, and outings to Leysin and Champéry are possible by rail or road. Many other resorts (such as Verbier) are within driving distance.

THE MOUNTAINS

The railway up from Bex goes on up to the **slopes**, terminating at Bretaye (1800m); a gondola from the other end of the village goes to one of the high-points of the slopes, Roc d'Orsay.

The col of Bretaye has intermediate slopes on either side, with a maximum vertical of 300m back to the col and much longer runs back to the village. To the east, easier open slopes (very susceptible to sun) go to La Rasse (1350m) to meet the otherwise separate Les Chaux sector, served mainly by a gondola up from a large car park at Barboleusaz.

Low altitude, lack of snowmaking and sunny orientation mean that Villars' **snow reliability** is not good.

This is not a resort for **experts**, although there are some steep pitches and several areas of worthwhile off-piste – now including the old route back from Les Diablerets.

For **intermediates** not worried about mileage or snow reliability, there are interesting pistes. Until recently, getting to the similarly appealing slopes of Les Diablerets meant some serious skiing on the way out and some walking on the way back. But now a chair provides a two-way link.

Beginners will feel comfortable on the village nursery slopes, and riding the train to Bretaye. There are gentle slopes here, too, but also lots of people charging about a crowded area.

There are **snowboard** fun-parks at both Bretaye and Les Chaux.

The **cross-country** trails up the valley past La Rasse are long and pretty, and there are further loops in the depression beyond Bretaye.

It is mainly at weekends that **queues** appear for the lifts at Bretaye.

The **mountain restaurants** are a mixed bag. The main one at Bretaye is characterless and very busy; the Golf Club is pricey but gets excellent reports; Lac des Chavonnes is worth the walk from the piste.

Villars' Ecole Moderne, started in 1974 and still using the ski évolutif method, was one of the first of the rare alternatives to the Swiss **ski school**. There is also a Bureau des Guides offering heli-trips. Both schools run **children's** nurseries. There is also a non-ski nursery in next-door Chesières.

STAYING THERE

Although the centre of Villars is quite compact, the gondola is quite a walk from the railway station. But there is an efficient, free shuttle bus (reliable but busy at times) and many **hotels** are between the two lifts. The 4-star Panorama is 'comfortable, with brilliant food' – but is awkwardly sited. The Alpe Fleurie and Renardière are our favourite 3-stars. The huge Palace is now occupied by Club Med. Some UK operators offer apartments.

For many visitors, **eating out** means regional specialities in the neo-rustic Vieux Villars; alternatives include a recommended pizzeria in the centre.

For **après-ski**, La Gourmandine is the place for crêpes. Charlie's is a very welcoming, pleasantly busy upstairs bar. Le Sporting has great olives. El Gringo is a proper disco.

There's plenty to keep you active **off the slopes**: tennis courts, walks, swimming, skating and curling; or trips on the train – to Lausanne for instance.

Wengen

1275m

Charm, stunning views and extensive intermediate terrain

WHAT IT COSTS

((③)

HOW IT RATES

The slopes

Snow	**
Extent	***
Experts	***
Intermediates	****
Beginners	***
Convenience	***
Queues	***
Restaurants	****

The rest

Scenery	*****
Resort charm	*****
Off-slope	****

➕ Some of the most beautiful scenery in the Alps

➕ Pretty, traditional, 'traffic-free' Alpine village reached only by cog railway

➕ Extensive slopes, ideal for intermediates

➕ Good for anyone wanting a relaxing break without pounding the slopes

➖ Limited terrain for experts

➖ Nursery slopes often short of snow

➖ Snow conditions unreliable, despite some artificial help

➖ Little nightlife for club- and disco-lovers

Wengen, like Mürren across the valley, is one of our favourite resorts. As an early intermediate, one of us went to Wengen on holiday for four successive years. It has ideal terrain for someone at that stage. Combine that with the charm of the village, the friendliness of the locals and the beauty of the scenery and you can see why the place entrances many people so completely that they never go anywhere else, whatever their standard.

So it's sad that its erratic snow record makes it risky to book a holiday in Wengen months in advance. The slopes are not high – little above 2000m – and current investment in snowmaking is not enough to ensure good coverage.

But the old-world charm of the place is difficult to beat. You have to be willing to accept an old-world pace too. The train up the mountain in the morning may be quaint, but quick it ain't. Wengen is a place for relaxing and enjoying winter amid Europe's most glorious scenery. It's not the place if you want to maximise mileage, catch the most efficient lifts or find great challenges. Relax and you'll love it. Stay tense – in working mode – and you'll find it very frustrating.

boarding *Wengen has put a lot of effort into becoming boarder friendly. Most lifts are chairs, gondolas, trains or cable-cars. Annoyingly, one of the few drags connects Kleine Scheidegg to Männlichen, where there's a fun-park – but it is also accessible directly from Wengen via the cable-car. There's also the 'Snow Valley' by the Wixi chair (above Wengernalp), a long, wide gully with obstacles and jumps (including a VW Beetle) and half-pipe. The nursery area is not ideal, but beginners have plenty of slopes to progress to, with lots of long blue and red runs from the top of the train from the village. Experts will tire quickly of the area, and hanker after the steeper slopes of Mürren, or the heli-boarding trips.*

What's new

For 1997/98 there is a new disco called The Bakery.

Planned for 1998/99 is the replacement of the old Gummi chair on the Männlichen by a high-speed quad, which may also open up some new terrain.

Recent reporters have been very complimentary about the efficient hands-free electronic KeyCard lift ticket system.

The resort

Wengen is set on a shelf high above the Lauterbrunnen valley, opposite Mürren, and reached only by cog railway from Lauterbrunnen – the railway carries on up the mountain as the main lift. Wengen was a farming community long before skiing arrived. Today its charming 'traffic-free' village remains small and fairly unspoilt.

The only traffic in Wengen is little electric hotel trucks, which gather at the station to pick up guests, and a couple of Range Rover taxis.

The main street is the hub of the village. Lined with chalet-style shops and hotels, it also has the ice rink, curling club and village nursery slopes giving it a pleasant open aspect. The nursery slopes double as the venue for floodlit ski-jumping and parallel slalom races on several nights a season.

The views across the valley are stunning. They get even better higher up, when the Eiger, Jungfrau and Mönch come into view. The Mönch (Monk) is between the other two and, mythology says, protects the Jungfrau (Maiden) from the Eiger (Ogre).

The main way up the mountain is the regular, incredibly punctual train to Kleine Scheidegg, from the southern end of the village. There's also a cable-car from above the nursery slopes up to the Männlichen area.

MOUNTAIN FACTS

Altitude 945m-2970m
Lifts 48
Pistes 183km
Blue 30%
Red 50%
Black 20%
Artificial snow 20km
Recco detectors used
— helicopter-based

The mountains

Although it is famous for the fearsome Lauberhorn World Cup Downhill course – the longest and one of the toughest on the circuit – Wengen's slopes are best suited to intermediates; early intermediates at that. There are no seriously steep pistes and the scariest part of the Downhill course, the Hundschopf jump, is shut to holiday makers. Most runs are gentle blues and reds, ideal for cruising. The slopes are shared with Grindelwald in the next valley, and on that side there are some long and beautiful runs down to the village. But the lower parts of these often suffer from poor snow conditions

↑ Wengen's traffic free main street

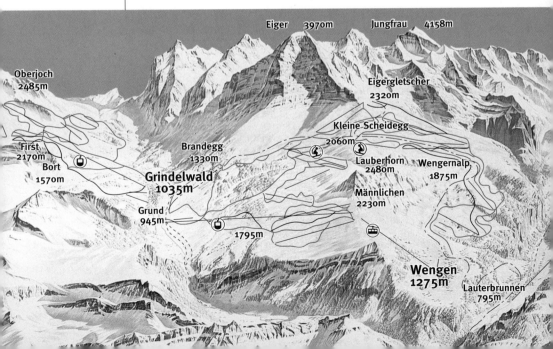

LIFT PASSES

97/98 prices in Swiss francs

Jungfrau Top Ski Region
Covers all lifts in Wengen, Mürren and Grindelwald, trains between them and Grindelwald ski-bus.

Beginners Points card (adult 100 points 46, lifts cost 4 to 10 points).

Main pass
1-day pass 50
6-day pass 232

Senior citizens
Over 62: 6-day pass 209 (10% off)

Children
Under 16: 6-day pass 116 (50% off)
Under 6: free pass

Short-term passes
Single ascent tickets for most lifts. Half-day pass for First (adult 38), Kleine Scheidegg-Männlichen (adult 40) and Mürren-Schilthorn (adult 38).

Alternative periods
3 days in 7 pass available (133).

Notes Day pass price for Kleine Scheidegg-Männlichen area only (100km of piste, 21 lifts), as Jungfrau Top Ski Region pass is only available for 2 days or over. Discounts for teenagers 16 to 20 (6-day 186) and groups.

Alternative passes
1- and 2-day passes available for First (adult 2-day 90), Mürren-Schilthorn (adult 2-day 90) and Kleine Scheidegg-Männlichen (adult 2-day 95).

and there is hardly any snowmaking on the Grindelwald side.

You can get to Mürren by taking the train down to Lauterbrunnen, and a funicular and connecting train up the other side. Mürren and Grindelwald are, like Wengen, covered by the Jungfrau pass.

THE SLOPES
Picturesque playground
Most of the slopes are on the other side of the mountain from Wengen. From the top of the train at **Kleine Scheidegg** (2060m) you can head straight down to Grindelwald or work your way across the mountain with the help of a couple of lifts to the top of the **Männlichen** (2230m). This area is served by drag- and chair-lifts, and can be reached directly by catching the little-used cable-car up from Wengen.

There are a few runs back down towards Wengen from the top of the **Lauberhorn** (2470m), but below Kleine Scheidegg there's really only one.

SNOW RELIABILITY
Poor
Most slopes are below 2000m, and at Grindelwald they go down to less than 1000m. Very few slopes face north and Wengen's snowmaking facilities are not up to protecting them. A reporter tells us that the snowmaking that is there isn't always used when it's needed.

All this can mean severe problems in a snow famine, and while we've found wonderful snow a couple of times in late March, we've also struggled to find any in January.

FOR EXPERTS
Few challenges
Wengen is quite limited for experts. The one genuine black run in the area takes you from Eigergletscher to Wixi. The steepest parts of the Lauberhorn Downhill course are normally shut to holiday makers. The main challenges are off-piste runs such as the Oh God from near Eigergletscher to Wixi and the White Hare from under the north face of the Eiger. There are a number of off-piste runs from the Jungfraujoch late in the season, but you must go with a guide.

For more challenges it's well worth going to nearby Mürren, an hour away by train and funicular. Heli-trips with mountain guides are organised if there are enough takers.

FOR INTERMEDIATES
Wonderful if the snow is good
Wengen has superb intermediate slopes. Nearly all are long blue or gentle red runs. From Kleine Scheidegg there's an easy scenic blue run all the way down through trees to Grindelwald – or you can stop at Brandegg and catch the train back up. The run back to Wengen is a relaxing end to the day, as long as it's not too crowded.

On the Männlichen there's a choice of gentle runs down to the mid-station of the gondola up from Grindelwald Grund. If conditions permit, you can get right down to the bottom. There's a piste from Männlichen to Grindelwald that is marked black but is perfectly fine for any competent intermediate.

For tougher pistes, head for the top of the Lauberhorn lift and then runs to Kleine Scheidegg, or to Wixi (following the start of the Downhill course). You could also try the north-facing run from Eigergletscher to Salzegg, which often has the best snow late in the season.

FOR BEGINNERS
Not ideal
There's a nursery slope in the centre of the village – it's convenient, but the snow is unreliable. There's a beginners' area at Wengernalp but, to get back to Wengen, you either have to climb up to the train or tackle the run down, which you may find tricky in places. There are good, long gentle slopes to progress to – especially the run down by the railway on the Grindelwald side.

FOR CROSS-COUNTRY
There is none
There's no cross-country skiing in Wengen itself. There are tracks down in the Lauterbrunnen valley, but the snow there is unreliable.

QUEUES
Can be bad – but improving
There can be some horrific bottlenecks in peak periods, and daily scrums to board the trains that the school uses. Weekend invasions can increase the crowds. Particular black spots are the train and gondola from Grindelwald.

However, queues up the mountain have been alleviated a lot in the last few years. Some of the old drag- and chair-lifts have been replaced by new, fast four-person chairs, and the capacity of the Männlichen cable-car has been increased.

SCHOOLS/GUIDES

97/98 prices in Swiss
francs

Swiss
Classes 6 days
3hr: am
6 half days: 204
Children's classes
Ages: 4 to 12
6 half days: 204
Private lessons
2hr or 5hr
125 for 2hr

CHILDCARE

The kindergarten on
the first floor of the
Sport Pavilion takes
children aged 3 to 7,
from 8.45 to 4.30.
Children can be taken
to and from lessons
with the ski school,
which starts at age 4.

A couple of 4-star
hotels have their own
kindergartens.

GETTING THERE

Air Zürich, transfer
3½hr. Bern, transfer
1½hr.

Rail Station in resort.

UK PACKAGES

Bladon Lines, Club
Med, Crystal,
Independent Ski
Links, Inghams,
Kuoni, Made to
Measure, PGL Ski
Europe, Plus Travel,
Ski Club of GB, Ski
Les Alpes, Swiss
Travel Service,
Thomson

Interlaken Kuoni,
SkiGower, Swiss
Travel Service

THE BRITISH IN WENGEN

*There's a very strong British presence at Wengen. Many Brits have been returning
to the same rooms in the same hotels in the same week, year after year and treat
the resort as a sort of second home. Wengen is also home to the Downhill Only
Club – so named when the first Brits persuaded the locals to keep the summer
railway running up the mountain in winter so they would no longer have to climb
up in order to ski down again. That amused the locals greatly, who until then had
regarded skiing in winter as a necessity rather than a pastime to be done for fun.
The Downhill Only Club is still going strong and organises regular events
throughout the season.*

*There's a great rivalry with the other long-standing British community over the
valley in Mürren, where another ski club, the Kandahar, is also still thriving.*

MOUNTAIN RESTAURANTS
Plenty of variety
A popular but expensive place for
lunch is Wengernalp, where the rösti is
excellent and the views of the Jungfrau
are superb. The highest restaurant is at
Eigergletscher. If you get there early on
a sunny day, you can nab a table on
the narrow outside balcony and enjoy
magnificent views of the glacier. The
station buffet at Kleine Scheidegg is
good value (a reporter raved about a
huge bowl of tasty 'Hopla Bopla' pasta
which fed three for 15SF in 1997). The
Café Oberland, just below Almend, is
popular at lunch-time and at the end
of the day for those who want to soak
up the last of the sun and a boozy
coffee before returning to Wengen.

On the Grindelwald side of the
mountain, the restaurants by the
Brandegg station and the top of the
Aspen drag are recommended. As is
the Grindelwaldenblick, a worthwhile
trudge uphill from Kleine Scheidegg,
with great food and views of the Eiger.

SCHOOLS AND GUIDES
Healthy competition
A recent reporter says, 'the Swiss
school is definitely trying harder than a
few years ago' – tuition and standard
of English are usually good. The
independent Privat school has been
praised for good-value tuition.

Snowboarders are well served. And
guides are available for heli-trips and
powder excursions.

FACILITIES FOR CHILDREN
Apparently satisfactory
Our recent reports on children's
facilities are from observers rather than
participants, but are all favourable. It is
an attractive village for families, with
the baby slope in the centre. The train
gives easy access to higher slopes.

Staying there

Wengen is small, so location isn't as
crucial as in many other resorts. The
main street is ideally placed for the
station.

The hotels on the home piste are
convenient for the slopes. Those who
don't fancy a steepish morning climb
should avoid places set well below the
station.

HOW TO GO
Wide range of hotels
Most accommodation is in hotels.
Plenty of tour operators organise hotel
packages here.

There is only a handful of catered
chalets (and, surprisingly perhaps, no
especially luxurious ones). Self-catering
apartments are thin on the ground too.
There is a popular Club Med right on
the main street.

Hotels There are about two dozen
hotels, mostly 4-star and 3-star, with a
handful of simpler places.

((((4) **Parkhotel Beausite** Unattractive
block at top of the village, near cable-
car. Good pool; kindergarten.

((((4) **Sunstar** Modern hotel on main
street. Comfortable rooms; lounge has
a log fire. Live music some nights. Pool
with views. Food very good. Friendly.

((((4) **Regina** Central position. Smart,
traditional atmosphere. 'Best food in
Wengen.' Carousel nightclub.

((((4) **Silberhorn** Comfortable modern 4-
star in excellent central position, with
choice of restaurants.

((((4) **Caprice** Small, smartly furnished
chalet-style hotel across the tracks
from the Regina. Kindergarten.

(((3) **Alpenrose** Long-standing British
favourite; eight minutes' climb to the
station. Good views; 'first-class' food;
friendly staff.

ACTIVITIES

Indoor Swimming pool (in Park Hotel), sauna, solarium, whirlpool, massage (in hotels), cinema (with English films), bowling, billiards
Outdoor Skating, curling, 20km cleared paths, toboggan runs, para-gliding, glacier flights, sledging excursions, hang-gliding

(((3) **Eiger** Very conveniently sited, overlooking the station. Focal après-ski bar. Renovated a few years ago – comfortable modern rooms.
(((3) **Falken** Further up the hill. Another British favourite, known affectionately as 'Fawlty Towers'.
((2) **Bernerhof** Wooden chalet on main street; jolly bar.
Self-catering The hotel Bernerhof's decent Residence apartments are well positioned just off the main street, and hotel facilities are available to guests.

EATING OUT
Lots of choice

Most restaurants in the village are in the hotels. They offer good food and service, and are open to non-residents. It's worth trying the Eiger which has a traditional restaurant and a stube with Swiss and French cuisine.

There's no shortage of fondues in the village. If all you want is a snack, then try the Pizzeria at the Victoria Lauberhorn, the Silberhorn or the Tanne Bar. You could book a table at Wengernalp's excellent restaurant – the last train back to Wengen leaves at 11.45pm. If you feel daring, you could take the piste back – perhaps on a toboggan.

APRES-SKI
Quietly lively

Wengen has a reputation for quiet nightlife which is rather misleading. Most British guests here want a relaxing time, hence reports tend to minimise what's on offer. But there are a number of places where a lively atmosphere is generated, largely by locals and visiting Germans. A number of reporters have been pleasantly surprised by the action available if you look around.

The stube at the Eiger and the tiny Eiger Bar, just round the corner, are popular at the end of the day. If you've still got energy, you could try the tea dancing at the Silberhorn or Belvedere.

The Tanne, Pickle and Sinam's are very popular bars, the latter with live music some nights and karaoke the rest. The bowling alley has the cheapest beer in town. There are a couple of discos (and a new one called the Bakery for 1997/98), a nightclub, dancing and live music in some hotels. The cinema often shows English-

language films. You can watch floodlit ski-jumping and slalom competitions for the locals on the slopes in the centre of the village. There are also ice hockey matches.

OFF THE SLOPES
Good for a relaxing time

Wengen is a superb resort for those who want a completely relaxing holiday. The unbeatable scenery makes just sitting around and soaking up the sun thoroughly enjoyable. And the train is ideal for pedestrians wanting to get up the mountain to meet friends for lunch (there's a special, though expensive, five-day pass).

For those who feel the need to take a little exercise there are some lovely mountain walks, ice skating, a curling club and bowling. Excursions to Interlaken and Berne are possible by train, as is the trip to the Jungfraujoch at 3455m (see the feature panel in the Grindelwald chapter).

STAYING UP THE MOUNTAIN
Great views

You can stay at two points up the mountain, reached by the railway: the pricey Jungfrau at Wengernalp – a favourite lunch spot with great views – and at Kleine Scheidegg, where there's a choice of rooms in the Kleine Scheidegg hotel or dormitory space above the station buffet.

STAYING DOWN THE VALLEY
The budget option

Staying in a 3-star hotel like the Schützen or Oberland in Lauterbrunnen will cost about half as much as similar accommodation in Wengen. Lauterbrunnen isn't exactly throbbing with nightlife, but the train from Wengen runs until 11.30pm and is included in your lift pass. Staying in Lauterbrunnen also improves your chances of getting a seat on the train to Kleine Scheidegg rather than joining the scrum at Wengen. Lauterbrunnen is also much better placed for Mürren.

You can save even more money by staying in the beautiful summer resort of Interlaken. Choose a hotel near Interlaken Ost station, from which you can catch a train to Lauterbrunnen (22 minutes) or Grindelwald (36 minutes). Driving takes about as long as the train on weekdays in good weather.

TOURIST OFFICE

Postcode CH-3823
Tel +41 (33) 855 1414
Fax 855 3060

Zermatt

1620m

Magical in many respects – both on and off the slopes

WHAT IT COSTS

((((5))))

HOW IT RATES

The slopes

Snow	****
Extent	****
Experts	*****
Intermediates	****
Beginners	*
Convenience	*
Queues	***
Restaurants	*****

The rest

Scenery	*****
Resort charm	*****
Off-slope	****

What's new

For the 1996/97 season a new 150-person cable-car replaced the earlier 80-person one from Blauherd to Unterrothorn, dramatically reducing queues here.

Shuttle buses in town are now free to lift-pass holders and larger and more frequent – though still crowded at times.

For 1997/98 six-day international passes will be available, covering Cervinia as well as Zermatt's slopes. Costing SF58 more than the Swiss pass, they will be cheaper than buying the SF31 daily supplement if you go to Italy twice in a week.

More snowmaking will be installed for 1997/98.

The chopper retreats, having made its 20th drop of the day →

➕ Wonderful high and extensive slopes for experts and intermediates

➕ Spectacular high-mountain scenery, dominated by the Matterhorn

➕ Charming, if rather sprawling, old mountain village, largely traffic-free

➕ Reliable snow at altitude

➕ World's best mountain restaurants

➕ Extensive helicopter operation

➕ Nightlife to suit most tastes

➕ Smart shops

➕ Linked to Cervinia in Italy

➖ Getting to main lift stations may involve a long walk, crowded bus or expensive taxi-ride

➖ Beginners should go elsewhere

➖ The three separate slope areas are not well linked – the system could do with updating

➖ Getting up the mountain and around the different areas can be a slow business

➖ Annoying electric taxis detract from the otherwise relaxed, car-free village ambience

You must try Zermatt before you die. Few places can match its combination of excellent advanced and intermediate slopes, reliable snow, magnificent scenery, Alpine charm and mountain restaurants with superb food and stunning views.

Many people complain that the car-free village is spoiled by intrusive electric carts and taxis, and some that the atmosphere is of Swiss efficiency and international tourism rather than mountain-village friendliness. But there's still a magical feel, particularly when you get away from the busy, modern-seeming main street into the winding snowy paths, with their old wooden buildings.

Most of Zermatt's flaws are minor compared to its attractions, which come close to matching perfectly our notion of the ideal winter resort. It is certainly one of our favourites, and we are not alone.

boarding *Boarders in soft boots have one big advantage over skiers in Zermatt – they have much more comfortable walks to and from the lift stations at resort level! The slopes are best for experienced freeriders, because the tough piste and off-piste action is what Zermatt is really about, and either a guide or a heli-trip, despite the expense, will be the ride of your life – there's a fun-park and half-pipe too. The main lifts are boarder-friendly: train, funicular, gondolas and cable-cars, but drag-lifts take over up on the glacier. The resort is not ideal for learning to board just as it isn't ideal for first-time skiers. The evenings have something for everyone.*

The resort

Zermatt started life as a traditional mountain village, developed as a mountaineering centre in the 19th century, then became a winter resort too. Summer is still as important as winter here.

Be warned – Zermatt is big business. Prices are high, and most restaurants and hotels are owned by a handful of families. Their employees don't always seem happy in their work.

The village sprawls along a narrow valley either side of a river, with mountains rising steeply on each side. It is a mixture of chocolate-box chalets and more modern buildings – most in traditional style. You arrive by mountain railway from Täsch, where cars have to be left. The main street runs past the station and is lined with large luxurious hotels and smart shops.

Zermatt doesn't have the relaxed, quaint feel of some other car-free resorts, such as Wengen and Saas-Fee. That's partly because the electric vehicles buzzing around are more intrusive and aggressive, and partly because the clientele is more overtly upmarket and jet-set, with large contingents from Japan and the US.

For a resort with such good and extensive slopes, there's a remarkably high age profile. Most visitors seem to be over 40, and there's little of the youthful atmosphere you get in rival resorts with comparable slopes, such as Val-d'Isère, St Anton and Chamonix.

The main street, with the station square near one end, is the focal point of village life. The cog railway to the Gornergrat area leaves from opposite the main station, and the underground funicular to the Sunnegga area is just a few minutes' walk away. The gondola to the Klein Matterhorn (and the link to Cervinia) is a 15-minute trek from here.

The school and guides office, tourist office and many hotels, restaurants, shops, bars and nightspots are on, or a short stroll from, the main street. There's another main street a few yards away, along the side of the river. To each side are narrow streets and paths, many of which are hilly and treacherous when icy.

MOUNTAIN FACTS

Altitude	1620m-3820m
Lifts	33
Pistes	245km
Blue	33%
Red	44%
Black	23%
Artificial snow	29km
Recco detectors used	

The mountains

There are slopes to suit all standards except absolute beginners, for whom we don't recommend the resort. For intermediates and experts Zermatt has few rivals worldwide. There are marvellously groomed cruising trails, some of the best moguls around, long, beautiful scenic runs out of view of the lift system, exciting heli-trips and off-piste possibilities if you hire a guide, as well as the opportunity to get down into Italy for the day and lunch on pasta and chianti.

THE SLOPES
Beautiful and varied

Zermatt consists of three separate areas, at best awkwardly linked and involving some uphill walks. The **Sunnegga-Blauherd-Unterrothorn** area is reached by the underground funicular starting about five minutes' walk from the station. This shifts large numbers rapidly but can lead to queues for the subsequent gondola – the cable-car above was rebuilt for the 1996/97 season, and has increased capacity. From this area you can make your way – via south-facing slopes that lose their snow and two gruelling steep drag-lifts – to the second main area, **Gornergrat-Stockhorn**. This link was shut when we were last there in 1996 because of lack of snow – very annoying. That meant the only way to Gornergrat was by the cog railway from opposite the main station. New 'high-speed' trains are supposed to cut the 45-minute ride to 25 minutes – but old trains still operate on the single-track railway, so new ones have to wait and end up taking just as long. A gondola makes the link back to Sunnegga.

From Gornergrat, if snow-cover permits, you can get below Furi to link up with the third and highest area, **Klein Matterhorn-Trockener Steg-Schwarzsee**. But you can't do the journey in the opposite direction: once on the Klein Matterhorn, moving to a different mountain means heading down and getting from one end of the village to the other to catch a lift up. The Klein Matterhorn gives access to Cervinia – you need to buy an 'international pass' or pay a daily supplement to your Zermatt lift pass and the high lifts are frequently shut because of high winds.

In theory you can get back to the

LIFT PASSES

97/98 prices in Swiss francs

Area Pass
Covers all lifts on the Swiss side of the border.
Beginners Coupon book (100 coupons 136). Pass for Riffelberg-Gornergrat beginner area (adult 6-day 218).
Main pass
1-day pass 60
6-day pass 296
Senior citizens
Over 65 male, 62 female: 6-day pass 222 (25% off)
Children
Under 16: 6-day pass 148 (50% off)
Under 9: free pass
Short-term passes
Single ascent tickets for most lifts.
Notes Daily supplement available to cover all lifts in Cervinia and Valtournenche (31).
Alternative passes
Passes for any period available for each area of Zermatt (Gornergrat-Stockhorn, Sunnegga-Rothorn, Trockener Steg-Klein Matterhorn-Schwarzsee), and combinations of areas. 1-day pass available for Zermatt, Cervinia and Valtournenche (62).

village from all three areas. But in practice the lower runs have often been shut or unpleasant on our visits.

SNOW RELIABILITY
Good high up, poor lower down
Zermatt has rocky terrain and a relatively dry climate. But it also has some of the highest slopes in Europe, and quite a few snowmakers.

All three areas go up to over 3000m, and the Klein Matterhorn cable-car is the highest in Europe, ending at over 3800m and serving a summer glacier. There are loads of runs above 2500m, many of which are north-facing, so guaranteeing decent snow except in freak years.

Artificial snowmaking machines serve some of the pistes on all three areas, from around 3000m to under 2000m. But the runs back to the resort are often closed or tricky, despite the artificial help.

FOR EXPERTS
Good – with superb heli-trips
If you've never been, Zermatt has to be on your short-list. If you have been, we're pretty sure you'll want to return.

If you love long, fluffy mogul

pitches the slopes at Triftji, below Stockhorn, are the stuff of dreams. From the top of the Stockhorn cable-car there's a run down to the T-bar that serves another two steep 2km runs – one each side of the lift. The whole mountainside here is one vast mogul field – steep, but not extremely so. Being north-facing and lying between 3400m and 2700m, the snow is usually the best around, which makes the huge moguls so forgiving that even we can enjoy them. The snag in early season is that this whole area is unlikely to open until well into January, and possibly later.

You can continue down from here to Gant and catch the gondola up to Blauherd. On that mountain there are a couple of wonderful off-piste 'downhill routes' from Unterrothorn, which used to be official black pistes and have spectacular views down towards the village and over to the Matterhorn.

On the Klein Matterhorn, the best area for experts is Schwarzsee, from where there are several steep north-facing gullies through the woods. Unfortunately, you can't try these repeatedly without taking the beautiful, but slightly boring, track down to Furi

409

Zermatt

THE WORLD'S BEST MOUNTAIN RESTAURANTS

We once met a man who had been coming here for 20 years simply because of the mountain restaurants. The choice is enormous (the tourist information says 30 but it seems more). Most of those we've tried have excellent food and many are in spectacular settings. It is impossible to list here all those worth a visit – so don't limit yourself to those we mention.

At Furi, the Restaurant Furi itself, Aroleid above it and Simi's on the road below all have large sun terraces and good reputations. The hotel at Schwarzsee is set right at the foot of the Matterhorn, at over 2500m, with staggering views of the mountain and the Trockener Steg slopes and serves endless variations of rösti. On the way back to the village in this area, a couple of cosy, stopping-off points are Zum See and Blatten.

The Kulmhotel, at 3100m at Gornergrat, has both self-service and table-service restaurants with amazing views of lift-free mountains and glaciers. Further down, the Riffelalp hotel has excellent pot-au-feu and pasta; the chef came from the 5-star Mont Cervin down in Zermatt.

The large terrace of the restaurant at Sunnegga offers decent food and a great view of children's classes falling down the steep ending of the blue piste nearby. Up at Rothorn, the new(ish) restaurant has excellent food – we had wonderful lamb. Down at Findeln are several attractive rustic restaurants, including Franz & Heidy's and Chez Vrony ('unbeatable on a snowy day'). And the restaurant at Tuftern sells good Heida white wine from the highest vineyard in Europe – just down the valley at 1200m.

Wherever you go, don't miss trying the local alcoholic coffee known as Schlümli Pflümli – but only if you've had enough of the slopes for the day!

SCHOOLS/GUIDES

97/98 prices in Swiss
francs

Swiss
Classes 6 days
4hr: 2hr am and pm
6 full days: 215
Children's classes
Ages: 6 to 12
6 full days including
lunch: 255
Private lessons
Half- or full-day
145 for half-day for 1
to 2 people; each
additional person 5

and catching the cable-car up again.

There are marvellous off-piste possibilities from the top lifts in each sector, but they aren't immediately obvious to those without local knowledge. They are also dangerous because of the rocky terrain.

We don't recommend anyone going off-piste without a guide. But in Zermatt the school doesn't run off-piste groups in the way they do in resorts such as Val-d'Isère and Méribel. You have to hire a guide privately for a full day, and that's expensive unless you have a fair-sized group. Much better value for individuals and couples is a half-day heli-trip – provided you know what you're in for.

Zermatt is the Alps' biggest heli-trip centre; the helipad resembles a bus station at times, with choppers taking off every few minutes. There are only three main drop-off points, so this can mean encountering one or two other groups on the mountain, even though there are multiple ways down. From all three points there are routes that don't require great expertise. The epic is from the Monte Rosa, at over 4000m, down through wonderful glacier scenery to Furi.

FOR INTERMEDIATES
Mile after mile of beautiful runs
Zermatt is ideal for adventurous intermediates. Both the blue and the red runs tend to be at the difficult end of their grading. There are some very beautiful reds down lift-free valleys from both Gornergrat and Hohtälli – we like these first thing in the morning, before anyone else is on them. The variant to Riffelalp ends up on a very narrow wooded path with a sheer cliff and magnificent views to the right.

On Sunnegga, the 5km Kumme run, from Unterrothorn to the bottom of the Patrullarve chair, also gets away from the lift system and has an interesting mix of straight-running and mogul pitches. On Klein Matterhorn, the reds served by the Hörnli and Garten drags and the fast four-person chair from Furgg are all long and gloriously set at the foot of the Matterhorn.

For the less adventurous intermediate, the best areas are the blues above Riffelberg (on Gornergrat), above Sunnegga, and the runs between Klein Matterhorn and Trockener Steg. Of these, the Riffelberg area often has the best combination of good snow and easy cruising, and is

popular with the school. Sunnegga gets a lot of sun, but the artificial snow means that the problem is more often a foot or more of heavy snow near the bottom than bare patches.

On the Klein Matterhorn, most of the runs, though marked red on the piste map, are very flat and represent the easiest slopes Zermatt has to offer, as well as the best snow. The problem here is the possibility of bad weather because of the height – high winds, extreme cold and poor visibility can make life very unpleasant. To get to Cervinia, you set off from Testa Grigia with a choice of blue or red routes – even an early intermediate should find the 10km blue route right down to the village manageable.

FOR BEGINNERS
Learn elsewhere
Zermatt is to be avoided by beginners. The easiest slopes are outlined above. And there's no decent nursery slope area. Unless you have a compelling reason to start in Zermatt, don't.

FOR EVERYONE
A spectacular cable-car ride
The Klein Matterhorn cable-car is an experience not to miss if the weather is good. The views down to the glacier and its crevasses, as the car swings steeply into its hole blasted out of the mountain at the top, are stupendous. When you arrive, you walk through a long tunnel, to emerge on top of the world for the highest piste in Europe – walk slowly, the air is thin here and some people have altitude problems. The top drag-lifts here are used in summer but normally shut in winter.

FOR CROSS-COUNTRY
Fairly limited
There's a 4km loop at Furi, 3km near the bottom of the gondola to Furi, and 12 to 15km down at Täsch (don't count on there being snow). There are also some 'ski walking trails' – best tackled as part of an organised group.

QUEUES
Some bottlenecks, and slow lifts
Zermatt used to have one of the worst reputations for queues in the Alps. The major problems have now been pretty well eliminated. There can still be a lengthy scrum for the gondola out of town towards Klein Matterhorn at the start of the day. And the lifts above the Sunnegga train can generate

CHILDCARE

There are nurseries in two upmarket hotels. The Kinderparadies in the Nicoletta (967 0151) takes children aged 2 to 8, from 9am to 5pm. The Kinderclub Pumuckel at the Ginabelle (967 4535) takes children from 30 months to 6, from 9am to 5pm, and ski tuition is available on the spot.

Ski school lessons start at age 6.

One day, the burghers won't be able to resist turning these byres into four-star hotels →

queues, especially at peak periods. Most complaints we get, however, are about the time it takes to get to the top, and the poor links between areas.

To avoid the queues, start out early – really early. Catch the Gornergrat train before 8.30am or so, and you shouldn't encounter queues until late morning at the earliest.

SCHOOLS AND GUIDES
Standards vary

The school has a poor reputation with a lot of people we've heard from over the last few years. Our most recent reporter has used the school over three years, and tells us, 'standards vary – this time it was good, but the instructors can be impatient and classes can be large'.

FACILITIES FOR CHILDREN
Good hotel nurseries

The Nicoletta and Ginabelle hotels have obvious attractions for families who can afford them (though their nurseries are open to others). Despite our exceptionally fat file of reports on Zermatt, we have no first-hand reports on these facilities. For children of ski-school age, the resort is difficult to recommend.

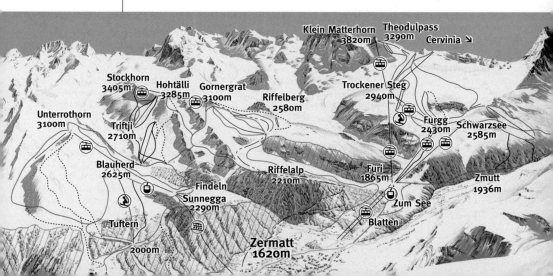

GETTING THERE

Air Geneva, transfer 4hr. Zürich, transfer 5hr.

Rail Station in resort.

UK PACKAGES

Bladon Lines, Chalets 'Unlimited', Fairhand Holidays, Independent Ski Links, Inghams, Kuoni, Lagrange, Lotus Supertravel, Made to Measure, Plus Travel, Powder Byrne, Ski Choice, Ski Club of GB, Ski Les Alpes, Ski Scott Dunn, Ski Total, Ski with Julia, SkiGower, Swiss Travel Service, Thomson, White Roc

Staying there

Choosing where to stay is very important in Zermatt. The solar-powered shuttle buses are crowded, but at least they are now free to lift-pass holders, larger and more frequent than they used to be. Walking from one end of the village to the furthest lifts can take 15 to 20 minutes and can be unpleasant because of icy paths.

The best spot for most people is near the centre and the Gornergrat and Sunnegga railways. Some of the accommodation is inconveniently situated, up the steep hill across the river from the centre. Winkelmatten can be particularly tedious unless you intend to head for the Klein Matterhorn area most days.

Getting up to the village from Täsch is no problem. The trains run on time and have automatically descending ramps which allow you to wheel luggage trolleys on and off. You are met at the other end by electric and horse-drawn taxis and hotel shuttles.

HOW TO GO
A wide choice, packaged or not
Chalets Several operators do have places here, many of the most comfortable contained in sizeable blocks of apartments.
Hotels There are over 100 hotels, mostly comfortable and traditional-style 3- and 4-stars, but including some luxurious and pricey and some more affordable places.
(((((5) **Mont Cervin** Biggest and perhaps best in town. Elegantly traditional inside, despite blocky looks. Central. Good pool.
(((4) **Alex** An established favourite, close to the station. Welcoming; charmingly decorated. Good facilities, including a pool.
(((4) **Ambassador** Peaceful position on northern fringe, near Gornergrat station. Large pool; fitness room.
(((4) **Monte Rosa** The original Zermatt hotel, towards southern end of village – full of climbing pictures and mementos, but well modernised. The Whymperstube is named after the British conqueror of the Matterhorn, who stayed here.
(((4) **Ginabelle** Smart pair of chalets, over the river, not far from Sunnegga lift; great for families – on-the-spot ski nursery as well as day-care.
(((4) **Nicoletta** Bright modern chalet quite close to centre, with nursery.
(((3) **Julen** Charming, modern-rustic chalet

over the river, with Matterhorn views from some rooms.
((2) **Atlanta** No frills, but good food; close to centre, with Matterhorn views from some rooms.
((2) **Alpina** Modest but very friendly, and close to centre.
Self-catering There is a lot of apartment accommodation in the village, but not much of it finds its way to the UK package market – so it sells out early. The hotel Ambassador apartments have excellent facilities. The large, comfortable Armina apartments are ideal for large families. The Malteserhaus apartments are comfortable, but sell early.

STAYING UP THE MOUNTAIN
Comfortable seclusion
There are several hotels at altitude, of which the pick is probably the Riffelalp, rebuilt from a ruin in 1988 and recommended for good food and a quiet time. It's at the first stop on the Gornergrat railway. The last train up from Zermatt is at 6pm, but if you fancy a night in town and there's room, you can stay at the Seilers' other hotels – the Schweizerhof for no extra charge, or the Mont Cervin or Monte Rosa for a supplement. At the top of the railway, at 3100m, is the Kulmhotel Gornergrat.

STAYING DOWN THE VALLEY
Attractive for drivers
In Täsch, where visitors must leave their cars, there are five 3-star hotels, costing less than half the price of the equivalent in Zermatt. The Täscherhof is next to the station; the City and Bellevue close by. It's a 13-minute ride from Zermatt, with trains every 20 minutes for most of the day; the last train down is 11.10pm.

EATING OUT
Huge choice at all price levels
There are 100 restaurants to choose from, ranging from top-quality haute cuisine to egg and chips. Among the most highly rated restaurants is the Mazot, which has prices to match the food. At the other end of the scale, Café du Pont has good-value pasta and rösti, and the Bahnhof Buffet offers good food at some of the lowest prices. For its rustic atmosphere and dried meats, try the Whymperstube.

The Chi-Ba-Bou, in the hotel Ambassador, specialises in fondue and has a good reputation. For pizza,

Tony's Grotta is hard to beat – we've had excellent food but surly service there. Taking the last lift up and strolling down to an early dinner in a mountain hut is worth considering – check their serving times first.

ACTIVITIES

Indoor Sauna, tennis, hotel swimming pools (some open to public), salt water pool, keep-fit centre, squash, billiards, curling, bowling, gallery, excellent Alpine museum, cinema, indoor golf **Outdoor** Skating, curling, sleigh rides, 30km cleared paths, helicopter flights, para-gliding, cycling

TOURIST OFFICE

Postcode CH-3920
Tel +41 (27) 967 0181
Fax 967 0185

APRES-SKI
Lively and varied
There's something for almost every taste, with a good mix of sophisticated and informal fun, though it certainly helps if you have deep pockets.

On the way back to the village from the Klein Matterhorn there are lots of restaurants below Furi for a last drink and sunbathe. In town, there are fewer places than you might expect to have an end of the day glühwein or hot chocolate. The Papperla is one of the most popular (it's busy after dinner, too). Elsie's bar, renowned for its snails and oysters, gets packed early and late. Promenading along the main street is popular, and gives the village a great atmosphere.

Later on, the hotel de la Poste complex is popular for eating, drinking, dancing and jazz. There is something for everyone in this remarkable establishment, from a quiet, comfortable bar (David's Boathouse) to a lively disco-bar (Le Broken); Pink Elephant is a popular but rather pricey jazz/piano bar; the Brown Cow is a friendly but otherwise uninspiring bar that's usually full of Brits, as it has some of the cheapest beer in town.

The dreary North Face is another cheap place, which is popular with tour reps. Two bars with dancing and a bit more atmosphere are the comfortable Grampi's and the Tschuggi – a smart cellar with karaoke. Z'Alt Hischi is an atmospheric bar for a quiet drink. The Hexenbar is a similarly cosy place. The hotel Alex appeals to over-30s for eating, drinking and dancing, with 'middle-of-the-road music, quality decor and candlelit tables'.

The Vernissage is an unusually stylish, modern place – the projection room for the cinema is built into the upstairs bar, and there are displays of art elsewhere.

OFF THE SLOPES
Considerable attractions
Zermatt is an easy place to spend time (and money). And if lunch up the mountain appeals, this is nearly as good a resort for pedestrians as it is for those on boards. The lack of a public swimming pool is no real problem, with 15 hotel pools, and there is a decent range of other activities for the energetic. The Alpine museum is recommended – as is a helicopter trip around the Matterhorn if you're feeling adventurous (and flush with cash). You can also try the ice-diving (they provide a wet-suit) at Trockener Steg.

United States

The number of reports we get on US resorts grows steadily every year. And one thing they all have in common – virtually without exception – is wholehearted praise for the US skiing experience. People are captivated by it and by the contrasts with European resorts. Wherever you go you'll be struck by the high standards of service and courtesy you receive, by the immaculate piste grooming that happens every night and by the top-quality accommodation. Depending on the resort you choose you may also be struck by the superb quality of the snow, the cute Wild West ambience and how easy it is to visit other nearby areas. But don't fall into the trap of lumping all US resorts together – they differ enormously. And there are distinct disadvantages, too.

It was snow that first took the British to America in large numbers, during the Alpine snow droughts of the late 1980s. The super-high Rockies had the reputation of getting limitless quantities of super-light snow, and in those crucial years they certainly did better than the Alps. The reputation went slightly beyond the reality, but in practice it doesn't matter – most American resorts have serious snowmaking facilities anyway. What's more, they use them – they lay down a base of artificial snow early in the season, rather than using snow-guns to make up for a lack of the real thing.

This is partly a reaction to the pattern of natural snowfall. A lot of the Rockies' snow arrives relatively late in the season – something that seems to be increasingly true in the Alps, but not traditionally what we expect. In January, or even February, you may encounter signs saying: 'Caution: Early Season Conditions Apply'. What they mean is that you may occasionally encounter a rock.

The state of Utah has staked a claim to the best snow conditions of all by adopting the slogan 'Greatest Snow on Earth'. The Utah resorts – particularly Snowbird and Alta – get very large amounts of snow, and it is by our standards superbly powdery stuff. But measurements of water content have shown that Colorado gets even lighter snow, justifying its 'Champagne powder' label. California, on the other hand, tends to have somewhat heavier snow, often referred to as 'Sierra Cement' – but it is more than acceptable by European standards. And New England has a reputation for hard and icy conditions and wild temperature fluctuations.

Piste grooming is taken very seriously – most American resorts set standards that Alpine resorts are only now beginning to attempt to match. Every morning you can expect to step out on to perfect 'corduroy' pistes. But this doesn't mean that there aren't moguls – far from it. It's just that you get moguls where the resort says you can expect moguls, and not where you're

‡ Direct charter flights to Denver.

‡ Best Group Offer Guaranteed; with up up to 1 in 6 travelling FREE!

‡ Excellent range of catered chalets in Breckenridge, Vail & Steamboat.

‡ Available from £299 based on room only for 4 people sharing at the Iron Horse Inn, Steamboat. Departing on the 17th Jan '98 for 7 nights from Gatwick.

‡ Specially selected Family Choice resorts.

THOMSON Ski & Snowboarding

To request a brochure phone: 0990 275 587 and quote 24 S GSG or call into your local travel agent to pick up a copy

414

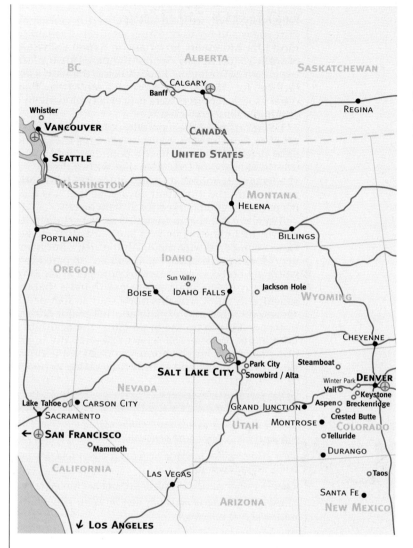

expecting an easy cruise. Indeed many resorts have now taken to grooming half the width of some runs and leaving the other half mogulled – so that you can dart in and out of the bumps as you like.

American resorts are well organised in lots of other respects, too. Many offer free guided tours of the area. Lift queues are short, partly because they are highly disciplined, and spare seats on chair-lifts are

religiously filled, with the aid of cheerful, conscientious attendants. Piste maps and boxes of tissues are freely available at the bottom of most lifts. Mountain 'hosts' are on hand to advise you about the best possible routes to take. School standards are uniformly high – with the added advantage of English being the native language. And facilities for children are impressive too – more than perhaps any other aspect, reporters were universally glowing in their praise about children's ski school classes.

US resorts have the reputation of not providing opportunities for off-piste, but this seriously misrepresents the position. It's true that areas practically always have a boundary, and that venturing beyond it is discouraged or forbidden. But within the area there is often challenging terrain that is very much like being off-piste in an Alpine resort – with the important advantage that it is much safer because it's patrolled and checked for avalanche risk.

There are drawbacks to the US as well, though. One is that many resorts (including big names) have areas that are very modest in extent compared with major Alpine areas. But many US resorts are very close to each other – so if you are prepared to travel a bit, you won't get bored. A more serious problem as far as we are concerned (and many of our reporters agree with us) is that the day is ridiculously short. The lifts often shut at 3pm or 3.30, even late in the season. That may explain another major drawback for those who like a good lunch on the mountain – the dearth of decent mountain restaurants. Monster self-service cafeterias doing pizza, burgers and other fast foods are the norm – so that people can spend as much time on the slopes and as little time eating as possible. Small

READERS' REPORTS SAY IT ALL

'Chalet superb – spacious, comfortable, well equipped and the master bedroom was particularly large, with panoramic views and its own Jacuzzi.'

'Piste grooming was immaculate velvet corduroy and new snow was genuinely like skiing whipped cream.'

'Queues – what queues? A wait of five minutes was quite exceptional.'

'Guest huts near top of main lifts were brilliant. They gave out coffee and cookies, water and even sun cream.'

'Our sons aged 9 and 11 went in different ski school classes. Both improved dramatically and loved every minute of it.'

'The best groomed pistes I've ever seen.'

'Hot cider and biscuits in bus queue at end of day.'

'One telephone call to the local transport and we had a bus at our door for the extra cost of $1 each.'

'The instructors make the classes FUN.'

'Brilliant is the only word to describe the ski school.'

'Quite simply, we adore skiing in the USA. The Americans are so organised and polite, the snow quality cannot be beaten, the grooming is an art form, lift lines are virtually non-existent and when they do occur are civilised and no-one stands all over your new skis. In mid-week the slopes are often deserted. We also found that it was better value for money, if not cheaper than a top resort in France or Switzerland. We first went in 1996 to Lake Tahoe and were immediately converted. Last year we skied Aspen, Vail, Keystone and Breckenridge.'

atmospheric restaurants with table service and decent food are rare – but growing in number as resorts try to attract more European guests.

It's also true that much of the terrain and many of the runs are monotonous. You don't get the spectacular mountain scenery and the distinctive high-mountain runs of the Alps – most are below the tree line (the upside of this is that your time on the slopes is very unlikely to be interrupted by bad weather because of the good visibility the trees give when it's snowing). And because most of the mountains have been developed specifically for the skiing and boarding with no old village or farming communities at the base, they can feel rather artificial.

The grading of pistes (or trails, to use the local term) is different from Europe. Red runs don't exist. The colours used are combined with shapes: green circles, blue squares, black diamonds. Greens correspond fairly closely to greens in Europe (that is, in France, where they are mainly found). American blues largely correspond to blues here, but also include tougher intermediate runs that would be red here; these are sometimes labelled as double blue squares, although in some resorts a hybrid blue-black grading is used instead. American blacks correspond to steeper European reds and easier European blacks. Many US resorts also have double black diamonds, which are seriously steep – often steeper than the steepest pistes in the Alps and including high, open bowls.

US resorts vary as widely in style and convenience as Alpine resorts. There are old restored Wild West towns such as Telluride, Crested Butte and Aspen, genuine cowboy towns such as Jackson Hole, purpose-built monstrosities such as Copper Mountain and Snowbird, and even neon-lit, skyscraping gambling dens such as Heavenly. But two important things that they all have in common

are good-value, spacious accommodation and good, reasonably priced restaurants.

Be prepared, though, for altitude problems. Most resorts are higher than the 2300m of Europe's highest (Val Thorens) and some are built at almost 3000m with runs going up to 4000m – we heard from several reporters who had serious altitude sickness problems.

In the end, your reaction to skiing and snowboarding in America may depend mainly on your reaction to America. If repeated cheerful exhortations to have a nice day wind you up, perhaps you'd better stick to the Alps. If you like the idea that the customer is king, give America a try. We love it and look forward to our annual visit.

A regular feature of steep slopes in the US is that part is groomed, and part is not ↓

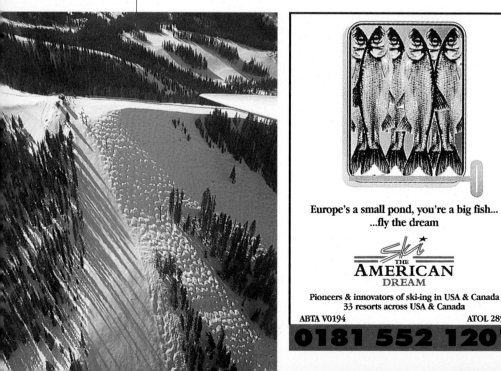

California

California? It means surfing, beaches, wine, Hollywood, Disneyland and San Francisco cable-cars. But it also has the highest mountains in continental USA and some of America's biggest winter resorts, usually reliable for snow from November to May (one often remains open until the Independence Day holiday, the 4th of July). What's more, winter holidays in California are tremendous value for money.

Holidays here are cheap because winter is low season for much of the accommodation and for scheduled flights from Britain into LA and San Francisco. Last season we met a family from Britain who had been on four skiing holidays in bargain-basement Bulgaria. They had decided to try California because it wasn't much more expensive (they paid £449 each for two weeks, including flights, accommodation and car hire) and it was 'something new'.

Not surprisingly, they were loving it. Heavenly and Mammoth, in particular, are impressive mountains, with something for all standards of skier or boarder. Our main reservation is the character of the resorts themselves; they don't have the traditional mountain-town ambience that we look for in the States. That's partly because this is California, the automobile state: the resorts have not been designed with walking in mind, which makes them rather soulless. You usually have to drive or take a bus to the lifts, which have little village development at their bases. This is about to change, with major new 'pedestrianised villages' being developed next to the slopes – but the results are still a few years away. On the plus side, Heavenly offers uniquely big-time entertainment in its casinos.

A common allegation is that the snow that falls in California is wet 'Sierra Cement'. Our fat file of reports from visitors has some complaints about that, but most people found the snow just fine – as we have whenever we've visited.

If you go to California, try a two-centre holiday, which will give you chance to see the very different styles of the different main resorts. Mammoth is a few hours' drive from the dozen or so resorts clustered around beautiful Lake Tahoe.

Heavenly

1995m

Knockout lake views, and gambling until dawn

WHAT IT COSTS

€€€€⑤

HOW IT RATES

The slopes

Snow	★★★
Extent	★★★
Experts	★★★
Intermediates	★★★★
Beginners	★★★★
Convenience	★
Queues	★★★
Restaurants	★

The rest

Scenery	★★★★
Resort charm	★
Off-slope	★★

What's new

For the 1997/98 season a new six-person high-speed chair is planned from mid-mountain on the California side to near the top of the Nevada side, along with two new runs. This is the first stage of a Master Plan which also features an eight-person gondola from near Stateline to the bottom of the new chair; when this is built, convenience of getting to the slopes will be much improved. There are also plans to redevelop and smarten up the area around the base of the proposed gondola.

● Amazing views across Lake Tahoe and arid Nevada

● Fair-sized area which (unusually for America) offers a sensation of travelling around

● Lots of easy off-piste among trees

● Some serious challenges for experts

● Numerous other worthwhile areas within driving distance

● Amazingly cheap package holidays

● A unique après-ski scene

● Impressive snowmaking facilities

● The base-town of South Lake Tahoe is quite unlike a traditional resort, and not attractive

● Very little traditional après-ski activity

● If natural snow is in short supply, there is very little challenging terrain

A resort called Heavenly invites an obvious question: just how close to Heaven does it take you? Physically, close enough: with a top height of 3060m and vertical drop of 1065m, it's the highest and biggest of the resorts clustered around scenic Lake Tahoe (see page 425 for the others). Metaphorically, it's not quite so close. The slopes have something for all standards, and having another dozen resorts within easy reach by car means that an interestingly varied holiday is assured. The problem we have with the place is aesthetic. One of the wonderful features is the amazing views, particularly across the lake; but those (like us) who value that feature are likely to be dismayed by the appearance and atmosphere of the town of South Lake Tahoe, at the foot of the slopes. If you can live with this drawback and you have a car, you can have a great holiday here. And you can have one at an amazingly low cost.

boarding *It's not surprising with the Californian surfing and snowboarding culture that snowboarding is popular in Heavenly. There's a big 'Airport' fun-park with half-pipe next to the Olympic chair, on the Nevada side of the slopes, and a great 'Whoopdeedoo' park (like a fun-park, but for skiers as well) on the Californian side, which we've enjoyed on skis. For experienced boarders, the off-piste in the trees and the double black diamond bowls make a great playground. Beginners and intermediates will enjoy great cruising runs and the chair-lifts which make travelling all over the mountain easy. Great deals on accommodation and flights make Heavenly one of the cheapest US resorts for budget boarders – though there's quite an absence of lively boarder-friendly bars.*

The resort

Heavenly is at the south end of Lake Tahoe, on the borders of California and Nevada, east of San Francisco. Heavenly's base-town – South Lake Tahoe – is unlike any other resort we know. The Stateline area at its centre is dominated by four monstrous hotel-casinos (located just inches on the Nevada side of the line). These brash but comfortable hotels offer good-value accommodation (subsidised by the gambling) and big-name entertainment as well as slot machines, roulette wheels, craps and endless card games. They are a conspicuous part of the amazing lake views from the lower slopes (though not from above mid-mountain, nor on the Nevada side). The area around the casinos is strangely devoid of 'downtown' atmosphere (never mind mountain resort atmosphere); there are few bars or shops, and the centre is bisected by US Highway 50. The rest of the town consists of low-rise motels, stores, wedding chapels and so on, spreading for miles along this busy, pedestrian-hostile highway; many are

MOUNTAIN FACTS

Altitude 1995m-3060m
Lifts 26
Pistes 4800 acres
Green 20%
Blue 45%
Black 35%
Art. snow 500 acres

LIFT PASSES

96/97 prices in dollars
Heavenly
Covers all lifts on
Heavenly mountain.
Beginners 3-day learn
to ski packages
include lift, pass and
rental (adult 130).
Main pass
1-day pass 47
6-day pass 240
Senior citizens
Over 65: 6-day pass
102 (58% off)
Children
Under 13: 6-day pass
102 (58% off)
Under 5: free pass
Short-term passes
Half-day passes
available from 12.30
to 4pm (adult 30)
Notes Passes of three
days or more allow
one non-skiing day;
6-day pass valid for 7
days, with one non-
skiing day.

rather shabby, though this is partly camouflaged by the tall trees that surround most of them.

More than any other US resort, South Lake Tahoe is a place for the car-borne. Your base may be within walking distance of a bar, a restaurant or a shop, but don't count on it. The casinos run free shuttle-buses to pull people in to the Stateline area at night, but many of the best bars and restaurants are tucked out of the way.

The place as a whole is surprisingly downmarket. The casinos have some swanky restaurants, but are basically places where Californians and other gambling-starved Americans flock to feed their quarters into slot machines. The accommodation away from the centre is not particularly smart. But most of it conforms to American norms, and (except at weekends) all of it is under-used in winter, which is one reason why you can get cheap deals.

Access to the slopes is currently via any of three base stations which can easily be reached by road. The major one is California Lodge, on the outskirts of South Lake Tahoe, beside a huge car park, a mile out of town, up a heavily wooded slope. There are plans to build a gondola, starting close to the casinos (see What's New). Boulder and Stagecoach Base lodges lie around the mountain in Nevada. There are a dozen other areas within an hour's drive.

The mountain

Most of Heavenly's slopes suit intermediates down to the ground. But there are also good beginner slopes at the California base area, and some splendid easy runs to progress to, while experts can find some genuine challenges at the two extremes of the area – as well as lots of fun in acre upon acre of easy off-piste tree-covered terrain. Keep in mind that there are many other worthwhile areas within easy reach by car or bus (or paddle steamer!). You'll want to try at least a couple during your stay, as well as Heavenly – see page 425.

THE SLOPES
Interestingly complex

Heavenly's mountain is quite complicated, and getting from A to B requires more careful navigation than is usual in the US.

There is a clear division into the

California side (the lifts and runs directly above South Lake Tahoe) and the Nevada side (above Stagecoach Lodge and Boulder Lodge). The new lift for 1997/98 will create a welcome second route from California to Nevada, cutting out a boring traverse. On both sides, the terrain is complicated by ridges. There are no really easy runs on the Nevada side, apart from limited nursery slopes at the bottom.

Directly above California Lodge is a steep slope of around 520m vertical, with broad black pistes down the fall line and the narrower Roundabout blue trail snaking down. A mid-sized cable-car and two chairs go up to the first ridge, and all these lifts can be ridden down again by novices. Short, easy runs go from this ridge down into a narrow wooded valley which is the starting point of the blue Roundabout run as well as the base of two further chair-lifts. These serve a variety of runs, and give access to the main bowl on the California side, above the Sky Deck restaurant. The blue and black runs here are served by three chair-lifts, including the Sky Express high-speed quad.

The Sky Express chair makes the link with the Nevada side of the area, via the Skyline Trail catwalk. And the new six-seater Tamarack Express will take you directly to the Nevada skiing. On this side there are three main bowls. The central one, above East Peak Lodge, is an excellent intermediate area served by two fast quad chairs, with a downhill extension of the bowl served by the Galaxy chair. On one side of this central bowl is the steeper, open terrain of Milky Way Bowl, leading to the seriously steep Mott and Killebrew canyons, served by the Mott Canyon chair. On the other side of the central bowl is the North Bowl, leading down to Nevada's two base lodges.

SNOW RELIABILITY
Impressive artificial backup

Despite a ten-year average snowfall of 250 inches (matching that of many Colorado resorts), Heavenly suffered badly from drought in the early 90s. And it has not been unusual for the resort to go for many weeks without a heavy snowfall. That, no doubt, prompted it to install a very impressive snowmaking system that now covers 65% of the area and ensures that most

SCHOOLS/GUIDES

96/97 prices in dollars

Heavenly
Classes 5 days
2hr: from 10am, noon
or 2pm
6 half days, including
rental and pass: 260
Children's classes
Ages: 4 to 12
5 5hr 45mins days
including pass, rental
and lunch: 270
Private lessons
1hr, 2hr, 3hr and 6hr
62 for 1hr

sections remain open most of the time. The resort sometimes operates an irritating policy of closing off areas on Thursdays and Fridays to keep them fresh for the weekenders.

FOR EXPERTS
Some specific challenges

Although the area as a whole is better suited to intermediates, there are some genuine challenges for the more advanced. The runs under the California base lifts – The Face and Gunbarrel (often used for moguls competitions) – are of proper black steepness, and very testing when the snow is hard. Ellie's Run, at the top of the mountain, may offer continuous moguls too. But the really steep stuff is on the Nevada side. Milky Way Bowl offers a fairly gentle introduction to this terrain, which in most respects resembles European off-piste slopes. At the extremity of the bowl, the seriously steep Mott and Killebrew canyons are roped off, with defined gateways to steer the less expert to the lower gates and less steep slopes, and to keep people out when the crucial Mott Canyon chair-lift is closed.

All over the mountain, there is

excellent off-piste terrain among widely spaced trees, which offers tremendous fun when the conditions are right.

FOR INTERMEDIATES
Lots to do

Heavenly is excellent for intermediates, who are made to feel welcome and secure by excellent piste grooming and signposting. The California side offers a progression from the relaxed cruising of the long Ridge Run, starting right at the top of the mountain, to more testing blues dropping off the ridge towards the Sky Deck restaurant. The confident intermediate may want to spend more time on the Nevada side, where there is more variety of terrain and some long, quite testing runs down to the base stations and to the Galaxy chair.

FOR BEGINNERS
An excellent place to learn

The California side is more suited to beginners, with gentle green runs served by the Pioneer and Powder Bowl lifts at the top of the cable-car, and good nursery slopes at base lodge level. The snow is well groomed and therefore easy to learn on.

SOUTH LAKE TAHOE

Even South Lake Tahoe looks good in the evening light ➜

CHILDCARE

Children between 4 and 12 can enrol in the Snow Explorers school programme which offers skiing from age 4 and a snowboarding option from 8 upwards. It is an all-inclusive day of supervision, lessons, lunch, lift access, equipment and snacks. The programme is based at the extensive Children's Ski Centre at California Lodge (which includes an indoor play area) or at the Boulder Lodge Centre. There are also 'Tag-along' private lessons where a parent can tag-along and observe their child's progress.

FOR CROSS COUNTRY
A separate world

The Spooner Lake Cross Country Area located close to Tahoe is an extensive meadow area of over 100km in 21 prepared trails. There are ample facilities for both instruction and rental. Organised moonlit tours are a popular alternative to the noise and bright lights of the casinos.

QUEUES
Some at weekends

Lift lines are generally not a problem at Heavenly, except during some weekends and public holidays when the entire Tahoe area is swamped with weekenders and day trippers. The key lifts moving people out from the base lodges are fast, reliable and comfortable.

MOUNTAIN RESTAURANTS
Not many options

The limited choice for lunch includes two that can be recommended on the California side. At The Top of the Tram is a table-service restaurant (Monument Peak) which makes up for its simple food with a calm atmosphere and the famous lake view (reservations necessary). And the outdoor Sky Deck has an excellent barbecue, where Californian rock music blasts out and the cool dudes hang out. On the Nevada side, East Peak Lodge has a fair-sized terrace with interesting views over arid Nevada, but it gets hideously overcrowded when the weather drives people indoors. There's an Italian-themed place at Stagecoach Lodge, and a Tex-Mex at Boulder.

Further up the slopes, the high-rise hotels disappear from view, leaving only the lovely lake ➜

GETTING THERE

Air San Francisco, transfer 3½hr. Reno, transfer 75 mins. South Lake Tahoe, transfer 15 mins.

UK PACKAGES

American Dream, Crystal, Funway Holidays, Inghams, Ski Activity, Ski Independence, Ski North America Direct, Skisar U.S., Skiworld North America, United Vacations Ski Freedom USA, Virgin Snow

ACTIVITIES

Indoor 6 casinos, 6 cinemas, cheap factory shops, ice skating, bowling, gyms, spas, Western museum
Outdoor Boat cruises, snowmobiling, horse-drawn sleigh rides, horse riding, ice skating, hot springs, ghost town tours

TOURIST OFFICE

Postcode NV 89449
Tel +1 (702) 586 7000
Fax 588 5517

SCHOOLS AND GUIDES
Good attitude
The school offers a full range of services. Midweek classes can be small, and therefore very good value. As well as normal lessons they offer a variety of special clinics for moguls, steeps and 'snow of the day', for example. They also have special lessons on the new shaped or carving skis, which can be rented from the Rossignol Demo Centre.

FACILITIES FOR CHILDREN
We lack reports on the childcare arrangements, but they seem to be up to the usual high American standard.

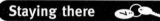

Staying there

When deciding where to stay, you need to give careful consideration to your plans for evening as well as daytime activity. If you have a car, your options are numerous; you could consider basing yourself out at one of the Nevada lift stations, and driving when you want entertainment. Night owls could scarcely do better than to stay in one of the casinos. Otherwise, stay away from the centre and try to tuck yourself away in the woods.

HOW TO GO
Hotel or motel?
Accommodation in the South Lake Tahoe area is both abundant and varied, ranging from the glossy casinos to small, rather ramshackle motels. Hotel and motel rooms are easy to find midweek, but can be sold out at busy weekends.
Hotels Caesars, Harrah's, Horizon and Harveys are the main casino hotels, in descending order of price. Rooms booked on the spot can be quite expensive; packages are good value.
((((④ **Embassy Suites** Luxury one-bedroom suites in a new, traditional-style building next to the casinos. We've had good reports on these.
(② **Tahoe Chalet Inn** Clean and friendly, close to casinos. Back rooms (away from busy highway) preferable.
(② **Best Western Timber Cove Lodge** Bland but well run, with lovely lake views from some rooms.
Self-catering There are lots of condominiums and chalets, with units ranging in size from one bedroom to four bedrooms or more. Some are available from tour operators.

Chalets Some good UK tour operator-run catered chalets have been introduced in the last few years including some lakeside ones.

EATING OUT
Good value
For those whose appetites are not diminished by the deafening ringing of hundreds of fruit machines, the casino hotels offer fantastic value in their buffet-style all-you-can-eat dining. They have some more ambitious 'gourmet' restaurants too – some high enough up their tower blocks to give superb lake views. Caesars casino has an in-house branch of Planet Hollywood. The sprawling resort area offers a great choice of international dining, from cosy little pizza houses to large, traditional American diners, Mexican tequila-and-tacos joints, and English and Irish pubs. We had excellent fish dishes at the New Dory's Oar).

APRES-SKI
Extraordinary
America's *Snow Country* magazine rates this area best in the US for nightlife, and it's easy to see why. What makes the area unique is the casinos on the Nevada side of the stateline. These aren't simply opportunities to throw money away on roulette or slot machines: top-name entertainers, pop and jazz stars, cabarets and Broadway revues are also to be found in them – designed to give gamblers another reason to stay. Other entertainments are also on offer – for example, 'hot buns' and 'tight jeans' competitions; Turtles, at the Embassy Suites, is the place for a bop to the latest hits; the Wild West Country Club has appropriate dancing.
   A more unusual way to spend the evening is to dance and dine your way across the lake aboard an authentic paddle steamer – not working in winter 1997 but due to re-open for 1997/98.

OFF THE SLOPES
Luck be a lady
There is little to enjoy apart from the casinos. Snowmobiling is available a short drive from South Lake Tahoe, and there are hot-air balloon rides. Pedestrians can use the cable-car to the Top of the Tram to walk in the surrounding area and view the lake and mountains below. When the sun is shining, it is a pleasant place to while away an afternoon.

Lake Tahoe

1890m

Slopes everywhere you look and magnificent lake views

WHAT IT COSTS

(((((5)

MOUNTAIN FACTS

Alpine Meadows

Altitude	2085m-2630m
Lifts	12
Pistes	2000 acres
Green	25%
Blue	40%
Black	35%
Art. snow	185 acres

Kirkwood

Altitude	2375m-2985m
Lifts	12
Pistes	2300 acres
Green	15%
Blue	50%
Black	35%
Art. snow	none

Northstar-at-Tahoe

Altitude	1930m-2625m
Lifts	12
Pistes	2220 acres
Green	25%
Blue	50%
Black	25%
Art. snow	200 acres

Squaw Valley

Altitude	1890m-2760m
Lifts	30
Pistes	4000 acres
Green	25%
Blue	45%
Black	30%
Art. snow	360 acres

UK PACKAGES

Chalet Snowboard, Crystal, Inghams, Ski Activity, Ski Independence, Skisar U.S., United Vacations Ski Freedom USA, Virgin Snow

Northstar-at-Tahoe
United Vacations Ski Freedom USA

Squaw Valley
Inghams, Ski Activity, Ski Independence, United Vacations Ski Freedom USA, Virgin Snow

---

Set high in the mountains 200 miles east of San Francisco, on the borders of California and Nevada, Lake Tahoe has the highest concentration of resorts in the US, with 14 downhill and seven cross-country centres. It is a very beautiful region, ideal for driving around on a tour, visiting a different area each day – as well as having two or three areas well worth spending several days exploring.

THE RESORTS

The slopes of the Lake Tahoe region are mostly just that – slopes, rather than fully fledged resorts with their own villages and vibrant nightlife. Some have no accommodation, others a little. But most of the areas earn their money from weekend or day-trippers from the local area, or from the big cities on the west coast.

Don't expect a 'resort' in the European sense of the word. And you may be surprised by the influence that gambling has in the area. The California–Nevada border cuts through the region and through Lake Tahoe itself. At the border you'll find a clutch of amazingly popular, bright, brash casinos. The biggest accommodation centre (and the biggest centre for gambling) is South Lake Tahoe – for a description of that, see the Heavenly chapter on page 420.

The next biggest resort is Squaw Valley – which has a limited amount of accommodation but little nightlife outside that. It is about a 90-minute drive from South Lake Tahoe; be sure to check whether the quickest route along the west bank of the lake is open – it's often shut at Emerald Bay due to avalanche danger.

Apart from those two, you'll find lots of B&Bs and motels dotted around the lake, and a couple of quite pleasant small towns.

THE MOUNTAINS

The choice of **slopes** to visit is enormous, with more than enough to keep even the keenest skier or boarder happy for a couple of weeks. You just need to be prepared to drive around to the different resorts. We once stayed at Squaw Valley for three days and were unable to use Squaw at all in that time because of the amount of snow falling. But we were able to go to other nearby areas which were more sheltered. And we had a great day at

Squaw a few days later by driving from our next lodgings at Heavenly.

The record for **snow reliability** isn't as good around here as in many other US resorts. But the area does have huge amounts of artificial snowmaking capacity, so lack of snow shouldn't be a problem.

Heavenly, at the southern end of the lake, has the greatest vertical drop of the region, with slopes to suit all standards and splendid lake views. See page 420 for more details.

Nearby **Sierra-at-Tahoe** is a smaller, tree-lined area – more sheltered, so useful in bad weather.

Kirkwood, also at the south end of the lake, is renowned for its steep runs – wonderful and uncrowded on powder days. It has fine intermediate groomed trails too (which in total account for 50 per cent of its area).

The major resort at the north end of the lake is **Squaw Valley**. It is unusual in having no named runs at all – and no trails marked on the piste map, just blue squares and black diamonds. The area is 4,000 acres of open, above-the-treeline bowls on six linked mountains.

The possibilities for experts are phenomenal, with lots of steep slopes, chutes and big mogul fields – many extreme skiing and boarding movies are made here. It is good for intermediates too, with lovely long groomed blue runs including a top-to-bottom three-mile cruise – 45 per cent of the terrain is rated as suitable for intermediates. Squaw is a big snowboarding centre and at night the half-pipe and run (for skiers too) down from mid-mountain is floodlit.

Alpine Meadows has the longest season and some of the most varied terrain in the Tahoe region – snow conditions can still be good in July some years. This area is excellent for all standards, with green runs and nursery slopes at the bottom, top-to-bottom blues and some varied blacks,

TOURIST OFFICE

Alpine Meadows

Postcode CA 96145
Tel +1 (916) 583 4232
Fax 583 0963

Kirkwood

Postcode CA 95646
Tel +1 (209) 258 6000
Fax 258 8899

Northstar-at-Tahoe

Postcode CA 96160
Tel +1 (916) 562 1010
Fax 562 2215

Squaw Valley

Postcode CA 96146
Tel +1 (916) 583 6985
Fax 581 7106

including high bowls and tree-covered terrain. The mountain has slopes facing in all directions, giving good conditions whatever the weather.

Northstar-at-Tahoe is a fairly small, almost entirely beginner and intermediate mountain close to Squaw. Although there are black runs marked on the trail map, none is seriously steep and the nine or so blacks on the back (served by a single high-speed quad) vary little in character and are really good long advanced intermediate cruises. Again, the area is very sheltered and good for bad weather days. There's a pleasant shopping, restaurant and bar area at the bottom of the mountain, with very convenient hotel rooms and condominiums. It would be a good family choice of a quiet place to stay.

Those are the six areas we'd most recommend visiting. But there are eight other areas in the Tahoe region in case you get bored, most of which are marked on our map. There are also **cross-country** possibilities at most of the downhill areas as well as in dedicated cross-country areas.

Queues are rare in all the areas, except at peak weekends when people pour in from San Francisco and Los Angeles. We have few reports of the **schools** or facilities for **children**, but have no reason to believe that they fall short of the generally excellent standards of other US resorts.

STAYING THERE

We'd recommend spending a few days at each end of the lake.

At the southern end there's little alternative to staying in the brash and rather tacky town of South Lake Tahoe – for more detail see our Heavenly chapter on page 420.

At the northern end there's more choice. Squaw Valley has three hotels, of which the Lodge at Squaw Creek is the biggest and most luxurious. It is huge, and often full of guests at conferences and seminars that allow them time off. It is out of town, with its own lift into the area and a piste back. It has all the facilities you'd expect – pools, hot tubs with great mountain views, spacious rooms, a few shops and a couple of bars. The cable-car itself runs in the evenings to serve the floodlit slopes and the dining facilities at the High Camp Bath and Tennis Club at the top. This is an incredible mid-mountain base, with several restaurants and bars, outdoor pool, ice skating, tennis and bungy jumping. There are plans to build a pedestrian-only resort at the bottom of the slopes – which would massively increase Squaw's attraction for a week's stay.

An alternative is to stay in the small town of Tahoe City, right on the lake, a short drive from both the Squaw Valley and Alpine Meadows areas. It has a fair number of hotels and bars, and some good restaurants. We liked Jake's– popular with locals, airy wooden decor, lake views and excellent modern American cooking.

There are also plenty of motels and condominiums dotted around the lakeside road.

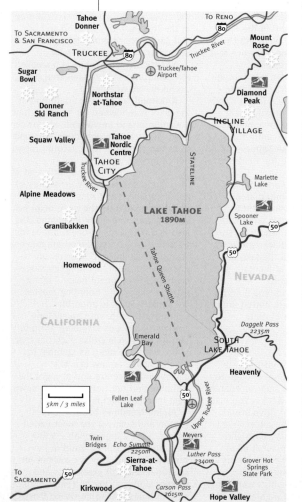

Mammoth Mountain — 2430m

Californian sun and snow with extensive, varied terrain

WHAT IT COSTS

(((((5)

HOW IT RATES

The slopes

Snow	****
Extent	***
Experts	****
Intermediates	****
Beginners	****
Convenience	**
Queues	****
Restaurants	*

The rest

Scenery	***
Resort charm	**
Off-slope	*

MOUNTAIN FACTS

Altitude	2430m-3370m
Lifts	29
Pistes	3500 acres
Green	30%
Blue	40%
Black	30%
Art. snow	300 acres
Recco detectors used	

➕ One of North America's biggest and best areas

➕ Can get a lot of snow – and there's extensive snowmaking

➕ Very extensive steep bowls at the top of the lift system

➕ Plenty of easy/intermediate cruising runs lower down, in the trees

➕ Good children's facilities

➕ Extensive, well kept, snowsure cross-country trails

➕ Amazingly cheap package holidays

➖ Mammoth Lakes is a rather diffuse place, lacking resort atmosphere and awkward if you don't have a car

➖ Most accommodation is miles from the slopes

➖ Weekend crowds from Los Angeles

➖ No mountain restaurants worth mentioning

➖ Poor trail map, especially for upper mountain

➖ Upper runs can be icy and windblown

Mammoth lives up to its name, more or less. It may not be a giant area in Alpine terms, but it is much bigger than most in the US, and big enough to provide a week's amusement for most people. It has everything from steep, high, experts-only chutes and bowls (with magnificent views) to long, easy cruising runs in the trees. During the week the slopes are often almost deserted. And on busy days you can always try Mammoth's smaller sister resort, June Mountain, a short drive away.

The resort currently lacks a cosy slope-side village – but that should change over the next few years. And it is something we guess most British visitors will put up with if they're paying bargain package prices.

boarding Mammoth set out long ago to attract the snowboarding crowd off the surfing beaches near LA, initially to its sister mountain June, where there's a good fun-park and half-pipe. But there's now also a fun-park and pipe near the main gondola on Mammoth Mountain and a specialist board shop and section of the school. And the slopes are ideal for all standards, with gnarly riding in the high bowls and perfect beginner and intermediate runs below. The lifts are almost exclusively chairs or gondolas and one of us had a great time here as an early intermediate boarder on the wide Stump Alley and Bowling Alley runs. There are some snowboard-friendly bars in town, lively at weekends.

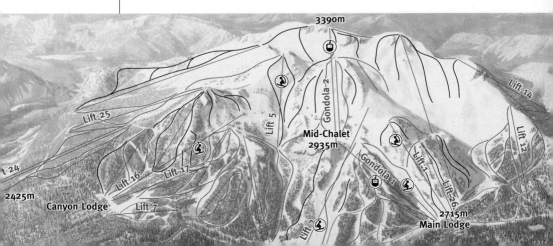

What's new

Three new high-speed quads are replacing three existing lifts – chairs 2 and 5 and the T-bar serving the racecourse. The fun-park and half-pipe will be floodlit for night boarding with loud music piped in. And there will be a new restaurant and floodlit tubing hill (you slide down on an inner tube – great fun) near the base of lift 2.

In the longer term, a much-needed pedestrian village will be developed at Juniper Ridge near chairs 15 and 24.

LIFT PASSES

96/97 prices in dollars
Mammoth Mountain
Covers all lifts at Mammoth.
Beginners 1- (63), 2- (144) and 3-day (235) learn-to-ski packages include pass, lessons and rental.
Main pass
1-day pass 45
6-day pass 229
Senior citizens
Over 65: 6-day pass 115 (50% off)
Children
Under 13: 6-day pass 115 (50% off)
Under 7: free pass
Short-term passes
Scenic ride on Mammoth Gondola (adult 10); afternoon pass available (adult 35).
Notes Main pass also covers the 8 lifts at June Mountain, 30km away. 13- to 18-year-olds get a discount on pass (6-day 172). Passes of over 2 days allow for one non-skiing day – 5-day pass is valid for 6 days, with one non-skiing day.

The resort

Most people stay in Mammoth Lakes, a small year-round resort town four miles from the slopes, and linked to them by efficient shuttle-buses. It sprawls along the very wide road (called Main Street) leading towards the slopes, and one or two major side-roads. Hotels, bars, restaurants and little shopping centres with well-stocked shops line the roadside – but it's not the place for a relaxing stroll. Mammoth may be short on resort ambience, but its setting among trees and its not unattractive buildings give a pleasant enough appearance. Even the ubiquitous McDonald's has been tastefully designed. The 'village' is usually under a blanket of snow, which also helps.

There is accommodation (but not much else) at the main base area – the Mammoth Mountain Inn complex. And along the road up to the slopes lie several hotels and condos. Shuttle-buses are efficient, but a car is useful, especially for getting to June Mountain for a change of scenery. There are ambitious plans by Intrawest (which has also developed other resorts) to build an attractive pedestrian village with accommodation, bars, restaurants and shops near the base of Chairs 12 and 24 – which will transform the attraction of Mammoth as a week-long destination in the longer-term.

The five- or six-hour drive up from Los Angeles, along a very good road, is spectacular. You pass through the San Bernardino mountains and Mojave Desert before reaching the Sierra Nevada range, of which Mammoth is part. Alternatively you can fly into Mammoth's own airport.

The mountain

Although Mammoth is one of America's largest areas, the resort's claim to have 150 trails should not be taken too seriously. The slightest variant of a run is given a separate name and number. Nevertheless, the 30 or so lifts access an impressive single area suitable for all standards. The highest runs are almost exclusively steep powder bowls and chutes, most of which are for experts only. In general, the lower down you go the easier the terrain.

Finding your way around is something else. The lifts are known by numbers allocated as they were built,

so the system has no geographic logic. Chair 26 is between chairs 1 and 19 and next to chair 11, and so on. And the trail map shows trails by means of occasional symbols, not continuous lines, which makes it difficult to see where a particular run takes you. But in the end it doesn't matter a lot: head downhill, and you'll eventually come to a lift. And if you get lost, there's a fair chance you'll come across a member of the helpful mountain host service.

Mammoth's area is still majority owned and actively run by its founder, Dave McCoy, who built the first lift here in the 1940s. Many people told him at the outset that it was too high, too remote and too stormy here to make it as a resort, so he is naturally proud that his dream of developing the inhospitable mountains of the area into one of America's top resorts has been turned into reality.

THE SLOPES
It's all here
There are three major lift-stations at regular intervals along the foot of the slopes, which mainly face north-east. An isolated fourth is also reachable by shuttle-bus.

The main base area, the **Main Lodge,** at the far end, has the biggest choice of lifts, including a gondola and a high-speed chair. These both connect with other lifts taking you straight to Mammoth's highest slopes.

At the centre of the area is Mid Chalet, the site of a huge restaurant and the mid-station of the gondola from Main Lodge, the second stage of which goes on up to the highest point of the area, at 3370m. The views from the top are splendid, with Nevada to the north-east and the jagged Minarets to the west.

From the top, there are essentially three ways down. The first, on which there are countless variations (including 15 shown on the trail map), is down the front of the mountain, which ranges from steep to very steep – or vertical if the wind has created a cornice, as it often does. The second is off the back, down to **Chair 14 Outpost,** whence chair 14 or 13 bring you back to lower points on the ridge. The third is to follow the ridge down to the Main Lodge area – a route that can hardly be detected on the idiotic trail map. This route brings you past an easy area served by chair 12, and a very easy area by chairs 11 and 27.

Main Lodge has an array of other lifts fanning out over the mountain. One of them links to a triple chair for speedy access to the summit ridge.

Mid Chalet can also be reached from **Chair 2 Outpost**, on the road up from town. Other lifts from here take you into the more heavily forested eastern half of the area – long, gentle runs served by lifts up from **Canyon Lodge** and **Chair 15 Outpost**, both on the fringe of town, and seriously steep stuff on the subsidiary peak, served by lifts 25 and 22.

A separate ski area called **June Mountain** is 30 minutes' drive away and is covered by the lift pass.

SNOW RELIABILITY
A long season
Mammoth has an impressive snow record, and, thanks to its height and its snowmakers, it enjoys a long season – opening as late as 4 July in many seasons. But the upper mountain can get icy and windswept – in both our and reporters' experiences.

FOR EXPERTS
Some very challenging terrain
The steep bowls that run the width of the mountain top provide wonderful opportunities for experts but the snow can suffer from high winds and it can be difficult to find your way around because of the inadequate piste map and marking. The steep chutes either side of Chair 22 are also very challenging, and being relatively sheltered, are often open in bad weather when the top is firmly shut. Above Main Lodge is another steep area ideal for the expert. A quiet little bowl behind the main mountain plunges down to Chair 14 Outpost. Many of the lower trails are short, by European standards, but can easily be repeated. And you can go virtually from top to bottom all day entirely on black runs. There are plenty of couloirs to try, some only for the very brave.

FOR INTERMEDIATES
Lots of great cruising
Mammoth's piste maintenance is such that intermediates can use runs they might consider too steep in European resorts where bumps are allowed to build up. And there is plenty for all standards of intermediate.

Some of the mountain's longest runs, served by Chairs 9 and 25, are ideal for good intermediates. There are

also a couple of lovely, fairly steep, tree-lined pistes running the length of Chair 10 down to Chair 2 Outpost.

Many of the tree-lined runs above Chair 15 Outpost and Hut 2 are flattering, while the piste between Mid Chalet and Chair 2 Outpost is the one real motorway on the mountain.

The less adventurous have some good, wide runs through trees in the triangle between Main Lodge, Chair 2 Outpost and Mid Chalet.

FOR BEGINNERS
Good tuition
Nursery slopes are adequate, and the excellence of tuition, piste grooming and snow quality usually makes progress very speedy. Hansel and Gretel are a couple of very easy pistes through the trees above Canyon Lodge.

FOR CROSS-COUNTRY
Very popular
Two specialist centres, Tamarack and Sierra Meadows, provide tuition and tours. There are 70km of well maintained trails, including some winding through the beautiful Lakes Basin area, and miles of pretty ungroomed tracks through forests.

QUEUES
Weekend invasions
During the week the lifts and slopes are usually very quiet, with no queues. But even the efficient lift system can struggle to cope with 15,000 visitors arriving from LA on fine weekends. That's the time to try June Mountain.

MOUNTAIN RESTAURANTS
Singular and inadequate
The only mid-mountain restaurant is at the mid-station of the gondola – a giant cafeteria lacking charm, atmosphere and interesting food. The Canyon Lodge cafeteria has been recommended for good 'home-made' style soups and the sundeck at Chair 14 Outpost for the barbecue and reggae music. For a civilised lunch go to the Yodler at Main Lodge.

SCHOOLS AND GUIDES
Excellent reports – mostly
Mammoth has a high reputation for tuition but we've had a report of ten in a class – large by US standards. We had a great snowboarding lesson here (from a Scotsman!). For experts and seniors there are some special once-a-month camps (eg steep terrain).

SCHOOLS/GUIDES
96/97 prices in dollars
Mammoth Mountain
Classes 7 days
4hr: 10am-noon and 1.30-3.30; 2hr: am or pm
5 full days: 194
Children's classes
Ages: 4 to 12
5 full days including lunch: 335
Private lessons
1hr, 3hr or 6hr
60 for 1hr; each additional person 10

CHILDCARE
Children's classes are handled by the Woollywood Ski and Snowboard School at the Main Lodge, which 'interfaces' with Small World Child Care (934 0646) based at the nearby Mammoth Mountain Inn. Small World Child Care takes children from newborn to age 12, from 8am to 5pm.

GETTING THERE

Air Los Angeles, transfer 5hr. Reno, transfer 3hr. Mammoth Lakes, transfer 20 minutes.

UK PACKAGES

American Dream, Crystal, Funway Holidays, Inghams, Ski Activity, Ski Independence, Skisar U.S., Skiworld North America, United Vacations Ski Freedom USA, Virgin Snow

ACTIVITIES

Indoor Mammoth museum, art galleries, theatre
Outdoor Snowmobiling, ski touring, bobsleigh, dog-sledding, tobogganing, sleigh rides, hot air balloon rides, snow shoe tours

TOURIST OFFICE

Postcode CA 93546
Tel +1 (760) 934 0745
Fax 934 0603

You have a choice of perfect corduroy (foreground) or steep and deep (background) ↓

FACILITIES FOR CHILDREN
Family favourite

Mammoth is keen to attract families. Children have a very caring Woollywood school which works closely with the nearby nursery. We've had one particularly glowing report of a 3-year-old who had 'a great time' in the Small World nursery and had a private lesson one day which was a big success: 'she came back with a huge smile'.

Staying there 🔑

Staying near Main Lodge is most convenient for the slopes. But there's a much greater choice of bars and restaurants in town, and the efficient, free shuttle-bus service means getting to and from the slopes is easy.

HOW TO GO
Good value packages

There's a good choice of hotels and condos. Condos tend to be either out near the lifts or along the road to them, rather than in town.
Hotels There's a wide choice but none especially luxurious or expensive.
(((4 Mammoth Mountain Inn Motel/hotel/condo complex at the foot of the slopes. Comfortable and spacious bedrooms, but rather gloomy public rooms.
((3 Quality Inn Good, main street hotel with the biggest hot tub in town. Shuttle-bus outside.
((3 Alpenhof Lodge Comfortable and friendly, in central location. Well liked by reporters. Shuttle and plenty of restaurants nearby.
((3 Jagerhof Lodge British-run, friendly; much praised by reporters. At the edge of town on bus route. Restaurants close by.
Self-catering The 1849 condos are spacious and well equipped and decorated, with the Canyon Lodge base-station only a couple of minutes' walk. The Mammoth Ski and Racquet Club, a 10-minute walk from the same lifts, are very comfortable. The Summit and Timber Ridge condos are similarly convenient though less luxurious. Meadowridge, 400m from chairs 15 and 24, is recommended by a reporter (but you need a car).

EATING OUT
Outstanding choice

There are over 50 restaurants in town, dotted around over a wide area. They cater for most tastes and pockets – Japanese, Chinese, Mexican, Italian, Cajun, steak, seafood. We had delicious dinners at Nevado's and Skadi (both 'modern American' food). Other good places are the atmospheric Slocum's, lively Whiskey Creek and Stonehouse Brewery. The Yodler does good hearty food at the Main Lodge area. Roberto's does Mexican food; the Shogun Japanese (and Karaoke). Angel's, Perry's and Grumpy's have been recommended by reporters. Schat's Bakery on the main street does delicious breakfasts and pastries.

APRES-SKI
Lively at weekends

The liveliest immediate après-ski spot is the Yodler, at the Main Lodge base area – a Swiss chalet, transported across the Atlantic. There is a pleasant evening sleigh-ride and dinner trip, but nightlife is essentially bars which come to life at weekends. Whiskey Creek has rock 'n roll and country and western bands and gets packed. Slocum's is popular with locals; Rafters has live entertainment; and Gringo's does the best margaritas in town. The Cellar has an especially good selection of beers.

OFF THE SLOPES
Mainly sightseeing

There is surprisingly little to do off the slopes except shop and sightsee by car. Sights include the pretty Mono Lake, the beautiful Yosemite National Park, and the Sequoia and Kings Canyon National Parks. Bear in mind that some of these trips will not be possible in midwinter. There's also a gold-mining ghost-town to visit. There are some diverting clothes shops, but Mammoth is essentially only a place for those keen to use the slopes.

Colorado

Colorado was the first US state to market its resorts internationally and is still the most popular American destination for UK visitors. And justifiably so. To our mind it has the most alluring combination of attractive resorts, slopes to suit all standards and excellent, reliable snow – dry enough to justify its 'champagne powder' label.

But you need to choose your resort carefully because they vary enormously both in the amount and variety of slopes on offer and in the character of the villages themselves. While the old parts of Telluride and Crested Butte are two of the dinkiest former Wild West towns around, they offer very limited terrain compared with purpose-built, mock-Tyrolean Vail and glitzy Aspen, for example. And some resorts have easy access to other major mountains nearby, while others are rather isolated.

For 1997/98 new non-stop charter flights from the UK to Denver will make Colorado resorts more easily accessible once again. The best alternative option for some resorts is to fly in to Eagle Vail.

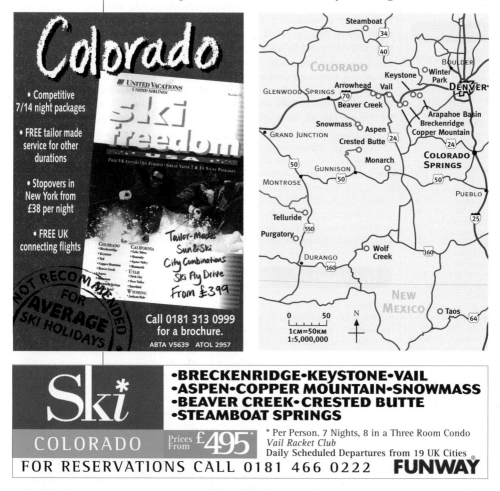

Aspen   2420m

Charming old town with four great mountains

WHAT IT COSTS

((((((6)

HOW IT RATES

The slopes

Snow	★★★★★
Extent	★★★★
Experts	★★★★
Intermediates	★★★★★
Beginners	★★★★★
Convenience	★★
Queues	★★★★
Restaurants	★★★

The rest

Scenery	★★★
Resort charm	★★★★
Off-slope	★★★★

What's new

A couple of seasons ago a new Two Creeks base lodge for the Snowmass area was opened, giving quicker access to the Snowmass slopes from Aspen.

For 1997/98 the existing Ruthie's lift on Aspen mountain will be replaced by the first high-speed two-person chair-lift in the US – the idea is to double the capacity but not overcrowd the slope. On Snowmass, a new button-lift will take people from Big Burn to the top of the Cirque, an area previously accessible only by snowcat or hiking. This will be the highest lift-served terrain in the US (3812m) and gives Snowmass the biggest vertical drop in the US (1342m).

- ➕ Extensive terrain to suit all standards
- ➕ Gets better every season, with new lifts opening up more good slopes
- ➕ Attractive, characterful old town, with lots of tempting shops
- ➕ Good for celebrity-spotting
- ➕ Lively, varied nightlife
- ➕ Slope-side accommodation at Snowmass

- ➖ Four separate mountains
- ➖ Rather sprawling town, so choice of accommodation important
- ➖ Can be very expensive (although certainly doesn't have to be)

Aspen is our favourite US resort and it certainly has a lot going for it. Its four mountains between them offer enough to keep people of every standard interested. It has a good snow record and the biggest vertical drop in the US. The town is a beautifully restored Victorian silver-mining town, with wide streets built in typical American grid fashion and a huge variety of restaurants, bars and plush shops. And the resort doesn't rest on its laurels – it is always devising new attractions and building new high-speed quads.

This year we've heard from more reporters about Aspen than any other US resort, and they were unanimous in their verdict – superb and surprisingly affordable. Of course, the resort has many rich and famous guests, lots of whom have holiday homes here and private jets parked at the local airport. But don't let that put you off. Most celebs are keen to keep a low profile.

boarding *Aspen has great snowboarding for every standard. Although Aspen Mountain in the centre of town bans snowboarding, the other three mountains welcome it wholeheartedly and there's a fun-park on Buttermilk and a half-pipe on Snowmass. 13–27 year-olds get a great deal on lift passes – $39 a day rather than $56 last season. All four mountains are served almost entirely by chairs or gondolas. Snowmass and Aspen Highlands both have some gnarly boarding for experts, while Snowmass is ideal for intermediate cruising and confidence building. Beginners should head for Buttermilk. With a good-sized boarding community, some of the bars can be quite entertaining at night.*

The resort

Just over a century ago Aspen was a booming silver-mining town of 12,000 inhabitants, boasting six newspapers, an opera house and a red light district. But Aspen's fortunes took a nose-dive when the silver price plummeted in 1893, and by the 1930s the population had shrunk to 400 or so. Elegant Victorian buildings – such as the Wheeler Opera House and the Hotel Jerome – had fallen into disrepair.

Aspen is a compact town with a typical American grid of streets. The historic centre has been beautifully renovated to form the core of what is now the most fashionable snow town in the Rockies. There's a huge variety of shops, bars, restaurants and galleries – some amazingly up-market, with prices to match. Spreading out from this centre, you'll find a mixture of developments, ranging from the homes of the super-rich on the outskirts to the mobile homes for the workers who now find it too expensive to buy or rent in Aspen.

Twelve miles away is Snowmass, with its own mountain and modern accommodation right on the slopes.

Day-trips to other resorts are rather a long slog, but a two-centre holiday is easily arranged.

MOUNTAIN FACTS

Altitude 2400m-3600m
Lifts 41
Pistes 4285 acres
Green 13%
Blue 44%
Black 43%
Art. snow 566 acres
Recco detectors used

LIFT PASSES

96/97 prices in dollars
Four Mountain Pass
Covers Aspen
Mountain, Aspen
Highlands, Buttermilk
and Snowmass, and
shuttle bus between
the areas.
Beginners Included in
price of beginners'
lessons; 149 for 3-day
learn-to-ski or
snowboard lessons.
Main pass
1-day pass 56
6-day pass 296
(low season 234 –
21% off)
Senior citizens
Over 65: 6-day pass
236 (20% off)
Over 70: free pass
Children
Under 18: 6-day pass
198 (33% off)
Under 7: free pass
Notes All passes of 2
days and over are
valid for a 10 day
period, eg 6 day pass
valid for 10 days, with
4 non-skiing days.
Alternative passes
Premier Passport is
designed for two-
centre holidays.
Covers all Aspen and
Vail and one-
way transfer between
the resorts. Allows
from 10 days skiing
out of 12 up to 18 out
of 21.

The mountains

Aspen has lots for every standard; you just have to pick the right mountain.

THE SLOPES
Widely dispersed

There are four mountains, only one accessible from Aspen town.

Development started in Aspen on a small scale in the late 1930s. The first lift (then the world's longest chair-lift) was opened shortly after the Second World War, and Aspen hasn't looked back since. By 1958, development of Buttermilk and Aspen Highlands had started. Snowmass opened in 1967.

Getting around between the areas by free bus is easy. Each area is big enough to keep you amused for a full day. And all of them have regular free guided tours.

The Silver Queen gondola takes you from right in the heart of town to the top of **Aspen Mountain** in 15 minutes. The alternative – to take three chair-lifts – is only worth considering if the queues are horrific for the gondola. A series of chairs serves the different ridges – Gentleman's Ridge along the eastern edge, the Ridge of Bell in the centre, and Ruthie's to the west – with valleys or gulches in between. There are no green runs at all. In general, there are long cruising blue runs along the valley floors and short steep blacks down from the ridges. The mountain is ideal for good intermediates or better.

Snowmass is an entirely separate resort some 12 miles west of Aspen. though there's now access via the relatively new Two Creeks base much nearer to Aspen. Snowmass is the largest of Aspen's areas – some 2,500 acres in all – fanning out from the purpose-built village at the base. Chair-lifts head off towards four separate peaks, the slopes of which are all interlinked. From left to right looking at the mountain, these are Elk Camp, High Alpine, Big Burn (named after the fire started by Ute Indians protesting against the mining that was ruining their terrain) and Sam's Knob. Many of the runs are wide, sweeping, and perfectly groomed, providing relaxing and scenic highways. But it also has some of the toughest terrain in the whole area.

Buttermilk – said to be the closest area to an airport in the world – is famous as a learning mountain,

although a fair proportion of the runs would suit intermediates too.

The runs fan out from the top in three directions. West Buttermilk, with long, gentle runs through the woods, is ideal for beginners, as is the Main Buttermilk area (though this also has some good intermediate runs); Tiehack, to the east, is a bit more demanding, but ideal for an intermediate to learn to use mogul, powder or tree-lined runs.

Aspen Highlands was, until 1993, separately owned and run, and famous for its slow and antiquated lifts. It is now run by the Aspen Skiing Company, and they have installed two successive high-speed quad chair-lifts that whisk you to the top in under 20 minutes – half the time it used to take. There is a strange mixture of tough blacks runs and easy greens and blues. And the views from the top are the best that Aspen has to offer – the famous Maroon Bells that appear on all the scenic postcards.

SNOW RELIABILITY
Never a problem

Aspen has a good natural snow record. In addition, all areas except Snowmass have substantial snowmaking capabilities. Immaculate grooming adds to the quality of the pistes.

FOR EXPERTS
Buttermilk is the only soft stuff

There's plenty to choose from – all the mountains except for Buttermilk offer lots of challenges.

Aspen Mountain has a formidable array of double black diamond runs. From the top of the Silver Queen gondola, try Walsh's, Hyrup's or Kristi, linking up with Gentleman's Ridge and Jackpot for a combination of steep slopes, moguls and trees – the longest black run on the mountain. Or head for the Ridge of Bell – and a chance to show off your mogul skills to those going up in the chair or gondola. Don't miss the expert tree and bump slopes running off the International into Spar Gulch – these are collectively called the Dumps, because they were formed out of slag and rubble dumped by the miners back in the silver-mining days. There are numerous other black challenges too – 65 per cent of the trails are black.

At Snowmass, our favourite area was around the Hanging Valley Wall and Glades – beautiful scenery and

wonderful tree-covered slopes, and steep enough everywhere to satisfy the keenest – well worth the short hike. The highest terrain of The Cirque area will be served by a drag-lift from the 1997/98 season; it is for the brave only and mainly above the tree-line, with steep, narrow, often rocky, chutes – Gowdy's is one of the steepest in the whole area, AMF ('Adios My Friend') speaks for itself. The runs back down under the High Alpine lift offer cruising, bumps and tree-lined runs within a small area. And, lower down, there's a network of long black trails down from Sam's Knob.

At Aspen Highlands, there are challenging runs from top to bottom of the mountain. At the top the Steeplechase area consists of a number of parallel natural avalanche chutes, and their elevation means the snow stays light and dry. The Olympic Bowl area, served by Chair 5, has great views of the Maroon Bells peaks and some serious moguls. Last time we were there we had a fantastic time in fresh chest-deep powder on runs we wouldn't have tackled in their normal state. Chair 8 takes you to more moguls. Chair 6 serves a nice varied area – you can cream down Thunderbowl, practice bumps on Powderbowl and enjoy good snow on the little-used Limelight.

FOR INTERMEDIATES
Grooming to die for

Snowmass is the best mountain for intermediates and the Big Burn is definitely the first place to head for. The huge open area is a cruising paradise. The runs merge into each other, though there's a satisfying variety of terrain and some trees to add interest. The easiest intermediate slopes are reached from the Elk Camp lift. There's a choice of runs from the top, through spruce trees. Naked Lady lift gives you access to yet more intermediate slopes – a little trickier and more varied including some moguls. The Sam's Knob sector offers slightly more advanced challenges. Finally, Green Cabin, accessed from the top of the High Alpine lift, is a magical intermediate run cruising from top to bottom of the mountain, with spectacular views on the way.

Most intermediate runs in Aspen

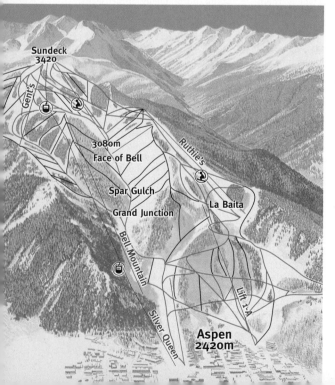

Sundeck
3420

Gent's

3080m
Face of Bell

Ruthie's

Spar Gulch

La Baita

Grand Junction

Bell Mountain

Silver Queen

Lift 1-A

Aspen
2420m

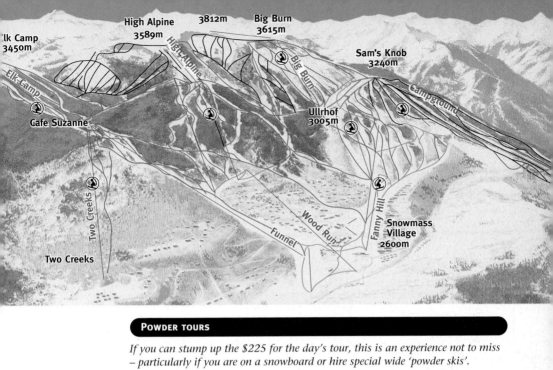

POWDER TOURS

If you can stump up the $225 for the day's tour, this is an experience not to miss – particularly if you are on a snowboard or hire special 'powder skis'.

Your day starts with you signing a form which relieves the Aspen Skiing Company of all responsibility for your safety and welfare, before you climb into the Silver Queen gondola just after 8am (while it is still shut to the rest of the public). At the top you are armed with an avalanche transceiver and instructed on how to search out your lost colleagues should they be buried under an avalanche. You then pile into a ten-passenger heated snow-cat and are driven off onto the 'backside' of Aspen Mountain. Away from the lifts and other skiers, your two guides search out untracked snow – there's 1500 acres to choose from.

The cat rejoins you at the end of each run and takes you off for the next. You're likely to squeeze in about 10 runs in all. At midday, you stop for a better-than-average buffet lunch at an old mountain cabin.

SCHOOLS/GUIDES

96/97 prices in dollars

Aspen Skiing Company
Snowmass and Buttermilk for all abilities; Aspen Mountain and Aspen Highlands for intermediate and advanced only

Classes 5 days
5hr: 10am-3pm; 2½hr: 10am-12.30 or 12.45-3.15
3 full days: 145

Children's classes
Ages: 6 to 12
5 5hr 45min min days: 280

Private lessons
half- or full-day
270 for half-day

Highlands are above the mid-mountain Merry-Go-Round restaurant. The most popular slope, Scarlet's Run, is directly above it. Grand Prix is a wide cruiser between trees – but watch out for the path to the right taking you back to mid-mountain, otherwise you hit a double black diamond run. Beyond Grand Prix, you can reach Picnic Point via Upper Robinson's – a table and views make it a good place to pause.

Aspen Mountain has its fair share of intermediate slopes, but they tend to be tougher than on the other mountains. Copper Bowl and Spar Gulch running between the ridges making up Aspen Mountain are great cruises early in the morning but can get crowded later. Upper Aspen Mountain, at the top of the Silver Queen gondola, has a dense network of well-groomed blues. Ruthie's has more cruising runs and less in the way of crowds. Ruthie's Run leads into the popular Snow Bowl, a wide, open area with moguls on the left but groomed on the right and centre. Buttermilk may not be the obvious choice for intermediates – yet it has quite a lot going for it. The Main Buttermilk runs offer good, easy slopes to practise on. And good intermediates should be able to handle the relatively easy black runs in the Tiehack area and gain the confidence to progress to the somewhat tougher black pistes on other mountains.

FOR BEGINNERS
Can be a great place to learn
Buttermilk is a great mountain for beginners, whether tackling skiing or snowboarding (banned on Aspen Mountain). West Buttermilk has

beautifully groomed, gentle and tree-lined runs – ideal for building up confidence. The easiest slope of all, though, is found in the central Main Buttermilk sector – Panda Peak.

The easiest beginner slope at Snowmass is the wide Assay Hill, at the bottom of the Elk Camp area. Right next to Snowmass Village Mall is the Fanny Hill high-speed lift and beginners' run of the same name. Further up, from Sam's Knob, a series of runs offer a long, gentle cruise.

Despite its mighty vertical rise, Aspen Highlands boasts the highest concentration of beginners' runs in Aspen, located below the Merry-Go-Round restaurant. Right by the base area, Chair 9 serves Half Inch – the easiest beginners' slope. The biggest problem is meeting up with more experienced friends for lunch – they may be on a different mountain.

FOR CROSS-COUNTRY
Back-country bonanza
There are 80km of groomed trails between Aspen and Snowmass in the Roaring Fork Valley – the most extensive maintained cross-country system in the US. And the Ashcroft Ski Touring Centre maintains around 30km of trails around Ashcroft, a mining ghost-town. Take the opportunity of eating at the Pine Creek Cookhouse, some 2.5km from the Ashcroft trailhead: excellent food and accessible by ski, board or sledge only. In addition, there are limitless miles of ungroomed trails. Aspen is at one end of the famous 230-mile Tenth Mountain Division Trail, heading north-east and almost linking up to Vail, with 13 huts for overnight stops.

24 HOURS OF ASPEN

Every year in November or December, Aspen kicks off its season with an amazing 24-hour-long race, lasting from 12 noon one day until 12 noon the next. Pairs of skiers from different nations continuously ride up the Silver Queen gondola to the top of Aspen Mountain (a 14-minute ride) and ski down as fast as possible (generally 2min 15secs to 2min 30secs).The winners usually complete around 80 runs, hitting top speeds of over 90mph, skiing a total distance of over 200 miles and a vertical drop equivalent to nine runs down Mount Everest.
Eating, drinking, massaging weary limbs and carrying out normal bodily functions all has to take place on the gondola rides. The former World Cup downhillers who generally compete are assisted by around 600 volunteers who organise the event, tune competitors' skis and cheer them through the long night. And hundreds of thousands of dollars are raised for charity in the process. Ordinary holiday skiers can follow the same route and marvel at the stamina and fitness of the 24-hour men and women.

CHILDCARE

The childcare possibilities are too numerous to list in detail.

A new children's 'learning center' was opened at Tiehack a couple of years ago – Fort Frog – with a special children's shuttle bus from Aspen. The Powder Pandas classes there take children aged 3 to 6. At Snowmass, the Big Burn Bears ski kindergarten takes children from age 4, and children aged 18 months to 3 have the Snow Cubs playschool.

There are several all-day non-skiing crèches, taking children from as young as 12 months.

GETTING THERE

Air Aspen, transfer ½hr. Eagle, transfer 1½hr. Denver, transfer 3½hr.

Rail Glenwood Springs (70km).

UK PACKAGES

Airtours, American Dream, Bladon Lines, Crystal, Funway Holidays, Independent Ski Links, Inghams, Lotus Supertravel, Made to Measure, Ski Activity, Ski Club of GB, Ski Independence, Ski North America Direct, Skisar U.S., Skiworld North America, Thomson, United Vacations Ski Freedom USA

Snowmass American Dream, Crystal, Funway Holidays, Lotus Supertravel, Made to Measure, Ski Independence, Skisar U.S., United Vacations Ski Freedom USA

QUEUES
Few problems

There are rarely major queues on any of the mountains. At Aspen Mountain, the Silver Queen gondola can have delays at peak times, but you have alternative lifts to the top. Snowmass has so many alternative lifts and runs that you can normally avoid any problems. But some long, slow chairs can be cold in mid-winter, and the home slope gets very busy. Aspen Highlands is almost always queue-free, even at peak times. The two lifts out of Main Buttermilk sometimes get congested. The main complaints that reporters had were of the mountains shutting down lifts too readily because of wind and too many slow lifts.

MOUNTAIN RESTAURANTS
Good by American standards

Even this smartest of US resorts can't compare with, say, Switzerland for mountain restaurants. But there are some good places.

On Aspen Mountain, try La Baita (an Italian-style restaurant), with good views down onto Aspen, and Sundeck, at the top of the gondola, with fabulous views. The Ajax Tavern at the bottom is a smart alternative.

At Snowmass, Gwyn's is an elegant restaurant serving excellent food. The best views of the mountains surrounding this area are from Sam's Knob restaurant and cafeteria.

Merry-Go-Round at mid-mountain at Aspen Highlands has great strudel and a great view of approaching freestylers on Fridays at noon (if they get a sponsor for the event this season).

SCHOOLS AND GUIDES
Special programmes

There's a wide variety of specialised instruction available – bumps, powder, mountain racing and so on – and a four-day Mountain Masters program on Aspen and Snowmass, where small, intermediate and advanced groups are led by the same instructor for five hours a day. There are also three-day Learn to Snowboard programmes, women's ski seminars and various free guided tours, including nature tours to learn about local plants and wildlife.

FACILITIES FOR CHILDREN
Choice of crèches?

There is no shortage of advertised childcare arrangements. We have no recent first-hand reports. But reporters'

observations were that, as usual in the US, all the kids were having the time of their lives. And past reports have always been first-class. The youngest children are taken from the gondola building each morning around 9am by the Max the Moose bus to Buttermilk's very impressive Fort Frog – a wooden frontier-style fort, with lookout towers, flags, old wagons, a jail, saloon and native American teepee village – and delivered back at 4pm.

Staying there 🔑

Aspen is the liveliest place to stay and near the Silver Queen gondola is the most convenient. Buses for the other areas also leave from nearby. Snowmass means slope-side convenience and the buses from Aspen run until 1am or later.

HOW TO GO
Accommodation for all pockets

Aspen Mountain and Snowmass between them have beds for some 16,000 guests in a mixture of hotels, inns, B&Bs, lodges and condos – and there are several catered chalets.

Chalets This year we've had two rave reviews of Skiworld's Alpine Springs chalet, near Aspen Highlands – go for the master bedroom with panoramic views and private Jacuzzi.

Hotels There are places for all budgets.

(((((5))) **Ritz-Carlton** Opulent city-type hotel, near the gondola. Fitness centre, outdoor pool, whirlpool spas, sauna.

(((((5))) **Little Nell** Stylish modern hotel right by the gondola. Fireplaces in every room, outdoor pool, hot tub, sauna and more.

(((((5))) **Jerome** Step back a century in history in one of Aspen's most famous hotels. Victorian authenticity combined with modern-day luxury; swimming pool, hot tub.

((((4))) **Sardy House** Elegantly furnished, intimate little hotel 10 minutes from the gondola, with comfortable, modern extension. Small outdoor pool, hot tub. 'Superb' says one reporter.

((((4))) **Lenado** Smart modern B&B place with open-fire lounge and individually designed rooms – we loved it.

((((4))) **Silvertree.** Large slope-side hotel at Snowmass. Pools, hot tubs.

(((3))) **Innsbruck Inn** 'Quite excellent' says a recent reporter. Tyrolean-style hotel, a fair walk from centre and lifts.

((2))) **Christmas Inn** More basic motel, on the edge of town.

ACTIVITIES

Indoor Aspen Athletic Club (racquetball, swimming, free weights, aerobics classes, sauna, steam, jacuzzi), skating
Outdoor Ballooning, para-gliding, snowcat tours, snow-shoe tours, sleigh rides, dog-sledding, snowmobiles, tours of mines

TOURIST OFFICE

Postcode CO 81612
Tel +1 (970) 925 1220
Fax 920 0771

Nowhere combines impressive slopes with mining-town charm like Aspen ↓

Self-catering The standards here are high, even in US terms. Many of the smarter developments have their own free shuttle-buses. We and some satisfied reporters have stayed at the luxurious Gant, with impressive communal facilities, and close to the gondola and the centre. The smart Aspen Club complex enjoys a prime position next to the gondola, with free entry to the excellent health and sports facilities. Chateau Roaring Fork and Eau Claire, four blocks from the gondola, are spacious, well-furnished and with the largest outdoor pool in Aspen. There are also some luxurious individual houses on offer.

Lots of restaurants take part in the 'A la Car' scheme: you order from a book of menus, and the meal is delivered.

EATING OUT
Dining dilemma

There is an exceptionally wide choice, including Japanese and Swiss, as well as the more usual options. The most

sophisticated and expensive food is in the top hotels, but there are some excellent upmarket restaurants around the town too. Piñons serves innovative American food in toned-down South-Western surroundings. Syzygy is a suave upstairs place with live jazz. Poppie's Bistro Cafe is famous for its breads and puddings. There are some excellent Italian places, including Mother Lode (where we had a great meal), Campo de Fiori and Farfalla. Cache Cache does good-value French with Italian options.

Cheaper places include: Boogies (a 50s-style Diner), Su Casa and La Cocina (both Mexican, the latter popular with locals), Hard Rock Cafe, Planet Hollywood, Main Street Bakery and Mezzaluna ($1.50 beer and $5 gourmet pizzas in happy hour.)

APRES-SKI
Party time

Immediately after a day on the slopes, Ajax Tavern next to the Little Nell (formerly Shlomo's) is the place to be in Aspen. At Snowmass and Aspen Highlands there are lively places when the lifts close at the base areas.

There are lots of other bars to move on to in Aspen itself, early or late in the evening. The trendiest place last season was the Cigar Bar, with comfortable sofas and smoking permitted! The J-bar of the Jerome hotel and the Red Onion still have a local feel to them, attracting a changing crowd throughout the evening. The Flying Dog is the local micro-brewery. Shooters Saloon is a splendid country and western place, with pool tables and (if you're lucky) line-dancing. Cantina serves the best margaritas in town. Tippler is a quite spacious disco-bar. For exclusive peace and quiet, wangle an invitation to the Caribou club.

OFF THE SLOPES
Silver service

Aspen has lots to offer, especially if you've got a high credit card limit and like shopping. Just wandering around town is pleasant. It's easy for pedestrians to get up the mountains to meet for lunch. Most hotels have excellent spa facilities.

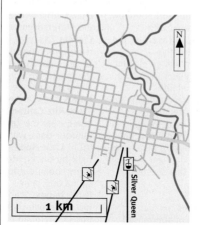

Breckenridge

Popular introduction to Colorado

WHAT IT COSTS

(((((6)

HOW IT RATES

The slopes

Snow	*****
Extent	**
Experts	***
Intermediates	****
Beginners	****
Convenience	***
Queues	****
Restaurants	**

The rest

Scenery	***
Resort charm	***
Off-slope	***

MOUNTAIN FACTS

Altitude	2925m-3960m
Lifts	18
Pistes	2031 acres
Green	14%
Blue	26%
Black	60%
Art. snow	369 acres

From the left, Peaks 10, 9, 8, and 7. Only on the last two of these do the slopes extend above the forest ↓

➕ Varied local mountains, with something for all standards

➕ Shared lift pass with nearby Keystone and not-so-nearby Vail

➕ Efficient lift system means few queues

➕ Lively bars, restaurants and nightlife by US standards

➕ Based on restored Victorian mining town, with many new buildings in attractive 19th-century style

➖ The local area is rather small, with few long runs

➖ At this extreme altitude there is an appreciable risk of sickness for visitors coming straight from lower altitudes

➖ The pseudo-Victorian style gets a bit overblown in places, giving the town the air of a theme park

Breckenridge is very popular with first-time visitors to Colorado. It's easy to see why: it is one of the closest resorts to Denver Airport, has slopes for all standards, usually excellent dry snow, good facilities for families, relatively lively nightlife and good-value slope-side accommodation. Add to that the image of a restored Wild West mining town and you have a very compelling package. And most of our reporters love it.

This season its attraction is increased by a link with Vail (it's now owned by the same company) and millions of dollars in improvements being pumped into it. It is true that the slopes do not cover a huge area (even by US standards) and that the town is rather spoiled by out-of-style buildings in parts and a rather Disneyesque feel to other parts. But there are lots of other areas to try nearby on day trips, some covered by a shared lift pass, some not – much more than you could cover in a week or ten days. And it is the liveliest place to stay to the east of Vail.

boarding *Breckenridge is pretty much ideal for all standards of boarder and played a leading role in the development of snowboarding in the US. Beginners have ideal nursery slopes and easy greens to progress to and intermediates have great cruising runs, all served by chairs. For good boarders there's one of the best fun-parks in the US on Peak 9, with a series of great jumps and obstacles and a half-pipe.The powder bowls at the top of Peaks 7 and 8 make for awesome riding – unfortunately accessed only by an awkward T-bar. Nearby Arapahoe Basin (no longer under the same ownership, so with no shared lift pass) is another area for hardcore boarding in steep bowls and chutes.*

For 1997/98 two new high-speed quad chair-lifts are replacing two slow double chairs, one serving the top half of Peak 9, the other the top half of Peak 8 below the bowls. Snowmaking is being installed on Peak 8, increasing the resort's snowmaking by 50 per cent. A new restaurant is being built between Peaks 9 and 10 and the Bergenhof Lodge at the base of Peak 8 is being upgraded.

There will be transport and interchangeable lift ticket arrangements with Vail, Beaver Creek and Keystone.

CHILDCARE

At each major lift base there is a Children's Center (453 3250), with 'fun facilities' and a complex array of options for all-day care from 8.30 to 4.30. Peak 8 takes children from 2 months, and runs a Snow Play programme for those aged 2 years; both Centers offer this for non-skiers aged 3 to 5. Special school classes are held for those aged 3, mornings only. Those aged 4 or 5 have their own junior school. Children aged 6 to 12 go into ordinary children's school, but all-day care is available at Kid's Castle meeting areas at each lift base.

There is also a separate Kinderhut children's school (453 0379) at Beaver Run Resort, with 'magic carpet' ski-lift, offering all-day care.

The resort

Breckenridge was founded in 1859 and became a booming gold-mining town in the latter part of the century. The biggest ever gold nugget, weighing nearly 14 pounds and named Tom's Baby, was unearthed here. The old wooden and clapboard buildings have been well renovated and form the bottom part of Main Street. Over 250 restored Victorian buildings are included in what is Colorado's largest national historic district. New shopping malls and buildings have been added in similar style – though they are obvious modern additions.

The town centre is attractively lively in the evening, with plenty of shops and over 100 restaurants and bars. Christmas lights and decorations remain on the lamp-posts throughout the season, giving the town an air of non-stop winter festivity. This is enhanced by a number of real winter festivals such as Ullr Fest – a carnival honouring the Norse God of Winter – and Ice Sculpture championships which leave wonderful sculptures for weeks afterwards.

Hotels and condominiums, generally built in more modern style are spread over a wide, wooded area and are linked by a regular Town Trolley. Breckenridge also boasts more slope-side accommodation than any other Colorado resort.

The mountains

There are four separate peaks, linked by lift and piste. Boringly, they are named Peaks 7, 8, 9 and 10 – going from right to left as you look at the mountain. Though there's something for all standards, the keen piste-basher will want to explore other resorts too. Breckenridge and Keystone down the road were bought in 1996 by the owners of Vail and Beaver Creek (around an hour away); there are plans for interchangeable lift tickets and luxury coach transport between all four areas. Copper Mountain and Arapahoe Basin are also nearby but no longer under common ownership; when we went to press details of shared lift tickets and transport between them had not been finalised.

Those with a car can also try Steamboat, less than two hours' drive away.

THE SLOPES
Small but fragmented

Two high-speed quad chair-lifts go from the top end of town up to **Peak 9**, one accessing mainly green runs on the lower half of the hill, the other mainly blues higher up. From there you can get to **Peak 10**, which has a large number of blue and black runs served by one high-speed quad.

The other flank of Peak 9 takes you to a lift up into the **Peak 8** area – tough stuff at the top, easier lower down. The base lifts of Peak 8 at the Bergenhof can also be reached by the town shuttle bus or the Snowflake lift from the edge of town. From the top T-bar of Peak 8, you can traverse to the all-black **Peak 7** slopes which have no lifts of their own – you go back to the base of Peak 8.

At the end of the day three trails lead back down to town from Peak 8 – Sawmill to the main Peak 9 lifts, Snowflake to the edge of town and Four O'Clock down towards the centre. A regular free shuttle runs around the resort to the Peak 9 and Peak 8 lifts.

SNOW RELIABILITY
Excellent

With the village at almost 3000m (the highest of the main North American resorts), the slopes going up to almost 4000m and a lot of east and north-east facing slopes, it's no surprise that Breckenridge boasts an excellent snow record. That is supplemented by substantial artificial snowmaking (increased by 50 per cent for 1997/98) mainly intended for pre-Christmas use.

FOR EXPERTS
Quite a few short but tough runs

A remarkable 60% of Breckenridge's runs are classified as 'most difficult' (single black diamond) or 'expert' (double black diamond) terrain. That's a higher proportion than the famous 'macho' resorts such as Jackson Hole, Taos and Snowbird. But remember that Breckenridge is not a big area by European standards, so most experts there for a week or more will want to spend some of their time exploring the other nearby resorts.

Peak 7 is an entirely off-piste area, which can only be reached by traversing or hiking up from the top of the T-bar. It's worth it – we skied it for the first time in 1997 and it has wonderful steep runs with good snow on north-east-facing slopes.

LIFT PASSES

96/97 prices in dollars
Breckenridge-Keystone
Covers all lifts in Breckenridge and Keystone.
Beginners 2 beginners' lifts. Beginners and novices have a reduced area pass in ski school.
Main pass
1-day pass 45
6-day pass 210
Senior citizens
Over 60: 6-day pass 162 (23% off)
Over 70: free pass
Children
Under 15: 6-day pass 72 (66% off)
Under 6: free pass
Alternative periods
Passes of 2 days and over allow one non-skiing day, eg 6-day pass valid for a 7-day period, with one non-skiing day.
Notes Breckenridge, Keystone and Arapahoe are all a ski-bus ride apart. Discounts for groups of over 20.
Alternative passes
Ski the Summit coupon booklets interchangeable for lift pass at Breckenridge, Copper Mountain, Keystone and Arapahoe Basin (6 days skiing out of 7 adult 215).

SCHOOLS/GUIDES

96/97 prices in dollars
Breckenridge
Classes 6 days
5hr: 9.45-12.15 and 1.30-4pm; 2½hr: am or pm
6 full days: 270
Children's classes
Ages: 3 to 12
6 full days including lunch and ski-pass: 374
Private lessons
1hr, 2hr, 3hr or 6hr
75 for 1hr

Peak 8 has some good open terrain in Horseshoe and Contest bowls, where the snow normally remains good and you can hike up to Imperial Bowl and Lake Chutes, where the steepest slopes are.

We particularly liked the back bowls of Peak 8. This is basically terrain among a thin covering of trees and bushes. Lots of runs, such as Lobo, Hombre, Amen and Adios, are marked on the trail map. But in practice you can easily skip between them and invent your own way down. It's picturesque and not too steep. Steep black mogul fields lead down under Chair 4 to the junction with Peak 9.

Peak 9 itself has nothing to offer experts except very steep blacks from the top down under Chair E on the North Face. These have had very patchy snow covering on each of our visits, conditions which probably account for their fearsome names such as Devil's Crotch and Satan's Inferno.

Peak 10 offers much more interest. Off to the right of the chair, at the edge of the area, is a network of interlinking black mogul runs by the side of the downhill course – consistently steep and bumpy. To the left of the chair is a lovely, lightly wooded off-piste area, The Burn.

FOR INTERMEDIATES
Nice cruising, limited extent
Breckenridge has some good blue cruising runs for all standards of intermediate. But dedicated piste bashers will find it very limited and will want to visit the other nearby resorts.

Peak 9 has the easiest terrain. It is nearly all gentle, wide blues at the top and greens at the bottom. Timid intermediates will find it delightful.

Peak 10 has a couple of more challenging runs graded blue-black, such as Crystal and Centennial, which make for good fast cruising.

Peak 8 has a choice of blues down through trails cut close together in the trees. We particularly liked the quiet Claimjumper, which is visited less than the others because of its position at the far northern end of the area, next to the boundary.

More adventurous intermediates will also like to try some of the high bowl runs (see above). And Keystone, Vail, Beaver Creek and Copper Mountain all offer miles of excellent intermediate terrain.

FOR BEGINNERS
Excellent
The bottom of Peak 9 has a big, virtually flat area and some good gentle nursery slopes. There's then a good choice of green runs to move on to. Beginners can try Peak 8 too, with another selection of green runs and a choice of trails which take you right back to town.

FOR CROSS-COUNTRY
Specialist centre in woods
Breckenridge's Nordic Center is prettily set in the woods between the town and Peak 8 (and is served by the shuttle bus). It has 38km of trails.

QUEUES
Not normally a problem
Breckenridge's six high-speed quads (three on Peak 9, two on Peaks 8 and one on Peak 10) make light work of peak-time crowds. We've never come across serious queues and neither have our reporters, except in exceptional circumstances, such as President's Day weekend.

MOUNTAIN RESTAURANTS
One place worth eating
Mountain eating is fairly typical of US resorts: large, efficient self-service cafeterias which serve standard fare of burgers, pasta, chillis in a rather utilitarian atmosphere – and very crowded at peak time.

Vista Haus, at the top of Peak 8, is the exception with a choice of three restaurants including the excellent Italian buffet at Piz Otto's.

SCHOOLS AND GUIDES
Excellent reports
Our reporters are unanimous in their praise for the workings of the school: classes of five to eight, doing what the class, not the instructor, wants, special clinics on, for example, bumps or powder.

FACILITIES FOR CHILDREN
Excellent facilities
This year we have had several reports on the children's ski school and the crèche, every one bubbling with enthusiastic praise. Typical comments: 'the instructors make the classes FUN', 'excellent teaching, combining serious coaching with lots of fun', 'our boys enjoyed every minute of it', 'kids got a daily report card which they liked', 'so much more positive than in Europe'.

GETTING THERE

Air Denver, transfer
2½hr.

Breckenridge's
historic district dates
from the 1800s ↓

Staying there

Breckenridge is quite spread-out. Although there is a lot of slope-side accommodation, there is also a fair amount away from Main Street and the lift base-stations. Free shuttle buses serve most of the area well, but less reliably in the evening than the day. The area between the base of Peak 9 and Main Street is the best location if you plan to go out in the evening.

HOW TO GO
Lots of choice

Over a dozen tour operators feature Breckenridge in their programme and it's easy to arrange your own holiday there too – there are regular transfers from Denver Airport to Breckenridge.

Chalets Several tour operators have very comfortable chalets, both in and out of town – there is more choice than in any other US resort.

Hotels There's a good choice of style and price range.

((((④ **Breckenridge Hilton** Prime location, vast rooms (it was built as condos) and good facilities make this recently renovated hotel very popular with Brits. Pool, tubs.

((((④ **Lodge at Breckenridge** Stylish luxury spa resort set out of town among 32 acres, with great views. Private shuttle bus. Pool, tubs.

(((③ **Beaver Run** Huge resort complex with 520 spacious rooms. Half this

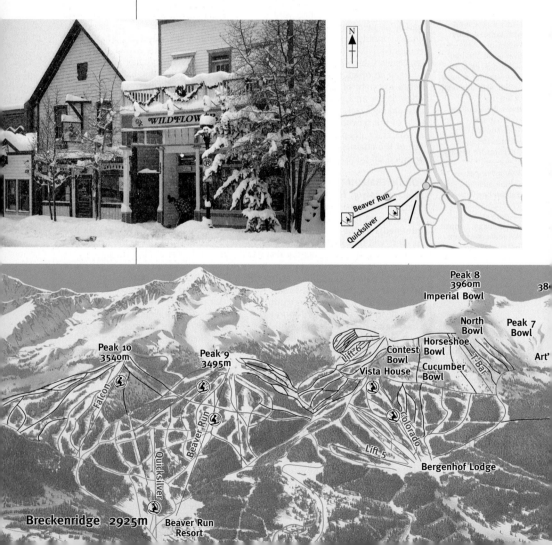

ACTIVITIES

Indoor Sports clubs, swimming, sauna, massage, jacuzzi, cinema, theatre, art gallery, library, indoor miniature golf course
Outdoor Heli-skiing, horse- and dog-sleigh rides, rafting, fishing, snow-mobiles, snow coach rides, toboggans, scooters, mountain biking

UK PACKAGES

Airtours, American Connections, American Dream, Bladon Lines, Chalets 'Unlimited', Crystal, Equity School Ski, First Choice Ski, Funway Holidays, Independent Ski Links, Inghams, Made to Measure, Neilson, Ski Activity, Ski Equipe, Ski Independence, Ski North America Direct, Ski-Val, Skisar U.S., Skiworld North America, Summit Chalets, Thomson, United Vacations Ski Freedom USA

Frisco Equity School Ski, Equity Total Ski

TOURIST OFFICE

Postcode CO 80424
Tel +1 (970) 453 5000
Fax 453 3202

year's reporters stayed here and all raved about its position right by one of the main lifts up Peak 9.

(((3)) **Williams House** Beautifully restored, charmingly furnished four-room B&B on Main St.

(2) **Fireside Inn** Cosy New England-style B&B. Historic part of town. Tub.

(2) **Breckenridge Mountain Lodge** Straightforward, good-value accommodation. Tubs.

(1) **Breckenridge Wayside Inn** Friendly budget place out of town by golf course. Tub.

Self-catering There is a huge choice of condominiums, many set conveniently along the aptly named Four O'Clock run. Comfortable, well equipped and conveniently located condos include Liftside Inn, Tannhaüser, Pine Ridge, River Mountain Lodge, Sundowner, Wedgewood, Tyra Summit and Wildwood. The Beaver Run resort has self-catering and hotel accommodation.

STAYING DOWN THE VALLEY
Good for exploring the area

Staying in Frisco makes sense for those touring around or on a tight budget. It's a small town based on a Victorian settlement, where the stage-coach used to stop. There are cheap motels (including the old stagecoach stop, now the Frisco Inn), some B&B places and a Best Western hotel.

EATING OUT
Over 100 restaurants

There's a very wide range of eating places, with pretty much everything you'd expect, from typical American food to 'fine-dining', and almost every ethnic cuisine you could wish for.

The Brewery is famous for its enormous portions of appetisers such as Buffalo Wings – as well as its splendid brewed-on-the-spot beers. We particularly liked the Avalanche beer.

The Whale's Tail has been highly recommended for its seafood, lively atmosphere and good, half-price children's portions. Poirier's Cajun Café has been recommended by several reporters. The Village Pasta Co serves good cheap fresh pasta and Mia Casa good cheap Mexican food. The Hearthstone has been recommended for 'lovely food in good surroundings'.

APRES-SKI
The best in the area

There's a lively atmosphere as soon as you come off the slopes, but things quieten down considerably later. The Breckenridge Brewery is the 'in' place at tea-time. Its main rival is Jake T Pounders at the Peak 9 base-station, which has live music. Jake is an unusual owner – he's a dog! The Gold Pan saloon dates from Goldrush days, and is reputedly the oldest bar west of the Mississippi. Shamus O'Toole's is popular with locals. Downstairs at Eric's is a trendy disco bar. Tiffany's is the livelier of the two main discos.

OFF THE SLOPES
Pleasant but quiet

Breckenridge is a pleasant place to wander around, and not without distractions. But those staying for a week or 10 days and not using the slopes would find it pretty limiting, and the excursion possibilities are few. One of the base-stations would be best for lunchtime meetings.

Copper Mountain

2960m

Great slopes for all standards above a soulless resort

Copper Mountain currently has little charm but great terrain – though there are ambitious plans to improve the village. It is well worth visiting for a day or two if you are staying in the more atmospheric resorts of Breckenridge or Keystone.

WHAT IT COSTS

⦅⦅⦅⦅⦅6

HOW IT RATES

The slopes

Snow	*****
Extent	**
Experts	***
Intermediates	****
Beginners	****
Convenience	****
Queues	****
Restaurants	*

The rest

Scenery	***
Resort charm	*
Off-slope	*

What's new

Copper was bought in 1997 by Intrawest, a company which is also involved in resorts such as Whistler, Keystone and Mammoth. It plans $26 million of mountain improvements and a $340 million village development over the next few years.

And over the past two seasons, Copper's expert ski terrain has been improved with new lifts and the opening of Copper Bowl.

MOUNTAIN FACTS

Altitude	2960m-3770m
Lifts	21
Pistes	2433 acres
Green	22%
Blue	37%
Black	41%
Art. snow	270 acres

UK PACKAGES

Club Med, The Ski Company, United Vacations Ski Freedom USA

TOURIST OFFICE

Postcode CO 80443
Tel +1 (970) 968 2882
Fax 968 2711

THE RESORT

Copper Mountain is a functional, purpose-built resort, high on convenience, low on charm – rather like some French purpose-built resorts. The apartment blocks are surprisingly spread out, making the free shuttle-bus pretty essential. There is currently little in the way of shops or ambience away from the area near the lifts.

The resort has a big conference market and the only Club Med ski village in North America. It's good for families and there's a fine sports club, with a huge pool and indoor tennis.

Copper was taken over in 1997 by Intrawest, who have also developed several other North American resorts, and they have plans to make the village much livelier and more attractive. Keystone, Breckenridge and Arapahoe Basin are all nearby and Vail, Steamboat and Winter Park within an hour or two.

THE MOUNTAIN

The **area** is quite sizeable by American standards, and it is very easy to work out where you want to go. As you look up at the mountain, the easiest runs are on the the right hand side and the terrain gradually gets steeper the further left you go. Two high-speed quads whizz you up to the tree line, from where numerous runs head back towards the base. Further lifts serve the resort's open bowls above.

Height and an extensive snowmaking operation give Copper very good **snow reliability.**

There is a lot of good **expert** terrain. In the last few seasons the steep and wild Copper Bowl on the backside of Copper's mountain and Western Union on the front side have been developed, and a new lift in Copper Bowl was opened in 1996/97. Experts will also enjoy the double diamond terrain of Spaulding Bowl, and there are great bump runs through the trees.

Good **intermediates** have the benefit of the steepest runs also being the

longest. These are in the Copper Peak section. The slightly less proficient can enjoy shorter, gentler runs on the middle section of mountain, while early intermediates have gentle cruising terrain in the Union Peak section.

The nursery slopes are excellent for **beginners**, and there are plenty of very easy green runs to graduate to.

A fun-park for **snowboarding** is due to open for 1997/98.

For **cross-country**, there are 25km of trails through the woods.

Copper has a lot of terrain served by few lifts and gets a lot of day visitors from Denver so **queues** can be a problem, especially at weekends.

The one **mountain restaurant** is mediocre, and many people prefer to go back to the base for lunch.

The **school** has a fine reputation, especially for teaching children.

The all-day kindergarten takes **children** from 3 years, and has its slopes right outside the nursery. The nursery takes children from 2 months old and, as well as the usual facilities, provides cooking and crafts. Evening babysitters are also available.

STAYING THERE

Copper Mountain is essentially a **condominium** resort and nearly all are of a high standard.

Copper's only **hotel** is Foxpine Inn. It has well appointed rooms and a swimming pool. There are hotels nearby, in Dillon and Frisco.

There are only half-a-dozen **restaurants**, but all are quite good. O'Shea's is an Old West-style barbecue place; Steak Out is good; Pesce Fresco's has an international menu that includes fine fish; and the sports club's restaurant does excellent salads.

Nightlife is very quiet. The 'pub' in Copper Commons is a wine bar. A multi-screen cinema is nearby. Evening sleigh rides take people out to a diner. Other **off-slope activities** centre around the The Racquet & Athletic Club and West Lake.

Crested Butte 2855m

Surprises galore in a Jekyll and Hyde resort

WHAT IT COSTS

(((((6)

HOW IT RATES

The slopes

Snow	****
Extent	**
Experts	****
Intermediates	***
Beginners	****
Convenience	***
Queues	****
Restaurants	*

The rest

Scenery	***
Resort charm	****
Off-slope	**

- ✚ Known for its 'extreme' terrain
- ✚ Enough non-extreme but steep runs to keep experts happy
- ✚ Excellent for beginners and for near-beginners, with long easy runs
- ✚ Charming, tiny, restored Victorian mining town with good restaurants
- ✚ Alternative of convenient resort village
- ✚ Excellent school, with special courses for the disabled
- ✚ Better-than-average scenery for Colorado

- ▬ Limited for confident intermediate piste-bashers
- ▬ Old town is ten minutes from resort village by shuttle bus
- ▬ Out on a limb, away from mainstream Colorado resorts
- ▬ Only one satisfactory mountain restaurant

Among experts who are at home on steep, unprepared runs – and 'extremists' who like their mountains as steep as possible – Crested Butte enjoys cult status, thanks to the extent and gradient of the slopes on the outer fringes of the area. Meanwhile, the commercial success of the place depends on beginners and timid intermediates, for whom the long, groomed slopes of the main area are ideal. These two groups can safely include Crested Butte on their short-lists. But avid piste-bashers should stay away – there isn't enough suitable terrain. That's a shame because the cute old town is one of our favourites for atmosphere.

What's new

For 1997/98, the Keystone chair-lift out of town to beginner and intermediate slopes will be replaced by a high-speed quad. And the East River lift will be upgraded from a double to a triple chair, easing the queues for those coming out of the Extreme Limits alive.

Some terrain on the way back to town will be recontoured to make it less steep for beginners.

boarding *Boarders with a taste for powder will love Crested Butte, as a large proportion of its area is unpisted and 'extreme'. It is also very pro-boarding, and attracts many to its mountain, not least for the extreme snowboarding competitions. Beginners will find a large section of easy, long, open green runs down to the base station. Unfortunately, there's little suitable terrain in between the two for progressing riders. There's a fun-park and quarter-pipe, the mountain is covered by chairs and easy to get around and there is a highly regarded specialist snowboard shop 'The Colorado Boarder'. The town has a couple of lively bars but is not bursting with night life.*

The resort

Crested Butte is a small resort in a remote corner of Colorado, well away from the Denver–Breckenridge–Vail mainstream. It takes its name from the local mountain – an isolated peak (a butte, pronounced 'beaut') with a distinctive shape. Crested Butte started life as a coal-mining town in the late 1800s; it is now one of the most attractive resorts in the Rockies – just a few narrow streets with beautifully restored wooden buildings and sidewalks, and the tiniest imaginable town jail, straight out of a Western. Elk Avenue, the main street, is a five-minute stroll from top to bottom, and is lined with bars, restaurants and

shops. There's even a classic general store, run by an old-timer.

The bars and restaurants are varied in price and character. But wherever you go you'll find genuinely friendly and hospitable locals. And mingled with them you'll find a fair share of down-to-earth celebrities.

The resort village of Mount Crested Butte, linked by regular free shuttle buses, is a huge contrast to the town of Crested Butte. Nearly all the buildings are modern and characterless, and the two main hotels have recently adopted Marriot and Sheraton chain identities. There is a cluster of bars and restaurants at the foot of the slopes, around the large Marriot hotel.

MOUNTAIN FACTS

Altitude	2775m-3620m
Lifts	13
Pistes	1160 acres
Green	13%
Blue	29%
Black	58%
Art. snow	380 acres

SCHOOLS/GUIDES

97/98 prices in dollars

Crested Butte
Classes 7 days
2½hr: 9.45-12.15 and
1.15-3.45
4 2½hr days: 120
Children's classes
Ages: 3 to 12
6 5½hr days including
rental, pass and
lunch: 384
Private lessons
2hr, 3hr or 6hr
110 for 2hr; each
additional person 35

The mountain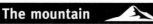

It's a small area, but it packs in an astonishing mixture of perfect beginner slopes, easy cruising runs and expert terrain. The only groups of people who might not be suited by this mixture are piste-bashing intermediates who like different groomed runs all the time and experts who don't fancy seriously steep terrain.

THE SLOPES
A Jekyll and Hyde mountain

Two high-speed quad chair-lifts leave the base area. The Silver Queen takes experts to black runs and lifts which access the steepest runs. Those just off the nursery slopes will take the new Keystone high-speed quad to the easiest runs. And intermediates can access cruising blue runs from either of these two lifts.

SNOW RELIABILITY
Excellent – usually

Crested Butte claims to benefit from snowstorms approaching from several directions, and it has a substantial snowmaking installation which covers groomed runs from most lifts. We've usually had superb snow here.

FOR EXPERTS
Some cult terrain

For those who like steep ungroomed terrain, Crested Butte is idyllic – see below. For the average black-run mogul lover the resort is much more limited. And be warned: The Extreme Limits needs a lot of snow cover and it

THE EXTREME LIMITS

Crested Butte's Extreme Limits makes up almost half its terrain, though you wouldn't dream it from looking up from the groomed trails. Two drag-lifts at the top of the ski area access all this. In particular, the North Face button lift, which takes only a couple of minutes to ride, is like Dr Who's Tardis. You get to the top and half the 550 acres of the Extreme Limits hidden from the blue runs below stretches before you beyond a sign which says: 'This terrain is the steepest lift-served terrain in North America. Experts only'. There are cliffs to leap off if you want them but good skiers and boarders can have the time of their lives on seriously steep but prettily wooded and safe terrain – there are guided tours twice a day. The High Lift, added a few years ago, opened up a whole new range of extreme possibilities previously reached only by long climbs.

LIFT PASSES

Crested Butte Mountain Resort
Covers all lifts in Crested Butte only.

Beginners Beginners' lessons in ski school includes lift pass.

Main pass
1-day pass 46
6-day pass 260

Short-term passes
Half-day pass available (adult 33).

Alternative periods
All lift passes of 4 days and over allow for one day off, eg 4 days skiing in 5, 6 out of 7 days

Notes Free lift passes for first and last weeks of season (21/11/97 to 20/12/97 and 6/4/98 to 19/4/98), with reductions on ski hire and lodgings. Children under 13 pay their age for each day's skiing.

is not unusual for it to be closed until the third week in January.

There is also Irwin Lodge up the road, which runs a snowcat operation on its slopes of virgin powder – see Staying up the mountain.

FOR INTERMEDIATES
Not a lot
Similarly, good intermediates are likely to find the area limited unless they enjoy perfecting their technique on the same few runs each day.

For early, unsure intermediates, Crested Butte has attractions. The east-facing runs down the Paradise, Teocalli and East River lifts are all wide, fairly gentle, well groomed and normally uncrowded cruising runs which can be taken fast or slow. There are usually several variations to choose from, ending up back at the same lifts.

A particularly gentle and uncrowded area is that served by the Gold Link lift, isolated from the rest of the slopes and good for near-beginners too.

FOR BEGINNERS
Excellent
There are excellent nursery slopes near the village. After that you'll be taking the Keystone chair-lift up to a choice of several long, easy green runs leading

We don't guarantee that it will be this quiet all the time ↓

back down again. Or you can stop off part-way down to catch the Painter Boy lift. This has green runs down again or you can try the easy blues down the Gold Link lift.

FOR CROSS-COUNTRY
Looks good
There are 30km of cross-country trails near the Nordic Ski Centre in the old town of Crested Butte.

QUEUES
No problem
Queues are virtually non-existent except at peak periods. The trails are quiet and uncrowded too.

MOUNTAIN RESTAURANTS
Only one worth visiting
Most people go back to the base-station for lunch – not a hardship. The main restaurant at the base of the Paradise lift is fairly civilised, with a wooden interior and good choice of food. There's even a table-service restaurant inside as well as the large self-service and outdoor barbecue areas. The other restaurant, at the base of the Twister lift, is accurately described as a warming house. The food is primitive, and many callers bring their own.

And we don't guarantee that main street will be this snowy ↓

CHILDCARE

The Children's Centre in the Whetstone building, at the foot of the slopes, offers a comprehensive range of care for children aged 6 months to 7 years, from 8.30 to 4.30. There are separate classes for children aged 2 to 3, 4 to 7, and 8 to 12, split into beginners and non-beginners.

GETTING THERE

Air Gunnison, transfer ½hr. Denver, transfer 4½hr.

UK PACKAGES

American Dream, Funway Holidays, Made to Measure, Ski Activity, Ski Equipe, Ski Independence, Skisar U.S., United Vacations Ski Freedom USA

ACTIVITIES

Indoor Racquetball, swimming, hot tubs, weight-training, aerobic classes, saunas
Outdoor Snow-cat skiing, snowmobiling, sleigh rides, ballooning, winter horse riding, mountain barbecues, snow shoe tours

TOURIST OFFICE

Postcode CO 81225
Tel +1 (970) 349 2221
Fax 349 2250

SCHOOLS AND GUIDES
A major asset

The school has an excellent reputation. and offers specialised clinics (including Ski the Extreme, carving skis, bumps, powder, telemark, learn to snowboard) as well as normal group and private lessons.

There are free daily mountain tours for intermediates or better, and the school has a high reputation for teaching people with disabilities.

FACILITIES FOR CHILDREN
Comprehensive

Crested Butte takes childcare seriously, and the facilities look excellent.

Staying there

Most of the accommodation is at the resort village. From some places you can stroll to the lifts; but many condos, in particular, are much further away and dependent on the bus. There is some accommodation in the town.

HOW TO GO
Plenty of choice

Practically all the tour operators with serious US programmes offer packages to Crested Butte, mainly in hotels.
Chalets We don't know of any.
Hotels You have a broad range of options, from international-style comfort to homely character.
⟨⟨③ **Grand Butte Marriot** Big, anonymous, comfortable, convenient (right at the foot of the slopes) and used by most of the British tour operators. Small swimming pool; sauna and hot tub.
⟨② **Nordic Inn** B&B. The oldest hotel in the mountain village, only a short walk from the lifts. It has an outdoor hot tub, friendly service from Alan Cox and his staff, and large rooms.
⟨② **Manor Lodge** Comfortable modern hotel close to the lifts, with live entertainment most evenings.
⟨② **Crested Butte Lodge** More modern, nearer the centre, with an indoor pool, sauna and outdoor hot tub – and much more personal than the Grand Butte.
⟨② **The Inn at Crested Butte** Brand-new non-smoking hotel on the edge of the old town. Outdoor hot tub.
⟨② **Elk Mountain Lodge** Renovated miners' hotel in old town with good rooms. B&B only.
⟨② **Gothic Inn** Five-room Alpine-style B&B in the town.
Self-catering There are literally

thousands of apartments available to rent, mainly in the village. Crested Mountain Village apartments are perhaps the most convenient and have pool, hot tubs, saunas and friendly and efficient reception facilities. The Buttes, the Gateway and the Plaza are also recommended. The Three Seasons condos have plenty of mod cons but are some way from the lifts.

EATING OUT
Better than you'd expect

For such a small place Crested Butte has a surprisingly high number of decent restaurants – nearly all of them in the old town. Top of the pile is undoubtedly Soupcon, a tiny place in an old log cabin just off the main street, serving refined French food. Le Bosquet and Timberline run it close and Bacchanale is a good Italian. The Idle Spur is the statutory micro-brewery, doing satisfying food as well as a range of beers.

APRES-SKI
Lively bars

The old town of Crested Butte has plenty of diversions for a short stay, provided you're not looking for great sophistication or variety. Kochevar's is an amusing Wild-West saloon, complete with shuffleboard (the American-size version of shove-ha'penny). Out at the resort village, Rafters usually has a lot going on.

OFF THE-SLOPES
Limited

Charming though it is, Crested Butte won't keep non-skiers/boarders amused for very long.

STAYING UP THE MOUNTAIN
A wilderness retreat

For experts, cross-country skiers, snowmobiling and those who simply like to get away from it all, Crested Butte has something special.

Irwin Lodge is a great wooden barn of a place in a remote back-country area, reached in winter only by snow-cat or snowmobile. It has an outdoor hot tub, great views and fairly simple rooms above a huge communal sitting room with open fire. Most people go there for the guided powder opportunities, with uplift by snow-cat. For details call 00 1 970 349 2773.

Keystone 2835m

Pampered cruising in the trees

WHAT IT COSTS

(((((6)))

HOW IT RATES

The slopes

Snow	*****
Extent	**
Experts	***
Intermediates	****
Beginners	****
Convenience	**
Queues	****
Restaurants	***

The rest

Scenery	***
Resort charm	**
Off-slope	**

What's new

The whole resort is currently being developed by Vail Resorts (which now owns Keystone) in conjunction with Intrawest, a company involved in resorts such as Whistler, Mammoth, Squaw Valley and Mont Tremblant – there are ambitious plans for building and developing six distinct districts.

There were new snowboarding facilities for 1996/97. For 1997/98, the improvements will centre around River Run, where there will be a new high-speed quad to supplement the gondola. A new children's centre and an additional beginner area served by a new chair are planned. There will also be a floodlit tubing hill and transport and interchangeable lift ticket arrangements with Vail, Beaver Creek and Breckenridge.

➕ Splendid intermediate area with immaculately groomed runs

➕ Almost half the runs are floodlit, and open until 9pm

➕ Lots of other nearby resorts and slopes to visit, including shared lift-pass with Breckenridge and Vail

➕ Efficient lift system – few queues

➕ Luxurious condominiums in woods

➖ Very quiet in the evenings

➖ Resort currently lacks a real centre, so very little village feel

Keystone is a splendid area for intermediates, with miles and miles of immaculately groomed tree-lined runs. It also has Colorado's biggest night operation, with 14 runs operating until 9pm, a huge computerised snowmaking system to supplement the natural stuff, and the best mountain restaurant in the US. Experts might find it a bit limited, but with other nearby areas to explore too, they should find enough to interest them for their stay.

The resort best suits people who are keen to make good use of the slopes but who aren't seeking lively nightlife. There are some excellent restaurants, but not much in the way of lively bars and dancing. Those who want nightlife would be better off staying in Breckenridge, and making excursions to Keystone.

boarding *Until the 1996/97 season, snowboarding was banned at Keystone. Then they decided to open up to boarders in a big way, investing $2.5 million in special snowboard facilities, including a 20-acre fun-park and several half-pipes, all floodlit to make the biggest night-snowboarding operation in Colorado, a new snowboarding learning area and a new snowboard rental shop which is the biggest in the US. The area is ideal for beginners and intermediates with mainly chair-lifts and gondolas, good beginner areas (though there are a couple of drag-lifts here) and superb, groomed cruising runs. Experienced boarders will love the open bowls and tree runs of The Outback and the steep bowls and chutes of nearby Arapahoe Basin, a favourite area with hardcore boarders. Evenings are devoid of traditional snowboard hang-outs.*

The resort

Keystone was the dream of Max Dercum. He gave up his university professorship to drop out with his wife, Edna, to Colorado in the 1940s. Max converted the old stage-coach stop into the Ski Tip Lodge, now the most atmospheric place to stay.

While Max and his wife ran the school in Arapahoe Basin, he worked on his plans to convert the mountains in front of his door into one of the best areas in the US. He saw his dream open for business in 1969, and it has been booming ever since. Max sold out long ago, but still lives locally.

Keystone is a sprawling resort of luxurious condominiums spread over wooded countryside at the foot of Keystone Mountain and without any real hub. Regular buses transport you between your accommodation and three main areas, which all have shops, restaurants and bars (though no supermarkets or liquor stores – they are on the main road). The Mountain House area lies at the foot of chair-lifts up the mountain. A couple of miles away (but not near the slopes) is the picturesque lake area – a huge natural ice rink in winter – where the large and luxurious Keystone Lodge is located. A new area is being developed at River Run, at the base of the main gondola, which will have an attractive and lively car-free centre with accommodation, shops, bars and restaurants. Other quieter neighbourhoods are also planned.

MOUNTAIN FACTS

Altitude 2835m-3720m
Lifts   24
Pistes   1739 acres
Green   13%
Blue   36%
Black   51%
Art. snow   851 acres

The mountains

Keystone has expanded rapidly in the last few years and now offers extensive intermediate intermediate slopes by US standards and some challenging steeper terrain. A high-speed quad chair goes up from the Mountain House base, and a gondola and new high-speed quad from River Run.

Keystone and Breckenridge down the road were bought in 1996 by the owners of Vail and Beaver Creek (around an hour away); there are plans for interchangeable lift tickets and luxury coach transport between all four areas. Copper Mountain is nearby and Arapahoe Basin (or A-Basin as it is known locally) a few minutes by road but both are now separately owned; when we went to press details of shared lift tickets and transport between them had not been finalised. In contrast to Keystone's superb modern lifts, A-Basin is still served by a series of slow old chairs.

Those with a car can also try Steamboat, less than two hours' drive.

THE SLOPES
A keen intermediate's dream
Three tree-lined, interlinked mountains form Keystone's local slopes – Keystone Mountain, North Peak and The Outback. The only one directly accessible from the resort is **Keystone Mountain**, accessed from Mountain House or River Run.

From the top you can choose from 55 runs, or drop over the back down to the foot of **North Peak** and take a chair-lift up. Or you can ride the Outpost gondola which links the top of Keystone Mountain to the top of North Peak (and stays open late into the night to ferry diners to and from the mountain-top restaurants up there).

From North Peak you can get back to the bases of both Keystone Mountain and the third peak, known as **The Outback**, served by another high-speed quad chair-lift.

SNOW RELIABILITY
Excellent
Keystone rarely suffers from a shortage of natural snow. But in case it does, it has one of the world's biggest snowmaking systems as back-up.

One of the main reasons for the snowmaking is to help form an early season base. Keystone traditionally vies with Killington to be the first US resort to open its runs for the season – normally in October.

A-Basin has no need for artificial snow. It has the highest lift-served area in the US, at almost 4000m, and the base-station is at an impressive 3285m. The slopes are normally open well into June.

FOR EXPERTS
Good if you're happy to travel
Keystone's own area has some good challenging runs but not in huge quantity. There are some good mogul runs, such as Ambush and Geronimo, and tree skiing on both North Peak

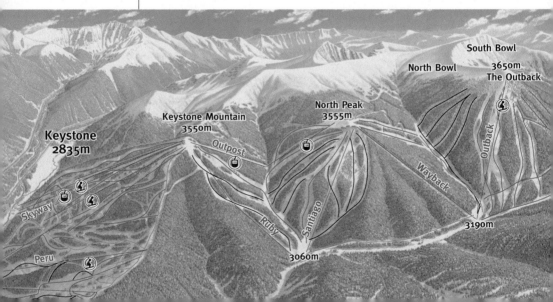

SCHOOLS/GUIDES
96/97 prices in dollars
Keystone
Classes 6 days
2½hr: 10.30-1pm or
1.30-5pm; 2hr
evening: 4.30-6.30
6 half-days: 216
Children's classes
Ages: 3 to 12
6 full days including
lunch and ski-pass:
384
Private lessons
1hr, 1½hr, 2hr, 3hr or
6hr
75 for 1hr

and The Outback. We particularly liked the North Bowl area and tree skiing on The Outback. But most runs on the mountains are intermediate cruisers.

Arapahoe Basin, down the road, is a good place for those looking for a challenge. The East Wall here has some splendid steep chutes. And the opposite side of the bowl is riddled with steep bump runs – although none of the runs is particularly long.

Copper Mountain and Breckenridge have some good challenging terrain too. To get the most out of the region you'll have to be prepared to travel around quite a lot.

FOR INTERMEDIATES
A cruiser's paradise
Keystone is ideal for intermediates. The front face of Keystone Mountain itself is a network of beautifully groomed blue and green runs through the trees. Enthusiasts who want to bash the pistes for as long as possible won't find anywhere better. Almost 50% of the mountain's runs are floodlit, and open until 9pm, and the whole mountain is served by snowmaking.

The Outback and North Peak also have easy cruising blues, with The Outback having some of the steepest

blue runs, including a couple of blue-black bump runs through the trees which are pretty much off-piste and unmarked.

On top of that there are the other resorts to explore. Vail, Beaver Creek and Copper Mountain all have some great intermediate terrain.

FOR BEGINNERS
Nice gentle greens
The front face of Keystone Mountain has some excellent easy green runs for beginners to try once they are off the nursery slopes. Schoolmarm goes right from top to bottom of the mountain.

FOR CROSS-COUNTRY
Extensive facilities
There's a special Cross-Country and Touring Center between Keystone and A-Basin which is served by a shuttle bus. There are 29km of groomed trails. And 57km of unprepared trails take you through spectacular scenery in the Montezuma area, with great views of the Continental Divide. Some trails lead to old mining ghost-towns. The Cross-Country and Touring Center runs guided tours, including a Full Moon evening tour.

QUEUES
Not a problem
Keystone has an efficient, modern lift system, and, except at the morning peak, there are usually few queuing problems.

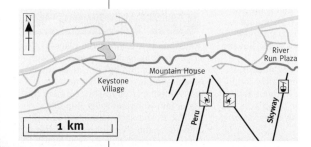

↙ Night Rider: Keystone's slopes are open until 9pm every evening

Gourmet mountain dining: the Alpenglow Stube is the best mountain restaurant in the USA ↓

LIFT PASSES

96/97 prices in dollars
Breckenridge-Keystone
Covers all lifts in Breckenridge and Keystone.
Beginners Beginners and novices have a reduced area pass in ski school.
Main pass
1-day pass 45
6-day pass 210
Senior citizens
Over 60: 6-day pass 162 (23% off)
Over 70: free pass
Children
Under 15: 6-day pass 72 (66% off)
Under 6: free pass
Alternative periods
Passes of 2 days and over allow one non-skiing day, eg 6-day pass valid for a 7-day period, with one non-skiing day.
Notes Breckenridge, Keystone and Arapahoe are all a ski-bus ride apart. Discounts for groups of over 20.
Alternative passes
Ski the Summit coupon booklets interchangeable for lift pass at Breckenridge, Copper Mountain, Keystone and Arapahoe Basin (6 days skiing out of 7 adult 215).

CHILDCARE

The Children's Center at the base of the mountain caters for children aged 2 months to 12 years and is open from 8am to 9pm. They can also provide evening baby-sitting in your own room. From age 3, children can join in the Snowplay programmes.

The school's Mini Minor's Camp takes children aged 3 to 4, the Minor's Camp those from 5 to 12.

Keystone has the biggest night skiing and snowboarding operation in the US, with Keystone Mountain open top to bottom. When the light begins to fade, the floodlights come on and you can carry on skiing or riding up to 9pm. A gondola, high-speed quad and drag lift serve 14 floodlit green and blue runs, with the longest top-to-bottom trail being over three miles long, and a 20-acre terrain park.

Cruising through falling snow illuminated by the bright lights can be delightful. On a cold, clear night, however, it can be really bitter.

You can combine the skiing with the best on-mountain dining in the US. The Alpenglow Stube, at the top of North Peak, stays open until 8.15pm for mountain-top dining for pedestrians, skiers and snowboarders alike. It serves haute cuisine with a Colorado flavour, featuring dishes such as rack of lamb, Atlantic salmon and wild boar. It is much more luxurious than almost any other mountain restaurant we have seen – you can even swap your ski boots for a pair of slippers. A cheaper option is next door's Der Fondue Chessel which features fondue, raclette and 'Bavarian' music and dancing.

You have to take a gondola to and from these restaurants from the top of Keystone mountain – there's no night skiing on North Peak.

MOUNTAIN RESTAURANTS
Includes the best in the US

There are only two mountain-top restaurant complexes – Summit House at the top of Keystone Mountain and The Outpost at the top of North Peak.

The Outpost, in particular, is streets ahead of most US mountain eating places. The whole place is beautifully designed in wood, with high ceilings, large picture windows and a big sun terrace. The self-service restaurant is well designed and sells good fresh pizza, pasta, salads and grills. But the real jewel is the table-service Alpenglow Stube (see box above). It has a luxury atmosphere rarely found in European, let alone US, mountain restaurants – they even swap your boots for slippers at the cloakroom.

SCHOOLS AND GUIDES
Typical American excellence

As well as the normal lessons, there are bumps, bowls and trees classes, courses run by Olympic medallists Phil and Steve Mahre, special carving ski clinics and snowboarding lessons designed specially for experienced adult skiers. Recent reporters have been full of praise for the children's ski school, particularly mentioning the 'fun' element of the classes and the daily reports (both written and verbal). 'French ski schools could learn a bit here,' said one.

FACILITIES FOR CHILDREN
Excellent

Childcare facilities are excellent, with programmes tailored to specific age groups, and nursery care going on into the evening. We're not surprised to learn that Keystone has twice been voted Family Resort of the Year by the magazine *Family Circle*. Another child centre opens at River Run for 1997/98.

Staying there

Keystone is a comfortable place to stay if you're looking for a quiet time with good restaurants but not much other evening atmosphere. The most convenient places to stay are near the Mountain House or River Run lifts.

But all the accommodation is well served by the shuttle buses. All the condominiums we've seen or heard about are large and luxurious – and we've stayed in some fabulous ones.

HOW TO GO
Independent booking easy

A few tour operators offer packages and booking independently is easy. There are regular shuttles from Denver Airport to Keystone. There are hotels but most accommodation is in condominiums.
Hotels There isn't a great choice but they're all of a high standard.
((((④ **Chateaux d'Mont** Small luxurious hotel near the lifts; only 15 suites, with private hot tubs and other luxuries. 'Outstanding' said one reporter.

GETTING THERE

Air Denver, transfer 2hr.

UK PACKAGES

American Connections, American Dream, Crystal, Funway Holidays, Made to Measure, Ski Independence, Ski North America Direct, Skisar U.S., United Vacations Ski Freedom USA

ACTIVITIES

Indoor Swimming, hot tubs, tennis
Outdoor Floodlit ice skating, sleigh and stagecoach rides, snowmobiling, horse-riding, dog-sledding, evening gondola trips

TOURIST OFFICE

Postcode CO 80424
Tel +1 (970) 453 5000
Fax 453 3202

(((④ **Keystone Lodge** Large, luxurious modern hotel in Keystone Village – a shopping and restaurant complex by the frozen lake. Pool and fitness centre.
((③ **Inn at Keystone** Modern, comfortable hotel a short walk from the lifts. Outdoor hot tubs. Liked by reporters who stayed there.
((③ **Ski Tip Lodge** Former stage-coach halt and home of Keystone's founder, Max Dercum, who restored and extended it and used broken ski tips found on the slopes as door handles – hence the name. Atmospheric old rooms, bar and lounge with log fires. Well out of town by the cross-country centre and some new development. Good restaurant.
Self-catering There are hundreds of well-appointed condominiums, most with use of a pool and hot tub. The Liftside condos are in the heart of the resort, close to the lifts, and come complete with all mod cons and good communal facilities. The equally comfortable and well positioned Frostfire condos have fewer in-house amenities but each unit has en suite whirlpool bath. The Resort condos enjoy a pretty location in the woods, a bus-ride from the lifts. The Cinnamon Ridge and Slopeside condos are other comfortable places. All the places we've stayed in have been large and luxurious, with nice touches such as log fires and two-storey floor-to-ceiling windows.

STAYING DOWN THE VALLEY
Possible, good for exploring
A couple of reporters stayed in **Silverthorne**. The Days Inn was thought comfortable but basic. The Alpen Hutte was friendly and had its own private bus transfer. **Frisco** was thought a better centre for visiting other nearby resorts.

EATING OUT
Generally very high standard
Whether you want to eat up the mountain or in the valley, there's a good choice.
The Summit House, at the top of the gondola on Keystone Mountain, remains busy at the end of the normal day because of the floodlit sessions at night. There's live country and western entertainment and simple food – hamburgers, ribs and so on.
The Outpost, on North Peak, is a hive of dining activity with the

Alpenglow Stube (see box on previous spread).
We had a delicious meal at the Ski Tip Lodge by the cross-country track (the menu changes daily). The building is a charming restored former stage-coach halt which the resort's founder used to live in.
The Keystone Ranch has an award-winning restaurant that serves six-course dinners in a building based on a 19th-century homestead built in an area which the Ute and Arapahoe Indians used as their summer campground for buffalo hunting.
There are simpler places in all three main accommodation areas, such as Gassy Thomson's and Ida Belle's for typical American-style burgers, ribs and grills, the Commodore for steak, seafood and pasta, and the Bighorn Steakhouse and Pizza on the Plaza for pizza, soup, salad and sandwiches.
You can take a dinner sleigh ride to Soda Creek Homestead, or a more unusual 'progressive dinner' – a stage-coach ride where you have each course in a different restaurant.
Less grandly, you can get takeaways delivered to your condominium.

APRES-SKI
Pretty quiet in the evenings
Immediately after coming off the slopes, it can be quite lively. The Summit House at the top of the gondola has live music and caters for people using the slopes at night as well as après-skiers. Keysters at the bottom of the gondola has karaoke and Montezuma has rock 'n roll. Some of the eateries double as bars with live music: Snake River Saloon has happy hour, 5–7pm; Ida Belle has ragtime music and a miners' tavern decor; and Dillon Inn has Country and Western.
But places empty out quite early and Keystone isn't really the place for late-night revellers.

OFF THE SLOPES
OK if you want a peaceful time
Keystone is one of the best places in Colorado for pedestrians getting around on the mountain. The gondolas make both mountain restaurant complexes easily accessible, and the transport system makes getting to Breckenridge and Vail easy.
There are plenty of other activities, including skating on the frozen lake (the largest outdoor maintained rink in the US) and indoor tennis.

Steamboat

2100m

Powder glade expansion above a cowboy town

WHAT IT COSTS

((((((6)

HOW IT RATES

The slopes

Snow	****
Extent	**
Experts	***
Intermediates	****
Beginners	*****
Convenience	***
Queues	****
Restaurants	***

The rest

Scenery	***
Resort charm	**
Off-slope	**

➕ Medium-sized area, in the middle of major expansion programme

➕ Excellent beginner and early intermediate terrain

➕ Good restaurants by US standards

➕ Some good slopeside lodging

➕ Famed for its gladed powder terrain

➖ Western cowboy hype rather overdone

➖ Resort separated from old cattle town, and much less characterful

➖ Area rather bland

➖ There is some tough terrain, but not a huge amount

Steamboat markets itself as a real cowboy town. Its brochures usually have horse-riding, stetson-wearing, lassoo-wielding cowboys on the cover. Even Billy Kidd, the head of the school (who skis every day with anyone who turns up to meet him at the top of the mountain at 1pm), is decked out in cowboy gear for the brochures. The area does still have genuine working cowboys but the old 'wagon train' atmosphere doesn't permeate the resort or old town much. Don't go there just for the Western atmosphere.

A better reason for going is its compact area of largely easy-to-intermediate terrain. And in good snow conditions Steamboat is also one of the best resorts around for powder skiing in among the trees. It is in the middle of an expansion programme which will add 40 per cent to its terrain when complete. But until then we'd recommend keen piste-bashers to combine a visit to Steamboat with a stay at another resort – they might find the current terrain limited.

What's new

Steamboat is in the middle of a large expansion programme – see opposite.

In addition, a new high-speed quad is replacing the existing Thunderhead lift and the Arrowhead lift nearby for the 1997/98 season. The area beneath this new lift is having snowmaking installed to allow it to open earlier in the season and trees are being thinned to create more good gladed terrain.

boarding *Steamboat is an ideal place to try boarding for the first time – there are great learning areas, ideal gentle slopes to progress to and you can get all over the mountain using chair-lifts and the gondola. The snowboard school even offers another lesson free if you can't ride from the top of the beginners' area after the first. Steamboat is also a great choice for experienced boarders, with several different fun-parks (including one especially for kids) and half-pipes and a choice of specialist snowboard shops. And the riding in the glades in fresh powder is unbeatable.*

The resort

The resort is a 20-minute bus-ride from the old town of Steamboat Springs – a long drive or short flight from Denver – and is much the most convenient place to stay. Near the gondola station there are a couple of shop- and restaurant-lined multi-level squares leading to the one main street; the buildings are all modern, but with plenty of wooden façades. Much of the accommodation is up the side of the piste, but some is a bus ride away, so the village does have a slightly sprawling feel to it.

The old town is a bit of a disappointment after the hype of the brochures. Its plus-point is that it's a genuine working cattle town. And you're likely to end up chatting to friendly locals if you try some of the bars. In mid-January the Cowboy Downhill is held and cowboys pour into town to compete in a fun slalom, lassooing and saddling competitiron. The rest of the season, there's much less of a real cowboy presence.

The main (and almost only) street is very wide, with multiple lanes of traffic each way – it was built that way to allow cattle to be driven through town. It is lined with bars, hotels and shops, built at various times over the last 120 years, in a wide mixture of architectural styles, from old wooden buildings to modern concrete shopping plazas.

The town got its name in the mid-1800s, when trappers going along by the Yampa river heard a chugging they thought was a steamboat. It turned out to be the sound of a hot spring bubbling through the rocks.

MOUNTAIN FACTS

Altitude 2100m-3220m
Lifts   21
Pistes   2929 acres
Green   14%
Blue   56%
Black   30%
Art. snow   400 acres

Classic Colorado
mountainscape ➔

STEAMBOAT'S EXPANSION PLANS

The 1996/97 season saw the first stage of a 950-acre expansion of Steamboat's terrain (an increase of almost 40 per cent) when the new Morningside Park area opened, with a triple chair serving intermediate and expert runs. In 1997/98 the first part of Pioneer Ridge opens – an area of advanced and expert terrain which you'll have to traverse or hike to until the new lift is built for 1998/99.

The yellow line shows the boundary of the new Pioneer Ridge area. There will be runs open here in 1998, and the resort's Ski into the Future programme will offer guided tours of the new area.

Morningside Park ↓

Storm Peak
3165m

Sunshine Peak
3165m

Sundown

Sunshine

Storm Peak

Rendezvous
Saddle

Pioneer Ridge

Burgess Creek

Thunderhead
2770m

Thunderhead

Silver Bullet

Christie

Steamboat

Christie Base

Gondola base
2100m

The mountain

Steamboat's area is prettily set among the trees, with splendid views down to the rolling hills below. Although it claims to be one of Colorado's biggest areas, a keen intermediate piste-basher could cover all the marked runs in a day. After its current expansion there will be more choice, especially for good intermediates and better – but it still won't rival the amount of terrain of places such as Aspen and Vail.

THE SLOPES
Four flanks on a mountain

The slopes divide naturally into four areas and all have runs to suit all abilities. The Silver Bullet gondola from the village rises to **Thunderhead**. One area lies on the face of this mountain, with runs back to the village and a variety of chairs to carry you back from various points. From Thunderhead you can go down to the left to catch a chair up to **Storm Peak** or to the right to go up to **Sunshine Peak**. From Storm Peak you can now drop over the back into the new **Morningside Park** area. Each of these has its own runs and lifts and you can go from one to the other.

If you have a hire car, **Vail-Beaver Creek, Copper Mountain, Keystone, Arapahoe Basin, Breckenridge** and **Winter Park** are all less than a two-hour drive.

SNOW RELIABILITY
Good despite low altitude

Steamboat is relatively low by Colorado standards; it goes from 2100m to 3225m. So its highest slopes are below the height of the base of Arapahoe Basin. Despite this it has an excellent snow record, getting as much in a year as most of the higher resorts. And many of the pistes have snowmaking facilities. We went there after snow hadn't fallen for a month and, though there were more rocks and icy patches than the other resorts we went to, it was still worth the visit.

FOR EXPERTS
Powder glades are the highlight

The main attraction of Steamboat for experts is the challenging off-piste terrain in the trees – its use in Europe is increasingly banned for ecological reasons. This is particularly wonderful after a fall of fresh powder.

A great area is on Sunshine Peak below the Sundown Express and Priest Creek lifts. There's a huge amount of choice here. You simply take off through the aspens and choose a route where the trees are spaced as you like them – wide or narrow. There are also black pistes marked on the map in this area. The two to the left of the lifts as you go up – Closet and Shadows – are only loosely pistes: the trees have just been thinned out a bit. On the right of the lift as you go up the blacks marked are more genuine cleared routes.

The new areas of Morningside Park and Pioneer Ridge also have excellent gladed terrain – there will be special guided tours of the latter for 1997/98.

On Storm Peak, experts can take a short hike up from the top of the lifts to the Chutes – where there's another wide choice of route and the steepest slopes on the mountain.

Elsewhere on the mountain, you'll find other blacks marked. But most are easy for good intermediates and make great fast runs if they've been groomed.

FOR INTERMEDIATES
Some long cruises

Much of the mountain is ideal intermediate territory, with long cruising blue runs such as Buddy's Run, Rainbow and Ego on Storm Peak and High Noon, One O'Clock and Two O'Clock on Sunshine Peak. We have a rave review of the new Morningside Park area after a fresh snowfall: 'Superb skiing in almost total silence down through the trees – highly recommended.'

Don't ignore Thunderhead either – there are a lot of good runs which it's easy to miss out on if you insist on being drawn up to the top of the mountain. At the end of the day, Vagabond is usually less crowded than Heavenly Daze right under the gondola.

Some of the black runs such as West Side and Lower Valley View also make good challenging intermediate runs when the bumps have been groomed out of them.

The runs at the far right-hand side of the area are very gentle – Tomahawk and Quickdraw are marked blue but are perfectly possible for those who normally stick to green. This area is known to locals as 'Wally World' because of the ease of the terrain.

CHILDCARE

The Kids' Vacation Center is run by the resort in the gondola station. The Kiddie Coral nursery takes children aged 6 months to 6 years, all day. Those aged 2 can opt for the Buckaroos programme with a one-hour private lesson (ski rental not included). Older children go on to the Sundance Kids group classes.

The school has a Rough Rider programme for children up to 15, with their own skiing skills playground area and lunchtime supervision.

The Adventure Club at Night offers evening childcare in the Vacation Center for ages 2½ to 12, from 6pm to 10.30.

GETTING THERE

Air Steamboat Springs, transfer ½hr. Yampa Valley regional airport, transfer 1hr. Denver, transfer 3½hr.

The main problem for keen intermediates will be the limited extent of the area – not really enough to keep you interested for a week unless you enjoy repeating the same runs.

FOR BEGINNERS
Excellent learning terrain

There's a big gentle nursery area at the base of the mountain served by four lifts. You progress from this to take the Christie chair-lifts to a variety of gentle green runs such as Yoo Hoo, Giggle Gulch and Right of Way.

FOR CROSS-COUNTRY
Plenty out of town

There's no cross-country in Steamboat itself but a free shuttle service takes you to the Touring Center, where there are 30km of groomed tracks and lessons available. There are also Forest Service trails on Rabbit Ears Pass.

QUEUES
Not a serious problem

There may be 10-minute queues for the gondola at the start of the day, but at least they are superbly organised. New fast quad chairs have cut out the worst bottlenecks up the mountain, though there can still be queues for the slow Sunshine lift serving the easiest top-of-the-mountain runs.

MOUNTAIN RESTAURANTS
Good by US standards

There are two main restaurant complexes on the mountain, both of which include unusually good table-service restaurants by US standards. The biggest is at Thunderhead. You can catch the gondola up from 8am and breakfast while waiting to start at 9am. At lunchtime there's a choice of a big BK Corral self-service cafeteria, a barbecue on the sundeck, the Stoker bar and restaurant, Hazie's table-service restaurant and the Café Thunderhead for children's ski and snowboard school classes.

At Rendezvous Saddle there's a slightly smaller alternative which has a self-service section including a pizza bar, another sundeck and barbecue and Ragnar's table-service Scandinavian restaurant. You can book for Ragnar's and Hazie's.

There's also a snack bar and sundeck at Four Points.

SCHOOLS AND GUIDES
Mixed views

The latest reports on the school have been very positive, both for adults and children. 'Instructors' attitude was a joy to behold – very friendly and outgoing. My standard improverd tremendously,' said one intermediate adult reporter. The adult programme includes special workshops such as on carving skis and bumps and you can join a Sunrise session where you get on the slopes before the public. There's also a Challenge course aimed at experts and learn to snowboard courses.

FACILITIES FOR CHILDREN
Kids Go Free

Steamboat has a Kids Go Free scheme – free lift pass for one child of up to age 12 per parent buying a pass. The school has a variety of courses for different standards and age groups. 'Our two boys in the Desperados ski week had the time of their lives and their skiing improved dramatically,' said one 1997 reporter. Childcare arrangements are comprehensive, including evening sessions in the Vacation Center – an excellent idea that ought to be widely copied. The one weak spot seems to be that school ends at 3pm, and there seem to be no facilities for looking after pupils after that time.

Staying there

Staying in the old town of Steamboat Springs is cheaper but much less convenient than staying at the resort itself. Our preference would be to stay on the slopes and make occasional excursions to the town in the evening. In case you're gripped by indecision, there is accommodation between the two – the worst of both worlds.

HOW TO GO
Plenty of packages

More tour operators go here than to many comparable mid-size US resorts. There's accommodation for all tastes, including more downmarket places than is the US norm and some catered chalets run by UK tour operators.
Hotels The smarter hotels out at the resort have less character than some of the in-town options.
⟨⟨⟨4 **Ptarmigan Inn** Ideally situated just above the gondola station and right on the piste, with an outdoor

UK PACKAGES

Airtours, American Dream, Bladon Lines, Crystal, First Choice Ski, Funway Holidays, Inghams, Lotus Supertravel, Made to Measure, Neilson, Ski Activity, Ski Independence, Ski North America Direct, Skisar U.S., Skiworld North America, Thomson, United Vacations Ski Freedom USA

ACTIVITIES

Indoor Ice skating, hot tubbing, swimming pools, tennis, gym, weights room, climbing wall, museum
Outdoor Ice driving school, dog-sledding, snowmobiling, ballooning, hot springs, dinner sleigh rides, horse-riding, skating, ice and rock climbing, fly-fishing, snowcat skiing

TOURIST OFFICE

Postcode CO 80487
Tel +1 (970) 879 6111
Fax 879 7844

pool and hot tub, a sauna and good après-ski bar with a happy hour.
((((4) **Sheraton** Big, anonymous, concrete hotel right on the main square at the foot of the slopes, with a pool and hot tub – just the sort of place we like to avoid.
(((3) **Harbor** The oldest hotel in the old town. All its rooms vary in size and character and there's a sauna, steam room and two hot tubs.
((2) **Alpiner Lodge** Bavarian style economy option in old town.
Self-catering The apartments we have seen have been universally high in quality. The best we saw were the Bear Claw condos – wonderfully spacious and individually furnished, and right on the piste at the top of the Headwall chair. The complex has a sauna, outdoor pool and hot tub, and an efficient shuttle bus system. Other recommendations include Timber Run, a short shuttle-bus ride from the centre with a number of hot tubs kept at different temperatures; the Lodge at Steamboat, close to the gondola station, also with good facilities; Thunderhead Condos; and the aptly named Ski Inn.

EATING OUT
Huge variety
There's a huge choice of places to suit all pockets. Steamboat specialises in mountain-top eating – there are three places to choose from. You start by going up the Silver Bullet gondola (with complimentary blankets). If you're going to Ragnar's, you then take a sleigh hauled by a snowcat for a Scandinavian meal. Or you stay put at Thunderhead. There you can go to BK's (the lunchtime self-service restaurant) for an as-much-as-you-can-eat buffet, accompanied by country and western music and dancing. Or you can try haute cuisine at Hazie's, where the menu goes somewhat upmarket from the lunchtime fare. In the resort itself, the Slopeside Grill has a good selection of pizza and pasta dishes and doubles as a bar, with live music some nights.
Down in the valley you can take horse-drawn sleigh rides to other dinner options, such as down Walton Creek canyon, to eat in heated tents with Western music.
In downtown Steamboat try L'Apogee, for French-style food, or the cheaper Harwig's Grill on the same premises. The Steamboat Yacht Club

on the riverbank is recommended for seafood and views of ski-jumping. The Chart House and Coral Grill, on the outskirts of town, are recommended for seafood. For more traditional American fare try the popular Old West Steakhouse or the atmospheric ranch-style Ore House. Antares is fairly new, hugely popular and has excellent international cuisine. Other options include Japanese, Russian, Chinese and Cajun.
In the resort, La Montana and Cantina are recommended for Tex-Mex, Mattie Silles for seafood, Cugnino's for Italian and The Butcher Shop for steaks and the like.

APRES-SKI
Fairly lively
The base lodge area has a few noisy bars, but things are much quieter and less brash in the old town. The liveliest place immediately after coming off the slopes is usually the Inferno, in the square. This has live music and a happy hour – and on Sundays it has a very popular 'Disco Inferno' night. Buddy's Run, near the gondola entrance, can also be fun, with live music or comedy. Dos Amigos is the place for jugs of margarita and half-price appetisers. Or try the Tugboat Tavern in the main street. The Ptarmigan Inn is for those who want a somewhat more sophisticated atmosphere.
The Old Town Pub in Steamboat Springs dates from 1904, has live music at weekends and does quintessential American food – burgers, steaks, etc.
There are popular micro-brewery bars in both the resort and the old town – the Heavenly Daze and Steamboat Brewery are worth trying.
There are plenty of evening activities too, including watching floodlit ski-jumping in the old town.

OFF THE SLOPES
Lots to do
Getting up the gondola to the restaurant complex is easy for pedestrians. Visiting town is too. And you can go and relax in outdoor hot springs seven miles from town or learn to drive on the special ice circuit. There are plenty of other activities too.

Telluride

2660m

Dinky old town, dinky little area

WHAT IT COSTS

HOW IT RATES

The slopes

Snow	****
Extent	**
Experts	****
Intermediates	***
Beginners	*****
Convenience	****
Queues	*****
Restaurants	**

The rest

Scenery	***
Resort charm	****
Off-slope	**

MOUNTAIN FACTS

Altitude	2660m-3625m
Lifts	12
Pistes	1050 acres
Green	21%
Blue	47%
Black	32%
Art. snow	155 acres

What's new

The long-awaited gondola linking the old town with the Mountain Village via the top of the mountain opened for 1996/97.

1997/98 sees the opening of a new snowboard fun-park with over 300m vertical of berms, gaps, hits and table-tops and a new building at the Mountain Village, with a nursery, ski shops and ski school.

UK PACKAGES

American Dream, Lotus Supertravel, Made to Measure, Ski Independence, Ski North America Direct, Skisar U.S.

TOURIST OFFICE

Postcode CO 81435
Tel +1 (970) 728 6900
Fax 728 6364

High-mileage piste-bashers may find Telluride rather small, but it's growing. We have great affection for the place – the San Juan mountains are stunning and set the resort apart from others in the Rockies, and the town has lots of character.

THE RESORT

Telluride is an isolated resort in south-west Colorado. The town first boomed when gold was found – some say its name is a shortened version of 'To hell you ride'. Now it looks like a typical small Wild-West town from the movies – except that the main street is busy with pick-up trucks not horses. The slopes and lifts go right into town.

Further up the hill, Mountain Village is a model American leisure resort with modern buildings, including The Peaks, a huge hotel.

THE MOUNTAINS

The **slopes** feature some fearsomely steep terrain, and also ideal beginner and intermediate areas – just not that much of any of them.

From town a new gondola and two chair-lifts climb the steep, wooded northern flank of the area. The gondola carries on down to the Mountain Village, from where chair-lifts also rise. Lifts from both bases meet at two points. From the higher point you can hike up to Gold Hill which peaks at 3735m. There are plans to develop a big area including this, building five new lifts. The terrain gets flatter towards the Mountain Village; below it is the long, gentle nursery slope. The world's longest high-speed quad chair serves the long easy runs of a separate mountain. **Snowboarders** will have a new Ride Park for 1997/98 – the biggest in the south-west of the US.

Snow reliability is good. Telluride has a high average snowfall and lots of well placed snowmaking.

The double black bump runs directly above the town made the area's reputation for **experts** – 960m of vertical. There are also great, steep gladed runs on the other side of the lift-system high-point, and on Gold Hill.

The **intermediate** terrain is mainly on runs served by the lifts just above Mountain Village. From the top of the mountain, See Forever is a glorious scenic cruise down the main ridge.

There is one easy way back to town – the winding Telluride Trail.

There are ideal **beginner** runs in the Meadows at Mountain Village, and more are accessed by lift 10.

The scenic beauty of the area makes it splendid for **cross-country** – The Telluride Nordic Center runs over 40km of trails, plus various adventure trips.

Queues are rarely a problem, but lift 6 is a slow double chair, and can be a bottleneck at peak times as it serves many classic tough runs.

As in many US resorts, **mountain restaurants** are fairly primitive and entirely self-service affairs. Gorrono, just above the Mountain Village, has a big outside terrace with a barbecue, and a separate bar in an old cabin.

As well as the usual, **ski schools** offer special mogul tuition, and free mountain orientation tours daily.

There is thorough provision for **children**. The school's Adventure Club provides indoor and outdoor play before and after lessons.

STAYING THERE

The resort is offered by only a few US specialist operators. You have to choose between the town or the less atmospheric Mountain Village, but the gondola link runs till late.

Most hotels are in and around the town, but the biggest, plushest and priciest is The Peaks in Mountain Village. The New Sheridan is one of the town's oldest hotels; Skyline Guest Ranch is a lovely old ranch-house with excellent food, a few minutes' drive from Mountain Village.

There are also plenty of self-catering condos and houses to rent.

There is a cosmopolitan choice of **eating out** with French, Greek–Italian, German–Austrian, Chinese plus Tex–Mex and typical American. Telluride has a lively bar-based **après-ski** scene too. Leimgruber's is popular immediately after leaving the slopes.

Off the slopes, a glider flight is spectacular for views, or there's riding.

Vail-Beaver Creek   2500m

Luxury living and the USA's largest area

WHAT IT COSTS

(((((6)

HOW IT RATES

The slopes

Snow	*****
Extent	****
Experts	****
Intermediates	*****
Beginners	*****
Convenience	***
Queues	***
Restaurants	**

The rest

Scenery	***
Resort charm	****
Off-slope	***

What's new

Beaver Creek's terrain was expanded by 30% for 1997 with the construction of the Bachelor Gulch chair-lift and other runs and lifts linking Beaver Creek to Arrowhead. For 1998, the Stump Park lift serving the top half of the main mountain is to be replaced by a fast six-seat chair. The Arrowbahn fast chair from Arrowhead will shift 50% more people. Construction work has started on the new Birds of Prey downhill race course, in preparation for the 1999 World Alpine Ski Championships.

Two fast new lifts out of Vail were built for 1996/97 – the Eagle Bahn gondola at Lionshead and the Riva Bahn chair at Golden Peak. 1997/98 will bring a 30%. increase in trail-grooming capacity. Looking ahead, there are exciting plans to develop the north-facing terrain beyond Vail's Back Bowls, starting in 1998/99.

➕ Biggest area in the US, and an impressive one by any standard – great for confident intermediates

➕ Beaver Creek's slopes are blissfully quiet and very varied, with serious double-blacks and beautifully groomed cruising runs

➕ Vail's Back Bowls are a big area of treeless terrain – unusual in the US

➕ Largely traffic-free resort villages, and a fair simulation of Tyrolean Alpine charm in Vail Village

➖ Vail's slopes can be crowded by American standards, with lift queues even in low season

➖ The famous Back Bowls face south, and the snow can suffer in warm weather

➖ Tyrolean-style Vail Village and rather dour Beaver Creek are far from the Wild West atmosphere you might look for on a trip to the US

➖ Expensive, especially Beaver Creek

➖ Disappointing mountain restaurants

Vail is one of the biggest and best resorts of the US, whichever way you look at it. And taken together with nearby Beaver Creek and Arrowhead, owned by the same company, it offers more mountain than anywhere else (as well as more high-speed quad chair-lifts and more instructors). Not surprisingly, it is one of the most popular destinations for visitors from abroad – the UK in particular.

The resorts cultivate an exclusive image – and central accommodation can be pricey. But what matters more to the visitors who send us enthusiastic reports is the resorts' convenience, civilised atmosphere and big area of great snow. Most of the terrain is ideal for novices and intermediates. Experts will also find runs to interest them in Vail's largely ungroomed Back Bowls, if the snow is good, and on the mogul fields of Beaver Creek.

We always enjoy visiting Vail and Beaver Creek, but in the end they can't compete with the distinctive atmosphere of rivals based on old mining towns or cowboy towns. If we're going that far West, we like it to be a bit Wild.

boarding *This slick pair of resorts are wooing boarders with excellent facilities and a positive attitude – there's even a special snowboard trail map showing which runs freeriders and freestylers should head for. With beautifully groomed, gentle slopes and no drag-lifts, these are great areas for beginners, but there's plenty of terrain for experts too – quality of snow in the famous but sunny Back Bowls being less of an issue for boarders. Both resorts have fun-parks with half-pipes, and Vail's main one (at Eagle's Nest) is open at night. There are specialist board shops in both villages, and tuition options include special camps for grown-ups – a great idea that we can recommend.*

The resort

Standing in the centre of Vail Village, surrounded by chalet-style buildings and bierkellers, you could be forgiven for thinking you were in a top Austrian resort. And that's just what Vail's founder, Pete Seibert, intended back in the 1950s. But Vail Village is now just part of an enormous resort, stretching for miles along the valley – most of it in anonymous modern style.

Beaver Creek, developed by the owners of Vail in the 1980s, is ten miles to the west. It is unashamedly exclusive, with a choice of top-quality hotels and condos right by the slopes. It centres on a huge pedestrian square featuring exquisite bronze statues and even an open-air fire to warm you up on evening promenades.

Arrowhead is the newest addition to Vail's portfolio. A secluded collection of luxurious chalets, it was bought by Vail a few years ago, and linked into the Beaver Creek lift network for the 1996/97 season, creating a sort of mini-three-valleys system.

MOUNTAIN FACTS

Beaver Creek

Altitude 2470m-3490m
Lifts	14
Pistes	1529 acres
Green	19%
Blue	43%
Black	38%
Art. snow	709 acres

Vail

Altitude 2475m-3490m
Lifts	26
Pistes	4112 acres
Green	32%
Blue	36%
Black	32%
Art. snow	347 acres

Recco detectors used

LIFT PASSES

96/97 prices in dollars
Vail and Beaver Creek
Covers all Vail and
Beaver Creek lifts,
and ski-bus around
resort.
Beginners 1- (98) and
3-day (294) Learn-to-
ski courses including
lift pass and
equipment rental.
Main pass
1-day pass 52
6-day pass 300
(low season 210 –
30% off)
Senior citizens
Over 65: 6-day pass
270 (10% off)
Over 70: free pass
Children
Under 13: 6-day pass
198 (34% off)
Short-term passes
Return trips on some
lifts for foot
passengers only. Half-
day pass from noon
available (adult 39).

The mountains 🏔️

Even leaving aside Beaver Creek, Vail
has a lot of terrain by US standards,
both prepared trails and ungroomed
powder skiing in the Back Bowls. And
Beaver Creek and Arrowhead offer the
nearest thing you'll find in the States
to the linked lift networks of the Alps.
Even so, there isn't the sheer extent of
terrain that you find in the biggest
Alpine areas such as Val-d'Isère/Tignes,
the Three Valleys or La Plagne.

There are runs to suit every taste,
from beginner or nervous intermediate
to powderhounds and mogul-freaks.
The resort stands out for our reporters'
enthusiasm for it. We've had many
reports on it, nearly all glowing with
praise. 'Brilliant', 'Excellent', 'Grooming
exemplary', 'Hazard marking superb'
are typical. The main criticism – made
by several correspondents – is that
some of the runs (especially single
black diamonds) are over-graded.

The Vail and Beaver Creek areas are
completely separate but linked by bus
and covered on the same lift pass.
They also feel very different; Vail gets
much more crowded than Beaver
Creek, which is overlooked by many
people staying in Vail. They're making
a mistake, in our view.

THE SLOPES
Something for everyone
The slopes above **Vail** can be accessed
via three main lifts. From right next to
Vail Village, the Vista Bahn fast chair
goes up to the major mid-mountain
focal point, Mid-Vail (3095m); the new
Riva Bahn fast chair goes up from the
Golden Peak base area just to the
east; and from the second major resort
centre, Lionshead, the new Eagle Bahn
gondola goes up to the fast-developing
Eagle's Nest complex (3155m).

The front face of the mountain is
largely north-facing, with well-groomed
trails cut through the trees. At altitude
the mountainside divides into three
bowls – Mid-Vail in the centre, with
Game Creek to the south-west and
Northeast Bowl to the, er, north-east.
Lifts reach the ridge at three points,
the highest at 3430m, all giving access
to the **Back Bowls** – mostly treeless
and ungroomed.

The terrain of **Beaver Creek** is now
almost as extensive as that of Vail. The
slopes immediately above the resort
divide into two sectors, each accessed

by a fast quad chair. The major sector
is centred on Spruce Saddle, with lifts
above it reaching 3485m. The other is
lower and smaller, but forms the newly
opened link with **Bachelor Gulch** and
Arrowhead. Up the valley a little, and
between these two sectors, is Grouse
Mountain, with seriously steep slopes.

Other resorts within a two-hour
drive include Aspen, Steamboat,
Breckenridge and Keystone. The last
two are now owned by Vail, and you
can expect some sort of lift-pass
sharing arrangements to apply.

SNOW RELIABILITY
Excellent, except in the Bowls
As well as an exceptional natural snow
record, Vail and Beaver Creek both
have extensive snowmaking facilities,
normally needed only in early season.
But one of the biggest
disappointments about Vail is that its
famous Back Bowls get too much sun.
In four visits we've never hit the
champagne powder conditions for
which the Back Bowls are ideal.

The steep Grouse Mountain slopes
in Beaver Creek can also suffer from
thin snow cover.

FOR EXPERTS
Enough to keep most folks happy
Vail's Back Bowls are vast areas,
served by three chair-lifts and a couple
of short drag-lifts. You can go virtually
anywhere you like in their 2,734 acres,
trying the gradient and terrain of your
choice. There are interesting tree-lined
areas as well as the more common
tree-free mogulled slopes. But the
Bowls are not particularly steep, and
they have disappointed some of our
more dare-devil correspondents.

On the front face there are some
genuinely steep, often mogulled,
double black diamond runs which
frequently have better snow than the
Back Bowls. The Highline lift on the
extreme east of the area serves three.

In Beaver Creek, Grouse Mountain is
the place for experts to head for. This
is almost entirely black-run territory,
with some intimidatingly steep double-
dimaond runs. Other good steep blacks
lead down to the bottom of Grouse
from the main mountain summit.

The Larkspur Bowl area has three
short steep mogul runs worth trying.

Beaver Creek is a great place to ski
fast, thanks to the lack of crowds.
Even by American standards, Beaver
Creek's runs are often deserted.

FOR INTERMEDIATES
Ideal territory

The majority of Vail's front face is great intermediate territory, with easy cruising runs. On the western side of the area, especially, there are excellent long blues – Born Free and Simba both go from top to bottom. Game Creek bowl, nearby, is excellent too.

As well, as tackling some of the easier front-face blacks, intermediates will find plenty of interest in the Back Bowls. Some runs are groomed, making it easy for groups of mixed ability to take different routes and ride the lifts together. Several of the runs are graded blue, including Silk Road which loops around the eastern edge

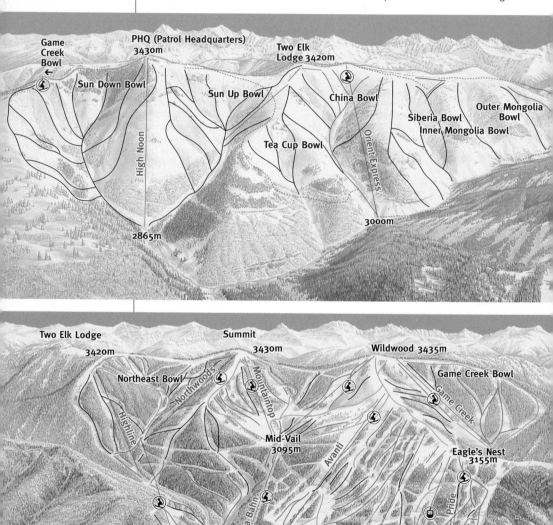

of the domain, with wonderful views. More adventurous intermediates can branch out to try some of the unpisted slopes, many of which can make the ideal introduction to powder.

Beaver Creek is an intermediate's dream. There are marvellous long cruising blue runs almost everywhere you look, including various ways from top to bottom of the main mountain – a vertical drop of just over 1000m. The Larkspur chair and the chairs going west from the village serve further cruising runs – and lead to yet more ideal terrain served by the Bachelor Gulch and Arrowhead fast chairs.

FOR BEGINNERS
Difficult to beat

There are good nursery slopes at Vail Village and Beaver Creek, but what makes both resorts rather special for absolute beginners and (especially) nervous novices is the gentle slopes at altitude. At Eagle's Nest, Vail has an extensive area of green and blue runs, including the nursery slope on which one of your editors took his first hundred falls on a snowboard. We recommend it. Beaver Creek's main mountain, similarly, has a superb gentle area of green runs at the top.

There are plenty of easy longer runs to progress to, including runs from top to bottom of the mountains. And Beaver Creek has very sensibly designated a couple of runs down from mid-mountain to the village as low-speed zones.

↑ Mid-Vail – the main focus of the front face of the mountains above Vail, with various eating options, from barbecue and food courts to the best food on the slopes (at Cook Shack)

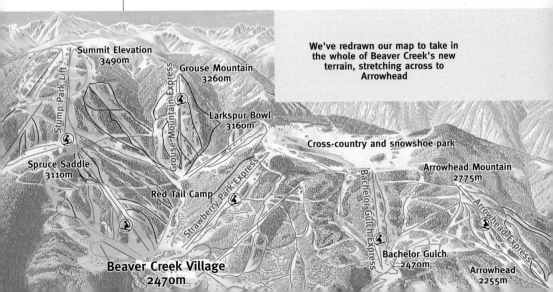

Summit Elevation
3490m

Stump-Park Lift

Grouse Mountain
3260m

Grouse Mountain Express

Larkspur Bowl
3160m

We've redrawn our map to take in the whole of Beaver Creek's new terrain, stretching across to Arrowhead

Cross-country and snowshoe park

Spruce Saddle
3110m

Red Tail Camp

Strawberry Park Express

Bachelor Gulch Express

Arrowhead Mountain
2775m

Arrowhead Express

Beaver Creek Village
2470m

Bachelor Gulch
2470m

Arrowhead
2255m

SCHOOLS/GUIDES

96/97 prices in dollars

Vail and Beaver Creek
At four locations -
Vail Village,
Lionshead, Golden
Peak and Beaver
Creek
Classes 7 days
5hr: 9.45-3.45 with
1hr lunch; 3hr 15mins:
12.30-3.45
3 full days: 260
Children's classes
Ages: 3 to 13
5 6½hr days including
rental, lift pass and
lunch: 370
Private lessons
1hr, 2hr, half- and
full-day
98 for 1hr, for 1 to 6
people

CHILDCARE

School tuition is
based at Children's
Ski Centers located at
Golden Peak and
Lionshead in Vail, and
at Beaver Creek
resort. There are
separate programmes
to suit children of
different ages and
competence – Mini-
Mice for children aged
3, Mogul Mice and
Superstars for those
aged 4 to 6.

Small World Play
Schools, located at
Golden Peak in Vail
and at Beaver Creek,
provide day-care for
children aged 2
months to 6 years,
from 8am to 4.30.

FOR CROSS-COUNTRY
Some of the best

Vail's cross-country areas are at the
foot of Golden Peak and at the Nordic
Center on the golf course. At Beaver
Creek, there's a splendid mountain-top
network of 32km of tracks at McCoy
Park, at the top of the Strawberry Park
chair-lift out of the resort.

QUEUES
Can be bad in Vail

Vail has some of the longest lift
queues we've hit in the US, especially
at weekends because of the influx from
Denver. As usual in the US, they move
quickly and are well disciplined.

The fast Riva Bahn chair from
Golden Peak has relieved the rush-hour
pressure on the Vista Bahn from Vail
Village, but at busy times you can still
expect to queue for mid-mountain lifts
and for the Back Bowl chairs when the
snow there is good. Weekends are the
worst times. There's a useful traffic-
light system at the main lifts to help
you avoid the worst queues.

Beaver Creek, on the other hand, is
virtually queue-free – it is amazing that
more people don't go there from Vail.

MOUNTAIN RESTAURANTS
Trying hard

Vail's mountain restaurants are not
bad by US standards, and the resort is
trying hard to bring its facilities up to
European standards, but it still has a
long way to go. The vast Two Elk
Lodge, for example, is an impressive
affair with massive wooden pillars and
a high roof – but you have to fight for
a table. At Eagle's Nest, similarly, the
main self-service restaurant gets
ridiculously overcrowded.

The only way to get a pleasant
lunch, it seems to us, is to pay a bit
more for table-service – Cook Shack at
Mid-Vail is best, or the Wine Stube at
Eagle's Nest. And reserve a table.

At Beaver Creek, Spruce Saddle
(rather like Two Elk Lodge) at mid-
mountain is the main place for lunch.
Beano's Cabin is a beautiful wooden
cabin in the woods near Larkspur
Bowl, serving superb food – but it's a
private members' club at lunchtime.

SCHOOLS AND GUIDES
Among the best in the world

The Vail-Beaver Creek school has an
excellent reputation. All the reports
we've had of it have again been
glowing. Class sizes are usually small –
as few as four is not uncommon.
Having tried three different instructors,
we can vouch for the high standard.
There are specialist half-day workshops
in, for example, bumps and powder.
You can sign up on the mountain.

FACILITIES FOR CHILDREN
Excellent

The comprehensive arrangements for
young children look excellent, and a
recent report on the children's school
says it is 'outstanding' with 'staff and
tuition excellent'. At both Vail and
Beaver Creek there are splendid
children's areas with adventure trails
and themed play areas.

Staying there

Vail is vast, and it's worth thinking
about where you want to be based –
although the free bus-service is very
efficient. The most convenient – and
expensive – places to stay are in mock-
Tyrolean Vail Village centre near the
Vista Bahn fast chair or in plain,
functional Lionshead, near the new,
powerful gondola.

But there is a lot of accommodation
further out – the cheapest tends to be
across the main I-70 freeway, but lacks
the real Vail atmosphere.

Beaver Creek can be reached by a
shuttle bus from Vail. Staying there is

MOUNTAINTOP BUSINESS

*The 1996/97 season saw a big expansion of facilities at Eagle's Nest, at the top of
the new Eagle Bahn gondola from Lionshead, particularly designed to offer
diversions in the evening. Floodlit facilities include a new ice-rink, half-pipe and
tubing hill (you slide down on a rubber inner-tube) as well as a nursery slope. You
can go snowmobiling or snowshoeing, and there are bars and restaurants open for
dinner. Vail prides itself on attracting America's top executives, so the Sprint
Communications Centre should be no surprise. With phones, PCs with Internet
access, videoconferencing facilities, fax and financial market information, it's
ideal for those who just can't bear being away from the office.*

GETTING THERE

Air Eagle, transfer 1hr.
Denver, transfer 2½hr.

UK PACKAGES

Airtours, American
Dream, Bladon Lines,
Crystal, First Choice
Ski, Funway Holidays,
Independent Ski
Links, Inghams, Lotus
Supertravel, Made to
Measure, Ski Activity,
Ski Club of GB, Ski
Equipe, Ski
Independence, Ski
North America Direct,
Skisar U.S., Skiworld
North America, The
Ski Company Ltd,
Thomson, United
Vacations Ski
Freedom USA

Beaver Creek
American
Connections,
American Dream,
Chalets 'Unlimited',
Crystal, Lotus
Supertravel, Made to
Measure, Ski
Independence, Skisar
U.S., United Vacations
Ski Freedom USA

an option for the wealthy. It is an unashamedly upmarket resort with a fair choice of luxurious, expensive hotels, all within an easy walk of the slopes. Nightlife and choice of bars and restaurants is much more limited.

HOW TO GO
Package or independent

There's a big choice of packages to Vail and a smaller one to Beaver Creek. It's also very easy to organise your own visit, with regular shuttles from Denver airport by Vans to Vail. Hiring a car would be worthwhile only if you wanted to visit other resorts such as Breckenridge.

Chalets Vail offers the widest choice of catered chalets in the US, available through a wide range of UK tour operators. Many are slightly out of the main resort at East Vail or West Vail.

Hotels Vail has a fair choice of hotels, ranging from luxurious to budget. In the more upmarket Beaver Creek you can go completely overboard.
At Vail:

(((((5) **Sonnenalp Bavaria Haus**
Generally considered best in town, with some very impressive suites. Large sports complex and splendid piano bar-lounge. The other Sonnenalp place – Swiss Haus, isn't so special.

(((((5) **Lodge at Vail** Swanky place, owned by Orient Express Hotels, right by the Vista Bahn in Vail Village. Huge buffet breakfast keeps most people going all day.

((((3) **Vail Village Inn** Condo and hotel complex, recently partly renovated and rebuilt. Complaints of unfriendly staff and scruffy decor from one recent reporter. Good position. Outdoor pool.

(((3) **Chateau Vail (Holiday Inn)** Not quite as central. Adequate comfort, with a pool.

((2) **Roost Lodge** A popular budget option in West Vail, with comfortable rooms and friendly, helpful staff. Pool, sauna, hot tub, constant free coffee and regular cheese and wine parties.
At Beaver Creek:

(((((5) **Beaver Creek Lodge** Luxurious all-suite hotel. Health club with pool, sauna and so on.

(((((5) **Hyatt Regency** Much better than your standard Hyatt, with impeccable service. Lively bar.

Self-catering There are numerous options. For those who want lots of in-house amenities, the Racquet Club at East Vail is superb – high-standard apartments and town houses with use

of pool, health centre and, of course, racket sports. There are plenty of cheaper options, and several tour operators have allocations conveniently close to the Lionshead gondola.

STAYING UP THE MOUNTAIN
Great if you can afford it

Trappers Cabin is a luxurious private cabin up the mountain, which a group can rent by the night ($500 each for a minimum of four people). You come in at the end of the day to a champagne welcome, make a snow-shoe excursion to see the sunset, soak in an outdoor hot tub and enjoy a gourmet dinner. The cabin-keeper then leaves until morning. We're told you can also stay on a similar basis at the exclusive Game Creek Lodge.

STAYING ALONG THE VALLEY
Cheaper but quiet

Staying out of central Vail is certainly cheaper but not so lively. If you rent a car, staying out of town and visiting nearby resorts makes for an interesting holiday. East Vail and West Vail both have reasonably priced accommodation. Another budget option is to stay in Avon at the foot of the approach road up to Beaver Creek. Day-trippers have to leave their cars here and take the shuttle bus up to the resort. It's not a very atmospheric town but it does have a number of reasonably priced hotels and motels. The Comfort Inn is used by a fair number of tour operators.

EATING OUT
Endless choice

Whatever kind of food you want, Vail has it. Burgers, Tex Mex, Chinese, Japanese, Moroccan, Italian, Thai and a big choice of European-style 'fine dining'. It's easy to pay a lot, but you don't have to – Vail needn't cost more than other US resorts.

Recommended fine-dining options in Vail include the Wildflower, in the Lodge, Ludwig's, in the Sonnenalp Bavaria Haus, the Left Bank and La Tour. The Saddleridge, in Beaver Creek, offers a marvellous night out. It is a luxurious wooden building packed with photos and Wild West artefacts, including old six-shooters and General Custer's hat. The Mirabelle, at the bottom of the access road, is also rather special.

The sleigh-ride to Beano's Cabin in Beaver Creek also makes a splendid

ACTIVITIES

Indoor Athletic clubs and spas, massage, museum, cinema, tennis courts, artificial skating rink, library, galleries

Outdoor Hot-air ballooning, skating, ice hockey, heli-skiing, sleigh rides, fishing, mountaineering, snowmobiles, snow-shoe excursions, snowcat tours, bob-sleighing, dog-sledding, paragliding, tubing hill

TOURIST OFFICE

Postcode 81658
Tel +1 (970) 845 5745
Fax 845 5728

evening out. The food and setting are several cuts above the average 'dinner sleigh-ride'.

For a budget option we liked the Hubcap Brewery in Vail Village, which has a choice of local ales and filling American food. For pasta, pancakes or high-fat breakfast at all hours (open 7am Tuesday to 7pm Sunday), head for DJ McCadam's in Concert Plaza.

Recommendations from readers this year include Lancelot (for steaks), Montauk (for fish), Vendetta (Italian), Blu's (varied menu, good value), Los Amigos (Mexican), Terra Bistro and Sweet Basil (quite pricey).

APRES-SKI
Lively after skiing, early to bed
Staying at high altitude plus the early opening and closing times of lifts makes Vail's nightlife a short pre-dinner affair. After an early dinner, tiredness sets in for most reporters.

Many have fallen into the handy but rather dire Red Lion, but there are plenty of better places: the Hong Kong Café is popular for its cocktails; the Swiss Chalet attempts to recreate

European 'gemütlichkeit'; King's Club is the place to go for high-calorie cake intake, and becomes a piano bar later; Louie's has live jazz; and Los Amigos and the Hubcap Brewery are other atmospheric places at around four o'clock. Club Chelsea is a piano bar with the only smoking room in town.

Cyrano's is one of the few places to stay lively, serving good food and becoming a disco later. Garton's saloon also stays open late and has live bands some nights. Garfinkel's at Lionshead is another place that's popular all evening.

Nick's is the key nightspot; the Club and Sheika's are other discos.

A couple of old-West-style places out of town have live entertainment including country and western bands, and line-dancing with instructions for the uninitiated.

OFF THE SLOPES
A lot to do
Getting around on the free bus is easy and there are lots of activities to try and walks available. Excursions to Denver are feasible.

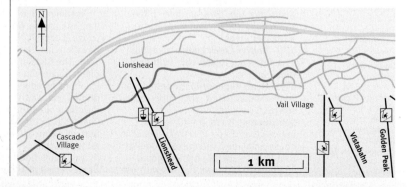

Winter Park

Colorado's best-kept secret, now becoming better known

WHAT IT COSTS

(((((5)

HOW IT RATES

The slopes

Snow	*****
Extent	***
Experts	****
Intermediates	****
Beginners	*****
Convenience	*
Queues	****
Restaurants	***

The rest

Scenery	***
Resort charm	**
Off-slope	*

MOUNTAIN FACTS

Altitude	2740m-3675m
Lifts	22
Pistes	2581 acres
Green	12%
Blue	47%
Black	41%
Art. snow	280 acres

➕ The best snowfall record of all Colorado's major resorts

➕ Slopes to suit all standards, from great beginner areas to some of the steepest chutes we've seen

➕ Town feels like a real American place rather than just a resort

➕ Spectacular views

➕ Cheap by US resort standards

➖ Not much resort ambience. There's no resort village at the bottom of the slopes (though one is planned) and the main town is a bus-ride away, strung out along a road, with no real focus

➖ The nearest big resort to Denver, so can get crowded at weekends

For over 50 years, Winter Park has been a favourite winter sports area for the residents of Denver, only a 90-minute drive (or weekend train-ride) away. To serve this local trade, the area has developed excellent runs for all standards, and an efficient lift system including seven high-speed quads. We have to admit to being surprised by what we found when we first visited a few years ago.

The downside for a 'destination' holiday is currently a lack of normal resort atmosphere. The town, with most of the accommodation, is strung out along the main US40 highway with no real focus, and no glitz or glamour. But it does have good, quiet condo accommodation set in the woods, bars and restaurants with a local feel and some lively nightspots. And there are plans to build a new pedestrian village at the foot of the slopes – when that is complete the resort will be a much more attractive place for a week's stay.

Parsenn Bowl
3675m

Vasquez Cirque

Timberline

Mary Jane
3415m

Sunnyside

High Lonesome Express

Vasquez Ridge
3260m

Winter Park
3260

The whole area between Vasquez Cirque and Vasquez Ridge will be opened up for the 1997/98 season – mainly expert terrain

Summit Express

Olympia Express

Pioneer Express

Zephyr Express

Mary Jane
base area
2880m

Winter Park Village
2745m

What's new

For 1997/98 435 acres of new advanced and expert terrain in Vasquez Cirque west of Parsenn Bowl – open bowls and chutes at the top, glades lower down – will be opened, served by the existing Timberline chair.

boarding *Winter Park has three great fun-parks and a big half-pipe, making it a favourite with many boarders. Two fun-parks are on Winter Park Mountain (Knuckle Dragon just above Snoasis and Madhatters just above that) and one amid the trees on Mary Jane (Stone Grove). The first two are created by trail-grooming machines and have rail slides, quarter-pipes and a series of jumps. Stone Grove is a gladed area where natural features such as drop-offs and gullies are great fun. There is also great advanced and extreme boarding terrain. Winter Park is an ideal beginner and intermediate boarder area, with excellent terrain for first steps on a board, a good school and a network of lifts which is entirely chairs. The bars and restaurants, which tend to be quiet mid-week, get crowded and lively at weekends – and snowboarders tend to hang out at Slade's Underground in downtown.*

LIFT PASSES

97/98 prices in dollars
Winter Park Resort
Covers all lifts in Winter Park, Mary Jane, Vasquez Ridge, Vasquez Cirque and Parsenn Bowl areas.
Beginners Pass for Galloping Goose beginner lift only on June Mountain (5 per day)
Main pass
1-day pass 45
6-day pass 245
(low season 156 – 36% off)
Senior citizens
Over 61: 6-day pass 132 (46% off)
Over 70: free pass
Children
Under 14: 6-day pass 90 (63% off)
Under 6: free pass
Short-term passes
Half-day passes up to or from 12.15pm (adult 28)
Alternative periods
Passes of 2 days and over allow one non-skiing day, eg 6-day pass valid for 7 days with one day off. 8- and 9- day pass allow 2 non-skiing days.
Notes Special rates for disabled skiers.

The resort

Winter Park is around 70 miles from Denver, over the Berthoud Pass, right on the Continental Divide – and straddling the US40 highway.

It started life around the turn of the century as a railway town, when Rio Grande railway workers started climbing up the slopes and skiing down. One of the resort's mountains, Mary Jane, is named after a legendary 'lady of pleasure' who is said to have received the land as payment for her favours.

The railway still plays an important part in Winter Park's existence, with a station right at the foot of the slopes and regular trains bringing day-trippers from Denver every Saturday and Sunday. The area around there is now known as Old Town Winter Park. There are ambitious plans to develop a new pedestrian-only Winter Park Village here and when that is complete, it promises to be an attractive and lively place to stay.

For the moment, however, most accommodation is a shuttle bus ride away in downtown Winter Park which straddles the main highway. Here some spacious condos are dotted around by the roadside and in the trees either side. There are also motels, bars and restaurants lining the road, which continues northwards to the neighbouring town of Fraser.

A car would be handy but is by no means essential. Other resorts within a two-hour drive include Steamboat, Breckenridge, Copper Mountain, Keystone and Vail.

The locals are very friendly and helpful – typical small town America.

The mountains

In the last few years Winter Park has become much better known on the international market and more and more UK tour operators are featuring it every season.

And it is well worth a visit. It has a fair-sized set of slopes (big by US standards) and a wonderful mixture of terrain that will suit all standards.

THE SLOPES
Interestingly divided
From 1997/98 there will be five very distinct, but well-linked, areas – each with its own special character. From the main base, a high-speed quad takes you up the original **Winter Park** mountain to the Sunspot restaurant area at 3,260m. From there, you can descend in virtually all directions. Runs lead down towards the main base and link to chairs back up, or you can head over to the **Vasquez Ridge** area on the far right. This is served by a high-speed quad which allows you to use that area continuously or get back to the Winter Park mountain. Both these areas are primarily beginner and intermediate terrain.

From the top of Winter Park mountain you can ski to **Mary Jane** mountain, which has much tougher runs. Mary Jane itself is served by six lifts, including two high speed quads to the summit (3414m). From there you can head over to **Parsenn Bowl** (3675m) which has intermediate and advanced terrain, much of it above the tree line. From here you can also access the new **Vasquez Cirque** area of advanced and extreme slopes to the west. A groomed run along the top of the cirque will allow you to drop in to ungroomed terrain – open bowls and chutes at the top, glades lower down.

SCHOOLS/GUIDES

97/98 prices in dollars

Skier Improvement Center
Classes 6 days
2½hr: from 9.30 or 11am
6 2½hr days: 210
Children's classes
Ages: 3 to 13
6 full days including pass and lunch: 313
Private lessons
1½hr, 3hr or 6hr
85 for 1½hr, for 1 or 2 people; each extra person 20

National Sports Center for the Disabled
Special programme for disabled skiers and snowboarders
Private lessons
3hr or 6hr, with pass and special equipment
40 for 3hr; 80 for 6hr

SNOW RELIABILITY
Among Colorado's best

Winter Park is situated right on the Continental Divide in the highest part of the Rockies. Its position means that its average yearly snowfall of almost 30ft is the highest of any major Colorado resort. As a back up, artificial snowmaking covers a high proportion of the runs on Winter Park mountain.

FOR EXPERTS
Some hair-raising challenges

Up till now, experts have headed for Mary Jane, which has some of the steepest mogul fields and hair-raising challenges in the US. The steepest chutes are on Mary Jane's Backside accessed by a control gate off a long black run called Derailer. Hole in the Wall, Awe Chute, Baldy's Chute and Jeff's Chute are all fearsomely steep, narrow couloirs, bordered by rocks. Peer down Awe Chute before backing off, as we did, and you'll understand why the locals have a slightly different name for it! More manageable, wider black mogul fields for most experts are Derailer, Long Haul, Brakeman, Railbender and Phantom Bridge. Coming down a notch of difficulty, there are some good blue/black runs on Mary Jane's front side. There are good challenges on Winter Park Mountain too.

The new Vasquez Cirque area promises excellent expert terrain – all ungroomed – with spectacular views.

FOR INTERMEDIATES
Choose your challenge

From pretty much wherever you are on Winter Park mountain and Vasquez Ridge you can choose a run to suit your ability. Most are well groomed every night giving you perfect early morning cruising on the famous Colorado 'corduroy' pistes.

For bumps try Mary Jane's front side, where long and perfectly formed mogul fields normally develop.

Parsenn Bowl has stunning views and some gentle, cruising pistes as well as more challenging unpisted bowls. It's an intermediate paradise and an ideal place to try your first steps off the marked pistes.

FOR BEGINNERS
The best we've seen

Several seasons ago, Winter Park built Discovery Park – a 25-acre mid-mountain area specifically for beginners served by a high-speed quad. It has another two lifts, a nursery area, gentle beginner runs, an adventure trail through the trees and a special terrain park. Once you are out of the Park, there are easy runs all the way down to the base.

FOR CROSS-COUNTRY
Lots of it

There are several different areas, all with generally excellent snow, adding up to well over 200km of groomed trails, as well as back-country tours.

NATIONAL SPORTS CENTER FOR THE DISABLED

If you are able-bodied, the most striking and humbling thing you'll notice as you ride your first chair-lift up the mountain is the number of people with disabilities of all sorts hurtling down the mountain faster than many of us could ever hope to. There are blind skiers, skiers with one leg, no legs, paralysis – whatever their problem, they've cracked it.

That's because Winter Park is home to the US National Sports Center for the Disabled (NSCD) – the world's leading centre for teaching winter sports to people with disabilities. As well as full-time instructors, there are 1,000 trained volunteers who help in the programme, using techniques and adapted equipment which the centre has pioneered the development of. People are placed with instructors trained to teach people with their particular disability – more than 40 disabilities are specially catered for. And since 1996/97 the centre has taught snowboarding as well as skiing.

If you are disabled and want to learn to ski or snowboard there's no better place to go. It's important to book ahead so that a suitable instructor is available. The centre can help with travel and accommodation arrangements: NSCD, PO Box 36, Winter Park, CO 80482, USA. Tel: 00 1 970 726 1540 Fax: 00 1 303 89 5823.

CHILDCARE

The ski school runs special classes for children aged 3 or more and provides lunch.
The Children's Center has a non-skiing programme for children aged 2 months to 5 years. The Children's Center is open 8am to 4pm. Lessons are 10am to 3pm.

GETTING THERE

Air Denver, transfer 2hr.

Rail Leaves Denver Sat and Sun at 7.15am and returns at 4.15pm. Journey time 2 hours.

UK PACKAGES

American Dream, Crystal, First Choice Ski, Inghams, Made to Measure, Neilson, Ski Independence, Ski North America Direct, Skisar U.S., Thomson, United Vacations Ski Freedom USA

ACTIVITIES

Indoor Cinema, swimming pool, roller skating, casino trips, amusement arcade, health club, comedy club, aerobics, raquetball
Outdoor Dog-sledding, sight-seeing flights, snow-shoe excursions, sleigh rides, 'tubing', ice skating, snowmobiling, snowcat tours, ice fishing

TOURIST OFFICE

Postcode CO 80482
Tel +1 (970) 726 5514
Fax 726 5993

QUEUES
Rarely a problem

During the week the mountain is generally quiet. At weekends the Denver crowds arrive. But even then the network of twenty lifts includes seven high-speed quads which make light work of the crowds.

MOUNTAIN RESTAURANTS
Some good facilities

For a resort which caters mainly for locals Winter Park has surprisingly good restaurant facilities. The highlight is the Lodge at Sunspot, at the top of Winter Park mountain. This beautifully built wood and glass building houses a welcoming bar with a roaring log fire, a table-service restaurant and a very good self-service section.

SCHOOLS AND GUIDES
A good reputation

The school consistently comes out well in US magazine surveys. There are comprehensive ski and snowboard programmes, including a free lesson for first-timers in January, carving and mogul clinics and a 'quick fix' video analysis (only $5).

FACILITIES FOR CHILDREN
Some of the best

There is a Children's Center at the Winter Park base area which houses day-care facilities for children and is the meeting point for children's ski and snowboard classes. Classes are available in four age groups.

 **Staying there**

Nearly all the accommodation is down in town, served by a free shuttle bus.

HOW TO GO
Big choice

Several UK tour operators now offer Winter Park and we suggest you try combining it with another resort in a two-centre holiday. That way you'd see the contrast between Winter Park's 'locals' atmosphere and a normal US 'destination' resort – try Steamboat, Breckenridge or Vail.
Hotels There are a couple of outstanding hotel/condo complexes.
《《《4 **Iron Horse Resort** The only slope-side accommodation. Comfortable, with outdoor pool and hot tub. Complementary local shuttle.
《《《4 **Vintage** Quarter mile from slopes Same facilities as Iron Horse.

There's some seriously steep terrain ↑

Self-catering There is a lot of comfortable condo complexes.

EATING OUT
A fair choice

There are lots of restaurants, with both ethnic and typical American food. You can also ride the lift up to eat at the Lodge at Sunspot on some evenings.
   Our favourite local restaurant is the Crooked Creek Saloon at Fraser – as much for the atmosphere as the food. It is popular with locals, has great Old West decor and photos and serves typical American food.

APRES-SKI
Surprisingly lively

As people leave the slopes, the hot spots are the Derailer Bar at the foot of Winter Park mountain and the Club Car at the bottom of Mary Jane. Later on, try The Slope (in Old Town) for live music and dancing or Adolph's, just across the road. Deno's, downtown, has nine big screen TVs. The favourite snowboard hang-out is Slade's Underground. There is a tubing hill at Fraser Valley where you can slide down an inner tube, spinning out of control if you go solo. It's more fun to join a big group, link arms and hurtle down en masse.

Utah

'The Greatest Snow on Earth' – that's what Utah claims on every car number-plate. It's a debatable claim: the Colorado resorts say that their famous powder is drier, and have figures to prove it. What they can't dispute is that some Utah resorts do get huge dumps of snow – and by Alpine standards it's wonderful stuff. If you like the steep and deep, the pilgrimage to Utah is one you can't put off forever.

There are big differences in snowfall. The biggest dumps are reserved for Snowbird and Alta, close together in Little Cottonwood Canyon; combined with some super-tough terrain, the snow record of these small resorts makes them the powder capitals of the world.

The 2002 Winter Olympics will be based in Salt Lake City, so you'll be hearing a lot about Utah. Park City, the main 'destination' resort of the area is hosting events such as bob-sleigh, jumping and slalom, but it's unknown Snowbasin that gets the prestige downhill and GS events. Our resort directory at the back of the book includes lots of others such as Sundance, Brighton and Solitude. An unusual and interesting holiday can be had by staying in Salt Lake City.

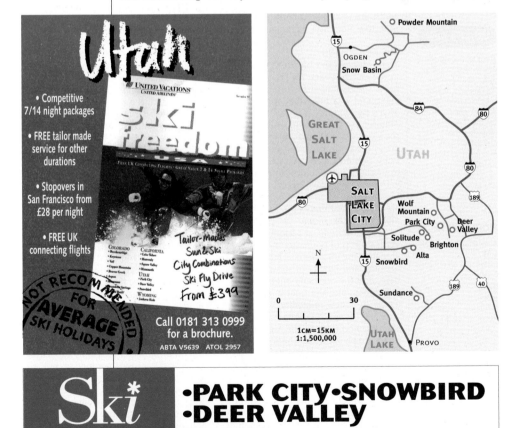

Alta

2605m

Simply the best powder snow in the known universe

Alta is famous for remarkable amounts of powder snow arriving with great regularity, for a stubborn refusal to develop the area and for one of the cheapest lift passes around. The resort is limited but the slopes are classy, and preserved for skiers – snowboarding is banned.

HOW IT RATES

The slopes

Snow	*****
Extent	*
Experts	****
Intermediates	***
Beginners	***
Convenience	****
Queues	***
Restaurants	**

The rest

Scenery	****
Resort charm	***
Off-slope	*

What's new

The great thing about Alta is that nothing much changes. For the 1996/97 season they replaced the Wildcat chairs, and for 1997/98 they're replacing the Germania chairs – but it is just the chairs we're talking about here, not the chair-lifts as a whole.

MOUNTAIN FACTS

Altitude	2605m-3245m
Lifts	13
Pistes	2200 acres
Green	25%
Blue	40%
Black	35%
Art. snow	50 acres
Recco detectors used	

UK PACKAGES

American Dream, Skisar U.S.

TOURIST OFFICE

Postcode UT 84092
Tel +1 (801) 742 3333
Fax 742 3333

THE RESORT

Alta sits at the craggy head of Little Cottonwood Canyon, 2km beyond Snowbird and less than an hour's drive from downtown Salt Lake City. The lovely peaceful location was once the scene of a bustling and bawdy mining town – long since flattened by avalanches and neglect. The 'new' Alta is a strung-out handful of lodges and parking areas, and nothing more; life revolves around the two separate lift base areas – Albion and Wildcat – which are linked by a bi-directional rope tow along the flat valley floor.

THE MOUNTAINS

Alta's **slopes** can't have changed much in the last 20 years; no high-speed lifts here. The dominant feature is the steep end of a ridge that separates the area's two basins. To the left, from Albion base at the head of the canyon, the slopes stretch away over easy green terrain towards the black runs of Point Supreme and Devil's Castle; to the right, a more concentrated bowl with blue runs down the middle and blacks either side. These two sectors are linked at altitude, and by a flat tow along the valley floor.

A base altitude of 2600m and a vertical drop of 600m are modest statistics for US resorts – but the quantity and quality of snow that falls here, and the northerly orientation of the slopes, put Alta right in the top drawer for **snow reliability**.

Small though it is, Alta is great for **experts**, who flock to the high ridges after a fresh snowfall. There are dozens of steep chutes through the trees on the front faces leading back to the Wildcat base area, and wide steep slopes around the Albion basin.

Adventurous **intermediates** do pretty well at Alta, too – there's good variety in the runs and the easier blacks offer a gradual progression. Piste-bashers hungry for mileage will find it limited.

Timid intermediates and **beginners** will be happy on the Albion side,

where the lower runs are broad, gentle and well groomed.

There's little provision for **cross-country** skiing; but it does go on, and the surrounding back-country offers adventures for those with guidance.

Queues are not unknown at Alta – the snow record, easy access from Salt Lake City and the rather slow chair-lifts see to that – especially in spring and on sunny weekends. At least the lift company limits the tickets sold.

There's a **mountain restaurant** in each sector of the slopes– the Alpenglow on the Albion side has a small, often busy, terrace and a slightly Alpine feel to it – and a couple of places in the valley are open for lunch.

The famous Alf Engen **ski school** naturally specialises in powder lessons – though all the regular classes and clinics are also available. The small classes, good teachers and low prices provide good value. The ski school organises **children's** lessons. Day-care for those over 3 months old is available at the Children's Center in the Albion ticket building.

STAYING THERE

There are about a dozen places to stay – simple **hotels and apartments**. None of the locations is bad, but for the best slope-side convenience the smart Alta Lodge and the comfortable modern Goldminer's Daughter take the honours. The latter has the main après-ski congregation bar. Snowpine Lodge is small and welcoming, close to the Albion lift.

Eating out in Alta is unusual: eating in is the routine. The lodges expect to provide dinner for their guests, but generally not for others. But there are one or two exceptions, including Rustler Lodge and Snowpine.

Après-ski is self-contained in the lodges and rarely goes beyond a few drinks and possibly a sports film.

Nor are there many **off-slope alternatives** other than a trip to Salt Lake City.

Park City

2105m

An entertaining base for excursions into Utah's deep powder

WHAT IT COSTS

ⓒⓒⓒⓒⓒ⑥

HOW IT RATES

The slopes

Snow	****
Extent	***
Experts	****
Intermediates	****
Beginners	****
Convenience	***
Queues	****
Restaurants	**

The rest

Scenery	***
Resort charm	***
Off-slope	***

➕ Atmospheric Wild West-style main street (complete with jail and museum), convenient for the slopes

➕ Good choice of lively bars and restaurants makes nonsense of Utah's image as a puritanical Mormon state

➕ Well maintained slopes, good snow record, and lots of snowmaking

➕ Major pampering opportunity at super-smooth Deer Valley

➕ Easy road access to other major Utah resorts

➖ Rest of town doesn't have same charm as main street – essentially an enormous sprawl of anonymous condos

➖ No long runs

➖ Little variation in terrain

➖ Park City doesn't get the spectacular amounts of snow that fall in Little Cottonwood Canyon, only a few miles away

➖ Lack of spectacular scenery

You'll be hearing a lot about Park City in the next few years. Nearby Salt Lake City is holding the 2002 Olympic Winter Games, with the events taking place in resorts at varying distances from the city – rather like Albertville in 1992 – and Park City is the venue for many of the events (although the prestige downhill and GS races will be held at unknown Snowbasin, away to the north).

At first sight, it isn't the most compelling of US resorts for a holiday. Its slopes include terrain to suit all standards, but they are not very extensive – and they don't get a full share of what Utah proudly claims on its car number-plates to be 'The Greatest Snow on Earth'. The best of the deep powder snow is reserved for Snowbird and Alta, in Little Cottonwood Canyon.

But those resorts have little accommodation and even less evening animation, and certainly nothing to match Park City's beautifully restored and developed main street, which grew up in the silver-mining boom years of the 1880s and makes this a much more interesting place to stay. If you're interested in visiting several Utah resorts, consider basing yourself here and making excursions by car. Alta is less than an hour's drive away.

boarding *Wolf Mountain (or The Canyon, as it's now called) has long been a haven for Utah boarders, with plenty of half-pipes and a flood-lit fun-park on the small mountain. This is in contrast to the better-known resorts: snowboarding is banned in urbane Deer Valley, and it's only this year that Park City ski area has opened up to boarders. Park City has the best of the freeride terrain, its higher lifts extending out of the timber line and up to some great powder bowls. Intermediates fair less well, as the main cruising runs tend to be short, but beginners are well catered for with a series of lifts in the base area. The town has plenty of bars, which the nightlife centres around.*

What's new

For 1997/98 two new six-seater chairs will replace the slow two-stage gondola that for years has been the backbone of the lift network. The Pay Day Triple chair up from the Resort Center is apparently also made redundant by this new route up the mountain. Four new runs are being cut on the 'back' side of the area, near Blueslip Bowl, all equipped with snowmaking.

Look for big changes in the near future at Wolf Mountain, close to Park City, which has been acquired by the dynamic New England-based American Skiing Company – and renamed for the second time in only a few years. It's now The Canyon.

The resort

Park City is in Utah's Wasatch Mountains, 45 minutes by road from Salt Lake City. It was born with the discovery of silver in 1872. By the turn of the century, it boasted a population of 10,000 (largely of Irish origin), a red-light district, Chinese quarter and 27 saloons. All this faded with the crash in the silver price. But careful restoration has left Park City with a splendid historic centre-piece.

The old wooden sidewalks and clapboard buildings of Main Street are now filled with a colourful selection of Park City's 15 art galleries, 100 smart shops and boutiques, a dozen bars and 80 restaurants. New buildings have been tastefully designed to blend

MOUNTAIN FACTS

Altitude 2100m-3050m
Lifts   14
Pistes   2200 acres
Green   16%
Blue   45%
Black   39%
Art. snow   475 acres

LIFT PASSES

97/98 prices in dollars
Park City
Covers all lifts in Park
City Mountain Resort,
with free ski-bus.
Beginners Beginners'
courses (1, 3 or 5
day) includes 1 day
free ski pass on First
Time Lift.
Main pass
1-day pass 49
6-day pass 256
(low season 154 –
40% off)
Senior citizens
Over 65: 6-day pass
128 (50% off)
Over 70: free pass
Children
Under 12: 6-day pass
119 (54% off)
Short-term passes
Half-day passes from
1pm (adult 36). Night
skiing pass 4pm-9pm
available.
Notes All passes of
over 2 days allow 1
non-skiing day; 6 day
pass valid for 7 days,
with 1 non-skiing day.
Reductions for groups
and students.
Alternative passes
Multi-area books
contain vouchers that
can be swapped for
day passes in Alta,
Brighton, Deer Valley,
Park City, Snowbird,
Solitude, and Wolf
Mountain (adult 6-day
288).

in smoothly, but away from the centre
the resort is spread over a wide area
and lacks the same charm.

The US National Ski Team
headquarters is in Park City, and with
the 2002 Winter Olympics imminent
there is a lot of development taking
place; facilities are set to improve
dramatically in the next few years.

The Resort Center is the main base
area, with its modern buildings and its
own bars, restaurants and
accommodation.

Deer Valley and The Canyon (Wolf
Mountain) are almost suburbs of Park
City, but all three retain quite separate
identities. Deer Valley is upmarket,
ready to pamper its clientele with
swish hotels, slope-side convenience
and some of the most swish lunch
spots of any US mountain resort. The
Canyon is (or has been up to now)
bold and breezy – day passes are
cheaper here, and snowboarders are
welcome. All three areas are linked by
the free ski-buses.

Road connections to other Utah ski
areas – including Snowbird, Alta,
Brighton, Solitude and Sundance – are
good.

The mountain

Although good enough to host World
Cup events, the terrain is generally
quite tame – smooth trails cut through
the trees on rounded, low mountains.
The bite in the system is in the bowls
at the top of the resort's slopes.

THE SLOPES
Nothing spectacular
The Town chair-lift goes up from one
end of Main Street directly into the
slopes, but the main lift base is the
modern purpose-built Resort Center
near a big parking lot. This is some
distance from Main Street, which is the
centre of town. The slow, old gondola
and the Pay Day triple chair up from
here have been replaced by one fast
six-seat chair-lift up from Resort
Center, and a second one beyond that
up to Summit House, the main
mountain restaurant.

Most of the runs lie between the
Summit House and the base area, and
spread along the sides of a series of
interconnecting ridges. Four new runs
are being prepared for the 1997/98
season, going down from Summit
House towards Mid Mountain
restaurant and Pioneer lift.

Virtually all the terrain above
Summit House is unprepared, and
accessed only by the Jupiter chair
which takes you to a high point of
3050m.

There are a few old, wooden mine
buildings left dotted around the
slopes, which add extra atmosphere.

A floodlit run – the longest in the
Rockies – is available until 10pm, but
you have to pay extra.

SNOW RELIABILITY
'The Greatest Snow on Earth?'
All Utah resorts make a lot of fuss
about the quality and quantity of their
snow. Park City's record may not be a
match for those of Alta and Snowbird,
but it's still impressive, and ahead of
what most Colorado resorts can claim.
A season from late November to early
April is normally scheduled but, with a
bit of luck and use of the extensive
snowmaking, the season is frequently
extended. Thirty per cent of runs are
covered by snowmaking.

FOR EXPERTS
Head for the top bowls
Jupiter Bowl is directly accessible by
chair-lift and gets churned up first after
a snowfall. After that it's a case of
hiking along the ridge to reach the
likes of Puma and McConkey's bowls.
All the bowls include some serious
terrain – with narrow couloirs, cliffs
and cornices as well as easier ways
down.

The side of Summit House ridge,
serviced by the Thaynes and
Motherlode chairs, has some little-used
black runs with occasional steep
pitches, plus a few satisfying trails in,
rather than cut through, the trees.
There's a zone of steep runs down into
town from further round the ridge,
including Willy's Run, which has seen
duty as a World Cup men's GS course.
And don't miss Blueslip Bowl near
Summit House – so called because ski
company employees used to go
through it although it was out of
bounds; if caught, they got a blue slip
which meant they were fired.

The Utah Interconnect will interest
those keen to see a little more of the
Wasatch Mountains back-country – it
can be completed in a day and links
Park City with four other Utah resorts.
Experts will also want to spend days at
the other nearby resorts, notably
Snowbird and Alta.

You may even want to try the Utah

It's a cute little mountain →

Winter Sports Park down the road. This is one of the few places where you can learn to ski-jump – starting on a baby jump and gradually working your way up. They have full-scale hills and freestyle jumps here too.

FOR INTERMEDIATES
Limited choice

There are blue runs everywhere, apart from Jupiter. The areas around the King Con high-speed quad and Silverlode high-speed six-seater chair have a dense network of great (but short) cruising runs. There are also more difficult trails close by, for those looking for a challenge. But there is little in between, and there are few opportunities for long cruising runs – most trails are in the 1km to 2km region. The Pioneer chair-lift is slightly off the beaten track and it serves some very pleasant, quiet runs – ideal for warming-up and for those not seeking too many thrills.

Intermediates will certainly want to visit Wolf Mountain and Deer Valley for a day each. Deer Valley has the best-

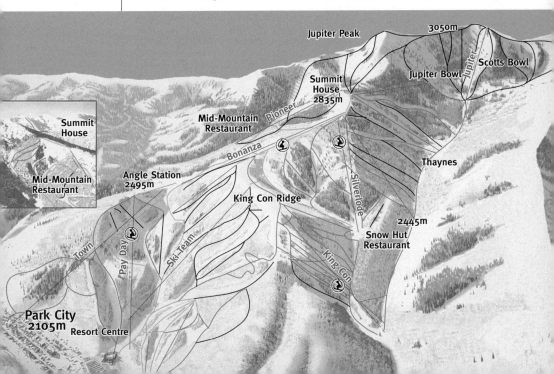

SCHOOLS/GUIDES

96/97 prices in dollars

Park City
Classes 5 days
4hr: 9.45-11.45 and
2.15-4.15; 2hr: noon-
2pm or 2pm-4pm
5 4hr days: 207
Children's classes
Ages: 7 to 13
5 6hr days including
lunch: 338
Private lessons
1hr, 2hr, half- or full-
day
82 for 1hr; each
additional person 15

CHILDCARE

The ski school's
KInderschule takes
children aged from 3
to 6, from 8.30 to
4.30, mixing tuition
with other activities.

There are a dozen
different nurseries in
the town.

groomed runs around and offers
flattering intermediate cruising –
though even here fresh snow will be
left ungroomed on some runs.

FOR BEGINNERS
A good chance for fast progress
Novices get started on the short lifts
near the base area. The beginners'
classes graduate up the hill quite
quickly, and there's an 'easiest way
down' clearly marked all the way from
Summit House. It's easy enough for
most beginners to manage after only a
few lessons, but it is quite long. The
Town chair can be used to descend.

FOR CROSS-COUNTRY
Some trails; lots of back-country
The scope for 'back-country' skiing is
enormous – several companies in town
arrange trips to some of the nearby
National Forests, including overnight
stays in log cabins or, for the hardy,
snow caves.

There are prepared trails on both
the Park City golf course, next to the
downhill area, and the Homestead
Resort course, just out of town. Both
centres can provide lessons and
equipment hire – they charge around
$5 a day for use of their trails.

QUEUES
Peak period problems only
Lift queues aren't normally a problem
and the new lifts replacing the gondola
should remove the only real bottleneck
in the resort. The queues that used to
form for the Prospector quad chair
were dealt with by the installation of
the Silverlode six-seater chair (Utah's
first) for 1996/97.

MOUNTAIN RESTAURANTS
Nothing exciting
There are three restaurants, all of
reasonable quality. The Mid-Mountain
restaurant is an old mine building
which was heaved up the mountain to
its present location near the bottom of
Pioneer chair. The food is standard
self-service fare. The Summit House is
café-style – good for chilli, pizza, soup
etc. The Snow Hut is a smaller log
building and usually has an outdoor
grill sending the smell of burgers half-
way up nearby runs. There's quite a
choice of restaurants back at the base
area, and that's where many people
head at lunchtime.

If it's a gourmet lunch you are after,
you'd be better-off in Deer Valley.

SCHOOLS AND GUIDES
Thorough, full of enthusiasm
The official ski school offers all sorts of
specialist programmes, and the usual
group and private lessons. Group
lessons can be excellent value: many
people choose private lessons, with
the happy result that four to six is the
normal size for groups.

FACILITIES FOR CHILDREN
Well organised; ideal terrain
For very young children, even babies,
there are a number of licensed carers
who operate either at their own
premises or at visitors' lodgings. The
ski school deals with children under
the umbrella of a separate
Kinderschule. Book in advance to
guarantee a place.

Staying there

It's quite practical to stay in Park City
and not bother with a car – choose a
location that's handy for Main Street
and either the Town chair or the free
shuttle bus. The bus goes from various
locations in town to the Resort Center,
it's frequent and runs till late. There's
also a trolley-bus along Main Street.
Regular buses serve Deer Valley and
The Canyon. If you plan to visit resorts
such as Snowbird and Alta a few times
a car would be useful, though there
are buses.

HOW TO GO
Packaged independence
Park City is the busiest and most
atmospheric of the Utah resorts, and a
good base for visiting the others.
Hotels The mass of chain motels on
the fringes of most American towns is
missing in Park City; and rooms at
typical motel prices are a little scarce.
Some of the following are upmarket
B&B places.
(((4 **Homestead** Relaxing country
resort hotel, with accommodation in
houses spread around the grounds.
Miles from the downhill, but well
placed for cross-country and
snowmobiling. Pool.
(((4 **Silver King** Deluxe hotel/condo
complex at base of the slopes, with
indoor-outdoor pool
(((4 **Washington School Inn** Another
historic building – there are quite a few
around – which doubles as a hotel. Big
breakfasts and après-ski snacks. Good
location.

GETTING THERE

Air Salt Lake City, transfer ½hr.

UK PACKAGES

American Dream, Crystal, Funway Holidays, Made to Measure, Ski Activity, Ski Independence, Ski North America Direct, Skisar U.S., Skiworld North America, United Vacations Ski Freedom USA, Virgin Snow

Deer Valley Funway Holidays, Made to Measure, Skisar U.S., Virgin Snow

ACTIVITIES

Indoor Park City Racquet Club (4 indoor tennis courts, 2 racquetball courts, heated pool, jacuzzi, sauna, gym, aerobics, basketball), Prospector Athletic Club (racquetball courts, weights room, swimming pool, aerobics, spa, massage and physical therapy, whirlpool, sauna), art galleries, concerts, theatre, martial arts studio, bowling **Outdoor** Snowmobiles, ballooning, sleigh rides, ski jumping, ice skating, bobsleigh and luge track, sports and recreation opportunities for disabled children and adults

TOURIST OFFICE

Postcode UT 84060
Tel +1 (801) 649 8111
Fax 647 5374

(((③ **Old Miners' Lodge** A 100-year-old building next to the Town lift, restored and furnished with antiques.
(((③ **Radisson Park City** Excellent rooms and indoor-outdoor pool but poorly placed for nightlife, out of town.
(② **Chateau Apres** Close to the slopes: comfortable, faded budget place.
(② **Imperial Inn** Quaint B&B at top of Main Street.
Self-catering There's a big range of self-catering units available, though only a small selection – typically from the larger condo-complexes – finds its way into the brochures of tour operators. The Shadow Ridge and Park Station apartments are typical. What they lack in character they make up for with their comfort and comprehensive facilities. Silver Cliff Village is adjacent to the slopes and provides spacious, serviced units. It also provides access to the facilities of the Silver King Hotel. Those travelling independently have a wider range of smaller places to choose from.

Food shopping in town is good and cheap, especially at Albertson's hypermarket; there are five liquor stores. There are also several take-away outlets – the Park City pizza company is recommended for fresh-made pasta, pizza and sandwiches, and Nacho Mamas for either take-out or stay-in Mexican food.

EATING OUT
Book in advance

Ethnic variation in the cuisine is much greater than might be expected – Szechuan, Cantonese, Japanese, Mexican, Vietnamese and Italian are all represented. They all get busy, so book in advance. Less surprisingly, there are more good steak places than the average digestive system can handle in a fortnight. The Carpetbagger at the Claimjumper is worth getting hungry for. Texas Red's does Tex-Mex grub and the Depot Restaurant does steaks and lots of other things – it's also in a fine old renovated railroad building. The Barking Frog is a trendy place with an open, spacious feel. Cisero's has the best Italian food and gets packed. At the base of the slopes the Baja Cantina does great margaritas and Mexican food. Denny's Restaurant at Kimball is open 24 hours for basic sustenance. Just to clarify, Irish Camel Ltd actually serves Mexican food and El Cheapo Grill is not that cheap.

APRES-SKI
Plenty of bars

Although there are still some arcane liquor laws in Utah, Park City seems to have adopted a fairly sensible attitude to their application, and – provided you're over-21 and have your ID handy – the laws are never a serious barrier to getting a drink. The Wasatch Brew Pub makes its own excellent ale on the premises and has a good supper menu.

At the bars and clubs which are more dedicated to drinking (ie don't feature food) membership of some kind is required. This may involve handing over $5 to cover a fortnight's membership – one member can then introduce numerous 'guests' – or else there'll be some old guy at the bar already organised to sign a bunch of people in for the price of a beer. The Claimjumper, the splendidly scruffy Alamo and Pop Jenks are the most lively places and there's usually live music and dancing, at the very least at weekends. Adolph's is a bit smarter.

Steeps Café, at the Resort Center, is the regular happening place after coming off the slopes – there's a disco and it tends to go on long into the evening.

OFF THE SLOPES
Should be interesting

Salt Lake City has a few points of interest, many connected with its Mormon heritage, and some good shopping – Trolley Square is worth a look, as much for the buildings as the shops. Scenic balloon flights and excursions to Nevada for gambling are both popular. And there are lots of snow-based non-skiing activities – sleigh rides, snow-shoeing, ice-skating; there's even an ice-sculpture festival. Snowmobiling is big – there are 150 miles of prepared trails in lovely countryside. In January there's Robert Redford's Sundance Film Festival.

There are a couple of clubs in town with a pool, gym etc and a fairly up-market range of shops and galleries selling antiques, Western goods, expensive paintings, stuffed animals, Indian artefacts etc. The museum and old jail house are worth a visit.

It's a cute little town ➔

The Canyon 2075m

This separate area, formerly known as Wolf Mountain, and formerly formerly known as Park West, is only four miles down the road, and an easy 15-minute transfer from Park City. It's a little lower, a little less than half the size and less than half the price to use the slopes. Snowboarding is not so much allowed as encouraged here – they even have boarders on the front of the trail map. The layout is much like that of Park City, but the bowls are reached only by hiking – no soft-option Jupiter chair here. Ironhorse peak should be avoided by beginners – one side of the ridge has good intermediate runs, the other side has only 'expert' runs. The area is almost always pleasantly uncrowded and there is a collection of lodgings, restaurants and shops at the base area.

It wouldn't be a particularly exciting place to stay, but it has quite a lively après-ski atmosphere – good music, grilled burgers and drinks. The lodge at the base site serves hearty breakfasts.

Deer Valley 2075m

Just a mile from the end of Main Street, this is the 'dude' capital of Utah – famed for the care and attention lavished on both slopes and guests. Valets unload your equipment in the car park, the chair-lifts are padded and it looks as if stones are hand-picked off the slopes – it's very obviously aimed at people who are used to being pampered and can pay for it. The eating places are particularly upmarket.

Some of the lodgings are similarly top-dollar, including the Stein Eriksen Lodge and Goldener Hirsch at Silver Lake Village at mid-mountain (but reachable by road). The terrace of Stein Eriksen and the Stag, lower down, offer excellent lunchtime cuisine unheard of in most US resorts.

The slopes are immaculate, though not all are easy – there are mogul runs and 'double black diamond' runs in the top bowls. And some runs are left ungroomed after a snowfall, creating the conditions that incompetent but ambitious intermediates dream about: a foot of powder on a completely smooth base. Deer Valley is a recommended cultural experience.

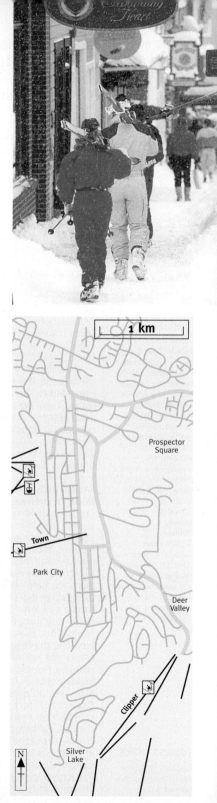

Snowbird 2470m

Alta-style snow, with city-style lodgings

WHAT IT COSTS

(((((6)))))

HOW IT RATES

The slopes

Snow	*****
Extent	*
Experts	*****
Intermediates	***
Beginners	**
Convenience	*****
Queues	**
Restaurants	*

The rest

Scenery	***
Resort charm	*
Off-slope	*

What's new

Good news: for 1997/98 a high-speed quad is to replace the Gad 1 double chair, the slow alternative to the queue-prone cable-car. Snowcat skiing is now available in Mineral Basin. And a 25m swimming pool is being built.

MOUNTAIN FACTS

Altitude	2410m-3355m
Lifts	9
Pistes	2500 acres
Green	20%
Blue	30%
Black	50%
Art. snow	none
Recco detectors used	

- ➕ Quantity and quality of snow unrivalled except by next-door Alta – and fully justify Utah's reputation
- ➕ A lot of widely varying runs crammed into a small area
- ➕ Some seriously steep ungroomed slopes to challenge experts
- ➕ Luxurious accommodation with excellent facilities
- ➕ Slopes-at-the-door convenience
- ➕ Airport nearby, and independent travellers need not hire a car

- ➖ Area is limited, particularly for energetic piste-bashers
- ➖ Tiny, claustrophobic resort
- ➖ Uncompromising modern architecture
- ➖ Main cable-car generates queues, despite its impressive size

There can be few places where nature has combined the steep with the deep better than at Snowbird, and even fewer places where there are also lifts to give you access. So despite the notably charmless appearance of the purpose-built village and the limited extent of the slopes– particularly confining for keen intermediates not yet comfortable off-piste – it remains one of the top US locations for hot-shots. For visitors from Britain it is the main destination in Little Cottonwood Canyon although Alta is, if anything, more compelling (see separate chapter) and anyone staying in Snowbird will certainly want to explore next door. There is no shared lift pass, but buying passes by the day does not add much to the cost.

boarding *Things are looking up. Alta next door continues to deny boarders access to the greatest snow on earth, but here the Gad 2 lift was opened to boarders for the first time in the 1996/97 season, meaning that the whole mountain is now open for boarders. The resort's managers now seem to perceive the slopes a one big fun-park, and have even created a half-pipe high up in the area, off Little Cloud lift. The ski school has a dynamic boarding section.*

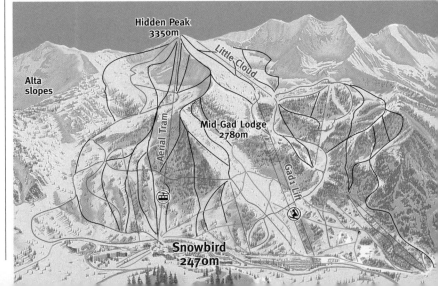

LIFT PASSES

96/97 prices in dollars
Snowbird
Covers lifts and aerial tram in Snowbird.
Beginners Chickadee chair pass (9 per day).
Main pass
1-day pass 45
6-day pass 216
Senior citizens
Over 65: 6-day pass 156 (28% off)
Children
Under 12: 6-day pass 156 (28% off)
Short-term passes
Half-day (am or pm) pass available (adult 37)
Notes Discounts for groups of 20 people or more.
Alternative passes
Day and half-day passes for chairlifts only (36 per day for adults, 25 for children)

The resort

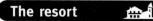

Snowbird lies 40km south-east of Salt Lake City in the Wasatch mountains, some 10km up Little Cottonwood Canyon – just before Alta. The setting is rugged and rather Alpine – though visitors from Europe may be reassured to hear that in these parts 'canyon' translates as 'valley', and doesn't imply precipitous sides. In contrast, the resort buildings are mainly block-like and dull – but they do provide high-quality lodgings and are convenient for the slopes.

The resort area and the slopes are spread along the road on the south side of the narrow canyon. Snowbird Center and the base-station of the main cable-car are towards the eastern, up-canyon end of the resort; much of the rest consists of car-parking areas. From the mouth of the canyon, there are good road links with downtown Salt Lake City, and other resorts.

The mountain

Snowbird's mountain is a small one by Alpine standards, but manages to pack in runs of all standards, with (broadly speaking) the tougher runs high up and easier ones low down.

THE SLOPES
Looming above the resort

The slopes rear up from the edge of the resort, covering the north-facing side of the canyon. The famed 125-person cable-car from Snowbird Center (the 'Aerial Tram') takes eight minutes to get up to Hidden Peak at 3355m. The toughest terrain is on the flanks of the ridge beneath the line of the tram, several coming off the rim of the Cirque, to the east. To the west of the tram, in Gad Valley, there are runs ranging from very tough to nice and easy – and six of the seven chair-lifts (all slow doubles, except the new Gad 1 fast quad).

SNOW RELIABILITY
Exceptional

With Little Cottonwood Canyon apparently acting as the local snowfall magnet, and with north-facing slopes and all the runs above 2400m, snow reliability is very good. Snowbird and Alta typically average about twice the snowfall of the Park City area or of most Colorado resorts.

SCHOOLS/GUIDES

96/97 prices in dollars
Snowbird
Classes 5 days
Half- (pm only) or full-day
5 5½hr days: 270
Children's classes
Ages: 3 to 15
5 full days including lunch: 320
Private lessons
1hr, 3hr or 6hr
60 for 1hr, for 1 person

FOR EXPERTS
Steep and deep – superb

Snowbird was created for and still appeals mainly to experts. For such a relatively compact area there is a lot of tough terrain. The trail map is liberally sprinkled with double black diamonds, and some of the gulleys off the Cirque ridge are at least that – Silver Fox and Great Scott are very narrow, very steep and frequently neck-deep in powder. Great Scott is considered to be one of the US's steepest trails. At the edge of the area, High Baldy is an expert trail that leads to an off-piste route over to next-door Alta. Lower down the mountain lurk the bump runs, including Mach Schnell – a great run straight down the fall line through trees. There is some wonderful off-piste terrain in the bowl beneath the high Little Cloud chair, and the Gad 2 lift opens up some attractive off-piste tree runs at the western extremity.

FOR INTERMEDIATES
Quality, not quantity

The winding Chip's Run on the east side of the Cirque ridge provides the only comfortable route down from the top of Hidden Peak for intermediates – at 5km, it's Snowbird's longest run, and a good place from which to enjoy the views towards the top of the canyon. Certain blue and green trails (including Chip's) are designated family runs – "for anyone wishing to ski with friends and family at a more relaxed pace'. Gad Valley is the best area for confident intermediates – there are some testing runs through the trees off the Gad 2 lift.

FOR BEGINNERS
Better than you'd expect

Beginners have the Chickadee lift right down in the resort – ideal for getting started – and then there's a small network of suitable trails on the lower slopes of Gad Valley. Big Emma is a lovely smooth trail, broad enough to accommodate the widest of turns.

FOR CROSS-COUNTRY
Go elsewhere

There are no prepared cross-country trails at Snowbird. All-terrain skiers can hike into the back country, but for loops you would have to travel to other resorts such as Solitude, where there are 20km.

GETTING THERE

Air Salt Lake City, transfer ½hr.

UK PACKAGES

American Dream, Crystal, Funway Holidays, Made to Measure, Skisar U.S., United Vacations Ski Freedom USA, Virgin Snow

ACTIVITIES

Indoor Snowbird Canyon Racquet Club (tennis, raquetball, squash, climbing wall, aerobics, weight training, fitness room), hot-tubs, The Cliff Spa (fitness room, aerobics, beauty centre, sauna, steam room, solarium), conference centre, art gallery
Outdoor Swimming pools, hot-tubs

TOURIST OFFICE

Postcode UT 84092-9000
Tel +1 (801) 742 2222
Fax 742 3344

QUEUES
Relief is imminent

At Snowbird nearly everyone wants to use the tram – if you can manage without it, you can buy a cheaper lift-pass, at least by the day. The lift system has been far too reliant on the Tram, and for much of the season queues of up to 40 minutes have been the result. The new Gad 1 fast quad is exactly what Snowbird needs, except that you can now expect queues for the Little Cloud chair above it.

MOUNTAIN RESTAURANT
Note the use of the singular

Choosing a mountain restaurant for lunch doesn't take long: it's the Mid Gad self-service cafeteria – or 'fuel stop', to use the resort's own description – or else it's back to base, where the lodges and the Snowbird Center offer a range of alternatives.

SCHOOLS AND GUIDES
Something for everyone

The ski school offers a quite progressive range of lessons and speciality clinics – including disabled skier programmes, women-only clinics and powder lessons using fat skis. The school also works to a maximum class size of eight, for all but Christmas and President's Weekend.

FACILITIES FOR CHILDREN
All ages well cared-for

Children from age 3 can be handed over to the ski school, and the Cliff Lodge will arrange childcare for those as young as 6 weeks. Camp Snowbird provides non-skiing activities for 3- to 12-year-olds, and there are occasional evening distractions like parties, games and movies to keep the kids happy.

Staying there 🔑

All the lodgings and restaurants are within walking distance of each other. The Tram station is central and the Gad lifts can be reached on snow. There are shuttle bus services linking the lodgings, the lifts and the car parks, and a regular service up to Alta.

HOW TO GO
It's easy independently

Salt Lake City airport is close, and well set up to handle independent travellers. There are several companies offering frequent transfers. If you plan to visit several other resorts, you'll want to hire a car, and it's worth considering Salt Lake City as a base – not least because avalanche danger can close Little Cottonwood Canyon after heavy snowfalls.

A few UK tour operators feature accommodation in Snowbird – mostly rooms in Cliff Lodge, the huge luxury hotel and restaurant complex just up the nursery slopes from the Center. Prices here are understandably high for twin rooms, but if you can bear to share a four-bed 'dorm' room they're great value, considering the facilities you can use. There are other lodges, and smaller condominuim blocks.

EATING OUT
A reasonable choice

Generally eating out revolves around Cliff Lodge and Snowbird Center – both house a number of restaurants. It's advisable for at least one member of a party to join the Club at Snowbird ($5) as most of the better restaurants are classed as private clubs. The Aerie and the Wildflower are quite upmarket venues, the Mexican Keyhole and the Forklift are easier on the pocket and better for families.

APRES-SKI
Very quiet weekdays

Après-ski in Snowbird tends to be a bit muted, especially during the week, though the comedy club may liven things up if you're lucky with the choice of acts. A sunset swim and a few cocktails at the rooftop pool in Cliff Lodge is reputed to be the best way to meet the in-crowd. It's quite feasible to head into downtown Salt Lake City for the occasional big night out on the town – lots of live bands and so on.

OFF THE SLOPES
Head down-canyon

People not using the slopes will be bored at Snowbird once they've tried the Cliff Spa and its massages, herbal treatments and the like. The new 25m swimming pool will make serious aquatic exercise possible. Best bet is to head towards the city – the Racquet Club down the valley is owned by Snowbird and has superb tennis facilities, and there are some attractions downtown, particularly around Temple Square. And there are various natural wonders, including the Great Salt Lake itself and, further afield, the Utah National Parks.

The Rest of the West

This section covers a varied group of isolated resorts in different parts of the great Rocky Mountain chain that stretches the length of the United States from Idaho down to New Mexico. Each has its own unique character – and each is well worth knowing about.

Sun Valley, Idaho, was America's first purpose-built resort, developed in the 1930s by the President of the Union Pacific Railway. It quickly became popular with the Hollywood jet-set and has managed to retain its stylish image and ambience over the years. But, because of its rather isolated location, limited hotel accommodation and poor reputation for snow (rectified by the world's biggest snowmaking installation) it hasn't become a big international destination. But if you want to indulge yourself a little and be pampered, bear it in mind – it has one of our favourite luxury hotels.

In winter Jackson Hole, Wyoming, is the nearest there is to a resort with a genuine Wild West cowboy atmosphere. The old town is lined with wooden sidewalks and there are lively saloons, where modern-day working cowboys drink, play pool and dance to country music. The mountain is a 15-minute drive away and offers some of America's most extreme terrain, with steeps, jumps and bumps to suit all – a sharp contrast to the tame, immaculately groomed runs typical of many US resorts. It does have those, but that's not why most people go there.

Taos, Mew Mexico, is the most southerly major resort in America, and because of its isolation is relatively unknown on the international market. There's a tiny resort development at the foot of the slopes, which are set high above the traditional adobe town of Taos, 18 miles away in the arid valley. The area was developed in the 1950s by a European and is still family-run, with a friendly feel to it. It is one of the few resorts still to ban snowboarders from its slopes, which have many very challenging runs, including some very long, steep mogul fields.

Also see our Resort Directory, at the back of the book, for a brief look at other western resorts such as Big Sky and Big Mountain in Montana.

Jackson Hole   1925m

Wild West cowboy town close to wild, untamed slopes

WHAT IT COSTS

(((((6)

HOW IT RATES

The slopes

Snow	★★★
Extent	★★
Experts	★★★★★
Intermediates	★★★
Beginners	★★★
Convenience	★★★
Queues	★★
Restaurants	★

The rest

Scenery	★★★
Resort charm	★★★★
Off-slope	★★

➕ Some of the toughest slopes in the US, including truly radical terrain

➕ Jackson town has genuine Wild West character

➕ People are friendly and hospitable – they want you to have fun

➕ Good variety of cross-country terrain

➕ Beautiful, unspoilt location in a remote part of the US, with several other attractions in the region

➖ There are too few lifts and some are old – but modernisation has begun

➖ Queues, especially for the aerial tram (cable-car), can be bad

➖ It's a long journey from the UK – though you can fly into Jackson

➖ Primitive mountain restaurants

➖ Snow can be poor on lower slopes

➖ Limited scope for improving beginners and the timid

If you're adventurous and want real American Wild West atmosphere, Jackson Hole is the place. The tiny town is 12 miles from the slopes, but cowboys roam wooden sidewalks, fall out of saloons, play pool, and dance to country music.

Jackson Hole has some serious terrain – steeps, jumps, narrow couloirs, bumps. Fifty per cent of the terrain is classed as 'expert' – black, double black and even blacker, and it takes an expert to get the most out of the area. It takes good snow too – so you've got to be lucky with the weather. Anyone below adventurous and competent intermediate standard may soon get bored – the area is not huge, and much of it will be beyond them. But the Bridger gondola, new for 1997/98, will make it quicker to reach some of the intermediate (and expert) terrain, and there's plenty else to see, including the beautiful winter wilderness of the nearby National Parks of Yellowstone and Grand Teton.

What's new

For the 1997/98 season, Jackson Hole opens its first major new lift for years. The Bridger gondola will go from the base area to the Headwall, opening up new expert and intermediate slopes and terrain that was previously accessible only by hiking. It will also take pressure off the tram (cable-car), reducing the often lengthy queues.

The amount of snowmaking is being increased by almost 40 per cent and Apres Vous mountain will now be served top to bottom.

The base area building is being completely rebuilt, including the childcare facilities and rental shops.

boarding *Jackson Hole is a cult resort for extreme snowboaders, just as it is for extreme skiers. The steeps and cliffs make for high-adrenalin thrills and great photos, there's a fun-park near the top of the Casper chair, a half-pipe near the bottom of Apres Vous mountain and the specialist Hole in the Wall snowboard shop. It's not a bad resort for having a go at boarding and for intermediates, with the beginner slopes served by a high-speed quad and only one drag-lift (at the bottom of expert-only terrain). The nightlife in the bars around the town square gets wild enough to keep hardcore boarders grinning.*

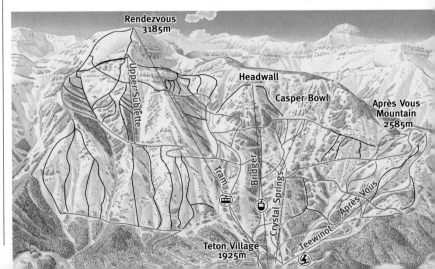

MOUNTAIN FACTS

Altitude	1925m-3185m
Lifts	10
Pistes	2500 acres
Green	10%
Blue	40%
Black	50%
Art. snow	110 acres

LIFT PASSES

97/98 prices in dollars
Jackson Hole
Covers all lifts and includes 'Tram'.
Main pass
1-day pass 48
6-day pass 258
Senior citizens
Over 65: 6-day pass 129 (50% off)
Children
Under 15: 6-day pass 129 (50% off)
Short-term passes
Afternoon pass from 12.30 (adult 36).
Notes 5 year-olds and under have free use on some lifts.
Alternative passes
Jackson Hole Ski Three 5-day voucher book covers Jackson Hole, Grand Targhee and Snow King resorts (215).

The resort

The town of Jackson, in the north-west corner of Wyoming, sits at the south-eastern edge of Jackson Hole – the 'hole' being the high, flat valley floor surrounded by mountain ranges. The town is real 'cowboy' territory. It is small and compact, with characterful western saloons, wooden sidewalks and good restaurants. Everywhere you look there are station-wagons and snowmobiles, skis, boards and stetsons, saloons and ski-bums – it's a strange mix and the effect is great. In among the cowboys and the log cabins there's a sprinkling of upmarket galleries and downmarket souvenir shops. But, in winter at least, it retains a genuine Western feel.

The slopes, a 15-minute drive north-east, stretch up the eastern flanks of the mountains above Teton Village – a small, modern collection of lodgings, shops and restaurants.

The mountains

Jackson Hole has finally started upgrading its slow, old lifts and revamping Teton village. The Bridger gondola for example, new for 1997/98, makes terrain around the Headwall easier to reach, and should ease the pressure on the cable-car. There's a move to change Jackson Hole's image, too – from that of a big, tough mountain to one that also suits intermediates and families – but it's still big and tough. Experts and good, adventurous intermediates will love the challenges on Rendezvous Mountain but there's not much for the less bold.

THE SLOPES
One big mountain, one small one
One big mountain makes Jackson Hole famous – **Rendezvous**. The cable-car ('Tram') is the only way to the summit. The peak provides a 1260m vertical drop and serves terrain riddled with chutes, cliffs, bumps and jumps. Signs saying 'experts only' tend to mean it. Taking the new gondola and then a couple of chairs will get you almost to the top.

Apres Vous mountain is adjacent to Rendezvous. Its peak is 600m lower and it has mainly blue and a few green trails, as well as a handful of blacks.

It takes two chairs to get from the base area to the summit of Apres Vous

– Teewinot (a fast quad), then Apres Vous (a double). Between the line of these chairs and the new gondola there are a couple of chairs serving Casper Bowl and the Amphitheatre. Linking runs connect Apres Vous and Casper Bowl, and you can work your way over to the two chairs on Rendezvous.

Hosts provide hourly tours from the top of Rendezvous. And at 1.30pm on weekdays you can usually take a tour with Pepi Stiegler, head of the school and Olympic gold medal winner.

Snow King is a small area of runs on the outskirts of Jackson town, floodlit in the evening. **Grand Targhee**, famous for its powder snow, is within one hour's drive – buses run daily.

SNOW RELIABILITY
Steep lower slopes can suffer
The claimed average of between 32ft and 38ft of 'mostly dry powder' snow sounds impressive, and for a core three-month season conditions are likely to be reasonable. But the base elevation here is relatively low for the Rockies, and if you're unlucky you may find the steepish lower slopes like the Hobacks shut. Snowmaking now covers Apres Vous top to bottom, however.

FOR EXPERTS
Best for the brave
After warming up on Apres Vous, most people want to take on Rendezvous. It's worth pausing at the top of the Tram to take in the views and pluck up courage – there's no gentle way down.

Take the East Ridge Traverse at least once to stare over the edge of the awesome Corbet's couloir – it flattens out to 50° after the vertical entry. Corbet's is one of many thrilling and potentially damaging features on a mountain that needs to be treated with great respect. It's the most famous because the Tram passes right above it, providing a great view of people throwing themselves off the lip.

From Corbet's – top or bottom – you can track over to Tensleep Bowl and the tricky Expert Chutes. Several more of the many steep, narrow chutes on Rendezvous are accessed via the Thunder chair.

Laramie Bowl, reached from the Upper Sublette quad and the Tram, has the Alta Chutes and, lower down, some good bump and tree-lined runs. Cheyenne Bowl has open slopes and, below, lovely runs through the trees.

SCHOOLS/GUIDES

97/98 prices in dollars

Jackson Hole
Classes 6 days
4hr: 9.30-11.30 and
1.45-3.45; 2hr: am or
pm
6 full days: 300
Children's classes
Ages: 3 to 14
5 full days including
lunch: 260
Private lessons
1hr, 2hr, half- or full-
day
115 for 2hr; 130 for 2
to 3 people

CHILDCARE

The Kids Ranch (739
2691) near the Crystal
Springs lift takes
children aged 2
months to 5 years,
from 8am to 5pm,
with indoor and
outdoor games and
one-to-one ski
lessons from age 3.

GETTING THERE

Air Jackson, transfer
½hr.

The new gondola will also open up
more expert terrain on the Headwall.

The lower runs, including the
Hobacks, at the edge of the area, are
generally bumpy and frequently have
less-than-ideal snow.

There are some heli-trip operations
and some serious back-country routes
from Teton Pass – use a guide. A day
in the powder of Grand Targhee, about
40 miles away, is worth the excursion.

FOR INTERMEDIATES
Exciting for some
There are great cruising runs all over
Apres Vous, and Casper Bowl and the
new gondola also offer quite gentle
runs. Many of the several blacks on
Apres Vous suit improving
intermediates testing their limits.

After that it's a case of checking out
the main mountain by trying the
steeper runs from the Bridger gondola
or traversing to the Thunder chair and
seeking out the few tough blues
among blacks and double-blacks.

FOR BEGINNERS
Not many suitable slopes
There's a choice of two lifts – the
Eagle's Rest and Teewinot chairs – and
four or five broad, gentle runs – fine
for getting started. The problem comes
thereafter and the leap to tackling the
runs off either the Apres Vous or
Crystal Springs chairs. Beginners would
be best served going to another resort.

FOR CROSS-COUNTRY
Lots of possibilities
There are six centres in the valley,
offering trails of various length and
difficulty. The Spring Creek Nordic
Centre has mainly beginner terrain and
offers moonlight tours. The Nordic
Centre at Teton has 22km of trails and
organises trips into the National Parks.

QUEUES
Should soon show improvement
There have often been long queues for
the 30-year-old Tram. But the Bridger
gondola, which can shift 2,000 people
an hour, should alleviate the pressure
– though it might overcrowd some of
the chair-lifts.

MOUNTAIN RESTAURANTS
Head back to base
There's only one restaurant on the
mountain – at the base of the Casper
chair-lift – and it's very ordinary. The
only other facilities are the snack-bars

and toilets at the base of the Thunder
chair and Corbet's Cabin, at the top of
the Tram. For a decent lunch, head to
the base area. Nick Wilson's in the
Clocktower, the Alpenhof restaurant
and the Mangy Moose are favourites.

SCHOOLS AND GUIDES
Learn to tackle the steeps
The school handles any standard of
skier and rider but there are also
special Mountain Experience classes on
steep and deep slopes and, on certain
dates, special Steep Skiing and Steep
Snowboard camps.

According to past reporters, classes
operate at all nine ability levels
regardless of how few pupils there are.
And at 1.30pm most days.

There are also back-country alpine
guides available.

FACILITIES FOR CHILDREN
Just fine
The area may not seem to be one
ideally suited to children, but in fact
there are enough easy runs and the
'Kids Ranch' care facilities are good.

Staying there

If you want to go straight from your
front door to the slopes, choose Teton
Village. If you're happy to drive 12
miles morning and evening, there's a
far better choice of lodgings in the
town of Jackson – and lots of other
attractions. There is a regular and
efficient bus service, and any lodging
in town is likely to be within a five-
minute walk of the town square.

HOW TO GO
In town or by the mountain
Hotels From economy motels to
expensive hotels and lodges there's
something to suit most tastes – though
nothing really luxurious. There are
quite a few small B&Bs – they tend not
to be cheap, but do give a bit of an
insight into the local lifestyle.
(((④ **Wort Hotel** The ritziest place to
stay: brick-built hotel right in the
centre of town and proud owner of the
Silver Dollar Bar. Hot tub.
(((④ **Inn at Jackson Hole** Comfortable,
functional Best Western in Teton
Village. Pool, sauna, hot tub.
(((④ **Alpenhof** Our favourite in Teton
Village. Tirolean-style, with lots of
wood and atmosphere. Good food.
Pool, sauna, hot tub.
(((④ **Rusty Parrot Lodge** A stylish

UK PACKAGES

American Connections, American Dream, Chalets 'Unlimited', Crystal, Funway Holidays, Inghams, Lotus Supertravel, Made to Measure, Ski Activity, Ski Club of GB, Ski Independence, Ski North America Direct, Ski Scott Dunn, Skisar U.S., Skiworld North America, United Vacations Ski Freedom USA

Grand Targhee
American Dream, Lotus Supertravel

ACTIVITIES

Indoor Art galleries, ice skating, swimming, theatre, concerts and live music
Outdoor Snowmobiles, mountaineering, horse riding, snow-shoe hikes, snowcat tours, floodlit skiing, heli-skiing, sleigh rides, dog-sledding, walks, wildlife safaris and tours of Yellowstone National Park

TOURIST OFFICE

Postcode WY 83001
Tel +1 (307) 733 4005
Fax 733 1286

place in Jackson town, with a rustic feel and handcrafted furniture. Hot tub.
(((3 **Sojourner Inn** At Teton Village. It is comfortable and convenient with pool, sauna and hot tub.
(((3 **Lodge at Jackson Hole** Western-style lodge in Jackson town. Pool, sauna, hot tub. Comfortable rooms.
(((3 **Parkway Inn** Friendly, family-run place in Jackson town; nice pool.
((2 **Forty-Niner Inn** Regular motel; hot tub and sauna.
Self-catering There is lots of choice at Teton Village, within and around Jackson and at more isolated locations. The Cowboy Village Resort has neat little log cabins on the edge of town. Teton Village Property Management control many of the condos at Teton Village. The Snow King Resort Condominiums have full hotel service facilities, next to the town slopes.

There's only one large supermarket in Jackson and a number of smaller stores and delis. Teton Village has good small stores but no supermarket.

EATING OUT
It's a pleasure in Jackson

Teton Village has pizza, Mexican, a Steakhouse and a number of hotel restaurants. They're all OK but most people favour the Mangy Moose and the Rocky Mountain Oyster downstairs – good value, good fun. In Jackson there's a load of places to try. The Cadillac Grille, with its art-deco interior, is the coolest place – there's a burger bar attached. The Blue Lion is small, cosy and casually stylish. The Cowboy Steakhouse is attached to the Cowboy Bar and can come in very handy after a few hours on the saddle stools. There's also Italian, Cajun, Chinese and several fast food chains. The Bunnery is great for breakfast and fresh-baked things; for bagels head for Pearl Street Bagels.

APRES-SKI
Check out the saloons

In Teton Village, Beaver Dick's and the Pub have their fans, but the biggest draw is the Mangy Moose – it's a big happy, noisy place often with good live music. The famous bars in Jackson are JJ's Silver Dollar Bar at the Wort hotel and the Million Dollar Cowboy Bar on the town square. The Silver Dollar is

the classier venue and has over 2,000 silver dollars inlaid into the counter. The Cowboy Bar features saddles as bar stools and a stuffed grizzly bear, and is usually the rowdiest place in town. The Rancher is a huge poolhall. And the Shady Lady Saloon sometimes has live music – country and western of course. The Virginian Saloon is a quieter watering hole. It's a good idea for those under 30 to carry passports – the drinking age is 21 and zealously enforced.

For a night out, try driving to Wilson, where the Stagecoach Inn has cowgirl waitresses, big portions of western food and live music on Sundays. Or spend the evening on the slopes on the local floodlit Snow King hill, on the outskirts of Jackson.

OFF THE SLOPES
Some great outdoor diversions

Yellowstone National Park is 100km to the north, and although most of the roads are closed to traffic in winter, snow-mobile and 'snow-coach' trips are permitted. The park is famous for its geysers, the wildlife and the general beauty of the surroundings. The National Elk Refuge, just outside Jackson, has the largest remaining elk herd in the US – around 8,000 strong. Visits to the Granite Hot Springs and to parts of the Grand Teton National Park are also possible. In town there are some 40 galleries and museums and a number of outlets for Indian and Western arts and crafts. Most of the larger hotels have swimming pools.

Grand Targhee 2440m

This 'resort' 42 miles north-west of Jackson has only 444 beds but is a great place to visit for a day-trip. It has a wonderful reputation for powder snow and has adopted the slogan 'Snow from Heaven not Hoses'. There are only three chair-lifts, but they give you access to unusually deserted pistes which often have splendid untracked powder nearby. There is also a good snowcat operation – you ride up in a snow grooming machine converted into a people carrier (10 plus a couple of guides) and descend on virgin slopes. Book in advance.

Sun Valley

1755m

Stylish resort with slopes to flatter its rich and famous guests

Millions of dollars have been spent in recent years building new facilities to maintain Sun Valley's reputation as America's original luxury purpose-built winter sports resort. For a peaceful, relaxing time, it's hard to beat.

WHAT IT COSTS

((((((6)

HOW IT RATES

The slopes

Snow	★★★
Extent	★★★
Experts	★★★
Intermediates	★★★★
Beginners	★★★
Convenience	★★
Queues	★★★★
Restaurants	★★★★

The rest

Scenery	★★★
Resort charm	★★★
Off-slope	★★★

MOUNTAIN FACTS

Altitude	1755m-2790m
Lifts	13
Pistes	2067 acres
Green	38%
Blue	45%
Black	17%
Art. snow	600 acres

UK PACKAGES

American Dream, Ski Activity, Ski Independence, Skisar U.S.

TOURIST OFFICE

Postcode ID 83340
Tel +1 (208) 726 3423
Fax 726 4533

THE RESORT

Sun Valley is based around the old mining village of Ketchum. It was built in the 1930s by Averell Harriman, President of the Union Pacific Railway, with the help of Count Felix Schaffgotsch of Austria. It quickly became a favourite with stars such as Clark Gable and Judy Garland. Over the last few years its current owner Earl Holding has pumped many millions of dollars into new high-speed lifts, new runs, the world's largest computer-controlled snowmaking system and amazingly plush on-slope restaurant complexes and base lodges with floor to ceiling windows, beautiful wooden decor, heated terraces so snow and ice instantly melt, and public loos with marble basins and gold-plated taps. Sun Valley still attracts the stars, including Clint Eastwood and Arnie Schwarzenegger. The town of Ketchum retains its old-world charm and is home to some atmospheric bars, restaurants and shops.

THE MOUNTAINS

The main **slopes** of Bald Mountain (known locally as Baldy) are accessed from one of two luxurious base lodge complexes at River Run and Warm Springs, a shuttle bus-ride from most accommodation. It serves mainly intermediate terrain. The separate Dollar Mountain is more of a beginners' mountain, though it has some good tougher runs and tends to be quieter because everyone heads straight for the bigger Baldy.

Snowboarding is now allowed on most of the mountain and the chair-lifts make getting about easy.

The resort has an erratic natural **snow reliability** record, which is why it installed 600 acres of snowmaking, covering over 70 per cent of the groomable runs.

There are a few tough runs and bowls for **experts**, but nothing beyond single black diamond pitch, including the two most famous mogul runs Exhibition and Limelight. Heli-skiing is available locally. Most of the terrain is ideal for **intermediates**, with lots of runs at a similar consistent pitch. There are good blue bowl runs with great views from the top ridge as well as groomed cruisers through the trees lower down.

Both Baldy and Dollar are good for **beginners**, with some very gentle, long green runs to progress to.

Forty kilometres of prepared **cross-country** skiing trails start at the Nordic Centre by the Sun Valley Lodge and there are more along the valley from Ketchum to Galena Lodge.

Queues are rarely a problem, with Sun Valley's network of high-speed quads whisking people around the mountain.

The **mountain restaurants** and base lodges have to be seen to be believed. They are way ahead of most US on-slope facilities.

The ski school Just For Kids and Playschool programmes cater for **children**.

STAYING THERE

One of our favourite **hotels** in any resort is the stylish Sun Valley Lodge, part of Harriman's original development. As well as magnificent rooms, there are a big outdoor ice rink and pool, and the corridors are lined with photos of film-star guests. Hemingway wrote *For Whom the Bell Tolls* here. But there are plenty of cheaper options, including some motels and **self-catering** options.

There is plenty of choice for **eating out**. We enjoyed excellent food at the relaxed Evergreen Bistro and had a great breakfast at The Knob Hill Café. There are some atmospheric **après-ski** places including the Sawtooth Club (popular with locals), Whiskey Jaques for live music and dancing and the Pioneer Saloon popular for its Prime Rib and Clint Eastwood spotting.

You can have a fine time relaxing **off the slopes**, including sleigh rides, walking, ice skating, swimming and strolling round the galleries and shops.

Taos 2800m

New Mexico adds spice to the slopes and resort

HOW IT RATES

The slopes

Snow	****
Extent	**
Experts	*****
Intermediates	***
Beginners	**
Convenience	***
Queues	****
Restaurants	*

The rest

Scenery	***
Resort charm	***
Off-slope	**

What's new

The resort has replaced some existing chairs with high-speed quads and expanded its snowmaking over the last few years. But the beauty of it is that it doesn't want to overdevelop its mountain, and it chooses to keep some of the best skiing for those willing to hike to get to it.

MOUNTAIN FACTS

Altitude	2800m-3600m
Lifts	11
Pistes	1100 acres
Green	24%
Blue	25%
Black	51%
Art. snow	496 acres

➕ Some very steep, challenging terrain

➕ Intermediates and beginners surprisingly well catered for

➕ Small, intimate resort nestled in splendour of New Mexico Rockies

➕ Two contrasting bases

➕ One of the best schools in the US

➖ Taos town a long drive from the resort

➖ Some of the best runs are a long hike from the top lifts

➖ Relatively small area of slopes

➖ Very little accommodation in the resort itself

Taos is unlike any other US resort. It is set high above an arid New Mexico valley, 18 miles from the adobe town of Taos, home to many famous artists and writers over the years, including DH Lawrence. Its culture and food is southern and it makes a good contrast with the Colorado resorts, a five or six hour drive away – you could consider it as part of a two-centre holiday.

The slopes are different, too. If you are after the steep and deep, Taos has some of the best in North America. Many runs are made deliberately awkward to reach to keep the numbers using them low and the quality of the snow high.

boarding *Taos is one of the few resorts that still bans snowboarding from its slopes. It remains to be seen how long it will be able to afford to continue to turn away this growing and lucrative segment of the market.*

The resort

Not far from Santa Fe in New Mexico, Taos Ski Valley is the most southerly mainstream resort in North America. It could be on a different planet from the town of Taos, some 18 miles away through red-brown desert scenery.

The resort is little more than a handful of lodges, built in chalet style – and a huge car park. It was founded in 1955 by Ernie Blake, who fulfilled his vision of building a European-style ski resort in the southern Rockies. The resort is still family-run.

Taos town, in contrast, is sizeable, and rich in cultural influences – native American, Spanish and classic South-Western. It's full of art galleries, museums, restaurants and bars, as well as hotels and B&Bs.

The mountain

When you hit Taos Ski Valley, the first thing that will strike you is Al's Run, a mogul pitch of formidable steepness rising sheerly out of the resort. Ernie Blake put up a sign saying 'Don't panic! You're looking at 1/30 of Taos Ski Valley. We have many easy runs too'. They do, but it is best for experts

nevertheless – Slim, a spread-eagled, life-like dummy, warns you to be careful on this steep terrain.

THE SLOPES
Small but expandable
Two chair-lifts take you into the mountains – one a high-speed quad. Once you're up, there are runs on three separate flanks of the mountain, served by a total of eight lifts. Most access green, blue and black runs. Many of the toughest runs (15 of those marked on the trail map), however, can be reached only via a lengthy climb.

SNOW RELIABILITY
Variable
Because of its southerly position Taos has a different weather pattern to the Colorado resorts. The snow record is generally good, and almost half the terrain is covered by snowmaking – but one recent season was a disaster.

FOR EXPERTS
Hike to the heights
Al's Run is the most obvious challenge, but the bottom section is often shut.

The best terrain is an energetic hike from the top of the mountain. Highline Ridge and West Basin Ridge both have

UK PACKAGES

American Dream, Chalets 'Unlimited', Made to Measure, Ski Independence, Skisar U.S.

CHILDCARE

The Kinderkäfig Center houses all the ski school's children's facilities under one roof. Kinderkare takes babies from as young as 6 weeks up to toddlers not quite ready to ski. Junior Elite takes pre-school children from 3 years, introducing them to skiing through games, and also does proper classes for children up to the age of 12, with lunchtime care and indoor supervised play after skiing.

TOURIST OFFICE

Postcode NM 87525
Tel +1 (505) 776 2291
Fax 776 8596

a collection of very steep and narrow chutes through the trees and rocks.

The other major challenge is a 75-minute-plus hike to Kachina Peak for magical off-piste bowls and powder.

If you don't want to hike, chairs 2 and 6 take you to the best challenges – mainly big bump runs through trees.

FOR INTERMEDIATES
Good but limited cruising
There are always easy-cruising, blue-run alternatives to the steeps, but they are limited. Try the lovely long blues at the western end of the slopes, and to the east the slopes accessed by the Kachina lift. Adventurous intermediates will enjoy the open Hunziker Bowl.

FOR BEGINNERS
Good facilities
Strawberry Hill at the base is devoted to novices, and there are easy green tracks all over the mountain.

FOR CROSS-COUNTRY
Not one of the best
There's no formal cross-country, but those with a guide can head off into parts of the National Forest.

QUEUES
Self-imposed limits
Taos restricts sales of lift passes to avoid crowds. Queues are rare except at the bottom lifts at peak times.

MOUNTAIN RESTAURANTS
Head back to base
There are just two restaurants, neither selling the world's greatest food, or much alcohol. If you want a decent lunch, head back to the resort – no great hardship. The large terrace of the hotel St Bernard is a favourite spot.

SCHOOLS AND GUIDES
Simply the best?
Taos' school is considered by many as one of the best there is. The aim is to push everyone as far and as fast as possible – but also to have fun. In addition to straight group classes and private lessons you can arrange whole-week packages and special workshops.

FACILITIES FOR CHILDREN
Childcare from 6 weeks old
The resort takes childcare just as seriously as it takes tuition, with programmes tailored precisely to different age groups.

Staying there

You need to decide whether to go for convenient but limited Taos Ski Valley, cultural but distant Taos town, or one of the many lodges between the two. Having a car is almost a necessity if you stay out of the resort.

HOW TO GO
Little choice
Only a couple of UK tour operators feature Taos. But any US specialist could put a package together for you.
Hotels There are no luxurious hotels, but lots of more modest places.
At Taos Ski Valley:
((((4) **Inn at Snakedance** Original Taos hotel, with panoramic, glass-walled bar, large sun terrace and spa facilities.
(((3) **St Bernard** At the base of Al's Run; fine food, après-ski scene. Also has condos in a separate building.
In Taos town itself:
((((4) **Historic Taos Inn** Indian influenced hotel with excellent restaurant and stylish Adobe Bar. Outdoor pool, hot tub.
(((3) **Sagebrush Inn** Adobe built in 1929. Excellent food, nightly entertainment, tennis, pool, hot tubs.
Self-catering There's a wide selection of self-catering condos, some between the town and the resort. The Quail Ridge Inn Resort is an unusual, large adobe-syle complex with comfortable rooms and suites and a lot of facilites.

EATING OUT
Spoilt for choice if you drive
At the resort, you'll find a couple of places to try out New Mexico dishes as well as more traditional US fare.

In Taos town you'll find South-Western food, seafood and steaks. The Historic Taos Inn has good food.

APRES-SKI
A quiet time
Some hotels and bars have live music, but you don't come here to rave.

OFF THE SLOPES
Plenty of sightseeing
There's not much other than skiing going on at the Ski Valley. In Taos itself there's ice skating, swimming, shopping and a walking tour.

Trips to historic, pretty Santa Fe, and to Taos Pueblo – four miles from Taos, and home of the Tiwá Indians for nearly 800 years – are recommended.

New England

You go to Utah for the deepest snow, to Colorado for the lightest powder and swankiest resorts, to California for the mountains and low prices. You go to New England for ... well, for what? Extreme cold? Rock-hard artificial snow? Mountains too limited to be of interest beyond New Jersey? Yes and no: all of these preconceptions have some basis, but they add up to an incomplete and unfair picture.

Yes, it can be cold: one of our reporters recorded –27°F, with wind chill producing a perceived temperature of –73°F. Early in the season, people wear face masks to prevent frostbite. But we got routine winter weather when we visited in February.

Certainly, New England doesn't get much super-light powder, and the resorts do have big snowmaking installations, designed to ensure a long season. But they make and groom their snow to produce a superb surface; and many of the resorts get impressive amounts of natural snow – the best of them on a par with Colorado resorts.

Sure, the mountains are not huge in terms of trail mileage. But several have verticals of over 800m (on a par with Keystone) and most have over 600m (matching Breckenridge), and are worth considering for a short stay, or even for a week if you like familiar runs. (For more novelty, a two- or three-centre trip is the obvious solution.) You won't lack challenge – most of the double black runs are seriously steep. And you won't lack space: most Americans visit over weekends, which means that you may have a whole run to yourself on weekdays – except during President's week, in late February. It also means the resorts are keen to attract long-stay visitors, so UK package prices are low.

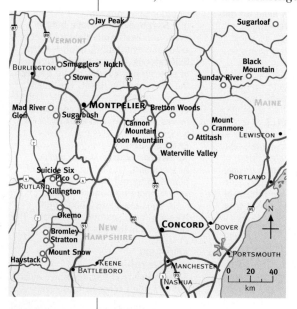

New England is easy to get to from Britain, as well as from New Jersey – a flight to Boston (a charming city, worth a stopover) then perhaps a three-hour drive to your resort. You pass through ramshackle hamlets with classic country stores selling maple syrup alongside gasoline, past people fishing on frozen lakes. It sure makes a change from the coach transfer from Geneva.

Killington 670m

The Beast of the East – one of the great US après-ski scenes

WHAT IT COSTS

(((((5)

HOW IT RATES

The slopes

Snow	****
Extent	**
Experts	***
Intermediates	***
Beginners	****
Convenience	*
Queues	****
Restaurants	*

The rest

Scenery	***
Resort charm	**
Off-slope	*

What's new

In 1996, Killington became part of the new American Skiing Company (which has now bought nearby Pico – 'Killington's 7th mountain'). For 1996/97 Rams Head and Skye Peak got fast quad chairs. A new Family Centre was built at Rams Head.

For 1997/98 a swish new hotel is being built at the Snowshed lift base.

- The biggest mountain in the East, matching some Colorado resorts
- Lively après-ski, with lots of bar-restaurants offering happy hours and late-night action
- Terrain to suit everyone, from long, easy trails to serious challenges
- Excellent nursery slopes
- Comprehensive snowmaking
- Good care and tuition for children, although it's not a notably child-oriented resort

- No real resort village – hotels, condos and restaurants are widely spread around the base of the mountain and along the 6-mile access road; you don't absolutely need a car, but it sure helps
- The trail network is complex and there are lots of trail-crossings
- Terminally tedious for anyone who is not a skier or boarder

It's difficult to ignore Killington. Even before its owners annexed next-door Pico, it was claiming to have: the largest mountain in the East, whether gauged in trail length, accessible area, vertical drop or top altitude; the most quad chairs in the East; the world's biggest snowmaking installation and the East's largest grooming fleet, and as a result the longest season in the East (in 1997 it stayed open until 22 June); America's longest lift and longest trail – a winding 16km for a drop of 945m (a gradient just steep enough to keep you moving); and allegedly New England's steepest mogul slope – Outer Limits, 800m long for a drop of 370m (a gradient steep enough to keep you moving all the way to the bottom if you fall). All quite impressive by local standards. But last season's trail map got a bit carried away: 'Killington is one of the largest ski areas in the world,' it says. Sorry guys: that's just silly.

Although they're building a swanky hotel/club at Snowshed (the main lift base) for 1997/98, the place will still lack anything resembling a village – a serious drawback for many visitors (from Europe, at least). But we kinda like the place. Once you get used to driving everywhere, it ceases to be a problem. And the vibrant nightspots weigh in the balance, even for us: in the early evening they're jolly places to eat, even if you're visiting with kids.

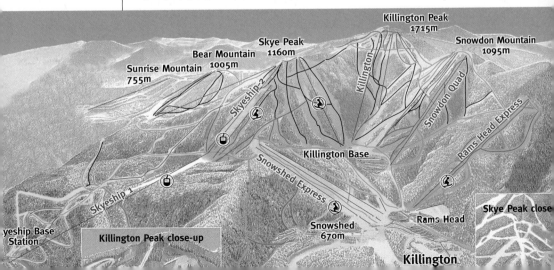

Killington

MOUNTAIN FACTS

Altitude	325m-1295m
Lifts	33
Pistes	1200 acres
Green	36%
Blue	32%
Black	32%
Art. snow	864 acres

LIFT PASSES

96/97 prices in dollars

Killington Lift Ticket
Covers all lifts in the Killington ski resort area.

Beginners 1- to 7-day Introduction-to-Skiing packages include limited area lift pass (4 lifts), rental and tuition (adult 6-day 288).

Main pass
1-day pass 48
6-day pass 257

Senior citizens
Over 64: 6-day pass 140 (46% off)

Children
Under 13: 6-day pass 140 (46% off)

Notes Pass also covers the other resorts owned by the company that owns Killington; Pico, Mount Snow/ Haystack, Sugarbush, Attitash/Bear Peak, Sunday River, Sugarloaf/USA

boarding *A cool resort like Killington has to take boarding seriously, and it does. There are two half-pipes on Killington Peak – a mini-pipe for easy initiation, and a full 12-footer for accomplished boarders – and a fun-park on the expert's area, Bear Mountain. And there are terrain features scattered around the area. There's a Ride Guide to take you to the best slopes, and recent reshaping has cut out some of the unpleasant flats on contouring green runs. Several big-name board events are held here. For less competent boarders, there are excellent beginner slopes, and plenty of friendly high-speed (ie slow-loading) chair-lifts – and the ski school does a Guaranteed Learn to Ride clinic.*

The resort

Killington is an extraordinary resort, especially to European eyes. Most of its hotels and restaurants are dotted along a six-mile approach highway, with just a small part of the accommodation (mainly apartments) concentrated in developments close to the slopes. The nearest thing you'll find to a focus is the occasional set of traffic lights.

The mountains

Killington has a densely woven mesh of runs that offers something for everyone. To some extent the terrain on its six sectors suits different standards – Rams Head is all easy-intermediate, Bear Mountain is all expert stuff – but there are also areas where a mixed ability group would be quite happy. There are easy runs from top to bottom of the mountain.

In 1995, Killington created four Fusion Zones – thinned-out forest areas, specially designed to give a range of challenge. These areas are, of course, not groomed, but they are also not patrolled. Trails on which there is no snowmaking (or grooming) are labelled 'Wild Thing'. Some runs of all levels are left to form bumps; there is half-and-half grooming on selected trails; and terrain features – ridges, bumps, quarter-pipes – are created.

THE SLOPES
Complicated

The runs spread over a series of wooded peaks, all quite close together but giving the resort a basis for claiming to cover six mountains – or seven, now that the small nearby resort of Pico is in the same fold. There are long-term plans to link the two resorts, but timing is unclear.

Killington's management has done a thorough job of cramming huge

numbers of runs and impressive numbers of lifts into a modest area. The result is a very complex network of runs, especially at the peaks.

For those staying in Killington, there are two main lift bases. Killington Base area has chairs radiating to three of the six peaks – **Skye**, **Killington** (the high-point of the area) and **Snowdon**. Novices and families head for the other, slightly lower base area, which has two parts: Snowshed is at the foot of the main beginner slope, served by several parallel chairs (see picture, page 494); just across the road that leads up to Killington Base (and now accessed by an underpass) is Rams Head, where the new Family Center has been developed at the foot of the entirely gentle **Rams Head** mountain.

The two remaining peaks are behind Skye Peak; they can be reached by trails from Killington and Skye, but each also has a lift base accessible by road. **Bear Mountain** is the expert's hill, served by two quad chairs from its mid-mountain base area. The sixth 'peak', **Sunrise**, is a slight blip on the mountainside, arrival point of a long triple chair up from the Sunrise base area in the valley, beside the main road. Not far away is another main-road access lift, the Skyeship gondola, up to Skye Peak.

The famous Skyeship, built in 1995, has cabins that are heated and wildly decorated. And it has a few rather vulgar deluxe Signature cabins with only four seats, plus cocktail cabinet and tinted glass; for a large premium, you can reserve one.

Pico (pronounce Pie-Co) is only a few minutes' drive from the Killington Road junction on US Route 4, on the way to the town of Rutland. It consists of little more than the mountain and a base lodge. Pico's mountain is quite small, and doesn't have much challenge, but suits intermediates well.

SCHOOLS/GUIDES

96/97 prices in dollars

Killington
Classes 7 days
1½hr: from 9.30, 10.30, 11.30 or 1.30: 25
Children's classes
Ages: 4 to 12
6 3hr days: 300
Private lessons
available on request

CHILDCARE

The new Family Center at Rams Head is 'home base'. The Friendly Penguin nursery takes kids from age 6 weeks to 6 years, and there are ski classes for several age groups. There's a special rental shop, and lockers for kids in ski school classes. Outside the door is the new Snow Play Park, with magic carpet lift and handle tow lift.

UK PACKAGES

American Connections, American Dream, Bladon Lines, Crystal, Equity School Ski, Equity Total Ski, Funway Holidays, Inghams, Made to Measure, Neilson, Ski Activity, Ski Independence, Ski North America Direct, Skisar U.S., Skiworld North America, Solo's, Virgin Snow

ACTIVITIES

Indoor Massage (at Cascades Lodge), Falls Brook fitness centre (cross country, skating, jacuzzi, sauna, weights), Mountain Green health club (swimming pool, jacuzzi, sauna, aerobics, weights), cinemas and bowling at Rutland, spas
Outdoor Skating, sledding, sleigh rides, cross country, sightseeing flights

SNOW RELIABILITY
Excellent

Killington's snowmaking system is comprehensive, and the product is impressively soft. The natural snowfall record isn't bad, either. The resort's famously long season is something of a con, though. Snow is built up throughout the season on the SuperStar trail on the front of Skye Peak, to form a sort of artificial glacier. At its peak, the snow depth approaches tree-top level, so it takes a long time to melt in the spring.

FOR EXPERTS
Plenty of challenges

The main areas that experts head for are Killington Peak, where there is a handful of genuine double-diamond fall-line runs under the two chair-lifts, and Bear Mountain. Most of the slopes here are single blacks but Outer Limits, under the main quad chair, is a double-diamond claimed to be 'the steepest mogul slope in the East'. We haven't measured their gradients, but we think there are steeper runs at Stowe and Smugglers' Notch. There are two or three worthwhile blacks on Snowdon, too. The lightly wooded Fusion Zones on Skye and Snowdon are well worth seeking out.

FOR INTERMEDIATES
Navigation problems?

There are lots of easy cruising blue and green runs all over the area, except on Bear Mountain, where the single blacks present a bit more of a challenge for intermediates. Snowdon is a splendid area for those who like to vary their diet. There's a blue-graded Fusion Zone on Rams Head.

FOR BEGINNERS
Splendid

The facilities for complete beginners are excellent, and improving. The Snowshed slope is one vast nursery slope served by three chair-lifts, and to one side of it is an area with a very slow Poma lift which is an ideal place to get started. Rams Head also has excellent gentle slopes.

FOR CROSS-COUNTRY
Two main options

Extensive cross-country loops are available at two specialist 'resorts' – Mountain Meadows down on Route 4, and Mountain Top Ski Touring, a short drive away at Chittenden.

QUEUES
Problem-free, usually

Killington gets a lot of weekend business, but at other times the slopes and lifts are likely to be quiet.

MOUNTAIN RESTAURANTS
Bearable base lodges

There is only one real mountain restaurant – at the top of Killington Peak, in what was the top station of the old gondola. Each of the lift base stations has some sort of eatery, of which the one at Killington Base Lodge is the least dreary.

SCHOOLS AND GUIDES
Impressive results

Like most US areas, Killington has a thoroughly professional ski school. The kids we took made great progress.

FACILITIES FOR CHILDREN
Fine in practice

We haven't seen the new family centre at the Rams Head base, but the facility it replaces at Snowshed was fine.

Staying there

Killington is the most spread-out resort we have come across, with lots of its accommodation literally miles from the lift bases. Provided you're taking a car, you're probably best advised to forget any ideas about being based near the slopes, and concentrate on other factors – being near one of the very lively nightspots, perhaps.

But even here it is possible to fix accommodation that is relatively close to the lifts, and some of it is reachable on snow when conditions are good – there are condos at the foot of the slopes to the left of Snowshed (looking at the trail map).

HOW TO GO
Wide choices

There is a wide choice of places to stay, whether booking independently or through UK tour operators. As well as hotels and condos, there are chalets and at least one chalet-hotel (Crystal's Club Hotel New England).

Bear in mind that tour operators sell accommodation miles from the slopes (some of it nearer Pico than Killington). Chalet Killington, a hotel in a good compromise position a mile or two down the Killington Road from the slopes, is not especially luxurious but has been recommended by visitors.

494

NEW ENGLAND

CRYSTAL

T **0181 399 5144** F **0181 390 6378**

A charming New England Inn where guests have ski lessons and use of the latest Rossignol Carve skis free of charge. All bedrooms are ensuite with TV, there is a jacuzzi and guests can use a swimming pool at a nearby hotel. One week prices start from £435 per person with return scheduled flights. Prices include a Crystal Club breakfast, afternoon tea and 3-course evening meals with free wine and coffee.

← CRYSTAL CLUB HOTEL NEW ENGLAND →

GETTING THERE

Air Boston, transfer 2½hr.

TOURIST OFFICE

Postcode VT 05751
Tel +1 (802) 422 3333
Fax 422 4391

Showshed, with the main beginners' slope stretching away behind ↓

EATING OUT
You name it

There are all sorts of restaurants spread along the Killington Road, from simple pizza or pasta through mainstream steak-seafood-chicken-smothered-in-cheese to one or two more ambitious 'fine dining' places. Many of the nightspots mentioned below serve food for at least part of the evening. The menu guide published locally is essential reading.

APRES-SKI
The beast of the East

Killington has a well-deserved reputation for a vibrant après-ski scene; many of its short-stay visitors are clearly intent on making the most of their few days (or nights) here.

Although there are bars at the base

lodges, keen après-skiers head down Killington Road to one of the lively places dotted along its six-mile length. Many of these places change their character more than once during the afternoon and evening. From 3pm it's cheap drinks and free munchies, then in the early evening it's serious dining time, then later on the serious action starts (and admission charges kick in). Most of the places mentioned here would also rate a mention in Eating Out, if we had the space.

The train-themed Casey's Caboose is said to have the best 'wings' in town, and the freebies served in the afternoon attract hordes of local rednecks. Charity's is another lively bar, with an interior apparently lifted from a turn-of-the-century Parisian brothel. The Wobbly Barn is a famous live-music place that rivals Jackson's Mangy Moose for the position of America's leading après-ski venue. The top-line rock bands it lays on fully justify the admission charge. The Pickle Barrel caters for a younger crowd, with theme nights (pyjama party, beach party) as well as rock bands and loud music. The Outback complex has something for everyone, from pizzas and free massages to disco and live bands.

OFF THE SLOPES
Take a good book

If there is a less amusing resort in which to spend time not skiing or boarding, we have yet to find it. Make sure you have a car, as well as a book.

Smugglers' Notch 315m

Fine fun for families

Smuggs hits the family target squarely, with a constant round of early-evening activities, sympathetic instructors, comprehensive childcare, a 'petting zoo' with sheep and goats, a generally child-friendly layout and some long, quiet, easy runs. There are challenging slopes, too, but it's a small domain and mileage-hungry intermediates should go elsewhere (as should nightbirds).

WHAT IT COSTS

(((((5)

HOW IT RATES

The slopes

Snow	****
Extent	*
Experts	***
Intermediates	***
Beginners	****
Convenience	*****
Queues	****
Restaurants	*

The rest

Scenery	***
Resort charm	**
Off-slope	*

MOUNTAIN FACTS

Altitude	315m-1110m
Lifts	10
Pistes	1000 acres
Green	20%
Blue	55%
Black	25%
Art. snow	100 acres

What's new

The trail/lift link with Stowe was revived for 1996/97.

A new snowboard park was built on Madonna Mountain, spread over 2km, including a half-pipe.

The nursery slope, Sir Henry's Hill, has been expanded and floodlit, and kitted out with gadgets to give skiing and boarding sensations.

UK PACKAGES

American Dream, Ski Club Europe

TOURIST OFFICE

Postcode
VT 05464-9599
Tel +1 (802) 644 8851
Fax 644 2713

THE RESORT

Smugglers' Notch is about the nearest thing you'll find in the US to a French-style purpose-built family resort – except that it doesn't look so bad. The village isn't genuinely traffic-free – you may have to tangle with traffic to get to the childcare centre, even – but it comes close, and once installed in your condo you can happily do without a car. Those not afflicted with children be warned: you may find it's difficult to get away from Billy Bob Bear.

THE MOUNTAIN

Smuggs has varied and satisfying **slopes**, spread over three hills, with some real challenges as well as easy cruising and a worthwhile vertical of 800m. And it's blissfully quiet on the mountain except at weekends and holidays. It's undeniably a small area, though. You can get to Stowe (see next page) by lift and trail, and a day there is covered by the Smuggs pass.

The amount of snowmaking is gradually increasing, and **snow reliability** is already good.

It's a great area for **beginners.** One of the chair-lifts out of the village runs at half speed, and the runs it accesses are of an ideal gradient. And the higher lifts take you to long easy runs that even novices can tackle by the end of their first week.

There are **intermediate** runs of every grade; there just aren't many of them. The link with Stowe adds variety.

There are challenges for **experts**. We were impressed by the two or three double-diamond runs on Madonna, but they have now opened The Black Hole – the only triple-diamond run in the East, they say. You can go off-piste in the trees anywhere within the resort boundary – but be aware that these areas are not patrolled.

Smuggs encourages **snowboarding**, and its new fun-park sounds impressive. Evening beginners' lessons

are available three times a week.

The **cross-country** trails are rather limited for a competent skier.

Except at holiday times, **ski school** classes are small, reports favourable.

Smuggs aims to be simply the best for **children**. The mountain is child-friendly, offering excitement with safety – with a special jolly kids' trail map. There's a terrain park for kids, and little forest glades where even tinies can be taken off piste. The school arrangements are very good, too, with childcare before, between and after skiing sessions, and carriage to the kids' chair-lift by horse-drawn sleigh. See our special report, below.

STAYING THERE

There are no **hotels** in the resort itself – though there are some within driving distance. There are lots of condos on or near the slopes, and none is very far from the snow.

There are a couple of **restaurants** in the resort, and others a short drive down the road to the outside world.

The adult **après-ski** possibilities are about the most limited we have come across. We hear good reports of the teen centre, and our kids loved the diversions laid on for them.

There is very little to do **off the slopes.** The pool (in a balloon building) is no more than adequate.

THE CHILD'S VIEW

Smuggs is a great place for children who like to ski. It has lots of little special trails for younger children like Laura, who was four years old when we went there, and fairly difficult runs for older children like me (I was 8). There are two ski clubs to look after children of different ages. My teachers were very friendly and they take you on slopes that are just right. There are very nice apartments that are quite close to the slopes.
By Alex Gill

Stowe

475m

Charming Vermont town, small but serious mountain

Stowe is one of New England's cutest little towns, its main street lined with dinky clapboard shops and restaurants. Its mountain, six miles away, is modest in size, but within its bounds there is everything from great cruising to fearsome mogul fields. For a short stay, it makes a very attractive proposition – especially if the trail/lift link and pass-sharing with Smugglers' Notch can be kept going.

WHAT IT COSTS

((((5)

HOW IT RATES

The slopes

Snow	****
Extent	*
Experts	***
Intermediates	****
Beginners	****
Convenience	*
Queues	****
Restaurants	**

The rest

Scenery	***
Resort charm	****
Off-slope	*

What's new

The trail/lift link with Smugglers' Notch was revived for 1996/97. The long Big Spruce chair that this uses is to be replaced by a fast quad, though it's not clear when.

A new daycare center has been opened, taking children from the age of 2mths.

MOUNTAIN FACTS

Altitude	390m-1110m
Lifts	11
Pistes	480 acres
Green	16%
Blue	59%
Black	25%
Art. snow	350 acres

UK PACKAGES

American Connections, American Dream, Bladon Lines, Crystal, Funway Holidays, Inghams, Made to Measure, Neilson, Ski Club Europe, Ski Independence, Skisar U.S., Skiworld North America, Virgin Snow

TOURIST OFFICE

Postcode VT 05672
Tel +1 (802) 253 3000
Fax 253 2159

THE RESORT

Stowe is a classic little New England town – a real community and a popular spot for tourists year-round, with bijou 'specialty' shops lining its sidewalks. You could find no sharper contrast to the two other New England resorts we feature in this edition. The slopes of Mount Mansfield, Vermont's snow-capped (although mainly wooded) highest peak, are a 15-minute drive away, and much of the accommodation is along the road out to it.

THE MOUNTAIN

The **slopes** are in three sectors, two linked by blue runs mid-mountain and green ones at the base, the third (Spruce Peak) a short shuttle-ride away (there are plans for a lift link).

The main sector, served by a trio of chair-lifts from Mansfield Base Lodge, is dominated by the famous Front Four – a row of seriously steep double-black-diamond runs. But there is plenty of intermediate and easy stuff, too, with some particularly easy long runs down to the outlying Toll House lift base, with its own hotel-restaurant.

A fast 8-seat gondola serves the next sector: easy-intermediate runs with one black alternative – plus the short but very steep Waterfall, under the gondola at the top.

The third area, Spruce Peak, has the main nursery area at the bottom, with a chair-lift to mid-mountain and another beyond that. The top of this sector gives access to Smugglers' Notch, over the hill (see previous page), and in 1996/97 the two resorts showed renewed interest in exploiting the link, with limited pass-sharing.

Snow reliability is well up to New England norms, with snowmaking on practically all the blue runs of the main and gondola sectors (and one or two blacks), and on lower Spruce Peak.

For **experts,** the 'front four' and their variants present a real challenge

– very few pistes in the Alps can match the steepest of these. For **intermediates**, the usual New England reservation applies: the terrain is limited in extent; there's also a severe shortage of ordinary black runs. For **beginners**, the nursery slopes and long green runs are great.

The resort is keen to attract **snowboarders**, with no less than four fun-parks and a half-pipe. Stowe has excellent **cross-country** centres dotted around the landscape (including the musically famous Trapp Family Lodge), with lots of connected trails.

The area is not entirely free of **queues** – particularly for the main chair on the main sector – but they move rapidly and, of course, courteously.

There are two **mountain restaurants**. At the top of the gondola, Cliff House is a lofty room with table service, sophisticated food and good views. The Octagon, at the top of the main sector, is a small cafeteria.

The excellent **children's** facilities are at the base of Spruce Peak.

STAYING THERE

Stowe is a long-established tourist town, which claims more 3- and 4-diamond **hotels** and **restaurants** than any other town or city in New England, except Boston. There are hotels in and around Stowe itself and at various points along the road to the mountain, some with Austrian or Scandinavian names and styles. Ye Olde England Inne sounds appalling, but is strongly recommended by a reporter, as are the Stowehof Inn and Green Mountain Inn. There are restaurants of all conceivable kinds. The Cliff House at the top of the gondola is open for dinner.

Après-ski is muted – Stowe reportedly goes to bed early. There's a good cinema with new releases.

Stowe is a pleasant town in which to spend time **off the slopes** – at least if you like shopping.

Canada

Canada was not on the British ski scene at all a few years ago and people only started going there after US resorts had established themselves in the brochures. But now Canada attracts British skiers in huge numbers. The 1996/97 season in particular saw a massive hike in the numbers going to Banff-Lake Louise because of attractive packages (starting at under £300) offered by tour operators who were making use of new charter flights laid on to Calgary and the fact that winter is low season for the area, meaning that accommodation can be picked up for rock-bottom prices. 1997/98 will see even greater expansion as charter flights are being flown into Vancouver (for Whistler resort) as well as Calgary. But if people are attracted there initially through price, they return because they like what they find.

Canada offers the service and courtesy that is so striking when you first visit the US – mountain hosts to show you around the slopes, immaculately groomed runs, civilised lift queues, lots of high-speed quad chair-lifts, piste maps available at the bottom of most lifts, and lift operators who seem happy in their job and appear to want you to have a good time.

But what distinguishes Canadian from American resorts – the ones in the West at least – is that the mountains resemble those of the Alps. You get spectacular scenery of the kind that is very rare in the US. And at the two resorts featured in most tour operators' brochures – Whistler-Blackcomb and Banff-Lake Louise – there are very extensive slopes. In fact, Whistler-Blackcomb has the biggest vertical drop and highest piste mileage in North America, and a lot of exciting runs above the tree line as well as through woodland.

Banff-Lake Louise has another big plus-point. It is surrounded by Canadian National Park land and an amazing variety of wildlife that you'd never come across in Europe. Herds of elk and big-horn sheep roam the streets and roadsides. You might even see a moose or bear. Winter is Banff's low season – hotel prices are half their summer levels and the resort offers excellent value for money.

Both resorts also have other attractions. They have excellent snowfall records and can be relied upon for good snow cover for a long season. Accommodation is usually high-quality and spacious and there is a wide variety of good-value restaurants serving generous helpings of a wide variety of different cuisines. Both are very cosmopolitan resorts with significant Japanese influences – Japan is just across the Pacific and the Japanese pour across in big numbers, especially to Whistler in winter and to Banff in summer. Don't be surprised to see shop signs and hotel notices in Japanese and to be served by people of Japanese origin in a lot of places.

But in Banff now, the majority of winter visitors are British. The resort estimates that in the 1996/97 season 30,000 of its 'destination' visitors (those who stayed at least three nights) were British – making up 40 per cent of all destination skiers.

There are down sides to both these resorts though. Whistler suffers from a lot of bad weather coming in from the Pacific Ocean – it is practically on the coast. While this normally means a lot of snow up top, it can also mean a lot of rain at resort level, and days on end without sight of the sun. Banff and nearby Lake Louise have a different problem – especially in early season, temperatures can be bitterly cold (–30°C not unknown). Riding a high-speed chair in very low temperatures isn't much fun. Banff suffers from the fact that there are no villages at the bases of the slopes – you have to stay a bus- or car-ride away.

Canada is also home to the world's most famous heli-skiing operations, where you can stay for a week in a luxurious lodge and be whirled up to virgin powder for several runs a day. We tried it a few seasons ago and came back addicted. Or you can try heli-trips for a day from most resorts – a much more affordable option.

There are numerous smaller resorts in Canada's Rockies that are now appearing on the British market, mainly through specialist Canadian and North American operators – see the Western Safari chapter on page 514.

As well as downhill skiing and snowboarding, Canada is famous for a wide variety of other activities such as snowmobiling, cross-country skiing, dog-sledding, snow-shoeing and ice fishing.

Eastern Canada is now beginning to attract British skiers and snowboarders too, including a fair number of school groups. Like the eastern US, it has the attraction of a somewhat shorter flight time but the disadvantage of extremes of weather – as in Banff, it can be bitterly cold in the eastern resorts. And the culture and language are quite different from western Canada – the main resorts in the east are in the heart of the province of Quebec, where the French influence is predominant – language, cuisine and culture are all dominated by French-Canadians and there's a strong political movement to gain independence from the rest of Canada.

The most popular eastern resort is Mont Tremblant, just 75 miles west of Montreal. With a base at just 265m and a top height of 910m, you might think it low but the cold winter temperatures and

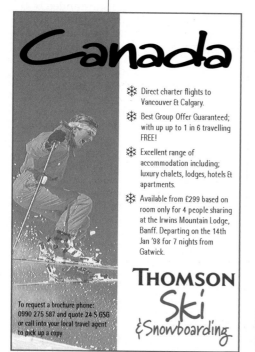

Canada's most extensive snowmaking system guarantee good snow cover. The ten lifts serve 74 runs for all standards but suiting intermediates and beginners best – and the small vertical drop (though it is the biggest in the east) means the runs are much shorter than those in the west. The resort at the base was largely developed by Intrawest (who also own Whistler and Blackcomb) and they have built an attractive, colourful pedestrian village with interestingly varied architecture. It suits families well (as long as they can stand the cold!) and has good all-day kindergartens – taking children from 12 months in the non-ski one and from the age of three in the ski kindergarten. Après-ski has a distinctly French feel to it, with fine restaurants and bars centred around the Place St-Bernard in the heart of the pedestrian village. Snowboarders have fun-parks on both the front and the back sides of the mountain.

Mont St Saveur is another much smaller area in a pretty setting, nearer to Montreal and catering for weekenders and city-dwellers wanting to do some night skiing – the majority of the trails are illuminated.

The other main resorts in the east are near the city of Quebec, with its historic, old, fortified centre which is full of life and a large number of restaurants, bars, shops, museums and galleries. If you fancy a city holiday with some skiing thrown in, you could consider basing yourself in Quebec. Mont Ste Anne, the biggest ski area, is a 30-minute drive away and Stoneham is 20 minutes. Both have snowmaking covering virtually all the pistes and both have big floodlit slopes to attract people from Quebec in mid-week. Both also have some accommodation at the base of the slopes but no real resort development. The trails suit beginners and intermediates best and there are snowboard fun-parks in both areas.

Banff-Lake Louise 1340m-1660m

Winter wonderland with wildlife

WHAT IT COSTS

((((4)

HOW IT RATES

The slopes
Snow	*****
Extent	****
Experts	***
Intermediates	****
Beginners	***
Convenience	*
Queues	*****
Restaurants	*

The rest
Scenery	****
Resort charm	***
Off-slope	***

➕ Three widely separated areas between them have a lot of runs

➕ Excellent snow record over long season (November to May)

➕ Really spectacular high mountain scenery – the best in North America

➕ Area teeming with wildlife

➕ Great value for money

➖ Can be extremely cold

➖ Separate areas are a long drive or bus ride from each other and there is no accommodation at their bases

➖ Lack of traditional ski resort atmosphere

➖ Lots of Brits there now because of cheap charter flight packages

Over 30,000 Brits visited Banff-Lake Louise in 1996/97, making up 40 per cent of all winter visitors to the area who stayed three or more nights. This was largely because of good value packages linking charter flights from the UK with accommodation that is tremendous value because winter is the area's low season. Most visitors are delighted with what they find.

Both Banff and Lake Louise (an hour or so apart) are set in the spectacular and unspoilt Banff National Park. The landscape is one of glaciers, jagged peaks and magnificent views and the valleys are full of wildlife that you'll never see in Europe. The slopes have something for everyone, from steep couloirs to gentle cruising. The snow is some of the coldest, driest and most reliable you'll find anywhere in the world and there's a lot of it. The people are friendly and welcoming. And the food is great value and served in generous portions.

Apart from the number of Brits around, we (and most of our reporters) have three reservations. It can be bitterly cold (–30°C is not unusual), a lot of time is spent getting to and from the three widely separated ski areas, and the resorts and the lodges at the base of the slopes lack a traditional resort atmosphere.

boarding *Boarders will feel at home in Banff-Lake Louise. All three areas have good fun-parks and half-pipes and all have some gnarly terrain for experienced riders. Several of our reporters had beginner lessons and all enjoyed them and made swift progress. If you are interested in lively bars and nightlife, Banff is the place to stay – Lake Louise village is deadly dull.*

What's new

At Sunshine Village a whole new mountain – Goats Eye – opened a couple of seasons ago, served by a high-speed quad. It now has the region's steepest runs. A high-speed quad was also installed to replace the slow Continental Divide lift.

At Norquay a huge new timber-framed Cascade base lodge was built for the 1996/97 season. Another is being built at Lake Louise for 1997/98.

Lake Louise also has ambitious plans to build lifts and open new runs opposite its current back bowls – on Richardson's and Wolverine Ridges. But no dates have yet been fixed.

MOUNTAIN FACTS

Altitude	1635m-2730m
Lifts	30
Pistes	6400 acres
Green	19%
Blue	47%
Black	34%
Art. snow	1600 acres

The resort

Banff is primarily a summer resort, which happens to have three separate ski and snowboard areas nearby – winter is their low season and hotel prices halve. Most people (including the people who work on the mountains) stay in Banff – which is a 45 to 60-minute drive from the largest area of slopes (Lake Louise), 20 to 25 minutes from the Sunshine area and 10 to 15 minutes from Mount Norquay. The buses to these areas are free to three-area lift pass holders.

Banff is spectacularly set, with several towering peaks rising up around its outskirts. There is lots of wildlife around. Don't be surprised to

find a herd of elk or long-horned sheep outside your hotel. And watch out for black (and even grizzly) bears on the drives to and from the slopes.

Banff gained its independence from the National Park authority in 1990. Since then it has grown substantially. But it still consists largely of one long main street and a small network of side roads built in the usual North American grid fashion. The main street is lined with hotels, condominiums, restaurants and tacky souvenir shops – many obviously catering for the Japanese market.

The buildings themselves have been successfully confined to low-rise developments. But despite many wooden clapboard buildings, it lacks

LIFT PASSES

97/98 prices in
Canadian dollars

Tri-area lift pass
Covers all lifts and
transport between
Banff, Lake Louise
and Sunshine Village.
Beginners First time
ski packages
including rental, pass
and tuition (35-43
depending on
mountain)
Main pass
1-day pass
6-day pass 303
Children
Under 13: 6-day pass
114 (62% off)
Short-term passes
Half-day pass for
individual areas of
Lake Louise, Sunshine
Village or Banff
Mount Norquay.
Notes Tri-area only
available for 3 days
or more.
Alternative passes
Day passes for
individual areas of
Lake Louise, Sunshine
Village or Banff
Mount Norquay, with
reductions for senior
citizens (over 65, and
over 55 at Norquay)
and teenagers (13-17).

genuine charm. It's not another Aspen or Telluride for atmosphere.

The only other place to stay is Lake Louise village, a five-minute drive from the slopes with the same name. But the village is not on the lake; that's another five-minute drive. And 'village' is rather too grand an expression for the tiny collection of hotels, condominiums, petrol station, supermarket, liquor store and few shops. If Banff lacks charm, Lake Louise village lacks it even more. But it does have one excellent hotel.

In marked contrast is Lake Louise itself, site of the Chateau Lake Louise hotel. In terms of scenery, you'd be hard-pressed to find a more beautiful resort. In 1882, Tom Watson, a surveyor for the Canadian Pacific Railroad, was the first white man to set eyes on this lake and the 3564m Victoria Glacier towering above it. On seeing the view, Watson exclaimed, 'As God is my judge, I never in all my exploration have seen such a matchless scene.' Neither have we – it is simply stunning.

The mountains 🏔️

In sharp contrast to our lack of enthusiasm for the villages, we find the snow hard to beat. Taking account of all three mountains, the area is big, and the views are the most spectacular that the Rockies have to offer, rivalling the best in the Alps.

THE SLOPES
A lot of moving around to do

The biggest of the three areas (claimed to be the biggest in North America in terms of acreage of slopes, but it certainly isn't in terms of marked pistes) is **Lake Louise**. This is a 45-minute drive or up to 60-minute bus-ride from Banff.

Two successive high-speed quads take you to the top of the main mountain. From here, as elsewhere, there's a choice of green, blue or black runs to other lifts. So people of varying standards can take the same lifts together. Almost all the mountain is wooded, good for when it's snowing.

From the top there's a stunning view of some of the high peaks of the Continental Divide (which runs from Canada to New Mexico), including Canada's uncanny Matterhorn lookalike, Mount Assiniboine.

Go over the back of this top ridge

and you're into Lake Louise's treeless back bowl runs. The bowl is predominantly north-facing and so keeps its snow in good condition.

From the bottom of the bowl runs you can take a lift back to the top again or up to the **Larch** area. This is the area's other mountain and was the original Lake Louise winter sports area. Served by one double chair, it has a number of pretty, wooded, relatively short runs. From the bottom you can return to the top of the main mountain or head back to the main base area along a lengthy green path.

There are plans to build lifts up both Richardson's Ridge and Wolverine Ridge, on the far side of the back bowls, and open up two new areas of lift-served slopes.

The Lake Louise area is owned by Charles Locke, who amassed his fortune in oil and on the stock market. He bought it in 1981 through his appropriately named company, Locke, Stock and Barrel. His wife is also appropriately named – yes, she's called Louise!

The second largest set of slopes is **Sunshine Village**, a 20 to 25 minute drive from Banff, 40 from Lake Louise village to the base of the gondola. Then it's another 25 minutes on the gondola to the main on-mountain base (though you can get out at the mid-station for the new Goats Eye area). It has the highest runs and best snow record in the area. It prides itself on not needing any artificial snow – we got right to the bottom in late April without seeing a bare spot.

Most of the slopes are above the tree line, up to 2730m. If the weather is bad, it is best to go elsewhere. But in good weather, this is a great area.

Sunshine has enough slopes to keep the keenest enthusiast happy for a day or two, with lifts fanning out in all directions and good snow throughout a long season. Its attraction for experts was increased a couple of seasons ago by the opening of Goats Eye mountain, which is very exposed at the top and can be bleak and windswept.

Norquay was Banff's first – and remains its smallest – area, 10 to 15 minutes' drive from town and served by just five lifts. It has wooded slopes to suit all standards and is recommended by recent reporters for being extremely quiet and under-rated – a good place for a warm-up day and

SCHOOLS/GUIDES

96/97 prices in
Canadian dollars

Club Ski
Guided tuition of the
three areas
Classes 6 days
4hr per day
3 full days: 144
Private lessons
Hourly
65 for 1 or 2 people

Lake Louise
Classes 6 days
1hr 45mins: 10.15 or
1.15
6 half-days: 150
Private lessons
Hourly
65 for 1 or 2 people;
each additional
person 16

Sunshine
Classes 6 days
2hr 15mins: 9.45 or
1.15
6 half-days: 150
Private lessons
Hourly
65 for 1 person

Banff Mount Norquay
Classes 6 days
2hr: 10am or 1pm
6 half-days: 150
Private lessons
Hourly
50 for 1 person; each
additional person 15

for poor weather days. There's a
scratch card on the back of the lift
ticket which almost always rewards
you with a free pint of beer or plate of
Nachos at the Cascade base lodge.
There's a floodlit piste once a week.

SNOW RELIABILITY
Excellent

When we were last there, we found
plenty of snow everywhere on both
Lake Louise and Sunshine in late April.
And that was at the end of what the
locals claim was the worst winter for
snow in many years. Norquay was shut
due to lack of customers rather than
snow. Wherever it's needed, there's
artificial snowmaking.

FOR EXPERTS
Widespread pleasure

Experts will want to spend most of
their time at the Lake Louise area. The
back bowls offer endless variations of
black mogul and powder runs. Many
people's favourite is Paradise Bowl –
one run is marked on the map but
there are scores of other variants.
Others prefer the runs on the far left,
which take you right away from all
signs of lifts. The two steepest are
Ridge Run and Whitehorn One. Again,
there are endless variations.

Because this is National Park, you
can go anywhere. But the areas
outside the boundaries aren't patrolled
and there's no avalanche control. A
guide is essential.

On the front of the mountain there
are more tough runs, including Outer
Limits, Sunset and the Men's and
Women's Downhills.

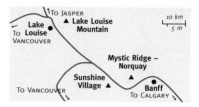

Sunshine has plenty of open, bump
runs above the tree line. One particular
novelty is a short, steep pitch, near the
mid-station, known as the Waterfall run
– because you do actually ski down
over a snow-covered frozen fall. The
new Goats Eye lift has opened up a
great area of expert double black
diamond trails and chutes, both above
and below the tree line.

Norquay also has a couple of
double black diamond runs, one a 35-
degree bump run, the other a steep
gunbarrel. There's a decent selection of
other blacks to keep you happy.

There is also heli-skiing and heli-
boarding available.

FOR INTERMEDIATES
Ideal runs wherever you go

In all three areas, at least 45 per cent
of the runs are classified as
intermediate. One thing which
characterises both Lake Louise and
Sunshine is that there is a wide choice
of runs from the top of virtually all
lifts. Wherever you look there are blue
and green ways down – some of the
greens as enjoyable (and pretty much
as steep) cruises as the blues.

On Louise, Meadowlark is a
beautiful tree-lined run from the top of
the Eagle chair to the base area.

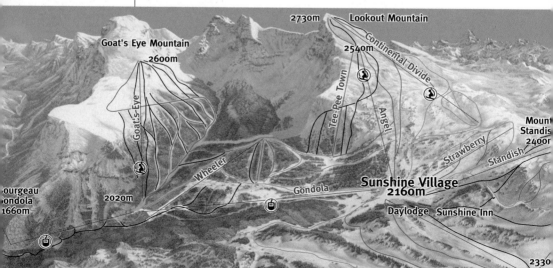

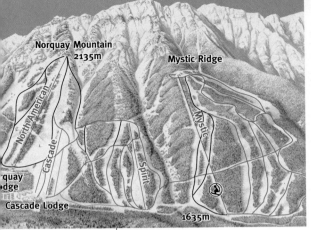

Norquay Mountain
2135m

Mystic Ridge

North American

Cascade

Mystic

Spirit

quay
dge

Cascade Lodge

1635m

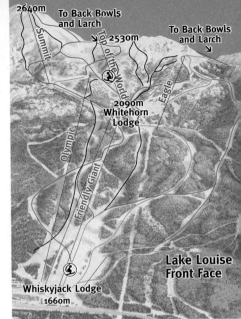

2640m
To Back Bowls
and Larch

2530m

To Back Bowls
and Larch

Summit

Top of the World

Eagle

2090m
Whitehorn
Lodge

Olympic

Friendly Giant

Lake Louise
Front Face

Whiskyjack Lodge
1660m

Juniper and Juniper Jungle are wonderful cruising runs on the western side. The Larch area has some short but enjoyable intermediate terrain. And the adventurous should try the blue-graded Boomerang which starts with a hike from the top of the highest lift, the Summit Platter drag. On many runs one side is groomed, the other left to develop moguls.

On Sunshine, we particularly liked the World Cup Downhill run, which goes right from the top of the slopes down to the mid-mountain base. And don't ignore the Wa-wa T-Bar, which gives access to the often quiet Wa-Wa Bowl and Tincan Alley.

The Mystic Ridge area of Norquay was developed especially to attract intermediates and has 11 tree-lined blues and a couple of sometimes-groomed blacks served by two high-speed quads. It's worth trying.

FOR BEGINNERS
Excellent terrain
Louise has a good nursery area near the base, served by a short T-bar; Sunshine has a good area by the mid-mountain base, which is served by an even shorter hand-tow. And Norquay has a small nursery area but no real runs for progressing beginners.

Recommended graduation runs for improvers on Louise are the gentle, wide Wixwaxy (designated a slow skiing zone, so there are no lunatics bombing past you) and the slightly more difficult Deer Run or Eagle Meadows. There are even greens round the back bowls and in the Larch area – worth taking for the views.

Sunshine has the beginners-only Meadow Park among other user-friendly greens.

If you're a complete beginner with a party of more experienced friends and you want to meet up with them regularly, we don't recommend this area as ideal. Each mountain has its own school and you'll want to stick to one, whereas the more experienced will probably want to split their days between the three areas.

FOR CROSS-COUNTRY
High in quality and quantity
It's a good area for cross-country. There are trails near Banff, around the Bow River, and on the Banff Springs golf course. But the best area is around Lake Louise, which has around 100km of groomed trails of all standards – watch out for wolf packs!

QUEUES
Deserted during the week
Half of the area's visitors come for the day from nearby cities such as Calgary – so it's normally quiet during the week. The worst weekend queues can be for the gondola up Sunshine in the morning.

The Lake Louise area is so confident it can handle numbers that it offers a full refund of your lift pass on any day you have to queue for more than 10 minutes at the base area.

More of a problem than queues is the cold. Temperatures as low as –30°C are not unusual. The fast chairs can then be extremely unpleasant.

GETTING THERE
Air Calgary, transfer 1½hr.

UK PACKAGES
Airtours, All Canada Ski, American Connections, American Dream, Bladon Lines, Canada's Best, Chinook-It, Crystal, First Choice Ski, Frontier Ski, Funway Holidays, Independent Ski Links, Inghams, Interworld Canada, Lotus Supertravel, Made to Measure, Neilson, Ski Activity, Ski Equipe, Ski Independence, Ski North America Direct, Ski Safari, Ski Vacation Canada, Skisar U.S., Skiworld North America, Thomson

Lake Louise Airtours, All Canada Ski, American Connections, American Dream, Canada's Best, Chinook-It, Crystal, First Choice Ski, Frontier Ski, Funway Holidays, Independent Ski Links, Inghams, Interworld Canada, Lotus Supertravel, Made to Measure, Neilson, Ski Activity, Ski Club of GB, Ski Independence, Ski Vacation Canada, Skisar U.S., Skiworld North America, Solo's, Thomson, Waymark Holidays

Sunshine Village Canada's Best

MOUNTAIN RESTAURANTS
Not bad for North America
All three mountains have eating facilities both at the base area and up the mountain. But most are cafeteria-style and serve the usual basics: burgers, hot dogs, sandwiches, soups.

On Louise, Temple Lodge, near the bottom of the Larch lift, is probably the most attractive, built in rustic style with a big terrace and choice of eating venues, including a table-service restaurant. Whitehorn Lodge, near the bottom of the Eagle chair, has excellent views from its balcony. At Whiskey Jack, at the base, the table-service restaurant is much better than the dire self-service cafeteria – but the whole area is being redeveloped for the 1997/98 season.

Sunshine Village has a choice of eating places at its mid-mountain base. The renovated Daylodge has improved its choice of food. And the new Mad Trappers saloon serves great beer, burgers and peanuts. The Sunshine Inn (an on-mountain hotel) has the best food – table-service snacks in the Chimney Corner Lounge or a full lunch in the Eagle's Nest Dining Room. There's also food service at the bottom of Goats Eye mountain.

At Norquay, the big new timber framed Cascade Lodge has great views and a table-service restaurant upstairs as well as a self-service cafeteria.

SCHOOLS AND GUIDES
Caught on film
The Club Ski Program takes you to all three mountains and offers a mixture of guiding and instruction, including free video analysis, a fun race and a group photo. We'd recommend it to anyone who wants to see the whole area while improving their technique. Reporters who've tried it rave about it: 'absolutely brilliant' and 'learnt more in three days than in my previous two weeks skiing'. All standards are catered for.

FACILITIES FOR CHILDREN
Each area has them
One recent reporter used the childcare facilities at all three areas and thought they were 'all excellent. I'd recommend all three and advise booking in advance at Lake Louise.'

Staying there

Wherever you stay (except at mid-mountain on Sunshine) it will be a drive or bus-ride to the slopes. Lake Louise village is the nearest place to major slopes. But don't expect any resort ambience or much nightlife.

HOW TO GO
Superb-value
There is a huge amount of accommodation available – especially hotels and self-catering, but also a few catered chalets run by British tour operators.

Hotels Summer is the peak season here. Hotel prices halve for the winter – so you can stay in luxury hotels at bargain rates.

In or near Banff:

《《《 **Banff Springs** The luxury option in Banff, a turn-of-the century, castle-style Canadian Pacific property. It's virtually a town within a town. It can sleep 2,000 people, has over 40 shops, 12 restaurants and bars, a night club and a huge free indoor pool. There's also a superb, new Health Club and Spa for which there's a charge.

FREE SKI-GUIDING

All three areas pride themselves on their free ski-guiding services. Just turn up at one of the two or three meeting times a day and meet your 'Ski Friend' – a volunteer who will show you around the area. You are divided into groups, according to ability and the type of runs you want to do.

You can use the service as many times as you want in order to get the chance to ski with people of similar ability to yourself.

This sort of service is common in the US now – but there it's normally seen as a mountain orientation tour and run once a day for a group of mixed ability. The Banff-Lake Louise service is another step forward – and they claim to have invented the idea which the Americans have copied. All the reports we've had of the guiding have been very positive.

CHILDCARE

Last year the nursery at Lake Louise took children aged 18 days to 6 years, from 8am to 4.30. The one at Sunshine Village takes children aged 19 months to 6 years, from 8.30 to 4.30. The one at Norquay's Cascade Lodge takes children aged 19 months, from 9am to 4pm. In all three, children aged 3 or more can take short ski lessons.

ACTIVITIES

Indoor Film theatre, museums, galleries, swimming pools (one with water slides), gym, squash, racquetball, weight training, bowling, jacuzzi, sauna, mini-golf, climbing wall
Outdoor Swimming in hot springs, ice skating, heli-skiing, horse-drawn carriage rides, sleigh rides, dog-sled rides, snowmobiles, curling, ice hockey, ice fishing, helicopter tours

(((3) **Caribou Lodge** On the main street, slightly out of town. It has a variety of wood-clad, interestingly and individually designed rooms, a sauna and hot tub complex and a good restaurant and bar. Highly recommended by several reporters.
(((3) **Rimrock** Spectacularly set, out of town on Sulphur Mountain, with outstanding views and a fully equipped health club.
((2) **Inns of Banff** About 20 minutes' walk from town centre; recommended by reporters for its large rooms and health club facilities.
((2) **Banff Park Lodge** In the town itself. Used by several British tour operators, large and central, with hot tub, steam room and indoor pool.
((2) **King Edward** Right in town centre, set above shops; recommended by reporters for large rooms and being surprisingly quiet for its position. An old hotel which has been recently renovated.
At Lake Louise village:
(((4) **Post** A member of the Relais & Châteaux chain, with the best cuisine in the area, wood-panelled rooms and even a few log cabins in the grounds. Indoor pool, hot tub and steam room. Go for a room facing away from the railway to avoid the worst of the hooting trains during the night.
((2) **Lake Louise Inn** The cheaper option in the village, still with pool, hot tub and sauna.
At Lake Louise itself:
(((3) **Chateau Lake Louise** With stunning views over frozen Lake Louise, this 515-room Canadian Pacific-owned hotel has undergone multi-million dollar restoration over the last few years and has a choice of restaurants and a health club with indoor pool, steam room and hot tub.
((2) **Deer Lodge** A simpler, cheaper option with a rooftop hot tub.
Self-catering The biggest complex is the Banff Rocky Mountain Resort, set in the woods on the edge of town, which has a wealth of in-house facilities including indoor pool, squash and hot tubs. The Douglas Fir resort was recommended by two reporters.

EATING OUT
Lots of choice in Banff
The best cuisine in the region is in the Post Hotel restaurant at Lake Louise. The Chateau Lake Louise has two Alpine-style restaurants – the Walliser Stube, serving fondue and cured

meats, and the Edelweiss, for more formal dining. It also has the Poppy Room, for family-style food and some other options. In the village, try the Station Restaurant and the Baker Creek Bistro. Two reporters also recommend the YMCA/ youth hostel, which has a cheap restaurant open to the public.
But there's much more choice in Banff, with over 100 different restaurants, from McDonald's to fine dining in the Banff Springs Hotel. Reporters were enthusiastic about lots of places but complained about them being busy and many places not taking bookings. Regular recommendations include Earl's (burgers and ethnic dishes, very popular and lively), Mellisa's (steaks), Balkan (a Greek), Joe BTFSPKLK's (a classic 1950s diner with jukebox), Magpie and Stump (Mexican, with Wild West decor), Giorgio's (Italian), Silver Dragon (Chinese), Sukiyaki (Japanese), Rose & Crown (pub grub), Hard Rock Café (burgers), Bumpers (huge portions of ribs), Keg (steaks, two branches – one in town and one in Caribou Lodge).

APRES-SKI
Liveliest in Banff
One of the drawbacks of the area is that tea-time après-ski is limited because the villages are a drive from the slopes.
But things liven up later, especially in Banff. Wild Bill's has live country and western music and line dancing. The Rose & Crown has live music and gets crowded. The Works, Outta Bounds and Silver City nightclubs are all popular and lively.
Lake Louise is quieter. The Glacier Saloon, in Chateau Lake Louise, with traditional Wild West decor, often has live music until late. Charly Two's pub, in the Lake Louise Inn, has dancing until 2am. The Outpost Pub, in the Post Hotel, is worth trying, as is the Saddleback lounge, in the Lake Louise Inn. The weekly dinner up the mountain and torchlit descent is another different option.

OFF THE SLOPES
Beautiful scenery
If you enjoy walking, the area has a lot of attractions. You can go snowshoeing and on organised Ice Canyon walks. There are museums to visit such as The Whyte Museum of the Canadian Rockies, The Natural History Museum and The Luxton Museum of the Plains

↑
The views around Lake Louise are the best in North America

Indians. And, of course, there's the wildlife and the natural hot springs.

There are sleigh rides, dog sledding, skating and tobogganing. Lake Louise has ice skating and broomball games.

STAYING UP THE MOUNTAIN
Worth considering
At Sunshine Village, the Sunshine Village Inn is the only slope-side hotel. It is well run, has a good atmosphere, a big outdoor hot tub, good food and small but attractive rooms with excellent views. Unlike every other hotel in the area, it closes in summer, and its winter rates are as high as any.

STAYING IN OTHER RESORTS
The road to Jasper is stunning
An attractive option is to spend a couple of days in Jasper, with its own small area at Marmot Basin. The three-hour trip on the Columbia Icefields Parkway, through the Banff and Jasper National Parks, is one of the most beautiful drives in the world. The best place to spend the night here is the Jasper Park Lodge, where log cabins are set around a frozen lake. On the walk to breakfast, you may well encounter a herd of elk grazing outside your cabin.

TOURIST OFFICE

Postcode ToL oCo
Tel +1 (403) 762 4561
Fax 762 8185

Selected chalets and club hotels in Banff-Lake Louise   ADVERTISEMENT

BRAND NEW • FOR • THIS EDITION

Jasper

1064m

Small area of slopes set amid glorious scenery and wildlife

Set in the middle of Jasper National Park, the small railroad town is surrounded by spectacular scenery and teeming with wildlife. The slopes, 30 minutes away, are fine, but Jasper best suits those looking for an all-round winter holiday.

WHAT IT COSTS

((((4)

HOW IT RATES

The slopes

Snow	****
Extent	*
Experts	***
Intermediates	***
Beginners	****
Convenience	*
Queues	****
Restaurants	*

The rest

Scenery	***
Resort charm	***
Off-slope	***

MOUNTAIN FACTS

Altitude	1705m-2600m
Lifts	7
Pistes	1000 acres
Green	35%
Blue	35%
Black	30%
Art. snow	10 acres

UK PACKAGES

All Canada Ski, American Connections, American Dream, Crystal, Frontier Ski, Inghams, Made to Measure, Neilson, Ski Activity, Ski Independence, Ski Vacation Canada, Skisar U.S., Thomson

TOURIST OFFICE

Postcode ToE 1Eo
Tel +1 (403) 852 3816
Fax 852 3533

THE RESORT

Jasper is an unremarkable, growing railway town which started life as a stopover for fur traders. There's little more to it than a couple of main streets. A fair amount of accommodation is out of town and the local slopes are a 30-minute drive away. Its main attraction is the beautiful scenery, and drives and walks in the surrounding unspoiled National Park land. The three-hour trip on the Columbia Icefields Parkway, past glaciers, frozen waterfalls and lakes to Lake Louise through the Banff and Jasper National Parks, is one of the most beautiful drives in the world. This makes Jasper a good place to stay for a couple of days as part of a two-centre holiday combined with a longer stay in Banff-Lake Louise or Whistler, both of which have much more extensive skiing and snowboarding. You can travel from Whistler to Jasper by overnight train from Vancouver and wake up to spectacular Rocky Mountain scenery.

THE MOUNTAINS

The **slopes** of Marmot Basin are 30 minutes' drive from town and right in the heart of the unspoiled National Park area. The small area has slopes for all standards with the runs graded evenly – roughly a third each for green, blue and black gradings. This is less intermediate terrain than is normally the case and adventurous intermediates might find the runs a bit tame unless they brave the blacks. There's good **snowboard** terrain here and the two T-bars are avoidable.

The resort has decent **snow reliability**, though when we were there at the end of the season the highest runs were shut because of poor snow and there isn't much artificial help.

There are some tough runs for **experts**, especially those willing to hike up from the top of the Knob chair. Virtually the whole of the left-hand side of the mountain as you look up is made up of single black diamond runs. There are some good, steep, long

mogul runs on both the top and bottom halves of the mountain, together with some excellent tree skiing from the Caribou Ridge area.

There is a fair amount of terrain for **intermediates**, but those who will enjoy it most are people willing to give some of the easier black runs a go.

Marmot Basin is good for **beginners**, with some very gentle, long green runs to progress to lower down.

There is some excellent, scenic **cross-country** skiing available close to Jasper itself rather than out at Marmot Basin, with the trails in the Jasper Park Lodge area being especially beautiful, round the lake and through the trees.

Queues are rarely a problem.

There are two basic **mountain restaurants**, one in the base lodge and another at mid-mountain.

The Little Rascals nursery at the base of the slopes caters for **children** from 19 months to five years. The ski school runs classes from four up.

STAYING THERE

There are some excellent **hotels** in and near Jasper. Our favourite is the excellent Jasper Park Lodge, a beautiful collection of luxurious log cabins set 4km out of town around a lake in the middle of 1,000 acres of land rich with wildlife. Room service is delivered on bicycles and you may well have to walk around grazing elk to reach your room or visit the outdoor pool and other leisure facilities. Chateau Jasper is another luxury hotel with pool nearer to town. There is **self-catering** available, though most tour operators concentrate on hotels.

There is plenty of choice for **eating out**, from fine dining at the Jasper Park Lodge to Cajun, pizza and Japanese. And there are some decent bars for **après-ski**, including the Astoria, O'Shea's and Nick's.

There is lots to do **off the slopes**, including beautiful walks, snowshoeing, ice skating, and there is a fine aquatic centre and indoor sports complex.

Whistler 675m

North America's biggest mountain set in Alpine-style scenery

WHAT IT COSTS

(((((6)

HOW IT RATES

The slopes

Snow	****
Extent	****
Experts	*****
Intermediates	*****
Beginners	****
Convenience	****
Queues	*****
Restaurants	*

The rest

Scenery	***
Resort charm	***
Off-slope	**

What's new

Ever since it was started Whistler has been improving and expanding its runs and bed base. Its mountains are now well served by three gondolas (the Whistler Creek one new for 1996/97) and 10 fast quads. Two of these (Green and Redline on Whistler Mountain) are being replaced by safer, more reliable ones for 1997/98. And new black runs have been cut through the trees from West Bowl to Whistler Creekside – though in 1996/97 they weren't officially open. On Blackcomb for 1997/98 there will be new beginner and intermediate trails.

Both mountains are now owned by the Vancouver-based resort developer Intrawest, and development looks set to continue apace – there is approval for a 54,000 bed base compared with the current 38,000.

➕ North America's biggest ski and snowboard area, with the largest vertical drop of over 1600m

➕ Spectacular 'Alpine' scenery with lots of above-the-tree-line bowls

➕ Good slopes for all standards

➕ Modern pedestrianised resort built in pleasant 'West Coast' style with varied architecture

➖ Proximity to coast and low altitude means it can rain at resort level

➖ Two separate mountains are linked only at resort level

➖ Mediocre (but improving) mountain restaurants

➖ Rapid expansion means village becoming large and lots of building going on

Whistler has North America's biggest and best skiing and snowboarding. Billions of Canadian dollars have been invested in developing two separate mountains (linked at their bases), both of which have miles of runs for all standards, the greatest vertical drops in North America, good snow guaranteed on the highest slopes, modern lift systems which whisk you rapidly back up the mountain and spectacular 'Alpine'-type scenery so often missing in US resorts. And further improvement is guaranteed now that both are owned by one company, which will put an end to the traditional rivalry between them.

This year Whistler has received rave reviews from every one of our reporters for all major aspects except one – the weather. Be warned: it rains a lot here at resort level as frequent storms roll in from the nearby Pacific ocean. As you go up the mountain, the rain normally turns to snow, but rain low down can dampen your spirits and visibility up high can be poor. Don't expect day after day of clear skies – we've been there twice and rarely seen the sun.

But if you are an all-weather skier or rider, you'll have the time of your life. And the pedestrianised villages are attractive, friendly and fun, with good bars and restaurants and some very comfortable accommodation. We love the place.

boarding *Both mountains are excellent for every standard of boarder, from beginner to expert. All the main lifts are chairs and gondolas and there is terrain for all – from gentle green runs to heart-stopping cliffs to jump off. There are T-bars up on the Glacier, but the discomfort is worth it for the powder! Both mountains have a fun-park and a half-pipe. It is a popular area with snowboarders and is well known for its summer boarding camps.*

The resort

Whistler village and its smaller neighbour, **Blackcomb**, a 10-minute walk away, are set at the foot of their separate ski areas, a scenic 75-mile drive inland from Vancouver on Canada's west coast.

Whistler started as a ski area in 1965 with the 'village' consisting of a few ramshackle buildings in what is now called Whistler Creekside, a few miles from Whistler proper. It catered largely for day-trippers from Vancouver.

Whistler village was built in the late 1970s on the site of what used to be the area's rubbish tip. Blackcomb

village was developed in the 1980s. Both are traffic-free.

The architecture is varied and, for a purpose-built resort, quite tasteful. There are lots of chalet-style apartments built on the hillsides. The centres have individually designed wooden and concrete buildings, blended together in a master plan and built around a series of squares. There are no monstrous high-rise blocks. But there are a lot of large five- or six-storey hotel and apartment buildings.

The resort has expanded rapidly and looks set to continue to now that property development company Intrawest has bought Whistler (it

MOUNTAIN FACTS

Altitude 650m-2285m
Lifts 28
Pistes 6997 acres
Green 20%
Blue 55%
Black 25%
Art. snow 70 acres
Recco detectors used

LIFT PASSES

96/97 prices in
Canadian dollars
**Dual Mountain Lift
Ticket**
Covers all lifts on
both Whistler and
Blackcomb
mountains.
Beginners Daily
program for beginners
includes 2hr lesson,
ski rental and pass
(adult 67 per day).
Main pass
1-day pass 51
6-day pass 276
Senior citizens
Over 65: 6-day pass
199 (28% off)
Children
Under 13: 6-day pass
150 (46% off)
Under 7: free pass
Short-term passes
Half-day pass for each
area separately.
Notes Dual mountain
pass of 5 days or
over gives one non-
skiing day; 6-day
pass valid for 7 days
with one day non-
skiing. Further
discounts for 13- to
18- year-olds, and
groups of over 25.

already owned Blackcomb mountain). Whistler is the main resort, with most of the bars, restaurants and shops and the two main gondolas (one going up each mountain). Whistler North is being developed a longer walk from the lifts and last year's visitors were surprised by the number of building sites around.

Blackcomb is much smaller and quieter with a limited range of shops and restaurants. Its 343-room Chateau Whistler hotel, built in true château style, dominates the views down into the village from the mountain.

Whistler Creekside, a 10-minute bus-ride from the main Whistler village, is rather out on a limb, with limited nightlife and eating and drinking places, though there are plans to develop it further.

There is a free bus service between Whistler and Blackcomb, with fares charged for going further out. But if you're staying centrally it's just as quick to walk between the two.

It is a very cosmopolitan resort, with many visitors from Japan and Australia as well as Europe and US.

The mountains

The area has acquired a formidable reputation among experts. And that reputation is well deserved. There are some fearsomely steep chutes and lots of off-piste bowls.

But both mountains also have enormous amounts of well-groomed intermediate cruising terrain. Together they have over 200 marked pistes, and they form the biggest area of slopes, with the longest runs, in North America. But the base villages are low (less than 700m) and many people 'download' in the gondolas from the mid-stations because of poor snow, especially in late season.

Perhaps surprisingly, both Whistler and Blackcomb mountains have their own devotees among regular visitors, who choose to use just one non-stop.

THE SLOPES
The best in North America
The main way up **Whistler Mountain** is from Whistler Village by a long two-stage, 10-person gondola which rises over 1100m from the village at 650m to Pika's and The Roundhouse, the main mid-mountain base at 1810m.

From there runs fan out in all directions back down through the trees

to a series of chairs which carry you back up again. There's no need to head back to Whistler until the end of the day.

But the jewel in Whistler's crown only reveals itself when you reach the top of the gondola. There, high above you, lie Whistler's five magnificent above-the-tree-line bowls which reach 2178m – from left to right, Symphony, Harmony, Glacier, Whistler and West. You can go more or less anywhere in these, and a few of the ways are pisted to make areas accessible for intermediates as well as experts. They are served by two chairs, one a high-speed quad.

A six-person gondola from Whistler Creekside also accesses Whistler Mountain.

Access to **Blackcomb Mountain** from Whistler village is by an eight-seater gondola, which is met by a high-speed quad chair. There is also a route up Blackcomb by a series of high-speed chairs starting from the Blackcomb base area. The 1610m vertical rise from Blackcomb village at 675m to the top of the Seventh Heaven Express at 2285m is the largest in North America (and impressive even by European standards).

One of the second-stage chairs, the Solar Coaster Express, takes you to the main mid-mountain base and the Rendezvous restaurant at 1860m. From here there's a wide variety of runs through the trees in all directions and for all standards. Two different peaks can be reached from a chair down to the right, or a chair and a T-bar to the left. Both access the summer slopes on the Horstman Glacier. And the T-bar also brings you (with a short climb) to the Blackcomb Glacier in the next valley – a beautiful run which takes you right away from all lifts and signs of civilisation.

On both mountains you can ride up (at extra cost) at 7.30am, have breakfast at the top and hit the slopes as soon as they open – very popular with reporters. And Blackcomb has floodlit slopes twice a week.

SNOW RELIABILITY
Good high up, poor low down
Snow conditions at the top are usually excellent. But because the resort is low and close to the Pacific, the bottom part of the mountains can be wet or unskiable.

FOR EXPERTS
Few can rival it

Whistler Mountain's bowls alone are enough to keep experts happy for weeks. Each of the five has endless possible variations, with chutes and gullies of varied steepness and width. The biggest challenges are around Glacier, Whistler and West Bowls, with runs such as The Cirque and Doom & Gloom – though you can literally go anywhere in this high and wide area.

Blackcomb has challenging bowls, too, but they aren't as extensive or set as dramatically as Whistler's. From the top of the Seventh Heaven lift you can traverse across to Xhiggy's Meadow, where there are good sunny bowl runs. Or if you're feeling brave you can drop over the ridge behind you down one of the extremely steep chutes here, including the infamous 41° Couloir Extreme (used to be Saudan Couloir).

Alternatively, you can hike up from the Glacier Express lift to Spanky's Ladder (look out for the sign saying 'Please do not urinate here as other people have to look at it').

On both mountains there are challenging black mogul runs on the lower part (including new ones down to Whistler Creekside).

If all this isn't enough, there's also local heli-skiing available.

FOR INTERMEDIATES
Ideal and extensive terrain

Both mountains are paradise. Good intermediates will enjoy the less extreme variations in the bowls on both mountains in good weather.

One of our favourite intermediate runs is the Blackcomb Glacier from the top of the mountain at almost 2300m down to the bottom of a high-speed quad at 1130m. This 5km run starts with a short two-minute climb up from the top of the Showcase T-bar over the ridge and into the valley hidden behind. You drop into a wide, wide bowl – the further you traverse, the shallower the slope becomes. A large part of the attraction of the run for us is being away from sight of all lifts.

You are guaranteed good snow on the Horstman Glacier runs, too. These are Blackcomb's summer slopes, with typically gentle top-of-the-mountain glacier runs. Lower down there are large numbers of perfectly groomed cruising runs through the trees – ideal for when the weather is bad.

On Whistler Mountain, there are easy blue pistes in Symphony, Harmony and Glacier bowls, which allow even early intermediates to try the bowls for themselves, always knowing there's an easy way down. The Saddle run from the top of the

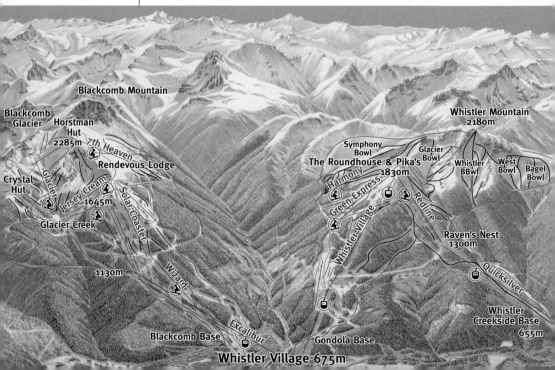

Whistler's traffic-free village has interesting, varied architecture →

Harmony Express lift was a favourite with many of our reporters. The blue path round the back from the top of the Peak chair, which skirts West Bowl, has beautiful views over a steep valley and across to Black Tusk (an apt name for the phallic-shaped top of this famous mountain).

Lower down the mountain there is a vast choice of groomed blue runs with a series of efficient fast chairs to bring you back up to the top of the gondola. It's a cruiser's paradise – especially the aptly named Ego Bowl. A great run to take at the end of the day is the Dave Murray Downhill all the way from mid-mountain to the finish in town. Although marked black on the map, it's a wonderful fast and varied cruise when it has been groomed.

FOR BEGINNERS
A great place to learn
Whistler has excellent nursery slopes by the mid-station of the gondola – and Blackcomb down at the base area. Both also have facilities higher up.

On Whistler, Upper Whiskey Jack is a gentle first run from the top of the gondola after progressing beyond the nursery slopes. You can return to its start by various chair-lifts or continue right down to the base area on simple greens. There is a variety of other easy green and blue runs.

On Blackcomb, Green Line goes right from the top of the mountain to

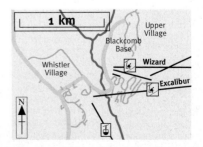

SCHOOLS/GUIDES

96/97 prices in Canadian dollars

Whistler and Blackcomb
Guided instruction with Ski Esprit course
Classes 6 days full-day from 8.45
6 full days: 360
Children's classes
Ages: 3 to 12
5 6hr days including lunch: 220
Private lessons
1hr, 2hr or 3hr
72 for 1hr

CHILDCARE

Ski Scamps at Whistler Mountain has the Mice and Bunnies room at the gondola base, and the Children's Learning Centre at Olympic station. Special learning areas and lifts are outside.

The Kids' Kamp at the base of Blackcomb has huge dining and nursery areas inside, snow garden and special lifts outside. It takes non-skiing children aged 18 months to 3 years, as well as acting as the base for ski tuition.

Both ski schools have special programmes for youngsters. Wee Scamps on Whistler and Wee Wizards on Blackcomb take children aged 2 to 3, from 8.30 to 3.30. Super Kids and Ski Scamps take older children, with different schemes for different levels of skiing competence.

Après-ski programmes – with a 'Kids' Night Out' – are offered during the season.

the bottom. The top part is a particularly gentle run, with a couple of steeper pitches lower down.

FOR CROSS-COUNTRY
Picturesque but low
There are over 15km of cross-country tracks starting in the valley by the frozen river, on the path between Whistler and Blackcomb, and heading off towards the Lost Lake. And there is more cross-country around the golf courses. But all this is at low altitude, so conditions can be unreliable. Keen cross-country merchants can catch the train to better areas.

QUEUES
Weekend invasions
During the week there's rarely a problem with queues. At weekends, crowds pour in from Vancouver and can create a delay getting up Whistler Mountain. But once up the mountain the only real bottlenecks are for the chairs to the Whistler bowls (20 minutes at worst).

MOUNTAIN RESTAURANTS
Blackcomb better than Whistler
The main restaurants sell decent good-value food but are charmless self-service refuelling stops and get incredibly crowded.

Whistler's main place is Pika's, at the top of the gondola – The Roundhouse, a few yards up the hill, is quieter and worth the walk. A reporter commends its stuffed burritos. Raven's Nest Café, at the top of the chair up from Whistler Creekside, is smaller and friendlier with good 'build your own' sandwiches. But in good snow you might prefer to go back to town, where the Garibaldi just above the Whistler gondola does decent 'pub' food.

Rendezvous is Blackcomb's massive mid-mountain base, with paper plates and plastic cutlery. Christine's, at the same location, is the only table-service restaurant around, serving an up-market selection of food (snails, smoked salmon, steaks) and offering an award-winning wine list.

The Glacier Creek Lodge at the bottom of the Glacier Express lift is the best self-service place on either mountain – an attractive building with good food and a wide choice including stir-fry, pasta and salad bars.

The two alternatives are tiny mountain huts built to resemble Alpine refuges. Crystal Hut, at the top of the

Crystal Ridge chair, has a wood oven and Horstman Hut, at the top of the mountain, attempts to create a Bavarian feel and does good strudels.

SCHOOLS AND GUIDES
Very high standards
The joint mountain programme, Ski Esprit, is as much a guiding service as it is instruction. We've had several excellent recent reports of it, from both intermediates ('you feel you are not being taught anything, but suddenly the skiing seems to come together') and experts ('he had most of us leaping off cornices on the first day').

As well as standard group and private lessons, both mountains offer specialist courses and clinics. There is also snowboard instruction.

Children are well catered for with a variety of different programmes for different ages.

There are also highly praised, free, twice-daily guided tours of each mountain.

FACILITIES FOR CHILDREN
Comprehensive
The facilities are as impressive as usual in North America. Blackcomb's base area has a special, slow-moving Magic Chair to get children part-way up the mountain. Whistler's gondola mid-station has a splendid dedicated kids-only area. Our main reservation about taking young children here would be the weather. Playing in a snow garden in falling snow is one thing; in falling rain, something else.

Staying there

The most convenient place to stay is Whistler village, where you can go straight up either mountain by gondola (much more pleasant than Blackcomb's chair if it's raining, says one reporter). A lot of chalets and apartments are an inconvenient walk or bus-ride from the villages and slopes. And Whistler Creekside, though convenient for Whistler's slopes, is less so for getting to Blackcomb and has much less life than the main villages.

HOW TO GO
High quality packages
A lot of British tour operators now go to Whistler and there are charter flights to Vancouver for the first time in 1997/98. They offer a wide range of very comfortable accommodation,

GETTING THERE

Air Vancouver, transfer 2hr.

UK PACKAGES

Airtours, All Canada Ski, American Connections, American Dream, Bladon Lines, Chalets 'Unlimited', Chinook-It, Crystal, First Choice Ski, Frontier Ski, Funway Holidays, Independent Ski Links, Inghams, Interworld Canada, Lotus Supertravel, Made to Measure, Neilson, Piste Artiste, Powder Byrne, Ski Activity, Ski Arrangements, Ski Club of GB, Ski Equipe, Ski Independence, Ski Miquel, Ski North America Direct, Ski Safari, Ski Total, Ski Vacation Canada, Ski Weekend, Ski Whistler, Skisar U.S., Skiworld North America, Solo's, The Ski Company, Thomson

Blackcomb Frontier Ski, Funway Holidays, Ski Independence

ACTIVITIES

Indoor Ice skating, museum, tennis, hot tubs
Outdoor Flightseeing, heli-skiing, para-gliding, snowmobiling, snow-shoe excursions, fishing, horse-riding, sleigh rides, guided tours

TOURIST OFFICE

Postcode VoN 1Bo
Tel +1 (604) 932 4222
Fax 932 7231

including some catered chalets.
Hotels There is a very wide range.
((((⑤ **Chateau Whistler** The top hotel, huge and impressive, modern but in traditional Canadian Pacific château-hotel style, right at the foot of Blackcomb Mountain. It has an indoor-outdoor pool, exercise machines, saunas etc.
((((④ **Delta** Big, modern, stylish, in the heart of Whistler village; health club, covered tennis courts, pool.
((((④ **Crystal Lodge** Formerly the Nancy Greene Lodge; centrally placed in Whistler, 140 rooms, recent reports less enthusiastic. Pool.
(((③ **Fairways** On summer golf course, but not far from lifts. Comfortable. Recommended by reporters. Pool.
(((③ **Glacier Lodge** In Blackcomb. Pool, hot tub and sauna.
Self-catering There are plenty of spacious, comfortable condominiums in both chalet- and hotel-style blocks available through British tour operators.

EATING OUT
High quality and plenty of choice
There is no shortage of good places to eat. Reporters were enthusiastic about the range, quality and value for money.

Umberto's is highly regarded for classy (but pricey) Italian cuisine and good service and the Wildflower restaurant in the Chateau Whistler serves excellent innovative dishes.

Down the price scale, Crab Shack, near the Fairways hotel was recommended by several reporters for its lively bar and good seafood (including spicy Creole dishes). Citta's was also popular for generous portions of steaks, burgers and Tex-Mex, and a fun, informal atmosphere. There are numerous Japanese restaurants catering for the substantial number of Japanese visitors. Sushi Village is good and reasonably priced.

Other reporter recommendations were Thai on One, Monk's Grill and the Keg for prime rib and steaks, Ole Mole's for Mexican and Brewhouse for home-brew beer and decent food.

APRES-SKI
Something for most tastes
With over 50 bars, night-clubs and restaurants, Whistler is very lively by North American standards. Two favourite bars immediately after a day on the slopes are the Longhorn at Whistler and Merlin's at Blackcomb,

both at the foot of the slopes. The former has a huge terrace that is particularly popular in spring; inside, the place rocks till after midnight. The Garibaldi Lift Co just above the Whistler gondola also rocks when the slopes close, sometimes with a live band. Black's, next to the Longhorn, is better for a quiet drink. Dusty's is the place to go at Whistler Creekside – good beer and nachos and loud music.

Back in Whistler, Citta's is a popular early evening bar. Buffalo Bill's offers free early evening appetisers, which pulls in early eaters on a tight budget, and is lively and loud later on.

The Mallard bar in Chateau Whistler and the Crystal Lodge Piano Bar are popular for a more relaxed and sophisticated time.

Later on, Tommy Africa's is good for a thumpin', pumpin' bop and vies with the Savage Beagle and Rogue Wolf for the younger clubbing crowd.

OFF THE SLOPES
Not ideal
Whistler is a long way to go if you aren't going to sample the superb slopes. The villages are quiet during the day. Those not using the slopes can get tickets for the gondolas and main chair-lifts. The health club in the Delta is open to non-residents, and there are some other activities available. Excursions to Vancouver and to Squamish (famous for its wild eagles) are easy. The Glacier Tours guided tour of Vancouver was especially recommended by one satisfied reporter.

STAYING DOWN THE VALLEY
We wouldn't
Staying out of town basically means staying at Whistler Creekside or along the road between there and the main village. There's a regular bus service until just after midnight.

Accommodation is cheaper but the ambience is not as nice and the nightlife not nearly as lively or varied.

Western Safari

Get there before the masses arrive

Western Canada has a huge number of small resorts as well as the big names of Whistler and Banff-Lake Louise. Combining several of these with a couple of days' heli- or snowcat skiing or boarding on virgin powder is an attractive proposition for those willing to rent a car and travel around bit. It certainly makes for an exciting and different kind of holiday and we have several enthusiastic reports in our files from reporters who have tried it. Rather than arrange the whole thing yourself, there are several tour operators who are happy to put an itinerary together for you.

Panorama is a small purpose-built resort, right on the slopes, two hours south-west of Banff and with the second biggest vertical drop in North America (1310m). As well as beginner and intermediate slopes, it expanded its terrain for the 1996/97 season to include double black diamond tree runs known as the 'Extreme Dream Zone' and a new snowboard park. It is also home to R K Heli-Ski, which offers one-day packages – it covers over 125 runs in the Purcell Mountains on varied terrain.

Kananaskis near Calgary was home to the 1988 Winter Olympics with many events being held at Nakiska five minutes away – a small, mainly intermediate ski area with artificial snow covering 80% of the terrain.

Big White is British Columbia's highest ski area and the next biggest to Whistler, with around 100 runs. Set in the spectacular Monashee mountain range, it has a reputation for Canada's best powder skiing. Last season saw the first phase of a massive $45 million expansion, creating 12 new runs served by a new high-speed quad which covers more vertical than any other in Canada. There are two snowboard fun-parks and some beautiful cross-country trails. It has slope-side accommodation.

Silver Star is a newly developed ski area, with its gaslight era base village built in 1890s style and the old town of Vernon nearby. Although especially good for family holidays, there are challenging ungroomed runs as well as ideal cruising terrain.

Sun Peaks, near the town of Kamloops, has developed rapidly in the last few years. It used to be known as Tod Mountain and had legendary steep skiing known largely to locals only. Now $100 million of investment has created slope-side accommodation and good intermediate and beginner terrain. Former Olympic gold medallist Nancy Greene and her husband did much to help develop Whistler. They have now moved to Sun Peaks, where they have built a hotel by the slopes and Nancy is Director of Skiing.

Fernie Snow Valley, three hours south of Banff, has a reputation for great powder. As well as its own ski area it is home to Island Lake Mountain Tours snowcat operation, which has its own isolated rustic lodge. Fernie itself is an old lumber town with 5,000 year-round residents and over 25 restaurants and bars.

Western Canada is also home to the world's most famous heli-skiing operations, where you can stay for a week in a luxurious lodge and be whirled up to virgin powder for several runs a day – at a cost of £2,000 or more (plus flights from the UK). Mike Wiegele and CMH are two of the most famous, both operating out of interior British Columbia. Tyax Lodge Heli-Skiing, 60 miles north of Whistler, is a similar operation. Or you can try heli-skiing for a day from most resorts – a much more affordable option.

UK OPERATORS

Most specialist North American operators can put together a tour for you – as can some of the bigger operators too.

Andorra

WHAT IT COSTS

②

- ➕ Excellent choice for beginners, with resorts that boast good tuition and ski areas that won't frighten
- ➕ Lively nightlife in most resorts, sometimes making it feel like a summer holiday package destination
- ➕ Resorts close enough to each other to sample at least one other during a week
- ➕ Tax-free status of country is a real boon – cheap alcohol, cigs and some electrical goods

- ➖ Small ski areas, with little to challenge experts
- ➖ Most resorts have little in the way of charm, and Soldeu and Pas de la Casa are sited on the busy main road through the country
- ➖ Nightlife tends to revolve around booze and clubs – little in the way of variety

More than most winter-resort countries, Andorra invites generalisations. Because it's such a small country, all the resorts are remarkably similar, having almost all the same pluses and minuses. Low prices (including duty-free goods), simple hotels, ugly villages, lively bars and clubs, good ski schools, fairly reliable snow, young clientele, a lot of Brits, small ski areas, easy slopes and awful mountain restaurants are all fairly typical of Andorran resorts across the board.

There's an immediate temptation to compare Andorra to Eastern Europe. Some of the above pluses and minuses would be appropriate to Borovets and company, too. Perhaps the main differences are that Andorra is somewhat more expensive (though still cheap by Alpine

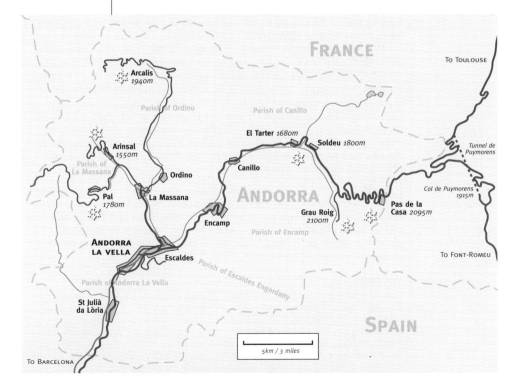

standards), has much livelier nightlife, attracts a mostly young and lively clientele rather than families, has more reliable snow and more ski areas within striking distance for those who want to travel.

Andorra has also proved a tough competitor, on the British market at least, for Austria. Many of the little Austrian resorts where so many learned to ski in the 1970s and 1980s are losing British custom, and this is partly because they can't compete with Andorra for providing first-time winter holidays that are not only cheap and cheerful, but also relatively snowsure. Andorra's snow reliability should not be underestimated. A combination of height and heavy investment in snowmakers puts it well ahead of much of Austria. You can book Andorra months in advance with some confidence. And an early reservation is necessary: late bookers can have difficulty finding an Andorra package.

Package holiday prices are low, as are prices once you arrive, notably for drinks and extras such as tuition and equipment hire. But some reporters have been disappointed to find duty-free luxury goods not the super-bargain they had expected. As for nightlife, it certainly is very lively, with lots of throbbing bars; but if you get bored with bar-hopping, there's little else.

The lack of variety in the nightlife and the small size of the individual areas means that most Andorran resorts are going to be of limited appeal if you have slightly more sophisticated tastes in evening entertainment, or are a 'high-mileage' skier or boarder. Pas de la Casa and Soldeu are relative neighbours and are easily reached by bus from each other, and the three western Andorran resorts (Arinsal, Pal and Arcalis) are also within reach of each other. But to do all five stations takes a significant feat of logistics. Unless you have your own car, or the tour operator provides the transport, you will be confined to one side of the country or the other – the bus service will deliver you to the resorts on the opposite side just in time to watch the lifts shut!

The only alternative is to stay in one of the towns in the middle of Andorra such as Canillo, Encamp, Andorra la Vella, La Massana or Ordino. They are all on the main roads to the resorts – the distance to each from Andorra la Vella is between 11km (Arinsal) and 26km (Grau Roig – connected to Pas de la Casa). The bus service is slow but straightforward, though a car or tour operator transport would be preferable, and every day will involve a journey. What they do offer is an antidote to the booze-fuelled nightlife of the mountain resorts and far more facilities for people who are less enthusiastic about sliding down the pistes.

boarding *As with most places that draw a young crowd, boarding has a big following in Andorra. Which is why it's slightly surprising to find that, apart from Pas de la Casa, no resort has invested in facilities for boarders, and many areas still rely on long drag-lifts to get people up the mountains. The drawbacks are, in part, compensated for by the excellent tuition, and the lively après-board scene, with good bars and pumping clubs.*

Arinsal 1550m

Lots of young people come here for the nightlife, and Arinsal does not disappoint. The numerous lively bars and discos are not as rowdy as in nearby Soldeu. But there is little to do apart from bar-hopping and clubbing, and the spread-out nature of Arinsal itself means there is little village atmosphere and a lot of cold walks between 'happening' places.

The slopes are very limited, and the resort is difficult to recommend to anyone except beginners who come as much for the bars as the slopes.

1

6Andorra

ARINSAL
HOW IT RATES

The slopes

Snow	★★★
Extent	★
Experts	★
Intermediates	★★
Beginners	★★★★
Convenience	★★★
Queues	★★★
Restaurants	★

The rest

Scenery	★★★
Resort charm	★
Off-slope	★

MOUNTAIN FACTS

Altitude 1550m-2560m	
Lifts	15
Pistes	28km
Blue	45%
Red	31%
Black	24%
Artificial snow	4km

UK PACKAGES

Airtours, Crystal, First Choice Ski, Inghams, Neilson, On The Piste Travel Ltd, Panorama, Thomson

Andorra La Vella
Inghams, Lagrange

La Massana Inghams, Snowcoach

TOURIST OFFICE

Tel +376 838438
Fax 838738

THE RESORT
Arinsal is a little village of Catalan slate and grey stone, near the head of a narrow valley north of Andorra la Vella. It has seen rapid development in recent years, giving the place a building-site appearance. Yet little new accommodation is available near the single resort-level lift, inconveniently situated a kilometre out of town. Most people face a long walk or a bus-ride to this chair. Fortunately, the village bus service is good. Arinsal is dominated by British holidaymakers.

THE MOUNTAIN
The very small area is a narrow, east-facing coomb of mainly open **slopes**, suitable for beginners, children and unadventurous intermediates. All runs lead straight back towards the mid-station area, ideal for parents to keep a watchful eye on children.

Proposed development of the Coll d'Ature mountainside, a move in the direction of Pal, will add not only size, but much needed variety, including some relatively snowsure tree-lined runs. A rarely used black run or a blue road down to the Arinsal chair are the only options in bad weather.

With most runs above 1950m and a fair number of guns, **snow reliability** is relatively assured. Most lifts above the mid-station are drags, keeping the mountain open when it's windy.

Progressive intermediates and **experts** shouldn't even think about Arinsal. But some slopes are not entirely easy and are suitable for **intermediates** who do not mind a limited area. Piste maintenance is good. Essentially, Arinsal is an area suitable for near-**beginners** or early intermediates. The nursery slopes are gentle, away from the main area and well covered by snow guns. They do not cover a particularly large area, and as a result can get very crowded in peak season.

Although everyone has to ascend the mountain by a single lift, **queues** are not a problem on weekdays. Spanish weekenders and local children can hit the slopes en masse at times.

If you rate a resort by its **mountain restaurants**, this isn't Zermatt. They're expensive, by local standards, and crowded. And they serve mediocre snacks – hamburgers and so on.

Arinsal's **ski school** is its pride and joy. It offers good technical tuition and patient instruction. English is widely

spoken; prices are low; and lessons are fun. Class sizes can, however, be very large in peak season. There is a ski kindergarten but no non-skiing crèche for young **children**.

STAYING THERE
Arinsal is essentially a cheap and cheerful small hotel resort.

The Crest is perhaps the best **hotel** in Arinsal, and has the advantage of being next to the chair-lift; it offers half-board or B&B terms. The studio-style rooms are geared towards families, sleeping up to five. The Solana has good food but simple rooms. it is much nearer the lifts than the peripheral St Gotthard. Apartments are generally of a higher standard that the hotels. The Velvet, Poblado and Rosa Blanca apartments are all quite comfortable.

There is a fair range of **restaurants** for a small resort. Cisco's is a lively restaurant/bar serving Mexican food, Borda specialises in Catalan dishes and La Calisa has Spanish cooking. Arguably the best in town is Il Neu.

For **après-ski**, Arinsal has very animated bars and discos, but if you get fed up with these, there isn't much else to do – a fondue evening is the best bet. Prices are low, but not as low as many expect of Andorra. Red Rock is a focal spot, popular for its large measures, videos and burgers.

Arinsal has few facilities for those **off the slopes**. The main thing to do is to shop in la Vella, half an hour away by infrequent bus.

Pal 1780m
Pal is a quiet and picturesque mountain village over the ridge from Arinsal (about 5km by road), with a small, wooded ski area a couple of kilometres further up the hill. It is remarkably different to its near-neighbour, and certainly worth a day-trip if you are staying in the area – it also shares the lift pass.

THE RESORT
Pal has escaped much of the attentions of the developers that other resorts in Andorra have succumbed to. However, no British tour operator has any beds in the village, and the inconvenience of the slopes being a bus ride away make it a less than ideal place to stay.

**PAL
MOUNTAIN FACTS**

Altitude 1780m-2360m
Lifts   14
Pistes   30km
Blue   35%
Red   60%
Black   5%
Artificial snow   7km

TOURIST OFFICE
Tel +376 838438
Fax 838738

THE MOUNTAIN

Pal has a small area of **slopes** which are the most wooded of the Andorran resorts, and the ample car-parking space makes it popular with the locals at the weekend. It is surprisingly different from Arinsal, which is tall and narrow with no trees; Pal is short and wide, and covered with greenery.

You can start from any one of the car parks on the road that skirt the slopes; most lifts seem to have one at the end of it. There is a main base lodge which has a couple of shops and a restaurant, and is attractively set amongst trees. **Snow reliability** is fair, with snow guns on the nursery slopes. The high altitude and north-facing slopes help to give a reasonably long season.

The only thing to attract **experts** will be fresh snowfall, when access to off-piste through well-spaced trees is best. Tree cover is so poor in other Andorran resorts that Pal is the only option for this. **Intermediates** should go high, where well-bashed reds come down from the summit to the mid-station area. There are a couple of quite steep reds leading off to the Coll de la Botella, one of which can grow moguls. **Beginners** start off on the very gentle nursery slopes just in front of the base lodge, and are able to progress to the short blues that are accessed by longer lifts that start in the same place.

Queues are not generally a problem, and mid-week the slopes are often deserted. As with Arinsal and Arcalis, the weekenders really do make their presence felt mid-season. By the end of the season the Spanish are already making for the seaside!

There are two **mountain restaurants**: the base lodge, which is modern and reasonable with a sun terrace, and a basic hut at the Coll de la Botella which serves drinks and snacks.

Pal seems to conduct its **ski school** in much the same fashion as the Arinsal school, with good class size and instruction, though there are few English-speaking instructors.

STAYING THERE

We have had no reports from anyone who has stayed in the village itself, as its development as a package destination has been overlooked by tour operators in favour of the Brit-dominated Arinsal. There is a regular bus service between the two resorts,

which is covered by the joint lift-pass. Buses to la Massana and Andorra la Vella are also available, if somewhat more erratically timetabled. There is little scope in the village for **après ski** or much in the way of **off the slopes** alternatives.

Arcalis 1940m

As the most remote resort in Andorra, it's easy to assume Arcalis is not a worthwhile day-trip. But that would be a shame, as the variety of the terrain is better than most of the other resorts, even if the extent is not up to much. Unfortunately, a day-trip is all it would be – with no accommodation for 15km, it's a long trek. And if you're staying in Pas de la Casa, kiss it goodbye now – it's 56km away.

THE RESORT

With no village at the resort, it does at least mean that Arcalis has not suffered the affliction of the usual collection of hotels and apartments that are 'thrown up' on the mountainside, as with other resorts in Andorra.

This lack of development may be due to Arcalis's publicly owned status – most Andorrans seem rather proud of the place. It also has some nice touches; it has the nicest base lodge (one of the few buildings) in Andorra, and even a couple of sculptures nestling in amongst the landscape.

The resort is very popular with weekenders, both from Andorra and Spain, and the ample car parking on the approach road soaks them up.

THE MOUNTAIN

The **slopes** are made up of two valleys which join with a central ridge, which creates a horseshoe shape. To the left of the ridge is the main valley, the Cercle d'Arcalis, which is bowl-shaped and is well populated on its left flank with trees. It also contains most of the lifts, which fan out from the base lodge. The ridge provides a couple of steep, sheltered, north-facing pistes back into the right of the bowl, and access to the south-facing runs off the side. These are long blues and reds which run down the second valley, the Cercle de la Coma, which is tree-free. These runs return to the base station around the end of the ridge.

Snow reliability is good. Artificial snow covers the base area and some pistes leading into it. The height of

ARCALIS
MOUNTAIN FACTS

Altitude	1940m-2600m
Lifts	12
Pistes	24km
Blue	54%
Red	38%
Black	8%
Artificial snow	8km

TOURIST OFFICE
Tel +376 838438
Fax 838738

the area, which starts a good 400m higher than Arinsal, also adds to the length of the season.

Of all the resorts in western Andorra, Arcalis has the most to offer **experts**. The black run that leads from the ridge back down towards the base is steep, and often mogulled, while the red run it connects to starts from the top of the main chair, going through a spectacular gully before widening out. There is also plenty of space between runs for off-piste forays, especially in the Cercle de la Coma. Arcalis is well-known for heli-skiing; the mountains facing the area are favoured by the guides.

Intermediates are well catered for, with smooth, long blues and reds being the main feature of Arcalis's slopes. These head through the trees in the Cercle d'Arcalis, and a couple of variations of wide, open runs on blues and reds down through the Cercle de la Coma. The **beginners'** slopes are conveniently located near the base lodge, with a couple of drag lifts leading to some longer blue runs.

Queues are not a problem; mid-week you can explore the resort and hardly see anyone. At the weekend the area is much busier, especially in good weather, but the approach road/car park has lifts at a number of different places, and with recent investment in high-speed chairs, there shouldn't be a long wait at the bottom.

The base station has a restaurant and facilities. Other **mountain restaurant** choices are limited; there is a snack bar at the top of the main lift, and a good – but rather busy at weekends – self-service restaurant in the Cercle de la Coma.

We have no reports on the **ski school**, but it seems well run, with a good range of options including snowboard (run by the very pierced ski school director) and Telemark lessons. There is a day nursery for children aged 1 to 5, and a ski kindergarten for 5 to 12 year-olds.

STAYING THERE
With no accommodation at the slopes, there is no option but to stay elsewhere – Ordino is a small town 15km down the valley, and the closest place where accommodation is available, while La Massana is a further 2.5km on.

Pas de la Casa 2050m
With Andorra's highest lift-served terrain, and the greatest amount of piste (though not the largest acreage – that accolade belongs to Soldeu), Pas de la Casa vies for the top spot with its near neighbour as best all-round area. With a convenient, if charmless resort base, and cheap and plentiful accommodation, it is proving to be a popular package destination.

THE RESORT
Sited right on the border between Andorra and France, Pas de la Casa is a sizeable collection of concrete-box style apartment blocks and hotels, and indicative of the rapid development Andorra saw in the late 60s and early 70s. At least some thought went into its development, with most accommodation conveniently near the main slopes, and it boasts plenty of cheap shops and bars in the town centre, and a sports centre. Reporters complain that it's starting to look a little tatty and run-down, and as it is on the main road into Andorra, it can suffer from traffic pollution. Pas de la Casa is less Brit-dominated than other Andorran resorts, and tends to attract more French and Spanish families.

THE MOUNTAINS
The **slopes'** main area is on a high, treeless, north/south ridge, with Pas de la Casa on the east side, Grau Roig on the west. Two other small areas radiate out from Grau Roig; to the south, towards the head of the valley is Mont Malús, a small wooded area served by a drag with a couple of pretty reds and a black run through the trees; to the west of Grau Roig, a drag leads over the ridge in the direction of Soldeu, and a recently completed third drag now leads up to the Colada d'Enradort (2447m), making the connection to Soldeu temptingly close.

Heavy investment in artificial snowmaking equipment, coupled with the area's height, makes for a very good **snow reliability** record and a season that often stretches into late April.

Piste marking seems to be a bone of contention with our reporters – most believe a lot of the red and black pistes to be over-rated. This will leave **experts** rather short of challenge, though the black runs heading back to

PAS DE LA CASA
HOW IT RATES

The slopes

Snow	***
Extent	**
Experts	*
Intermediates	***
Beginners	****
Convenience	****
Queues	***
Restaurants	***

The rest

Scenery	**
Resort charm	*
Off-slope	*

What's new

For the 1997/98 season a new six-seater high-speed chair back from Grau Roig, replaciing a slow chair, will eliminate the end-of-day bottleneck. The link to Soldeu gets a little closer with the installation of the drag up to the Colada d'Enradort, and the installation of yet more snowmaking should help keep the punters happy

MOUNTAIN FACTS

Altitude	2050m-2640m
Lifts	27
Pistes	85km
Blue	25%
Red	60%
Black	15%
Artificial snow	10km

UK PACKAGES

Airtours, Bladon Lines, Crystal, Fairhand Holidays, First Choice Ski, Inghams, Lagrange, Neilson, Panorama, Thomson, Top Deck

TOURIST OFFICE

Tel +376 820399
Fax 823036

the resort, including the Slalom, are of a steep pitch and can be mogulled, though they are groomed before the bumps grow very large. The black run leading down from the top of the Mont Malús drag is also a favourite.

The slopes cater for aspiring **intermediates** far better, with plenty of top-to-bottom reds and blues on the main ridge, though the criticism that they are a little bland, being of consistent gradient most of the way down, is not wholly unjustified.

There are two areas for **beginners**, though the area in Grau Roig is little use to people staying in Pas de la Casa. The area on the resort side of the mountain is a short but inconvenient bus ride out of town, though there are plenty of gentle slopes in the main area to progress to.

Snowboarding is popular with the young crowd that Pas de la Casa attracts, and there is a small, lift-served board-park and half-pipe on the Grau Roig side of the mountain.

Queues occasionally build up, mainly at the resort base in the mornings, and late afternoon in Grau Roig. At the resort, the two high-speed quads now get through the queues efficiently, and over the other side the new six-seater high-speed chair along with the existing high-speed quad should see an end to missed tea.

The **ski school** has an excellent reputation, with good English language classes.

STAYING THERE

There's a wide choice of apartments and **hotels** on offer, and even a few chalets and chalet hotels. We can't make any special recommendations, as we've had no especially glowing reports of any of the accommodation. The main thing to watch out for is the location, as some is not in town, but higher up on the col over to Soldeu, about 5km out of the resort.

The **après-ski** scene and **eating out** tend to gel into one: there are numerous bars, restaurants and nightclubs. The tour operators take over one bar (the Marselles) as a focal point for British activity. In the popular Milwaukee bar and, later on, the Billboard club, there's more of an international flavour. **Off-the-slopes** activity is limited to shopping, the leisure centre, or taking a trip to Andorra La Vella.

Soldeu 1800m

Soldeu has a lot in common with other resorts in Andorra – limited slopes, low prices, great ski school, grim-looking village, lively bar-based nightlife. But its slopes are some of the best in the region, and are fairly convenient – the walk to the lifts, although irritating, is relatively short.

THE RESORT

The village is a small, though ever-growing, ribbon of ugly modern buildings along a busy road, most of them hotels and bars. Other than sleeping, eating, drinking, and getting onto the slopes there is nothing to do, and the poor transport facilities make excursions difficult. The long metal bridge which you used to have to cross to get to the chair-lift can now be avoided by taking the gondola.

THE SLOPES

The **slopes** are shared with El Tarter. There are a few challenges – the runs are most suited to timid or early intermediates. A chair-lift rises over wooded, north-facing slopes to Espiolets, a broad, extensive nursery area. From here, a short gentle run to the east takes you to a lift up to Solana (2440m). A longer, gentle run in the opposite direction takes you to the foot of the open bowl of Riba Escorxada and the arrival point of the lift up from El Tarter. Lifts ascend to both Solana and the high-point of Llosada (2560m), with blue and red runs back down. All main routes have very easy options, so all but complete beginners can get around the area.

Soldeu enjoys fairly **reliable snow**. Most slopes are north-facing, with artificial snow on the descents to Soldeu. Should runs to the village be incomplete, the area as whole is not unduly affected.

It's a limited area for **experts**. There are short off-piste trails down the bowl beneath Llosada, and sometimes you can play in powder among the trees above El Tarter. The most direct of the wooded runs down to El Tarter and Soldeu are suitable for good **intermediates**, while those of moderate ability will enjoy the relatively long pistes from Llosada. Timid skiers have gentle cruises throughout the area. Riba Escorxada is a fine section for mixed ability groups.

This is a good resort for **beginners**.

SOLDEU
HOW IT RATES

The slopes

Snow	***
Extent	**
Experts	*
Intermediates	***
Beginners	****
Convenience	***
Queues	***
Restaurants	*

The rest

Scenery	***
Resort charm	*
Off-slope	*

What's new

The big news in Soldeu is that the gondola started last season from the town up to the Espiolets area has been completed, so the weak-kneed no longer have to cross the vertigo-inducing suspension bridge over the ravine.

MOUNTAIN FACTS

Altitude	1680m-2560m
Lifts	22
Pistes	60km
Blue	53%
Red	20%
Black	26%
Artificial snow	14km

UK PACKAGES

Airtours, Bladon Lines, Crystal, Fairhand Holidays, First Choice Ski, Inghams, Lagrange, Neilson, Panorama, Ski Club of GB, Thomson, Top Deck

Canillo Panorama, Top Deck

El Tarter Panorama

Encamp First Choice Ski, Thomson

TOURIST OFFICE

Tel +376 851151
Fax 851337

The Espiolets nursery area is adequate and relatively snowsure, and there are numerous easy pistes to move on to.

Despite the new gondola out of town, the lift system is generally antiquated and inefficient, and free of **queues** on weekdays only because of the high proportion of beginners. When there is an influx at weekends, there can be waits up the mountain.

The **mountain restaurants** are poor. The one at the top of El Tarter chair is the best of a bad bunch.

The **ski school** has a high reputation for standards of English, quality of tuition and friendliness. **Children** aged three to eight can attend a non-ski nursery. Children's ski school starts from six years old, but lunchtime supervision is not available.

STAYING THERE

The central 3-star Sporthotel is by far the best **hotel** in Soldeu – tastefully designed in local stone and stained pine, with good bedrooms and a pleasant and well equipped sauna/gym. Buffet breakfast is good. The popular Naudi offers good value provided you stay in the main hotel, not the more basic annexe.

The Edelweiss apartments are spacious and generally pleasant, and well placed opposite the Sporthotel, the facilities of which are available.

Though standards are not particularly high, there is plenty of choice of places for **eating out**. The Pussycat is an atmospheric restaurant with reasonable food and good service. The Duc hotel restaurant has arguably the best food in town.

Although **après-ski** is lively, it consists mainly of bars and reporganised outings. The Sol Y Nieve bar at the foot of the slopes starts things off at the end of the day, while later on the Edelweiss, Bruxelles and Bonnel bars are the most popular. Aspen is the main snowboard hangout. The Naudi has a quieter locals' bar. The El Duc is the best disco.

There is little to amuse **non-skiers**. There is a very smart sports centre in Canillo (erratic bus service) with pool, ice rink, squash and gym. It is closed in the afternoons. The Sporthotel has sauna and gym, and the only all-day bar (the 'excellent' Piccadilly).

La Massana

La Massana is a small and well preserved town, on the junction of two valleys, one which leads to Pal (9km) and Arinsal (5km), and the other to Arcalis (18km). The valley leads on down to the capital of Andorra la Vella (6km), and there are regular buses in all directions. There is plenty of reasonable accommodation, and the nightlife is much more sedate than the likes of Arinsal; there are a number of far more cultural diversions such as the National Auditorium.

Andorra la Vella

For anyone not using the slopes, the lack of facilities in the resorts is a major drawback. The main alternative is to travel to Andorra la Vella – or, if the skiing is less important to you than the facilities, stay here and travel to the resorts.

There are plenty of high-quality, if slightly expensive, hotels. Andorra la Vella is not a big place, and most are within easy walking distance of the centre of the town.

The town itself has many attractions. The duty-free shopping could fill a page, but probably the most interesting place is Caldea. This neo-cathedral style building in the centre of the town has everything (bar the cost) to pamper yourself with. The interior is laid out in a 'Hanging Gardens of Babylon' style, and the facilities really are impressive – linked indoor and outdoor pools, fountains and waterfalls in the pools, saunas, Jacuzzis, Turkish baths, hydrotherapy, sunbeds, massage ... even a grapefruit bath! There are plenty of other sports facilities available around la Vella.

There is plenty of choice when it comes to dining out, as you would expect in a capital city. Andorrans love seafood, and the traditional Catalan restaurants delight in providing it, which seems odd in the mountains; it is delivered fresh from the coast daily. Nightlife is also well catered for – there are plenty of bars and nightclubs, and most stay open until 4am. However, the clientele is generally a more sophisticated bunch, mainly Andorrans and Spaniards, and the 'drink-until-you-drop' attitude of the mountain resorts is rare.

Spain

The Spanish Pyrenees were a popular British budget destination a decade ago, but then Andorra and Eastern Europe succeeded in capturing much of the Spanish trade. It's easy to see why. The mass-market resorts often struggled for snow and, even when conditions were good, there was a tendency for high winds to close the lifts. Although prices were low, they were lower elsewhere, and Spain also gained a reputation for low standards – poor hotels, ancient hire equipment, old lifts and so on.

But it's dangerous to generalise about Spanish resorts. There is more to the country than its downmarket image suggests. There are now some well-equipped Pyrenean resorts with fine, snowsure slopes that compare favourably with mid-sized places in the Alps. Two resorts are certainly not downmarket – Sierra Nevada and Baqueira-Beret are both frequented by the king of Spain. Winter sports are becoming more popular with the prosperous Spanish themselves, and as a result many of the smaller resorts are continually improving.

Furthermore, the general ambience of Spanish resorts is attractive – not unlike that of Italy. There's plenty of animation, with eating, posing and partying taken seriously. Large families often lunch together, creating much merriment while huge amounts of food are consumed. Dinner starts late after such a blow out so, in turn, nightlife doesn't get going before many a British punter has retired, disgruntled at the lack of action.

The 1995 World Championships were due to take place in **Sierra Nevada** (2100m) in the extreme south of Spain; but at the eleventh hour they had to be postponed to 1996, due to lack of snow – with high temperatures rendering the resort's state-of-the-art snowmaking installation useless. The resort's natural snow arrives via completely different weather patterns from those supplying the Alps and Pyrenees; in 1990, when the Alps were disastrously snowless, Sierra Nevada had the best conditions in Europe. The mostly intermediate slopes are very exposed to the elements. When the wind blows, as it does, the slopes close, and the strong sun makes the pistes either icy or soft in late season. The resort is very ugly but user-friendly, and its restaurants, bars and shops are nicely gathered around a central square. Granada's proximity means good outings but overcrowding at weekends and holidays. Hotels are comfortable and good value.

Baqueira-Beret (1500m) is the best of the Pyrenean resorts – a user-friendly place with high-standard accommodation, modern lifts and a sizeable, fairly snowsure area. Spanish prices make it a real bargain. The mountain seems bigger than its claim of 90km of piste would suggest, thanks to its variety. The runs are mostly above 1800m, much of them northish-facing, backed up by snowmakers. Queues are rare because most of the lifts are high-capacity chairs. There are runs for all grades, including some steep challenges. Ski Miquel has a good chalet and hotels available, and this year we have received more reports about this resort than most Andorran resorts.

Candanchu/Astún (1500m), with 88km of piste, is probably the biggest resort you have never heard of. It is on the package market for the first time this year, with an appearance in the Inghams brochure. With a wide range of accommodation set in some of the Pyrenees' most stunning scenery, and a local reputaion for tough runs, a visit to the area by the editors cannot be avoided for long.

The smaller Pyrenean resorts are best toured by car: spend a day in each and drive to more sheltered places if the wind blows. The best-known, **Formigal**, has a good ski school but is windswept. Our favourite is nearby **Panticosa**, a charming old village with sheltered, if limited slopes. **La Molina** has a sizeable set of slopes. It's an old place, preferable to its dreary purpose-built satellite, **Supermolina**.

Bulgaria

Bulgaria attracts those on a tight budget: the basic package, equipment hire, school and lift pass are all very cheap. Drawbacks include limited slopes, old lifts, and mountain food that has you reaching for the Mars bars. But there are compensations other than simply low prices: all of our reporters have been struck by the friendliness of the local people, the ski schools are excellent, the tour op-organised nightlife is good fun, and from Borovets an excursion to Sofia is recommended.

The resorts also try hard to provide the sort of amenities 'Westerners' require from a holiday resort. Many of the hotels have the potential to be perfectly adequate places to stay and Bulgaria, like the rest of Eastern Europe, is struggling to raise standards. Unfortunately, economic conditions limit what can be achieved and progress is slow. Reports of the resorts get more positive each year, and many visitors are return bookings. The low prices have not attracted huge numbers of young drinkers away from Andorra. Bulgaria receives young and old, families and singles alike. Consequently the atmosphere is cosmopolitan, with people of different ages and walks of life mixing in together.

Bulgaria's two main resorts are some way apart, served by different airports, with similarly short transfer times (less than two hours). They are similar places in some ways; both have good tuition, low prices (though not as low as in the days of Communism) and poor mountain restaurants ('mostly caravans with outside seating'). But the two areas suit people of different levels of ability.

Borovets (see over the page for a full report) has intermediate slopes made rather awkward for improving beginners and leisurely cruisers by a combination of steepness and poor piste grooming.

Pamporovo (1450m) is far better for beginners and early intermediates, with mostly easy runs. Others may find 25km of short runs too limited. But the slopes are pretty and sheltered, with pistes cut through pine forest. Getting around is easy, with no bottlenecks or hazards, and getting lost is difficult even in the worst weather. Beginners should book a 'learn to ski' package through their tour operator. It's a good deal, saving up to 80% of the cost of booking extras locally. (You can also get Bulgarian lift passes at half the local price by booking them from the UK.) Despite having to bus to the slopes, families praise Pamporovo. Not only are the slopes suitable but the English-speaking crèche is well regarded, and the purpose-built village has 'everything to hand'. The ski school's instructors are patient, enthusiastic and speak good English, and class sizes are usually quite small. At the heart of the village are the two hotels, Perelik, which has a pool, and Mourgaret, both of which are good by Bulgarian standards. The food is monotonous, though the buffet offers a fair choice. The organised evening events are popular, and there are some bars, but Pamporovo is quieter and less commercialised than Borovets. Late season snow-cover is unreliable.

Vitosha (1810m) is no more than a few widely scattered hotels with limited, bland runs, and on our visit, we were unable to find any nursery slopes, which was a surprise given the resort's five-star rating for beginners in one brochure. The hotels are mostly dour, and all but one are a bus-ride from the lifts. Sofia is close by, allowing short transfers and easy excursions, but the slopes get overrun at weekends. Vitosha's main saving grace is its good snow record.

Borovets 1300m

Cheap but not especially cheerful

WHAT IT COSTS

(1)

HOW IT RATES

The slopes
Snow	**
Extent	*
Experts	*
Intermediates	**
Beginners	****
Convenience	****
Queues	**
Restaurants	*

The rest
Scenery	***
Resort charm	**
Off-slope	*

What's new

Some people say the food has improved by at least 100 per cent in the last couple of years. But it still leaves a lot to be desired.

➕ Still very cheap, despite growth of economy

➕ A completely different winter holiday, with the chance to experience a fascinating, although depressed, culture

➕ Very good ski school

➕ Compact village – little walking to lifts

➕ Beautiful setting among thick pine forest

➖ Low standards of comfort, particularly food

➖ Archaic airports, airline, coaches can cause long travel delays (We strongly recommend a Sofia flight – Plovdiv airport is a disaster)

➖ Not particularly snowsure, yet no artificial back-up

➖ Small, yet steep, slopes relatively unsuitable for many grades

➖ Poor piste and lift maintenance

➖ Limited off-slope facilities

➖ Ugly hotels

➖ Problem with theft of equipment

Borovets is typically Balkan, with all that implies – keen piste-bashers, gourmets, posers – and those wanting creature comforts should look elsewhere. However, it is one of the few resorts to meet the needs of those on a budget seeking reasonable slopes, pretty scenery, and convenient village lifts. Borovets is also developing, with much-needed infrastructure being provided in response to market demands. These assets put it ahead of Bulgarian and Romanian rivals, making it the best all-round resort in Eastern Europe. It also has had an excellent snow record in recent years.

Since the fall of Communism it is no longer true to say 'You can't spend your money', but prices are still at least half those of the Alps. Theft, however, is becoming a major problem. A few years back, we heard about one couple having the contents of their hotel room loaded into their suitcases and stolen. Theft of snowboard and ski equipment now appears to be rife as well. It pays to take extra precautions and always keep an eye on all your gear.

boarding *Borovets, though a budget destination, has yet to catch on with boarders, probably because of the lack of facilities. Board hire is available, and the Crystal brochure offers snowboard instruction as well. The main lift, from resort level to Yastrabets, is a cable car, but the lifts above it are all drags. The other slopes, Sitnayakovska Skala, is serviced by two chairs, one from bottom to top, the other from bottom to half-way, with the rest of the lifts being drags. The resort will not appeal to boarders over good intermediate ability as there is just not enough challenge – but at least the beer's cheap.*

The resort

Borovets is little more than a compact collection of large, ugly, modern hotels, with most of the essentials of a resort – bars, restaurants, shops etc – housed within them. This said, there has been new development every year since the fall of the Communist regime; some regulars believe the place is becoming too commercial and is now

not as ultra-friendly or cheap as its Bulgarian rival, Pamporovo. This is relative, of course. It's still inexpensive by the standards of most resorts.

The beautiful wooded setting of the place provides a degree of Alpine-style charm, and trees do hide some of the worst architectural excesses.

Despite the very low prices, including cheap beer, Borovets is not dominated by young people looking to

MOUNTAIN FACTS

Altitude 1300m-2700m
Lifts   15
Pistes   40km
Green/Blue   30%
Red   61%
Black   9%
Artificial snow   some

LIFT PASSES

96/97 prices in sterling
Borovets area
Covers all lifts in the resort.
Main pass
1-day pass 12
6-day pass 59
Children
Under 12: 6-day pass 51 (14% off)
Notes Pass and school prices are local price in sterling. They are significantly cheaper (almost half-price) when booked as part of a package.

SCHOOLS/GUIDES

96/97 prices in sterling
Borovets Ski School
Classes 6 days
4hr: 10am-noon and 2pm-4pm
6 full days: 64
Children's classes
Ages: up to 12
6 full days: 46
Private lessons
Hourly
11 for 1hr

---

whoop it up. Many of the visitors are families on low budgets. Evening animation is centred mainly within the Rila hotel, leaving the rest of Borovets to have a muted atmosphere.

There are two focal points to the resort. The first is a central cluster of large hotels. The main village lift (a gondola) goes from here to two of the three ski sectors. A couple of minutes' walk takes you to the top of the resort, where an enormous hotel overlooks the remaining village lifts, all conveniently close to one another. There are no resorts near enough to justify an excursion.

The mountains

THE SLOPES
Biggest in Eastern Europe

The 40km of piste are spread over three sectors, two of which are loosely connected. The two largest have fairly steep slopes made more awkward by poor piste maintenance. A gondola rises over 1000m from the edge of town to service both the small, high, easy slopes of the Markoudjika sector, and the mainly long, steepish Yastrebets pistes that lead back to the same lift station. A little drag lift and path connect the two. The Baraki sector is within easy walking distance of the gondola bottom station, even in ski boots, starting conveniently in front of the biggest of the village hotels, with several base lifts to choose from. Runs are short, with a range of just 550m up to a top station at 1850m.

SNOW RELIABILITY
Remarkably good

Borovets has enjoyed an excellent snow record in recent years. One reporter this year enjoyed up to two metres of snow in April. The small Markoudjika section is the most snowsure, but the area as a whole is markedly reduced when runs to the village are incomplete – there are few runs between the top and middle stations of the gondola, and Baraki's section is drastically reduced. Despite advertisements to the contrary, there is little snowmaking.

FOR EXPERTS
One run doesn't make a holiday
The long, fairly challenging piste, and its variants, beneath the gondola is where you'll be practising those turns.

FOR INTERMEDIATES
Some variety

Good intermediates will enjoy the red runs, most of which are fairly tough. Average performers have a lovely long blue run, dropping 1000m, from Yastrebets. The less-confident are not well provided for, although the short runs at Markoudjika have good snow. The lack of grooming tends to mean there are few leisurely cruises available.

FOR BEGINNERS
Not ideal

The nursery slopes are conveniently positioned at the foot of the Baraki section, but are inadequate. The excellence of the ski school is some compensation. Markoudjika is good for near beginners, though again we have to emphasise that poor grooming does not make for easy progression. Overall, the nursery slopes tend to get very overcrowded even when the resort itself is only a quarter full. And it is difficult to progress on to more challenging slopes without going straight on to reds.

FOR CROSS-COUNTRY
Not appealing

Officially, there are 20 trails, but the area covered is small. Few people come here to do the sport, so trails are either pleasantly or unpleasantly lonely, depending on your point of view. Trails are poorly maintained.

QUEUES
Can be dreadful

There are weeks when queues form only at ski school start and finish times, but when the resort is full and/or lacking complete snow-cover lines can be long in places. The gondola and a single-person chair are the main bottlenecks. When the attractions of the higher slopes are particularly apparent, delays to reach Yastrebets can be serious (up to two hours). At such times people bussed in from Pamporovo have added to the chaos. Lifts also have a tendency to shut regularly 'for maintenance', putting strain on the others. One visitor found that the gondola was open for only two days a week, even though the snow-cover at the time was excellent. High winds were blamed, but our reporter thought a desire to save money was probably the real reason.

CHILDCARE

The kindergarten in the hotel Rila takes children aged 2 to 5, from 9am to 4.30 and in the evening from 7pm.

GETTING THERE

Air Sofia, transfer 1¼hr.

MOUNTAIN RESTAURANTS
Basic and inadequate

These are mostly basic little snack bars with limited seating, serving good-sized portions of very simple fare. It helps if you like chips. Lunchtime queues can be more time-consuming than lift delays. Most reports say the mountain restaurants continue to be dreadful. And although some brochures claim there are 12 of them out there in the slopes, this seems like a bit of wishful thinking. You can get some unusual items on the menu, such as calf's brain, pig's heart and tongue fried in eggs. It's probably safest to stick to pizza.

It is not inconvenient to return to Borovets for lunch – and probably advisable. The Ela hotel is close to the Yastrebets slopes and has bearable food.

SCHOOLS AND GUIDES
A justly high reputation

The Borovets ski school gives caring, patient, fun tuition four hours per day. Standards of English are surprisingly high, and classes are not too large. There is also a new co-operative school, which offers similar prices and services.

FACILITIES FOR CHILDREN
Generally approved of

Reports of ski kindergarten have been complimentary, although supervision is suspect. The non-ski nursery is situated in hotel Rila.

Staying there

The compact nature of the resort, with everything (including lifts) within easy walking distance of everything else, makes location of hotel relatively unimportant. This said, there is some accommodation out in the countryside which relies on quite a poor bus service and/or taxis (very cheap). Horse-drawn sleighs also provide a taxi service around the village; it is cheap enough to use frequently, but scarcely needed.

HOW TO GO
On a hotel package, probably

Borovets is essentially a hotel resort. Apartments are available, but cooking is difficult: there is no supermarket and nothing like the range of food you would expect to be available in shops. There are now two catered chalets in the resort, the Mariela (available through Crystal) and the Deya.

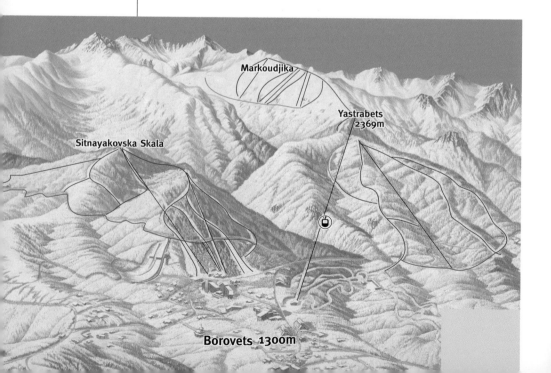

Markoudjika

Yastrebets
2369m

Sitnayakovska Skala

Borovets 1300m

UK PACKAGES

Balkan Holidays, Crystal, First Choice Ski, Inghams, Neilson, Ski Balkantours

ACTIVITIES

Indoor Sauna, fitness centre, swimming pools, gym
Outdoor Sleigh rides, helicopter trips, mountain walks, excursions to Samokov, Sofia, Rila monastery and Plovdiv

TOURIST OFFICE

Postcode 1040
Tel +359 (2) 980 5297
Fax 981 0114

The view from a piste of the Sitnayakovska Skala area to the Rila hotel →

Hotels The big, modern monstrosities are conveniently close to the lifts, and there is also an attractive Scandanavian-style development out in the forest.

① **Rila** Low marks for virtually everything, especially food; not recommended.

① **Samokov** Much the better of the two big conference hotels, though its four-star rating should not be taken too seriously. Plenty of amenities but little atmosphere or character. The 25m pool is a major asset in a resort with few off-slope facilities.

① **Ela** and **Mura** Friendly sister hotels, both with plenty of hot water (an important consideration here) The food at the Mura has declined dramatically – and is now almost inedible.

① **Edelweiss** Comfortable in recently refurbished rooms (not all rooms); 10-minute walk from lifts.

① **Breza** Rather spartan, but small and friendly, with lots of hot water; more rustic character than anywhere else.

① **Bor** One of the less well positioned places, and rather basic – but popular for its friendliness.

① **Yagoda Chalets** Studio apartments sold on a half-board basis. Part of an attractive Finnish-designed development of log cabins in the forest 3km out of town. Buses every 20 minutes during the morning rush, then hourly. Taxis about £2 each way.

Self-catering The Rila studios are clean and comfortable, but hot water can be erratic.

EATING OUT
Organised events best

Food is generally poor. The Maritsa restaurant in the hotel Samokov attempts French cuisine at the bargain price of £5 per head, but the best food of the week is likely to be on the folklore and local village dinner evenings arranged by tour reps. Restaurants worth a mention include Krima, Ela Tavern, and Francos.

APRES-SKI
Limited, but a varied range

Events organised by tour operator reps include trips to sample Bulgarian folklore and a visit to a local village for dinner. Sleigh rides and tobogganing are available. Many consider the entertaining ski school show the highlight of the week. Others prefer the sumo wrestling! There are several discos. Hotel bars are generally large and impersonal.

OFF-SLOPE ALTERNATIVES
Not a lot

There isn't enough to keep anyone not using the slopes happy for long, but there are a few intriguing options. Excursions to the Rila monastery by coach and to Sofia by coach or helicopter are interesting. There may also be the opportunity of a visit to the ballet in Sofia. Borovets has little to offer, but the Samokov pool is open to the public. The Piano Bar art gallery has some good works at bargain prices.

Romania

⊕ Extremely cheap

⊕ Interesting excursions and friendly local people

⊕ Good standard of affordable tuition

⊖ Primitive facilities

⊖ Poor food

⊖ Limited slopes with few real challenges

Like Bulgaria, Romania sells mainly on cost. On-the-spot prices, in particular, are very, very low. Provided you have correspondingly low expectations – and provided you go to Poiana Brasov and not Sinaia – you'll probably come back content. If you have any interest in good living, and particularly good lunching, stay away. It's a place for beginners and near-beginners – the slopes are limited in extent and challenge, but the tuition is good (and cheap, of course).

There is another dimension to a holiday here, which is the experience of visiting (and supporting) an interesting and attractive country with a traumatic recent history. Reporters have commented on the friendliness of the people, and most recommended exploring beyond the confines of the resorts. Bucharest is 'not to be missed'.

Romania's two resorts are in the Carpathian mountains, about 120km north-west of the capital and arrival airport, Bucharest. They are very different places, but have one or two things in common apart from low prices: tuition, with excellent spoken English, small classes and a patient, friendly approach; and very basic mountain restaurants, with primitive sanitary arrangements that would 'shock the toughest of characters'.

The main resort is **Poiana Brasov** (1020m), near the city of Brasov. It is purpose-built, but not for the convenience of those using the slopes: the hotels are dotted about a spacious, pretty wooded plateau, served by regular buses and cheap taxis. There is no village as such.

The main slopes consist of decent intermediate tree-lined runs of about 750m vertical, roughly following the line of the main cable-car and gondola, plus an open nursery area at the top. There are also some nursery lifts at village level. A black run takes a less direct route down the mountain, which means that on average it is gentler than the red run under the lifts; it has one steepish pitch towards the end. The more adventurous would need to seek opportunities to go off-piste. The resorts gets weekend business from Brasov and Bucharest, and the main lifts can suffer serious queues.

The Bradul and Sport hotels are handy for the lower nursery slopes and for one of the cable-cars, but you can't be certain that it will be operating. None of the hotels is special, but the Alpin gets the best reports and the Ciucas is a 'good, basic' place with satellite TV. Après-ski revolves around hotels; they have bars and discos which can be quite lively at times. The Hotel Sport has a popular disco. The two nightclubs put on cheap cabarets, including Russian ballet dancers attempting to be erotic. Off-slope facilities are limited; there is a good-sized pool, and bowling. Excursions are 'surprisingly expensive', but are none the less well worth investigating. A trip down to Brasov is worth the £4 taxi fair, especially as prices there are even lower than in the resort.

One or two companies offer holidays in **Sinaia** – a small town on the busy road from Bucharest to Brasov. When we visited it we were impressed by the modest intermediate slopes, on largely treeless hills next to the town. The town was a rather depressing place, and to judge by reports, it is even more so now – one reporter was shocked and saddened by the evident poverty, and upset by the number of stray dogs around.

The abiding impression we brought back from Romania was one of resources stretched to their limits. To judge by the reports we have received, post-revolutionary Romania has not made much progress. One report tells of the loos at Bucharest airport, where three sheets of toilet paper were issued to each person on entry.

Norway

- ⊕ Probably the best terrain and facilities in Europe for serious cross-country skiing
- ⊕ The home of Telemark – plenty of opportunities to learn and practise
- ⊕ Complete freedom from the glitziness often associated with downhill resorts, and from the ill-mannered lift queues of the Alps
- ⊕ Quiet atmosphere that suits families and older people
- ⊕ Usually reliable snow conditions throughout a long season

- ⊖ Very limited downhill areas – small, with few challenges
- ⊖ Unremarkable scenery – nothing like the drama of the coastal fjords
- ⊖ Mountain restaurants are little more than pit-stops
- ⊖ Prohibitively high prices (because of high taxes) for alcoholic drinks
- ⊖ Very little lively après-ski
- ⊖ Short daylight hours in midwinter
- ⊖ Highly changeable weather
- ⊖ Limited off-slope activities

Norway and its resorts are very different from the Alps, or for that matter the Rockies. Our list of ⊕ and ⊖ points makes the Norwegian recipe clear. Some people find it very much to their taste. For cross-country there is nowhere like it, and for downhillers who dislike the usual resort trappings and long for a simpler approach to winter holidays, it could be just the place.

But it is quite difficult to imagine the kind of dedicated downhiller who would happily spend a week in a Norwegian resort. And speaking for ourselves – well, any one of the first four ⊖ points we've listed would probably be enough to put us off; when these are combined in a single destination, along with four other non-trivial drawbacks, you can count us out.

From the 1960s to the 1980s, Norway's popularity with British skiers declined steadily, until it was attracting only 1,500 or so – about one-tenth of the peak number. So in 1988 the tourist agencies launched an initiative to reverse the trend. Aided by the Alpine snow shortages at the turn of the decade and the award of the 1994 Olympic Winter Games to Lillehammer, the campaign has been a success. Bookings from the UK have grown appreciably in recent seasons.

There is a traditional friendship between Norway and Britain, and we think of Norwegians as welcoming people, well disposed towards British visitors. Some reporters find the reality bears this out: 'a warm welcome awaits,' says one. Sadly, our visit a few years ago left us underwhelmed by the warmth of welcome, and we're not alone. One report, for example, speaks of a 'lack of enthusiasm from townspeople – a take it or leave it approach'. But at least English is widely spoken; you'll find British TV programmes on local channels.

Prices in Norway tend to be high even by Alpine standards. Alcohol is particularly expensive. Wine cannot be bought in regular shops, but only from the state-controlled monopoly stores, which are few and far between and never open when you need them.

Cross-country skiing comes as naturally to Norwegians as walking; and even if you're not that keen, the fact that cross-country is normal, and not a wimp's alternative to 'real' skiing, gives Norway a special appeal. Here cross-country is both a way of getting about the valleys, and a way of exploring the hills. Although you can plod around short valley circuits as you might in an Alpine resort, what distinguishes Norway for the keen cross-country skier is the network of long trails across the gentle uplands, with refuges along the way where backpackers can pause for refreshment or stay overnight.

This network of mountain huts offers cheap, if primitive, accommodation which can turn touring into a week-long adventure with the chance to really get away from the crowds. Several operators now offer ski-touring packages or they can be arranged on the spot.

More and more Norwegians now use Telemark equipment and technique for back-country skiing trips like this, instead of cross-country skis. Telemark (named after the region of Norway where it has been used for generations) is, in some respects, a hybrid of cross-country and downhill skiing. It is a tricky, but eventually elegant, technique.

For Alpine runs, the country is not nearly so attractive. Despite the fact that it is able to hold downhill races, and despite the recent successes of its own Alpine racers, Norway's Alpine areas are of limited appeal. Another drawback is that the majority of lifts in Norway are still T-bars. This can make things awkward for boarders but the sport is nonetheless popular, particularly with local youths who swarm on to the slopes at weekends.

The site of the 1994 Olympics, the little lakeside town of **Lillehammer** (200m) is not actually a downhill resort at all. There is plenty of cross-country terrain around, but the nearest downhill runs are 15km north at Hafjell. This is a worthwhile little area, with a vertical of 850m, eight lifts, and pistes totalling 20km with a longest run of 5km. The Olympic slalom events were held here; but the planned women's downhill and super-G races were moved elsewhere after the racers judged the course too easy. They went to Kvitfjell, about 35km further north, developed specially for the men's downhill and super-G. It's steeper but smaller – 12km of pistes.

Norway's other internationally known resort is **Geilo** (770m) – a small, quiet, unspoilt community on the railway line that links Bergen on the coast to Oslo. It provides all the basics of a resort – a handful of cafés and shops clustered around the railway station, ten hotels more widely spread around the wide valley, children's facilities and a sports centre.

Geilo is a superb cross-country resort. As the Bergen–Oslo railway runs through the town it is possible to go for long tours – Ustaoset is a nice trip – and then catch the train back at the end of the day.

But Geilo is very limited for downhillers. The 24km of piste are spread over two small hills – one,

Vestlia, a bus-ride away, with a good, informal hotel and restaurant at its foot – offering a maximum vertical of 265m and a longest run of 1.5km. None of the runs is difficult.

Clearly the best hotel, and one of the attractions of staying in Geilo, is the Dr Holms Hotel – smartly white-painted outside, beautifully furnished and spacious inside. This is the centre for après-ski, but prices are steep. The luxurious Bardola hotel is also recommended. The resort is quiet at the end of the day but the main hotels often provide live entertainment.

The most rewarding resort for keen downhillers is **Hemsedal** (650m), about 30km north of Geilo. The runs here, totalling about 35km, are more varied and longer – up to 6km, and almost 800m vertical – and the rather more craggy terrain provides testing off-piste runs (accessible from the lifts) as well as better-than-usual scenery. As usual, there are extensive cross-country trails in the valleys and up at altitude. The slopes are some distance from the town, and the bus service is infrequent and sometimes crowded, although reliable. Reporters are impressed by the main hotel, the Skogstad.

A long way north of the other resorts is **Oppdal** (550m), which claims more downhill runs than any of its rivals (about 80km – as much as a small Alpine resort). The total vertical is also impressive (about 900m) but this is a bit misleading – most of the runs are short.

There are almost equally extensive slopes at **Trysil** (600m), off to the east on the border with Sweden, and the runs are longer (up to 4km and 650m vertical). The runs here are all around the conical Trysilfjellet, some way from Trysil itself – though there is some accommodation at the hill.

In complete contrast to all of these resorts is **Voss** (50m), a sizeable lakeside town quite close to Bergen and the sea. A cable-car links the town to the slopes on Hangur and Slettafjell, with a total of 40km of pistes. Snow reliability can be poor for Norway. There are plenty of excursion possibilities, in particular the spectacular Flåm railway, which plunges down the side of a mountain to fjord (sea) level. From there you can take a fjord trip by boat to link up with a bus back to Voss. Nearby Bergen is an historic, beautiful city which is well worth a visit.

Sweden

WHAT IT COSTS

(((((5)

- ➕ Snowsure season from December to May
- ➕ Unspoilt, beautiful landscape
- ➕ Uncrowded pistes and few lift queues
- ➕ Vibrant après-ski and nightlife scene
- ➕ Excellent selection of off-the-slopes activities

- ➖ Limited challenging downhill terrain
- ➖ High prices for alcohol
- ➖ Lacks the dramatic peaks and vista of the Alps
- ➖ Short days during the early season

First-time visitors to Sweden could be in for a surprise. En route from the airport you travel along deserted roads amid captivating scenery of forests and lakes. This huge wilderness gives an entirely different feel from the grandeur and peaks of the Alps or Dolomites. As you would expect in a country with a high standard of living, accommodation, food and service are good. And the people are welcoming, lively and friendly. Scandinavians enjoy the outdoor life and there are plenty of off-slope activities. You could try dog or reindeer sledding, visit frozen waterfalls or a genuine Sami village. And it is excellent for cross-country skiing. Its downhill areas are limited in size and challenge but the main resort of Åre will keep a moderate intermediate happy. As a destination for a holiday, Sweden is likely to appeal most to those who want an all-round winter holiday in a different environment and culture from a normal Alpine resort.

There has been a surge in interest in Sweden in recent years and for the 1997/98 season Crystal is running a charter flight to a local airport to cut down on transfer times.

Although British packages to Sweden are more expensive than those to Norway, Sweden is significantly cheaper for things like cigarettes and alcohol, as well as food and clothing. And when we went to press you were getting 13 kroner to the pound rather than 10 a year ago. Apart from alcohol (which remains expensive), prices are pretty much on a par with the main Alpine countries.

The British skiers and boarders we met in Sweden were mainly experienced and well-travelled. The majority were there because of a desire to try a different destination.

One of the most important advantages of skiing in Scandinavia is the reliability of snow for a long season. Easter weekend is traditionally the main skiing time for most Scandinavian families – it is possible to get good snow as late as mid-May. In places, you can ski all year round.

Scandinavians love their cross-country and back-country skiing, and there are lots of opportunities for

getting off-piste and away from the tracks. Snowboarding is also popular, with parks and pipes available in the main resorts. On the down side, the lift systems tend to be dominated by T-bars and there is nowhere which can really match the huge Alpine resorts for extent of pistes.

There is plenty to do off the slopes, be it exploring the landscape on foot or by car, or perhaps visiting a traditional Sami settlement. The Sami are the indigenous people of northern Scandinavia and Siberia (never call them 'Lapps' – it is now considered a term of abuse). They traditionally lead a nomadic lifestyle – following huge herds of reindeer – and can often still be seen wearing traditional costumes. If you get the chance to hear some of their music and singing, it is an experience you are unlikely to forget (although you may not rush to buy the CD). Popular Sami souvenirs include jewellery made out of reindeer droppings. Impress your friends.

By far the biggest ski and boarding resort in Sweden is **Åre**, positioned beside the lake of the same name. It is a small town made up of typical coloured wooden buildings and some larger, ugly apartment blocks. There are several outlying villages around if you prefer a quieter location, and buses to all of them.

Åre describes itself as the largest ski area north of the Alps and it has 90km of piste and 44 lifts (35 of them drags). There are two separate areas of slopes – the main one goes up from Fjallby and a blue run comes back between buildings right down into the main square, where you can get the small mountain railway back out again for access to the main lifts about 200 metres uphill from the square.

The top area here does not open until the daylight hours lengthen in February – and it needs lots of snow to cover its rocky terrain. The area is very often closed because of poor weather. But there are good slopes lower down too, with pistes and drags sheltered and surrounded by trees. As many of the runs are also very quiet (especially the Rodkullen and Bjornen sectors), you really feel away from it all. The most congested area is at the base of lift four, the Fjälgardsliften.

The second Duved/Tegefjäll area is smaller, with only nine main lifts and a couple of baby ones. It tends to be even quieter than the main area.

Generally, the slopes are best suited to intermediates. Experts may find the lack of good, long black runs frustrating, although the world cup run will be of interest. There are plenty of safe off-piste possibilities on the back of Åreskuten.

It is a snowboard-friendly resort and there is a half-pipe at Åre and a fun-park near Rodkullen. It is not the best place in Sweden for cross-country – but there are 70km of marked tracks. Telemark skiing is also very popular here, as it is in most of Scandinavia.

There is a good ski school in Åre, run by English-born Toni Koning. There is a money-back gaurantee if you cannot learn to ski within five lessons. As in most of Sweden, standards of English tend to be exceptionally good.

There are plenty of hotels of a high standard in and around Åre. Crystal offers various apartments and hotels, both in the town centre, which is best for nightlife, or in the quieter outlying areas. Après-ski in Åre itself is awesome. The nightclub scene is 'thumping' – and rated among the top six of all Europe's winter resorts.

Storlien is a village at the top of a pass near the border with Norway. It has a compact ski area of 17 runs on the same mountain, with 16km of piste served by seven T-bars. The vertical drop is a mere 191 metres and the longest run only 1,400 metres. Its main attraction is the excellent snow reliability. The stuff is often still bucketing down in April. The king of Sweden has a chalet in the area. The main hotel is the Högfjällshotel which has lots of character, but is expensive, a bit shabby for some tastes, and we've had reports of food being disappointing.

Salen in mid-west Sweden is really four resorts and two sets of slopes. It is essentially a family resort, and very child-friendly. There are 85km of piste and a well-developed lift system. Beginners are well catered for with 35 nursery slopes. Intermediates will appreciate the flattering, well-groomed pistes through the forests. There are 20 black runs listed in the sector, although experts will want to try some of the off-piste descents, especially The Wall which, like its namesake in the Portes du Soleil, deserves to be taken seriously.

For boarders, there are two half-pipes and more than 20 jumps in the Lindvallon and Hogfjället areas.

There is plenty of self-catering accommodation and some good-quality hotels close to the lifts. Après-ski is quiet and tends to be centred around the hotels. Off-slope activities include snow-scooter safaris and ice-hole fishing – one for the very, very patient.

Riksgransen, 200km north of the Arctic Circle, is an area of jagged mountain peaks and narrow fjords. It used to be a mecca for visitors wanting to see the midnight sun and the northern lights. Now it is a mecca for snowboarders and off-piste enthusiasts. The season starts in mid-February and ends in June – when you can be on the slopes during the night under the midnight sun.

There are 20km of piste, nineteen generally short runs and some decent off-piste to explore. There's also midnight heli-skiing!

Björkliden, also above the Arctic Circle, has a ski season which actually starts in mid-May. There are 15km of piste, but the area's main claim to fame is its subterranean skiing inside Scandinavia's largest cave system. You need to go with a guide, but it is a breath-taking experience.

Scotland

- It's easy to get to from northern Britain
- It is possible to experience perfect snow and stirring skiing
- Decent, cheap accommodation and good-value packages are on offer
- Mid-week is rarely crowded
- There are extensive ski-touring and ski-mountaineering possibilities
- Few travel hassles
- Lots to do off the slopes

- Weather is extremely changeable and sometimes vicious
- Snowfall is erratic, and has been poor in several recent seasons
- Ski areas are small; runs tend to be short
- Queueing can be a problem – though usually only at peak times and if lifts are closed
- Little ski village ambience and few memorable mountain restaurant

Scotland is different! If you want reliable snow, perfect pistes, blue skies, sunshine and charming mountain restaurants, forget it. Conditions in Scotland are unpredictable, to say the least. If you are willing to take a chance, or if you live nearby and can go at short notice when things look good, fine. But don't look on it as a replacement for your usual week in the Alps. If you try it, you'll love it or hate it; but at least you'll know. And you'll have something to talk about in the pub.

Scotland's five ski areas are surprisingly different from one another, although they do share some characteristics. Snow conditions and the weather can vary dramatically – especially from west to east; up-to-date and accurate information on conditions and the latest weather forecast are particularly important for those contemplating a trip at short notice. Conditions can be testing. Rain, gales, icy slopes, slush, fog, rocks and heather are not unheard of, but those who ski regularly in Scotland tend to finish up as strong, versatile skiers.

For novices who are really keen to learn – and who are prepared for the possibility of less than ideal conditions – Scotland could make sense, especially if you live nearby. One option is to book instruction via one of the outdoor centres, many of which also provide accommodation.

For intermediates, a tour by car that takes in the five main areas is an amusing way to spend a week if you are lucky with the weather. Most of the slopes in most of the areas fall somewhere around the intermediate level. But all areas, apart from the Lecht, offer the occasional piece of tough or very tough skiing. Much of the terrain is suitable for ski touring and ski mountaineering; Cairngorm especially is something of a centre of expertise for mountain activities.

Snowboarding is popular in Scotland but conditions may not allow half-pipes and fun-parks to be built.

Apart from weather, Scotland's style, ambience and attitude is not to everyone's taste. All these elements are better than they were – the relatively new Nevis Range area has probably had a lot to do with that – but Aviemore is still ugly, Fort William is hard to like, and cosy, charming café-bars and restaurants are still too few in number. Licensed restaurants have appeared at the slopes in the last few years, bringing not just alcohol but also much better catering. The limited facilities at the base areas (none has accommodation) mean that après-ski there is poor. By 5pm almost everybody has gone. There is nightlife – there are reasonable pubs and bars – but it's like Scotland not Switzerland.

March 1998 should see Scottish skiing finally put on the map, when Cairngorm and Nevis Range host the Europa cup finals for Alpine skiing. It will be the largest and most prestigious skiing event ever held in Britain, with up to 150 of Europe's top winter sportspeople taking part. Let's hope the conditions are okay.

Cairngorm is the biggest and best known resort in Scotland. Aviemore is the main centre but a significant amount of Cairngorm business also comes in from other villages in the

What's new

The ski area at the Nevis Range has been doubled in size thanks to the addition of three new lifts (two chairs and a T-bar) in the last couple of years.

The long-awaited funicular railway at Cairngorm is still on the drawing board.

CAIRNGORM MOUNTAIN FACTS

Altitude	555m-1245m
Lifts	17
Pistes	2085 acres
Green	32%
Blue	32%
Red	32%
Black	4%
Artificial snow	none

Cairngorm Chairlift Company

Postcode PH22 1RB
Tel +44 (1479) 861261
Fax 861207

NEVIS RANGE MOUNTAIN FACTS

Altitude	655m-1220m
Lifts	12
Pistes	1560 acres
Green	20%
Blue	34%
Red	31%
Black	15%
Artificial snow	none

Tourist Office

Postcode PH33 6SW
Tel +44 (1397) 705825
Fax 705854

GLENCOE MOUNTAIN FACTS

Altitude	305m-1120m
Lifts	7
Pistes	494 acres
Green	25%
Blue	25%
Red	38%
Black	12%
Artificial snow	none

Glencoe Ski Centre

Postcode PA39 4HZ
Tel +44 (1855) 851226
Fax 851233

GLENSHEE MOUNTAIN FACTS

Altitude	610m-1070m
Lifts	26
Pistes	1952 acres
Green	26%
Blue	34%
Red	34%
Black	6%
Artificial snow	3 acres

Glenshee Ski Area

Postcode AB35 5XU
Tel +44 (1339) 741320
Fax 741665

THE LECHT MOUNTAIN FACTS

Altitude	610m-825m
Lifts	12
Pistes	600 acres
Green	15%
Blue	50%
Red	25%
Black	10%
Artificial snow	15 acres

The Lecht Ski Area

Postcode AB36 8YP
Tel +44 (1975) 651440
Fax 651426

Spey Valley. Ambitious plans to install a top-to-bottom funicular railway are still in the planning stage – but are expected to go ahead eventually.

The slopes, which lie between 555m and 1145m, are accessed from car parks about a mile apart at the base of two corries – Coire Cas (the main area) and Coire na Ciste (a narrow gulley with the toughest skiing in it). The two sectors come together at the Ptarmigan beginners' area just below the summit of Cairn Gorm. There are chair-lifts operating from both base areas and, as the snowline recedes up the hill, they provide access to the skiing.

There are mountain restaurants at each of the base areas, at the Shieling (midway up Coire Cas) and at the very top. There's no accommodation at the ski area. The Stakis Coylumbridge, the nearest hotel, offers good-value packages. The Red Mcgregor Hotel is centrally located in Aviemore. There are chalets, cottages, houses and caravans – and even the occasional castle – to rent on a self-catering basis. For the après-ski late in the evening, Crofter's Show Bar is the best dance haunt. Chevvy's features alternative music and is a focal point for snowboarders. The Winking Owl tends to be preferred by skiers.

Nevis Range is the newest and the highest Scottish resort and it occupies the north-facing slopes of Aonach Mor – a 4000-foot peak, Britain's eighth highest and in close proximity to the Ben itself. The resort, which openend in 1989, has invested in three new lifts in the past couple of years (two chairs and a T-bar), which have opened up the North East facing Corries in the Coire Dubh area and doubled the amount of available slopes to 631 hectares. The new area also holds its snow well because of its orientation. A new beginners' area has been built higher up the mountain, which has more reliable snow than the original, low nursery slopes.

A long gondola ride in comfortable six-seater cabins is something of a novelty in Scotland and a fair indicator of the relative sophistication of the facilities here. The chair-lift – a few minutes' walk from the gondola station – arrives at an altitude of 900 metres and is crucial to keeping skiing going late in the season – the upper runs are expected to last until late May.

When the sun shines and the views of Ben Nevis and Carn Mor Dearg are at their most spectacular, intermediates should head for the summit and take it all in – it's superb. The main mountain restaurant, the self-service Snowgoose Restaurant and Bar, shares a building with the gondola top station and is frequently the most popular location on the mountain. Gondola trippers as well as skiers hang out here looking for warmth.

Fort William is only a 15-minute drive from the skiing. The town provides everything that the visitor needs; some hotels arrange transport to the slopes. There are many B&Bs and hotels in and around Fort William that offer accommodation. Self-catering units are plentiful.

Glencoe's slopes lie between 305m and 1108m, on the Meall A Bhuiridh mountain at the edge of Rannoch Moor and just east of Glen Coe – a moody and magnificent setting if ever there was one. The base area is a car park and a few buildings housing the café, ticket office and a museum. The Access lift, a double chair, rises to the Plateau tow, which opens up the main nursery area and provides access to the other tows and the bulk of the slopes. The upper slopes enjoy good snow cover, often for a season that lasts from December to May. The only hotel nearby is the isolated Kings House Hotel a mile away. They also have a bunkhouse and an area for tents.

Glenshee has expanded into a system that now boasts 26 lifts and has comfortably the biggest area and uplift capacity of the Scottish resorts. It remains primarily a venue for day trippers because of the lack of a major accommodation centre. Most of the slopes, which lie between 640m and 1070m, are suitable for intermediates and beginners.

The Lecht is largely a beginners' area, 32 miles from Aviemore. The slopes (610m–823m) are on the gentle east-facing side of a high pass with a series of parallel drag lifts and runs just above the car parks. The main area includes five beginner tows and five others, each with a run or two back down towards the road. With a maximum vertical of only around 200m, runs are short. There is a floodlit dry ski slope which ensures some evening skiing and a bit of summer business. The nearest place to stay, Tomintoul, is six miles away from the slopes. It is a typical Highland village with a few hotels and B&Bs.

Australia

➕ Offers skiing and boarding during the European summer

➕ In one holiday you can also take in a visit to tropical northern Australia

➖ It's a long way from anywhere except New Zealand and south-east Asia

➖ Mountains are rather low, and lift/trail networks small by Alpine standards

Even more than New Zealand, Australia offers resorts that are basically of local interest, but which might amuse people with other reasons to travel there – catching up with those long-lost relatives, say. The mountains are certainly more entertaining than most of the glacier areas on which snow-starved Europeans must normally rely in the summer. The resorts (unlike those in New Zealand) mainly offer some accommodation close to the slopes.

The major resorts are concentrated in the populous south-east corner of the country, between Sydney and Melbourne, with the biggest and best in New South Wales, in the National Park centred on Australia's highest mountain, Mt Kosciusko (2230m), about six hours' drive from Sydney. Skiing has been going on here since the early years of the century – as in the next-door state of Victoria, where there are also several lower resorts within three or four hours' drive of Melbourne. Should you be visiting Tasmania, you might want to check out the possibilities there, too – though they're limited.

The season generally runs from mid-June to mid-October, but may be extended at either end if snow conditions allow.

The best-known Australian resort is **Thredbo**. In many respects it is rather like a small and quite smart French purpose-built resort – user-friendly, mostly made up of apartments (though there are some lodges) and few off-slope activities. But there are many more bars than you would find in the French equivalent. It's a steep little place, with stiff climbs to get around from one part to another. Road access is easy, but the toll is high – and, indeed, prices have struck some reporters as generally high.

The slopes, prettily wooded with gum trees, rise up across the valley from the village, served by a regular shuttle bus through the resort. They are well laid out, with better connections between runs than in many areas – and the resort as a whole gives the impression of good organisation. The 12 lifts include four fast quad chairs, and the trails include Australia's highest (2035m) and longest (6km). There is a decent vertical of 670m, and a good range of runs; the blacks are not difficult, but they offer some variety, and on the higher lifts there are off-piste variants.

Not far away is the **Perisher Blue** complex, with a pass covering more lifts than anywhere else in Australia – but a vertical of less than 400m. The main area is **Perisher/Smiggins**, where lifts and runs – practically all easy or intermediate – range over three lightly wooded sectors. The resort is reachable by road, but is also served by the Skitube, a rack railway that tunnels its way up from Bullocks Flat and goes on to the second area, **Blue Cow/Guthega**, where the slopes offer more challenges. There is some accommodation in Perisher, but more down in the town of Jindabyne.

A snow cat can take you on to the isolated chalets of Australia's highest resort, **Charlotte Pass** (1760m), with five lifts but only 200m vertical.

In Victoria, **Mt Buller** is an isolated peak with a proper resort village near the summit. Draped around the mountain is a quite extensive network of over 25 chairs and drags.

Another mountaintop resort is **Mt Hotham**. At 1750m, the village has a reputation for powder snow. The 10 lifts serve a complete range of runs, and the village is not without life.

New Zealand

The number of keen skiers and boarders from New Zealand found kicking around the Alps gives a clue that there must be some decent slopes back home – and indeed there are. The resorts are rather different from those of the Alps or the Rockies, and the networks of lifts and runs are rather limited by those exalted standards. However desperate you are for snow during the northern summer, we wouldn't advise travelling half-way round the world from Europe or the US just to get access to the likes of Coronet Peak, Mount Hutt or Whakapapa. But resorts like these could make an interesting part of a wider-ranging visit to New Zealand, and if you're starting from somewhere nearer – Australia, or even south-east Asia – the resorts of New Zealand may be the best option you have. For Europeans already spending a lot to travel to New Zealand, the extra cost of a day or two's heli-drops is well worth while, if conditions are right.

There are exceptions but, broadly speaking, the system in New Zealand is that you stay in towns at fairly low altitude – usually below the snow-line – and drive up each day to a base lodge where there will be a simple restaurant, equipment hire and one or two shops as well as the main lifts, but usually no accommodation.

There are resorts on both North Island and South Island. The main concentration on South Island is around the lakeside town (and year-round resort) of Queenstown, covered in detail in a separate chapter starting on page 538. Queenstown has become known as the adrenalin capital of New Zealand – and probably the world – by offering a range of dangerous (or at least thrilling) activities, of which the best-known is bungy jumping. Most are available in winter as well as summer (see page 540).

In what follows, we describe the most prominent resorts (apart from Queenstown and its two local mountains), but there are a number of other possibilities. The main commercial ones are described briefly in our Directory, at the back of the book, but there are also other ski-fields run by clubs – so if you're visiting New Zealand and going anywhere near the mountains, it's worth enquiring what's available locally. But don't expect groomed trails, or other luxuries: some of these fields are pretty primitive, involving stiff walks to get to the base and crude rope tows when you get there.

Any of the major resorts is worth a day or two of your time if you're in the area and the conditions are right. But if your credit card is also in good condition, don't miss the heli-skiing; even if you're no expert off-piste, with powder skis it's a doddle, and tremendously satisfying. There are several companies operating on South Island, based in Queenstown, Wanaka and Methven. Try to leave the arrangements loose, to cope with the highly changeable weather. An alternative adventure is to fly by plane to ski the length of a glacier.

As in the northern hemisphere, the season doesn't really get underway until about midwinter – mid or late June – and runs until some time in October. Mount Hutt aims to open first, in mid-May, and disputes the longest-season title with Whakapapa, which generally stays open until mid-November.

Snowboarding is very popular in New Zealand, and most of the major resorts have special terrain parks including half-pipes, as well as boarding classes and hire equipment.

WHAKAPAPA MOUNTAIN FACTS

Altitude	1625m-2300m
Lifts	25
Pistes	988 acres
Blue	30%
Red	45%
Black	25%
Art. snow	20 acres

TOURIST OFFICE

Tel +64 (7) 892 3738
Fax 892 3732

MOUNT HUTT MOUNTAIN FACTS

Altitude	1420m-2075m
Lifts	10
Pistes	902 acres
Green	25%
Blue	50%
Black	25%
Art. snow	103 acres

TOURIST OFFICE

Tel +64 (3) 308 5074
Fax 308 5076

TREBLE CONE MOUNTAIN FACTS

Altitude	1200m-1860m
Lifts	5
Pistes	1359 acres
Green	15%
Blue	45%
Black	40%
Art. snow	125 acres

TOURIST OFFICE

Tel +64 (3) 443 7443
Fax 443 8401

CARDRONA MOUNTAIN FACTS

Altitude	1505m-1895m
Lifts	5
Pistes	790 acres
Green	20%
Blue	55%
Black	25%
Art. snow	none

TOURIST OFFICE

Tel +64 (3) 443 7411
Fax 443 8818

Although South Island has most of the resorts, the most developed resort – almost on an Alpine scale – is **Whakapapa** (pronounced Fukapapa), on the slopes of Mt Ruapehu on North Island. Sadly, volcanic Mt Ruapehu has been misbehaving recently, and both the 1995 and 1996 seasons were spoilt by eruptions which left the slopes black with volcanic ash rather than white with snow.

Mt Ruapehu is in the middle of North Island, and therefore within driving distance (about four hours) of both Auckland and Wellington, the two main towns. Whakapapa, on the north-facing slopes, offers a top height of 2300m and a serious vertical of 657m, served by 14 drags and chair-lifts, including one fast quad. The terrrain is mixed, including some challenging off-piste, wide open cruising runs. Next to the base lodge is an extensive, but often crowded, dedicated beginners' area, Happy Valley, with half a dozen rope tows and the resort's only snowmaking (so this area may open long before the rest of the mountain). The lifts and runs spread across quite an area of mountainside, and there are no less than three mountain restaurants. Although most people drive up for the day, there is accommodation only 7km away at Whakapapa village – including a very welcoming, traditional-style 'grand' hotel.

On the south-western slopes of Mt Ruapehu (reachable on snow by going off-piste from Whakapapa after a stiff climb) is **Turoa** – smaller, but still quite a serious resort, with 10 lifts, New Zealand's biggest vertical of 720m and runs of up to 4km in length. It's an open, mainly gentle mountainside, but there are some black runs at the side of the area, and plenty of scope for exploration off-piste. Accommodation is 20 minutes away in Okahune.

South Island has more resorts, in several clusters. It's arguable that the single most impressive ski-field – 655m vertical, with an excellent range of trails including blues and blacks top-to-bottom – is **Mount Hutt**, directly west of Christchurch. Even so, its lift system is about half the size of Whakapapa's. The main area is an open bowl with gentle terrain in the centre, served by chairs and drags, and steeper terrain around the sides, reached by traversing from the top drag. There is snowmaking over a large area of the central bowl.

Mount Hutt has a big base lodge, but has no accommodation near the lifts. You can stay a half-hour drive away (down a worryingly exposed road) in **Methven**, but the South Island capital of Canterbury is only another half-hour or so away.

There are two resorts accessible from the quiet little lakeside town of **Wanaka**, an hour or two's drive from Queenstown but in a different, more peaceful world. The lakeside Edgewater Resort is a comfortable, relaxing base.

At present the more impressive of these two areas is **Treble Cone** – named after a trio of peaks above the slopes. Treble Cone provides amazing views of Lake Wanaka, its shores usually green or brown rather than white; the main mountainside – now served by the southern hemisphere's first six-seat fast chair, giving uplift of 500m vertical – faces the lake, which is great therapy if you spend too much time looking at your ski tips.

Within its limits, this is an good mountainside for a competent skier or boarder. Both on the main flank and off to the side in Saddle Basin – served by a slow chair and then a T-bar – there are long, natural half-pipes with a lot of entertainment value when snow is good, as well as smooth, wide runs for cruising. There is snowmaking on two runs from top to bottom, and on the lower half of a third one.

Cardrona (pronounced Cudrohna) projects itself as a family ski area, but its three chair-lifts give access to a good range of open terrain (as much of it below as above the 1630m 'base' station) including some serious if short chutes – the total vertical is a modest 390m. The resort attracts quite a range of competitive events, including the national snowboarding and the national extreme skiing championships. If plans to develop next-door Arrow Basin come to fruition – adding 50% to the present accessible area – by 1998 Cardrona could be the most compelling of the four Southern Lakes resorts.

Cardrona has some accommodation at the modern base station – a handful of pleasant apartments, strictly for self-catering fans (the restaurant isn't open in the evening). And it has one simple restaurant on the slopes, away from the base lodge. Assuming you're not staying up at the base lodge, a great way to end the day is to collapse into the Cardrona Inn, on the valley road.

Queenstown

310m

A lively base for sampling a range of resorts

HOW IT RATES

The slopes

Snow	**
Extent	*
Experts	***
Intermediates	***
Beginners	***
Convenience	*
Queues	***
Restaurants	*

The rest

Scenery	****
Resort charm	**
Off-slope	*****

➕ For Europeans, more interesting than summer skiing on glaciers

➕ For Australians, conveniently close

➕ Huge areas of off-piste terrain accessible by helicopters, with excellent snow at the right time

➕ Lots to do off the slopes, especially for adrenalin junkies

➕ Lively town, with lots going on

➕ Grand views locally, and the spectacular 'fjord' country nearby

➖ Slopes (in two separate areas locally) are a drive from town

➖ Limited lift-served slopes in each area

➖ It's a long way from anywhere except Australia

➖ Mountain restaurants are little more than pit-stops

➖ Highly changeable weather

If you want a single destination in New Zealand – as opposed to visiting a few different mountains on your travels – Queenstown is probably it, especially if you can cope with the cost of a few heli-drops. Although the resorts of North Island are impressive, the Southern Alps are, in the end, more compelling – and their resorts are free of volcanic interruptions. Mount Hutt may be a slightly more impressive area than either of Queenstown's local fields – Coronet Peak and The Remarkables – but it's a rather isolated field. From Queenstown you have a choice of the two local fields plus the option of an outing to Treble Cone and Cardrona. The best way to take them in would be to plan on a night or two in Wanaka, an hour or two away (see Introduction to New Zealand).

boarding Boarding is popular in New Zealand, and although the two mountains close to Queenstown don't seem to have quite such a hold on the boarding market as Cardrona, they have everything you need, including equipment, tuition and (at Coronet Peak) a new terrain park with half-pipe. You needn't go anywhere near a drag-lift, and there are no flats to worry about except on the lowest green run at The Remarkables.

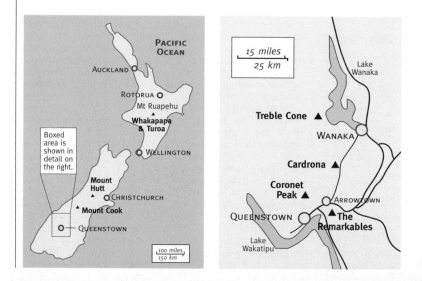

The resort

Queenstown is a winter-and-summer resort on the shore of Lake Wakatipu. Although the setting is splendid, the town itself is no beauty – it's touristy and commercial, and parts of it have the uncontrolled, shacky feel of small-town America. But it has a lively, relaxed feel to it and makes a satisfactory base, with some good restaurants, plenty of entertaining bars, and lots of touristy clothes shops.

The mountains

There are four ski areas – all small by Alpine standards – that you can get to from Queenstown. The two described here are close by, the others a more serious drive away, and best visited from Wanaka (see Introduction). At each base area you'll find a mini-resort – a ski school, a ski rental shop, a functional self-service restaurant.

All these areas have something for all standards of skier or boarder, with off-piste opportunities as well as prepared and patrolled trails. Kiwi ski areas use the American green/blue/black convention for run gradings.

THE SLOPES
Not the height of convenience
The Remarkables, true to their name, are a dramatic range of craggy peaks visible across the lake from some parts of Queenstown. The slopes are tucked in a bowl behind the peaks, over half-an-hour's drive from town.

Two chairs go up from the base. The slow Alta lift serves easy runs and accesses the higher Sugar Bowl chair, which serves mainly long easy runs plus a couple of black chutes. The Shadow Basin chair accesses steeper terrain, and the Homeward Runs – a broad, fairly gentle, unprepared slope down to the resort access road, where a shuttle truck goes back to the base.

Coronet Peak is about 20 minutes from Queenstown. Again, there are three main chair-lifts, the central one a fast quad that accesses practically all the runs. The main mountainside is a pleasantly varied intermediate slope, though it steepens near the bottom. A fourth lift, a T-bar, serves another mainly intermediate area to one side.

SNOW RELIABILITY
Good at Coronet
The New Zealand weather is highly variable, so it's difficult to be confident about snow conditions. But Coronet Peak has snowmaking on practically all its intermediate terrain.

FOR EXPERTS
Challenges exist
Both areas have quite a choice of genuinely black slopes. Coronet's Back Bowls is an experts-only area, and The Remarkables' Shadow Basin chair serves some excellent slopes inside and outside its basin, including some serious chutes you have to hike to.

THE REMARKABLES MOUNTAIN FACTS

Altitude	1620m-1980m
Lifts	5
Pistes	543 acres
Green	30%
Blue	40%
Black	30%
Art. snow	25 acres

TOURIST OFFICE
Tel +64 (3) 442 4615
Fax 442 4619

Lake Wakatipu and the outskirts of Queenstown, seen from the road up to the slopes of The Remarkables ↓

CORONET PEAK MOUNTAIN FACTS

Altitude	1210m-1650m
Lifts	6
Pistes	690 acres
Green	20%
Blue	50%
Black	30%
Art. snow	200 acres

TOURIST OFFICE

Tel +64 (3) 442 4620
Fax 442 4624

CHILDCARE

At both areas there is a Penguin Club for children aged 4 to 6, and a Kea Club for those aged 7 to 16. Both have morning and afternoon sessions. The Queenstown Crèche can take younger children all day.

FOR INTERMEDIATES
Fine, within limits

There's some very enjoyable intermediate skiing in both areas – rather more at Coronet, where there are also easy blacks to go on to.

FOR BEGINNERS
Excellent

There are gentle areas at both areas served by rope tows, and longer green runs served by chair-lifts.

FOR CROSS-COUNTRY
Unremarkable

There is a short loop around a lake in the middle of The Remarkables area, but the only serious area is the plateau of Waiorau, near Cardrona.

QUEUES
It depends

We lack reports on high-season crowds, but there are enough beds locally to lead to queues in the peak.

MOUNTAIN RESTAURANTS
Er, what mountain restaurants?

Both areas have a simple cafeteria in the base lodge.

SCHOOLS AND GUIDES
All the usual classes

The schools are well organised, with a wide range of options, including 'guaranteed' beginner classes.

FACILITIES FOR CHILDREN
Look good

We lack evidence of how the childcare works in practice, but it looked OK to our parental eye.

Staying there

Given that you're going to be driving or taking a bus to the slopes every day, location isn't important. Some hotels are quite some way from central Queenstown – inconvenient for après-ski unless there's a shuttle bus.

HOW TO GO
Stay out of town?

The hotels range from the very simple to the glossily pretentious Millennium. One of the most welcoming places – with more of a 'ski-lodge' atmosphere than many in town – is Nugget Point, a few miles out.

EATING OUT/APRES-SKI
Lots of choice

Queenstown is a lively little town, with a range of bars and clubs that stay open late with disco or live music. There are said to be over 100 restaurants – Chinese, Italian, Malaysian, Lebanese ... The Moa is a particularly stylish bar-restaurant, with live music sometimes. McNeill's is an excellent brew-pub.

OFF THE SLOPES
Scare yourself silly

There are lots of scary things to do – see below. Just to the west of Queenstown is New Zealand's fjord country, and you can go on independent or guided walks into it or at least towards it. Tourist flights by plane or helicopter are also popular. Arrowtown, a cute, touristy old mining town, is interesting for a quick visit.

GET THAT ADRENALIN RUSH

The streets of Queenstown are lined by agencies offering various forms of artificial thrill, mainly bungy jumping, whitewater rafting, parapenting, skydiving, jetboating or various combinations, with or without plane or helicopter rides.

AJ Hackett's bungy jump at Kawarau Bridge is where this crazy activity got off the ground, as it were, and although there are now much bigger jumps to be done, this one looks quite scary enough for most purposes – you plunge towards the icy river, but are pulled up short by your bungy cord and lowered into an inflatable boat.

The Shotover Jet Boat experience is a better bet if you want a little shot of adrenalin rather than a big one. You get chauffeured at high speed along the rocky river Shotover in a boat that can get along in very shallow water, execute high-speed 360° turns and pass very close to cliffs, overhanging trees and the like. They say they haven't had an accident in the many years they've been doing this, which means either that it's not as dangerous as it seems or that you have the opportunity to become the first casualty. It's probably more fun in summer than in temperatures of –10°C, when any spray that hits your hair freezes as it lands.

Reference section

Tour operators

Arranging your own accommodation in a resort is not difficult. But most people still prefer the convenience of a package holiday, which is what most of the companies listed below are set up to provide. We've also included a list of operators that offer accommodation without travel arrangements.

AA Ski-Driveaway
Ski drive specialist
PO Box 128, Fanum House,
Basingstoke, Hants RG21 7DT
Tel 0990 655555
Fax 01256 493875

ABT Ski
Chalet in St-Martin
Shepperton Marina, Felix Lane,
Shepperton, Middlesex
TW17 8NJ
Tel 01932 252025
Fax 01932 246140

Airtours
Mainstream operator
Wavell House, Holcombe Road,
Helmshore, Rossendale,
Lancashire BB4 4NB
Tel 01706 260000
Fax 01706 232977

All Canada Ski
Holidays in Canada
Sunway House, Raglan Road,
Lowestoft, Suffolk NR32 2LW
Tel 01502 585825
Fax 01502 500681

Alpine Action
Chalets in the Three Valleys
3 Old Salts Farm Road,
Lancing, West Sussex BN15 8JC
Tel 01903 761986
Fax 01903 766007

Alpine Options Snowtrain and Skidrive Holidays
Les Deux-Alpes specialist
Haland House, 66 York Road,
Weybridge, Surrey KT13 9DY
Tel 01932 828668
Fax 01932 840005

Alpine Tours
Austria, Italy and Slovenia
54 Northgate, Canterbury, Kent
CT1 1BE
Tel 01227 454777
Fax 01227 451177

Altours Ski
Wide-ranging programme
Diamond Destinations, 41A
Church Street, Staveley,
Chesterfield S43 3TL
Tel 01246 471234
Fax 01246 471999

American Connections
US and Canadian operator
10 York Way, Lancaster Road,
High Wycombe HP12 3PY
Tel 01494 473173
Fax 01494 473588

American Dream
Major North America operator
1-7 Station Chambers, High
Street North, London E6 1JE
Tel 0181-552 1201
Fax 0181-552 7726

Austrian Holidays
Hotel holidays in Austria
5th Floor, 10 Wardour Street,
London W1V 4BQ
Tel 0171-434 7399
Fax 0171-434 7393

Balkan Holidays
Holidays in Bulgaria
Sofia House, 19 Conduit Street,
London W1R 9TD
Tel 0171-543 5555
Fax 0171-543 5577

Barrelli Ski
Eclectic French selection
19 Sefton Park Road, St
Andrews, Bristol BS7 9AN
Tel 0117-940 1500
Fax 0117-940 1500

Bigfoot
Chamonix holidays
186 Greys Road, Henley on
Thames, Oxon RG9 1QU
Tel 01491 579601
Fax 01491 576568

Bladon Lines
Major chalet operator
10-18 Putney Hill, London
SW15 6AX
Tel 0181-780 8800
Fax 0181-780 4405

Borderline
Specialist in Barèges
Les Sorbiers, Rue Ramond,
65120 Barèges, France
Tel 01963 250117
Fax 00 335 62 92 83 43

Chalet Beaumont
Large chalet in Chamonix
Derwent House, 35, South Park
Road, Wimbledon, London
SW19 8RR
Tel 0181-544 0404
Fax 0181-544 0404

Chalet Snowboard
Boarding in France and US
31 Aldworth Avenue, Wantage,
Oxon OX12 7EJ
Tel 01235 767182
Fax 01235 767182

Chalet World
Chalets in big name resorts
PO Box 260, Shrewsbury
SY1 1WX
Tel 01952 840462
Fax 01952 840463

Chinook-It
Adventure in Canada and US
30 Sansom Street, Camberwell,
London SE5 7RE
Tel 0171-252 5438
Fax 0171-252 5438

Club Med
All-inclusive 'ski villages'
106-110 Brompton Road,
London SW3 1JJ
Tel 0171-581 1161
Fax 0171-581 4769

Collineige
Chamonix valley specialist
30-32 High Street, Frimley,
Surrey GU16 5JD
Tel 01276 24262
Fax 01276 27282

Color Line
Holidays in Norway
International Ferry Terminal,
Royal Quay, North Shields,
Tyne and Wear NE29 6EE
Tel 0191-296 1313
Fax 0191-296 1540

Contiki
Coach holidays for 18-35s
Wells House, 15 Elmfield Road,
Bromley, Kent BR1 1LS
Tel 0181-290 6422
Fax 0181-225 4246

Crystal
Major mainstream operator
The Courtyard, Arlington Rd,
Surbiton, Surrey KT6 6BW
Tel 0181-399 5144
Fax 0181-390 6378

Equity School Ski
School group holidays
Dukes Lane House, 47 Middle
Street, Brighton, East Sussex
BN1 1AL
Tel 01273 298298
Fax 01273 203212

Equity Total Ski
Family holidays, many in Italy
Dukes Lane House, 47 Middle
Street, Brighton, East Sussex
BN1 1AL
Tel 01273 299299
Fax 01273 203212

Erna Low
Holidays to France
9 Reece Mews, London
SW7 3HE
Tel 0171-584 2841
Fax 0171-589 9531

Fairhand Holidays
Ski-drive holidays to France
Suite 5, 216-218 Main Road,
Biggin Hill, Kent TN16 3BD
Tel 01959 540796
Fax 01959 540797

Fantiski
Holidays in France
c/o 1st Choice Travel Services,
Warmlake Estate, Maidstone
Road, Sutton Valence, Kent
ME17 3LR
Tel 01622 842555
Fax 01622 842458

Finlays
Mainly chalets in France
The Barn, The Square, Ancrum,
Borders TD8 6XH
Tel 01835 830562
Fax 01835 830550

First Choice Ski
Major mainstream operator
Olivier House, 18 Marine
Parade, Brighton BN2 1TL
Tel 0990 557755
Fax 01273 676410

FlexiSki
Specialists in flexible breaks
Crogen Stables, Corwen,
Denbighshire LL21 0SY
Tel 0171-352 0044
Fax 01490 440446

Freedom Holidays
Flexible-length Swiss holidays
30 Brackenbury Road,
Hammersmith, London W6 0BA
Tel 0181-741 4471
Fax 0181-741 9332

Frontier Ski
Holidays in Canada
3rd Floor, Broadmead House,
21 Panton Street, London
SW1Y 4DR
Tel 0181-776 8709
Fax 0181-778 0149

Funway Holidays
North American programme
One Elmfield Park, Bromley,
Kent BR1 1LU
Tel 0181-466 0222
Fax 0181-313 3547

Hannibals
Serre-Che and Val Cenis
Farriers, Little Olantigh Road,
Wye, Ashford, Kent TN25 5DQ
Tel 01233 813105
Fax 01233 813432

Headwater Holidays
Cross-country skiing holidays
146 London Road, Northwich,
Cheshire CW9 5HH
Tel 01606 48699
Fax 01606 48761

Huski
Holidays in Chamonix
63a Kensington Church Street,
London W8 4BA
Tel 0171-938 4844
Fax 0171-938 2312

Icelandair
Holidays in ... Iceland
172 Tottenham Court Rd,
London W1P 9LG
Tel 0171-388 5599
Fax 0171-387 5711

Independent Ski Links
Mainly France
Little Arram Farm, Bewholme
Lane, Seaton, Hull HU11 5SX
Tel 01964 533905
Fax 01964 536006

Inghams
Major mainstream operator
10-18 Putney Hill, London
SW15 6AX
Tel 0181-780 4444 or
0181-780 6600
Fax 0181-780 4405

Inntravel
Cross-country skiing holidays
Hovingham, York YO6 4JZ
Tel 01653 628811
Fax 01653 628741

Interski
Holidays with tuition in Italy
Acorn Park, St Peter's Way,
Mansfield, Nottinghamshire
NG18 1EX
Tel 01623 456333
Fax 01623 456353

Interworld Canada
Hotels/self-catering in Canada
Acorn House, 60 Bromley
Common, Bromley BR2 9PF
Tel 0181-313 0690
Fax 0181-466 0653

Kuoni
Holidays in Switzerland
Kuoni House, Dorking, Surrey
RH5 4AZ
Tel 01306 742500
Fax 01306 744222

The Ski-Drive Specialist to France

LAGRANGE

Apartments, Chalets & Hotels in more than 30 Top Resorts

Tel: 0171 371 6111

ABTA

543

Tour operators

Lagrange
Self-catering in France
168 Shepherds Bush Road,
Hammersmith, London W6 7PB
Tel 0171-371 6111
Fax 0171-371 2990

Le Ski
Courchevel/Val d'Isère chalets
25 Holly Terrace, Huddersfield
HD1 6JW
Tel 01484 548996
Fax 01484 451909

Lotus Supertravel
USA, France, Switzerland
Sandpiper House, 39 Queen
Elizabeth Street, London
SE1 2BT
Tel 0171-962 9933
Fax 0171-962 9965

Made to Measure
Tailor-made holidays
43 East Street, Chichester,
West Sussex PO19 1HX
Tel 01243 533333
Fax 01243 778431

Mark Warner
Chalet-hotel holidays
20 Kensington Church Street,
London W8 4EP
Tel 0171-393 3168
Fax 0171-393 0093

MasterSki
Christian holidays
Thames House, 63-67 Kingston
Road, New Malden, Surrey
KT3 3PB
Tel 0181-942 9442
Fax 0181-949 4396

Meriski
Chalet specialist in Méribel
The Old School, Great
Barrington, Oxon OX18 4UR
Tel 01451 844788
Fax 01451 844799

Momentum Travel
Tailor-made specialists
4 Cortayne Road, London
SW6 3QA
Tel 0171-371 9111
Fax 0171-610 6287

Moswin Tours
Small German programme
Moswin House, 21 Church
Street, Oadby, Leics LE2 5DB
Tel 0116-271 9922
Fax 0116-271 6016

Motours
French ski-drive operation
Buckingham House, Longfield
Road, Royal Tunbridge Wells,
Kent TN2 3DQ
Tel 01892 518555
Fax 01892 518666

**Mountain and Wildlife
Ventures**
Nordic ski-touring
The Adventure Traveller,
Compston Road, Ambleside,
Cumbria LA22 9DJ
Tel 015394 33285
Fax 015394 34065

Neilson
Major mainstream operator
71 Hough Side Road, Pudsey
LS28 9BR
Tel 0990 994444
Fax 0113-239 3275

On The Piste Travel Ltd
French group coach holidays
Manitron House, Millbuck Way,
Sandbach CW11 3GQ
Tel 01270 764171
Fax 01270 763160

Panorama
Italy and Andorra budget hols
29 Queens Road, Brighton,
East Sussex BN1 3YN
Tel 01273 206531
Fax 01273 205338

Passage to South America
Tailor-made holidays
Fovant Mews, 12 Noyna Road,
London SW17 7PH
Tel 0181-767 8989
Fax 0181-767 2026

Peak Ski
Chalets in France/Switzerland
White Lilacs House, Water
Lane, Bovingdon, Herts
HP3 0NA
Tel 01442 832629
Fax 01442 834303

PGL Ski Europe
Specialist in school holidays
Alton Court, Penyard Lane,
Ross-on-Wye HR9 5NR
Tel 01989 768168
Fax 01989 768376

PGL Teenski
School trip specialist
Alton Court, Penyard Lane,
Ross on Wye HR9 5GL
Tel 0500 749147
Fax 01989 766306

Plus Travel
Specialises in Swiss resorts
9 Eccleston Street, London
SW1W 9LX
Tel 0171-259 0199
Fax 0171-259 0190

Poles Apart
Holidays in France
Ermington Mill, Ermington,
Ivybridge, Devon PL21 9NT
Tel 01548 831183
Fax 01548 831113

Powder Byrne
Luxury holidays
4 Alice Ct, 116 Putney Bridge
Road, London SW15 2NQ
Tel 0181-871 3300
Fax 0181-871 3322

**Powder Skiing in North
America Limited**
Heli-skiing holidays in Canada
61 Doneraile Street, London
SW6 6EW
Tel 0171-736 8191
Fax 0171-384 2592

Ramblers
Cross-country holidays
Box 43, Welwyn Garden City,
Herts AL8 6PQ
Tel 01707 331133
Fax 01707 333276

Silver Ski
Chalet holidays in France
Conifers House, Grove Green
Lane, Maidstone ME14 5JW
Tel 01622 735544
Fax 01622 738550

Simon Butler Skiing
Chalet holidays in Megève
5 Woodbine Cottages, Shalford
Common, Guildford GU4 8JF
Tel 01483 502897
Fax 01483 452001

Simply Ski
French and Swiss holidays
Chiswick Gate, 598-608
Chiswick High Rd, London
W4 5RT
Tel 0181-742 2541
Fax 0181-995 5346

COURCHEVEL
MÉRIBEL
LA PLAGNE
VAL D'ISÈRE
VERBIER

SIMPLY *Ski*

Chalet holidays ranging from the comfortable to
the luxurious in Europe's top resorts.

Excellent child care facilities.
Free Ski leader service. Scheduled BA flights.

Friendly, personal service by
specialists in quality skiing holidays.

For our informative brochure, please call
0181 995 9323

ABTA V1337   ATOL 1922   AITO

PEAK Ski

VERBIER, TIGNES & CHAMONIX

★ CATERED CHALETS
★ WEEKEND SPECIALS
★ ACCOMMODATION WELL SITUATED

White Lilacs House, Water Lane, Bovingdon, Herts
01442 832629 Fax: 834303 Email: peakski@which.net

Ski Activity
Holidays in big-name resorts
Lawmuir House, Methven,
Perthshire PH1 3SZ
Tel 01738 840888
Fax 01738 840079

Ski Amis
Mainly chalets in France
Alanda, Hornash Lane,
Shadoxhurst, Ashford, Kent
TN26 1HT
Tel 01233 732187
Fax 01233 732769

Ski Balkantours
Schools/groups to E Europe
61 Ann Street, Belfast BT1 4AA
Tel 01232 246795
Fax 01232 234581

Ski Barrett-Boyce
Chalet in Megève with tuition
14 Hawthorn Road, Wallington,
Surrey SM6 0SX
Tel 0181-647 6934
Fax 0181-647 8620

Ski Beach Villas
Small Italian programme
29-31 Elmfield Road, Bromley,
Kent BR1 1LT
Tel 0990 992222
Fax 01132 393275

Ski Beat
Plagne/Tignes/Méribel chalets
Metro House, Northgate,
Chichester, West Sussex
PO19 1BE
Tel 01243 780405
Fax 01243 533748

Ski Bon
Chalets in Méribel
Hilldale, Radnor Cliff Crescent,
Folkestone, Kent CT20 2JQ
Tel 01303 241560
Fax 01303 241560

Ski Chamois
Holidays in Morzine
18 Lawn Road, Doncaster
DN1 2JF
Tel 01302 369006
Fax 01302 326640

Ski Choice
Mainly hotel and self-catering
Travel Choice, 27 High Street,
Benson, Wallingford, Oxon
OX10 6RP
Tel 01491 837607
Fax 01491 833836

Ski Club Europe
Schools and group holidays
Fairway House, 53 Dartmouth
Road, London SE23 3HN
Tel 0181-699 7788
Fax 0181-699 7770

Ski Club of GB
Holidays for club members
The White House, 57-63
Church Road, Wimbledon,
London SW19 5DQ
Tel 0181-410 2000
Fax 0181-410 2001

Ski Equipe
Upmarket chalet operator
27 Bramhall Lane South,
Bramhall, Stockport, Cheshire
SK7 2DN
Tel 0161-440 0010
Fax 0161-440 0080

Ski Esprit
Chalet holidays for families
Oaklands, Reading Road North,
Fleet, Hampshire GU13 8AA
Tel 01252 616789
Fax 01252 811243

Ski Famille
Family holidays in Les Gets
Unit 9, Chesterton Mill,
French's Road, Cambridge
CB4 3NP
Tel 01223 363777
Fax 01223 361508

Ski France
Chalets/catered apartments
Acorn House, 60 Bromley
Common, Bromley, Kent
BR2 9PF
Tel 0181-313 0690
Fax 0181-466 0653

Ski Hillwood
Family holidays
2 Field End Road, Pinner,
Middlesex HA5 2QL
Tel 0181-866 9993
Fax 0181-868 0258

Ski Independence
North American holidays
Osprey Holidays, Broughton
Market, Edinburgh EH3 6NU
Tel 0990 550555
Fax 0990 502020

Ski Leisure Direction
Mainly self-catering in France
Image House, Station Road,
London N17 9LR
Tel 0181-324 4042
Fax 0181-324 4030

Ski Leogang
Leogang specialist
6 Palace Street, London
SW1E 5HY
Tel 0171-730 7234
Fax 0171-730 1180

Ski Les Alpes
Holidays in the Alps
20 Lansdowne Gardens,
London SW8 2EG
Tel 0171-720 7127
Fax 0171-720 7134

CHALET HOLIDAYS

Atmospheric chalets in the best ski resorts

**ST ANTON • LECH
WHISTLER • ZERMATT
LES GETS • MERIBEL
LES CONTAMINES**

Call For Brochure: **0181 948 6922** ABTA V4104 ATOL 2271

Ski Mates
Coach holidays to Verbier
Ingledon House, Allenbrooke Road, Rosehill Estate, Carlisle CA1 2UT
Tel 01228 404303
Fax 01228 404309

Ski Miquel
Small but eclectic programme
33 High Street, Uppermill, Nr Oldham OL3 6HS
Tel 01457 820200
Fax 01457 872715

Ski Morgins
Chalet holidays in Morgins
The Sett, Badger, Burnhill Grn, Wolverhampton WV6 7JS
Tel 01746 783005
Fax 01746 783005

Ski North America Direct
Holidays to US and Canada
Station Chambers, High Street, North London E6 1JE
Tel 0181-552 6003
Fax 0181-470 4822

Ski Olympic
Chalet holidays in France
Pine Lodge, Barnsley Rd, Doncaster, South Yorks DN5 8RB
Tel 01302 390120
Fax 01302 390787

Ski Partners
Schools programme
Friary House, Colston Street, Bristol BS1 5AP
Tel 0117-925 3545
Fax 0117-929 3697

Ski Peak
Vaujany specialist operator
The Old Bakery, Dockenfield, Farnham, Surrey GU10 4HX
Tel 01252 794941
Fax 01252 794942

Ski Rosie
Apartments in Châtel
Squirrels, 127 Marlins Turn, Hemel Hempstead HP1 3LW
Tel 01442 235142
Fax 01442 235142

Ski Safari
Canadian specialist
13 Leinster Gardens, London W2 6DR
Tel 0171-262 5069
Fax 0171-262 1301

Ski Safe Travel
Mainly coach trips to Flaine
Unit 4, Braehead Estate, Old Govan Road, Renfrew, Scotland PA4 1XX
Tel 0141-812 0925
Fax 0141-812 1544

Ski Scandinavia
Holidays in Scandinavia
Whetstone Lodge, The Dicken, Whetstone, Leicester LE8 6LE
Tel 0116-275 2750
Fax 0116-275 2751

Ski Scott Dunn
Upmarket holidays
Fovant Mews, 12 Noyna Rd, London SW17 7PH
Tel 0181-767 0202
Fax 0181-767 2026

Ski Total
European chalet holidays
3 The Square, Richmond, Surrey
Tel 0181-948 6922
Fax 0181-332 1268

Ski Vacation Canada
Holidays in Canada
Cambridge House, 8 Cambridge Street, Glasgow G2 3DZ
Tel 0141-332 1511
Fax 0141-353 0135

Ski Valkyrie
European programme
56 Bower Street, Maidstone, Kent ME16 8SD
Tel 01622 763745
Fax 01622 690964

Ski Weekend
Weekend and ten-day holidays
2 The Old Barn, Wicklesham Lodge Farm, Faringdon, Oxon SN7 7PN
Tel 01367 241636
Fax 01367 243833

Ski Whistler
Specialists in Whistler
2 The Old Barn, Wicklesham Lodge Farm, Faringdon, Oxon SN7 7PN
Tel 01367 244911
Fax 01367 243833

Ski trek
Self-drive holidays to France
Old Road, Braunston, Daventry NN11 7JB
Tel 01788 890049
Fax 01788 890049

Ski-Val
France, Austria and USA
41 North End Road, West Kensington, London W14 8SZ
Tel 0171-371 4900
Fax 0171-371 4904

SkiGower
Mainly Swiss school trips
2 High Street, Studley, Warwickshire B80 7HJ
Tel 01527 854822
Fax 01527 857236

Skisar U.S.
Hotels and B&Bs in N America
Suite 5, 216-218 Main Road, Biggin Hill, Kent TN16 3BD
Tel 01959 540796
Fax 01959 540797

Skiworld
European programme
Skiworld House, 41 North End Road, West Kensington, London W14 8SZ
Tel 0171-602 4826
Fax 0171-371 1463

Skiworld North America
American part of Skiworld
41 North End Road, West Kensington, London W14 8SZ
Tel 0171-602 7444
Fax 0171-371 1463

Sloping Off
Schools/tailor-made by coach
31 High Street, Handley, Salisbury, Wiltshire SP5 5NR
Tel 01725 552247
Fax 01725 552489

Snowbizz
Holidays in Puy-St-Vincent
69 High Street, Maxey, Cambridgeshire PE6 9EE
Tel 01778 341455
Fax 01778 347422

Snowcoach
Andorra, Austria and France
Holiday House, 146-148 London Rd, St Albans, Herts AL1 1PQ
Tel 01727 866177
Fax 01727 843766

Snowise
Holidays in Châtel
The Farmhouse, Nix Hill, Manea Road, Wimblington, March, Cambridgeshire PE15 0RR
Tel 01354 741403
Fax 01354 740493

Snowline Skiing
French and Swiss programme
Collingbourne House, Spencer Court, 140-142 High Street, Wandsworth, London SW18 4JJ
Tel 0181-870 4807 or 0321 754377
Fax 0181-875 9236

Snowman Holidays
Hotel near Mègeve (Le Bettex)
The Business Centre, Llangarron, Ross-on-Wye, Herefordshire HR9 6PG
Tel 01989 770766
Fax 01989 770011

VAUJANY ALPE D'HUEZ MERIBEL
Ski PEAK
Chalets • Hotels • Apartments • Ski Guiding • Personal Service • Superb Cuisine • Child Care
01252 794941
PLEASE CALL FOR A BROCHURE
ATTO 2697 1029

Solo's
Singles' hols: 30-49 or 50-69
54-58 High Street, Edgware,
Middlesex HA8 7ED
Tel 0181-951 2800
Fax 0181-951 1051

St Anton Ski Company
Hotels and chalets in St Anton
Rafaut 65, St Anton am
Ahlberg, A-6580, Austria
Tel 0831 822 878

Stanford Skiing
Holidays in France
213 Sandcross Lane, Reigate,
Surrey RH2 8LL
Tel 01737 242074
Fax 01737 242003

Stena Line Holidays
Ski-drive to France and Italy
Charter House, Park Street,
Ashford, Kent TN24 8EX
Tel 0990 747474
Fax 01233 202351

STS
School group holidays
Miry Lane, Wigan, Lancaster
WN3 4AG
Tel 01942 823503
Fax 01942 322749

Swiss Travel Service
Hotels in Switzerland
Bridge House, 55-59 High
Road, Broxbourne, Herts
EN10 7DT
Tel 01992 456123
Fax 01992 448855

The Ski Company
France and US, with tuition
13 Squires Close, Bishop's
Park, Bishop's Stortford, Herts
CM23 4DB
Tel 01279 653746
Fax 01279 654705

The Ski Company Ltd
Luxury chalets
c/o Abercrombie & Kent,
Sloane Square House, Holbein
Place, London SW1W 8NS
Tel 0171-559 8585
Fax 0171-730 9376

Thomson
Major mainstream operator
Greater London House,
Hampstead Rd, London
NW1 7SD
Tel 0990 329329
Fax 0171-387 8451

Timescape Holidays
Coach/self-drive to Mayrhofen
581 Roman Road, London
E3 5EL
Tel 0181-980 7244
Fax 0181-980 7157

Top Deck
Lively, informal holidays
131-135 Earls Court Rd, London
SW5 9RH
Tel 0171-370 4555
Fax 0171-373 6201

Travelscene Ski-Drive
Self-drive, mainly in France
11-15 St Ann's Road, Harrow,
Middlesex HA1 1AS
Tel 0181-427 4445
Fax 0181-861 4154

UCPA
All-inclusive budget trips
c/o Action Vacances, 30
Brackley Road, Stockport,
Cheshire SK4 2RE
Tel 0161-442 6130
Fax 0161-442 6130

United Vacations
US programme
PO Box 377, Bromley, Kent
BR1 1LY
Tel 0181-313 0999
Fax 0181-313 3547

Val d'Isère Properties
Specialist in Val d'Isère
Collingbourne House, Spencer
Court, 140-142 High Street,
London SW18 4JJ
Tel 0181-875 1957
Fax 0181-875 9236

Vantage Point
Corporate specialists
12 Franconia Road, London
SW4 9ND
Tel 0171 622 6700
Fax 0171 622 6701

Virgin Snow
Holidays to America
Virgin Holidays Limited, The
Galleria, Station Road, Crawley,
West Sussex RH10 1WW
Tel 01293 617181
Fax 01293 536957

Waymark Holidays
Cross-country skiing holidays
44 Windsor Rd, Slough SL1 2EJ
Tel 01753 516477
Fax 01753 517016

White Roc
Weekends and short breaks
69 Westbourne Grove, London
W2 4UJ
Tel 0171-792 1188
Fax 0171-792 1956

Winterski
Holidays in Italy
31 Old Steine, Brighton
BN1 1EL
Tel 01273 702222
Fax 01273 620222

YSE
Holidays in Val d'Isère
The Business Village, Broomhill
Rd, London SW18 4JQ
Tel 0181-871 5117
Fax 0181-871 5229

ACCOMMODATION-ONLY OPERATORS

AGD Travel
Les Gets catered apartments
Rails Farmhouse, East
Hanningfield, Chelmsford,
Essex CM3 8AU
Tel 01245 400684

avant-ski
Holidays in France
49 Knoll Rise, Gateshead, Tyne
and Wear NE11 9QQ
Tel 0171-603 3138 or
0191-460 1440
Fax 0171-603 3138 or
0191-460 1440

Aravis Alpine Retreat
Chalet in La Clusaz
Les Hirondelles, 74450,
Saint-Jean-de-Sixt, France
Tel 00 33 4 50 02 36 25
Fax 00 33 4 50 02 39 82

Canada's Best
Tailor-made holidays
170 Fulford Road, York
YO1 4DA
Tel 01904 658436
Fax 01904 634598

Chalet Freestyle
Deux-Alpes chalet specialist
7 Burlington Road, Leicester
LE2 3DD
Tel 0116-270 3063

Chalets de St Martin
Chalets in St-Martin
1-3 Vine Lane, High Street,
Christchurch, Dorset BH23 1AB
Tel 01202 473255
Fax 01202 480042

Chalets 'Unlimited'
*Chalets in France, Switzerland
and US*
White Lilacs House, Water
Lane, Bovingdon, HP3 0NA
Tel 01442 834303
Fax 01442 834303

Challenge Activ
One chalet in Morzine
49 Eastwick Road, Walton-on-
Thames, Surrey KT12 5AR
Tel 01932 254501
Fax 01932 254501

Le Relais
Chalet in Ste-Foy
95 Dora Road, London
SW19 7JT
Tel 0181-944 9762
Fax 0181-944 9762

Mountain Highs
Chalet specialist in Morzine
Lower Buttsbeare, Bridgerule,
Holsworthy, Devon EX22 7HB
Tel 01288 381457
Fax 01288 381457

Peisey Holidays
One chalet in Peisey-Nancroix
Chalet Les Sapins, Peisey-
Nancroix, Aime 73210, France
Tel 01252 836186 pm or
01737 223488
Fax 01737 223499

Piste Artiste
Holidays in Champéry
Chalet Piste Artiste, 1874
Champery, Switzerland
Tel 0171-436 0100
Fax 00 41 24 479 3344

Ski Addiction
Chalets and hotels in Châtel
The Cottage, Fontridge Lane,
Etchingham, East Sussex
TN19 7DD
Tel 01580 819354
Fax 01580 819354

Ski Arrangements
Chalets/apartments in France
10 Surgery Lane, Crich,
Matlock, Derbyshire DE4 5BP
Tel 01773 853300
Fax 01773 853311

Ski Aval
Chalets in Val d'Isère
La Legettaz, PO Box 90, 73151
Val d'Isère, France
Tel 00 33 479 41 94 46
Fax 00 33 479 41 94 62

Ski Bumpy Trails
Chalet in Argentière
72 Camden Mews, London
NW1 9BX
Tel 0171-485 8519

Ski Etoile
Chalet in Montgenèvre
28A Water Lane, Newport,
Shropshire, TF10 7LD
Tel 01952 820155
Fax 01952 812835

Ski Hiver
Peisey chalets
119A London Road,
Waterlooville, Hants PO7 7DZ
Tel 01705 428586
Fax 01705 428904

Ski Trois Vallées
Courchevel and Méribel chalets
Chalet Blanc Chardon, Rue des
Beauforts, 73120 Courchevel,
France
Tel 0800 961470
Fax 00 33 479 08 44 95

Ski Verbier
Specialises in Verbier
172 Eversleigh Road, London
SW11 5XT
Tel 0171-738 0878
Fax 0171-924 2620

Ski with Julia
Swiss hotels and apartments
East Lodge Farm, Stanton,
Broadway, Worcs WR12 7NE
Tel 01386 584478
Fax 01386 584629

Snowfocus
Chalet in Châtel with nannies
Lavendar Lodge, Hurling
Burrow, 7 Milestone, St Agnes,
Cornwall TR5 0PG
Tel 01872 553003
Fax 01872 553050

Summit Chalets
Holidays in Breckenridge
53 Town Road, Croston,
Lancashire PR5 7RA
Tel 01772 601866
Fax 01772 601509

Vanilla Ski
Chalets in France
Maison La Foret, Villard
Dessus, 73700 Seez, Savoie,
France
Tel 01932 860696 or
00 33 479 410873
Fax 00 33 479 410873

Weekends in Val d'Isère
Weekends in Val d'Isère!
95 Dora Road, London
SW19 7JT
Tel 0181 944 9762
Fax 0181 944 9762

Black-and-white pages

A classified listing of the names, numbers and addresses you are likely to need.

BREAKDOWN INSURANCE

AA Five Star Service
Automobile Association,
Freepost, Erskine, Renfrewshire
PA8 6BR
Tel 0345 555577

Autohome
202-204 Kettering Road,
Northampton NN1 4HE
Tel 01604 232334
Fax 01604 231304

Britannia Continental
Britannia Rescue, St Georges
Square, Huddersfield, West
Yorkshire HD1 1JF
Tel 01484 514848
Fax 01484 518961
Only available to members

Europ Assistance
Sussex House, Perrymount Rd,
Haywards Heath, West Sussex
RH16 1DN
Tel 01444 442211
Fax 01444 455204

Green Flag
Green Flag House, Cote Lane,
Leeds LS28 5DG
Tel 0113-236 3236

International Assistance Services
32 High Street, Purley, Surrey
CR8 2PP
Tel 0181-763 1550
Fax 0181-668 1262

Leisurecare Insurance Services
Shaftesbury Centre, Percy
Street, Swindon, Wilts SN2 2AZ
Tel 01793 514199
Fax 01793 481333

Mondial Assistance UK
Mondial House, 1 Scarbrook
Rd, Croydon, Surrey CR0 1SQ
Tel 0181-681 2525
Fax 0181-680 2769

RAC Travel Services
RAC Enterprises Ltd, P.O. Box
499, Croydon CR2 6ZH
Tel 0800 550055
Fax 0181-681 8710

CAR WINTER EQUIPMENT

Barford Boxes
7 High Street, Barford, Warwick
CV35 8BU
Tel 01926 624151

Brindley Chains Ltd
1 Tatton Court, Kingsland
Grange, Warrington WA1 4RR
Tel 01925 825555
Fax 01925 825338
Pewag

Discount Autoparts
122 Newmarket Road,
Cambridge CB5 8HE
Tel 01223 323488
Fax 01223 324952
Thule, Kar Rite, Skandibox

GT Towing Ltd
6 Hatfield Rd, Potters Bar,
Hertfordshire EN6 1HP
Tel 01707 652118
Fax 01707 644638

Kar Rite Europe Ltd
One and Two Falconer Road,
Haverhill, Suffolk CB9 7XU
Tel 01440 712829
Fax 01440 712843

Latchmere Motor Spares
93-97 Latchmere Road, London
SW11 2DR
Tel 0171-223 5491
Fax 0171-228 3907

Motor Traveller
225 St Leonards Road,
Windsor SL4 3DR
Tel 01753 833442
Fax 01753 832495
Thule, Milz

Snowchains Ltd
Wrotham Road, Borough
Green, Kent TN15 8DG
Tel 01732 884408
Fax 01732 884564
Thule, Weissenfels

Thule Ltd
Units 4 & 5 Concorde Drive, 5c
Business Centre, Clevedon,
Bristol BS21 6UH
Tel 01275 340404
Fax 01275 340686

DRY SKI SLOPES

SOUTH-WEST ENGLAND

Avon Ski Centre
Lyncombe Lodge, Churchill,
Avon BS19 5PQ
Tel 01934 852335/852828
Fax 01934 853314

Christchurch Ski Centre
Matchams Lane, Hurn,
Christchurch, Dorset BH23 6AW
Tel 01202 499155
Fax 01202 483564

Exeter and District Ski Club
Belmont Road, Exeter EX1 2DJ
Tel 01392 211422

John Nike Leisuresport
Plymouth Ski Centre, Alpine
Park, Marsh Mills, Plymouth
PL6 8LQ
Tel 01752 600220
Fax 01752 228404

Radnor Golf and Ski Centre
Radnor Road, Redruth,
Cornwall TR16 5EL
Tel 01209 211059
Teaching machine, not a slope

Warmwell Leisure Resort
Warmwell, Near Weymouth,
Dorset DT2 8JE
Tel 01305 853245

Wellington Sports Centre
Corams Lane, Wellington,
Somerset TA21 8LL
Tel 01823 663010
Fax 01823 663018

Wessex Ski Club
Barton Hall, Kingskerswell
Road, Torquay, Devon TQ2 8JY
Tel 01803 313350
Fax 01803 313350

Yeovil Ski Centre
Addlewell Lane, Yeovil,
Somerset BA20 1QW
Tel 01935 421702

SOUTH-EAST ENGLAND

Alpine Ski Centre
Gallwey Road, Aldershot, Hants
GU11 2DD
Tel 01272 25889
Fax 01252 348561

Beckton Alpine Centre
Alpine Way, London E6 4LA
Tel 0171-511 0351
Fax 0171-473 0770

Bishop Reindorp Ski Centre
Larch Avenue, Guildford,
Surrey
Tel 01483 504988

Borowski Ski and Snowboard Centre
New Road, Newhaven, East
Sussex BN9 0EH
Tel 01273 515402
Fax 01273 611171

Bowles Outdoor Centre
Eridge Green, Tunbridge Wells
TN3 9LW
Tel 01892 665665
Fax 01892 669556

Bromley Ski Centre
Sandy Lane, St Paul's Cray,
Orpington, Kent BR5 3HY
Tel 01689 876812
Fax 01689 826077

Calshot Activities Centre
Calshot Spit, Fawley,
Southampton SO45 1BR
Tel 01703 892077
Fax 01703 891267

Crystal Palace National Sports Centre
PO Box 676, Upper Norwood,
London SE19 2BL
Tel 0181-778 9876
Fax 0181-676 8754

Folkestone Ski Slope
Radnor Park Avenue,
Folkestone, Kent CT19 5HX
Tel 01303 850333
Fax 01303 240842

Hillingdon Ski and Snowboard Centre
Park Road, Uxbridge,
Middlesex UB10 9NH
Tel 01895 255183/258506
Fax 01895 255458

John Nike Leisuresport
Bracknell Ski Centre, John Nike
Way, Amen Corner, Bracknell,
Berkshire RG12 8TN
Tel 01344 860033
Fax 01344 860023

John Nike Leisuresport
Chatham Ski Centre, Alpine
Park, Capstone Road,
Chatham, Kent ME7 3JH
Tel 01634 827979
Fax 01634 814075

Sandown Ski Centre
More Lane, Esher, Surrey
KT10 8AN
Tel 01372 467132
Fax 01372 466979

Southampton Ski Centre
Basset, Southampton,
Hampshire SO16 7AY
Tel 01703 790970
Fax 01703 782291

WALES

Cardiff Ski Centre
Fairwater Park, Fairwater,
Cardiff CF5 3JR
Tel 01222 561793
Fax 01222 561793

Dan-yr-Ogof Ski Slopes
Abercrave, Upper Swansea
Valley, Powys SA9 1GJ
Tel 01639 730284
Fax 01639 730293

Plas y Brenin
Capel Curig, Gwynedd
LL24 0ET
Tel 01690 720214
Fax 01690 720394

Pontypool Ski Centre
Pontypool Park, Pontypool,
Gwent NP4 8AT
Tel 01495 756955

Rhiwgoch Ski Centre
Bronaber, Trawsfynydd,
Gwynedd LL41 4UR
Tel 01766 540578
Fax 01766 540305

Ski Centre Pembrey
Pembrey Country Park, Llanelli,
Carmarthenshire SA16 0EJ
Tel 01554 834443
Fax 01554 834443

Ski Llandudno
Great Orme, Llandudno,
Gwynedd LL30 2QL
Tel 0149 2874707

MIDDLE ENGLAND

Gloucester Ski/Board Centre
Robinswood Hill, Gloucester
GL4 6EA
Tel 01452 414300
Fax 01452 307212

John Nike Leisuresport
Swadlincote Ski Centre, Hill
Street, Swadlincote, Derbyshire
DE11 8LP
Tel 01283 217200
Fax 01283 550359

North Staffs Ski Club
Kidsgrove, Stoke ST7 4EF
Tel 01782 784908

Richard Herrod Leisure Centre
Foxhill Road, Carlton,
Nottingham NG4 1RL
Tel 0115-961 2949
Fax 0115-987 2075

Skew Bridge Ski School
Northampton Road, Rushden,
Northants NN10 9AW
Tel 01933 359939
Fax 01933 410750

Stoke Ski Centre
Festival Park, Stoke-on-Trent
ST1 5PU
Tel 01782 204159
Fax 01782 204157

**Tallington Ski and Snowboard
Centre**
Tallington Lakes Leisure Park,
Barholm Road, Tallington, Nr
Stamford, Lincs PE9 4RJ
Tel 01778 344990
Fax 01778 345321

Tamworth Snowdome
Leisure Island, River Drive,
Tamworth, Staffordshire
B79 7ND
Tel 01827 67905
Fax 01827 62549

Telford Ski Centre
Court Street, Madeley, Telford,
Shropshire TF7 5DZ
Tel 01952 586862
Fax 01952 586862

The Ackers
Golden Hillock Road, Small
Heath, Birmingham B11 2PY
Tel 0121-771 4448
Fax 0121-766 7870

Wycombe Summit
Abbey Barn Lane, High
Wycombe, Bucks HP10 9QQ
Tel 01494 474711
Fax 01494 443757

EASTERN ENGLAND

Brentwood Park Ski Centre
Warley Gap, Brentwood, Essex
CM13 3DP
Tel 01277 211994
Fax 01227 220734

Gosling Ski Centre
Stanborough Road, Welwyn
Garden City AL8 6XE
Tel 01707 391039
Fax 01707 373620

Harlow Ski School
Hammarskjold Road, Harlow,
Essex CM20 2JF
Tel 01279 444100
Fax 01279 413556

Hemel Ski Centre
St Albans Hill, Hemel
Hemstead HP3 9NH
Tel 01442 241321
Fax 01442 234871

Norfolk Ski Slope
Whitlingham Lane, Trowse,
Norwich, Norfolk NR14 8TW
Tel 01603 662781
Fax 01603 662781

Suffolk Ski Centre
Bourne Terrace, Wherstead,
Ipswich IP2 8NG
Tel 01473 602347
Fax 01473 602347

NORTHERN ENGLAND

Alston Training/Adv Centre
High Plains Lodge, Alston,
Cumbria CA9 3DD
Tel 01434 381886

Halifax Ski Centre
Bradford Old Road,
Swalesmoor, Halifax HX3 6UG
Tel 01422 340760
Fax 01422 367000

Kendal Ski Club
Thorney Hills, Kendal, Cumbria
LA9 4AR
Tel 01539 733031

Oldham Ski Centre
Counthill Road, Moorside,
Oldham OL1 3HA
Tel 0161-911 4081

Pendle Ski Club
Clitheroe Road, Sabden,
Clitheroe, Lancs BB7 9HN
Tel 01200 425222

Sheffield Ski Village
Vale Road, Parkwood Springs,
Sheffield S3 9SJ
Tel 0114 276 9459
Fax 0114-276 0413

Ski Rossendale
Haslingden Old Road,
Rawtenstall, Rossendale,
Lancashire BB4 8RR
Tel 01706 222426
Fax 01706 226457

Ski Runcorn
Town Park, Palace Fields,
Runcorn, Cheshire WA7 2PS
Tel 01928 701965
Fax 01928 710009

Spectrum Leisure Complex
Hunwick Lane, Willington,
Crook, Co Durham DL15 0JA
Tel 01388 747000
Fax 01388 747098

Sunderland Ski Centre
Sports Complex, Silsworth
Lane, Sunderland SR3 3AN
Tel 0191-553 5785
Fax 0191-553 5789

The Oval
Wirral, Old Chester Road,
Bebington L63 7LF
Tel 0151-645 0551
Fax 0151-644 1673

Whickham Thorns Centre
Market Lane, Dunston
NE11 9NX
Tel 0191-460 1193

SCOTLAND

Aberdeen Ski Centre
Garthdee Rd, Aberdeen
AB10 7BA
Tel 01224 311781

Alford Ski Centre
Greystone Road, Alford,
Aberdeen AB33 8TY
Tel 01975 563024

**Ancrum Outdoor Education
Resource Centre**
10 Ancrum Road, Dundee,
Tayside DD2 2HZ
Tel 01382 435911
Fax 01382 435915

Aviemore Mountain Resort
Aviemore PH22 1PF
Tel 01479 810624
Fax 01479 810862

Bearsden Ski Club
The Mound, Stockiemuir Road,
Bearsden, Glasgow G61 3RS
Tel 0141-943 1500
Fax 0141-942 4705

Firpark Ski Centre
Tillycoultry FK13 6PL
Tel 01259 751772

Glasgow Ski Centre
Bellahouston Park, 16
Dumbreck Road, Glasgow
G41 5BW
Tel 0141-427 4991
Fax 0141-427 3679

Glenmore Lodge
Aviemore PH22 1QU
Tel 01479 861256
Fax 01479 861212

Loch Rannoch Activity Centre
Kinloch Rannoch PH16 5PS
Tel 01882 632201
Fax 01882 632203

Lochanhully Woodland Club
Carrbridge PH23 3NA
Tel 01479 841234
Fax 01479 841682

Midlothian Ski Centre
Hillend, Edinburgh EH10 7DU
Tel 0131-445 4433
Fax 0131-445 5549

Newmilns Ski Slope
High St, Newmilns KA16 9EB
Tel 01560 322320
Fax 01560 322320

Polmonthill Ski Centre
Polmont, Nr Falkirk FK2 0YE
Tel 01324 503835

**Stakis Royal Deeside and
Craigendarroch Country Club**
Ballater AB35 5XA
Tel 01339 755858
Fax 01339 755447

NORTHERN IRELAND

Craigavon Golf and Ski Centre
Turmoyra Lane, Silverwood,
Lurgan BT66 6NG
Tel 01762 326606
Fax 01762 347272

Mount Ober Ski Centre
Ballymaconaghy Road,
Knockbracken, Belfast BT8 4SB
Tel 01232 795666
Fax 01232 705862

EQUIPMENT DISTRIBUTORS

Ardblair Sports Ltd
Yard Rd, Blairgowrie,
Perthshire PH10 6NW
Tel 01250 873863
Fax 01250-875289
Leki, Dolomite, Diamir Fritschi

Big Bear Sports
Harkness Ind Est, Station Rd,
Borehamwood, Herts WD6 1DQ
Tel 0181-207 0377/5553
Fax 0181-207 4232
Look, Dynastar, Lange

Blue Ridge
Unit 25, 12 Wadsworth Road,
Perivale, Middlesex UB6 7LD
Tel 0181-991 9244
Fax 0181-991 9255
Tecnica; Vokl

Europa Sportsystems
Ann Street, Kendal LA9 6AA
Tel 01539 740083
Fax 01539 730955
*Nordica, Kastle, Marker,
Killerloop*

Euroski
66 North Rd, Brighton BN1 1YD
Tel 01273 688258
Fax 01273 701004
Alpina

Glacier Imports
74 Prospect Rd, Southborough,
Tunbridge Wells, Kent TN4 0EH
Tel 01892 543952
Fax 01892 535464

Mast Co
24 Albert Road, Caversham,
Reading RG4 7PE
Tel 0118-947 1735
Fax 0118-946 1213
*Fischer, Dynafit, Tyrolia,
Raichle, Scott*

Outdoor Leisure
Moac Hse, Demmings Rd Ind
Est, Cheadle, Cheshire SK8 2PE
Tel 0161-428 1178
Fax 0161-428 1243
K2

Salomon
Annecy House, Loddon Centre,
Wade Rd, Basingstoke
RG24 8FL
Tel 01256 479555
Fax 01256 479357

Sportline Ltd
Dominion House, Kennet Side,
Bone Lane, Newbury RG14 5PX
Tel 01635 48387
Fax 01635 38682
Head

Ultra Sport
Acton Road Ind Est, Long
Eaton, Nottingham NG10 1FY
Tel 0115-973 1001
Fax 0115-946 1067
Generics, Palmer & Flow, Blax

Vango (Scotland) Ltd
70 East Hamilton Street,
Ladyburn, Greenock PA15 2UB
Tel 01475 744122
Fax 01475 742333
Rossignol

INSURANCE COMPANIES

Accident and General
ISIS Bldg, Thames Quay, 193
Marsh Wall, London E14 9SG
Tel 0171-512 0022
Fax 0171-512 0602

Apple Booking Company
Apple Barn, Smeeth, Ashford,
Kent TN25 6SR
Tel 0800 414141
Fax 01303 812893

BUPA Travel Services
PO Box 2878, Russell Mews,
Brighton BN1 2NZ
Tel 0990 858585
Fax 01273 866191

Bishopsgate Insurance
Bishopsgate House, Tollgate,
Eastleigh, Hants SO53 3YA
Tel 01703 313030
Fax 01703 644614

**British Activity Holiday
Insurance Services**
Security House, Frog Lane,
Tunbridge Wells, Kent TN1 1YT
Tel 01892 534411
Fax 01892 511980
For groups of 4 or more only

**Columbus Travel Insurance
Direct**
17 Devonshire Square, London
EC2M 4SQ
Tel 0171-375 0011
Fax 0171-375 0022

Commercial Union
PO Box 420 St Helens, 1
Undershaft, London EC3P 3DQ
Tel 0171-283 7500
Fax 0171-662 8140

Cork, Bays & Fisher
66 Prescot Street, London
E1 8HG
Tel 0171-481 0707
Fax 0171-464 3340

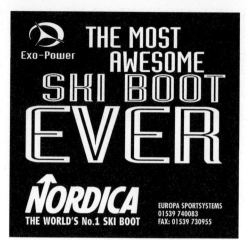

Douglas Cox Tyrie
Central House, 32/66 High
Street, Stratford, London
E15 2PF
Tel 0181-534 9595
Fax 0181-519 8780

Europ Assistance
Sussex House, Perrymount Rd,
Haywards Heath, West Sussex
RH16 1DN
Tel 01444 442211
Fax 01444 459292

General Accident
Pitheavlis, Perth PH2 0NH
Tel 01738 621202
Fax 01738 621843

**Hamilton Barr Insurance
Brokers**
Bridge Mews, Bridge Street,
Godalming, Surrey GU7 1HZ
Tel 01483 426600
Fax 01483 426382

JS Insurance Management Ltd
196-197 High Street, Egham,
Middlesex TW20 9ED
Tel 01784 430043
Fax 01784 472601

Jardine Insurance Brokers
23rd Floor, Sunley Tower,
Piccadilly Plaza, Manchester
M1 4BT
Tel 0161-228 3742
Fax 0161-228 6475

Ketteridge SkiGuard Insurance
26 Cromwell Avenue, Billericay,
Essex CM12 0AE
Tel 01277 630770
Fax 01277 630770

Matthew Gerard
MG House, 7 Westminster
Court, Hipley Street, Old
Woking, Surrey GU22 9LQ
Tel 01483 730900
Fax 01483 730969

**McKlean, Kent and Coomber
(MKC)**
Nevendon Hall, Nevendon
Road, Basildon SS13 1BX
Tel 01268 590658
Fax 01268 590860

P J Hayman & Co
Forestry House, New Barn
Road, Buriton, Nr Petersfield,
Hants GU31 5 SL
Tel 01730 260222
Fax 01730 266655

Perry, Gamble & Co
Tuition House, 27/37 St
George's Road, London
SW19 4XE
Tel 0181-879 1255
Fax 0181-879 1767

Snowcard
Lower Boddington, Daventry,
Northants NN11 6XZ
Tel 01327 262805
Fax 01327 263227

SportsCover Direct Ltd
62 Prince Street, Bristol
BS1 4QD
Tel 0117-922 6222
Fax 0117-922 1666

Suretravel
The Pavilions, Kiln Park
Business Centre, Kiln Lane,
Epsom, Surrey KT17 1JG
Tel 01372 749191
Fax 01372 749701

Whiteley Insurance Consultants
Kingfisher House, Portland
Place, Halifax HX1 2JH
Tel 01422 348411
Fax 01422 330345

NATIONAL TOURIST OFFICES

Andorran Delegation
63 Westover Road, London
SW18 2RF
Tel 0181-874 4806

Argentinian Tourist Board
27 Three Kings Yard, London
W1Y 1FL
Tel 0171-318 1340
Fax 0171-318 1349

Australian Tourist Commission
Gemini House, 10/18 Putney
Hill, Putney, London SW15 6AA
Tel 0181-780 2227
Fax 0181-780 1496

Austrian National Tourist Office
30 St George Street, London
W1R 0AL
Tel 0171-629 0461
Fax 0171-499 6038

Canadian Tourism Commission
62-65 Trafalgar Square,
London WC2N 5DY
Tel 0891 715000
Fax 0171-839 1149

Chile - Consulate General
12 Devonshire Street, London
W1N 2DS
Tel 0171-580 1023
Fax 0171-436 5204

**French Government Tourist
Office**
178 Piccadilly, London
W1V 0AL
Tel 0891 244123
Fax 0171-493 6594

German National Tourist Office
65 Curzon St, London W1Y 8NE
Tel 0891 600100
Fax 0171-495 6129

Italian State Tourist Office
1 Princes St, London W1R 8AY
Tel 0171-408 1254
Fax 0171-493 6695

Japanese Tourist Commission
Tel 0171-734 9638

New Zealand Tourism Board
Haymarket, London SW1Y 4TQ
Tel 0839 300900
Fax 0171-839 8929

Norwegian Tourist Board
Charles House, 5/11 Lower
Regent St, London SW1Y 4LR
Tel 0171-839 6255
Fax 0171-839 6014

Romanian Tourist Office
83A Marylebone High Street,
London W1M 3DE
Tel 0171-224 3692
Fax 0171-224 3692

Scottish Tourist Board
23 Ravelston Terrace,
Edinburgh EH4 3EU
Tel 0131-332 2433
Fax 0131-343 1513

Slovenian Tourist Office
2 Canfield Place, London
NW6 3BT
Tel 0171-372 3844
Fax 0171-372 3763

Spanish Tourist Office
57/58 St James's Street,
London SW1A 1LD
Tel 0171-499 1169
Fax 0171-629 4257

Swedish Travel Council
11 Montague Place, London
W1H 2AL
Tel 0171-724 5868
Fax 0171-724 5872

Switzerland Tourism
Swiss Centre, Swiss Court,
London W1V 8EE
Tel 0171-734 1921
Fax 0171-437 4577

Visit USA Association
Tel 0891 600 530
Also 0897 508 922
Fax: 0897 508 990

RETAILERS

SOUTH-WEST ENGLAND

Aqualeisure
2 Market Place, Melksham,
Wiltshire SN12 6EX
Tel 01225 706604

Team Ski & Leisure
37 High East Street,
Dorchester, Dorset DT1 1HN
Tel 01305 268035

SOUTH-EAST ENGLAND

Captain's Cabin
93 High Street, Chatham,
Chatham, Kent ME4 4DL
Tel 01634 819777

Captain's Cabin
19 Wincheap, Canterbury, Kent
CT1 3TB
Tel 01227 457906

Carters
99-113 Caversham Road,
Reading, Berkshire RG1 8AN
Tel 0118 959 9022
Fax 0118-950 0618

Eurosport (The Board Room)
66-67 North Road, Brighton,
East Sussex BN1 1YD
Tel 01273 688258
Fax 01273 701004

Folkestone Sports Centre Shop
Radnor Park Avenue,
Folkestone, Kent CT19 5HX
Tel 01303 850333
Fax 01303 240842
*Ski and boot hire, ski wear
and accessories*

John Pollock
157 High Road, Loughton,
Essex IG10 4LF
Tel 0181-508 6626

John Pollock
67 High St, Barnet EN5 5UR
Tel 0181-440 3994

Landau Ski & Sports
111 Sandgate Road,
Folkestone, Kent CT20 2BN
Tel 01303 257511

Ski Occasions
The Studio, 50A Friern Barnet
Lane, Near N Finchley, London
N11 3NA
Tel 0181-368 1212
Fax 0181 368 1212
Mobile 0378 513413

Ski Rental Shop
Unit 10, Oakwood Industrial
Park, Gatwick Road, Crawley,
West Sussex RH10 2AZ
Tel 01293 515248
Fax 01293 553536
*Gatwick/Heathrow pick-up and
drop-off*

Snow & Rock
188 Kensington High Street,
London W8 7RG
Tel 0171-937 0872

Snow & Rock
99 Fordwater Road, Chertsey,
Surrey KT16 8HH
Tel 01932 569569

Snow & Rock
150 Holborn, Corner of Grays
Inn Road, London EC1N 2LC
Tel 0171-831 6900

Snow Boats
8-10 The Street, Wrecclesham,
Farnham, Surrey GU10 4PR
Tel 01252 715169

Snowshoes
133 Worplesdon Road,
Guildford, Surrey GU2 6XA
Tel 01483 573032
Fax 01483 573032

Surf & Ski Sports Limited
1-2 Regent Street, Brighton,
East Sussex BN1 1UL
Tel 01273 673193

WALES

Barry Ski Lodge
Cardiff Road, Barry, South
Glamorgan CF63 2QW
Tel 01446 741870

MIDDLE ENGLAND

Attwoolls Ski Shop
Bristol Road, Whitminster,
Gloucestershire GL2 7LX
Tel 01452 740278

Beans
86 Sheep Street, Bicester,
Oxfordshire OX6 7LP
Tel 01869 246451

Canyon Mountain Sports
92 Granby Street, Leicester,
Leicestershire LE1 1DJ
Tel 0116-255 7957

Lockwoods Ski Shop
125-129 Rugby Road,
Leamington Spa CV32 6DJ
Tel 01926 339388
Fax 01926 470408

Outdoor Shop
27-31 High Street, Stony
Stratford, Milton Keynes
MK11 1AA
Tel 01908 568913
Fax 01908 265253

Snow & Rock
14 Priory Queensway,
Birmingham B4 6BS
Tel 0121-236 8280

Solihull Ski Centre
100 Widney Rd, Solihull
Tel 01564 774176

Two Seasons
42 Harpur Street, Bedford
MK40 2QT
Tel 01234 350720

Two Seasons
203 Wellingborough Road,
Northampton NN1 4ED
Tel 01604 27377

EASTERN ENGLAND

Countryside Ski & Climb
118 High Street, Stevenage,
Hertfordshire SG1 3DW
Tel 01438 353086

John Pollock
Harlow Ski Slope, Harlow
Sports Centre, Hammarskjold
Way, Harlow, Essex CM20 2JF
Tel 01279 425009

Ski Exchange
27 Dry Drayton Inds, Scotland
Road, Cambridge CB3 8AT
Tel 01954 210984
Fax 01954 212220

Snow & Rock
Hemel Ski Centre, St Albans
Hill, Hemel Hempstead
HP3 9NH
Tel 01442 235305

Top Gear
3/5 Broadway, Leigh on Sea,
Essex
Tel 01702 713165

NORTHERN ENGLAND

Alpine Centre
193 Church Street, Blackpool,
Lancashire FY1 3NY
Tel 01253 24307

BAC Outdoor Leisure
Central Hall, Coronation Street,
Elland, Halifax HX5 0DF
Tel 01422 371146
Fax 01422 371146

H D Cocker and Sons
58 Keirby Walk, Burnley,
Lancashire BB11 2DE
Tel 01282 425830

Mountain & Marine
157-159 London Road South,
Poynton, Cheshire SK12 1LQ
Tel 01625 859863
Fax 01625 859878

Snow & Rock
Sheffield Ski Centre, Vale
Road, Parkwood Springs,
Sheffield S3 9SJ
Tel 0114-275 1700

SCOTLAND

David Low Sports
21 Commercial Street, Dundee,
Tayside DD1 3DD
Tel 01382 224501
Fax 01382 221752

NORTHERN IRELAND

Topping Leisure
2 High Street, Comber, County
Down BT23 5HL
Tel 01247 873590

SKI/BOARDING ORGANISATIONS

Artificial Ski Slope Instructors (ASSI)
The English Ski Council, Area
Library Building, Queensway
Mall, The Cornbow, Halesowen,
West Midlands B63 4AJ
Tel 0121-501 2314
Fax 0121-585 6448

British Association of Ski Instructors (BASI)
Glenmore, Aviemore PH22 1QU
Tel 01479 861717
Fax 01479 861718

British Ski Association
19 Market Street, Carnforth,
Lancashire LA5 9JR
Tel 01524 720920
Fax 01524 720087

British Ski Club for the Disabled
Springmount, Berwick St John,
Shaftesbury SP7 0HQ
Tel 01747 828515

British Ski Federation
258 Main Street, East Calder,
West Lothian EH53 0EE
Tel 01506 884343
Fax 01506 882952

British Snowboarding Association
5 Cressex Rd, High Wycombe,
Bucks HP12 4PG
Tel 01494 462225
Fax 01494 462225

English Ski Council
Area Library, Queensway Mall,
Cornbow, Halesowen, West
Midlands B63 4AJ
Tel 0121-501 2314
Fax 0121-585 6448

Scottish National Ski Council
Caledonia House, South Gyle,
Edinburgh EH12 9DQ
Tel 0131-317 7280
Fax 0131-339 8602

Ski Club of Great Britain
The White House, 57-63
Church Road, Wimbledon,
London SW19 5DQ
Tel 0181-410 2000
Fax 0181-410 2001

Ski Council of Wales
240 Whitchurch Road, Cardiff
CF4 3ND
Tel 01222 619637
Fax 01222 522178

The Uphill Ski Club
12 Park Crescent, London
W1N 4EQ
Tel 0171-636 1989
Fax 0171-436 2601
For disabled skiers

TRANSPORT

AIRLINES

Air Canada
Tel 0990 247226

Air France
Tel 0181-742 6600

Air UK Ltd
Tel 0345 666777

Alitalia
Tel 0171-602 7111

American Airlines
Tel 0181-572 5555
Linkline 0345 789789

Austrian Airlines
Tel 0171-434 7300

British Airways
Tel 0345 222111

Canadian Airlines
Tel 0345 616767

Continental Airlines
Tel 0800 776464

Delta Airlines
Tel 0800 414767

Lauda Air
Tel 0171-630 5924
Freephone 0800 767737

Lufthansa German Airlines
Tel 0181-750 3500

Northwest Airlines
Tel 01293 561000

Swissair
Tel 0171-434 7300

United Airlines
Tel 0181-990 9900
Freephone 0800 888 555

Virgin Atlantic Airways
Tel 01293 747747

AIRPORTS

Aberdeen
Tel 01224 722331

Belfast
Tel 01849 422888

Birmingham
Tel 0121-767 5511

Bournemouth
Tel 01202 364000

Bristol
Tel 01275 474444

Cardiff
Tel 01446 711111

Dublin
Tel 00 353 1 8444900

East Midlands
Tel 01332 852852

Edinburgh
Tel 0131-333 1000

Exeter and Devon
Tel 01392 367433

Glasgow
Tel 0141-887 1111

Leeds-Bradford
Tel 0113-250 9696

London Gatwick
Tel 01293 535353

London Heathrow
Tel 0181-759 4321

London Luton
Tel 01582 405100

London Stansted
Tel 01279 680500

Manchester
Tel 0161-489 3000

Newcastle
Tel 0191-286 0966

Teesside
Tel 01325 332811

CAR HIRE

Alamo Rent-a-Car
Tel 0990 994000
Fax 01273 223315

Avis
Tel 0181-848 8765
Fax 0181-561 2604

Budget Rent-a-Car
Tel 0541 565656
Fax 01442 276000

Eurodollar
Tel 0990 565656
Fax 01895 256050

Europcar Interrent
Tel 01923 811000
Fax 01923 811010

Hertz
Tel 0990 996699
Fax 0181-679 2448

Holiday Autos International Ltd
Tel 0990 300400
Fax 0990 300430

Suncars
Tel 0990 005566
Fax 01444 441234

CROSS-CHANNEL TRAVEL

Brittany Ferries
Tel 0990 360360
Fax 01752 661308
Portsmouth–Caen

Holyman Sally Lines
Tel 0990 595522
Fax 01843 589329
Ramsgate–Dunkerque or Ostend

Hoverspeed Fast Ferries
Tel 0990 240241
Fax 01304 240088
Dover–Calais, Folkestone–Boulogne

Le Shuttle
Tel 0990 353535
Fax 01303 288784
Folkestone–Calais (tunnel)

P & O European Ferries
Tel 0990 9890980
Fax 01304 863464
Dover–Calais, Portsmouth–Le Havre, Portsmouth–Cherbourg, Felixstowe–Zeebrugge

P & O North Sea Ferries
Tel 01482 377177
Fax 01482 706438
Hull–Zeebrugge or Rotterdam

Stena Line
Tel 0990 707070
Fax 01233 202349
Routes: Dover–Calais, Harwich –Hook, Newhaven–Dieppe

RAILWAYS

British Rail International
Tel 0990 848848
Fax 0171-922 9874

French Railways
Tel 0990 300 003
Fax 0171-409 2408
Motorail: 0171-203 7000

German Rail
Tel 0181-390 8833
Fax 0181-399 4700

Swiss Federal Railways
Tel 0171-734 1921
Fax 0171-437 4577R

Resort directory / Index

As well as the resorts we've covered in detail there are literally hundreds more in the Alps and North America, most of them much smaller than those we've covered in full, but still worth a short visit. Many are covered by multi-resort lift passes, so that you can easily visit a number in one week. Here we give brief details on another 750-plus. We also list the pages on which you'll find the in-depth coverage of the main resorts. Note: all places named after saints are ordered in a single sequence, regardless of local spellings of Saint, San, Sankt or whatever.

Key
- ⛟ *Lifts*
- ⛷ *Pistes*
- ⊠ *UK Tour operators*

49 Degrees North   USA
Inland area with best snow in Washington State including 120-acre bowl reserved for powder weekends.
1193m; slopes 1193–1754m
⛟4 ⛷920 acres

Abetone   Italy
Resort in the exposed Appenines, less than two hours from Florence and Pisa.
1390m; slopes 1390–2160m
⛟27 ⛷50km
⊠ *Alpine Tours*

Abtenau   Austria
Sizeable village in Dachstein-West region near Salzburg, on large plain ideal for cross-country for which it's known.
712m; slopes 712–1260m
⛟7 ⛷15km

Achenkirch   Austria
Unspoilt, low-altitude Tirolean village close to Niederau and Alpbach, in a beautiful setting overlooking a lake.
930m; slopes 950–1800m
⛟7 ⛷25km ⊠ *Ramblers*

Adelboden   **348**

Les Aillons   France
Traditional village near Chambéry, attractive on bad-weather.
1000m; slopes 1000–1900m
⛟25 ⛷50km

Aix-les-Thermes   France
Sizeable spa village with own train station near Font-Romeu and Andorra. Near Carcassone and Lourdes.
1400m; slopes 1400–2400m
⛟17 ⛷26km

Akakura   Japan
Old spa of some oriental charm, 150km from Tokyo, with a modern lift system serving mostly easy runs.
770m; slopes 770–1500m
⛟41 ⛷85km

Alagna   **319**

Alba   Italy
Picturesque Dolomite village with a small, quiet area, with access to the Sella Ronda at nearby Canazei.
1515m; slopes 1515–2430m
⛟5 ⛷10km ⊠ *Chalets 'Unlimited', Crystal*

Alleghe   Italy
Dolomite village in a pretty lakeside setting. Cheap base near Cortina.
980m ⛟24 ⛷80km
⊠ *Altours Ski*

Alpbach   **84**

Alpe-d'Huez   **167**

Alpe des Chaux   **401**

Alpe-du-Grand-Serre   France
Tiny resort near Alpe-d'Huez and Les Deux-Alpes. Good for bad-weather days.
1400m; slopes 1400–2200m
⛟20 ⛷34km

Alpendorf   Austria
Hamlet-cum-base-station 4km from St Johann im Pongau, with immediate access to the Salzburger Sportwelt area.
800m; slopes 800–2185m
⛟59 ⛷200km

Alpental-Snoqualmie-Ski Acres-Hyak   USA
One of the few American places with interlinked lifts, European-style. Damp weather and wet snow are drawbacks.
slopes 972–1640m
⛟33 ⛷1916 acres

Alpine Meadows   **425**

Alps   Korea
Korea's most northerly, snow-reliable resort. An hour from Seoul. Enormous ski-to-the-door condo high-rise complex.
⛟5

Alta   **472**

Altenmarkt   Austria
Unspoilt village well placed just off the Salzburg-Villach autobahn for numerous resorts including snowsure Obertauern and Wagrain.
855m; slopes 855–2240m
⛟28 ⛷150km
⊠ *Alpine Tours, Made to Measure, Sloping Off*

Alto Campoo   Spain
Barren, desolate place with undistinguished slopes but single hotel is superb and wilderness views from mountain magnificent.
1700m; slopes 1650–2125m
⛟6

Alt St Johann   Switzerland
Old cross-country village with Alpine slopes connecting into Unterwasser area near Liechtenstein.
900m; slopes 900–2260m
⛟21 ⛷50km

Alyeska   USA
Alaskan area 60km from Anchorage, with luxury hotel. Spring best for weather.
94m; slopes 94–960m
⛟7 ⛷1200 acres

Aminona   **356**

Andalo   Italy
Atmospheric Dolomite village near Madonna, with low wooded slopes well equipped with snowmakers; best for novices.
1050m; slopes 1040–2125m
⛟17 ⛷40km ⊠ *Alpine Tours, Equity Total Ski, First Choice Ski, PGL Ski Europe, STS, Sloping Off, Winterski*

Andermatt   **349**

Andorra La Vella   **515**

Angel Fire   USA
Intermediate neighbour of Taos, New Mexico. Height usually ensures good snow. Interesting sightseeing.
2582m; slopes 2582–3245m
⛟6 ⛷320 acres

Les Angles   France
Characterless Pyrenean resort with a good sports centre and varied slopes, worth a day-trip from nearby Font-Romeu.
1600m; slopes 1650–2375m
⛟19 ⛷40km ⊠ *Lagrange*

Annaberg-Lungötz   Austria
Peaceful village in a pretty setting, sharing a sizeable area with Gosau, close to Filzmoos.
780m; slopes 780–1700m
⛟35 ⛷50km

Antagnod   Italy
Weekend day-tripper area on way up to Champoluc, above Aosta valley. No village.
1710m; slopes 1710–2000m
⛟4 ⛷7km

Anzère   Switzerland
Sympathetically designed modern resort on a sunny balcony near Crans-Montana, with slopes suited to leisurely intermediates.
1500m; slopes 1500–2460m
⛟12 ⛷40km
⊠ *Fairhand Holidays, Lagrange, Made to Measure*

Apex Alpine   Canada
Modern village built on Wild West theme, in Disneyesque style. More limited slopes than other resorts in region.
1575m; slopes 1575–2178m
⛟4 ⛷505 acres
⊠ *Ski Safari, Skisar U.S.*

Aprica   Italy
Ugly, straggling village between Lake Como and Brenta Dolomites, with bland slopes and limited facilities.
1175m; slopes 1175–2575m
⛟30 ⛷60km
⊠ *Equity School Ski, PGL Ski Europe, STS, Ski Club Europe, Winterski*

Arabba   **333**

Aragnouet-Piau   France
Purpose-built mid-mountain satellite of St-Lary best suited to families, beginners and early intermediates.
1850m; slopes 1420–2500m
⛟32 ⛷80km

Arapahoe Basin   **449**

Arcalis   **515**

Les Arcs   **175**

Ardent   **181**

Åre   **531**
380m; slopes 380–1275m
⛟44 ⛷90km ⊠ *Crystal*

Arêches   France
Pretty resort with low wooded slopes, tucked away off the Bourg-Albertville 'B' road.
1080m; slopes 1080–2100m
⛟13 ⛷35km ⊠ *Inntravel*

Big Powderhorn　　USA
Area with most 'resort' facilities in south Lake Superior region – highest lift capacity too. Extensive regional lift pass but areas suffer from winds.
370m; slopes 370–559m
🚡 9　🎿 215 acres

Big Thunder National Ski Training Centre　Canada
Steep slopes for would-be Olympians on north shore of Lake Superior. Two other areas nearby. Cross-country layout hosted 1995 Nordic World Championships.
🚡 5

Bischofshofen　　Austria
Working town cum mountain resort near St Johann im Pongau with limited runs on local hill and main slopes starting nearby at Muhlbach.
547m; slopes 790–1900m
🚡 42　🎿 160km

Bivio　　Switzerland
Quiet village near St Moritz with easy slopes opened up by a few drag lifts.
1780m; slopes 1780–2600m
🚡 4　🎿 35km

Bizau　　Austria
One of two main areas in low Bregenzerwald region north-west of Lech.
680m; slopes 680–1640m

Bjorkliden　　531
🚡 5　🎿 15km
✉ Ski Scandinavia

Blackcomb　　508

Blatten-Naters　Switzerland
Stunning glacial scenery, immediately above Brig, with larger Aletsch slopes nearby.
675m; slopes 1325–2880m
🚡 9　🎿 60km

Bled　　Slovenia
Beautiful lakeside base from which to drive to several nearby areas. Its own slopes are very limited.
503m; slopes 503–1265m
🚡 5　🎿 16km
✉ Alpine Tours, Crystal

Blue River　　Canada
Base of world-famous Mike Wiegele heli-ski operation in Cariboo and Monashee mountains. High standard in-the-mountains retreat with all mod cons.
✉ Chinook-It, Ski Scott Dunn

Blue Cow　　535
1900m; slopes 1620–1980m
🚡 14　🎿 889 acres

Blue Mountain　　Canada
Largest area in Ontario, with glorious views of Lake Huron. High-capacity lift system. 96% snowmaking. Worthwhile excursion from nearby Toronto or Niagara Falls.
229m; slopes 229–448m
🚡 15　🎿 310 acres
✉ All Canada Ski

Bluewood　　USA
Particularly remote area even by American north-west standards. Worth a visit if you're in Walla Walla.
1374m; slopes 1374–1716m
🚡 3　🎿 430 acres

Bogus Basin　　USA
Idaho's most extensive area (bigger than Sun Valley). Large floodlit operation; wooded slopes.
1762m; slopes 1762–2309m
🚡 10　🎿 2600 acres

Bohinj　　Slovenia
Lakeside village near Bled set in a beautiful valley, with lovely views from its plateau area of short runs high above.
540m; slopes 1535–1880m
🚡 6　🎿 20km
✉ Alpine Tours, Crystal

Bois-d'Amont　　France
One of four resorts that make up Rousses area in Jura region. Useful stopover.
1050m; slopes 1120–1680m
🚡 40　🎿 43km

Bolognola　　Italy
Tiny area in Macerata region near Adriatic Riviera.
1280m; slopes 1280–1844m
🚡 7

Bolton Valley　　USA
Neighbour of Vermont's loveliest ski village, Stowe. Amtrak run ski train to nearby Waterbury and Burlington. Mostly intermediate slopes.
463m; slopes 463–957m
🚡 6　🎿 150 acres

Le Bonhomme　　France
One of several areas near Strasbourg, relatively close to Channel. Like most resorts in region, has snowmakers.
830m; slopes 830–1235m
🚡 11　🎿 13km

Bonneval-sur-Arc　France
Unspoilt old village in the Haute Maurienne valley with many of its slopes above 2500m (and fanciful ambitions to link to Val-d'Isère).
2000m; slopes 1800–3000m
🚡 10　🎿 40km　✉ Inntravel

Boreal　　USA
Closest area to north Lake Tahoe town, Truckee. Limited slopes best for novices but has largest snowboard park in California. Northstar, Squaw Valley, Diamond Peak nearby.
2187m; slopes 2187–2370m
🚡 9　🎿 380 acres

Bormio　　301

Borovets　　524

Bosco Chiesanuova　Italy
Weekend day tripper's place near Verona. A long drive from any other resort.
1190m; slopes 1190–1805m
🚡 13　🎿 30km

La Bourboule　　France
Spa village cum cross-country centre with Alpine slopes of Le Mont-Dore nearby. Amid spectacular extinct-volcano scenery.
850m; slopes 1050–1850m
🚡 41　🎿 80km　✉ Lagrange

Bourg-St-Maurice　　175

Bourg-d'Oisans　　France
Pleasant valley town on main Grenoble-Briançon road. Civilised, inexpensive base from which to visit Alpe-d'Huez and Les Deux-Alpes.

Boyne Highlands　　USA
Area with impressive, high-capacity lift system for weekend Detroit crowds. Fierce winds off Lake Michigan a major drawback.
226m; slopes 226–391m
🚡 11　🎿 200 acres

Boyne Mountain　　USA
Weekend Detroit crowds. Not as windy as sister Boyne Highlands. Shared lift pass.
188m; slopes 188–340m
🚡 10　🎿 115 acres

Bramans　　France
Old cross-country village (50km of trails) near Modane. Well placed for touring numerous nearby resorts such as Val-Cenis and Valloire.
1230m;　🚡 1

Bramberg　　Austria
Village near Pass Thurn (Kitzbühel area). Shares odd area with Neukirchen – only valley lift in Neukirchen with best runs to liftless Bramberg.
820m; slopes 855–2130m
🚡 13　🎿 35km

Brand　　Austria
Old family favourite, unpopular these days, perhaps because it lacks the charm to compensate for its small, low area.
1035m; slopes 1035–1920m
🚡 7　🎿 29km

Les Brasses　　France
Collective name for six hamlets with some of the closest slopes to Geneva, but known for cross-country.
900m; slopes 900–1600m
🚡 17　🎿 50km　✉ Lagrange

Braunwald　　Switzerland
Sunny but limited area, a funicular ride above Linthal.
1300m; slopes 1300–1910m
🚡 8

Breckenridge　　439

Brentonico　　Italy
Little resort just off Verona-Trento motorway. Worth half-day visit in conjunction with a look at Lake Garda.
1160m; slopes 1160–1520m
🚡 16　🎿 11km

La Bresse　　France
Largest of ski areas near Nancy and Strasbourg. Relatively close to Channel. 200 snow cannon help.
630m; slopes 630–1635m
🚡 30　🎿 60km　✉ Lagrange

Bretton Woods　　USA
Area with best snowfall record in New Hampshire; mostly easy slopes. Attractive base lodge, good views.
486m; slopes 486–941m
🚡 5　🎿 180 acres
✉ Virgin Snow

Briançon　　265

Brian Head　　USA
Utah area south of Salt Lake City, too far from Park City for day trip.
2917m; slopes 2917–3318m
🚡 6　🎿 825 acres

Brides-les-Bains　　233

Bridger Bowl　　USA
Area near Big Sky and Bozeman, best for experts – only a third of area is groomed. Good powder!
1853m; slopes 1853–2461m
🚡 6　🎿 1200 acres

Brighton　　USA
Near Salt Lake City, and better all-round area than neighbour Solitude, with challenging runs and superb powder areas.
2660m; slopes 2660–3190m
🚡 7　🎿 850 acres
✉ Skisar U.S.

Brixen　　151

Brodie Mountain　　USA
Largest Massachusetts area. Popular with young singles for its lively Irish folk music après-ski. 100% snowmaking. Mostly easy slopes.
440m; slopes 440–820m
🚡 6　🎿 325 acres

Ellmau 91

Encamp 515

Enego Italy
Limited weekend day-trippers' area near Vicenza and Trento.
1300m; slopes 1300–1443m
🚡 7 🎿 30km

Engelberg 367

Entrèves 314

Essert-Romand 245

Etna Italy
Scenic, uncrowded, short-season area on the volcano's flank, near Nickolossi.
1800m; slopes 1800–2350m
🎿 5km

Evolene Switzerland
Charming rustic village in unspoilt, attractive setting south of Sion. Own little area, with Verbier's slopes accessed at nearby Les Masses.
1350m; slopes 1300–3330m
🚡 100 🎿 400km

Faak am See Austria
Limited area, one of five overlooking town of Villach.
840m; slopes 840–1050m
🚡 4 🎿 3km

Fairmont Hot Springs Canada
Major luxury spa complex ideal for relaxing holiday with some gentle skiing thrown in.
1276m; slopes 1276–1580m
🚡 2 🎿 60 acres

Faistenau Austria
Cross-country centre close to Salzburg and St Wolfgang. Limited Alpine area.
786m 🚡 5

Falcade Italy
Largest of many little ski areas close to but not part of Sella Ronda.
1145m; slopes 1145–2168m
🚡 11 🎿 39km
✉ *Alpine Tours, Winterski*

Falera 368

Le Falgoux France
One of the most beautiful old villages in France. In very scenic Volcano National Park. Several ski areas nearby.
930m; slopes 930–1350m

Falkertsee Austria
Base area with bleak, open slopes in contrast to nearby Badkleinkirchheim.
1690m; slopes 1690–2385m
🚡 5 🎿 15km

Falls Creek Australia
Euro-style modern on-mountain family resort, five hours from Melbourne, with a fair network of short intermediate runs.
1600m; slopes 1500–1780m
🚡 22 🎿 1115 acres

Farelones-La Parva Chile
Chile's best and most well liked ski area, an hour from Santiago. Crowded at weekends.

La Feclaz France
One of several little resorts in remote Parc des Bauges. Close to Chambéry by crow flight but miles from anywhere by road.

Fernie 514
1065m; slopes 1065–1800m
🚡 7 🎿 800 acres
✉ *All Canada Ski, Chinook-It, Frontier Ski, Ski Safari*

Fieberbrunn 96

Fiesch Switzerland
Traditional Rhône valley resort close to Brig, with a lift into the beautiful Aletsch area.
1050m; slopes 1925–2710m
🚡 26 🎿 90km
✉ *SkiGower*

Filzmoos Austria
Charming, unspoilt, friendly village; leisurely slopes, ideal for novices. Good snow record for its height.
1060m; slopes 1060–1645m
🚡 16 🎿 32km
✉ *Inghams, Made to Measure*

Finkenberg 115

Fiss 149

Flachau Austria
Quiet village in a pretty setting at one end of three-valley lift network.
925m; slopes 800–2185m
🚡 59 🎿 200km
✉ *Ski Club Europe*

Flachauwinkl Austria
Well placed within the Salzburger Sportwelt area, but with the Salzburg-Villach autobahn carving through it.
930m; slopes 800–2185m
🚡 59 🎿 200km

Flaine 215

Flims 368

Flumet France
Surprisingly large resort, well placed for whole Mont Blanc area. Cheap big-village alternative to Megève.
1000m; slopes 1036–2070m
🚡 50 🎿 150km

Flumserberg Switzerland
Collective name for villages sharing a varied area an hour south-east of Zurich.
1220–1400m; slopes 1220–2220m
🚡 16 🎿 40km

Folgaria Italy
Largest of several resorts east of Trento. Old lift system (90% drags).
1175m; slopes 1175–1880m
🚡 18 🎿 24km
✉ *Alpine Tours, Crystal, Equity School Ski, STS*

Folgarida 325

Foncine-le-Haut France
Major cross-country centre with 220km of trails, relatively close to Channel.
✉ *Lagrange*

Fonni Gennaragentu Italy
Sardinia's only 'ski area'. Barely exists.
🚡 1 🎿 5km

Font-Romeu France
Family resort set in woodland, with the biggest snowmaking set-up in the Pyrenees.
1800m; slopes 1750–2220m
🚡 33 🎿 30km
✉ *Lagrange*

Foppolo Italy
Relatively unattractive but user-friendly village, a short transfer from Bergamo, best for families on a budget.
1510m; slopes 1105–2300m
🚡 15 🎿 47km
✉ *Crystal, Equity School Ski, Equity Total Ski, First Choice Ski, Winterski*

Forca Canapine Italy
Limited area near Adriatic and town of Ascoli Piceno. Weekend day-tripper spot.
1450m; slopes 1450–1690m
🚡 11 🎿 20km

Formazza Italy
On Swiss border close to Jungfrau by crow flight but miles from anywhere by road.
1280m; slopes 1280–1810m
🚡 5 🎿 10km

Formigal 522
1520m; slopes 1510–2250m
🚡 20 🎿 50km
✉ *Inghams, Thomson*

Le Fornet 277

Forstau Austria
Secluded hamlet above Radstadt-Schladming road. Very limited area with old lifts, but nice and quiet.
930m; slopes 930–1880m
🚡 8 🎿 14km

Fortress Mountain Canada
One of two areas near Kananaskis (17km away). Renowned for powder snow, dramatic scenery, uncrowded (weekdays) slopes, snowcat excursions.
2133m; slopes 2133–2468m
🚡 6 🎿 320 acres

La Foux-d'Allos France
Purpose-built resort that shares a good, intermediate area with Pra-Loup.
1800m; slopes 1500–2600m
🚡 63 🎿 230km
✉ *Fairhand Holidays, Lagrange*

Frabosa Soprana Italy
One of numerous little areas south of Turin, well placed for combining winter sports with Riviera sightseeing.
891m; slopes 891–1741m
🚡 9 🎿 30km

Frisco 439

Frontignano Italy
Best lift system in Macerata region near Adriatic Riviera.
1340m; slopes 1340–2000m
🚡 8 🎿 10km

Fügen Austria
Unspoilt village with limited area best suited to beginners, poorly placed for other Zillertal resorts.
560m; slopes 560–2310m
🚡 17 🎿 48km

Fulpmes Austria
Sizeable village in a beautiful valley, with a small area of its own, close to Neustift and the Stubai glacier.
960m; slopes 960–2260m
🚡 9 🎿 25km
✉ *Alpine Tours, Crystal*

Furano Japan
Small Hokkaido resort. One of the few Japanese areas to get reasonable powder.
🚡 19

Furasdalen Sweden
Cross-country Mecca. Home of world's longest ski trails, with 300m vertical of Alpine runs. Top-class facilities throughout.
🚡 33 🎿 72km

Fusch Austria
Across golf course from Kaprun and Schuttdorf. Cheap(er), quiet place to stay when visiting Zell am See.
805m; slopes 760–2000m
🚡 55 🎿 130km
✉ *STS*

Fuschl Austria
Attractive, unspoilt, lakeside village close to St Wolfgang and Salzburg, 30 minutes from its slopes. Best suited to part-time skiers-cum-sightseers.
670m; slopes 750–1350m
🚡 9 🎿 17km
✉ *Crystal*

Haus in Ennstal 144

Haute-Nendaz 393

Heavenly 420

Hebalm Austria
One of many small areas in
Austria's easternmost ski
region near Slovenian border.
No major resorts in vicinity.
1050m; slopes 1050–1400m
🚡 6 🎿 10km

Heiligenblut Austria
Picturesque village in
beautiful surroundings with
mostly high terrain. Its remote
position west of Bad Gastein
ensures crowds don't invade.
1300m; slopes 1300–2900m
🚡 12 🎿 55km
✉ Inghams

Hemlock Resort Canada
Area 75 miles east of
Vancouver on way to Sun
Peaks, with amazing snowfall
(600 inches a year) . Mostly
intermediate terrain. Lodging
at base area.
972m; slopes 972–1337m
🚡 4 🎿 350 acres

Hemsedal 529
650m; slopes 650–1450m
🚡 16 🎿 35km
✉ Crystal, Inghams, Ski
Scandinavia

Heremence Switzerland
Quiet village in unspoilt
attractive setting south of
Sion. Verbier slopes accessed
a few minutes' drive away at
Les Masses.
1250m; slopes 1300–3330m
🚡 100 🎿 400km

Hermagor Austria
Carinthian village below the
Sonnenalpe ski area. Franz
Klammer rates this one of the
best areas in Austria.
600m; slopes 1210–2005m
🚡 23 🎿 101km

Himos Finland
1995 Finnish ski resort of the
year. Varied Alpine skiing,
half-pipes and snowboard
park, cross-country.
🚡 9

Hintersee Austria
Very close to Salzburg.
Several long top-to-bottom
pistes and lifts, so size of
area greatly reduced if
snowline high. Easy slopes.
746m; slopes 750–1570m
🚡 10 🎿 40km

Hinterstoder Austria
Quiet, unspoilt traditional
village, 80km east of
Salzburg, with a good snow
record for its height.
600m; slopes 600–1860m
🚡 15 🎿 35km

Hintertux 97

Hippach Austria
Hamlet near a queue-free lift
into Mayrhofen's main area.
600m; slopes 625–2095m
🚡 33 🎿 64km

Hochgurgl 121

Hochsölden 150

Hochybrig Switzerland
Purpose-built complex only
64km south of Zurich, with
facilities for families.
1050m; slopes 1050–2200m
🚡 16 🎿 50km

Hohuanshan Taiwan
Limited ski area with short
season in high wild
inaccessible Miitaku
mountains.
3275m 🚡 1

Hollersbach Austria
Pass Thurn hamlet near
Mittersill. Uncrowded base
from which to visit Kitzbühel
if snowline low; Kaprun,
Gerlos, Matrei and Uttendorf if
high.
806m; slopes 1265–2000m
🚡 8 🎿 45km

Homewood USA
Area with unsurpassed Lake
Tahoe views, near
accommodation centre Tahoe
City. Most sheltered slopes in
vicinity so a good choice in
bad weather.
1893m; slopes 1893–2394m
🚡 10 🎿 1260 acres

Hoodoo Ski Bowl USA
Area east of Eugene with
plans to expand, but snow
record isn't as good as
competitors near Portland.
Typical Oregon area –
sizeable but short runs.
1418m; slopes 1418–1732m
🚡 4 🎿 600 acres

Hopfgarten 151

Horseshoe Resort Canada
Toronto region resort with
high-capacity lift system,
100% snowmaking. Second
mountain – The Heights –
doubles size of area but is
open to members only.
311m; slopes 311–405m
🚡 7 🎿 60 acres

Hospental 349

Les Houches 185

Hovden Norway
Big, modern luxury lakeside
hotel in wilderness midway
between Oslo and Bergen.
Cross-country centre with
Alpine slopes as side-line.
759m; slopes 759–1206m
🚡 2

Hunter Mountain USA
New Yorkers' favourite area
so it gets very crowded at
weekends – and also
Wednesdays. OK slopes by
eastern standards.
303m; slopes 303–607m
🚡 16 🎿 210 acres

Hüttschlag Austria
Hamlet in dead-end valley
with lifts into Gastein area at
neighbouring Grossarl.
1020m; slopes 840–2685m
🚡 53 🎿 250km

Hyundai Sungwoo Korea
21 slopes. Massive high-rise
monstrosity with plans for
future expansion, two hours
from Seoul. 🚡 8

Idre Sweden
Collective name for four areas
whose lifts and buses are on
one pass. Snowsure but only
300m vertical.
🚡 32 🎿 25km

Igls Austria
Traditional resort near
Innsbruck, with tall but
limited area.
895m; slopes 895–2250m
🚡 6 🎿 14km
✉ Austrian Holidays,
Inghams, Lagrange, Made to
Measure

Iizuna Japan
Tiny area one hour from 1998
Olympic site Nagano, four
hours from Tokyo.
🚡 5

Incline Village 425

Indianhead USA
South Lake Superior area with
most snowfall in region.
Intermediate cruising terrain
too. Winds are a problem.
394m; slopes 394–587m
🚡 9 🎿 160 acres

Inneralpbach 84

Innerarosa 350

Innsbruck Austria
Lively and interesting city at
Alpine crossroads, surrounded
by small areas, each ideal for
a day-trip.
575m; slopes 870–2350m
🚡 33 🎿 92km
✉ Austrian Holidays, Made
to Measure, Ramblers

Interlaken 402

Ischgl 98

**Ishiuchi Maruyama-Yuzawa
Kogen** Japan
Sizeable resorts a few
minutes from one another
that share lift pass offering
largest area in central Honshu
region. Only 1.5 hours from
Tokyo. 🚡 56

Isola 2000 222

Iso-Syote Finland
Southernmost downhill skiing
in Finland. Finnish
championship venue, but
mostly easy skiing. Main hotel
at top of mountain.
432m; slopes 240–432m
🚡 11 🎿 21km

Itter 151

Jackson Hole 483

Jasper 507

Jay Peak USA
Vermont resort near Canadian
border with best snowfall
record in the east. Tree-lined
intermediate slopes.
551m; slopes 551–1205m
🚡 6 🎿 325 acres

Jochberg 103

La Joue-du-Loup France
Purpose-built little ski-in/ski-
out family resort. Shares
sizeable intermediate area
with Superdévoluy. High
proportion of drags.
1470m; slopes 1470–2510m
🚡 31 🎿 105km

Jouvenceaux 328

Jukkasjarn Sweden
Centuries-old resort with
unique hotel – rebuilt every
December out of 3,000 tons
of snow and ice.

June Mountain USA
Well liked by day-visitors from
nearby, lift pass-sharing
Mammoth. Quiet slopes and
superb school.
2295m; slopes 2295–3090m
🚡 9 🎿 500 acres

Juns 97

Kals am Grossglockner
Austria
Village in remote valley north
of Lienz. Planned link with
Matrei will transform area to
sizeable proportions.
1325m; slopes 1325–2065m

Kaltenbach Austria
Village with one of the larger,
quieter Zillertal areas, with
plenty of slopes above
1800m.
560m; slopes 560–2300m
🚡 12 🎿 59km

Kananaskis 514
slopes 1525–2468m
🚡 12 🎿 605 acres
✉ All Canada Ski, Canada's
Best, Crystal, Frontier Ski,
Made to Measure, Skisar U.S.

Lienz Austria
Pleasant town-cum-resort in pretty surroundings.
720m; slopes 730–2280m
⛷ 12 ✝ 55km

Lillehammer 529
180m; slopes 180–1050m
⛷ 13 ✝ 35km ✉ Inntravel

Limone Italy
Pleasant old railway town not far from Turin, with a pretty area, far from snowsure. A taste of the 'real' Italy.
1010m; slopes 1000–2040m
⛷ 33 ✝ 80km
✉ Neilson, STS

Lindvallen-Hogfjallet Sweden
Largest ski area (but two unlinked mountains) in Scandanavia. Start of Vasalopp, world's largest cross-country race. Also has world's first ski-through McDonald's!
623m; slopes 623–926m
⛷ 72 ✝ 85km

Livigno 320

Lizzola Italy
Small base development in remote spot north of Bergamo. Several other little areas nearby.
1250m; slopes 1250–2070m
⛷ 9 ✝ 30km

Llaima Chile
Exotic, popular ski touring area (Alpine and Nordic) around and below a mildy active volcano with trails through dense trees.
1500m

Loch Lomond Canada
Shares lift pass with neighbour Candy Mountain near Thunder Bay on shores of Lake Superior. Third area close-by. Challenging slopes – steep, narrow, bumpy.
228m; slopes 228–471m
⛷ 7

Lofer Austria
Quiet, traditional Brit-free village close to Salzburg with a small area of its own, and Waidring's relatively snowsure Steinplatte nearby.
640m; slopes 640–1745m
⛷ 14 ✝ 30km

Longchamp 286

Loon Mountain USA
New Hampshire's premier area (there's no resort as such), set amid scenic wilderness, renowned for immaculately groomed intermediate slopes.
290m; slopes 290–910m
⛷ 9 ✝ 234 acres
✉ Virgin Snow

Lost Trail USA
Remote Montana area, open only Thursday-Sunday and holidays. Mostly intermediate.
2005m; slopes 2005–2370m
⛷ 4 ✝ 600 acres

Loveland USA
High, varied slopes, a day-trip from Keystone and renowned for snow. Long season, good for all standards.
3220m; slopes 3220–3731m
⛷ 10 ✝ 836 acres

Luchon France
Sizeable village with plenty of amenities and train station, with gondola (8 minutes) to its ski area. Superbagnères purpose-built at top.
650m; slopes 1450–2260m
⛷ 16 ✝ 35km ✉ Lagrange

Lurisia Italy
Sizeable spa resort. Good base for visits to surrounding little ski areas and Nice.
660m; slopes 660–1750m
⛷ 7 ✝ 18km

Luz-Ardidon France
Spa village below its ski area. Cauterets and Barèges nearby. Near Carcassone.
710m; slopes 1680–2540m
⛷ 19 ✝ 33km

Macugnaga Italy
Two pretty villages, 1km apart, set amid stunning scenery. Staffa has high intermediate slopes, Pecetto has sheltered novice runs.
1330–1390m; slopes 1330–2970m
⛷ 12 ✝ 40km ✉ First Choice Ski, Neilson, Thomson

Madesimo 324

Madonna di Campiglio 325

La Magdelaine Italy
Neighbour of Cervinia, good on bad weather days.
1644m; slopes 1644–1870m
⛷ 4 ✝ 4km

Maishofen Austria
Cheap(er) place to stay when visiting equidistant Saalbach and Zell am See.
764m

Malbun Liechtenstein
Quaint, civilised, user-friendly little family resort, 16km from the capital, Vaduz. Limited slopes, with short easy runs.
1600m; slopes 1595–2100m
⛷ 6 ✝ 16km

Malcesine Italy
Large summer resort on Lake Garda with fair area.
1430m; slopes 1430–1830m
⛷ 8 ✝ 12km

Malga Ciapela Italy
Resort at the foot of the Marmolada glacier massif, with a link into the Sella Ronda, and Cortina nearby.
1445m; slopes 1445–3340m
⛷ 8 ✝ 18km

Mallnitz Austria
Village in a pretty valley close to Slovenia, with two varied areas providing a fine mix of wooded and open runs and good off-piste.
1200m; slopes 1300–2650m
⛷ 12 ✝ 30km

Mammoth Mountain 427

Manigod France
Small valley village over the Col de la Croix-Fry from La Clusaz.

Marble Mountain Canada
Area near charming Newfoundland town Corner Brook and Gros Morne National Park wilderness. One of highest snowfall records on east coast.
84m; slopes 84–570m
⛷ 5 ✝ 126 acres

Maria Alm Austria
Charming unspoilt village east of Zell am See with a varied area that stretches impressively over five linked mountains.
800m; slopes 790–1900m
⛷ 42 ✝ 160km ✉ STS

Mariapfarr Austria
Village at centre of one of longest, most snowsure cross-country networks in Europe, and next to major St Michael-Mauterndorf Alpine area.
1121m ✉ Waymark Holidays

Mariazell Austria
Traditional Styria village with an impressive basilica, that has a real antiquated feel to it. Limited slopes.
870m; slopes 870–1265m
⛷ 15 ✝ 20km

Marilleva 325

La Massana 515

Le Massif Canada
Quebec area with potential (and plans) to become star of the east coast. Big vertical drop, high snowfall, steep mostly unpisted slopes, marvellous St Lawrence views.
slopes 33–836m
⛷ 2 ✝ 144 acres

Matrei in Ostitirol Austria
Large market village south of Felbertauern tunnel. 16 planned lifts will double area. Mostly high slopes.
1000m; slopes 1000–2350m
⛷ 6 ✉ Alpine Tours

Mauterndorf Austria
Village near Obertauern with tremendous snow record. Surprisingly undeveloped – high number of T-bars. Claimed 200km of piste is overstatement.
1122m; slopes 1075–2360m
⛷ 44 ✝ 200km
✉ Sloping Off

Maverick Mountain USA
Plenty of terrain accessed by few lifts. Cowboy Winter Games venue – rodeo one day, ski races the next.
2157m; slopes 2157–2801m
⛷ 2 ✝ 500 acres

Mayens de Riddes 393

Mayens-de-Sion Switzerland
Tranquil hamlet off road up to Les Collons (in Verbier area).
1250m; slopes 1300–3330m
⛷ 100 ✝ 400km

Mayrhofen 115

Meaudre France
Small resort near Grenoble with good snowmaking to make up for low altitude.
1000m; slopes 1000–1600m
⛷ 10 ✝ 17km

Megève 225

Meiringen Switzerland
Conan Doyle's deathplace for Sherlock Holmes. Varied terrain, a good outing from the nearby Jungfrau resorts.
595m; slopes 1050–2245m
⛷ 15 ✝ 60km ✉ Made to Measure, PGL Ski Europe

Les Menuires 230

Merano Italy
Purpose-built base on high plateau near Bolzano.
2000m; slopes 2000–2240m
⛷ 18 ✝ 28km

Méribel 233

Metabief-Mont-d'Or France
Twin villages in Jura region. Worthwhile stopover for self-drivers en-route to Geneva.
900m; slopes 900–1430m
⛷ 33 ✝ 30km

Methven 536

Mijoux France
Pretty wooded slopes between Dijon and Geneva. Shares lift pass with neighbour Lelex.
1000m; slopes 900–1700m
⛷ 31 ✝ 50km

Mission Ridge USA
Area in a dry region that gets higher-quality snow than other Seattle resorts but less of it it. Good intermediate slopes.
1388m; slopes 1388–2057m
⛷ 6 ✝ 300 acres

Misurina Italy
Tiny village near Cortina.
Cheap alternative base.
1756m; slopes 1756–1900m
🎿 4 🎿 13km

Mittersill Austria
Valley-junction village near
Pass Thurn. Uncommercialised
base from which to visit
Kitzbuhel if snowline low;
Kaprun, Gerlos, Matrei and
Uttendorf if high.
789m; slopes 1265–2000m
🎿 8 🎿 45km

Moena Italy
Large village between
Cavalese and Sella Ronda
resorts, ideally located for
touring Dolomites area.
1184m; slopes 1184–2489m
🎿 21 🎿 29km
✉ *Waymark Holidays*

La Molina 522
1700m; slopes 1600–2535m
🎿 29 🎿 85km

Molltall Glacier Austria
Little-known high slopes other
side of Tauern tunnel from
Bad Gastein. Worthwhile trip
when snowline high.
slopes 2570–3122m
🎿 4 🎿 11km

Monarch USA
Wonderfully uncrowded area,
a day-trip from Crested Butte.
Great powder. Good for all
levels except expert.
3278m; slopes 3278–3628m
🎿 4 🎿 637 acres

Monesi Italy
Southernmost of resorts south
of Turin, surprisingly close to
Monaco and Nice.
1310m; slopes 1310–2180m
🎿 5 🎿 38km

Le Monêtier 265
La Mongie 296
1800m; slopes 1750–2550m
🎿 56 🎿 100km
✉ *Crystal, Lagrange*

Montalbert 251
Montana Snow Bowl USA
Area renowned for powder,
outside lively university town
Missoula. Intermediate pistes
plus 700 acres of extreme
slopes. Grizzly Chute is the
ultimate challenge.
1519m; slopes 1519–2309m
🎿 4 🎿 1900 acres

Montchavin 251
Mont-de-Lans 210
Le Mont-Dore France
Largest resort in beautiful
volcanic Auvergne region.
Attractive traditional village.
1050m; slopes 850–1850m
🎿 41 🎿 80km ✉ *Lagrange*

Monte Bondone Italy
Essentially a Trento
weekenders' area (some of
the lifts are closed weekdays).
slopes 1300–2100m
🎿 9 🎿 10km
✉ *Alpine Tours, Solo's*

Monte Campione Italy
Tiny purpose-built resort. 80%
snowmaking helps offset low
altitude. Area spread thinly
over four mountainsides.
100km of piste overstated.
1200m; slopes 1200–2010m
🎿 14 🎿 100km ✉ *Equity
School Ski, Equity Total Ski*

Monte Livata Italy
Closest resort to Rome, with
plenty of accommodation for
weekenders.
1429m; slopes 1429–1750m
🎿 8 🎿 8km

Monte Piselli Italy
Tiny area with highest slopes
of the many little resorts east
of Rome.
2100m; slopes 2100–2690m
🎿 3 🎿 5km

Monte Pora Italy
Tiny resort near Lake d'Iseo
and Bergamo. Several other
little areas nearby.
1350m; slopes 1350–1879m
🎿 8 🎿 20km
✉ *Equity School Ski*

Mont Gabriel Canada
Montreal area with runs on
four sides of mountain,
though two south-facing sides
rarely open. Two short but
renowned double black
diamond bump runs.
🎿 9

Montgenèvre 241
Mont Glen Canada
Least crowded of areas south
of Montreal, so sensible
weekend choice.
682m; slopes 682–1033m
🎿 4 🎿 110 acres

Mont Grand Fonds Canada
Small area sufficiently far
from Quebec not to get
overrun at weekends.
400m; slopes 400–735m
🎿 4

Mont Habitant Canada
Very limited area (215m
vertical) but with nicest base
lodge of any resort in
Montreal region. Excellent
restaurant.
🎿 3

Mont Olympia Canada
Small two-mountain area near
Montreal, one mostly novice
terrain, the other best suited
to experts. 🎿 6

Mont Orford Canada
Cold, windswept lone peak
(there's no resort), worth a
trip from nearby Montreal on
a fine day.
🎿 8

Mont Ste Anne 497
150m; slopes 150–800m
🎿 15 🎿 420 acres
✉ *All Canada Ski, Canada's
Best, Ski Vacation Canada,
Skisar U.S.*

Mont St Sauveur 497
🎿 9

Mont Sutton Canada
Varied area with perhaps the
best glade skiing in the East,
including some for novices.
Quaint Sutton village nearby.
🎿 9

Mont Tremblant 497
265m; slopes 265–910m
🎿 10 🎿 500 acres
✉ *All Canada Ski, American
Connections, American
Dream, Crystal, First Choice
Ski, Frontier Ski, Inghams,
Made to Measure, Neilson,
Ski Club Europe, Ski
Independence, Ski Vacation
Canada, Skisar U.S.,
Thomson*

Morgins 351
Morillon 215
Morin Heights Canada
One of best areas in Montreal
region. 100% snowmaking.
Attractive base lodge.
🎿 6

Morzine 245
Les Mosses Switzerland
Uninteresting resort and area,
best for a day-trip.
1450m; slopes 1450–2350m
🎿 12 🎿 60km

Mottaret 233
Mottarone Italy
Closest slopes to Lake
Maggiore. No village – just a
base area.
803m; slopes 803–1491m
🎿 8 🎿 10km

Mt Abram USA
Small, pretty, tree-lined area
renowned for its immaculately
groomed easy runs.
295m; slopes 295–608m
🎿 5 🎿 130 acres

Mountain High USA
Best snowfall record and
highest lift capacity in Los
Angeles vicinity – plus 93%
snowmaking. Mostly
intermediate cruising.
2005m; slopes 2005–2491m
🎿 11 🎿 205 acres

Mt Arrowsmith Canada
On Vancouver Island, short
drive from city ferry. Limited
for skiers but impressive
1500-foot half-pipe.
1276m; slopes 1276–1592m
🎿 3

Mt Ashland USA
Arty town renowned for
Shakespeare (winter season
starts February). Boutiques,
galleries, nice restaurants.
Mountain includes glaciated
bowl rimmed with steeps.
Best for experts.
1929m; slopes 1929–2278m
🎿 4 🎿 110 acres

Mt Bachelor USA
Interesting 360 degree area
(there's no resort) on an
extinct volcano in central
Oregon. Gets a lot of rain.
1825m; slopes 1825–2755m
🎿 13 🎿 3200 acres

Mt Baker USA
Holds official world snowfall
record for a ski resort despite
low altitude, almost on the
coast near Seattle. Plenty of
challenging slopes. Known for
spectacular avalanches.
1139m; slopes 1139–1595m
🎿 9 🎿 1000 acres

Mt Baldy Canada
Tiny area but worthwhile
excursion from Big White.
Above Canada's only desert –
gets ultra light snow. Great
glades/powder chutes for
boarders and good skiers.
slopes 1698–2142m
🎿 2 🎿 150 acres

Mt Baldy USA
Some of the longest and
steepest runs in California.
Near Los Angeles, but 20%
snowmaking and antiquated
lifts are a major drawback.
1975m; slopes 1975–2613m
🎿 4 🎿 400 acres

Mt Baw Baw Australia
Small but entertaining
intermediate area in attractive
woodland, with great views.
Closest area to Melbourne –
2.5 hours. Nearest town –
Noojee.
1480m; slopes 1338–1563m
🎿 8 🎿 61 acres

Mt Buffalo Australia
Site of Australia's first ski lift.
Plateau area best suited to
beginners. Short season. On-
mountain accommodation. 4
hours from Melbourne.
1400m; slopes 1453–1610m
🎿 8 🎿 66 acres

Mt Buller   535
1600m; slopes 1600–1790m
🚡 24   🎿 990 acres

Mt Cranmore   USA
One of several Mt Washington
valley resorts in New
Hampshire, near factory-
outlet-shopping town North
Conway. Mostly easy slopes.
100% snowmaking.
151m; slopes 151–515m
🚡 5   🎿 185 acres

Mt Dobson   New Zealand
Best of smaller Kiwi areas.
Mount Cook and Pacific
views. Wide treeless basin
with long runs by NZ
standards. Good snowcover
record. Mostly intermediate.
1630m; slopes 1630–2045m
🚡 4   🎿 990 acres

Mt Hood Meadows   USA
One of several sizeable areas
amid magnificent Oregon
scenery. Impressive snowfall
record but snow tends to be
wet, and weather damp.
1374m; slopes 1374–2218m
🚡 11   🎿 2150 acres

Mt Hood Ski Bowl   USA
Sizeable area set amid
magnificent Oregon scenery.
Weather can be damp.
1093m; slopes 1093–1536m
🚡 9   🎿 910 acres

Mt Hotham   535
1750m; slopes 1452–1846m
🚡 9   🎿 30km

Mt Hutt   536
slopes 1420–2075m
🚡 10   🎿 902 acres

Mt Lemmon   USA
Southernmost area in North
America. Close to famous Old
West town Tombstone.
Reasonable snowfall plus
100% snowmakers.
2515m; slopes 2515–2780m
🚡 3   🎿 80 acres

Mt Lyford   New Zealand
Limited but developing area
close to the superb whale-
and seal-watching centre,
Kaikoura, 140km north of
Christchurch.
1200m; slopes 1200–1640m
🚡 6   🎿 395 acres

Mt Olympus   Greece
Ski mountaineering site with
chain of huts on both faces.
Best visited in late winter.

Mt Rose   USA
Only 22 miles from Reno.
Good slopes of its own and
well placed for trips to other
Tahoe resorts.
2509m; slopes 2509–2947m
🚡 5   🎿 900 acres

Mt Selwyn   Australia
Popular with beginners and
families. Surprisingly good lift
system. 6 hours from Sydney.
1520m; slopes 1489–1610m
🚡 13   🎿 111 acres

Mt Snow/Haystack   USA
Twin southern Vermont areas,
a couple of miles apart, with
a lot of intermediate trails
and some stiffer glades. Some
condos at Mount Snow base,
and lodgings down the valley.
580m; slopes 580–1095m
🚡 24   🎿 750 acres
✉ Crystal

Mt Spokane   USA
Little intermediate area
outside Spokane with cheap
lift pass.
1160m; slopes 1160–1787m
🚡 5   🎿 350 acres

Mt St Louis/Moonstone
Canada
Premier area in Toronto
region, spread over three
peaks, with very high-capacity
lift system. 100%
snowmaking.
🚡 13   🎿 175 acres

Mt Sunapee   USA
Closest area of any size to
Boston; primarily intermediate
terrain. Suffers lack of
investment through being
state-owned – only 80%
snowmaking.
253m; slopes 253–833m
🚡 7   🎿 210 acres

Mt Washington Resort Canada
Main area in remote part of
Vancouver Island. Beautiful
scenery. Impressive snowfall
record but rain is problem.
1106m; slopes 1106–1584m
🚡 6   🎿 970 acres

Mt Waterman   USA
Small Los Angeles area where
kids ski free. 20%
snowmaking is a drawback.
2136m; slopes 2136–2439m
🚡 3   🎿 135 acres

Mühlbach   Austria
Village near Bischofshofen, a
short bus-hop from one end
of an impressive five-
mountain area that stretches
for miles towards Maria Alm.
855m; slopes 790–1900m
🚡 42   🎿 160km
✉ PGL Ski Europe

Mühltal   120

Muhr   Austria
Village by Katschberg tunnel
well placed for visiting areas
that get different weather
patterns – St Michael, BKK,
Flachau, Obertauern.
1107m

Muju   Korea
Largest area – 30 slopes – in
Korea and the furthest from
Seoul (3.5 hours south). Daily
shuttles from the capital. Not
as ugly or crowded as most
Korean resorts.
🚡 13

Mürren   378

Mutters   Austria
Innsbruck satellite resort,
good base for exploring the
whole area.
850m; slopes 900–1800m
🚡 7   🎿 11km

Myoko Kogen   Japan
Japan's best all-round area.
Extensive slopes spread over
five distinct, interconnected
sections with longer, wider
runs than Japanese norm.
Magnificent scenery.
🚡 57

Naeba   Japan
Attracts the fashion
conscious. North of Tokyo.
🚡 38

Nakiska   Canada
One of two areas near
Kananaskis (4km away). 1988
Olympic site but 70%
intermediate. Spectacular
scenery, uncrowded
(weekdays) slopes, state-of-
art snowmaking.
1525m; slopes 1525–2253m
🚡 5   🎿 285 acres

Nasserein   133

Nauders   Austria
Attractive village near Italy
with a high, sunny
intermediate area with lots of
snowmakers.
1365m; slopes 1400–2750m
🚡 16   🎿 55km

Nax   Switzerland
Quiet sunny village in balcony
setting overlooking Rhône
valley. Own little area and
short drive from Veysonnaz.
1300m; slopes 1300–3330m
🚡 100   🎿 400km

Nendaz   393

Neukirchen   Austria
Quiet, pretty beginners' resort
with a fairly snowsure plateau
at the top of its mountain.
Intermediates have the Ziller
valley nearby.
855m; slopes 855–2150m
🚡 13   🎿 30km

Neustift   119

Nevegal   Italy
Weekend day-trippers' place
near Belluno, south of
Cortina.
1030m; slopes 1030–1652m
🚡 14   🎿 28km

Nevis Range   533

Niederau   120

Niedernsill   Austria
Astute choice for crowd-free
slopes when snowline high,
Kaprun queues long. Tucked
behind Kaprun. Also well
placed for visiting uncrowded,
snowy Gerlos and Matrei.
768m; slopes 1483–2600m
🚡 6   🎿 20km

Niseko Kogen   Japan
Hokkaido's main resort. Very
exposed with unpredictable
weather, little skied until
February. Small area with very
short runs. 🚡 22

Nockberge Innerkrems Austria
Area just south of Katschberg
tunnel. Gets weather from
east (Tirol gets it from west).
1500m; slopes 1500–2300m
🚡 10   🎿 33km

Nordic Valley   USA
Utah cross-country area close
to Salt Lake City. Powder
Mountain and Snowbasin are
nearby Alpine areas.

Nordseter   Norway
Cluster of hotels in deep
forest close to Lillehammer.
Basic Alpine facilities but
better cross-country centre.
1002m

Norefjell   Norway
120km north-west of Oslo.
Has Norway's toughest run, a
very steep unpisted 600m
drop.
751m; slopes 140–1000m
🚡 4

La Norma   France
Traffic-free purpose-built
resort near Modane and Val-
Cenis, with mostly easy
terrain.
1350m; slopes 1350–2750m
🚡 17   🎿 65km
✉ Fairhand Holidays,
Lagrange, On The Piste
Travel Ltd, Ski trek

Northstar-at-Tahoe   425

Nosawa Onsen   Japan
Shinetsu spa village with
good hot springs. Pistes cut
out of heavy vegetation.
🚡 27

Nôtre-Dame-de-Bellecombe
France
Pleasant village spoilt by the
busy Albertville-Megève road.
Inexpensive base from which
to visit Megève, though it has
fair slopes of its own.
1135m; slopes 1150–2070m
🚡 40   🎿 120km
✉ Barrelli Ski

Nova Levante   Italy
Little area used mostly by
weekend day-trippers.
1182m; slopes 1182–2200m
⛟ *14* ⛷ *20km*

Nub's Nob   USA
One of the most sheltered
Great Lakes ski areas (many
suffer fierce winds). 100%
snowmakers; weekend crowds
from Detroit. Wooded slopes
suitable for all levels.
276m; slopes 276–406m
⛟ *8* ⛷ *160 acres*

Oberau   120
Obereggen   Italy
Tiny resort used mainly by
weekend day-trippers.
1550m; slopes 1550–2200m
⛟ *6* ⛷ *10km*

Obergurgl   121
Oberlech   109
Oberndorf   140
Oberstdorf   Germany
Attractive winter-sports town
with famous ski jumping hill,
near the Austrian border, with
three small areas.
835m; slopes 800–2225m
⛟ *26* ⛷ *30km*
✉ *Moswin Tours*

Obertauern   126
Ochapowace   Canada
Main area in Saskatchewan,
east of Regina. Doesn't get
huge amount of snowfall but
75% snowmaking helps.
⛟ *4* ⛷ *100 acres*

Ohau   New Zealand
Some of NZ's steepest slopes
served by long T-bar. Great
views of Lake Ohau.
Unusually for NZ, base has
accommodation.
1425m; slopes 1425–1825m
⛟ *3* ⛷ *310 acres*

Oppdal   529
540m; slopes 540–1300m
⛟ *15* ⛷ *80km*
✉ *Ski Scandinavia*

Orcières-Merlette   France
Good family resort;
convenient snowsure nursery
slopes, longer runs mostly
funnel safely back to town,
good village facilities.
1850m; slopes 1850–2650m
⛟ *27* ⛷ *100km*
✉ *Fairhand Holidays,
Lagrange, Motours*

Oropa   Italy
Little area just off Aosta-Turin
motorway. Easy change of
scene from Courmayeur.
1180m; slopes 1180–2490m
⛟ *6* ⛷ *11km*

Les Orres   France
Friendly modern resort that
enjoys great views and varied
intermediate terrain; but snow
is unreliable, and it's a very
long transfer from Lyon.
1600m; slopes 1550–2770m
⛟ *24* ⛷ *50km*
✉ *Fairhand Holidays, First
Choice Ski, Lagrange*

Orsieres   Switzerland
Traditional, sizeable winter
resort near Martigny. Well
positioned base from which
to visit equidistant Verbier
and Chamonix valley.

Ortisei   333
Oslo   Norway
Capital city with cross-country
ski trails in its parks. Alpine
slopes and lifts in Nordmarka
region, just north of city
boundaries.

Otre il Colle   Italy
Smallest of many little resorts
near Bergamo.
1100m; slopes 1100–2000m
⛟ *7* ⛷ *7km*

Oukaimeden   Morocco
Slopes 75km from Marrakesh
with a surprisingly long
season. A few simple hotels
and equipment available.
2630m; slopes 2630–3310m
⛟ *4* ⛷ *15km*

Ovindoli   Italy
One of smallest areas in
L'Aquila region east of Rome,
but has higher slopes than
most and one of the better
lift systems.
1375m; slopes 1375–2220m
⛟ *9* ⛷ *10km*

Ovronnaz   Switzerland
Pretty village set on a sunny
shelf above the Rhône valley,
with a good pool complex.
Limited area but Crans-
Montana and Anzère close.
1350m; slopes 1350–2425m
⛟ *8* ⛷ *25km*

Owl's Head   Canada
Steep mountain rising out of
a lake that affords superb
views, in a remote spot
bordering Vermont, away from
weekend crowds.
⛟ *7*

Oz-Station   167
Pajarito Mountain   USA
Los Alamos area laid out by
nuclear scientists. Atomic
slopes too – steep,
ungroomed. Open
Wed/Weekend/Hol. Fun day
out from Taos.
2686m; slopes 2686–3172m
⛟ *5* ⛷ *220 acres*

Pal   515
Pamporovo   523
1650m; slopes 1620–1925m
⛟ *18* ⛷ *17.5km*
✉ *Balkan Holidays, Crystal,
Neilson, Ski Balkantours*

Panarotta   Italy
Smallest of resorts east of
Trento. Higher altitude than
nearby Andalo.
1500m; slopes 1500–2000m
⛟ *6* ⛷ *7km*

Panorama   Canada
Pretty, convenient family
resort, two hours west of
Banff, renowned for its big
vertical drop, top tuition, and
superb heli-skiing.
1080m; slopes 1080–2590m
⛟ *9* ⛷ *1600 acres*
✉ *All Canada Ski, Frontier
Ski, Inghams, Ski Safari,
Skisar U.S.*

Panticosa   522
1165m; slopes 1165–1885m
⛟ *7* ⛷ *25km*

Park City   473
Parnassus   Greece
Biggest and best area in
Greece with surprisingly good
slopes and lifts, 30km from
Delphi. Wonderful sea views.
slopes 1600–2250m
⛟ *10*

Parpan   Switzerland
Pretty village linked to the
large intermediate area of
Lenzerheide.
1510m; slopes 1230–2865m
⛟ *38* ⛷ *160km*

Partenen   Austria
Traditional village in pretty
setting at end of Montafontal
(dead-end in winter). Slopes
start at neighbour Gaschurn
with lots more in vicinity.
1050m; slopes 900–2370m
⛟ *26* ⛷ *100km*

Pas de la Casa   515
Pass Thurn   103
Passo Lanciano   Italy
Closest area to Adriatic.
Weekend crowds from nearby
Pescara when snow good.
1305m; slopes 1305–2000m
⛟ *13*

Pebble Creek   USA
Small area on Utah-Jackson
Hole route. Blend of open and
wooded slopes.
1914m; slopes 1914–2522m
⛟ *3* ⛷ *600 acres*

Pec Pod Snezkou   C
Republic
Piste skiing very limited.
Strictly for ultra-tight budgets.
769m; slopes 710–1190m
⛟ *5* ⛷ *12km*

Peisey-Nancroix   175
Pejo   Italy
Unspoilt traditional village in
a pretty setting, with a limited
area. A cheap base for nearby
Madonna.
1340m; slopes 1340–2800m
⛟ *6* ⛷ *15km*
✉ *Ski Club Europe, Winterski*

Perisher/Smiggins   535
slopes 1680–2055m
⛟ *30* ⛷ *2340 acres*

Pescasseroli   Italy
One of numerous areas east
of Rome in L'Aquila region.
Summer camping spot.
1250m; slopes 1250–1945m
⛟ *6* ⛷ *25km*

Pescocostanzo   Italy
One of numerous areas east
of Rome in L'Aquila region.
Summer mountain retreat.
1395m; slopes 1395–1900m
⛟ *4* ⛷ *25km*

Pettneu   133
Petzen   Austria
One of many little areas in
Austria's easternmost ski
region near Slovenian border.
600m; slopes 600–1700m
⛟ *6* ⛷ *13km*

Peyragudes-Peyresourde
France
Small Pyrenean resort with its
ski area starting high above.
Better snow record than
neighbouring Barèges.
1000m; slopes 1600–2400m
⛟ *15* ⛷ *37km*

Pfunds   Austria
Picturesque valley village
close to several resorts in
Switzerland and Italy, as well
as Ischgl in Austria. Ski
school runs safari weeks to
explore the possibilities.

Phoenix Park   Korea
Characterless golf complex
with 12 ski slopes to keep
things ticking over in winter.
Two hours from Seoul.
⛟ *7*

Piancavallo   Italy
Uninspiring yet curiously
trendy purpose-built village,
an easy drive from Venice.
1830m; slopes 1300–2000m
⛟ *17* ⛷ *45km*
✉ *Equity School Ski, PGL Ski
Europe, STS, Ski Club Europe*

Piani delle Betulle   Italy
One of several little areas
near east coast of Lake Como.
730m; slopes 730–1850m
⛟ *6* ⛷ *10km*

Piani di Artavaggio Italy
Small base complex rather
than village. One of several
little areas near Lake Como.
876m; slopes 876–1874m
⛷ 7 ⛷ 15km

Piani di Bobbio Italy
Largest of several tiny resorts
above Lake Como.
768m; slopes 768–1856m
⛷ 10 ⛷ 20km

Piani di Erna Italy
Small base development – no
village. One of several little
areas above Lake Como.
600m; slopes 600–1636m
⛷ 7 ⛷ 6km

Piau-Engaly France
User-friendly St-Lary satellite
similar in appearance to Les
Arcs 1600, in one of the best
areas in the Pyrenees.
1850m; slopes 1420–2500m
⛷ 32 ⛷ 70km
✉ Crystal, Lagrange

Piazzatorre Italy
One of many little areas in
Bergamo region.
868m; slopes 868–2000m
⛷ 6 ⛷ 15km

Pico 491

Piesendorf Austria
Cheap(er), quiet place to stay
when visiting Zell am See.
Tucked behind Kaprun near
Niedernsill
782m; slopes 760–2000m
⛷ 55 ⛷ 130km

Pievepelago Italy
Much the smallest and most
limited of Appenine ski
resorts less than 2 hours from
Florence and Pisa.
1113m; slopes 1113–1410m
⛷ 7 ⛷ 8km

Pila 326

Pilion Greece
350m vertical. Pleasant slopes
cut out of dense forest, only
15km from holiday resort
Portaria above town of Volos.
⛷ 3

Pinzolo Italy
Atmospheric village with
slopes well equipped with
snowmakers. Cheap base for
nearby Madonna.
800m; slopes 800–2100m
⛷ 6 ⛷ 30km

Pitztal Austria
Long valley with good glacier
area at its head, accessed by
underground funicular.
1250m; slopes 1735–3440m
⛷ 12 ⛷ 40km

Pla-d'Adet France
Purpose-built complex at foot
of St-Lary (original village
down at 830m) ski area.
Limited but has restaurants,
childcare, disco.
1680m; slopes 1420–2450m
⛷ 32 ⛷ 80km ✉ Lagrange

La Plagne 251

Poiana Brasov 528
1020m; slopes 1020–1770m
⛷ 8 ⛷ 15km
✉ Crystal, Inghams, Neilson,
Ski Balkantours

Pomerelle USA
Small area on Utah-Sun Valley
route.
2430m; slopes 2430–2734m
⛷ 3 ⛷ 200 acres

Pontechianale Italy
Highest, largest area in
remote region south-west of
Turin. Day-tripper place.
1614m; slopes 1614–2750m
⛷ 8 ⛷ 40km

Ponte di Legno Italy
Attractive sheltered
alternative to bleak, ugly
neighbour Tonale. Linked by
piste and bus.
1257m; slopes 1257–1920m
⛷ 5 ⛷ 15km
✉ PGL Ski Europe, STS

Pontresina 387

Porter Heights New Zealand
Closest skiing to Christchurch
(one hour). Open, sunny
bowl. Mostly intermediate
plus back bowls for powder
hounds. Snowmakers have
improved snow reliability.
1300m; slopes 1300–1980m
⛷ 5 ⛷ 200 acres

Porterillos Argentina
Limited area near Mendoza,
just over the border from
renowned Chilean resort
Portillo.

Portillo Chile
Little more than a luxury hotel
150km north-east of Santiago,
with more snowsure, less
crowded pistes than Las
Leñas in Argentina.
2850m; slopes 2510–3350m
⛷ 11 ⛷ 25km
✉ Passage to South America

Powderhorn USA
Area in west Colorado
perched on world's highest
flat-top mountain, Grand
Mesa. Sensational views. Day-
trip from Aspen.
2491m; slopes 2491–2977m
⛷ 4 ⛷ 300 acres

Powder King Village Canada
Most remote, northerly of
Canadian resorts, between
Prince George and Dawson
City. Well named – great
powder. Plenty of lodging.
Feasible two-centre
destination with Jasper.
881m; slopes 881–1519m
⛷ 3 ⛷ 160 acres

Powder Mountain USA
Sizeable Utah area, a feasible
day out from Park City.
Wonderfully uncrowded locals'
secret, renowned for bowls of
fluffy virgin powder. Snowcat
operation too.
2309m; slopes 2309–2704m
⛷ 6 ⛷ 1600 acres

Pozza di Fassa Italy
Pretty Dolomite village with
its own slopes, three other
small areas on its doorstep,
and access to the Sella Ronda
at nearby Campitello.
1320m; slopes 1320–2215m
⛷ 13 ⛷ 20km
✉ Crystal, Winterski

Pra-Loup France
Convenient, purpose-built
family resort with an
extensive, varied intermediate
area linked to La Foux-d'Allos,
south-east of Gap.
1600m; slopes 1500–2600m
⛷ 55 ⛷ 160km
✉ Airtours, Fairhand
Holidays, Lagrange, STS, Ski
Club Europe, Thomson

Pragelato Italy
Inexpensive base short drive
east of Sestriere. Own area
worth a try for half a day.
1524m; slopes 1524–2936m
⛷ 5 ⛷ 10km

Prägraten am Grossvenediger
Austria
Traditional mountaineering/ski
touring village in lovely
setting south of Felbertauern
tunnel. Ski slopes at
neighbouring Matrei.
1312m; slopes 1000–2350m
⛷ 6

Prali Italy
Tiny resort east of Sestriere.
Worthwhile half-day change of
scene from Milky Way.
1455m; slopes 1455–2540m
⛷ 6 ⛷ 25km

Pralognan-la-Vanoise France
Unspoilt traditional village
with pistes overlooked by
spectacular peaks.
Champagny (La Plagne) and
Courchevel are close by.
1410m; slopes 1410–2355m
⛷ 14 ⛷ 25km ✉ Fairhand
Holidays, Lagrange

Prati di Tivo Italy
Sizeable resort by southern
Italy standards. East of Rome
near town of Teramo.
Weekend day-trip place.
1450m; slopes 1450–1800m
⛷ 6 ⛷ 16km

Prato Nevoso Italy
Purpose-built resort with
rather bland slopes. Novel
mountain-top skidoo transfer
to/from Artesina.
1500m; slopes 1500–1928m
⛷ 13 ⛷ 35km

Prato Selva Italy
Tiny base development – no
village – way east of Rome
near Teramo. Weekend day-
trip place.
1370m; slopes 1370–1800m
⛷ 4 ⛷ 10km

Le Praz 202

Les Praz 185

Praz-de-Lys France
Little known snow-pocket
area near Lake Geneva that
can have good snow when
nearby resorts (eg La Clusaz)
do not.
1500m; slopes 1200–1800m
⛷ 22 ⛷ 50km ✉ Lagrange

Praz-sur-Arly France
Traditional village in a pretty,
wooded setting just down the
road from Megève, with its
own varied slopes.
1035m; slopes 1035–2000m
⛷ 14 ⛷ 60km ✉ Motours

Le Pré 175

Predazzo Italy
Small quiet place between
Cavalese and Sella Ronda
resorts. Well positioned for
touring Dolomites area.
1018m; slopes 1018–1454m
⛷ 8 ⛷ 17km

Premanon France
One of four resorts that make
up Rousses area in Jura
region. Useful stopover en-
route to resorts beyond
Geneva.
1050m; slopes 1120–1680m
⛷ 40 ⛷ 43km
✉ Lagrange

La Presolana Italy
Large summer resort near
Bergamo. Several other little
areas nearby.
1250m; slopes 1250–1650m
⛷ 6 ⛷ 15km

Punta Arenas Chile
Most southerly organised
slope in the world, on the tip
of Patagonia, not too far from
Cape Horn.
⛷ 1

Purgatory USA
Limited Colorado resort with enough good terrain to make it a useful day out from nearby Telluride.
2670m; slopes 2670–3290m
📶 9 🎿 692 acres

Puy-St-Vincent 260

Pyha Finland
Finland's steep and deep resort (280m vertical), popular with good skiers and boarders. Youthful atmosphere in its only hotel.
📶 6 ✉ Crystal

Pyrenees 2000 France
Tiny resort built in pleasing manner. Shares pretty area of short runs with Font-Romeu. Impressive snowmaking.
2000m; slopes 1750–2250m
📶 32 🎿 52km ✉ Lagrange

Quebec 497

Queenstown 538

Radium Hot Springs Canada
Resort amid beautiful countryside near Panorama offering alternative to limited purpose-built slopeside village. High-quality lodging with lots of facilities available.
slopes 975–2135m
📶 8 🎿 300 acres

Radstadt Austria
Interesting, unspoilt medieval town near Schladming that has its own small area, with the Salzburger Sportwelt accessed from nearby Zauchensee or Flachau.
855m; slopes 855–1700m
📶 10 🎿 17km
✉ Ski Club Europe

Rainbow New Zealand
Northernmost ski area on South Island, 90 minutes from Nelson. Wide, undulating, treeless. Mostly novice and intermediate.
1440m; slopes 1440–1760m
📶 4 🎿 865 acres

Ramsau Austria
Charming village overlooked by the Dachstein glacier. Renowned for cross-country, it also has Alpine slopes locally, on glacier and at Schladming.
1200m; slopes 1100–2700m
📶 21 🎿 40km
✉ Waymark Holidays

Rauris Austria
Old roadside village close to Kaprun and Zell am See, with a long narrow area that has snowmakers on lower slopes.
950m; slopes 950–2200m
📶 10 🎿 25km

Ravascletto Italy
Resort close to Austria in a pretty wooded setting, with most of its terrain high above on open plateau.
920m; slopes 920–1735m
📶 12 🎿 40km
✉ PGL Ski Europe

Reallon France
Traditional-style village, with splendid views from above Lac de Serre-Ponçon.
1560m; slopes 1560–2115m
📶 6 🎿 20km ✉ Lagrange, On The Piste Travel Ltd

Red Mountain Canada
Area renowned for its steep and deep powder, eight hours east of Vancouver, 3km from Rossland, a charming old mining town.
1185m; slopes 1185–2040m
📶 6 🎿 1100 acres
✉ Frontier Ski, Ski Safari

Red Lodge USA
Lively Western town with rich history. Intermediate area. Good 2- or 3-day excursion from Big Sky.
2248m; slopes 2248–2861m
📶 6 🎿 500 acres

Red River USA
New Mexico western town – complete with stetsons and saloons – with slopes above. Neighbour of Taos.
2658m; slopes 2658–3145m
📶 7 🎿 135 acres

Reichenfels Austria
One of many small areas in Austria's easternmost ski region near Slovenian border. Only resort not in regional lift pass share arrangement.
809m; slopes 809–1400m
📶 4 🎿 8km

The Remarkables 538

Rencurel-les-Coulumes France
One of seven little resorts just west of Grenoble totalling 200km of piste.

Reutte Austria
500-year old market town with many suitably traditional hotels, and rail links to nearby Lermoos, Innsbruck.
855m; slopes 855–1750m
📶 9 🎿 18km

Revelstoke Canada
Town from which you can heli-ski the Monashees without staying in a remote mountain lodge, with local terrain on Mt McKenzie for bad-weather days.
460m
✉ Powder Skiing in North America Limited

Rhêmes-Notre-Dame Italy
Unspoilt village in the beautiful Rhêmes valley, south of Aosta. Courmayeur and La Thuile within reach.
📶 2 🎿 5km

Riederalp Switzerland
Pretty, car-free village perched high above the Rhône valley amid the glorious scenery of the Aletsch area. Access by cable-car from near Brig.
1925m; slopes 1925–2710m
📶 26 🎿 90km

Rigi-Kaltbad Switzerland
Resort on a mountain rising out of Lake Lucerne, with superb all-round views, accessed by the world's first mountain railway.
1440m; slopes 1195–1795m
📶 9 🎿 30km

Riihivuori Finland
Unusual in having its 'base' area at the top of the mountain. 20km from city of Jyvaskyla.
📶 4

Riksgränsen 531
600m; slopes 600–910m
📶 7 🎿 10km
✉ Ski Scandinavia

Riscone Italy
Dolomite village sharing pretty area with San Vigilio. Good snowmaking. Short easy runs.
1200m; slopes 1200–2275m
📶 35 🎿 40km

Risoul 261

Rivisondoli Italy
Sizeable summer mountain retreat east of Rome, with one of the better lift systems in vicinity.
1350m; slopes 1350–2050m
📶 7 🎿 16km

Rjukan Norway
Gateway to ultimate cross-country region – Hardanger Vidda. Trails to Voss take a week.
300m

Roccaraso Italy
Largest of the resorts east of Rome, at least when snowcover is complete.
1280m; slopes 1280–2200m
📶 12 🎿 56km

Rohrmoos 144

La Rosière 262

Rougemont 377

Ruka Finland
Finland's best-known ski resort. Most slopes have snow cannon – season starts October. Spacious area by Finnish standards.
📶 18 ✉ Crystal

Russbach Austria
Secluded village tucked up side valley, linked into Gosau-Annaberg-Lungotz area. Slopes spread over wide area.
817m; slopes 780–1700m
📶 34 🎿 50km

Saalbach-Hinterglemm 127

Saalfelden Austria
Venue for 1991 World Championship cross-country events (snowmakers in use). Ideally placed for touring eastern Tirol. Maria Alm, Saalbach nearby.
744m

Saanen 377

Saanenmöser 377

Saas-Almagell Switzerland
Compact village up the valley from Saas-Grund, with good cross-country trails and walks, and limited Alpine area.
1670m 📶 17

Saas-Fee 382

Saas-Grund Switzerland
Sprawling valley village below Saas-Fee, with separate, small but high Alpine area.
1560m; slopes 1560–3100m
📶 17 🎿 45km ✉ SkiGower

Saddleback USA
Small area between Maine's premier resorts. High slopes by local standards.
665m; slopes 665–1251m
📶 5 🎿 120 acres

Sahoro Japan
Ugly, purpose-built Hokkaido Island complex with a limited area, but one of the most exotic package destinations.
400m; slopes 400–1100m
📶 10 🎿 15km ✉ Club Med

St Andrä im Lungau Austria
Valley-junction village ideally placed for one of longest, most snowsure cross-country networks in Europe.
1044m

St Anton 133

S Bernadino Switzerland
Pretty resort south of the road tunnel of the same name, close to Madesimo, with a fair amount of terrain opened up by its few lifts.
1595m; slopes 1595–2515m
📶 7 🎿 50km

S Candido Italy
Austrian border resort on road to Lienz.
1175m; slopes 1175–1580m
📶 4 🎿 15km

S Carlos de Bariloche
Argentina
South America's only year-round community-cum-resort, with five areas nearby. Cerro Catedral is the best but gets crowded in August.
790m; slopes 1050–2050m
⛷ *32* 🚡 *26km*
✉ *Passage to South America*

S Cassiano 333

Sta Caterina Italy
Pretty, user-friendly village near Bormio, with a snowsure novice and intermediate area.
1740m; slopes 1740–2725m
⛷ *7* 🚡 *25km* ✉ *Airtours, First Choice Ski, Thomson*

St Cergue Switzerland
Limited resort less than an hour from Geneva, good for families with young children.
1045m; slopes 1045–1700m
⛷ *9* 🚡 *20km*

St Christoph 133

St-Colomban-des-Villards
France
Small resort in next side valley to La Toussuire. Good base for visiting largest areas in vicinity (Valloire and Val-Cenis).

Sta Cristina 333

Ste-Foy 264

St-François-Longchamp 286

St Gallenkirch Austria
Smaller, less attractive village than Gaschurn, with which it shares a sizeable intermediate area near Schruns.
900m; slopes 900–2370m
⛷ *26* 🚡 *100km*

St-Gervais 225

St Gilgen Austria
Neighbour of St Wolfgang in beautiful lakeside setting. Own slopes with more nearby, but best for relaxing holiday.
546m; slopes 546–1540m
⛷ *14* 🚡 *20km*

S Gree di Viola Italy
Easternmost of resorts south of Turin, surprisingly close to Italian Riviera.
829m; slopes 829–1756m
⛷ *11* 🚡 *50km*

St Jakob in Defereggen Austria
Unspoilt traditional village in a pretty, sunny valley close to Lienz and Heiligenblut, with a good proportion of its slopes above 2000m.
1390m; slopes 1390–2520m
⛷ *9* 🚡 *35km*

St Jakob in Haus Austria
Snowpocket village with its own slopes, and a shared lift pass with nearby Fieberbrunn, Waidring and St Johann.
855m; slopes 855–1500m
⛷ *4* 🚡 *30km*

St-Jean-de-Sixt France
Traditional hamlet, a cheap base for La Clusaz and Le Grand-Bornand (3km to both).
963m ⛷ *2*

St-Jean-Montclar France
Small village at foot of thickly forested slopes. Good day out from nearby Pra-Loup.
1300m; slopes 1300–2500m
⛷ *18* 🚡 *50km*

St Johann im Pongau Austria
Bustling, lively town with a small area of its own, but the impressive Salzburger Sportwelt area starts only 4km away at Alpendorf.
650m; slopes 800–2185m
⛷ *59* 🚡 *200km*
✉ *PGL Ski Europe*

St Johann in Tirol 140

St-Lary 296
890m; slopes 1420–2500m
⛷ *32* 🚡 *70km*
✉ *Crystal, Fairhand Holidays, Inghams, Lagrange*

St Leonhard in Pitztal Austria
Village beneath a fine glacier in the Oetz area, accessed by underground funicular.
1250m; slopes 1735–3440m
⛷ *12* 🚡 *40km*

St Luc Switzerland
Quiet, unspoilt rustic village on the south side of the Rhône valley, with plenty of high, easy pistes.
1650m; slopes 1650–3025m
⛷ *16* 🚡 *75km*
✉ *Ski Les Alpes*

St Margarethen Austria
Village near Obertauern in remarkable snow pocket. Claimed 200km of piste is overstatement.
1064m; slopes 1075–2360m
⛷ *44* 🚡 *200km*

Sta Maria Maggiore Italy
South of Simplon Pass from Rhône valley, near Lake Maggiore.
820m; slopes 820–1890m
⛷ *5* 🚡 *10km*

St Martin bei Lofer Austria
Traditional village in lovely setting beneath impressive Loferer Steinberge massif. Cross-country centre with Alpine slopes at Lofer.
634m; slopes 900–1745m
⛷ *14* 🚡 *35km*

St-Martin-de-Belleville 263

S Martin de los Andes
Argentina
Limited area on the slopes of Cerro Chapelco. Neighbour to Argentina's main resort, Bariloche, near the Chilean border.
⛷ *6*
✉ *Passage to South America*

S Martino di Castrozza Italy
Plain village in the southern Dolomites with varied slopes in four disjointed areas, none very extensive.
1465m; slopes 1450–2385m
⛷ *25* 🚡 *50km* ✉ *Crystal*

St Martin/Tennengebirge
Austria
Highest village in Dachstein-West region near Salzburg. Limited slopes of its own but close to Annaberg which has interesting area.
1000m ⛷ *6* 🚡 *4km*

St-Maurice-sur-Moselle France
One of several areas near Strasbourg relatively close to Channel. Unlike most resorts in region, no snowmakers.
550m; slopes 900–1250m
⛷ *8* 🚡 *11km*

St Michael im Lungau Austria
Quiet, unspoilt village in the Tauern pass snowpocket with an uncrowded but disjointed intermediate area. Close to Obertauern and Wagrain.
1075m; slopes 1075–2360m
⛷ *11* 🚡 *60km* ✉ *Alpine Tours, Ski Club Europe*

St Moritz 387

St-Nicolas-de-Véroce 225

St-Nizier-du-Moucherotte
France
One of seven little resorts just west of Grenoble totalling 200km of piste. Unspoilt, inexpensive place to tour. Villard-de-Lans is main resort.

St-Pierre-de-Chartreuse France
Second oldest French ski resort (after Chamonix). Locals' weekend place near Grenoble. Unreliable snow.
900m; slopes 900–1800m
⛷ *20* 🚡 *25km*

S Simone Italy
Tiny purpose-built development north of Bergamo. Lift pass shared with unappealing Foppolo area, 10 minutes drive away.
2000m; slopes 1600–2100m
⛷ *8* 🚡 *25km*
✉ *Equity School Ski*

St Stephan Switzerland
Unspoilt old farming village at the foot of the largest area in the Gstaad Super Ski region.
995m; slopes 950–2155m
⛷ *69* 🚡 *250km*

St Veit im Pongau Austria
Spa resort with limited slopes at neighbouring Goldegg but Wagrain (Salzburg Sportwelt) and Grossarl (Gastein valley) are nearby.
763m ⛷ *6* 🚡 *12km*

St-Veran France
Highest 'real' village in Europe, full of rustic character. Close to Serre-Chevalier and Milky Way. Lots of snow-reliable cross-country skiing in the area.
2040m; slopes 2040–2800m
⛷ *15* 🚡 *30km*

S Vigilio Italy
Charming, atmospheric Dolomite village with a delightful, sizeable area well covered by snow guns.
1200m; slopes 1200–2275m
⛷ *35* 🚡 *40km*

S Vito di Cadore Italy
Sizeable village on way up to Cortina. Cheap alternative place to stay. Own slopes of negligible interest.
1011m; slopes 1011–1380m
⛷ *9* 🚡 *12km*

St Wolfgang Austria
Charming lakeside resort near Salzburg, some way from any slopes, best for a relaxing winter holiday with one or two days on the slopes.
540m; slopes 665–1350m
⛷ *9* 🚡 *17km* ✉ *Airtours, Austrian Holidays, Crystal, Inghams, Neilson*

Les Saisies France
Traditional-style Albertville Olympics cross-country venue in a pretty setting, surrounded by varied four-mountain Alpine slopes.
1500m; slopes 1150–1975m
⛷ *24* 🚡 *70km*

Salen 531
550m; slopes 550–950m
⛷ *73* 🚡 *85km* ✉ *Crystal*

Salzburg-Stadt Austria
Single long challenging run off back of Salzburg's local mountain, accessed by spectacular cable-car ride.
425m; slopes 450–1805m
⛷ *1* 🚡 *8km*

Samedan Switzerland
Valley town, just down the road from St Moritz.
1720m; slopes 1720–2276m
🚡 *21km* ✉ *Kuoni*

Siviez   393

Sixt   France
Traditional village near
Samoëns, at foot of new piste
down from Flaine area. Own
little area across valley, too.
770m; slopes 700–2560m
⛟ *80* ⛷ *260km*

Ski Apache   USA
Apache-owned area south of
Albuquerque noted for
groomed steeps. Panoramic
views. Nearest lodging in
charming Ruisodo.
2917m; slopes 2917–3494m
⛟ *10* ⛷ *300 acres*

Ski Sunlight   USA
Quiet little area worth the
easy trip from Vail to get
away from its crowds for a
day. Varied terrain. Good
snowboard park.
2395m; slopes 2395–3006m
⛟ *4* ⛷ *465 acres*

Ski Windham   USA
Two hours from New York City
and second only to Hunter for
weekend crowds. Decent
slopes by eastern standards.
486m; slopes 486–941m
⛟ *8* ⛷ *220 acres*

Smokovec   Slovakia
Spa town near Poprad, with
three small areas on its
doorstep, known collectively
as North Tatras.
1020m; slopes 850–2005m
⛟ *21* ⛷ *10km*

Smuggler's Notch   495

Snowbasin   USA
Scenic day resort (no lodging)
17 miles from Ogden, with
delightful tree-lined skiing
and some high bowls. Soon
to have new pistes, lifts,
base, approach road – it's
hosting the 2002 Olympic
downhill events.
1944m; slopes 1944–2552m
⛟ *5* ⛷ *1800 acres*

Snowbird   479

Snowmass   432

Snow Summit   USA
San Bernadino National Forest
ski area near Palm Springs.
Lovely lake views. 100%
snowmaking. High-capacity lift
system for weekend crowds.
2127m; slopes 2127–2491m
⛟ *11* ⛷ *230 acres*

Snow Valley   USA
Area quite near Palm Springs.
Fine desert views. High-
capacity lift system copes
with weekend crowds better
than nearby Big Bear.
2035m; slopes 2035–2382m
⛟ *13* ⛷ *230 acres*

Solda   Italy
Other side of Stelvio Pass
from Bormio. Very long
airport transfers.
1906m; slopes 1906–2623m
⛟ *19* ⛷ *25km*

Sölden   150

Soldeu   515

Solfonn   Norway
Tiny development two hours
west of Geilo with some of
Norway's most challenging
Alpine slopes. Extensive,
interesting cross-country trails
too, amidst lakeland.
548m; slopes 548–762m
⛟ *2*

Solitude   USA
Steep but short powder runs
for experts, while the lower
slopes cater for beginner and
intermediate tastes only.
2430m; slopes 2435–3060m
⛟ *7* ⛷ *1600 acres*

Söll   151

Sommand   France
Purpose-built base that
shares area with Praz-de-Lys.
1420m; slopes 1200–1800m
⛟ *22* ⛷ *50km*

Sorenberg   Switzerland
Popular weekend retreat
between Berne and Lucerne,
with a high proportion of
steep, low pistes.
1165m; slopes 1165–2350m
⛟ *18* ⛷ *50km*

South Lake Tahoe   425

South Tatras   Slov
Republic
An area (there's no resort)
covering both sides of Mount
Chopok near Poprad.
slopes 1240–2005m
⛟ *19* ⛷ *20km*

Spindleruv Mlyn   Slov
Republic
Largest Giant Mountains
region resort but few
facilities. Several scattered
little low areas.
750m; slopes 750–1300m
⛟ *11* ⛷ *25km*

Spital am Pyhrn   Austria
Limited village east of
Schladming, 4km from its
easy intermediate slopes.
Nearby Hinterstoder is more
interesting.
650m; slopes 810–1885m
⛟ *10* ⛷ *18km*

Spittal/Drau   Austria
Historic Carinthian town with
a limited area starting a
cable-car ride above it. A
good day-trip from BKK.
555m; slopes 1650–2140m
⛟ *12* ⛷ *22km*

Sportgastein   85

Squaw Valley   425

Srinagar   India
Himalayan resort in trouble-
torn Kashmir, with a small
pisted area but excellent heli-
skiing.
2720m; slopes 2645–3645m
⛟ *7* ⛷ *5km*

Stafal   319

Steamboat   454

Steinach   Austria
Pleasant village in
picturesque surroundings, an
easy outing from Innsbruck,
just off the autobahn near the
Brenner Pass.
1050m; slopes 1050–2005m
⛟ *5* ⛷ *16km*
✉ *Alpine Tours*

Stevens Pass   USA
Mostly intermediate slopes, a
day-trip from Seattle.
Accommodation 60km away
in Bavarian-style town
Leavenworth. Low snowfall
and no snowmakers.
1223m; slopes 1223–1762m
⛟ *13* ⛷ *1125 acres*

Stoneham   Canada
Leading Quebec resort, better
equipped and more sheltered
than most neighbours, with
pistes across four mountains,
including the largest night
operation in Canada. 92%
snowmaking.
175m; slopes 175–590m
⛟ *9* ⛷ *300 acres*
✉ *Canada's Best*

Stoos   Switzerland
Small, unspoilt village an
hour from Zurich.
Overcrowded weekends.
Amazing views of Lake
Lucerne from summits.
1300m; slopes 569–1922m
⛟ *7*

Storlien   531
⛟ *7* ⛷ *17km*
✉ *Ski Scandinavia*

Stowe   496

Stratton   USA
Smart, purpose-built, car-free
village at foot of fair-sized
mountain with efficient lifts,
and accommodation
spreading widely around.
570m; slopes 570–1180m
⛟ *12* ⛷ *500 acres*

Strobl   Austria
Neighbour of St Wolfgang in
beautiful lakeside setting.
Slopes at nearby St Gilgen
and Postalm, but best for
relaxing winter holiday.
544m; slopes 546–1540m
⛟ *14* ⛷ *20km*

Stuben   133

Sugar Loaf   USA
Developing Maine resort, five
hours from Boston, with the
US East's best open terrain.
425m; slopes 405–1295m
⛟ *14* ⛷ *433 acres*
✉ *Crystal*

Sugar Bowl   USA
Exposed area north of Lake
Tahoe with highest snowfall
in California, best for experts.
Accommodation in Truckee
but Squaw Valley nearby.
Weekend queues.
2091m; slopes 2091–2547m
⛟ *8* ⛷ *1100 acres*

Sugarbush   USA
Dynamic resort in upper
Vermont, with two mountains
linked by fast chair, and
something resembling a
village at the foot of one of
them. Good range of runs,
including some real
challenged.
480m; slopes 450–1260m
⛟ *18* ⛷ *412 acres*
✉ *Crystal, Funway Holidays,
Inghams, Made to Measure,
Neilson, Virgin Snow*

Sun Peaks   514
1255m; slopes 1210–2152m
⛟ *6* ⛷ *1073 acres*
✉ *All Canada Ski, Frontier
Ski, Inghams, Ski
Independence, Ski Safari, Ski
Vacation Canada, Skisar U.S.*

Sun Alpina   Japan
Collective name for three tiny
neighbouring areas that share
lift pass. Four hours from
Tokyo, three from Osaka.
⛟ *23*

Sundance   USA
Robert Redford-owned,
tastefully designed family
resort set amid trees in
snowsure Utah, with a fair
amount of mostly
intermediate terrain.
2505m; slopes 2505–3160m
⛟ *4*

Sunday River   USA
One of the more attractive
resorts in the East, four hours
from Boston, best for
intermediate cruisers.
245m; slopes 245–957m
⛟ *17* ⛷ *645 acres*
✉ *Crystal, Inghams, Neilson,
Skisar U.S.*

Sunrise Park   USA
Arizona's largest area, run by
Apaches. Slopes on three
mountains; best for novices,
leisurely intermediates.
2795m; slopes 2795–3342m
⛟ *11* ⛷ *800 acres*

Sunshine Village 500

Sun Valley 487

Suommu Finland
No village – just a lodge right on the Arctic Circle. A few pistes but mostly ski-touring centre. 60km from Rovaniemi.
140m; slopes 140–408m

Super Molina 522
🚠 *93km*

Superbagnères France
Little more than a particularly French-dominated Club Med, best for a low-cost, low-effort family trip to the Pyrenees.
1880m; slopes 1450–2260m
🚠 *15* 🎿 *15km* ✉ *Lagrange*

Super-Besse France
Purpose-built resort amid spectacular extinct-volcano scenery. Shares area with Mont-Dore. Limited village.
1350m; slopes 1050–1850m
🚠 *41* 🎿 *80km*

Superdévoluy France
Ugly, purpose-built, user-friendly family resort, an hour south-east of Grenoble, with a sizeable intermediate area.
1500m; slopes 1500–2510m
🚠 *32* 🎿 *105km*
✉ *Fairhand Holidays, Lagrange, Motours, Ski trek*

Super-Lioran France
Purpose-built satellite of Le Lioran, Auvergne village. Spectacular volcano scenery.
1160m; slopes 1160–1850m
🚠 *24* 🎿 *40km*

Susjoen Norway
Cluster of hotels in deep forest close to Lillehammer. Basic Alpine facilities but better cross-country centre.
884m

Tahko Finland
Largest resort within 500km of Helsinki. Plenty of intermediate slopes. Snowboard championships venue. Attractive wooded, frozen-lake setting.
235m; slopes 235–418m
🚠 *8*

Tahoe City 425

Talisman Mountain Resort Canada
One of best areas in Toronto region but relatively low lift capacity suggests inevitable long weekend queues. 100% snowmaking.
235m; slopes 235–418m
🚠 *7* 🎿 *75 acres*

Tamsweg Austria
Large village with railway station in ultra snowy region. Cross-country centre.
1021m

La Tania 202

Taos 488

Tarnaby-Hemaran Sweden
Twin resorts where Stenmark learned his trade. Only Swedish area with its own airport. Snowsure.

El Tarter 515

Tarvisio Italy
Interesting, animated old town bordering Austria and Slovenia. A major cross-country centre with fairly limited Alpine slopes.
750m; slopes 750–1860m
🚠 *12* 🎿 *15km*
✉ *PGL Ski Europe*

Täsch 407

Tauplitz Austria
Traditional village at the foot of an interestingly varied area north of Schladming.
900m; slopes 900–2000m
🚠 *19* 🎿 *25km*
✉ *Ski Club Europe*

Tazawako Japan
Small area four hours from Tokyo. One of the few Japanese areas to get reasonable powder.
🚠 *10*

Telluride 459

Temu Italy
Sheltered hamlet near Tonale. Worth visit in bad weather.
1155m; slopes 1155–1956m
🚠 *4* 🎿 *5km* ✉ *STS*

Tengendai Japan
Tiny area three hours from Tokyo with one of Japan's best snow records, including occasional powder.
🚠 *5*

Termignon France
Traditional rustic village. Good slopes of its own, and good base for touring Maurienne valley resorts – Valloire, Val-Cenis etc.
1300m; slopes 1300–2500m
🚠 *6* 🎿 *35km* ✉ *Fairhand Holidays, Lagrange*

Terminillo Italy
Purpose-built resort 100km from Rome with a worthwhile area when snow is good.
1500m; slopes 1500–2700m
🚠 *13* 🎿 *40km*

Thollons-les-Memises France
Attractive base for relaxed holiday. Close to Evian, Lake Geneva, Portes du Soleil. Own little area too.
950m; slopes 1600–1960m
🚠 *18* 🎿 *14km*

Thredbo 535
1365m; slopes 1365–2035m
🚠 *13* 🎿 *405 acres*

La Thuile 342

Thyon 2000 393

Tignes 271

Timberline (Palmer Snowfield) USA
East of Portland, Oregon, and the only lift-served summer skiing in USA: winter snow maintained by spreading vast amounts of salt to harden it.
slopes 1516–2576m
🚠 *6*

Togari Japan
One of several areas close (one hour) to 1998 Olympic site Nagano.
🚠 *16*

Tonale Italy
Ugly resort in a bleak setting with guaranteed snow at a bargain price. Pretty Madonna is nearby.
1885m; slopes 1885–3015m
🚠 *28* 🎿 *80km* ✉ *Airtours, Altours Ski, Crystal, Equity School Ski, Equity Total Ski, First Choice Ski, Inghams, PGL Ski Europe, STS, Ski Club Europe, Thomson*

Torgnon Italy
Neighbour of Cervinia, good for bad weather.
1500m; slopes 1500–1965m
🚠 *4* 🎿 *6km*

Torgon Switzerland
Old village in a pretty wooded setting, with a lift connection to the Portes du Soleil.
1095m; slopes 975–2275m
🚠 *219* 🎿 *650km*

Le Tour France
Charming, unspoilt hamlet at the head of the Chamonix valley with much easier terrain than neighbours.
1465m; slopes 1465–2185m
🚠 *9* 🎿 *40km*
✉ *Poles Apart*

La Toussuire France
Dreary, downmarket modern resort off Maurienne valley with a large, uncrowded intermediate area.
1700m; slopes 1280–2265m
🚠 *44* 🎿 *120km*
✉ *Fairhand Holidays, Lagrange*

Trafoi Italy
Quiet, traditional (Austrian-style) village near Bormio, worth a day-trip if snow low-down is good.
1570m; slopes 1570–2550m
🚠 *6* 🎿 *10km* ✉ *STS*

Treble Cone 536
1200m; slopes 1200–1860m
🚠 *5* 🎿 *1359 acres*

Troodos Cyprus
A good outing from Greek-sector coastal resorts, with interesting old villages en route. Pretty, wooded pistes and fine views.
1920m 🚠 *4* 🎿 *5km*

Trysil 529
400m; slopes 400–1130m
🚠 *20* ✉ *Headwater Holidays, Mountain and Wildlife Ventures*

Tschagguns Austria
Village with a varied little area of its own and the slopes and town life of Schruns close by.
700m; slopes 655–2085m
🚠 *12* 🎿 *50km*

Tsugaike Kogen Japan
Sizeable resort four hours from Tokyo, three hours from Osaka. Helicopter service to top station March to May.
🚠 *27*

La Tuca Spain
Purpose-built development near Viella with lift to slopes. Worthwhile excursion from nearby Baqueira-Beret, especially in bad weather.
1050m; slopes 1270–2250m
🚠 *7*

Tulfes Austria
Hamlet on mountain shelf close to Innsbruck, with small main area above the trees and long runs back to base.
950m; slopes 950–2305m
🚠 *8* 🎿 *19km*

Turoa 536
slopes 1600–2320m
🚠 *10* 🎿 *2225 acres*

Turracher Höhe Austria
Tiny, unspoilt resort on a mountain shelf, with varied intermediate slopes above and below it. A good outing from Bad Kleinkirchheim.
1765m; slopes 1400–2200m
🚠 *11* 🎿 *40km*
✉ *Alpine Tours*

Tyax Lodge Canada
Heli-skiing operation in Chilcotin mountains. Transfers from Whistler or Vancouver. High-standard in-the-mountains retreat.

Uludag Turkey
Surprisingly suave, laid-back, well equipped, purpose-built resort near Bursa, popular with posers.
1800m; slopes 1800–2500m
🚠 *14* 🎿 *15km*

Unken Austria
Traditional village with closest slopes to Salzburg, hidden in side valley.
564m; slopes 1000–1450m
⛷4 🚡 *12km*

Untergurgl 121
Unternberg Austria
Riverside village with trail connecting into one of longest, most snowsure cross-country networks in Europe. Large St Margarethen Alpine area on doorstep.
1028m

Unterwasser Switzerland
Old but not especially attractive resort 90 minutes from Zurich. Fabulous lake and mountain views. More challenging half of area shared with Wildhaus.
910m; slopes 900–2260m
⛷21 🚡 *50km*

Uttendorf-Weiss-See Austria
Astute choice for crowd-free slopes when snowline high, Kaprun queues long. Tucked behind Kaprun.
807m; slopes 1483–2600m
⛷6 🚡 *20km*

Vail 460
Val Gardena 333
Valbella Switzerland
Convenient but characterless village sharing large intermediate Lenzerheide area.
1540m; slopes 1230–2865m
⛷38 🚡 *160km* ✉ *Club Med, Made to Measure*

Valberg France
Surprisingly large Alpes Maritimes resort (bigger than better-known Isola 2000) close to Nice. Shares area with much smaller Beuil-les-Launes.
1650m; slopes 1400–2100m
⛷27 🚡 *58km*

Val-Cenis 223
Val d'Illiez Switzerland
Peaceful, unspoilt village a few minutes below Champoussin. Nice open-air thermal baths. Good views of impressive Dents du Midi.
950m; slopes 1050–2280m
⛷228 🚡 *650km*

Val-d'Isère 277
Val Ferret Switzerland
Old climbing village near Martigny, with spectacular views. Own tiny area.
1600m ⛷4

Valfréjus 223
Vallandry 175

Valloire 223
Valmeinier 223
Valmorel 286
Val Senales Italy
In the Dolomites near Merano; not so much a resort as a top-of-the-mountain hotel, the highest in the Alps.
3250m; slopes 2005–3250m
⛷10 🚡 *24km*

Val-Thorens 291
Valtournenche 304
Vandans Austria
Sizeable working village well placed for visiting all the Montafon areas.
654m; slopes 654–2085m
⛷12 🚡 *50km*

Vars 295
Vaujany 167
Vent Austria
High, remote Oztal village with just enough pistes to warrant a day trip from nearby Obergurgl.
1900m; slopes 1900–2680m
⛷4 🚡 *15km*
✉ *Sloping Off*

Ventron France
One of several areas near Strasbourg relatively close to Channel. Unlike most resorts in region, no snowmakers.
630m; slopes 900–1110m
⛷8 🚡 *10km*

Verbier 393
Verchaix France
Charming hamlet in lovely surroundings, next to Morillon, at foot of Flaine area. Inexpensive British-run hotel Chardon Bleu recommended by reporters.
700m; slopes 700–2560m
⛷80 🚡 *260km*

Verditz Austria
One of several small, mostly mountain-top areas overlooking town of Villach.
676m; slopes 676–2167m
⛷5 🚡 *17km*
✉ *Sloping Off*

Vermion Greece
Oldest ski centre in Greece, in central Macedonia 60km from Thessaloniki. Barren but interesting slopes.
⛷5

Verndalsskalet/Bjornrie Sweden
Twin areas (same pass) 20 minutes apart. 385m vertical. Former said to have hottest après-ski in Sweden.
⛷16 🚡 *28km*

Vex Switzerland
Major village in unspoilt, attractive setting south of Sion. Verbier slopes accessed nearby at Mayens-de-l'Ours.
900m; slopes 1300–3330m
⛷100 🚡 *400km*

Veysonnaz 393
Vic-sur-Mere France
Charming village with fine architecture, beneath Super-Lioran ski area. Beautiful extinct-volcano scenery.
680m; slopes 1250–1850m
⛷24 🚡 *60km*

Viehhofen Austria
Cheap(er) place to stay when visiting Saalbach. 3km from Schönleiten gondola, piste back to village from Asitz section.
859m; slopes 930–2095m
⛷60 🚡 *200km*

Vigo di Fassa Italy
Best base for Fassa valley, with Sella Ronda access via nearby Campitello.
1390m; slopes 1320–2215m
⛷13 🚡 *20km*

La Villa 333
Villacher Alpe-Dobratsch Austria
One of several small, mostly mountain-top areas overlooking town of Villach.
500m; slopes 980–2167m
⛷8 🚡 *12km*

Villard-Reculas 167
Villard-de-Lans France
Unspoilt, traditional village west of Grenoble, full of life and character with animated cafés etc. Snowsure, thanks to snowmaking.
1050m; slopes 1160–2170m
⛷36 🚡 *130km*
✉ *Fairhand Holidays, Inntravel, Lagrange*

Villar-d'Arêne France
Tiny area on main road between La Grave and Serre-Chevalier. Empty, immaculately groomed, short easy runs, plus a couple of hotels.
1650m

Villaricas Chile
Vies with New Zealand's Mt Ruapehu resorts for the title of most active volcanic ski area in the world. Eruption-damaged.
1200m

Villaroger 175
Villars 401

Vipiteno Italy
Well known year-round bargain-shopping town close to Brenner Pass.
958m; slopes 958–2100m
⛷12 🚡 *25km*

Virgen Austria
Traditional village in beautiful valley south of Felbertauern tunnel. Slopes at Matrei.
1194m; slopes 1000–2350m
⛷6

Vitosha 523
1800m; slopes 1515–2290m
⛷8 🚡 *29km*

Vorderlanersbach 115
Voss 529
6om; slopes 150–945m
⛷10 🚡 *40km* ✉ *Color Line, Ski Scandinavia*

Vuokatti Finland
Small mountain in remarkable setting, surrounded on three sides by dozens of little lakes. Good activity centre with plenty of indoor sports.
⛷8

Wagrain Austria
Traditional village at the heart of the intermediate three-valley area linking Flachau and St Johann im Pongau.
900m; slopes 800–2185m
⛷59 🚡 *200km*
✉ *Ski Club Europe*

Waidring 140
Waiorau Nordic New Zealand
Specialist cross-country centre just over an hour from Queenstown. All levels of trails through valley floors, bowls, ridges. Spectacular views. Overnight huts.
1600m 🚡 *50km*

Wald Austria
Cross-country centre surrounded by Alpine areas – Gerlos, Krimml and Neukirchen – with Pass Thurn also nearby.
864m

Wanaka 536
Waterville USA
Popular New Hampshire area with spread-out village built in pleasing wooden low-rise style. Lift pass sales limit and high lift system capacity keep weekend queues down.
602m; slopes 602–1216m
⛷13 🚡 *255 acres*

Weinebene Austria
One of many gentle flat areas in Austria's easternmost ski region near Slovenian border.
1560m; slopes 1560–1836m
⛷5 🚡 *12km*

573

Resort directory / Index

Weissbach bei Lofer Austria
Traditional resort between
Lofer and Saalfelden. No
slopes of own but well placed
for touring Tirol. Kitzbühel,
Saalbach, St Johann, Zell am
See nearby.
666m

Weissensee Naggeralm
Austria
Famous for Europe's largest
frozen lake. Every conceivable
ice sport played including ice-
golf. One of many little areas
in eastern Austria.
930m; slopes 930–1400m
⛷ 4 ⛷ 7km

Weisspriach Austria
Hamlet in very snowy pass
near Obertauern which shares
surprisingly undeveloped area
with Mauterndorf and St
Michael.
1120m; slopes 1075–2360m
⛷ 44 ⛷ 150km

Wengen 402

Wentworth Canada
Long-established Nova Scotia
area with largest accessible
acreage in Maritime
Provinces. Harsh climate
ensures snow arrives and
stays at such low altitude.
53m; slopes 53–301m
⛷ 6 ⛷ 150 acres

Werfen Austria
Traditional village spoilt by
Tauern autobahn passing
between it and slopes.
Limited Alpine area – claimed
40km overstated. Good
touring between peaks to
Dachstein West region.
600m; slopes 1000–1836m
⛷ 14 ⛷ 40km

Werfenweng Austria
Hamlet with advantage over
main village Werfen of being
away from autobahn, by
slopes. Best for novices.
1000m; slopes 1000–1836m
⛷ 14 ⛷ 40km

Westendorf 156

Whakapapa 536
1650m; slopes 1625–2300m
⛷ 25 ⛷ 988 acres

Whistler 508

Whitecap USA
Largest, snowiest area in
Wisconsin, close enough to
Lake Superior and
Minneapolis to ensure winds
and weekend crowds.
435m; slopes 435–557m
⛷ 8 ⛷ 390 acres

White Pass Village USA
Closest area to Mt St Helens.
Remote and uncrowded with
a good snowfall record.
Mostly intermediate cruising.
1367m; slopes 1367–1823m
⛷ 6 ⛷ 635 acres

Whitewater Canada
Ski area 20km from Nelson.
Known for steep slopes (40%
advanced).
1641m; slopes 1641–2036m
⛷ 3 ⛷ 400 acres

Wildhaus Switzerland
Undeveloped farming
community in stunning
scenery, near Liechtenstein,
popular with families and
serious snowboarders.
1050m; slopes 900–2260m
⛷ 21 ⛷ 50km

Wiler Switzerland
Main village in particularly
remote, picturesque dead-end
valley near Lotschberg rail
tunnel north of Rhône valley.
Very limited slopes.
1380m; slopes 1380–2700m
⛷ 6

Willamette Pass USA
US speed skiing training
centre in national forest near
beautiful Crater Lake, Oregon.
Small but varied piste area
popular with weekenders.
1555m; slopes 1555–2030m
⛷ 5 ⛷ 210 acres

Williams USA
Tiny area above the main
accommodation centre for
Grand Canyon.
2278m; slopes 2278–2536m
⛷ 2

**Windischgarsten und
Umgebung** Austria
Large working village on same
railway line as Schladming.
Slopes at nearby Hinterstoder
and Spital. Lacks holiday
atmosphere.
600m; slopes 810–1870m
⛷ 10 ⛷ 18km

Winter Park 467

Wolf Creek USA
Remote area with highest
snowfall record in Colorado.
Uncrowded; good for all
levels; wonderful powder.
Great stop (accommodation
30km away) en route between
Taos and Telluride.
3144m; slopes 3144–3577m
⛷ 5 ⛷ 800 acres

Xonrupt France
Cross-country centre only 3km
from nearest Alpine slopes to
Channel at Gérardmer.
715m; slopes 666–1150m
⛷ 20 ⛷ 40km ✉ Lagrange

Yangji Pine Korea
Modern, ever-growing resort
with pistes cut out of dense
forest. Eight slopes. 40
minutes south of Seoul. Gets
very crowded.
⛷ 7

Yllas Finland
Largest ski centre in the Arctic
area (463m vertical), 170km
from Lapland's capital
Rovaniemi. Unusually open
slopes for Finland, popular
with boarders and telemarkers
for off-piste.
⛷ 18
✉ Inghams, Ski Scandinavia

Yong Pyeong Korea
Largest resort in Korea,
200km east of Seoul, with
snowmakers on all 18 of its
exclusively short runs.
750m; slopes 750–1460m
⛷ 16 ⛷ 20km

Zakopane Poland
An interesting old town near
charming medieval Cracow
and moving Auschwitz. Mostly
intermediate pistes.
685m; slopes 685–1990m
⛷ 7 ⛷ 10km

Zao Japan
Three interconnected areas.
Unpredictable weather and
very cold temperatures.
Renowned for 'chouoh' –
pines frozen into weird
shapes.
⛷ 38

Zauchensee Austria
Purpose-built resort with lifts
fanning out into the
Salzburger Sportwelt area that
surrounds it.
855m; slopes 800–2185m
⛷ 59 ⛷ 200km ✉ Alpine
Tours, Made to Measure

Zell am See 157

Zell am Ziller Austria
Sprawling valley town with
pistes on two nearby
mountains – modest areas,
mainly easy and intermediate.
575m; slopes 930–2410m
⛷ 25 ⛷ 47km

Zermatt 407

Zinal Switzerland
Rustic village, pretty but for
some incongruous modern
building, with high slopes.
1700m; slopes 1660–2895m
⛷ 9 ⛷ 70km

Zug 109

Zürs 109

Zweisimmen Switzerland
Limited but inexpensive base
for slopes around Gstaad,
with its own delightful little
easy area too.
950m; slopes 950–2005m
⛷ 6 ⛷ 25km

MONEY BACK VOUCHER – PART 1

TO BE SENT (NORMALLY WITH YOUR DEPOSIT) TO
THOMAS COOK SKI DIRECT, DEPT. WTSS, UNITS 1, 2, 3, MERLIN BUSINESS PARK,
CONINGSBY ROAD, NORTH BRETTON, PETERBOROUGH PE3 8BL

Name _____

Address _____

_____

_____

_____

I have bought a copy of Where to Ski and
Snowboard and claim a refund of the
£14.99 cover price. I understand this
amount will be deducted from the cost of
the holiday I am booking through Thomas
Cook. Offer valid for 1997/98 or 1998/99
winter season holidays.

Departure Date _____

Tour Operator _____

MONEY BACK VOUCHER – PART 2

TO BE SENT TO
WHERE TO SKI AND SNOWBOARD, THE OLD FORGE, NORTON ST PHILIP, BATH BA3 6LW

Name _____

Address _____

_____

_____

I have booked a 1997/98 or 1998/99
winter holiday through Thomas Cook
and claimed a refund of the price of
Where to Ski and Snowboard.

Departure Date _____

Tour Operator _____

Have you booked any other winter sports holiday
through Thomas Cook in the last two seasons?   Yes ☐   No ☐

Where did you hear about Where to Ski and Snowboard
(please tick all that apply)?

Daily Mail Ski magazine ☐

Other magazine ☐

Daily newspaper ☐

Sunday newspaper ☐

Saw in book shop ☐

Where to Ski and Snowboard mailing ☐

Reports on resorts help us
make Where to Ski and
Snowboard as useful and up-
to-date as possible. Please
tick here if you would be
willing to fill in a
questionnaire about your
holiday and about how the
book could be made even
more useful to you. We will
then send you one shortly
before your departure date.

Yes, please send me a questionnaire ☐

CUT ALONG DOTTED LINE

WHERE *to* SKI
and Snowboard

WHERE *to* SKI
and Snowboard

WHERE *to* SKI
and Snowboard

WHERE *to* SKI
and Snowboard

WHERE *to* SKI
and Snowboard